Tenth Edition

Labor Relations and Collective Bargaining

PRIVATE AND PUBLIC SECTORS

Michael R. Carrell

Founding Director
Alternative Dispute Resolution Center
Northern Kentucky University

Christina Heavrin, J.D

Former Labor Negotiator and Special Counsel to the Mayor
Louisville/Jefferson County Metro Government
Louisville, Kentucky

PEARSON

Boston Columbus Indianapolis New York San Francisco Upper Saddle River
Amsterdam Cape Town Dubai London Madrid Milan Munich Paris Montreal Toronto
Delhi Mexico City Sao Paulo Sydney Hong Kong Seoul Singapore Taipei Tokyo

Editorial Director: Sally Yagan
Acquisitions Editor: Brian Mickelson
Director of Editorial Services: Ashley Santora
Director of Marketing: Maggie Moylan
Editorial Project Manager: Sarah Holle
Senior Marketing Manager: Nikki Ayana Jones
Marketing Assistant: Ian Gold
Production Project Manager: Clara Bartunek
Creative Art Director: Jayne Conte
Cover Designer: Suzanne Behnke
Cover Art: Alamy.com
Full-Service Project Management: Integra Software Services Pvt. Ltd.
Printer/Binder: Edwards Brothers Incorporated
Cover Printer: Lehigh/Phoenix-Hagerstown
Text Font: Times, 10/12

Credits and acknowledgments borrowed from other sources and reproduced, with permission, in this textbook appear on the appropriate page within text.

Library of Congress Cataloging-in-Publication Data
Carrell, Michael R.
Labor relations and collective bargaining : private and public sectors / Michael R. Carrell, Christina Heavrin. — 10th ed.
p. cm.
9th ed. has subtitle: Cases, practice, and law.
Includes bibliographical references and index.
ISBN-13: 978-0-13-273001-3 (alk. paper)
ISBN-10: 0-13-273001-4 (alk. paper)
1. Collective labor agreements—United States. 2. Collective bargaining—Law and legislation—United States. 3. Industrial relations—United States. I. Heavrin, Christina. II. Title.
KF3408.C37 2013
344.7301'89—dc23

2011033786

10 9 8 7 6 5 4 3 2 1

PEARSON

ISBN 10: 0-13-273001-4
ISBN 13: 978-0-13-273001-3

DEDICATION

We dedicate this work to the thousands of former students who inspired us to write yet another edition of this book!

In addition, we dedicate it to our colleagues on both sides of the negotiation table, from whom we have learned through practice much of the material presented in this book.

Finally, we dedicate it to our families, who have given us time on weekends, holidays, and evenings to write books:

Colleen Sue, my wife, loving mother of our girls, and 2011 "Employee of the Year"
Shari Diane, my firstborn and a model parent and homeowner
Amber Maureen, my Hanover College graduate and Oregon graduate student
Lexi Savannah, my NKU Accounting and Spanish major, and her new husband Sean Toon
Annabelle Michael, my Dixie Heights High School 2011 Valedictorian
Autumn Rain, Boompa's dance partner and first grader

Michael R. Carrell

As always, this is dedicated to my husband, Mike Ward, my son and his wife, Jasper and Amanda, Jax, my grandson, and my son, Kevin.

Christina Heavrin

Reviewers:

We also dedicate this tenth edition to the following reviewers who provided insightful suggestions:

Tenth edition reviewers:

Jerry Carbo, Shippensburg University
Diane Galbraith, Slippery Rock University
Bob Hoell, Georgia Southern University
David Jacobs, Morgan State University
Gundars Kaupins, Boise State University
Louis J. Manchise, Northern Kentucky University
Sophie Romack, John Carroll University
Josh Schwarz, Miami University
David Strecker, Oklahoma State University

Reviewers of prior editions:

Robert Hatfield, Western Kentucky University; Anthony Chelte, Western New England College; Dawn Addy, Florida International University; James Browne, Colorado State University–Pueblo; Ross Prizzia, University of Hawaii West; Jim Hall, Santa Clara University; Jack Dustman, Northern Arizona University; Douglas McCabe, Georgetown University; Mel Schnake, Valdosta State University; James Kyle, Indiana State University; James Castagnera, Rider University; Joe Benson, New Mexico State University; Ronald Atkins, Salve Regina University; Katie Laskowitz, Purdue University; Jeffrey Bailey, University of Idaho; Kenneth Kovach, George Mason University; Richard Posthuma, University of Texas–El Paso; James Wanek, Boise State University; Steve Briggs, DePaul University; Thomas Lloyd, Westmoreland

County Community College; J. Dane Partridge, Virginia Polytechnic Institute; Virginia C. Rogers, University of South Dakota; Ronney Vandeveer, Purdue University; Lane Tracey, Ohio University; Deborah Kottel, University of Great Falls; Debra J. Cohen, George Mason University; R. Richard Sabo, California State Polytechnic University; Robert A. Figler, University of Akron; Deb Buerkley, Southwest State University; William Sharbrough, The Citadel; David R. Bloodsworth, University of Massachusetts; Larry Donnelly, Xavier University; Roger Wolters, Auburn University; Louis White, University of Houston at Clear Lake; Steven Willborn, University of Nebraska at Lincoln; John Vahaly, University of Louisville; and Robert C. Miljus.

BRIEF CONTENTS

CONTENTS

The glossary for this text can be found at *http://www.prenhall.com/carrell.*

PREFACE

FOCUS OF THE BOOK

Welcome to the tenth edition of *Labor Relations and Collective Bargaining*, which over the past 30 years has become the standard for labor relations textbooks. The *PHR and SPHR Certification Guide* lists only one textbook for the employee and labor relations functional area for students preparing for the **Society for Human Resource Management (SHRM)** professional exams—this textbook! This new edition includes several significant changes from the ninth edition, including two entirely new chapters and a focus on labor relations in the public sector as well as private sector. We sincerely thank the reviewers of prior editions for suggesting many of the changes. The tenth edition contains over 100 updates derived from both court and NLRB decisions and recent labor events. At the same time, it maintains the hallmark features of past editions.

NEW TO THIS EDITION!

- Chapter 1 is a totally **new introduction to the field of labor relations**, which defines the field of labor relations and explains why all students will learn important organizational concepts that are relevant to many fields of interest. In addition the chapter discusses the pros and cons of labor unions, and why people join unions. Types of unions and labor–management cooperation are also covered.
- Chapter 3 is a totally new chapter that defines **public sector labor relations** (local, state, federal government) and provides its history. In addition, the chapter outlines important contrasts between private and public sector labor relations.
- Chapter 5 includes an explanation of the two primary methods of negotiation: **distributive bargaining and integrative bargaining**. Practical "real-life" examples of both methods are included in the chapter. These negotiation techniques can be utilized by students in a variety of personal and professional situations.
- Chapter 5 includes a discussion of **ethics** in negotiations. In collective bargaining, people are faced with difficult and unique ethical situations as they strive to conceal their "bottom-line" interests while building trust through open, honest negotiations.
- Chapter 6 includes a new section on **conflict resolution techniques—mediation**, **arbitration**, and **fact-finding**. As an alternative to an impasse, these techniques are explained and their advantages and disadvantages presented.
- Chapter 9 includes coverage of **social media** usage by employees, which has become a growing job security issue. Increasing use of Facebook, Twitter, You Tube, and so on has caused employers to develop and negotiate new policies to address productivity and legal concerns.
- ***New NLRB and Court Decisions.*** This edition includes over 100 changes from the prior edition that reflect new NLRB and court decisions as well as recent union and labor relations events.
- Appendix C is a **Labor Media Guide** which includes a brief summary of a mixture of award-winning documentaries, popular Hollywood first-run movies, and other unique media which focus on labor events and can "bring to life" the human element and circumstances of American labor history. Each is available on DVD, and the Instructor's Manual contains suggested scenes, labor issues presented, suggested relevant text chapters, and relevant discussion questions.

Labor Relations and Collective Bargaining: Private and Public Sectors, tenth edition, introduces students to collective bargaining and labor relations with an emphasis on application, as well as a thorough coverage of labor history, laws, and practices. Drawing on over 60 years of experience in negotiating, labor law, and teaching, we have developed a text for readers who need a practical working knowledge of labor relations in the private and/or public sectors. The text focuses on collective bargaining and labor relations with an emphasis on the real-world situations one faces on the job, including a chapter on negotiating strategies and tactics that can be used in any professional or personal situation. Sections of actual labor agreements as well as arbitration cases and decisions of the National Labor Relations Board (NLRB) and the courts illustrate and emphasize contemporary issues of collective bargaining and labor relations. In addition, experts in the fields of labor law and arbitration have contributed tips on how the concepts learned can actually be applied.

The focus of the book is as follows:

a. ***Appropriate Courses.*** This text is designed for and has been adopted in both graduate and undergraduate courses in labor relations and collective bargaining in both public sector courses (political science, public administration, etc.) and private sector business management courses.
b. ***Text Focus.*** This text provides an applied approach while including thorough coverage of significant court and NLRB decisions as well as labor events.
c. ***Approach.*** This text provides an applied, practical approach to labor relations based on the authors' 60-plus years of experience. The approach is illustrated by the many examples of provisions from current labor agreements and the inclusion of NLRB and court decisions within each chapter, as well as cases for students at the end of each chapter, "Tips from the Experts," "You Be the Arbitrator" sections at the end of each chapter, and a thorough coverage of all issues contained in collective bargaining agreements.
d. ***Prerequisites.*** No specific courses need to be taken before a course that uses this text at the graduate or undergraduate level. Most students have little or no knowledge of the subject before taking such a course.
e. ***SHRM.*** This text provides coverage of the employee and labor relations functional areas of the SHRM certification exams.
f. ***AACSB.*** This text can be used in a course that is designed to provide coverage of managerial content.

PEDAGOGICAL FORMAT

A student-oriented chapter format was designed to integrate theory with the bread-and-butter issues at the core of most actual negotiations. This integration, which includes the following material, provides a sense of how issues in the real world are resolved:

- ***Labor News.*** These chapter-opening articles summarize current labor relations activities to help students relate current events to the day-to-day labor practices discussed in the chapter
- ***In-Chapter Marginal Definitions.*** Terms unique to labor relations and collective bargaining are defined in the margins of pages where the term first appears for the convenience of students. A complete glossary of all labor relations and collective bargaining terms and concepts appears online at www.prenhall.com/carrell.
- ***Chapter Cases.*** Several short cases, which include the decisions of the arbitrator or judge, illustrate those points discussed within each chapter while bridging the gap between theory and practice.
- ***Tips from the Experts.*** In several chapters labor relations professionals answer questions about the collective bargaining process and point out pitfalls for employers and employees involved in the labor relations field.

- ***Labor Profiles.*** In many chapters, a number of profiles of labor leaders or of innovations in the labor relations process help the student understand the concepts in the chapter and the history of labor relations in the United States.
- ***Contract Provisions.*** Illustrating key provisions with numerous new examples from contracts, including *Agreement* between General Electric Aviation and Lodge No. 912, International Association of Machinists and Aerospace Workers, AFL-CIO, 2007–2011; *Agreement* between the Kroger Company and the United Food and Commercial Workers International Union AFL-CIO, 2007–2010; *Agreement* between Louisville/ Jefferson County Metro Government and Fraternal Order of Police Lodge # 614, 2008–2011; *Agreement* between Duke Energy Ohio, Inc. and local Union 1347 International Brotherhood of Electrical Workers, AFL-CIO, 2006–2009; and *Agreement* between C. Lee Cook Division, Dover Resources, Inc. and Lodge No. 681, International Association of Machinists and Aerospace Workers, AFL-CIO, 2007–2012.

Chapter-end and end-of-text materials include the following:

- ***"You Be the Arbitrator."*** A real-world arbitration case at the end of each chapter allows students to assume the role of arbitrator who is presented with the facts, relevant provisions of a labor agreement, and the positions of the union and management. Students are asked to decide an award and opinion, cite the most relevant facts, and decide what actions might have taken to avoid the conflict.
- ***Case Studies.*** Case studies help students understand both sides of the issues. The case studies describe the facts and lawsuits, but actual decisions are not provided. These cases are taken from court and NLRB decisions and allow students to play the role of the arbitrator or judge in deciding cases.
- ***Key Terms and Concepts.*** A list of the important terms and concepts discussed in the chapter, including the vocabulary unique to labor relations, is provided. The student should be able to recognize, define, and discuss the terms after completing the chapter. Key terms appear in boldface and are defined in context.
- ***Review Questions.*** Straightforward questions focus on the major areas covered. If the review questions present any difficulty, the student should reread the appropriate material.
- ***Glossary.*** A glossary of all key terms that appear in bold print in the chapters can be found online at www.prenhall.com/carrell.
- ***Texts of Major Labor Legislation.*** The text of the National Labor Relations Act and the Labor Management Relations Act, as amended, is included at the end of this book to provide a ready reference to these important documents.

COMPREHENSIVE COVERAGE

This text comprehensively treats the environment of labor relations, the activity of collective bargaining, and the need for administrating an agreement after it has been signed. The text explores labor relations issues in both the private and public sectors, the impact of diversity in the workplace, and how global labor relations affect U.S. interests.

Part One traces the development of collective bargaining. Chapter 1 outlines exactly what is the field of labor relations and why students should study it. Also, the pros and cons of unions and why people join unions are discussed. Chapter 2 focuses on the roots of the American labor movement and discusses the laws that led to and finally established the collective bargaining process. Chapter 3 discusses the history of public sector labor relations (local, state, federal governments). In addition significant contrasts between the private sector (for-profit small to large businesses) and public sector are explained.

Part Two examines the collective bargaining process. Chapter 4 discusses how bargaining units are formed, the organizational campaigns by both unions and employers, and the representation election process. The rights of unions to represent members as well as the obligations of unions to their members are also explored in this chapter. Chapter 5 outlines the bargaining process "at the table" including the two most common negotiating methods, distributive and integrative bargaining, as well as the critical elements of time, information, power, and BATNA. In addition the unique ethical challenges faced by negotiators are discussed. Chapter 6 provides a detailed discussion of the collective bargaining process, including preparation and bargaining subjects, strikes, and key contract provisions. Part Three covers the costs of collective bargaining agreements. Chapter 7 covers wage and salary issues including the different types of compensation provisions that are negotiated in collective bargaining agreements. Chapter 8 looks at the benefits negotiated in most contracts, including forms of pay for time not worked, pensions, health care, premium payments, and employee services. Chapter 9 presents the critical issues of job security and employee seniority and alcohol and drug testing. In addition new important issues including employee social media usage and employee teams are presented.

Part Four presents the operational processes involved in enforcing collective bargaining agreements. Chapter 10 explores unfair labor practices, protected and prohibited employee activities, duty to bargain in good faith, and the NLRB. Chapter 11 presents widely used grievance and disciplinary, types of employee misconduct, and procedures to resolve grievances between employers and employees. Chapter 12 describes the types of arbitration used in labor relations, the historical and legal state of arbitration, and the arbitration process Chapter 13 is a timely look at globalization and its impact on U.S. workers. The chapter contains a comparative review of the worldwide labor movement as well as the state of industrial relations in other countries, including Great Britain, Germany, Japan, and China.

INSTRUCTOR SUPPLEMENTS

The site http://www.pearsonhighered.com/educator is where instructors can access the resources available with this text in downloadable, digital format.

It gets better. Once you register, you will not have additional forms to fill out or multiple user names and passwords to remember to access new titles and/or editions. As a registered faculty member, you can log in directly to download resource files and receive immediate access and instructions for installing Course Management content to your campus server.

Need help? Our dedicated Technical Support team is ready to assist instructors with questions about the media supplements that accompany this text. Visit http://247pearsoned.custhelp.com/ for answers to frequently asked questions and toll-free user-support phone numbers. The following supplements are available to adopting instructors.

To access the supplements listed here, please visit the Instructor's Resource Center (IRC) Online at www.pearsonhighered.com/carrell.

Power Points

Instructor's Manual

Test Bank

Collective Bargaining Simulation

Appendix B provides a collective bargaining simulation of an actual agreement negotiated by the authors. The instructor can access the following: the entire agreement, a list of the priorities of both the union and management that were involved in the negotiations, a summary of the changes agreed to in the actual negotiation, and the entire new agreement at www.pearsonhighered.com/carrell.

This bargaining exercise is based on a real-world negotiation involving the renegotiation of a contract between the Fraternal Order of Police union and management of the Louisville Metro Police Department. Students can negotiate an agreement in which several pay and benefits issues as well as noneconomic issues are addressed. The instructor may share with students the actual new agreement negotiated by the parties after their own negotiations have been completed.

Exercises

Student exercises that appeared at the end of chapters in prior editions are now available to the instructor in the Instructor's Manual.

STUDENT SUPPLEMENTS

The website www.pearsonhighered.com/carrell features an interactive and exciting online student study guide. Students can access multiple-choice, true/false, and Internet-based essay questions that accompany each chapter in the text. Objective questions are scored online, and incorrect answers are keyed to the text for student review.

CourseSmart eTextbooks

Developed for students who want to save on required or recommended textbooks, CourseSmart eTextbooks online save students money off the suggested list prices of the print text. Students simply select their eText by title or author and purchase immediate access to the content for the duration of the course using any major credit card. With a CourseSmart eText, students can search for specific keywords or page numbers, make notes online, print out reading assignments that incorporate lecture notes, and bookmark important passages for later review. For more information or to purchase a CourseSmart eTextbook, visit www.coursesmart.com.

ACKNOWLEDGMENTS

We wish to thank the collective bargaining, labor law, and arbitration experts who so graciously agreed to contribute to the text. They are Kay Wolf and Thomas C. Garwood, Jr., formerly of Garwood, McKenna & McKenna, P.A., Orlando, Florida; Nancy E. Hoffman, general counsel, Civil Service Employees Association, Inc., Local 1000, AFSCME, AFL-CIO, New York; Phyllis Florman, arbitrator, arbitration office of Volz & Florman, Louisville, Kentucky; Scott D. Spiegel of Lynch, Cox, Gilman & Mahan, P.S.C., Louisville, Kentucky; Steve Barger, executive secretary-treasurer, Kentucky State District Council of Carpenters, AFL-CIO; Kenzie Baker, vice president, Local Union 1347 International Brotherhood of Electrical Workers, AFL-CIO; Richard A. Ille, vice president, General Electric Aviation, Evendale, Ohio; Mr. Lennie Wyatt, president, Local 1099, United Food and Commercial Workers Union, Monroe, Ohio; Kevin Garvey, director collective bargaining UCFW Union, Local No. 1099, Monroe, Ohio; Lisa Crain, director human resources, C. Lee Cook, Louisville, Kentucky; Frank E. Warnock, City Solicitor, City of Covington, and for his numerous and significant contributions, a special acknowledgment of Louis J. Manchise, vice-chair, Alternative Dispute Resolution Center, NKU, and former director, Federal Mediation Service, FMCS.

ABOUT THE AUTHORS

Michael R. Carrell

Dr. Carrell is the founding director of the Alternative Dispute Resolution Center at Northern Kentucky University, located in the greater Cincinnati area. In 2010 Dr. Carrell received the prestigious Lifetime Achievement Award at the Annual Labor–Management Conference for his career as a negotiator, author, and teacher in the field of human resource management and labor relations. From 1998 to 2007, he served as the dean of the NKU College of Business. Carrell received his doctorate from the University of Kentucky, and his MBA and BA in economics from the University of Louisville. In addition he received professional certification from the Harvard Law School Program on Negotiation. His professional career has included positions as a personnel director, labor negotiator, and mediator. In addition, he was elected to the City of Louisville Board of Aldermen for five terms, and served as president of the board and mayor pro tem for three terms. His academic career spans four decades and includes positions at the University of Louisville, as well as serving as business dean at California State University, Bakersfield; University of Nebraska–Omaha; Morehead State University; and Northern Kentucky University.

Dr. Carrell has authored over 50 scholarly works in some of the leading management and human resource journals including *The Academy of Management Journal*, *The Academy of Management Review*, *The Dispute Resolution Journal*, *Organizational Behavior and Human Performance*, *Personnel Journal*, *The Personnel Administrator*, *HR Magazine*, *Labor Law Journal*, *Business Forum*, *Personnel*, *The Journal of Accountancy*, *Training*, and *Public Personnel Management*. Dr. Carrell has also published several books in the fields of negotiation, collective bargaining and labor relations, organizational behavior, and human resource management. During his academic career he has received awards for both outstanding research and teaching.

Christina Heavrin

Ms. Heavrin has practiced law for 32 years primarily in the public sector as an attorney for local government in her hometown of Louisville, Kentucky. In addition to negotiating numerous litigation settlements and contracts, she has negotiated a number of major agreements, such as a multimillion-dollar property exchange that relocated major industries and railroads from the city's downtown wharf, resulting in the development of both an award-winning public park and a successful industrial park in the city's enterprise zone; an agreement between the state of Kentucky, Jefferson County, the City and a for-profit hospital for guaranteed indigent health care services for city residents; a tax-sharing agreement between the City of Louisville and Jefferson County that enabled the two governments to share revenue of over $200 million and to combine their economic development programs; and a multimillion-dollar expansion of Waterfront Park that included a major environmental cleanup and the construction of a minor-league baseball stadium in downtown Louisville. When voters approved the merger of the City of Louisville and Jefferson County Governments, Ms. Heavrin was appointed special counsel to the first mayor of the Metro Government. Her duties included negotiating over 40 collective bargaining agreements between Louisville Metro Government and unions that represent about 6,000 employees. Recently Ms. Heavrin was appointed General Counsel to the Kentucky Cabinet for Health and Family Services by Governor Steve Beshear.

PART I Labor Relations Overview

CHAPTER 1

Introduction to Labor Relations

The rights of public sector employees to form unions and collectively bargain came under attack in Wisconsin, Indiana, and Ohio as Republican governors sought large wage and benefit concessions to balance state budgets. *Source:* David Joles/The Star Tribune/AP Images.

Workers have a right to organize into unions
and to bargain collectively with their employers . . .
and a strong free labor movement is an invigorating
and necessary part of our society

DWIGHT D. EISENHOWER (34TH U.S. PRESIDENT)

Chapter Outline

LABOR NEWS

Collective Bargaining Rights and Public Unions in Historic Fight!!!

In 2011 public sector unions' very right to exist was challenged in a fashion unlike any other in modern times! Midwestern states including Indiana, Ohio, and Wisconsin—the state that gave birth to public sector unions in the 1950s—witnessed Republican governors and state houses not only demanding large cuts in wages and benefits to balance state budgets, but also go so far as to try and strip government employees of their right to form unions and bargain collectively. In Wisconsin, for example, union leaders agreed to accept the cuts needed to balance the state budget, but Governor Scott Walker still demanded that public employees' right to bargain collectively be ended by state law. Many including Republican Pat Wellnitz asked why it is necessary to strip employees of their rights if they are willing to make the necessary concessions; "ending collective rights is pretty drastic, even for a staunch Republican," said Wellnitz. Newly elected Republican Ohio governor John Kasich, citing budget problems, also supported a bill that would end the collective bargaining rights for 35,000 state workers and 20,000 university employees in his state. In addition, police and firefighters would lose the right to binding arbitration required to end a negotiation impasse. However, Hamilton County commissioner Todd Portune testified before a legislative committee that in Cincinnati local unions had "pitched in" to make the cuts needed to balance the budget. These events in states generally believed to be pro-union made national news as pro- and antiunion forces around the country watched to see what the final outcome would be, which was possibly the start of a sea change in public sector collective bargaining.

Perhaps it is ironic that the events in Wisconsin, Indiana, and Ohio took place shortly after, for the first time in U.S. history, in 2009, more union members were government workers (7.9 million) than were private sector workers (7.4 million), according to the U.S. Bureau of Labor Statistics. The blue-collar worker is no longer the real stereotype. The steady rise in public sector union membership (today 37.4 percent of all government workers and 43.3 percent of local government workers) combined with a sharp decline in private sector union membership due to the "Great Recession" of 2008 caused the historical event years earlier than forecasted. Substantial losses in manufacturing and construction jobs accounted for a great percentage (2.2 million) of the private sector decline in recent years. Another trend in union membership is the rise in female union membership (7.7 million), which has made gains on male union membership (9.2 million); males suffered a much larger decline in overall union membership, 11.4 percent in 2009, compared to females, only a 3.3 percent decline.

Union workers, however, continued to receive higher average weekly wages, $908, than their nonunion counterparts, who received $710 average weekly wages. Labor officials and economists were uncertain if the rebound of the U.S. economy would enable private sector union membership to outnumber public sector membership, as it had every year in the past. Private sector unions had realized modest membership gains in the two years prior to 2009, after several years of decline, but could not sustain the gains in the wake of the slide in the economy.

Source: Adapted from S. Sulzberger and Monica Davey, "Union Bonds in Wisconsin Begin to Fray," *The New York Times* (February 22, 2011), pp. A1, A17; Jon Craig, "Ohio Labor Unions Ramp Up Protests," *The Cincinnati Enquirer* (February 23, 2011), p. B7; and Steve Greenhouse, "Most U.S. Union Members Are Working for the Government," *The New York Times* (January 22, 2010), p. A1.

The purpose of this book is to introduce students to the field of labor relations and collective bargaining. This goal is achieved by providing a thorough coverage of important labor laws, labor history, and important cases. In order that the material is useful to all students regardless of their level of knowledge and experience in Human Resource Management (HRM) and labor relations, the book was written with an emphasis on application and real-world practical knowledge gained from the authors' 60-plus years of professional experience, as well as many interviews and materials provided by other labor relations professionals. This focus is intended to enable students to apply concepts and knowledge gained from the book to their everyday professional and personal lives. For example, in the chapter on negotiating strategies, the strategies and tactics presented have been utilized by former students in personal negotiation situations such as buying a house or an automobile, negotiating a new employment position, and even resolving disputes between friends and spouses.

SHRM CERTIFICATION Students interested in obtaining certification as a Professional in Human Resources (PHR) or a Senior Professional in Human Resources (SPHR) through the Human Resource Certification Institute (HRCI), the credentialing organization founded by the Society for Human Resource Management (SHRM), will find that this book contains all the required content in the employee and labor relations functional area. In fact, the HRCI's *PHR and SPHR Certification Guide* by Raymond B. Weinberg (HRCI; Alexandria, VA, 2008) lists only one textbook for the employee and labor relations functional area (p. 25) for students preparing for the exams—this textbook! Both the HRCI guide and this textbook can be found online in the SHRM bookstore: www.shrm.org.

WELCOME!

As the authors of this book we welcome you to the field of labor relations and collective bargaining! We have drawn upon our "real-world" experience in negotiating labor contracts and other business and professional contracts, as well as our teaching courses in labor relations, negotiations, and human resource management. To help students relate the material to their own lives and interests we have included several unique features. For example, each chapter contains sections called "Tips from the Experts," contributed by several professional management and labor negotiators. Summaries of the most significant labor laws, National Labor Relations Board decisions, and court cases are provided in easy-to-comprehend terms. Also provided are many examples of actual provisions from labor agreements so students can directly learn from these "real-world" examples which are discussed in the chapters.

The field of labor relations contains many terms that may be new to readers, and thus to help them identify and easily learn these critical terms, they have been located in the margins of the chapter pages. In addition, the power of media such as films, videos, and documentaries can be utilized with this text as well! Appendix C provides a list and summary of recommended media that will help students learn the sometimes tragic human stories and historical labor relations events, and provide insights into content of the chapters. One example is the film *Norma Rae*, with Sally Field in the Academy Award–winning title role. The film is based on the real-life events experienced by a union organizer in a J. P. Stevens & Co. textile mill in South Carolina—at that time the largest employer in the state. By viewing the hardships endured by Norma Rae, a struggling single mother of young children, students can better understand why she risks her job and much more to gain recognition from management. Also, the end of each chapter contains a section, "You Be the Arbitrator," in which the facts of an actual labor relations grievance (complaint filed by either the union or management) and the positions of management and the union are presented. Students perform the role of arbitrator (similar to a judge) and decide the outcome of the case.

In addition, Appendix B includes a "real-world" collective bargaining simulation based on an actual contract negotiated by the authors themselves. The simulation is about the renegotiation of an existing labor agreement between a Fraternal Order of Police (FOP) local chapter and management representatives of a city government. Toward the end of this course students will have gained the skills, knowledge, and abilities necessary to successfully renegotiate the FOP/city contract, exactly as professional negotiators would in real life. Thousands of past students after using this text in a course have successfully negotiated a new collective bargaining agreement judged by professional labor negotiators to be almost equal in professional quality to the ones actually negotiated!

WHAT IS LABOR RELATIONS AND WHY STUDY IT?

LABOR RELATIONS

Any activity between management and unions or employees concerning the negotiation or implementation of a collective bargaining agreement.

Labor relations is the term which generally refers to the process between management and a representative of employees (a union) utilized to make decisions in the workplace. The decisions include issues such as wages, benefits, working conditions, hours of work, safety, job security, and grievance procedures, to name some of the most common provisions. When representatives from management and the employees sit down to formally negotiate these issues and put in writing their agreed provisions, the process is called collective bargaining—because the employee representatives represent the collective interests of the employees.

During negotiations the two sides may reach an agreement on individual issues—these are called "tentative agreements" because, once negotiations have successfully concluded, the members of the union must ratify (approve by vote) the proposal consisting of all the tentative agreements presented by the union negotiators. After ratification by the members, the union and management officials sign a written agreement (if requested by either party). This signed agreement is usually titled **Collective Bargaining Agreement**, often called *CBA* for short, or just *Agreement*, between the two parties. Figure 1-1 contains examples of two agreements and lists the major subjects contained in most CBAs. The written agreement is then a *contract* between the employer and the employees. In this textbook, as in life generally, we use all three terms—*contract*, *collective bargaining agreement*, and *CBA*—interchangeably to refer to the written and signed document negotiated under the provisions of the National Labor Relations Act (NLRA).

COLLECTIVE BARGAINING AGREEMENT

A written and signed document between an employer entity and a labor organization specifying the terms and conditions of employment for a specified period of time.

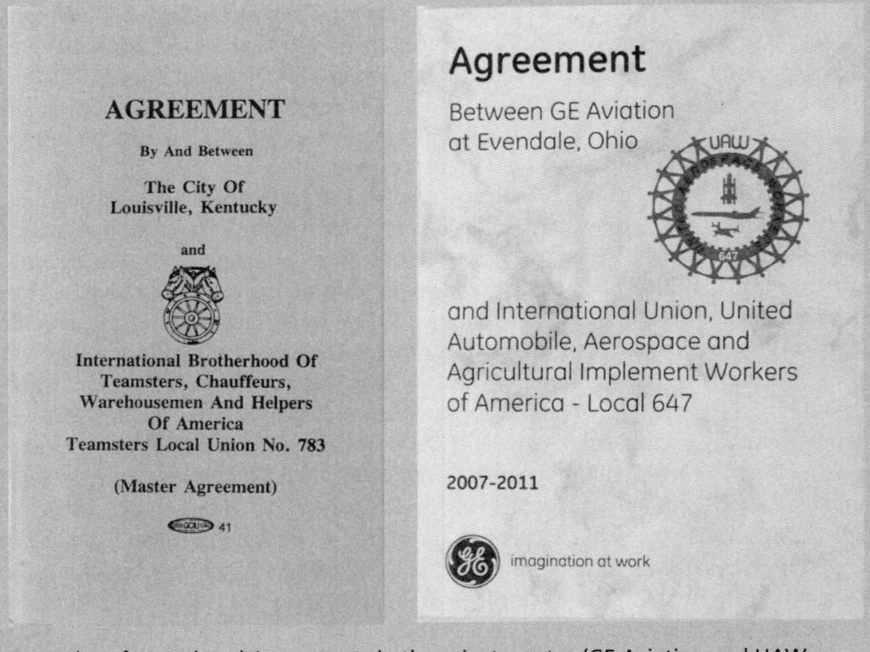

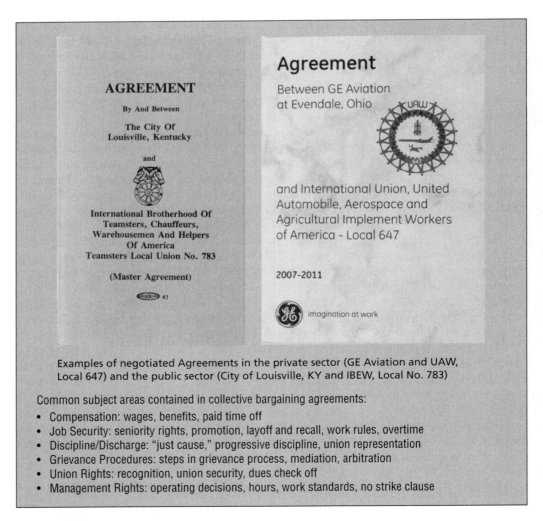

Examples of negotiated Agreements in the private sector (GE Aviation and UAW, Local 647) and the public sector (City of Louisville, KY and IBEW, Local No. 783)

Common subject areas contained in collective bargaining agreements:

- Compensation: wages, benefits, paid time off
- Job Security: seniority rights, promotion, layoff and recall, work rules, overtime
- Discipline/Discharge: "just cause," progressive discipline, union representation
- Grievance Procedures: steps in grievance process, mediation, arbitration
- Union Rights: recognition, union security, dues check off
- Management Rights: operating decisions, hours, work standards, no strike clause

FIGURE 1-1 Collective Bargaining Agreement. *Source:* Michael Carrell.

Collective bargaining in the private sector is the process by which union leaders representing groups of employees negotiate specific terms of employment with designated representatives of management. The term *collective bargaining* originated in the British labor movement. But it was a labor union president in the 1800s, Samuel Gompers, who developed its common use in the United States. The following is a modern-day definition:

> Collective bargaining is defined as the continuous relationship between an employer and a designated labor organization representing a specific unit of employees for the purpose of negotiating written terms of employment.[1]

According to the definition, collective bargaining must be recognized as a *continuous* process, beginning with the negotiation of a contract through the life of the contract with almost daily interpretation and administration of its provisions. In recent years the process has also come to include the handling of employee grievances in most labor agreements and, if necessary, arbitration of such grievances in a final and binding decision. The *employer* referred to in the definition may be one or more related employers joined together for purposes of collective bargaining and required by law under the NLRA to recognize employee representatives. The **labor organization** or union is selected by a group of employees to represent them at the bargaining table. The election process undertaken to select a union, the specific *unit of employees*, or the bargaining unit to which employees belong is also determined by the NLRA.

LABOR ORGANIZATION

Defined in Sec. 2. [§ 152] of the NLRA and means any employee committee or other organization of any kind in which employees deal with employers concerning grievances, labor disputes, wages, hours, or working conditions.

The *terms of employment* negotiated generally include the price of labor, for example, wages and benefits; work rules, including hours of work, job classifications, effort required, and work practices; individual job rights, such as seniority, discipline procedures, and promotion and layoff procedures; management and union rights; and the methods of enforcement and administration of the contract, including grievance resolution. Heated confrontations—the "screw the boss" and "keep the union in its place" syndromes—have sometimes characterized the American system of collective bargaining and labor relations.[2] However, most union and management officials today view collective bargaining as a rational, democratic, and peaceful way of resolving conflict between labor and management.

Why should I study labor relations if I don't belong to a union or ever intend to join one—may be what you are thinking! You are correct that if you spend your entire career in the private sector (for-profit businesses), then the odds of your belonging to a union are small. However, *all* workers in the private sector have rights under federal and state laws whether they choose to form a union or not. All workers as well as members of management in private sector nonunion businesses need to know the rights enjoyed by their employees, as well as management's rights, should employees attempt to unionize. Also, if you ever work in the public sector (local, state, federal government), then the odds of your becoming a union member are almost one in two! Thus students regardless of their chosen careers are highly likely to be directly affected by many of the issues explained and discussed in this book.

Even if you are not directly involved as a member of management or a union during your career, you are very likely to be indirectly affected by events in labor relations. For example, you may have been one of millions of Americans who were upset when their favorite television show *Grey's Anatomy*, *Desperate Housewives*, or *The Tonight Show with Jay Leno*, to list a few, halted production of new episodes in 2008 due to the strike by the Writer's Guild of America in Hollywood, California, or you might have been 1 of 7 million New Yorkers who was stranded when the subways and busses stopped running for three bitter cold days in December 2005 during the transit strike. Or you may have been one of the millions of grocery shoppers who found their favorite Albertsons, Vons, or Ralphs store closed when the Kroger's west coast chains had to suspend operations in 860 stores during the United Food and Commercial Worker's strike. In the future if the proposed new federal law *The Employee Free Choice Act* (EFCA) is enforced, you may be one of millions of nonunion workers directly affected by the act. Finally, the history of the labor movement in the United States, discussed in the next two chapters, is one that any student of American history will find interesting and useful, and will help them better understand many facets of today's workplaces and many aspects of our society.

KNOW YOUR RIGHTS! Another reason to study labor relations is to learn the employee labor rights which are provided to you under federal and states laws. Many laws that provide important individual rights, such as those provided by the Equal Pay Act, Civil Rights Act, Americans with Disabilities Act, Family and Medical Leave Act, and Age Discrimination in Employment Act, are discussed in detail in human resources management courses, and are summarized in Table 1-1. Additional important rights, however, such as those provided by the National Labor Relations Act, Taft-Hartley Act, Fair Labor Standards Act, Landrum-Griffin Act, as well as many others, are also important for you to know, and are discussed in detail in this book. In addition, landmark decisions by the National Labor Relations Board (NLRB) and landmark court decisions that affect your labor rights are also presented.

TABLE 1-1 Major U.S. Employee Rights Laws

Year	Title	Major Provisions	Locate Online
1963	*The Equal Pay Act*	Requires "equal pay for equal work" in the same workplace, regardless of gender, and makes it unlawful to retaliate against a person who complained about pay discrimination, or participated in a lawsuit.	www.eeoc.gov
1964	*The Civil Rights Act (Title VII)*	Makes it illegal to discriminate against someone on the basis of race, color, religion, national origin, or sex, and it is illegal to retaliate against a person who complained about discrimination, or participated in a lawsuit. Also requires employers to reasonably accommodate sincerely held religious practices, except in cases of undue hardship.	www.eeoc.gov
1965	*E.O. 11246 (Affirmative Action)*	Federal contractors and subcontractors; affirmative action must be taken by covered employers to recruit and advance qualified minorities, women, persons with disabilities, and covered veterans.	www.dol.gov
1967	*Age Discrimination in Employment Act (ADEA)*	Protects people aged 40 and older from discrimination because of age, and makes it unlawful to retaliate against a person who complained about pay discrimination, or participated in a lawsuit.	www.eeoc.gov
1978	*Pregnancy Discrimination Act*	Makes it illegal to discriminate against a woman because of pregnancy, childbirth, or a related condition, and makes it unlawful to retaliate against a person who complained about pay discrimination, or participated in a lawsuit.	www.eeoc.gov
1988	*Employee Polygraph Protection Act*	Prevents employers from using lie detector tests, either for preemployment screening or during the course of employment, with certain exemptions. Also, employers may not discharge, discipline, or discriminate against an employee or job applicant for refusing to take a test.	www.dol.gov
1990	*Older Workers Benefit Protection Act*	Prohibits employers from age discrimination in employee benefits.	www.eeoc.gov
1990	*Americans with Disabilities Act (ADA)*	Makes it illegal to discriminate against a qualified person with a disability in the private sector and in state and local governments, and makes it illegal to retaliate against a person because the person complained about discrimination, or participated in a lawsuit. Also requires that employers reasonably accommodate the known physical or mental limitations of an otherwise qualified individual with a disability, unless doing so would impose an undue hardship.	www.disabilities.gov

1993	*Family and Medical Leave Act*	Requires that all public agencies, all public and private elementary and secondary schools, and companies with 50 or more provide an eligible employee with up to 12 weeks of unpaid leave each year for any of the following reasons: (1) for the birth and care of the newborn child of an employee; (2) for placement with the employee of a child for adoption or foster care; (3) to care for an immediate family member (spouse, child, or parent) with a serious health condition; or (4) to take medical leave when the employee is unable to work because of a serious health condition.	www.dol.gov
2008	*Genetic Nondiscrimination Act*	Makes it illegal to discriminate against employees or applicants because of genetic information—including information about an individual's genetic tests and the genetic tests of an individual's family members, as well as information about any disease, disorder, or condition of an individual's family members. Also makes it illegal to retaliate against a person who complained about discrimination, or participated in a lawsuit.	www.eeoc.gov

LABOR UNIONS TODAY: PROS AND CONS

What exactly is a labor union? Are labor unions "good or bad"? What are the pros and cons of unions? These questions should be answered before we begin the thorough coverage of labor relations provided in this book. First, the term "labor union" or just "union" refers to a group of employees who join together to discuss and usually positively affect their employment relationship. Why? Often the initial meeting is due to a recent event in the workplace that has caused them alarm—the discipline of a coworker, a wage or benefit reduction, or concern over a perceived unsafe working condition. The employees feel that when they meet with management about the issue, they will benefit from "strength in numbers"—a core belief of why employees decide to work as a group rather than taking individual action. Many times in organizations across the United States every year a similar scenario occurs and the meeting between management and the employees resolves the issue, and the group does not meet together again, or very seldom.

However, in some cases the issue(s) is not resolved to the satisfaction of the employees, and at some point they seek another method of addressing the issue. Then, as it often happens, someone in the group contacts a formal labor union official and asks for assistance. In other cases a labor union official contacts the employees as part of a union organizing effort. Regardless of how the initial contact is made, in most cases the group is informed of their rights under federal and state laws. One very important right that is available to most private sector employees under the National Labor Relations Act (and available to many public sector employees under similar federal, state, and local laws) is the following:

> Sec.7. Employees shall have the right to self-organize, to form, join, or assist labor organizations. To bargain collectively through representatives of their own choosing . . . "[3]

Notice that the act does not say "labor union" or "union," but instead refers to such as "labor organizations." In fact the term "union" does not appear in the federal act. Labor organizations, as they are called in the act, are most often referred to as unions (e.g., The United Food and Commercial Workers Union), but also use other descriptors such as *brotherhoods* (The International Brotherhood of Teamsters), fraternal orders (The Fraternal Order of Police), *guilds* (The Writer's Guild of America), *associations* (The National Association of Letter Carriers), *federations* (American Federation of Teachers), or some unique designation (United Auto Workers). All are labor organizations, and thus their members enjoy all of the rights provided by federal or state labor laws.

TABLE 1-2 The General Pros and Cons of Union Membership

Perspective	Pros	Cons
Members	* Higher wages * Representation in discipline/discharge cases * Greater job security * Better health care, pension, and paid time-off benefits	* Union dues * Fewer individual rewards based on performance
Management/owners	* System for grievance handling * Fewer individual requests/ complaints * Standard rules reducing friction at the workplace	* Higher personnel costs reduce competitive position * Less flexible work rules * Greater time spent on grievances * Less competitive than nonunion
Society	* Increased middle class * Leadership in passing major employment laws	* U.S. firms less competitive in global markets * Image of union leaders * Less relevant in today's global marketplace

The answer to the other question presented, what are the pros and cons of unions (thus are they good or bad)? depends on who you are; as the old saying goes—where you stand depends on where you sit! Thus we will answer the question from three different perspectives—union members, management/owners, and society as a whole. A summary of the major pros and cons from these three perspectives is presented in Table 1-2. First, from the members' viewpoint, unions are good because through collective bargaining they have provided members higher wages and better benefits than their nonunion counterparts in other organizations. This fact alone for many members is reason enough to view unions as good. Wages and benefits are sometimes called the "bread and butter issues" for unions—their core reason for existence. However, for many, many years members have also cited job security as just an important reason to view their union as good. They believe the knowledge and expertise their union representatives provide them in cases involving discipline, and sometimes discharge, and grievance handling are important to their job security, as are contract provisions that provide for seniority in cases of recall after layoff and in cases of promotions. Other benefits that might be cited by members include negotiated paid time off, health care, and pensions that are generally greater than those received by nonunion employees. Some of the "cons" members might cite include union dues that usually average about two hours' pay per month. Some might point to the lack of individual organizational rewards based on their individual performance, because unions tend to negotiate rewards that are across-the-board or are based on seniority, not individual performance.

Management, of course, would have a different perspective in answering the question about the pros and cons of unions. The "cons" list would be longer—and would start with the flip side of members' higher wages and benefits. These additional personnel costs cause a business to be less competitive than their nonunion competition and/or global competition. Management also would cite the cost of the time and effort required in dealing with unions, particularly in the discipline and grievance processes provided under most agreements. Work rule inflexibility due to provisions in agreements is another major "con" often cited by management. The inflexibility causes, according to management, wasted time and sometimes increased costs, and lower productivity. Management would cite few, if any, "pros." If pressed, some managers would admit that having an effective system for handling employees' grievances can make their jobs easier because they know exactly how to proceed when a grievance is presented. Additionally, many managers would point to the benefit of having standard work rules to manage their facility which the union has agreed to and employees must follow. Many nonunion employers, it might be noted, also have similar systems in place for handling employee grievances for exactly that reason. Managers who have worked in both union and nonunion environments might cite as another "pro" the fact that they receive fewer, if any, employee individual requests for pay increases, additional time off, or other favors because such issues are included in the contract and thus a manager has no authority to grant such requests.

Society as a whole has a unique perspective on the question about the pros and cons of unions. Some people would answer that unions in the past played a significant role in the creation of the American middle class—whose purchasing power is critical to the U.S. economy—a very important historical "pro." Another historical "pro" would be the critical political efforts of unions to gain passage of the important federal legislation presented in Table 1-1, including the Fair Labor Standards Act that banned child labor, and set the standard 40-hour workweek and the national minimum wage; the Equal Pay Act that requires employers to provide "equal pay for equal work" regardless of gender; the Civil Rights Act which prohibits employers from discrimination based on color, race, gender, religion, or national origin; and the Age Discrimination Act which prohibits discrimination against individuals over the age of 40, as well as other important laws, such as the Occupational Safety and Health Act (OSHA) and the Family and Medical Leave Act (FMLA). On the other side, some people in society today would claim that the negative image of union workers as less productive and demanding of greater rewards is valid and has caused many American employers to lose jobs or even close their operations. Yet others may also contend that unions today are simply "out of touch" or "not relevant" in today's global economy.

Communities in some cases have unique perspectives on unions because the actions of a union may have significant impact on a particular community. Consider, for example, Fond du Lac, Wisconsin, a city of 43,000 people on Lake Winnebago whose largest employer is Mercury Marine. Mercury Marine, a division of Brunswick Corporation, made outboard engines in Fond du Lac for over 30 years in 2009, when the community was severely shaken because the company announced it would move the plant and its 2,000 jobs to Stillwater, Oklahoma. Why the unexpected exit from Wisconsin? Because the members of the International Association of Machinists and Aerospace Workers' Local 1947 had rejected a labor contract that required significant health care cost increases for the workers and a three-year wage freeze. The night after the workers voted to reject the deal, Mercury announced it would begin moving operations to another facility in Stillwater, Oklahoma. Larry Brown, president of the Chamber of Commerce in Stillwater, announced the next day that preparations for the move had begun and Stillwater was excited about the new jobs. But then union workers in Fond du Lac, without the approval of their leadership, began a petition for a new vote—and thus the two communities in Wisconsin and Oklahoma were confused, angry, and hopeful because the outcome meant prosperity or severe hardship with 2,000 jobs and millions of development dollars at stake.[4] This scenario or similar ones occur every year across the United States when the interactions between union and management impact the location of facilities and jobs vital to the economic health of communities.

"Are unions good or bad?" Perhaps what is most important when considering the pros and cons of unions is for you to think deeply about all three of these perspectives, as well as others that will be presented in this book, and then form your own opinion. You should be able to form your own opinion by understanding the different viewpoints and the multiple perspectives, facts, and reality, rather than the opinions of others.

WHY JOIN A UNION?

When employees are given the option of voting in a secret-ballot election to have a union represent them with management, or to not have union representation, or in other situations when they can choose to join the union which does represent them, or choose not to join, why do some decide in favor of a union, and others do not? Labor research has not provided an exact answer to this question, but it has provided a list of issues that are influential to workers' decisions:[5]

- ***Job security.*** Above all, employees want protection from unfair or arbitrary decisions by management. In cases of layoffs they expect seniority to be followed, and in cases involving discipline and discharge, they expect the union to provide them with experienced advice and counsel.
- ***Wages and benefits.*** This is the "bread and butter" issue for many workers. They expect contract negotiations to provide them with better wages and benefits than their nonunion counterparts—at least by a difference that exceeds their union dues.
- ***Working conditions.*** Workers expect the union to protect them by negotiating for a safe and healthy working environment.
- ***Fair and just supervision.*** Workers expect that the grievance and disciplinary process negotiated by the union in the CBA will provide them protection against biased or unreasonable supervisors. Most CBAs require the "just cause" standard in disciplinary cases, which is a basic principle followed by arbitrators and judges.
- ***Need to Belong.*** A strong need in many individuals is the need to belong to a larger group that shares one's values and concerns. A union often gives employees a mechanism for bringing them together and social network.
- ***Collective voice.*** A basic principle of unionization is "**strength in numbers**," and therefore the individual employee believes he or she has a more powerful voice when dealing with management. To a large extent the labor union is an entity developed as a means by which individuals could unite and have the collective power to accomplish goals that could not be accomplished alone. Whether that power was used to increase take-home wages, to ensure job protection, to improve working conditions, or simply to sit across the bargaining table as an equal with the employer, members believed that in union there is strength.[6]

HARD AND SOFT ISSUES Some people view all union–management issues as either "hard"—meaning economic gain (wages and benefits) and job security—or "soft"—meaning how they are treated by management and coworkers. Unions have often been viewed by their members and others as pragmatic organizations primarily seeking to improve the hard issues—the economic conditions of their members. For example, the average 2010 union hourly wage was $22.75, or 19 percent more than the average nonunion wage of $19.04 an hour. However, even greater is the difference in benefits between union workers at $13.88 an hour and nonunion workers at $7.33 an hour, as seen in Table 1-3. The success of their unions' activities can be measured by the improvements in members' working conditions and the perception members have of the union's effectiveness. As the workforce changes, unions need to change the way they attract members But first, they need to understand what has attracted workers to unions in the past and why many of those now in the workforce have not been attracted to unions.

TABLE 1-3 Union v. Nonunion Hourly Wage and Benefit Differences, 2009 (Average of U.S. Workers)

Per Hour Compensation	Union ($)	Nonunion ($)	Difference ($)	Difference (%)
Total compensation	36.62	26.37	10.25	38
Wages and salaries	22.75	19.04	3.71	19
Benefits	13.88	7.33	6.55	89

Source: *U.S. Bureau of Labor Statistics. Employment and Earnings* (January 2009).

In addition to the economic benefits unions provide their members, in comparison with nonunion workers, Joe Twarog, associate director of Labor Education, has summarized other benefits. These noneconomic benefits generally include job security, protection against discretionary actions, and due process and are summarized in Table 1-4.

In a survey of labor leaders around the country, the four most important factors affecting the health of the American labor movement were the following:

1. Collective bargaining rights
2. Leadership in the labor movement
3. Union member solidarity
4. Action of the NLRB

TABLE 1-4 Union Members' Perceived Differences Between Union and Nonunion Workplace Benefits

Benefit	Union	Nonunion
Due process	The union contract provides each bargaining unit member with access to "due process" through the grievance and arbitration procedure.	No formal grievance process with arbitration. In some cases, there may be an internal, self-policing "appeals" process that is ultimately unenforceable.
Wages, benefits, and working conditions	These are negotiated. All members have the opportunity to improve their working conditions through contract negotiations at the bargaining table.	All are unilaterally set by the employer. No avenue for employee input. Management gives what it wants to.
Hiring, promotions, transfers, layoffs	All are governed by the contract. Seniority and other objective standards apply.	All are determined unilaterally and subjectively by the employer.
Changes in working conditions	The negotiated contract establishes all working conditions. These can only be changed by negotiations between the parties.	Changes can be made at any time, without warning, by the employer alone.
Discipline	Any disciplinary action is usually subject to the "just cause" standard, meaning that there is a burden of proof on the employer to justify the discipline.	Workers are "employees at will," meaning that they are subject to discipline and termination for no reason at all, depending on the desires of the employer. No just cause standard applies.
Weingarten rights	These rights allow an employee to have a union representative present during investigatory meetings when discipline may result.	No such rights. Recently, the National Labor Relations Board reversed its position and took away these rights in nonunion facilities.
Voice in the workplace	Employees have a real and formal voice in their working conditions at the bargaining table.	Employers may listen to the employees and then do whatever they choose to do, regardless.
Access to information	The union, through its officers and representatives, has access to information to investigate grievances and for contract negotiations.	Employees have no rights of access to information. The employer tells employees what it wants to do. Information is closely guarded.
Voice in patient care	Through the contract, RNs can negotiate enforceable language on staffing levels, mandatory overtime, floating, and other issues that impact directly on patient care and the quality of health care.	In some facilities, RNs may be afforded the opportunity to make suggestions on some issues that management is then free to ignore. None of the nurse input is enforceable.

Source: Joe Twarog, "The Benefits of Union Membership: Numerous and Measurable," *Massachusetts Nurse 76*, no. 4 (May 2005), p. 6. Used by permission.

The assessment of these labor leaders certainly coincides with the demands of the workers.[7] The Louis Harris survey of 1,500 union and nonunion workers tried to answer the basic questions of how members believe they benefit from union representation. The following questions were asked of individuals of both groups: What conditions in the workplace would change if workers lost their unions? Would conditions get better, worse, or stay the same? The results (Table 1-4) showed a substantial difference between union and nonunion workers.

Union leaders view the active participation by members in union activities as critical to maintaining strong unions. Union participation, according to a significant body of research, is determined largely by members' commitment, which is determined by two factors: their pro-union attitudes in general and their belief that the union is instrumental in improving their economic well-being (wages and benefits) and general working conditions.[8] Pro-union attitudes are generally developed over several years and are influenced by external factors, including family members, work history, the media, and direct observation. Their instrumental beliefs can more easily be affected by direct union efforts at the negotiating table and in resolving grievances.

Although most supervisors believe that employees are initially attracted to unions over the hard issues such as wages and benefits, many labor experts, including labor attorney Jonathan A. Segal, believe it is the "soft" issues that often first lead employees to unionize. The soft issues include the following:

- ***Recognition.*** Many employees feel overworked and underappreciated. If supervisors do not give them recognition, a union might give them the recognition they desire.
- ***Protection from humiliation.*** Some supervisors discipline or correct employees in the presence of their peers. The humiliated employee can easily become a union organizer.
- ***Hopelessness.*** Many employees, especially Generation X members, feel they will never be promoted. The pie of good career jobs is shrinking, but the union organizational positions offer an alternative career.
- ***Double standards.*** Reserved parking spaces for management, executive dining rooms, country club membership, and paid noontime lunches are visible manifestations of a double standard that union organizers can easily point out during an organizing campaign.
- ***Lack of control.*** Many managers still do not "empower" employees to make decisions about their jobs, but collective bargaining can give them some control.
- ***Job insecurity.*** Most nonunion employees work "at will," whereas union employees can be terminated only with "just cause." Only one perceived unfair firing could cause employees to question their own job security.
- ***Broken promises.*** Once an organizing campaign is under way, employers cannot make promises to influence a union election and can only ask for a "second chance" if they have broken promises in the past.
- ***Representation.*** If supervisors and human resource professionals do not represent employee needs and stand behind them when asked, employees may seek help from an outside source, such as a union.[9]

CAPITALISM AND COLLECTIVE BARGAINING The rise of capitalism is often traced to the classic economics book *The Wealth of Nations* by Adam Smith, first published in 1776. The book and the idea of capitalism certainly influenced the American founding fathers and those that followed them. The creation of private ownership of property is a cornerstone of Smith's capitalism. The freedom to enter into contracts and to decide the use of one's economic resources such as capital and labor are essential concepts in capitalism. Owners of capital are free to invest their economic resources in raw materials, plant and equipment, machinery, and so on, as well as invest in the "labor" of workers which is available through the "labor market." Just as employers are free to seek employees and offer them economic resources such as wages and benefits in exchange for their labor, employees are free to enter into contracts, or not, for their labor. Thus owners have property rights to utilize their capital and employees have property rights over their labor and a right to decide when to exchange it for wages and benefits. The interest of employers, representing owners of capital, is to maximize return on their investment, and thus minimize the price of labor—wages and benefits. At the same time the interests of employees, as owners of labor, is to maximize the price of labor—their wages and benefits. This basic conflict of interests, between owners and employees, has existed from the very start of capitalism and continues to define a key component of labor relations and collective bargaining.

Employers are free to contract, or not, with individuals for their labor. At the same time individuals' rights of freedom to contract also means they have the right to join other individuals and bargain collectively with an employer over the terms for their wages, benefits, and other conditions of employment. The right of workers to bargain collectively is consistent with the principles of freedom of contract, as well as owner and worker property rights.[10] Exactly how employers and employees may lawfully engage in collective bargaining evolved over a period of several years, and it is discussed in the next chapter.

UNION MEMBERSHIP

Who are members of unions? If you are thinking of a cigar-smoking, older white male assembly line worker, then you have identified the stereotype—but not the typical union member of today! Today a union member is just as likely to be a young female governmental worker. In fact 2009 marked a significant historical event in U.S. labor relations. For the first time, the number of union members working in the public sector exceeded the number of union members working in the private sector! This change resulted from years of declining or stagnant union membership in the private sector—particularly in manufacturing, where the globalization effect of outsourcing American manufacturing jobs to other countries has significantly reduced the total number of jobs in the United States, together with a steady rise in union membership in all levels of government which began in the 1960s when President Kennedy issued an Executive Order that first allowed federal employees to organize into unions and the steady progression of state and local governments that passed similar laws from the1960s through the 1980s. Furthermore, the trend is likely to continue. A U.S. Department of Labor analysis of the growth and declines of union membership from 2003 to 2008 found that the five unions with the largest increase in membership were in public service industries—elementary and secondary schools (367,204), hospitals (158,058), justice/public safety (153, 603), colleges and universities (98,271), and health care nonhospitals (61,508). And it should be noted that in 2008, unions gained almost 500,000 new members in the United States—gains that were quickly lost in the Great Recession that followed. During the same period, 2003–2008, the five industries with the largest loss in union membership were all in the private sector.[11] Thus the trend of public sector union membership growth outpacing that of the private sector may very well continue.

Figure 1-2 illustrates how the decline in private sector membership and the rise in public sector membership came to a historic crossroads in 2009, when for the first time in history the number of public sector union members was greater. The figure also reveals four important trends in U.S. union membership. First, union membership in the private sector increased dramatically in the 1930s and 1940s after the National Labor Relations Act was passed in 1935, because it first gave employees the lawful right to organize and use collective bargaining to increase wages and benefits as well as provide job security. Second, public sector union membership remained very low (around 2 percent) until the early 1960s when it climbed sharply following President Kennedy's Executive Order. From 1980 through the present public sector total membership thus continues to rise, but at a slow rate. A third trend concerns **union density**

UNION DENSITY

The number of union employees in proportion to the total number of employees in a state or other area.

FIGURE 1-2 Trends in U.S. Union Membership

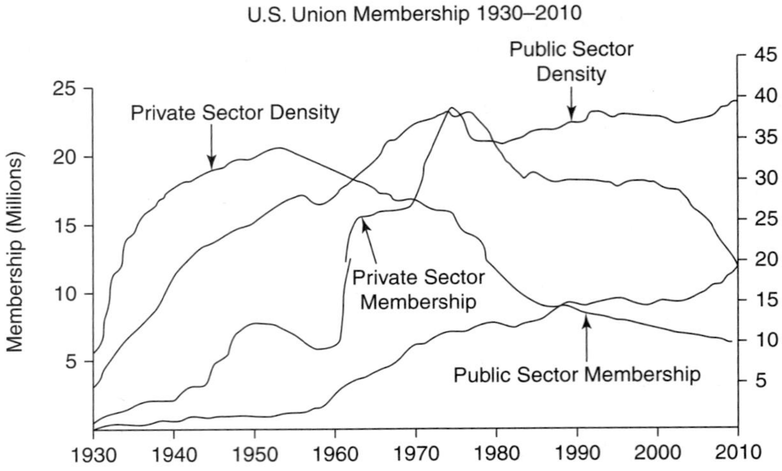

(percentage of workers that belong to unions), which peaked in the private sector in 1955 at 35 percent, when about one in three workers belonged to unions—and thus some would argue their political clout as well as their general public support also peaked. Private sector union density then after 1955 began a sharp and steady decline for over 50 years to its level of around 7 percent in 2010. Figure 1-2 also shows a fourth trend, public sector union density, which grew sharply in the 1960s and 1970s as more states and local governments passed laws that first allowed their public workers to unionize, and has remained relatively high, between 35 and 40 percent in recent years. In fact, the union membership rate was higher in all three levels of government (local 42 percent, state 31 percent, federal 27 percent) than the highest private sector industry, transportation and utilities (22 percent). The highest union membership rate in an industry, private or public sector, is the protective services industry with 35 percent union membership (police officers and firefighters).[12] Thus, the overall steady decline of private sector union membership together with the steady rise of public sector membership came to what many forecasted as an inevitable crossing point in 2009 when for the first time in U.S. history more union members worked in the public sector than in the private sector!

In 2009, union membership totaled 15.3 million workers or 12.3 percent of the labor force. More public sector employees (7.9 million) belonged to a union than did private sector employees (7.4 million). Unions represent 16.9 million wage and salary workers. This group includes both union members and other workers whose jobs are covered by a union contract, but do not belong to that union. Union membership and representation varies greatly by industry, as illustrated in Table 1-5, with the greatest concentration in government (41.1 percent of all government workers), transportation and utilities (23.4 percent), construction (15 percent), manufacturing (11.9 percent), and telecommunication (11.2 percent). In 2008, however, as national unions pushed to organize new members, union membership rose by 428,000 members, a reversal from recent years when they lost numbers. About two-thirds of that growth, 275,000, was in the public sector. The number of union members dropped in 2009, but that decline is largely reflective of the overall drop in employment due to the Great Recession of 2008.

UNION LEADERS Who are union leaders? Just to name a few whose names you might recognize: former U.S. president Ronald Reagan (twice president of the Screen Actors Guild), Susan B. Anthony (former president, Workingwomen's Central Association), Derek Fisher, Los Angeles Lakers (president, National Basketball Players Association), Jimmy Hoffa (former Teamsters Union president), Cesar Chavez (founder, United Farm Workers—formerly the National Farm Workers Association), Melissa Gilbert, actress and star of the television series *Little House on the Prairie* (former president Screen Actors Guild).

TABLE 1-5 Union Members and Workers Represented by Selected Industry, 2009

	Union Members (in Thousands)	Percentage of Employed	Workers Represented by Unions (in Thousands)	Percentage of Employed
Agriculture and related industries	12	1.1	14	1.4
Mining	57	8.6	63	9.5
Construction	958	14.5	993	15.0
Manufacturing	1,470	10.9	1,595	11.9
Wholesale and retail trade	937	5.3	1,032	5.8
Transportation and utilities	1,144	22.2	1,210	23.4
Telecommunications	280	10.0	312	11.2
Financial activities	150	1.8	193	2.3
Professional and business services	256	2.3	314	2.8
Education and health services	1,655	8.6	1,912	9.9
Other services	182	2.3	182	3.2
Public sector	7,896	37.4	8,677	41.1
Federal government	1,005	28.0	1,192	33.2
State government	2,025	32.2	2,222	35.3
Local government	4,867	43.3	5,263	46.8

Source: *U.S. Department of Labor, Employment and Earnings* (January 2010).

Derek Fisher of the 2010 NBA Champion Los Angeles Lakers is also a union president—President of the National Basketball Players Association. *Source:* NBAE/Getty Images.

WORKPLACE CHANGES It is easy to understand why workers in many manufacturing industries chose to unionize after the passage of the 1935 National Labor Relations Act. At that time many manufacturing plants were oppressive places of employment. Each morning men lined up at the gate. If there was no work, they were sent home; if they were hired, it was for that day only. There was no continuous employment. The men never knew when their workday would end until the whistle blew. Workdays often lasted 10, 12, and even 14 hours. One autoworker recalls that some foremen were so intimidating that workers had to do the foremen's yard work on the weekends and had to bring along their daughters to provide sexual services. The foremen managed by terror and hired prizefighters to keep control. Workers could not talk while at their position or even during lunch, and had to raise their hands to go to the bathroom. The bathrooms did not have doors, and foremen followed workers who took a bathroom break to make sure the break was needed; such indignities, as well as poor wages and unsafe working conditions, made workers ready to join unions.[13]

In response to these conditions and in frustration over issues such as wages, benefits, and fair treatment, union membership grew quickly in the 1930s, from 3.4 million members in 1930 (12 percent of nonfarm payrolls) to more than 10 million in 1941. Union density peaked in 1954, when 35 percent of workers were union members. Although the percentages began to fall, the number of union members continued to grow, from 17 million in 1954 to a peak of 20.2 million in 1978, and 15.3 million in 2010.

In the past 30 years, the demographic makeup of union membership has gradually changed to about 75 percent white, 15 percent black, and 11 percent Hispanic. The gender composition has changed—female workers rose from 34 percent of union membership to about 43 percent during a period in which the female proportion of the total workforce remained stable. The classic U.S. union member in 1980 was a white, blue-collar, middle-aged male construction or manufacturing worker. Today, however, the union worker image is changing, and the classic union worker is somewhat more likely to be a man or woman, public sector or private sector worker, and far less likely to be employed in manufacturing, transportation, or construction.[14] U.S. union membership also varies greatly by region. The West Coast, middle Atlantic, New England, and the east-north central states have higher rates of membership; southern states and mountain states are lower (see Figure 1-3).

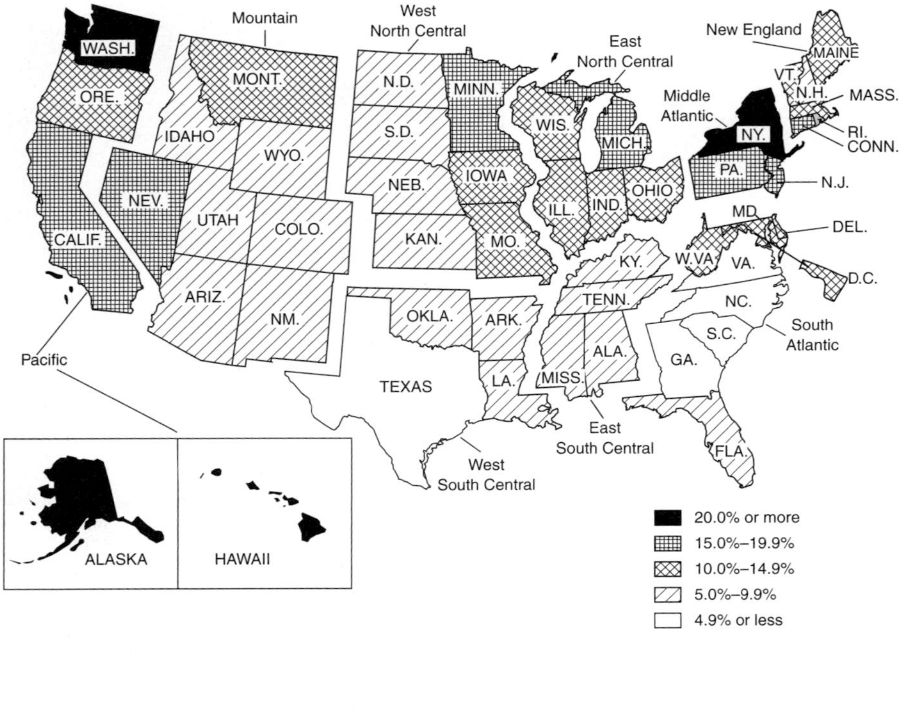

FIGURE 1-3 Union Membership Rates by State, 2007 Annual Average. *Source*: U.S. Bureau of Labor Statistics (2008). Available at www.bls.gov/news.release. Accessed February 16, 2008.

TABLE 1-6 Union Density Rates, Major Industrial Countries (Percentage)

	1970	1990	2008	Change 1990–2008
Australia	44.2	40.0	18.6	−21.4
Austria	62.8	46.9	28.9	−18.0
Belgium	42.1	53.9	51.9	−2.0
Canada	31.0	34.0	27.1	−6.9
Denmark	60.3	75.3	67.6	−7.7
Finland	51.3	72.5	67.5	−5.0
France	22.7	10.3	7.7	−2.6
Germany	32.0	31.2	19.1	−12.1
Ireland	50.6	48.5	32.3	−16.2
Italy	37.0	38.8	33.4	−5.4
Japan	35.1	25.4	18.2	−7.2
Netherlands	36.5	24.3	18.9	−5.4
New Zealand	56.5	49.5	20.8	−28.7
Norway	56.8	58.5	53.3	−5.2
Spain	n/a	12.5	14.3	+1.8
Sweden	67.7	80.0	68.3	−11.7
Switzerland	28.9	22.7	18.3	−4.4
United Kingdom	43.0	38.2	27.1	−11.1
United States	27.4	15.5	11.9	−3.6

Source: Online OECD Employment Database, "Trade Union Density (%) in OECD Countries (1960–2008)," Organization for Economic Co-operation and Development, 2009. Available at http://www.oecd.org. Accessed August 16, 2010.

Why has union membership in the United States declined? A Stanford University study provided several key reasons. First, it noted that declining union membership is not unique to the United States. In fact, of the 20 major industrial countries of the world, only **one** did not record a decrease in the percentage of workers belonging to unions (**union density**) from 1990 to 2008 (see Table 1-6). As will be discussed in a later chapter, the union density in many countries has declined as it has in the United States due to greater global competition, management demands, and shifts from manufacturing to service economies. In addition, most of the developing regions of Asia, Africa, and Latin America experienced declining union membership. The study found the major reasons for the decline in union membership in the United States include the following:[15]

- The growing attrition of existing members from their unions. This may be caused by frustration with union leadership or be related to a surprising result of the study: Union workers feel they have *less* self-direction in the workplace than do nonunion workers. In addition, union workers have increasingly witnessed layoffs and the use of replacement workers, which may have eroded their belief that unions can provide job security.
- Reduced nonunion member interest in joining a union, possibly because of increased similarity between union and nonunion employers.
- Increased efforts by management to remain nonunion through worker-friendly human resource management policies and actively fighting organizing efforts.
- Union organizing efforts have largely been the responsibility of individual national unions while the American Federation of Labor–Congress of Industrial Organizations (AFL–CIO) pursued labor's political agenda in Washington, D.C. This issue was largely responsible for the 2005 split from the AFL–CIO by several national unions that formed the Change to Win Coalition, a new union federation focused on increasing membership.
- Global marketplace changes, including increased competition from non-U.S. employers and the rapid, continued practice of sending U.S. jobs to other nations, have negatively affected U.S. unions.

Employee Free Choice Act

Union leaders do have reason to hope for a reversal in their declining numbers. A 2007 poll by Peter D. Hart Research Associates indicated that 53 percent of all nonunion workers would vote for union representation if given the opportunity. According to Stewart Acuff, director of organizing for the AFL–CIO, the results indicate that "[t]he gap between those who have a union and want a union is tremendous." The key to giving those workers the chance to unionize, according to labor leaders, is to change the legal process by which workers can choose a union. Thus labor union leaders have supported the proposed new law, the Employee Free Choice Act, which would require the National Labor Relations Board to certify a union to represent workers if a majority signs cards that authorize the union. Current law usually requires a secret-ballot election process. Union leaders believe organizing would be much easier under the proposed new law.[16]

Union–management relations in the United States are in a divisive period, which is evident by a series of significant strikes and other actions in several industries that have traditionally had strong union bases, such as the airlines, newspapers, grocery/food stores, and communications. This is the central question in all the current labor problems: Is this simply a passing phase caused by economic problems, which started with the 2000 downturn in the U.S. stock market and was enhanced by the terrorist events of September 11, 2001, and furthered by the Great Recession of 2008 or is it a fundamental restructuring in the U.S. workplace? About 30 years ago a similar economic period in U.S. history, the rapid changes caused by technology—such as robotics in manufacturing and the introduction of computers in several industries, which replaced many clerical/office jobs, caused a significant downsizing in many U.S. industries, which then enabled many companies to operate more "lean and mean" and fuel the economic boom of the 1990s to 2007. Today, however, according to Peter Rachleff, a labor consultant, pressures on these unionized industries are "both cyclical and, as they say in MBA classes, secular: We're . . . stuck at this . . . intersection between secular or structural changes in the economy . . . the lack of real growth of good jobs and the increased global competition." Is this period only a cyclical adjustment, or is it another true secular, permanent change as the economy experienced in the 1970s and 1980s? Only time will determine.[17]

OPPORTUNITIES FOR GROWTH

The effect on the American workforce of these major changes in the way business is done has been predictable. Layoffs, subcontracting, and relocations have hit every manufacturing industry. Because union jobs had been concentrated within trades and manufacturing industries since the 1950s, unions have lost thousands of members and influence. Unions, however, have tried to focus on certain industries and groups of workers to increase membership.

STRATEGIC INDUSTRY FOCUS The new union federation Change to Win aims to build membership and union strength by focusing on a few strategic industries—building services, hospitals, long-term health care providers, express shipping, and the leisure/hotel/lodging industry. The leadership of the federation believes the labor movement should reorganize from a few large unions and many small ones (40 AFL–CIO national unions have fewer than 100,000 members) to about 15–20 large unions, each concentrated on a specific industry or sector. This could provide the unions with greater leverage in negotiations as well as the ability to organize new members. The strategy is very similar to the early craft unions of the AFL and industrial unions of the CIO.[18] One industry target, for example, is express shipping, which is dominated by three large carriers: UPS, DHL, and FedEx. The International Brotherhood of Teamsters in 2004 began an organizational effort to organize DHL's delivery workforce of about 25,000 employees. The Teamsters already represents thousands of UPS workers (FedEx is nonunion). In less than a year, the Teamsters recruited over 1,500 new DHL workers by stressing salary, health care, and pension issues, to represent about 9,000 total DHL employees in the United States.

The organizational effort at DHL, however, will be difficult because the union will need to organize about 420 local DHL employers, and the delivery agents are independent cartage contractors (ICCs), not full-time DHL employees. At UPS, by comparison, the delivery agents are direct employees of only one employer: UPS.[19]

Hospitality Industry

In recent years, the North American hotel and lodging industry has become a target for union organizing. This focus is probably owing to historically low wages and benefits for work that is needed 24 hours per day, seven days a week, and 365 days a year. In the past, a union would negotiate an agreement with a council of hotel owners in a metropolitan market. The owners could withstand a work stoppage in one area because they operated hotels in ten or more markets. However, the national hotel union, Unite Here, began a movement to "consolidate contract expiration dates," so most or all of the contracts with the major hotel companies—Marriott, Starwood, Hilton—would be renegotiated at the same time. The strategy is that it would be much harder for these hotels to face a strike in the same year in several major markets—Las Vegas, New York, Los Angeles, Washington, San Francisco, Atlantic City, and Detroit. This innovative union strategy has been successful when public response is supportive and convention and vacation trade in those cities is affected.[20]

Health Care Industry

The health care industry, and in particular long-term care, has experienced an unprecedented growth in recent years as the baby boomer generation enters the market in large numbers. The unions in the health care industry have also experienced substantial growth. The Service Employees International Union (SEIU), for example, grew by over 150,000 new members in one year! Health care, along with the government sector (all levels), has been called the "shining exception" to the decline in union membership experienced in other industries. In addition, the rate at which unions are winning NLRB representation elections is climbing, from less than 50 percent in 1995 to almost 69 percent in 2005. Why has the health care industry become the "shining example"? According to John Lyncheski, director of the Healthcare Practice Group of the Cohen and Grigsby law firm, there are several reasons: First, employers are driving employees to unions by providing low take-home pay and turning away from employee demands for better working conditions and patient care, as well as less overtime. Second, unions are using more sophisticated organizing methods including "home visits," professionally produced ads, DVDs, and "salts" (union members presenting themselves as applicants, then upon hiring organize from within the employer). Third, some employers forget that their supervisors are the key to positive employee relations and should be attuned to the warning signs of union activity.[21]

A recent report by the American Society for Healthcare Human Resources Administration for the American Hospital Association revealed that workers in the healthcare industry were far more likely to join a new union than workers in other industries. In 2008, for example, unions won 75 percent of worker certification elections in health care, thus forming a new union, while unions in other industries won only 45 percent. Jeffrey Payne, a vice president for human resources at the Lakeland Florida Regional Hospital, stated, "I've been in healthcare for 16 years and I haven't seen it (potential for new unions) taken this seriously among my peers . . . ."[22] Healthcare unions have realized this opportunity, and in order to more easily organize new healthcare workers two of the labor movements' longtime enemies, the Service Employees International Union (SEIU), which is the largest in the industry with over 1 million members, and the National Union of Healthcare Workers (NUHW), signed a formal "truce" agreement in 2009. The agreement provides that only the NUHW will organize nurses, while the SEIU will organize units of all other healthcare workers including service workers, maintenance workers, nonprofessional staff, and clerical workers.

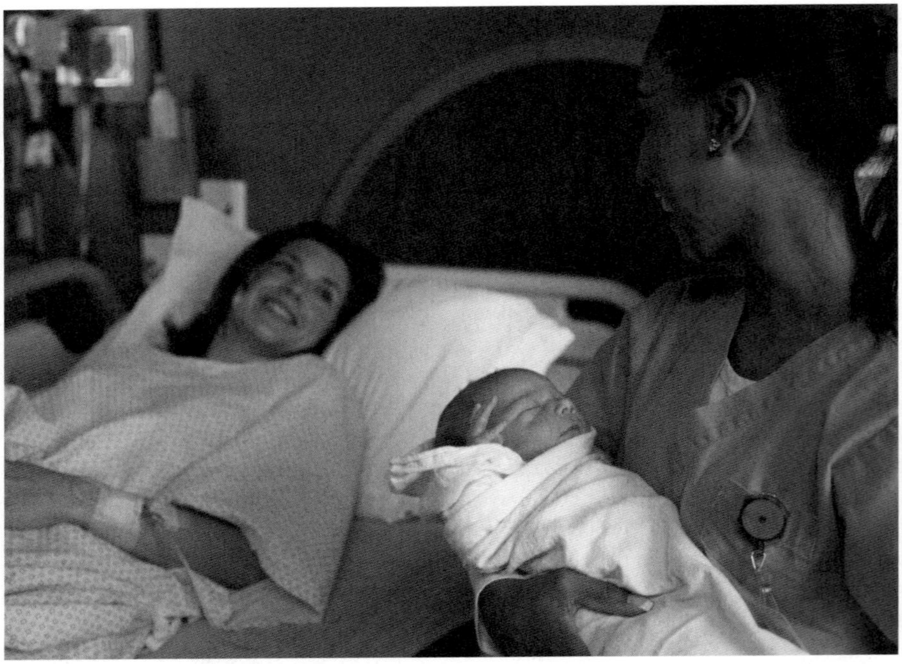

Healthcare workers, particularly those in hospitals, such as nurses, are the most likely group of employees to vote in favor of union representation.
Source: Rubberball Productions/Getty Images.

Airline Industry

The airline industry is one of the most heavily unionized industries in the United States. However, since the September 11, 2001, terrorist attacks, the industry, once one of the most economically sound, lost over $35 billion and 100,000 jobs in the following six years. Five of the major carriers, U.S. Airways, Delta, United, Northwest, and American Trans Air, were forced into bankruptcy to regain financial viability. Southwest Airlines, the most heavily unionized airline, was the only major carrier to post annual profits and/or growing market share. The bankruptcies forced a major cost restructuring in the industry, with unions and their members accepting dramatic cuts in wages and benefits. Thomas Kochan, an MIT industry labor expert, predicts the troubled labor relations that resulted from the cuts, as well as the shaky financial condition of the airline, have caused an industry-wide labor relations crisis. Pat Friend, president of the Association of Flight Attendants union, calls it an industry "Armageddon."

This crisis is also fueled by higher jet fuel costs, greater pressure from smaller carriers and foreign carriers, and the multiyear collective bargaining agreements that were signed in the wake of September 11, 2001, with unions representing pilots, flight attendants, and mechanics, but the contracts must be renegotiated at about the same time in 2008 and 2009. Thus the airline unions and carriers will be in a position to bargain with a united front and possibly set a new course for labor relations within the industry. This is the critical question: Can they follow the Southwest Airlines' model of success through union and employee involvement and customer service?[23] Perhaps the best predictor of the future of unions in the airline industry came in 2010 when over 42,000 Delta Air Lines flight attendants and ground crews voted against union certification. The election was caused by the 2008 merger of Delta and Northwestern Airlines. Before the merger the Northwestern 20,000 workers had been members of the Association of Flight Attendants and International Association of Machinists unions while Delta's 22,000 workers had been nonunion. Some labor leaders called the 2010 vote the most significant labor election in decades due to the large number of workers and the importance of the airline industry to organized labor.

Casino Industry

Because of tremendous growth, a 2007 federal court decision, and rising worker concerns, the U.S. casino industry, with 670,000 workers, is a source of potential union growth. The rapid increase of Indian tribe casinos has increased the number of locations and workers in recent years to more than 400 casinos in 28 states with annual revenues over $7 billion. Until a 2007 decision by the U.S. Court of Appeals, however, it was not clear if the casino workers were subject to the National Labor Relations Act.[24] The Court of Appeals decided in a precedent case that "tribal sovereignty is not absolute autonomy, permitting a tribe to operate in a commercial capacity without legal restraint." The case involved a 1999 complaint by the Hotel Employees and Restaurant Employees International Union that alleged a San Manuel, California, casino interfered with employee collective bargaining rights. The tribe claimed sovereign immunity, making the NLRA not applicable.[25]

In 2010, however, members of United Auto Workers Local 2121 voted by a 75 percent majority to approve a landmark—the first CBA negotiated under tribal law with Mashantucket Pequot Gaming Enterprise at the Foxwoods Resort Casino in Mashantucket, Connecticut. The contract may become a model for Native American–owned casinos across America because it shows that tribal sovereignty can be maintained. The tribe continued to assert that the NLRA does not have jurisdiction over tribal lands—an issue that may not be finally resolved until the U.S. Supreme Court makes a decision. The landmark CBA provided for a 12 percent wage increase over two years, seniority during layoffs, and cooperation between labor and management on a study of dealer repetitive stress injuries. The contract, however, in keeping with tribal law prohibits strikes, but does provide for the arbitration of disputes.[26]

The United Auto Workers (UAW) now represents over 8,000 casino workers in five states. Why would the UAW and other unions want to organize casino workers? Elizabeth Burn, secretary and treasurer of the UAW, explains that casino dealers who earn an average of $60,000 annually have similar interests as autoworkers: "Middle-class jobs that can sustain a family are the heart of union organizing." In Las Vegas, Nevada, the Transport Workers Union of America also moved quickly after the court decision and organized the dealers at Wynn Casino and Caesars Palace. Another reason unions view casinos as a potential source of new members: They can't outsource the services to other countries.[27]

In 2010, the UAW and Foxwoods/MGM signed the first CBA under tribal law—for the largest casino in the United States. *Source:* © Neville Elder/Corbis.

Shipping Industry

The two U.S. shipping industry unions, the International Longshoremen's Association (East Coast) and the International Longshore and Warehouse Union (West Coast), together represent over 100,000 members. They are also a potential modern model of success for other unions to follow. The average salary of their members is over $124,000 per year, foremen over $192,000—the highest of any blue-collar occupation in the United States. The keys to their recent success include (1) master contracts that cover large territories and thus keep the shipping industry firms on an equal-fee basis—and give the unions substantial leverage; (2) they embraced technology: shipping containers the size of railroad cars are moved by ten-story cranes; thus their jobs are a far cry from those portrayed by Marlon Brando in the 1954 film *On the Waterfront* (see Appendix C), where men manually moved large boxes, bags of coffee, and produce; and (3) the 2002 West Coast lockout by the Pacific Maritime Association that included 29 ports was thwarted in only ten days owing to pressure by other industries, such as automotive that had to shut down plants because of "just-in-time" logistics.[28]

Professional Workers

A professional and technical workforce requires union organizers to become attuned to changing worker concerns and aspirations. Those changes may be having an effect. The historic resistance of professional workers to unionism may be weakening, as evidenced by higher union success rates in professional unit elections than in all other units.[29] The successful unionization of doctors in Los Angeles County and nurses in Cleveland, Ohio, signaled to many labor leaders the change in attitudes toward unions by health care professionals. At the American Medical Association convention, physicians voted to unionize, claiming they could then negotiate better with the managers of hospitals, Health Maintenance Organizations (HMOs), Preferred Provider Organizations (PPOs), and so on. The move came only a month after the doctors in Los Angeles voted to unionize. In the nation's largest election for physicians in 18 years, nearly 800 physicians employed by Los Angeles County voted overwhelmingly to join the Union of American Physicians and Dentists (UAPD), an Oakland-based affiliate of American Federation of State, County and Municipal Employees (AFSCME). With the victory, the UAPD boosted its membership to 6,000 doctors, making it the nation's largest union of post-residency physicians.

The Service Employees International Union (SEIU) in recent years has successfully organized thousands of service workers who often receive low wages and no medical or pension benefits. In 2005, for example, the SEIU began organizing 1,300 janitors working for commercial cleaning employers in Ohio. The janitors typically work about 20 hours per week for $7,200 annually, which is below the federal poverty level of $18,660 annually for a family of four. Most janitors work two or three part-time jobs for $6 to $8 per hour.[30]

Immigrant Workers

Immigrant workers are the fastest growing segment of the working class. Unions recognize the potential substantial number of new members in these workers and are pouring resources into organizing them. They include Mexican construction workers in Seattle, Dominican hotel and nursing home workers, and Haitian cab drivers in Connecticut. A major win for unions was the 1999 victory in Los Angeles to represent 75,000 home health care workers, mostly immigrants. But immigrant organizing efforts can run into unique cultural and language problems. For example, Russian workers often had bad experiences with unions in Russia, Vietnamese workers in Georgia were afraid the union organizers were part of the U.S. government and would send them home, and some so-called union members in Europe persecuted Hungarians and Poles.[31]

Foreign-Owned U.S. Auto Plants

Over the past 30 years, out of 33 automobile assembly, engine, and transmission plants wholly owned by foreign auto manufacturers, none, zero, not one has been organized by the United Auto Workers (UAW) despite repeated attempts. Many foreign-owned auto plants located in southern states have right-to-work laws (see Chapter 6 for more discussion) that make it harder for unions to organize workers. However, the plants in Ohio, Kentucky, and Indiana are *not* under state right-to-work laws and yet have not been organized. In 2007, Honda Motor Company announced that its new plant in Greensburg, Indiana, would only accept applicants from 20 of the state's 92 counties. The decision was quickly criticized by the UAW as an illegal form of discrimination against workers with a union affiliation. The National Labor Relations Act does make such discrimination against union members unlawful. However, it allows employers to restrict hiring to certain geographic areas for business reasons. Honda's policy is to require that workers live within an hour's drive of the plant. UAW members believe the decision by Honda was intended to exclude thousands of current or former union workers from Indiana auto plants recently closed or scheduled to close.[32] Between the split of the Canadian UAW members in 1986 and the decline of Detroit's "Big Three" automobile companies' share of the market and thus union members, the UAW has sustained an almost unbelievable loss of over 1.5 million members in a 35-year period from its membership peak in 1971 to 2007. The new foreign-owned auto plants include Toyota (Kentucky, Indiana, and West Virginia), Honda (Ohio, Indiana), BMW (South Carolina), Nissan (Mississippi), and the Daimler Chrysler Mercedes-Benz plant in Alabama. The UAW in 2000, after repeated organization campaign failures in other states, targeted the new German-owned Mercedes-Benz plant. After several months of trying to collect authorization cards from enough workers, the union gave up. Why?

According to "Wa Wa" Walters, president of a United Steelworkers of America local union in an Alabama tire plant, "It's kind of hard to organize a guy driving a Mercedes to work every day." For example, Wade Smith, a 32-year-old worker at the Mercedes plant, made over $100,000, including overtime, and drives a Mercedes Sport Utility Vehicle to work. Another reason, however, was the continuing campaign organized by the local business community that included billboards that read, "No UAW: Save Our Jobs for Alabamians," which refers to the suspicion that if the UAW won, future new jobs might be filled by UAW members from Detroit or other cities who could bid on the jobs.[33]

LABOR–MANAGEMENT COOPERATION

Management and labor work in cooperation in a number of ways discussed throughout this book, although examples of their adversarial relationship are more common and receive more media attention. Why? Because a union going on strike is usually viewed as "news," while a union and management peacefully resolving a grievance or settling a new contract, which occurs about 98 percent of the time, is not as newsworthy. However, increased globalization and increased pressure from nonunion competitors has in recent years caused a new sense of urgency for labor–management cooperation because both sides often realize they both gain from it in the long run. This cooperation may take any number of forms, including the following:

- **Voluntary recognition of the union.** While an unusual occurrence, in some cases management will agree to voluntarily recognize a union as the bargaining representative for a group of workers and begin contract negotiations, rather than resist the union and insist on a secret-ballot election. For example, in 2008 when United Parcel Service (UPS) purchased Overnite Transportation, UPS decided not to fight any organizing effort by the Teamsters union which then began to represent workers in nine former Overnite locations. Why did management choose a cooperative alternative? A UPS executive explained: "UPS Freight and UPS have always respected the wishes of the employees and will continue to do so."[34] (See Chapter 4.)

- **Performance-based incentive systems.** A growing number of CBAs contain provisions that base future employee pay increases on increased specified employer performance measures such as increased productivity, reductions in cost-per-unit, or overall profits. Such plans include profit-sharing plans, scanlon plans, and gain-sharing plans. (See Chapter 7.)
- **Employee teams.** Increasingly CBAs contain provisions for employee teams. Such teams most often take one of three forms: (1) permanent self-managed teams that are given greater decision making over an entire work process or operation. Success with such teams has been reported by Ford Motor Co., General Electric, Boeing Aircraft, and LTV Steel to name but a few; (2) problem-solving teams or "quality circles" are created to improve quality and develop solutions for particular problems; (3) and special project teams which are usually 10–15 people from different functions brought together to design and develop a new process or product. (See Chapter 9.)
- **QWL programs.** Quality of work life (QWL) programs involve union and management representatives that meet to improve communications and their general quality of life in the workplace. The General Motors' (GM) and United Auto Workers' QWL is often cited as an early successful labor–management cooperation effort. The GM/UAW program was installed at 18 GM plants, and a study of their first ten years indicated improved product quality and lower grievance and absence rates were achieved.[35]
- **Federal government.** National Partnership Council teams of union and management officials representing over 310,000 federal unionized employees developed improved systems of communication and efficiency. (See Chapter 3.)
- **Integrative collective bargaining.** When a positive labor–management climate allows for integrative collective bargaining (as opposed to the more common and adversarial distributive method), the union and management negotiation team members work in collaboration to seek mutually acceptable proposals on issues on common concern and brainstorm "outside-the-box" solutions to problems. The Federal Mediation and Conciliation Service (FMCS) has reported that their integrative (or interest-based) training programs for negotiators has become the type of training most often requested of the agency.[36] (See Chapter 6.)

In 2005, about 20 percent of all major collective bargaining agreements provided at least one cooperative article. Typical of agreements that exhibit labor–management cooperation is the 2005–2010 agreement between AK Steel and United Steelworkers Union Local 1865. AK Steel CEO James L. Waincott called it a model for "new era" agreements because both sides gained their primary objectives and the company will be more competitive. The management gains included (1) the consolidation of 100 job classifications into only five, which provides greater workforce flexibility; (2) the elimination of a workforce guarantee (minimum number of workers), which allows for a reduction in force; and (3) greater health care cost sharing by workers. The union gains included (1) an enhanced profit-sharing plan, which should provide increased worker pay, and (2) a guaranteed defined pension plan, which preserves future pension payments through higher pension contributions.[37] A historic, pioneering example of labor–management cooperation was the California NUMMI plant.

GM/NUMMI

In 1962, General Motors (GM) built a new Chevrolet plant in Fremont, California. By 1982, the plant's constant labor problems were blamed for poor quality, low productivity, high absenteeism, and GM's decision to close the plant. But the plant reopened in 1983 as New United Motor Manufacturing, Inc. (NUMMI), a unique international joint effort between GM and Toyota and the UAW. It was one of the first major examples of labor–management cooperation in the United States. It also was the first example in the United States of the Japanese-style team management with U.S. workers. Over the next several years, the new Japanese management combined with UAW members to make U.S. labor history. For years, GM had complained that the UAW was the cause of its problems at the Fremont plant. But 85 percent of the NUMMI

The GM-Toyota NUMMI Plant demonstrated that American union workers can compete successfully with Japanese and European workers, in a time when some questioned their productivity.
Source: AP Images.

workers were those same union workers who, when combined with Japanese management, produced high-quality Toyota Corollas and Chevrolet Novas (then Prizm). The NUMMI plant convinced many Americans that the old problems were with American management, not with American labor. Exactly how did the new Japanese management change one of the least productive U.S. auto plants into one of the finest? Several factors combined may provide the answer:

- ***Cooperation.*** The most significant change was the spirit of cooperation that began with the UAW/NUMMI "letter of intent," including these broad guidelines:
- ***Fewer job classifications.*** In the old GM plant were 95 job classifications that generally produced routine, boring jobs. NUMMI has four classifications: one unskilled and three skilled.
- ***Fewer supervisors.*** With teams performing routine management functions and a focus on building quality (rather than inspecting for it), fewer supervisors and inspectors were needed.
- ***Work teams.*** The 2,400 hourly employees were organized into teams of 5–10 members who rotate among as many as 15 tasks.[38]

The unique GM/Toyota NUMMI plant, however, closed in April 2010, a victim of the Great Recession of 2008 that caused GM to close many U.S. plants including the Fremont, California, plant. Toyota announced that it was not interested in operating the plant alone. Over 4,700 workers lost their jobs, but received an average of $50,000 severance package as provided by their GM/UAW agreement. The NUMMI plant was successful for over 26 years, and it was the only Toyota plant with unionized workers, thus some industry experts guessed that may have contributed to the decision by Toyota not to keep it operating, but the state of the economy as well as other Toyota problems were likely factors as well.

TYPES OF UNIONS

CRAFT UNION

A labor union whose membership is organized in accordance with their craft or skills.

INDUSTRIAL UNION

A labor union whose membership is composed primarily of semiskilled or unskilled workers, such as automobile workers and steelworkers, who are organized on the basis of the product they produce.

Skilled craft workers formed the original unions in America. **Craft unions** represent a group of workers who share a skill or an occupation, such as electricians, carpenters, and bricklayers. Unions such as the United Brotherhood of Carpenters and Joiners of America and the International Brotherhood of Electrical Workers are examples of such craft unions. The year 2006 marked a historic first for craft unions when the All China Federation of Trade Unions (ACFTU) successfully organized the first union Walmart store in China. The historic July 29, 2006, event in Jinjiang, China, soon led to the ACFTU organizing 62 Walmart stores in 30 China cities. Ironically, the ACFTU, with over 130 million members is the world's largest union, and Walmart with over 1.5 million employees is the world's largest employer.

Industrial unions found their start in factories where largely unskilled laborers worked. Organizing the entire plant in one union gave the workers the necessary leverage to counteract

Profile 1-1

Melissa Gilbert, Union President

Most people today recognize her as cute, little Laura Ingalls on the hit dramatic television series *Little House on the Prairie* (1975–1984), on which Michael Landon played her father Charles Ingalls. Melissa Gilbert, however, has also worked as a union president. She was elected president of the Screen Actors Guild (SAG) in 2001, together with Elliott Gould who was elected recording secretary and Kent McCord who was elected treasurer. Gilbert defeated Valarie Harper, known to many as *Rhoda*, from the television series of that name as well as the same character on the hit television series *Mary Tyler Moore.* The heated contest resulted in the second most ballots ever cast in the 75-year history of the union.

The union, with 120,000 members, includes principal and background performers in both the film and television industries (www.sag.org). Ms. Gilbert was only 38 years old when she was elected president, but she quickly earned respect from members when she negotiated with MGM, Warner Brothers, Paramount Studios, and others to keep jobs for SAG members. Gilbert served as president until 2005, when she was succeeded by Alan Rosenberg.

the availability of unskilled nonunion workers. Early industrial unions include the United Auto Workers and the United Mine Workers.

Unions in the **entertainment and professional sports** industries are growing and are often highlighted in the media when the public is directly affected by their labor activities. For example, in 2008 millions of Americans were distraught when several popular television series were cancelled due to the Hollywood Writer's Guild strike, and millions of sports fans were upset in 1994 when a strike by the Major League Baseball Players Association led to the owners cancelling much of the season and the World Series. The Screen Actor's Guild (SAG) is the largest entertainment industry union representing the rights of over 120,000 artists in the entertainment field. Past SAG presidents include Ronald Reagan, Charlton Heston, Patty Duke, Ed Asner, and Melissa Gilbert (see Profile 1-1). In 2009 actors Tom Hanks and George Clooney

Former Screen Actors Guild president Melissa Gilbert defeated Valerie Harper in a heated 2001 election to head the powerful union. *Source:* AP Images.

actively led the contract talks between SAG and studio executives. After over a year of stalled negotiations and fears of a strike like the Writer's Guild strike in 2008, Hanks and Clooney were able to convince SAG members to approve by a 78–22 percent vote a new contract that provided for 3 percent wage increases and a first-time provision for residuals to be paid for free streaming shows.[39]

Transportation unions in the railroad and airline industries, such as the United Transportation Union and the Air Line Pilots Association, are governed by the Railway Labor Act, which differs somewhat from the National Labor Relations Act. After the 1981 strike by the Professional Air Traffic Controllers Organization, the public became more aware of the impact of unionization on the airline industry. In 2007, after years of pilots focusing only on negotiations with their own carrier, members of the Air Line Pilots Association began to support each other to show solidarity within their profession. For example, when Comair pilots began picketing at airports, pilots from Delta Air Lines, Alaska Airlines, Northwest Airlines, and United Airlines joined them. The unity was a major shift for pilots who in prior years stayed within their own airline's issues. "It was inspirational" said Captain Paul Denke, spokesman for the Comair pilots union.[40]

Finally, unions of agricultural workers, like the United Farm Workers founded by Dolores Huerta and Cesar Chavez, do not have the protections of the National Labor Relations Act, but they do have rights under California law and still organize and gain recognition through concerted activities, as discussed in Profile 1-2.

In June 2005, the United Farm Workers (UFW) union in California announced a historic boycott of Sonoma, a subsidiary of E & J Gallo Winery. The UFW followed past boycotts organized by Cesar Chavez, the labor leader who organized the union. Chavez founded the UFW in 1962 and led a successful national boycott of grapes in 1965–1966

Profile 1-2

Cesar Chavez and the Rise of the United Farm Workers

Although the passage of the 1935 National Labor Relations Act gave most employees the right to organize and collectively bargain over wages and the conditions of their employment, agricultural workers were excluded from the act. In 1962, Cesar Chavez founded the National Farm Workers Association (later called the United Farm Workers [UFW] after merger with the Agricultural Workers Organizing Committee) and began his lifelong struggle to gain collective bargaining rights for these unrepresented workers. Using techniques of nonviolence such as boycotts, pickets, and strikes, Chavez spearheaded *La Causa* (the cause), the struggle for decent wages and working conditions for the mainly migrant workforce in California's agribusiness farms.

One of his most successful boycotts involved a nationwide boycotting of grapes. In the summer of 1965, grapes were ripening in the fields around Delano, California. Getting the grapes picked and to market them quickly is crucial to the grower's profit. A group of migrant farmworkers who were coming from harvesting grapes in southern California demanded a wage of $1.25 an hour, but the growers would not agree. A strike of nine farms organized by the Agricultural Workers Organizing Committee, an AFL–CIO organization, was begun. Chavez's union joined the strike, and within a month the strike had spread to more than 30 farms. Under pressure from the strikers, the growers, who had always been able to end strikes with a small wage concession, offered to raise wages to $1.25. This time the workers said no.

Shortly after the strike began, Chavez called on the public to refrain from buying grapes without a union label. Union volunteers were sent to big cities where boycott centers were established. The strike was still on when in March 1966, Chavez led strikers on a 340-mile march from Delano to Sacramento, the state's capital. The walk started with 70 strikers, but by the end of the 25-day walk, Chavez addressed a crowd of 10,000 who rallied in support of the farmworkers. One of the two major growers bowed to the pressure and signed an agreement with the NFWA. The other major grower agreed to hold a representation election. However, before the election could be held, the International Brotherhood of Teamsters offered itself as an alternative to the UFW (the union resulting from the merger of the National Farm Workers Association (NFWA) and the Agricultural Workers Organizing Committee (AWOC). Angered by this betrayal by another union, Chavez called for a boycott of the election. More than half the workers refused to vote, and the

(continued)

Ceasar Chavez led the first successful farm workers organizational fight in California.
Source: Getty Images.

issue was sent to an arbitrator appointed by California's governor. Another election was held under the auspices of the arbitrator, and the UFW won the election. By 1970, with grape shipments down 40 percent, the UFW had effectively organized most of the grape growers industry, claiming 50,000 dues-paying members. Chavez's vision of an organization that was both a union and a civil rights movement gave its members both a sense of mission and a depth of moral pressure to enable it to succeed. For the first time in U.S. history, 25,000 farmworkers had higher wages, health care, and retirement benefits that placed them above the federal poverty level. The boycott succeeded, despite a $2 million advertising campaign by the growers that urged people to "Eat California Grapes, the Forbidden Fruit" and efforts by President Richard Nixon, who called the boycott "clearly illegal" and whose Department of Defense increased grape shipments to Vietnam troops by 40 percent, to 2.5 million pounds.

Source: Adapted from "The Rise of the UFW" and "The Story of Cesar Chavez." (2002). Available at www.ufw.com. Accessed August 15, 2011; and Cynthia Crossen, "Against All Odds, 1960s Grape Pickers Win Right to Bargain," *Wall Street Journal* (May 1, 2006), p. B1.

(see Profile 1-2). These boycotts relied on farmworkers and supporters who walked picket lines in front of grocery stores across the United States, urging customers to boycott grapes, wines, and lettuce. Forty years later, the UFW used the Internet and e-mail lists of 50,000 union, political, and environmental groups to reach consumers directly and urge them to boycott Gallo wines. After three months the boycott led to a new contract with the Gallo Winery, in Sonoma, California.

UFW president Arturo Rodriguez called the boycott "the only thing that hopefully is going to bring them [Gallo] to the table." Gallo spokesman John Segale, however, responded that the UFW "delays and their actions continue to hurt the workers they represent." The central issues in the dispute are wages, medical coverage, vacation leave, and grievance procedures for seasonal contract workers. The UFW boycott won support from the Los Angeles City Council as well as national labor leaders. A 1975 UFW boycott led California lawmakers to adopt the nation's only law giving agricultural workers the right to organize.

Rodriguez noted, "Cesar always said the good thing about a boycott is that's something you can do every single day. . . . Everybody can participate in a boycott."

Shortly after the Gallo Boycott, the UFW successfully organized America's largest table grape producer, Giumarra Vineyards.[41]

Many working men and women could have trouble sympathizing with baseball players because the average player's salary is 77 times that of an average worker and the average basketball player's salary is 136 times that of an average worker. How does your salary compare with these national averages?

Occupation	2010 Average Salary ($)
U.S. worker	43,303
Baseball player	3,340,133
Football player (NFL)	1,800,000
Basketball player (NBA)	5,854,000
Hockey player (NHL)	4,300,000

FIGURE 1-4 How Does Your Salary Compare? *Source*: U.S. Department of Labor, Major League Baseball Players Association, National Football League Players Association, National Basketball Players Association, and National Hockey League Players Association.

UNIONS IN PROFESSIONAL SPORTS

As the numbers of jobs in most traditionally unionized industries continue to drop, a generation of American sports fans is learning about collective bargaining through the news media instead of around the dinner table. Collective bargaining and unions have had a substantial impact on Americans through professional sports. Through contract negotiations, players in recent years have received an increasing share of gate receipts and television revenues. Some sports fans may complain that the days when athletes "played because of their love for the game" are gone forever; however, others recognize that today's players are able to make a career from their profession and are sharing in the wealth they generate through their accomplishments. Still other sports fans blame the high players' salaries (see Figure 1-4) for the high stadium prices, and they miss the days when players stayed with one team for their entire careers. In addition, collective bargaining has resulted in some strikes and lockouts and has disrupted several seasons.

In general, the sports industry can be viewed as a part of the larger entertainment industry, which enthralls the American public. In this respect, star athletes are similar to musicians, stage bands, actors, and other performers. The principal common features among these professionals are technology, media, market constraints, and societal power. The televising of sporting events, including cable and satellite distribution, has become the largest source of revenue for professional sport franchises. Schedules, locations, and times of games are quickly changed to meet the needs of the television industry. Similar influences can be found in other entertainment fields. Both sports and other professional entertainment areas are highly subject to the "star system," in which a few stars command a substantial influence on their professions and derive substantial income from outside sources such as product endorsements. Like the older unions in entertainment—the Screen Actors Guild, the National Association of Broadcast Engineers and Technicians, and the American Federation of Television and Radio Artists—sports unions are concerned about the welfare of the other players (nonsuperstars), who are more subject to the desires of management.[42]

The key elements of labor relations in professional sports are shown in Figure 1-5. The three principal participants are management (leagues and team owners), labor (players and unions), and government. The federal government performs the regulatory function under the National Labor Relations Act in the same capacity that it oversees all private commerce. A body of NLRB and court decisions unique to collective bargaining in professional sports has been compiled since 1935. In this respect, the sports industry is similar to many other American industries—steel, auto, service, and clothing—in that it falls under the NLRA, but it contains past practices, unions, and historical events unique to the industry.

Management in the sports industry operates through league structures. The leagues negotiate collective bargaining agreements, set rules for drafting players, determine management rights,

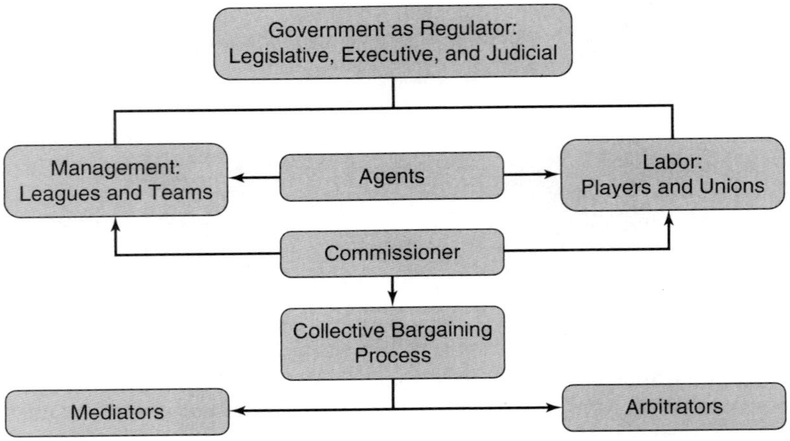

FIGURE 1-5 Models of Labor Relations in the Sports Industry.
Source: Reprinted from *Industrialization and Labor Relations: Contemporary Research in Seven Countries,* edited by Stephen Frenkel and Jeffrey Harrod. Copyright © 1995 by Cornell University. Used by permission of the publisher, Cornell University Press.

and negotiate national television agreements. Thus, club owners yield a great deal of the traditional management authority to the leagues. They do, however, retain decision making over front-office personnel, local television contracts, and stadium management, and they negotiate individual player contracts.

Labor unions in the sports industry operate much like other unions. They organize the players for the purpose of collective bargaining, promote solidarity, negotiate contracts, use power tactics such as strikes and picketing if necessary, file and administer grievances, collect dues, and lobby for the interests of their members. The roles of the commissioners and agents are unique to the sports industry. In general, commissioners serve both management and labor and act as the public spokespeople for the league. Because they are hired and paid by management, however, they tend to be viewed as part of the management structure.

Agents serve as representatives of individual players and negotiate their contracts with individual team owners. Some agents also manage the assets of their players and negotiate their outside contracts. Many observers believe that agents have become a destructive force in the sports industry and have caused the colossal salaries of some players, whereas the unions have concentrated on increasing the salary, benefits, and working conditions of all players. Unless the unions take over the role of negotiating individual contracts, a change that superstar players are unlikely to support, the influence of players' agents is likely to continue to grow. The other major participants are the mediators and arbitrators. The common use of individual player **salary arbitration** in the sports industry has had a significant influence on player salaries and has developed a highly specialized field of collective bargaining.[43]

SALARY ARBITRATION

A process specified in a sport's CBA that provides if a player and team cannot agree on a new salary for a future, they agree to submit the issue to an arbitrator who will make a final and binding decision.

BASEBALL In baseball the National and American Leagues of Professional Baseball Clubs represent management for purposes of collective bargaining. The Major League Baseball Players Association (MLBPA), formed in 1952, has represented players for collective bargaining since 1966. Under a 1922 Supreme Court decision, upheld in the 1972 *Curt Flood* decision, the Court excluded professional baseball from federal antitrust acts. The Court cited baseball's unique needs as an industry and its place in U.S. history.[44] For many years the collective bargaining agreements for professional baseball teams limited the areas of negotiations to primarily salary, insurance, and pensions. Then in 1970, a new provision provided for a tripartite grievance arbitration panel to replace the commissioner as the last step in resolving disputes.

The "modern era" of professional sports and collective bargaining began in the mid-1970s. Arbitration of salary disputes in baseball (after three years of service) was first provided in the 1973 agreement. The arbitrator, however, must choose the final salary offer of either the player or the team without any compromise. The 1976 baseball agreement first allowed players

TABLE 1-7 Major-League Baseball Salaries, 1970–2010

Year	Average Salary ($)
1970	29,303
1975	44,676
1980	143,756
1985	371,157
1990	597,537
1996	1,156,666
2001	2,138,896
2010	3,340,133

Source: Major League Baseball Players Association.

to become **free agents** (after six years of service) and thus limited to newer players the "reserve clause" status, under which teams reserve the sole right to negotiate a contract with the player. The reserve clause is a most unusual labor–management principle in that it takes from players a basic right enjoyed by other American workers—to sell their services to any employer. The NBA limited its reserve clause contract language in 1980, the NFL in 1993. As a free agent, the player can sign with the highest bidder or whoever he chooses. These major changes in the 1970s began what is called the "modern era" of professional sports as other sports unions followed the lead of baseball.[45] In 2010, baseball players' salaries averaged over $3.3 million, 75 times what they received in 1975, the last year before free agency, and the minimum player's salary was $400,000. By comparison, the average U.S. worker's 2010 income of $43,303 was only four times what it was in 1975.

FREE AGENTS

Players who are you permitted to negotiate contract terms with any club. Players are not usually eligible for unrestricted free agency until they turn a certain age. They could become unrestricted free agents earlier if a club exercised its walk-away rights or if their contract was bought out or terminated.

Table 1-7 shows the effect of free agency and salary arbitration on average players' salaries.

In 2005, 89 baseball players used arbitration and received an average salary of $2.8 million. Although this amount is about five times larger than the average player's salary only 15 years earlier, it was down 126 percent from 2004, which is important to note because players sometimes lose when they use arbitration. In fact, in about 66 percent of the cases, the arbitrator award was lower than the owner's last offer. For example, Jeremy Affeldt was awarded $950,000 rather than the Kansas City Royals' last offer of $1.2 million. Cincinnati outfielder Adam Dunn received the largest percentage increase through arbitration, 934 percent (from $445,000 to $4.6 million), and Houston Astros pitcher Roger Clemens won the largest single-season salary for a pitcher in baseball history: $18 million![46]

NATIONAL LABOR RELATIONS BOARD (NLRB)

The National Labor Relations Board (NLRB) oversees most labor relations activities in the private sector and was created by the 1935 National Labor Relations Act. The purpose of the National Labor Relations Act (NLRA) was to minimize industrial strife interfering with the normal flow of commerce. Congress created a federally protected interest in the internal operations of certain industries.[47] That interest was in setting the legal process by which labor and management would engage in collective bargaining. To that end, the NLRA gave employees certain protected rights. Section 7 of the act enumerates these rights: (1) to self-organize; (2) to form, join, or assist labor organizations; (3) to bargain collectively through representatives of their own choosing; (4) to engage in other concerted activities for the purpose of collective bargaining; and (5) to refrain from any or all of the earlier-mentioned activities.[48]

The act also lists employer activities considered **unfair labor practices** in violation of those rights: interfering with employees' rights earlier enumerated, interfering with the

UNION MEMBERSHIP

Employees of an organization that belong to a labor organization.

formation or administration of a union, discriminating against union members and refusing to bargain with employees' representatives.[49]

When labor disputes arise, the parties turn to the enforcement agency for the NLRA, the National Labor Relations Board.

The National Labor Relations Board (NLRB) is a five-member body appointed for five-year terms by the president of the United States, with the advice and consent of the Senate. The NLRB has the authority to investigate and prevent unfair labor practices and, through a wide range of remedies, "to protect the rights of the public in connection with labor disputes affecting commerce."[50] Four basic principles guide the NLRB's administration: encourage collective bargaining, recognize majority representation, enforce the law through administrative procedures, and impose penalties for violations.[51]

From January 2008 to March 2010 the NLRB operated in a "period of great uncertainty" according to Chairman Wilma B. Liebman. Due to politics in Washington, the board operated for 27 months with only two of the five members because Presidents Bush and Obama were not able to get their nominees approved by Congress.[52] The two members continued, however, to function as the board even with three vacancies, relying upon a legal opinion issued by the U.S. Department of Justice that said two members were sufficient for the board to render decisions. The two-member board issued almost 600 decisions during the two months. Then on June 17, 2010, the U.S. Supreme Court in *New Process Steel, LP v. NLRB* ruled that the board was "not authorized to issue decisions" with three vacant seats because the board did not have a quorum.[53] In March 2010 President Obama appointed two new board members during a congressional recess (thus they did not require Senate approval to be seated) and ended the deadlock.

Jurisdiction of the NLRB

The NLRB has jurisdiction over persons when there is a labor dispute affecting commerce or when there is a controversy involving an employer, employee, or a labor organization.[54] This jurisdiction has been found broad enough to include all representation and unfair labor practice proceedings. The following tests must be met before the board is empowered to act.

PERSONS The definition of a person under the National Labor Relations Act is all-inclusive and involves "one or more individuals, labor organizations, partnerships, associations, corporations, legal representatives, trustees, trustees in bankruptcy, or receivers."

LABOR DISPUTE A labor dispute must exist for the board to exercise jurisdiction. The act defines **labor dispute** as "any controversy concerning terms, tenure, or conditions of employment." Labor disputes have been held to include employee-concerted activities such as strikes, walkouts, and picketing; unfair labor practices, such as employers' refusal to bargain; and interference in employee rights.

AFFECTING COMMERCE A broad definition of *commerce* under the statute gives the board authority in all but purely local disputes. The board has jurisdiction if the labor dispute directly affects commerce. In addition, if the employer's operation affects commerce, any labor dispute involving that employer falls within the board's jurisdiction. The NLRB, using this authority, has taken jurisdiction over a manufacturer whose goods were to be transported interstate, even though the manufacturer was not engaged in out-of-state commerce. For practicality, the board has established jurisdictional standards using annual specific dollar amounts for different types of businesses: for nonretail enterprises, a gross outflow or inflow of at least $50,000 in revenue is required for the NLRB to take jurisdiction, whereas retail establishments need gross business volumes of at least $500,000 per year and substantial interstate purchases or sales.

The NLRB is often called on to decide the limit of its own jurisdiction. In *San Manuel Indian Bingo and Casino*,[55] the NLRB reversed previous board decisions and asserted jurisdiction over a casino owned by an Indian tribe and located on its reservation. The board reasoned that the act did not expressly exclude Indian tribes as employers and that because the particular undertaking was a typical commercial enterprise employing and catering to non-Indians, it was within the "affecting commerce" clause of the act.

EMPLOYEES The definition of employee is liberally construed, so exclusions in the definition become important in determining who is not an employee. The types of workers not covered are agricultural workers, domestic servants, persons employed by a spouse or a parent, independent contractors, supervisors, individuals who work for employers subject to the Railway Labor Act, and employees of the U.S. government, the Federal Reserve Bank, the states, or their political subdivisions.

In 2006, the NLRB reiterated its position that *undocumented workers* are employees entitled to protection under the act because there is no explicit exclusion for such employees and to include them assures that lawful residents are not adversely affected by the competition of illegal alien employees.[56] Employees of U.S. employers who are permanently stationed in another country, however, do not have rights under the act according to a Supreme Court decision, *EEOC v. Arabian American Oil Co. (ARAMCO).*[57] The court reasoned that the act has domestic application, and workers permanently stationed in a foreign country should fall under the laws of the host country.[58]

EMPLOYERS The definition of *employer* also takes on broad connotations by listing those persons who are not employers: the U.S. government or a wholly owned government corporation (with the exception of the U.S. Postal Service by virtue of another federal law), the Federal Reserve Bank, a state or political subdivision, anyone subject to the Railway Labor Act, or any labor organization.[59]

LABOR ORGANIZATIONS Labor organizations are most commonly labor unions, but the NLRB recognizes other kinds of employee committees that represent their employees to employers.[60] Labor organizations are also subject under the act to the unfair labor practices section that places some limitations on strikes supported by the organization.

Preemption

A question of **preemption** arises when a field of activity, such as collective bargaining or labor relations, is subject to regulation by both the federal and state governments and a decision must be made as to whether concurrent jurisdiction exists or if the federal government enjoys exclusive jurisdiction. The Constitution is clear that federal law is the supreme law of the land, so a factual determination must be made as to whether Congress has entered and completely covered a field or activity.

PREEMPTION

A legal theory in which federal law takes precedence over state law.

The U.S. Supreme Court decided the preemption issue as it relates to the labor–management relationship in a series of cases.[61] If an activity is clearly protected under Section 7 of the National Labor Relations Act, the state is totally preempted from the field and federal law controls. Section 7 provides employees the rights to self-organization; to form, join, or assist labor organizations; to bargain collectively; to engage in other concerted activities; or to refrain from doing all of these.

Also, if Section 8, the unfair labor practice section, clearly prohibits the activity sought to be regulated by the state, the state is totally preempted from the field. The Court went even further when it decided that the state would be preempted if the activity was arguably protected or prohibited by the act. However, the *arguably protected or prohibited* test was not to be applied in what the Court described as a rigid manner.[62]

Throughout the text we will be referring to the decisions of the NLRB that have formulated the current practices and procedures of collective bargaining under the NLRA.

Summary

Labor relations generally refers to the process between management and a representative of employees (a union) that is utilized to make decisions in the workplace concerning issues such as wages, benefits, working conditions, hours, safety, job security, and grievance procedures. Negotiations between the two sides may reach an agreement on individual issues—tentative agreements (TAs), and once negotiations have successfully concluded, the members of the union must ratify (pass by vote) a proposal consisting of all the tentative agreements presented by the union negotiators. Then usually union and management officials sign a written agreement titled *Collective Bargaining Agreement*, or *CBA* for short or just *Agreement*.

It is important to study labor relations even though only a small percentage of workers belong to unions, because all workers in the private sector have legal rights which they should be aware in case they need to utilize those rights. In addition, members of management need to know the rights enjoyed by their employees—as well as management's rights should employees attempt to unionize. One very important right that is available to most private sector employees under the National Labor Relations Act (and available to many public sector employees under similar federal, state, and local laws) is the right to organize, join, or form a labor organization. Today people often believe that labor organizations are either good or bad—depending on their viewpoint—as a member, a manager, or member of society. Union membership in the United States has gradually declined since its peak in the 1950s until today only about 7 percent of private sector and 40 percent of public sector employees belong to unions. However, several industries provide opportunities for growth by unions including professional workers particularly in the healthcare industry, immigrant workers, the airline industry, hotel and lodging, and the casino industry.

In America today there are several different general types of unions including craft unions which represent workers in a particular skill or occupation; industrial unions which include semiskilled and unskilled workers in a particular plant or facility; transportation unions which include airline, railroad, and subway workers; and the unions which sometimes represent high-profile workers in the entertainment and professional sports fields.

The National Labor Relations Act regulated the industrial relations of employers whose activities affect interstate commerce. The act guaranteed employees the right to self-organization and required the employer to bargain collectively with employee representatives. The NLRB was established to enforce the act. The board, to protect the employee rights guaranteed by the act, determines the appropriateness of the selected bargaining units. The board also regulates and conducts union elections to ensure that employees exercise their freedom of choice. Labor relations, as regulated by the National Labor Relations Act, is considered the exclusive domain of federal law. With a few exceptions, the NLRB has primary jurisdiction in any labor dispute affecting commerce.

CASE STUDIES

Case Study 1-1 Job Performance

The company manufactures ovens. During the period 1982 to 1996, nonbargaining unit, salaried employees did the testing of the ovens. In 1996, the company told the union they would like to see the oven testing work done by members of the bargaining unit. The union reluctantly agreed. The company and union entered into a "sidebar agreement" that provided that "the move of the oven tester position from salaried to hourly is contingent upon a smooth transition with no reduction in product quality. (We are confident that this will be the case.)" By 1997, when the collective bargaining agreement (CBA) expired, there were four bargaining unit testers. The company and union successfully negotiated a new contract, and the only discussion regarding the testers in those negotiations was where to place them in the new agreement.

In 1999, however, the company met with the union and voiced concern about the job performance of the testers. The company contended that because the testers were not doing their jobs, oven quality problems had risen significantly. The company told the union it was taking the tester positions out of the bargaining unit. The union objected. It was the union's position that the company could not unilaterally take the job classifications at issue out of the bargaining unit. It was the company's position that under the "experimental" language in the December 31, 1996, sidebar agreement, an agreement that was in effect when the current CBA was negotiated and remained in effect, the company had the authority to take the jobs out of the bargaining unit because the experimental program had failed. The union filed an unfair labor practice charge, and a hearing was held.

At the hearing, the company testified that after the job classifications were put into the bargaining unit, there were ongoing problems with output, quality, refusals to work overtime, neglect, and possible sabotage. After the jobs were removed from the bargaining unit, quality improved. It was undisputed that the four testers were properly trained to perform the full range of job duties of a tester/assembler. Given this fact, the company attributed their poor job performance to behavioral problems as opposed to competency deficiencies. The company contended it never disciplined the testers for anything related to job performance because it could never get sufficient proof to identify specific individuals who might be responsible for the problems. The record very convincingly shows that the company believed that by taking the job classifications at issue out of the bargaining unit, they could better control the people who would fill the jobs.

The union testified that not only did the company never discipline the four testers for poor job performance, but it also offered the jobs to these same four testers after the jobs were removed from the bargaining unit. Furthermore, the union contended that although the job classifications were put into the bargaining unit on an experimental basis and the company retained the sole authority to take them out of the bargaining unit if the experiment failed, the company had an obligation to negotiate that change in the new CBA. The evidence showed that the company knew the experiment was not going well before negotiations for the current CBA began. The record clearly established that at no time during the negotiations did anyone in the company tell the union that the experiment was not going well and could be declared a failure. Given the company's silence in this regard during the negotiations, the union believes that the sidebar agreement was replaced by the CBA, which included the tester positions as regular positions.

Source: Adapted from *Lincoln Foodservices Products, Inc. v. Sheet Metal Workers International Union Local 237*, 114 LA 1745 (October 19, 2000).

QUESTIONS

1. Why would the placement or removal of the job classifications in a bargaining unit have any impact on the quality of the job performed?
2. If the company knew that the tester "experiment" was not going well during the negotiations on a new contract, should it have negotiated the issue?
3. Was the company justified in attempting to remove the positions from the union?

Case Study 1-2 Grooming Standards at Southwest Airlines

Ramp agents of Southwest Airlines load and unload baggage from aircraft and also collect baggage from customers as they board the aircraft. The union states that Grievant B, a ramp agent with 13 years of experience, is being discriminated against because management at its Love Field Operation in Dallas, Texas, requires him to wear his long hair tucked beneath a cap, but female ramp agents and male maintenance employees are not required to wear caps.

At an arbitration hearing, the company testified that its grooming rules have been enforced on a uniform basis. All male ramp agents have been treated the same, and all female ramp agents have been treated the same. The company argues that discrimination is permissible as long as it is not unlawful and as long as differences in grooming standards that do not unreasonably inhibit work opportunities are permissible under Title VII of the 1964 Civil Rights Act. The company also states that the issue of an alleged discrimination with respect to male maintenance employees is beyond the scope of this grievance because a separate labor agreement exists between maintenance employees and the company.

Source: Adapted from *Southwest Airlines*, 97 ARB 3036 (2003).

QUESTIONS

1. How realistic is the company's argument regarding grooming standards?
2. Can an employer unilaterally impose a grooming rule over the objections of its employees or their bargaining agent?
3. How valid is the company's argument that the labor agreement with maintenance employees is "beyond the scope of this grievance"?

Key Terms and Concepts

Review Questions

1. At this point in your reading of the text, what do you believe are the major pros and cons of unions today?
2. What are the names of three national labor unions that you are aware of and what are the general work activities of their members?
3. What do the terms "collective bargaining agreement (CBA)" and "contract" generally refer to in labor relations?
4. The year 2009 was a significant year in the trends of union membership in the United States, why? Do you believe this event will reverse itself? Why or why not?
5. Which U.S. industry do you believe is likely to grow in union membership in the next decade, why?
6. By what means did Cesar Chavez successfully organize the United Farm Workers in California? Do you believe the same means could be utilized successfully today? Why or why not?
7. What provisions in the agreement between the Major League Baseball Players Association (MLBPA) and the team owners began what is called "the modern era" of professional sports? Why? Do you agree it began the modern era?
8. In general how do jobs in craft unions differ from those in industrial unions?

YOU BE THE ARBITRATOR

Should an Employee's File Be Expunged?

Introduction: This grievance concerns the warning memo placed in the file of a college professor.

CBA ARTICLE XV DISCIPLINE/DISCHARGE PROCEDURES

The Employer shall not discipline or discharge any Employee without just cause.

The following procedure of progressive discipline shall be applied by the Employer, except the Employer need not follow progressive discipline before suspension or discharge if the suspension or discharge is for theft, deliberate damage to Company property, gross insubordination, physical violence, or other similar offenses.

The Employer may issue an oral warning(s) prior to written warnings or suspensions, which shall be imposed for related offenses as follows:

First Offense: Written warning(s)

Second Offense: One (1) day suspension without pay

Third Offense: Suspension of up to three (3) days without pay

Fourth Offense: Further suspension or discharge

Warnings and one-day suspensions as herein provided shall be null and void after six (6) months and shall not be used as a basis for further disciplinary action. Suspensions of more than one day as herein provided shall be null and void after nine (9) months and shall not be used as a basis for further disciplinary action.

These procedures herein provided are subject to the terms of the grievance procedure.

Facts

An Alternative Calendar Committee (ACC) of the employer's college met to discuss a proposal to shorten the calendar at the college from 171/2 to 16-week semesters. Professor L testified that the proposal to shorten the calendar had been discussed at an Academic Senate meeting and that he had been appointed chair of the ACC. The grievant, Professor W, was president of the Faculty Association at that time. Although he was not a member of the ACC, the meeting was open. The proposal to shorten the academic calendar was considered controversial by the faculty. During the meeting, there was a discussion of whether the ACC or the Faculty Association should survey the faculty on the issue. There was a considerable amount of discussion regarding this issue. At the end of the meeting the other faculty members had moved to the other end of the room.

There is general agreement that L and W stayed at the back of the room and engaged in a heated discussion. W said that L was trying to circumvent the contract by having ACC survey the faculty rather than the Faculty Association. L retorted that the contract the Faculty Association had negotiated was lousy. L admitted stating at the meeting that W "was acting like a jerk" and that he had criticized the contract W had negotiated. At the end of the discussion they grabbed their things and walked to the end of the room to join the other faculty members. According to witnesses, during the heated discussion L and W were loud but not shouting. No one witnessed W using inappropriate language, nor was he observed making any threatening gestures. No one witnessed W shove a chair into L. However, according to L, W had shoved a chair into him.

L reported the incident, and W was sent a warning memorandum regarding the incident that stated:

> An incident was reported and investigated that occurred on Tuesday, August 28, 2001, at the end of an Alternative Calendar Committee meeting in the Staff Lounge. Apparently, your behavior towards L was physically menacing, as you were shouting inches away from his face while continually pushing a chair against L. Both Security personnel and my office took statements from those present at the meeting.
>
> W, this memorandum is intended as a warning. The College is concerned about the safety of its employees. Another incident of this kind of behavior may warrant disciplinary action. You are to conduct yourself in a professional and respectful manner, even though you may not agree with others.
>
> This memorandum will be placed in your personnel file. I trust you will see that any form of physical intimidation is not to be tolerated on campus.

W grieved the warning memorandum, and a meeting was held. At the end of the meeting the supervisor issued the following grievance memorandum:

> At the grievance meeting held Monday, October 22, 2001, there was agreement that an altercation occurred in which you and L exchanged statements related to the proposed alternative calendar. There was not agreement that you pushed a chair into the legs of L.
>
> You insist you did not push a chair. Upon further discussions with L, he insists that you did push a chair into his legs. The incident could have resulted in an injury. Since there is no corroboration that a chair was pushed into L's legs, it would be inappropriate for disciplinary action to be taken. However, a memorandum of warning to you is appropriate and appropriately included in your personnel file. Placing the memorandum of warning in your personnel file does not violate the contract agreement in any way.
>
> If there are no subsequent altercations or incidents of a similar nature the memorandum of warning will be removed from your personnel file on June 30, 2003.

In light of the finding at the grievance meeting, W appealed the decision to leave the warning memorandum in his personnel file.

Issue

Should a warning memorandum in an employee's file that contains false and/or erroneous information as to facts or conclusions be expunged?

Position of the Parties

The *grievant's position* is that the warning memorandum should be removed from his file immediately. If the warning memorandum is read together with the grievance memorandum, it is clear that the warning memorandum is defective, as the grievance memorandum states that there was no corroboration that a chair was pushed against L. Grievant contends that the warning memorandum cannot be minimized as "a mere warning." In progressive discipline, disciplinary action progresses from verbal or written warnings to more serious discipline such as suspension and, ultimately, discharge. The purpose is to put an employee on notice that if the behavior continues, more serious discipline may follow. The contemplation of further disciplinary action is set forth in the warning memorandum, in which it is stated that the warning will remain in the grievant's personnel file until June 30, 2003, and will then be removed if, and only if, "there are no subsequent altercations or incidents of a similar nature." As there was no "incident" as alleged by L in the first place, the grievant should not be left on an initial stage of a disciplinary action by having the memorandum left in his file.

The *college's position* is that the warning memorandum and the grievance memorandum read together create an accurate report of the incident. Even though the "shoving" was not proven, there was significant evidence that the grievant and L engaged in a verbal altercation. The college does not agree that leaving the information in the grievant's file is an inappropriate disciplinary action under the CBA.

Source: Adapted from *Citrus College Community Dist.*, 117 LA 26.

YOU BE THE ARBITRATOR INSTRUCTIONS

At the end of each chapter is the summary of an actual grievance case that could not be decided by management and union representatives and thus as provided in the CBA (Collective Bargaining Agreement) at the request of either party was referred to an arbitrator to make a "final and binding" decision that both parties have agreed to accept. You are required to perform the duty of an arbitrator (judge) and carefully read the facts, relevant section(s) of the CBA which are provided, and the positions of the parties, and then make a decision. Arbitrator decisions contain two parts: an "award"—one side or the other has asked for something that the other has not agreed to, for example, in cases involving a terminated employee, the union may have asked that the employee be reinstated in their former position and be given back pay equal to the pay he or she missed—thus the award might or might not grant one or both requests; the second part is an "opinion"—a statement explaining why the arbitrator made the award, often citing critical facts of the case, a position of one of the parties, or even common sense. Arbitrators, as discussed in a later chapter, in making their decisions, usually look first to the relevant section(s) of the CBA (which may be silent on the issue, vague, or contain two relevant sections that are in conflict). The language of the CBA is the most important factor to be considered by an arbitrator. If the CBA language does not enable the arbitrator to make a decision, then he or she looks at the facts and other evidence presented, past practice (what actions were taken in similar cases in the past), relevant facts from past negotiation sessions, and common industry practice to reach a decision.

Keys to making good arbitration decisions are as follows: (1) start and remain objective—set aside any feelings about unions, management, and so on, (2) first look to the provisions of the CBA for direction—if the language is vague or if two sections are in conflict consider what was the likely intention of the negotiators, (3) carefully consider past practice—the lack of consistency compared to similar cases may be significant, and (4) does the penalty equal the offense—in some cases guilt is not the issue, instead the issue is the penalty applied equal to the level of the offense—especially in employee termination cases. Also consider whether the penalty was applied equally to others in similar past cases.

You can, with the experience of deciding these cases, become a good arbitrator!

QUESTIONS

1. As arbitrator, what would be your award and opinion?
2. Identify the key, relevant section(s), phrases, or words of the collective bargaining agreement (CBA), and explain why they were critical in making your decision.
3. What actions might the employer or the union have taken to avoid this conflict?

CHAPTER 2

Private Sector Labor Relations: History and Law

Katherine Heigl, star of Grey's Anatomy, walked the picket line in support of striking writers in 2009. The Screen Actors Guild sought to avoid another industry strike in 2009 and was able to negotiate a new contract without a strike. *Source:* Getty Images.

Chapter Outline

. . . the labor movement did not diminish the strength of the nation but enlarged it. By raising the living standard of millions, labor . . . lifted the whole nation.

MARTIN LUTHER KING, JR. (AMERICAN CIVIL RIGHTS LEADER)

LABOR NEWS

Hollywood Writers Guild Strike

Technology was the key issue that ignited the unprecedented 2007–2008 strike by the Writers Guild of America that represents 12,000 screenwriters. The strike was against the Association of Motion Picture and Television Producers that include the major entertainment companies: CBS Corp., Walt Disney Co., NBC Universal, News Corporation, Time Warner (CW), and Viacom (Paramount Pictures). The strike focused on writers' future residuals on downloaded and online streaming and other new technology formats that simply did not exist only a few years ago when the last contract was signed. Thus the old contract didn't provide the writers royalties from the new formats. The writers demanded 2.5 percent of revenues from original or recycled online work. The strike cost to the Los Angeles economy alone was $1.4 billion and possible long-term loss of market share. For example, in 1988, when the last strike took place, ratings of the three major networks fell by 4.6 percent. The TV industry lost over $500 million in commercial revenues during the 2008 strike.

The strike produced a quandary for actors and actresses who were members of the Screen Actors Guild (SAG) union and sympathetic to the writers but, like the owners, were economically affected by the action because many shows, including late-night talk shows, *Desperate Housewives*, and *Grey's Anatomy* among others, halted production. Some shows, including reality shows such as *American Idol*, were able to air as usual because they don't rely on unionized writers. Some top Hollywood names, including *Grey's Anatomy* actress Katherine Heigl and Tina Fey of *30 Rock*, walked the picket lines in support of the writers. Heigl even carried a banner that read "Nick Counter Is a Weiner," a reference to the president of the producers' association.

Writers Guild president David Young believes that writers' strength, like other unions, is their ability to stay united and was the key to negotiating a more favorable new contract that gave writers a share of Internet revenues. Patrick Verrone, president of the West Coast branch of the Guild, said, "This is the best deal the Guild has bargained for in 30 years." The turning point in negotiations came when actors refused to cross the picket lines at the Golden Globe Awards, which showed solidarity with the writers, and then a similar action by the actors threatened the Academy Awards program.

In 2009 members of the Screen Actors Guild (SAG), which represents over 120,000 artists, wanted to avoid another disruptive industry strike. When negotiations stalled, actors Tom Hanks and George Clooney actively led a new effort in the contract talks between SAG and studio executives. They were able to convince SAG members to approve a new contract by an impressive 78–22 percent vote that provided for 3 percent wage increases and a first-time provision for residuals to be paid for free streaming shows.

Source: Adapted from Lynn Elber, "Writers Strike May End," The Associated Press, *National Examiner* (February 11, 2008), p. A1; Nick Timiraus, "Striking Out: Are the Oscars Next?" *Wall Street Journal* (January 12–13, 2008), p. A7; Merissa Marr, "Cracks in Producers' United Front," *Wall Street Journal* (December 5, 2007), p. B1; and Richard Verrier, "SAG Members Finally Approves Contract," *The Los Angeles Times* (June 9, 2009), p. A1.

Every day in millions of workplaces throughout the United States, employers and employees interact in what is referred to as *labor–management relations*. For some, in addition, their working relationship has been structured around a process known as labor relations and collective bargaining. This process has existed in the United States for more than 220 years. It began in 1792 when the Philadelphia Cordwainers (shoemakers) formed a local trade union to bargain for higher wages. The history of the labor movement in the United States is the story of people who sought to find balance between the interests of employers and the interests of employees. Early struggles were often violent and threatened a nation on its rise to become an industrial giant and resulted in excesses on both sides. In this chapter we explore the historical events that over the past 220-plus years formed modern U.S. labor relations. Our labor relations and collective bargaining as it exists today was formed largely by federal statutes enacted during and since the 1930s, and court decisions interpreting those statutes. This legal framework for labor–management relations in the private sector of the U.S. economy (for-profit businesses) was greatly affected by and can best be understood when viewed within its historical context presented in this chapter. In government workplaces, however, labor relations practices developed 30 years later than in the private sector, largely because of the success of labor unions in improving the life of their members and a historic decision by President John F. Kennedy. The history of public sector labor relations is discussed in Chapter 3.

THE ROOTS OF THE AMERICAN LABOR MOVEMENT

Pre-Revolutionary America was overwhelmingly rural, with nearly 90 percent of the population living in the countryside.[1] A majority of the population earned their living as farm owners, tenants, or hired hands. Supporting these agricultural workers, however, was a workforce of craftspeople and unskilled laborers. Craftspeople included carpenters and masons, shipwrights and sailmakers, tanners, weavers, shoemakers, tailors, smiths, barrel makers, glassmakers, and printers. These artisans at first plied their trades independently, but as demand increased, a master worker would set up a small retail shop and employ journeymen and apprentices in America's original workplace. Prior to permanent trade unions, these workers joined together in combinations of master workers to maintain monopolies.

The original craftspeople came from free laborers, those immigrants who paid their way to the New World and established homes and families and passed on their trade to their children. The increased need for such skilled workers, however, led to the London Company's recruitment of indentured servants for colonial America. Many of these indentured servants were eager to leave England and northern Europe because of the homelessness and unemployment caused by their declining economy. Convicts willing to migrate as an alternative to English prisons also joined the indentured servant pool. Many of these laborers supplemented the craftsmen's workers and learned, by the end of their indentured period, a marketable skill.

Indentured servants, as well as slaves brought from Africa, also supplied the unskilled workforce necessary for farming, the expansion of the colonies into the wilderness, and the distribution of goods. The craftspeople of colonial America supplied some familiar names in the American Revolution: Benjamin Franklin (printer and inventor), Paul Revere (silversmith), and George Washington (surveyor).

After the American Revolution, craftspeople also supplied the first **labor unions** in America. The Federal Society of Journeymen Cordwainers (shoemakers) formed in 1792, the Journeymen Printers in New York (1794), and the New York Cabinetmakers (1796) are prime examples. These "trade societies," as the craftsmen's unions were called, grew of necessity as the volume of goods produced caused a clear separation between worker and employer. Thus, the employers and workers began their struggle for control over the bottom line. The availability of competing craftspeople meant that consumers would no longer pay any price for the crafted goods.

LABOR UNIONS

An organization of workers dedicated to protecting their interests in the workplace and improving wages, hours, and working conditions.

To increase profits, the employer needed to decrease cost, and to do that, the employer needed to decrease wages. The organization of skilled craftspeople allowed wage security for the artisans. When all available shoemakers committed to work only for the wage they believed fair, the solidarity of the worker, so necessary for success, was born. As the employer moved away from hands-on involvement with the making of the product, the merchant–capitalist emerged. That merchant–capitalist expanded the manufacturing of handicrafts.

These expanded workplaces were the first sites for American unions and consisted primarily of craftspeople that were white men. In the early 1800s, slavery still found African Americans in servitude, primarily on plantations in the South. Women worked primarily in the home—their own or someone else's. Even though the demographics of the American workforce for the past two centuries have undergone great transition, the profile of American unions has stayed amazingly homogeneous. As the number of workplaces for skilled laborers increased, so did the need for organizing those workers. During the 1830s, the American factory system was emerging, and the struggle between employer and employee intensified. Factories substituted mechanical power and machinery for muscle power and skills. Industrialization necessitated large capital outlays and a concentration of labor. Mass production for national and even international markets began to develop. By the time the Civil War erupted, the textile, boot and shoe, and iron industries were ready to take the final step to a modern mechanized operation.

In the Northeast, textile mills opened, and in contrast to skilled labor operation, unskilled laborers peopled an American factory in significant numbers. The workers chosen for these factories were often young women recruited from the neighboring rural areas. In the 1840s, these young women found a relatively safe and promising environment in textile mills such as those in Lowell, Massachusetts, and Pawtucket, Rhode Island. Originally, these young women came from the rural New England countryside to work to save enough money for a marriage dowry, to move west, or to preserve the family farm. The work was hard and consumed their days with 11- to 13-hour schedules. But the time of their lives devoted to this work could be measured in months, not years. The 1850s, though, saw an influx of women immigrants from Ireland and Germany who took these hard low-paying jobs with little, if any, chance to move on to something better.[2]

The impact of this influx of immigrant labor on American workers between 1846 and the Civil War was not limited to young women in New England. Almost 3 million immigrants entered the country between 1846 and 1855, providing an abundant supply of both skilled and unskilled labor. Workers who had previously protected their wages by agreement not to work for less than their fellow workers were faced with competition from immigrants willing to work for much less. As skilled trades became mechanized, the availability of cheap labor to run that machinery greatly reduced wage rates.

This influx of millions of immigrants over a 100 years ago may be equaled in America today and in the near future. After an initial resistance to these intruders, American labor formed a partnership with some of those immigrant groups.[3] The challenge to today's labor movement may be to repeat that alliance.

After the Civil War, there was another influx of immigrants to the United States. Nearly 5 million immigrants arrived in the last decade of the nineteenth century. These immigrants arriving on the East Coast were, by and large, from southeastern Europe—Italians, Poles, Czechs, Slovaks, Hungarians, Greeks, and Russians. On the West Coast, immigrants from China were welcomed to help build the Transamerican Railroad. During this period the United States grew rapidly, primarily as a result of the creation of national corporations, such as E. H. Harriman's railroads, Andrew Carnegie's steel mills, and John D. Rockefeller's oil refineries.

The monopolistic practices of the employer encouraged the employees to unionize.[4] The need for the joint action of laborers in this newly mechanized environment was expressed by Jonathan C. Fincher, an organizer of a union for machinists and blacksmiths:

> In the early days of mechanism in this country but few shops employed many men. Generally the employer was head man; he knew his men personally. . . . If aught went astray, there was no circumlocution office to go through to have an understanding about it. But as the business came to be more fully developed, it was found that more capital must be employed and the authority and supervision of the owner or owners must be delegated to superintendents and under foremen. In this manner men and masters became estranged and the gulf could only be bridged by a strike, when, perhaps, the representatives of the working men might be admitted to the office and allowed to state their case. It was to resist this combination of capital, which had so changed the character of the employers that led to the formation of the union.[5]

GROWTH OF NATIONAL UNIONS

Unions, People, Incidents

TRADE UNIONISTS

Like-skilled workers, such as printers, shoemakers, tailors, and bakers, who organized the earliest unions in the United States.

It was at this point that the unionization of workers left its infancy of informal local communities of like-skilled laborers and tried to find its place in the changing American economy. The idealism of those leaders credited with creating the American labor movement can be seen in the original national unions. For years, **trade unionists** had tried to develop a national trade union.

In 1866, seventy-seven delegates from various local organizations attended the first National Labor Congress held in Baltimore, Maryland. The Congress resulted in the formation of the **National Labor Union**, which allowed membership for skilled and unskilled workers alike. The National Labor Union saw itself as a political force nationwide and advocated the creation of local unions of workers.

NATIONAL LABOR UNION

Founded in 1866, this was the first union to allow skilled and unskilled workers to join in one union. It pursued a political as well as a workplace agenda.

Active at a time when reformists such as Elizabeth Cady Stanton and Susan B. Anthony advocated women's suffrage, a Farmers' Alliance sought government support for farmers' produce, and religious organizations worked in tenements to save lives as well as souls, the National Labor Union advocated reforms to help the workers. It demanded adoption of laws establishing an eight-hour workday and sought restrictions on immigration and the abolition of convict labor. It was the first to ask for the creation of a Department of Labor at the national level. It initially supported women's unions, and it recognized the need to organize African Americans, although it did not invite them to join the National Labor Union. As the suffragettes' cause gained ground, the willingness to accept women's trade unions in the National Labor Union diminished. And by 1872, most of the women's labor organizations disappeared. The National Labor Union's reluctance to admit African Americans to full membership led to the creation of the National Colored Labor Union (NCLU). The NCLU hoped to affiliate with the National Labor Union but was refused in the 1870 Congress.[6]

As the National Labor Union's political agenda grew, its effectiveness as a "national union" diminished. When it finally converted to the National Labor Reform Party in 1872 and nominated a candidate for the presidency who withdrew from the election, the National Labor Union ended its days.

Although the National Labor Union could not boast of passing many of the reforms it advocated, it did spur the formation of numerous national trade unions, including spinners, shoemakers, railway conductors, locomotive firemen, and coal miners. When the depression of 1873 hit, these trade unions formed the core of two major national unions and nurtured two legendary labor leaders: Eugene Debs and Samuel Gompers. The depression of 1873 placed employees at the mercy of their employers and ushered in a violent period for the American labor movement. Following are some examples.

Molly Maguires

In January 1875, coal miners who were members of the Miners' and Laborers' Benevolent Association went on strike against the anthracite mine owners. Because of hunger, the miners went back to work in June 1875 and took a 20 percent pay cut. The Benevolent Association's leaders were forced to leave the area, and the local miners' unions essentially ceased to function.

After the strike there were a series of murders, assaults, robberies, and acts of arson around the minefields. Authorities blamed a legendary group of union organizers known as the **Molly Maguires** for the criminal acts. Twenty-four members of the Molly Maguires were brought to trial after the Philadelphia and Reading Railroad hired a Pinkerton private investigator to infiltrate the group. Ten were convicted and executed; the rest were sentenced to prison. The fairness of the trial was suspect, but the result was plain. The labor movement was portrayed as a violent and criminal movement.[7] Throughout this period, as seen in Profile 2-1, owners used hired detectives to challenge the labor movement.

MOLLY MAGUIRES

A group of union organizers who were prosecuted and either executed or imprisoned after an 1875 strike against anthracite mine owners failed.

Railway Strike of 1877

The treatment of workers by railroad companies is another good example from this period. Railroad companies had, through various capitalization schemes, produced large dividends for wealthy stockholders while consistently losing money. To compensate, the companies increased railway rates and reduced wages. The workers' discontent reached desperation after a 35 percent wage cut in three years; irregular employment; increases in railway, hotel, and transportation costs (the use of which was necessitated by work schedules); and a suppression of union activities.

RAILWAY STRIKE OF 1877

The bitter and violent strike involving railroad workers from Maryland to Missouri who protested 10 percent wage cuts after a 35 percent cut years earlier.

Profile 2-1

"Labor Spies"

The use of the Pinkerton Agency by employers to infiltrate labor unions in 1875 was just the beginning of more than 65 years of such activities in the United States. Robert Pinkerton, son of Allan Pinkerton, the agency's founder, realized the potential for industrial espionage work and began sending operatives to union meetings.

Between 1890 and 1910, business was so good that he established 15 new offices. The activities of the labor spies included gathering advance warning of strike plans, investigating labor incidents, listing union sympathizers for retaliation purposes, and sowing dissent and unrest within the union ranks.

The Pinkerton Agency was not alone in this type of work. Between the late 1890s and the early 1940s, various governmental or labor investigatory bodies had documented extensive spy activities. In 1912, the U.S. Commission on Industrial Relations reported approximately 275 detective agencies with active antiunion operatives. And in 1936, a congressional investigative committee headed by Senator Robert M. LaFollette, Jr., uncovered the following costs paid by employers for the detective agency's services:

- General Motors, January 1934–July 1936: $994,000
- Chrysler Motor Company, 1935: $72,000
- Remington Rand Corporation, 1936: $81,000

The committee also reported the income of various agencies:

- Burns Agency, 1934: $580,000
- Pinkerton, 1935: $2,300,000

The LaFollette committee documented the correlation between increased espionage activities and union membership drives. At the end of its investigation, the LaFollette committee proposed sweeping legislation to prohibit employers from using such tactics as violations of the Wagner Act. Although the legislation did not pass, the exposure of the detective agencies' tactics caused many employers to stop using them. Later the National Labor Relations Board cracked down on such tactics as unfair labor practices, and at least publicly, the use of espionage ceased.

Source: Adapted from Robert M. Smith, "Spies against Labor," *Labor's Heritage 5*, no. 2 (Summer 1993), pp. 65–77.

Employers in the late 1800s through the 1940s often hired the Pinkerton Agency or one of over 270 similar agencies. The Pinkerton agents served as spies on labor organization, armed guards, or strikebreakers. *Source:* © Dorling Kindersley, Courtesy of the H Keith Melton Collection.

In 1877, numerous eastern lines announced a new 10 percent cut in wages, and the workers in Maryland began a strike. The railway strike spread quickly and violently to West Virginia, Kentucky, Ohio, Pennsylvania, New York, and Missouri. State militia dispersed one gathering in Pittsburgh, killing 26 people. A militia was called out in Kentucky, and federal troops fought with workers in Maryland, Ohio, Illinois, and Missouri. The strike lasted less than 20 days, but more than 100 workers were killed and several hundred badly wounded.[8] For the first time in the history of the U.S. labor movement, a general strike swept the country, and federal troops were called out to suppress it.

The embryonic labor movement realized that the failure of the largely spontaneous strike stemmed from lack of organization. Propertied classes, terrified by the events of 1877, strengthened support of the state militia. The construction of armories in major East Coast cities coincides with this period.[9]

The Railway Strike of 1877 ignited a wave of work stoppages between 1880 and 1900. As America's labor force quickly became more centralized in big cities, it also became more organized—and the Railway Strike gave it a new weapon to achieve its goals. The U.S. Labor Bureau's first estimate of strikes and lockouts is for the period of 1880–1900, which was included in the 1900 census. The estimate was astounding—from the first strike in 1877, the total for the 20-year period was 117,000 strikes and other work stoppages at U.S. employers. One of the first methods employers sought in response to strikes was to purchase strike insurance. But only one insurer—Mutual Security Company of Waterbury, Connecticut—would write strike insurance, and it was expensive.[10]

The Haymarket Square Riot

The **Haymarket Square Riot** took place in Chicago in 1886. Laborers had called a general strike on May 1, 1886, to demand an eight-hour day. The May 1 day-long strike passed quietly, but a subsequent demonstration on May 3 at the McCormick Harvester plant in Chicago caused a confrontation with police and resulted in the deaths of four strikers. A peaceful meeting, held to protest the police shooting, ended when a bomb was thrown into a group of police, killing one policeman and injuring others. The police opened fire, and more strikers were killed or injured. Eight so-called anarchists, some of whom had not even been at the meeting, were tried and found guilty not because of complicity in throwing the bomb but because they held political beliefs that threatened accepted ideas.[11] One account describes the trial as follows:

HAYMARKET SQUARE RIOT

A meeting held in Chicago in 1886 to protest the police shooting of striking workers that ended with the bombing of police officers and the subsequent trial and conviction of eight defendants. The Knights of Labor did not participate, but because of their previous violence, they were associated with the riot and began to lose public support.

> Proceedings began before Judge Joseph E. Gary on June 21. The jury, consisting largely of businessmen and their clerks, was a packed one and the trial judge prejudiced. . . .
>
> These witnesses, all of them terrified and some of them paid, testified that the defendants were part of a conspiracy to overthrow the government of the United States by force and violence and that the Haymarket bomb and Degan's murder were the first blow in what was to have been a general assault on all established order. But their testimony was so filled with contradictions that the State was compelled to shift its ground in the midst of a trial. The core of the State's charges then became the allegation that the unknown person who had thrown the bomb was inspired to do so by the words and ideas of the defendants . . .
>
> The press was there, of course, in all its glory, from every great city of the country. Thousands of words were printed daily in all parts of the country. From these dispatches we learn of the graceful, laughing society people beside Judge Gary on the bench, learn of the wives of the defendants, pale and haggard, their restless, bewildered children clinging to them, as they crowded together in the front row. We are informed that the courtroom was hot and suffocating, that the people packed together had scarcely room enough to wave the fans with which they had supplied themselves, and that the length of trial, dragging on week after week, reflected the justice of American jurisprudence wherein even the guilty get all the impressive forms of the law before hanging. . . .
>
> The verdict was almost a formality, and the trial's big day arrived when the condemned men arose in court to accuse the accuser, to say why a death sentence should not be passed upon them by Gary, and why it was not they but society that was guilty. They dominated the courtroom and they dominated the country that day. No newspaper was so conservative that it did not admit that the defendants in defying death and in defending the working class were both dignified and impressive.[12]

Four of the eight defendants were executed, one committed suicide, and the remaining three were sent to prison.[13]

Knights of Labor

KNIGHTS OF LABOR

An organization open to skilled and unskilled laborers, formed in 1869 as The Noble Order of the Knights of Labor (KOL). It sought economic and social reform through political action rather than strikes.

Although the **Knights of Labor** (KOL) was formed in 1869, the KOL grew to prominence between the Railway Strike of 1877 and the Haymarket Square Riot of 1886. Once seen as the future of the American labor movement, it sought to promote a national union embracing both skilled and unskilled workers in a single labor organization. It recognized that industrial workers, the so-called unskilled workers, would soon outnumber trade unionists. The KOL was begun by trade unionists, who had decided it was safer to keep its membership secret. Members were less likely to be blackballed by antiunion employers. The secrecy of the organization both limited its growth and brought it under suspicion. When it was forced to go public in 1881, it benefited from a rash of labor victories brought about by strikes against the Union Pacific Railroad, the Southwest System Railroads, and the Wabash Railroad. The latter resulted in face-to-face negotiations between powerful financier Jay Gould and the KOL—the first instance of bargaining with a specific employer by a nationwide labor organization.

The success of the KOL led to a huge influx of members—so many that the president, Terence V. Powderly, felt overwhelmed.[14] Unfortunately, the KOL began experiencing a number of defeats in 1886, when some 100,000 workers were involved in unsuccessful strikes and lockouts attributed to their organization. The KOL was also blamed for the Haymarket Square Riot, which contributed to its continuing decline. And finally, although the KOL had advocated an eight-hour workday, its leadership refused to support the May 1, 1886, general strike of some 170,000 workers that was called to pressure employers to institute it. Membership in KOL dropped dramatically when trade unionists turned elsewhere for a national union, and industrial workers simply disbanded the locals they had formed. As support for the KOL declined, a coalition of over 100 skilled trade unions formed the Federation of Organized Trade and Labor in 1881 and rejected the Knights' philosophy of one big union and social reform and focused instead on economic issues. The new federation, however, was short-lived and in 1886 became the American Federation of Labor (AFL).[15]

Homestead, Pennsylvania, 1892

HOMESTEAD, PENNSYLVANIA

An 1892 strike at a steel plant owned by Andrew Carnegie. The plant operator responded with paid police and strikebreakers. The strike ended when martial law was declared and the state militia was sent in by the governor.

PINKERTON AGENCY

A detective agency used by various employers and the government in the late 1800s to infiltrate and spy on unions.

The Amalgamated Association of Iron and Steel Workers and the Carnegie Steel Company's plant in **Homestead, Pennsylvania**, had enjoyed a relatively friendly relationship while under a three-year agreement that expired in 1892. Andrew Carnegie, although professing satisfaction with the relationship between his plant and the union, turned negotiations over to the local plant manager, Henry Clay Frick. Frick's preparation for negotiations included arranging for both strikebreakers and more than 300 armed guards. With a declared goal of breaking the union, Frick locked the workers out when they refused the wage cuts proposed at the bargaining table and then brought in the armed **Pinkerton Agency** guards.

The guards and the workers engaged in a gun battle resulting in three dead Pinkerton guards and seven casualties on the workers' side. After an uneasy cease-fire, the governor of Pennsylvania sent 8,000 state militiamen to Homestead and established martial law. The plant reopened under militia protection with strikebreakers replacing the union workers. The union organizers were prosecuted for rioting and murder. The Carnegie Steel Company had successfully crushed the steel workers union not only at this plant but also in other Pennsylvania mills. In Profile 2-2, the spirit of the labor movement in Homestead is remembered.

Pullman Strike, 1894

Interest was again focused on the railroads when workers in Illinois went on strike in 1894. These workers lived in Pullman's town, where wages were low and rents high. A group of employees who made the Pullman cars demanded wages be restored to previous levels and rents be lowered. When the demands were refused, these workers struck. In sympathy, another group of workers refused to switch Pullman cars. When switchers were fired, even more classifications of railway workers went on strike. This new solidarity among railway workers was the result of

Profile 2-2

The First Labor Day: *"Old Beeswax"* Taylor *(1819–1892)*

Thomas W. Taylor, nicknamed Old Beeswax, was a colorful leader of the U.S. labor movement at the height of the power of the Knights of Labor. He was also a founding member of the American Federation of Labor (AFL). In 1892, he was serving as mayor of Homestead, Pennsylvania, one of the nation's preeminent labor towns.

In June 1882, ten years before the Homestead lockout, the Amalgamated Association of Iron and Steel Workers and the Knights of Labor had organized a peaceful "Grand Labor Demonstration" in which 30,000 workers marched and a crowd of 100,000 attended. Old Beeswax rode at the head of the parade. The demonstration, which some call the first Labor Day in the United States, was held to rally support for ironworkers who had recently won a bitter strike with the local mine owners.

Old Beeswax, with many of his contemporaries, believed that the struggle undertaken by labor was one of freedom—a freedom from slavery imposed by the owners. The rally song penned by Old Beeswax and sung on that first Labor Day captured the spirit of the cause.

Source: Adapted from Paul Krause, "The Life and Times of 'Beeswax' Taylor," in *Labor History 33*, no. 1 (New York: Taiment Institute, New York University, 1992), pp. 32–54.

the establishment of the **American Railway Union** in 1893 by Eugene V. Debs. His was a new kind of industrial union that placed all workers into one organization, instead of dividing them into hostile craft unions, fulfilling the goal of KOL.

The **Pullman strike** was peaceful and well organized under Debs's leadership. It shut down Illinois Central along with the Southern Pacific and Northern Pacific railroads. The boycott spread from Illinois to Colorado.

With the help of the federal government, railroad owners added mail cars to all trains. The strikers were then charged with interfering with mail delivery. Federal troops were brought in to break the strike. Although violence ensued, the strike continued. The court ordered the strikers back to work by applying the Sherman Antitrust Act.[16] This 1890 act declared that contracts, combinations, and conspiracies formed in restraint of trade and commerce were illegal. Theoretically directed at business, the court's injunction caused much controversy when applied to labor unions. Yet, along with contempt-of-court sentences and fines, the injunction finally broke the Pullman strike. Debs was sentenced to six months in prison for contempt of court as a result of his participation.

AMERICAN RAILWAY UNION (ARU)

An industrial union of railway workers founded by Eugene Debs in 1843. It was one of the first unions organized on an industry rather than a craft basis.

PULLMAN STRIKE

The strike in 1894 by Pullman Car Company employees who were demanding higher wages and lower rents. The strike was honored by other groups of railroad workers, who shut down railroads from Illinois to Colorado until the strike was broken by a federal court injunction and the use of federal troops.

Eugene Debs led the Pullman strike of 1893 which utilized a new type of union—industrial union—which organized all the workers under one labor union, rather than several unions organized by craft or trade. *Source:* Getty Images.

Eugene Debs

EUGENE VICTOR DEBS

(1855–1926) An American union leader, one of the founding members of the Industrial Workers of the World (IWW), and several times the candidate of the Social Democratic Party for President of the United States. Debs led the American Railway Union in the Pullman Strike. After the strike was broke, Debs and other union officials were sentenced to a year in jail for having violated injunction against the strike.

Eugene Debs was the son of an immigrant. He left school when he was 14 years old and became a railroad shop worker for 50 cents a day. At age 16 he joined the Brotherhood of Locomotive Firemen and began his work as a union organizer. Although he served as both a city and state elected official, his devotion was to the labor movement. In 1893 he broke away from the Brotherhood and formed the American Railway Union. Frustrated by the inability of the numerous railroad craft unions to maintain solidarity during a strike, Debs hoped this union of employees across craft lines would prove able to sustain a job action. The resulting success and then failure of the Pullman strike was a watershed for both Debs and the labor movement. The labor movement realized that government involvement in support of employers was their nemesis. At that point the focus of national unions turned to creating a different government agenda.

The six months in prison radicalized Debs. There he read Marx's *Das Kapital* and came to believe that the labor struggle in the United States represented a struggle between the classes. "The issue is Socialism versus Capitalism. I am for Socialism because I am for humanity."[17]

When Debs started out as a labor organizer, he decried strikes and violence. But years of strikebreaking by Pinkerton agents and rival unions and the futility of intraunion struggles led to a change of heart. He is quoted as saying, "The strike is the weapon of the oppressed, of men capable of appreciating justice and having the courage to resist wrong and contend for principle."[18]

For the next 30 years, Debs led the democratic socialist movement among the workers of America. He espoused industrial unionism in the economic realm and socialism in the political realm to protect workers from the unbridled capitalism facing the United States in the last decade of the century. As the Socialist Party of America's presidential candidate in 1900, 1904, 1908, 1912, and 1920, he waged a campaign for such so-called radical ideas as the abolition of child labor, the right of women to vote, a graduated income tax, the direct election of U.S. senators, an unemployment compensation law, a national Department of Education, and pensions for men and women.

Debs's objection to U.S. entry into World War I was stated frequently in speeches around the nation. In Canton, Ohio, in 1918, his speech pointed out that the burden placed on the workers during a war far exceeded that placed on the business owners. The federal government indicted Debs for that speech under the Espionage Act and convicted him. Debs was again incarcerated and, in fact, he was in jail during the 1920 presidential election, in which he received a million votes. Although Debs continued to espouse democratic socialism until his death in 1926, he rejected the Communist Party, which had come into power in 1917 in Russia after overthrowing the czar.[19]

Eugene Debs led the historic Pullman Strike in 1914 and was later a five time Socialist Party candidate for president of the United States. *Source:* © Stapleton Historical Collection / HIP / The Image Works.

American Federation of Labor

The **American Federation of Labor** (AFL) was formed in 1886 under the leadership of Samuel Gompers. Its sole policy was to improve the position of skilled labor. The AFL's program included standard hours and wages, fair working conditions, collective bargaining, and the accumulation of funds for union emergencies. More important, the AFL introduced the concept of business unionism to union management and leadership. A decentralization of authority allowed trade autonomy for national unions, enabling them to make decisions for themselves. A particular craft or trade union had exclusive jurisdiction to ensure protection from competition. The AFL rejected formation of a political labor party, preferring to work as a voting bloc within existing parties. At one of its initial meetings, the AFL prepared the following declaration of principles that embodied the spirit of the national labor movement:

AMERICAN FEDERATION OF LABOR (AFL)
A federation of unions made up of skilled workers formed in 1886 by Samuel Gompers. The AFL offered trade unions local autonomy because the national union operated as a decentralized organization. Eventually the AFL merged with the CIO.

> Whereas, a Struggle is going on in the nations of the civilized world, between the oppressors and the oppressed of all countries, a struggle between capital and labor which must grow in intensity from year to year and work disastrous results to the toiling millions of all nations, if not combined for mutual protection and benefits. The history of the wageworkers of all countries is but the history of constant struggle and misery, engendered by ignorance and disunion, whereas the history of the non-producers of all countries proves that a minority thoroughly organized may work wonders for good or evil. It behooves the representatives of the workers of North America in congress assembled, to adopt such measures and disseminate such principles among the people of our country as will unite them for all time to come, to secure the recognition of the rights to which they are justly entitled. Conforming to the old adage, "In union there is strength," a formation embracing every trade and labor organization in North America, a union founded upon the basis as broad as the land we live in, is our only hope. The past history of trade unions proves that small organizations, well conducted, have accomplished great good, but their efforts have not been of that lasting character which a thorough unification of all the different branches of industrial workers is bound to secure.[20]

It was perhaps ironic that the unification of workers during the Haymarket Square Riot caused the AFL to monopolize the labor scene, overshadowing its predecessors. Although the KOL had participated in neither the general strike nor the Haymarket Square incident, their notoriety for other successful strikes led to the assumption that they had engineered the Haymarket upheaval. The public began to associate the KOL with violence and anarchy. Such criticism caused the KOL to lose support. The AFL began to dominate the labor movement.[21]

With the AFL in a dominant position, labor's goals jelled. Leaders kept labor's ultimate goal—participation in the decision-making process—in sight. This goal meant collective bargaining and an arbitration system to resolve disputes with individual employers. On a national level, labor sought legislative actions to gain an eight-hour day, to prohibit child labor, and to provide for workers' compensation in case of injury on the job. Thus, the American labor movement was largely based on two competing ideas. One was community: People with common interests can best collectively work to solve their problems—that is, there is strength in numbers. The second idea was individualism: People can become successful through their own hard work and ingenuity. The founders of the AFL were distrustful of the KOL's belief that only the elimination of the wage system could guarantee individual respect within one collectively active political community. The AFL founders believed instead that individual respect and dignity could be achieved through economic rewards for work and that a better life could be achieved through a new class of skilled workers. Thus, through collective action, individuals could achieve better individual rewards, such as higher pay, better hours, and better working conditions. The KOL was pursuing political equality, not individual equality, through collective action.[22]

Samuel Gompers, founder and president of the American Federation of Labor. *Source:* AP Images.

Samuel Gompers

Samuel Gompers, at age 13, emigrated with his family from England in 1863. His father was a cigarmaker, and Samuel joined his first cigarmakers' union in 1864. Steeped in British trade unionism, Gompers saw the burgeoning labor movement in the United States go from an idealist, reformist cause to a daily bread-and-butter struggle for an improved workplace. It was this focus he brought to the AFL that caused it to survive when the KOL and the Socialist Labor Party lost ground. Gompers, with two other labor leaders, began the AFL after reorganizing the Cigarmakers International Union in 1875. This reorganized union charged initiation fees and dues to fund sick and death benefits for its members, thus ensuring a stable membership base. Members of the trade locals wanted to copy the revitalization of the Cigarmakers Union, and Gompers supplied the model.

In 1881, the same year the KOL decided to go public with its organization, a meeting of labor leaders from national and international trade unions and the KOL was held in Pittsburgh. Originally, and against Gompers's wishes, the vision for an alliance of unions as a result of this meeting was to include both trade and industrial unions. The resulting Federation of Organized Trades and Labor Unions embraced the idea of the solidarity of all workers and the single-mindedness of the trade unionist who chose a workplace agenda as opposed to a societal overhaul agenda. Although the federation did not survive five years, it was a transition from the KOL's organization to the new unionism espoused by Gompers.

SAMUEL GOMPERS

(1850–1924) British-born U.S. labor leader, founder, and first president of the American Federation of Labor (AFL). He was a union organizer known for his opposition to radicalism and political involvement. Believed that unions should focus on economic goals, bringing about change through strikes and boycotts.

Gompers's AFL placed the major emphasis on economic or industrial action as opposed to political action. Although the member trade unions retained their autonomy, the unity of labor was promoted through education and through support of striking locals. Gompers is credited with practically forming the federation by himself. He worked tirelessly, traveled extensively, and devoted his entire life to it for 38 years until his death.

Bunker Hill & Sullivan Mining Incident, Coeur d'Alene, Idaho

COEUR D'ARLENE MINING INCIDENT

In 1899 the WFM demanded that Bunker Hill & Sullivan Mining, the last holdout that employed nonunion workers, recognize the WFM to represent its miners. The owners refused by firing all WFM miners at other mines. The WFM then responded by dynamiting the mine. Martial law was declared, and federal troops restored order. The miners were rounded up into barracks that were surrounded by barbed wire.

In contrast to the demise of the trade unionists in the steel mills of Pennsylvania after Homestead, a similar confrontation led to a strengthening of union organizations in the mining country of the West. In 1892, miners in the Coeur d'Alene area of Idaho were locked out when they refused significant wage reductions. The mine owners brought in strikebreakers and armed guards who were confronted and driven out by the miners. Armed federal troops were called in, and they restored order, reopened the mines with strikebreakers, and arrested the union men. The reaction from union members was to form the Western Federation of Miners (WFM) and begin a series of strikes: Cripple Creek, Colorado, 1894; Leadville, Colorado, 1896; Coeur d'Alene, Idaho, 1899; and Telluride, Colorado, 1901. Each strike involved a determined reaction from mine owners, who employed strikebreakers and armed guards and finally the state militia, when necessary, to squelch the strike. The union members were arrested and blacklisted. Nevertheless, the WFM continued to grow.

The **Coeur d'Alene incident** is of particular interest because the unprecedented acts there came to occupy an important and unique role in the history of the American labor movement. In 1885, Noah S. Kellogg, looking for gold in the South Fork of the Coeur d'Alene River,

Bill Haywood - Charles Moyer - George Pettibone outside Boise, Idaho Sherrif's office awaiting trial for murder of ex-governor Frank Steunenberg. *Source:* Library of Congress.

discovered lead ore in what became known as the Bunker Hill lode in Milo Gulch. In 1898, the Bunker Hill & Sullivan Mining and Concentrating Company purchased interest in a manufacturing plant and expanded it into a facility for smelting ores. Almost immediately, trouble with the Western Federation of Miners began—and continued for 12 years. The conflict peaked in 1899 when the WFM demanded that Bunker Hill & Sullivan Mining, the last holdout that employed nonunion workers, recognize the WFM to represent its miners. The owners refused by firing all WFM miners at other mines. The WFM then responded by dynamiting the mine, the largest in the world. Governor Frank Steinenberg, once a friend of the union, declared martial law and asked President McKinley to send in federal troops from Montana to restore order. The miners were rounded up into barracks that were surrounded by barbed wire—an area referred to as the **bull pen**—a term later used in baseball to refer to the enclosed area for relief pitchers. The miners never forgave Governor Steinenberg, who constantly received threatening letters. Then in 1905, as he opened the garden gate at his home, a bomb exploded. As he lay dying in his home, he told family members that the miners finally got him. Three WFM leaders were arrested for the murder.[23]

Industrial Workers of the World

What emerged from the meeting in 1905 was the Industrial Workers of the World (IWW). Forming the nucleus of the IWW, the WFM joined with 42 other labor organizations with an aim of uniting all skilled and unskilled workers into one great industrial union of the workforce. Like the National Labor Union, the KOL, and the Socialist Labor Party, the IWW embraced both a workplace agenda—to organize all labor into industrial unions—and a political agenda—to overthrow capitalism for a cooperative society. The IWW's members, who were commonly called **Wobblies**, organized industrial workers in a Lawrence, Massachusetts, textile mill and led a long and bitter strike there in 1912. The Wobblies, however, suffered the same fate as its predecessors, who had dual agendas, when its membership went from at least 30,000 at the time of the Lawrence strike to 10,000 in 1930 to less than 1,000 in the mid-1990s.[24] The tragic turn of many labor struggles can be seen in the life of Fannie Sellins (Profile 2-3).

WOBBLIES

Nickname for members of the Industrial Workers of the World (IWW) organization. Founded in 1905, the IWW hoped to organize all the workers of the world into one union. Its political agenda included the overthrow of capitalism.

Profile 2-3

Fannie Sellins (1870–1919): Labor's Martyr

The story of Fannie Sellins's life is not so different from that of other workers in her time. Sellins was of Irish descent; she lived and worked as a dressmaker in St. Louis at the turn of the century. As recorded in the 1910 census, she was a widow, with three children at home and one already living away from home. She was a union member; in fact, she served as president of the St. Louis Local 67 of the United Garment Workers of America (UGWA). She came to national prominence as a result of a lockout of the members of the UGWA locals by the firm of Marx & Hoas in 1909. Sellins traveled to Chicago to solicit support for the striking union members. Her eloquent and inspirational pleas gained assistance from the Women's Trade Union League, Jane Addams of Hull House, and the United Brotherhood of Carpenters. The striking union was able to stand its ground during the lockout, and in 1911, agreement was reached with the company on union recognition.

A 1919 strike of Allegheny Coal & Coke Company miners brought Sellins to the Alle-Kiski region of Pennsylvania. Deputies hired by the coal mine owners to protect company property engaged in a number of confrontations with the striking workers. Sellins witnessed an assault by a deputy of a mine worker and took pictures of it. A melee ensued when Sellins attempted to leave the area with the pictures to have the deputy arrested. An investigation of the incident found that Sellins was shot in the back and killed while trying to get away from the deputies. The story the deputies told was that Sellins was shot while attacking the deputies.

Fannie Sellins became a martyr of the labor movement. Pictures of her lifeless body were used as propaganda material in coalfields and steel mills from Gary, Indiana, to West Virginia. She was buried in Union Cemetery, Pennsylvania.

Source: Adapted from John Cassedy, "A Bond of Sympathy," *Labor's Heritage 4,* no. 4 (Winter 1992), pp. 34–47.

From the turn of the century to the end of World War I, the labor movement struggled through any number of victories and defeats: strikes that broke unions and strikes that solidified union membership, political victories for its reform agenda and a significant split with other reform movements, and court injunctions and the passage of protective laws. By the end of the war, the IWW was no longer a major labor association, but its stated objective—to organize industrial workers—resulted in the creation of major national industrial unions, such as the United Mine Workers, the Ladies Garment Workers, and the Amalgamated Clothing Workers.[25] The IWW, however, still operates today, and has organized campaigns against Starbuck's, the coffee giant, and in 2010 The Jimmy John's Worker's Union, an IWW affiliate, filed an election petition with the NLRB. It was the first fast-food union in the United States.

Women's Trade Union League

WOMEN'S TRADE UNION LEAGUE

The original name of the National Woman's Trade Union League, this union was begun between 1903 and World War I by middle-class reformers and working-class women to support unionization of women workers.

The first national association dedicated to organizing women, the **Women's Trade Union League** (WTUL), emerged after a 1903 meeting of the AFL at which some women labor leaders believed the AFL did not intend to involve women fully within its ranks. Samuel Gompers shared society's belief that a woman's place was in the home. He stated, "It is wrong to permit any of the female sex of our country to be forced to work, as we believe that men should be provided with a fair wage in order to keep his female relatives from going to work."[26] The WTUL was a community-based network formed through an alliance between elite and working-class women to investigate women's working conditions and promote the creation of women's trade unions. Mary Kenney O'Sullivan, an organizer for the AFL; Mary McDowell, founder of a Chicago settlement house; Lillian Wald, founder of the Visiting Nurse Service; and Jane Addams, founder of Hull House, among others, founded the League as a way of uniting women from all classes to work for better working and living conditions. The WTUL advocated for an eight-hour workday, a minimum wage, and the abolition of child labor.

Ludlow, Colorado, Massacre, 1914

April 20, 1914, has been called "a day that will live in infamy" in the history of the American labor movement. Coal miners in Colorado and other western states had been trying to join the

"A day that will live in infamy"; April 20, 1914 when 20 men, women and their children were massacred. The Ludlow Monument lists the names of the victims, and was designated a National Historic Landmark in 2009. *Source:* © David Muenker/Alamy.

United Mine Workers of America. The coal operators, however, had strongly opposed their joining the UMWA. In April 1914 in Ludlow, Colorado, the miners went on strike, and the coal operators evicted them and their families from their company-owned houses. The miners, in response, quickly erected a tent colony on public property. The coal operators called in the Colorado militia, and together with an army of thugs hired as strikebreakers, they staged a well-planned attack. At 10 A.M. on April 14, 1914, without warning, they surrounded the tents and massacred 20 men, women, and small children in the tent colony. Many others were seriously injured. Kerosene was poured over the tents, which were set on fire. Some died from randomly fired gunshots; others were found burned to death in their tents. The gunshots were from machine guns mounted on an armored car, called the "Death Special." The exact date of April 14 was chosen because the miners had planned a celebration—it was Greek Easter. Many of the miners who survived were blacklisted by the coal operators and never worked in the coal industry again. Not one of the militia or hired thugs was ever prosecuted.[27] The Ludlow Tent Colony site was dedicated a national historic landmark in 2009.

John L. Lewis

The 1920s were seen as a crisis period for the labor movement. The postwar prosperity, coupled with completing their economic shift to mass production, left U.S. bureaucratic firms in a dominant position. Workplaces with large craft unions became overshadowed by workplaces with

JOHN LLEWELLYN LEWIS

(1880–1969) An American leader of organized labor who served as president of the United Mine Workers of America from 1920 to 1960. He was a major player in the history of coal mining. He was the driving force behind the founding of the Congress of Industrial Organizations and helped organize millions of other industrial workers in the 1930s. After resigning as head of the CIO in 1941, he took the Mine Workers out of the CIO in 1942, then back into the American Federation of Labor.

unskilled and unorganized industrial workers. The inability of the AFL to change and organize the industrial worker doomed it to lose membership during this decade.

The antiunion position of many employers also crippled attempts of national industrial unions to increase their membership. The United Mine Workers was one such industrial union. Emerging from its leadership in 1924 was John L. Lewis, the next giant in the history of the American labor movement. Lewis was a great labor leader who inspired millions to join America's new industrial unions. However, in the 1920s, some labor leaders viewed Lewis as a ruthless autocrat who was as intent on stifling rank-and-file union members who dared to challenge him as he was intent on defeating the coal companies. In 1926, for example, John Brophy challenged Lewis in his campaign for president of the Mine Workers Union. Powers Hapgood, a Brophy supporter at the miners' convention, challenged the election. Hapgood was first pummeled in his hotel room by Lewis men and then on the convention floor until he fell silent. Lewis saw the stock market crash of 1929 and the ensuing Great Depression as an opportunity to organize the unorganized workforce. With the passage of the Wagner Act in 1935, which gave government protection to collective bargaining, industrial unionism became possible. Lewis set out to make that possibility a reality.

Lewis was the son of Welsh immigrants. He, along with his father and two brothers, worked in the coal mines of Cleveland, Iowa. He joined the United Mine Workers in 1900. He left mining and, after failed attempts at other careers, ended up as an organizer for the AFL (1910–1916) and then an official of the United Mine Workers (1916–1920).

Congress of Industrial Organizations

In 1935, John L. Lewis and leaders of the Ladies Garment Workers and the Clothing Workers set up the **Congress of Industrial Organizations (CIO)**. Industrial workers, unlike their fellow craft workers, could not rely on the solidarity based on their skill for union strength. Industrial unions had to build such loyalty from the results of their organization. Reacting to the trade unionization of the AFL, Lewis led the formulation of the CIO. The CIO focused on a workplace

John L. Lewis (standing at the left) founded the Congress of Industrial Organizations (CIO) for workers who did not have the advantages that craft skills gave workers in other unions. *Source:* AP Images.

agenda, as did the AFL, but unlike the AFL, it organized and encouraged industrial unions. Although originally associated with the AFL, by 1938 the CIO was a separate and growing organization. The CIO also differed from the AFL by promoting solidarity with African American workers and with the women and immigrants in the workforce.

The CIO attracted the autoworkers, and in Flint, Michigan, in 1936, the United Auto Workers (UAW) staged the first sit-in strike. The nation watched for weeks as this first display of passive resistance by the union members caused General Motors major problems. When the governor of Michigan was asked to intervene with the militia, he instead called for a meeting between General Motors and Lewis, representing the UAW. A compromise was reached, and although General Motors did not recognize the UAW as the exclusive representative of its employees, it did recognize representation of UAW members to management.

After the auto industry experience, the CIO had similar successes in the steel industry when U.S. Steel recognized the union and signed a contract without the need for a strike. The use of the "sit-down strike" during this brief period forced management to honor the collective bargaining process put into law by the Wagner Act. Most workers identified these successes with the CIO and Lewis. CIO union membership began to increase, but even the AFL membership grew. The competition for union members between the leadership of the CIO and the AFL intensified.

The political activities of the labor movement that resulted in pro-labor legislation are detailed next. The results can be seen in the rise of union membership from the 1930s to its high in the 1950s when 33 percent of all nonagricultural workers were part of a labor union.

CONGRESS OF INDUSTRIAL ORGANIZATIONS (CIO)

A federation of unions made up of industrial workers formed in 1935 by John L. Lewis. The CIO organized unions within industries, such as the auto and steel industries, and included all the workers at a work site rather than restricting membership to one trade. Eventually the CIO merged with the AFL.

EARLY JUDICIAL REGULATION

As previously discussed, pre-Revolutionary America saw little division between the employers and employees. The economy of the colonies was primarily agricultural, with some handicraft trade. Basic goods were supplied by skilled laborers: shoemakers, tailors, carpenters, printers, smiths, and mechanics. The growth of the economy benefited these laborers, who, because their skills were scarce, could enjoy relatively high wages and job security. They were largely self-employed and dealt with consumers on an equal footing. After the American Revolution, some of these skilled workers became shop owners, employing others to fill orders that became more frequent as the economy began to build. Their need to produce goods in an increasingly competitive market demanded cheaper production costs and lower wages. Thus, a clearer distinction between employer and employee began. Skilled workers of a single craft formed associations and societies to protect their handiwork and their livelihood. Their method of action was to agree on a wage scale and then pledge to work only for an employer who would pay those wages. The response from the employer to this erosion of management rights was swift and decisive. Using a very supportive court system, those workers were charged with criminal conspiracy in a series of cases known as the Cordwainers conspiracy cases.[28]

CORDWAINERS CONSPIRACY CASES

A series of court cases that challenged the association of cordwainers and their wage agreement, ruling their action to be an illegal conspiracy and a conspiracy to impoverish others. The 1806 Supreme Court ruling that found the mere combination of workers to conspire to raise their wages to be illegal was later overturned.

The Cordwainers Conspiracy Cases

In the **Cordwainers conspiracy cases**, the state courts stated that the common law of criminal conspiracy was the law of the United States. In other words, if two or more people conspired to commit an illegal act, they were then guilty of conspiracy whether or not they ever completed the particular illegal act. Early American labor law was interpreted by judges and based on English common law. Whereas English judges had relied largely on statutes to find criminal conspiracy in labor cases, U.S. judges, who often shared a common background with employers, chose to find legal precedents in the common law for protecting the employer's property rights over the employee's job rights.[29] In the 1806 Philadelphia Cordwainers case, the court considered

CONSPIRACY

A legal tenet that if two or more people conspire to commit an illegal act, they are guilty of conspiracy whether or not they ever complete the illegal act itself.

the mere "combination" of workers to raise wages an illegal act. The court believed that such combinations were formed to benefit the workers and to injure nonparticipants. Public outcry over judicial interpretation of combinations led later courts to find other grounds for declaring them illegal.

In a New York Cordwainers case three years later (*People v. Melvin*), the court dismissed the idea that it was illegal merely to combine. But it denounced using a combination of workers to strike because it deprived others, primarily the employers, of their rights and property. Further, in an 1815 Pittsburgh case, the court clearly characterized the offense involved in organizing workers as conspiracy to impoverish a third person, be it the employer or another worker willing to work against the combination's rules. The threat of criminal conspiracy charges and the depression following the War of 1812 practically destroyed the fledgling labor movement. When prosperity returned, the demand for skilled labor put the employees in a better bargaining position, and combinations of skilled laborers began again.

Employers responded to this attempt by labor to again enter the decision-making process by taking employee combinations to court. Conspiracy cases against the New York Hatters (1823), Philadelphia Tailors (1827), and Philadelphia Spinners (1829) questioned the legality of the means used to force the employer to meet labor's demands: picketing, circulation of scab lists, and the sympathetic strike. Before labor could rally from such attacks by the courts, another depression weakened the demand for labor, and the combinations lost their bargaining power.

The development of the American factory system and the monopolies created by the robber barons in the later part of the nineteenth century softened public opinion for a while; to some extent there was sympathy to the needs of the worker. Because of this need for the worker to meet the employer as an equal, the courts began to move away from finding workers guilty of criminal conspiracy.

The conspiracy doctrine was further narrowed during *Commonwealth v. Hunt* (1842), which involved a stubborn journeyman who worked for less than union scale and repeatedly broke other union rules.[30] Union members caused his dismissal by refusing to work with him, and his complaint led to the criminal conspiracy charge. The court found that criminal conspiracy required either an illegal purpose or a resort to illegal means. In this instance, the purpose was to induce workers to become union members and abide by union rules; hence, it was not illegal. In addition, the means—refusing to work with a worker who did not comply—was not unlawful because no contract was breached. The court upheld the workers' right to organize and to compel all workers to comply with the union scale.

Use of Labor Injunctions

Abandonment of the criminal conspiracy doctrine by the courts did not signal judicial acceptance of unions, nor did it enhance the employers' relationships with unions. Indeed, judicial and business attitudes toward union activities became even more hostile as viable union organizations sought to use economic measures to regulate the terms and conditions of worker employment, as demonstrated by the Court's decision in Case 2-1.

CASE 2-1

Injunction

The Hitchman Coal & Coke Company had reluctantly accepted unionization in 1903. For the next three years it was plagued with strikes over mine workers' pay scales, causing considerable losses to the company. A two-month strike in 1906 prompted a self-appointed committee of employees to inform the company that they could not afford to stay off the job, and they asked the company on what terms they could return to work. The company said they could come back—but without the union. The employees agreed and returned to work.

Prospective employees were told that, although the company paid the same wages demanded by the union, the mine was nonunion and would remain so, that the company would not recognize the United Mine Workers of America, and that the company would fire any worker who joined. Each worker employed assented to those conditions.

The United Mine Workers of America wanted to expand union mines in the area because nonunion mines tended to keep the cost of production low. Union mines could not compete and still grant workers the pay increases they demanded.

Union organizers repeatedly declared the need to organize the nonunion mines by means of strikes. They were determined to protect themselves from the unorganized mines. A plan was devised whereby the unionized mines would stay open while the nonunion mines would strike. The working miners would provide strike benefits for the strikers to ensure their cooperation.

The Hitchman Company refused to grant recognition when approached by union officials and informed the union of the employment agreements not to unionize. Representatives of the union began organizing the miners with the express intent of shutting down the mine until the company recognized the union. Their organizational means were limited to orderly and peaceful talks with individual workers and a few unobtrusive public meetings. The company sought and received an injunction against the union's activities. The union appealed.

Decision

The injunction was upheld on appeal. The U.S. Supreme Court reasoned that the company was within its rights in excluding union workers from its employ and that even though the union was within its rights in asking workers to join, it could not injure the company when exercising that right. The court found that the express intent of the union—to organize the workers to strike for recognition—would injure the company in two ways. It would interfere with the employer–employee relationships, and it would cause a loss of profits.

Source: Adapted from *Hitchman Coal & Coke Co. v. Mitchell*, 62 L. Ed. 260 (1917).

The labor incidents cited earlier coincided with the growth and development of national labor organizations. Employers' use of court **labor injunctions** to stop these acts, supported by court reaction to these incidents, took on national importance and to a large extent created the need for a national labor policy.

LABOR INJUNCTION

A court order that prohibits any individual or group from performing any act that violates the rights of other individuals concerned. Until 1932, injunctions were primarily used by employers to end boycotts or strikes.

The ability of railway workers to cripple the national railroads during the Pullman strike caused alarm in the government and among employers. A state court invoked the Sherman Antitrust Act, which declared monopolies illegal against the striking workers. The U.S. Supreme Court later confirmed the lower court's application of the Sherman Antitrust Act to the Pullman strike in the *Danbury Hatter*'s case.[31] The Supreme Court stated that the act was designed to prevent conspiracies in restraint of interstate commerce and that a boycott was a form of this interference and therefore prohibited.

The Erdman Act

A key by-product of the Pullman strike was the passage of the Erdman Act of 1898.[32] President Grover Cleveland had formed the U.S. Strike Commission to investigate the cause and results of the Pullman strike. The commission recommended a permanent federal commission to conciliate and, if necessary, decide railway labor disputes. Congress used this recommendation as its basis for passage of the Erdman Act. This act gave certain employment protections to union members and offered facilities for mediation and conciliation of railway labor disputes. Although the legislation was limited to employees operating interstate trains, its mere passage suggested that federal regulation of the employer–employee relationship might be necessary to ensure peace in interstate industries.

Unions Gain a Foothold

The courts continued to use the injunction as a way to regulate union activity. But not all court actions against organized labor were successful in discouraging union actions. In 1902, the United Mine Workers organized a strike of anthracite coal miners, demanding an increase in wages and union recognition. With the widespread support of boycotts and money for the workers, the United Mine Workers withstood federal troops and antitrust lawsuits. President Theodore Roosevelt stepped in and offered to establish a president's commission to arbitrate. The workers accepted the offer almost immediately, but the mine owners balked. Threatening to seize the mines unless the coal operators accepted a plan of arbitration, the president gained acceptance of his offer.[33] The commission's recommendation included wage increases but fell short of union recognition. Textile workers conducted another successful strike during this period in Lawrence, Massachusetts, in 1912. Again the strikers were supported by contributions from around the country. After nine and a half weeks, mill owners capitulated and met most of the workers' demands.

COMPANY UNIONS

An employee organization formed by an employer and recognized within a company, often it will offer employer-conceived reforms, such as health benefits and better living conditions, to discourage employee unionization. This type of union usually does not meet the requirements of the National Labor Relations Act and thus is not considered a true union.

The deadly1913–1914 strike by mine workers in Ludlow, Colorado, spurred the start of **company unions**. The mine owner, John D. Rockefeller, Jr., realized the inevitability of such workers' organizations. By instituting his own recognized employee organization and initiating reforms such as health funds and better living conditions, Rockefeller sought to eliminate the need for union recognition. Such company unions created the illusion of participation but lacked the essential element whereby labor and the employer meet as equals at a bargaining table.

These successes increased the resolve of organized labor to establish viable collective bargaining relationships with employers. But the employers were not ready to yield control to their employees. When faced with an employee strike, employers resisted, seeking and often receiving support from the courts in the form of labor injunctions (see Table 2-1 for events in the era of strong union opposition).

TABLE 2-1 Chronology of the Most Significant Events in U.S. Labor Relations

Era of Union Opposition

1790	*New York Printers strike.* First strike by employees.
1790s	*First unions.* Craft workers formed first known unions, including printers, shoemakers, tailors, carpenters, and bakers.
1806	*Philadelphia Cordwainers case.* Court found combination of employees illegal.
1837	*Severe depression.* Mass unemployment reduced union membership.
1842	*Commonwealth v. Hunt.* The conspiracy doctrine greatly narrowed.
1860s	*Civil War.* Buildup of coal, steel, and other war-related industries.
1866	*National Labor Union.* Advocated consumer cooperatives, immigration restrictions; disbanded in 1872.
1869	*Knights of Labor.* National social union formed to organize farmers and skilled and unskilled workers.
1875	*Molly Maguires.* After a strike by coal miners, union organizers were tried and executed for strike-related violence.
1877	*Railway strike.* More than 100 workers were killed, and several hundred were wounded in the first national strike.
1886	*American Federation of Labor (AFL).* Samuel Gompers led the first national trade union to advocate collective bargaining, trade autonomy, exclusive jurisdiction, standard hours, and better wages and working conditions.
1886	*Haymarket Square riot.* Several workers were killed; others were found guilty of anarchism. The Knights of Labor suffered the blame for the riot, shifting much of their support to the AFL.
1890	*Sherman Antitrust Act.* Designed to break up corporate monopolies.
1892	*Homestead, Pennsylvania.* A strike by steel workers against Carnegie Steel Company ended with the town being placed under martial law.

TABLE 2-1 *(Continued)*

1894	*Pullman strike.* Rail workers demanded higher wages and lower rents. The strike was ended by court orders under the Sherman Act. The strike led to passage of the 1898 Erdman Act giving railroad employees employment protection.
1905	*Industrial Workers of the World (IWW).* The "Wobblies" were organized in response to the strong opposition to the labor movement. They advocated including all workers in one union and the end of capitalism.
1914	*Ludlow, Colorado, massacre.* Twenty men, women, and children killed by fire and bullets in a tent colony.
1919	*Boston Police Strike.* Walkout led to the police union's separation from the AFL and set back the national police union movement.
Era of Union Support	
1914	*Clayton Act.* Congress attempted to limit use of court injunction. First national pro-union legislation.
1914–1918	*World War I.* President Wilson created the National War Labor Board to mediate labor disputes. The board also recognized employee collective bargaining rights during the war.
1926	*Railway Labor Act.* Railroad employees were given collective bargaining rights and the right to use voluntary arbitration.
1929	*Stock market crash.* Beginning of Great Depression and 33 percent national unemployment.
1931	*Davis-Bacon Act.* Required federal contractors to pay "prevailing wages," which are usually union wages.
1932	*Norris-La Guardia Act.* Limited use of court injunction; made yellow-dog contracts unenforceable.
1935	*Wagner Act.* The Magna Carta of U.S. labor history. Within 12 years, union membership tripled in the United States. Upheld by the Supreme Court in 1937. Created the NLRB.
1935	*Committee for Industrial Organizations.* John L. Lewis led industrial unions to split with the AFL.
1936	*Flint, Michigan.* The UAW staged the first "sit-in" strike, occupying the GM auto plant.
1936	*Walsh-Healey Act.* Required federal contractors to pay time and a half for overtime, over an eight-hour day.
1938	*Fair Labor Standards Act.* Provided minimum wage, 40-hour week, overtime pay, and the abolition of child labor.
1941–1945	*World War II.* Widespread labor strikes during and after the war harmed the war effort and caused strong antilabor public sympathy.
Era of Union Stabilization	
1947	*Taft-Hartley Amendments.* Amended Wagner Act to equalize the balance between labor and management. Also created the Federal Mediation and Conciliation Service (FMCS) and right-to-work states.
1952	*No-raiding pact.* After 17 years of bitter fighting, new labor chiefs in the AFL and CIO signed a no-raiding pact.
1955	*AFL-CIO merge.* New unity spurred labor hopes for membership gains, which failed to materialize (25 percent of labor force in 1955, 12.5 percent in 2004).
1959	*Landrum-Griffin Act.* U.S. Senate hearing on labor union corruption led Congress to establish stricter controls on union operations.
1962	*President Kennedy's Executive Order 10988.* The order gives federal employees the right to bargain collectively and join or refrain from joining unions. Begins period of substantial growth by public unions.
1978	*Civil Service Reform Act.* Creates Federal Labor Relations Authority, which oversees labor practices in the federal government.

(continued)

TABLE 2-1 *(Continued)*

Era of Union Stabilization	
1981	*Air traffic controllers (PATCO) strike.* President Ronald Reagan uses replacement workers to end the first declared national strike against the federal government. The success of his action spurs a period of increased use of replacement workers in private and public sectors, reducing the number of strikes.
1986	*President Reagan's Executive Order 12564.* The order initiates random drug testing of federal employees and contains "zero tolerance" of illegal use.
1987	*Teamsters Union.* Rejoins AFL-CIO after 30 years of separation. Many other unions merge in the 1980s to increase their strength.
1993	*Family and Medical Leave Act.* Law requires employers to give employees up to 12 weeks of unpaid leave for family reasons. The act was strongly supported by unions.
1994	*Baseball players' strike.* The most unpopular strike in sports history cancels the 1994 World Series and costs the industry many fans.
1997	*UPS strike.* The Teamsters Union strike idled over 180,000 workers, crippled delivery of packages worldwide, and focused national attention on the plight of part-time workers.
2002	*West Coast dock strike.* Over 10,500 longshoremen stage a costly strike ($1 billion a day) that closes 29 West Coast docks. President Bush invoked the Taft-Hartley Act to reopen the ports temporarily. A new six-year agreement ended the strike and provided higher wages and pension benefits, as well as the use of new technology on the docks that will replace jobs over time.
2005	The *AFL-CIO split.* During its 50th anniversary year, the AFL-CIO endures a major split as seven national unions, including the Teamsters, SEIU (the largest union in the AFL-CIO), and UNITE HERE create a rival federation, the Change to Win coalition.
2007–2010	*Employee Free Choice Act.* Congressional bill that would make it easier for unions to organize new members, achieve a first contract, and increase certain penalties fails in the Senate in 2007. President Obama promised to sign if it passed Congress.

PRO-LABOR LEGISLATION

The Clayton Act

Public criticism of the use of the injunction against labor unions caused Congress to pass the Clayton Act in 1914.[34] This act sought to limit the court's injunctive powers against labor organizations. The **Clayton Act** stated that labor was not a commodity; that the existence and operation of labor organizations were not prohibited by antitrust; and that individual members of unions were not restrained from lawful activities. The act provided that neither the labor organization nor its members were considered illegal combinations or conspiracies in restraint of trade.

CLAYTON ACT

Passed by Congress in 1914, this law was designed to limit the use of the Sherman Antitrust Act in labor disputes and to limit the court's injunctive powers against labor organizations, stating that labor was not a commodity and union members were not restrained from lawful activities. Strict interpretation by the courts limited the effectiveness of the act.

Still, courts continued to apply the Sherman Antitrust Act after passage of the Clayton Act by narrowly interpreting its provisions. The courts felt that secondary strikes, boycotts, and picketing were not covered by the Clayton Act because of the employee–employer language and because legitimate objects of labor would not include strikes and activities if their purpose or effect was the unreasonable restraint of trade. Although the Clayton Act was practically ineffective, its passage signaled a hopeful period for labor organizations. With other political victories behind them, such as child labor laws, workers' compensation, and some limitations on working hours, members of the labor movement believed that a new era was upon them.

The National War Labor Board

During World War I, President Woodrow Wilson formed the National War Labor Board to prevent labor disputes from disrupting the war effort. Formed to provide a means of settlement by mediation or conciliation of labor controversies in necessary war industries, it adopted self-organization and collective bargaining as its basic policy.[35] Federal recognition of labor rights continued and expanded when the federal government began to operate the railroads. After World War I, the National War Labor Board was abolished, and railroads were returned to their owners. Despite the economic sense of avoiding labor disputes through cooperation, the federal government no longer protected collective bargaining.

The labor movement sustained losses in the early 1920s. Another postwar depression and labor's alleged association with American sympathizers for Russian communism eroded public support. Even though the Clayton Act supposedly exempted labor unions from injunctions, the courts interpreted the Clayton Act as granting immunity only if an injunction was not necessary to prevent irreparable injury to property or its rights. In the broadest sense, any labor action could injure property or property rights.[36] Trade union leadership and the rank and file turned to political action and industrial unionism to counteract their losses. They allied with the Progressive movement, a loose coalition of farmers, socialists, and reformers who represented a populist view. Many people, fearing that the use of militia, federal troops, and court injunctions against unions represented a threat to the democratic process, adopted the Progressive doctrine. That doctrine espoused the control of the political activities of corporations, graduated income and inheritance taxes, stringent conservation measures, federal regulations of the labor of women and children, and workers' compensation laws. The movement, although not widely embraced, successfully supported the passage of the Railway Labor Act. In 1942, President Roosevelt reestablished the National War Labor Board to oversee labor issues during World War II. Many of its members became instrumental in the creation of the postwar labor policies.

The Railway Labor Act

RAILWAY LABOR ACT

Passed in 1926 to prevent disruptions in the nation's rail service, it required railroad employers to negotiate with employees union. In 1936 it was expanded to include the airline industry.

In an effort to avoid the interruption of commerce, the Railway Labor Act (RLA) was passed in 1926 with the support of both labor and management.[37] It required railroad employers to negotiate with their employees' duly elected representatives. It provided for amicable adjustment of labor disputes and for voluntary submissions to arbitration. As a result of the RLA, Congress again fostered peaceful settlement of labor disputes through negotiation and mediation. The Supreme Court case upholding that act removed major judicial obstacles by supporting a national labor policy based on the affirmative legal protection of labor organizations.[38] Under the umbrella of the

The Railway Labor Act was expanded in 1936 to include the airline industry. In 2010 under the RLA, the National Mediation Board oversaw a historic union election involving over 42,000 workers of the merged Northwestern Airlines and Delta Air Lines. The election was viewed as one of the most important in decades due to the number of workers involved and the importance of the airline industry to organized labor
Source: Getty Images.

commerce clause of the U.S. Constitution, the Court said that Congress could facilitate settlements of disputes and that "the legality of collective action on the part of employees in order to safeguard their proper interests is not to be disputed. . . . Congress . . . could safeguard it and seek to make their appropriate collective action an instrument of peace rather than of strife."[39]

In 1936, the RLA was expanded to include the fledgling airline industry. The RLA listed four purposes: avoid interruptions to commerce, protect employee right to join a union, ensure independence of carriers and employees to resolve issues between them, and settle grievances and disputes growing out of the RLA contracts. Because RLA contracts do not expire but can be modified only through negotiations, the RLA set up a multistage mediation procedure that included a "cooling-off" period and the appointment of presidential boards to investigate disputes and push for settlements.[40]

THE CREATION OF A NATIONAL LABOR POLICY

In 1929, the stock market crashed, and the United States plunged into a major depression. The impact of the Great Depression on the workers was devastating. A third of the country's workforce was unemployed. President Hoover's programs to combat unemployment served mainly to highlight the deprivation. The labor movement made more emphatic efforts to organize and demand recognition and became more politically active. The severity of conditions led to public sympathy for workers' problems. For years the nation struggled over the right of workers to organize and to negotiate collectively with employers. Judicial solutions to the struggle were ineffective. Court decisions, by their nature, were confined to particular parties, to narrow situations, and to fixed time frames. Such decisions could not give national guidance. The judicial process was also time consuming; neither labor nor management wanted disputes to drag on while the wheels of justice ground to a decision.

State legislation was also ineffectual because organized labor transcended state boundaries. With few exceptions, the disruption of an industry in any one state affected industries throughout the country.

The Norris-La Guardia Act

Congress recognized the need for a national labor policy. The Erdman Act and the Clayton Act were the first steps in ensuring industrial peace based on the balanced bargaining relationship of worker to owner. The Davis-Bacon Act, passed in 1931, was another attempt to support the fledgling union movement. This act put into place a requirement that companies using federal dollars for construction projects use the "prevailing wage rate" of the area as the minimum-wage rate on their construction project. Because the trades needed for construction—carpenters, plumbers, and electricians—were generally organized, the prevailing wage rate would most often be the union wage rate. Companies are selected to do federally funded jobs through a competitive bidding process. The Davis-Bacon Act meant that companies who used union labor did not lose their competitive advantage when bidding on federal jobs by paying their workers union wages.[41]

NORRIS–LA GUARDIA ACT

Passed in 1932, this act restricts the federal courts from issuing injunctions in labor disputes, except to maintain law and order. The act also made yellow-dog contracts illegal.

The **Norris-La Guardia Act** (1932) was the next step in formulating a comprehensive national labor policy.[42] This act, like the Clayton Act, sought to restrict federal judicial intervention in labor disputes, thereby giving the unions an opportunity to grow. Courts could not enjoin strikes without actual violence, nor could they restrict the formation of a union or associated activities. The act also made illegal "yellow-dog" contracts, in which employees pledged to refrain from union membership. These protections were extended to secondary boycotts and strikes by expanding the employer–employee language of the Clayton Act.

The National Labor Relations Act (The Wagner Act)

The Great Depression and the election of Franklin D. Roosevelt with strong labor support set the stage for passage of national legislation. Roosevelt quickly proved his interest in the plight of the worker. The National Industrial Recovery Act (1933) recognized workers' rights in selecting their own representatives.[43] Well intentioned but poorly constructed, the National Recovery Administration had no power to enforce the act, and industry largely ignored it. Within two years the National Industrial Recovery Act was declared unconstitutional.[44]

Relief of the unemployment problem continued by creation of such New Deal programs as the Civilian Conservation Corps, unemployment insurance, the Social Security program, and the Works Progress Administration. But these measures alone were not enough.

By 1935, the judiciary policy toward labor was one of selective suppression of organized labor's activities whenever they trampled too heavily on the interest of any other segment of society. Commercial interests must not be injured by disruption of the interstate flow of goods, consumers and unorganized laborers must not be injured by wage standardization, and employees and the public at large must not be injured by expansion of labor disputes through secondary boycotts.[45]

Senator Robert Wagner, a champion for labor, proposed an act that recognized employee rights to organize and bargain collectively. A quasi-judicial tribunal with the power and authority to enforce its own orders would be created. Although the act was purported to protect the public from the disruption of interstate commerce resulting from labor disputes, Senator Wagner stated that the act would also give the employee freedom and dignity.[46]

The **National Labor Relations Act** (also known as the **Wagner Act**) gave most private sector employees the right to organize.[47] It required employers to meet with accredited representatives of a majority of their employees and to make an honest effort to reach agreement on issues raised. Employees now had the right to strike, and the employer's retaliatory powers were limited under the act's unfair labor practice provisions. The **National Labor Relations Board (NLRB)** was created to enforce provisions of the act.

WAGNER ACT

The cornerstone of U.S. Federal labor law. The act was the first in history to give most private sector employees the right to organize into unions, to bargain collectively with employers, to define unfair labor practices by employers, and to create the NLRB.

NATIONAL LABOR RELATIONS BOARD (NLRB)

An independent agency of the federal government that serves to investigate unfair labor practices, determine appropriate bargaining units, certify unions that legally represent a majority of employees, and administer the provisions of the National Labor Relations Act.

By legislating the recognition of employee representatives and protecting the right to strike, Congress forced the employer to share the decision-making power with employees. Labor no longer depended on work stoppages to get to the bargaining table or on economic factors to determine its equality.

The entire thrust of the Wagner Act was to protect employees from employers and to establish a balance of bargaining power between the two. Later it was criticized for its one-sided nature, but at the time it was passed, organized labor had no leverage to pose a threat to management; thus, equal protection for management seemed unnecessary. Critics claimed that the act was unconstitutional because, although it was based on the commerce clause, the latter did not specifically allow Congress to dictate the relationship between employers and employees. The NLRB was careful in its activities, delaying adjudication on the constitutionality question until the Supreme Court upheld the act in the 1937 case of *Jones and Laughlin Steel Corporation*.[48] Labor–management relations improved somewhat under the Wagner Act but still remained uneasy. Figure 2-1 outlines the major provisions of the Wagner Act.

The creation of a national labor policy dominated the labor scene in 1935, but the character of the national labor union was also undergoing changes. The AFL, a confederation of craft unions, had been the principal union model for half a century. In 1935, however, the Committee of Industrial Organizations, later called the Congress of Industrial Organizations (CIO), challenged the leadership of the AFL by successfully supporting industrial unions. Membership in industrial unions was based on employment in a particular industry, such as automobile, steel, or clothing, rather than on a particular skill.

The CIO grew to 5 million members in less than 20 years under the leadership of John L. Lewis. This growth was attributed to the passage of the Wagner Act, the increased shift of the American economy from agriculture to manufacturing, and the heightened economic activity of World War II and the Korean War.

The Fair Labor Standards Act

The National Labor Relations Act was followed by the passage of the Walsh-Healey Act and the Fair Labor Standards Act (FLSA). The Walsh-Healey Act, passed in 1936, foreshadowed the

Findings and Policy

- Denial by employers of employee collective bargaining leads to strikes, industrial unrest, and obstruction of commerce
- Inequality of bargaining power between employees and employers affects the flow of commerce and aggravates recurrent business depressions
- Protection of the right of employees to organize and bargain collectively safeguards commerce
- Policy of the United States to encourage practice and procedure of collective bargaining and the exercise of employees of their right to organize and negotiate

Rights of Employees

- To organize into unions of their own choosing
- To assist such labor unions
- To bargain collectively with their employer through representatives of their own choosing
- To strike or take other similar concerted action

Employer Unfair Labor Practices (illegal)

- Interfering with employee rights guaranteed by the act
- Refusal to bargain in good faith with employee representatives
- Discrimination against union members or employees pursuing their rights under the act, including retaliation for exercising rights under the act
- Any attempt to dominate or interfere with employee unions

Representatives and Elections

- Employee representatives shall be exclusive representatives of the appropriate unit
- NLRB decides appropriateness of unit for bargaining purposes
- NLRB shall conduct secret-ballot elections to determine employee representatives

National Labor Relations Board

- Members appointed by president of the United States
- Conducts elections to determine employee representatives of appropriate unit
- Exclusive power to prevent employer unfair labor practice

FIGURE 2-1 Major Provisions of the Wagner Act (NLRA)

FAIR LABOR STANDARDS ACT (FLSA)

Passed in 1936, it requires employers to pay covered employees at least the federal minimum wage and overtime pay of one-and-one-half-times the regular rate of pay for work exceeding a 40-hour week.

passage of the FLSA. It again imposed rules on employers who received federal dollars. It required those employers with federal contracts to pay time and a half to any employee working more than eight hours per day.[49] The Fair Labor Standards Act, passed in 1938, applied primarily to employees engaged in interstate commerce and provided a federal minimum wage and a 44-hour week to be reduced to 40 hours in three years.[50] Passage of the act secured three main objectives of the labor movement: wages adequate to maintain a decent standard of living, shorter hours, and the abolition of labor by children younger than age 16.

World War II and the war effort resulted in a shortage of labor and more labor demands. Strikes brought charges that labor unions were unpatriotic. Congress, reacting to pressure, passed the Smith-Connally Act to control strikes injurious to the war effort.[51] Passage of this act showed a shift in political forces against strong federal support of union activities. The Wagner Act, however, was still in place at the end of the war, and labor entered the postwar economic slump with considerable legal protection. The collective bargaining rights mandated by the act forced business to deal with labor on an equal footing. Supported by two Supreme Court decisions in the early 1940s, labor unions were allowed the use of peaceful picketing to inform the public of their alleged grievances and to elicit support for their cause.[52]

The Fair Labor Standards Act has been amended several times since 1938. The minimum wage has been raised several times to $7.25 in 2009. In 2004, the FLSA received a major amendment by the Bush administration and the U.S. Congress. The amendment strengthened and clarified the criteria for the "exempt" classification, adding both a salary-level test and a duties test. To be exempt from the overtime provision (time and a half for hours worked over 40 per week), a worker must be paid a salary of $455 per week ($23,660 per year) and meet a bona fide job duties test. Specific job exemptions include executive, administrative, professional, outside sales, and some computer-related jobs in which the employee's primary duty includes exercising discretion and independent judgment.[53]

The Labor-Management Relations Act (Taft-Hartley Amendments)

For 12 years, the Wagner Act gave unions the time and ability to grow strong. From 1935 to 1947, union membership went from 3 million to 15 million, with some industries having 80 percent of their employees under collective bargaining agreements.[54] The image of organized labor in Congress was one of power—power to stop coal production during World War II and to shut down steel mills, seaports, and automobile assembly plants after the war. That image was personified by isolated instances of placard-carrying strikers attempting to stop **scabs**, or strike-breakers, from passing through a picket line.

SCABS

A derogatory term to describe workers who cross a union picket line to perform the jobs of striking workers.

Widespread strikes during 1945–1946 and wage drives in 1946–1947 caused critics of the Wagner Act to increase the political pressure for amendment. The amendment's stated goal was to equalize its impact on employers. The relentless campaigning of the Chamber of Commerce and the National Association of Manufacturers, resentment over wartime strikes, and internal union irregularities began to turn the tide against organized labor.

Numerous bills were introduced to change the Wagner Act, to weaken the powers of the NLRB, to redefine appropriate bargaining units, to outlaw a closed union shop, to subject unions to unfair labor practices charges, and to limit strikes and other concerted activities.

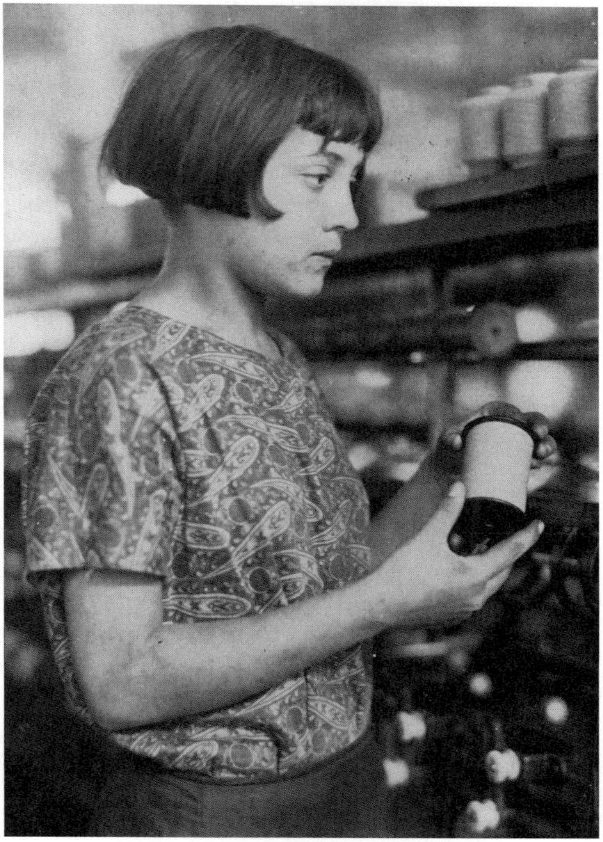

The 1935 FLSA achieved a long-time goal of early labor unions—the abolishment of child labor. *Source:* Library of Congress.

TAFT-HARTLEY AMENDMENTS

Also known as the Labor Management Relations Act of 1947, it generally was created to counterbalance the provisions of the National Labor Relations Act of 1935. The law declared closed shops and automatic check-offs illegal, cited unfair labor union practices, and protected the rights of employees who chose not to unionize. The law also created the Federal Mediation and Conciliation Service, restricted secondary boycotts and strikes, and gave states the right to outlaw union shops.

Although these bills did not pass, they laid a foundation for the passage of the **Taft-Hartley Amendments** in 1947. Table 2-1 includes a brief chronology of the era of strong union support in the United States.

A Republican Congress in 1946 introduced 200 bills on labor relations during its first week, and President Harry Truman proposed some revision of the nation's labor laws in his State of the Union Address. After extensive hearings by both the House and the Senate, the 1947 Labor-Management Relations Act (known as the *Taft-Hartley Act*) was passed.[55] Although President Truman vetoed it, Congress overrode his veto, and the bill became law on August 22, 1947.

Management saw the Taft-Hartley Amendments as a shift to a more balanced approach to labor relations. Labor unions were subjected to many of the same duties as employers. Whereas the Wagner Act gave employees the right to organize, the Taft-Hartley Amendments recognized their right not to organize. Under the Wagner Act, employers were required to bargain in good faith; under Taft-Hartley, that duty was extended to unions. The unfair labor practices section protected employees and employers from labor unions' unfair labor practices. The Wagner Act had protected employees from being fired for joining a union; the Taft-Hartley Amendments protected employees from losing their jobs for not joining a union. The 1947 amendments recognized and gave preference to state right-to-work laws over bargained-for provisions in collective bargaining agreements that required union membership as a condition of employment. Figure 2-2 outlines the major provisions of the Taft-Hartley Amendments.

Organized labor immediately began to work for the repeal of Taft-Hartley. Labor had, by opposing any change to the Wagner Act, shut itself out of congressional decision making and demanded that Taft-Hartley be repealed before even discussing possible changes in the Wagner Act.

Findings and Policy

- Certain practices of labor organizations, such as secondary strikes, burden and obstruct the free flow of commerce
- Elimination of such practices is necessary to guarantee rights of act

Rights of Employees

- To refrain from any and all union activities except union shop provision (which a majority must approve) in valid collective bargaining agreements
- Closed shops requiring workers to join unions before being hired became unlawful

Union Unfair Labor Practices

- Restraint or coercion of employees in exercise of their rights
- Refusal to bargain in good faith with employer
- Discrimination against employee for not engaging in union activities
- Unions can be sued for breach of contract

Restrictions on Strike Activities

- No secondary strikes and boycotts
- Prohibits strikes conducted by one labor union to dislodge another labor union
- Outlaws strikes to force employers to make work for union members
- Prohibits strikes during the term of a valid collective bargaining agreement unless employees give 60 days notice to employer and 30 days notice to the Federal Mediation and Conciliation Service (FMCS)
- Provided 80-day injunction for strikes that threaten national security

Right-to-Work Laws

- Give states the right to outlaw union shop requirements in collective bargaining agreements so employees can refrain from joining the union representing them at the bargaining table

FIGURE 2-2 Major Provisions of the Taft-Hartley Amendments

This all-or-nothing approach backfired, and Taft-Hartley was left unchanged. Labor legislation did not receive national attention again until 1957.

Certainly one response of the labor community to the passage of the Taft-Hartley Amendments was a reemergence of the "in union there is strength" approach to organized labor. The AFL-CIO merger in 1955 ended a 20-year separation of the two dominant national labor organizations and enabled the united group to claim a total membership of 16.1 million workers: 10.9 million members from 108 AFL unions and 5.2 million members from 30 CIO unions.

The Labor-Management Reporting and Disclosure Act of 1959

The internal affairs of unions from the early 1800s until 1959 were not the subject of any federal law. Thus, legal disputes were settled inconsistently through the application of common law and state court interpretation of a union constitution. The 1959 Labor-Management Reporting and Disclosure Act abruptly changed that situation. It was the first federal law passed with the objective of regulating the conduct of internal union affairs. At first the act covered only private sector employees, but a 1978 amendment included public employees. These are the major provisions of the act:

- Member freedom of speech
- Member right to participate in union activities
- Mandatory secret-ballot election of officers
- Limits on the use of union funds[56]

The famed McClellan hearings in 1957 set the stage for the second major change to the national labor policy since the Wagner Act. Initiated to investigate wrongdoings in the labor–management field, the Senate committee soon unearthed corruption in some major unions. Charges of racketeering centered on threats that strikes would be called against employers and on incidents in which union officials sold out the interests of union members for cash.[57] Political leaders noticed the public outcry for labor legislation to protect the internal operations of unions, and congressional bills offering sweeping reforms were introduced. Labor supported reforms as long as amendments to Taft-Hartley were included. Management also supported them as long as their amendments to Taft-Hartley were included. The mood created by the McClellan hearings was in management's favor, and the **Labor-Management Reporting and Disclosure Act of 1959** (known as the **Landrum-Griffin Act**) was passed.[58]

LANDRUM-GRIFFIN ACT

Passed in 1959 to help regulate internal union operations, the act amended the Wagner Act and the Taft-Hartley Act and resulted in the limitation of boycotts and picketing, the creation of safeguards for union elections, and the establishment of controls for the handling of union funds.

The Landrum-Griffin Act provisions amending the Wagner and Taft-Hartley Acts further eroded the power of labor unions by limiting such economic activities as boycotts and picketing. In regulating the internal operation of labor unions, the Landrum-Griffin Act introduced controls on internal handling of union funds. It established safeguards for union elections and in certain cases gave members the right to bring suit against the union. Under the act, unions were required to have a constitution and bylaws and to file these and other disclosure documents with the secretary of labor. It also established due process rules for disciplining members. For example, in 1995, a union member was expelled from his union after working to remove his union and put another in its place. After he was expelled from the union, he stopped paying dues. The union notified him that under the collective bargaining agreement, they would have him terminated for failure to pay dues. He appealed, and the NLRB upheld the union.[59]

The Landrum-Griffin Act protects the democratic nature of unions. The act ensures full and active participation by the rank and file in the affairs of the union. It accords protection of union members' rights to participate in the election process. It requires high standards of responsibility and ethical conduct by union officials and protects members from the arbitrary and capricious whims of union leaders. The first major case involving the rights of union members in an election was in *Wirtz v. Local 6*. The issue in that case was whether a union could require a member to have been elected to a lesser office within the union before standing for a higher office. The U.S. Supreme Court found that to be an unreasonable requirement and thus a violation of the Landrum-Griffin Act.[60]

The Bill of Rights of Members of Labor Organizations established the machinery necessary to enforce this act. The rights under this Title I section include the right to nominate candidates and to vote in union elections, to attend membership meetings, and to participate in the deliberation of those meetings. Freedom to speak about union affairs and to assemble with union members was also reaffirmed. Title I protects union members from excessive charges because dues, fees, and assessments are decided by a majority vote of the membership. Members are given the right to sue the union and are ensured due process protections in the union's disciplinary actions.

Under subsequent titles of the Landrum-Griffin Act, union members gained access to union financial reports, local unions received protection from their national organization in the assertion of trustee rights, the fair and democratic conduct of union elections was ensured, and the fiduciary duty of union officials to their members was clearly outlined. With passage of the Landrum-Griffin Act, the legislation that established the national labor policy—a policy characterized by strong support of collective bargaining as a means of ending industrial strife—was in place. Successive chapters will discuss how that bargaining process is to be carried out under the provisions of the act. See Table 2-1 for highlights of events in the modern era of unionization.

The Employee Free Choice Act

Wilma B. Liebman, Chair of the National Labor Relations Board (created by the NLRA to oversee the Act), has written that the 1935 Act which was "intended to encourage collective bargaining and equalize bargaining power between labor and capital" . . . "is now out of sync with a transformed economy" . . . and that the fact that "organized labor as a percentage of the private sector workforce is at a historic low" validates her opinions. Liebman, and other labor historians, point out a number of significant changes which together changed the American labor market over the years since the 1935 Act, including the decline of manufacturing combined with the surge of the service economy, shifting demographics of the workforce—primarily more women, minorities, and part-time workers, technology which changed how people work and communicate at the workplace, and global competition which shifted to focus for management and labor away from American competitors to international, often nonunion and low-paying competitors. But, perhaps the single watershed event was the 1981 firing of the federal air-traffic controllers by President Ronald Reagan (see Chapter 3) which awakened private sector employers to fully recognize a power they had seldom used before—the right to hire replacement workers during an economic strike.[61] In recent years labor leaders have often agreed with Liebman, especially concerned about the historic low percentage of union members in the United States. They also contend the act does not provide for a basis for labor–management relations in today's U.S. employment market, and that it needs to be substantially updated. The answer to this problem, they generally agree, is the **Employee Free Choice Act** (EFCA). The EFCA was introduced in the U.S. Congress in 2007 when it passed the House of Representatives, but failed in the Republican-controlled U.S. Senate. During the 2008 presidential race Senator John McCain opposed the EFCA, while Senator Barack Obama pledged his support of the EFCA and thus gained substantial union support. Thus far, however, President Obama has not put forth the EFCA during his administration. The bill is the top legislative priority of organized labor.

EMPLOYEE FREE CHOICE ACT

Congressional bill that would make it easier for unions to organize new members, achieve a first contract, and increase certain penalties fails in the Senate in 2007.

The Employee Free Choice Act, a proposed amendment to the National Labor Relations Act, is surprisingly short and direct, and contains three primary provisions:[62]

1. **"Card-check recognition."** Certification of a union to represent a group of employees for purposes of collective bargaining if a majority of the employees sign authorization cards. Currently employers may ask for a secret-ballot election, in which the union must win a majority of those voting.
2. **First contract.** If after a union is recognized to represent an appropriate unit of employees, an employer and a union are not able to reach a first contract (CBA) within 90 days, then either side may request mediation for 30 days from the Federal Mediation and Conciliation

Service (FMCS), and if mediation is not successful, then the dispute will be referred to arbitration, and the arbitrator's decision is binding on the parties for two years. Currently the parties must "bargain in good faith"; however, there is no requirement that they reach agreement, and about one-third to one-half of first contract negotiations do not settle a first contract.

3. **Increased penalties.** The act provides stronger penalties for law violations during a union organizing campaign or first contract negotiations that include treble back pay for affected employees, civil fines up to $20,000 per violation, and the NLRB must seek a court injunction if it has reasonable cause to believe an employer has interfered with the organizing campaign or first contract negotiation process.

Supporters to the EFCA contend that it is needed to balance the relationship between employers and labor organizations, that currently the process involving secret-ballot elections is too long and gives employers an unfair advantage, and that when the critical first contract negotiation process fails to produce a contract, it implies the wishes of the employees have been ignored. In addition, employers during organizational campaigns under current law commit unfair actions because the penalties are too low—compared to the costs of losing the election and facing negotiated increased wages and benefits.

Opponents of the EFCA contend that the secret-ballot election is the "gold standard" for determining the wishes of individuals and should not be replaced with authorization cards—which may be signed under pressure, whereas the voting booth allows employees to express their wishes in complete privacy. Even former Democratic presidential candidate and U.S. senator George McGovern wrote that there have been "many documented cases where workers have been pressured, harassed, tricked and intimidated into signing cards," and thus McGovern opposed the replacement of the secret-ballot process.[63] However, survey research involving workers who were involved in card check campaigns or NLRB representation elections did not support the "undue pressure by unions" argument presented by Senator McGovern and other critics of the proposed EFCA. Instead, the interviewed workers reported "little undue union pressure to support unionization in card check campaigns" while also reporting "management pressure to oppose unionization" in both card check campaigns and NLRB representation elections.[64]

Opponents of the EFCA also believe that allowing arbitrators to decide critical first contract issues such as wages, health care benefits, pensions, and so on for a two-year period could be extremely harmful to employers, and they note that nothing similar in the U.S. private sector has been utilized—thus it a largely untested proposal. However, research on the effects of a similar labor law in Canada produced interesting results—not those proposed by critics of the proposed EFCA. Instead the research on the effects of the Canadian law requiring first contract arbitration found that it reduced work stoppages by about 50 percent, that unions rarely utilized the arbitration provision, and that the primary result was that both management and unions were more motivated to settle a first contract.[65] The increased penalties section of the EFCA is the one section that opponents have expressed the least criticism. The future of the proposed EFCA may be the future of organized labor in the United States and thus it will be watched closely by those on both sides.

WORKFORCE DIVERSITY

The labor movement has at times been caught between the proverbial rock and a hard place in its relations with the groups that make up the new diverse workforce. In the past, the labor movement had a number of opportunities to seek out these groups: for African Americans during abolition and the 1960s' civil rights movement, for women during the suffrage movement and the various stages of the women's movement, and for immigrants at the turn of the twentieth century and after World War I.

Union leaders know that minorities and women benefit economically from union membership. Union workers earn 22 percent more in annual wages than nonunion workers, according to the Department of Labor's Bureau of Labor Statistics. The union wage difference is even greater for

FIGURE 2-3 Median Weekly Earnings of Full-Time Wage and Salary Workers, 2009. *Source:* U.S. Department of Labor, Employment and Earnings (2009). Accessed August 18, 2011.

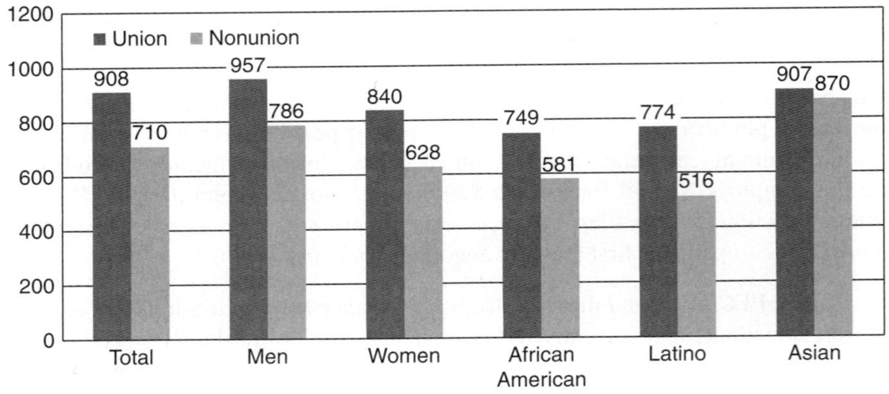

minorities and women. Union women earn 25 percent more than nonunion women, African American union members earn 22.5 percent more than their nonunion counterparts, and for Latino workers the union advantage totals 33 percent (see Figure 2-3).

African Americans and Unions

The abolitionist movement could not claim major support from American white workers. Trade unionists protested the move the federal government was making toward war over the issue of slavery in 1861 with the slogan "Concession, Not Secessions."[66] After the Civil War, the labor movement struggled with the influx of cheap labor into the labor pool, eroding its power to keep wages high. Freed slaves and immigrants were a part of that cheap labor pool. The National Labor Union (NLU) originally encouraged freed slaves to unionize, but they were not invited to actually join the NLU.[67] The relationship between the freed slaves and the white workers in the industrial centers deteriorated. African Americans began forming their own trade union locals, including the **National Colored Labor Union** (NCLU). Headed by Isaac Myers, the NCLU organized in the South in 1870 and applied for affiliation with the NLU, stating, "The day has passed for the establishment of organizations based upon color."[68] Unfortunately, the white labor movement did not agree.

NATIONAL COLORED LABOR UNION

Organized in 1870, this union was a response to the segregated National Labor Union and the American Federation of Laborers.

Although labor leaders were seen as supportive of the civil rights movement, such support did not go deep into union membership. Trade unions that sponsored apprenticeship programs excluding African Americans were not alone in their discrimination. Industrial unions did not help the African American worker. Reacting to this treatment, civil rights leaders and organizations simply regrouped and organized African American workers into unions as part of their civil rights activities. The **Maryland Freedom Union** (MFU) and the **Mississippi Freedom Labor Union** organized and engineered strikes and demonstrations to improve the lot of African American workers who had been shunted to low-paying jobs. A boycott of a small retail chain in a white neighborhood of Baltimore, Maryland, in 1966 led to the MFU's first success. When AFL-CIO officials learned that the MFU had been recognized as the exclusive bargaining agent for the employees of the retail chain, they objected. Walter Reuther, then head of the AFL-CIO's Industrial Union Department, pressured the leadership of the Congress of Racial Equality, a major civil rights organization, to sever its support of the MFU.[69] The MFU, like the activist civil rights organizations, peaked in the late 1960s and disappeared in the 1970s.

MARYLAND FREEDOM UNION

In 1966 with the Mississippi Freedom Labor Union organized and engineered strikes and demonstrations to improve the lot of African American workers who had been shunted to low-paying jobs.

Although the AFL had supported African American membership in affiliate unions, it was not until 1964 that the last affiliate of the AFL-CIO removed the "whites only" clause from its bylaws and constitution. African Americans today are more unionized (13.9 percent) than the workforce as a whole (12.3 percent). In the future, African Americans are likely to increase their role in union leadership and membership. The labor movement has been an important vehicle in the growth of the African American middle class and partially explains the proclivity of black Americans to join unions.

At the same time, there is a shift away from heavy industry and manufacturing in the American economy, and union workers are losing their jobs and are being left unprepared for the new high-skilled labor market. Whereas blacks in 2009 showed a greater preference for union membership than whites, 13.9 to 12.1 percent, Hispanics trailed with 10.2 percent membership. Membership among women, 11.3 percent, has always trailed that of men, which was 13.3 percent in 2009.[70]

Women and Unions

Women today provide almost two-thirds of the new entrants into the job market. The two major areas of potential growth for unionization are in the health industry and among clerical workers. Both of these industries are made up mostly of women workers. The reluctance of unions to include women fully and women's reluctance to unionize may have the same basis. During the post–Civil War period, women who had entered the workforce during the war continued to work. The National Labor Union found itself in the center of controversy for recognizing representatives of women's unions into its Congress. Because unions did not welcome women into their organizations, protective unions and trade associations for women were formed. Sometimes women and men working right next to each other had separate unions. Most men workers viewed women as competition, so they decried their employment. The NLU allowed representatives of a number of the women's protective unions to join their 1868 congress, including Susan B. Anthony, the most famous suffragette. When Anthony admitted that her protective union was used as a strikebreaking organization because the women's movement needed to do so, the NLU expelled her. After that, protective unions for women lost support from their fellow male workers, and by 1872 most had died out.[71]

As discussed earlier, the years between 1903 and World War I found the women's labor unions forging an alliance between middle-class reformers and working-class women. These reformers and workingwomen formed the **Women's Trade Union League**[72] and in 1907 adopted the following six-point platform:

1. Equal pay for equal work
2. Full citizenship for women
3. An eight-hour workday
4. A minimum wage
5. Organization of all workers into unions
6. The economic programs of the American Federation of Labor

During the early 1900s, the league supported unionization of women workers in many industries, but it had its major successes in the garment industry. Unfortunately, the AFL, led by Samuel Gompers, gave no more than lip service to support of the league's activities.

The Great Depression greatly damaged the Women's Trade Union League, which had no convention from 1929 to 1936. Following the passage of the Wagner Act and the strong growth of the CIO, women's auxiliaries to CIO unions became a major factor in the success of the CIO's organization. The famous and effective sit-down strikes of that period in the auto, steel, and mine industries were possible because of the support that wives, mothers, and sisters gave to the strikers. These women were rewarded by a promise from the CIO that women should be taught about unionism as "an effective means of mobilizing support for unionism among the families of union members."[73] Although the CIO never overtly denied admission of women into unions, as had the AFL, neither had it ever encouraged women to organize.

During World War II, women continued to invade the man's working place—first of necessity and then by choice. When the war ended, men expected women to go back home and give the jobs to men, just as had occurred previously. Many women tried not to do that, but the pattern of layoff was such that twice as many women as men lost their jobs during the spring and summer of 1945. The CIO's Reemployment Plan, adopted at its 1944 convention, failed to mention women workers. Despite layoffs, women did not leave the job market, although to a large extent they did leave the factories. The real expansion in women's employment took place in clerical and service operations such as education and the health fields. Because those workers were not targets of union organizing, the history of the women's movement for equality and their interest in labor unions began to branch off into different directions.

As the women's movement focused on improving the position of women in the United States, including women in the workforce, the goal was legislation to ensure equal treatment, equal pay, and equal rights. The success of that movement can be seen in the passage of the 1963 Equal Pay Act and Title VII to the Civil Rights Act of 1964, which prohibited job discrimination on the basis of gender (among other provisions).

With that law theoretically protecting women in the workforce from employers, women had the ability to turn to unionization again to increase their power in the workforce. In 1974, women within the U.S. labor movement organized the founding conference of the **Coalition of Labor Union Women** (CLUW) to promote a renewed interest among women to unionize.

COALITION OF LABOR UNION WOMEN

Founded in 1974, this union was formed to promote the unionization of women in the workforce.

Immigrants and Unions

Except for American Indians and their descendants, all the people of the United States are immigrants or descendants of immigrants. Despite this fact, the history of the American labor movement chronicles both the inclusion and the exclusion of immigrants from the ranks of organized labor.

Skilled laborers of whatever background were included in trade unions in the earliest days of organization. But as the industrial revolution converted many trade industries to industrial factories, competition with immigrant labor was keenly felt. When trade unionism first experienced the challenge of industrial unionism, the organizing of immigrants, who had largely migrated from England, Iceland, and northern Europe, swelled the ranks of those unions. It was not until after World War I that industrial labor unions took a negative stand on immigration, especially regarding people from Italy and southern Europe. Unionists supported the Immigration Acts of 1921 and 1924, which restricted immigration, because those acts reduced the nation's labor supply. Union members believed that they would reap the benefit of these policies with higher wages and job security.

Today, both American employers and unions recognize that new unskilled immigrants are changing workplaces across the United States. Union leaders and managers are realizing they must abandon old assumptions of how these new workers will view organized labor and instead adopt new strategies to gain the loyalty of each new wave of immigrants.

The 1999–2001 strike by 750 Mexican immigrant members of Teamsters Local 890 in King City, California, against Basic Vegetable Products is an excellent example of a new strategy that has been viewed as a "model of labor movement revival." The strike lasted 27 months and was successful against not one but two formidable employers (Basic Vegetable Products was sold to ConAgra Corporation during the strike). The union and its workers employed several key strategies to retain representation as well as wages and benefits:

- "Reframing" the issue to one of workers' rights to unionism and racial justice.
- Making the work stoppage "a strike for our families and our community" to preserve jobs for future generations.
- Building coalitions with regional Chicano and Mexican merchants to oppose the permanent replacement workers.
- Affiliating with the regional labor council and the National Teamsters Union to raise over $2 million in benefits for the strikers.
- Building a successful boycott of Basic potato products in regional schools, cafeterias, hospitals, and jails.
- Defeating a decertification election by encouraging enough strikers to return to work so they could vote.
- Building support from ConAgra unions and top corporate management as well as shareholders until ConAgra changed course and returned to the bargaining table to negotiate a settlement and hire back the strikers to replace the permanent replacement workers.[74]

Summary

The labor union movement in the United States is the history of individuals struggling to survive. As the country grew and developed, the needs of owners and workers intertwined, and the struggle for control caused both strife and cooperation. During that struggle, the labor movement faced hostile court decisions, economic depressions, and internal power struggles. Labor unions had to decide whether to follow a social, political, or economic agenda. The emergence of the AFL and the CIO, with collective bargaining as their most important goal, meant that labor unions picked an economic agenda.

In 1935, Congress articulated the foundation of today's national labor policy with the passage of the Wagner Act (National Labor Relations Act [NLRA]). That act was the culmination of more than 100 years of organized labor's efforts to recognize the employees' rights in the workplace. The disruptive nature of work stoppages caused political leaders to seek a national solution to labor's problems. Under the NLRA, employees were free to organize and bargain collectively and were given the right to strike, and employers were required to bargain with employee representatives. The Great Depression and the New Deal set the stage for Congress to pass legislation that not only protected organized labor but also promoted its growth. Although the Taft-Hartley Amendments and the Landrum-Griffin Act modified the NLRA, its basic support of collective bargaining was not changed.

Today, union supporters recognize that labor membership, public support, and union clout in Washington, D.C., has waned in recent decades. The resulting need to focus on organizing new members led to the historic 2005 split by seven unions from the AFL-CIO to form Change to Win. In addition, labor supporters in Washington are seeking a new organizing law—the Employee Free Choice Act—to make it easier to win new members.

The workforce of the new millennium poses its own challenges and opportunities for unions, which have historically attracted blue-collar white men. Professional men and women, people of color, and those of diverse ethnic backgrounds are the workforce of today. The concerns of workers continue to be wages, working conditions, job security, and respect. It remains to be seen if unions can step into today's workplaces and represent today's worker with the same kind of success they experienced in the past.

CASE STUDIES

Case Study 2-1 Interfering with the Employee's Right to Unionize

The employer sells automotive replacement parts at wholesale from warehouses and distribution centers in the eastern United States. Ms. Fortin began work at the company's Miami warehouse in 1986, and from that time until her layoff in October 1994, she held a number of customer service positions. Because of her excellent reputation for providing service to customers, she was assigned to staff the Metro-Dade account, a separate account established to provide exclusive service to approximately 24 governmental customers in the metropolitan Dade County area. In 1994, Fortin had been commended for increasing sales in the Metro-Dade account.

On June 1, 1994, Fortin appeared under subpoena to testify on the union's behalf at a representation hearing concerning the organizational efforts being undertaken at her workplace and was quoted in the *Miami Herald* as saying the workers "want to better ourselves."

When she returned to work later that day, she received her first disciplinary warning ever. The employer issued four additional disciplinary warnings to Fortin during June, three within two days of the hearing. The employer also removed an exclusive telephone number with its voice mail capabilities used by the customers of the Metro-Dade County account to reach Fortin directly and ceased the special van deliveries to those customers. Fortin was held accountable for the ensuing decreased sales in that account. Notwithstanding this discipline, Fortin remained one of the union's most prominent vocal supporters, appearing in a group photo on a union flyer distributed during the campaign, passing out leaflets and petitions, and serving as one of the union's two observers at the election held on July 7 and 8, 1994.

In early August 1994, her supervisor gave Fortin a negative performance evaluation in which she received an overall rating of "2," indicating "improvement needed." On October 27, 1994, Fortin was laid off. Her new supervisor relied on the negative performance evaluation in deciding to lay her off.

The union charged the employer with an unfair labor practice for fabricating disciplinary actions and a poor performance evaluation and for unlawfully laying off Fortin because of her union activities.

The employer contended that each of the disciplinary actions it took against Fortin was *unrelated* to her union activity and that in each case Fortin was disciplined for being away from her workstation and in an area of the warehouse where she did not belong. Furthermore, one of the employer's outside salesmen told Fortin's supervisor that customers were complaining of poor service from her. And finally, Fortin's new supervisor based his layoff decision on her poor performance evaluation and was not even aware of her union activity.

The union contended that Fortin had business reasons to visit the warehouse and had done so routinely in the past and that the employer began to restrict her movements only after it learned of her support for the union. Moreover, other employees were not similarly disciplined, even those employees who were talking to Fortin on the very occasion for which she was disciplined. Given this disparity of treatment and the fact that Fortin's movements were not restricted before the employer learned of her union activity, the reasonable inference, according to the union, is that Fortin's union activity was a motivating factor in the employer's discipline of her. As to the poor performance evaluation, the union noted that the evaluation covered a one-year period from August 1993 to August 1994, during which time Fortin was selected for the Metro-Dade account and commended for increasing the Metro-Dade sales. If there was any problem with the Metro-Dade account, as noted earlier, the employer caused it by removing the special phone line voice mail service, and special delivery van dedicated to Metro-Dade customers rather than any fault of Fortin. Finally, because the performance evaluation was based on the employer's union animus, basing the layoff on it was unlawful, even if the supervisor knew nothing of her union activities.

Source: Adapted from *Parts Depot Inc. v. NLRB,* 170 LRRM 1005 (September 29, 2000).

QUESTIONS

1. Do you believe Fortin was the victim of antiunion discrimination by her employer? Why or why not?
2. Fortin's supervisor had no knowledge of her union activity but laid her off on the basis of her poor performance evaluation. Give reasons why a court should uphold or override the supervisor's decision.
3. Explain why you think employers still resist unions 70 years after the passage of the National Labor Relations Act.

Case Study 2-2 Discriminating Against Union Members

The company, a nursing home, provides nursing, rehabilitation, and therapy services. The union represents all regularly scheduled nonprofessional employees, including nurse's aides, housekeeping employees, laundry employees, dietary employees, medical records clerks, and janitor-maintenance employees. The company employs 80 full-time personnel to operate the facility, of which about 50 are included in the bargaining unit. The company and the union had a long-standing collective bargaining relationship, but the current contract was due to expire on September 10, 1999, and negotiations were not going well.

In the midst of the negotiations, the grievant, a nurse's aide, a longtime employee of the company and *a member of the union negotiating team,* was injured on the job. After a doctor's examination, she was placed on "light duty" and referred to physical therapy. At the time, the company did not have a light-duty policy. However, the company ordered the grievant back to work for assignment to light duty and threatened to fire her if she did not return. Grievant did not report to work for light duty. She claimed that because the contract contained no light-duty provision, the company did not have the authority unilaterally to institute such a policy.

In addition, the company scheduled members of the union negotiating team, including the grievant, for part-time work on days when contract negotiations were to take place. The grievant did not report for work on days when negotiations were to take place because she claimed that under the "past practice" of the company and union, union negotiating team members were not required to work the day of negotiations but rather were allowed to meet to prepare for the actual negotiations' session. The grievant was terminated for failure to report for work as ordered.

The union filed a grievance protesting the discharge as unjust and in violation of the National Labor Relations Act. The union contended that the company's imposition of light duty on the grievant and the scheduling of members of the negotiating committee to work on the day of negotiations were unfair labor practices.

According to the union, historically members of the negotiating committee have been scheduled off—unpaid—on the days of contract negotiations, thereby establishing a "past practice" the company had to honor. The union asserts that members of the negotiating committee were improperly scheduled to work on November 1 and 2, and when they rightfully attended to union business as they had always done in preparation for bargaining sessions, they were severely disciplined for not reporting to work as directed. As noted by the union, had the negotiating team members worked those days, it would have interfered with their duties as members of the negotiating committee. Furthermore, the company did not have the right unilaterally to institute a light-duty policy and impose it on a union negotiating team member. Such a policy affected the terms and conditions of the employees' work and is therefore a mandatory subject for bargaining.

The company argues *economic privilege* in the preceding instances of unilateral action. According to the company, the purpose of the change in the scheduling and attendance policy was to require people to come to work to make certain that adequate staffing was maintained. The purpose of requiring union officials to work part time on days of union negotiations, although perhaps previously unnecessary, was to fill the work schedule, not adversely affect union negotiators, and the purpose of the light-duty work assignments was to save money by having medically restricted employees on the job. The policy was not instituted for or directed at the members of the negotiating team. Thus, the company has not violated the NLRA.

Source: Adapted from *HCM, Inc. v. United Food and Commercial Workers Union, Local 1529,* 116 LA 1200 (January 8, 2002).

QUESTIONS

1. Active union members often have two jobs to do—as an employee and as a union member. How far do you think an employer should be required to go to allow the member to do both jobs?
2. The nonprofessional jobs at a nursing home are often hard to fill, and there can be a lot of employee turnover. Do you think having a union at a nursing home helps or hinders in the employment and retention of employees?
3. Do you think the company has evidenced an antiunion attitude by instituting in close proximity a light-duty policy that directly impacts one of the union negotiators and by requiring the union negotiating team to work part time on negotiating days?

Key Terms and Concepts

American Federation of Labor *49*
American Railway Union *47*
Clayton act *60*
Coalition of Labor Union Women *72*
Coeur d'Alene incident *50*
company unions *58*
Congress of Industrial Organizations (CIO) *54*
Cordwainers Conspiracy Cases *55*
Employee Free Choice Act *68*
Haymarket Square Riot *45*
Homestead, Pennsylvania *46*
Knights of labor *46*
labor injunctions *57*
Labor-Management Reporting and Disclosure Act of 1959 (Landrum-Griffin Act) *67*
Maryland Freedom Union *70*
Molly Maguires *43*
National Colored Labor Union *70*
National Labor Relations Act (NLRA) *63*
National Labor Relations Board (NLRB) *63*
National Labor Union *43*
Norris-La Guardia Act *62*
Pullman Strike *47*
scabs *65*
Taft-Hartley Amendments *66*
Wagner Act *63*
Women's Trade Union League *52*

Review Questions

1. What factors in the 1800s contributed to the growth of U.S. labor unions?
2. Did the Great Depression have any impact on the U.S. labor movement? If so, what?
3. Why is Fannie Sellins called "Labor's Martyr"?
4. Describe the federal and court actions against union workers in the 1800s.
5. Why did the Wagner Act have a major impact on employees' rights?
6. What circumstances prompted Congress to pass the Taft-Hartley Amendments? The Landrum-Griffin Act? What are the key provisions of these acts?
7. What were common objectives of the early labor unions?
8. Why was April 20, 1914, "a day that will live in infamy" in labor history?
9. Why was the relationship between unions and African Americans one of advances and defeats?
10. In which industry did women enjoy the most organizing success in the early 1900s?

YOU BE THE ARBITRATOR
Management rights

CBA ARTICLE II MANAGEMENT

SECTION 1. MANAGEMENT FUNCTION

1. The Management of the Plant and all Company operations shall be vested exclusively in the Company, including the direction of the work forces; the right to modernize and install new equipment and to rearrange production schedules; the right to hire; the right to suspend or discharge employees for just cause; the right to relieve employees from duty because of lack of work or for other reasonable causes; all subject to the provisions of this agreement.
2. All employee job descriptions will be evaluated against standards of the industry to include, but not exclusive, the "Job Competencies Analysis System" agreement.

SECTION 6. NEW JOB CLASSIFICATION

1. 1. When a new job classification is established, the Company will develop a Job Description, Labor Grade, and Rate. These will be explained to the JLRC. The rate will then be installed. When a wage rate for a new job classification is installed, the employee or employees affected may object to the rate, and at any time within ninety (90) days from receipt of the Labor Grade and rate, file a grievance, and such grievance shall be processed under the grievance procedure of this Agreement. If such grievance is settled at any step of the grievance procedure, the decision shall be effective as of the date when the employee or employees were assigned to the new job classification.

Facts

The Company manufactures corn syrup, corn syrup solids, and sweeteners at its plant in Iowa. The Union is a bargaining unit representing 238 production workers including the Grievant at the Company's facility. The Company and Union are parties to a Collective Bargaining Agreement (CBA) which was in full force and effect at all relevant times herein. The Company announced that it was discontinuing three job classifications in the Sanitation Department and establishing one new job classification in that Department. As a result of the Company's actions five bargaining unit jobs were affected. Two of these five bargaining unit members bid into the new job classification of Material Handler in the Sanitation Department. The other three bargaining unit members bid into other jobs with the Company. No bargaining unit member was laid off or lost his or her job as a result of the Company discontinuing these three job classifications and establishing one new job classification.

Some of the work previously done by bargaining unit members in that department was now being performed by outside contractors. Several of these outside contractors already were performing work for the Company including ice and snow removal, janitorial, landscaping, and trucking.

Following the Company's actions, the Union filed a grievance alleging that the Company violated the CBA without first negotiating with the Union before making these job classification changes and by subcontracting out the work of the bargaining unit.

Issue

Did the Company violate the CBA by discontinuing three job classifications in the Sanitation Department and establishing one new job classification in the Sanitation Department without first negotiating with the Union? Did the Company violate the CBA by subcontracting the work previously done by the union members?

Positions of the Parties

The Company has the right pursuant to the Management Rights Clause to discontinue job classifications and establish new job classifications. The job classifications eliminated were not "core jobs" in that the Company was not in the business of truck driving, yard maintenance or janitorial work. The Company also had legitimate business reasons for discontinuing these job classifications and contracting out these duties. First, trash dumped on Company premises caused sanitation problems. Second, by eliminating the trash dump the Company could use that area for wet feed. Third, the Company no longer was required to pay landfill fees or purchase a new trash truck. The Company estimated it had an immediate savings of $60,000 to $90,000.

The Company did not negotiate the discontinuance of these job classifications as there was nothing in the CBA requiring them to do so. There had been five previous instances wherein the Company discontinued job classifications and established new job classifications and the Union did not grieve any of those Company actions. As a result of the Company's actions in this dispute, the five employees whose job classifications were eliminated were not laid off nor did they lose employment.

As to the subcontracting, the Company pointed out that there is no contractual provision preventing the Company from subcontracting work. And that the Company had been contracting out work for a number of years without any protest or grievance filed by the Union. Under the Management Rights Clause, the Company had legitimate business purposes to contract out certain work that was not core work of the Company's business.

The Union's position is that the Company violated the CBA by unilaterally eliminating three job classifications and establishing one new job classification and subcontracting out the work without negotiating with the Union. This is a contract interpretation case, and it is the Arbitrator's duty to determine the mutual intent of the parties as expressed in the language of the CBA. If the disputed CBA language is clear and unambiguous, the Arbitrator will give such language its plain meaning. However, if the disputed CBA language is reasonably susceptible to more than one meaning, the language may be considered ambiguous and the Arbitrator may rely on other interpretative aids such as bargaining history or past practice of the parties.

The Union contends that the phrase "the right to relieve employees from duty because of lack of work or *for other reasonable causes*" in the Management Rights Clause is susceptible to more than one meaning. First, there was no lack of work, the Company still needed the services performed by the bargaining unit employees, as demonstrated by the fact that the Company contracted out the work. So, that leaves the issue of what is "reasonable causes"? The only reasons cited by the Company to support their action was to save money. But the Management Rights Clause speaks to specific operational and not financial decisions. Furthermore, because the CBA specifically provides for the creation of *new* job classifications, but says nothing about eliminating job classifications, the Union argued that eliminating job classifications was not contemplated by the "relieve employees from duty" language.

As to subcontracting, if the Management Rights Clause is interpreted to allow for subcontracting out bargaining unit work, then there would be nothing to prevent the Company from dismissing all of its employees and contracting for all of the plant's work. That was certainly NOT the intent of the Union when it agreed to the very specific Management Rights Clause in the CBA.

Source: Adapted from *Roquette America, Inc., [Keokuk, Iowa] and Bakery, Confectionery, Tobacco, Workers and Grain Millers International Union, Local 48G*, 128 Lab. Arb. (BNA) 103 (2010).

QUESTIONS

1. As arbitrator, what would be your award and opinion in this arbitration?
2. Identify the key, relevant section(s), phrases, or words of the collective bargaining agreement (CBA), and explain why they were critical in making your decision.
3. What actions might the employer and/or the union have taken to avoid this conflict?

CHAPTER 3

Public Sector Labor Relations: History and Law

Thousands of faculty, students, and staff on ten University of California campuses turned out to protest against state budget cuts. The budget reductions increased tuition by 32 percent and cut faculty pay by 10 percent through unpaid furlough days, among other action needed to balance university budgets. *Source:* Jae C Hong/AP Images.

Chapter Outline

The American Labor Movement has consistently demonstrated devotion to the public interest. It is and has been good for all America.

JOHN F. KENNEDY (35TH PRESIDENT OF THE UNITED STATES)

LABOR NEWS

Thousands Protest University of California Budget Cuts

Thousands of students, faculty, and staff on ten campuses of the University of California participated in protests of the size not seen on that campus since the protests against the Vietnam War in the 1960s. The issue which fueled the protests was the California Legislature's approval of Governor Arnold Schwarzenegger's proposed 20 percent reduction in state funds. The budget cut caused the ten campuses of the University of California system to adopt massive tuition increases and cuts in faculty and staff pay. An online walkout petition signed by 1,221 faculty then quickly spread across the ten UC campuses and the union representing over 11,000 professional and technical staff supported the walkout which caused classes to be canceled. The budget action caused tuition increase of 32 percent and faculty and staff pay cuts of 10 percent through unpaid furlough days. UC, Berkeley, theatre professor Catherine Cole, who canceled classes and attended the rally, said: "We've hit a tipping point [in higher education]." Chancellor Robert J. Birgeneau concurred and predicted that "in the future UC would rely less on state support and more on higher tuition and student fees . . . and that in the future paying for public education is going to be increasingly difficult for middle-class families."

Source: Adapted from Malia Wollan, "Thousands Protest University of California Finances," *The New York Times* (September 25, 2009), p. A17.

The IRS agent who is auditing your taxes, your postal carrier, your favorite teacher, the clerk at the drivers' license bureau, the firefighters you see rushing to the scene of a fire, the police officer who pulls you over for speeding—what do they have in common? They are all public (government) employees, and there's more than a 38 percent chance that they are union members and engaging in collective bargaining with government officials, elected or appointed, at the federal, state, or local level. The National Labor Relations Act gave private sector employees substantive rights to organize into labor unions and required private sector employers to meet with their employees at the bargaining table to discuss the terms and conditions of the job.

Public employees, however, were not guaranteed rights under the National Labor Relations Act. The development of labor relations in the public sector has followed a completely different route, which only started in earnest in the 1960s; however, today there are more union members in the public sector than in the private sector, despite there being five times more workers in the private sector. In 2009, 37.4 percent of public employees were union members, with 7.9 million union members working in all levels of government. By comparison, only 7.2 percent of employees in the private sector were union members and the number of private sector union members dropped to 7.4 million, lower than the public sector for the first time in U.S. history. What is remarkable about this dramatic growth of public sector unions over the past 40 years is that it has occurred at the same time private sector unions realized a sizable loss of members.

MEMPHIS SANITATION STRIKE

African American sanitation workers went on strike in order to be paid minimum wages. It became a Civil Rights issue when Martin Luther King Jr. joined in the marches and demonstrations. Rev. King was assassinated in Memphis after delivering his famous "I have been to the mountaintop" speech. The strike ended eight days after his death.

Much of the growth, however, came during the so-called tidal wave of the 1960–1970s period following President Kennedy's 1962 Executive Order that first recognized public employees' right to join a union, and the many similar state and local laws that followed. The unionization of public employees since then reflects a basic change in the character of the American labor movement. For instance, in 1966, 915,000 public employees were union members. Then in 1968, the **Memphis Sanitation Strike** ignited a burst of public sector union organizing efforts at all levels of government. Their success gave momentum to the public sector union movement.[1] The membership of public employee unions skyrocketed to 2.9 million by 1975, 7 million by 1993, and 7.9 million by 2009.[2]

The Memphis strike was staged by 1,300 African American sanitation workers who refused to work until they were paid *minimum wage*! As public sector employees they were not covered by minimum wage laws. Over 64 days, the strike grew into a major civil rights struggle, with AFSCME and the workers demanding union recognition, wage increases, and an end to discrimination. The presence of national Civil Rights leaders and the participation of local clergy members and community leaders in boycotts and civil disobedience garnered national attention to the strike. On April 3, 1968, the day before he was assassinated, Dr. Martin Luther King Jr. delivered his now famous "I've been to the mountaintop" speech in support of the striking sanitation workers at Mason Temple in Memphis, Tennessee on:

> The issue is injustice. The issue is the refusal of Memphis to be fair and honest in its dealings with its public servants, who happen to be sanitation workers . . . We've got some difficult days ahead. But it doesn't matter with me now. Because I've been to the mountaintop. And I don't mind. Like anybody, I would like to live a long life. Longevity has its place. But I'm not concerned about that now. I just want to do God's will. And He's allowed me to go up to the mountain. And I've looked over. And I've seen the promised land. I may not get there with you. But I want you to know tonight, that we, as a people, will get to the promised land. And I'm happy, tonight. I'm not worried about anything. I'm not fearing any man. Mine eyes have seen the glory of the coming of the Lord.

The strike ended nine days later with a settlement that included union recognition and a wage increase. Figure 3-1 lists a brief chronology of the strike's major events.

Dr. King delivers his "I've been to the mountaintop" address to a crowd in Memphis the day before he is killed by an assassin's bullet. *Source:* © Bettmann/CORBIS.

Monday, February 12—Memphis sanitation and public employees strike after last-minute attempts to resolve grievances fail. Newspapers claim 200 workers of 1,300 remain on the job but only 38 of 180 trucks move. Mayor Loeb says strike is illegal but says "this office stands ready . . . to talk to anyone about his legitimate questions at any time."

Tuesday, February 13—An International Union official flies in from Washington to meet with the mayor. He calls for union recognition, dues checkoff, and negotiations to resolve the workers' grievances. The mayor says he'll hire new workers unless the strikers return to their jobs.

(continued)

Wednesday, February 14—The mayor delivers a back-to-work ultimatum for 7 A.M. Feb. 15. Police escort the few garbage trucks in operation. Negotiations between the city and the union break off. Newspapers say more than 10,000 tons of garbage is piled up.

Saturday, February 24—Black leaders and ministers form citywide organization to support the strike and the boycott. City obtains court injunction to keep union from staging demonstrations or picketing.

Tuesday, March 5—Ministers announce the Rev. Dr. Martin Luther King Jr. will come to Memphis, as 116 strikers and supporters are arrested for sitting in at city hall.

Thursday, March 14—National NAACP leader Roy Wilkins addresses meeting of 10,000 or more and expresses support for a firm, peaceful protest. Six pickets are arrested and charged with blocking the Democrat Road sanitation depot entrance.

Thursday, March 28—March from Clayborn Temple, led by Dr. King, is interrupted by window breaking. Police move into crowds with nightsticks, mace, tear gas and gunfire. A 16-year old boy, Larry Payne, is shot to death. Police arrest 280, report about 60 injured, mostly blacks. State legislature authorizes 7 P.M. curfew and 4,000 National Guardsmen move in.

Friday, March 29—Some 300 sanitation workers and ministers march peacefully and silently from Clayborn Temple to City Hall—escorted by five armored personnel carriers, five jeeps, three huge military trucks and dozens of Guardsmen with bayonets fixed. President Johnson and AFL-CIO President George Meany offer assistance in resolving the dispute. Mayor Loeb turns them down.

Wednesday, April 3—Dr. King returns to Memphis and addresses rally, delivering his "I've been to the mountaintop" address.

Thursday, April 4—A sniper, later captured and identified as James Earl Ray, assassinates Dr. King as he stands on the balcony outside his room at the Lorraine Hotel.

Friday, April 5—Federal troops and Atty. Gen. Ramsey Clark are in Memphis as FBI begins international manhunt for assassin. President Johnson instructs Undersecretary of Labor James Reynolds to take charge of mediation to settle the strike.

Saturday, April 6—Reynolds meets with Mayor Loeb in the first of a long string of meetings—first with one side, then the other, rarely together.

Tuesday, April 16—AFSCME leaders announce that agreement has been reached. The strikers vote to accept it. The strike is over.

FIGURE 3-1 1968 AFSCME Memphis Sanitation Workers' Strike Chronology. *Source:* Excerpts from AFSCME Local 1733 pamphlet. Available at http://www.afscme.org (1970). Accessed August 20, 2011.

DEFINING THE PUBLIC SECTOR

The public sector consists of a myriad of levels and jurisdictions of governmental units providing basic services. The three levels of government are federal, state, and local. The United States has a federal system of government with a national government and subnational entities officially called states. Local governments include cities, counties, towns, and villages, and such entities as local school boards and public utilities. All three levels of government have two roles as it relates to collective bargaining: in the private sector as creator and protector of collective bargaining rights, and in the public sector as employer. The federal government through the National Labor Relations Board, state governments through similar State Boards or Labor Departments, and many local governments through local labor–management organizations, and/or through the appropriate courts at all levels, are those to whom employees and employers will turn to when there are labor issues to address. In this chapter, and in the context of labor relations, however, we view these governments as employers, or management.

THE FEDERAL GOVERNMENT The federal government is divided into three main branches: the legislative, the judicial, and the executive. These branches have the same basic shape and perform the same basic roles defined for them when the Constitution was written in 1787. Congress, the legislative branch, passes the laws. The president is the elected chief executive officer and is charged with faithful execution of the laws. The Supreme Court and all other federal courts have the judicial authority vested in them by the Constitution to interpret the law. A system of checks and balances prevents power from being concentrated in any one of the three branches. During the centuries since the Constitution first defined the federal system, the federal government has grown and evolved in response to economic and political events. There are certain areas where a national policy is clearly required, such as foreign relations, defense, the monetary system, and foreign and interstate commerce. The National Labor Relations Act, for example, was passed in the interest of ensuring peaceful interstate commerce.

Other areas once thought to be in the domain of state or local government, or the private sector, have become national concerns and have resulted in federal intervention, such as social security, the environment, agriculture, and race discrimination. The day-to-day administration of federal laws is in the hands of the various federal executive departments, created by Congress to deal with specific areas of national and international affairs, such as the Department of State, the Department of Defense, and the Treasury Department, three original departments created by Congress. There are also independent agencies that are a part of the federal governmental structure, such as the National Labor Relations Board, the United States Postal Service, and the Central Intelligence Agency (CIA). Between World War I and World War II, as a result of the Great Depression, dozens of new agencies and new programs were created to deal with the U.S. economy. Because of the federal government's increased role in domestic and foreign affairs, its widespread regulatory systems, its authority and responsibilities have grown tremendously. This growth is reflected in the number of federal civilian employees, which increased from 391,000 in 1916 to 1.9 million in 1950 to 3,594,000 in 2009.[3] Over *one million of those employees* are represented by unions, although all are not union members as you can see in Table 3-1. Because the law allowing federal employees to form bargaining units and enter into negotiations does not require that they become union members, many do not. Even though they are not union members, the negotiated contract still applies to them.

Now looking at the role of the federal government in the private sector, there will be references throughout this text to both the National Labor Relations Board and the federal courts. The National Labor Relations Board has the authority to enforce the NLRA, to order remedial actions, that is, remedies to make whole those who have been harmed by violations of the act. If the offending party fails to abide by the board's order, or wishes to challenge the board's order, the issue goes to federal court. The federal court has three levels, district court, court of appeals, and the Supreme Court. A ruling from a district or court of appeals that is not challenged is legally binding; if challenged and heard by the Supreme Court, then that decision is legally binding.

TABLE 3-1 Union Affiliation of Public Sector Employees, 2009

	Total	Members of Unions	Percent of Employed	Represented by Unions	Percent of Employed
Public Sector	21,133,000	7,896,000	37.4	8,677,000	41.1
Federal Government	3,594,000	1,005,000	28.0	1,192,000	33.2
State Government	6,294,000	2,025,000	32.2	2,222,000	35.3
Local Government	11,244,000	4,867,000	43.3	5,263,000	46.8

DUAL SOVEREIGNTY

The sharing of governmental power between the federal and state governments. Under the U.S. Constitution, all powers not granted to the federal government are reserved for the states.

STATE GOVERNMENT A state government is the governing body of one of the 50 states. State governments and the federal government are legally **dual sovereigns**. The *sovereign* nature of government is one of the major issues discussed further in this chapter—it explains why collective bargaining in the public sector differs from that in the private sector. State governments share power with the federal government, and under the U.S. Constitution, all governmental powers not granted to the federal government are reserved for the states. The framers of the Constitution recognized the potential for conflict between the two levels of government, especially in the use of concurrent or shared powers, so they adopted strategies to avoid it. The U.S. Constitution was made supreme over state constitutions and included a clause that declared the actions of the federal government supreme whenever its constitutional use of power clashed with the legitimate actions of the states. As discussed in Chapter 1, the *preemption* of the federal labor law over state laws on the same subject is a result of this constitutional provision. The Constitution also established ground rules for relationships among states by listing the reciprocal obligations the states owed each other—primary respect for each other's laws.

All states have a written constitution and a three-branch government modeled on the U.S. federal government. The executive branch of every state is headed by an elected governor, and the legislative branch is typically a bicameral legislature made up of a senate and a house of representatives (except Nebraska, which has a unicameral body). The judicial branch is typically headed by a supreme court which hears appeals from lower state courts. Most states are subdivided into counties, which are considered subsets of state government and share in the state's sovereignty. Like the federal government, state and county governments need money to function. States rely primarily on sales and/or property taxes, but also on grants from the federal government for administering programs such as retirement, unemployment compensation, and other social insurance systems, and fees such as tolls, lottery ticket sales, and income from college tuition. Counties can exercise such functions and impose such taxes as their respective state constitutions allow.

Historically, the tasks of public safety, public education, public health, transportation, and infrastructure have generally been considered primarily state responsibilities, although all of these now have significant federal funding and regulation as well. One of the largest issue areas left to the discretion of the states is education. The public education system is administered mostly on the state and local levels. Elementary and secondary schools receive funding from all the different levels of government: about 45.6 percent from the state government, 37.1 percent from local governments, and 8.3 percent from the federal government.[4]

Workers in some states, such as these highway workers, are given the right to organize, join unions, and bargain collectively, while similar workers in other states are not given such rights. *Source:* Bloomberg via Getty Images.

Some states, such as California and Hawaii, have expanded bargaining rights in the private sector to those employees not covered by the NLRA, specifically agricultural workers. State Labor Relation Boards are usually created to enforce the respective state labor law by ordering remedial actions and enforcing the same through the state court system.

LOCAL GOVERNMENT A *municipal corporation* is the legal term for a local government. A municipal corporation is a political creation of a state that is composed of the citizens of a designated geographic area and which performs certain state functions on a local level. These political entities are called corporations because, unlike the federal or state governments, they are not considered *sovereign* entities. Rather they are created by the state as an entity capable of conducting business but only as to such powers as are conferred upon it by the state. They fall into two categories—those with general jurisdiction, such as cities or towns, and those with specific jurisdiction, such as school districts or public utilities.

States give municipalities the power to create an official governing body, such as a board or council. In many local government structures, the legislative body also serves as an executive body, directing the day-to-day operation of its activities. Some local government separates the executive and legislative duties with a mayor or a "chief executive" who manages the government. The governing members of the local government are elected by voters who live within the voting boundaries of the municipality. The local body has the power to pass ordinances, or local laws. These laws may not conflict with state or federal laws. The responsibility to carry out those laws falls on the mayor/chief executive if there is a separate executive authority.

Some states grant so-called **home rule** powers to municipalities in the state constitution or state statutes. Home rule is a flexible grant of power from the state to municipalities to determine their own goals without interference from the state legislature or state agencies. It allows municipalities to act on issues of local concern because they do not have to seek approval for their actions from the state legislature. Although home-rule powers are broad, in no event may a municipality enact a law that is specifically precluded by state law or that is contrary to state law. As discussed later in this chapter, the grant or prohibition of collective bargaining rights of local government employees is often the result of decisions made at the state and not the local level.

HOME RULE

A flexible grant of powers from the state to municipalities to determine their own goals without interference from the state legislature or state agencies.

The governmental authority most commonly exercised by municipalities is the exercise of what is called *police powers*, that is, the power to enact laws governing health, safety, morals,

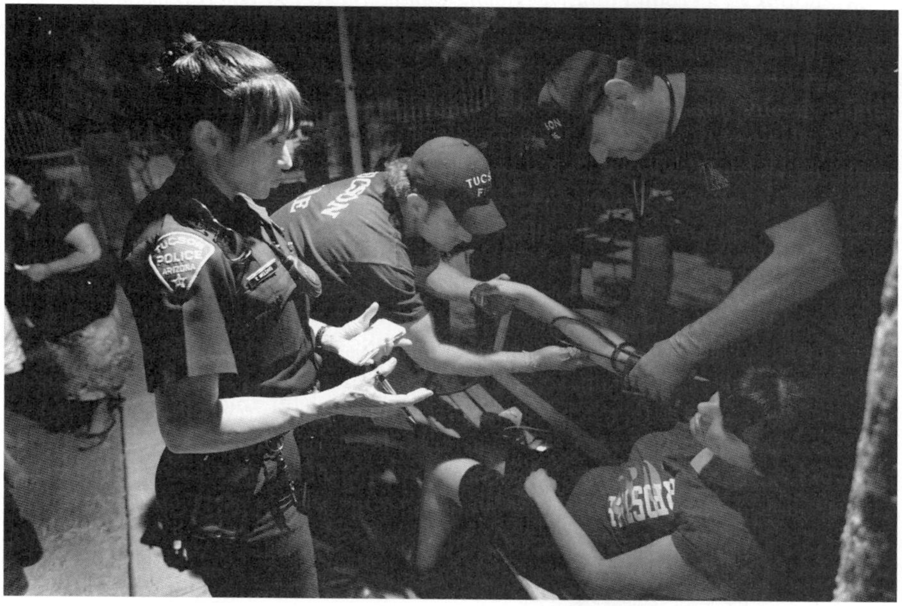

Police officers and firefighters are often represented by local chapters of the Fraternal Order of Police (FOP) and International Association of Fire Fighters (IAFF). *Source:* Scott Olsen/Getty Images

and general public welfare. States also commonly give their municipalities the power to enter into contracts. This power can be exercised only by action of the local governing body. So in the event a local government does enter into collective bargaining with its employees, its governing body, usually a city council, must approve that agreement. This adds a *political* aspect to labor relations in the public sector that does not usually exist in the private sector. Municipal corporations may impose taxes and/or user fees depending upon their statutory authority. The services usually provided by local government include schools, police and fire protection, parks and recreational facilities, and traffic lights.

Just as employment in the federal government grew, state and local governments' employment increased over fourfold, from approximately 4 million in 1950 to around 12 million in 1976 and to 17.5 million in 2009.[5]

HISTORY OF PUBLIC SECTOR LABOR RELATIONS

Congress excluded federal, state, and local government employees from the provisions of the National Labor Relations Act. In the traditional sense, Congress viewed government not as an employer but as a representative of the people, supplying certain necessary services. Therefore, government-employed people were not employees but public servants, and already existing systems protected them from the arbitrary actions of private employers. Such systems addressed basic employee concerns—wages, benefits, and job security—even as the sovereignty of the government was maintained.

PENDLETON ACT Such was not always the case. In the early 1800s, citizens were scandalized by the use of party patronage in federal, state, and local governments. This **spoils system** caused a turnover of government workers on the basis of their political affiliation, not on their ability or dedication. Government workers were expected to support political candidates with time and money or fear losing their jobs. The government lost continuity and efficiency because of the repeated replacement of trained employees.

SPOILS SYSTEM

CIn the early 1800s, this patronage system for the federal government meant that workers were hired on the basis of who they supported in elections. Employees were expected to support political candidates or lose their job.

PENDLETON ACT

Created the federal merit system to address the abuses of the spoils system; administered open competitive examinations; protected employees from being fired for political reasons; and provided that Congress set the wages for federal workers.

In 1883, Congress passed the **Pendleton Act**, which provided for a bipartisan three-member Civil Service Commission to draw up and administer competitive examinations to determine the fitness of appointees to federal office. The act protected federal employees from being fired for failure to make political contributions and actually forbade political campaign contributions by certain employees. The Pendleton Act affected only about 10 percent of the federal employees at the time, but it enabled the president to broaden the merit system and was the foundation of the present federal civil service system. Many states followed the federal government's lead and instituted civil service merit systems for their employees. A civil service or "merit" system provides job security for government workers. Rules governing hiring, firing, and discipline protect workers from arbitrary actions, and due process hearings give workers a forum to protest employment actions by government managers.

EARLY PUBLIC SECTOR UNIONS The Pendleton Act also gave Congress the right to regulate wages, hours, and working conditions of public employees. To a large extent, the response to the Pendleton Act by both the executive and legislative bodies in the early 1900s demonstrates the hydra-headed nature of public sector labor relations. Two early federal employee organizations, the New York Letter Carriers (1863) and the National Association of Letter Carriers (1890), engaged in intense lobbying for improved salaries, better working conditions, and greater security for letter carriers and their families. In 1895, the Postmaster General prohibited postal employees from visiting Washington to influence legislation. President Theodore Roosevelt followed in 1902 with his infamous "gag order," forbidding postal and federal employees, either individually or through associations, to solicit members of Congress for wage increases or for other legislation. In reaction, Congress enacted the Lloyd-LaFollette Act of 1912 with the intention of conferring job protection rights on federal employees and a restriction on the authority of the executive branch of government to discharge a federal employee for talking to Congress. The purpose of this act, from the legislative perspective, was to allow Congress to obtain uncensored, essential information from federal employees or their associations. Congress intended to allow the federal workers direct access to Congress in order to register complaints about conduct by their supervisors and to report corruption or incompetence.[6] However, from the executive perspective, the unfettered access to Congress by federal employees played havoc with the ability to manage federal agencies and the federal budget.[7]

Following upon the success of the Letter Carriers, other organizations of government employees, such as the National Federation of Federal Employees (NFFE) formed in 1917, the American Federation of Government Employees (AFGE) formed in 1932, and the National Association of Government Employees (NAGE) formed soon after, concentrated on lobbying to obtain legislation favorable to their members. For most government workers, such lobbying proved to be successful. Although income was modest, fringe benefits such as vacations, paid holidays, paid sick leave, and pensions offered the public employees rewards not found in the private sector. So before the National Labor Relations Act was passed, federal employees, represented by employee associations and organizations, could boast of an indirect participation in decisions affecting their employment. Unlike their counterparts in the private sector, their employer also could be reached in the legislature and at the ballot box. However, the growth of public employment at every level soon began to erode that accessibility.

Although most public sector unions began and grew in strength and number in the 1960s and 1970s, a few of today's major local government public unions have much older roots. Firefighters and police officers, for example, first formed "**fraternal organizations**" or "social clubs," similar to unions in the late 1880s. The firefighters formed the International Association of Fire Fighters (IAFF), which was chartered by the American Federation of Labor (AFL) in 1918. It is the oldest noneducation nationally affiliated state or local union. Police fraternities chartered at the same time suffered a setback in 1919 in Boston, Massachusetts. That year the Boston police commissioner refused to meet with the Boston Social Club to discuss wages and working conditions, which caused a walkout by 1,200 police officers. However, the Boston Social Club's AFL charter included a promise of "no strike." The officers were all fired, and the American Federation of Labor revoked the charter. Massachusetts governor Calvin Coolidge, a future U.S. president, stated, "There is no right to strike against the public safety by anybody anywhere, anytime," a position that took hold nationally and set back the cause of police unionism for many years.[8] Today, however, the Fraternal Order of Police (FOP), formed in 1917, is the world's largest organization of sworn law enforcement officers with over 325,000 members in 2,100 lodges.[9]

FRATERNAL ORGANIZATIONS

A union that represents public employees in one profession and began as a professional organization before widespread collective bargaining by public employees.

Teachers were another group to form early public sector unions. The National Teachers Association, today known as the National Education Association(NEA), formed in 1857, and the American Federation of Teachers (AFT) formed in 1916. These organizations, first set up by school administrators to advance the interest of the teaching occupation, grew more aggressive in championing the repeal of laws that forbade teachers from smoking, placed restrictions on their dress, or imposed curfews.[10] The American Federation of State, County and Municipal Employees (AFSCME) traces its origins to the Wisconsin State Employees Association formed in 1932. AFSCME began as a number of separate locals organized by a group of Wisconsin state employees. By 1935, 30 locals had become a separate department within the American Federation of Government Employees. In 1936, the American Federation of Labor chartered AFSCME.

The Push for Public Sector Collective Bargaining

During the 1930s and 1940s, private sector unionization flourished under the protection of the National Labor Relations Act. These unions sought job security, higher wages, improved benefits, grievance procedures, arbitration rights, and, more important, recognition as participants in the decision-making process.

HATCH ACT

Passed in 1939, amended in 1993, the Hatch Act limited the political activities of federal employees to shield workers from political pressure and ensure that the resources of the federal government were not used to favor a political party.

CIVIL SERVICE SYSTEM

A governmental system of employment based on merit. Employee selection is based on examination scores or an assessment of experience and abilities. Promotion, advancement, and discipline are based on job performance.

Unionization grew later and more slowly than the public sector for a number of reasons. One, unions held less attraction for many public employees because they already enjoyed some of the protections sought by private employees—job protection through the civil service system, benefits like sick and annual leave days (1893), and an eight-hour day (1888). In addition, the nature of government employment was predominately white collar, while unionization in the 1930s and 1940s was by and large a blue collar activity. And finally, the sovereign issue, discussed in more detail later, and a legal environment that was highly unfavorable to public employee collective bargaining, kept employees at all levels of government from being able to approach government employers and engage in collective bargaining. The successes of private unions, however, began to surpass the public employees' ability to lobby. In the private sector, wages and benefits improved year after year, and job security was increased through the establishment of grievance and arbitration procedures in collective bargaining agreements. The organized worker also became cognizant of the respect a union could demand from an employer. Because strikes were protected under the act, the employer did not hold all the bargaining strength.

Public employees discovered that lobbying efforts alone could not provide them with the controls and benefits of collective bargaining. Their swelling ranks made the lobbying process increasingly cumbersome.[11] The organizational size and complexity of government contributed to mismanagement and job dissatisfaction. It became increasingly difficult for employees to influence legislative action because the numerous layers of bureaucracy freed politicians from responsibility. For example, the passage of the Classification Act of 1923 (superseded by the Classification Act of 1949), which provided a personnel and pay structure for federal employees based on duties assigned a job rather than the qualifications of the person holding the job, and the 1939 **Hatch Act**, which limited the political activities of most federal workers, took a great deal of flexibility away from sitting politicians. (See Profile 3-1.) In addition, the **civil service systems** that had been developed to protect public employees

Profile 3-1

Hatch Act (1993 Amendment)

In 1993, President Bill Clinton signed a bill amending the Hatch Act and removing restrictions on federal workers' partisan political activity that had been in place for over 50 years. The Hatch Act was passed in 1939 after politicians used their control over Works Progress Administration (WPA) programs to influence elections. Workers were solicited for contributions and pressured to change their party registration and to work for the election of candidates selected by the WPA politicians. In an effort to clean up the WPA, the Hatch Act was proposed. The act placed prohibitions on the federal employees, limiting their rights to take an active part in partisan elections rather than placing any strictures on those who solicited the employees. The act passed and President Franklin Roosevelt signed it into law. Almost immediately, it was amended to include state and local government employees working under federal contracts and was put under the U.S. Civil Service Commission for enforcement.

Labor unions seeking to organize federal employees in the 1950s found the Hatch Act to be a deterrent. The threat, or perceived threat, of being accused of violating the Hatch Act because of union organizing activities became a major issue. One union, the United Federal Workers of America, decided to challenge the law. Arguing the case two times to a divided Supreme Court, the union contended that the Hatch Act went too far. The act's infringement on the First Amendment rights of federal employees was not necessary to guard against corruption. The Court disagreed and upheld the act as a reasonable restriction on activity necessary to ensure orderly management of the federal government free of political partisanship.

After years of seeking amendment, federal employees can now engage in a wider range of political activities off duty, including managing political campaigns. In addition, federal sector union members may solicit other union members for contributions to union-based PAC funds. However, federal employees are still barred from running for office and from soliciting for other types of political contributions.

Source: Adapted from Gilbert Gall, "The CIO and the Hatch Act," *Labor's Heritage 7,* no. 1 (Summer 1995), pp. 4–21; "Federal Service Labor and Employment Law," *Labor Lawyer 10,* no. 3 (Summer 1994), p. 373. See also Stephen Barr, "The Hatch Act Meets the Digital Age," *Washington Post* (October 19, 2007), p. D4.

were perceived as employer-recruited, employer-directed personnel mechanisms. As one expert observed, "It is the labor–management inadequacy of the civil service system that has been a prime cause of the remarkable thrust of union organization among public employees in recent years."[12]

PUBLIC SECTOR LABOR LAWS

The Sovereignty Doctrine

As discussed in Chapter 2, the key to employers' resistance to collective bargaining in the private sector was the desire to protect their private property rights. The National Labor Relations Act tried to balance the employer's private property rights against the employee's right to organize and to bargain collectively. Although the purpose of the act was to place employees in an equal bargaining position, employers still held all rights not taken from them at the bargaining table.

In the public sector, governments, backed by judicial decisions, were able to resist collective bargaining for many years by relying on the **sovereignty doctrine**. Sovereignty is defined as "the supreme, absolute, and uncontrollable power by which an independent state is governed."[13] In a democracy, the source of that supreme power is the people who have vested their government with rights and responsibilities as caretakers of that power. The sovereignty doctrine requires that the government exercise its power unfettered by any force other than the people—all the people.

SOVEREIGNTY DOCTRINE

The unrestricted and paramount power of the people to govern. In the public sector, this doctrine is presented as a basic reason for not allowing employees to have collective bargaining rights or the right to strike their public employers.

Collective bargaining was seen as a threat to that sovereignty doctrine for if government was to share decision-making authority with employees, it would affect the way government provides services and the amount those services would cost the taxpayer. In the absence of laws allowing public sector employees to join unions and negotiate with their employers, courts had held that public employers could not delegate any power to a private body such as a union. Specifically, delegating to labor the power to bargain or to arbitrators the power to bind governments would violate sovereignty doctrines and, ostensibly, threaten democracy.

But the sovereignty doctrine had numerous weak points. First, government contracted extensively with the private sector contractors, and the negotiation of those contracts took place bilaterally. This practice undermines a claim that government always makes its decisions unilaterally. Second, the sovereignty doctrine can no longer be used to support the theory that government—the ruler—can do no wrong when the Supreme Court has allowed citizens to claim civil rights violations against state and local governments, and torts and contract violations against local governments and other municipal corporations, subjecting them to monetary damages and remedial actions.

It was the federal courts that finally supported the right of public employees to organize and join unions. In the landmark case *McLaughlin v. Tilendis*,[14] the U.S. Court of Appeals held that in firing teachers in Cook County, Illinois, for joining the American Federation of Teachers violated the employees' First Amendment right of free association and free speech. Subsequent decisions discarded the sovereignty-based doctrine that prohibited collective bargaining in the public sector, although it is still a factor in how bargaining and resolution of bargaining disputes are governed.

EXECUTIVE ORDER (E.O.) 10988

The executive order signed by President John F. Kennedy in 1962 allowing federal employees bargaining representation, forms of employee recognition, and the right to collective bargaining.

Federal Employees

EXECUTIVE ORDERS In January 1962, the President's Task Force on Employee-Management Relations reported that a third of the federal employees belonged to labor organizations. It recommended that the government officially acknowledge this fact and respond affirmatively to employees' desire for collective bargaining. President John F. Kennedy signed **Executive Order (E.O.) 10988**, which recognized the rights of federal employees to join or to refrain from joining

President John F. Kennedy's Executive Order 10988 gives federal workers collective bargaining rights. It also began a wave of similar state and local actions that stimulated the growth of public sector unions at all levels. *Source:* Getty Images.

labor organizations, granted recognition to those labor organizations, and detailed bargaining subjects. Although this executive order can be cited as having established the framework for labor–management relations in the federal government, in comparison to its private sector counterpart, the National Labor Relations Act, it contained glaring deficiencies.

What is important about Kennedy's original order of 1962 is the lightning effect it had on organizing drives among federal, state, and municipal employees. The order served as a signal to organize public workers as much as the Wagner Act of 1935 had stimulated the growth of industrial union membership in the CIO and AFL. The effect of E.O. 10988 was to send public sector union membership rolls soaring. Before 1962, only 26 union or association units in the executive branch of the federal government had union shops, and they represented only 19,000 workers. Six years after the Kennedy order, there were 2,305 bargaining units, with a total membership of 1.4 million employees. A number of unions represented federal workers. The largest was the American Federation of Government Employees (AFGE). From 1962 to 1972, the AFGE grew from 84,000 members to 621,000. The Postal Workers and the Letter Carriers unions also experienced growth in that period. For state and local public employees, the 1962 Kennedy order also spawned growth in unionization, although the order did not apply to them directly. The fact that union membership grew, however, did not mean that all state or local governments recognized or bargained with unions.[15]

As in the National Labor Relations Act, the right to organize was granted to federal civilian employees under E.O. 10988. However, the head of an agency could determine that a bureau or office was primarily performing intelligence, investigative, or security functions, and the employees of that bureau or office could be excluded from the executive order for national security reasons.

Another deficiency in E.O. 10988 was the lack of a central authority to determine bargaining unit recognition and to resolve disputes. Many decisions were left to agency heads who were the immediate supervisors of the labor organization's members. The most significant difference between the National Labor Relations Act and E.O. 10988 was the right to engage in work stoppages. Strikes were specifically denied to the public labor organizations, and no substitute for a strike was provided, which left much of the "power" with the employers.

To address these deficiencies, President Richard Nixon issued Executive Order 11491 in 1969, which established a Federal Labor Relations Council and an Assistant Secretary for Labor–Management Relations to manage the labor relations system and to resolve disputes such as which employees could be represented by unions, how elections for selecting union representatives should be run, and whether any of the provisions of the Executive Orders were violated. To resolve issues in lieu of strikes, the Executive Order offered mediation and arbitration through two new entities: the Federal Mediation and Conciliation Service (FMCS) and the Federal Service Impasses Panel (FSIP). A subsequent Executive Order made the use of negotiated grievance procedures for settling contract disputes mandatory.[16]

POSTAL REORGANIZATION ACT OF 1970 Another initiative of the Nixon Administration was the passage of the Postal Reorganization Act of 1970 that made the U.S. Postal Service (USPS) an independent agency of the executive branch. USPS was permitted to operate using business principles, and charged with generating enough revenues to support the costs of the service it provides by allocating those costs among the many users of the postal system. Implementing the 1970 Postal Reorganization Act did not come without a struggle, however. The unions regarded the reform as privatization, and a Letter Carriers Union local in New York started a strike that soon included one-third of the postal workforce, the first major strike by federal workers in U.S. history! The impact was immediate and crushing; huge parts of the business sector ground to a halt. Nixon declared a national emergency and announced that he would send the National Guard into New York City to move the mail. Within two days, the strike was over. The impasse was broken when postal workers were granted full NLRB collective bargaining rights with the exception of the right to strike or the right to require all employees to become union members.[17]

THE CIVIL SERVICE REFORM ACT OF 1978, TITLE VII, also known as the Federal Labor Relations Act, and Reorganization Plan No. 2 of 1978 govern federal employee labor relations. The act is modeled after the National Labor Relations Act; it gives federal employees the right to join or not join unions and to engage in collective bargaining; and it places central authority in a three-member panel, the Federal Labor Relations Authority, who are appointed by the president of the United States. The Federal Labor Relations Authority (FLRA) oversees creation of bargaining units, conducts elections, decides representation cases, determines unfair labor practices, and seeks enforcement of its decisions in the federal courts. The president also appoints a general counsel empowered to investigate alleged unfair labor practices and to file and prosecute complaints. The unfair labor practice provision of the act generally mirrors the unfair labor practice provision in legislation for private employers and employees. And the act mandates inclusion of a grievance procedure with binding arbitration as a final step in all federal collective bargaining agreements. The Federal Service Impasse Panel was continued by the act and provides assistance in resolving negotiation impasses. The Federal Labor Relations Act, however, excludes from scope of negotiable issues wages and benefits, job duties, or classifications, and it prohibits political activities or requiring union membership. The act covers most federal employees with the exception of supervisors and members of the armed forces and other security agencies. Profile 3-2 provides an interesting look at an FLRA ruling.

CIVIL SERVICE REFORM ACT OF 1978

Act designed to reform the outdated federal civil service structure, modeled after the NLRA. Created the Federal Labor Relations Authority to oversee labor–management relations within the federal government.

NATIONAL SECURITY PERSONNEL SYSTEM In 2002, President George W. Bush, in the wake of the September 11, 2001, terrorist attacks, created the Department of Homeland Security (DHS). The new department consolidated under one agency several federal agencies with a central mission to protect America from terrorists. The DHS and the Department of Defense (DOD) were given their own personnel system, which included some civil service law provisions, except the president was given the authority to "exclude federal agencies, subdivisions and units . . . from relevant labor subsections." The National Security Personnel System (NSPS) was to oversee about 760,000 federal government civilian employees. The unions successfully objected in court actions

Profile 3-2

Appropriate Bargaining Unit for the NLRB

In June 2007, the general counsel of the NLRB, Ronald Meisburg, objected to a ruling of the Federal Labor Relations Authority (FLRA) that the National Labor Relations Board Union represented employees from both the board side and the general counsel side of the NLRB. The FLRA had recently certified the combined unit, even though the two separate bargaining units had existed for over 40 years. Meisburg's objection stemmed from the roles the general counsel and the board play in enforcing the NLRA. The general counsel is an independent prosecutor of labor cases before the board, which sits as a court. To combine the two bargaining units into one would mean that the general counsel and board would be bargaining together and that the general council would bargain with the union about the board's staff and the board about the general counsel's staff. In voicing these objections Meisburg said, "The FLRA's consolidation decision is in conflict with this statutory directive and blurs the lines of supervisory authority that are set out in the National Labor Relations Act."

In 2010, the U.S. Court of Appeals reversed the decision of the FLRA combining NLRB attorneys, investigators, and support staff into one unit. The principal issue was whether putting the National Labor Relations Board-side and the NLRB's General Counsel-side employees in the same unit impermissibly interferes with the General Counsel's independence created under the NLRA. The court answered in the affirmative and vacated the FLRA's decision.

Source: Press Release R-2630, "NLRB General Counsel Seeks Court Review of Combined Unit of Board-Side and General Counsel-Side Employees," (June 28, 2007). Available at http://www.nlrb.gov. Accessed February 22, 2008; *N.L.R.B. v. Federal Labor Relations Authority*, 613 F.3d 275 (C.A. D.C. 2010).

to the changes in the labor relations sections of the NSPS because they did not "protect the collective bargaining rights or ensure fair treatment of employees facing major disciplinary action."[18] The National Defense Authorization Act for Fiscal Year 2010 repealed the statutory authority for the NSPS and directed the Secretary of Defense to provide for the conversion of all NSPS employees and positions back to their original status by January 1, 2012.

Table 3-2 provides a chronology of the major events in federal public sector labor relations.

TABLE 3-2 Federal Public Sector Collective Bargaining History

1871	The first Civil Service Commission was established to prohibit public employees from losing their jobs with every change of administration.
1883	The Pendleton Act was passed protecting about 10 percent of federal employees from being fired for failure to make political contributions and forbade political activities by certain employees.
1912	Lloyd-LaFollette Act was passed; it allowed public employees to lobby Congress for better wages and working conditions.
1923	Passage of the Classification Act of 1923 which provided a personnel and pay structure for federal employees based on duties assigned a job rather than the qualifications of the person holding the job.
1932	The American Federation of Government Employees, one of the first public sector unions, was formed to lobby for legislation favorable to their members.
1939	The Hatch Act was passed limiting the political activities of most federal workers.
1962	Executive Order 10988 was signed by President John F. Kennedy. The order recognized the rights of federal employees to join unions and granted recognition to those unions and allowed limited bargaining rights.
1970	The Postal Reorganization Act was passed allowing postal workers to come under the National Labor Relations Act.
1978	The Civil Service Reform Act replaced previous executive orders concerning federal employee bargaining rights. Title VII of that act established the Federal Labor Relations Authority and modeled bargaining rights in the federal government after the NLRA.
1993	The Hatch Act was amended to lift some of the restrictions against political activities of public employees.

State and Local Government Employees

There is no federal law currently governing the collective bargaining relationship between states and local governments and their employees. Although Congress recently considered a bill, the *Public Safety Employer-Employee Cooperation Act*, which would have given local government *public safety officers* the right to join a union, to have the union recognized by their employer, and to bargain collectively over hours, wages and terms of employment. The measure would allow the parties to seek mediation to resolve their differences, but it would not permit the workers to strike or to force their employers into binding arbitration. In July 2010, the bill died in the Senate. Any attempt to pass federal legislation affecting state employee collective bargaining rights may be thwarted by the *dual sovereignty* of the federal and state governments. The Supreme Court in five cases from 1968 to 1999 addressed the power of Congress to regulate public employment by states and local governments. The Court first applied the Fair Labor Standards Act in 1968 to public employees but reversed that decision eight years later by holding that the U.S. Constitution barred Congress from applying the FLSA to public employees.[19] But in 1985, the Court reversed itself again and reasserted the right of Congress to regulate certain state government issues.[20] The Supreme Court may have backed away from that opinion in two cases in the 1990s—one limited the application of federal employment laws to states relying on the theory of dual sovereignty[21] and the other reasserted the Court's power to set limits on Congress' authority to invoke the Commerce Clause to regulate in areas that have only an insignificant connection with interstate commerce.[22]

Rather than a comprehensive nationwide approach to collective bargaining, then, what exists is a myriad of state statutes and local ordinances that address collective bargaining rights on the state and local level. Forty-two states have enacted legislation granting public sector collective bargaining rights as shown in Figure 3-2. The state laws generally fall into three categories: comprehensive public sector collective bargaining rights; targeted public sector collective bargaining rights; or restrictions to public sector collective bargaining rights.

Comprehensive laws allow all state and municipal employees to join unions and to collectively bargain with their governmental employer. Most of these comprehensive statutes mirror the NLRA by creating a state or local labor relations authority, which plays the same role

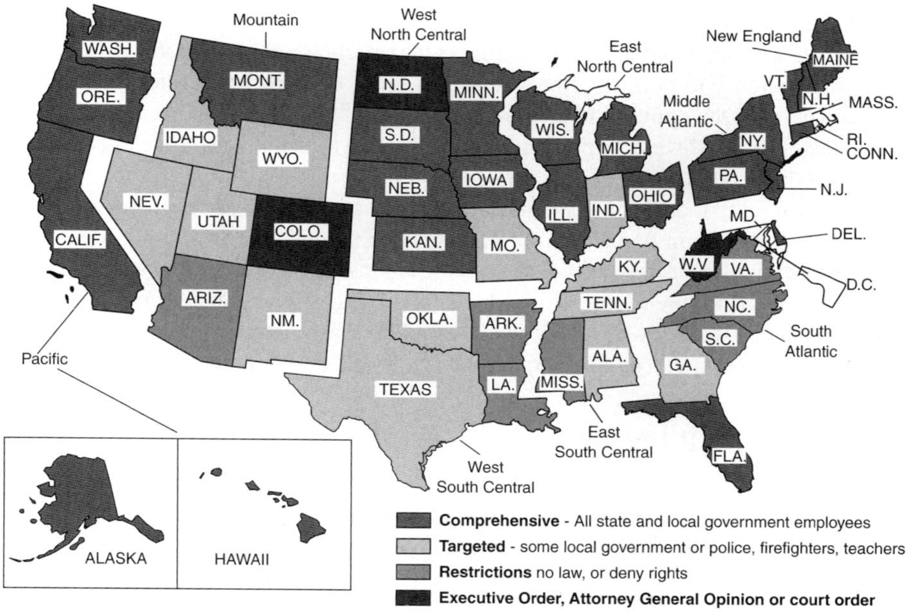

FIGURE 3-2 Status of Employee Collective Bargaining Rights by State. *Source:* Adapted from Richard Kearney, *Labor Relations in the Public Sector*, 4th ed. (Boca Raton, FL: CRC Press, 2009), pp. 62–64; AFSCME webpage, Available at http://www.afscme.org/members. Accessed August 20, 2011.

the NLRB and FLRA do on the national level, and most mirror the provisions of the NLRA and the Federal Labor Relations Act and prohibit public employers from:

- interfering, restraining, or coercing public employees in the exercise of their rights to form, join, or assist labor organizations, or to refrain from such activity;
- encouraging or discouraging membership in labor organizations;
- sponsoring, dominating, or otherwise assisting their employees' labor organizations; and
- refusing to negotiate, or to meet and confer, with the duly recognized representative of its employees.

Targeted collective bargaining laws either grant rights to most state and local employees but exclude some by name, or grant such rights exclusively to one or more classes of public employees, such as firefighters, policemen, or teachers. Targeted collective bargaining statutes often refer to the labor relations process as "meet and confer" rather than collective bargaining. Such legislation usually includes bargaining over wages, hours, terms of employment, and working conditions. Unfair labor practices and limits on, or prohibitions of, the right to strike also are legislated. The bargaining obligation is enforced by an existing administrative agency and procedures are established should there be an impasse.[23]

Restrictive collective bargaining rights either prohibit public sector collective bargaining or are silent on the subject, which means the government employees have no right to negotiate with their employers. In the absence of a state law, state governors may issue an *executive order* similar to the one issued by President Kennedy that gave federal employees collective bargaining rights or an Attorney General might issue an official Attorney General's Opinion (OAG) granting such rights. The order or opinion can give state or local workers collective bargaining rights if no state law prohibits such rights. However, workers seeking collective bargaining rights would prefer a state law grant them because laws are more difficult to change than an executive order or an OAG. For example, in 2007, Indiana governor Mitch Daniels, in one of his first official acts, voided the collective bargaining rights of about 25,000 state employees represented by three unions. His executive order made all existing labor contracts null and void. The collective bargaining rights had been granted by an executive order of a previous governor, not state law, and thus could be revoked by the new Republican governor, without approval by the legislature. The affected state workers included 8,638 represented by AFSCME 62, 14,654 represented by Unity Team Local 9212, and 1,377 Indiana State Police represented by IUPA Local 1041.[24]

Local, county, and municipal governments may also adopt collective bargaining laws or, by practice, recognize and bargain with employee organizations.

Although state and local laws differ as to particulars, some patterns do emerge. Legislation is more favorable to collective bargaining in the northern, northeastern, Midwestern, and far western parts of the United States. The Sunbelt states located along the lower Atlantic coast, the Southeast, the Southwest, and the southwestern Rocky Mountain States generally do not have comprehensive public sector labor laws.

In 2007, the U.S. Supreme Court in *Davenport v. Washington Education Association*[25] gave states new authority in regulating public employee unions. The unanimous decision allows state laws to curb political activity by public sector unions by requiring them to obtain written consent from nonmembers they represent in a bargaining unit before spending fees collected from them for electioneering expenses. The decision upheld a Washington state law that bans public unions from spending nonmembers' fees to "influence an election or to operate a political committee."[26]

PUBLIC SECTOR UNIONS

Public sector unions today fall roughly into three categories: associations or fraternities, public sector–only unions, and mixed unions. As discussed earlier, many public sector unions have their roots in professional *associations and fraternities* that developed before widespread public sector collective bargaining. The National Education Association (NEA) is the largest professional organization in the world, with over 3.2 million members and affiliates in every state as well as in over

14,000 communities.[27] NEA state affiliates regularly lobby state legislators, seek to influence education policy and professional standards for educators, and act to protect academic freedom and the rights of school employees. At the local level, affiliates perform a variety of activities, which may range from raising funds for scholarship programs to bargaining contracts for school district employees. At the national level, the NEA lobbies Congress and federal agencies on behalf of its members and public schools and provides training and assistance to its affiliates. The International Association of Fire Fighters (IAFF) is a labor union representing professional firefighters in the United States and Canada. The IAFF is affiliated with the AFL-CIO in the United States and the Canadian Labour Congress in Canada. Currently, the IAFF has 289,000 members in 3,100 locals. The Fraternal Order of Police (FOP) is an organization of sworn law enforcement officers in the United States. It claims a membership of over 325,000 members organized in 2,100 local chapters (lodges), organized into local lodges, state lodges, and the national Grand Lodge. The FOP lobbies Congress and regulatory agencies on behalf of law enforcement officers, provides labor representation, promotes legal defense for officers, and offers resources such as legal research. These three organizations focus on one group of employees in the public sector—teachers, firefighters, and police, respectively.

The American Federation of State, County, and Municipal Employees (AFSCME) is an example of a *public sector–only union* that organizes multiple sectors of public employees. AFSCME is the second-largest public union in the United States and the fifth-largest national union in the AFL-CIO, with over 1.4 million members. It represents public employees and health care workers throughout the United States, Panama, and Puerto Rico. They include employees of state, county, and municipal governments; school districts; public and private hospitals; universities; and nonprofit agencies that work in a cross section of jobs ranging from blue collar to clerical, professional, and paraprofessional. The American Federation of Teachers (AFT), which in the 1960s pioneered collective bargaining for Pre-K through 12th-grade teachers, has grown into a 1.5 million-member union representing workers not just in education, but also in government, health care, and public service. The Association of Federal Government Employees (AFGE) is a federal employee–only union with just under 300,000 members. AFGE represents employees in agencies such as the Department of Defense, the Department of Veterans Affairs, the Social Security Administration, and the Department of Justice.

PUBLIC SECTOR-ONLY UNION

A union that organizes multiple sectors of public employees but does not organize in the private sector.

Many public sector employees are represented by unions that organize in both the public and private sectors. The Service Employees International Union, which claimed 2.2 million members in 2010, has more than 1 million members in local and state governments including public school employees, bus drivers, and child care providers.[28] Another example of a **mixed union** is the International Brotherhood of Teamsters. Teamsters, which originally was organized by drivers of horse teams, currently represents such public service employees as deputy sheriffs, corrections officers, and those who provide security in public buildings; nurses, blood collection personnel, and aides who care for the elderly and veterans; school janitors and bus drivers; and workers who maintain roads and public utility systems.[29]

MIXED UNION

A union that represents both public and private sector employees.

As detailed in Table 3-3, public sector unions are prominent in the list of all U.S. unions (private and public sectors) with 100,000 or more members, with 10 of the 32 unions

TABLE 3-3 Unions with 100,000 or More Members, 2007

Union	Members
National Education Association	3,167,612
Service Employees International Union	1,575,485
American Federation of State, County, and Municipal Employees	1,470,095
International Brotherhood of Teamsters	1,398,573
United Food and Commercial Workers International Union	1,304,061
United Steelworkers of America (with PACE)	975,947
American Federation of Teachers	832,058
International Brotherhood of Electrical Workers	697,863

(continued)

TABLE 3-3 *(Continued)*

Laborers' International Union of North America	657,197
International Association of Machinists and Aerospace Workers	646,933
Communications Workers of America	559,083
International Union, United Automobile, Aerospace, and Agricultural Implement (UAW)	538,448
United Brotherhood of Carpenters and Joiners of America	523,126
Union of Needletrades, Industrial and Textile Employees	458,901
International Union of Operating Engineers	397,348
Maritime Trades	370,444
United Association of Journeymen and Apprentices of the Plumbing and Pipe Fitting Industry of the United States and Canada	332,205
National Association of Letter Carriers	287,236
International Association of Fire Fighters	283,932
American Postal Workers Union	283,279
American Association of Classified School Employees	260,000
National Postal Mail Handlers Union	249,509
American Federation of Government Employees	229,248
Amalgamated Transit Union	182,109
Screen Actors Guild	176,455
American Nurses Association	157,055
Building and Construction Trades	150,000
Sheet Metal Workers International Association	149,149
International Association of Bridge Structural, Ornamental and Reinforcing Iron Workers	134,134
International Union of Painters and Allied Trades	129,499
Transport Workers Union of America	115,145
National Rural Letter Carriers' Association	111,893
Office and Professional Employees International Union	104,596

Source: U.S. Department of Labor, 2007.

listed, and two of the three largest unions, being public sector unions. For example, the National Education Association ranked first; the American Federation of State, County and Municipal Employees (AFSCME) ranked third; and the American Federation of Teachers ranked seventh.[30]

CONTRASTING PUBLIC AND PRIVATE SECTOR LABOR RELATIONS

While federal and state statutes covering public sector collective bargaining may be modeled after the NLRA, there are still laws or practices that differ greatly from the act and from each other. Similarities and differences between how collective bargaining is carried out in the public and private sectors are generally covered throughout this text. Those comparisons deal with the mechanics of organizing employees and negotiating agreements, of determining bargaining issues and positions, costing wage and benefit proposals, and the processing of grievances and arbitrations. Collective bargaining in the private sector is largely shaped by market forces. A private concern is driven by the profit motive—its assets and income must exceed its liabilities and expenses or it will not be in business for long. The private sector must be responsive to its customers because it operates in a competitive arena, and unless it provides its customers with the best value for the price, the customers will go elsewhere.

Collective bargaining in the public sector, however, is ultimately shaped by political forces. The services that are provided by government are generally not available from any other organizations, and are critical to health, safety, and welfare such as education, public safety, public health and social services, and public utilities. It is important to recognize that government, unlike private sector employers, has no competitors, and generally has a "monopoly" position in the market it serves. In addition, governments seldom go out of business, merge, or get acquired by competitors. The public sector is financed by taxes and fees assessed against individuals equally regardless of the quality or quantity of the services provided to an individual. The core difference between the public and private sectors that raises some unique and troublesome problems for both unions and employers when bargaining in the public sector is that *government is not a business*. The following explores some of the issues that impact collective bargaining in the public sector that are not in the private sector because of the nature of government.

Collective Bargaining's Impact on Governmental Budgeting

While federal employees do not bargain on wages, most state and local employees can bargain over wages and benefits—a critical difference between collective bargaining at the federal level versus the state and local levels! Budget-making for state and local governments is a political process in which various interest groups seek to have larger shares of the budget allocated for particular purposes. Within this budget-making process public employees constitute one interest group. In the absence of collective bargaining, they are one among many interest groups. When a union becomes the exclusive representative of all employees in the bargaining unit, it gives those employees increased influence in the budget decision-making process. Collective bargaining provides them with a *special procedure* through which they can participate in decision making in a way not made available to others both with the executive branch and with the legislative branch.

The chief executive of a state or local govenment—a mayor or a governor—is usually authorized to bargain on behalf of the city or state. The executive may delegate the negotiating task to a surrogate, for example, a human resources director or labor negotiating team. But nevertheless, the negotiations are undertaken at the direction of the chief executive, who must bargain in good faith with the union until either an agreement or an impasse is reached. This means that the chief executive enters into a dialogue with the union face-to-face on substantive issues of money and services. Management's proposals for pay and benefits must be argued with explanations and supporting facts, in a way not usually done about the allocation of tax resources with other interest groups. Once a collective bargaining agreement is entered into, its employment terms are binding for the duration of the agreement, unlike terms established by ordinance or regulations, which may be changed without the consent of the employees.

If a government has multiple unions, the bargaining process will create pressures for uniformity. The high visibility of settlements in the public sector creates almost compelling pressures on the chief executive to treat all groups the same, regardless of their relative value to the mission of the state or city. The bargaining process strengthens the position of bargaining groups which are politically weaker. This does not mean that all groups will necessarily be given identical pay or benefits, but differences must be perceived as fair and not based solely on differences in political or negotiating power.

Legislatures at the federal, state, and local level pass budgets, so ultimately the wages and benefits granted to public employees come within their control and authority. Unions in the public and private sectors are often experienced at lobbying on behalf of their members. But for public sector unions, the lobbying goes beyond just seeking favorable labor legislation and often includes lobbying directly for increased pay and benefits, either in support of an agreed-upon contract with the executive or as an alternative to it. Employee organizations also affect the budgeting process through the election process. Public employees are highly motivated to vote, to support candidates, and to be seen as a political force in order to be in a position to have a seat at the table when government resources are allocated. Because governmental resources are not unlimited, substantial increases in one area, such as public safety, can cause decreases in other areas such as parks or sanitation. So public employees, when engaged in the collective bargaining process, are influencing the budget-making process as well.

PATTERN BARGAINING Pattern bargaining in the private sector refers to national or international unions, such as the United Auto Workers, entering into agreements that set the bar for pay or benefit increases across the industry. In the private sector, neither an employer nor a union is free to insist, as a condition of reaching an agreement in one unit, that the negotiations also include other units, or that the terms negotiated in the first unit be extended to other units.[31] **Pattern bargaining** in the public sector, however, generally involves one government's bargaining stance with its multiple unions—police, fire, public health workers, and so on; in this process the principle of "equal treatment" virtually ensures that every *visible benefit* granted one group will be given in some form to all. The public employer's refusal to settle with other unions until it has settled with the "pattern-setting" unit would be, according to traditional notions, bad-faith bargaining. But since employee costs in the public sector are a significant figure for budgetary purposes, some techniques such as pattern bargaining often must be devised to control the ultimate budgetary impact. The political and economic realities of public sector bargaining means that the wages and terms and conditions of employment granted one union may determine the bargaining parameters for all others. The power of the historic "**me too**" negotiating stance can be great because it is very difficult for government officials to deny one group of workers what they have granted another group—especially pay raises. Thus union members as well as nonunion workers can be expected to say "me too" after the first union has settled. Occasionally, a less influential union is willing to negotiate assurances that they will receive equal benefits ("most favored nation clause"), if the settlement entered into later with any other union is more favorable. The first union then becomes the pattern-setting union. A pattern-setting union may object to being responsible for benefits to employees not in its bargaining unit, but if pattern bargaining is unacceptable, the unions can propose two-level bargaining where they negotiate together those terms they are willing to be determined by a pattern and those that fall outside that agreement.

PATTERN BARGAINING

A collective bargaining practice in which a national union strives to establish equal wages and benefits from several employers in the same industry. The union uses the negotiated contract of one company to serve as a model contract for the entire industry.

"ME TOO"

Public sector union demands for equal treatment when one union receives something of value.

INABILITY TO PAY In the NLRA the obligation to bargain in good faith requires that employers and unions exchange relevant information when necessary to substantiate assertions made during collective bargaining. If an employer bases its bargaining position on an inability to pay increased wages, then that employer must allow a union to examine the company's books in order to verify the claim. A company that asserts an inability to pay and then refuses to furnish substantiating financial information upon request fails to bargain in good faith. In the public sector, financial information of a public entity is generally available to everyone under typical open records or so-called **FOIA**, freedom of information acts. When a government employer does not offer pay raises that meet the expectations of their union employees, or otherwise engage in concession bargaining to reduce the employees' economic benefits, furnishing information in support of that position is generally not an issue. What is at issue is whether local and state governments are allowed to set funding priorities with the revenues they have available when those priorities reduce funds available for employees' wages and benefits.

FOIA

So called "freedom of information acts" or "open records" makes documents of public entities generally available to all citizens. In public sector collective bargaining often financial information of a public entity is generally available to all bargaining units.

Recently a federal court in Maryland threw out a county's furlough plan that was put in place to save $20 million to meet a revenue shortfall of approximately $57 million.[32] The court ruled that while the county had the right to impose furloughs on all of its workers, even though the contracts with its unions did not include furloughs, it had to demonstrate that cutting the budget through furloughs, which reduced the negotiated pay of employees, was reasonable and necessary. The court examined the financial situation facing the county and how it decided to address the tax revenue deficits and said that in light of other options open to it, the decision to recoup $20 million of the needed $57 million shortfall from union employee pay was not reasonable. The court concluded that the county had available to it $97 million in reserve funds, had budgeted $8 million for real estate and equipment purchases that were not under contract; could have reduced funding to the Community College or the County Hospital; or asked for additional funds from the Parks and Planning Commission. The Court stated that "[t]he choice of which revenue-saving measure the County selected is outside the Court's purview, however the menu of alternatives does not include impairing contract rights to obtain forced loans to the [County] from its employees."[33]

Bargaining Differences in the Public Sector

MULTILATERAL BARGAINING In the private sector, the expectation of the union is that the representative of management at the bargaining table speaks for the employer, so that if an agreement is reached, only the union goes back to its membership and asks for approval. But in the public sector, that is not always the case. The public sector negotiator for management may find the role similar to that of the negotiator for labor, that is, charged with returning a negotiated agreement for approval to the final authority. This is known as **multilateral bargaining**. In an **executive-legislative** form of government, such as the federal government, state governments, and most large cities, both the executive and the legislature are considered management, but with different roles. The executive manages personnel policies on a day-to-day basis under directives, particularly budgetary directives, of the legislative body. During labor negotiations, however, when the decisions affecting the collective bargaining agreement are being made by the executive, but subject to either budgetary approval or approval of the contract itself by the legislative body, conflicts between the two parts of management in the public sector can arise. If the legislative body disapproves of a proposed agreement after the executive and the union have agreed, the collective bargaining process is undermined. If the legislative body seeks to join in the negotiations, it undermines the executive's authority at the bargaining table and puts the public entity in a weak bargaining position. If the negotiations are at an impasse and the legislative body seeks to play the role of mediator, it in effect simply starts a new level of negotiations.

MULTILATERAL BARGAINING

Generally refers to negotiations in the public sector where the authority to commit to a collective bargaining agreement may be shared by the executive and legislative branches, and thus three parties are involved in negotiations.

EXECUTIVE-LEGISLATIVE

A form of government, such as the federal and state governments and most large cities, when both the executive and the legislature are considered management, but with different roles. The executive manages the government on a day-to-day basis under directives, particularly budgetary directives, of the legislative body.

OPEN NEGOTIATIONS Public employee collective bargaining makes news. Press coverage of public employee collective bargaining can harm the bargaining process in several ways. If an impasse is reached, the parties may try to explain their side to the media, hoping to influence public opinion and in turn the negotiating process. Rushing for media coverage may cause a party to present proposals publicly before it has presented them to the other party at the negotiating table. By emphasizing the differences between the parties instead of the points of agreement, reporters can actually prolong the posturing stage. In the normal course of events, agreement of public employees and employers at the collective bargaining table is not newsworthy; therefore, media coverage often is confined to reporting on the items separating the parties and not the items of agreement. Publicity might also encourage the negative tactic of turning to the legislative body for impasse resolution. Coverage reinforces the bad feelings too often present in negotiations in a way the private sector rarely experiences.

Sunshine laws may require that collective bargaining sessions be open to the public, often thwarting the parties' ability to compromise.[34] Sunshine laws require public bodies, such as city councils, to conduct their official business in public sessions open to citizens and the press (see Case 3-1). Some initial posturing is necessary on both sides so that the negotiator's constituency is assured that he or she is acting on their behalf. Negotiators may find it difficult to stop posturing if they are under constant scrutiny. At any particular juncture during the negotiation process, it may seem as if one side or the other is winning or losing. A fear of "loss of face" by either side may endanger the fair compromise so necessary to successful negotiations.

SUNSHINE LAWS

Statutes requiring that the official business of government be conducted in public, sometimes requiring that public-sector collective bargaining sessions be open to the public.

However, press coverage of public sector collective bargaining is necessary because the ultimate decision does rest with the public. Without contribution by the public at some point during the process, the parties will not be able to gauge its reaction. By making the progress of negotiations public, elected officials and union members are able to get a response and so can modify their positions. For example, if a union representing teachers learned through news coverage of their negotiations that the public would support tax increases to improve the teacher–student ratio but not to raise salaries, its posture during the negotiations might change.

CASE 3-1

Negotiating under Sunshine Laws

During 1985, the city's collective bargaining contracts with its police union and its general employees' union were being renegotiated. Before each negotiating session, the city posted notice of the meetings on the city's calendar at City Hall. Additionally, the city's representatives usually communicated directly with the newspaper's reporters concerning such meetings. The city and the unions were unable to agree on a wage level as well as a few other minor economic matters for the new contract. The city and the unions declared that negotiations were at an impasse, and a mediator was appointed to hear the disputes. The mediator scheduled the hearing for the police union on December 10 and the other union for December 11, 1985.

On December 9, the city's bargaining team member contacted his counterpart on the police union's team and arranged a meeting between the representatives for both sides to be held at 7 P.M. in a conference room at City Hall. No notice was posted; the press was not notified. The purpose of the meeting was an attempt to settle the impasse. The meeting was futile.

The city had posted public notice of the mediation, which was convened on the morning of December 10. The reporter and other media representatives were present. Shortly after the mediator convened the hearing, the police union's representative requested a recess so that the city's representative could step out into the hall to speak with him. The reporter, covering his first mediator hearing, did not follow the attorneys as they left the conference room. Out in the hall, the union's representative offered another settlement proposal, which the city's representative accepted. The two representatives agreed not to reveal the terms of the settlement offer until the following day to avoid prejudicing the mediator because she was to hear the general employees' dispute the next day. The two bargaining representatives reentered the conference room and announced to the mediator that a settlement had been reached. The mediator adjourned the proceedings but retained jurisdiction in the event of a later disruption regarding the settlement. The reporter next asked the two representatives to tell him the terms of the settlement. Both declined, citing the need for confidentiality.

The next day the mediation began with the general employees' union with the same mediator presiding. Once again, the representatives for the city and for the union met outside the hearing room in the hall for a private meeting. The same reporter followed the parties out of the hearing room, and the two representatives made no effort to exclude him from this "off-the-record" encounter. After the second day's mediator hearing was terminated, the reporter was informed of the settlement terms between the city and the police union. The membership of the police union and the general employees ratified the settlements. The city council, at a public meeting with notice, subsequently approved the contracts, including the terms of the settlement agreed to during the private meeting on December 10.

The newspaper sued the city charging that it had violated the Florida sunshine law by carrying out negotiations with the police union on a collective bargaining agreement without notice to the public and an opportunity for the public to attend. The city argued that the Florida sunshine law specified that "collective bargaining negotiations" were to be open to the public, but once an impasse was reached, that provision no longer applied.

Decision

The court did not accept the city's interpretation of the Florida sunshine law. The court noted that "impasse" only means a deadlock during negotiations when the parties refuse to compromise further to reach agreement. An impasse does not relieve the parties of the duty to negotiate in good faith. An impasse is a part of "negotiations" and, therefore, subject to the sunshine law.

Source: Adapted from *City of Fort Myers v. Newspress Publishing Company, Inc.*, 127 LRRM 3051 (1987).

Lack of "Union Security" in the Public Sector

Union security refers to the ability of the union to grow and to perform its collective bargaining role without interference from management or other unions. As the exclusive representative of certain employees, a union enjoys a high degree of security. But unions seek even more security. In the private sector, union security provisions include requiring an employee to stay a union member during the term of the contract (maintenance of membership); become a member of a union or lose the job (union shop); require an employee to support a union financially even if not a member (agency shop); and/or an automatic dues deduction provision. (There is an exception for states which prohibit union shops. See Chapter 6 discussion of "right-to-work" states.) These provisions ensure support for the union's work as well as a dependable source of revenue.

UNION SECURITY

The provisions of collective bargaining agreements that directly protect and benefit the union, such as dues check-off and union shops.

One significant challenge for public sector unions is the lack of union support because of "free riders" and "cheap riders." **Free riders** are employees who are in a unit represented by a union and are covered by a collective bargaining agreement but cannot be required to join the union or pay any union dues or fees. **Cheap riders** are employees who are covered by a collective bargaining agreement but cannot be required to become union members, but they are required to pay something, or "**fair share**," to the union for the bargaining and representation services they receive. In both cases, the collective bargaining agreement is binding on them, and the union is required to provide them with the same benefits as union members.

FREE RIDERS

Employees within a bargaining unit who choose not to join the union that bargains for an agreement for the unit. Although the employees receive all negotiated benefits, they pay no costs associated with the union.

CHEAP RIDERS

Employees within a bargaining unit who choose not to join the union that bargains for an agreement but are required to pay a fee to the union to provide their share of the costs associated with negotiations (usually 80 to 85 percent of the regular union dues).

Federal employees under the Federal Labor Relations Act cannot be required to either become union members or pay *any* money in the form of fees or dues in support of the union's representation.[35] As a result of that, AFGE, for example, represents over 600,000 employees but has a little less than half that many dues-paying members. State and local employees in states without right-to-work statutes cannot be required to join unions but may be required to contribute their "fair share" for union representation under a 1977 Supreme Court decision, *Abood v. Detroit Board of Education*.[36] In *Abood,* a Michigan statute authorizing union representation of local governmental employees permitted an "agency shop" arrangement, whereby every employee represented by a union, though not a union member, must pay to the union, as a condition of employment, a service charge equal in amount to union dues. Eight teachers filed actions challenging the validity of the agency shop clause alleging that they opposed collective bargaining in the public sector, that the Union was engaged in various political and other ideological activities that appellants did not approve, and that the agency shop clause deprived them of the freedom of association, or in this case, nonassociation protected by Bill of Rights. The Supreme Court ruled that insofar as the service charges were used to finance collective bargaining, contract administration, and grievance adjustment purposes, the agency shop clause was valid. Otherwise, the employees cannot be required to pay for the activity of the Union with which they disagree. This decision established the criteria for a **fair share** arrangement in the public sector.

FAIR SHARE

A sum of money paid in lieu of union dues, which represents the benefit a nonunion member of the bargaining unit gets from collective bargaining and contract administration by the union.

Supervisors In Bargaining Units

Under the NLRA and the Federal Labor Relations Act concerning federal employees, "supervisors" are not given collective bargaining rights. In the private sector and, presumably in the federal government, a supervisor is seen as a vital part of management, so collective bargaining with supervisors makes no sense. On the state and local levels, the inclusion of supervisory personnel within the bargaining unit has presented a difficult question. While many state or local laws may exclude "supervisors" from collective bargaining rights, when those laws have been challenged, courts and/or labor relation boards have applied the NLRB test for what makes a supervisor a true supervisor and decided they were not supervisors. The nature of the actual duties of the positions can make the decision difficult. Should, for example, police lieutenants and sergeants be part of a police officers' bargaining unit if the only major difference is their rank and the fact that they have no managerial duties?

Those in favor of such inclusion point to the need to consolidate employees into groups to limit the number of unions with which a public employer is to negotiate. It has been suggested that supervisors moderate demands and create less-militant organizations. In some instances, supervisory titles in the public sector do not reflect actual supervisory authority because of the way decisions are made in the public sector. In addition, all supervisory and nonsupervisory career employees share common interests, especially in financial issues. Those who oppose the inclusion of supervisory personnel point out that supervisors face a potential conflict of interest when they themselves are affected by a contract they must enforce. Also, in pursuing grievance procedures, the distinction between management and employee needs to be clear, and supervisors may need to continue an operation during a work stoppage by the bargaining unit.

Size of Public Sector Bargaining Units

The size of a public employee bargaining unit can give a strategic advantage to either management or labor. The public employer may encourage a larger unit, hoping the diverse interests and backgrounds of a larger unit will prevent the union from gaining majority status. Larger units prevent or reduce the possibility that multiunion negotiation will be used against the employer. The time and cost of bargaining are greatly reduced with larger units. Still, employers realize that the political power of public employee unions may be increased if the unit is very large. Because unions seek to represent the unit most likely to give it majority status, size is not the only determining factor in their organization efforts. In addition, because of the mix of service and clerical employees being organized on a local or state level, the employees often have to choose between two labor organizations—a trade union and an employee association. Their choice will have significant impact on the labor–management relationship.[37]

The Right to Strike

In the private sector, an impasse in collective bargaining negotiations can result in a strike. The National Labor Relations Act reserves that right to the employee as an economic weapon. In the public sector, the **right to strike** is usually denied to the public employee either by statute or by court action.

RIGHT TO STRIKE

For employees in the private sector, the right to strike is guaranteed by the National Labor Relations Act, but public employees are generally prohibited from striking, making the right to strike a major issue for public-sector unions.

The primary reason for prohibiting public employee strikes is that most of the services provided by public employees are essential to the public general welfare. Public safety, police, fire, and emergency medical services are often cited as examples of why public employees should not be allowed to strike. But some less obviously critical services should also be considered, such as maintenance of public parks. The nature of public parks is that they are open to the public, generally 24 hours a day, 365 days a year. Park maintenance is not just about esthetics but also safety. While a strike by park workers might not generate immediate concern, over the long run a community could feel the negative impact.

Another reason cited for prohibiting public employees to strike is that giving unions the right to strike places too much power in the hands of the employees rather than in the elected representatives of the people, which violates the sovereignty doctrine. Because there are no market controls on government services, the strike threat could cause public employers to make unwise agreements at the expense of the taxpayer.[38]

Those who believe the public employee should have the right to strike argue that despite legislation to the contrary, public employees do go on strike.[39] When that happens, attention is focused on the strike issue and not on the reason for the disagreement, thereby thwarting the resolution of a bargaining impasse. Strikes, or at least credible strike threats, can facilitate agreements at the bargaining table by equalizing the parties' bargaining power.[40] In addition, strikes test the union's strength as a bargaining representative; their strength or weakness can be used as a bargaining strategy. Finally, proponents of public employees' right to strike contend that nonessential public employees should have the same rights to strike as their counterparts in the private sector.[41]

THE PROFESSIONAL AIR TRAFFIC CONTROLLERS' (PATCO) STRIKE The Professional Air Traffic Controllers Organization (PATCO) represented air traffic control employees of the

Federal Aviation Association (FAA). As federal employees, the air traffic controllers could not legally strike. But PATCO gained a reputation of being an independent and feisty union when several hundred controllers conducted a work stoppage in 1969,[42] and 3,000 controllers informally went on strike in 1970. While some members were fired or suspended, some of the members' feelings of independence were rooted in the belief that they were highly skilled professionals who could not easily be replaced.

Then in 1981, PATCO leaders called the first declared national strike against the federal government. The 13,000 strikers thought they were irreplaceable. President Ronald Reagan quickly warned that such direct disobedience of the law against public employee strikes would not be tolerated. He stated, "There is no strike; what they did was to terminate their own employment by quitting."[43] Reagan gave workers a deadline that most ignored; then *he fired all but the few who returned to work.* Not one controller was given amnesty or rehired until 12 years later when President William Clinton took office in 1993, but by then most of the controllers had retired or found other careers.

The success of the Reagan administration in replacing such highly skilled workers, together with widespread public support, left little doubt in the minds of government workers as to what might happen if they went on strike. PATCO miscalculated its ability to gain concessions by striking. It sacrificed substantial pay, a generous benefits package, and its very existence in its attempt to legitimize strikes in the public sector.[44] The **PATCO strike** began a new era in both public and private sector labor relations, one in which employers view permanent replacement workers as a serious option to striking union workers.

PATCO STRIKE

The first declared national strike against the federal government resulted not only in the firing of all striking PATCO workers but also in the prohibition of any PATCO striking worker from ever working again as an air traffic controller.

Despite the arguments against public employees' right to strike, some states allow public workers to strike either directly or by not prohibiting it as shown in Table 3-4.

TABLE 3-4 States That Allow Public Employee Strikes

State	Police and Fire	State Workers	Teachers	Local Governments
Alaska	Strikes prohibited	Strikes allowed nonessential workers	Strikes allowed only after advisory arbitration	Strikes allowed
California	Strikes allowed unless they threaten health and safety	Strikes allowed unless ruled as an unfair labor practice (ULP)	Strikes allowed unless ruled as ULP	Strikes allowed unless ruled as ULP
Colorado	Court held strikes legal	Court held strikes legal	Court held strikes legal	Court held strikes legal
Idaho	Strikes prohibited	No bargaining	Strikes not prohibited; voluntary fact-finding	No bargaining
Hawaii	Strikes allowed after exhausting impasse proceedings	Strikes allowed after exhausting impasse proceedings	Strikes allowed after exhausting impasse proceedings	Strikes allowed after exhausting impasse proceedings
Illinois	Strikes prohibited	Strikes allowed; after required mediation	Strikes allowed; after required mediation	Strikes allowed; after required mediation

(continued)

TABLE 3-4 *(Continued)*

Louisiana	Court held strikes legal	Court held strikes legal	Court held strikes legal	Court held strikes legal
Minnesota	Strikes not allowed	Strikes allowed after mediation	Strikes allowed after mediation	Strikes allowed after mediation
Montana	Strikes prohibited	Strikes allowed; mandatory fact-finding; voluntary arbitration	Strikes allowed; mandatory fact-finding; voluntary arbitration	Strikes allowed; mandatory fact-finding; voluntary arbitration
New Jersey	Strikes prohibited	Strikes allowed	Strikes allowed	Strikes allowed
Ohio	Strikes not allowed	Strikes allowed	Strikes allowed	Strikes allowed
Oregon	Strikes prohibited; binding arbitration	Strikes allowed after mandatory fact-finding	Strikes allowed after mandatory fact-finding	Strikes allowed after mandatory fact-finding
Pennsylvania	Strikes prohibited if safety involved	Strikes allowed, with restrictions	Strikes allowed, with restrictions	Strikes allowed, with restrictions
Vermont	No mention	Strike prohibited	Strikes not allowed; binding arbitration	Strikes allowed
Wisconsin	State prohibited Local option	Strike prohibited	State prohibited Local option	Local option

Source: Various state and legal websites.

Resolving Impasse in the Public Sector

Because most public employees are not vested with the right to strike, reaching an impasse in the public sector follows a slightly different path. In most local legislation granting public employees the right to collectively bargain, impasse cannot occur as a matter of law until the parties have completed a protocol of some Alternate Dispute Resolution (ADR) process: mediation, fact-finding, and/or arbitration. The rationale for this additional element of impasse lies in the restrictions placed on public employees. Since the law eliminates the most common form of employee impasse resolution, the strike, the lawmakers add to the duty of good-faith bargaining the burden of completing an ADR regimen. This addition offsets the union's right with a burden most often borne by management.

In Case 3-2, involving the Maine School District, the court held that unilateral implementation of changed contract terms prior to completion of the statutory ADR regimen would be a perse violation of the duty to bargain in good faith.[45] The court explained that the "peaceful" third-party intervention procedures are intended as substitutes for strikes and work stoppages "and are designed to provide escalating pressure on both parties to produce a voluntary settlement." The court in that case pointed out, however, that the ADR regimen ended in a voluntary and not a mandatory finding. If both parties engaged in a typical public sector collective bargaining process agree that they have reached an impasse and are ready to mediate, arbitrate, or fact-find, then they can proceed through the applicable ADR with the knowledge that at the end of it, they may still be at impasse. It is at that point that an employer can unilaterally impose changes that are reasonably comprehended within the employer's pre-impasse proposals, that is, the employer cannot impose terms and conditions that the union had no knowledge of or chance to negotiate.

CASE 3-2

Unilateral Action: Last Best Offer

The union and the school board began negotiations in June 1990 for an initial contract for a combined unit of teacher aides and assistants. The negotiations were long and included the parties participating in three mediation sessions and in fact-finding. Thereafter, the parties submitted several issues, including wages, health insurance, and duration of the contract to arbitration. Following a hearing, the arbitration panel issued a report on July 9, 1992, making nonbinding recommendations on wages, retirement payment, and health insurance but imposing a two-year duration of contract for the school years 1991–1992 and 1992–1993.

In September 1992, the school board sent a proposal on wages and insurance to the union. The terms were not in complete accord with the arbitrators' recommendations. The parties met, but the union rejected the offer and made counterproposals. In November 1992, the school board notified the union of its last best offer on wages and insurance. The union immediately filed for mediation. The school board thereafter implemented its wage and insurance proposals. The union filed a prohibited practice complaint with the state labor board alleging that the school board violated the state bargaining act by unilaterally implementing its proposal on wages and insurance.

The labor board ruled that the school board committed no violation of the act by unilaterally imposing its wage and insurance proposals. State law, as well as federal law, imposes the obligation to bargain in good faith as part of the statutory definition of collective bargaining. The law requires employers' and employees' representatives in the public and private sectors to bargain in good faith with respect to the mandatory subjects of bargaining, namely, wages, hours, and other terms and conditions of employment. To support the bargaining process and prevent it from being circumvented or disparaged, labor law has long been interpreted to prevent either party from unilaterally changing wages, hours, or working conditions. Thus, while bargaining and before impasse, an employer is prevented from "going over the head" of the bargaining agent by unilaterally increasing or decreasing wages. The parties are required to maintain the status quo while bargaining.

When negotiations reach a bona fide impasse, however, a party is allowed to implement unilaterally its last best offer. Once the parties have in good faith exhausted the prospects of reaching an agreement, unilateral change that reasonably relates to the pre-impasse proposals does not violate the law. After impasse, however, the duty to bargain is not extinguished. Rather, it is temporarily suspended until changed circumstances indicate that the parties are no longer inalterably deadlocked. Under state law, public employees, who do not have the right to strike or engage in work stoppages, are required to engage in such "peaceful" third-party intervention procedures as mediation, fact-finding, and arbitration. Impasse cannot occur until these forms of intervention have been exhausted. These procedures are designed to provide escalating pressure on both parties to produce a voluntary settlement.

The union argued that allowing the school board unilaterally to put its last best offer in place frustrates the purpose of the collective bargaining act. It is, in effect, forcing the union to accept the terms and conditions of employment that it had affirmatively rejected. It undermines the bargaining process because it says to the school board that the "peaceful" third-party procedures available in the public sector as an alternative to a strike are merely delays in the process, not meaningful impasse resolution measures.

(continued)

Decision

The court disagreed with the union and found that the school board did not violate the state law concerning collective bargaining by implementing its last best offer after reaching an impasse. In its opinion, the union missed the point. The wage and insurance provisions implemented by the school board did not end the negotiations between it and the union—it simply created a new "status quo" from which the parties would have to begin bargaining when the duty to bargain was no longer dormant.

Source: Adapted from *Mountain Valley Education Assoc. v. Maine School Admin. Dist. No. 43*, 148 LRRM 2862 (1995).

If, however, there is no agreement that "impasse" has been reached, to avoid remaining in limbo, employers must be able to prove that an actual impasse has occurred. Courts and the NLRB have pointed to specific conduct which evidences that there is an impasse in the private sector that can be applied in the public sector such as:

- The parties must disagree over a "key issue" to validly assert impasse.
- Delaying tactics of the union may be justification for unilateral action by the employer.
- But since the burden to prove the "good faith" rests on the employer who is claiming impasse to impose a contract, the employer should generally demonstrate its good faith, as opposed to the union's bad faith, in its attempt to show impasse.[46]
- The length of time over which the parties have negotiated may be used to prove impasse. However, in the public sector where elected officials take or leave office based upon elections, the length of bargaining may not indicate an impasse, but just the necessity of dealing with a change of administrations.
- Important issues upon which the parties *agree* may have an impact on whether there is an impasse. If these issues offer the parties an opportunity to trade-off and compromise, then it suggests that ultimate agreement on all issues is more likely.
- If the union declares an impasse and the employer's offer to meet again is declined, the employer may be allowed to take unilateral action.[47]

MEDIATION

The introduction of a neutral third party into a grievance situation or collective bargaining impasse. Although mediators have no decision-making powers, they use their skills and work actively to achieve a settlement that is mutually agreeable to both sides.

FACT-FINDING

A dispute resolution procedure in which a neutral third party reviews both sides of a dispute and then publicly recommends a reasonable solution.

ADVISORY ARBITRATION

A For public For Often in public sector collective bargaining the parties submit an unresolved dispute to an unbiased third party who examines the impasse and issues findings and recommendations. While not binding, the findings may move the process along by making reasonable recommendations.

Alternative Dispute Resolution Procedures

Legislation that allows public sector collective bargaining but prohibits strikes often details the procedures available to resolve an impasse.

Mediation provisions are provided in most states with collective bargaining in the public sector. As with the private sector, the mediator has no independent authority but uses acquired skills to bring the parties back together and reach an agreement. Mediation may be provided by the Federal Mediation and Conciliation Service (FMCS), state labor departments, or local mediation boards. Experienced mediators in a majority of cases can resolve disputed issues and often help the parties reach a settlement.

Fact-finding and **advisory arbitration** can be far more successful in the public sector than in the private because of political pressures. Under fact-finding and advisory arbitration, an unbiased third party examines the collective bargaining impasse and issues findings and recommendations. The findings may move the process simply by eliminating the distrust one party feels for the other party's facts or figures. Reasonable recommendations may also pressure a party to accept an offer that otherwise would not have been considered. Because the findings are generally made public, one side or the other runs the risk of losing public support for their position if the "finders of fact" make a reasonable recommendation.

Interest arbitration allows usually an arbitration panel to make a **final and binding decision** on a negotiation dispute. Interest arbitration has been used in the public sector to resolve impasses as an alternative to the economic pressure of a strike used in the private sector. Many states provide for interest arbitration, although it is not without critics.

INTEREST ARBITRATION

A process used to resolve an impasse in negotiations where the parties submit the unresolved items to a neutral third party to render a binding decision.

Opponents contend that binding arbitration discourages the "give and take" necessary for good-faith collective bargaining. Knowing that the arbitrators will "begin" the deliberations with where the parties "ended" their negotiations, both sides will hold something back. And the process is inherently unbalanced since it makes a no-risk or low-risk step available to a union or employee organization since it is unlikely that the arbitrators will give the employees less than the employer offered. More importantly, it places decisions that affect the taxpayers in the hands of nonelected officials, who are not even accountable to elected officials and may not be a taxpayer of the community affected by the decision. Due to the nature of pattern bargaining in the public sector, an arbitration decision could have a ripple effect on other collective bargaining negotiations with other bargaining units that are not in front of the arbitration panel. In addition, there are serious questions of constitutionality as an unconstitutional delegation of legislative authority.[48]

Proponents of interest arbitration, however, believe that the threat of arbitration, like the threat of a strike, provides an incentive to negotiate when the parties understand and appreciate the final and binding procedure. In jurisdictions with interest arbitration, the majority of collective bargaining contracts are settled voluntarily by the parties without resorting to arbitration, which according to one study was only used to resolve between 6 and 29 percent of negotiations.[49] And in jurisdictions which allow for strikes, or where strikes still happen even if they are not legal, interest arbitration reduces conflict and builds consensus between the two parties as an alternative to a strike.[50]

Enforcement of Collective Bargaining Rights

The Federal Labor Relations Authority (FLRA) and many state-created labor authorities perform the same role in public sector labor relations as the NLRB performs in the private sector, that is, determining appropriate bargaining units, conducting elections, and hearing unfair labor practice complaints. However, unlike the NLRB, the Federal Labor Relations Authority has jurisdiction in all the arbitration awards appealed to it regardless of the issue involved. The authority performs a quasijudicial role when it determines whether the arbitrator's award is contrary to any law, rule, or regulation or is deficient "on other grounds similar to those applied by federal courts in private sector labor–management relations."[51]

CURRENT PUBLIC SECTOR CHALLENGES

Privatization

Perhaps the greatest threat to public unions and their members today is outsourcing, or **privatization**. Privatization refers to a process in which governmental employees are replaced with private sector workers through a contract with an outside employer for the purpose of reducing overall costs. In the past, outsourcing full-time public sector jobs was unheard of; it was something "big business does, not us." In the 1980s and 1990s, however, as public agencies became strapped for funds, governments looked to lower their personnel costs. In Indianapolis, for example, outsourcing reduced the city's number of public employees by 40 percent in only three years. Sunnyvale, California, used a temporary manpower company for 25 percent of its workforce. Some states, such as Pennsylvania, have developed their own pool of temporary workers, and large state community college systems use as many as 66 percent contract workers instead of full-time faculty.

PRIVATIZATION

When governmental employees are replaced with private sector workers through a contract with an outside employer for the purpose of reducing overall costs.

Outsourcing has become so widely used so quickly in the 1990s that many public employee unions and some public officials have become alarmed. The most effective response by unions is to negotiate a provision in their agreements that prevents any civil service status employee from losing his or her job to such action. Although legal, these provisions are difficult to negotiate if management intends to outsource. Managers recognize that privatized workers can be treated quite differently from permanent employees; some make as little as a third the wages of full-time public sector employees, and they get no health benefits, paid vacations, holiday pay, or sick leave. Some observers see outsourcing as another factor eroding the middle class. "Everyone sees outsourcing as a way of gaining for the government the advantages and flexibility of the private sector, but this creates problems for society," says Frank McArdle, managing director of the General Contractors Association of New York. "When you drive down wages through outsourcing, you undermine your tax base and you add to the burden on government services." Adds Sal Albanese, a New York City Council member, "In the past, the government provided a tremendous opportunity for people to elevate themselves into the middle class. We're in danger of losing that."[52]

While privatization is often thought of as a local government issue, the federal government has also looked at privatization as an option. President George W. Bush advocated the privatization of military housing and the expansion of opportunities for private organizations to provide social and community services as part of his government management agenda.[53]

Advocates of privatizing government services contend that contracting out public services does the following:

- Produces better management of programs by bringing sophisticated cost-cutting techniques.
- Frees public administrators from managing day-to-day operations, and allows government to focus on its "core activities."
- Provides specialized skills otherwise too costly for government to recruit and hire.
- Reduces capital outlays for facilities and equipment, which enables government to be more flexible in revising programs.
- Motivates private sector managers to perform well because they are motivated by opportunities for financial gain.
- Private firms can provide goods and services "better, faster, and cheaper" than government.
- Spurs economic growth by opening new areas of activity to entrepreneurs.
- Dispels criticisms with government's performance as a provider of services.

Some governmental services such as parking garage attendants have been privatized to reduce costs. *Source:* Seth Wenig/AP Images.

- Addresses concerns over "waste, fraud, and abuse."
- Budget deficits require government to develop new sources of revenue and to reduce costs.

Opponents of privatization cite the following downsides to contracting out public services:

- Savings are often illusory because the costs for government to bid, administer, and monitor the results of outside contracts are not considered.
- Depending on outside contractors for facilities and equipment makes government vulnerable to cost increases because it is unable to step in and provide the service.
- Private contractors expect to earn a profit and must also make enough to pay taxes.
- Laying off public employees costs the government unemployment compensation, a loss of tax revenues, and low employee morale.
- Contracting out lowers the quality of services provided because the private contractor's goal is to maximize profits, which often leads to overburdening its employees.
- Contracting out means losing in-house expertise required to carry out governmental activities and makes oversight of contractors more difficult, again, resulting in lower quality of services.[54]
- It's a union-busting strategy intended to weaken unions by decreasing the number of unionized government employees.
- Adversely affects women and minorities.
- Shift of functions to the private sector may transfer governing discretion into the hands of private parties.
- Contracting out can promote conflict-of-interest relationships between government employees and the private sector.
- Competitive markets can fail, especially if there are too few firms to compete for government contracts. For example, when a company operating charter schools in California became defunct in August 2004, the parents of 10,000 children had but a few weeks to locate new schools for their children.[55]
- Overseeing outside work creates management challenges for government administrators.[56]

The American Federation of State, County and Municipal Employees (AFSCME) recommends a number of strategies for employees to fight efforts to privatize public services. The first suggestion is to address the issue in the collective bargaining agreement by either prohibiting any contracting-out or severely limiting it. Because such provisions are not always attainable, AFSCME suggests employees try to negotiate a "successorship" clause covering the contracting-out of any particular service so the contractor would have to retain the employees for the duration of the contract and then negotiate with the union.

AFSCME suggests employees explore legal challenges to contracting out. Such unilateral actions on the part of the public employer may violate its duty to bargain if a collective bargaining law similar to the National Labor Relations Act covers it. In some jurisdictions, contracting-out has been seen as a violation of civil service laws, which protect public employees from adverse job actions not based on merit. Finally, AFSCME urges public employees to lobby elected officials and to seek community support for maintaining the provision of public services by public servants, as opposed to private, for-profit entities.[57]

School Vouchers

But outsourcing is not the only threat to job security for public sector employees. Both the National Education Association (NEA) and the American Federation of Teachers (AFT) have cited "school voucher" programs as a major concern for the public employee. Critics of public schools have advocated tuition voucher programs, which provide families with public funds that could be used for private school tuition, including religious-based school tuition. Advocates of school vouchers contend that giving families a choice will force public schools to improve to stay competitive.[58]

The NEA and AFT raise questions regarding the constitutionality of using public money for religious schools and whether private schools would provide equal access to all children. They cite the lack of public oversight of private schools as undermining the need for accountability to the public for the expenditure of tax dollars or point out that appropriate oversight by government will create a new bureaucracy and erode the autonomy and independence of private and religious schools. NEA president Bob Chase sees a voucher program as a threat not just to public employees but also to the entire public school system:

> America established public education to level the playing field, to provide equity of the most basic opportunity, the opportunity to learn. . . . The children in our country represent great diversity of race, religion, and income, and we cannot afford to replace public education, our single most important and unifying institution, with a system of private schools that pursue private agendas at taxpayer expense.[59]

Despite these concerns, the Supreme Court in 2002 upheld an Ohio state voucher program in *Zelman, Superintendent of Public Instruction of Ohio, et al. v. Simmons-Harris, et al.*[60] The state of Ohio had established a pilot program designed to provide educational choices to families with children who reside in the Cleveland City School District, which has about 75,000 students, the majority of whom are from low-income and minority families. Cleveland's public schools had been among the worst performing public schools in the nation and had been placed under state control by the federal district court. The district failed to meet the state standards for minimal acceptable performance. More than two-thirds of high school students either dropped out or failed before graduation. Of those students who managed to reach their senior year, one of every four still failed to graduate. Of those students who did graduate, few could read, write, or compute at levels comparable with their counterparts in other cities.

Against this backdrop, Ohio enacted its Pilot Project Scholarship Program, which provided tuition aid for students in kindergarten through third grade, expanding each year through eighth grade, to attend a participating public or private school of their parents' choosing and tutorial aid for students who chose to remain enrolled in public school. The Court noted that the Ohio program was enacted for the valid secular purpose of providing educational assistance to poor children in a demonstrably failing public school system. So the only legal question presented to it was whether the Ohio program nonetheless has the forbidden "effect" of advancing or inhibiting religion. The Court did not draw a distinction between government programs that provide aid directly to religious schools and programs of true private choice, in which government aid reaches religious schools *only as a result* of the genuine and independent choices of private individuals.[61]

According to the School Choice Yearbook 2010, student enrollment in private school choice programs, which include school voucher programs and scholarship tax credit programs, has increased by 86 percent over the past five years.[62] States with school choice programs are increasing as well, as can be seen in Table 3-5.

In 2005, teachers' job security and pay were central issues in a special election called by California governor Arnold Schwarzenegger. The initiatives were opposed by the California Teachers Association and the largest state employee union, the California State Employees Association, as well as other unions. The defeat of the initiatives was viewed as a victory for job security for teachers and support for unions in general. The initiatives were as follows:

- ***Proposition 75.*** This initiative would have required unions to obtain annual written consent from government union employees before union dues could be spent for political purposes.
- ***Proposition 74.*** This initiative would have increased the period required for teachers to become a permanent employee (become tenured) from two years to five years. In addition, it would have changed the process by which school boards can terminate a permanent teacher. Thus, opponents criticized the measure as a threat to the job security of teachers.

TABLE 3-5 States with School Choice Programs, 2010

Arizona	Corporate Tax Credits for School Tuition Organizations Personal Tax Credits for School Tuition Organizations Displaced Pupils Choice Grants Scholarships for Pupils with Disabilities
Florida	Tax Credits for Scholarship Funding Organizations McKay Scholarships Program for Students with Disabilities
Georgia	Georgia Special Needs Scholarships Tax Credits for Student Scholarship Organizations
Iowa	Tax Credits for Educational Expenses Tax Credits for School Tuition Organizations
Illinois	Tax Credits for Educational Expenses
Louisiana	Personal Tax Deduction
Maine	Town Tuition Program
Minnesota	Tax Credits and Deductions for Educational Expenses
Ohio	Autism Scholarship Program Cleveland Scholarship and Tutoring Program Educational Choice Scholarship Pilot Program
Oklahoma	Special Needs Vouchers
Pennsylvania	Educational Improvement Tax Credit Program
Rhode Island	Corporate Tax Credits for Scholarship Organizations
Utah	Carson Smith Special Needs Scholarship Program
Vermont	Town Tuition Program
Washington D.C.	Opportunity Scholarship Program
Wisconsin	Milwaukee Parental Choice Program

Source: Adapted from The Friedman Foundation for Educational Choice. Available at www.friedmanfoundation.org. Accessed October 13, 2010.

- ***Proposition 76.*** This initiative, called the "Live within Our Means" Act, would have limited state and school spending, prohibited state borrowing, and given the governor the power to reduce public employees' compensation.

The initiatives were placed on the November 2005 ballot despite opposition from 60 percent of California, according to public opinion surveys. The surveys apparently were fairly on target because all three initiatives failed despite the $250 million spent by supporters. The League of Women Voters as well as public employee unions campaigned against the initiative.[63]

Taxpayer Revolt

When the Great Recession of 2008 caused a drop in tax revenues, cash-strapped state and local governments were forced to find ways to cut costs while continuing to provide the services taxpayers had come to expect. With wages and benefits for state and local government workers totaling 50 percent of state and local government expenditures, it wasn't long before officials were trying to find ways to cut personnel costs.[64] Across the country governments began shutting down offices for a day or more or cut back on staff with unpaid **furloughs**. The use of furloughs by local and state governments, which are actually salary cuts for public employees, placed unions representing government workers between the preverbal "rock and a hard place." If they supported, or at least didn't oppose furloughs, they were accepting pay cuts outside of the collective bargaining process. If they did not

FURLOUGHS

Involuntary, unpaid and temporary leaves of absence from employment, recently used by governments to balance budgets without laying off employees.

support furloughs, and in fact fought the furloughs, they were forcing governments to take the more drastic step of eliminating the jobs altogether. Response by public sector unions, not surprisingly, ran the gamut of opposing and supporting. In Rhode Island and California unions took state governments to court but in Arizona, union leaders accepted furloughs as preferable to layoffs.[65] In Cincinnati, Ohio, a deficit of nearly $28 million in 2009 caused city officials to propose 6 furlough days to keep from having to lay off employees. When the unions said no, the city laid off employees, including police officers, and closed four fire companies. Furloughs, however, did not result in the significant savings some officials had hoped for because with the employees still on the payroll, health care and pension costs continued to rise. Also, many unions were successful in stopping furloughs or even recovering lost wages when courts or arbitrators deemed the furloughs a breach of contract.[66] The use of furloughs, however, put a spotlight on public employment. With unemployment reaching 10.1 percent in October 2009, all public sector spending, including compensation for public employees became a high-profile issue for cash-strapped taxpayers.

As elected officials grappled with acute revenue shortfalls, some prominent public officials targeted public employee compensation as excessive and mobilized the public and legislatures to cut public employee pay, reduce benefits, and modify collective bargaining procedures. New York mayor Michael Bloomberg eliminated two years of teachers' pay raises;[67] Michigan governor Jennifer Granholm proposed changes in state employee retirement and health care benefits that would save the state $450 million in the first year;[68] and New Jersey governor Chris Christie urged voters to reject budgets in school districts where teachers have not agreed to a one-year wage freeze and increased contributions toward their health insurance.[69]

The issue broadened from calls for changes to balance the governments' budgets to a debate on whether or not public employee compensation, with the help of unionization, is excessive, or affordable, or higher than the private sector. There is little debate that prior to the rise of unions in government in the 1960s and 1970s public employee pay was lower than for similar workers in the private sector, but governments offered enhanced benefits to attract and retain skilled workers. The U.S. Bureau of Labor Statistics in 2009 released a comparison of compensation in the public and private sectors that has been relied upon by both those who say public sector compensation is excessive and those who say it is not. (See Table 3-6.) One explanation for this dichotomy is that the nature of the work of government and the nature of work in the private sector does not make comparisons simple.

The Federal Reserve Bank of Chicago and the Civic Federation hosted a forum in February 2009 to discuss the differences in wages and benefits in the public and private sectors and listed the following as the reasons why comparing public and private sector compensation is not an exact science.

- The occupational mix for public and private sectors is different. Around 66 percent of public sector jobs are professional and administrative while there are 50 percent in the private sector. And while retail sales and food service jobs are 20 percent in the private sector, they are only 2 percent in the public sector.
- The survey itself is voluntary and more public sector employers participated than from the private sector, so the numbers might be skewered to the public sector.

TABLE 3-6 BLS Comparison of Public and Private Sector Compensation, 2009

	State and Local Government ($)	Private Sector ($)
Total compensation	39.74	27.64
Wages and salaries	26.13	19.53
Total benefits	13.62	8.11

Note: Averages for all workers

- More public sector employees are represented by unions than private sector employees, and negotiated wages and benefits are higher for unionized workers.
- Public sector employees stay in their jobs longer so that their compensation is increased over a longer period of time than in the private sector.
- Wages in low-skill jobs pay more in the public sector than in the private sector, but high-skill jobs pay less.
- Retirement benefits are higher in the public sector, but approximately 25 percent of public employees do not participate in Social Security, so their government retirement is all they will receive.[70]
- A better comparison between public and private sector employee compensation is made when employee characteristics are used rather than job descriptions. For example, education level is the single most important earnings predictor and public sector employees have more education than private sector employees; 54 percent of public sector employees hold at least a four-year college degree compared to 35 percent of the private sector.[71]

Summary

Widespread unionization in the public sector developed later than in the private sector largely in the 1960s and 1970s in response to President Kennedy's Executive Order 10988. Presently, public sector unionization is still somewhat limited because of the sovereignty doctrine curtailing the scope of collective bargaining in the public sector. Under Executive Order 10988, as updated under the Civil Service Reform Act of 1978, federal employees are granted limited collective bargaining rights, whereas public employees in state and local governments must look to individual state and local legislation for those same rights.

Public sector collective bargaining offers unique challenges due to the nature of the work, the organization of government, and the role of taxpayers in the process. Without the right to strike, most public sector unions rely upon mandatory dispute resolution provisions to maintain a balance in bargaining power at the table.

Privatization by government is seen as a growing threat to public sector employees. Public employee unions question the real cost savings or benefits of contracting out public services and urge their members to lobby against privatization and engender community support for maintaining public services by public servants.

CASE STUDIES

Case Study 3-1 Collecting Union PAC Money

Idaho's Right to Work Act, which covers both public and private employees, says that the "right to work" means that no employee will be required to join or support a labor organization as a condition of employment. Prior to 2003, employees could authorize both a payroll deduction for union dues and a payroll deduction for union political activities conducted through a political action committee. In 2003, the Idaho Legislature amended the Right to Work Act by adding a prohibition on payroll deductions *for political purposes*. A union representing Idaho public employees challenged this limitation.

The union argued that the State was seeking to stifle the "speech" of the unions concerning politics and that this violated their First Amendment rights. The State's Attorney General defended the law by pointing out that the State was not limiting the rights of the union to say or do anything they wanted politically, but the State ought *not* to "subsidize" the "speech" of the unions. Because it cost the State to set up and maintain the payroll deduction program, if it honored the union's request the State would be giving financial support to the union.

The District Court agreed, but distinguished between state employees and local government employees. It concluded that the unions' right to speak politically was not abridged by the law because the First Amendment does not compel the State "to subsidize speech." So

(continued)

since the State had a legitimate purpose for not allowing for the deductions for the political activities of the unions, the statute was valid. However, the court held that since the State failed to identify any State funds used by local governments to administer payroll deductions, the act was invalid for local governments. The ruling as to the state was not appealed by the unions, but the State appealed the decision as to local governments.

The Court of Appeals agreed with the District Court: Since there were no state funds used for the payroll deduction systems of local governments, there was no basis for the state's prohibition applying to local governments. The State appealed to the U.S. Supreme Court.

The State argued that a political subdivision is a subordinate unit of government created by the State to carry out delegated governmental functions. As a political subdivision created by the state, it has no privileges or immunities under the federal constitution so the State could dictate that it could not collect union political money. Given the relationship between the State and its political subdivisions, it is immaterial whether the State allocates funding to the local governments or not. The question is whether the State must affirmatively assist political speech by allowing public *employers* at any level to administer payroll deductions for political activities.

The Union argued that it was clear the State's goal was to restrict the "speech" of the union members because the "legitimate reason" the State argued for NOT collecting at the State level was financial hardship. Since there was no financial hardship for the State in the collection of union political money by the local government, there was no legitimate reason for the law.

Source: Adapted from *Ysursa v. Pocatello Education Association*, 129 S.Ct. 1093 (2009).

QUESTIONS

1. The deduction of union dues and support for the political action activities of the union was a negotiated provision of local governments' contract with its unions. Do you think that the State should be allowed to dictate to local governments how they should negotiate with their employees? Explain.
2. Why would taxpayers have a problem if they knew that the state or local governments were collecting political action committee money for the unions?
3. What would be the basis for the Supreme Court to rule in the State's favor? In the Union's favor?

Case Study 3-2 Resolving Impasse by Binding Arbitration

The Employer is a government agency which seeks to enhance health, lengthen life, and reduce the burdens of illness and disability. The Union represents approximately 100 police officers whose job is to ensure the safety and security of the Employer's facilities, employees, and visitors. While negotiating a renewal of their Collective Bargaining Agreement, the Parties disagree over whether bargaining unit employees should be prohibited from using tobacco products on the Employer's premises. Executive Order 13058, issued by President Clinton on August 9, 1997, prohibits "the smoking of tobacco products in all interior space owned, rented, or leased by the executive branch of the Federal Government, and in any outdoor areas under executive branch control in front of air intake ducts," with certain exceptions that are not relevant to the issue in this case.

The Employer proposed to the Union a Memorandum of Agreement that prohibited tobacco use of any kind, in any of the Employer's owned or leased buildings, on all outside property or grounds, including parking areas and in government vehicles. Employees who failed to comply with the policy would be subject to discipline. The Union's proposal was to prohibit smoking in government buildings and vehicles, within 25 feet of building entrances, and 50 feet of Hospital entrances, and near building air intakes. Members will still be able to smoke in their privately owned vehicles while on government property and still be able to use smokeless tobacco products. The Parties agree they are at an impasse over the tobacco issue and have asked for binding arbitration by the Federal Service Impasses Panel. The Panel asked both sides to submit their final offers and single written statements of position on the tobacco ban policy.

According to the Employer, the nation looks to it for leadership and direction in all areas of health research, developments, administration, and action. It also cites numerous studies that establish that tobacco use is the leading preventable cause of death in the United States. By implementing its tobacco-free policy on its entire campus, Employer is setting an example, protecting its employees from secondhand smoke, increasing productivity, decreasing absenteeism, and lowering the cost of medical expenditures associated with tobacco use. Accepting the Union proposal to allow them to continue to use tobacco products on the campus would pose health risks to other employees and force the Employer to accept a proposal counter to its mission of good health, and cause confusion for employees viewing officers using tobacco in public areas in seeming violation of the known policy.

The Union's interest is to have the employees it represents treated like all other federal employees. The adoption of its proposal would continue the *status quo* with respect to the employees it represents by prohibiting smoking in government buildings, vehicles, and within established setback or designated areas near the hospital and building air intakes. This practice is consistent with Executive Order 13058 which applies to most other federal employees. Furthermore, Employer is required to negotiate with the Union, and during that process it proposed a one-sided position demanding an absolute ban of tobacco where no real dialogue occurred and its interests were not shared with the Union. The Union contends that banning smokeless tobacco serves no purpose because it is not always apparent that an employee uses smokeless tobacco. Finally, the Employer's attempt to control an employee preference that does not impact his/her ability to perform assigned responsibilities creates an unnecessary infringement on the employees' behavior.

Source: Adapted from *Department of Health And Human Services, National Institutes of Health, Bethesda, Maryland And D.C. Lodge #1, Fraternal Order of Police*, 10 FSIP 087 (October 5, 2010).

QUESTIONS

1. Which party has the most risk in turning this question over to a third party to resolve? Why?
2. How could the FSIP decide this issue and give something to both sides?
3. Do you think it is a valid concern of the Employer that agreeing to the Union proposal would reflect badly upon it since the public looks to it for guidance on health matters? Explain.

Key Terms and Concepts

advisory arbitration *106*
cheap riders *101*
Civil Service Reform Act of 1978 *91*
civil service system *88*
dual sovereignty *84*
executive-legislative *99*
fact-finding *106*
"fair share" agency shop *101*
FOIA *98*
fraternal organization *87*
free riders *101*
furlough *111*
Hatch act *88*
"home rule" *85*
interest arbitration *107*
Kennedy E.O. 10988 *89*
Memphis Sanitation Strike *80*
mediation *106*
me-too *98*
mixed union *95*
multilateral bargaining *99*
PATCO strike *103*
pattern bargaining *98*
Pendleton Act *86*
privatization *107*
public sector-only union *95*
right to strike *102*
Sovereignty Doctrine *89*
spoils system *86*
sunshine laws *99*
union security *101*

Review Questions

1. How are public employees provided the right of collective bargaining? Do state and local government employees have the same rights as federal employees?
2. Why did government resist collective bargaining?
3. How do public employees' rights generally differ from those of private sector employees?
4. How do "school voucher programs" threaten public sector employees?

5. How might a public sector union use multilateral bargaining to its advantage?
6. Should some public sector employees be given the right to strike? If so, which ones? If not, what rights might they be given to help balance the bargaining process?
7. Do you believe binding arbitration should be used to settle a public sector collective bargaining impasse? Why or why not?
8. When, if ever, should a government privatize a service?
9. How does the "monopoly position" of a government affect the collective bargaining process?
10. Will the taxpayer revolt that began during the Great Recession of 2008 affect labor relations in the public sector in future years? If so, how? If not, why not?

YOU BE THE ARBITRATOR

Bereavement Leave

ARTICLE 23
BEREAVEMENT LEAVE

Section 23.1. If a death occurs in the employee's immediate family (spouse, children), employee's family (mother, father, stepparents), a grandfather, grandmother, father-in-law, mother-in-law, person in loco parentis, and any member of the employee's family residing in the employee's residence, such employee shall be granted three (3) days' funeral leave, consecutive and contiguous to the death without loss of pay, benefits, days off, holidays, or vacation time, provided that such leave may be extended, within discretion of the Sheriff, based on individual circumstances. If the death requires that the employee travel more than 200 miles, the Sheriff may, at the request of the employee, allow up to two (2) additional workdays as a bereavement leave.

Facts

The employer provides the statutory law enforcement services to the citizens of Fulton County, Ohio. The grievant is a deputy. The grievant worked on the night shift, and his days off were Wednesday and Thursday. On the evening of Thursday, June 21, the grievant's paternal grandmother died. The grievant was not informed of her death until after he had finished his shift on Friday, June 22. He was also informed that the funeral was going to be Sunday, June 24. The grievant reported for work for his regular shift on Saturday, June 23. The grievant then informed his supervisor of the death and indicated that he would be taking Sunday, June 24, off to attend the funeral. The grievant's request was approved, and the grievant then requested two additional days of bereavement leave, that is, Monday, June 25, and Tuesday, June 26, which was made known to the grievant's supervisors. The grievant filled out a "Request for Leave" form as required. However, after the fact, the employer reviewed his request in light of the collective bargaining agreement (CBA) and decided the grievant was not entitled to bereavement pay for Tuesday on the ground that the three days of bereavement leave here should have been Friday, Saturday, and Sunday. Nevertheless, the employer chose only to disallow the Tuesday bereavement pay. The grievant appealed.

Issue

Did the employer violate the provisions of the CBA when it denied bereavement leave to the grievant?

Position of the Parties

The employer argues that under the CBA, the grant of three days' funeral leave must be consecutive and *contiguous* to the death (see Article 23, Bereavement Leave). So grievant was entitled to bereavement pay only for Sunday, as the death occurred on Thursday. The approval of any extension of that leave is within the discretion of the sheriff, who in this instance approved one day of the extension, Monday. Therefore, the grievant is not entitled to bereavement pay for Tuesday.

The union argues that the CBA does not require that the three bereavement days begin on the "first day" after the death, just that the days be near the death and be consecutive and contiguous to each other. When the employer approved the grievant's request for Sunday off, the three days of bereavement began, which means Monday and Tuesday should also count as bereavement days.

QUESTIONS

1. As arbitrator, what would be your award and opinion in this arbitration?
2. Identify the key, relevant section(s), phrases, or words of the collective bargaining agreement (CBA), and explain why they were critical in making your decision.
3. What actions might the employer and/or the union have taken to avoid this conflict?

Source: Adapted from *Fulton County Sheriff,* 116 LA 1773 (Arb. 2002).

CHAPTER 4

Establishing a Bargaining Unit and the Organizing Campaign

United Parcel Service (UPS) voluntarily recognized new Teamster members after it purchased Overnite Transportation. Voluntary recognition by an employer, like UPS in this situation, is a seldom-used alternative to a secret-ballot election as a means for a union to obtain the right to represent employees. *Source:* © Jim West / Alamy.

Chapter Outline

You can't do it unless you organize!

SAMUEL GOMPERS (FOUNDER AND FIRST PRESIDENT OF THE AMERICAN FEDERATION OF LABOR)

LABOR NEWS

UPS Freight Workers Peacefully Join Teamsters

UPS has had a generally positive relationship with the Teamsters Union. Thus, when UPS purchased Overnite Transportation (which became UPS Freight), management decided not to fight any attempt by the newly acquired workers to join the Teamsters Union, which already represented UPS employees. Instead, management chose to remain "neutral" and to recognize any Teamsters local union that collected signed authorization cards from a majority of its workers and not to require a secret-ballot election. The result was majorities of UPS Freight workers signed cards and were recognized in Milwaukee, Minneapolis, Southern California, Oakland, Seattle, New England, Memphis, Detroit, and Louisville. By 2010 the Teamsters represented over 12,400 UPS Freight workers in 42 states. Ira Rosenfeld, UPS executive, explained why management chose to recognize the new workers voluntarily: "UPS Freight and UPS have always respected the wishes of the employees and will continue to do so."

Source: Adapted from Bill Wolfe, "UPS Freight Workers Sign Up for Teamsters," *Louisville Courier-Journal* (January 26, 2008), p. A1.

The collective bargaining process is at the heart of the employer–employee relationship. That process, however, is not a simple one. The 1935 National Labor Relations Act, as subsequently amended, defines the process and limits the parties to it. A group of employees cannot simply present their requests to the employer. Procedures must be followed to determine if those particular employees are protected by the act. A union purporting to represent the employees must prove that it does indeed represent them. And any particular group of employees who feel they have similar interests and desires and therefore should negotiate together may not satisfy the requirements of the act as an "appropriate" unit of employees for collective bargaining purposes. This chapter explores the process by which a group of employees can organize for purposes of collective bargaining and be recognized by the NLRB as a bargaining unit. The organizational campaign strategies of both the union (in support) and management (in opposition) and representational election process are also discussed.

BARGAINING UNIT DETERMINATION

APPROPRIATE BARGAINING UNIT

The group of employees determined by the NLRB to be an appropriate unit for collective bargaining purposes. After a bargaining unit is identified, the employees of that unit have the right to select their bargaining representative, usually a labor union.

The NLRB, in carrying out its lawful responsibilities, decides representation cases. That is, Section 9(b) of the Labor-Management Relations Act authorizes the board to decide on a case-by-case basis the **appropriate bargaining unit** of employees for collective bargaining purposes. The board exercises this power to guarantee employees the fullest freedom under the act—mainly, employees' right of self-organization. The NLRB does not have rigid or constrictive regulations for dealing with recognition cases. It has wide discretion in its decisions, which courts will uphold unless they find that the board acted arbitrarily.[1] Both the board and the courts recognize that more than one unit sometimes may be appropriate for collective bargaining. The board is not required to choose the *most appropriate unit*, only *an appropriate unit*, as demonstrated in Case 4-1 which involves the service technicians and lube workers at a Ford truck dealership. Although there are no hard-and-fast rules in the act to determine appropriateness, there are certain limitations on the types of units and on workers to be included and excluded from units. The NLRB generally follows certain fundamental and logical policies in determining an appropriate bargaining unit.

CASE 4-1

Appropriate Bargaining Unit: Ford Truck Dealership

The company is a truck dealership that sells, modifies, and services light-duty and heavy-duty trucks. The company operates two facilities. The Main Facility is the primary location for sales and service of trucks. The second, known as the Annex, is across the street and operates under a different name. The Annex specializes in servicing, equipping, and modifying trucks. The central issue in dispute is whether the union designated an appropriate collective bargaining unit under the National Labor Relations Act.

At the Main Facility, the service department consists of several service advisers who deal with customers seeking truck service, approximately 14 service technicians who diagnose and repair trucks, and two lube workers who perform lubes, oil and filter changes, and the like. The service technicians work either day or evening shifts. They are responsible primarily for the actual servicing and repairing of customer vehicles. Service technicians are paid an hourly wage, receive commissions based on their efficiency, and can receive commissions for additional work authorized by a customer on a technician's recommendation. Service technicians are certified and are required to provide their own tools, wear blue uniforms with a company logo, and attend regularly scheduled meetings with management. The lube workers also work either day or evening shifts. They work alongside the service technicians and are responsible primarily for oil and filter changes and lubes. The lube workers are not certified and are paid hourly. One lube worker owns his tools; the other does not. The lube workers report to the same supervisor as the service technicians.

At the Annex are several installer/fabricators, a parts employee, and an estimator. The installer/fabricators are technically part of the company's service department. The Annex employees are responsible primarily for installing custom beds and other features on trucks sold by the company and those brought in for service or other work. Sometimes work is performed on the same truck at both locations, as when modifications are made to trucks bought at the main location, and some of the work is performed at the Annex, such as air conditioner and hitch installation. Installer/fabricators employed at the Annex must be able to weld and are administered a welding test prior to employment. Like the service technicians, the installer/fabricators are required to provide their own tools. There is only one shift at the Annex, however, and Annex workers have a different supervisor than the service department employees. Annex employees wear a different uniform and are paid an hourly wage without any commission or bonuses.

The company employs one human resources manager for both facilities. The company's parts and service director also interviews all applicants for either facility. Employees at both facilities are on the same payroll and have the same vacation and benefit policies as well as use the same break room, though there is an additional break room in the Annex. Employees are rarely transferred from one facility to the other. All the company employees attend occasional safety meetings and company functions.

The union filed an election petition to represent a unit of employees at the Main Facility consisting of all full-time and regular part-time service technicians and lubricators. The NLRB certified the 16 employees at the Main Facility as an appropriate unit, and an election was held. The union won by a vote of nine to seven and was certified. The company, however, refused to bargain, contending that the group of employees designated as the bargaining unit was not the appropriate unit for collective bargaining.

The company claimed that the board erred in its unit determination because there were other appropriate units. For example, the company believed that a pure "craft" unit consisting of the service technicians was a more appropriate unit because the lube workers have limited responsibilities and do not receive technician training or that a broader unit that included all the service department personnel at both locations would be a more appropriate unit because the employees performed functions related to the repair of trucks.

Decision

The Court noted that the National Labor Relations Act delegates to the NLRB the power to determine what an "appropriate" employee unit is for collective bargaining purposes. The Court will uphold an NLRB's unit determination as long as the identified unit is appropriate and the decision is supported by evidence. The company's position was that the unit certified by the NLRB was not appropriate because there were other potential units that could also be appropriate. But the existence of other "appropriate" units will not in and of itself invalidate a finding of the NLRB that the unit requesting recognition is an appropriate unit. In this case, placing the lube workers in the same unit as the service technicians made sense because of all the workers at the Main Facility, these were two groups of workers who actually performed mechanical work. And although there might have been similarities between the workers in the Main Facility and in the Annex, there were also differences. The Annex workers performed different functions and were required to have different skills. They worked different shifts and were compensated differently. The Court upheld the NLRB decision that the service technicians and the lube workers were an appropriate unit.

Source: Adapted from *Country Ford Trucks, Inc. v. NLRB and International Assoc. of Machinists and Aerospace Workers, AFL-CIO, Local 1528*, 165 LRRM 2649 (2000).

Most contracts contain an article that specifies the recognition of the union as the representatives of the bargaining unit, such as this example:

ARTICLE I
Recognition

> Section 1. (a) The Company recognizes the Union, during the term of this Agreement, as the sole and exclusive representative of the employees in the bargaining unit defined as "The Electrical Workers Unit" by the National Labor Relations Board in its Decision and Direction of Election dated August 12, 1944, for the purpose of collective bargaining with respect to rates pay, wages, hours of employment and other conditions of employment.[2]

Bargaining Unit

The bargaining unit is defined as the particular group of employees represented by the union in collective bargaining. The union has exclusive bargaining rights for all employees within the unit, whether they join the union or not; and it has no rights for those employees outside of the bargaining unit. The determination of exactly which employees are within the bargaining unit may have a great effect on the outcome of the organizing campaign. The union seeks a unit in which it feels it can win a majority of the vote in a representation election. When the employer and union cannot agree on the unit, the NLRB, under Section 9 of the National Labor Relations Act, decides on "the unit appropriate for the purposes of collective bargaining."[3]

Appropriate Unit

The basic underlying principle for the NLRB's determination of an appropriate unit is that only employees having a substantial mutuality of interest in wages, hours, and working conditions can be appropriately grouped in that unit. The logic is that the greater the similarities of working conditions, the greater the likelihood the unit's members can agree on priorities and thus make the collective bargaining process successful.[4]

The criteria that are most often used in deciding what constitutes a rational unit include community of interest, history of bargaining, desire of employees, prior unionization, relationship of the unit to the organizational structure, and public interest.

COMMUNITY OF INTEREST The **community-of-interest doctrine** attempts to quantify, by means of descriptive criteria, when workers should feel that their individual interests are so similar that collective bargaining will be fruitful. The board has at various times enumerated these criteria: similarity of job functions and earnings, in benefits received or hours worked, and/or in job training or skills required; a high degree of contact and interchange among the employees; and/or geographic proximity and common supervision.[5] All these factors can indicate a common interest or interests that, coupled with the other listed criteria, establish an appropriate unit.

COMMUNITY OF INTEREST

Criteria used by the NLRB to evaluate a group of employees and determine whether they constitute an appropriate bargaining unit, including; similarity of jobs, and wages & benefits; degree of contact and proximity; and common supervision.

The NLRB's decisions in this area are subject to change, however. For example, in a 2000 decision, the NRLB ruled that a group of temporary employees at *M. S. Sturgis, Inc.* showed "a sufficient community of interest" with permanent employees to be added to the bargaining unit.[6] The "temporary employees" were subject to the same supervision, worked the same hours, and performed the same work side by side with the permanent workers who were part of a bargaining unit. This ruling reversed a 1990 NLRB ruling and was widely touted as giving about 5.7 million temporary employees collective bargaining rights for the first time.[7] In 2004, the NLRB *reversed* its decision in *M. S. Sturgis* in *Oakwood Care Center* and ruled that full-time employees of one employer could not be in the same bargaining unit as employees who were jointly employed (i.e., as temporary employees with a joint but separate employer). Oakwood, a long-term residential care facility, had its own employees, and it used a temporary service for additional employees. All the employees were supervised and disciplined by Oakwood supervisors, and Oakwood and the temporary service jointly determined the pay and benefits of the temporary employees. The NLRB acknowledged that under the *Sturgis* case, the temporary employees would have been a part of the bargaining unit. In overruling *Sturgis,* the NLRB, in a 3–2 opinion, stated that grouping employees of different employers into the same bargaining unit violates the act's purpose of protecting employee rights by subjecting the employees to fragmented bargaining and inherently conflicting interests.[8]

HISTORY OF BARGAINING If a bargaining unit and a particular employer have a history of bargaining, the board will recognize the appropriateness of the unit, in the absence of compelling reasons to the contrary, to ensure the employees' right of self-organization and most importantly to provide a climate of stable labor relations. History of bargaining usually becomes a question when the board receives a request for decertification to allow for smaller or different bargaining units or when a new class of employer has come under the board's jurisdiction, such as when the National Labor Relations Act was extended to the health care industry. Although the board favorably considers prior bargaining relationships, such histories are not absolute. The board has disregarded history of bargaining in several cases when that history contravened the board's policy of mixing clerical and production and maintenance personnel, when it was based on oral contracts, and when it reflected racial or sexual discrimination.[9]

EMPLOYEE WISHES The **Globe doctrine** established the NLRB policy to give weight to employee wishes when determining an appropriate bargaining unit.[10] Although the board cannot delegate the selection of a bargaining unit to employees, it may use the election process as a way to consult employees. In the *Globe* case, the board provided for special balloting to determine the representation wishes of the employees. The situation involved both a small craft unit and a large industry unit, and both could be appropriate. By permitting the employees in the smaller unit to indicate their preference, the board was able to decide whether to leave the craft group in the smaller bargaining unit or to combine it with the larger group.[11] Such consultation is especially helpful if two or more bargaining units are considered about equally appropriate by the board's otherwise objective standards.

GLOBE DOCTRINE

The policy set by the NLRB to help it determine the representation wishes of employees when establishing an appropriate bargaining unit. The board may use the secret ballot election process as a means of giving weight to the desires of a group of employees, such as a smaller craft group within a larger industrial group.

EMPLOYEE UNIONIZATION The NLRB considers the extent of unionization by a bargaining unit as one factor in unit determination but not as a controlling factor. The question is still one of appropriateness and not of whether the wishes of a union can be honored. If the bargaining unit is otherwise appropriate, prior unionization can be considered to indicate employee wishes.

THE UNIT AND EMPLOYER ORGANIZATIONAL STRUCTURE As discussed earlier, the considerations used to determine appropriateness are not legally binding formulas but an exercise in rational examination of the facts of an individual case. The NLRB recognized this distinction from its earliest decision. In *Bendix Products Corporation,* the board stated, "The designation of a unit appropriate for the purposes of collective bargaining must be confined to evidence and circumstances peculiar to the individual case."[12] Under such a philosophy, an employer may, because of its relationship to branch offices or particular reporting policies, make an otherwise inappropriate unit appropriate for its employees. Thus in some cases the organizational structure and geographic locations may affect the decision on the bargaining unit. The board must examine, in some cases, the internal operations of a company to ascertain those peculiarities.

PUBLIC INTEREST One consideration added by the courts for review by the board is the public interest. Without much guidance provided by the courts, the board is to ascertain when its decision will serve the public interest. In making this determination, the NLRB must not be affected by the desires of the parties involved.[13]

ACCRETION

The practice of allowing the addition of new employees and jobs to existing bargaining units provided their work satisfies the same criteria of the original unit.

ACCRETION When new employees or positions are added by an employer, **accretion** allows the NLRB to consider adding the new groups of employees directly to existing units if their work satisfies the same criteria as the original unit, that is, community of interests, bargaining history, interchange of employees, geographic proximity, common supervision, and union wishes. However, such a determination is not automatic. If the new class of employees retains a separate identity, perhaps by virtue of its newness, it can be determined an additional appropriate unit. Accretion usually occurs when an employer expands operations, builds a new facility, or merges with another employer. It is often to the advantage of the union to have an accretion since it adds more employees to the bargaining unit.[14] Accretion offers the board a conflicting choice. Adding new employees to an established union preserves the stability so important under the act, but squeezing in new employees, under perhaps narrow similarities, constricts the employees' freedom of choice.

For example, in 2009 the NLRB ruled that baristas working at a Starbucks franchise in a Hilton hotel restaurant should be a separate bargaining unit, and not accreted to the existing restaurant employees unit. The board found there was not sufficient community of interest between the Starbucks and hotel employees because there was no common supervision, no regular contact, and a lack of integration of work with the hotel restaurant workers. Starbucks exercised significant control over its own operation, including service rules, food supplies, and training of employees. In addition to specialized coffee drinks, Starbucks employees sold merchandise while other hotel employees did not. The hotel employees' handbook, however, did cover the baristas as well as other employees in the bargaining unit and hotel management hired all the employees. UNITE HERE, the union that represents the other hotel employees, had requested that the baristas be accreted; the hotel, however, opposed the accretion.[15]

STIPULATED UNITS The board's authority to determine an appropriate unit is not without limitations. A company and a union may stipulate to the board what they consider an appropriate unit. The courts have said that the board may not alter the bargaining unit in such cases. However, a stipulated unit may not violate principles in the National Labor Relations Act or established board policy, for example, by including supervisors.[16]

SUPERVISORS Supervisors, by the nature of their work, generally are considered management under the NLRA and thus excluded from any bargaining unit—or from the collective bargaining

The NLRB in a 2009 case decided that Starbucks employees working inside the Hilton Milwaukee City Center should not be accreted to an existing restaurant bargaining unit, but instead should have their own bargaining unit.
Source: Getty Images.

rights granted under the act. As the workplace has become more complex and jobs more varied, the exact definition of a "supervisor" under the NLRA has become an issue debated in the U.S. Congress and by labor experts. The National Labor Relations Act defines a supervisor as "someone using independent judgment to assign and direct the work of other employees in the interest of the employer."

In 2007, the Re-employment of Skilled and Professional Employees and Construction Tradeworkers (RESPECT) Act was filed in Congress to amend the NLRB definition of supervisors. The bill would delete the words "assign" and "responsibility to direct" from the definition and would require that employees must be in a supervisory role for at least 50 percent of their work time to be classified as a supervisor under the NLRA. Supporters of the RESPECT Act believe that employees, including team leaders, contraction foremen, and nurses, are not primarily management and should have collective bargaining rights. Opponents believe the bill would make a significant change from the past 60 years.[17]

The lines drawn by court rulings and board interpretations are never exact. In *National Labor Relations Board v. Yeshiva University*, it was determined that the faculty members were managerial employees because of their input into the academic product of the university. As managerial instead of professional employees, they did not come under the protection of the National Labor Relations Act and could therefore not be recognized. Such a determination has a negative effect on unionization in the academic sector.[18] In 2004, the NLRB ruled that graduate teaching assistants are students and thus have no right to organize. This ruling overturned a 2000 NLRB decision that required New York University to recognize a graduate teaching assistants' union. The 2000 NLRB ruling sparked a wave of union organizing efforts on private university campuses across the Northeast, including Brown, Columbia, Temple, Harvard, Cornell, Tufts, and the University of Pennsylvania: 24 campuses altogether with over 40,000 teaching and researching assistants represented by unions. Then, in 2004, a new NLRB "loaded with Bush appointees reversed the 2000 ruling."[19]

Types of Units

Certain types of units have evolved within the established principles of appropriateness. The act itself lists employer units, craft units, plant units, or their subdivisions.

CRAFT UNIT

A bargaining unit composed exclusively of workers with a specific and recognized skill, such as electricians or plumbers.

CRAFT UNITS Workers whose jobs primarily require a recognized skill, such as electricians, machinists, and plumbers may compose a **craft unit**. Recognition questions for craft units usually come before the board when a group of craft employees wants to break away from an existing industrial union which included many different skills job functions—this action is called *craft severance*. Congress has established the policy that the board cannot determine a craft unit inappropriate on the grounds that a different unit has been established by prior board determination, unless the majority of the employees in the craft unit vote against separate representation. Despite this legislative policy, the NLRB has severely limited craft severance elections through a number of decisions. Under the *National Tube* doctrine,[20] the board identified certain industries whose operations were so integrated that craft workers could not be taken from the unit without affecting the stability of labor relations. And in the *Mallinckrodt Chemical Works* decision, the board outlined the criteria it would use to allow craft severance; the application of these standards has greatly reduced incidents of craft severance.[21]

The NLRB requires that the craft group be distinct from others in the unit by virtue of the skilled, nonrepetitive nature of its work. The board examines the extent to which the group has retained its identity or, as the alternative, actually participated in the affairs of the larger unit. The impact of separating the craft unit from the whole is also a factor in the board's determination. Consideration of the particular bargaining history of the larger unit, as well as the history of collective bargaining in the industry as a whole, must be part of the board's deliberations. In some instances, the NLRB decision is influenced by the degree to which the craft work is integrated with the unskilled work and therefore essential to the production process. Finally, the board may examine the qualifications of the union seeking to represent the craft union for its experience as an agent for similar groups.[22]

The International Brotherhood of Electrical Workers (IBEW) is known as a craft union because most of the members have a recognized skill—they work with electrical components and equipment as line technician, repairers, machine operators, meter installers, boiler operators, cable splicers, welders, and the like. *Source:* AP Images.

DEPARTMENTAL UNITS Similar to a craft unit, a **departmental unit** is composed of all the members of one department in a larger organization. The board uses standards similar to those used for craft severance in determining one department to be an appropriate unit separate from the entire plant or company. An examination of the difference in skills and in training, the degree of common supervision, the degree of interchange with employees outside the department, and different job performance ratings have been used to allow a departmental unit to exist.[23]

DEPARTMENTAL UNIT

Similar to a craft unit, a departmental unit is composed of all the members of one department in a larger organization.

ONE EMPLOYER, MULTIPLE LOCATIONS Many employers have plants, facilities, or stores at more than one location. And the NLRB must determine if a single location can be an appropriate unit or whether all locations should constitute a single unit. It is well established that a petitioned-for single facility unit is *presumed* to be an appropriate bargaining unit.[24] That presumption, however, is rebuttable on a showing that the single facility has so effectively merged into a more comprehensive unit, or is so functionally integrated, that it has lost its separate identity. To determine whether the single-facility presumption has been rebutted, the board looks at such factors as the centralized control over daily operations and labor relations; extent of autonomy of the local management to handle the facility's day-to-day ordinary operations and to supervise the employees' day-to-day work; similarity of employee skills, functions, and working conditions; extent of employee interchange; geographic proximity; and bargaining history, if any.[25] The party *opposing* the single-facility unit has the burden of rebutting its appropriateness. However, the board does not require overwhelming evidence of such integration. In one, the board determined that the employer had successfully rebutted the presumption of a single-facility unit when the union sought to represent employees at one of the two facilities of the employer, and the board determined that the two facilities operated as one even though they were 100 miles apart.[26] The board reached the opposite conclusion in a case in which the facilities, in this case Kroger stores, were merely 8 miles apart, but there was minimal interchanges between them.[27]

MULTIEMPLOYER UNITS Although the Wagner Act favors localizing a unit within one employer, collective bargaining can be conducted between a group of related employers and representatives of their employees.[28] Factors to be considered in such a designation are whether there is an express or implied approval of all parties to enter into such bargaining relationship or if the history of the bargaining in the industry implies intent to consent to multiemployer units. The employer can withdraw from a multiemployer collective bargaining relationship before the date for modification or negotiation of a new contract. After bargaining has begun, an employer may withdraw only with the union's consent or on showing unusual circumstances. The union consent ensures the stability necessary under the National Labor Relations Act, and the board has found unusual circumstances when there is a genuine bargaining impasse.[29]

RESIDUAL UNIT

Employees left unrepresented after the bulk of the employees are organized, such as janitors and sales people, may be entitled to separate representation by a residual unit.

RESIDUAL UNITS Workers do not always fit into neat packages, and the board has sometimes given recognition to odd collections of employees because of their common working situations or the proximity of their working sites. The NLRB policy is that employees are entitled to separate representation if they are left unrepresented after the bulk of employees are organized. Employees who do not fit anywhere else—such as sales and service personnel, porters, janitors, and maids—are combined into **residual units**.

REMAINING UNIT

An employee group separate from the primary production and maintenance units in their job duties, such as professional, technical, guard, and clerical units.

REMAINING UNITS Employee groups that are separate from primary production and maintenance units can be classified as **remaining units**. Because of exclusions contained in the act itself, professional employees and guards often have professional and guard units. Technical units contain employees with a high degree of skill and training who exercise independent judgment but fall short of professional status. The factors to be considered in determining a technical unit are the desires of the party, the bargaining history, the existence of a unit seeking self-representation, the separate supervision of the technical employees, the location of the workplace, similarity of work hours, and employee benefit packages. It often becomes a question of who should be included on the basis of the level of skill and training, employee contact and interchange, and similarity of working conditions. Departmental units are treated the same as craft units in severance cases. Office clerical units are commonly separated from production and maintenance units in a large plant because the board recognizes the common interest of office clerical employees, regardless of previous bargaining history.

CONSTRUCTION INDUSTRY UNITS Due to the unusual nature of the U.S. construction industry—seasonal, temporary, or project-based—it is given unique treatment in the act:

> Sec. 8. [§158.] (f) [Agreements covering employees in the building and construction industry] It shall not be an unfair labor practice . . . for an employer . . . to make an agreement . . . with a labor organization . . . because the majority status has not been established under Section 9 of this Act prior to the making of such an agreement, or (2) such an agreement requires as a condition of employment membership in such a labor organization after the seventh day following the beginning of such employment . . . or (3) such agreement requires the employer to notify such labor organization of opportunities for employment with such employer . . .

Thus in the construction industry an employer may begin to bargain with a union before any employees are hired for a new project. The union, unlike unions in other industries, is not required to show it represents a majority of the employees in an appropriate bargaining unit before it bargains with the employer. These negotiated agreements are called "pre-hire" or Project Labor Agreements (PLAs).[30] However, the NLRB has held that a PLA is unenforceable if it requires the use of only union labor on a project or if it gives a union leverage in securing necessary permits resulting in a "labor monopoly" on the project.[31]

HEALTH CARE INSTITUTION UNITS The 1974 Health Care Amendments extended coverage of the act to employees of nonprofit hospitals. In hearings concerning the amendments, Congress directed the NLRB to give "due consideration . . . to preventing proliferation of bargaining units in the health care industry." However, this direction was not specified in the language of the act itself. The board applied the usual standards for unit determination for a number of years but eventually passed an administrative rule approving eight basic appropriate *health care units* for the health care industry in 1987:

1. Physicians
2. Registered nurses (rns)
3. All other professional employees, including licensed practical nurses
4. Technical employees
5. Business office clerical employees
6. Skilled maintenance employees
7. Guards
8. All other nonprofessional employees

The American Hospital Association brought action to enjoin the board from enforcing the newly promulgated rule. The Supreme Court upheld the board's ruling.[32] Unions blamed the delays caused through the litigation brought by hospitals challenging the bargaining units for stymieing union efforts to organize the health care industry.[33]

Management objection to nurses' bargaining units continued. In *NLRB v. Health Care & Retirement Corporation*,[34] the Supreme Court reversed an NLRB ruling regarding nurses' units and severely reduced opportunities for growth of unions in the health care industry. In that case the health care corporation had challenged the certification of a nurses' unit on the grounds that the nurses acted as "supervisors" and were therefore exempt from the act. The Court agreed and pointed out that the NLRA defines a supervisor as someone using independent judgment to assign and direct the work of other employees in the interest of the employer. Under that definition, most nurses were supervisors and, therefore, exempt from the act. In response, the NLRB tried to carve out an exception stating that nurses were not supervisors exercising "independent judgment" if their judgment was no more than using their professional or technical training or experience to direct less-skilled employees to deliver services in accordance with employer-specified standards. The Court rejected the NLRB exception in *NLRB v. Kentucky River Community Care, Inc.*,[35] holding that just because a nurse's exercise of supervision was limited by professional standards did not mean the nurse was not a supervisor. In 2006, the NLRB again tried to clarify the issue of supervising nurses' collective bargaining eligibility. In the first case, *Oakwood Health Care Inc.*, the NLRB ruled that nurses in acute care facilities who use "independent judgment" in a "non-routine" manner to direct the work of other employees should be considered supervisors. The board found that "permanent charge nurses" (as opposed to temporary charge nurses) exercised independent judgment when "assigning" other nursing personnel to care for specific patients and that such supervisory activity was a substantial part of their work time.[36] The NLRB decision in *Oakwood Health Care* was controversial and led to members of Congress introducing bills that sought to overturn the decision. In the second case involving nurses at a nursing home, the board found that the charge nurses did *not* exercise sufficient supervisory authority to exclude them from the act; in fact, the charge nurses were not evaluated on how they did or did not direct other employees.[37]

UNION STRUCTURE

The structure of labor unions reflects the reasons they were formed and the influences of the times in which they grew. Unions seek to secure a better living standard for their members through higher wages and fringe benefits and to enhance job security through tenure, layoff provisions, and seniority rights. In addition, labor organizations have broadened their interests to seek legislative protections for workers such as occupational health and safety laws, workers' compensation, and unemployment insurance. To meet the unions' objectives, a two-tiered labor organizational structure has evolved. On the local level, job-oriented units form the basis for bargaining with employers. On the national level, a network or federation of unions pursues broader goals.

Types of Unions

CRAFT UNIONS Craft unions are made up of workers who have been organized in accordance with their craft or skill. "One craft, one union" is their slogan. For example, in the building construction industry, skilled workers include electricians, carpenters, bricklayers, and ironworkers; in the printing industry, printers, typesetters, and engravers; in the service industry, barbers, cooks, and telephone workers; and in the manufacturing industry, millwrights, machinists, and tool-and-die makers. The craft union, as an organization of skilled workers, is able to approach an employer on a much different footing than the industrial union. A craft union local typically seeks to organize all practitioners of its trade employed by a certain employer or within a specific geographic area. By doing so successfully, the craft union creates a union shop. Employers who need the services of a skilled laborer must employ a union member. Craft unions also seek to restrict the supply of skilled laborers so they can demand higher wages. Stringent apprenticeship programs consisting of several years of classroom instruction and on-the-job training limit craft union membership. State or local licensing boards composed of members of the trade union can often restrict the number of licenses issued.

CRAFT UNION
A labor union whose members primarily perform jobs of one particular skill.

Labor agreements entered into by craft unions usually cover a geographic region rather than one employer. Union members may work for more than one employer within a year and still be covered by that same agreement. This practice is common when the building trade unions have negotiated a labor agreement with all the major construction companies in the area. Electricians, plumbers, drywall installers, and other trades can go from job to job under the same agreement.

Since carpenters have a particular skill they are often in a craft union. *Source:* Levent Konuk/ShutterStock.

INDUSTRIAL UNION

A labor union whose membership is composed primarily of semiskilled or unskilled workers, such as automobile workers and steelworkers, who are organized on the basis of the product they produce. Usually all production and maintenance (not management) workers within an organization belong to the same industrial union.

INDUSTRIAL UNIONS Industrial unions are generally composed of unskilled and semiskilled workers or all the nonmanagement personnel in a plant or facility and due to their numbers often have a wider and stronger base than craft unions. The slogan "One shop, one union" typifies the **industrial union** seeking to organize workers at one workplace with the same employer, regardless of their skills or jobs. The industrial union seeks to increase membership to ensure its influence.

Typical industrial unions include organizations of autoworkers, rubber workers, textile workers, commercial workers, steelworkers, miners, and truck drivers. Increasingly, government employees such as firefighters, police, and hospital workers are organizing industrial-type unions. However, a study of industrial unions' organizing efforts in recent years revealed that they have transitioned into more "general" unions as they have sought to expand their membership outside their traditional industry, which in most cases has seen a declining number of employers and employees. For example, the United Automobile Workers (UAW) Union conducted in one year 47 campaigns—nearly half of all its organizing campaigns and certification elections—in nonautomobile industries including transportation, wholesale retail sales, and services.[38]

The local industrial union most often is affiliated with a national or international union. Some national unions negotiate master agreements, which are regional or national labor agreements covering wages, transfers, pensions, layoffs, and other benefits. The local agreement must be negotiated separately to cover matters of specific concern to the local union and the plant. An example of such an agreement is the labor agreement between the United Auto Workers and Ford Motor Company.

Members of an industrial union often join the union after being hired simply because of a provision in the collective bargaining agreement. Members regard their union as their voice with the employer, and when employment ends, their membership usually ends as well.

Levels of Unions

The four levels of unions are local unions, national (or international) unions, intermediate unions, and the federation of unions.

LOCAL UNIONS Unionized workers are members of a local union, which is the organizational component of the labor union. It handles the day-to-day operations of the collective bargaining

The United Auto Workers (UAW) is known as an industrial union because it represents almost all the employees in one workplace: "one shop, one union." *Source:* MCT via Getty Images.

agreement, disposes of most grievances, manages strikes, and disciplines members. A local union may fill a social role in the lives of its members, sponsoring dances, festivals, and other functions. It may be the focal point of the political organization and activity of its members.

A local union usually meets once a month to conduct business. At such meetings, annual elections are held, union issues are discussed, and activities are organized. Although this level is the most important to its members, attendance at the union meetings varies and is highest at times of crisis. Unlike paid **business agents** for craft unions, elected officials of local industrial unions are compensated by being given time off the job when conducting union business. Local unions usually adopt bylaws that specify their jurisdiction, meetings, and election process, as well as the duties and salaries of officers (see Figure 4-1).

BUSINESS AGENT

The full-time administrator of a local union paid to handle the negotiation and administration of the union contract as well as the daily operation of the union hiring hall.

LOCAL OFFICERS Officers of local unions are usually elected positions for fixed terms. The positions often include president, vice-president, secretary/treasurer, sergeant-at-arms, business manager (or agent), and steward (See Figure 4-1). The local officers often serve on the negotiating committee with other members elected by the membership or chosen by the officers. This role is their most important, and when two slates of candidates run for officer positions, how well they perform at the bargaining table may determine which slate is selected. The same officers may serve for several terms—unless the members become dissatisfied with the terms of a new contract, and then look to elect new officers whom they believe "can deliver the bacon." The second major role of officers is the handling of daily union–management business, in particular resolving grievances. These functions may be handled by the union business manager and shop stewards. The business manager is usually a full-time employee of the union who handles daily administration of the contract. Local unions usually have several shop stewards. **Stewards** have a unique and critical role in the union. They are either appointed or elected by the membership and serve in a unique role—as

STEWARD

An on-the-job union representative who carries out the responsibilities of the union in the plant at the departmental level.

BY LAWS
OF
LOCAL UNION 1347
INTERNATIONAL BROTHERHOOD
OF
ELECTRICAL WORKERS
CINCINNATI, OH

INDEX

FIGURE 4-1 Bylaws of Local Union. *Source:* Kenzie Baker, IBEW Local Union 1347, permission granted by Stephen Feldouse Business Manager, (December 2005).

an employee of the employer who then represents a union member when the employees have a grievance against the employer! They are the "eyes and ears" of the officers and alert them to issues of concern. To the members of the union the steward is the personification of the union. Many members' only direct weekly contact with the union is the steward, and thus stewards often hold great influence with members. Thus stewards become a buffer between management and the union, and their ability to facilitate grievances is critical to their success. Unions often, therefore, provide training programs to their stewards in areas such as communication skills, handling difficult people, searching for the true interests that underlie an issue, and techniques to resolve grievances at their lowest level- which is beneficial to both the union and management. For example, in Ohio the United Food and Commercial Workers Union (UFCW) Local 1099 provides steward certificate training during quarterly business meetings. This difficult **dual commitment** of stewards—to both management and the union members is likely the cause of high turnover in steward positions. Successful stewards are highly regarded by both sides and often are elected to officer positions in the union. Some union leaders believe the role of steward and thus his/her ability to successfully meet the dual commitment is the most important factor, perhaps next to the terms of a new contract, in membership satisfaction with their union, and therefore the officers.

NATIONAL (OR INTERNATIONAL) UNIONS Typically, but not always, the local union is affiliated with a national or international union. Craft and industrial unions organize on a national basis and designate local unions by region. The national union serves as the local's parent, having created it. But a local union is considered a separate and distinct voluntary association owing its existence to the will of its members. The union's constitution, bylaws, and charter determine the relationship between a national union and its subordinate local unions. The charter is a contract between the national and local organization and its members. The constitution and bylaws authorize the national union not only to function but also to protect individual rights.

The national union provides services to the locals, and the fundamental relationship is based on the services rendered. Services include organizing the nonunion workers within the jurisdiction of the local union. In appropriate circumstances, the national union negotiates master agreements with nationwide employers and then assists the local union in negotiating a local agreement. Even if no national contract is entered into, the national union assists the local unions in their contract negotiations through its research and educational services and may provide an expert negotiator. A national union helps with grievance and arbitration administration and provides support in strike activities. National unions play an important role organizing new members, as well as a representative role on behalf of their locals in national and statewide political interests. Local unions support the national unions with dues and send members to participate in national conventions.

INTERMEDIATE ORGANIZATIONAL UNIONS Intermediate organizational unions consisting of regional or district officers, trade councils, conference boards, and joint councils lie between national and local unions. For industrial unions, the intermediate office serves to bring the national office closer to the local unions to provide better services. For craft unions, joint councils often bring the various crafts together to give them better negotiating power with local construction employers, to coordinate their activities, and to assist in resolving jurisdictional disputes between craft unions.

FEDERATION OF UNIONS From 1955, when the American Federation of Labor (AFL) and Congress of Industrial Unions (CIO) merged to create the AFL-CIO, until 2005, the AFL-CIO was the only **federation of unions** in the United States. In 2005, however, seven national unions split from the AFL-CIO to create Change to Win.

FEDERATION OF UNIONS

The uniting of many national unions to increase union power and recognition. The federation serves as a national spokesperson for its members although it is not a union itself. Two federations in the United States are the AFL-CIO and the Change to Win Coalition.

The AFL-CIO today is composed of 56 national and international unions; has approximately 39,000 local unions; and 10.5 million members including plumbers, machinists, teachers, musicians, engineers, bottlers, firefighters, editors, and farmworkers. Figure 4-2 illustrates the AFL-CIO structure. Federations were formed to increase union power. Although the AFL-CIO is itself not a union, it represents U.S. labor in world affairs and coordinates union activities such as lobbying, voter registration, and political education. For example, the AFL-CIO worked with local unions to defeat two Los Angeles campaigns to break up the city. The secession issues appeared on the ballot in Hollywood and the San Fernando Valley in 2002. Supporters hoped to create new smaller cities and cut the costs and taxes for municipal services such as police, fire, sanitation, public works, and housing. The city of Los Angeles at the time had 35,500 workers, most of who belonged to labor unions. Miguel Contreras, head of the Los Angeles County Federation of Labor, AFL-CIO, noted that Los Angeles had "progressive" labor laws, which might not be passed in the new cities. The new cities would be required to honor existing union contracts for one year only. With over 810,000 California members, the federation distributed leaflets and manned telephone banks against the succession ballots.[39]

FIGURE 4-2 AFL-CIO Organization Chart.
Source: Available at www.aflcio.org (2008). Accessed May 2, 2009.

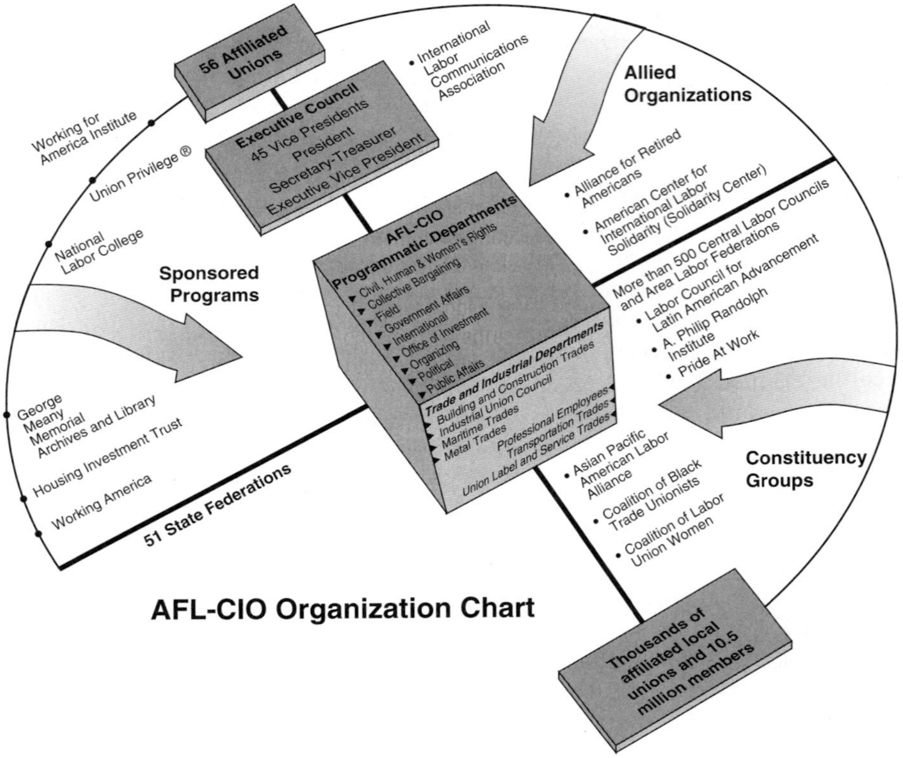

Change to Win

CHANGE TO WIN

A new union federation of national unions dedicated to growing their membership through strategic organizational campaign and improving the living standards of workers.

In 2005, seven national unions split from the AFL-CIO to form the **Change to Win** Coalition, a new union federation of national unions dedicated to growing their membership through strategic organizational campaign and improving the living standards of workers. The three national unions that led the split were the International Brotherhood of Teamsters, the Service Employees International Union, and the United Food and Commercial Workers. The new federation started with six million members and elected Anna Burger as the first woman in history to lead a labor federation in the United States (see Profile 4-1). In 2010 Change to Win represented over 5.5 million members, and was known for aggressive organizational campaigns. The affiliate member unions include the International Brotherhood of Teamsters (IBT); Labor's International Union of North America (LIUNA); Service Employees International Union (SEIU); United Farm Worker of America (UFW); and United Food and Commercial Workers International Union (UFCW). The mission statement of Change to Win provides a clear focus—"to unite the 50 million workers in affiliate industries, whose jobs cannot be outsourced, and who are vital to the global economy." This focus on organizing certain workers is less broad and less political than the mission of the AFL-CIO. Yet in recent years rumors that the two federations might join back together have continued to spread, but thus far the merger has not happened. Certainly the two have worked together on many issues vital to labor such as passage of the Employee Free Choice Act (See Chapter 1.).

INDEPENDENT UNIONS As stated earlier, not all local unions are affiliated with a national or an international union that in turn is a part of the AFL-CIO or Change to Win. Local independent unions are characterized by smaller memberships, more limited funds, and a lower profile. Independent unions are generally not designed along either the craft or the industrial unit model, preferring to open their membership to employees of a specific professional occupation.

Profile 4-1

Rival Unions Split from AFL-CIO, End 50 Years of Unity

On the eve of the 50th anniversary of the historic 1955 merger of the two major American unions, the American Federation of Labor and the Congress of Industrial Organizations, seven national unions split from the AFL-CIO to form a rival labor organization, Change to Win Coalition. Led by the Teamsters Union and its powerful president, James P. Hoffa, the Service Employees International Union, the largest AFL-CIO union, the United Food and Commercial Workers (UFCW), and UNITE (textile, restaurant, and hotel employees) boycotted the 2005 AFL-CIO annual convention in Chicago and announced the creation of their new labor coalition. Other unions began to follow, and the AFL-CIO lost over 4 million of its 13 million members and 7 of its 56 national unions.

Why the split? At a time when organized labor is fighting to remain an important force in American society, many labor experts questioned the motive behind the split. UFCW president Joe Hansen claimed, "The world has changed and workers' rights and living standards are under attack . . . and tradition and past successes are insufficient to meet new challenges." Hansen further stated that a primary goal of the new coalition is to organize employees and bring new members into organized labor, and that the split was more about strategies than goals. The AFL-CIO in the past placed too much emphasis on backing political candidates in Washington.

A second possible cause for the split is the rivalry between AFL-CIO president John J. Sweeney, who was reelected at the convention in Chicago, and Andrew L. Stern, president of the Service Employees International Union, who had been mentored by Sweeney when he headed the union. Stern began a campaign several months before the convention to convince members of his own union and other unions to leave the AFL-CIO.

Leo Gerard, president of the United Steelworkers of America, agreed that the split was a power struggle between the two union leaders, Sweeney and Stern, and stated, "This is not about creating better lives for our children and grandchildren. This is nothing but a disguised power grab. They [the unions that split] should be ashamed of it."

Source: Adapted from Steven Greenhouse, "Ambitions Are Fueling a Division of Labor," *New York Times* (July 26, 2005), pp. A1, 17; Will Lester, "UPCW Is Third Union to Abandon AFL-CIO," *The Associated Press* (July 29, 2005).

In 2005 seven national unions split from the AFL-CIO and formed Change to Win—a new labor organization focused on increasing membership in targeted industries.
Source: James Finley/AP Images.

The independent unions resemble other unions in that they do target membership, albeit often a wider target. They may hold national conventions and elect national officers, although the conventions are more frequent and seemingly more democratic among the independent unions.

BARGAINING UNIT DETERMINATION IN THE PUBLIC SECTOR

As discussed in Chapter 3, the Federal Labor Relations Authority must determine an appropriate bargaining unit for federal agencies. Borrowing from court decisions under the National Labor Relations Act, the federal law applies a community-of-interest test to identify an appropriate unit on an agency, plant, installation, functional, or other basis. At the federal level, confidential employees, managers, supervisors, and personnel employees are excluded from the bargaining unit. Professional employees are excluded from nonprofessional units unless the professional employees vote in favor of their own inclusion.

A community-of-interest test is also used in state and local governments that recognize the right of the public employees to organize. However, as many states recognize only specific groups of employees who might become organized—teachers, police officers, firefighters—determining an appropriate unit is generally moot. However, when necessary to define community of interest in the public sector, the following criteria have been developed by the Advisory Committee on Intergovernmental Relations:

1. Similar wages, hours, working rules, and conditions of employment
2. Maintaining a negotiating pattern based on common history
3. Maintaining the craft or professional line status
4. Representation rights, which involve the inclusion or exclusion of supervisors or nonprofessionals (this refers to organizations such as police or fire departments)[40]

PUBLIC SECTOR UNIONS

While some unions are uniquely focused on public sector employees, such as the National Education Association (NEA), International Association of Fire Fighters (IAFF), American Federation of Government Employees (AFGE) and the American Federation of State, County and Municipal Employees (AFSCME), many state and local government employees are represented by the same unions as employees in the public sector, including Teamsters, Service Employees International Union (SEIU) and International Brotherhood of Electrical Workers (IBEW). And while these unions can provide local organizations with assistance in organizing employees and administering agreements, the national unions are generally not able to provide any type of "master agreement" due to the fragmented nature of public sector organizations.

THE ORGANIZING DRIVE

The impetus to organize employees may originate from either of two general sources. First, the workers may be dissatisfied with their pay or work conditions and thus they initiate contact with the union. Although some supervisors believe that most organizing drives focus on wages and benefits, in reality most drives are caused by "soft issues," such as employees feeling overworked and underappreciated; humiliation or harassment by supervisors, clients, or coworkers; employees' sense of double standards for management and workers; perceived job insecurity possibly caused by the unjust termination of a worker; or simply protection from change or broken promises by management.[41]

Second, a **union organizer**, a full-time salaried staff member who generally represents a national union, may contact workers. As the job title suggests, the union organizer increases union membership and strength by organizing groups of workers who are not presently unionized. An **organizing drive** usually follows the series of events shown in Figure 4-3.

UNION ORGANIZER

A full-time, salaried staff member of a union who generally represents a national union who organizes work places to increase union membership.

ORGANIZING DRIVE

A movement initiated by dissatisfied employees or a union organizer to submit a representation petition to the NLRB and win a representation election, thus providing union certification and collective bargaining.

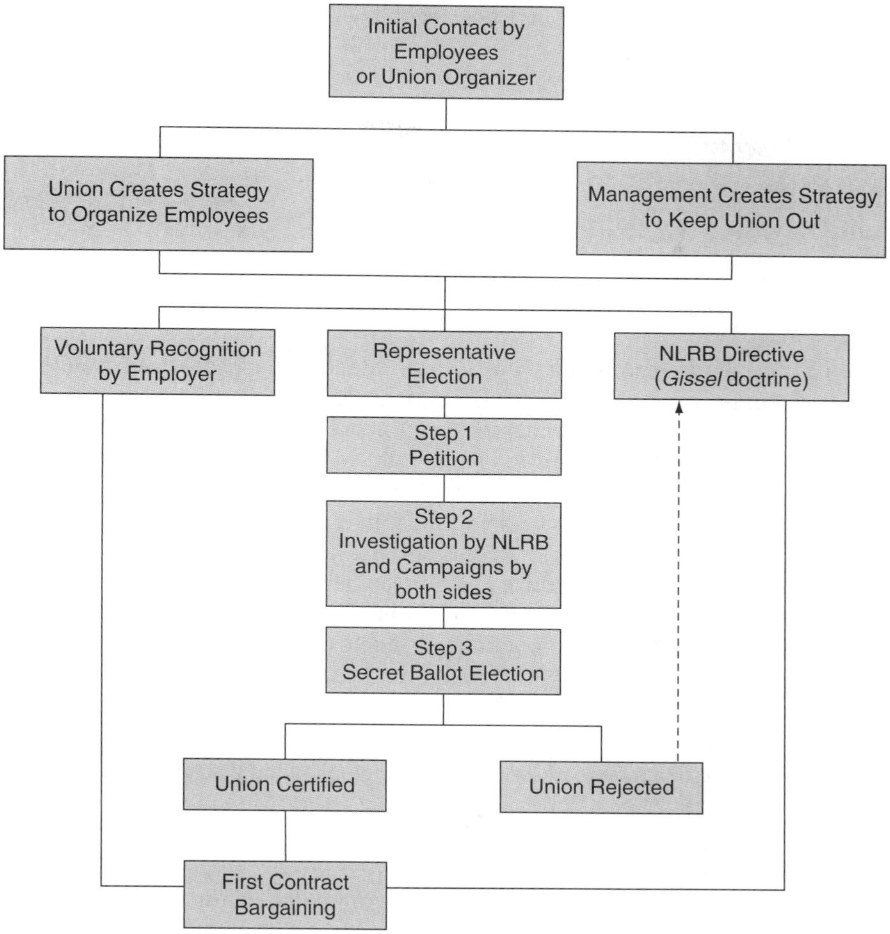

FIGURE 4-3 The Organizing Process

The union's goal is to organize workers and bring them into the union. Labor's strategy is to convince the workers that union membership will bring them benefits they do not presently enjoy. Union organizers may suggest that union representation will result in higher pay, more benefits, better working conditions, and greater fairness in promotions, job transfers, and layoffs. Speaking proudly of the benefits and work improvements they have achieved for other workers, union organizers often cite impressive and convincing statistics about wage gains achieved through collective bargaining. Labor advocates hold formal meetings at the local union hall and encourage supporters to spread the word informally about the benefits a union would bring to the employees' place of work. Pro-union handbills and flyers are often passed to workers as they leave work or go to lunch.

If management's goal is to keep the union out of the workplace, then its strategy may be to convince the workers that unionization will do them more harm than good. Management may attempt to ensure workers that their present pay and benefits are competitive and may show data to prove it. Emphasizing a philosophy of fair dealings with all employees, management may discuss the union's involvement in violent or corrupt activities if such has been the case. Management also enumerates the costs of union membership, which include initiation fees, dues, and other assessments. The workers are reminded that wages will be lost should a strike occur. A discussion of how far management can go to discourage unionization and not violate the National Labor Relations Act can be found in Chapter 10.

There are three different methods by which a union may obtain the right to represent employees in a bargaining unit from the NLRB: (1) through a secret-ballot representation election, the most common process; (2) voluntary recognition card check by an employer; (3) an NLRB directive (in rare cases where the NLRB has decided holding a fair election is impossible).

UNION ORGANIZING STRATEGIES

Although every workplace is different, some basic steps are involved in launching a union organizing campaign as seen in these suggestions by the Industrial Workers of the World:[42]

Step 1 Build an Organizing Committee Identify the leaders and establish an organizing committee representing all major departments and all shifts, which reflect the racial, ethnic, and gender diversity in the workforce. Committee members must be prepared to work hard to educate themselves and their coworkers about the union and to warn and educate coworkers about the impending management antiunion campaign. The employers will most likely engage in a well-organized, well-funded antiunion campaign. The organizing committee must be educated about the workers' right to organize and must understand their union's policies and principles of democracy and rank-and-file control. Also at this step, basic information about the workplace must be gathered, including: the organizational structure, information about the employees, employer data and financial information, work issues of concern, and so on.

Step 2 Determine the Issues The committee develops a program of union demands (the improvements they are organizing to achieve) and a strategy for the union recognition campaign. A plan for highlighting the issues to the workers is carried out through various organizing campaign activities.

Step 3 Choose a Union Recognition Strategy Workers are asked to join the union and support the union program by achieving union status. A union recognition strategy needs to be chosen:

- ***Card-check recognition:*** The Organizing Committee and/or a representative from the union informs the employer that a sizable majority (at least 50 percent plus one person but ideally 60 percent or more) has signed union authorization cards. If successful, the employer voluntarily agrees to recognize the union as the legal bargaining agent for the designated bargaining unit.
- ***Strike for recognition:*** A sizable majority (at least 50 percent plus one person but ideally 60 percent or more) may agree to a short strike to force the employer to recognize the union. If successful, the employer voluntarily agrees to recognize the union as the legal bargaining agent for the designated bargaining unit.
- ***Call for an NLRB-sponsored election:*** The Organizing Committee convinces coworkers to sign union authorization cards. This is the most common of the three strategies. The goal is to sign up a sizable majority; however, only 30 percent of the workforce needs to sign authorization cards to qualify for an NLRB-sponsored election. This "card campaign" should proceed quickly once begun and is necessary to hold a union election. If successful, the employer is legally required to recognize the union as the legal bargaining agent for the designated bargaining unit.

SECRET-BALLOT REPRESENTATION ELECTION

A private, confidential vote by employees, overseen by the NLRB, which allows employees to cast their vote for or against union representation confidentially without pressure or coercion from the union or employer.

Step 4 Union Recognition Status To hold an NLRB-sponsored **secret-ballot** election, the signed authorization cards are required to petition the state or federal labor board to hold an election. The labor board determines who is eligible to vote and schedules the election. The union campaign continues and intensifies during the period before the election. If the union wins, the employer must recognize and collectively bargain with the union, but is not required to agree to any issue or a contract.

Salting

SALTING

Members are encouraged by their union to seek employment at a nonunion company. Once hired, they promote unionization. The union may supplement their regular pay to provide equity with a "union" wage.

In response to union membership decline, unions in recent years initiated a program commonly called **salting**. Union members are encouraged to seek employment with target companies that are not unionized. The union members receive permission from the union through "salting resolutions" to work nonunion without being subject to disciplinary action by their union.

There are three types of salting. First, in cases in which union jobs are not available, the union members are urged to seek employment at nonunion companies, and on their own time, they talk with their fellow workers about the benefits of unionizing. In these cases, the union members are not compensated by the union for their activities. A second type of salting is when union members seek employment with nonunion companies at the request of the union. Again, on their own time, they promote unionization. As compensation, the union supplements the regular pay they get from the employer to equal a "union" wage. Often, when union jobs open up or when it is clear that the company will not become unionized, the union encourages these members to move on. A third type of salting is when regular full-time employees of a union seek employment with a nonunion company for the sole reason of organizing the workers. The union makes up the difference between their organizers' pay and what the employer pays the employees of the union while being employed at the nonunion company.

UNION AVOIDANCE STRATEGIES BY MANAGEMENT

In many workplaces, management's goal is simply to keep the union out, and as the example shows in Profile 4-2, a company need not be shy about saying so. The strategy is to convince the workers that unionization will do them more harm than good. Management may attempt to ensure workers that their present pay and benefits are competitive and may show data to prove it.

In reality, management routinely subjects workers to threats and harassment during an organizing campaign. A review of over 1,000 NLRB elections found that it is "standard practice for workers to be subjected to threats, interrogation, harassment, surveillance, and retaliation for union

Profile 4-2

Union Avoidance Program at Walmart

Walmart, Inc., is the world's largest employer, with over one million workers in 3,372 stores, and the world's largest retailer, with over $220 billion in annual sales. In fact, Walmart revenues are over 2 percent of the entire gross domestic product of the United States. Sam Walton opened his first Walmart in 1962 on the philosophy of "Service to our customers."

In 1970, the Retail Clerks Union (RCU) initiated the first serious organizational campaign of Walmart stores in Missouri. Sam Walton hired a professional union buster, John Tate, who lectured workers on the negative aspects of unions and encouraged Walton to implement a profit-sharing program. After defeating the union, Walton hired a consulting firm to develop a union avoidance strategy. Martin Levitt describes the program as "whatever it takes to wear people down and destroy their spirit. Each manager is taught to take union organizing personally . . . anyone supporting a union is slapping the supervisor in the face."

In 2000, the United Food and Commercial Workers Union (UFCW) initiated a new union organizing campaign. The union won the representation election—and the meat-cutting department of Walmart in Jacksonville, Texas, became the first in the history of the company to organize a union successfully. Two weeks later, however, Walmart announced the elimination of the meat-cutting departments in all its stores and fired four of the workers who voted for the union. Dotty Jones, a former Jacksonville meat cutter, said Walmart managers held a meeting and told the employees there was nothing they could do; "they would hold it up in court until we were old and gray."

(continued)

Walmart workers face serious opposition to unionization by the retail giant.
Source: Ruaridh Stewart/ZUMA Press/Newscom.

Despite Walmart's successful union avoidance program, in recent years workers in over 100 stores in 25 states have started organization campaigns. Why? Greg Denier, an official with the UFCW union, says, "Americans can't live on a Wal-Mart paycheck . . . and Wal-Mart is the dominant employer, and what they pay will be the future of working America." The average Walmart employee earns $18,000 a year—only about 40 percent receive health care coverage—which costs employees up to $2,844 a year plus deductibles.

Another issue is the employment of women in top store positions. Although women account for two thirds of all Walmart employees, they account for less than 10 percent of top store managers, the same percentage as in 1975.

Can unions successfully organize Walmart in the future? Not according to Bernie Hesse, a UFCW organizer in Minneapolis, who claims, "They'll close the frigging store," or Martin Levitt, author of *Confessions of a Union Buster;* "In my 35 years in labor relations, I've never seen a company that will go to the lengths that Wal-Mart goes to, to avoid a union."

Source: Adapted from Karen Olsson, "Up against Wal-Mart," *Mother Jones* (March–April 2003), pp. 54–59.

activity." The study found that in 57 percent of cases reviewed employers threatened to close the business, fired workers in 34 percent of the cases, and threatened wage cuts in 47 percent, and workers were forced to attend antiunion sessions with a supervisor in 66 percent of the cases. However, the study also concluded that many such employer tactics are, in fact, legal.[43]

Management "TIPS" and "FORE" in Campaigns

One company that had a corporate-wide policy against unionization instructed its managers on how to avoid unions legally by enumerating certain do's and don'ts. These instructions have been put into useful acronyms for managers and supervisors facing union organizing campaigns as shown in Table 4-1. For the things a manager *may not do,* they are told to remember **"TIPS"**: threaten, interrogate, promise, and spy. Or, as the management consultant in Profile 4-3 terms it: "SPIT"—spy, promise, interrogate, or threaten. For the things a manager *may do,* they are told to remember **"FORE"**: facts, opinions, rules, and experience.[44]

Among things managers *cannot* do to discourage unionization are the following:

TABLE 4-1 Common Arguments Made by Proponents of Card-Check Recognition and Mandatory Secret Ballots

Proponents of Card-Check Recognition	Proponents of Mandatory Secret Ballots
Card-check recognition requires signatures from over 50 percent of bargaining unit employees. A secret-ballot election is decided by a majority of workers voting.	Casting a secret ballot is private and confidential. A secret-ballot election is conducted by the NLRB. Under card-check recognition, authorization cards are controlled by the union.
During a secret-ballot campaign, the employer has greater access to employees.	Under card-check recognition, employees may only hear the union's point of view.
Because of potential employer pressure or intimidation during a secret-ballot election, some workers may feel coerced into voting against a union.	Because of potential union pressure or intimidation, some workers may feel coerced into signing authorization cards.
Employer objections can delay a secret-ballot election.	Most secret-ballot elections are held within two months after a petition is filed.
Allegations against a union for unfair labor practices can be addressed under existing law. Existing remedies do not deter employer violations of unfair labor practices.	Allegations against an employer for unfair labor practices can be addressed under existing law. Existing remedies do not deter union violations of unfair labor practices.
Card-check recognition is less costly for both the union and employer. If secret-ballot elections were required, the NLRB would have to devote more resources to conducting elections.	Unionization may cost workers union dues; higher union wages may result in fewer union jobs.
Card-check and neutrality agreements may lead to more cooperative labor–management relations.	An employer may be pressured by a corporate campaign into accepting a card-check or neutrality agreement. If an employer accepts a neutrality agreement, employees who do not want a union may hesitate to speak out.

Source: Adapted from Gerald Mayer, "Labor Union Recognition Procedures: Use of Secret Ballots and Card Checks," *CRS Report for Congress* (May 23, 2005), p. 13. Available at http://digitalcommons.ilr.cornell.edu/key_workplace/237/. Accessed February 21, 2008.

T—Threaten

- Don't threaten or imply the company will take *adverse action* of any kind for supporting the union.
- Don't threaten to *terminate* employees because of their union activities.
- Don't threaten to *close the facility* if a union is voted in.
- Don't threaten to *transfer employees* to other locations because of their union affiliation.
- Don't threaten employees with *loss of their wages* and benefits during negotiations.
- Don't threaten employees with *loss of their job* if they sign a union authorization card.
- Don't threaten employees by saying, "With the union there will be *a strike*."
- Don't threaten to penalize employees who actively support the union for *violations of company policies* that nonunion employees are permitted to commit without being disciplined.
- Don't make *work assignments* with the intent of causing an employee who has been active on behalf of the union to quit his or her job.
- Don't take any action that is intended to *impair the employee's job or pay* because of his or her activity on behalf of the union.
- Don't intentionally *assign work or transfer employees* so that those active on behalf of the union are separated from those you believe are not interested in the union.
- Don't *reduce hours* of employees with the intention of curtailing the union's strength of organizing.

I—Interrogate

- Don't interrogate or ask employees their *position concerning unions.*
- Don't ask employees how they are *going to vote in an election.*
- Don't ask employees if they or anyone else *signed a union authorization card.*
- Don't ask employees if they are *going to the union meeting* or who else may be attending.

Profile 4-3

Union Buster

Peter List's job title is not "union buster," but that is how many of his employers refer to him. List is hired by employers to persuade workers not to join a union because it is not in their best interests. His background is surprising. For eight years his career was handling heavy spools of telephone cable on the factory floor of an AT&T factory in Phoenix, Arizona. He joined the Communications Workers of America his very first week at AT&T, rose to the rank of chief shop steward within the union, and edited the local union newspaper.

Today, however, List is hired to fight union organizing campaigns, and in 2003 he won 32 of 35 campaigns. List estimates that 60–70 percent of his clients are small business owners because unions have sought to organize more small businesses in recent years, and he averages a 57 percent "win rate" against them. Why did List switch sides? In 1992, AT&T outsourced his job to Mexico and thus he went back to college to complete a degree in labor relations. In his senior year he had an "epiphany" when researching a thesis on the history of unions. List decided unions blamed their decline on everyone—but themselves. He developed a strong pro-capitalist Ayn Rand philosophy of radical individualism and opposed all governmental regulation of labor relations. List then started his own company, the North American Employers Group, which advises employers who are engaged in an organized campaign.

For example, in 2001, the Teamsters collected authorization cards from a majority of 35 employees at Mazza & Sons in Tinton Falls, New Jersey. The recycling and demolition firm had hired a "salt," or Teamster member, who began organizing from the inside. The company had not given workers a raise in several years and thus was vulnerable. The Teamsters began picketing Mazza & Sons and created what Dominick Mazza called a "battle zone" that disrupted business. Mazza called List, who immediately started distributing handouts to the employees. List also coached Mazza on what he legally could and could not say or do during the organizational campaign. He emphasized that a manager or owner should never "SPIT" on workers: *S*py, *P*romise, *I*nterrogate, *T*hreaten. In addition, List suggested that managers explain critical facts such as these: If a union is certified, management is under no obligation to sign an agreement; if negotiations reach an impasse, management has the right to impose its final offer unilaterally; and if the workers strike, management can hire permanent replacement workers. After a few months the picketing stopped, and the Teamsters lost interest in Mazza & Sons.

Source: Adapted from Richard Murphy, "The Persuaders," *Fortune Small Business 14,* no. 4 (May 2004), pp. 74–82.

- Don't ask employees their *opinion of the union organizer.*
- Don't *visit employees' homes* for the purpose of asking questions about the union or urging them to reject the union.

P—Promise

- Don't promise employees a *pay increase, better benefits,* or *special favors* if they vote against the union.
- Don't promise employees a *promotion* if they vote against the union.
- Don't promise employees that *all the concerns* they brought to management before the election will be corrected to their advantage if they vote against the union.
- Don't engage in *favoritism* of employees who are antiunion.

S—Spy

- Don't spy on any *union activities* the employees may be involved in, such as attending union meetings.
- Don't *attend a union meeting,* even if invited.

Among the things managers *can do* to discourage unionization are the following:

F—Facts

- Do tell employees that by signing a union authorization card, they may have authorized the union to become their *legal representative* in all matters pertaining to wages, hours, and working conditions.
- Do tell employees that if they sign a union authorization card, it *does not mean they must vote for the union* in an election. An election is a secret-ballot process.
- Do tell employees that if a union is voted in, everything (their wages, benefits, and working conditions) would go *on the bargaining table*. It is much like the game show *Let's Make a Deal!* They could get more, they could get the same, or they could get less. Regardless, they will be responsible for dues, fees, fines, and assessments.
- Do tell employees that they *can actively campaign against the union*—you just cannot help them in any manner.

O—Opinion

- Do tell employees that *management does not believe the employees need* third-party representation.
- Do tell employees that *management believes in the open-door policy* and are willing to discuss any subject with them.

R—Rules

- Do tell employees that the *law permits the company to permanently replace them* if there is a strike.
- Do tell employees that the *union cannot make the company agree to anything it does not want to* during negotiations.

E—Experience

- Do share any *personal experiences* you may have had with a unionized workplace.

Countersalting Steps

Companies that have been "salted" have also come up with countermeasures. For example, one company suggests that employers take the following steps to prevent hiring "salts":[45]

1. Prescreen as many applicants as possible to ensure you are hiring the most qualified person for any opening you have available. The National Labor Relations Act prohibits an employer from refusing to hire an applicant because of his or her union affiliation. However, the law does not prevent a company from selecting the most positive, dedicated, and enthusiastic applicant available.
2. Use "consensus" interviewing. Several members of management should interview applicants and then compare notes and recommendations for hiring.
3. An application should say, "List entire employment history, starting with present employer. For any unemployed or self-employed periods, show dates and locations. (Attach additional sheets when necessary.)" If there are only three spaces on the application to list existing or former employers, ask applicants if they have completed their entire employment history. If they have not, ask them to attach additional sheets.
4. Ensure that applications show entire work history with no gaps in employment. If you notice gaps, question them. Then ask applicants to fill in those gaps.
5. Check references thoroughly.

ORGANIZING AT THE WORKPLACE The right to engage in organizational campaigns in and around the workplace obviously affects the employer's right to maintain a work environment. The NLRB and the courts have devised rules to balance the two interests. Here, briefly, are some of those rules. In Chapter 10 we discuss how violating these rules lead to charges of unfair labor practices either against the employer or a union.

SOLICITING UNION SUPPORT Employees on their own time, even on the employer's property, can solicit union support by talking about the union. This includes lunchtime, break time, rest periods, and before and after the regular workday. A nonemployee, usually a union organizer, does not have the right to solicit union support on the employer's property if there is ***any other means*** to reach the employees.

- ***Distributing Union Material.*** Distribution of union literature is restricted to nonworking times and areas because such literature could clutter the workplace. No rule, however, is without exceptions. If justified by the nature of the business, a no-solicitation rule restricting employees even on nonworking time can be defended. Examples include department stores, restaurants, and patient care areas of hospitals where the public nature of the working area would prohibit normal interaction between employees, so that leaving literature is allowed.
- ***Union Buttons or Insignias.*** Employees may wear union buttons or insignias. This right is balanced against the employer's right to conduct business. If a button or insignia should in particular circumstances cause a disturbance, present a health hazard, distract workers, cause damage to a product, or offend or distract customers, it may be prohibited.
- ***Bulletin Boards, Meeting Hall, and Mailboxes.*** Employees have no statutory right to use an employer's bulletin board, meeting halls, or mailboxes. However, if the employees are allowed access to the bulletin board, the employer cannot censor the material to exclude union solicitation. Meeting halls fall under the same rule. If access has been allowed to employees on an unrestricted basis, use by employees for union organization cannot be the only exception.
- ***E-mail Solicitation.*** Employees may use company e-mail for discussions relating to wages, hours, and working conditions, assuming the use does not violate a legitimate employer policy regarding the use of work time or equipment.
- ***No-Solicitation Policy.*** An employer may implement a "no-solicitation" or "non-use" nondiscriminatory policy for both employees and nonemployees during work or nonwork hours in the workplace and restrict the use of bulletin boards, meeting halls, e-mails, and mailboxes if that policy extends to all types of solicitation. If it is applied only to union solicitation, it is likely to be an unfair labor practice. However, the NLRB has created a distinction between allowing employees *personal* use such as "for-sale" notices or birthday announcements and allowing *organizational* purposes such as union material.

PICKETING DURING AN ORGANIZATIONAL CAMPAIGN During an organizational campaign, the "target-employer" is the primary employer. Under the act, a union can picket a primary employer but for only 30 days before being required to file a petition for an election with the NLRB. Mass picketing, violence, or threats of violence are not allowed; nor is secondary picketing—picketing a neutral party in order to have that neutral party pressure the targeted employer on the union's behalf. If the employer shares premises with other neutral employers,

TABLE 4-2 Union Organizing Campaign: TIPS and FORE

Managers and Supervisors Should Follow These TIPS and FORE Guidelines:

DON'T	*DO TELL*
THREATEN	**F**ACTS
INTERROGATE	**O**PINION
PROMISE	**R**ULES
SPY	**E**XPERIENCE
These actions are **prohibited** by the National Labor Relations Act.	These actions are **permitted** by the National Labor Relations Act.

in "informational" picketing that is simply informing the public that the target employer does not pay union wages.

Table 4-2 outlines some of the common issues in pickets.

REPRESENTATION ELECTION PROCEDURES

While there are three different methods by which a union may become the representative of a group of employees for the purposes of collective bargaining, the most common is the secret-ballot election. Why? It has been called, by supporters, "the gold standard" of providing employees freedom of choice—as to whether or not they want union representation. The steps in a **secret-ballot representation election** are described in the following paragraphs.

Step 1 Representation Petition The first step in the election process is to file a representation petition at the office of the appropriate regional director (see Figure 4-4). A union must present evidence of employee support before a representation election is held. The NLRB requires designation by at least 30 percent of the bargaining unit employees, usually in the form of signed and dated authorization cards. The NLRB also accepts designations in the form of signed petitions and union application cards.[46]

Board actions have several kinds of petitions. An employee, a group of employees, or a union representing employees can file an **RC petition** seeking certification of an appropriate unit. An employer can file an *RM petition* if one or more labor organizations claim representation status in an appropriate unit and the employer questions the representative's status. Also, when an employer has objective proof that the union no longer represents the majority of the employees, he or she may file an RM petition. An employer, employee, other individual, or a union may also use a decertification or *RD petition* to determine whether a recognized union still has the support of employees.

Other types of petitions available are the *UD petition*, which 30 percent or more of the employees file to rescind a union shop agreement; a *UC petition*, requesting clarification of the composition of a bargaining unit currently certified; and an *AC petition,* requesting that a change of circumstances be recognized, such as a change of union name or affiliation on a previous NLRB certification.

Petitions demonstrate sufficient employee interest or the actual type of representation case so that the board may decide if it has jurisdiction. The board assumes the requisite employee interest and accepts an expedited election petition if it is filed within 30 days of the beginning of a recognitional or organizational picket. The board normally accepts petitions requesting certification or decertification only if 30 percent of the employees in a unit favor such an election. Presenting cards authorizing the union to act as the employees' agent for collective bargaining usually demonstrates this 30 percent. It can also be shown by a certification listing at least 30 percent of the employees of the represented unit as members in good standing of a union.

Another union may enter an election with a **showing of interest** that represents 10 percent of those in the unit in question. A cross petition from another union may also be filed claiming representation of an appropriate unit different from the original unit but including some of the same people.[47]

SHOWING OF INTEREST

The demonstration of employee support, usually in the form of petitions or authorization cards, that a union is required to compile before a representation election can be considered.

Step 2 Investigation The second step occurs when the regional director conducts investigations and a hearing, if necessary, to determine whether to proceed with an election. The employer's business must sufficiently affect commerce so as to rest jurisdiction in the NLRB. An actual representation question must exist, and sufficient employee interest must be demonstrated. The requested unit is deemed appropriate and the bargaining agent qualified. Certain statutory time periods must be honored.

FORM EXEMPT UNDER 44 U.S.C.

INTERNET
FORM NLRB-502
(2-08)

UNITED STATES GOVERNMENT
NATIONAL LABOR RELATIONS BOARD
PETITION

DO NOT WRITE IN THIS SPACE	
Case No.	Date Filed

INSTRUCTIONS: Submit an original of this Petition to the NLRB Regional Office in the Region in which the employer concerned is located.

The Petitioner alleges that the following circumstances exist and requests that the NLRB proceed under its proper authority pursuant to Section 9 of the NLRA.

1. PURPOSE OF THIS PETITION (if box RC, RM, or RD is checked and a charge under Section 8(b)(7) of the Act has been filed involving the Employer named herein, the statement following the description of the type of petition shall not be deemed made.) (Check One)

- ☐ **RC-CERTIFICATION OF REPRESENTATIVE** - A substantial number of employees wish to be represented for purposes of collective bargaining by Petitioner and Petitioner desires to be certified as representative of the employees.
- ☐ **RM-REPRESENTATION (EMPLOYER PETITION)** - One or more individuals or labor organizations have presented a claim to Petitioner to be recognized as the representative of employees of Petitioner.
- ☐ **RD-DECERTIFICATION (REMOVAL OF REPRESENTATIVE) - A substantial number of employees assert that the certified or currently recognized bargaining representative is no longer their representative.**
- ☐ **UD-WITHDRAWAL OF UNION SHOP AUTHORITY (REMOVAL OF OBLIGATION TO PAY DUES)** - Thirty percent (30%) or more of employees in a bargaining unit covered by an agreement between their employer and a labor organization desire that such authority be rescinded.
- ☐ **UC-UNIT CLARIFICATION**- A labor organization is currently recognized by Employer, but Petitioner seeks clarification of placement of certain employees: (Check one) ☐ In unit not previously certified. ☐ In unit previously certified in Case No. ____________
- ☐ **AC-AMENDMENT OF CERTIFICATION**- Petitioner seeks amendment of certification issued in Case No. ____________ Attach statement describing the specific amendment sought.

2. Name of Employer	Employer Representative to contact	Tel. No.
3. Address(es) of Establishment(s) involved *(Street and number, city, State, ZIP code)*		Fax No.
4a. Type of Establishment (Factory, mine, wholesaler, etc.)	4b. Identify principal product or service	Cell No.
		e-Mail
5. Unit Involved *(In UC petition, describe* **present** *bargaining unit and attach description of proposed clarification.)*		6a. Number of Employees in Unit:
Included		Present
Excluded		Proposed *(By UC/AC)*
		6b. Is this petition supported by 30% or more of the employees in the unit?* ☐ Yes ☐ No *Not applicable in RM, UC, and AC

(If you have checked box RC in 1 above, check and complete EITHER item 7a or 7b, whichever is applicable)

7a. ☐ Request for recognition as Bargaining Representative was made on (Date) ____________ and Employer declined recognition on or about (Date) ____________ (If no reply received, so state).

7b. ☐ Petitioner is currently recognized as Bargaining Representative and desires certification under the Act.

8. Name of Recognized or Certified Bargaining Agent *(If none, so state.)*		Affiliation	
Address	Tel. No.	Date of Recognition or Certification	
	Cell No.	Fax No.	e-Mail

9. Expiration Date of Current Contract. If any *(Month, Day, Year)*	10. If you have checked box UD in 1 above, show here the date of execution of agreement granting union shop *(Month, Day and Year)*
11a. Is there now a strike or picketing at the Employer's establishment(s) Involved? Yes ☐ No ☐	11b. If so, approximately how many employees are participating?

11c. The Employer has been picketed by or on behalf of *(Insert Name)* ____________, a labor organization, of *(Insert Address)* ____________ Since *(Month, Day, Year)* ____________

12. Organizations or individuals other than Petitioner (and other than those named in items 8 and 11c), which have claimed recognition as representatives and other organizations and individuals known to have a representative interest in any employees in unit described in item 5 above. (If none, so state)

Name	Address	Tel. No.	Fax No.
		Cell No.	e-Mail

13. Full name of party filing petition (If labor organization, give full name, including local name and number)

14a. Address *(street and number, city, state, and ZIP code)*	14b. Tel. No. EXT	14c. Fax No.
	14d. Cell No.	14e. e-Mail

15. Full name of national or international labor organization of which Petitioner is an affiliate or constituent *(to be filled in when petition is filed by a labor organization)*

I declare that I have read the above petition and that the statements are true to the best of my knowledge and belief.

Name *(Print)*	Signature	Title *(if any)*
Address *(street and number, city, state, and ZIP code)*	Tel. No.	Fax No.
	Cell No.	eMail

WILLFUL FALSE STATEMENTS ON THIS PETITION CAN BE PUNISHED BY FINE AND IMPRISONMENT (U.S. CODE, TITLE 18, SECTION 1001)

PRIVACY ACT STATEMENT

Solicitation of the information on this form is authorized by the National Labor Relations Act (NLRA), 29 U.S.C. § 151 *et seq.* The principal use of the information is to assist the National Labor Relations Board (NLRB) in processing unfair labor practice and related proceedings or litigation. The routine uses for the information are fully set forth in the Federal Register, 71 Fed. Reg. 74942-43 (Dec. 13, 2006). The NLRB will further explain these uses upon request. Disclosure of this information to the NLRB is voluntary; however, failure to supply the information will cause the NLRB to decline to invoke its processes.

FIGURE 4-4 National Labor Relations Board Petition

Internet Form NLRB-4551
(11-94)

UNITED STATES OF AMERICA
NATIONAL LABOR RELATIONS BOARD

REQUEST TO PROCEED

In the matter of____ ____________________

(Name of Case) *(Number of Case)*

The undersigned hereby requests the Regional Director to proceed with the above-captioned representation case, notwithstanding the charges of unfair labor practices filed in Case No. ____________________. The alleged unlawful conduct in the above (unfair labor practice) case that occurred after the filling of the petition may constitute the basis of objections.

Date____________________ ____________________

By____________________

____

(Title)

FIGURE 4-5 Request to Proceed with an Election

Once the NLRB has determined an election petition is valid, the employer is obligated to furnish to the petitioning union a list of eligible voters' names and addresses. In an unusual case, the union requested e-mail addresses because the bargaining unit members were crew members on a ship and would be at sea during the preelection period.[48]

Step 3 Secret-Ballot Election The third step is the secret-ballot election (see Figure 4-5). The NLRB has the responsibility to ensure that a representative election is fairly and honestly conducted. In a 1948 case, the board stated that its function in representation proceedings was "to provide a laboratory in which an experiment may be conducted, under conditions as nearly ideal as possible, to determine the uninhibited desires of the employees."[49] But the board recognized that the standards for election cases had to be judged against realistic standards of human conduct. When improprieties occur, certain factors should be weighed, such as the size of the unit, the circumstances of any alleged misconduct, and the real or apparent influence of the interfering party.

The NLRB has traditionally favored direct or manual ballots (voting machines, voting boxes, etc.) over mail ballots in representational elections. The board's policy has been to use only mail ballots when manual ballots are "infeasible." Manual ballots are favored because they provide (1) greater secrecy, (2) integrity of the voting process, (3) absence of coercion, and (4) greater participation by employees. Mail balloting is cheaper than manual balloting, but the National Labor Relations Act clearly states employees should be given a "free choice" in representational elections, which can be more easily guaranteed in manual balloting. Yet in recent years the NLRB has used mail balloting more often, establishing appropriate procedures to ensure the fairness and validity of the election. These include precise procedures for casting and returning the ballots, and when those procedures are not followed, the election may be set aside. For example, the election was set aside in a runoff election between two unions, because a union representative collected the ballots from the employees rather than have the ballots mailed in as directed.[50]

Doctors and medical professionals gather to protest against Congress' and President Barack Obama's health care reform efforts during a rally at the U.S. Captiol September 10, 2009 in Washington, DC. Organized by The Association of American Physicians and Surgeons, the rally drew about 150 people in lab coats and surgical scrubs. *Source:* Chip Somodevilla/Getty Images.

Prohibited Conduct During an Election

Through its rulings over the years, the NLRB has determined that activities that constitute violations of the act, or prohibited conduct while an election is being conducted, include the following:

1. ***Campaign propaganda and misrepresentation*** Campaign rhetoric by either side is routinely ignored because it is part of any election campaign and usually will be disregarded by employees in making decisions. But the NLRB would intervene in cases in which forgery or misleading information is rendered in such a way that the voters are unable to discern the propagandistic nature of a publication.
2. ***Threats and loss of benefits*** Unlike mere campaign rhetoric, the actual reduction or withholding of benefits or the direct threats of economic reprisals as a method of combating an organizational drive is prohibited. These include discharge, loss of pay or benefits, more onerous working conditions, and threats of plant closure, physical violence, or permanent replacement of strikers.

   An employer is not prohibited from communicating general views about unionism or predictions of the effect of unionization on the company as long as such predictions involve consequences outside the employer's control.
3. ***Promise or grant of benefit*** The promise of economic benefits by the employer if employees reject unionization will violate the National Labor Relations Act, as will the promise or grant of economic benefits during an organizational campaign to influence the outcome of an election or to discourage organizational activities. However, the granting of benefits during a union campaign may not interfere with the employee's right to organize when the timing, amount, and application of the increase were consistent with past practice.
4. ***Interrogation and polling of employees*** Absent unusual circumstances, the polling of employees by an employer is prohibited unless the following safeguards are observed: The purpose of the poll is to determine the truth of a union's claim of majority—this purpose is communicated to the employees, assurances against reprisals are given, the employees are polled by secret ballot, and the employer has not engaged in unfair labor practices or otherwise created a coercive atmosphere.

A long-standing NLRB precedent provides that an employer who entertains a *good-faith reasonable doubt* whether a majority of its employees supports an incumbent union has three options:

- To request a formal board-supervised election
- To withdraw recognition from the union and refuse to bargain
- To conduct an internal poll of employee support for the union

5. *Surveillance* Surveillance in almost any form has been held a violation of the unfair labor practices section of the National Labor Relations Act. The board has such an aversion to surveillance that it will uphold findings even if the employees know nothing about it or the surveillance was only an employer's attempt to foster an impression of scrutiny. Encouraging surveillance and eavesdropping by union members has also been condemned by the NLRB.

6. *Poll Activity* The NLRB prohibits any electioneering at or near the polls in a campaign. And in a 1953 case, *Peerless Plywood Co.*,[51] the board detailed a *24-hour rule*, which prohibits employers and unions from making organizational campaign speeches on company time to large assemblies of employees within 24 hours of a scheduled election. It does not prohibit voluntary assemblies on or off company time or the distribution of written material.

In cases in which an election involves three choices—for example, Union A, Union B, or no union—a **runoff election** may be required if none of the choices receives a majority of the votes cast. The two top vote getters are placed before the members of the bargaining unit again, and the one receiving a majority vote can be certified:

RUNOFF ELECTION

The successive election held when a representation election involving three or more choices results in no one choice receiving the majority vote. The choices receiving the most votes are again voted on until one receives the majority of the votes cast.

> Under NLRB rules and regulations, "A runoff election is conducted only where: (a) the ballot in the original election contained three or more choices [i.e., two labor organizations and a *neither* choice]; and (b) no single choice received a majority of the valid votes cast. Thus there can be no runoff where the original ballot provided for: (1) a *yes* and *no* choice in a one-union election; or (2) a *severance* election." The ballot in the runoff election provides for a selection between the two choices receiving the largest and second largest number of votes in the original election.[52]

In 2002, for example, a representation election was held for office and service employees at the University of Baltimore. The initial ballot had three options: (1) no representation, (2) AFSCME, and (3) the MCEA, a local independent union. None of the three won a majority, and thus a second, runoff election was held, and AFSCME won with 64 percent of the runoff vote to 35 percent for MCEA.[53]

Step 4 Certification of Election Results If the board is satisfied that the election represents the employees' free choice, the election is certified, the fourth step. Either no union is victorious or, if a union has gained a majority of those voting, that union is certified as the bargaining agent for the unit. If, however, the NLRB finds that the preelection period did not meet the "laboratory conditions" doctrine as it enunciated in the *General Shoe*[54] case, then the election result can be declared void. The NLRB describes "laboratory conditions" during the preelection period as those that provide employees an atmosphere in which they have a "free choice" of being represented by a bargaining representative or not. In general, the NLRB has found that actions that violate the "laboratory conditions" fall into three categories: coercion, threats of reprisal, and promises of benefits.[55]

CERTIFICATION

The determination by the National Labor Relations Board that a union represents the employees' free choice and therefore that the union can become the official bargaining agent for a bargaining unit.

Certification benefits a union in a number of ways. It closes any challenges to the union's status as the exclusive bargaining agent for the particular unit. Its status is binding on the employer for at least one year, during which time the employer must bargain with it. After the first year the employer must continue to bargain unless there is reasonable doubt that the union will continue to enjoy a majority vote of the unit. The board will not entertain petitions regarding rival certification for that unit within the one-year certification or within three years if a valid contract is in effect. The certified union may strike against the employer under certain circumstances without fear of an unfair labor practice charge. A 2005 study of newly certified bargaining units found that about 90 percent of the time the union was successful in negotiating the first contract with the employer within the first year. In previous years between 1996 and 2003, the annual success rate ranged between 73 and 95 percent, with a trend of higher rates in recent years. In previous decades the annual rates were as low as 60 percent. First contract negotiations are often more contentious than renewals because the NLRA provides no penalty for failure to reach a contract and no mandate for mediation.[56]

The number of representation elections held each year varies greatly by state. In 2009, for example, the five states with the most elections were New York, 214 (61.2 percent won by the union); California, 165 (67.8 percent); Illinois, 110 (63.6 percent); New Jersey, 99 (57.5 percent); and Pennsylvania, 85 (62.3 percent). The states with the fewest elections were Nebraska and Vermont, both with 5; South Dakota 4, Maine 3, Wyoming 2, and North Dakota, 1. In all 50 states and territories 1,633 representation elections were held in 2009, and unions won 63.8 percent.[57]

A union may seek recognition by the board to obtain the benefit of certification even if its status as an exclusive bargaining agent has not been challenged and the employer has agreed to bargain. The NLRB considers such a request as raising a question of representation.

Voluntary Recognition

VOLUNTARY RECOGNITION

An employer recognizes a union as the bargaining agent of the employees without requiring a secret ballot election.

Election, although the most accepted way by which employees select their representatives, is not the exclusive method condoned by the NLRB. An employer may recognize the union as the bargaining agent without an election: This **voluntary recognition** is rare but increasing in use by some unions. By publicity, picketing, friendly politicians, or boycotts, these unions pressure employers into recognizing a union without an election. In one such 2001 case, the Union of Needletrades, Industrial and Textile Employees, with the support of hotel and medical center workers (major clients of the targeted employer and the Baltimore City Council), convinced the laundry to recognize the union voluntarily and then negotiated a $1.25-per-hour raise for the $6-per-hour employees as well as better health and pension benefits.[58] As another example, in 2002, the University of California at Los Angeles (UCLA) voluntarily recognized AFSCME to represent food and service workers. The university agreed to recognize the union after several weeks of student and worker protests and a heated UCLA board meeting. AFSCME represents over 15,000 food and service workers on nine University of California campuses and five medical centers.[59]

NEUTRALITY/CARD-CHECK RECOGNITION

The employer and union agree in advance—before the union obtains cards signed by a majority of the employees—that the parties will use a card check by a neutral third party as a means of determining majority support and the employer will voluntarily recognize the union if the card check shows majority support for a union.

In a Supreme Court decision upholding a board bargaining order, the Court recognized two other valid means by which a union may establish majority status and thereby place a bargaining obligation on the employer: (1) through a show of support through a union-called strike and (2) when a union collects authorization cards from a majority of the unit members. The cards must be submitted to a third party for a "card check" to verify the names against payroll. If an employer agrees to the card check, then, if the third party finds a majority for the union, the employer must bargain.[60] In recent years employers agreeing to a card check include UPS, Cingular Wireless, Costco, Harley Davidson, Kaiser-Permantee, Hilton Hotels, Marriott, Freightliner, and Rite-Aid. Examples of Union Authorization Cards can be seen in Figure 4-6. Some labor experts believe that NLRB-conducted secret-ballot elections are "the gold standard" of employees' freedom of choice and view the card-check process as open to manipulation. They believe the **neutrality/card-check recognition** agreement process creates a tension between two

IWW AUTHORIZATION CARD

We believe that through collective bargaining we can gain a legal voice in our workplace, achieve fair treatment for all, establish job security and better benefits, wages and working conditions. Therefore, this will authorize the Industrial Workers of the World solely and exclusively to represent me in Collective Bargaining with my employer.

PLEASE PRINT:

NAME DATE

ADDRESS

CITY STATE ZIP CODE PHONE

EMPLOYER NAME HOURLY WAGE

SHIFT DEPARTMENT

SIGNATURE

IMPORTANT: This Authorization was signed and dated in the employee's own handwriting. YOUR RIGHT TO SIGN THIS CARD IS STRICTLY PROTECTED BY FEDERAL LAW.

SOURCE: www.iww.org (December 2005). Used with permission.

IAEP AUTHORIZATION CARD

I hereby authorize the **INTERNATIONAL ASSOCIATION OF EMTS & PARAMEDICS (IAEP) (NAGE, SEIU)** to act as my representative and exclusive bargaining agent for the purpose of collective bargaining.

SIGNATURE DOES NOT COMMIT YOU TO MEMBERSHIP

Name (print): ______ Email: ______
Address: ______
City: ______ State: ______ Zip: ______
Employer: ______ Worksite/Station: ______
Signature: ______ Date: ______
Home phone: ______ Shift: ______
Job Classification: ______

FIGURE 4-6 Typical Union Authorization Cards

important principles of federal law: the freedom of employers and unions to sign contracts and employee-free choice of union representation.[61] A neutrality/card-check agreement generally includes a statement from the employer indicating that it will remain "neutral" during the card drive, not oppose union organizing efforts, and recognize the union once it has obtained signed cards from a majority of employees. However, the agreement may also contain terms that equate to unlawful prerecognition bargaining that is a violation of the NLRA. For example, in 2006, several parties questioned the neutrality agreement between the UAW and Dana Corporation. The agreement contained, in addition to Dana voluntary recognition based on a majority of signed cards, certain "principles" that would be contained in the future collective bargaining agreement, including four-year terms, no-strike/no-lockout language, health care premium sharing and maximum deductibles, and flexible compensation programs. Those parties that supported the NLRB decision to accept the agreement as lawful contended that it was a "constructive, problem-solving" framework, an important step in implementing employees' "freedom of choice," and that it would help conduct the organizing drive by providing specifics to the employees before they sign cards. Opponents, however, claimed the principles amounted to the prenegotiation of mandatory issues by a union that has not been certified to represent the employees. In addition opponents note that such principles may encourage employers to seek a preferred union that will agree to a "sweetheart deal" that is not in employees' best interests.[62]

Legislation was introduced in the 109th Congress as a result of the movement by unions to seek voluntary recognition in all representation cases. The *Employee Free Choice Act* would amend the card-check process by placing a bargaining obligation on an employer if a majority of workers sign cards authorizing union representation. Thus the employer could not insist on a secret-ballot election, as is the case currently. Supporters of the bill claim: "It should be the employees' choice (for a secret-ballot election), not the employers', and that is really what the heart of this bill is all about." Opponents, however, claim the change in the card-check process would subject workers to intimidation from unions because they would be forced to make their preference known.[63] The pros and cons of card-check recognition versus a secret-ballot election are summarized in Table 4-3.

NLRB Directive

The third method by which a union may be certified to represent employees (in addition to election and voluntary recognition) is by an NLRB directive. Such cases are rare and only occur in situations where the NLRB has determined that an impartial election in which employees can express their "free choice" is not possible. The cases usually involve employer interference in a secret-ballot election that makes holding a second fair and impartial election unrealistic. Such NLRB directives are called a "Gissel bargaining order," based on a landmark 1969 case.[64]

In the *Gissel* case, the Court gave a stamp of approval for authorization cards as a substitute for an election *when an employer's actions amounted to an unfair labor practice*. The Court recognized that if traditional remedies could not eradicate the lingering effects of the employer's conduct and permit the holding of a fair election, the union's authorization cards were a more reliable indicator of the employees' desires than an election, and a bargaining order should be issued. Known as the **Gissel Doctrine**, the board is strictly limited in imposing a *Gissel* bargaining order to cases in which the union actually gained majority status through the authorization cards. Regardless of how outrageous the employer's actions, unless such a majority is demonstrated, no order to bargain can be issued.[65] The board has also issued bargaining orders when the employer has gained independent knowledge of the union's majority status or has acknowledged the union's right to represent employees or, as in Case 4-2, when it is demonstrated that the employer hoped that if it ignored the union, it would just go away.

GISSEL DOCTRINE

The Supreme Court decision that allows the use of authorization cards as a substitute for a certification election when an employer shows unfair labor practices and when the results of an election may be unreliable.

FIRST CONTRACT BARGAINING Once the NLRB has certified a union as the bargaining agent for a unit, then bargaining for an initial contract begins. For both sides, negotiating a first contract is, according to NLRB General Counsel Ronald Meisburg, a "critical stage of the negotiation process because it forms the foundation for the parties' future labor–management relationship." Unfortunately, the initial bargaining sessions are often heated because the parties recently completed a contentious election. In many cases the employers' negotiators don't want to be at the bargaining table and are well aware they cannot be forced to accept any proposal. Thus, heated first contract negotiating sessions may lead to charges of unfair labor practices being filed with the NLRB (discussed in detail in Chapter 10). During initial contract negotiations, almost half of all employers refuse to bargain. The NLRB protects the "free choice" that the employees have expressed in the recent election designating the union as its bargaining representative and thus may seek an interim court injunction under Section 10(J) of the National Relations Act against the employer. About 28 percent of the employer refusal to bargain cases filed during first contract negotiations are found "meritorious."[66]

TABLE 4-3 Organizational Picketing Issues

Type of activity	Purpose	Restrictions	Reasoning
Organizational Picketing/ Leafleting of Targeted Employer	Purpose is to force Employer to recognize or bargain with Union or is to force employees to accept the union as their collective bargaining representative	May not exceed 30 days without filing for recognition with NLRB; or if Employer has recognized another union; or if valid election held within 12 months	Must show actual organizing activity by having sufficient employee interest in unionization
Informational or Publicity Picketing	Purpose to advise the public that the Employer does not employ union members; or have a contract with a union; or pay union wages	Message must be truthful, picketing is directed to the public and not employees and can't interfere with other parties coming and going	Rights are based on First Amendment Free Speech
Secondary Picketing (Hot Cargo)	Purpose is to force a nontargeted employer not to do business with Targeted Employer	ONLY allowed in construction industry and garment industry; Otherwise is ULP by Union	Unions shouldn't be allowed to embroil a neutral employer in a dispute between Union and Targeted Employer
Secondary Picketing at a Construction Site (Hot Cargo)	Purpose is to force a nontargeted employer not to do business with the Targeted Employer	If both employers share a site, Union must target entrance used by Targeted Employer (Separate Gate Doctrine); unless nontargeted employer is "essential" to the operations of the Targeted Employer, then the Union can direct picketing at it as well	If Unions cannot picket at locations with "shared" activities, then being able to reach a construction employer would be nearly impossible
Leafleting	Peaceful, consumer handbilling without pickets, to convince consumers to boycott the Targeted Employer	Can't include picketing or targeting only employees of nontargeted employer	Rights are based on First Amendment Free Speech
Bannering	Holding a large banner publicizing the dispute to force nontargeted employer not to do business with Targeted Employer	Can't include picketing or targeting only employees of nontargeted employer	Rights are based on First Amendment Free Speech

CASE 4-2

Authorization Cards Honored Four Years after Signing

The company operates a plastics recycling facility. Its business is to recycle used plastic containers into plastic pellets that are then sold as raw material to manufacturers. The company employed 64 people at its inception and reached a peak workforce of 92 in February 1994. At the time of the events that were the subject of the instant complaint, the company employed 68 nonsupervisory employees, but since then the workforce has dwindled to 36.

In the fall of 1994, some of the company's employees contacted the International Ladies Garment Workers Union (ILGWU). In early October, the ILGWU began a campaign to unionize the company's workers. In January 1995, the company laid off 29 employees and then another 10 in July. Since 1995, the workforce of the company has remained at around 35 employees.

The ILGWU filed a charge with the NLRB, alleging various unfair labor practices, including charges that the layoffs were motivated by a desire to quash the unionization campaign. The general counsel of the NLRB issued a complaint against the company on March 21, 1995. The complaint was heard in 1995 and a decision issued in 1996. The administrative law judge (ALJ) found that the company had committed numerous violations of the NLRA and recommended the imposition of a bargaining order under the *Gissel* doctrine. The company timely appealed the ALJ's decision to the NLRB.

For some unexplained reason, the NLRB did not issue its decision and order until 1999, more than three years after the ALJ's decision. The board affirmed the ALJ's findings. The board agreed with the ALJ that the severity of the company's conduct required the imposition of a bargaining order under *Gissel*. Under the bargaining order, the company was directed to bargain with ILGWU's successor union, the United Needletrades, Industrial and Textile Employees (UNITE).

When the board's order was issued, the company's original attorney on this matter had retired, and the company was in the process of finding a replacement. The company filed a motion to reopen the case, arguing that circumstances had changed since the ALJ's decision, including the restructuring of its business, a high turnover rate (only five employees who were working at the time of the complaint still worked for the company), and the passage of four and a half years. The company asked for reconsideration of the bargaining order in light of these changed conditions. The board refused, and the company contested the order in court.

Decision

Courts are almost unanimous in holding that the NLRB must take current conditions into account when it determines whether to issue a bargaining order under the *Gissel* doctrine. Relevant changed circumstances include passage of time and turnover in the workforce. If the board had before it evidence that circumstances at the company's plant were in relevant respects significantly different from those at the time of the ALJ's decision recommending a bargaining order, the board erred when it refused to take the changes into account in determining whether a bargaining order should issue.

However, the Court found that the board was not required to seek out changed circumstances. Both the company and the NLRB agreed that the board's procedural rules would have permitted the company to update the record at any time after the ALJ's recommendation and prior to the board's decision. The company made no such motion until a month after the board's decision. The Court held that the party seeking to benefit from changed circumstances bears the burden of providing the information to the board. The board is entitled to assume, in the face of the party's silence, that the facts are as initially presented. Because the changes to the company were gradual over a number of years and not a sudden event, the company had no excuse for its failure to so inform the NLRB.

Source: Adapted from *NLRB v. U.S.A. The Company Corporation*, 168 LRRM 2897, (2001).

Decertification Elections

Also allowed under the act and supervised by the NLRB are decertification elections, whereby the members of the unit vote to terminate an existing union's right to represent them in collective bargaining. The NLRB honors a bar to a decertification election within the first year of representation after a secret vote election to give a new union time to reach agreement with the employer. Decertification elections most commonly occur, therefore, when the initial year of union representation ends with no collective bargaining agreement. If there is a valid contract in place, then a decertification petition can be filed within 60–90 days of its expiration, or if a contract has expired and no new agreement is being negotiated. The NLRB, in 2007, modified prior board rulings and held that voluntary recognition, unlike a secret-ballot election, does not bar a decertification petition from being filed by employees or a rival union for the first year after the recognition. The majority opinion stated that the "uncertainty" surrounding voluntary recognition based on an authorization card majority, as opposed to an election, justifies delaying the election bar for a brief period—45 days—during which unit employees can decide whether they prefer a board-conducted election.[67]

The rules for a **decertification election** are similar to those for certification, with some exceptions. Only employees can file a decertification petition, which must include 30 percent of the eligible members of the unit. Again, the NLRB investigates the validity of the petition. If the union feels there is a problem with the petition or that an employer has unlawfully helped in the petition, it may file a blocking charge and delay the election until the unfair labor charge is resolved. And, similar to when a majority of employees sign recognition cards, the NLRB has accepted a petition to decertify a union signed by more than 50 percent of the employees in the unit without an actual election.[68]

DECERTIFICATION ELECTION

The process of removing a union as the certified representative of employees within a bargaining unit. A secret-ballot election is conducted by the NLRB to determine a majority opinion.

Although an employer can in no way aid the filing of a petition, afterward, the employer, the employees who filed the petition, and the union may all engage in an election campaign. The rules for conducting a decertification election are the same as those for a representation election.

After the votes are counted, if a majority of the employees vote against the union, it is decertified. A tie vote counts against the union because it no longer enjoys a majority status. If the union wins, it continues to represent the unit, and another election is barred for at least a year. Why do workers vote to decertify their union? One or more of the following factors are usually present in situations in which unions are decertified:

1. The employer has recently treated employees better.
2. The employer waged an aggressive antiunion campaign.
3. The employer moves to a traditionally nonunion geographic area.
4. The union is perceived by a majority of its members as being unresponsive.
5. Female, minority, and younger workers lose confidence in the union because of its declining public image and aging leaders.[69]

The decertification election or representatives' decertification (RD) is similar to, but different from, a **deauthorization election** or union deauthorization election (UD). In a UD, the bargaining unit members decide if they want to nullify the union shop provision in their agreement. Thus if a union loses a UD, the union still represents the employees in the bargaining unit and the rest of the collective bargaining agreement remains intact. However, if a union loses an RD election, it no longer represents the employees in the bargaining unit, obviously a much more serious outcome. The UD election process in the NLRA is unique in that a majority of the employees in the bargaining unit must vote to rescind the union shop provision, compared with only a majority of those voting required in certification and decertification elections.[70]

DEAUTHORIZATION ELECTION

The bargaining unit members decide if they desire to nullify the union shop provision in their agreement, which must be passed by a majority of the bargaining unit members. Thus if a union loses a deauthorization election (UD), the union still represents the employees in the bargaining unit and the rest of the collective bargaining agreement remains intact, but emloyees are not required to join the union.

A 2003–2004 study by Clyde Scott and Edwin Arnold of decertification (RD) elections and deauthorization (UD) elections as well as certification of representation (RC) elections for a 40-year period (by decades, 1959–1998) indicated a few election trends: (1) although decertification (RD) elections and deauthorization (UD) elections together account for under 20 percent of all elections held by the NLRB, the percentage of RDs more than tripled (from 5.6 to 16.5 percent) and the percentage of UDs more than doubled (from 0.8 to 2 percent); (2) the number of RD and UD elections peaked in the 1980s (RD = 18.7 percent, UD = 2.8 percent); the number of representation elections (RCs) peaked in the decade of the 1970s (133,506) and fell by over half during the 1990s (61,515); (3) union victories in RDs rose from 34.8 percent during the 1960s to 56.5 percent during the 1990s while union victories in UDs remained stable around 31 percent; (4) unions were generally more successful in winning UD and RD elections in larger bargaining units.[71]

Representation Elections in the Public Sector

Although modeled after private-sector campaigns, union elections conducted in the public sector have some differences. Public-sector employers may not be able to prohibit nonemployee union agents' access to the workplace because the workplace is a public area.[72] Rules governing public employer preelection activities during an organizational campaign generally mirror private-sector restrictions, although some state and local governments have encouraged less restrictive standards, particularly when applied to employers expressing an opinion on the effect of unionizing. In effect, this approach balances the employer's right of free speech with its duty not to be coercive.[73]

Exclusive Representation

When a labor union is recognized as the exclusive bargaining agent for a unit of employees, two major issues come into play. The first is union security, which is preserving the union's continued representation of the employees. The second is what representation by a union means to an individual employee.

EXCLUSIVE REPRESENTATION

Having been certified as the collective bargaining agent for a particular unit, the union has the legal right to bargain for all the employees within the unit, nonunion as well as union.

Exclusive representation is both a practice and a principle of law. The practice predates the law. As discussed in earlier chapters, the very roots of the labor–management relationship depended on the workers' agreement to join together to make demands on the employer. Without such solidarity, employers would have gone to other workers willing to work for what the employer wanted to pay. Before this practice became law in the Wagner Act, labor organizers and union members had to "strong-arm" some employees who might otherwise break ranks.

Because part of the goal of the Wagner Act was to eliminate labor unrest, the lawmakers agreed that if a majority of the employees working in a defined unit voted to be represented by a union, then all the employees would be covered. This rule gives real power to the union's bargaining position and simplifies the bargaining process. The value of exclusive representation in negotiating collective bargaining agreements cannot be overemphasized. Without it, the process simply does not work. If even a few employees ignore the union and gain individual benefits from the employer, the need for a union can be questioned. Likewise, if individual members of a bargaining unit take unsanctioned action, an employer's confidence that the union can speak for the workers is undermined. For example, if employees engage in a wildcat strike, the agreement the union made *not* to strike in exchange for gains at the negotiation table becomes meaningless. And if exclusive representation was not the rule, the administration of a contract among like employees in an inconsistent manner would be disruptive to the labor–management relationship.[74] What are the keys to a union successfully organizing a workplace, and the keys to management successfully resisting a drive? The "Tips from the Experts" are provided by experienced labor and management professionals.

Tips from the Experts

Union

A union organizer can generate sufficient interest at a workplace to organize employees in the three following ways.

Organizing at the workplace is not much different from organizing in the community, on campus, or anywhere else for that matter. The key to successful organizing efforts is finding the connection between the prospective "members" and the "organization" seeking their allegiance. For employees, traditionally this connection was easy: better compensation for their labor, health benefits, and job security. Today, this connection must be based on other things as well. The basics exist for many workers, whether by existing collective bargaining or by legislation. Where the basics do exist, the emphasis must shift to (1) employment security, (2) employee–employer partnership in providing quality products and services, and (3) employee political power in the elective and legislative processes. It is necessary to find out what the workers want and to show them how the union is the vehicle for attaining what they want.

Management

What are three ways an employer can legally discourage employees from organizing?

a. Good communication, from suggestion programs (boxes for employees to write questions to be answered by top management, e.g., Winn-Dixie's "I want to know" program, in which the chief executive officer personally responds to any question within 24 hours; anonymous questions can be answered in company newsletters or publications specifically geared for that purpose) to reward programs. In the latter, employees compete for the best idea for cost-cutting or similar measures to simply training supervisors in how to best field questions and issues around which union organizing attempts focus and how to proclaim the company's union-free philosophy without interrogating the employee in the process.

b. Active participation, from joint employee–management quality teams dealing with specific workplace issues to bonus incentives for every employee when both the company and the individual employee exceed their performance objectives to employee representation in the development of critical personnel policies (e.g., the disciplinary system).

c. Instituting an internal grievance appeal process to remove the last (assuming "a" and "b" are followed) appeal the union has.

Summary

Employees under the National Labor Relations Act have the right to organize into labor organizations and to seek representation for the purpose of collective bargaining with their employers. The NLRA and subsequent court and NLRB decisions define the processes for this representation. The NLRB is given wide authority to determine on a case-by-case basis an appropriate unit of employees—one of similarities and interests for collective bargaining purposes. In the public sector the question of appropriate is often moot since employees' right to organize is specified by profession—teachers, police officers, fire fighters, and so on.

The initial step is usually taken by a group of employees or a union organizer. Unions generally have three methods by which they can be recognized to represent employees: voluntary recognition by an employer when a majority of the employees sign authorization cards; an NLRB directive; or, the most common, a secret-ballot representation election. The organizing drive conducted by a union wishing to represent a unit of employees is very important. Tactics used by unions to organize and by companies to resist unionization have become much more sophisticated—such as salting an employer. Management can, and usually does, try to convince the employees to vote against the union in an election, but must carefully follow "TIPS" and "FORE" during the campaign. The NLRB strives to hold a fair election—one in which all employees have a "free choice" without undue pressure by either the union or management. If a union receives a majority of those voting in the election, it is certified by the NLRB as the exclusive bargaining agent for the bargaining unit of employees for at least one year, and then begins to bargain a first contract with the employer.

Unions are structured into four levels; locals, nationals, internationals, intermediate, and federations. In the past most unions were either craft or industrial, however more recently the differences have become blurred as many national unions have organized workers outside of their traditional roots, and thus today many are mixed unions, and include not only workers of different crafts and unskilled industries but private and public sector members in some cases. Local union officers include president, vice president, secretary/treasurer, business manager, and stewards—for many members the union person they interact with most. Stewards, because they serve a dual commitment to both management and the union and handle most grievance issues, are highly valued.

CASE STUDIES

Case Study 4-1 Salting

The Company is engaged in the business of removing or cleaning hazardous waste. Most of its employees fall into three categories; (1) field technicians who are unskilled laborers; (2) drivers and operators of trucks; and (3) field supervisors who go out into the field and are in charge of jobs. The driver and equipment operator positions require commercial driving licenses (CDL). All parties agree that the people who are called field supervisors are employees and *not* supervisors within the meaning of Section 2(11) of the act.

The Union was engaged in organizing companies in the area handling hazardous materials. The Union sent a letter dated March 9 to the Company indicating (a) that it was commencing an organizing drive; (b) that the NLRA precluded the employer from restraining or coercing its employees; and (c) that it would be distributing literature to its employees at various projects. Subsequently, the Union began leafleting to the Company's employees on their way into and out of the workplace.

On March 21, the Company placed a help-wanted ad, seeking to hire operators who had CDL licenses and H&T (hazardous material handling endorsements). The Union sent two members, Castillo and Rivera, to apply for a job. And even though neither had the required commercial driver's license, they were allowed to fill out applications and were interviewed. They both were told that they could have jobs as field technicians, and arrangements were made for them to get a drug test. Neither informed the Company that they were members of a union or that they intended to organize employees on behalf of the Union. They were "covert" salts and were instructed to keep their union membership secret until the appropriate time. Castillo and Rivera were told by the Union that if they obtained jobs, the Union would make up the difference in the wage rate paid by the Employer and the wage rate that they had been getting from being employed as shop stewards at union employers. Also, the Union agreed to provide them with any benefits not provided by the Company. They started as field techs on April 16 or 17.

On the morning of April 13, the Union sent teams of union agents into the Company's office to apply for work at the Company as "overt" salts. The overt salts went to the Company's facility in pairs, wearing union clothing and carrying recording devices to record what was said during the application process. When the overt salts entered the facility, they asked the Company's receptionist for employment applications and advised her that it was their intention to organize the Company. She responded that the Company was not interested in becoming a union shop, but informed the applicants that they could apply for one of the available driver positions but that, in order to apply for such positions, they would have to produce driver's licenses with CDLs and HAZMAT endorsements. Although some of the applicants indicated to the Receptionist that they possessed those licenses, it is undisputed that, in fact, none of them did. When none of the individuals were able to produce the required licenses, she advised them that they could come back and fill out applications when they had obtained them. One of the applicants then inquired whether he could fill out an application for a field technician position. She told him that the Company did not have openings for field technicians at that time, but that he could complete an application and she would keep it on file. He did not, however, complete an application. None of the applicants returned to the Company after April 13, nor did they make any further attempt to apply for employment with the Company.

The Union filed an unfair labor practice charge against the Company for refusing to hire or consider for hiring the union members in violation of the NLRA.

In order to establish a refusal-to-hire violation the Union must establish the following elements: (1) that the Company was hiring, or had concrete plans to hire, at the time of the alleged unlawful conduct; (2) that the applicants had experience or training relevant to the announced or generally known requirements of the positions for hire, or in the alternative, that the employer has not adhered uniformly to such requirements, or that the requirements were themselves pretextual or were applied as a pretext for discrimination; and (3) that antiunion animus contributed to the decision not to hire the applicants. In order to establish a refusal-to-consider violation the Union has to show (1) that the Company excluded applicants from a hiring process; and (2) that antiunion animus contributed to the decision not to consider the applicants for employment.

The Company argued that none of these applicants had the qualifications necessary to be hired as drivers. Nor were these "overt salts" actually looking for employment. All of them had full-time jobs at the Union, as business agents, organizers, or dispatchers. When they were invited by the office person to submit applications for nondriver jobs, accompanied by their social security cards and driver licenses, they never followed up on this invitation and not one made any further attempt to apply for employment. Furthermore, the Company, having recently decided to hire around four laborers (including union salts Castillo and Rivera), did not immediately need any field technicians. Put simply, they were not qualified for the jobs advertised and they did not apply for jobs for which they were qualified, but which were not immediately available.

The Union argued that the Company's decision not to hire or consider for hire the "overt salts" was clearly motivated by antiunion animus for when the two "covert salts" applied for jobs for which they were not qualified, the Company allowed them to complete the application process and they were, in fact, hired as field techs. In addition, the Receptionist's statements that the Company did not want to be a union shop clearly showed the antiunion animus amid the ongoing organizing drive.

Source: Adapted from *Allstate Power Vac, Inc. and Laborers International Union of North America, Local 78*, 354 NLRB No. 111 (2009).

QUESTIONS

1. Explain how the Company's treatment of both the "covert" and "overt" salts applications for jobs compares to the recommended counter-salting steps for employers.
2. Would either the "covert" or the "overt" salts in this case satisfy the NLRB ruling that applicants for employment bust be genuinely interested in seeking employment before claiming protection under the NLRA?
3. Does the Company's opposition to becoming a union shop indicate that there was antiunion animus in refusing to consider the "overt" salts for employment?

Case Study 4-2 Exclusive Representation

In 1981, the company laid off more than 100 employees because of an economic recession. The existing contract already provided that laid-off employees would accrue "continuous service" credit for two years and would retain continuous service credit for an additional five-year period. In addition, the union negotiated additional benefits for these laid-off employees. One of the benefits was a commitment by the company that these laid-off employees would be "offered future employment opportunities" with the company in the event positions opened up.

Eleven years later, in 1992, the company needed employees, and it notified the former employees and offered them interviews. Some were rehired. However, 16 former employees who were still union members were not rehired. They sought the help of their union in filing a grievance against the company, claiming that the company had violated the contract by not rehiring them. The union declined, saying that because these union members were no longer employees of the company, they were not part of the bargaining unit and the union had no duty to represent them. The 16 former employees argued that under the agreement negotiated by the union while they were employees, they had acquired certain protections and that it was now the union's duty to enforce those protections. Because the former employees could not pursue the grievance without the union, the negotiated protections would be meaningless if the union failed to represent them. The 16 former employees sued the union.

Source: Adapted from *Smith v. ACF Industries*, 149 LRRM 2693 (1995).

QUESTIONS

1. If the court rules that the union has no duty to represent these former employees, they cannot pursue their grievance against the company. Discuss why this result is fair or unfair to all three parties: the company, the union, and the former employees.

2. When the union bargained for the laid-off employees, the employees were told they would have future employment opportunities with the company. Do you think it was unreasonable for these laid-off employees to expect the union's help 11 years later? Why or why not?
3. If the company and the union had known that 11 years would pass before positions opened up at this plant, do you think they would have provided the "future employment opportunities" provision?

Key Terms and Concepts

accretion *122*
appropriate bargaining unit *118*
business agent *129*
certification *148*
community-of-interest doctrine *121*
craft unit *124*
deauthorization election *153*
decertification election *153*
departmental unit *125*
exclusive representation *154*
federation of unions *131*
gissel doctrine *150*
globe doctrine *121*
industrial union *128*
neutrality/card-check recognition *148*
organizing drive *134*
remaining unit *125*
residual unit *125*
runoff election *147*
salting *137*
secret-ballot representation election *136*
showing of interest *143*
stewards *129*
TIPS and FORE *138*
voluntary recognition *148*

Review Questions

1. What criteria does the NLRB consider when determining whether an appropriate unit of employees has a substantial mutuality of interests?
2. How does the National Labor Relations Act limit the board's determination of the appropriate bargaining unit?
3. What are the steps the NLRB follows in a representation election?
4. How does certification benefit a union? Under what circumstances might the NLRB invalidate a certification election?
5. What factors might contribute to employees' voting to decertify a union?
6. What are the rules that employers and union organizers must follow during an organizational campaign?
7. Compare bargaining unit determination in the public and private sectors.
8. Discuss the issues from the employer's standpoint on union "salting" efforts.
9. Explain the respective roles of the four levels of unions: local, national, intermediate, and federation.
10. What steps are commonly used by unions to organize a workplace?

YOU BE THE ARBITRATOR
"Just Cause" for Termination

ARTICLE VII
SENIORITY

Section 2. Seniority shall be lost for the following reasons:

b. if the employee is discharged for cause.

ARTICLE XVII
GRIEVANCE AND ARBITRATION PROCEDURE

Section 3. Step 3.

4) The arbitrator shall not have the authority to amend or modify this agreement or establish new terms

or conditions under this agreement. The arbitrator shall determine any question of arbitrability.

ARTICLE XXII
DISCHARGE OR SUSPENSION

Section 1. The following disciplinary policy is hereby established:

Step 1. A written notice describing the nature of the employee's problem(s) will be given to the employee, an opportunity will be provided to correct these problems.
Step 2. A second written notice will be sent and a two (2) day suspension without pay will be imposed, affording the employee some time to reflect on the problem and on ways to correct them. . . .
Step 3. Termination—Management reserves the right to waive this policy, if, in their opinion, it is in the best interest of the company to do so. . . .

Facts

A truck driver was discharged for failing to make timely deliveries and not using the quickest, most direct route as previously instructed. The company warehouses and distributes wholesale floor covering products and operates from several locations. The driver was hired in November 2000 and during his relatively short, eight-month tenure with the company received a total of four other employee warning reports. According to the employer, the driver demonstrated a continuing pattern of failing to follow orders, company policies, and supervisory instructions involving the use of a global positioning system (GPS) mounted in his truck, completing daily driving logs, and utilizing toll roads for the best way to make deliveries in a timely fashion. On two occasions the employee simply failed to complete his deliveries, costing the company extra expense and a loss of customer satisfaction. The triggering event for his termination was his refusal to use the toll road to make a delivery even though he was offered an advance of the toll road fee. In response, the union claims that the employee's failure to use toll road was justified because he was already owed $87.32 in post-toll reimbursements. One of the employee's prior warning reports was grieved and settled in his favor, and he was disputing the remaining three at the time of his discharge. In this grievance he is challenging his discharge, seeking reinstatement with back pay, seniority, and benefits.

Issue

Does the collective bargaining agreement (CBA) require the employer to have "just cause" to fire an employee, even if the language is not in the CBA?

Position of Parties

The employer argues that this discharge is not subject to arbitration because the CBA does not contain a "for cause" requirement (see Article XVII, Grievance and Arbitration Procedure, and Article XXII, Discharge or Suspension, printed earlier). Therefore, there is no standard against which the arbitrator may test the employer's actions.

In response, the union argues that the company position ignores the plain language of the agreement stating that seniority "shall be lost. . . . if the employee is discharged for cause." According to the union, in a unionized work environment, the termination of seniority equates to the termination of employment (see Article VII, Seniority).

QUESTIONS

1. As arbitrator, what would be your award and opinion in this arbitration?
2. Identify the key, relevant section(s), phrases, or words of the collective bargaining agreement (CBA), and explain why they were critical in making your decision.
3. What actions might the employer and/or the union have taken to avoid this conflict?

Source: Adapted from *Superior Products,* 116 LA 1623 (2002).

CHAPTER 5

Negotiation Models, Strategies, and Tactics

Chapter Outline

UAW vice president Bob King, who directs the union's Ford Department, shakes hands with Ford CEO Alan Mulally at the opening of contract bargaining. *Source:* © Jim West/CORBIS.

Negotiations are about changing the status quo. Unless both parties can receive something more than what the status quo provides, there is nothing for them to negotiate.

THEODORE W. KHEEL (NOTED AMERICAN NEGOTIATOR AND MEDIATOR)

LABOR NEWS

United Auto Workers and Ford, GM, and Chrysler Provide Possible New Direction for U.S. Labor Contracts

In July 2007, the United Auto Workers Union (UAW) started what many U.S. labor experts saw as the most difficult round of auto industry contract negotiations in 50 years. After all, Ford, GM, and Chrysler, the U.S. "Big Three" automobile manufacturers, had lost market share and billions of dollars in recent years. The UAW staged brief strikes against GM and Chrysler to demonstrate its determination to preserve jobs, health care, and pensions. By December 3, 2007, the UAW finalized historic new four-year contracts, all of them with the Big Three—in less than five months!

So how did the UAW save jobs, health care provisions and pension benefits while enabling the auto manufacturers to realize billions in cost reductions? By agreeing to radical new changes in their labor contracts:

1. *Wage freeze.* Current workers received a four-year wage freeze.
2. *Lower wages for new workers.* In a new "two-tier" wage scale, new workers will be hired at wage levels between $14 and $16 per hour compared to an average of $26 per hour for current workers.
3. *Concessions.* No more COLAs, one paid holiday, no overtime after eight hours, and education benefits (paid tuition).
4. *Job Guarantees.* The UAW gained guarantees to keep plants open that were selected for closure as well as ideally keeping thousands of other jobs that might have been lost if the Big Three cannot regain financial success.

The UAW in past years has been credited with many other contract firsts, including paid health care, pensions, paid holidays, and job security provisions. With the new 2007–2011 agreement, the UAW and Ford again provided a new direction for American labor with a four-year wage freeze and a new "two-tier" wage system that includes starting salaries of about half of current workers—in exchange for job security. The 2011–2014 CBA included a $6,000 signing bonus and $3,700 in profit-sharing, but kept the two tier pay system.

In 2011, UAW locals and members were becoming angry over the concessions made in 2007. As Ford returned to profitability, and GM and Chrysler rebounded after receiving federal bailouts—which the UAW supported—UAW sought to end the "two-tier" wage systems and was successful at the GM Lordstown, Ohio, plant, where the new Chevrolet Cruze is built and at Ford's Michigan plant, where the new Ford Focus is built. Why did management agree to give up the two-tier?—Ford CEO Alan Mulally pointed out, "There are so many ways to create efficiencies without looking at wages!" Thus the future of "two-tier" wage rates for UAW/Ford, GM, and Chrysler appears uncertain.

Source: Adapted from Jere Downs, "New UAW Contracts May Have Wide Effect," *Louisville Courier Journal* (December 16, 2007), pp. D1, 2; Joseph R. Szczesny, "UAW Anger at Concessions on the Rise," *Time* (February 23, 2010); and Trademarkets (October 9, 2010). Available at www.Time.com. Accessed August 23, 2011.

Labor and management meet across a negotiating table because the National Labor Relations Act requires that the parties bargain in good faith. The NLRA also provides that neither party has to agree to any particular proposal as long as it continues to bargain in good faith. Thus, the act establishes the boundaries of the negotiation process but leaves the internal workings to the parties involved. No particular negotiation model, strategies, or tactics are required by law.

Over the years, the labor–management bargaining process has largely changed from an adversarial confrontation between the forces of "capital" and "worker" into a stylized ritual between the representatives of management and labor in which, more often than not, both parties come to the bargaining table with realistic expectations, and the understanding that their own interests are interdependent with the interests of the other party.

Whether or not that observation is correct, collective bargaining has certainly changed from mere confrontation to a process by which labor and management sincerely attempt to address conflicting interests. Respect for the process, however, does not change the fact that the collective bargaining process is adversarial, and it involves conflict resolution and compromise. The parties interact on the issues using whatever advantage they have to achieve their goals. The key to successful bargaining lies in flexibility, understanding the interests of both parties, and using the process.

In this chapter we discuss the major bargaining models of distributive and integrative bargaining and the types of strategies and tactics employed at the negotiation table. Although examined here in the field of labor relations, these models, strategies, and tactics are commonly used by negotiators in many business, professional, and personal bargaining situations.

NEGOTIATING SESSIONS: "AT THE TABLE"

When two parties sit down at the bargaining table, the exact process they choose to follow depends on their past history together and their individual skills and negotiating styles. Although no two labor–management negotiations follow the exact same steps, Figure 5-1 describes the bargaining process generally used during collective bargaining, followed by a brief explanation of these steps. The negotiation concepts listed in each step are discussed throughout the chapter. The chapter also presents the two major bargaining models and tactics that are commonly used "at the table" by negotiators. First, distributive bargaining, which is the traditional and primarily adversarial approach, is explained. Then a more collaborative approach, generally called integrative bargaining, is discussed.

Opening Session

In the opening session of most negotiations, time is devoted to establishing the details of the negotiation process. The parties begin with introductions of the negotiating team members and exchanging lists with the names and contact information of team members. Neither side may dictate

1. The Opening Statement

- **A.** Describe the **"Big Picture"** of the negotiation situation. The past relationship between the parties, current issues to be presented during negotiations, as well as the major external factors and the concerns of both parties may be discussed.
- **B.** Suggest **Ground Rules** that will facilitate the process (start with the 5 Ws: Who speaks for each party; Where will negotiations take place; When will sessions begin and for how long; What form of agreement is acceptable; How will formal proposals be made and agreed upon).
- **C.** List the **"Key Issues"** that must be resolved to reach a settlement and ask for a list of the other party's key issues. These issues are often economic in nature and thus involve wages, benefits, or costs. However other noneconomic issues such as seniority, grievance handling, or subcontracting might also be a key issue in a particular negotiation.

2. The First Negotiation Session: Presenting the Proposals

- **A.** Ask the **other party to present its proposals first**. Listen intently to determine its true, genuine interests on issues which underlie its opening positions on those issues.
- **B.** Utilize **"active listening"** tactics as the other party presents its case; acknowledge what he or she is saying with reflective statements, and open-ended questions such as **"Why . . ."** to better understand the other party's interests.
- **C.** Where possible, identify **common interests** which might easily be resolved.

3. Negotiate Minor Issues First

A. Identify the minor issues that should be easier to resolve and try to build momentum. Suggest logical **"trade-offs"** or **packages** of issues that provide some gains for both sides.

B. Include **"throwaways"** in your list of issues to build momentum and provide you leverage to make trade-off for issues of greater value.

C. Frequently mention that both sides need to satisfy some interests and realize mutual gains to reach an agreement. Ask the other party to brainstorm new options together.

4. Negotiate "Key Issues"

A. With "Key issues," of economic value such as wages or health care, **frame** each proposal with persuasive arguments and use relative **norms** when appropriate.

B. When a distributive process is utilized, make the first offer to **anchor** the negotiation, or let the other party make the first offer to enable you to respond with an offer to create a favorable **settlement range**.

C. Once the settlement range for an issue is established, make small **incremental concessions** that lead to your desired settlement value.

D. Only make **large concessions if matched** by the other party. Try to never counter your own proposal.

5. Responding to Proposals

A. Always take **time to evaluate** a proposal, rejecting immediately may signify a lack of sincerity on your part.

B. When **rejecting a proposal** explain why it does not meet your interests.

C. If time is available ask to **suspend the negotiation** to research data or information which may support your interests or question the other party's interests, or clarify a fact in dispute.

D. **Caucus** often to re-think your interests, evaluate the other party's proposal, or simply "regroup" your team. Never allow team members to express conflicting views at the table.

E. **Avoid possible impasse**, by suggesting that issues which appear to defy resolution be placed on the "back burner" until the end of negotiations.

6. The Closing Stage

A. To facilitate the closing, in the Ground Rules provide that issues agreed to during negotiations be **"signed-off, dated" and removed from the table** for further discussion.

B. A **written**, signed, and dated agreement or contract is standard in collective bargaining negotiations. One party can offer to prepare the first draft of all the signed-off and agreed provisions, and the other party then proofreads the draft.

C. Expect many of the **"Key Issues" to be settled at the end**, in the last 10 percent of negotiations, that is the normal process.

D. When it appears a deal is close, expect the other party to try a **"Nickel & Dime"** tactic to close the deal. Be prepared to "**walk away**" rather than make a last minute major concession just to achieve **"the over factor"**—desire to get the process over with. After all issues are agreed upon, the union will offer it to its membership.

FIGURE 5-1 A Model for Negotiating Sessions *Source:* Courtesy of Lou Manchise, former director of mediation services, Federal Mediation and Conciliation Service, "A Helpful Model for Negotiations," unpublished manuscript (2008). Used by permission.

the membership of the other's negotiating team, but rules may be established as to how many members are allowed on each side and as to their official roles, such as spokesperson, recording secretary, and doorkeeper, who makes sure only authorized persons attend the negotiations. Negotiating teams may be kept as small as possible to allow for productive discussion. Each side must have a designated leader who makes commitments for the respective parties. Traditionally, union negotiating teams can only agree to propose the contract to the membership for acceptance. Final approval generally depends on a secret-ballot vote of the members, depending on the rules of the union.

If the parties have negotiated previously, they often use the first session to discuss the "big picture" of the current situation, which may include critical issues such as deadlines, outside influences, and general economic conditions. A general discussion may take place on how they intend to proceed: using a traditional distributive bargaining process or a more collaborative process. If the parties, or people at the table, have not negotiated together before, this process and the discussion of ground rules may take some time as they jointly determine how to proceed.

A bargaining agenda might be set to establish the exchange of initial proposals and the order of discussion of bargaining items. If possible, the agenda includes how long to continue with one item if agreement is not made because a stalemate in the early stages of bargaining can unnecessarily sour the process. If feasible, the agenda provides that less controversial issues are discussed first so an atmosphere of progress and agreement is fostered.

Usually a decision is made on how to keep records of the negotiations. An accurate record keeps both parties honest during negotiations and facilitates drafting the final contract. A single outline of items discussed, proposals made on those items, and what was agreed to or where disagreement arose is often prepared by one party and initialed by the other. The site of the negotiations needs to have private spaces to allow for a caucus by either party. The caucus and adjournment rights of both parties are often decided in the ground rules or initial session. Misunderstanding as to the caucus rights can lead one or the other party to stage a needless walkout when a strategic retreat could have served as a positive catalyst to settlement. Finally, the role of a mediator, if they intend to use one in case of an impasse, may be included in the ground rules or initial session.

GROUND RULES Usually at the opening session, the parties set the rules of the collective bargaining process. If the parties have a long-standing relationship, establishing procedures can be very routine. But when the collective bargaining process is relatively new or when the parties have had poor labor relations, setting ground rules can be as difficult, and as important, as bargaining on the issues. The parties decide the "**5 Ws**": *who* speaks for the parties; *where* the parties will meet; *when,* how often, and how long will they meet; how *will* formal proposals and responses be made; and *what* form of agreement will be acceptable. The number and length of bargaining sessions may indicate a party's reluctance to bargain in good faith. These and other procedures are often agreed to in writing as **ground rules** for negotiations. Exactly what is included in the ground rules varies greatly according to the desires of the negotiators and the bargaining history of the two parties.

5 WS

The who, where, when; what form of agreement; and how will proposals be made as agreed to in the ground rules.

GROUND RULES

The general procedures and policies that each party agrees to adhere to during negotiations. These are usually agreed to in writing before the negotiations and may include such items as the time, date, and location for the negotiating session.

The following are examples of useful common ground rules:

1. All negotiation sessions will commence on the time, date, and location heretofore agreed on by the parties.
2. The chief negotiator for the company and the chief negotiator for the union shall be the chief spokespersons for the respective parties' interests. However, others present may speak as required or be called on by the chief negotiators.
3. Insofar as practical and reasonable, the data introduced by either party at negotiations shall be made available to the other party.
4. If either the company or the union intends to add a new member to its respective bargaining committee, the party adding the new member will notify the other party.
5. Proposals and counterproposals will be made on typed copies as reasonable and will be signed and dated by the appropriate party. The parties shall simultaneously exchange initial noneconomic and economic proposals at the appropriate times.

6. Individual items agreed to by both parties shall be signed and dated, and removed from the table with a "tentative agreement." Any attempt to reintroduce or discuss those items shall be viewed as a breach of good faith. However, the parties have agreed that all "tentative agreements" are subject to a total agreement being reached.
7. Management's chief negotiator and the union's chief negotiator shall have the authority to agree in substance on contract language and provisions. However, any agreement is preliminary and contingent on a final contract. All preliminary agreements made regarding individual contract provisions shall be initialed and dated by both chief negotiators.
8. If mediation is agreed to by both parties in the case of an impasse, the mediator shall be someone who is agreeable to both parties.
9. The current labor agreement will be extended on a day-to-day basis until a new one is reached, or until one party serves notice to the other party to end negotiations.

   Even an oral commitment by both parties to extend the current contract until a new one is reached can be binding—according to a 2009 NLRB decision.[1]

Recognizing Common Bargaining Tactics

The typical atmosphere of a collective bargaining session largely depends on the attitudes of the parties involved and the negotiating model they choose to use. As discussed later in this chapter, both attitude and negotiating model are greatly influenced by the parties' prior relationship, the economic circumstances of the employer, the employer's basic attitude toward unionization, and the leadership of the union.

Traditionally, the initial working sessions of collective bargaining are no more than monologues in which both parties present their list of demands and provide data and arguments to support their positions. The laundry list proposed by the parties purposely includes bargaining items that can and will be bargained away during the negotiations with varying degrees of reluctance. This **posturing** in the first sessions is very important. It allows a certain amount of **face-saving** to the party who comes to the bargaining table with the least amount of bargaining power. Posturing also provides members of the negotiating teams the opportunity to "let off steam" or "have their say" about issues that have caused raised emotions.

POSTURING

The pattern established during the initial bargaining session in which each negotiating party demonstrates its willingness to negotiate, identifies its basic bargaining positions, and generally sets the tone of the negotiations.

The participants should anticipate several common bargaining tactics if traditional bargaining is used including:

CONFLICT Negotiations by nature contain conflict, which can cause tempers to rise, name-calling, and anger. However, both sides are aware that their goals are *interdependent*. Neither side can achieve success at the table, or in future years, without a relationship with the other side.

CONCEALMENT During negotiations, parties often *conceal* their real goals and objectives to enhance their opportunity for the best possible settlement. This is a characteristic of the distributive negotiation process and should be expected. Every negotiator must decide how open and honest to be in communicating needs and preferences. If a negotiator is completely open and honest, he or she might settle for less than if he or she conceals goals and fights harder for a better settlement. However, if a negotiator is completely deceptive about goals, the talks may never move in the direction of a settlement. Thus, negotiators must present and discuss their goals, but without revealing their exact goal or acceptable outcome, to move negotiations forward.

PACKAGING It is difficult to achieve an agreement on all issues at one time. As many as 50 economic and noneconomic issues may be involved during labor negotiations. If all 50 issues are left on the table and discussed at the same time, the process would become unwieldy. Instead, a few items may be packaged together, agreed to, and removed from further discussion, allowing both sides to achieve their goal on one or more items and thus establish trust in the process, and

PACKAGING

A negotiation tactic of putting a few items together and allowing both sides to achieve gains on one or more items to establish trust and decrease the number of unresolved issues.

THROWAWAY ITEMS

A negotiating tactic in which a party introduces items of low priority to its side to trade for items of higher priority.

decrease the number of unresolved issues. These packages of items, therefore, move negotiations toward completion. **Packaging** may at least narrow the list of disputed items to the high-priority issues for each side. The ground rules may require each chief negotiator to "sign off" on a package—signing and dating a written counterproposal detailing the items agreed to—thereby removing them from further discussions.

THROWAWAY ITEMS Negotiators, in their list of initial demands, may include items of little or even no real value to their side, thus providing some items to trade in exchange for others of high priority to their side. Throwaways can be the basis of a successful bluff if the other side believes it has won a concession on an important item. The **throwaway items** may have some real value, but they simply are not of high priority in comparison with other issues. A throwaway item for one side may, in fact, be a high-priority item for the other side.

CAUCUSING Much of the negotiating time is spent with each party meeting separately. After a proposal or counterproposal is received, a team usually asks for a **caucus**. In caucuses, team members can openly discuss the merits of the proposal and their willingness to accept it, or they can formulate a counterproposal. One common strategy is to not reveal at the table how the party feels about a proposal received from the other side. Even an obviously desirable proposal may be taken to a caucus, and when the team returns to the table it accepts the proposal without emotion. An expression of happiness over a proposal may lead the other side to feel remorse or believe they need not give on further items. Caucusing is also used for resolving disagreement among members of the same team and gathering additional information about unanticipated or costly proposals.

FLEXIBILITY The successful negotiation process requires the exchange of many proposals and counterproposals. The parties should be prepared to be *flexible*. Every proposal received should be studied and responded to by acceptance or a counteroffer. The quick, immediate rejection of a proposal implies inflexibility and a response of "we will only accept our position." This attitude may anger the other side and may, in fact, be bad-faith bargaining if one party consistently rejects offers without serious thought. Also, most proposals must be carefully evaluated before their merits can be accurately estimated.

The parties to a negotiation often need to break out into private sessions, or a caucus, to discuss the various options discussed at the table. *Source:* © Blend Images/Alamy.

COMPROMISE The key to successful negotiations is *compromise* by both parties. If either side believes it will achieve its position on every goal, then most likely no settlement will be reached. Instead, both parties must realize that many of their goals are in direct conflict; what one side gains on an issue, the other side loses. If one side loses on too many issues, it may not sign the agreement, or, if forced to sign then, it certainly will be looking to "even the score" during the next round of negotiations.

SAVING FACE It is important to recognize the need for both parties to **save face**. The face-saving process at the end of labor–management negotiations typically involves the union negotiator claiming victory while management remains silent. The parties recognize that the union must win ratification by the membership. If management boasted about the gains it made at the table (and both sides always make some gains), then the union negotiators might lose face and the members reject the deal, sending their negotiators back to the table for more management concessions. Getting a final deal—the ultimate goal—is also the most effective way of putting all disputes and face-saving issues in the past.[2] Face saving also means that a negotiator needs to reconcile the stand that he or she has taken during a negotiation or in an agreement with his or her past words and deeds. One cannot take a firm stand on an issue and then agree to something totally different without a reasonable explanation. The importance of face saving to the negotiation process cannot be underestimated.[3]

SAVING FACE
Allowing negotiators to present the end product of a negotiation in the best light, with neither party publicizing individual wins or losses to ensure ratification of an agreement as well as the ability to ensure more positive relationships in the future.

Tips from the Experts

What are three classic mistakes to be avoided at the negotiations table?

Union

1. Make certain that when an employer claims it is unable to meet your wage demands, you demand information on the financial condition of the company. Under the National Labor Relations Act, you are entitled to financial information if the employer claims a lack of funds, an inability to stay competitive, or the loss of a necessary profit margin.
2. Remember that if negotiations reach an impasse and such an impasse is not the result of an employer's bad-faith negotiations, an employer may unilaterally implement its last offer. Such an action allows the employer to bypass the bargaining unit's representatives and deal directly with employees, thereby undercutting your ability to represent your members.
3. Make certain that any issue brought up at the negotiating table is either completely resolved or explicitly reserved for future negotiations. A so-called zipper clause in many collective bargaining agreements precludes reopening negotiations on any mandatory or permissive bargaining subject that could have been brought up at the negotiations table.

Management

1. Unless you want to provide the union with all the company's financial information, make certain you do not claim a financial inability to meet the union's wage demands. The U.S. Supreme Court has ruled that if management rejects a union's proposal on grounds of "inability to pay," the employer's financial condition then becomes relevant to the negotiations, and the employer must provide the union with financial statements, including profit and loss, assets, and liabilities. To avoid this problem, management can simply state, "We are not willing to agree" with the union's wage demands. Such unwillingness may be based on a number of factors and does not require management to reveal financial information.[4]
2. Make it clear at the beginning of the negotiations what authority you do or do not have to reach a binding agreement on behalf of the employer. If you need to check with higher authorities before making a commitment, make sure you have explained that to the union's negotiators. Otherwise, springing the need to go back to management can be seen as a delaying tactic that may be deemed an unfair labor practice.
3. Take care in labeling a proposal as the "last, best" offer because if an impasse is reached and there is no bad-faith bargaining on the part of the employer, the employer may implement its last offer unilaterally. However, it is not permissible in such circumstances to implement a proposal that is in any way different from what was previously offered to and was rejected by the union.

Before negotiations begin, the parties separately decide what overall strategy should be employed in the negotiation. To do this the negotiators for each side should first identify and weigh the critical elements of any negotiation: *information*, *time*, and *power*.[5] These factors may or may not be directly discussed at the table, but often significantly influence the outcome.

CRITICAL ELEMENTS IN A NEGOTIATION: INFORMATION, TIME, POWER

Information

The first critical element, information, has been called "the heart of negotiations." Why? Information shapes individuals' assessment of reality, their negotiation strategy, and their expectations of what can be achieved, and thus the outcome of a negotiation. Consider, for example, how information shapes the appraisal of the price of a new Ford Escape Hybrid SUV. The sticker price on one with the desired options is $36,000. A saleswoman contends the brand-new Escape Hybrids are hot-selling models, and a newspaper article, noting the high price of gas, says some people are paying over the sticker price. With this information, one would expect to pay *more* than $36,000 for a new Escape Hybrid. However, a week later, the dealer advertises a "special weekend" price on all Escape Hybrids of $1,500 off the sticker price. A neighbor buys an Escape Hybrid on a "great deal" through a friend and paid $2,000 below sticker. A *Consumer Reports* article advises buyers to go online to find the best price for new Escape Hybrids. An Internet search turns up an offer at $3,000 below sticker a mere 89 miles away. Now the expectation is to buy a new Escape Hybrid for at least $3,000 below sticker price. The appraisal of a "good deal" changed as more *information* was received.

BATNA

A negotiator's best alternative course of action if no settlement is reached.

WATNA

A realistic assessment of the worst alternative to not reaching an agreement that affects what a party is willing to agree to in order not to reach an impasse.

BATNA To a negotiator, *the most important single piece of information in a negotiation is one's* **BATNA**: **B**est **A**lternative **T**o a **N**egotiated **A**greement, or a party's alternative course of action if they walk away.[6] Before entering into any negotiation, a party must realistically assess the risk and reward of reaching, or not reaching, agreement. Key goals of what one wants or expects from the negotiations should be identified. If those key goals are not being met, then a buyer can walk away from a salesperson, a manager can search for a new vendor, a lawyer can go to court instead of settling a case, or an investor can seek other uses of his funds. In collective bargaining, a BATNA may be a union's ability to stage a successful strike or management's ability to hire replacement workers. It is also, however, very important that negotiators evaluate their **WATNA**: **W**orst **A**lternative **T**o a **N**egotiated **A**greement. That is, if negotiations falter, what is the worst possible outcome? Too often people are optimistic and can easily think about their BATNA but fail to consider their WATNA. In a failed labor negotiation, the WATNA may be, for example, the permanent closure of a facility, loss of all management and union jobs, and economic crisis for the local community.

RELATIVE BATNA One's BATNA does not have to be objectively "better" than the other party's BATNA to give one negotiating power. If a negotiator *believes* the range of possible negotiated outcomes of a particular transaction is inferior to the alternative of not reaching agreement, the negotiator may decide to quit the negotiation. This can cause the opposing party to question the range or advisability of his or her BATNA. Like a self-fulfilling prophecy, if a negotiator believes he or she has power within the negotiation because of available alternatives, then what the negotiator sees and hears in the negotiation tends to confirm that belief.[7] If a party is convinced that its BATNA is better than its opponent's, and that conviction is conveyed to the opponent, the party has increased its leverage in the negotiation.[8]

Time

Time plays a critical role in many negotiation situations, and Pareto's law, or the "80/20 rule," often applies. **Pareto's law** simply states that 80 percent of what is accomplished occurs as a result of 20 percent of the effort while the remaining 20 percent of what is accomplished takes 80 percent of the effort. In negotiation this often results in 80 percent of the deal being agreed to in the last 20 percent of the time spent in bargaining. Timing causes the chronological course of the negotiations and may force the negotiators to make the difficult decisions at the end because they are about to face the consequences of not reaching an agreement.

Negotiators who effectively use deadlines or careful timing can cause the last 20 percent of the time used to produce better results. For example, in the historic 1999 NBA negotiations between the owners and the player's union, the team owners had locked out the players in 1998, and several months of negotiations produced no progress. NBA commissioner David Stern set a deadline of January 7, 1999, after which he would be forced to cancel the season to provide the notice required by the league's contracts. On January 6, within only a few hours of the deadline, both sides reached agreement and season play resumed.[9]

In most negotiations both sides have some deadline or general preference as to when they would like or need to reach a settlement. Negotiators can use deadlines to their advantage.[10] Unless it is an initial union contract, in labor negotiations the deadline is almost always the date of the expiring contract. But even in those cases, the parties may be prepared to bargain past the point of the expired contract. Time and deadlines can favor either party and significantly alter the outcome of a negotiation.

Power

The third critical element is *power*. Patrick J. Cleary, former chair of the National Mediation Board, noted, "More than anything else—yes, even more than money—the negotiation process is about power, ego, leverage, and saving face."[11] *The most essential source of bargaining power in any negotiation is the ability to walk away.* A BATNA can determine who has more bargaining power in a negotiation. For example, in a 2002 negotiation of a collective bargaining agreement between the United Parcel Service (UPS) and the Teamsters, the Teamsters, by appointing Ken Hall as the lead negotiator, signaled that their best alternative to an unfavorable labor agreement was a strike. Why? In the prior contract talks, Hall helped lead the Teamsters to victory against UPS by staging a successful 16-day strike. The strike lasted three weeks and caused UPS to lose $750 million in revenue, and many longtime customers switched to its competitors Federal Express and DHL. Thus, in 2002, by appointing Ken as the renegotiation time neared, UPS experienced a decline in business as customers, fearing another strike, began using UPS's competitors. UPS could not afford another strike and needed a settlement quickly, giving the Teamsters significant leverage. The Teamsters were seeking major improvements, such as a 25 percent increase in wages for drivers and 50 percent for part-time workers, no reduction in health care or retirement benefits, converting 10,000 part-time jobs to full-time jobs, and a six-year agreement to provide job security. In a weak economic climate and while many employers were reducing health care and pension benefits in new contracts, the Teamsters were able to gain a historic contract because of its bargaining power.[12]

In contract negotiations management and labor need to understand the "**power balance**" that exists when they sit down to negotiate. For example, UAW president Ron Gettlefinger in 2007 was well aware of the fact that the U.S. Big Three automakers, GM, Ford, and Chrysler, had lost billions of dollars in recent years as well as invaluable market share. The union threatened strikes to show solidarity, but in reality realized the balance of power was not in their favor because the automakers all had excess plant capacity, months of inventory on dealer lots, and significant losses in recent years that seriously threatened their survival. The result was new agreements with the automakers that included two-tier wage rates that paid new workers at a rate of about half of the current workers. Only about ten years earlier, the power balance was reversed as the Big Three were experiencing record profits and sales and thus didn't want any loss of production because of strikes. At that time the UAW was able to negotiate historic job security provisions.

POWER BALANCE

External factors that affect the relative strength of the parties and the outcome of the negotiations.

These examples point out a critical aspect of power: It is situational, and the balance in many cases changes over time. Thus, negotiators who believe they clearly hold the power advantage year must also consider they may be on the other side in future years and thus not exploit their favorable balance. In addition, they must consider the value of maintaining a positive long-term relationship.

ETHICS IN NEGOTIATIONS

Ethics is the study of morality—the worth of moral judgments and principles of conduct that influence behaviors. A person's ethical belief system provides a basis for the **values** they develop. Values reflect a person's belief about "ends" to be achieved and about the "means" for achieving desired ends.[13] That is, they determine what one wants to accomplish and they determine what means one will be willing to use to reach that end.[14] In addition, adherence to particular values establishes behavioral rules. **Behavioral rules** are the accepted customs, standards, or models one expects of oneself in the conduct of one's life and what we expect of others with whom we interact. Thus, in a negotiation situation, a person's ethics, values, and behavior rules are important because they influence how each party views the other, how they evaluate the negotiation, and how they act during the negotiation.

In Western Civilization, three ethical theories have been used to describe alternate views of human nature, and have withstood the test of time. One ethical theory was developed by Aristotle (384–322 B.C.), a Greek philosopher, who believed that the inherent nature of human beings was "good."[15] And that no matter what the action, a human being's ultimate nature was to try to realize a truly *good* end. And, as it is inconsistent with "goodness" to use a "bad" means to achieve a good end, both the means used and the ends achieved must be "good." Aristotle promoted a *fairness* or justice approach to ethics, **ethics of purpose**. In labor negotiations the employer wants a contract it could afford and the employees want a contract that maximizes wages and benefits. Employees realize that if their employment contract is not affordable, the employer will go out of business and the employees will be unemployed. Employers realize as well that an unfair agreement will not foster the type of workplace that is good for business. The *means* the parties used to reach a fair and affordable contract is collective bargaining. If the parties conduct their bargaining under acceptable behavioral rules then, arguably, the means are good, even if the tactics that might be used at the table include concealment or posturing.

A second ethical theory was developed by Immanuel Kant (1724–1804), a German philosopher, who believed that each person could, by reasoning, recognize that one should treat each person as he or she wished to be treated. Therefore, human beings would devise rational rules of conduct by which to live. Any other approach would be inconsistent and irrational. Kant supported the classic rule of "do unto others as you would have them do unto you," **ethics of principle.** However, the rational thought process is complex. Two people may evaluate the same information and reach totally opposite conclusions because each receives and judges the information by using his own unique knowledge and experiences. Kant's theory relies upon a collective rationalization that establishes moral rules. Under Kant's theory, a negotiator who has manipulated information at the bargaining table has to ask himself or herself whether he/she would think the *other* side unethical if he or she withheld information at the bargaining table.

A third theory was developed by John Stuart Mills (1806–1873), an English philosopher and political economist, who believed that one could only judge the moral value of an action by its result. If an action benefits more people than it harms, then it is a moral action. Mill's utilitarianism suggested that ethical actions are those that provide the greatest balance of good over evil. Mill supported the theory that the "end justifies the means," **ethics of consequence**. Under Mill's theory if the employer and the employees reach agreement at the table, and both sides are satisfied by the results, then the tactics used at table were ethical. These three ethical theories can be summarized as follows:

Aristotle	Ethics of purpose	People are inherently **good** Will strive to reach a **good end** Will use **good means** to do so
Kant	Ethics of principle	People are inherently **rational** Will see the **right way** to do things Will pursue **rational means**
Mills	Ethics of consequence	People will determine **outcome of an action** Will do that which does the **most good** Will use **means necessary** to reach good end

With business ethics much in the news today, the topic of ethical tactics in negotiations has become a complex topic. As noted earlier, even philosophers disagree about the correct compass to use to measure our actions—can we reach good ends if the *means* are questionable? Do unto others, as we would have them *do unto us*? Or do the *ends justify the means*? Each of those measures requires subjective analysis, and people often disagree about what is good, right, or harmful. But even if parties know what's right, they may be motivated by self-interest to do otherwise. Self-interest, defined as pursuing an opportunity for private gain or avoiding personal loss or hardship, is a powerful motivator.[16] The essence of much bargaining involves persuasion—convincing the other side of what you will or will not agree to in order to reach an agreement. Since concealing your bottom line while still moving the negotiations forward may result in a better outcome for you, you have an incentive, or at least may be tempted, to use various misleading tactics. There is nothing unfair about such tactics if both of the parties to the negotiations understand that such tactics are a part of the process.

Often the ethical dilemmas in labor negotiations involve one or more of the following lapses in truth telling: (1) deception, (2) misrepresentation of one's position, (3) bluffing, and (4) falsification.[17]

Deception. In negotiations there are plenty of opportunities to deceive one another about the matters under negotiation. There are, however, disincentives to deceiving the other party to negotiations that also spring from self-interest. Opportunities for deception in negotiations about the matters under negotiation are greater when the *information disparity* between the parties is great. There is always some difference in the amount or type of information each party has when they begin a negotiation. If that difference is great, then unless the more knowledgeable party volunteers information, the other party might not know enough to ask the right questions. So through passive concealment, the more knowledgeable party can be deceptive. There is more opportunity for deception when the truth of the facts presented in the negotiations is *difficult to verify* by any objective standard. Other instances when deception is likely are when a party has *insufficient resources* to make the kind of inquiry necessary to verify information, when interaction is a *one-shot deal* so the time available to confirm information is limited, and when the intent to deceive is hard to establish.

Misrepresenting one's position. Another opportunity for unethical tactics in negotiations concerns concealing one's settlement preferences, that is, exactly what you will settle for in a given negotiation. There is a fundamental clash between moral theory and negotiations practice embodied in the settlement-issue deception.[18] While lying about one's bottom line is arguably unethical in many situations, it is a widely condoned negotiations strategy and considered "shrewd" when successful.

Bluffing. There is a significant opportunity for unethical behavior in negotiations when bluffing about future actions, that is, false representations embodied in threats and promises. Threats are often a part of traditional pressure bargaining, ranging from a threat to leave the bargaining table to threats on closing a business and laying off workers. Likewise, promises are often made during a

TABLE 5-1 Ethical and Unethical Bargaining Tactics

Appropriate Tactics	Marginal	Inappropriate Tactics
Gain information about opponent by asking associates and contacts	Make an unrealistically high or low first offer	Misrepresent factual information to support one's own position
Make an unrealistically high opening demand	Lead opponent to believe you are the only game in town, when you are not	Falsely threaten your opponent
Hide your real bottom line		Promise good things with no ability to deliver
Give false impression you aren't in a hurry to pressure your opponent		Bypass your opponent's negotiator to undermine opponent's confidence in him
		Gaining confidential information from your opponent

Source: Adapted from Roy J. Lewicki and Robert J. Robinson, "Ethical and Unethical Bargaining Tactics, An Empirical Study," in Carrie Menkel-Meadow and Michael Wheeler, eds., *What's Fair, Ethics for Negotiators* (San Francisco, CA: John Wiley & Sons, Inc., 2004), pp. 221–45.

negotiation to reach agreement. Deceptive threats and promises differ somewhat from those discussed earlier of either not offering information to the other party or concealing one's bottom line, because they are acts of commission. That is, a party affirmatively makes threats or promises that he or she does not intend to act upon in order to get the other party to concede something in the negotiations.

Falsification. Negotiation involves the exchange of information. False information leads to bad deals and it is bad for business. Unethical negotiating tactics may induce someone to reach an agreement to which he or she cannot be truly committed. Reluctant parties make undependable partners. Ethical negotiation, like good business, furthers and strengthens the relationships of the parties, giving value to all of the participants.[19]

Therefore, which common tactics of negotiation are generally considered appropriate and which inappropriate? The answer might be found in the results of two surveys in which M.B.A. students were asked to rate tactics used in a variety of negotiation settings and with differing levels of dishonesty, on perceived ethical appropriateness, and the likelihood they might use the tactic.[20] In both studies, the students generally agreed on the lists shown in Table 5-1.[21]

BARGAINING STRATEGIES

Collective bargaining generally involves one of two strategic approaches: distributive or integrative, both of which are discussed in this chapter. When considering which approach might be best for a given collective bargaining situation, and since none is the best for all situations, a negotiator should first review the issues just presented: information, timing, and power. Other significant factors to be considered include the specific issues to be negotiated, the people involved, and the general context of the negotiations. Of these, the specific issues are probably the most important.

If only one issue is likely to dominate the negotiation, such as wage increase, then distributive bargaining is more likely to be used because it is a "zero-sum" process. If there are multiple issues and a positive bargaining history between the parties, however, a more collaborative approach, such as integrative (sometimes called "win-win"), might be more appropriate. In actuality, most real-world labor negotiations have elements of both models but rely heavily on one or the other. The parties involved and their relationships are also key factors to be considered. If they have had an adversarial relationship in past negotiations and used distributive bargaining in the past, then it is highly likely they will use that approach again. If, however, the parties have no past relationship, or have a relationship that is generally open and honest, and multiple issues are involved, the integrative approach may be used and might help them negotiate a mutually beneficial settlement.[22] Finally, the general context of the negotiations may determine which model is used. In management–labor relations, for example, unless the two parties make a significant commitment to changing the way things have always been done, using other than the distributive model would be rare.

DISTRIBUTIVE BARGAINING

The negotiation model known today as distributive bargaining was first identified by R. E. Walton and R. B. McKersie in their seminal work on negotiation theory, *A Behavioral Theory of Labour Negotiations* (1965).[23] In their work they defined the differences between *distributive bargaining* and *integrative bargaining* (discussed in the next section) in the field of labor–management relations. Today the terms *distributive* and *integrative* are commonly used in all discussions of negotiation theories and practices. **Distributive bargaining** is a negotiation method in which two parties strive to divide a fixed pool of resources, such as money, each trying to maximize its share of the distribution. It is a "fixed-sum" game, and often the limited resource is termed a "fixed pie." It is also called a "zero-sum" process because the other party loses the amount gained by one party. For example, if a union realizes a $1,000 gain, then management realizes a $1,000 loss, and the sum of the two is zero. The most easily identified distributive examples for many people are the sale or purchase of a big-ticket item such as a house or car.[24] In such a purchase situation, the major factor is price, and funds are "distributed" between the two parties, and what one gains, the other loses.

DISTRIBUTIVE BARGAINING

A negotiation method described as a "win-lose" situation, in which resources are viewed as fixed and limited, and each side wants to maximize its share.

Negotiators need to be prepared to use distributive bargaining tactics successfully and be prepared to respond to them if the other side uses them because, for many people, distributive bargaining **is** negotiation. When hearing the word *negotiation*, the classic car-buying situation comes to mind: a single-deal negotiation in which only one issue is key—price, and both sides view it as a zero-sum game. Or collective bargaining comes to mind: a union seeking to share limited resources, such as the company's monetary assets, which can be used for a variety of purposes: new equipment or machinery, dividend payments, higher wages, and so on. Or a union hoping to fill available unfilled positions with new union members, so the process of deciding who is selected to be promoted or transferred can be the subject of distributive bargaining. Other noneconomic issues, such as the terms of seniority, employee grievance procedures, and plant rules, might be bargained in a distributive manner. Both labor and management often view any increase from the current contract as something to be gained at the negotiating table and as a loss to the other party. In distributive bargaining the fact that an issue is *framed* as a distribution by one party may cause the other to respond in a distributive manner.

Because many negotiators view any situation as distributive and therefore always use distributive strategies and tactics, one must be prepared to do likewise. And in labor–management collective bargaining, if the negotiators for one side choose to use a distributive bargaining process for each issue, it will be very difficult for those on the other side to not use a distributive process also.

Distributive bargaining is also referred to in general as "win-lose" bargaining because whatever one side gains is made at the expense of the other party. Thus, what is "won" by one is "lost" by the other. It is also referred to as "hard bargaining" because it is usually a highly competitive process designed to reach a formal written agreement, such as a labor agreement. The objective of the parties involved is to maximize their share of the fixed resource. Thus, each party may use a variety of tactics, including making threats, concealing their true objectives, misrepresenting information—or even lying, and using leverage or power if they perceive it is balanced in their favor. A common example in labor relations would be when management stages a lockout or a union threatens a strike when it perceives management could not afford the loss of production.

In general, the distributive bargaining model is identified by three components: (1) the parties involved largely view each other as *adversaries,* not necessarily away from the table, but still one party views the other as an opponent in the collective bargaining process at the table; (2) the objective of both parties is to *maximize their self-interest* or grab a larger "share of the pie"; and (3) they are *mostly concerned about the current negotiation* and interact with each other with a minimum concern for their past relationship and their future relationship. In collective bargaining, the reality is that both parties are well aware their future relationship is one of interdependence.[25] Thus, it is important to recognize that when they use the distributive model and bargain strictly as adversaries, they may suffer later when one or the other party takes the opportunity to "even the score" by filing numerous or frivolous grievances, subcontracting out work, or coming to the next round of contract talks with unrealistic demands.

When only one issue is involved, such as wages, the distributive bargaining process can best be explained by five key elements:

1. ***Target point.*** The most desired outcome or objective a negotiator sets for an issue, the target point, is the point at which the negotiator would prefer to end the negotiation, and would accept an offer.
2. ***Resistance point.*** The resistance point is a maximum or minimum beyond which the negotiator will not accept a proposal. This is the negotiator's bottom line (or reservation price).
3. ***Initial offer.*** This is the first number or offer the negotiator presents as a written formal proposal, which is accepted as reasonable starting point by the other side.
4. ***Settlement range.*** The difference between the resistance points of labor and management is the range in which actual bargaining occurs because anything outside the range will be quickly rejected by one party. This **settlement range** is also known as the **zone of possible agreement**, or ZOPA. In reality any point within the ZOPA may become the settlement value because all the points meet both the resistance points, for example, above a minimum price set by a seller, and below the maximum price set by a buyer.
5. ***Settlement point.*** The heart of negotiations is the process of reaching agreement on one point within the settlement range: the settlement point. The objective of each party is to achieve a settlement point as close as possible to its target point.[26]

SETTLEMENT RANGE

In the negotiation of a specific issue, this is the difference between the resistance points of labor and management, also known as the zone of possible agreement, because anything outside of the range would be clearly unacceptable to one side or the other.

THREE KEY STARTING VALUES When negotiating an issue of economic or numerical value, one very useful negotiating tactic is for the negotiator to decide three key values, or numbers, before starting the bargaining, to guide their actions; (1) target point, or the most **desired outcome**, or simply where you would like to end (settlement point); (2) resistance point, or **bottom line**—the absolute maximum or minimum value you will accept, and beyond which you will walkaway; (3) initial offer, or **opening offer**, which when "put on the table" with justification is viewed by the other side as the true first number—not a "lowball or highball" offer, and therefore sets one end of the settlement range. For example, in a wage negotiation the union negotiating team decided that it could not sell any wage cut to their members, and thus a wage increase of 0 was their bottom line. At the same time they decided an increase of 2 percent was the highest they could reasonably expect to achieve and therefore it became their desired outcome. The union chose 4.5 percent as their opening offer because it was the highest wage increase they could find a similar union had negotiated, and thus could be defended. Thus the union's three key values, decided before negotiations began, were 0, 2, 4.5.

Figure 5-2 illustrates an example of the distributive bargaining process. First, both sides develop and keep confidential their target and resistance points. Labor has surveyed its members, reviewed similar contracts recently negotiated, and estimated the company's financial situation. Within a generally favorable economic climate (which may allow higher wage increases), the labor negotiators set 4.5 percent as their wage rate target point but are willing to consider any offer above 3 percent, the resistance point, if the total package contains other economic benefits. They honestly believe that the members would vote against any contract with less than a 3 percent increase because inflation since the last negotiation has averaged 4 percent, and recent contracts in the industry have included raises between 3 and 5 percent. Management negotiators set their target point at 3 percent, the lowest increase negotiated by any of their competitors. The company president has authorized negotiators to

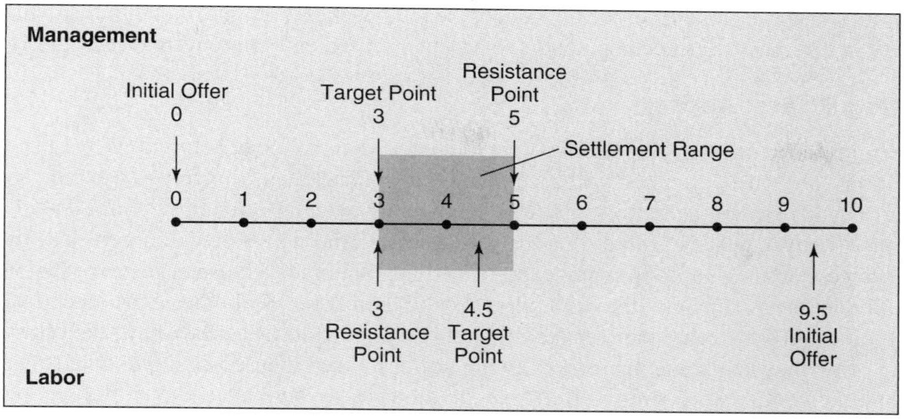

FIGURE 5-2 Distributive Bargaining Negotiation Model: First-Year Base Wage Increase (percentage)

accept an offer of up to 5 percent, the resistance point, if the total economic package is within a certain dollar amount.

Next, both sides choose their initial offers. Management decides that a proposed wage giveback (decrease in base wage) might be considered bad-faith bargaining because the company is in a reasonably good financial condition, so it initially offers a 0 percent increase, the lowest possible given the circumstances. Labor knows that no similar union has received more than 6 percent and therefore feels that 9.5 percent (just under double digits) is as high an initial offer as can be made within the context of good-faith bargaining. Both sides realize that their initial offers must be different from their target point to allow room for negotiation "give-and-take" while also staying within what the other side would consider a reasonable and good-faith offer. At the same time, both sides realize that the other side's initial offer has left them room to negotiate and is not their last, best, or final offer.

Negotiations between the two sides now center on the 0 to 9.5 percent range. Each side begins trying to convince the other to move from its initial offer. Neither side knows the target or resistance point of the other side. Both sides will, however, through bargaining table discussion, begin to estimate the target and resistance points of the other side to determine if a settlement range exists and therefore a settlement point can be found. At the same time, each side strives to convince the other of the validity of its own position. By presenting factual information such as company records, copies of recent contracts, and industry data—as well as persuasive information such as employee survey data—negotiators hope to influence the perceptions of the other party. Management may try to convince labor that to remain competitive and avoid layoffs, the company cannot afford an expensive settlement and is willing to take a strike if necessary.

Labor may try to convince management of the members' determination to negotiate a high increase and their willingness to put on a successful strike. Eventually, both sides believe that they know, indirectly or directly, the other side's resistance point. For example, management might state, "We will seriously consider an offer under 5 percent if the total package is right," or labor might indicate, "Our members know that no other local has settled for less than 3 percent." Now the negotiations center on the settlement range; both sides realize there are many possible settlement points within the range.

Now the "hard" bargaining begins. Within the 2 percent settlement range, each side carefully proposes a settlement point that, especially when wages are considered, may include other economic items in a package. And, most important, each negotiator is careful to propose only a settlement that he or she is prepared to accept. Within this range any offer might be accepted if both sides have a settlement point. Once the settlement point has been proposed and accepted, it is too late to "hold out for a little more."

The settlement point is finally reached when one side achieves its target point or when both are willing to accept something less than their target points but within the settlement range.

Factors such as the arguments of the other side, the total package, fatigue, or belief that "this is the best we can do" may influence negotiators to accept a settlement different from their target point.

Opening Offers: Anchors

The opening offers on an issue effectively set the outer limits of the bargaining. Why? In contract negotiations, obviously no union will accept less than management's opening offer, and no management negotiator will agree to more than the union's opening offer. Just as in a buyer–seller situation, no buyer will pay more than the asking price, and no seller will accept less than the buyer's lowest offer. Therefore, many experienced negotiators often prefer to make the opening offer and then try to "anchor" the discussion around their offer. Still other experienced negotiators prefer to have the other party make the first opening offer. Once they have the other side's opening offer, they can adjust their own opening offer to keep their desired outcome somewhere in the middle of the two opening offers. Negotiation researchers have shown that people irrationally fixate on the first number put on the table in a negotiation, and thus the offer becomes an **anchor** for the following negotiations, regardless of how arbitrary it may be. In fact, even when people know the anchor has little or no relevance, it still influences their decision making.

ANCHOR

An opening offer, often a number, and not necessarily a realistic number, that can influence the parties' assessment of the zone of possible agreement in the negotiation.

The curious phenomenon of anchoring is illustrated in Figure 5-3, "The Power of Random Numbers." Experienced negotiators know that the first offer on the table, especially in situations

With the spin of the wheel a number is selected purely at random. *Source:* Photos.com/ JupiterImages.

In an experiment on the effects of anchoring, Daniel Kahneman and Amos Tversky spun a wheel marked with random integers ranging from 0 to 100. Participants were then asked whether they thought that the percentage of UN member countries that were from Africa was greater than or less than the number just spun on the wheel. Participants were then asked for their best estimate of the proportion of UN member countries that were from Africa.

For one group of the subjects, the wheel stopped at 10. The vast number of these subjects said that the proportion of the UN member countries that were from Africa was more than 10 percent; on average, they guessed that the actual percentage was 25 percent.

For another group of the subjects, the wheel stopped at 65. Almost all of these participants said that the proportion of the UN member countries that were from Africa was less than 65 percent. In contrast to the first group, this group's average guess was that 45 percent of UN member countries were from Africa.

The only difference between the two experimental conditions was the number on the wheel, yet the groups' best estimates differed by 20 percentage points! The purely random number the subjects were given by the wheel dramatically—and irrationally—anchored their assessments.

FIGURE 5-3 The Power of Random Numbers. *Source:* Adapted from Daniel Kahneman and Amos Tversky, *Negotiation 7*, no. 9 (2004), p. 10.

of great uncertainty, can substantially influence the other party's perception of the ZOPA, and thus the outcome of the negotiation. Remember that in fact there are two ZOPAs because each side estimates the ZOPA based on its own resistance point, and the resistance point each party guesses has been set by the other party. Thus, if an opening offer causes the other party to change its perceived ZOPA, then it has anchored the bargaining in a most effective manner. Negotiators often make opening offers, with one of three types of anchors:[27]

1. ***Facts***: Statement of what is presented to be a fact: Example: "Our offer is based on this list of other industry contracts settled in this region; the lowest wage increase in the past year was 3.5 percent."
2. ***Extreme offer***: Example: "We believe our officers are special public servants who put their lives on the line every day and thus deserve a 10 percent wage increase this year."
3. ***Precedent***: Example: "In the past 30 years, management has always, every time, agreed to retroactivity as a ground rule; we expect you to honor this practice."

Once the opening offers are made, the real haggling process, often called bracketing, occurs. **Bracketing** is the process of moving toward a middle point between the opening offers (or brackets), which is the logical bargaining process.[28] Consider, for example, the negotiation described in Figure 5-4, "Grievance Settlement." Management and union representatives both want to negotiate the settlement of an employee's grievance involving discharge and reinstatement, and they have verbally agreed to a onetime payment; the amount, however, is the issue to be negotiated. The union made an opening offer of $12,500, and management responded with an opening offer of $7,500. The two sides then begin bargaining in the bracket range between the opening offers ($7,500 and $12,500). Thus, in general, a negotiator may "bracket" its initial offer, or initial counter, which is equal distance away from their desired objective as the offer made by the other party. So if the other person makes the first offer, a good response strategy is to bracket the negotiation and possibly end up splitting the difference, as is often the case, and therefore getting your desired objective. Some negotiators, when they feel bracketing might work, therefore, want the other party to make the first offer so they can bracket the negotiation. Realtors when counseling clients commonly apply bracketing.

BRACKETING

The process of moving toward a middle point between the opening offers (or brackets), which is the logical bargaining process.

For example, a house is listed for $370,000 and potential buyers ask their agent, "What offer should we make?" They already told the agent they don't want to go over $350,000 on any house. The agent responds, "Offer them $330,000, and let's hope they counter with $360,000 and then you can counter with $350,000."

DESIRED OUTCOME STRATEGY In the Figure 5-4 example, if management's desired outcome or target point is to settle for no more than $9,000, then instead of an initial offer of $7,500, they should have made a more extreme opening offer of $5,500, creating a midpoint of $9,000. Why? By keeping their desired value, $9,000, in the middle of the two offers that are on the table, it is far

FIGURE 5-4 Grievance Settlement Negotiation

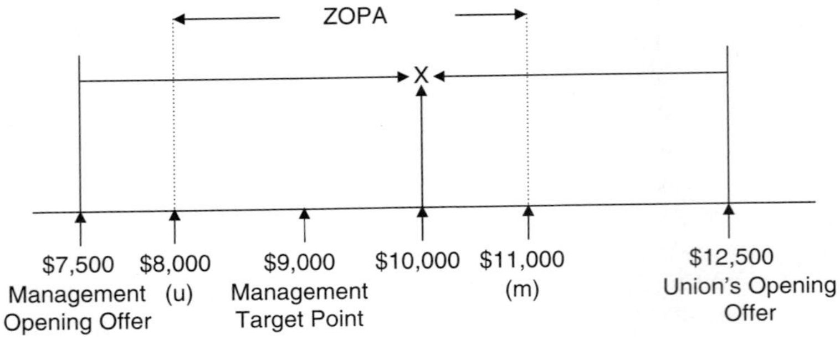

X, negotiated price; u, union's resistance point; m, management's resistance point

Summary of negotiation:

Union's initial offer: $12,500
Management's initial offer: $7,500
Union's resistance point (u): $8,000
Management resistance point (m): $11,000
Zone of possible agreement (ZOPA): $8,000–$11,000
Union's counteroffer: $11,000
Management counteroffer: $ 9,250
Union's second counteroffer: $10,000
Management accepted and thus negotiated final value: $10,000

more likely to become the settlement point, or very close to it! To best utilize the desired outcome strategy management will continue to make counter offers that keep $9,000 exactly in the middle. In collective bargaining, the key "number" in negotiations is often the percentage wage increase. Both union and management negotiators often carefully choose an opening offer that will create a bracket that contains what they believe is a middle range that includes their target point or most desired outcome. For example, if management's desired outcome is a 3 percent wage increase, and in negotiations the union's opening offer is a 6 percent increase, then management might make an opening offer of 0 percent, thus creating a midpoint of 3 percent. However, if the union had opened with an 8 percent offer, management might have responded with a concessionary opening offer of 2 percent to create the midpoint of 3 percent. Then, whatever counter offer the union makes, management will counter with a number that keeps 3 percent as the midpoint of the range of the offers on the table.

RESISTANCE POINT

The maximum or minimum beyond which a negotiator will not accept a proposal—a bottom line.

Both sides have also decided their **resistance point**; the union will not accept less than $8,000—which is the minimum they have decided and if offered any lower amount they will take the case to the next step, arbitration. Management decided $11,000 is their resistance point, or absolute limit to resolve the grievance, or they will ask for arbitration. Obviously, in most negotiations, both sides do not reveal their resistance points. The distance between the two therefore becomes the ZOPA because any agreed-to final price will be between the two points because they are the limits each party has determined.

The final, negotiated settlement point (X) usually is a point approximately in the middle of the two opening offers (if both sides accept the other's opening offer as reasonable) because although the opening offers are known, the resistance points have not been revealed. In this example, the midpoint is $10,000. If the final point is larger than the midpoint, say $11,000, then the union may perceive a "negotiated gain" of $3,500, and management a "negotiated gain" of only $1,500. Why? The union has haggled for $3,500 more than the management's opening offer, but management only realized a $1,500 drop from the union's opening offer. Neither wants to realize a smaller negotiated gain than the other side, and thus both sides often try to move to the midpoint.

A critical mistake some novice negotiators make is to fail to make an opening offer that does not place their desired outcome near the midpoint, for fear of offending the other party. Then if the other party makes concessions and demands roughly equal reciprocal concessions, it becomes very difficult to achieve. The best strategy for an opening offer may be to allow for adequate negotiating room between the two initial positions by setting an opening offer, which both anchors a minimum position and provides an acceptable midpoint. When making such an offer, however, a negotiator must prepare a supportive argument to give the offer creditability, or else it may be ignored by the other side and thus not function as an anchor. A strong defense of an initial offer can achieve two objectives: (1) it convinces the other party that the offer has merit, and (2) it begins to call into question the credibility of the other party's opening offer. A labor negotiator, for example, may begin to question the union's position and thus be more willing to move toward management's opening offer.[29]

If a negotiator must give the first opening offer, or choose to do so for strategic reasons, then they should choose *the most extreme offer, which can logically be defended* and then carefully gauge the reaction to the offer. Perhaps the worst scenario of an opening offer is when the other side quickly accepts the offer immediately. This situation is, again, the **winner's curse**: The offer is accepted, but the party is "cursed" with worry over why the offer was accepted so quickly without even one counteroffer.

WINNER'S CURSE

Negotiators who accept an offer too quickly and later experience remorse because they believe that (true or not) even though they left value on the table (gave too much or too little).

NORMS Once the two parties have exchanged initial offers, as in the grievance settlement example just presented, and each party has determined its reservation point and its initial offer, they are presented with the issue of how to arrive at a value somewhere in the range between the two initial offers, \$7,500 and \$12,500. This situation represents the basic distributive bargaining question: How to *distribute* the possible gain available to both parties? How does each negotiator proceed? What motivates them to make a particular counteroffer or accept/reject a counter offer made by the other party?

The parties negotiating this deal are trying to convince the other side as to the value of the offer being made. *Source:* AP Images.

Negotiations seldom take place in a vacuum, but instead they are often guided by social **norms** and accepted practices that are based on the context of the situation. The two negotiators in this situation might proceed according to one or more common norms, which, research and practice indicate, will most likely guide their behavior. Four common **negotiation norms** that might influence their behavior include (1) relational norms, (2) fairness norms, (3) reciprocity, and (4) good faith norm. Figure 5-5 provides a summary of each norm and the basis on which a negotiator develops and reacts to a proposal.

NEGOTIATION NORMS

Social beliefs or attitudes that affect one's behavior in a negotiation, such as a relational norm that values the relationship between the parties, a fairness norm that seeks consistency or equality, a reciprocity norm that reacts in kind to an action, and a good-faith norm that values integrity, honesty, and willingness to compromise.

RELATIONAL NORM In a negotiation situation, the parties may be involved in a pure "exchange" relationship, such as a onetime car purchase, in which there was no prior purchase or relationship between the parties and no future one expected. The parties are only concerned with maximizing their outcomes in this instance. However, in reality, in most bargaining situations the parties involved do have a "communal" relationship: They are coworkers, family, friends, neighbors, or management and a union who recognize they have a continuing interrelated workplace relationship. The collective bargaining relationship rests upon iterative social processes, and the parties recognize the value of their relationship—and thus may be hesitant to exploit each other's vulnerabilities. This critical relationship creates a cycle that starts with a high level of trust which causes both sides to consider an expanded scope of possibilities to settle thorny issues. This high-trust relational norm is critical to successful "win-win" bargaining processes, and any violation of the trust can easily lead to a very difficult "win-lose" bargaining behaviors.[30] This desire is referred to as a **relational norm** and can easily cause tension between a negotiator's desire to maximize outcomes and a desire to maintain a positive relationship. Relational norms can cause

FIGURE 5-5 How Norms May Affect Counteroffers. *Source:* Adapted from Michael R. Carrell and Christina Heavrin, *Negotiating Essentials* (Upper Saddle River, NJ: Pearson/Prentice Hall, 2008), p. 64.

Norm	*Negotiator's Use of the Norm*
Relational	Desires to maintain a positive long-term relationship. Especially important in most labor–management relationships.
Fairness	**1. Equality** Evenly splits the difference between opening offers (50–50). The union, for example, proposed a new provision for shift differential equal to $1/hour. Management responds with an initial offer of .20/hour, and they agree on .60/hour, evenly dividing the .80/hour difference.
	2. Equity Split the difference between offers based on proportional inputs. For example, a profit-sharing proposal includes 60 percent net gain in productivity to be divided among the bargaining unit members because a study of productivity found that labor accounted for 60 percent of the gain, and capital and equipment 40 percent.
	3. Need Splits the difference between offers based on proportional needs of the parties.
	4. Status Quo Leaves the current situation unchanged. Many contract provisions are not changed during the negotiation of a new agreement because the impetus to keep current language, especially if it is working, is great.
Reciprocity	Responds to a counteroffer or action with one of equal value. For example, the union has increased its health insurance copay offer by $5, and thus management responds with a $5 decrease in the proposed copay.
Good-Faith	Negotiators will (1) honor and not retract an offer, (2) meet and discuss issues, (3) make sincere proposals, (4) provide copies of any data or information used during negotiations and share sources of information.

negotiators to overlook maximum outcomes in favor of suboptimal or less efficient trades that are considered important in providing a more positive long-term relationship.

Why is the relationship norm important? Too often people, especially novice negotiators, view a negotiation situation in a purely exchange mode or as a onetime interaction, without regard for the future relationship between the parties. Therefore, their objective is "winning at all costs" or maximizing the gain in a purely distributive bargaining context. This onetime "car-buying" situation may be valid in many negotiation situations, but in many other situations it is not a valid assessment because the parties do have an important future relationship. Two major changes in the past 20 years have contributed to the increase of negotiations in which relationships are important. First, because work organizations have fewer levels between top management and entry-level jobs, bargaining unit employees are often given greater decision-making autonomy, and thus they are increasingly empowered to negotiate work issues with others within the organization. Second, organizations have become more inclined to develop partnerships with suppliers and other outside organizations, and therefore they are more inclined to maintain a long-term relationship. Thus, between union and management, the relationship norm is more important for the following reasons:[31]

1. Future negotiations with the same party should be anticipated; therefore negotiators seek to avoid harming the future relationship between the parties. Thus, the relationship norm affects the negotiation outcomes.
2. People usually expect negotiated "favors" to be repaid at a later date.
3. Trust is critical to a long-term relationship; thus, agreements must include less nit-picking, what-ifs, or contingency clauses and a higher level of trust.

FAIRNESS NORM The negotiation process involves one of human nature's most basic psychological drives: a need to maintain an appearance of consistency and fairness in both words and deeds (see Figure 5-5). Psychologists call this need to appear reasonable "the consistency principle."

Negotiations of all types provide many situations in which people seek consistency owing to the high level of uncertainty. The use of a norm to provide consistency in a bargaining situation can give a negotiator what is called "normative leverage." If negotiators correctly anticipate the other party's norm and therefore frame their proposal within that context, they can gain an advantage.[32] Negotiation researchers have concluded that the fairness norm may be the most commonly employed norm. It includes four major forms: (1) the **equality norm**, which negotiators often call the "50–50" or "split the difference"; it certainly sounds fair because both sides gain an equal amount. However a 50–50 split may not be fair unless the initial offers were equally fair to both parties, which is highly unlikely; (2) the **equity norm** or a distribution based on the proportional input of the parties: Employees compare the ratio of their own organizational rewards/efforts to the perceived ratios of other employees' rewards/efforts where rewards include pay, recognition, bonuses, and so on, and efforts include level of work, hours, ideas, and so on. If they perceive the ratios are roughly equal, then they experience feelings of equity or job satisfaction. However, if they perceive the ratio is unequal, they feel unfairly treated by the employer and usually seek to balance the ratio by either increasing the rewards received or, more likely, reducing their efforts or level of work, or even seeking another job; (3) the **need norm**, which can be a powerful social norm—for example, a union may stress the need of their members to receive a pay increase that equals recent increases in cost of living to maintain their living standard; and (4) **maintaining the status quo**, or keeping all significant issues in their current state. This fairness norm of maintaining the status quo is often employed by labor negotiators and arbitrators.[33] Many labor negotiations, for example, leave provisions of the expiring contract unchanged and only change a few key ones. It's not always assumed that the status quo is fair, but if it was accepted and used once, then it may be acceptable to both parties. And sometimes, it's easier not to change than to reach an agreement on a change.

Most negotiators expect the other side to act with fairness in both words and actions. *Source:* Stocklite/ Shutterstock.

Note that the common use of fairness norms in negotiations should not be confused with what is the "right," "best," or "fairest" solution. A fairness norm or any other norm is simply an external standard that people often employ to support their proposals or guide them in negotiations. However, the effective use of norms may provide a very convincing argument in support of a proposal and enable negotiators to convince the other side of the validity of their position.

Using norms or other justifications of proposals does not always provide negotiators with a means of reaching the desired outcome. Reasonable people can use different norms and facts to reach different solutions. However using norms or standards can assist negotiators in their efforts to reach an agreement in at least three ways: (1) making decisions based on a norm such as fairness is easier than making decisions on offers that are randomly tossed out; (2) an offer based on a norm is more persuasive than an arbitrary number, and thus more likely to receive serious consideration; and (3) it is easier to agree to the other party's offer if it is based on a norm because you are agreeing to a principle, not a pressure tactic.[34] For example, would a negotiator find it easier to agree to "That is my final offer, it's what I want, and I don't have to explain it!" or " I can't agree to increase the uniform allowance anymore; it provides for the purchase of two new uniforms per year as well as weekly cleaning, which is what is needed."

RECIPROCITY NORM The tendency to respond to the actions of others with equal or similar actions is the source of the reciprocity norm. Someone who believes that "an eye for an eye" is the most reasonable response to another party is practicing the reciprocity norm. In social relationships, such as negotiations, people are often governed by "rules of reciprocity" meaning they seek to minimize the difference between the benefits they provide others, and the benefits received from others.[35] The underlying cause of this norm is a person's *sense of obligation*—people often feel a strong need to respond in kind when they are given something of value from someone else—even a negotiator! For example, a union negotiator who drops her wage increase offer by 0.5 (one-half) percent may expect or even demand that management to counter with a 0.5 percent higher offer.[36]

GOOD-FAITH BARGAINING NORM In labor negotiations, good-faith bargaining is mandated as a part of the collective bargaining process by the National Labor Relations Act. The act requires the representatives of labor and management to meet at reasonable times and confer in *good faith* on wages, benefits, hours, and working conditions. This requirement includes active participation with an intention to reach an agreement and to sign binding agreements on mutually acceptable terms. It does not, however, require either party to make a concession or agree to a proposal. The **good-faith bargaining norm** is, however, a part of most negotiations. Parties expect certain behaviors from those who they are negotiating with such as (1) honoring what they propose in bargaining, not retracting an offer once made and accepted, and signing written agreements reached at the bargaining table; (2) willingness to meet at reasonable times and places to discuss issues; (3) making proposals on the issues at hand; (4) engaging in a process of give-and-take or compromise; and (5) providing honest information and, if necessary, sharing sources of information. A negotiator's greatest asset in a negotiation is integrity because few parties will continue to meet with someone they no longer trust to be negotiating in good faith. Without such trust the parties cannot expect to reach an agreement, or if one is reached, may fear it will not be implemented as negotiated. For example, in one recent negotiation, management offered the union the exact amount of back pay the union had requested in its last offer. The union negotiator, however, surprised by the offer and fearing he may have asked for too little, turned it down, and said, "We've decided our numbers were wrong!" Management negotiators saw the rejection as bad-faith bargaining, and withdrew the offer. Unfortunately, in most negotiation situations, reasonable people can disagree as to exactly what behaviors define good faith. Thus, one party may feel the other has violated its rules of good-faith bargaining, and tempers rise or discussions are prematurely terminated.

FRAMING POSITIONS The issues have been identified, initial offers have been made, and now the parties attempt to persuade each other in an effort to maximize their gains. One way to do that is to "frame" each issue (or group of issues) carefully, using a norm or other justification to support a certain position. That is, decide exactly how the issue will be presented to the other side in a context that is convincing. **Framing** is recognized as a key tactic in the negotiation process.

FRAMING

Presenting an issue to the other side in a negotiation in a way that is convincing and causes the other side to "see" the proposal in a different light.

People often view the same issue quite differently, especially when they sit across from each other in negotiations. They naturally bring different perspectives, expectations, biases, and experiences to the table. So how should an issue be framed to persuade the other party to accept it? One can frame an issue in a *slanted manner*, one that puts their position in the best possible light: "A fair wage increase is 6 percent because that is what others have received over the past two years"; or in a *nonjudgmental manner*, which states the issue as a question and invites the parties to search for a solution: "How can we objectively estimate a wage increase?" This method of framing is less antagonistic and moves discussions toward a process of creative problem solving if both parties are open to using it.[37] It is extremely effective in solving the underlying problems of language, issues such as seniority, overtime distribution, or shift selection. Four different types of frames that one can consider using when presenting a proposal are described in Table 5-2.

The framing of an issue can greatly affect the outcome of the bargaining. Even a one-word change can significantly alter how both sides view the issues. For example, in the negotiations between two unions to merge the union employees of two organizations, the parties were reviewing the list of people. In some cases only one person could be retained at the salary and in position now held by two. In the case of one position, a negotiator stated, "Now in thinking about Taylor, he is too valuable not to keep in the foreman job." The second negotiator who wanted his own person in that position needed to quickly reframe the issue of Taylor and repeated the statement with a one-word insertion, "In thinking about Taylor, he *thinks* he is too valuable not to keep him in the foreman job!" The issue of Taylor's worth in the new organization was totally changed from fact to only his lofty opinion of himself by a one-word change in the framing.

REFRAME OFFERS One effective method of reframing an issue is to use a "unifying, open-ended, and problem-solving suggestion" starting with a "what-if" or "how." For example, "How can the employees' desire to honor their seniority standing when assigning overtime and the companies need for efficiency and productivity guide the overtime distribution language?"

TABLE 5-2 Four Types of Frames (Applied to Grievance Settlement)

Type of Frame	Goal of union's approach to framing the issue	In response to management's initial position: "The union's request of $12,000 is too high . . ."
Reframing	Change management's context from a cost decision to an employee morale decision.	Union: "Other employees are very interested in how management handles this case; the outcome will certainly affect morale!"
Focus frame	Change management's context from a cost decision by focusing on the uniqueness of the grievance.	Union: "This is the only grievance of its kind in the past 50 years, and we both know there will never be another."
Contrast frame	Change management's context from a single payment of $12,000 to a much smaller, monthly stipend.	Union: "If we agree to add the amount to his base pay over 12 months, then your concern of his salary becoming the highest in the department is resolved."
Negative frame	Change management's context from winning to avoiding a loss.	Union: "You can wait to decide—but if we don't come to agreement, then the union's grievance committee will meet next week to decide if the issue should go to arbitration."

Source: Adapted from David Venter, "Framing—An Important Negotiation Tool," *The Negotiator Magazine* (March 2006), p. 1.

This statement brings together or unifies the positions of the two parties into an open-ended suggestion that focuses the discussion on finding a solution to the joint problem.

The value of two offers can be identical, but the manner in which they are framed or worded can substantially affect how they are received and thus possibly accepted. For example, in a research study people were asked to choose between two plans of action when three plants were scheduled to be closed and 6,000 employees laid off:

Plan A: This plan will save one of the three plants and 2,000 jobs.

Plan B: This plan has a one-third probability of saving all three plants and all 6,000 jobs but has a two-thirds probability of saving no plants and no jobs.

Then they were asked to choose between Plan B (same wording) and Plan C:

Plan C: This plan will result in the loss of two of the three plants and 4,000 jobs.

The two pairs of choices contained the exact same values or facts—plans A and C both will save only one plant of the three, and 2,000 of 6,000 jobs. Yet 80 percent of the people in the study choose Plan A in the first set of options, but then 80 percent chose Plan B in the second set. The only difference was the positive framing of Plan A compared with the negative framing of Plan C.[38]

Negotiators should, whenever possible, not simply reject an opponent's offer, but instead *reframe* it or literally "change the frame around the picture" so it satisfies the interests of both parties.

Use of Framing Questions

Negotiators can use framing statements, as just discussed, when presenting offers, or they can use framing questions to change the context of an offer made by the other party. Examples of effective reframing questions include the following:[39]

- ***Ask why:*** Instead of treating your opponent's offer as an adversarial position, use it as an opportunity to better understand his or her interest or to test the firmness of the position.

For example, "Why did you choose that exact number?" or "Why are you so determined to settle on that number; where did it come from?" A powerful "why" question can invoke the fairness norm: "Why is that health care copay fair?" Even if the other party refuses to defend the fairness of their number directly, the very fact it cannot be easily defended can insert in their mind a strong doubt in their own position, and thus make it easier to achieve a concession.

- ***Ask why not:*** If your opponent will not reveal the source of his or her position, asking "why not" can help uncover the real interests of the other party. For example; "Why not simply divide the difference equally?" or "Why not change the retirement fund assumptions and see what figure the actuary gives us?" The answer to your question may reveal important information about the true interests of the other party.
- ***Ask what if:*** Instead of disagreeing with the offer of the other party, acknowledge it, and respond with an option. For example, "I understand you believe you must have a 6 percent wage increase. What if we agreed to that figure, but to help pay for it, health care premiums and copays were changed?"
- ***Ask for advice:*** If asked in a constructive manner, the other party may develop an option that represents positive movement toward a settlement. For example; "How would you suggest I present that offer to top management when their past policy restricts us from offering a contract beyond one year?" or "I can agree to your wage increase, if you can find a way to cover our health insurance." Opponents often appreciate the opportunity to help develop mutually agreeable options, and once involved, they may even develop a sense of ownership in the options suggested and thus help one of them become a settlement point.

Effective questioning and listening to responses is a critical negotiation skill. In the alternative, if negotiators spend more time arguing for their positions and defending their stance on issues than they do asking questions, they cannot gain important insights into the implicit needs and concerns of the other party, and therefore cannot respond with proposals that are likely to reach a settlement. Effective use of questions can break a pattern of arguing for and against positions and move negotiations into conversations that uncover the true interests of the parties, and therefore potential positive outcomes. Disagreement on how overtime assignments are made is a typical collective bargaining issue in which such questioning might be helpful. In this example, employees in separate work areas share the same job title with similar job requirements. They do not want to be shifted from their assigned areas to cover for absent coworkers and have had a contract that limits such movement. This results in increased overtime costs for the employer because when workers are absent and those on duty cannot be moved, off-duty workers must be called in to cover the work. Management assumed the union had this provision in its contract as a way to maximize overtime pay; but the effective use of questions by both sides may uncover a different motivation. For example, the employees might object to being moved to a different location because although they may hold similar jobs, they question if they can, in fact, do the other job well; or they may believe the other work location has a more rigid schedule that could cause discipline problems. Uncovering these concerns could give management a way to address them during the negotiations, such as providing remedial training before moving a worker from one location to another, or by changing the hours of work where necessary to avoid tardiness.

Applying Norms and Frames

Applying the norms and framing just discussed to the grievance settlement illustrated in Figure 5-4 shows how a negotiation can progress from its opening offers to agreement. The union made an opening offer of $12,500, and management made an opening offer of $7,500. Each party then decided, but kept confidential, its bottom line or reservation point. The union decided they could accept a minimum of $8,000 or they would take the case to arbitration. Management decided their absolute limit was $11,000, and thus the range of possible settlement amounts, or zone of possible agreement (ZOPA), became $8,000–$11,000, although neither side could know the range because both didn't know the other party's reservation point. Management made a first offer of $7,500, so it is likely that the union would make the first counteroffer. If the union used the "good-faith bargaining norm" and decided to show a willingness for give-and-take by making a counteroffer of $11,000, and frame the offer with; "We are very pleased that management is willing to settle this unique grievance rather than go to arbitration. To try and resolve the issue today, we are willing to come down $1,500–$11,000." The management negotiators realize that $11,000 is their reservation price, and if they are particularly anxious to close the deal and avoid arbitration, or perhaps if they are inexperienced negotiators, they might agree to $11,000. But they likely would rely on the "equality fairness norm" and offer to split the difference evenly of $3,500 ($11,000–$7,500) and thus offer $9,250. They would decide to make this counteroffer because it is an equal sacrifice by both parties and it's not a round number and it is based on a defensible position, which makes them more comfortable in offering it to the union. Because the new counteroffer of $9,250 is higher than their reservation price, the union might accept it if the grievant was significantly motivated to settle. Or, the union might decide that because management has only made one counteroffer, they have not made their "highest and final offer," and thus the union offers to make a second, but smaller concession of $1,000. At this point management might agree to the union's second counter of $10,000 and thus close the negotiation. Both parties will likely believe they have negotiated a "good deal." The union gained $2,500 over management's opening offer and realized $2,000 more than its reservation price. Management also perceived they gained because the final price was $2,500 less than the union's opening offer, and they paid $1,000 less than their own reservation price.

INTEGRATIVE BARGAINING

The integrative bargaining technique, like the distributive technique, was largely developed within the field of collective bargaining and labor negotiations. Today it has evolved into a popular alternative to distributive bargaining. Integrative bargaining is a more cooperative approach to negotiation or conflict resolution. It is often referred to as a "win-win," "mutual-gains," or "interest-based" approach. Unfortunately, the term "win-win" today has become a cliché in our society, and thus it may refer to any collaborative approach. The integrative approach, like distributive bargaining, involves making concessions to reach an agreement, but in addition, it involves searching for mutually profitable options and logical trade-offs. It is also called an "expanded-pie approach" (in comparison with the distributive *fixed-pie* approach) because negotiators search for better proposals than the obvious ones that might only meet their own interests. Integrative techniques include a clear understanding of the issues, open sharing of information, and the joint exploration of solutions that benefit both parties.[40] In an integrative bargaining process, the parties generally cooperate to achieve maximum total benefit of the final agreement while also competing to divide the value of the package.

The essence of the integrative process is described in the classic story of two sisters who each coveted the same, and last, orange. They decided to share it and used the distributive tactic of splitting it into halves. After each sister took half of the orange home, one sister, who wanted only the juice, squeezed out the juice, drank it, and threw out the peel. The other sister, who only wanted the peel for a cake she was baking, threw out the pulp and added her half peel to the cake batter. Neither sister considered expressing her *true interest* in the orange but rather chose to negotiate for the whole orange. Both sisters would have realized a greater settlement—one sister all of the juice, the other all of the peel, if only they had chosen to be open and truthful about their real interests.

INTEGRATIVE BARGAINING

A negotiation method in which both sides seek ways to integrate the interests of both sides into mutually agreeable options.

Integrative bargaining can be broadly defined as a negotiating process in which the parties strive to *integrate their interests* as effectively as possible in the final agreement. The integrative negotiator generally strives to achieve two goals: (1) to *create* as much value as possible for both sides, and (2) to *claim* as much value as possible for their own interests. It does not require a negotiator to give in to any demands made by the other party or to sacrifice any of their own objectives. It does require the parties to seek out creative options and not simply focus on trading concessions on issues. It generally requires the existence of several issues to be negotiated, which enables the negotiators to find common ground on some issues, trade-off positions on some issues, and claim value on some issues. To create value and discover mutual benefits or common ground on some issues requires the parties to share information and present more options than is typical of distributive bargaining.[41]

Integrative versus Distributive Bargaining

The integrative bargaining process differs from the distributive process in many aspects, although neither are rigid concepts, and therefore in practice a negotiator might use aspects of both in a given negotiation. However it is helpful to recognize that the two methods begin with distinctly different strategies. In distributive bargaining both sides view their own goals as being in direct conflict with those of the other side. Thus, whatever one side gains, the other side loses, on each issue. The negotiators approach each issue as a "fixed pie." Thus, the larger one piece is, the smaller the other. Each side wants to maximize its share of the resources, or pie. Generally all the negotiators involved are prepared to use distributive bargaining because many negotiators use the method, and if one side uses it exclusively, then the other is usually forced to adopt it as well. Negotiators who wish to triumph over the other party or maximize their outcome at all costs often choose the distributive or "win-lose" approach. In negotiations involving lawyers, and the majority of lawsuits is resolved through negotiation and not the courts, distributive bargaining is often the method utilized. Lawyers either through training or choice, or both, often believe they can gain more for their clients by using distributive tactics rather than through integrative tactics. Their legal training is focused on the "win-lose" thinking of conflict resolution. Lawyers will focus more on improving options away from the table and/or utilizing social norms to gain an advantage. Thus one lawyer advises other lawyer-negotiators to think of distributive bargaining as the "cake" and integrative bargaining as the "frosting"—rather than the reverse as many skilled negotiators believe![42] In integrative bargaining, both parties begin with a spirit of collaboration and seek to identify mutual gain options, or "an expansion of the pie," as well as a gain in their share of the resources. To help recognize the differences, consider the factors and common strategies of the two methods in Table 5-3.

TABLE 5-3 Common Differences between Distributive and Integrative Bargaining Techniques

Factor	Distributive Bargaining	Integrative Bargaining
1. Number of issues	Usually consider one issue at a time	Several issues are negotiated
2. Common name	"Win-lose"	"Win-win"
3. General strategy	Maximize share of a "fixed pie"	"Expand the pie" by creating innovative solutions that meet some interests of both parties
4. Relationship of the parties	One time	Continuing, long term
5. Interests	Kept hidden	Shared with other party
6. Possible options	One expressed position for each issue	Many options; create new options for maximum mutual gain
7. Information	Kept hidden	Share with other party; explain the "why" of their position—explain their interests

THE INTEGRATIVE NEGOTIATION PROCESS Complex negotiations, such as the collective bargaining process between management and union representatives, usually involve multiple-issue negotiations. Negotiators might use the single-issue distributive process described in the prior section for each of the 10, 20, or more items at issue, settling each one separately, one at a time. By comparison, an alternative method would be to consider all the issues together simultaneously and only reach agreement on all issues at the same time, but that can easily become unwieldy. Thus, negotiators using an integrative model try to divide the issues into general groups, such as highly important, somewhat important, and those of little value. Usually negotiators prefer to start negotiations by quickly resolving a few of the issues of little value, which creates a positive atmosphere and a sense of progress.[43] Another integrative approach is for both parties to agree to bring only their ten most critical issues to the table, in addition to the economic issues. This may save time and help the negotiation process focus on fewer, more important issues and causes the parties to drop some of their less important issues from the discussions.

Principled Negotiations

Roger Fisher and William Ury in their landmark negotiation book *Getting to Yes* discussed four key components of integrative or interest-based bargaining with the strategy they called "principled negotiation." Those four key components are as follows: (1) Emphasize positions versus interests, (2) separate people from issues, (3) focus on objective criteria, and (4) develop mutual gains options. Fisher and Ury explain how most traditional negotiators use the distributive model of negotiating or a strategy of distributive bargaining in which each side makes an opening offer, determines their resistance point, guesses the resistance point of the other side, and then begins to haggle over the perceived difference. Each side gives reasons why its position is the "best" and offers to make small concessions until an agreement is reached. Each side continues to make concessions, giving up part of its interests, until it uncovers a settlement point. The entire negotiation process is about each negotiator presenting and defending his or her position. Often the negotiators in defending their positions tend to get emotionally involved and locked into arbitrary positions. The more negotiations focus on positions, the less they discuss what they are really interested in: issues.

KEY #1: POSITIONS VERSUS INTERESTS Many negotiators engage in distributive bargaining because they mistakenly believe they must keep their real interests hidden. Therefore they only reveal their positions—often a specific value to the other party—and assume the other party will only reveal its position. Then they proceed to the "ritual dance" of trading concessions and trying to find a middle-ground number both will accept. Principled negotiations require both parties to go beyond their stated positions, and instead discuss their desires, needs, and fears that led them to their stated position. These factors are called their *interests*.

POSITIONS VERSUS INTERESTS

The specific demand a party makes at the bargaining table (position) as compared with the party's underlying needs, desires, fears, or concerns (interest).

A **position** may be defined as the specific demand a party has chosen, whereas their **interest** includes the underlying needs, desires, concerns, and fears that caused the party to choose the position. Principled negotiations involve revealing and reconciling interests rather than simply defending *and* exchanging positions on issues. It works because in most cases several positions exist that may satisfy an interest. Thus, if the other side's stated position is unacceptable, then it is likely that other positions exist which are acceptable but can only be found by discussing each side's underlying interests. By openly discussing their true interests, both sides have a greater probability of reaching a settlement.

Consider the negotiations between the union and employer on job assignment. The employer's position was that employees with the same job titles and job requirements should be moved to any work location when the need arose. Furthermore, the employer's position was that assigning employees to work locations was an essential management rights issue and yielding to the union's stand was unacceptable. The employer's real interest, however, was to reduce overtime costs, and management knew that if employees could be moved from their primary work location to cover

TABLE 5-4 The Positions and Interests of Work Assignments

Party	Positions	Interest
Management	Change work assignment clause of the contract. Maintain management rights.	Reduce overtime costs.
Union	Work assignment clause was a gain in a prior negotiation.	Keep employees from being disciplined for failing to perform in temporary assignments.

for an absent coworker, such costs would go down. The union's position was that it had negotiated the current job assignment in prior negotiations and it had no incentive to give it up. The union demanded that the employer hire more people if coverage was an issue. The union's interest, however, was quite different. Union members were reluctant to move to other work locations because, although job duties were similar, they were not exactly the same. The employees felt they lacked the necessary training to perform some of the work assigned and feared being disciplined if they could not perform.

Table 5-4 presents a summary of their positions and interests.

KEY # 2: SEPARATE PEOPLE FROM ISSUES *People* conduct negotiations, and they have feelings and egos and often experience anger and fear, which can interfere in, if not in fact prevent, a settlement from being reached. Unfortunately, some negotiators allow their feelings about someone on the other side to influence their behaviors. Such responses to the positions taken by other parties can easily derail a bargaining situation that might otherwise be successful. This is particularly true if the parties are in a long-term relationship. The classic case is between a wife and husband who are discussing where to spend Labor Day weekend. The husband wants to play golf with friends, but the wife wants to go to their cabin on a nearby lake.

These are the keys to separating the people involved from their positions: First, avoid emotional outbursts or anger, which is likely to be viewed as a personal attack on the other party—thus you are discussing the people, not the issues. Second, don't discuss an issue as a personal basis, such as, "You always want to go to the lake." Instead discuss the issue: "I understand you want to go to the lake. What is it exactly you want to do at the lake?" Third, try to see the situation from the other side's perspective and recognize its goals. In almost any negotiation, this skill can be critical. Most people have reasons for their positions. If you can "step into their shoes" and view the situation from their perspective, you gain an appreciation for their position and can often find mutually agreeable solutions. Thus, if the wife responds with "I need the peace and quiet of sitting on the porch and reading uninterrupted for hours, but still want to be with you for dinner and walks along the lake." Then the husband might respond with "I understand what you are saying, how about if we go to the lake, but I invite my friends down for rounds of golf at the course nearby on Saturday and Monday?"

KEY # 3: FOCUS ON OBJECTIVE CRITERIA Distributive bargaining is a contest of wills and emotions, often decided by which party can bluff the best, shout the loudest, or talk the longest. A party can make an arbitrary demand such as, "The wage offer is 2 percent because I say it is." Then the other party counters with its own arbitrary demand, "We won't take less than 4.5 percent; that's it." Too often the side with the greatest power prevails or no settlement is reached. In interest-based bargaining, the parties present offers based on objective criteria such as facts, principles, or an outside standard. Objective criteria include such factors as financial data, cost of living changes, past precedent, documented industry examples, and similar results from other settlements. The key to interest-based negotiations is that when parties propose a solution they provide the objective criteria on which they based their number. They can answer a key question: "Why is that a reasonable number?"

By sharing third-party information, the participants in an integrative bargaining situation can create a collaborative atmosphere conducive to reaching mutually satisfying results. *Source:* Andersen Ross/ Getty Images.

MUTUAL GAINS OPTIONS

Negotiation offers that include some items or interests sought by each of the parties, thus both sides realize some of their goals.

KEY # 4: DEVELOP MUTUAL GAINS OPTIONS Parties will not agree to a proposed settlement unless they perceive it to be superior to no agreement. If negotiators only view a negotiation as the haggling over one issue, such as wages, then often no settlement satisfies both parties and thus negotiations end unsuccessfully. Negotiations often fail to have multiple options for several reasons:[44] (1) it is not natural; what is natural is to think, "This is what we want, now how do we get it"; (2) people view bargaining as simply narrowing the gap between two initial offers; (3) the "fixed pie" constraint—people assume there exists a limited amount of resources to distribute; and (4) people see the problems of the other party as *their* problems and don't easily recognize the need to find mutually satisfactory solutions.

To create multiple options, the first step is to agree to discuss openly *the true interests* of both parties. Once true interests and not just positions are known, the parties can consider different ways each party's interest might be satisfied. Consider, for example, a situation in which the union desired a guaranteed across-the-board annual bonus, but management insisted on one that varied according to the company's net profit level, which provided workers an incentive to increase performance. Union negotiators insisted that the employer had the "ability to pay" higher bonuses because in the last few years it had experienced higher profits and revenue. And management insisted that it had the "ability to pay" only if the bonus increase was linked to future increased net profits. Management, in an attempt to present a mutual-gain option, proposed a bonus formula with a fixed bonus amount per year of $100,000 plus a variable amount that rose as the company's net profit increased: 6 percent of net up to $300,000; 8 percent of net between $300,000 and $1.0 million, and 10 percent of net above $1.0 million. The key to the proposal was that it provided a mutual gain for both sides; the union achieved a minimum bonus of $100,000 but also a higher bonus as net profits rose. And the company was not required to increase the bonuses unless it had the profit to pay for it. Interestingly, a profit sharing plan or a onetime bonus clause now appears in approximately 25 percent of all U.S. labor contracts as a means of providing higher wages if an employer experiences greater profits during the life of a contract.[45]

THE CATEGORIZATION METHOD Although several negotiation processes could be described as integrative, the **categorization method** is a basic one that can be easily learned. Once the categorization method is understood, one can build on and expand this basic interest-based method into a more robust interest-based method. There are five steps of the categorization method of integrative or "win-win" bargaining (Figure 5-7). The process is presented here as a linear process, one in which the first step must be followed by the second step, and the second by the third, and so on. However, in reality, negotiators experienced in interest-based bargaining may not use a linear model but instead choose to follow a process that best meets their interests in a given situation.

CATEGORIZATION METHOD

An integrative negotiation method that includes: exchanging information, developing a common list of issues, agreeing on compatible issues, exchanging equal value issues and resolving remaining issues using distributive bargaining.

Unlike the distributive process, the parties generally do not begin by tossing out a number—their opening offer or anchor on an issue. The *first step* is for the parties to begin by exchanging information and seeking to identify all of the issues to be negotiated, listing them, and each side explaining their interests on those issues. The negotiators seek to learn about the other party's concerns and interests and to identify potential issues of mutual interest. Rather than treating the dialogue as requiring a response to any particular issue, a negotiator is focused on listening and interpreting what is presented. Key techniques in this first step include the following:[50]

- Use ***active listening.*** Active listening is perhaps the single most useful interest-based bargaining skill because it indicates that one genuinely seeks to understand what the other person is thinking, feeling, and needing. Listen closely to the other party's explanation without interrupting, disputing a fact or belief, or objecting to a statement, even if it may be critical of your position on an issue. Take notes of their discussion and watch body language. Perhaps most important, ask reflective questions to show you are listening: "So your members are concerned about job security in the future because of the proposed merger?" and probing questions: "Are you concerned about the merger because it may cause layoffs or because your members may end up in lower positions on the merged seniority list?"
- Ask ***open-ended questions*** about the level of need, interest, or concern of the other party on each issue discussed. Ask "why" an issue is important to help better understand the position presented: "Why have you proposed a 20 percent increase, why not 10 percent or 25 percent?"
- Express empathy for the other party's feelings, using ***reflective statements*** such as, "I can see why it is important that you have delivery by that date" but without agreeing to their position.

STEP 1: Exchange information and identify all of the issues to be negotiated. Each side explains its interests and concerns on the issues.

STEP 2: Develop a **common list of all issues** that were discussed by either side during the first step and seek to classify each issue as (1) compatible—similar interests; (2) exchange—approximately equal value that may be traded; (3) distributive—those issues that are not compatible, cannot be traded, and therefore whose value must be distributed.

STEP 3: Reaching final agreement on each of the **compatible issues** and removing them from further negotiation.

STEP 4: Trading, or **exchanging issues of approximately equal value**; in some cases several issues may be included in a single exchange.

STEP 5: Resolution of any remaining issue(s), which often is accomplished through the distributive bargaining on each separate issue.

FIGURE 5-7 The Five Steps of the Categorization Method of Integrative or "Win-Win" Bargaining

- Probe for the other side's willingness to ***trade off*** an issue for another issue—a key to interest-based bargaining. Ask questions such as, "Would you be willing to give up the new subcontracting language if we added language to guarantee no layoffs?"
- **Assert your own needs:** Explain your interests and positions on issues: "Because of EPA requirements it costs us three times as much to paint the housings ourselves compared with outsourcing like our competitors."
- **Refrain from making personal attacks** on the other people or criticizing their positions.

The *second step* in the categorization method of interest-based bargaining negotiations generally begins with the parties developing a common list of all issues of possible interest that were discussed by either side during the first step. They do not assume they have opposing goals on all issues. Instead, together they review the issues and classify them as one of three types: (1) compatible issues, those with identical or very similar goals and thus agreement can be reached quickly and the issue settled; (2) *exchange* issues, those of generally equal priority that can be traded one for the other. Therefore one party achieves its goal on one issue and the other party achieves its goal on another issue; or (3) the remaining *distributive* issues, often few in number but important, such as wages, health insurance, pensions, and so on, which may be settled in a distributive process as discussed earlier.

The *third step* involves listing, discussing, and then reaching final agreement on the compatible issues and therefore removing them from further negotiation. This step often passes quickly because the parties are essentially in agreement as to substance and usually only need to record the specifics of the issues. However, this step can be critical in establishing a positive climate for the entire negotiation process. By first identifying at least some issues and reaching mutual agreement, the parties involved begin the process with a sense of openness, collaboration, and accomplishment.

The *fourth step* involves the "trade-off" of issues, the heart of the integrative process. Both parties review the list of issues identified in the first step, with the compatible issues removed in the second step, which leaves the remaining unresolved issues that might be resolved through the exchange of one issue for another. In an open "brainstorming" process, either party can suggest exchanges of issues of approximately equal priority or value. In the process one party receives its position on an issue, but in return gives the other party its position on another issue. In some cases, two or more issues might be exchanged for a single issue if the approximate values are equal. If all remaining issues can be exchanged, the negotiation process is over, but in most situations one or more unresolved issues are left on the table. Negotiators may package several issues to create gains for both sides.

The *fifth step* is the resolution of the last issue(s), which often is accomplished through distributive bargaining. However, because the prior steps have resolved most of the issues involved, both parties are less likely to walk away from the table over the last issue. Why? First, they have reached agreement on several important issues that will be lost if they walk away; second, the integrative process has established a positive bargaining climate that is more conducive to resolving the last issue; and third, both parties have invested time and effort into the negotiation and therefore are more motivated to reach a final settlement.

Now we apply the five steps of the categorization method of interest-based bargaining just presented (see Figure 5-6) to a labor–management contract negotiation. The Ohio Metals Company and Local 56 of the Primary and Sheet Metal Workers of America, AFL-CIO, developed a positive labor–management climate over their 50-year relationship. As their current three-year contract is about to end they begin negotiation talks for a new contract. In general, the company, the union, and the workers have experienced prosperity in recent years, and certainly they expect to continue their positive relationship for many more years. In their first meeting they openly share several important sources of information. Management provided the company's financial information for each of the past three years as well as sales projections for the current year. The union negotiators provided copies of contracts negotiated within the past year within the industry and for similar regional employers within other industries. In addition, the union shared the results of a recent survey of its members that indicates what issues are important to them and their rank priority.

In their second meeting, the union and management negotiators lay their issues "on the table" or openly discuss each issue they would like to negotiate, and explain their interests or position on each issue. Management explains it is seeking a five-year contract that would enable it to enter into longer-term contracts with buyers, which they have discussed often over the past several months. Management would also prefer a drug-testing program in cases involving accidents or injuries to protect the interests of employees, the owners, suppliers, and customers. In exchange for any wage increase, management also wants workers in the bargaining unit to pay a greater portion of their health insurance, which has risen sharply since the last contract negotiation. Finally, management presents a proposal that would allow it to subcontract work to outside firms under certain conditions. The union negotiators present several economic items that they believe are needed to increase the total value of the contract until it is closer to other contracts in the region. Those items include a wage increase of 5 percent, the initiation of a profit-sharing plan to include 15 percent of net profits annually, an increase in the pension benefit formula, three days of paid funeral leave annually, a monthly clothing allowance, and an increase in the current shift differential provision. In addition, the union leaders present three noneconomic job security issues of importance to their members: a no-layoff provision, overtime assignment based on seniority, and a no-lockout provision.

In their next meeting (the third step) the negotiators review the common list of items developed in the previous meeting and agree they have compatible interests on three of the 13 issues. Both sides desire the security of a long-term contract and thus agree to a five-year term for the new contract. Both also agree that a new drug testing policy is needed and that testing should only be conducted in cases involving accidents or injuries. Finally, both agree that disruptions over contract disputes that can be settled through the grievance arbitration process provided in the contract are harmful to all parties involved, and thus should be prevented through a "no-strike/no-lockout" provision. With ten issues left on the table, the two sides began looking for items that they could exchange, the fourth step.

In general, this exchange process involves one side receiving its desired position (or something close) on one issue by giving the other party its position on another issue. In the first exchange, both sides agreed to the union's proposal on job security—a no-layoff clause, in exchange for management's proposal on subcontracting—which allows up to 10 percent of the bargaining unit jobs to be subcontracted to outside firms for economic reasons. Next, they exchanged economic issues of approximately equal value; first, the union's pension increase proposal of 2 percent for future retirees in exchange for management's shift differential proposal (no change); and second, the union's new clothing allowance proposal is traded ($50 per month) for management's funeral leave proposal, which combined funeral leave with personal leave and reduced the total number of days per year by two. Then after several proposals were presented on the remaining issues, management's profit-sharing proposal, which changed the current program to 10 percent of net profits, was exchanged for the union's proposal for overtime to be voluntary and assigned based on seniority. After these four trades involving eight issues, only two issues remained on the table: wages and health care insurance. The negotiators on both sides at this point felt a sense of accomplishment because 11 of the 13 issues had been resolved. However, they also recognized that the two remaining issues were critical ones that both sides at the start had listed as top priorities and were high-value items. The issues were recognized as zero-sum economic issues. Thus, they began a distributive bargaining process on each item independently. Eventually, by making counterproposals with concessions, a settlement point was reached on both issues, and thus with all 13 resolved, an agreement was reached. Table 5-5 summarizes the issues involved, positions of both sides, and bargaining category (compatible, exchange, distributive) used in the bargaining.

TABLE 5-5 Labor Contract Negotiations Through the Categorization Method

Issue Number	Description of Issue	Management's Initial Position	Union's Initial Position	Categorization Bargaining Category
1.	Length of contract	5 years	4 years	Compatible
2.	Pension increase	None	2%	Exchange (for #9)
3.	Wage increase	1%	5%	Distributive
4.	Profit sharing	10% of net	15% of net	Exchange (for #13)
5.	Drug-testing program	For cause only	For cause only	Compatible
6.	Health insurance	Employees pay 20%	Continue current program co-pay	Distributive
7.	Paid funeral leave/ Personal leave	4 days	6 days	Exchange (for #12)
8.	No strike/No lockout	Continue current provision	Continue current provision	Compatible
9.	Shift differential	10%	15%	Exchange (for #2)
10.	Subcontracting	10%	0%	Exchange (for #11)
11.	Job security	No provision	No layoff provision	Exchange (for #10)
12.	Clothing allowance	$25/month	$50/month	Exchange (for #7)
13.	Overtime	Management Right to assign personnel to overtime	Voluntary and based on seniority	Exchange (for #4)

Source: Adapted from Michael R. Carrell and Christina Heavrin, *Negotiating Essentials: Theory, Skills, and Practices* (Upper Saddle River, NJ: Pearson Education, 2008), p. 93.

INTEREST-BASED BARGAINING

In recent years a new collaborative negotiation process called interest-based bargaining (IBB) has emerged and is gaining support. Some experienced negotiators see IBB as an entirely new process, different from distributive and integrative, while others see it as an evolutionary form of integrative bargaining. The Federal Mediation Service is credited with developing the steps of IBB, in which parties (1) share information; (2) agree to search for mutually agreeable solutions; (3) use brainstorming to create new options; (4) focus on the facts and issues, not personalities or leverage; (5) negotiate and focus on parties' real interests, not positions as suggested in *Getting to Yes*; and (6) commit to IBB training and use of IBB principles.[46] John Beck of Michigan State University has successfully trained negotiation teams in IBB from a variety of industries, including General Motors, Kraft Foods, Lansing, Michigan's Sparrow hospital, and the Michigan Nurses Association. Rosemarie Kraeger, superintendent of Rhode Island's Middletown Public Schools decided "there had to be a better way" to negotiate contracts, which had always been painful and required several days. Thus Kraeger sent her teams to the Harvard University Program on Negotiation for training in IBB principles. The result? Kraeger said the teams successfully settled two contracts—in "a matter of hours"—because the teams learned to work together to find mutually agreeable solutions![47]

IBB STEPS The IBB process includes five steps, as illustrated in Figure 5-6. The first step involves bringing the parties together in joint sessions to identify and clarify the issues to be resolved. In this step, positions such as "we need a 5 percent salary increase across the board" are

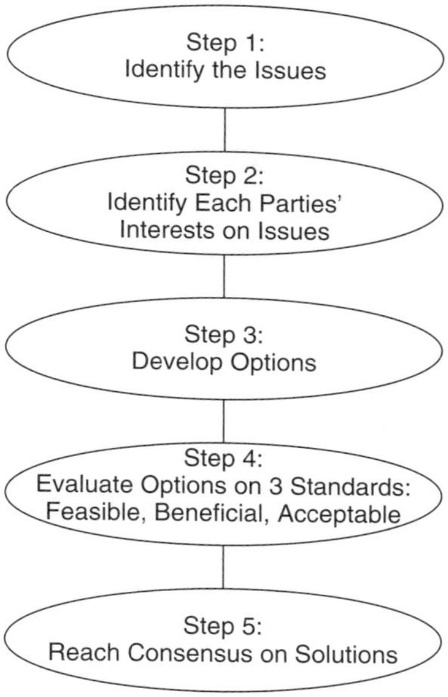

FIGURE 5-6 Steps in the Interest-Based Bargaining Negotiating Process. *Source:* Jerome T. Barrett and John O'Dowd, *Interest-Based Bargaining: A User's Guide* (Victoria, BC, Canada: Trafford Publisher, 2005), p. 70. Used by permission.

avoided, and instead each issue is carefully written, and the parties reach agreement on the list of issues to be resolved. The second step involves the parties caucusing separately to specify their own interests on each issue listed in step 1. Then the parties come together and present their list of interests without justification or criticism of the other party's interests. Step 3 involves brainstorming for as many creative options as possible to solve each issue. No option is judged, nor is any option rejected at this step. Step 4 is the evaluation of all the options developed in step 3. The standards for the evaluation of each option are as follows: (1) Is it *feasible:* Can the option be actually implemented? (2) Is it *beneficial:* Will it satisfy the interests of one or both sides? and (3) Is it *acceptable:* Do both the union and management teams agree to the option? Only if an option passes all three standards is it adopted; thus, neither side is ever required to accept an option.

In the Rhode Island Middletown Public Schools management and union negotiators were trained in interest-based bargaining principles and were able to settle new contracts "within hours"! *Source:* Yellow Dog Productions / Getty Images.

If no option is found for a particular issue, the brainstorming begins again. Step 5 includes the two sides in a joint session agreeing by consensus on the options that satisfy interests.[48]

The advantages of IBB compared with traditional negotiation methods may include the following: (1) By focusing on interests and not stating positions, negotiators will have improved communications and thus are more likely to fully understand the underlying interests of the other party, allowing them to do most of their work in joint open sessions; (2) the joint development of options through brainstorming is more likely to uncover additional ideas and thus superior solutions to problems; (3) traditional methods that focus on defending stated positions are more likely to break down because the parties become too invested in their positions instead of trying to uncover new options; and (4) the focus on interests is more likely to cause the parties to explain the critical "why" behind an interest or proposal. Potential disadvantages of the IBB method may include the following: (1) The method may use a great deal of time discussing interests and possible options when a mutual solution could be reached just as quickly using more traditional methods, (2) IBB negotiators may have difficulty transferring a proposed creative option into a practical, concrete solution; and (3) the standards suggested by IBB negotiators are often not precise, and are subjective, thus not easily agreed to by both parties.[49]

REACHING AGREEMENT

Point of Crisis

Finally, negotiators reach a decision. Once all the proposals and counterproposals have been presented, and both sides believe they can't give any more, the parties either reach an agreement on all issues or stop talking. If agreement cannot be reached, this may be the point of crisis. Various techniques involving neutral third parties such as mediation and arbitration are available to bring the parties back to agreement. Job actions such as strikes and lockouts may be utilized, and although they receive a great deal of publicity, they are seldom used to resolve contract disputes. Noted mediator Ted Kheel refers to this crisis point in negotiations as **the crunch**, or a point of no return that occurs when both sides realize that "some deadline will cause no decision to become the final decision." Up to this point both parties may feel little pressure to move significantly from their position. The crunch, however, is a signal that it is time for a decision to resolve the remaining issues or to declare an impasse. As an example, Kheel offers the tactic of CIO founder John L. Lewis, who, when negotiating for the United Mine Workers, practiced a "no contract, no work" strategy, meaning that the termination date of the current contract would not be extended. Thus, if a new contract was not reached by that date, the members would immediately strike. Then both sides felt "the crunch" to settle before the old contract expired—management wanted to avoid lost production and workers, lost wages. Most UAW negotiations during the Lewis period reached a settlement before the termination of the old contract, but the others experienced a strike, as Lewis had promised.[51]

The Closing Stage

Knowing that an agreement has been reached, the people involved become psychologically committed to the agreement and are often eager to move quickly to sign the papers, shake hands, exchange money for goods, and so on. However, it is very likely that additional concessions will be made after the parties think they are done.

Consider the quote often attributed to Yankee great Yogi Berra, "It ain't over till it's over!" If one party senses that the other party is *overly anxious* to close the deal, then they may try to extract last-minute concessions. Patience at this point is critical. A negotiator must take time to finalize the deal, remembering that *both sides* want the agreement; not make last-minute concessions just to close the deal, remembering that these concessions may be just as, or maybe more, valuable than any of the initial concessions. Also, consider that every once in a while, after months of fruitful talks, when "mutual gains" have been achieved, one side or the other might reject a "win-win" deal at the last minute for no apparent reason. As one negotiator explained, it may simply be because of "the knucklehead theory": The knuckleheads fail to recognize and accept a good deal.[52]

If any last-minute concessions are requested (e.g., if the other side makes a last-minute demand such as, "I forgot one item that we can handle easily. . . ."), consider one of three responses:[53]

1. ***Silence*** At this stage of the negotiations, judicial use of *silence* is advisable. Say nothing; any response may be perceived as a sign of weakness. Continue to close the deal at hand with no changes.
2. ***The Walkaway*** A skilled negotiator may be able to project a *personal indifference* to settling that will concern the opposing side that has certainly become invested in reaching an agreement. This may be the best time to suggest you can—and will—use **the walkaway** and retreat from the deal if the other side tries to extract a final concession.
3. ***Reciprocate*** This response technique involves inducing the other party to change a position, by indicating that if he or she will change his or her position on an issue, you will *reciprocate* and make another approximately equal concession. You should respond to their final demand for concessions by indicating your willingness to agree if they make a similar concession, and conclude the negotiations. Thus, "To accept this last item of yours, we agree to a signing bonus of $100, if you decrease the final cost of the clothing allowance by $100.

Of course, at the conclusion of a negotiation either party should not only be prepared to respond to last-minute demands by the other party, they might also consider making a demand, using the classic **nickel-and-diming** tactic, also called "the nibble." If a party believes the other side is too anxious to settle, before signing any papers they might insist on the addition of one small overlooked item—a "nickel or dime" item, which might be one the other side can easily agree to, thereby increasing the value of the negotiated settlement. For example, the tactic is often used when buying a car when the car's price has been set by the company and the salesperson has limited authority to alter it. However, the salesperson can usually provide something of value (e.g., next-day delivery, a higher price on a trade-in). If one misjudges the situation, however, the nickel-and-dime item could become a deal breaker when the other party walks away, unless the nickel-and-dime request is quickly withdrawn.[54]

NICKEL-AND-DIMING TACTIC

A last minute demand by one party made to take advantage of the other party when they are about to reach agreement.

Tentative Agreement

TENTATIVE AGREEMENT

In labor negotiations the agreements on issues reached at the table are only tentative agreements—that is subject to ratification by the bargaining unit members.

It is important to realize that all tentative agreements (TAs) reached by representatives of management and the union are just that: *tentative*. At this point, the union leadership holds informational meetings to present the details of the tentative agreement to the members and to answer questions. Then, according to the rules of the union, the agreement must be ratified (receive a majority positive vote) by the members of the union. If the union negotiators have done a good job determining the priorities of the members, informing them during the negotiation process, and estimating what they will or will not accept in a new contract, then this step is routine. To show solidarity with their leadership, members usually accept the contract offered to them as the "last, best, and final" one. The ratification process involves a secret-ballot process that can take several days to allow all members at all locations the opportunity to vote. The process can be complicated, however; for example, in 1996, the International Longshoreman's and Warehouse Union rules required a 60 percent majority of all voting members across the United States. The vote failed because the Los Angeles and San Francisco local union leaders led a successful campaign against the proposed contract, and the 60 percent vote required was not reached.[55]

The degree of formality and detail required of a final agreement depends on the value, length of time, and past relationship of the parties involved. However, this often requires that the individual and packages of articles and provisions that have been agreed to, signed-off on, and thus taken off the table over several weeks or months must now be carefully combined into one document: the final agreement. As explained in Chapter 10, a written agreement is required by the National Labor Relations Act, but even if it wasn't, it would be advisable because it serves three purposes:

1. ***Communication.*** People often hear what they want to hear, they don't listen carefully to details, or their memories of verbal agreements fade quickly. A written agreement can eliminate many of these problems.
2. ***Commitment.*** Reducing an agreement to writing often causes the parties to commit themselves to the agreement. Just seeing the terms in "black and white" can cause one to understand issues better than just hearing them. If a union steward or supervisor doubts what the correct grievance step is, showing them the contract language signed by both parties can quickly increase their commitment.
3. ***Contract.*** Putting the many individual agreements made on issues during negotiations into one written, signed, and dated document creates an enforceable agreement. The final document will be referred to daily as issues arise during the term of the new agreement and what was said at the table, intended, or even signed off on by both parties may not be remembered.

With a written, signed, and dated document in hand, the parties involved can feel confident their negotiating produced an agreement that achieves gains for both sides. In addition, they have a document that can be referred to by the many people involved in administering the agreement. A typical management policy is not to implement the new wage or other economic changes until the new agreement has been signed by both parties to avoid any possible disagreements.

The party who drafts the document should reflect the actual agreements made at the table, all of them. The nondrafting party should read the document carefully to verify that the language being used is clear and represents the understanding of the parties. This usually entails reviewing notes and signed provisions from the negotiations and making sure they and the written document are consistent. Finally, if "boilerplate" or standard contract terms have been included, even though those items were not actually discussed or agreed to, they should be reviewed to make sure these standard terms do not adversely affect the deal that was made. Often, the inclusion of such terms in the final agreement will cause the parties to discuss those details, which could help avoid problems in the future.

Summary

The core of collective bargaining guaranteed by the National Labor Relations Act is the actual negotiations of an agreement. Before they begin, negotiators for both management and labor should identify and weigh the critical elements of any negotiation: *information*, *time*, and *power*. The most important single piece of information in a negotiation is the BATNA or WATNA—best or worst alternative to a negotiated settlement. Understanding both one's own and the other party may provide bargaining power in the negotiations. Negotiators should also understand that some actions that occur during bargaining might be considered unethical in another context, but are not always so considered in labor negotiations. Before negotiating critical economic issues, a negotiator often decides three critical values; opening offer, desired outcome, and reservation point (maximum or minimum acceptable value to guide their actions during bargaining.

Collective bargaining generally involves one of two strategic approaches: distributive or integrative. Factors to be considered when deciding which approach will work include the specific issues to be negotiated, the people involved, and the general context of the negotiations.

Distributive bargaining, in general, is a negotiation method in which two parties strive to divide a fixed pool of resources, such as money, each trying to maximize its share of the distribution. It is called a "fixed-pie" or "zero-sum" process because the other party loses the amount gained by one party. In distributive bargaining, the parties often view each other as adversaries, try to maximize their self-interest or grab a larger "share of the pie," and are mostly concerned about the current negotiation, not future relationships. In collective bargaining the distributive strategy means that the parties seek to maximize their gain on each and every issue, and thus generally do not consider making logical trade-offs or finding possible compatible interests. If one side decides to only use the distributive approach, the other side usually has no choice but to also use distributive bargaining.

Integrative bargaining is a more cooperative approach to negotiation. It is often referred to as a "win-win," "mutual-gains," or "integrative" approach. The integrative approach, unlike distributive bargaining, involves seeking compatible issues by moving beyond stated positions or demands and instead discussing underlying interests to reach an agreement, and searching for mutually acceptable options and logical trade-offs. Negotiators generally strive to develop proposals that meet some interests of both sides because as Ted Kheel stated in the chapter-opening quote—unless both sides can receive something more than what the status quo provides, there is nothing for them to negotiate!

CASE STUDIES

Case Study 5-1 Good-Faith Negotiations

The Company owns and operates a nursing home for the elderly at its facility in Los Angeles, California. Jeoung Lee (J. Lee) is president of the Company. Although the Company is a corporation, witnesses spoke of J. Lee as the "owner." The Company and the Union were parties to one collective bargaining agreement that expired on June 30. The Company and the Union conducted six negotiating sessions over the terms of a new agreement. The Union was represented by Estrada and the Company by Yokoyama and Jarvis, neither of whom had previously negotiated a collective bargaining agreement for the Company. According to Jarvis, prior to commencement of negotiations, J. Lee, who speaks broken English, met with him and Yokoyama. She told them to go to the negotiating meetings and bring back information. Yokoyama testified that his role was to represent J. Lee at negotiations, to give information requested by the Union during negotiations, and to collect any information or agreement and present it to J. Lee.

According to the Union, Jarvis told the negotiating group that Yokoyama had the authority to negotiate and that J. Lee had empowered Yokoyama with the authority to reach final agreement for the Company. The Union denied there was any discussion that a final agreement would need to be approved by J. Lee.

Yokoyama, testifying for the Company, said that Estrada asked at each negotiation session why J. Lee was not present, and they answered that she was extremely busy and could not attend but that J. Lee would be the final person to approve any contract.

The last negotiations lasted eight to nine hours and, with a federal mediator's help, the parties reached a final agreement. The parties initialed a six-page document entitled "Tentative Agreement, Summary of the Agreement," which included an appendix of wage rates effective July 1. According to the Union, the parties discussed the fact that the bargaining unit employees needed to vote on the provisions before the agreement could be considered final but there was no discussion about J. Lee or anyone else in management having to approve any agreement.

According to Yokoyama and Jarvis, after the parties reached a tentative agreement, the Union asked if the Company was going to sign the contract. Yokoyama told them that he could not sign the contract without J. Lee signing the contract, that she would be the final person to approve the contract. Yokoyama testified that he reminded the Union he would initial each point, but the final approval would have to be made by J. Lee and then the Union asked, "When is J. Lee going to look at this?" One union bargaining team member confirmed that the Company's representatives said they would have to show J. Lee the agreement.

Yokoyama personally left the draft agreement in J. Lee's office in her absence and also gave a copy to the payroll office, explaining that it was a tentative agreement. On July 1, the Company implemented the wage provisions set forth in the tentative agreement. In early August, upon her return from Korea, J. Lee told Yokoyama that she did not approve of the wage increases and that she wanted to change wages back to what they were prior to July 1. J. Lee then held a meeting with employees and told them that the increases were not part of the agreement, that the increase was too costly, and nobody had told her that they had signed a contract on her behalf. Without notifying the Union, the Company rescinded the wage increases.

The Union filed an unfair labor practice for refusing to sign the negotiated agreement and for not notifying the union that the wage increase was being rescinded. The Union pointed out that the duty to bargain carries an obligation to appoint a negotiator with genuine authority to carry on meaningful bargaining on key issues. And while an employer is not required to appoint an individual possessing final authority to enter into an agreement, the law is clear that an agent assigned to negotiate a collective bargaining agreement is clothed with *apparent authority* to bind the principal unless notice is given to the contrary. Therefore, if the agent does not have authority to bind his principal, notice of that must be clearly and unambiguously given. If an employer's agent does not clearly communicate the existing condition precedent of his principal's approval of any agreement, the refusal to sign the agreement is unlawful. The Union testified that Yokoyama and Jarvis repeatedly said they could negotiate on behalf of the Company. There was no "clear or unambiguous" notice that the agreement reached at the bargaining table would have to be approved by J. Lee. Therefore, refusing to sign the agreement was an unfair labor practice.

The Union also objected to J. Lee's failure to notify the union that the wage increase was being rescinded. It is an unfair labor practice to change benefits without notice to the union and an opportunity to negotiate the change.

The Company responded on the bargaining in bad faith claim that if negotiators on the other side are apprised in advance of a requirement that any final and binding agreement is dependent on approval by the employer and that the agreement fashioned by the parties is only a tentative one, then either party has the right to reject it after presentation to its principal. So the issue in this case is what authority Yokoyama and/or Jarvis possessed to bind the Company by their negotiations and whether they conveyed to the Union that J. Lee's approval was a condition precedent to any final and binding collective bargaining agreement. The Company further argued that in spite of the conflicting testimony as to what was said at the negotiation sessions, the circumstances of the negotiations support a conclusion that not only did Yokoyama communicate the necessity of preapproval by J. Lee but also that the Union understood that to be the case. Both Jarvis and Yokoyama were inexperienced in labor negotiations and therefore it was unlikely that they would be given carte blanche to bind the Company. The Union admitted that in responding to wage and benefit proposals, Yokoyama referred to J. Lee's opinion on the subject and at one point, the Union negotiator demanded that J. Lee be present at negotiations. The persistent urging to have J. Lee present suggests that the Union was aware that J. Lee's approval of contract terms was necessary. All the testimony agreed that the Company representatives only claimed the authority to "negotiate" or "bargain." The authority to negotiate is not intrinsically equivalent to the authority to reach final agreement. Finally, the document initialed on the last day of negotiations specifically stated it to be a *tentative* agreement.

On the issue of an unfair labor practice for failing to notify the Union of the Company's decision to rescind the wage increase, the Company argued that because the wage increase had not been agreed to and was simply an error, it was not a benefit. There is no requirement to meet with or negotiate with the Union on correcting a mere bookkeeping error.

Source: Adapted from *JPH Management,* 169 LRRM 1001 (NLRB 2001).

QUESTIONS

1. Do you believe the company was or was not bound to sign the agreement? Explain.
2. Explain why it might be an unfair labor practice for the company to rescind the pay raise without first meeting with the Union.
3. It is not an unfair labor practice for an employer to send negotiators to the bargaining table without the authority to give final approval to the negotiated terms, but is it a good or a bad idea? Explain.

Case Study 5-2 Selection of Bargaining Team Members

The Company is an information services company providing a wide range of services to other companies throughout the United States. One of the specific services the Company provides is a call-in employee assistance program by which employees of its clients may obtain advice and referrals related to financial and/or legal matters, substance abuse programs, and mental health assistance. The Company's call-in center is staffed 24 hours a day, 7 days a week, and 365 days a year exclusively by the bargaining unit employees.

The Union and Company commenced negotiations toward a first collective bargaining agreement for the employees, and one of the first topics discussed was accounting for time spent by employee-members of the Union's negotiating team attending negotiations. The Union requested that the six employee-members of its negotiating committee be allowed to take leave without pay to attend bargaining sessions, and the Union would compensate those members directly or reimburse the Company if the Company paid the employees through the payroll system. The Company, however, insisted that absences incurred by employees while attending contract negotiations be charged against the employees' PDO (personal day off) accounts, in full-day segments, in the same manner as any other personal leave taken. The Company's written leave policy provides for PDO as paid time off to be used for absences such as leisure, personal business, and short-term personal or family illness. PDO is accrued based on length of company service and is operated on a "no fault" type arrangement where employees can take PDO for any or no reason. The Company also has a "Personal Leave of Absence Policy," the stated intent of which is to recognize reasonable requests for unpaid leave providing the requests will not impact normal business operations. Otherwise, the Company does not give unpaid time off for personal reasons under any circumstances and would not treat employee negotiators any differently. The Company explained that because of scheduling concerns regarding the call-in center, it was unwilling to permit employees on the negotiating committee to simply take unpaid leave in lieu of PDO, and that the efficient operation of its call-in center depended, for the most part, on dependable staffing.

The Union continued to seek to have its employee negotiators be permitted to take leave without pay for time spent participating in negotiations. The Union also proposed meeting outside normal work times, but the Company refused to set any night or weekend bargaining times. The Union argues it is the Company's position that it would be unreasonable to ask its managers to devote their nights and weekends to negotiations. The Union notes the Company had three valid options it could have taken consistent with applicable case law, namely: (1) it could have paid employee-negotiators to attend negotiations with no loss of PDO; (2) it could have granted unpaid leave to employee-negotiators to attend bargaining; or (3) it could have agreed to meet after hours for negotiations.

The Union charged the Company with an unfair labor practice for refusing to meet with the union representatives outside working hours and by simultaneously refusing to allow members of the bargaining committee leave without pay to participate in negotiations.

The Union argues that the Company has unlawfully interfered in the selection of Union's bargaining representatives by only bargaining during the working day and forbidding employees from taking *unpaid* time to participate in negotiations. According to the Union, the Company advanced no extraordinary circumstances to support its insistence on charging employees PDO, nor for its unreasonable refusal to meet after hours for negotiations. The Union argues that the absence of the six (or less) employee-negotiators from work to attend bargaining did and will not unduly disrupt the Company's scheduling because the employee-negotiators involved come from different work groups in a workforce of approximately 130. The Union asserts meeting on weekends could have eliminated this concern of the Company altogether. Furthermore, the Company's reliance on its past practice with respect to its PDO policy is invalid because there has never been a union at the Company prior to this time, so there could not have been any past practice with regard to the type of leave that would be appropriate to cover employee absences for the purpose of participating in collective bargaining.

The Company contends it has consistently applied its PDO policy in a lawful manner when dealing with employee absences from work including its requirement that employee-members of the Union's negotiating committee be charged PDO for the time they spend at negotiations. The Company points out that because employers are not required to pay employees for time spent attending negotiations, there is no meaningful distinction between that and its practice of paying its employees for time spent at negotiations but then deducting PDO for such time. The Company further notes that an employer is free to insist that negotiations take place during business or evening hours so long as it does not interfere with a union's ability to designate its employee negotiating representatives. The Company argues it has in no way interfered with the Union's right to designate its representatives by application of its PDO policy to the employee-members of the Union's negotiating committee. The Company strongly asserts it has never, by any of its actions, attempted to dictate or control which employees the Union chooses to bring to the bargaining table. The Company notes it has agreed to grant negotiating representatives of employees as much leave with pay as needed to attend negotiations, but that it merely requires the leave be charged against the employee representative's PDO account in the same manner that other employee nonbusiness time off from work is charged. In addition, the Company has placed no limitations on the ability of employee representatives to trade shifts with coworkers to attend contract negotiations.

The Company agrees that if an employer insists on bargaining during working hours it cannot simultaneously refuse employees *time off* to attend negotiations; however an employer is not required to grant *unpaid* time off to avoid violating the act. The Company has never denied any employee-member of the Union's bargaining committee *time off* for negotiations.

The Company contends the Union's allegation that it has refused to meet at times when employee-members of the Union's bargaining committee are not scheduled to work is false as a factual matter. The bargaining committee consists of employees who work all three shifts at the Company; thus, there is no time during which all of the Union's employee representatives are available to attend negotiations during nonworking times. And the Company argues charging PDO for negotiations is necessary to ensure staffing levels remain predictable and not create unnecessary staffing problems for the Company.

Source: Adapted from *Ceridian Corp. and Service Employees International Union Local 113*, 343 NLRB No. 70 (2004).

QUESTIONS

1. Do you think that the Company's insistence on treating the employee-members of the bargaining team the same as all other employees requesting unpaid time off was just a bargaining tactic? Explain.
2. Explain how using the categorization method of integrative bargaining might have helped these parties in their negotiations.
3. Identify the "positions" and "interests" of both parties on the use of PDO for employee-members of the bargaining team attending negotiations.

Key Terms and Concepts

anchor *176*
BATNA/WATNA *168*
bracketing *177*
categorization method *192*
caucusing *166*
desired outcome strategy *177*
distributive bargaining *173*
ethics principles (Purpose, Principle, Consequence) *171*
face-saving *165*
framing *183*
ground rules *164*
interest-based bargaining *191*
interests v. positions *188*
integrative bargaining *186*

mutual gains options *190*
nickel-and-diming tactic *197*
norms (relational, fairness, reciprocity, good faith) *180*
opening offer *174*
packaging *166*
Pareto's Law *168*
posturing *165*
power balance *169*
resistance point *178*
saving face *167*
settlement range *174*
tentative agreement (TA) *197*
"the crunch" *196*
"the walkaway" *197*
throwaway items *166*
"winner's curse" *179*
zone of possible agreement (ZOPA) *174*

Review Questions

1. What are the three key elements to a negotiation situation that should be evaluated before bargaining begins? Why is each a key to the process?
2. How might negotiators use timing to their advantage in a negotiation?
3. Define BATNA. How can one use a strong BATNA during negotiations?
4. Which of the ethical and unethical tactics in Figure 5-1 do you disagree with, and why?
5. Describe in general the distributive and integrative bargaining approaches. How do these methods differ? When would a negotiator likely choose each?
6. What are the three values one should decide before negotiating an economic issue such as wage rates?
7. List and explain each of the norms a negotiator might use to justify an offer. Which do you believe would be the most useful in negotiations? Why?
8. Instead of rejecting a proposal, what are three general reframing questions one might use as a response?
9. Why do you believe the categorization method of integrative bargaining might help two sides reach agreement on a new contract more easily than the distributive approach?
10. Give an example that clearly illustrates the difference between positions and interests. Why is the difference important to interest-based bargaining?

YOU BE THE ARBITRATOR
Negotiations

CBA ARTICLE XXXIV, SECTION 2

Should either party desire to discontinue or modify the existing agreement upon any termination date, at least thirty (30) days prior written notice of such intent must be given to the other party hereto. In the event of notice of cancellation or modification of the agreements, it shall be the duty of the parties to meet in conference not less than ten(10) days prior to the expiration date of said agreement for the purpose of negotiating new or modified agreements.

It is further agreed that proposed changes or new agreements shall be presented not later than the first day of the conference by the party serving notice.

Facts

The parties were signatories to a collective bargaining agreement ending June 15, 2009. Faced with labor costs $10 an hour over its major competitors in the flat glass market, the Company wished to modify the collective bargaining agreement and engage in concessionary bargaining. The Company sent a letter, dated April 22, 2009, to the Union stating that the Company intended to open negotiations for the existing labor agreement and suggested that the parties begin negotiations on June 1, 2009. At approximately the same time as the letter was sent, the Company's chief negotiator telephoned the Union's chief negotiator and requested a meeting. The meeting took place on May 14, 2009. Two Company officials accompanied the Company's negotiator; the Union's negotiator was the sole Union representative. The Company's negotiator stated the purpose for the meeting was to update the Union regarding the economic state of the Company's plant. He explained that the Company's competitors had labor costs of \$22 and \$26, while the Company carried labor costs of \$37. He explained that labor costs had to be brought below \$27 if the Company was to remain viable. He referenced negotiations concluded at a sister plant in Fresno, California, where a two-tiered wage system had been introduced. The Company's negotiator indicated that the

Company intended to introduce at the upcoming negotiations the two-tiered wage system and that they hoped to buyout some current employees and that new hires would be placed on the second [lower] tier of the two-tier system.

At the meeting, the Union negotiator requested that the Fresno settlement be given to him and that the Company provide "blended" labor costs for the proposed two-tiered wage system. The Company provided the Union with the information requested.

Negotiations between the parties began on June 1, 2009. The Company negotiator made an opening statement in which he stressed the flat glass market was depressed, that the Company's competitive advantages had eroded, and that the Company needed to get labor costs down to $27. He also stressed the need for the Company to obtain a two-tier wage system. Thereafter, he announced that he was prepared to present "noneconomic" proposals. Those proposals also indicated a reference to a revised two-tier wage system and overtime. The explanation of the proposals consumed the bulk of the day and the session effectively ended at 4:00 P.M. At that point, the Company's negotiator indicated that he may have one more noneconomic proposal. When asked what time the proposal would be ready, he replied that he could be ready at approximately 4:30 P.M. The Union did not wait to hear the proposal. There were no Union bargaining proposals made on June 1, 2009.

The parties met the next day, June 2, 2009, at which time the Union agreed to the noneconomic proposals offered by the Company the day before. However, the Union negotiator indicated that pursuant to Article XXXIV of the current contract, the Union was not obligated to bargain regarding proposals which followed the first day of bargaining, that is, June 1, 2009. The Company negotiator disagreed and presented the economic proposals that included a two-tier wage system. When the Union refused to bargain, the Company took the issue to arbitration.

Position of the Parties

The Union argued that Article XXXIV, Section 2, is clear and unambiguous. The provision mandates that a party serving notice of its desire to modify the contract must provide the other side with its specific proposed modifications to the contract by the end of the first day of formal bargaining. It was further argued by the Union that the term "proposed changes" unambiguously refers to specific proposed modifications to the contract. A proposed change means an offer by one person to another of terms and conditions with respect to some work or undertaking and the acceptance thereof will make a contract between them. The wording of Article XXXIV, Section 2, clearly requires the party serving notice of its desire to modify or terminate the agreement "shall present" its proposed changes. The word "shall" is a mandatory one and does not give the moving party in negotiations leave to delay the presentation of its proposals. The Company presented its specific noneconomic proposals on June 1, 2009, but failed to present any specific economic proposals until the second and third days of bargaining. The overviews of thoughts regarding negotiations during the May 14, 2009, preliminary meeting, and the opening statement on June 1st were not sufficiently specific or sufficiently tied to the language of the agreement to meet the requirement of Article XXXIV.

The Company argued that the unmistakable intent of Article XXXIV, Section 2, was to preclude late introduction of new bargaining topics. It points out that the language in question requires the party wishing to amend the agreement to provide 30 days' notice to the other side and directs that the parties "shall . . . meet in conference" at least ten days before the contract's expiration in order to negotiate changes or a new agreement. The Union's position focuses on the next sentence which states that the party giving notice shall present "proposed changes or new agreements . . . not later than the first day of conference." The Company asserts that these words do not require that proposed changes or new agreements either be in writing or be presented with a particular level of specificity. It maintains the word "conference" to mean formal table bargaining. As the language refers to presenting proposed changes or agreements "not later than the first day of conference," it clearly contemplates that presentation may be made **before** the first day of conference. Because the Company informed the Union's chief negotiator on May 14 and at the beginning of June 1 negotiating session that it would be proposing to reduce its labor costs from $37 to $27 per hour and that it would need a two-tier wage system that would apply to new hires to do that, the Union could not say that it was surprised regarding the Company's economic proposals.

QUESTIONS

1. As arbitrator, what would be your award and opinion in this arbitration?
2. Identify the key, relevant section(s), phrases or words of the collective bargaining agreement (CBA), and explain why they were critical in making your decision.
3. What actions might the employer and/or the union have taken to avoid this conflict?

Source: PPG Industries, Mt. Zion, Illinois and United Steelworkers of America Local 193-G, 127 LA 174 (2009).

CHAPTER 6

Negotiating a Collective Bargaining Agreement

In July 2010 Chicago area union construction workers staged a three-week strike which in the end gained them a 9.75 percent increase in wages and benefits over three years.
Source: © Chicago Tribune Company.

Chapter Outline

Somebody must be boss; somebody has to run the plant!

ARTHUR GOLDBERG (U.S. SUPREME COURT JUSTICE)

LABOR NEWS

Chicago Construction Strike Idles Hundreds of Projects

On July 2, 2010, just before the Fourth of July weekend, the Chicago Laborers District Council and Local 150 of the International Union of Operating Engineers walked off hundreds of construction sites in the Chicago, Illinois, area. For three weeks the projects remained idle as negotiators failed to agree to a new contract. The prior contract had expired weeks earlier. The core issues were wages and health care. When the strike began, the unions were asking for a 15 percent increase over three years, and the contractors offered a 1 percent increase. After three weeks the strikers appeared to achieve their goal when the negotiators agreed to a 9.75 percent increase in wages and health care benefits over three years—a far greater gain than many workers had realized during the Great Recession which caused record unemployment and wage freezes.

Central to the collective bargaining process are the actual **negotiations** carried out by the parties to reach an agreement. Artful use of this process can improve the relationship between an employer and the employees and result in a useful agreement for both parties. Unsuccessful negotiations can possibly lead to work stoppages and a loss of profits, wages, and benefits. This chapter examines details of the collective bargaining process and potential solutions to a bargaining impasse.

The bargaining process usually begins when a contract has reached the end of its term or one party wants to terminate or amend an existing contract. Most agreements provide for the automatic extension of an existing contract past the expiration date, usually for one year. Either party may initiate new negotiations by providing written explicit notice to the other party. A clause specifying automatic renewal and the process to begin new negotiations is included in 90 percent of labor agreements.[1]

Today even amicable union–management relationships often need to take a new approach to the negotiation process. Both sides are faced with difficult and complex issues that require greater preparation, professional analysts, and flexibility to create mutually acceptable solutions. These external factors may include economic pressure from international, lower-cost competition, soaring health care costs, and expensive retirement plans. Successful negotiators must think less about "beating the other side" and more about developing proposals that meet the needs of both sides. While some issues can be resolved by using trade-offs, other issues, especially more costly and complex ones, cannot and instead must be resolved by a problem-solving method.[2]

THE BARGAINING PROCESS

The collective bargaining process begins long before the parties meet across the bargaining table. As discussed in Chapter 4, the organization of units and the selection of the bargaining agent or union is a lengthy process necessary in determining the parties to a collective bargaining relationship.

The People Who Bargain

UNION REPRESENTATIVES Although there are as many types of negotiators as there are negotiations, some generalizations can be made. National agreements require large negotiating teams, with members from several union offices, staff, and locals. The majority of negotiations take place at the local level—either after a national agreement decides certain issues or because no national agreement exists.

A local union's negotiating team is made up of certain ex officio members, such as the president or one or more elected officers of the local union, a chief steward or grievance committee

Negotiations for new contracts covering 1,400 staff workers began in August 2011 between the University of Rochester Hospital and Service Employees International Union, Local 1199. *Source:* Ted Warren/AP Images.

member, and several union members representing various departments or job classifications. In most negotiations involving craft unions, the business agent is part of the negotiating team and often the chief negotiator. For industrial unions, an international union representative who is a professional negotiator is often available to guide and counsel local union officials.

Although international representatives have no official status during local negotiations, their experience often puts them in a leadership role. They give guidance on the grievance process and set the tone for negotiations and, in the case of impasse, for pressure tactics. They play the role of mediator or assume a militant stand to allow the local representatives to appear reasonable.

The authority of the union's negotiating team, however it is formed, is somewhat limited by the membership. The union members usually delegate only provisional and temporary authority to the negotiating team to make a settlement. In most situations, any final tentative settlement must be presented to the total membership for a vote.

MANAGEMENT REPRESENTATIVES The negotiation authority of the management negotiating team is derived directly from top management—the president, CEO, mayor, principal, and so on. In negotiations involving a single employer, representatives may include the labor relations director, human resources director, financial officer, production/operations manager, and a labor lawyer, as well as top managers. When a multiemployer association is involved, the management often employs a labor relations adviser and negotiator who is equivalent to the international representative. This professional serves a role similar to that of the union counterpart by promoting the multiemployer organization, by preparing management counterproposals, and by conducting negotiations.

NEGOTIATING SKILLS Successful negotiations depend on the knowledge and skill of the negotiators. They must, through careful preparations, become knowledgeable about their own and the other side's interests in the bargaining issues. They prepare and propose workable, attainable, and realistic proposals within the framework of the negotiations. To use the acquired knowledge wisely, a negotiator must develop an understanding of the opposition. Listening skills and the ability to communicate clearly are two cultivated techniques. A thick skin also may be helpful because the other side may engage in personal attacks at some point in the negotiations. A negotiator realizes that such attacks may only be necessary to satisfy a constituency—showing the members their negotiators are hard-nosed negotiators!

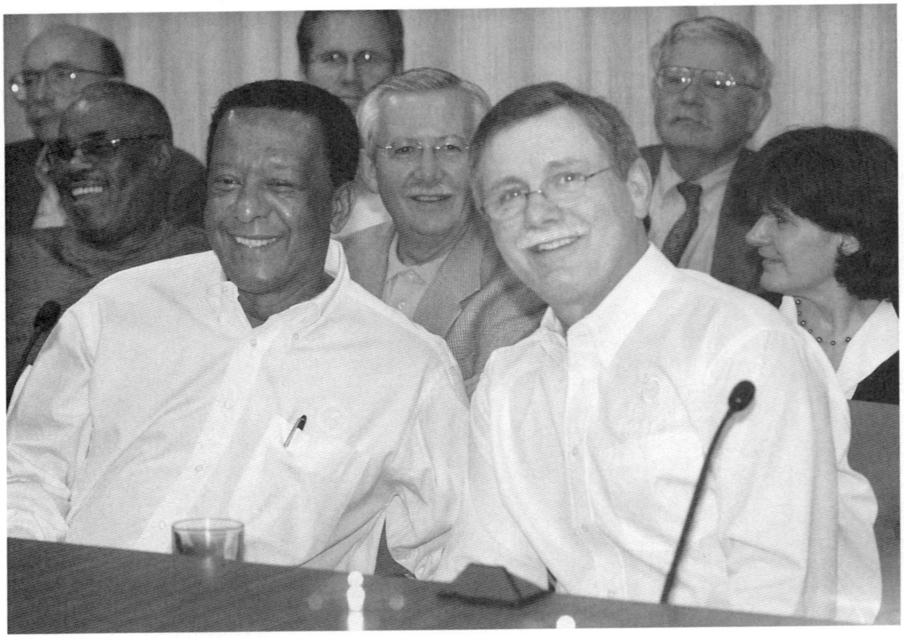

Former United Auto Workers (UAW) (from left), Vice Presidents Nate Gooden, Gerald Bantom, and Richard Shoemaker, President Ron Gettelfinger, and Secretary-Treasurer Elizabeth Bunn are shown at the negotiating table at Ford World Headquarters. *Source:* Carlos Osorio/AP Images.

PREPARATION STAGE

Many unions affiliate with larger international unions. If a master agreement is negotiated by the international, then the international controls all but local concerns. Preparation for negotiations on a master agreement is virtually nonstop, and time consuming. Preparation for contract negotiation on a local level, although not as intense, is still extensive.

The first stage, preparation, involves analysis and planning. In analysis, information is gathered, and the potential bargaining issues are selected, followed by a process of narrowing the list of issues to a manageable size. Planning forces the parties to evaluate and set priorities and to make realistic decisions about their demands. The parties' attention is focused on achievable goals. The parties are then ready for the second stage, the bargaining stage, which leads to the final stage, resolution (see Figure 6-1).

Categories of Bargaining Subjects

It is a function of law and common practice to decide what items to include in the collective bargaining session. The National Labor Relations Act provides that bargaining will include rates of pay, wages, hours of employment, and conditions of employment.[3] Under enforcement of the unfair labor practice charge of refusal to bargain, the National Labor Relations Board (NLRB) determines which subjects fall under the law. The board and later the courts recognized three categories of bargaining subjects: those that will be discussed, those that might be discussed, and those that cannot be discussed.

In the early years of the act, the board based its decisions on what constituted bargaining subjects by evaluating the history of the agreements. However, to protect unions and the collective bargaining process in its formative stage, the board found the discussion of union recognition clauses compulsory. Hence, union shops, dues check-offs, and the treatment of employees after a strike became part of the collective bargaining discussion.

In a case-by-case method, the board began to establish the list of subjects to be covered. In 1958, the Supreme Court decided the ***Borg-Warner*** **case**, which distinguished between the treatment accorded subjects determined by the board to be *mandatory*, and the treatment accorded

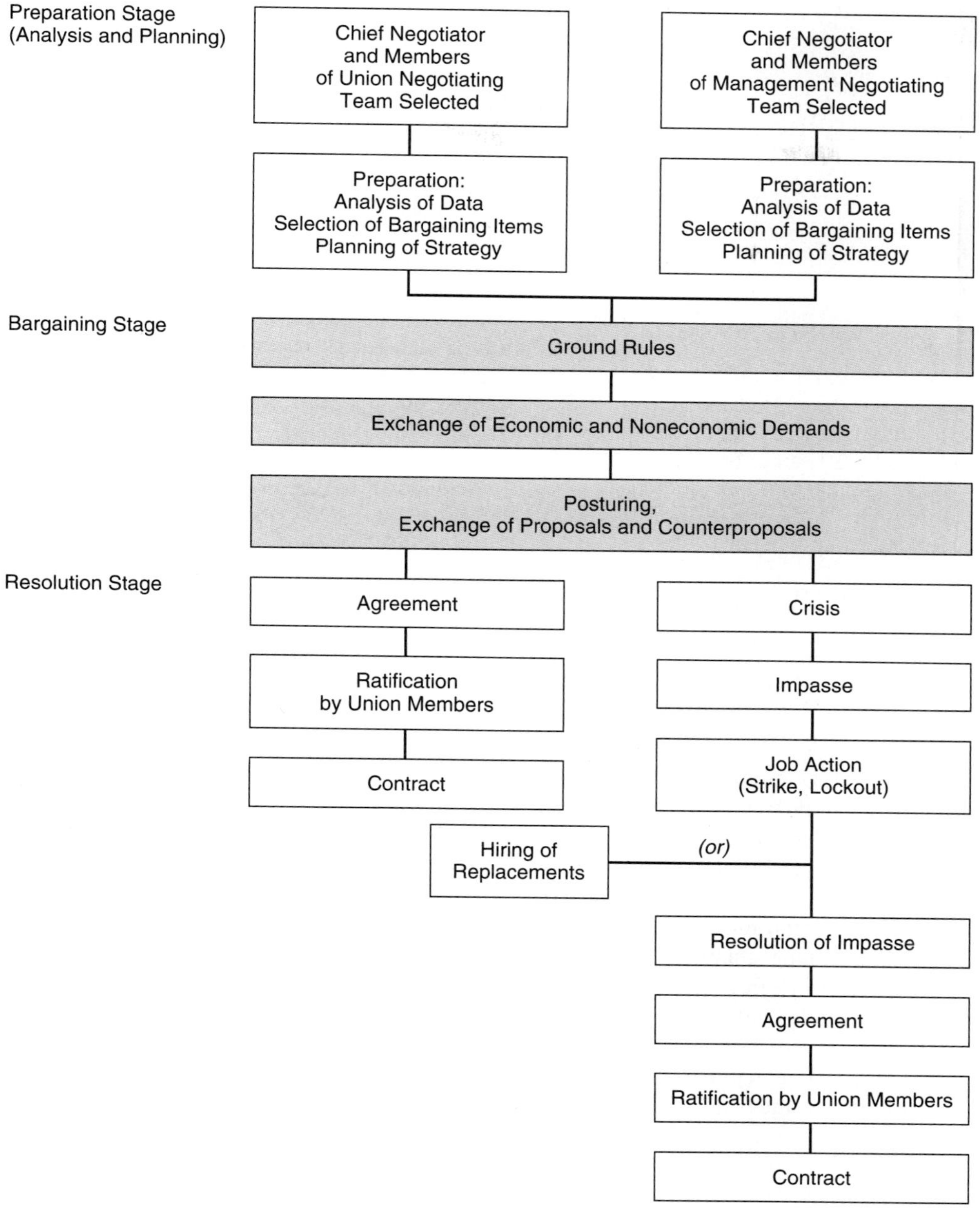

FIGURE 6-1 The Three Stages of the Bargaining Process

subjects determined to be *permissive*, and those subjects determined to be illegal. The Court noted that although the attitude of the parties is important in determining the good faith required by the act, the issues being discussed are also important.[4] It became a legal question of whether a proposal was one the parties were obliged to discuss. The U.S. Supreme Court identified two criteria for the NLRB to use in determining if an issue is a mandatory subject:[5]

1. Whether the issue is "plainly germane" to the "working environment" and
2. Whether the issue is "not among those 'managerial decisions which lie at the core of entrepreneurial control.' "

For example, in 2004, in the *Anheuser-Busch* case, the NLRB found that the employers use of hidden surveillance cameras in work and break areas, which led to employees receiving

Tips from the Experts

Union

What are the three most important things for a union to do to prepare for negotiating a collective bargaining agreement?

1. Its homework as far as defending its own proposals
2. Its homework as far as anticipating management's proposals
3. Its homework as far as the politics of the negotiations: its own negotiating team as well as management's

You can never be overprepared for negotiations. Whether it is an art or a science, effective negotiation takes tremendous understanding of the substantive issues, a lot of creativity, and thoroughness as well as keen understanding of people and power. Successful negotiations require looking beyond what is in place to what is possible to achieve a result that gives everyone what they need in a way that they can say "yes."

Management

What are the three most important things an employer must do in preparing for negotiations?

1. Select a spokesperson both for the team and for public statements: someone familiar with labor law as well as the company/industry/labor relations issues and someone who has the respect of both the union and management teams (whether in-house or an outside counsel or consultant).
2. Establish specific goals and directions, including "drop-dead" points.
3. Gather input from line management in terms of what is or is not working in current collective bargaining agreement (or practice, if this is the first collective bargaining agreement to be negotiated) and from budget personnel as to cost of changes and impact of same.

discipline for misconduct, was a mandatory subject because the use of cameras does affect employees' work environment—their right to privacy—and is not a core managerial right.[6] When the NLRB determined that the use of video surveillance cameras is a mandatory subject, it reasoned that their use is similar to the use of medical examinations and drug testing: They are all investigatory employer tools primarily used to find evidence of employee misconduct. Arbitrators, in deciding surveillance cases, have generally sought to balance the employer's legitimate need to control misconduct with employees' privacy interests.[7]

MANDATORY ITEMS

The items that must be bargained in good faith, if either party so requests, such as wages, hours, and benefits, based upon the Borg-Warner case that outlined categories of bargaining subjects.

If the subject is **mandatory**, a party may insist on its inclusion, and the other party cannot refuse to discuss it. Although compelled to bargain in good faith, neither party is legally obligated to compromise its stated position on a mandatory subject, and each party may even push the bargaining situation to an impasse. A legal impasse in negotiations can occur only when the parties cannot agree on a mandatory issue. The employer can, if there is a bona fide impasse, unilaterally implement its final offer to the union. If any permissive issues are also unresolved at the time of impasse, they can be implemented with the mandatory issue.[8]

Subjects deemed mandatory by the NLRB include those issues actually listed in the act: rates of pay, wages, hours of employment, and other conditions of employment. Also included are issues the NLRB considers related to the subjects listed in the act. After the *Borg-Warner* decision, the Supreme Court refined the definition of mandatory bargaining subjects to include subjects that "vitally affect" employees.[9] In recent years, several issues critical to unions, such as liquidation of a business, partial plant closings, subcontracting work, and plant relocations have been litigated to determine whether they are mandatory or permissive subjects of bargaining.

After some confusion that was generated by board decisions during Ronald Reagan's presidency, board rulings listed subcontracting and plant relocations in the mandatory list if such are a means to substitute other workers for the bargaining unit members. Partial plant closings or other "going-out-of-business" decisions are not subjects of mandatory bargaining because there is no intention to replace the bargaining unit members.[10] Table 6-1 delineates mandatory, permissive, and illegal subjects. The NLRB continues to add new issues to the lists of subjects as they become important. For example, employee drug testing was not an issue on any of the three lists until the 1980s when the subject came to the forefront.

Concessions are seldom made regarding permissive subjects because the parties cannot bargain to an impasse over them.[11] Designating plant closings and other business issues that

TABLE 6-1 Bargaining Items

Mandatory	Permissive	Illegal
Rates of pay	Indemnity bonds	Featherbedding
Wages	Management rights as to union issues	Whistle-blowing
Hours of employment		Discrimination by race, creed, color, religion, or national origin
Overtime pay	Preferential hiring	
Shift differentials	Pension benefits of retired employees	Interfering with union affairs or officials
Holidays		
Vacations	Scope of bargaining unit	Closed shop
Severance pay	Including supervisors in the contract	Hot cargo clause
Pensions		Separation of employees by race
	Additional parties to the contract, such as the international union	
Insurance benefits		Discriminatory treatment
Profit-sharing plans	Use of union label	
Christmas bonuses	Settlement of unfair labor charges	
Company-provided housing, meals, anddiscounts	Prices in cafeteria	
Employee security	Continuation of past contract	
Job performance		
Union security	Membership of bargaining team	
Management–union relationship	Employment of strikebreakers	
Alcohol and Drug testing	Employer child care	
Subcontracting or relocating union members' work	Plant closings	
Medical exams		
Employee surveillance		

Source: Based on information from Patrick Hardin, John E. Higgins, Christopher T. Hexter, and John T. Neighbors, *The Developing Labor Law*, 4th ed. (Washington, DC: Bureau of National Affairs, 2001).

focus on the economic profitability of a business as permissive[12] has had a profound impact on unions' ability to win concessions on such issues at the negotiating table or to alter major decisions affecting union security.

WAGES The board has defined wages as "direct and immediate economic benefits, flowing from the employment relationship."[13] Included in the discussion of wages are hourly pay rates, overtime pay, piece rates, incentive plans, shift differentials, paid holidays and vacations, and severance pay. Other forms of compensation are also included by the NLRB under the wage category and are therefore considered mandatory; they include the following:

1. ***Pensions and insurance benefits.*** Whereas employers considered pensions and insurance benefits as separate from wages, the NLRB considered them as payment

for services rendered and found an inseparable nexus between employees' current compensation and future benefits. However, retirement and pension plans are mandatory subjects for active employees only and not for retired members.

2. ***Profit-sharing plans.*** Profit-sharing plans are also considered as payment and enhancement of economic benefit. Such plans are usually structured to increase benefits to employees when company profits go up.
3. ***Christmas and other bonuses.*** A onetime or performance bonus may be a mandatory subject. The board has devised a test to determine whether such a bonus is a gift or part of the employees' compensation. Generally if the bonus has been given intermittently over the years, is not tied to salary, is not uniform, and depends on the employer's financial condition, it is a gift, and not a mandatory issue.
4. ***Stock purchase plans.*** Employers contend that stock purchase plans are not employee benefits but simply an incentive for the employee to invest in the company. The NLRB rejects that argument and deems such plans a form of compensation that is a mandatory subject for collective bargaining.
5. ***Merit wage incentives.*** A company may consider merit increases management's prerogative, but the NLRB has said that because merit raises involve the formation and application of standards affecting all wages, they must be considered a mandatory bargaining subject.
6. ***Company housing, meals, and discounts.*** The inclusion of these in the list of mandatory subjects depends on the situation. Such items would be mandatory if the job required living or eating on company-owned premises.

Provisions detailing hours, daily and weekly work schedules, and requirements for overtime premiums are found in virtually all contracts.[14] Specific start and stop times, lunch and rest periods, and other scheduling rules are usually included. Although scheduling work is normally a management prerogative, any change from the hours specified in the contract, no matter how minimal, is considered an unfair labor practice, even if it does not affect the employee's pay.

CONDITIONS OF EMPLOYMENT The board has stated that the phrase "conditions of employment" refers to terms under which employment status is given or withdrawn, rather than physical working conditions. Conditions must have a material and significant impact directly affecting the employment relationship. Four major areas include the following:

1. ***Employment security.*** This covers all aspects of hiring and firing and granting tenure. Hiring and probationary periods, seniority, job-bidding procedures, promotions, and transfers must all be bargained, except for the nondiscriminatory promotion of employees to supervisory positions. The order and manner of layoffs and recalls, issues surrounding the discharge and retirement of employees, and contracting out work normally performed by members of the bargaining unit are also mandatory. In some instances, plant closings and relocations must be bargained. Although courts have said that a company is not required to negotiate an economically motivated decision to close or relocate a plant, the effects of such an action must be bargained.
2. ***Job performance.*** The day-to-day relationship between employer and employee is a mandatory subject of bargaining and includes absenteeism, work breaks, lunch periods, discipline, and dress codes. Although safety practices must be discussed, management may still have the final say. Decisions concerning workloads and the number of employees necessary for a task are considered mandatory, and under recent board and court decisions, drug testing of employees is considered a mandatory bargaining subject, although the decision to test job applicants is not.[15]
3. ***Union security.*** The protection of the union's representation status is a mandatory subject for bargaining. Such protection requires a 30-day grace period before an employee must join the union, discontinuance of a union shop according to majority vote,

UNION SECURITY

The provisions of collective bargaining agreements that directly protect and benefit the labor organization (union), such as dues checkoff and union shops.

and a prohibition against discharge of an employee for nonmembership in a union for any reason other than failure to pay dues.

4. ***Management–union relationships.*** All principles governing the discharge of collective bargaining duties and enforcement of collective bargaining agreements, including grievance and arbitration procedures, are considered mandatory.

If the subject is **permissive**, a party must withdraw it from bargaining if the other party does not voluntarily agree to its inclusion in the discussion. Both parties must agree for permissive subjects to be bargained. Examples of permissive subjects include performance or indemnity bonds, which protect the employer from liabilities in the quality of the union's work, and management's right to have an impact on the internal affairs of the union.

PERMISSIVE ITEMS

Those items not related to wages, benefits, working conditions, or other mandatory subjects that may be negotiated in collective bargaining if both parties agree; If one party refuses to negotiate a permissive item, the other party cannot claim bad-faith bargaining or declare an impasse in negotiations over the item.

Subjects deemed **illegal** by the act or the NLRB may not be proposed for discussion and, even if agreed to by both parties, would not be enforced by any court. These include violations of public policy, otherwise unlawful issues, and items inconsistent with the principles of the National Labor Relations Act. A closed shop requiring union membership before an employee is hired, racial separation of employees, and discrimination against nonunion members are illegal bargaining subjects.

If in the future a portion of the contract becomes illegal under a state or federal law, the **severability clause** in the contract becomes effective. A severability clause allows for the terms of the contract to be independent of one another, so that if a term in the contract is deemed unenforceable by a court, the contract as a whole will not be deemed unenforceable. If there were no severability clause in a contract, a whole contract could be deemed unenforceable because of one unenforceable provision. Severability clauses appear in 68 percent of all contracts. About half provide that the offending section is null and void; the other half call for renegotiation of the issue.[16]

SEVERABILITY CLAUSE

A contract clause stating that any portion of a contract declared invalid by state or federal law shall be declared null and void while still holding the remainder of the contract valid.

Sources of Bargaining Issues

In general, it is the union that introduces most of the issues to be discussed at a collective bargaining session, and management reacts to such proposals. Management can and usually does, however, initiate some issues for negotiation.

Union negotiation teams solicit member input in formulating demands. This solicitation can be done at general union meetings, at meetings with union stewards, or through written or electronic questionnaires. Some bargaining items are formulated through analysis of the types of grievances filed and from recent arbitration awards. Problems detected at a lower level are passed on to be included in the collective bargaining talks. Management often adds line supervisors' suggestions on workforce rules and operations to its economic positions during negotiations.

Both union and management can also look to external sources for bargaining items. Recent contracts within the same industry or region can give both parties ideas on realistic, attainable proposals. Often the overall economic condition of the nation and that of the particular industry limit or expand bargaining demands.

In addition to general sources, each party is entitled to certain types of information from the other. Under the duty to bargain in good faith, a union may demand relevant information from the employer in preparing wage demands.

Planning may be the most critical element in successful negotiations. In general, negotiators plan effectively in the following ways:

1. ***Anticipation.*** Each side, through research and members' input, must correctly assess those issues critical to both sides. The general mood greatly affects the early stages of negotiations. The key issues for each side and the possibility of a strike or other actions should be anticipated and a response prepared. A response, such as a detailed counterproposal or a package of several items, can center the conflict on the issues rather than personal emotions.

2. ***Realistic objectives.*** Preparation on all items of interest can help avoid costly mistakes during heated and lengthy negotiations. Negotiators should prioritize all objectives and develop a settlement range. Logical trade-offs among items of interest can be analyzed and prepared.
3. ***Strategy.*** Each party must evaluate the opponent's current needs as well as its own, review the bargaining history between the two parties, and prepare an overall strategy for negotiations. Important aspects to consider include personalities of negotiators, current financial and political position of each party, and outside influences, such as the economy, product sales, and public support of unions. Strategy formulation helps both sides develop realistic expectations of how negotiations will proceed and what the final agreement will be. For example, senior union employees may be most unhappy with the current pension program, but a significant increase in the pension formula would require costly increases for all future retirees. Thus, in developing its strategy, management could develop an economic package including alternative combinations of onetime lucrative early retirement options with pay increases loaded toward younger employees.
4. ***Agenda.*** Both parties should develop an agenda for discussing all items in a logical manner and incorporate it into the written ground rules. For example, after settling problems with the current contract's wording (which may have arisen through grievance), negotiators can exchange noneconomic proposals and settle as many as possible. They should follow this settlement with an exchange of economic proposals dealing with smaller-cost items first, keeping on the table the highest priority economic and noneconomic items.

Expectations must be established at the same time priorities are set. Successful collective bargaining may be impossible if the highest priority of one party is an item the other party is unlikely to negotiate.

To establish realistic objectives, the party considers patterns and trends in contract settlements of other employers in the industry and the local community. In an economy where a 2 percent cost-of-living raise is almost universal, a request for 8 percent would be unrealistic. The parties also examine their current and past bargaining relationship along with their relative strength. For example, if contract negotiations have already been concluded with other employers in the same industry and this employer in the past followed that pattern, it may be unrealistic to expect major deviations.

BARGAINING STAGE

As identified in Figure 6-1, the second phase of the negotiation process may be called the "bargaining stage" when the union and management negotiating teams sit down at the table to negotiate a collective bargaining agreement. Based on the particular needs and interests of the parties, both sides come to the table with a list of issues, concerns, demands, and often complaints. In the first session the members of both negotiating teams are introduced, and both chief negotiators usually make opening statements. In addition, ground rules for the negotiation that provide a framework of the "who, when, where" of the negotiation sessions are usually discussed and agreed upon. If the parties have a long-standing relationship, establishing procedures can be very routine. But when the collective bargaining process is relatively new or when the parties have had bad labor relations, setting procedures can be as difficult, and as important, as bargaining on the issues.

In one of the first sessions both sides usually, in accordance with their ground rules, exchange a list of all the mandatory and permissive (although not so identified) issues they wish to negotiate or "put on the table" in future sessions. These issues are often divided into two lists: economic issues (wages, health insurance, pension, paid time off, etc.,) and noneconomic (grievance process, seniority, work rules, etc.) issues. Then the heart of the collective bargaining process takes place: the exchange of proposals and counterproposals over a period of weeks, months, and sometimes even years. The different strategies, tactics, and techniques commonly used in the bargaining stage are discussed in detail in Chapter 5.

PRESSURE BARGAINING: POSSIBLE STRIKES

An understanding of the use of perceived leverage, or **pressure bargaining,** during labor negotiations is necessary in any study of collective bargaining. Often the final settlement in the collective bargaining process is greatly affected by the relative bargaining power of each party. Simply stated, if it costs more to disagree than to agree, the party will agree. It is therefore an objective during collective bargaining to determine the costs of putting on or responding to an economic strike.

The ultimate test of strength in the negotiating process is the union's ability to strike and the company's ability to take a strike. Before such action is undertaken, or even seriously planned, both sides carefully estimate the external factors that may influence the balance of power, and therefore the success of a strike or other action such as management hiring permanent replacement workers if the union declares a strike. For example, in 1996 when the UAW and the "Big 3" U.S. automobile manufacturers began negotiations, the economy was strong, and the companies were making record profits and wanted to avoid even one day of lost production—the result was significant wage increases and job security. About 11 years later, however, the balance of power was reversed and the "Big 3" were losing millions of dollars, had excess capacity, and needed to gain concessions just to remain in business. The result was record wage and benefit concessions by the UAW. The external economic factors had changed 180 degrees in only 11 years, and had completely shifted the balance of power—and thus greatly affected the outcome!

REACHING IMPASSE

STRIKES No matter what method of negotiations is followed, the parties at some point reach an agreement or face an **impasse** (a stalemate). There are many reasons why negotiations could result in an impasse. The most obvious is that the interests of the two parties have not been reconciled. Another reason is that one party has no real intention of settling. Their overall strategy might include going to an impasse to show how inflexible the other party is. Also, during pressure bargaining, a strategic impasse may appear necessary to move the two parties closer together, and a genuine impasse results simply by miscalculating how close the parties really are.

Usually, the employees initiate economic pressures during negotiations because the union's goal in contract negotiations is to increase benefits, whereas management's goal is to maintain the status quo or gain concessions. In the private sector, the threat of a **strike** by the union employees is the union's most effective means of showing power, putting pressure on management, and possibly realizing gains at the bargaining table if successful. In the public sector, strikes are usually unlawful, although they still occur on occasion. A strike, however, may be called and endured for reasons other than a genuine inability to reach an agreement. One party may merely have miscalculated the breaking point of the opposition and increased a demand or refused a request once too often. Errors in strategy or in the interpersonal relations of the negotiator could preclude an opportunity for compromise. Management may want to liquidate surplus inventory while production is stopped by a strike. Union leaders may want to consolidate workers' support for their leadership, proving that a future strike threat has to be respected. Union leaders may feel the need for union solidarity that can be fostered only by a picket line. Often a strike is needed to vent member frustration over an inevitable but unsatisfactory contract settlement.[17] On occasion an impasse may result after the negotiation teams have reached a tentative settlement and union membership rejects the contract. Such rejection may stem from a misjudgment of membership wishes by union officials or an inability to sell the agreement.

STRIKE

A work stoppage by a number of employees caused by a disagreement with management over certain issues such as contract negotiations, grievances, or unfair labor practices.

CALLING A STRIKE The right to strike is one of the rights made available to employees expressly provided by the National Labor Relations Act. It "lies at the core" of the congressional intent to promote collective bargaining in the private sector.[18] Usually, but not always, in the public sector employees are banned from striking by law. Whatever the reason for an impasse, a decision to strike is not made lightly. In many instances the union negotiating team has asked members to support a strike vote early in the negotiating process to prove its bargaining power when it becomes necessary to apply pressure. Although such a vote strengthens the negotiator's position, it needs to be carefully worked so that a strike deadline is not imposed, thereby tying the negotiator's hands. Slow-moving negotiations could become deadlocked; the deadline could destroy the negotiating atmosphere.

"Nobody wins in a strike, but there comes a point in time when somebody can push you off a cliff," said United Auto Workers former president Ron Gettelfinger. Gettelfinger and his negotiating team representing 73,000 members called for a strike against General Motors in September 2007, demanding job security and health care assurances.[19] A union must weigh the cost of a strike against the probable benefit. A strike means loss of wages when wages may be quite high after years of successful union negotiations. Strike benefits can also be a drain on union funds. Workers risk losing their jobs, and even if they return to work, a strike can damage or destroy a good relationship with the employer. In addition, a union risks the loss of public sympathy. The success or failure of previous strikes and the availability of other jobs must also be considered. In addition to lost wages, union members today are also almost equally concerned about lost health insurance during a strike, which can leave their family without health care coverage. For example, Smart Papers LLC, a Hamilton, Ohio, company, refused to extend health care benefits to striking workers as a means of putting added pressure on them to return to the table. The company also did not extend COBRA health care benefits and began advertising for replacement workers.[20] Today, union leaders are far less likely to call a strike than in past years. In fact, the Bureau of Labor Statistics reports that in 2009, the number of major U.S. strikes (1,000 or more employees) fell to 5, the fewest since 1947, when it began recording strike data, and far less than the 424 in 1974, the modern record (see Figure 6-2). The number of major U.S. strikes has remained remarkably low in recent years. The loss of wages and potential permanent loss of their jobs are reasons why fewer union members and leaders are willing to call for a strike. Employers have demonstrated their willingness to hire and train replacement workers to defeat a strike. Finding qualified replacement workers just is not as difficult as in past years. However, today both sides realize that a strike isn't in either's best interest.[21]

MANAGEMENT RESPONSE The majority of strikes in the private sector occur when the existing contract expires; then employers have ample notice to prepare a strike plan. However, many

FIGURE 6-2 Number of Major Strikes (Involving 1,000 or More Workers)

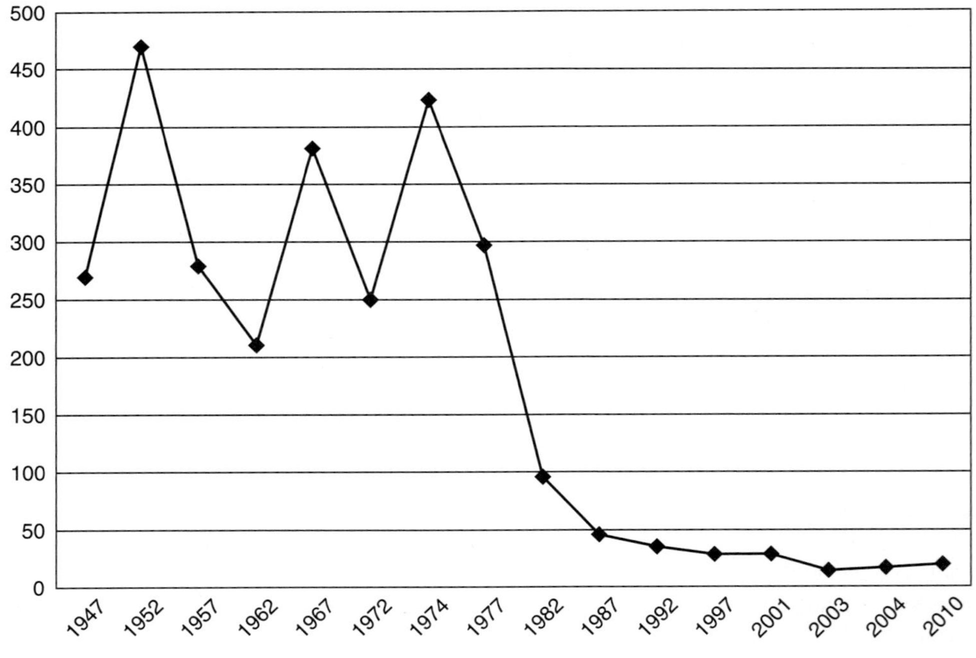

wait until negotiations begin to break down, which is too late. A strike plan often focuses on how the employer will shut down operation during the strike, continue to operate with only management personnel, or hire replacement workers. Strikers may not be fired during a strike, but they can be replaced with permanent replacement workers.

Employers may not lawfully discharge a striking worker until they have hired a replacement worker to fill the position. In one case, supervisors telephoned bargaining unit employees to see which would be striking. The employees were told that if they did strike, replacements had been hired. A federal appeals court upheld the company's actions when the union filed an unfair labor practices charge because contract negotiations were underway.[22]

Both sides should keep in mind the possibility of an eventual settlement calling for the recall of striking workers, even after replacements have been hired, and the possibility of "bonuses" being paid to them to compensate them for lost income. Although such events are rare, the Steelworkers Union, in 1996, reached an agreement with Bridgestone-Firestone two years after the union workers went on strike. The agreement provided for the recall of almost all the workers at five U.S. plants and the payment of $15 million in bonuses to them. The Steelworkers charged the Japanese-owned company with illegally replacing the 6,000 striking workers.[23]

WHY STRIKES OCCUR Labor relations researchers have presented three basic models that explain why strikes actually occur. The first is the *accident model*, which suggests that negotiators (both union and management) act rationally and have substantial incentives to avoid strikes. Thus, they usually seek to reach a settlement without a strike. Strikes, therefore, occur only accidentally because of bargaining errors, such as unrealistic expectations by union or management leaders, misperception of bargaining goals, or a substantial difference between union negotiators and their rank-and-file membership. The second theory focuses on *joint strike costs* and suggests that strikes are more likely to occur when the joint costs to management and the union are relatively low, for example, when management has substantial inventories and can use management or other personnel to keep operating for a substantial period of time without union members. The third theory views strikes as *rational tactics* in the bargaining process and suggests that they generally occur when the two parties have substantially different information. For example, a firm with a low ability to pay higher wages and remain solvent may have the incentive to endure a lengthy strike and convince the union of its financial condition. Research on strikes in the manufacturing industries for an 18-year period revealed that strikes were most often the result of bargaining errors or the accident model. Examples of strikes under the other two models, however, were also found.[24]

The circumstances that cause workers to strike and form a picket line are often tense and thus can easily provoke strikers to "let off steam," an impulse that can easily lead to serious misconduct. Workers on strike may resort to conduct that the employer believes is improper—conduct that causes damage to property or, in some cases, even bodily harm. The NLRB has held that activities of striking employees constitute serious misconduct when they "reasonably tend to coerce or intimidate employees."[25] The application of this standard has led the courts and the NLRB to consider physical acts or threats of physical harm directed at nonstriking employees (called scabs) to be serious and warrant possible discharge. Actions that have been ruled as serious misconduct include the throwing of rocks or eggs, vandalizing a supervisor's car, carrying a gun or a club on the picket line, and threatening physical harm.[26] In *Clear Pine Mouldings, Inc.*,[27] the NLRB ruled that verbal threats alone could warrant the discharge of a striker who, while carrying a gun, threatened to kill a nonstriking employee. In most cases, the isolated instance of obscenities or name-calling alone is not considered serious strike misconduct. If an employer fires striking employees because of serious misconduct, the employer is not required to show that all the employees were engaged in the activity if they were "actively cooperating" in the misconduct. And violent activity can result in the removal of the participants from the protection of the National Labor Relations Act. An examination of misconduct cases led one labor attorney to conclude that arbitrators are generally tolerant of strikers' misconduct, particularly if the employer provoked the incident.[28]

PRIMARY STRIKE

A strike called by a union against the direct employer of its members when a labor dispute exists.

ECONOMIC STRIKE

An employee strike over the failure to negotiate economic issues such as wages, benefits, or other conditions of employment. During an economic strike, the employer is entitled to replace strikers permanently and need only reinstate those for whom it has vacant positions.

UNFAIR LABOR PRACTICE STRIKE

A strike called over an employer's action determined by law to be an unfair labor practice, such as employee discrimination because of union activity. Employers cannot hire permanent workers during a ULP strike.

TYPES OF STRIKES Economic weapons such as a strike are necessary to the collective bargaining process. The **primary strike** is a strike between an employer and employee. For employees to be protected under the act, a labor dispute must exist between the striking employees and their employer.

The act recognizes two types of strikes and handles them differently. An **economic strike** is called to affect the economic settlement of a contract under negotiation. An **unfair labor practice strike** is called to protest an employer's violation of the National Labor Relations Act. For example, if a union member was fired for union activities, workers could stage a strike until the discriminatory practice was remedied.

Under either strike action, the worker retains status as an employee and thereby remains under the protection of the National Labor Relations Act. The worker's right to reinstatement after a strike depends on the type of strike. After an economic strike, the employee is not entitled to reinstatement if the employer filled the job with a permanent employee during the strike. However, if the job has not been filled or becomes vacant when a replacement leaves, the worker can reclaim it. Employees are entitled to reinstatement after an unfair labor practice strike even if the employer has filled their positions. Strike misconduct by the employee in either case can disqualify the worker from reinstatement. A strike intended as an economic strike can become an unfair labor practice strike by the union if the goal is not legal as in Case 6-1.

CASE 6-1

Hot Cargo Contract

On April 21, 1998, the board certified the union as the exclusive collective bargaining representative of full-time and regular part-time building service employees employed by the company. The union and company subsequently met on four occasions in an unsuccessful attempt to negotiate a collective bargaining agreement. At the first meeting, the union representative presented the company representative with a contract proposal containing, among other terms and conditions, the following picket line clause:

> No employee covered by this agreement should be required by the employer to pass picket lines established by any Local of the SEIU in an authorized strike.

During the four bargaining sessions, the parties agreed to various changes in the contract proposal but disagreed as to other provisions. The parties *did not* discuss the picket line clause during any of the bargaining sessions. At the end of the final bargaining session, the union stated that if the company did not accept the proposal then on the bargaining table, the union would strike. It is undisputed that the union's proposed contract included the picket line clause.

After the company refused to sign the proposed contract, the union struck. The union's business agent testified that an object of the strike was to get the company to sign the collective bargaining agreement. During the strike, the strikers informed the union that they wanted to return to work. The agent replied that he "would prefer [the strikers] to stay out for a little longer because we would have a better chance of getting a contract signed." The parties knew that the contract contained the picket line clause, but this clause *was never* a topic of discussion or controversy during the negotiations. Rather, the parties disagreed over other contract terms, and it was those disagreements that provoked the strike.

Nonetheless, the company filed an unfair labor charge against the union alleging that because the union's contract proposal contained a picket line clause prohibited by Section 8(e) of the act and the union engaged in a strike to force or require the company to enter into a contract containing that clause, the strike violated Section 8(b)(4)(ii)(A) (prohibiting secondary boycott agreements).

The administrative law judge found that Section 8(e) prohibited the picket line clause. He nevertheless recommended dismissal of the Section 8(b)(4)(ii)(A) allegation because he did not believe that *the object of the strike* was to force or require the company to enter into an agreement containing the picket line clause. The company appealed.

Decision

Like the ALJ, the NLRB agreed that Section 8(e) prohibited the picket line clause. Unlike the ALJ, however, the board found that the object of the strike was to force or require the company to enter into a contract containing the picket line clause, and therefore the union violated Section 8(b)(4)(ii)(A). The board noted that it is undisputed that the union engaged in a strike to obtain an agreement. Further, it is well established that a strike constitutes "coercion" within the meaning of the statute. The union proposed an agreement containing a picket line clause prohibited by Section 8(e). The union insisted that the company sign the contract or else the union would strike. When the company refused to sign the contract, the union began a strike. The strike was to compel the company to sign a contract, which, at all relevant times, included the clause prohibited by Section 8(e). Accordingly, the NLRB found that the union's strike, which began on February 22, 1999, had as *an object* forcing or requiring the company to enter into an agreement proscribed by Section 8(e) and that such conduct violated Section 8(b)(4)(ii)(A) of the act.

Source: Adapted from Local 32B-32J, *Service Employees v. Pratt Towers Inc.*, 169 LRRM 1185.

A strike that begins as an economic strike may become an unfair labor practice strike if the union can prove that an employer is refusing to bargain in good faith. It is obviously to the union's advantage to do so, as it is to management's advantage to keep the strike an economic strike by continuing to negotiate in good faith. Management then has the option to hire replacement workers during the strike and keep the plant open, thereby lessening any adverse impact caused by the strike. At the end of the strike, the replacement workers can be retained, and the employer may have upgraded the workforce with minimal disruption.[29] Unlike economic strikers, who may be replaced, unfair labor strikers have a substantially unqualified right to return to their jobs, even if the employer hired replacements. Thus, the type of strike may be a critical issue to both parties and may be in dispute.[30]

A strike technique that has recently gained favor with unions whose members work at numerous locations for the same employer is the rolling strike. A **rolling strike** targets one location at a time for a union walkout. The location, however, can change daily, making hiring replacements or covering locations with management nearly impossible.[31] For example, on August 11, 2005, baggage handlers and loaders represented by the Transport and General Workers Union staged a one-day walkout at Heathrow Airport in London, England, which stranded about 70,000 summer travelers. The walkout was to demonstrate support for workers fired by the airport catering firm and represented by the same union.[32]

ROLLING STRIKE

A strike technique used by unions that moves a strike against an employer from location to location so that hiring replacement workers becomes more difficult.

It is interesting to note that courts will not allow an employer to assume that permanent replacement workers hired during a strike are antiunion. In *NLRB v. Curtin-Matheson*, the Supreme Court upheld the board's rule that permanent replacement workers must be treated as any other group of employees when determining whether they wish to be represented by a union. That they took jobs while union employees were on strike does not create a presumption that they are antiunion.[33]

Permanent Striker Replacement

This distinction between how striking employees are treated as a result of either an economic or an unfair labor practice strike was established by a Supreme Court decision in 1938.[34] In the

Mackay case, the Court decided employers could permanently replace striking workers without violating the (then three-year-old) Wagner Act. The case involved a group of radio employees who decided to go on strike at midnight. The employer, believing it critical to stay "on the air" and provide continuous service, quickly filled the strikers' positions. The strikers then realized their strike was not having the desired outcome and asked for their jobs back. Management decided to reinstate them only if their replacements chose to resign—and 11 replacements did not. The union employees then filed suit claiming the employer had "interfered with, restrained, and coerced" them and thus violated their rights under the National Labor Relations Act. The NLRB agreed with the employees but also agreed with the employer that the act did not prohibit the hiring of permanent striker replacements.

MACKAY DOCTRINE

A court decision rule that interprets the NLRA as allowing employers to replace striking workers with permanent workers unless it is determined that the strike was an unfair labor strike. Striking workers who apply for reinstatement may be placed on a waiting list and hired as jobs become available.

The Supreme Court agreed, and the **Mackay doctrine** was established in one of the most important cases in labor law history. The Court noted that although Section 13 of the National Labor Relations Act prohibits the interference with employees' right to strike, an employer has the right to continue the operations of a business and replace strikers. The *Mackay* doctrine has been somewhat limited by three NLRB decisions: (1) employers cannot permanently replace strikers who are striking over an unfair labor practice, (2) strikers who apply for reinstatement unconditionally must be placed on a "waiting list" and hired as jobs become available if they do not acquire other employment, and (3) employers cannot grant pay raises to replacements not offered to strikers.[35]

Before the 1980s, however, companies seldom replaced striking workers with permanent replacements for a number of reasons. Frequently, an economic strike was determined, after the fact, to be an unfair labor practice strike, and the replacement workers were displaced. Often the company used the issue of allowing the strikers to return to their jobs as a way to settle an economic strike.

PERMANENT REPLACEMENT WORKERS

Under the National Labor Relations Board, when workers are engaged in an economic strike, management can hire permanent replacements. After the strike, the striking workers cannot claim their jobs back.

Economic factors of the 1980s first led companies to use **permanent replacement workers** more than ever before.[36] Mergers, downsizing, and companies going out of business may provide many employers with available trained workers during a strike. High unemployment and a weakening of union membership caused workers to cross picket lines willingly and to take jobs at wage rates lower than union-bargained rates. Two high-profile strikes in the 1980s, the 1981 PATCO strike in the public sector, and the 1986 Hormel strike in Austin, Minnesota, in the private sector both resulted in the hiring of permanent replacement workers in situations where many observers thought it would be impossible, and therefore awakened employers to the power of using replacement workers to negate a strike. The documentary *American Dream* provides actual footage of the Hormel strike in a powerful presentation of the Hormel 25-week strike that gained national significance. Today many employers have found that the mere threat of hiring replacements can cause a strike to be avoided. For example, in 2008 the United Food and Commercial Workers Union, Local 1099, cancelled a planned strike after the Kroger Company ran full-page advertisements in the Cincinnati Enquirer seeking replacement workers. The hiring of permanent replacement workers can also lead to the decertification of a union. The NLRB ruled that workers on strike for over one year are not eligible to vote in a decertification election. Thus, an employer, in an effort to win a decertification election, might force a strike, employ permanent replacement workers for over a year, and then seek a decertification election knowing the union strikers are no longer eligible to vote in the election. This employer tactic grew in popularity after the 1981 PATCO strike.[37]

If an employer has hired permanent replacement workers during a strike, then the union may want to negotiate a **strike settlement agreement** if a new contract is later approved. For example, in 2007, the Appalachian Regional Healthcare (ARH), which includes nine hospitals, hired replacement workers during a three-month strike by nurses. When a new contract was put before the striking nurses, ARH president Jerry W. Haynes announced that 150 replacement nurses would be permanent, and the 500 striking workers would be placed on a waiting list. Pat Tanner, chief negotiator for the nurses' union, declared the decision "an outrageous insult" and insisted on a separate strike settlement agreement that provided for hiring back the striking nurses and letting go the replacement nurses. The ARH also stipulated that such an agreement would need to state the strike was over wages—thus, an economic strike—while the union insisted it was primarily over staffing levels and mandatory overtime.[38]

In the past several years there has been a growing debate over a proposed amendment to the NLRA that would ban the hiring of permanent replacement workers during a strike. Supporters of the proposal contend that the escalating practice of hiring permanent replacement workers has weakened workers' ability to bargain collectively as expressly provided by the NLRA and has become a significant cause of the decline of unionization in the United States. Opponents of the proposed ban respond that it would tip the scale in favor of unions and even lead to more strikes that would disrupt the economy. Why? Individuals would be less likely to cross a picket line for jobs that were only temporary and end once the strike was settled. Both sides have legitimate points, and the issue may be central to the future of union–management relations in the United States. One "middle-ground" proposal would prohibit employers from hiring permanent replacement workers for a specified number of days after a strike had begun and thus provide both sides some bargaining leverage.[39] Congress, which thus far has chosen not to act, ultimately will decide the issue, and therefore employers remain free to hire permanent replacement workers.

PICKETING The use of **picket lines** during a strike varies according to the type of union involved. A craft union strike generally uses only two or three pickets. The purpose of the picket is simply to inform other craft union members that a strike is in progress. Because craft union workers are skilled laborers, workers who will not honor a picket line cannot easily replace them. Craft unions may use larger picketing groups when protesting the use of a nonunion contractor.

PICKET LINES

A line or procession of union members or union supporters staging a public protest outside an employer concerning a labor dispute—often due to failed contract talks.

An industrial union strike, however, often requires an active and large picket line to discourage unskilled laborers from keeping the production lines in operation. Mass picketing generally takes place at least at the start of a strike to persuade union members to join the strike and to keep strike-breakers away. In 2003, for example, almost 2,000 clerical, maintenance, and food service workers at Yale University rallied supporters in New Haven, Connecticut, by picketing. On one day in September, the workers' demonstration closed down the center of the city as well as the university with over 5,000 supporters of the Hotel Employees and Restaurant Employees International Union. As the demonstration became unruly, about 100 people were arrested, but the activity led to a new eight-year contract with 4–5 percent annual wage increases and sizable pension increases.[40]

An employer may respond to mass picketing by obtaining a court injunction against the union to refrain from certain activities. An injunction, usually in the form of a temporary restraining order, is possible if the strike activities have included incidents of violence, personal injury, or damage to property. In such cases, the court can order specific restraints on the union's use of pickets—limiting, for instance, their number and location.[41]

In *Overstreet v. United Brotherhood of Carpenters* (2005),[42] the union had a dispute with three contractors and tried to coerce them by putting pressure on 18 retail establishments that did business with the three contractors. The pressure was applied by the union erecting 4 × 15 foot "banners" near each retailer that read: SHAME ON [name of retailer], LABOR DISPUTE. Union members then placed the banners outside the entrances to the 18 retail businesses, even though their dispute was not with the retail businesses but with the contractors. They did not block the store entrances or talk to customers. The U.S. Ninth Circuit Court held the *bannering* was not unlawful secondary picketing. The court found that the union's actions did not "threaten or coerce, or restrain" because there was no picketing or one-on-one communication with employees or customers. Nor was there any unlawful "signal picketing," communication to employees, because the banners were directed at customers.

Today, picket lines have lost the power they once provided unions. In years past, a picket line in front of a plant, store, or construction site could cause a major financial loss to the employer. Many union and nonunion workers and their families and friends would "honor" the picket line. Crossing the line was the equivalent of pushing an old lady off a curb. Labor sympathizers would refuse to enter picketed workplaces as employees or customers. When unions represented 36 percent of the labor force, almost every adult had at least one union member in the family—and thus was sympathetic to labor's cause. Today, that just is not the situation. Even Rachelle Pachtman, the daughter of a union man, raised on union wages and benefits, crosses picket lines. "If there's a meeting in a hotel where workers are striking. . . . I'm going to the meeting. . . . But I feel terrible."[43]

LOCKOUT Although less frequent than strikes, an employer **lockout** may also be used in a labor dispute. The employer may withhold employment to resist union demands or actually to force concessions from the union. Layoffs, shutting down, or bringing in nonunion workers can accomplish the lockout. For example, in July 2005, management at NuTone Inc. in Madisonville, Ohio, notified 450 members of the United Auto Workers Local 2029 that they were locked out of their jobs. The union members were working without a contract after their contract with NuTone expired in June, and they had rejected the company's last offer. The locked-out employees were eligible for unemployment benefits.[44] The employer again must measure the same factors involved in withstanding a strike when deciding to lock out the employees: loss of profits, cost of continued operations, possible loss of customers, and the effect on future labor negotiations. Employer lockouts can be in violation of the National Labor Relations Act as an unfair labor practice if they are invoked to prevent unionization or to preclude collective bargaining before it begins.

Courts have supported both defensive and offensive employer lockouts under the Taft-Hartley Amendments. In defensive actions, employers are justified in a lockout if a threatened strike caused unusual economic loss or operational difficulties. In multiemployer bargaining, a strike against one employer can justify a lockout by the others to preserve the integrity of the multiemployer bargaining unit. Offensive economic lockouts have been justified after an impasse has developed during collective bargaining negotiation or if the lockout was used to pressure employees to end the labor dispute on grounds favorable to the employer. The courts reasoned that an economic strike by employees seeks the same end, and therefore the lockout is protected.[45]

The use of replacement workers during a lockout is governed by the same rule as using replacements during a strike. Permanent replacements may be hired during a lockout to affect the economic outcome of a contract under negotiations but not if the lockout is a result of an unfair labor practice by the employer.[46]

NO-STRIKE, NO-LOCKOUT PROVISIONS Most agreements in the private sector contain provisions restricting both the union's ability to call a strike and management's ability to stage a lockout, such as this Agreement between C. Lee Cook Division, Dover Resources, Inc., and Lodge No. 681, International Association of Machinists and Aerospace Workers AFL–CIO, 2007–2012:

> **ARTICLE XIII**
>
> **Strikes, Stoppages, and Lockouts**
>
> During the life of this Agreement, the parties hereto agree that there will be no lockout of employees or strikes, direct or sympathetic, or work stoppages, or slowdowns of any type or character, except where either party hereto willfully refuses to abide by a decision duly rendered and handed down by an arbitrator acting under authority of the provision of Article VII.[47]

Usually either both or neither type of provision is negotiated because they are reciprocal in nature. No-strike and no-lockout clauses often contain similar, if not identical, language, falling into two general categories: (1) unconditional bans (63 percent of agreements) on interference with production during the life of the contract, and (2) conditional bans that permit strike or lockout under certain circumstances, usually one or more of the following:[48]

NO-STRIKE, NO-LOCKOUT PROVISION

A contract clause restricting both the union's ability to call a strike and management's ability to stage a lockout.

Exhaustion of grievance procedure

Violation of arbitration award

Refusal to arbitrate dispute

Noncompliance with portion of agreement

Deadlocked contract reopener

The discipline or discharge of employees participating in illegal strikes under a no-strike provision may be permitted in the agreement. Most of these clauses provide for appeal by the employee.[49]

No-strike clauses are usually highly sought by industry, but severe circumstances may alter their value. For example, the U.S. steel industry had enjoyed an industry-wide no-strike agreement for 36 years when in 1986, the six major U.S. steelmakers decided to bargain separately with the United Steelworkers of America. The firms' fierce competition for survival forced them to give up the safety of joint negotiations and the continuance of the no-strike pact. The result was the longest U.S. steel industry strike in history.[50]

RESOLUTION STAGE: BEYOND IMPASSE

Because both management and union negotiators seek to successfully negotiate a new agreement that meets their interests, they usually want to resolve an impasse. They can decide early on before the contract has expired to seek a facilitator or mediator to assist them in the negotiation process, or they can request assistance after the contract has expired. Entering into negotiations long before the contract expiration date, however, can relieve some of the deadline pressure. The use of joint labor–management study committees before and during the contract negotiations also can alleviate much of the conflict present in traditional bargaining sessions.

Still, sometimes an impasse cannot be avoided, and impasse resolution becomes one of the stages of negotiations. Sometimes a pressure tactic such as a strike, lockout, or the hiring of permanent replacement workers is effective in bringing the other party back to the table. Often informal communication through a neutral third party enables the parties to resume talks to a successful conclusion. Traditionally, however, an impasse is often resolved by resorting to **mediation**, **arbitration**, or **fact-finding**.

MEDIATION

The introduction of a neutral third party into a grievance situation or collective bargaining impasse. Although mediators have no decision-making powers, they use their skills and work actively to achieve a settlement that is mutually agreeable to both sides.

MEDIATION Mediation is a voluntary process selected by both parties to assist them in moving beyond impasse to a settlement. Mediation services are usually provided by a third-party neutral, experienced and trained in dispute resolution techniques. A mediator has no authority to decide the unresolved issues, and instead relies on personal powers of persuasion, tenacity, creativity in suggesting alternatives to issues, and experience in labor relations disputes. The lack of authority to impose a decision on the parties is both a major strength and weakness of mediation. It is a strength because the parties are fully aware that they will directly participate in the formulation of the terms of any agreement on any issue. Thus the parties, to some extent, believe they control the outcome of the process—and they know that should the dispute go to arbitration, they will have no control over the decision, which is often final and binding. However, the lack of authority to decide issues is also a major weakness of mediation because there is no guarantee of a settlement.

Another major advantage of mediation is that it is confidential. The mediator usually destroys all papers and evidence of the case immediately after it is resolved, and cannot be required to testify in court—which often enables the parties to be more flexible in their efforts to find a settlement. By contrast, arbitration and court hearings take place in public forums.

For these reasons, control of any decision and confidentiality, as well as others, mediation is increasingly used to resolve labor disputes, and is generally preferred over other methods by the parties. In fact, about 85 percent of labor–management grievance disputes are resolved through mediation.[51] In addition, about 90 percent of management and 92 percent of union representatives reported a positive experience when using Federal Mediation and Conciliation Services' mediators to resolve a collective bargaining impasse.[52] How do mediators resolve

Tips from the Experts

Successful Mediator Practices

Create a Positive Atmosphere!

Simple, but effective, tactics include: (1) change the seating of the parties—even seat them on the same side of the table across from the mediator, (2) move the parties to separate rooms to break tension, (3) create a deadline on an issue—and resolve it before moving on to the next issue.

Maintain Neutrality

Above all else mediators must project neutrality! Treat both sides the same—even treat the hostile person the same as the polite person.

Absorb Conflict

Let the parties know you are listening; "I hear your anger," but don't respond, and instead absorb their hostility—negotiators will not argue for very long with a mediator who won't argue with them.

Provide Reality Checks

One of a mediator's most useful tactics. If a proposal, idea, or fact is unreasonable or extreme, ask for a reality check—"What evidence can you present the other side to support your proposal?" Or, "Do you really want to jeopardize the progress made thus far by offering a value that is triple the last one?"

No Conscience

A mediator's job is to get an agreement—not to decide if an offer is "fair" or "just." If the parties agree to it, then it is right, no matter how bizarre it might appear to the mediator! Avoid the "novice's curse"—drafting what a mediator believes is a neutral proposal—ask the party making the proposal to draft it and thus avoid any possible blame by the other party if they don't agree with the language.

Source: Adapted from Patrick J. Cleary, *The Negotiation Handbook* (Armonk, NY: Sharpe Pub., 2001), pp. 137–62.

labor disputes in most cases? Patrick J. Cleary, former chairman of the National Mediation Board, suggests several common mediator practices in "Tips from the Experts."

Mediation services are available through the Federal Mediation and Conciliation Service (FMCS: www.fmcs.gov) and similar state agencies. A mediator such as Louis Manchise in Profile 6-1 assists in rescheduling negotiation sessions, reopening discussions, and making suggestions on possible areas of agreement. If a mere misunderstanding of the parties' positions has caused an impasse, an unbiased third party can often show them how close they actually are to agreement. If the substantive distance between the parties causes the impasse, a mediator will use a variety of techniques to find a proposal both sides can agree on.[53]

Profile 6-1

Louis J. Manchise: Mediator

Louis J. Manchise has worked as a mediator in the Greater Cincinnati, Ohio, region for the past 33 years. Most recently, before joining the faculty at Northern Kentucky University, he served as director of mediation services for the Federal Mediation and Conciliation Service (FMCS) in Cincinnati. He is known in the conflict management community as a dedicated, hardworking, fair, and creative problem solver. Throughout his career he has mediated a wide spectrum of disputes. The cases he has been involved in include labor–management negotiations, employee–employer matters, commercial disputes, court cases, grievances, equal employment opportunity complaints, peer conflict, and inter- and intragovernmental conflicts at all levels: federal, states, counties, and cities.

Louis J. Manchise, national award-winning federal mediator.

Source: Courtesy of Louis J. Manchise, Vice Chair, Board of Directors, The Alternative Dispute Resolution Center, Northern Kentucky University. Accessible at www.adr.nku.edu. Used by permission.

A FMCS survey of 1,168 pairs of union and management leaders found that mediation is in greater demand today than in past years. Possible reasons include the economy and increased polarization of labor–management relations which often lead to an impasse over major issues such as wages, job security, and health care. Fifty percent of the leaders responded that mediation is needed to resolve differences and prevent work stoppages.[54]

INTEREST ARBITRATION

A process used to resolve an impasse in negotiations where the parties submit the unresolved items to a neutral third party to render a binding decision.

INTEREST ARBITRATION **Interest arbitration** is a distinctly different process from mediation. Like mediation it involves a neutral third party (or panel), but unlike mediation the arbitrator is given the authority to make a final and binding decision on the unresolved issues in a stalled contract negotiation. It is important to realize that interest arbitration is different from grievance arbitration (see Chapter 12) which utilizes arbitration to resolve rights disputes that have arisen during the life of a contract. Labor negotiators generally prefer to use mediation in resolving a contract negotiation impasse because they maintain control of the outcome, and therefore interest arbitration is infrequently used in the private sector to resolve a contract impasse.

But when negotiation and mediation have failed to produce a settlement, and both parties prefer a settlement to a continued impasse, or other possible outcomes, then they may agree in writing to utilize interest arbitration. Why? The primary benefit of interest arbitration is that it will produce a settlement of unresolved issues which is "final and binding."

The most common criticism of interest arbitration is that arbitrators too often simply "split the difference" or "meet in the middle" on key issues such as wages. This possibility may cause the parties to take only extreme positions—thus the middle if chosen will be closer to their real position. Another criticism is the there is little incentive to reach an agreement during negotiations if the parties believe the issue will end up in arbitration—thus the anticipation of arbitration has a "**chilling effect**" on their motivation to settle. In addition, some critics of arbitration believe that in some cases it has a "**narcotic effect**" on negotiations—that is, the parties become more reliant on arbitration to achieve their desired gains as they become more knowledgeable of the arbitrator's decisions.[55] These criticisms of interest arbitration may cause negotiators to avoid arbitration, even when in a specific situation they believe it would be useful. They don't want the other party to anticipate the use of interest arbitration, and then bargain at the table under the chilling or narcotic effect, which may greatly prejudice their bargaining proposals. Yet another criticism of interest arbitration is that it does not offer the confidentiality of mediation.

In the United States three federal laws govern private sector arbitration of disputes: the 1947 Labor–Management Relations Act (LMRA), which provides for the use of interest arbitration to resolve collective bargaining disputes; the 1926 Railway Labor Act, which has jurisdiction over labor disputes involving railroad, airline, and mass transit industries; and the 1925 Federal Arbitration Act, which provides for the arbitration of disputes in commercial cases. Interest arbitration usually begins when one or both parties submit a request for arbitration to the American Arbitration Association (AAA), the Office of Arbitration Services (OAS) of the Federal Mediation and Conciliation Service, or a state or local agency.

FACT-FINDING This is a semijudicial method of dispute resolution, which is primarily used in the public sector. A hearing, similar to the one used in the arbitration process, is used to assemble and make the facts public through the media. But the fact-finding panel, like a mediator, can only recommend how an impasse may be resolved. **Fact-finding** can be used to delay a strike, bring an unreasonable demand to the public's attention, create an atmosphere for new ideas, and if reasonable recommendations are made, pressure a party into acceptance. This technique is used where such pressure may force the parties to reach an agreement, especially if the facts show that one side is unreasonable.

FINAL-OFFER ARBITRATION This method of dispute resolution requires both parties to submit their final offer on an unresolved issue to an arbitrator or a panel that has the authority to select one of the proposals. Final-offer arbitration gives the parties the motivation to make their final offers reasonable. Both parties realize that a less reasonable offer has a lower chance of selection. Therefore, they strive to make their offer appear as fair and reasonable as possible. Final-offer arbitration may take one of two forms: final-offer total package, which restricts the arbitrator to selecting either the management's or union's entire final proposal on all unresolved issues, or final offer issues by issue, which allows the arbitrator to select either the management's or union's final proposal on each issue separately. In recent years final-offer arbitration has received a great deal of media coverage because it is used to resolve salary disputes between major league baseball players and the club owners. The collective bargaining agreement between the club owners and the union specifies the use of final-offer arbitration:[56]

ARTICLE VI.—SALARIES

> Sec. F. The arbitration panel shall be limited to awarding only one or the other of the two (salary) figures submitted. There shall be no opinion.

The final-offer salary arbitration process has resulted in roughly an even number of decisions won by players and the clubs from 1974 to 2010, with the clubs winning 52.6 percent of the cases decided by three-member panels. In 2010, for example, the players won three of eight arbitration hearings. Ryan Theriot's, of the Chicago Cubs, final offer was $3.4 million, the Cubs' final offer was $2.6 million, and the panel chose the Cubs offer. Cory Hart's, of the Milwaukee Brewers, final offer was $4.8 million, and the Brewers' final offer was $4.15 million, and the panel chose Hart's offer.[57]

MEDIATION–ARBITRATION As a combination of mediation and arbitration, the parties agree to bring in a mediator with authority to arbitrate any unresolved issues, should the mediation, which occurs first, fails. This method can, if it goes well, combine the best of the two methods—it provides a mediation in which the parties together develop a mutually agreeable settlement, but if that fails, then the parties are guaranteed a decision by an arbitrator. Since the arbitrator is the same person, he/she knows the issues well and may arrive at a more informed decision more quickly. A potential disadvantage of this method is the parties not fully participating in the mediation, since they believe it will lead to arbitration.

REDUCING AN AGREEMENT TO WRITING

At some point agreement is reached on wages, hours, and other terms and conditions of employment. Today the agreement is written, but when the National Labor Relations Act was passed, it did not expressly require that a collective bargaining agreement be reduced to writing and signed by the parties. Nor did it address whether bargaining was to be a process of continuing negotiations or even what the legal status of a signed agreement might be. These questions were left to the National Labor Relations Board (NLRB), the courts, and Congress to answer in piecemeal fashion.

DUTY TO SIGN

The obligation of both parties to reduce to writing and sign any agreement reached through the collective bargaining process. Refusal to sign can be declared an unfair labor practice.

As early as 1941, the Supreme Court imposed a **duty to sign**, or a duty on the parties in a collective bargaining relationship to reduce to writing and sign any agreement reached through the bargaining process. A refusal to sign was declared a refusal to bargain collectively and an unfair labor practice because, the Court found, a signed agreement had long been informally recognized as a final step in the bargaining process. The Court thought it obvious that the employer's refusal to sign an agreement "discredits the [labor] organization, impairs the bargaining process, and tends to frustrate the aim of the statute to secure industrial peace through collective bargaining."[58] In the Taft-Hartley Amendments, Congress recognized the need for a written agreement and defined the bargaining duty as including "the execution of a written contract incorporating any agreement reached if requested by either party."[59] Part of the negotiator's role in the collective bargaining process is drafting the final agreement. The negotiator should try to

Tips from the Experts

Arbitrator

What are the three most common drafting errors in collective bargaining contracts that cause problems for an employer or the union?

1. *Failure to define a contractual term or phrase.* Arbitrators give words their ordinary and usual meaning unless there is an indication that the parties intended a special meaning.
2. *Failure to specify the scope of the arbitrator's authority.* For example, is the award binding or merely advisory? Does the arbitrator have the usual authority to review the penalty imposed once he or she determines that the grievant did commit the offense with which he or she was charged?
3. *Failure to encourage resolution of grievances at the earliest possible step.* Such a failure would encourage open and full discovery and exchange of information in the lower grievance steps and could enhance the prospects of settlement or avoid the element of surprise at the arbitration hearing.

be clear and concise while accurately reflecting the agreement and the understanding of the parties. One author suggests that before it is signed, the final agreement should be circulated for comment among nonnegotiating union and management personnel it will affect:

> Once contract provisions are committed to paper, a good test of their meaning is to have a wide variety of different individuals, wholly unfamiliar with what has transpired during negotiations, read and interpret each provision of the contract. Particularly appropriate candidates for this **provisional intent test** are those who enforce, administer, police, or are governed by the terms of the agreement—stewards, foremen, department superintendents, shop chairmen, plant managers, grievance committeemen, rank-and-file members, etc. If provisional meaning is misconstrued, revision is in order.[60]

PROVISIONAL INTENT TEST

When knowledgeable but uninvolved parties read the draft of a collective bargaining agreement after it has been reached to determine whether the drafting accurately reflects the interests of the parties.

KEY PROVISIONS OF A CBA

The agreement between a union and an employer is not an employment contract. The employment contract is between the employer and the employee. It may be expressed verbally or in writing, or it may simply be a function of the employer's job offer and the employee's acceptance. The union is not a party to this employment contract, but the agreement between the union and the employer does shape the terms of that independent employment contract by establishing company policy in the areas covered by the agreement. The labor agreement also serves to define the union's relationship with management and provides the means to enforce its provisions. Each labor agreement is unique in terms and language, but all have basic similarities. Most labor contracts contain four main sections: union security, wages and benefits, management rights, and administration. Union security and management rights are discussed in the following sections of this chapter, wages and benefits are presented in Chapters 7 and 8, and contract administration in Chapters 10, 11, and 12.

Union Security

Union security refers to a union's ability to grow and to perform its exclusive collective bargaining role without interference from management, other unions, or other sources. A key element to a union's security is a provision in the collective bargaining agreement requiring employees to join the union and pay union dues as a condition of continued employment. Such a provision assures the union and its members that all the employees who share the benefits of collective bargaining agreements pay for the union's cost. Required union membership increases the financial base of the union and may increase its ability to represent its members at the bargaining table.

Unions are concerned about their security for many reasons. For instance, a union is certified as the exclusive bargaining agent for only one year following a representation election.

ARTICLE II
Union Security

1. Agency Shop

a. Subject to applicable law, all employees who, as of the date of this Agreement are members of the Union in good standing in accordance with the constitution and by-laws of the Union or who become members of the Union following the effective date of this Agreement, shall, as a condition of employment, remain members of the Union in good standing insofar as the payment of an amount equal to the periodic dues and initiation fees, uniformly required, is concerned.

b. Subject to applicable law, all present employees who are not members of the Union and all individuals hired after the effective date of this agreement, shall, beginning on the thirtieth day following the effective date of this agreement or the thirtieth day following employment, whichever is later, as a condition of employment, either become and remain members of the Union in good standing insofar as the payment of an amount equal to the periodic dues and initiation fees, uniformly required, is concerned, or, in lieu of such Union membership, pay to the Union an equivalent service charge.

FIGURE 6-3 Union Security Clause. *Source*: Agreement between General Electric Aviation and Lodge No. 912, International Association of Machinists and Aerospace Workers, AFL-CIO, 2007–2011. Used by permission.

Rival unions may not seek to organize its members during that short time. Although a union security provision cannot prevent such raiding after the year, loyalties are developed and strengthened by participation in the union for that year.

UNION SECURITY CLAUSE

A CBA provision that requires employees to be members in good standing of a union.

UNION SECURITY CLAUSE Many collective bargaining agreements contain a union security clause similar to the one in Figure 6-3. The clause requires that all employees within the bargaining unit become and remain members in good standing as a condition of employment. This phrase "members in good standing" means that employees have the option to choose either *full membership*, which includes the payment of all dues, fees, and assessments as well as prescribed membership obligations, or *limited membership*, which requires the payment only of those dues and fees directly needed to support the union in performing representation duties such as collective bargaining and grievance settlement. Thus, the costs of limited memberships are normally lower than those of full membership. The union, as the exclusive bargaining representative of all employees in the bargaining unit, is required to inform employees of their membership rights. These rights include the option to refrain from supporting union activities other than those involved in collective bargaining, contract administration, and grievance arbitration. The employer is not the representative of the employees and thus has no obligation to inform employees of their membership rights. Unions, to maintain solidarity and secure greater funding, strongly encourage employees to maintain full membership. It is also important to note that the clause specifies the employer's right to "secure new employees from any source"—not only union members or applicants referred by the union. Also note the employer agrees to terminate any employee—upon request from the union—for failure to become a member in good standing.

The 1935 National Labor Relations Act protected union security in several ways. Company unions were prohibited because the act's proponents saw them as a major threat to employee rights.[61] Yellow-dog contracts, whereby employees agreed not to join unions in order to get hired, and blacklisting of union sympathizers were made illegal. The act allowed an employer to make an agreement with the union requiring union membership as a precondition to employment. As a result, the closed shop clause became common.

Union security increased union membership. Automatic **check-off provisions** in the contract authorizing the employer to withhold dues from a member's wages ensured that the union would receive payment. For example, see Figure 6-4. Dues "check-off" is a common method by which the union collects the monthly dues and fees from members through payroll deduction. Employees must voluntarily authorize the payments, in writing, and their authorization cannot be irrevocable for more than a year or the life of the contract, whichever is shorter. The check-off is often renewed automatically each year unless the employee revokes it. A dues check-off provision can be critical to a union, and no longer can be considered a guaranteed concession from employers. In 2005, for example, Indiana stopped collecting dues from teachers and by 2011 dues-paying members had declined by 90 percent. Other states including Colorado, Utah, and Washington experienced similar declines after enacting state laws .[62]

CHECK-OFF

A contract provision requiring that the employer deduct union dues directly from union employee paychecks. The collected dues are then deposited in the union treasury.

Public reaction to the growth of union membership and numerous labor–management conflicts following World War I led to the 1947 passage of the Taft-Hartley Amendments to the National Labor Relations Act. Added to Section 7, which guaranteed freedom of organization, was a guarantee of the employee's right not to organize and engage in union activity. The closed shop was outlawed, although the amendments allowed union shops to be negotiated in future contracts. A union shop required union membership on or after 30 days of employment. The hiring power, therefore, was restored to the employer. However, although the act allowed union shops, it also permitted states to outlaw union shops by passing right-to-work laws that prohibit agreements requiring membership in a labor organization as a condition of employment (see next section). The Taft-Hartley Amendments also limited the dues check-off practice by requiring a written authorization from each union member.

ARTICLE 3
Union Shop Conditions and Check-off

Union Shop—It shall be a condition of employment that all employees of the Employer covered by this Agreement who are members of the Union in good standing on the execution date of this Agreement shall, on the sixty-first (61st) day following the execution date of this Agreement become and remain members in good standing in the Union. It shall also be a condition of employment that all employees covered by this Agreement and hired on or after its execution date shall, on the sixty-first (61st) day following the beginning of such employment become and remain members in good standing in the Union. The Employer may secure new employees from any source whatsoever.

During the first sixty (60) calendar days of employment, a new employee shall be on a trial basis and may be discharged at the discretion of the Employer, and such discharge shall not be subject to the Grievance and Arbitration Procedure.

Check-Off—The Employer agrees to deduct weekly Union dues and/or service fees and uniform assessments from the wages of employees in the bargaining unit who individually certify in writing, authorization for such deduction in a form authorized by law. The Employer agrees, in the case of new Union members, to deduct the Union initiation fee and in the case of a non-member, an initial service fee from the wages of any new or non-member Union employee who certifies in writing authorization for such deduction in a form authorized by law.

In the event no wages are then due the employee, or are insufficient to cover the required deduction, the deduction for such week shall nevertheless be made from the first wages of adequate amount next due the employee and thereupon transmitted to the Union.

Upon written request by an authorized representative of the Union, the Employer agrees to dismiss any employee within five (5) days from receipt of such request for failure to comply with Article 3, Section 3.1, limited only by the Labor Management Relations Act of 1947.

FIGURE 6-4 Automatic Withholding of Union Dues Source: Agreement between The Kroger Co. and the United Food and Commercial Workers International Union AFL-CIO, 2007–2010. Used by permission.

Finally, court decisions have limited the application of a union shop provision by narrowing the meaning of union membership. The Supreme Court has long held that being a union member for the purpose of complying with a union shop provision could not require more of a person than paying dues or limited membership. A union could not require attendance at meetings or participation in union activities.[63]

In a historic decision, *CWA v. Beck*, the Supreme Court limited a union shop requirement for the paying of dues as a union member to *only that portion of the union's dues that represented the cost of bargaining and representation*. This important decision covered both private and public sector unions, therefore individual union members can choose not to pay any funds to support "noncore" matters such as political contributions or lobbying efforts.[64] In 1995, the NLRB expanded the *Beck* holding to include an affirmative duty on the part of a union to inform its members of their rights under *Beck* to object to the expenditure of their dues for political or fraternal activities.[65]

CLOSED SHOP

A union security arrangement that requires employers to hire only union members. Closed shops were generally made illegal under the Taft-Hartley Act.

OPEN SHOP

A form of union security in which the workers within a bargaining unit may decide whether to join a union. Those who choose not to join are not required to pay union dues or fees or amounts equal to dues or fees.

UNION SHOP

A union security provision that all new employees must become union members in good standing.

AGENCY SHOP

A labor contract provision that requires employees to contribute a sum of money equal to union membership dues but does not require the employee to join the union. The employee benefits from collective bargaining by the union and in turn gives financial support to the union for negotiations, contract administration, and other actions.

FORMS OF UNION SECURITY Union security clauses may take several basic forms:

1. ***Closed shop.*** Outlawed by the Taft-Hartley Amendments, the *closed shop provision* allowed the employer to hire only union members. To get a job, a person first had to join the union.
2. ***Open shop.*** No employee is required to join or to contribute money to a labor organization as a condition for employment under the *open shop*.
3. ***Union shop.*** A **union shop** provides that within a specific period of time, usually 30–90 days, an employee must join the union (full or limited membership) to continue the job with the employer. Union membership under such a provision must be available on a fair and nondiscriminatory basis, and fees and dues must be reasonable and can be limited to an amount reflecting only the cost of bargaining and representation (see Figure 6-4).

   Although the National Labor Relations Act seems to allow a union to negotiate contracts requiring membership in the union as a condition of employment, in *NLRB v. General Motors Corporation*, the Supreme Court held that "membership" means paying union dues—the amount needed by the union to pay the costs to conduct collective bargaining. Thus, an employee cannot be required to sign a membership card or take an oath of membership. Despite the *General Motors* decision, many union leaders tell employees they must join the union.[66]

   Employees can petition the NLRB to hold a deauthorization poll—in which they can vote to revoke a union shop clause. Such petitions are rare however.
4. ***Union hiring hall.*** A *union hiring hall* provision is lawful and common in the construction, trucking, and longshoring trades. This form requires an employer to hire employees referred by the union, provided the union can supply a sufficient number of applicants. As long as the union refers union and nonunion members alike and does not require membership before the seventh day of employment, such provisions are legal. A hiring hall run by the International Brotherhood of Electrical Workers Local 48 (IBEW) in Portland, Oregon, was determined to be illegal by the NLRB because it dispatched workers based on their willingness to (1) engage in union organizing, (2) leave a nonunion employer and join the union, and (3) reward those who join the union with additional jobs.[67] And a refusal by the IBEW in Indiana to refer an electrician who was qualified and the next in line for referral because he owed the union back dues was declared an unfair labor practice because the labor agreement in question did not contain a union security clause.[68]
5. ***Agency shop.*** **Agency shop** provisions require employees to contribute a sum equal to membership dues to the union, but they are not required to join the union. The union is

provided with the financial support of employees who benefit from their collective bargaining, but the employee's right not to join the union is retained.

6. ***Maintenance of membership.*** The *maintenance of membership* provision requires those who are union members at the time a union contract is entered into to remain union members but only for the duration of the agreement. Nonunion members are not required to join.
7. ***Miscellaneous forms of union security.*** A *preferential shop* requires the employer to give hiring preference to union members. The *check-off* of union dues from an employee's paycheck operates as a union security form because it protects the source of union funding and automatically keeps the employees in good standing with the union. This form of union security is often the only legal device available in right-to-work states. *Superseniority* gives union leaders top seniority for layoff purposes and indirectly increases union security by ensuring the continuity of its leadership.

NLRB and court decisions have altered some of these traditional areas of union security. Agency shop nonunion members are increasingly challenging the amount of representation fees they are charged. A 1998 Supreme Court decision, *Air Line Pilots Association v. Miller et al.,* held that such challengers may not be required to use the arbitration process provided in a contract but can challenge a union's calculation of agency shop fees in a federal court. Citing its previous ruling in *Teachers v. Hudson*, the Court outlined three procedural protections for nonunion workers who object to the agency-fee calculation: They must be given (1) sufficient information to determine the fees estimation, (2) the escrowing of any amount in dispute driving the challenge, and (3) a reasonably prompt opportunity to challenge the amount of the fee before an "impartial decision maker." According to the Court, the impartial decision maker can be a federal judge.[69] In a follow-up to the guidance in *Hudson,* the Supreme Court upheld a Washington state law that requires a union to seek and obtain from employees who pay an agency-fee *affirmative authorization* before it can spend those fees for any noncollective bargaining purpose.[70]

Right-to-Work Laws

The Taft-Hartley Amendments to the NLRA also added to Section 14(b) of the National Labor Relations Act the following:

> Nothing in this act shall be construed as authorizing the execution and application of agreements requiring membership in a labor organization as a condition of employment in any state or territory in which such execution or application is prohibited by state or territorial law.

This provision allows states to enact laws prohibiting the union or agency shop forms of union security. Only 22 states, mostly in the West and the South, have done so (see Figure 6-5).

Right-to-work legislation understandably evokes great emotions from both proponents and opponents.[71] A significant research study published in 2004, however, concluded that states with right-to-work laws have 9 percent lower levels of union membership (union density) with all other significant factors held constant. Union membership varies greatly from state to state with the highest levels in New York (24.6 percent), Alaska (22 percent), Michigan (21.8 percent), California (18.4 percent), and the lowest levels in North Carolina (3.1 percent), South Carolina (4.2 percent), Utah (5.2 percent), and Arizona (5.2 percent). Although several factors influence union density, including "social capital" or workers' attitudes toward unions, and other social and political factors, the existence of a right-to-work law within a state has the most significant impact on the level of union membership within the state, and therefore it is an issue that raises strong emotions.[72]

RIGHT-TO-WORK

The federal law permitting states to prohibit agreements requiring membership in a labor organization as a condition of employment.

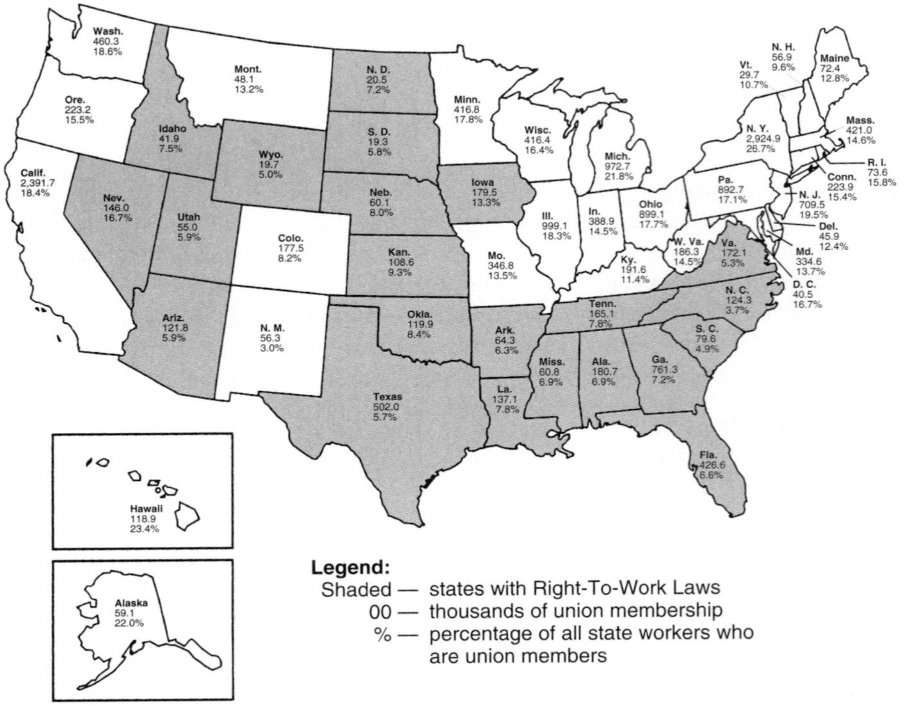

FIGURE 6-5 Union Membership and State Right-to-Work Laws. *Source:* Union Membership data derived from Additional Earnings and Union Membership Data, Companion to *Union Membership and Earnings Data Book:* Compilations from the Population Survey(2002).

Opponents contend that right-to-work legislation is an attempt to change the bargaining power at the negotiating table in management's favor. In addition, "right-to-work" as a slogan is misleading. As civil rights leader Martin Luther King once said:

> In our glorious fight for civil rights, we must guard against being fooled by false slogans as "right-to-work." It provides no "rights" and no "works." Its purpose is to destroy labor unions and the freedom of collective bargaining."

State right-to-work laws guarantee no one a job and in the opinion of opponents confer rights only on employers.[73] The phrase implies the union's concomitant right to prevent a person from working. According to union advocates, the requirement of union membership as a condition of employment is no more restrictive of an individual's freedom than the requirement of specific hours of work or of certain minimal job qualifications. Union members contend that employees should support the union primarily because of the benefits that union and nonunion employees alike receive through collective bargaining agreements.[74] Finally, opponents point out that the per capita income in states not having right-to-work laws is higher.

Proponents of the right-to-work legislation believe that it affirms the basic rights of a person to work for a living whether he or she belongs to a union or not.[75] They contend that no private organization should be able to tax a person and use that money to support causes with which all the members may not agree. Compulsory union membership can mean that a union does not need to be responsive to its members. And, according to proponents, right-to-work legislation encourages economic development because employers are not as likely to lose income from strikes over union security issues. A 2004 study confirmed that union membership density is significantly lower in right-to-work states in comparison to non-right-to-work states. The study also confirmed the belief that right-to-work states have lower wages overall in comparison with other states.[76]

A 1986 right-to-work referendum (RTW) election was held in Idaho. Both sides waged extensive media campaigns and focused the debate on the issues of lower wages and growth in the Idaho economy. Whether someone should be forced to join a union became a peripheral issue in the campaign. The National Right-to-Work Committee had targeted Idaho since 1976, when it successfully pushed passage of the Louisiana right-to-work law.[77] Right-to-work states have several characteristics that differ from union shop states. These characteristics include (1) low union membership, (2) little heavy industry, and (3) a high level of agriculture. Idaho shared these characteristics with the 20 right-to-work states.[78]

Union membership in Idaho was about 70,000 out of a population of one million. Idaho is surrounded by other right-to-work states: Wyoming, Utah, and Nevada. The referendum election was initiated by organized labor in an effort to overturn a 1985 law that was passed despite the governor's veto and made Idaho the 21st right-to-work state. Opponents of right-to-work began their campaign with the message, "The real intent of right-to-work is to damage unions and lower wages for all Idaho employees—both union and nonunion." Supporters of right-to-work pushed the message, "Should you be free to hold a job . . . whether you belong to a union or not?" Each side then began to muddle the issues by bringing in actors from Hollywood—Charlton Heston for the right-to-workers, Patty Duke for the opposition. The final vote was in favor of retaining the new right-to-work law by 30,514 votes of the 385,324 total votes cast.[79]

RESEARCH ON RIGHT-TO-WORK How did the new RTW law affect Idaho? A 2002 study published by the Federal Reserve Bank of St. Louis concluded: (1) Idaho is "an interesting case study" because it was a late adopter of a RTW law and because it is bordered by three RTW states and by three non-RTW states; (2) a decline in the unionization within Idaho began in 1981, four years prior to the law, and continued after passage until now it is similar to the border RTW states, but this decline was significantly faster after passage of the law; and (3) Idaho realized a significant and constant growth in manufacturing after passage of the law, suggesting that the state became more attractive to plants in comparison with the rest of the region.[80] A 2005 report on wages in Idaho for the 15-year period following the 1985 passage of its right-to-work law concluded that the wages of nonunion workers in the state fell by 4.2 percent while the wages of union workers remained unchanged. This result supported the hypothesis that the law reduced the level of unionization and the wages of nonunion workers, resulting in an increase in the union–nonunion wage gap in the state.[81] In 2002, Oklahoma became the 22nd right-to-work state. Colorado might have become the 23rd right-to-work state in 2008, but voters rejected the ballot measure after a spirited fight by both sides. It was a "notable victory for organized labor" because it was the first defeat of a right-to-work movement in many years. Members of the Coors Brewing Company family were active on both sides of the issue, with the patriarch Bill Coors making a strong television commercial appeal saying about the measure, "I'm not for it."[82]

Court rulings and right-to-work states have had the effect of creating two new categories of employees: free riders and cheap riders. **Free riders** are employees who are in a unit represented by a union and are covered by a collective bargaining agreement but do not join the union. The collective bargaining agreement is binding on them, but they may not have any influence over its creation. Because unions are prohibited from negotiating union-shop and agency-shop agreements in right-to-work states, these states tend to have more "free riders," which pose a problem for unions because they cannot collect dues from them but must provide them the same benefits as union members.[83] **Cheap riders** are employees who, again, are covered by a collective bargaining agreement but are not union members, but they are required to pay something to the union for the bargaining and representation services they receive. The share employees pay under union and agency shops where nominal membership or financial support is required ranges from 20 to 85 percent of a regular member's dues.

FREE RIDERS

Employees within a bargaining unit who choose not to join the union that bargains for an agreement for the unit. Although the employees receive all negotiated benefits, they pay no costs associated with the union.

CHEAP RIDERS

Employees within a bargaining unit who choose not to join the union that bargains for an agreement but are required to pay a fee to the union to provide their share of the costs associated with negotiations (usually 80 to 85 percent of the regular union dues).

TABLE 6-2 Length of Contract Term (2009 Contracts)

Duration in Years	% of Contracts
1	11
2	20
3	42
4 or more	27
	100% all contracts

Source: Adapted from Bureau of National Affairs, *2010 Source Book on Collective Bargaining* (Washington, DC: Bureau of National Affairs, 2010), p. 180. Copyright © 2010 by The Bureau of National Affairs, Inc., Washington, DC 20037. Used by permission.

OPENER CLAUSE

A clause in a collective bargaining agreement that allows negotiations to take place during the term of the contract on certain mandatory items, such as wages or insurance coverage.

LENGTH OF THE COLLECTIVE BARGAINING AGREEMENT A contract must run for a specific term. Most contracts contain renewal provisions, with prior notice of termination or of a time for reopening negotiations. Contracts can have **opener clauses** that allow for negotiations to proceed during the term of the contract on one or more items, generally wages.

A majority of contracts (about 69 percent) contain three-year terms or more, as shown in Table 6-2. The NLRB in a general ruling that extended the contract bar rule (see next section) to a three-year period aided the increase from one-year to three-year terms for most contracts.[84] In recent years, the number of contracts with periods extended to four years or more has steadily increased to 25 percent, up from only 5 percent in 1986. The desire by both union and management negotiators to provide greater long-term stability in labor relations has motivated negotiators toward longer multiyear agreements.[85] For example, Yale University and the Hotel Employees and Restaurant Employees International Union signed an eight-year agreement, the longest in the history of the university. The new agreement followed a bitter strike that closed down the center of New Haven, Connecticut, and resulted in 100 arrests. Richard C. Levin, president of Yale University, said he hoped the longer term of the agreement would provide "time to build a more cooperative relationship."[86] In a similar private sector example, in 2009, Harley-Davidson workers agreed to a seven-year contract to preserve their jobs, and management gained a long-term peaceful workforce.

Management Rights

The area of labor relations known as *management rights* has evoked more emotion and controversy than any other single issue. At the core of the debate is the concept of management's right to run the operation versus the union's quest for job security and other protections for its members.[87] Management rights provisions are found in almost all contracts in a section labeled *management rights*. Union rights are often considered to include those negotiated rights scattered throughout a contract according to subject matter.[88]

Of course, the question of who controls the workplace is of great interest to both management and labor. Management rights generally include decisions governing the working environment, including supervising the workforce, controlling production, setting work rules and procedures, assigning duties, and using plant and equipment. Management generally believes that if it is to operate efficiently, it must have control over all decision-making factors of the business. Management usually contends that any union involvement in the area is an intrusion on its inherent right to manage. Union advocates respond that where the right to manage involves wages, hours, or working conditions, labor has a legal interest under federal law.[89] Arthur Goldberg, former secretary of the Department of Labor and Supreme Court justice, summarized the management rights issue like this:

> Somebody must be boss; somebody has to run the plant. People can't be wandering around at loose ends, each deciding what to do next. Management decides what the

> employee is to do. However, the right to direct or to initiate action does not imply a second-class role for the union. The union has the right to pursue its role of representing the interest of the employee with the same stature accorded it as is accorded management. To assure order, there is a clear procedural line drawn: the company directs and the union grieves when it objects.[90]

A management rights clause often appears at the beginning of a contract following the union recognition and security clauses. Here is an example of a common management rights clause:

ARTICLE 5

Management Rights

> The management of the business and the direction of the working forces, including the right to plan, direct and control store operations, hire, suspend or discharge for proper cause, transfer or relieve employees from duty because of lack of work or for other legitimate reasons, the right to study or introduce new or improved production methods or facilities subject to the provisions of Article 20 of this Agreement, and the right to establish and maintain reasonable rules and regulations covering the operation of the store, a violation of which shall be among the causes for discharge, are vested in the Employer; provided however, that this right shall be exercised with due regard for the rights of the employees, and provided further, that it will not be used for the purpose of discrimination against any employee or for the purpose of invalidating any contract provision.[91]

RESERVED RIGHTS In addition to explicit management rights specified in the contract (as illustrated in the example), there are also residual, implied, or **reserved rights** not found in the language of the agreement. The reserved rights theory generally contends that management retains all rights except those it has expressly agreed to share with or relinquish to the union.[92] Management, under the reserved rights concept, does not review the agreement to determine which rights it has gained but instead reviews the agreement to ascertain which rights it has conceded to labor. All rights remaining reside with management.[93]

RESERVED RIGHTS

The generally accepted contention that all rights not specified in an agreement or shared with a union remain the unwritten or implied rights of management.

One area of management rights that has received a great deal of attention since the 1980s involves a management decision to *relocate* its operation, in whole or in part. Previous Supreme Court decisions had decided that if a company planned to "subcontract" work currently being done by union workers, that decision was a mandatory bargaining subject.[94] However, if the company was deciding to close down part or all of its operation, such a decision was not a mandatory bargaining subject.[95]

The NLRB, therefore, first likened management's decision to relocate part or all of its facility to the decision to close a plant, and it ruled in *Otis Elevator Co.* that relocating was not a mandatory bargaining subject.[96] After the federal court rejected that comparison, the NLRB, in *Dubuque Packing Co.*,[97] compared relocating to subcontracting and reversed itself, deciding it was a mandatory bargaining subject.[98]

RESTRICTED RIGHTS Restrictions of management rights are common in contracts (87 percent) as union negotiators strive to delineate the union's rights in specific areas of decision making. Contracts may contain these **restricted rights** in a general statement restricting management from "taking actions in violation of the terms of the agreement." Specific restrictions of management rights or, conversely, the providing of union rights are most often found in the following contract clauses:[99]

RESTRICTED RIGHTS

Contract provisions that place specific limitations on areas generally considered management rights.

- *Subcontracting of work* to outside firms (contained in 55 percent of all contracts)

- *Supervisory performance* of bargaining unit work, except for training, in an emergency, conducting experiments, and developing new products (58 percent)
- *Technological changes* in work methods or equipment (e.g., robots) without union approval or the retraining of displaced workers (26 percent)
- *Plant shutdown or relocation* without advance notice and transfer rights to a new location (23 percent)
- *Union rights of access* to bulletin boards, pertinent information, and company premises (94 percent)

GRIEVANCE AND ARBITRATION Most contracts provide for the machinery necessary to enforce the terms of the agreement. Union shop stewards and officials give on-the-job representation that includes grievance administration (see Chapter 11). External enforcement is provided through arbitration provisions.

Contract Bar

CONTRACT BAR

The general rule followed by the National Labor Relations Board stating that a current and valid labor contract can prevent another union from petitioning for an election and being certified as the exclusive representative for the term of the existing contract.

Through its decisions over the years, the NLRB established a **contract bar** doctrine stating that a current and valid contract can prevent another union from petitioning for an election and being certified as the exclusive representative. The board developed this doctrine as a balance between two competing interests under the National Labor Relations Act: the right of employees to choose their bargaining representatives and the need to achieve stability in labor relations through negotiation of collective bargaining agreements.

It is the NLRB's theory that if a union has negotiated and signed an agreement on behalf of its members, another union should not be allowed to seek recognition during the life of that agreement. Certain elements must be present to ensure that the contract acts as a bar to a representational election:

1. The contract must be in writing and signed by the parties. An oral agreement cannot be a bar.
2. The contract must be for a fixed term. An indefinite term expiring on some happening in the future cannot bar an election, nor will the board honor a contract with an unreasonably long term. Currently, the NLRB views a three-year contract as reasonable. Any contract of longer term will not bar an election to change representation at the end of the three-year period.
3. The contract must provide substantive terms and conditions to ensure a stable employer–employee arrangement. If a contract covered wages alone, it probably would not operate as a bar.
4. The contract must be duly ratified if ratification by the membership is required.
5. The contract must contain only legal provisions. Clauses that discriminate on the basis of race, religion, and so on, or that clearly violate union security provisions of the act cannot bar a new election.
6. The contract must not be prematurely extended. The NLRB allows employees the right to change representation during the **open period**—the first 30-day period in the 90 days before termination of the original contract.

OPEN PERIOD

The first 30-day period in the last 90 days before the termination of a collective bargaining agreement during which employees can vote to change their bargaining agent.

A 1996 case provides an example of the right to change representation. The Supreme Court unanimously ruled that an employer had violated Section 8(a)(1) of the National Labor Relations Act, which protects the union's rights, when the employer disavowed a contract. The union in the case had accepted the company's last contract proposal, but the employer disavowed the contract the next day because 16 (of 23) employees had complained about the union, and 13 had resigned from the union. The Court ruled that to preserve industrial peace and stability, the NLRB presumes that a union has majority support during the term of any contract, once negotiated, up to three years. Only at the end of the contract, during the open period, can employees seek to change representation.[100]

Under the contract bar doctrine, if a rival union wants to win the bargaining rights of a unit, it must petition for an election and win it during the open period—that is, between the 90th and 60th day prior to the contract's expiration. Once the end of an open period arrives without the filing of a petition, the incumbent union becomes insulated from another union's petition, and if a new agreement is reached before the old one expires, the new one presents a new contract bar.[101]

Once contract negotiations begin, the employees cannot petition for a change in representation. This **insulated period** begins 60 days before the contract is due to expire. Therefore, negotiations must not take place during the open period so that employees will have an opportunity to change representation.

INSULATED PERIOD

The last 60 days before a collective bargaining agreement is due to expire in which the existing bargaining agent cannot be subject to an employee vote to change bargaining agents.

BARGAINING IN THE PUBLIC SECTOR

For many of the reasons discussed in Chapter 3, negotiating a collective bargaining agreement in the public sector differs in significant ways from negotiating in the private sector: the nature of public employment as providing essential services with no real competition; the source of funding coming from taxpayers and not consumers; working at the direction of "elected" managers who report, ultimately to citizens; and limitations on negotiable issues. These differences certainly influence the context of contract negotiations. However, fundamental ideas regarding bargaining theories and the bargaining process in the private sector generally hold true for the public sector with a few important variations.

MULTILATERAL BARGAINING In the private sector, union negotiators derive their authority to negotiate from their membership. That authority is generally limited in that the contract must be taken back to the membership for a vote. However, management negotiators in the private sector have the authority to commit to a negotiated agreement at the bargaining table. This situation is often referred to as *bilateral bargaining*. In the public sector, where management's authority to negotiate flows from the people, the decision cannot generally be made by one official and is referred to as *multilateral bargaining*. In a multilateral bargaining situation a third party such as a city council must approve the tentative agreement negotiated by management.

PRESS INTEREST In the private sector there is press coverage of strike threats or actual strikes, but while the negotiations are being carried out, they are largely confidential. Public employee collective bargaining makes news even when there is no crisis. Press coverage can harm the bargaining process in several ways. If an impasse is reached, the parties may try to explain their side to the media, hoping to influence public opinion and in turn the negotiating process. Rushing for media coverage may cause a party to present proposals publicly before it has presented them to the other party at the negotiating table. By emphasizing the differences between the parties instead of the points of agreement, reporters can actually prolong the stalemate. When public employees and their employers reach agreement, it is not newsworthy; therefore, media coverage is often confined to reporting on the items separating the parties and not the items of agreement. Coverage reinforces the bad feelings too often present in negotiations in a way the private sector rarely experiences.

SUNSHINE LAWS Some states require public bodies, such as city councils, to conduct their official business in public sessions open to citizens and the press. Some initial posturing is necessary on both sides so that the negotiator's constituency is assured that he or she is acting on their behalf. Negotiators may find it difficult to stop posturing if they are under constant scrutiny. At any particular juncture during the negotiation process, it may seem as if one side or the other is winning or losing. A fear of "loss of face" by either side may endanger the fair compromise so necessary to successful negotiations.

NO RIGHT TO STRIKE In the private sector, an impasse in collective bargaining negotiations can result in a strike. In the public sector, the **right to strike** is usually denied to the public employee either by the collective bargaining statute or by court actions. As discussed in Chapter 3, the right-to-strike issue is to the public sector what the right-to-work issue is to the private sector. Despite the traditional bias against public employees' right to strike, some states allow public workers to strike either directly or by not prohibiting it.[102] In 1981, in a very pivotal case, PATCO (Professional Air Traffic Controllers) leaders called the first declared national strike against the federal government. The 13,000 strikers thought they were irreplaceable. President Reagan quickly warned that such direct disobedience of the law against public employee strikes would not be tolerated. He stated, "There is no strike; what they did was to terminate their own employment by quitting."[103] Reagan gave workers a deadline that most ignored; then he fired all but the few who returned to work. Not one controller was given amnesty or rehired until President Clinton took office in 1993.

The success of the Reagan administration in replacing such highly skilled workers, together with widespread public support, left little doubt in the minds of government workers as to what might happen if they went on strike. PATCO miscalculated its ability to gain concessions by striking. And the PATCO strike without question began a new era in both public and private sector labor relations, one in which employers view permanent replacement workers as a serious option to striking union workers.

RESOLVING AN IMPASSE Legislation that allows public sector collective bargaining but prohibits strikes often details the procedures available to resolve an impasse, usually, mediation, arbitration, and fact-finding. As with the private sector, the mediator has no independent authority but uses acquired skills to bring the parties back together and reach an agreement. Mediation may be provided by the Federal Mediation and Conciliation Service (FMCS), state labor departments, or local mediation boards.

Fact-finding and advisory arbitration can be far more successful in the public sector than in the private because of political pressures. Under fact-finding and advisory arbitration, an unbiased third party examines the collective bargaining impasse and issues findings and recommendations. The findings may move the process simply by eliminating the distrust one party feels for the other party's facts or figures. Reasonable recommendations may also pressure a party to accept an offer that otherwise would not have been considered.

Interest arbitration allows a panel to make a final and binding decision on a negotiation dispute and has been used in the public sector to resolve impasses. However, the legality of allowing a third party to set the terms of the contract has been questioned.[104]

Summary

Individuals representing labor and management are involved in the collective bargaining process. Negotiators prepare for the negotiations, set priorities, and proceed in an honest and thorough manner. The National Labor Relations Act delineates areas of mandatory, permissive, and illegal negotiations. A good negotiator must also understand and value the human element, which is an integral part of the negotiating process. For some parties, the give-and-take relation is as important as the end result. Knowing that, although every demand was not met, the position and point of view at least being heard by the other party can be part of a successful negotiation.[105]

When the collective bargaining process breaks down, an impasse is reached. The parties can react to that impasse in various ways. Strikes are the most widely publicized reaction. Most often, however, mediation, arbitration, and fact-finding are used to resolve impasses.

When the parties reach agreement, they reduce that agreement to writing. Some of the key provisions that are a part of most collective bargaining agreements include union security, management rights, as well as the wages and benefits.

Public sector negotiations differ in a number of ways because of the nature of public employment and the responsibility the public employer and employees have to members of the public they serve.

CASE STUDIES

Case Study 6-1 Surface Bargaining

The company was charged with an unfair labor practice for failure to bargain in good faith. The union alleged that the company was engaged in surface bargaining with no intention of entering into a collective bargaining agreement. The company had begun meeting with the union after the NLRB had certified it. Eighteen bargaining sessions were held over an 11-month period. The negotiations did not result in a contract. The parties did reach agreement on a recognition clause; the numbers, rights, and duties of union stewards; the use of a bulletin board by the union; pay for jury duty and other leaves of absence; a procedure for processing grievances and arbitrations; and plant visitation by union representatives.

The administrative law judge hearing the case found that the company met at regular intervals and bore no antiunion animus. The company's conduct away from the bargaining table did not indicate that the company had no intention to conclude an agreement with the union. As there was no evidence of a failure to meet to discuss terms and conditions, the arbitrator had to examine the proposals by the company and by the union to see whether their substance indicated good-faith bargaining. The company's proposals are briefly outlined as follows:

1. ***Wages.*** The company insisted that it remain in total control over wages. Wage increases were to be determined on the basis of semiannual merit reviews, in which the union would have no participation. The union had proposed a specific wage schedule, but the company would not adopt it.
2. ***Management rights.*** The company retained absolute right to subcontract work, to assign it to supervisors, to abolish jobs, and to transfer, discontinue, or assign any or all of its operations to others. It required the union to relinquish the employees' statutory right to notice in bargaining over such actions and their effects. Actions taken under the management clause were subject to the grievance procedure only if that right was limited by express contract provision, and there was no such limitation.
3. ***Zipper clause.*** The company proposed a zipper clause, which waived the union's right to bargain during the life of the agreement over anything that could have been considered mandatory or permissive under existing law.
4. ***No-strike clause.*** The company proposed a no-strike clause, including prohibition against a strike for unfair labor or unfair employment practices.
5. ***Discipline and discharge.*** The company rejected the union's proposal of a standard right to discipline an employee for "just or sufficient cause only." The company intended to reserve exclusive authority over discharges and discipline in the management rights clause.
6. ***Layoff and recall.*** The company proposed that the layoff and recall of employees would be at the company's sole discretion.
7. ***Dues check-off.*** The company rejected a union proposal that a dues check-off clause be included in the contract.
8. ***Nondiscrimination clause.*** The company rejected a union proposal that stated the company was not allowed to discriminate against union members. The company's position was that because discrimination was illegal, a clause forbidding it did not need to be included in the contract.

Source: Adapted from *A-1 Kingsize Sandwiches,* 112 LRRM 1360.

QUESTIONS

1. Was the company bargaining in good faith? Explain your answer.
2. Which company proposal was the most important in determining the "in good faith" issue?
3. Suggest how principled negotiations techniques could be used in this case.

(continued)

Case Study 6-2 Impasse in Negotiations

For more than 20 years, the Union has been the exclusive bargaining representative of production and maintenance employees of the Company. The most recent of a series of collective-bargaining agreements expired on February 28, 2006. The union representative requested certain information from the Company by letter in anticipation of upcoming negotiations, which the Company provided. For the Company the high cost of health insurance was, from the first negotiation session, a major issue. The Union presented a comprehensive contract proposal that dealt with most terms and conditions of the expired contract, including its proposal to eliminate the "right to change" provision under the "Medical-Hospital-Physician" clause of the expiring contract. The Union's position was that this change was necessary to prevent the Company from reducing its health care plan benefits during the term of the contract.

The Company gave the Union information on the costs incurred by the Company for the employee's health insurance and brought two representatives from a *new* insurance carrier to present their plans at a negotiation session. The Company's position was clear: Current health care costs were excessive, and the negotiations depended on reaching agreement on an acceptable insurance policy. At the third negotiating session, the Company presented additional and detailed information on health care costs, a contract proposal for the renewal of the current agreement, and a new comprehensive medical plan offered by the new provider. At their fourth session, the parties continued to discuss the alternatives to the employees' medical insurance. The Union adhered to its position that the current plan/provider be retained, and the Company submitted more information to the Union about the new plan. In the meantime, the Company had presented the Union, in advance of the session, with detailed information about the two health insurance plans, sending comparative charts showing monthly costs under the old and proposed plans, detailed charts showing covered medical services, deductible expenses, and prescription drugs. The Union acknowledged that the benefits offered by the new plan were similar to those under the existing plan, but again stated that proposal was unacceptable. The Union proposed *again* that the "right-to-change" language be taken out of the contract. When the parties next met, the Company agreed not to make substantial changes in the level of health benefits and to discuss any changes with the Union before implementing them, provided the Company retained the right to change insurance carriers. The Company's proposal also reflected improvements on other terms, such as wages and grievance procedures. The Union insisted again on eliminating the "right-to-change" provision contained in the expired contract.

At the next session, the Union finally expressed acceptance of the new insurance plan, provided that the current benefits be retained. To ensure this, the Union insisted that the "right-to-change" language of the old contract be deleted. The Company presented its final offer for renewal of the labor agreement, which contained better and enhanced terms, especially an increase in wages and an improved split on health care premium costs between the Company and the employees. The Company expressed hope that the Union would submit the package to its membership for approval. Instead the Union requested additional information on the Company's cost of the final proposal and promised to examine the Company's final offer and submit a counteroffer. The Company showed the Union another monthly cost comparison for each employee under the two health insurance plans but also stated that any counterproposal by the Union greater than the Company's final offer would underscore the current impasse in the negotiations. It advised the Union that the new provider had offered a reduction in rates, effective May 1, 2006, which would not be extended to June 2006 and requested the Union's approval of the implementation of the new health care plan as a substitute for the current plan.

In response, the Union informed the Company by letter it was not interested in agreeing to the implementation of the new health care plan and that the Union needed additional information for further negotiations. In addition, the Union charged that the Company's position to retain "the right-to-change" insurance benefits during the life of the contract amounted to an unfair labor practice.

The Company provided the Union with the additional information, but informed the Union that in light of the existing impasse in the negotiations, it would implement the new health care plan from May 1. The Company stated that one reason for the "impasse in the negotiations" was the Union's insistence on deleting "the right-to-change language" and to condition its acceptance of the health plan on that proposal. The Union filed an unfair labor practice charge against the Company.

Discussion

An employer's unilateral change to a mandatory subject of collective bargaining, such as health insurance, during the course of a collective-bargaining relationship is unlawful. A recognized exception to this rule is when an impasse is reached. The issue in this case is whether the parties have reached a lawful impasse. A party that prematurely declares an impasse and makes unilateral changes in, for example, health care coverage violates the act. Whether or not an impasse is reached is a question of various factors including (1) the background and relationship of the parties, (2) their willingness to negotiate, (3) the extent and frequency of bargaining, (4) the integrity of the bargaining, and (5) the good or bad faith of the parties. Here, the parties had a well-established and successful bargaining relationship, as exemplified by a series of collective-bargaining agreements. The parties' willingness to negotiate is shown by the Company's cooperation in agreeing to set dates and in attending meetings. Both parties presented proposals based on the expired contract and made concessions. The Company furnished detailed information, especially on the health insurance plan, and gave serious consideration to the Union's proposals.

The integrity of the bargaining was shown by the sincerity of the parties in attempting to arrive at an agreeable solution to their differences. There is no dispute that the Company was faced with increasing cost of the existing health plan and tried to involve the Union from the outset in the negotiations, by supplying financial information, by presenting insurance representatives, and by making significant concessions.

Finally, as to the good faith of the parties, it is clear that the parties were deadlocked on two issues and unable to overcome their differences. At one point the Union had indicated its acceptance of the new health plan after the Company had agreed to substantially identical benefits with those of the existing plan, but the Union changed its position and rejected the Company's request to accept the proposal. The record suggests that the Union conditioned its acceptance on the elimination of "the right-to-change" language. That issue was never resolved, although the parties had come close to an agreement at one point on the health plan. The parties resumed negotiations with revised proposals on two occasions but were unable to overcome their fundamental differences and remained deadlocked. A deadlock on certain issues does not free an employer to implement changes to the terms of an agreement, unless an overall impasse is reached. An overall impasse is reached if it is clear that further meetings would not be productive.

Source: Adapted from *Clarke Manufacturing, Inc. and United Steel, Paper and Forestry, Rubber, Manufacturing, Energy, Allied Industrial and Service Workers International Union, Local 2–200*, 352 NLRB No. 25 (2008).

QUESTIONS

1. Would the Company's willingness to share financial information on the health care plans with the Union help the board decide whether there was an impasse? Explain.
2. What other options were available to the parties to break the deadlock in these negotiations?
3. What would be the effect on the bargaining relationship between these two parties if the board finds that a legal impasse had occurred? If the board finds that a legal impasse has not occurred?

Key Terms and Concepts

arbitration (interest) *223*
Borg-Warner decision (bargaining subjects: mandatory, permissive, illegal) *208*
contract bar *236*
dues check-off provision *229*
duty to sign *226*
fact-finding *223*
final offer arbitration *225*
impasse *215*
Insulated period *237*
lockout *222*
Mackay Doctrine *220*
management rights *234*
mediation *223*
multilateral bargaining *237*
no-strike, no-lockout provision *222*
open period *236*
Opener clause *234*
permanent replacement workers *220*
picket lines *221*
primary strike *218*
provisional intent test *227*
Reserved rights *235*
Restricted rights *235*
Right-to-work laws *231*
Rolling strike *219*
Severability clause *213*
shop provisions: open, closed, union, agency *230*
Strikes; economic & unfair labor practice *215*
Sunshine laws *237*
Union security *212*

Review Questions

1. Who are the people directly involved in the collective bargaining process? What are their roles?
2. What is the purpose of a management rights clause? Do you agree with the reserved rights theory, why or why not?
3. Discuss how negotiators prepare for negotiations.
4. Why have the number of major economic strikes in the United States declined?
5. What is the purpose of a union picket line? Why are they less successful today than in past years?
6. Generally why do both management and the union favor no-strike, no-lockout provisions?
7. Describe commonly used methods for peacefully resolving a negotiation impasse, the advantages and disadvantages of each.
8. How do negotiators meet the "provisional intent test"?
9. Describe different union security provisions found in CBAs.
10. What are the pros & cons of state right-to-work laws?

YOU BE THE ARBITRATOR
School Bus Drivers

ARTICLE VII

MANAGEMENT RIGHTS, ITEM E

Maintain the efficiency of operations in the New Lebanon School District and the personnel by which such operations shall be carried out.

ARTICLE VII

MANAGEMENT RIGHTS, ITEM F

Exercise any other power or prerogative given it under the Revised Code of the State of Ohio or any reasonable inference to be therefrom.

ARTICLE XXXI

TRANSPORTATION, PARAGRAPH H

All field trips shall be offered on the basis of seniority rotation as follows:

1. There shall be two rotation lists made containing the names of all drivers in order of their seniority (those drivers only desiring to take field trips), the most senior driver being No. 1. One list will consist of daytime trips; the other after school and weekend trips.
2. The first trip of the school year shall be assigned to driver 1. The second being assigned to driver 2

and so on. Driver 1 shall not be eligible for another field trip until all the remaining drivers have had an opportunity to take a field trip on each individual rotation list.

3. If more than one field trip is offered on Monday (or whatever day), driver who is up for the next trip on the seniority list may have their choice of field trips; next drivers will have the same option until all trips have been exhausted.
4. Any driver becoming eligible may have the option to refuse the trip to be passed over in favor of the less senior driver. However, the driver refusing shall not be eligible again until the rotation is complete. There will be no trading of field trips.
5. Field trips shall be assigned to regular classified bus drivers only. In the event that the rotation has been exhausted and no regular drivers are available, the substitute drivers shall be permitted to take field trips.
6. Only classified bus drivers that are contract drivers with the Board shall be assigned to any route or extra trips.
7. When a field trip requires early departure and last all day or overnight, regular school bus drivers will have the option of taking the trip. The school bus drivers will drive their own bus on the trip or the best available. The Supervisor may assign any bus from the fleet to a field trip which is more than 100 miles one way. The regular bus drivers will relinquish their regular pay rate for the field-trip rate. Field trips will stay on the same rotation basis.
8. If drivers have a field trip canceled, they will be offered the first field trip from the same list (either day or after school) as long as they do not have another field trip assigned. Should they already have a field trip assigned, they will be offered the next field trip available. Receiving the makeup trip cannot cause one to lose a trip from the normal list.
9. Every effort will be made to provide drivers with a gas card to those assigned field trips that are beyond a 100-mile round trip.
10. When a field trip is available and after exhausting the regular rotation field trip list and substitute list, that trip becomes an "emergency field trip" situation. Under the earlier stated guidelines, regular and/or substitute bus drivers may take the participants to the field trip event and return to the school district. At the completion of the field trip, the same driver or an alternate driver may be assigned to pick up these participants and return to the school district; the driver being paid for the time needed to accomplish this.
11. Summer Field Trips/Summer School—For the purpose of determining the rate of pay, a summer field trip is defined as transporting students with a teacher/advisor/designee in charge, and the driver of this trip will be paid FIELD-TRIP RATE. Summer school transportation is defined as transporting students to a school or designated area where the driver has the same responsibility as transporting students to school during the regular school day (no adviser/coach/designee in charge), and the driver of this trip will be paid the REGULAR DRIVING RATE for which they are employed.

Facts

The employer is a public school district. In the past, the superintendent of the district had used his private van to transport students to sporting events. After the district purchased a van, the school van was used to transport students to sporting events. The union grieved the use of the van because the school bus drivers were not being used to drive the van, and the collective bargaining agreement (CBA) required the school bus drivers to drive students on any field trips.

Issue

Did the employer violate its CBA that requires school bus drivers to transport students on field trips when it did not require them to transport students to sporting events?

Position of the Parties

The school district's position was that the CBA's management rights clause gave the superintendent the authority to determine what vehicles to use to transport students when the trip is not a field trip. If the superintendent does not determine that a school bus should be used, then the CBA's provision is not applicable. The CBA does not define "field trip," so "field trip" is defined in the school district's policy as "any planned journey by one or more students away from district premises, which is under the supervision of a professional staff member and an integral part of a course of study." Under the district's definition, no sporting or after-school trip is a field trip.

The union's position was that the drivers should be assigned to drive the van whenever school trips are being taken. Even though the CBA does not define "field trip," the union does not accept the use of the definition in the district's policy or the narrow reading of the term "field trip." Any trip taken under the auspices of the district is a field trip for purposes of the CBA.

Source: Adapted from *New Lebanon Local Bd. of Ed.*, 114 LA 952 (Arb. 2000).

QUESTIONS

1. As arbitrator, what would be your award and opinion in this arbitration?
2. Identify the key, relevant section(s), phrases, or words of the collective bargaining agreement (CBA), and explain why they were critical in making your decision.
3. What actions might the employer and/or the union have taken to avoid this conflict?

Part III **Cost of Labor Contracts**

CHAPTER 7

Wage and Salary Issues

Starbucks paid $18 million to settle an overtime dispute with its employees. The U.S. Department of Labor in 2010 reported a record number of class action lawsuits in which workers won millions of dollars in overtime wages. *Source:* AP Images.

Chapter Outline

Men work for two reasons. One is for wages, and one is for fear of losing their jobs.

Henry Ford (Founder and President, Ford Motor Company)

LABOR NEWS

Overtime Cases Won by Workers

Mark R. Thierman, a Reno, Nevada, attorney and Harvard Law School graduate was a "union buster" management labor attorney for 20 years. Not anymore! Today, he is called the "trailblazer" of what has become a hotbed of U.S. employment cases: the overtime provision of the Fair Labor Standards Act (FLSA). From 2001 to 2010, the number of cases filed in federal courts more than doubled. The U.S. Chamber of Commerce describes it as the "FLSA litigation explosion," which has led to over $1 billion annually in settlements in recent years. The cases are usually filed against employers on behalf of a large group of employees and have included the following:

- ***Starbucks:*** $18 million settlement to store managers in California
- ***UPS:*** $87 million settlement to 23,000 drivers
- ***Walmart:*** $172 million jury award to California workers and $78.5 million jury award to Pennsylvania workers
- ***Sony:*** $8.5 million settlement to video-game employees
- ***Citigroup/Salomon Smith Barney:*** $98 million settlement to 20,000 stockbrokers
- ***IBM:*** $65 million settlement to 32,000 technical and support workers
- ***Unite Here:*** The labor union has been charged with failing to pay organizers overtime
- ***Abbott Laboratories:*** A federal judge ruled pharmaceutical reps are due overtime

The core issue of the cases is employers' failure to pay workers time-and-a-half pay for hours worked over 40 per week as required by the federal law—overtime. About 86 percent of the U.S. workforce is entitled to overtime according to the U.S. Department of Labor, or 115 million workers. Only certain workers are exempt from the law: mostly supervisors, professionals, and executives.

Why the recent deluge of cases? In 2010 the U.S. Department of Labor cited the following as possible reasons for the increase in class action suits for overtime violations:

- Successful employees are receiving double damages plus attorney fees—making it worth their efforts.
- Some employers are unclear about new overtime guidelines.
- Workers are more informed of their rights and willing to file suits.
- Competitive economic forces are increasingly causing employers to seek ways of cutting costs.

Source: Adapted from Michael Orey, "Wage Wars: Workers from Truck Drivers to Stockbrokers Are Winning Huge Overtime Lawsuits," *Business Week* (October 1, 2007), pp. 52–60; Tracy Staton, "Abbott Sales Reps Win Overtime Pay Lawsuit," *FiercePharma Newsletter* (June 15, 2010); and Joanne Deschemaux, "Wage and Hour Class Actions on the Rise," *HR Magazine 55*, no. 7 (July 2010), p. 11.

Wages and other economic benefits for employees are undoubtedly the "meat and potatoes" of collective bargaining in labor relations. To the employee, they represent not only their current income and standard of living but also potential for economic growth and the ability to live comfortably during retirement. Wages are often considered the most important and difficult collective bargaining issue. When newly negotiated settlements are reported to the public, often the first item specified is the percentage wage increase received by employees. In fact, in many cases that may be the only item employees consider critical or an absolute must as they vote to ratify a tentative agreement. They focus on "the number"—the percentage wage increase in the contract.

According to industrial research, historically pay level has been positively related to employee satisfaction.[1] Employees consider their pay to be a primary indicator of the organization's goodwill. Many individuals in our society consider the salary or income one receives a measure of one's worth. Employees can get an exact measure of their salary, which can easily be compared with the salaries of fellow employees and those in other organizations and occupations. Therefore, most of us consciously or subconsciously compare our income levels not only with inflation and our cost of living but also with incomes of other individuals.

Wages and benefits are also a prime collective bargaining issue to the employer. They represent the largest single cost factor on their income statement. Although many management negotiators would like to pay higher wages to employees, the reality of competition and the knowledge that competitors may be able to secure less expensive labor can make it difficult for a business to survive. Unlike many costs, such as capital and land, wages constantly rise, and they are not as easy to predict. Wages paid to employers in an area are also key issues to governments because they often are the largest source of tax revenue to federal, state, and local governments and in general are a strong indicator of the economic vitality of a community.

The total economic package of wages and benefits may be negotiated as one item rather than individual items, enabling both sides to estimate accurately the total cost of the contract to the organization in terms of increases over current salary and benefits. In this chapter we discuss wage issues; employee benefits are covered in Chapter 8. Wages and benefits are separated to draw a distinction between the two; however, negotiators consider both a part of the total economic package.

Labor and management negotiators normally define pay by either time worked or units of output. **Pay for time worked**, or an *hourly wage* or *annual salary*, has become the predominant means of employee compensation in the United States. Most labor contracts contain specific job titles and associated wage scales agreed on by labor and management. Table 7-1 shows an example.

PAY FOR TIME WORKED

Employee wage rate based on the time actually worked (hours, days, shifts, etc.).

TABLE 7-1 Job Classifications and Wage Rates

	Hire Rate ($)	Group	Department
I	19.80	Die Repair	Maintenance
II	19.62	Maintenance	Maintenance
III	19.30	Cage Attendant	Material Handling
		Head Loader	Shipping
		Crane Operator	Material Handling
IV	18.60	Material Handler	Material Handling
		Utility	Door and Window
		Loading	Shipping
		Plant Truck Driver	Shipping
V	18.30	Salvage	Material Handling
		Material Handler	Material Handling
VI	17.50	(None)	
VII	17.10	Glass Cutter	Insulated Glass
		Sample Builder	Sample
		Glass Washer and Assembler	Insulated Glass
		Spacer Assembly	Insulated Glass
		Door Prehanger	Door
VIII	16.50	Small Punch Press Operator	Door
		Processor	Door
		Window Wrapper	Shipping
IX	16.20	Packaging	Material Handling
XXIII	12.60	Equipment Operator	Paint Line
XXIV	11.00	Assistant Equipment Operator	Paint Line

Source: Adapted from *UAW-Chrysler Newsgra* (October 2007). Available at www.uaw.org. Accessed February 23, 2007. Used by permission.

Pay for units produced, usually referred to as **piecework**, is still used in many industries as not only a means of wage determination but also a motivational technique. Many piecework systems today provide a guaranteed salary with an additional rate established for units of output above a certain production level.

UNION WAGE CONCERNS

"A fair day's pay for a fair day's work" is a commonly used phrase summing up the expectations of many employees. Employees expect and even demand to be treated fairly and honestly by the organization. Although most are reasonable in their pay expectations, a few often believe they are being underpaid. If employees perceive that they are unfairly treated by the organization, particularly in pay matters, they typically react by leaving the workplace either temporarily through absenteeism and tardiness or permanently through seeking employment at another organization, by reducing the quantity or quality of their production, or by filing a grievance or enacting a work stoppage through the union. Eventually their pay dissatisfaction will be brought to the bargaining table, leading to demands for higher wages. Or they may change their perceptions of pay inequity by simply accepting the inequity, although this response may become a permanent morale factor.[2]

PAY EQUITY

A historic union doctrine of "equal pay for equal work" that provides one standard pay rate for each job and all employees who perform it.

Obtaining **pay equity** in the workplace is difficult. The slogan "equal pay for equal work" is a guide that union and management leaders follow and that employees expect to be maintained. Obviously not all jobs involve work of equal value to an organization. The first-year bookkeeper does not expect the same pay as a tax accountant; the same is true for a punch press operator and a maintenance attendant. Employees understand that the value of the work leads to different pay grades and classifications for different jobs. As shown in Table 7-1, labor agreements commonly provide for different job classifications being assigned different pay grades according to level of skill and work demanded. As long as pay grades are fairly structured and evenly applied, employees usually have no trouble accepting differential pay based on job classification and internal wage levels, unless, as seen in Case 7-1, pay differentials are not based purely on job classifications.

CASE 7-1

Wages: Extra Compensation

The company operated a centralized facility to provide public transportation. The bargaining unit consisted of the vehicle operators, excluding supervisors, substitutes, guards, and office personnel. The collective bargaining agreement (CBA) was in effect from October 1, 1996 to June 30, 1999.

The operation was decentralized in April 1997 when the company opened seven suburban service center locations. Because the company had acted before hiring the management supervisory personnel at each site, it decided to assign certain unit drivers to temporary positions titled "coordinator." These persons had limited supervisory authority but functioned as leaders in each service center. These positions were opened to the company's unit member drivers, who applied and filled the positions. The company paid a $1 an hour stipend in addition to the regular contract rates for drivers for the additional leader duties. The additional duties specified for such coordinators were listed as opening and closing the facility, coordinating the work and assignments of drivers, and overseeing that proper service was provided. Additionally, these persons dispatched drivers and handled answering the telephone. This move and the temporary assignments were negotiated with the union, but no agreement was reached, nor was any objection raised to the procedure.

By July 1998, the service centers had been staffed with managers, and the company acted to eliminate the leader duties previously done by coordinators. However, certain duties, such as dispatch and telephone answering, were still assigned to the classification now known as "service provider," which was a change from the former "driver" title. This realignment of duties was not negotiated with the union. When the company made this realignment of duties, those who had previously served as coordinators were continued at the $1-per-hour stipend out of recognition of the commitment those people had made to help the company. It viewed this as a grandfathering of the wage for those individuals. However, the company did not apply the $1 stipend to other individuals who served thereafter as service providers.

Ultimately, the union grieved extra duties assigned to the former driver classification and that certain employees who were classified as service providers were entitled to the $1 stipend because of the duties that they were performing, particularly the dispatching. The union complained that the company violated the contract and the law by unilaterally establishing terms and conditions of a new classification. The effectuation of such terms and conditions, including the assignment of duties and the payment of additional wages, is clearly contrary to the contract. Employees who are assigned such duties as telephone and dispatch should be paid at the same rate as others who formerly performed as coordinators.

The company insisted that it has the management right to assign duties to the drivers that are not inconsistent with the classification and the general purpose of the operation. In establishing coordinators on a temporary basis, it did exactly that and, in addition, compensated them for certain leader/supervisory obligations. When the need for the performance of such duties ended, the company properly removed such assignments. The fact that such employees and others later performed the function of dispatch and telephone should not be considered leader/coordinator duties for which an additional $1 stipend was paid but rather normal assignments permitted the company under the contract. All employees are paid equally for the same work within the classification, including dispatching and telephone. The only distinction is that those employees who formerly served as coordinators had been granted a special continuing rate of pay in light of their willingness to make the previous commitment to assist. In no respect did the company ever commit to pay an additional $1 for all drivers performing such nonleader/supervisory duties. There is no disparity in pay.

Discussion

A key to this dispute is the question of whether the company would have, in the past, prior to the new service centers, violated the contract by assigning to members of the unit such duties as dispatching and telephone as are now done by certain service providers.

Under the management rights clause, there is certain flexibility and discretion allowing the company to assign related duties. The contract does not have any clear limitation on the assignment of such additional work. As long as such tasks are not supervisory and are reasonably related to the purpose—providing customer transportation—they may be included. In setting up the service centers, the company acted in somewhat of a hurry, so it did not have the managers and, hence, had to make use of drivers by assigning them temporarily to additional duties of a leadership nature. There was no objection to the process of application and interview and placement, nor was there any objection to the fact that the company paid an extra $1-per-hour stipend. The company never indicated that this move was intended to be permanent. The company saw certain leadership duties as beyond the scope of the classification and was willing to pay, but that did not create an obligation to continue it indefinitely.

When the company put managers in place, it no longer required the coordinators to perform supervisory tasks. However, there still was a need for nonmanagerial duties, such as dispatch and telephone answering, to be done. The question is whether after the managers were in place it was improper for the company to assign such duties to unit members without the additional compensation.

The fact that some former coordinators continued to do such tasks and received the $1 stipend is not determinative of the company's commitment because, as the company

(Continued)

explained, it felt committed to those people who had helped in the transition. Payment to such former coordinators does not, under the circumstances, establish any right of others who are assigned such duties. The issue is whether the company was obligated to "pay equally" everyone within the classification who performs the same duties.

Decision

The court found that the company did not violate the contract by adding nonsupervisory duties to the service provider classification under its management rights clause because those duties are reasonably connected to the operation of transporting customers and therefore within the scope of the prior driver classification. Furthermore, when the company filled the management positions, the company rightfully discontinued the leader/supervisory duties of the employees designated as coordinators. However, the duties attributable to their status as service providers—dispatch, telephone, and so on—were not leader/supervisory duties and properly were retained within the scope of the service provider classification. Continuing assignment of such work to former coordinators with the $1 stipend and to others without such extra compensation did not create a new compensation level or disparate treatment of persons within the classification because the company had the right to continue to pay those individuals $1 more an hour in appreciation of their service.

Source: Adapted from *The Mass Transportation Authority v. AFSCME Local 1223,* 115 LA 521 (2000).

Worker/CEO Pay Gap

In recent years a new pay equity issue has emerged—the worker/CEO pay gap. The gap is growing, according to a study by the National Bureau of Economic Research. In 1970, the average full-time worker earned $32,522, whereas the average CEO or top corporate executive earned $1.25 million (adjusted to 1998 dollars). By 2007, the average worker's pay increased by 24.2 percent to $40,409, while the average Standard & Poor's 500 Company CEO pay increased by more than 3,720 percent to 15.06 million.[3] The difference in CEO pay and worker pay can irritate all workers, but poor timing of pay decisions can further strain management–union relations. For example, in 2003, as American Airlines asked three unions to accept deep pay and benefit cuts of about $10,000 per year per worker, or almost 20 percent of their total compensation, American Airlines disclosed special payments to 45 top executives of about $100 million of the $1.8 billion in concessions gained from the workers. Six top executives received a bonus equal to twice their base salaries. One union member, Joseph Szubryt, who supported the pay cuts to save union jobs exclaimed, "This feels like a stab in the back. . . . On the day we voted for all this stuff (pay and benefit cuts) . . . they disclose this? How the heck could these guys do that?"[4]

Some wage systems provide for higher wages to employees with more longevity. Thus, seniority helps employees not only in bidding for open jobs but also in receiving higher pay. Even though less senior employees perform the same work, everyone realizes that longevity pay serves as an incentive to stay with the organization. But pay inequities can develop for any number of reasons, as seen in the discussion of mergers in Profile 7-1.

Union Wage Objectives

How have unions, as organizations, affected the wages of their workers through the collective bargaining process? What primary objectives have unions held when negotiating wages? An extensive review of the related research by Bruce Kaufman, Department of Economics and the W. T. Beebe Institute of Personnel and Employment Relations at Georgia State

Profile 7-1

Pay Equity In Company Mergers

Mergers and acquisitions are common in today's malleable business climate and have a significant impact on a wide range of employee issues. One major area of concern, of course, is how merging two organizations' compensation plans affect employees' pay. Experts advise that companies need to see the issue as more than just coordinating two payroll systems. "You have to make sure that you're doing it in a holistic way, not just nailing one company to the other," said Ken Ransby, a principal in the San Francisco office of Towers Perrin. Ransby went on to suggest that although it might be ideal to use the best aspects of each organization's pay systems, such an approach might be too costly.

Before deciding how to approach compensation issues, the merged company should examine the underlying business reasons for the merger. If full integration of the two or more organizations was the goal, then the compensation systems must be aligned. Aligning pay systems requires a detailed analysis of the pay systems, consideration of how the organizations define pay, and recognition of geographic factors that cause pay disparities.

When Pfizer Animal Health Group acquired SmithKline Beecham Animal Health Business, the two compensation systems offered comparable pay, but Pfizer relied more on base pay whereas SmithKline offered incentive pay. The merged company wanted a single pay system, so it needed to integrate the SmithKline system into Pfizer's without having the SmithKline workers feel they were losing out. The solution was to fold into those former SmithKline workers' base pay an average annual incentive payout based on the three years prior to the merger.

Source: Adapted from "Company Mergers and Acquisitions Present New Pay Equity Considerations for Employers," *Labor Relations Reporter,* 158 LRR 393 (July 27, 1998).

University, produced eight dimensions of the effects union wage negotiations have caused in the past 56 years:

1. ***Union goals in wage bargaining.*** Lynn Williams, former president of the United Steelworkers Union, summarized union wage goals as (1) "achieving the maximum level of wages and benefits for its members" and (2) "maintain[ing] all the jobs it could within as viable an industry as possible."
2. ***The union–nonunion wage differential.*** In the United States the size of the union versus nonunion wage differential, on average, is currently about 19 percent. Thus compared to nonunion workers on similar jobs, union workers receive more pay. However exceptions exist. Some nonunion workers at Delta Air Lines, for example, before the merger with Northwestern airlines, were paid more than the union workers at Northwestern.
3. ***Union wage differentials over time.*** From the end of World War II to the early 1980s, the union–nonunion wage differential in the United States continued to increase, but since the early 1980s, it has had a modest decline.
4. ***Union wage rigidity and wage concessions.*** Unions have historically tried to hold to the principle of no "givebacks" or "backward steps" in wages, even to the point of letting a company go out of business rather than accept a cut in wages.
5. ***Wage structure.*** Unions have also affected the structure of wage scales among workers within one employer or industry, negotiating for differences in working conditions, skills, seniority, age, and job classification. They have typically "flattened" or "compressed" the wage structure among workers in a plant or company and between skilled and unskilled workers.
6. ***The form of compensation.*** Unions in most cases have bargained for wages based on time or hours worked. They have opposed pay systems based on output, such as a merit or piece-rate systems or merit evaluations by supervisors. They have also bargained for additional forms of compensation that are awarded across the board, such as bonuses based on seniority, overtime, and pensions.

When Pfizer acquired Smithkline, Pfizer found it needed to align the two pay systems both accomplish its goals for the merger and to be fair to employees. *Source:* Mark Lennihan/AP Images.

7. ***Employment effects.*** Unions have in general negotiated for practices and work rules that create or maintain more jobs. Examples include restrictive work rules limiting what duties persons can perform in their job description and "make-work" or "featherbedding" jobs.
8. ***Pattern bargaining.*** Unions have generally strived to pattern bargain or obtain similar wage gains from separate employers within the same industry or sometimes within similar industries or a community. The extent of pattern bargaining has declined somewhat since the 1980s.[5]

Industrial Differentials

Industrial wage differentials also provide a logical basis for differences in pay among employers in the same labor market. Employees recognize that the relationship between labor and total production costs affects their wage levels. Organizations in highly labor-intensive industries are usually less able to provide wage increases than organizations that are in more capital-intensive industries. For example, if a specialized chemical processing plant that has few competitors increased its wage rates by 10 percent, it would need to raise prices by only 0.6 percent to absorb the wage increase because only 6 percent of its total production costs would be attributable to labor. However, if a southern textile firm raised its wages by 10 percent, it would need to raise prices by 7 percent because its labor costs would equal 70 percent of total production costs. A 7 percent price increase could be disastrous to the highly competitive textile organization. Employees accept and understand that not all employers, because of their profitability or current competitive position within the marketplace, can be the highest-paying organization in the industry. If profits decrease so much that the organization suffers losses, wage demands usually reflect the reality of the economic times.

MANAGEMENT WAGE CONCERNS

Wage and benefit changes have an impact on the cost of the production of goods and services. Management must consider how a change in wages will affect its pricing policy and ability to compete in the marketplace. It is often mistakenly inferred that management wants to minimize its labor costs for no particular reason or because employees are not appreciated. The reality is that management needs to maintain competitive labor costs to produce and price their products successfully within their industry. Thus, maintaining a competitive industry position is a primary aim of management in negotiations.

This practice, known as **pattern bargaining**, can be highly successful for both management and labor.

PATTERN BARGAINING

A collective bargaining practice in which a national industry or union strives to establish equal wages and benefits from several unions or employers in the same industry.

The steel and auto industries, airline, petroleum, meatpacking and food industries, among others, have used pattern bargaining. Typically, the union leaders choose what they perceive as the weakest company—the one most susceptible to granting wage increases—and begin negotiations. Once negotiations are completed, the union insists that other firms in the industry agree to equal wage and benefit increases. However, another pattern strategy is to start with the largest employer in an industry, negotiate an agreement, and expect the other, smaller employers to follow suit. In 2001, for example, the United Mine Workers (UMW) ratified a new agreement with the Peabody Coal Company, the nation's largest coal producer, a year before the old contract expired. The early ratification provided a $600 "early signing" lump-sum bonus to workers before the old agreement expired as well as wage, health-care, and pension increases, signaling to all other, smaller coal companies the strength of the UMW. This enabled the union to negotiate similar contracts with smaller companies, calling them **"me-too" agreements**.[6]

"ME-TOO" AGREEMENTS

Agreements that contain pay increases equal to that of another CBA or received by another group. The rationale is that if management can afford to increase pay for one group, it can for another; or one group is as worthy as another.

In some situations a single union can use joint bargaining to the same wage package with all major employers simultaneously and thus not advantage or disadvantage any one employer. In 2003, for example, the Teamsters union in Chicago, Illinois, was able to stage a successful strike against the 17 private garbage haulers and then reach a settlement with each that provided a 30 percent increase in wages, up to $25.70 per hour, or an average of $42,000 per year. Instead of negotiating with the 17 employer-members of the Chicago Refuse Haulers Association individually, the Teamsters jointly negotiated the same wage package with all the haulers—who were then able to pass the identical increased costs on to their customers and not suffer any competitive disadvantage. The ability to use joint bargaining, like pattern bargaining, gives a union enormous bargaining power, but it is not often a realistic possibility.[7]

Pattern bargaining, however, does not prevent firms from negotiating differences according to local labor conditions and the profitability of a particular employer. Instead, when negotiated wage and benefit increases are equal for several employers, they maintain their same relative competitive position with regard to labor costs.

The uncertain economy that followed the terrorist attacks of September 11, 2001, caused a renewed interest in pattern bargaining by some employers. In 2002, about 30 percent of labor professionals negotiating new contracts said they closely watched the patterns set by competitors' settlements. This was significantly more than ten years earlier in the wake of the Caterpillar strike.[8] For example, in 2003, the United Steelworkers of America signed a five-year agreement with the U.S. Steel Corporation covering 13,000 workers. The agreement was patterned after similar contracts with LTU Steel Corporation and was identical to one with National Steel.[9]

Wage Laws

A number of federal laws outside the National Labor Relations Act affect wage rates. The major compensation legislation regulating employers is the Fair Labor Standards Act (FLSA) of 1938, as amended. It governs the items discussed in the following sections.

MINIMUM WAGES Under the FLSA, employers must pay an employee at least a minimum wage per hour, as shown in Table 7-2. The minimum wage per hour in 1938 was $0.25 and has been increased several times to $7.25 in 2009. Exempted from the act are small businesses whose gross sales do not exceed $500,000. Also exempted are organizations that operate within one state. However, some states have enacted minimum wage laws that are higher than the federal minimum, although most set the state minimum wage equal to the federal rate. Those with higher rates include California ($8.00), Connecticut ($7.65), and Massachusetts ($8.00).[10] The amendments to FLSA

TABLE 7-2 U.S. Minimum Wage Changes Under Fair Labor Standards Act

1938	1945	1950	1956	1962	1967	1974	1978	
$0.25	$0.40	$0.75	$1.00	$1.15	$1.40	$2.00	$2.65	
1979	**1980**	**1985**	**1990**	**1991**	**1996**	**1997**	**2008**	**2009**
$2.90	$3.10	$3.35	$3.80	$4.25	$4.75	$5.15	$6.55	$7.25

also provided for a training wage for employees less than 20 years of age set at 85 percent of the minimum wage. Critics of increases in the minimum wage often contend that employers are forced to lay off employees when the minimum is increased to control labor costs. However, three studies conducted after the increase in the minimum-wage rate and the creation of a training wage for teenagers showed that increases in the minimum wage caused no increase in unemployment.[11]

EXEMPT

Employees that are not subject to the overtime provisions of the FLSA, including most executive, administrative, professional, and outside sales employees.

NONEXEMPT

Employees who are subject to the overtime provisions of the FLSA and thus must be paid time and a half their normal rate of pay when they work more than 40 hours per week.

OVERTIME COMPENSATION The FLSA stipulates that certain employees must receive overtime pay of one and a half times the normal rate when they work over 40 hours per week. Certain kinds of employees are **exempt** from the overtime provision of the act. A job title is not a sufficient basis for exemption. Rather, the actual work performed and the primary duties of the employee determine exempt or nonexempt status. A person with an executive title who does not primarily manage a department or a function may not meet all conditions for exemption. In 2004, the U.S. Department of Labor issued new regulations to determine if an employee is classified as exempt. To be exempt an employee must be paid a minimum salary of $455 per week ($23,660 per year). An employee who is paid by the hour or who makes a salary of less than $455 per week is **nonexempt** regardless of the type of work performed. An employee paid $455 per week must also meet the "duties test" to be exempt from overtime provisions:

- Primary duty is the management of the organization.
- Regularly direct two or more full-time employees or equivalent.
- Authority to hire/fire or recommend the hiring or firing, or promotion of others.

Or meet the administrative exemption provision:

- Primary duty of office work directly related to the management of the organization or customers.
- Exercise independent judgment on matters of significance.

Or meet the professional exemption provision:

- Primary duty of performing work requiring advanced knowledge in a field of science or learning customarily acquired by a prolonged course of specialized, intellectual instruction; or performing work requiring invention, imagination, originality, or talent in a recognized field of artistic or creative endeavor.

Employees earning over $100,000 per year do not receive overtime if their duties are executive, administrative, or professional.

The 2004 rules were the first major changes in the 1938 act since 1949 and were hotly debated in Washington, D.C; labor unions claimed they would reduce the number of people receiving overtime by several million, and President Bush and supporters believed that the new rules would be easier for employers to implement.

About 98 percent of all agreements contain some premium pay for overtime above the FLSA requirement. Daily overtime premiums are provided in 93 percent of agreements. Sixth-day premiums—the sixth consecutive day of work is eligible for a premium payment—and seventh-day premiums are found in about 26 percent of contracts. The **pyramiding** (being paid for more than one premium pay on the same hours) of overtime pay is prohibited in 69 percent of contracts because of management's concerns that the same hours might either become eligible for both daily and weekly overtime or become eligible for more than one type of premium.

PYRAMIDING

The payment of overtime on overtime that occurs if the same hours of work qualify for both daily and weekly overtime payment. Most contracts prohibit this type of payment.

An example of the latter might be holiday pay plus double time on a seventh day worked. Most agreements also specify how overtime should be distributed among workers: "Equal distribution as far as practical" or on a strict seniority basis are common provisions.[12]

In some industries today, the aspect of overtime that unions view as a key issue is the use of *mandatory overtime*. They believe that the excessive use of mandatory overtime keeps many of their members from having enough time with their families and can cause shortages of full-time positions as management tries to minimize the total number of employees in certain jobs. For example, in 2002, the Registered Nurses Association of University Hospital in Cincinnati, Ohio, was ready to strike because they believed mandatory overtime had become routine. Nurses were often ordered to work a second shift at the end of their first shift and were commonly called in on their off days. In addition, the union stressed that mandatory overtime may not be good for patient care. The strike was averted when hospital management agreed to end mandatory overtime by 2004.[13]

In another case, the Communication Workers of America (CWA) walked off the job in 2003 over forced overtime. The 37,000 CWA members' strike against Verizon was the largest concerted labor action against a telecommunications employer in U.S. history, and it was not over pay or health care—but mandatory overtime. The union eventually won a limited overtime provision. Why do unions today view excessive hours as a critical issue? AFL-CIO industrial hygienist Bill Kojola says the way work is organized in the United States is changing and requires longer hours. Research, according to Kojola, indicates that longer hours have the following effects on the workers:

- Have an adverse impact on the cardiovascular systems of workers.
- Increase the blood pressure of workers.
- Increase the risk of accidents exponentially to the point it is double for a 12-hour shift compared with an eight-hour shift.
- Increased risk of accident is highest on a night shift, higher on an afternoon shift, and lowest on a morning shift.[14]

THE DAVIS-BACON ACT The Davis-Bacon Act of 1931 regulates employers who hold federal government contracts of $2,000 or more for federal construction projects. It provides that employees working on these projects must be paid the **prevailing wage** (PW) rate. In most urban areas, the union wage is the PW for that particular geographic area. Some state and local governments have similar laws. For example, in 2007, in Ohio the PW for electricians was $25.56 per hour; the average of all merit shop (nonunion) electricians was $19.17, a difference of about 25 percent. Similar differences for carpenters were $21.01 (merit), $23.27 (PW); bricklayers, $15.19 (merit), $22.20 (PW), whereas the PW for plumbers, $27.96, was less than that for merit: $30.04. Supporters of PW believe that in the long run the (PW) project saves costs by hiring more qualified workers. Opponents believe the higher costs, often between 8 and 15 percent of total costs, are unnecessary.[15] The U.S. Department of Labor calculates the prevailing wage for each region. The reasoning behind the Davis-Bacon Act is that governments often award contracts to the firm submitting the lowest bid for certain construction specifications. By requiring all employers in construction projects to pay the prevailing wage, the Davis-Bacon Act puts bidders on an equal basis and ensures that craft workers will not be underpaid.[16]

PREVAILING WAGE

The hourly wage, usual benefits and overtime, paid to the majority of workers, laborers, and mechanics within a particular area. Prevailing wages are established, by the Department of Labor & Industries, for each trade and occupation employed in the performance of public work.

Opponents of the Davis-Bacon Act have consistently claimed that it is difficult to administer and substantially increases the cost of public construction projects. Supporters contend, however, that contractors trying to win construction bids will underbid by cutting wages and then hiring less-skilled nonunion labor. Many congressional bills have been introduced that would repeal or amend the Davis-Bacon Act. None have passed.

WALSH-HEALEY ACT The Walsh-Healey Act of 1936 covers employees with federal contracts of over $10,000. It requires employers to pay overtime for any hours worked over eight per day at a rate of one and a half times the normal hourly rate. If an employee works days of more than eight hours within a 40-hour week, he or she will receive greater compensation for the same total hours worked.

NEGOTIATED WAGE ADJUSTMENTS

Standard Rate, Pay Range Systems

STANDARD RATE

The flat or hourly rate of pay established for each job classification or occupation within a plant or employer, effective for the duration of the collective bargaining agreement.

How wage rates are to be defined in the agreement is a critical issue. Many agreements contain a **standard rate**, or flat rate, of pay for each job classification effective during the life of the agreement, as in Table 7-1. Some agreements provide a pay range for each job: The person may be paid one of several steps within the range. Usually management will seek flexibility in wage administration by using a range of pay for each grade or category. A common practice in the nonunion sector, this allows management to reward individual differences in employees according to seniority, merit, or quality and quantity of production.

Management usually wishes to hire new inexperienced employees at the minimum pay rate and allow them to advance during their tenure with the company through merit and seniority increases. Management may argue that it makes little sense to pay exactly the same wage rate for a job regardless of the performance level of the employee. Union leaders may argue that merit increases, which are the primary reason to have pay ranges instead of one standard rate for each job, are useful management tools in theory but in practice run into severe problems. Union leaders feel that because these systems normally are based on a supervisor's performance appraisal, they are subject to supervisor bias. The subjectivity and imperfections of performance appraisal systems lead many union leaders to argue against a merit pay increase system.

Piece-Rate Systems

PIECE-RATE SYSTEM

A wage system in which employees receive a standard rate of pay per unit of output. The rate of pay is usually based on the average level of production, with bonus rates given on output units exceeding the average level.

An alternative pay system is a **piece-rate system**. Straight piecework is the most common and easily understood individual incentive plan. If an employee is paid $0.1 per unit produced and completes 100 units in an hour, then the hour's gross earnings will be $10.00. Variations of straight piecework include falling piece rate and rising piece rate. If designed effectively, a piece-rate system can reduce labor costs per unit, reward employees based on their productivity instead of the number of hours worked, and help attract and retain dedicated employees. An effective piece-rate system thus can benefit both the employer and the worker. One study, for example, found that when workers were paid piece rates instead of hourly wages, their productivity increased by 20 percent in comparison with workers performing the same job, but given a daily production standard, or goal.[17]

Plans that use a *falling piece rate* involve a standard time and rate of production. If the employee produces more than the standard, the gain is shared between the employer and the employee. The employee's hourly earnings increase with output above a standard of 100, but the rate per piece falls at various predetermined levels. Thus, an employee who has produced 140 units (40 percent above standard) might receive only $12.88 (29 percent more) and not $14.00, which would be the case if the $0.1 rate were maintained. The employer receives the remainder of the gain, effectively lowering the overhead cost per piece. Plans that use a *rising piece rate* also involve a standard time and rate of production.

Piece-rate systems have the advantages of being easily understood, simple to calculate, and motivational. But many jobs do not easily lend themselves to such a pay system because the output of the employee cannot be directly and objectively measured. Also, most employees' output is affected by the output of others, so their productivity is not directly proportional to their input. Finally, union and management negotiators may have a difficult time agreeing on what is a fair production standard. Changes in standards by management can easily lead to union grievances.

Standard hour plans are similar in concept to piece-rate plans except a "standard time" is set to complete a particular job, instead of paying the employee a price per piece. For example, an auto mechanic might be given a standard time of two hours to tune up an eight-cylinder car. If the worker's hourly rate is $16 per hour and three eight-cylinder tune-ups are finished in six hours, the employee earns $96. If a so-called Halsey 50/50 incentive plan is used, the worker and employer share equally in time saved by the employee. Thus, after completing the three tune-ups in five hours, the employee would be paid $104.00 ($96.00–$8.00 [a half hour saved at $16 per hour]), and the employer has an additional hour's work time.

Deferred Wage Increases

Many multiyear collective bargaining agreements provide increases in wage rates that are deferred to later years rather than taking effect immediately. Such **deferred wage rate increases**, together with the preferred use of cost-of-living adjustments (see next section), often make multiyear contracts desirable for both sides. Management can predict labor costs further into the future with a greater degree of accuracy, and union members feel that their buying power is protected for a longer period of time and do not have to worry annually about possible strikes. An example of a four-year deferred wage increase provision appears in Figure 7-1. In slang terms the deferred wage increases in Table 7-1 could be called a "3 - 2.5 - 2.5 - 3" for the four years.

DEFERRED WAGE RATE INCREASES

Wage rate increases that become effective on later dates as specified in a collective bar-gaining agreement.

Deferred wage provisions specify increases in the base pay to take effect on future dates during a multiyear contract. Negotiating multiyear increases often hinges on whether they are evenly distributed over the life of the contract or whether they are front-end loaded.

Front-end loading refers to a deferred wage increase with a larger proportion of the total percentage increase in the first year of the agreement. Thus, a three-year total wage increase package might be evenly distributed, with an equal percentage provided at the beginning of each year: 5-5-5 percent; or it could be front-end loaded: 10-3-2 percent. Contracts may provide front-end loading, including providing the total increase in the first year: 15-0-0.

FRONT-END LOADING

A deferred wage increase in which a larger proportion of the total increase occurs in the first year of a multiyear contract.

Management generally prefers to spread the increases over the life of the agreement for cash flow purposes and because the total cost of the agreement is substantially less because

WAGE AGREEMENT

This Wage Agreement is entered into this 18th day of June 2007 between the General Electric Company, for its Plant located in Evendale, Ohio (hereinafter referred to as "Company") and the International Association of Machinists and Aerospace Workers, AFL-CIO, for itself and in behalf of its Lodge No. 912 (hereinafter referred to as the "Union").

The Company and the Union hereby agree as follows:

This Wage Agreement shall be in full settlement of all wage issues between the Company and the Union up to and including June 19, 2011.

The Company will provide general wage increases as follows:

1. General Increase

Effective Date	Increase
June 18, 2007	Three percent (3.0%) applied to rates in effect on June 17, 2007.
June 23, 2008	Two and one half percent (2.5%) applied to rates in effect on June 22, 2008.
June 22, 2009	Two and one half percent (2.5%) applied to rates in effect on June 21, 2009.
June 21, 2010	Three percent (3.0%) applied to rates in effect on June 20, 2010.

FIGURE 7-1 Deferred Wage Agreement. *Source*: Agreement between General Electric Aviation and Lodge No. 912, International Association of Machinists and Aerospace Workers, AFL-CIO, 2007–2011. Used by permission.

higher wages paid only in later years are avoided in early years. For example, the two alternatives for the three-year 15 percent increase when applied to a $20,000 current wage produce the following wages paid:

Year	Equal Increases, 5%-5%-5% ($)	Front-End Loaded, 10%-3%-2% ($)	Difference Each Year
0	20,000	20,000	—
1	21,000	22,000	+ $1,000
2	22,050	22,660	+ $ 610
3	23,153	23,113	− $ 40
			+ $1,570

Union negotiators often prefer front-end-loaded wage rate increases so that their members receive the additional wages ($1,570) and realize a large increase in pay the very first year. However, negotiators acknowledge from past experience that front-end loading may produce long-term problems. Members who were quite happy with a 10 percent increase during the first year of an agreement can easily become dissatisfied with the two subsequent years of small increases, especially during periods of high inflation. Thus, "What have you done for me lately?" becomes a real problem for union and management leaders alike. Also, the annual wage rates at the end of the agreement can easily be lower under a front-end-loaded provision than under an evenly distributed provision, as in the previously cited examples. The union may demand a **wage reopener** provision providing for the reopening of contract talks to discuss only wage rates. Such a discussion during the later years of the agreement may become necessary because of unpredictable inflation or company financial success. Management is not obligated to agree to higher wage rates under such a reopener but realizes that this agreement may be necessary to obtain a long-term contract.

WAGE REOPENER

A collective bargaining provision, effective for the term of the contract, which provides for contract talks to be reopened only for the renegotiation of wage rates.

Also, management negotiators realize they will likely be faced with the demands, particularly when they are valid, during the next negotiating session anyway.

Before the 1980s, virtually all collective bargaining agreements with multiyear settlements included front-end-loaded wage increases. However, foreign and domestic nonunion competition in the 1980s forced management negotiators to seek a variety of cost-curbing measures including back-loaded contracts. A **back-loaded contract** provides a lower wage adjustment in the first year with higher increases in later years of a multiyear contract. For example, a 10 percent three-year wage adjustment could be 2-4-4. In many back-loaded contracts, workers receive no wage increase in the first year. For example, a 1997–1999 UAW–Chrysler collective bargaining agreement provided for a 0-3-3 distribution with a $2,000 bonus.[18]

BACK-LOADED CONTRACT

A multiyear contract that provides a lower wage adjustment in the first year with higher increases in later years.

Cost-of-Living Adjustments

Union negotiators may emphasize the need for **cost-of-living adjustments (COLAs)** during the life of an agreement. They contend that the real wage—the purchasing power negotiated in an agreement as a wage rate—is eroded by inflation during the life of the agreement. For example, in 2006, inflation in the United States, as measured by the Historical Consumer Price Index for Urban Wage Earners and Clerical Workers (CPI-W), was 3.2 and 19.1 percent in the seven years from 2000.[19] Thus, an employee would need to have received a 19.1 percent pay increase over the period to break even or "keep up with inflation." Therefore, labor may contend it is necessary to provide the COLA in an escalator clause so that wage rates will keep pace with inflation. General Motors first proposed a COLA clause during negotiations with the UAW in 1948.

COST-OF-LIVING ADJUSTMENT (COLA)

The negotiated compensation increase given an employee based on the percentage by which the cost of living has risen, usually measured by a change in the consumer price index (CPI).

Unions and employers were leery of COLAs until the 1950s. Both feared that COLAs would include pay cuts, which might have occurred because declines in the consumer price index (CPI) were at the time quite possible. Union leaders also disliked COLAs because they represented a "substitute for bargaining," meaning they would receive less credit for increases with a COLA. Unions preferred wage reopeners that put them back at the bargaining table. However, by the mid-1950s, both sides worried less about deflation and more about their ability to estimate correctly rising inflation. In addition, in 1950, General Motors and the United Auto Workers signed a historic wage formula that combined deferred wage adjustments with a COLA—a practice previously avoided by GM but soon followed by many negotiators.[20] The percentage of agreements that contained COLAs steadily increased and peaked in 1979 at 48 percent, but low CPI increases from the 1990s until today have caused the percentage slip to about 18 percent of agreements.[21] The combination of two factors—low inflation rates and the increasing use of multiyear contracts—has decreased the need for quarterly or monthly COLA adjustments to be made if annual base-wage rate adjustments have been negotiated in the contract.

Both labor and management negotiators are careful to specify exact COLA provisions during the agreement. Several critical issues must be carefully spelled out.

1. ***Inflation index*** Most provisions use the consumer price index determined by the Bureau of Labor Statistics (BLS) as a standard for measuring change in inflation. Increases in the CPI are linked to increases in wages by an adjustment formula. The two most commonly used formulas are a cents-per-hour increase for each point increase in the CPI or a percentage increase in wage rates equal to some percentage increase in the CPI. The most commonly used formula provides for a 1-cent increase in wages for each 0.26-of-a-point increase in the CPI.
2. ***When the increases are to be provided*** The majority of agreements provide for inflation adjustment four times a year subsequent to the reported increase in the CPI. This quarterly increase provision is also included in the UAW–Ford agreement. Other labor agreements provide for adjustments to be made twice a year (semiannually) or once a year (annually).
3. ***Change in base pay*** If COLAs are treated as additions to the base pay, then other wage adjustments, such as shift differential and overtime, will increase after a COLA because they are usually a fixed percentage of a base pay. Thus, the company will find its personnel cost increased by an amount greater than the percentage COLA. The alternative is to treat the COLAs given during the life of the agreement as a lump-sum payment and not as an addition to the base pay (see Figure 7-2 for an example).

a. Cost-of-Living Adjustments effective on the dates shown below in the amount of one cent ($.01) per hour for each full **eight** hundredths of one percent (**.08 percent**) by which the National Consumer Price Index for Urban Wage Earners and Clerical Workers (CPI-W; Base 1982–84 = 100), as published by the United States Bureau of Labor Statistics, increases in the applicable measurement period.

Effective Date	Measurement Period
December 17, 2007	June 2007–October 2007
June 23, 2008	October 2007–April 2008
December 15, 2008	October 2007–October 2008
June 22, 2009	October 2008–April 2009
December 21, 2009	October 2008–October 2009
June 21, 2010	October 2009–April 2010
December 20, 2010	October 2009–October 2010
April 18, 2011	October 2010–February 2011

b. No adjustment, retroactive or otherwise, shall be made in pay or benefits as a result of any revision which later may be made in the published figures for Index for any month on the basis of which the cost-of-living calculation shall have been determined.

FIGURE 7-2 Cost-of-Living Adjustments. *Source:* Agreement between General Electric Aviation and Lodge No. 912, International Association of Machinists and Aerospace Workers, AFL-CIO, 2007–2011. Used by permission.

4. ***COLA maximums*** Some labor agreements provide for a maximum COLA increase made by the company during the life of the agreement. This maximum is usually referred to as a cap put on the cost-of-living provision. The cap assures management that wage increases because of CPI increases will not go beyond a certain total.

A significant problem with COLA adjustments that concerns both union leaders and management is that, once given, the increases are taken for granted by employees. Members may believe that the wage increases they receive on the basis of COLA provisions are not negotiated increases, and therefore they want further wage increases. Union and management negotiators may believe that they are not given credit for these negotiated increases. Because members come to expect automatic adjustments for inflation, they tend to ask labor negotiators and management, "What have you done for me lately?" Finally, management complains that COLA provisions prevent them from forecasting future labor costs. Management contends that it cannot predict the total product cost adequately and that COLA costs hamper the ability to bid successfully on projects or priced items.

Profit Sharing

PROFIT SHARING

A pay incentive system in which employees receive a share of the employer's profits in addition to their regular wages. A precise formula specifying how profits will be distributed to employees is the heart of a profit-sharing plan.

Compensation systems whereby management agrees to make a lump-sum payment to employees in addition to their regular wages are termed **profit-sharing** or bonus plans. The payments may be based on the profits of the company using an agreed-on formula (profit sharing) or an amount specified in the contract based on production or sales levels. The UAW–Ford CBA, for example, provided a sliding scale of profits to be paid out, ranging from 6 to 17 percent of net profits that exceed certain sales levels. Both are preferred by management over base-wage increases because profit-sharing bonus increases do not carry over to future years and do not increase the cost of associated benefits such as overtime rates and pension payments, which are typically based on base-wage earnings. Profit-sharing plans appear in about 10 percent of agreements.[22]

Management favors profit sharing to COLAs as a wage supplement for several reasons: (1) payments are made only if the company makes a profit and thus is usually financially strong; (2) unlike COLAs, payments are not tied to inflation, which is not related to the company's financial status and may require increases during difficult times; (3) workers' pay is linked to their productivity and not just to the number of hours they work, giving them a direct incentive to see the company become more profitable; and (4) workers may feel more a part of the company and develop increased interest in reducing waste and increasing efficiency in all areas as well as their own jobs.

In 2001, for example, the Ford Motor Company distributed millions in annual profit-sharing checks to U.S. employees. The average worker received $6,700. Peter Pestillo, Ford's personnel chief and chief labor negotiator, noted, "We think it's money well spent. They get more, and they get more done. We think we get a payback in the cooperation and enthusiasm of the people." Only a few years later, for most of the decade, Ford was losing billions of dollars, and thus there were no profits to be shared.[23] However, 2010 produced record profits for Ford and General Motors, which resulted in over $400 million in profit-sharing payments to UAW workers, an average of over $5,000 per worker. Then in 2011 UAW president Bob King offered to bargain for increased profit sharing rather than higher hourly wages as new contract talks began. The offer was a historic first because like other unions the UAW had always resisted giving up sure pay increases in exchange for potential profit-sharing checks. The automakers were pleased since they could keep fixed costs competitive with other, nonunion manufacturers such as Toyota, Honda, and Nissan.[24]

The concept of profit sharing within the auto industry is not new, however. Douglas Frasier, former president of the UAW, noted that the union first asked for a profit-sharing plan more than 40 years prior to the first agreement in 1984 and during several other negotiations, but none of the U.S. auto giants were interested in profit-sharing plans until they were losing money in the 1980s.[25]

VARIABLE WAGE FORMULA One public sector equivalent to profit sharing is the variable wage formula. Similar to a profit-sharing provision, under a *variable wage formula* provision, future wage rate increases depend, at least in part, on the employer's future ability to pay—or future tax revenues. Also like a COLA provision, the wage increase is directly indexed to a specific tax revenue number. The primary advantage of a variable wage formula is that both sides can negotiate a long-term agreement because it provides for unknown future swings in tax revenues. Management knows that it will only pay increased wages if it has the ability to pay due to greater tax revenues, and a union knows that future revenue increases will be shared due to the formula. An example of a variable wage formula is provided in the Collective Bargaining Agreement By and Between Louisville/Jefferson County Metro Government and Louisville Professional Firefighters Association Local Union 345, IAFF AFL–CIO–CLC (October 10, 2009–June 30, 2013):

VARIABLE WAGE FORMULA

A public sector deferred wage increase that is indexed to the growth of future governmental tax revenues.

ARTICLE 20

Schedule of Pay

> Section 1. c. On July 1, 2012, the hourly base pay rates shall be increased by a percentage equal to one-half of the percentage increase in the occupational license fee revenue received by Metro Government from the Revenue Commission for the then most recently concluding fiscal year as estimated in Metro Government's Annual Budget Document and confirmed within 90 days of the close of the fiscal year and retroactively added to the hourly rate so to be effective on July 1 of the respective fiscal year or 2 percent whichever is more.

The above example contains three key values for negotiators to focus on during negotiations: (1) the definition of the exact tax revenue value that will trigger a wage increase (occupational license fee revenue), (2) the percent of tax revenue growth to be "shared" as a wage rate increase (50 percent), and (3) a minimum or "floor" wage increase in future years (2 percent). The variable wage formula negotiated between the city of Eugene, Oregon, and police, by comparison, provided for future wage rate increases of exactly 1 percent, 2 percent, or 3 percent depending on tax revenue growth, rather than a percentage of growth which could provide a wage increase of 2.15 percent or 2.50 percent and so on.[26]

Scanlon Group Incentive Plans

Joseph Scanlon developed a group incentive plan designed to achieve greater production through increased efficiency with accrued savings divided among the workers and the company. Scanlon at the time was the research director of the United Steelworkers and later joined the faculty at the Massachusetts Institute of Technology.[27] The **Scanlon plan** became the popular standard in U.S. group incentive plans. It has since become a basis for labor–management cooperation above and beyond its use as a group incentive plan. The plan contains two primary features: (1) departmental committees of union and management representatives meet together at least monthly to consider any cost-savings suggestions and (2) any documented cost savings resulting from implemented committee suggestions are divided 75 percent to employees and 25 percent to the company.[28]

SCANLON PLAN

A group incentive plan designed by Joseph Scanlon in which greater production is achieved through increased efficiency, with the accrued savings being distributed among the workers and the employer.

Most other group incentive plans involve programs that set expected levels of productivity, product costs, or sales levels for individual groups and then provide employee bonuses if the targeted goals are exceeded. One widely recognized example is the Nucor Corporation. In one year the company reported a staggering growth of 600 percent in sales and 1,500 percent in profits over ten years due to a production incentive program. The company actually developed four separate incentive programs: one each for production employees, department heads, professional employees, and senior officers. Their theory was that "money is the best motivation."[29]

A popular derivation of the Scanlon Plan is *gain-sharing*. Under a gain-sharing plan an organizational performance goal is agreed to, and if the performance exceeds the goal, the "gain" is "shared" by the parties according to an agreed-upon formula. The purpose of gain-sharing is to increase employee involvement and thus productivity—because they realize they will benefit economically if the goal is exceeded. In a process similar to "quality circles," groups of employees work together with members of management to develop and implement ideas that should improve efficiency. Monthly bonuses are then awarded based on the gain-sharing results.

Two-Tier Wage Systems

TWO-TIER WAGE SYSTEM

A wage system that pays newly hired workers less than current employees per-forming the same or similar jobs.

A wage system that pays newly hired workers less than current employees performing the same or similar jobs is termed "two tier." The **two-tier wage system** was established in 1977 at General Motors Packard Electric Division in Warren, Ohio.[30] The basic concept is to provide continued higher wage levels for current employees if the union will accept reduced levels for future employees. Union leaders believe that they must accept the two-tier system or accept pay cuts for current workers or face greater layoffs in the future. Management usually claims that the system is needed to compete with nonunion and foreign competition. Two-tier systems appeared in about 41 percent of manufacturing contracts in 1995, but fell to only 33 percent by 2002 and in 2005 appeared in only 27 percent of all contracts. The Great Recession of 2008 ignited a rebound in negotiated two-tier systems. In 2007, for example, the United Auto Workers and GM, Ford, and Chrysler agreed to a dramatic two-tier wage package that paid new workers only $14–$16 per hour, down from $26 per hour in prior contracts. The UAW agreed to the substantial pay reduction for new hires in exchange for job guarantees and decisions not to close plants that had been scheduled for closure. William C. Ford, executive chairman of the Ford Motor Company, confirmed, "If we didn't have that (the two-tier wage package) in this contract, the number of autoworkers would have dwindled."[31] In 2010 Ford hired the first shift of employees under the new two-tier agreement—creating 1,200 new jobs at the Chicago assembly plant. The new "second-tier" employees earned just over $14 per hour on average—about half what current workers on the same jobs were paid. In addition the new "second-tier" employees also do not receive the pension benefits of other workers, but instead receive 401 (k) accounts.[32]

During the Great Recession of 2008, two-tier agreements also spread to the public sector for the first time as governments sought ways of reducing costs. For example, in New York City the 121,000-member District Council 37, American Federation of State, County and Municipal Employees (AFSCME), approved in 2008 a contract that set wages for new hires for their first two years of employment 15 percent less than that of current employees.[33]

Industries in which two-tier wage systems are most common include food retail, airlines, manufacturing, chemical, rubber, plastic, and transportation.[34] And, in highly competitive industries such as food retailing, where nonunion employers such as Walmart compete directly with unionized employers, two-tier agreements are gaining ground. In 2005, for example, members of the United Food and Commercial Workers union in Colorado voted (60–40 percent) to accept a two-tier agreement with King Soopers and City Market Stores to avoid a strike. The union's negotiating committee had recommended rejecting the contract and going on a strike. Management maintained the two-tier pay system could have provided cost savings to remain competitive. Top-pay-scale union workers were required to pay higher health insurance premiums as their concession.[35]

Although a two-tier system is contrary to the historical union doctrine of "equal pay for equal work," or pay equity, when a system is first negotiated, the union representatives can claim that they have avoided disaster and saved the jobs or wage levels of current members (who must vote on the contract). It is relatively easy to sell such a concept because no workers at that point are accepting the "lower tier." However, five or ten years later, when many workers are paid lower wages for the same work as their affiliated union members, it can become a source of conflict and resentment. In some cases the lower-paid workers express their feelings with lower product quality and productivity records than their higher-paid counterparts.[36] In these bargaining units, the conflict could present even greater problems to both union and management as the number of lower-tier workers approaches 51 percent of the bargaining unit and they demand equity.

Do employees hired into a lower-tier pay position perceive their treatment as equitable? Concessions gained at the bargaining table do not guarantee cost savings and can cause problems for both sides. UAW workers at the General Motors (GM) plant in Lansing, Michigan, certainly think their new two-tier wage system has caused mixed emotions. In 2010 Steve Barnas, the UAW plant bargaining chairman, commented, "It's sure difficult to look across the line at someone getting paid more for doing the same job you're doing." Under the new two-tier contract GM workers at the GM Buick assembly plant average about $35,000 annually, or $14/hour or about half of what workers on the higher tier earn. Today the new hires average about 20 percent less than the average American manufacturing worker. Another union leader, Saladin Parm, said workers are the angriest he has ever seen them in his 23 years with GM. Still, former UAW president Ron Gettelfinger agreed to the concessions because ". . . you can have the best contract in the world, but if you don't have a job to go with it, what have you got?"[37] At the same time GM during the first three years of the four-year contract did not realize any significant cost savings because the Great Recession caused the manufacturer to lay off over 5,000 employees of the total 51,000 UAW factory workers—and only hire 2,000 on the new lower-tier wage system. Thus, due to poor timing the new contract started just before the recession, the key concession provision of the 2007–2011 agreement didn't help GM's bottom line as anticipated.[38]

Studies also indicate that the high-tier employee may be dissatisfied with the two-tier system. In a survey of over 1,000 employees in a 14-store food outlet company, researchers found that employees at the high end of a two-tier pay scale feared replacement by the lower-tiered employees. In addition, they believed the two-tier system had a detrimental effect on any wage increases they might feel entitled to receive.[39]

One method of minimizing the morale problems of low-tier employees is to provide eventual merging of the two tiers. Temporary two-tier wage systems allow newly hired employees to reach the higher tier within 90–180 days or more. Some two-tier systems are permanent because the contract does not provide for any means by which employees hired at the lower-tier wage can progress to the higher tier. The presence of permanent systems in a contract puts a great deal of pressure on union negotiators to achieve a merger of the two tiers, which is found in about 60 percent of all two-tier contract clauses.[40] Thus two-tier pay systems have produced mixed results. Table 7-3 outlines the pros and cons of the two-tier wage system.

Lump-Sum Payments

As illustrated in Table 7-4, of the major alternatives to increasing base pay, **lump-sum payments** and two-tier systems are methods to provide general wage increases and are increasing in their use, whereas COLAs and wage reopeners have declined in use. The most common form of lump-sum payment is a flat dollar amount per worker.

LUMP-SUM PAYMENTS

A method of providing a general wage increase as a onetime payment rather than adding the increase to the hourly or annual salary of the employee.

The 2005 collective bargaining agreement between Caterpillar, Inc. and the United Auto Workers was heralded as a landmark "return" of two-tier pay systems combined with lump-sum increases as a major change in direction for negotiated wage increases. In highly competitive industries such as retail grocery, airlines, and manufacturing, employers seek a means of lowering

TABLE 7-3 Pros and Cons of the Two-Tier Wage System

Pros	Cons
Significantly reduced labor costs	Resentment, low quality, and low productivity from low-tier employees
Maintenance of higher employment levels	Higher absenteeism and turnover of low-tier employees
Relief from wage compression between senior and junior employees on the same job	Intensification of the preceding problems as low-tier employees increase in number

TABLE 7-4 Wage Trends in Contracts (frequency expressed as percentage of contracts)

	1954	1961	1971	1979	1986	1992	1995	2004	2009
Deferred increases	20	58	87	95	80	89	88	77	75
Cost-of-living adjustments	25	24	22	48	42	34	34	18	16
Wage reopeners	60	28	12	8	10	5	8	7	7
Lump sums	—	—	—	—	—	23	22	17	13
Two-tier pay	—	—	—	—	17	27	41	27	25

Sources: Bureau of National Affairs, *Basic Patterns in Union Contracts,* 14th ed. (Washington, DC: BNA Books, 1995), p. 111; and Bureau of National Affairs, *2010 Source Book on Collective Bargaining* (Washington, DC: BNA Books, 2010). Used by permission.

or "resetting" wage rates to meet low-wage global competition. By negotiating lump-sum increases for current employees together with a two-tier system for new employees, an employer can effectively lower base-wage rates and total labor costs.[41] Management may prefer lump-sum payments to COLAs, or higher wages because their total cost during the contract is easier to predict, and they do not increase hourly wage rates. Unions may prefer they be paid early in the weeks of a new contract to provide quick benefit to members. Lump-sum payments do not preclude the negotiation of a wage rate increase, but usually management will offer a larger total compensation package in the first year if a lump sum is included instead of a larger base-wage increase. Common lump-sum awards include "signing" or "ratification" bonuses designed to give workers an immediate onetime payment between when the agreement is ratified and the first paycheck is issued under the new contract. In 2004, lump-sum payments were most common in manufacturing contracts (28 percent) versus nonmanufacturing (13 percent).[42]

CONCESSION BARGAINING

The 1980s recession ushered in a new era in negotiated wages—concession bargaining. High levels of unemployment prompted unions in severely affected industries to seek ways to protect jobs. Through collective bargaining, unions tried to stop further layoffs. Employers were willing to agree to increased employment security only at the high price of wage or benefit cuts. In several cases, reductions in benefits, particularly paid time off work, are required to guarantee employment levels.[43] Thus, *givebacks*, or **concession bargaining** techniques, were born out of necessity. During the 1990s concessions declined as the economy prospered. However, following the events of September 11, 2001, a new era of concession bargaining began, and in 2005, the Bureau of National Affairs estimated that over two-thirds of all employers negotiating contracts sought some concessions, primarily in health care, overtime, and pension benefits. In addition, 59 of the employers were willing to trade wage gains for benefit concessions. Table 7-5 illustrates areas in which employers seek to gain concessions.[44] It is important to remember that under the NLRA, during the life of a CBA employers are required to maintain negotiated wages and benefits—unless a union agrees to a new concession during a contract which is highly unlikely. Then concessions can generally only be gained during negotiations for a new agreement.[45]

CONCESSION BARGAINING

Collectively bargained reductions in previously negotiated wages, benefits, or work rules, usually in exchange for management-guaranteed employment levels during the term of a contract.

Concession bargaining first gained national headlines when the Chrysler Corporation negotiated more than $200 million in givebacks in November 1979. On the brink of bankruptcy, Chrysler used the United Auto Worker (UAW) concessions to negotiate more than $1 billion in long-term federal government loans. Although some concessions were in the area of deferred wage increases, the majority of the savings came in the reduced employee benefits of paid holidays, paid sickness and accident absences, and pension funds.[46] In return, Chrysler gave the UAW a seat on its board of directors and a no-layoff guarantee.

TABLE 7-5 Areas Where Employers Strive to Gain Concessions

	Percentage of Employers Seeking Concessions
Wages	49
Job Security	9
Paid Leave Benefits	22
Pensions/Retirement	31
Health Care/Insurance	50

Source: "Employees Take the Upper Hand in Wage Concessions," *HR Focus* (May 2009), p. 8.

PUBLIC SECTOR CONCESSIONS. The Great Recession which began in 2008 caused the first national spread of public sector concession bargaining. While many private sector unions and employers had experienced the Great Depression, most public sector unions had only first negotiated contracts in the 1970s and 1980s, when most states and local governments followed the lead of the federal government and first allowed employees to organize and collectively bargain. Thus the Great Recession of 2008 was the first time that many state and local governments experienced severe revenue decreases and thus needed to negotiate concessions to balance their budgets. A few had negotiated wage freezes or minor concessions in benefits during past recessions, but those negotiations were not as widespread or cuts as deep as those reflected in contracts negotiated during the years of 2008–2011.[47] Most negotiations forced government and union negotiators to choose among very painful alternatives such as raising taxes—which few elected bodies of government were willing to do during a recession, cutting wage rates, layoffs, reductions in employer benefit contributions, furloughs (unpaid leave days), and early retirement programs (then leaving jobs unfilled), and even two-tier wage and benefit programs which were unheard of in the public sector. Examples of such public sector concessions are presented in Profile 7-2.

Profile 7-2

Examples of Public Sector Concessions

A common pattern across the United States during the Great Recession was cities and states striving to avoid massive layoffs by "sharing the pain" of budget cuts through one or more of the following negotiated concessions:

- ***Chicago, IL:*** Mayor Daley offered unpaid furlough leaves to unions to avoid layoffs; two unions refused and suffered 431 layoffs.
- ***Detroit, MI:*** Mayor Dave Bing offered unions the choice of 26 unpaid furlough days to avoid layoffs of over 1,000 workers (one-tenth of the workforce).
- ***Los Angeles, CA:*** The city and unions together developed a concession plan that included increased worker pension and health care contributions.
- ***Eugene, OR:*** A negotiated 18 percent personnel cost decrease with AFSCME due to health care cuts (with 3 percent pay gains) and police agreeing to variable wage hikes (1–3 percent) based on inflation.
- ***Kokomo, IN:*** Firefighters agreed to layoffs for 1.5 percent pay hikes v. AFSCME FOP plus city workers; wage freeze with no layoffs.
- ***Lockport, NY:*** New "two-tier" wage scale with police starts new hires $2,700 less and saves city $20,000 per hire over 20 years.
- ***Tulsa, OK:*** Police rejected pay cut offer and accepted layoffs of 89 officers, but firefighters voted 422–177 to accept 5.2 percent pay cuts and 8 unpaid furlough days, and clothing allowance cuts in exchange for no layoffs of 147 members.
- ***Illinois:*** Newly hired employees must work up to 12 years more than current employees to receive full pensions.
- ***San Francisco:*** Twenty local unions accepted pay cuts of $100 million/year to avoid further layoffs.
- ***New Jersey:*** The state required employees increase their share of health care costs and banned part-time employees from drawing pensions.

Sources: Adapted from Stephane Fitch and Christopher Steiner, "Critical Mess," *Forbes 185,* no. 10 (June 7, 2010), p. 24–26; and M. R. Carrell and C. Heavrin, *International Municipal Lawyers Association Conference Proceedings*, Miami, FL (October 2009).

(continued)

Concessions demanded by mayors and governors including wage and benefit cuts, unpaid furloughs, and layoffs, caused many public sector workers like these Chicago police officers to stage public protests during the Great Recession of 2008–2011.
Source: Charles Rex Arbogast/AP Images.

ARENA BARGAINING

A process when management meets with representatives of all the bargaining units at one time to discuss difficult economic issues.

During the Great Recession of 2008, a new method of dealing with concession negotiations that increased in popularity was **arena bargaining**—a process when management meets with representatives of all the bargaining units at one time to discuss difficult economic issues. The method has been particularly useful in the public sector, such as school boards and local governments, where other stakeholders including elected officials and the public can hear the same discussions, which often include outside experts. Often arena bargaining will focus on one issue, such as health care insurance costs, rather than entire contracts or multiple economic issues.[48]

LEGACY COSTS

Contract costs for retiree benefits increases in retirement and health care provided in earlier contracts.

A key issue during the precedent-setting 2007 UAW–GM, Ford, and Chrysler contract negotiations were the **legacy costs** (retiree benefits increases provided by prior contracts) for retiree pension and health care benefits. It was estimated that about 10 percent of the price of a new vehicle was paid to retirees. Legacy costs also roughly equaled about $25 per hour. Although the nonunion Japanese competitors—Toyota, Honda, Nissan—pay roughly the same wages to current workers as the Detroit Big Three automakers, they do not have the retiree legacy costs, and thus, according to management at GM, Ford, Chrysler, they realize a significant cost advantage. A tough question is this: Which side is responsible for legacy costs: the union, whose members receive the benefits, or management, which agreed to them in past negotiations?[49]

Management's ability to convince labor of an impending financial crisis, one that could cause a significant loss of jobs or total shutdown of an operation, is a necessary element for successful concession bargaining.[50] In 2009 for example, the Hearst Corporation threatened to close the 144-year-old *San Francisco Chronicle*—the largest circulation daily newspaper in the city, if the California Media Workers guild and Teamsters local union did not approve major wage, benefit, and staff reductions. The *Chronicle* had been losing money for eight years straight, including over $50 million in 2008. The union members by a 10-1 margin approved the concessions and the elimination of 150 jobs to save the newspaper.[51] If a union is convinced that the employer may, in fact, file for bankruptcy, then it is motivated to agree to concessions in wages and benefits rather than allow a bankruptcy court judge to impose cuts. Courts have made cuts or allowed employers to abandon contracted wages and benefits in about 90 percent of U.S. bankruptcy proceedings.[52] However, economic adversity alone may not be enough to bring about concessions. Union negotiators expect management concessions and programs to enhance labor–management relationships. Thus, employers as well as unions have made concessions during giveback negotiations, many aimed at increasing quality of work life and worker participation in decision making. Economic concessions have often centered on management's sharing of future "good times" through profit sharing or gain sharing in exchange for immediate union givebacks.[53] For example, in 2010 new UAW president Bob King warned that in upcoming contract talks with Ford, GM, and Chrysler he expected some of the givebacks to be reversed—"at least to the extent that management and other stakeholders get rewarded." Why? King emphasized a core philosophy of union concession bargaining: "When there's equality of sacrifice, there's got to be equality of gain . . . We just want to make sure when things turn up we share in the upside."[54]

In many cases concessions are not directly called "concessions," so that neither side appears to have lost or won in negotiations. Most negotiations involving givebacks require both labor and management to make some concessions in a true give-and-take process.[55] Often, for example, if management demands givebacks in wages and benefits, union negotiators demand similar reductions in management salaries and benefits. If management requests greater flexibility in work rules and scheduling, labor negotiators might demand greater union participation in management decisions. During particularly hard economic times, such as the recent Great Recession, an employer may ask a union to accept concessions during a contract, even though the NLRA requires the employer to continue paying the negotiated wages and benefits in the CBA. In 2009, for example, Ford Motor Co. offered to invest $500 million in the Louisville, Kentucky, assembly plant—thus guaranteeing the plant would not close—if members of UAW Local 862 voted to accept wage increases contained in the 2007–2011 contract. The members voted 84 percent against, 16 percent in favor of the offer. UAW Local 862 President Rocky Comito said, "We heard from the silent majority . . . We gave so much already [in 2007 negotiations]." Troy Lee, a Ford electrician, perhaps best summarized the feelings of the workers when he said, "They should have given us three ways to vote. Yes, no, and hell no!"[56]

84 percent of UAW Local 862 members in Louisville, Kentucky, voted against a 2007–2011 contract proposal by Ford Motor Co. to accept concessions in exchange for Ford's promise to invest $500 million in the assembly plant—guaranteeing it would stay open. Troy Lee, a Ford electrician, commented, "They should have given us three ways to vote. Yes, no, and hell no!" *Source:* Bloomberg via Getty Images.

Executive Pay

The issue of *executive pay* has become a hot negotiation topic in recent years. Union members want senior management executives to "share their pain." For example, in 2004, union employees at US Airways Group Inc. were forced to accept a 21 percent pay cut to save the company from bankruptcy, but CEO Bruce Lakefield didn't lower his own $425,000 salary, which caused union leaders to confront him and ask why they were "asked to make sacrifices and he wasn't even making a token sacrifice." At Delta Air Lines, executives were given a 10 percent pay cut when pilots accepted a 32.5 percent pay cut and five-year wage freeze in 2005. But then six top Delta executives were given $1.9 million in stock options, causing John Malone, the union leader, to claim, "The generals are dining while the troops are toiling."[57] The issue has also caused problems in the public sector. In 2007, for example, about 2,300 University of Cincinnati faculty members approved a three-year contract that included a total 8.5 percent wage increase and economic concessions in health care that almost offset the salary gains. Then, only a month later, UC president Nancy Zimpher received an 8 percent one-year salary increase, plus a 30 percent bonus! The American Association of University Professors (AAUP) gave UC an "F+" in faculty relations and said the president's increase left them "appalled and demoralized."[58] In 2010 several thousand utility workers protested the "out of control" executive pay given to members of management who were at the same time at the bargaining table demanding concessions in healthcare. The workers were members of Utility Workers of America and Local 223 and employees of DTE Energy; they generate, deliver, and restore power and supply gas to Michigan customers. DTE had posted record first quarter profits of $230 million, and the chairman and CEO was awarded a $2 million bonus. James Harrison, president of Local 223, commented the company only had to bargain in good faith—instead of demanding concessions during a period of record profits.[59]

Payback Agreements

Employers may try to protect the investment they have made in their employees by including *payback agreements* in the negotiations. Payback agreements require an employee who voluntarily quits before a specified period of time (usually one year) to pay the employer the cost of certain benefits. The most common benefits specified include relocation costs for newly hired employees, training program costs, and tuition assistance costs. Companies such as American Airlines (pilot training costs of about $10,000), Electronic Data Systems Corporation (relocation costs), and Lockheed Corporation (tuition assistance) have successfully sued employees who refused to honor their payback agreements.[60]

Some unions have criticized payback agreements: The AFL-CIO has noted their similarity to indentured servitude (a person required to work for another as a servant). However, not all unions dislike the concept. The Sheet Metal Workers Union has required those who complete the union training program to repay the program costs if they work for a nonunion shop within ten years.

Employer Concessions

Union concessions generally involve wage, benefit, or work rule changes, with reduced benefits generally more acceptable to employees than wage concessions, although future wage increases may be renegotiated. Often work rule changes are easier to sell to employees and have a more lasting effect. Employers, however, must expect to pay the price of these concessions through one or more of five areas of negotiation:

1. ***Increased job security.*** The union will most likely try to extract a promise not to close plants or not to subcontract with nonunion producers. Another example of providing job security is the 2005 agreement between Comair and its pilots union, the Air Line Pilots Association. The agreement provided that Comair would add 36 new jet planes to its fleet

and a hiring freeze for three years. The pilots believed the new planes were needed to maintain the current number of Comair flights—and their job.[61]

2. ***Increased financial disclosure.*** The employer will have to make a claim of inability to pay or financial hardship. Although the company's financial information normally need not be disclosed in collective bargaining, when the employer puts profitability or financial condition in contention, the financial data must be provided to substantiate the position.
3. ***Profit-sharing plans.*** Union members generally feel that sharing losses during lean years should mean sharing profits in good years. For example, Chrysler Corporation's employees demanded a share of the record profits after the UAW made major concessions to guarantee the federal loan to Chrysler. Workers were pleased to receive the profit-sharing check during a slumping economy, and they expressed their feelings to the national union leaders who had negotiated the benefit in an unusual newspaper advertisement on April 13, 2001. The 103,000 hourly Ford workers under the national agreement received an average payout of $6,700 in 2001. The highest payout under the profit-sharing program that started with the 1982 contract was $8,000 in 1999.
4. ***Equality of sacrifice.*** Employers must demand the same sacrifices from management and nonunion employees as union employees. For instance, General Motors tried to increase its executive bonus program just after the UAW made major concessions in 1982. The UAW and its members demanded and got the increases rescinded.
5. ***Participation in decision making.*** Unions may seek greater participation in various management decisions, including plant closings and the use of new technological methods.

WAGE NEGOTIATION ISSUES

During the negotiation process one or both sides may use different wage-level theories to stress their economic proposals. One or both sides will bring to light one or more wage theories and issues having an impact on the negotiation of rates. Which issues might be stressed during negotiations and whether they are even presented depend on the history of the company's labor relations and the personalities of the negotiators. In general, either side would utilize an issue it felt was valid or simply useful in providing a significant point for its list of arguments.

Productivity Theory

One of the oldest and broadest negotiation issues concerning wages involves the **productivity theory** that employees should share in increased profits caused by greater productivity. At the heart of the issue is the commonly accepted proposition that the organization's production is a combination of three factors: machinery and equipment, employee labor, and managerial ability. Union and management leaders agree that all three share in the creation of profits because they contribute to the organization's productivity.

PRODUCTIVITY THEORY

The negotiating position that employees should share in increased profits gained by the greater productivity achieved because of their efforts.

Whenever figures show that productivity or profits have risen, then the question becomes, "What percentage is attributable to employees' labor as opposed to machinery and equipment or managerial ability?" Labor leaders commonly request that their members get their fair share of the increased profits. Management may request that the **value-added concept** be applied.

VALUE-ADDED CONCEPT

The theory that wages should equal the contribution of labor to the final product.

Determining labor's fair share then becomes the problem. Management may contend that all it asks is for employees to perform assigned work at stated times and at accepted levels of performance. The union usually counters that employees seek to improve the quality and quantity of output, reduce cost, and minimize the waste of resources. If specific production standards are established through negotiation, it is much easier to negotiate accepted wage increases. Yet separating out and measuring profit resulting from individual and group productivity as compared with management and capital equipment is almost impossible.

Ability to Pay

ABILITY TO PAY

The financial position of a company and its ability to change its wage rates are general factors involved in negotiations. They are usually a reflection of company profits and will be a basis of a negotiator's wage proposal.

The issue of **ability to pay** is commonly expressed during wage negotiations. In principle, this issue is similar to the productivity theory. Union leaders emphasize that labor is one of the primary inputs into a company's productivity and therefore profitability. Labor negotiators conclude that if the company is experiencing high profits, it can better pay its employees who have contributed to the good financial conditions. For example, 1996 was the most profitable year in the history of the airline industry. Thus, when it came time to renegotiate labor contracts, "a spirit of militancy" swept through the ranks of airline workers. "American Airlines is making record profits, and it's time our wages reflect that," said Rob Held, a pilot. American Airlines pilots, in fact, overwhelmingly rejected a contract offer that their own union leaders had called generous. United Airlines mechanics rejected an offer of a 10 percent wage increase. However, only a few years earlier these same unions had accepted layoffs, wage cuts, and longer hours during hard financial times in the airline industry.[62]

The ability-to-pay concept, however, has severe limitations according to management negotiators. First, unions will not press this issue during hard times when profits have decreased or when the company is suffering temporary losses. Unions seldom want to apply the ability-to-pay doctrine consistently in both good and hard times; instead, they expect wage levels to be maintained during hard times and increased during good times. Second, management will argue that higher profits must be applied back into the company in capital investments. Finally, although profit levels fluctuate greatly, negotiated wage rates do not vary accordingly. If higher wage rates were negotiated on the basis of a six-month crest of high profits, the company might find it extremely difficult to maintain the higher wages during a period of sluggish profitability. Unfortunately, wage rates are negotiated for the future, and real profit information is available only for the past, causing management to use "estimated profits" when negotiating. (See Table 7-6) Thus, estimating the company's future ability to pay during the life of the new contract is quite difficult.

TABLE 7-6 Estimated Profits Available under a New Contract

	Potential Profits Available from Current Operations	Current	Projected
1.	Sales revenue	$46,324,064	$52,056,000
2.	Production costs	–23,100,000	–26,565,000
3.	Labor costs (wages and benefits)	–14,390,064	–15,890,000
4.	Labor costs as a percent of sales	30.4%	30.52%
5.	Administrative and selling costs	–2,800,000	–3,080,000
6.	Overhead	–1,550,000	–1,705,000
7.	Net profits before taxes	5,484,000	4,816,000
8.	Income tax	–2,020,000	–1,774,000
9.	After-tax profit	3,464,000	3,042,000
10.	Dividends paid	–400,000	–400,000
11.	Profits with current operations	3,064,000	2,642,000
	Potential Increased Cost Savings Due to New Equipment	**Current**	**Projected**
12.	Increased output: 10% (reduced product costs: $23,100,000 × 0.10)	2,310,000	2,656,500
13.	Costs of new equipment = $6,400,000 × 0.10 (current interest rate)	–640,000	–640,000

TABLE 7-6 *(Continued)*

14.	Related new equipment costs	−640,000	−660,000
15.	Total cost of new equipment	−1,280,000	−1,300,000
16.	Savings due to new equipment (savings available to all organizational needs)	1,030,000	1,356,500

Potential Profits Available from Future Operations and Savings Due to New Equipment

		Projected
17.	Potential profits available for all corporate needs (11 + 16)	$3,998,500
18.	Percent of profits available for labor	35%
19.	Profits available for increased labor costs under new contract	1,399,475

NOTE: This example might be used by either management or labor to calculate the dollar amount each believes will be available for labor under the new contract. Of course, each side might make different assumptions about the firm's future sales, profits, and productivity.

Job Evaluation

Job evaluation is the process of systematically analyzing jobs to determine their relative worth within the organization. The process is generally part of job analysis—the personnel function of systematically reviewing the tasks, duties, and responsibilities of jobs, usually to write job descriptions and minimum qualifications as well as to provide information for job evaluation. In general, the result of a job evaluation effort is a pay system with a rate for each job commensurate with its status within the hierarchy of jobs in the organization.[63]

JOB EVALUATION

A systematic method of determining the worth of a job to an organization. This is usually accomplished by analysis of the internal job factors and comparison to the external job market.

Job evaluation procedures do not include analyzing employee performance; that is referred to as performance evaluation or performance appraisal. Rather, in a job evaluation the position is reviewed for several carefully selected criteria to determine the relative worth of the job to the organization in comparison with other jobs in the labor market. Union leaders as well as members of management can use job evaluation techniques as guides to negotiate wage agreements and explain paid differentials to employees. An example of how an agreement can provide for the use of job evaluation procedures during the life of a labor contract is shown in the following labor agreement between the Duke Energy Company and the International Brotherhood of Electrical Workers:

ARTICLE V

k. The Company's Evaluation Committee will be responsible for evaluating all new and revised job classifications. The Union will appoint two (2) members to the Company's Evaluation Committee. The evaluation that is established by this Committee is used to determine the maximum wage rate for each new or revised job classification. Results of the evaluation will be communicated to the Union two weeks before the new or revised job classification becomes effective.

l. The Union shall maintain a Job Evaluation Advisory Committee consisting of not more than five members who may review the evaluation and wage rate of any job classification which undergoes a substantial change in qualifications or duties. The Union's Committee may, by request, meet with the Company's Committee, at a mutually convenient time within thirty (30) days after the effective date of the new or revised job classification, to present any information relevant to the evaluation of the job classification which has been included in the previous written comments of the Union representative. The Union will be notified after the Company's Committee has reviewed the additional information presented by the Union. All wage rates so established shall be final and binding and not subject to the grievance and arbitration procedure. However, if any revised wage rates are reduced as a result of the evaluation(s), they will not be placed into effect until the Company and the Union have had an opportunity to negotiate them during full contract negotiations, even though the revised job classification will be in effect.

Source: Agreement between Duke Energy Ohio, Inc. and Local Union 1347 International Brotherhood of Electrical Workers, *AFL-CIO*, 2006–2009. Used by Permission.

Job classification is common in labor agreements, and when an agreement contains a rigid classification, the employer may not unilaterally change it. When no explicit provision exists, it is generally recognized that management has the right to make classification changes or to add new jobs. However, even if the agreement contains a job classification, arbitrators have recognized management's need—and right—to make changes as long as established pay rates are used, the union is allowed to file complaints through the grievance procedure, and management follows any procedures agreed to in the contract.[64] Case 7-2 illustrates a typical dispute over job classification.

CASE 7-2

Reclassification of Jobs

The company manufactures refrigerators and dehumidifiers. The grievance concerns assembly-line workers who installed foil wrap around the wired socket on certain food liner tops. The company instituted an operational modification that substituted fiberglass insulation for foil in the assembly operation. The grievants were classified as Class III Assemblers. Their grievance was a request to be reclassified to the high classification of Hand Pack Insulation workers. The Hand Pack Insulation classification was specifically created in the early 1960s to cover personnel who must work with fiberglass insulation.

It was the union's position that the grievants regularly worked with fiberglass insulation and therefore should be classified to the higher classification. The workers do not have to spend more than 50 percent of their time handling fiberglass insulation before they can be classified as Hand Pack Insulators because there are Hand Pack Insulators who cut up fiberglass insulation on only two days per week. By creating the new classification, the parties had recognized that employees generally do not like to work with fiberglass insulation because it causes the workers to itch.

Using the management rights clause as its basis, the company contended that it had the right to change the materials being used in particular operations and to assign different tasks to appropriate classifications. The company pointed out that many assembly-line workers had occasionally come into contact with fiberglass materials during the 20 years preceding this grievance and that no prior claims or grievances had been made regarding reclassification. It contended that the jobs performed by the two grievants were not meaningfully changed by the substitution of fiberglass for foil. In fact, the job description for the Class III Assemblers mentions that the personnel must deal with insulation, indicating that they may be expected to handle some fiberglass.

Decision

The arbitrator found that, although it is apparent that the Hand Pack Insulation classification was created to cover personnel who spend a significant amount of their time handling fiberglass insulation, the history of the plant indicates that numerous assembly-line workers in other classifications continued to handle some fiberglass insulation without job reclassification. The arbitrator cited the basic rule that when jobs are classified by titles and the parties have not negotiated a detailed description of job content, management are permitted wide authority to assign work that is reasonably related or incidental to the regular duties of the job. The arbitrator also put heavy emphasis on the fact that other personnel had not previously sought reclassification of their jobs to Hand Pack Insulator, even though they did handle some fiberglass insulation.

Source: Adapted from *Magic Chef, Inc.*, 84 LA 15 (1984).

WAGE SURVEYS

WAGE SURVEY

The collection and appraisal of data from various sources used to determine the average salary for specified positions in the job market.

Both labor and management conduct their own **wage surveys** to provide information on external labor market conditions. The job evaluation process is used to maintain internal equity for wage rates, but it is also important to maintain external equity. That is, both sides want to offer wages competitive with the labor market and industry so that the firm can attract and retain qualified, productive employees.

Union leaders want to provide evidence during negotiations to management and their own members that the wage rates they are negotiating are fair and justified by market conditions.

Negotiators seek wage survey information from three general sources. The first source is published labor market information from federal agencies, primarily the U.S. Department of Labor, which provides wage and salary information to all organizations by metropolitan statistical area. In general, the government's employment information is considered complete and accurate. Negotiators in specialized industries may wish to use the second source, industry wage surveys, published by various interested parties within the industry. Or negotiators may choose a third source, their own survey, which is a costly and time-consuming process. One side of the table is less likely to accept the figures produced by the other side unless they have a very strong working relationship or have participated in the survey process.

Using wage surveys in negotiations may involve two types of problems. First, because survey information is available from many sources, including industry data, the BLS employer associations, and union groups, it is often difficult to agree which source contains jobs and data applicable to a particular firm. This problem may be compounded if negotiators use survey information from different cities and therefore must agree on an acceptable cost-of-living difference between the areas as well. One solution is to combine relevant data of two published surveys to determine averages.[65] But even if negotiators agree on wage survey information, a second problem involves the question of how the negotiating company should compare itself with other firms. Survey information usually provides an average as well as a range of wages paid for different jobs. Negotiating parties must then agree on whether they want to pay higher, average, or lower wages than the competition.

Thus, wage survey information will not resolve the issue of appropriate wage rates but will at least provide ballpark information to negotiators. Management may argue that what it lacks in wages, it makes up in liberal benefits, working conditions, or advancement opportunities. Labor leaders may counter that these advantages are available in higher-paying organizations and do not make up for the lack in take-home pay.

COSTING WAGE PROPOSALS

Many of the changes in contract language may result in indirect or direct long-range cost to the company. However, most changes in wages, benefits, and COLAs are direct and usually substantial cost increases. Other types of changes, such as layoff provisions, seniority determination,

COSTING

The methods of determining the financial impact of a contract change, such as total annual cost, cost per employee per year, percentage of payroll, and cents per hour.

and subcontracting, may result in indirect cost increases to the company. The process of determining the financial impact of a contract provision change is referred to as **costing**.

The costing of labor contracts is obviously a critical aspect in collective bargaining negotiations. Both sides need to estimate accurately the cost of the contract provision so that it can be intelligently discussed and bargained for by either side. If it is an item that ultimately is given up by one side so that another provision can be gained, then its relative weight is best estimated by knowing its costs.

All economic provisions can be reduced to dollar estimates, whereas noneconomic items cannot be as easily valued by either side. The costing process enables both sides to compare the value of different contract provisions and, it is hoped, helps them arrive at a contract agreement. In most cases, accurate costing processes will be accepted by both sides with little disagreement over the methods employed.

The largest single cost incurred by most corporations is labor cost. Even in capital-intensive organizations such as commercial airlines, labor costs account for about 42 percent of total cost; but in labor-intensive organizations, such as local police departments, labor may account for more than 80 percent of total cost. Figure 7-3 shows how a typical company might cost the wage provisions of a contract.

Data
90 employees at $16.00/hr
60 employees at $13.00/hr
20 employees at $11.50/hr

Proposed wage increase = 6% across the board = 1,900 average number of production hours per year

Annual Cost

Current:	90 × $16.00	=	$1,440
	60 × 13.00	=	780
	20 × 11.50	=	230
		=	$2,450/hr

Current annual cost is $2,450 × 1,900 hr = $4,655,000

Proposed:	90 × $16.96	=	$1,526.40
	60 × 13.78	=	826.80
	20 × 12.19	=	243.80
			$2,597/hr

Proposed annual cost is $2.597 × 1,900 = $4,934,300

Total cost of proposed increase is $4,934,300 − $4,655,000 = $279,300

Cents per Hour

$16.96 − 16.00 = $0.96/hr for 90 employees
$13.78 − 13.00 = $0.78/hr for 60 employees
$12.19 − 11.50 = $0.69/hr for 20 employees

Roll-up (Average ÷ Employee)

Cost of benefits per person = $4.00/hr
$2,450 current cost ÷ 170 employees = $14.41 cost of wages/hr
$4.00 benefit cost ÷ $16.40 wages = 27.77% roll-up

Total Cost of Proposed Wage Rates ÷ Roll-up

$279,300.00 + 77,583.33 (27.77% × 279,300.00) = $356,883.33 wages + roll-up

FIGURE 7-3 Costing a Wage Proposal

Accountant Michael Granof outlines the four most commonly used methods of costing union wage provisions:

1. ***Annual cost.*** This is the total sum expended by the company over a year on a given benefit; usually the sum excludes administrative costs. Most companies make computations similar to those illustrated in Figure 7-3 to arrive at the annual cost of a wage agreement or benefit.
2. ***Cost per employee per year.*** This is determined by dividing the total costs of the benefit by either the average number of employees for the year or the number of employees covered by a particular program.
3. ***Percentage of payroll.*** This is the total cost of the benefit divided by the total payroll. Companies may include all payments to all employees in the total payroll, but some exclude overtime, shift differential, or premium pay.
4. ***Cents per hour.*** This is derived by dividing the total cost of the benefit or wage provision by the total productive hours worked by all employees during the year.[66]

The two most commonly discussed economic figures are the annual cost figure and the cents-per-hour figure. When the contract is being negotiated, the total value of all additional wages and other economic items is included so that the annual cost of the entire package can be estimated accurately. All sides want to know the exact figure of the negotiated wages and benefits. The management negotiator may even offer a lump-sum amount, giving the union negotiators the choice of how to divide it among the various proposed economic enhancements. The cents-per-hour figure is perhaps the single most important item to employees in the new contract. Because employees can quickly estimate their additional take-home pay by using the cents-per-hour figure, it becomes vital when they vote on contract ratification. Granof found that most management negotiators agree that the primary goal in bargaining is to minimize the cents-per-hour direct wage increase.[67]

Employers are usually aware that any negotiated economic increases may be duplicated for nonunion and management personnel. This spillover effect can be quite costly. However, most costing models do not include the spillover costs because unions do not consider them part of the negotiated wage increase.

Base

The first step in determining compensation costs is to develop the **base compensation** figure. During negotiation, this figure is essential in determining the percentage value of a requested increase in wages. For example, a $500 annual wage increase means a 2.5 percent wage increase on a $20,000 base and a 5 percent increase for an employee with a $10,000 base. The base may be thought of as the employee's annual salary; however, it seldom represents the total payroll costs incurred by the company for that employee. For example, the average salary cost, or base salary, for a nurse in a city hospital was $28,200. Under the terms of the contract, a nurse may have also received an average of the following: longevity pay of $1,000, overtime of $2,400, shift differential of $2,100, vacation cost of $1,272, holiday pay of $1,120, hospitalization insurance of $2,100, a clothing allowance of $300, and pension benefit of $1,970. The total additional paid benefits were $9,837 for each nurse, equal to about 34 percent of base pay. These additional costs, when added to the base of $28,200, produced what many think of as the nurse's true gross salary of $38,037.[68]

BASE COMPENSATION

An employee's general rate of pay per unit or hour, disregarding payments for items such as overtime, pension benefits, and bonuses.

Figure 7-4 illustrates the Chrysler Corporation–UAW agreement on base rates for three jobs. At the end of the old agreement the base rates were $22.98, $23.57 and $27.70 for the janitor, assembler, and tool-and-die job classifications, respectively. At the start of the new negotiation it was agreed to "fold in," or add to the old base rates, the COLAs that had been given, thereby creating new base rates that would stay in effect during the new three-year agreement. If the CPI increased each year, the new COLA adjustment and negotiated deferred wage increases of 3 percent in the second and third years would cause the hourly wage rates to increase, as reflected in Figure 7-4, to $27.81, $28.43, and $33.09 or about 21 percent each!

TABLE A
Examples of Total Hourly Wage Increases

	Janitor	Assembler	Tool and Die
Base Rate-Contract End	**$22.98**	**$23.57**	**$27.70**
Skilled trades tool allowance			.30
COLA Fold-In	2.00	2.00	2.00
New Agreement Base	**$24.98**	**$25.57**	**$30.00**
Beginning COLA float	.05	.05	.05
1st-year COLA	.32	.32	.32
End 1st-year Base Rate plus COLA	**$25.35**	**$25.94**	**$30.37**
2nd-year COLA	.40	.40	.40
End 2nd-year Base Rate plus COLA	**$25.75**	**$26.34**	**$30.77**
3rd-year 2% base rate Increase	.50	.51	.60
3rd-year COLA	.44	.44	.44
End 3rd-year Base Rate plus COLA	**$26.69**	**$27.29**	**$31.81**
4th-year 3% base rate Increase	.76	.78	.92
4th-year COLA	.36	.36	.36
End 4th-year Base Rate plus COLA	**$27.81**	**$28.43**	**$33.09**

(Projected COLA assumes annual nonmedical Inflation averaging 2.2 percent)

FIGURE 7-4 Chrysler–UAW Examples: Base Rate, COLA Adjustments, and Wage Adjustments. *Source: DaimlerChrysler Media Briefing Book*, (Auburn Hills, MI: Media Center, 2007), pp. 15–16. Available at http://chryslerlabortalks07.com/Media_Briefing_Book.pdf. Accessed August 26, 2011.

The one absolutely essential figure that every negotiator should have in mind at all times is how much a *wage increase of 1 percent* will cost the employer in thousands of dollars per year. Although the overall dollar cost of a contract settlement is important for budget purposes, most negotiators do not consider such costs to be especially pertinent. They find the total cents-per-hour cost of the negotiated wage increase more relevant, and they bargain in those terms. Settlements are also evaluated by their superiors in terms of cents per hour, but they need to be able to convert cents per hour to total dollars for accurate costing.[69]

Roll-Up

ROLL-UP

The direct increase in the cost of benefits that results from a negotiated increase in wage rates, such as Social Security, overtime pay, and pensions.

As hourly wages increase, many benefits also directly increase because they are directly tied to the wage rate or base pay of employees. This direct increase in benefits caused by a negotiated wage increase is referred to as the **roll-up**. Roll-up may also be called *add-on* or *creep*. All three terms refer to other costs incurred, which automatically increase as wage rates are increased. These costs must be "rolled up into" the total cost of the negotiated wage package to reflect accurately the total costs that will be incurred.

Examples of some of these benefits are the following:

1. ***Social Security and unemployment insurance contributions.*** The employer's contribution is computed as a percentage of each employee's wage up to a maximum annual figure. Any negotiated wage increase up to this maximum will cause a direct increase in the employer's contribution.
2. ***Life insurance.*** Often the amount of life insurance coverage paid by the employer is based on the employee's annual earnings. Therefore, as annual earnings are increased, the cost of the insurance automatically increases.
3. ***Overtime pay and shift premium.*** Overtime compensation and shift premium are often computed as a percentage of the base wage. Thus, these also increase with the base wage.

Tips from the Experts

Union

What are three wage issues union negotiation team members should look for at the negotiating table?

1. Fairness at both ends of wage/salary scale
2. Rewards for performance as well as for service
3. Equal pay for equal work

Management

What are some practical forms of wage concessions to use at negotiations that will not break an employer?

1. Swap indirect benefits and apply to direct labor (e.g., switch a holiday for a specific wage increase).
2. Lengthen the term of the collective bargaining agreement (perhaps in combination with item 3).
3. Stagger wage increases with minimum or no increase at the front end but load up near the end of contract (perhaps in combination with item 2).
4. Give concessions in an area that will be used infrequently but is a big morale booster, such as extended family leave (unpaid, event).

4. ***Pension benefits.*** The pension benefit formula normally includes employees' average annual wages. An increase in wages increases the employer's funding liability for the pension.[70]

Negotiators often determine an agreed-on percentage attributable to roll-up. The roll-up percentage is computed by dividing the cost of the directly increased benefit by the cost of the wage rate increase. For example, if a $2-per-hour increase in the base wage directly causes a $0.40-per-hour increase in benefits, then the roll-up percentage is $0.40 divided by $2, or 20 percent. Therefore, if negotiators agreed to increase employees' base wage by $2 per hour, from $20 per hour to $22 per hour, the 10 percent negotiated wage increase would cause a direct cost increase of 12 percent when the roll-up costs were added: $20 + $2 + .40 = $22.40/hour.

Total Negotiated Costs

At all times during negotiations, both labor and management maintain their estimated cost of wage and benefit items on which they have reached agreement. Therefore, as additional economic items are proposed, both sides know exactly the total cost of the new contract; they can then decide whether the cost of the new items would increase the total cost of the agreement beyond an affordable level. In Table 7-7, the total cost of all new wage and benefit enhancements for the

TABLE 7-7 Estimated Costs of Negotiated Wage and Benefit Increases

Item	First Year New Contract	Estimated Additional Cost
Wages (wage rate + roll-up)	3%	$361,000
Paid holidays	1 new day	40,505
Funeral leave	New provision: 3 days/death	121,515
Health insurance	Increase in employer share: ($120/year)	128,100
Clothing allowance	Additional year: ($50/employee)	33,500
Profit sharing	New provision: 10% of net	399,850
Pension benefits	Additional $50/month	100,000
Paid vacation	Two additional days/year for employees with less than two years service	24,712
Shift differential	Increased from 10% to 12%	108,867
Total cost of negotiated wage and benefit increases		$1,318,049

metals firm example in 7-6 is $1,318,049 at some time in the negotiations. Management had previously determined that the profits available for increased labor costs under a new contract were $1,399,475 (also shown in Table 7-6). Therefore, management would likely agree to the total package of items presented in Table 7-7 or might even be willing to agree to additional economic enhancements if their total cost is less than $81,426.

The union might, for example, propose increasing the clothing allowance by another $150 per year to reach a final agreement. Although the total cost of this proposal would be only $100,500, or about half of 1 percent of the total wages and benefits that management estimates would be paid under the new contract, it would increase the total costs of all negotiated items to $1,418,549. Thus, the new total would exceed the maximum management believes it can afford under a new contract. In such a situation, management might (1) reject this proposal and therefore signal to the union that the total cost is close to the maximum; (2) respond with a counteroffer of an additional $50 clothing allowance, which would be less than the $81,426 that management believes it has left to bargain; or (3) accept the final proposal by the union if it would secure a contract and hope that the $19,074 by which management exceeded its estimate will not critically affect future operations. If management believed that the union would press other economic issues after the clothing allowance increase was accepted, management would most likely reject the proposal. Otherwise, the union could keep proposing small additional increases and possibly exceed the maximum cost estimate by a large amount.

Summary

Wages and benefits represent the heart of the collective bargaining process. Guarantee of a certain standard of living and a reasonable return for their productive efforts is the major concern for most union members. At the same time, management realizes what large percentages of its total costs are wages and benefits. Through job evaluation, wage surveys, and other methods, both sides negotiate either a standard rate or a pay range for each job covered in the agreement. Also, future deferred wage increases are negotiated. Both labor and management begin negotiations by estimating sales, production costs, overhead costs, and other significant economic variables that can then produce the predicted total revenue available for negotiated wage and benefit enhancements. This figure can be used as a target figure during negotiations and can therefore be constantly compared against estimated total cost of negotiated increases. Management can thus ensure that the organization will be able to afford negotiated future labor costs, and the union can obtain a fair share of future profits for its members.

The accurate costing of all negotiated wage changes is critical to successful bargaining and to management's cost-containment efforts as well as to predictions of future labor cost. Roll-up costs must be included in any estimate when wage increases have been agreed on. The computer has given both management and labor a negotiating tool to add speed and accuracy to the costing of proposals.

Negotiated wages can take many forms including changes in base hourly rates, COLAs, two-tier pay systems, lump-sum payments, and profit-sharing plans. Concession bargaining which began in the 1980s has increased dramatically in recent years due to the Great Recession of 2008—and employers needs to adjust their personnel costs to remain competitive or, in the public sector, stay within budgets.

CASE STUDIES

Case Study 7-1 Premium Pay Rates

For at least 21 years, the company has paid double the straight-time pay rate for work after 50 hours in any given workweek to all plant employees, whether they worked a five-day, eight-hour schedule ("5/8 employees") or a four-day, ten-hour schedule ("4/10 employees"). The collective bargaining agreement (CBA) provided for such payment after 50 hours to the 4/10 employees but not the 5/8 employees. The employer, in December 2000, put the union and all hourly personnel on notice that effective January 1, 2001, overtime would be paid in accordance with the CBA; that is, the practice of paying double time after 50 hours to 5/8 employees would cease. The union objected and brought this grievance.

The union argued that the practice of paying 5/8 employees double time for hours worked over 50 hours in one workweek has been in effect for over 20 years. The current CBA has a provision that protects employees from any deduction in pay. It says, "No employee shall suffer a deduction in wage rates or working conditions as a result of this agreement." Allowing the company to change its overtime pay policies while this CBA is in effect violates that term. Furthermore, there have been some five CBAs negotiated since that practice has been in effect, and the company has never sought to negotiate or clarify the practice of how it pays overtime or the CBA provision regarding no reduction. Finally, the union pointed out that the length of time the practice was in place would certainly qualify it as a "past practice" that the company could not change unilaterally.

The company contended that the payment of overtime at double the straight-time rate for 5/8 employees is in direct conflict with the language of the CBA. An employer may abandon past practice that is in direct conflict with the clear language of the CBA. Also, the general CBA provision regarding "no reduction in pay" cannot be interpreted as controlling the specific overtime provision of the CBA.

Discussion

In nondisciplinary matters, the party complaining of a violation of a CBA has the burden to prove that the other party is violating a specific requirement of that agreement. In this case the parties do not dispute that the CBA does not include 5/8 employees in the overtime provision. The union contends, however, that both past practice and the provision of the CBA "maintenance of benefits" clause entitle these employees to the overtime.

The court recognizes the following as primary elements necessary for an activity to qualify as a past practice:

1. A pattern of conduct that is clear and consistent
2. Longevity and recognition of the activity
3. Acceptability and mutual acknowledgment of the pattern of conduct by the parties

Applying those standards to this case, paying double time to 5/8 employees would certainly qualify as a past practice.

The company argues, however, and points to case law to support it, that if it can be proven that a past practice directly conflicts with a provision of a CBA, the company can abandon it unilaterally. Because the CBA's provision specifically excludes the 5/8 employees and because the union has never sought to have them covered under that provision, the union cannot claim that the CBA provides for the overtime pay.

The issue for the court to determine is which side is correct as to which provision of the CBA applies. Both sides presented cases that had been decided that supported its position. The union argued that the court should avoid an interpretation of the CBA that renders the bargained-for benefits meaningless. A long-standing practice of paying double overtime wages would certainly be the type of "wages" the union sought to protect in its "no reduction" clause. The company argued, however, that the court should look to the unambiguous language of the CBA that governs overtime for the 5/8 employees as "trumping" the more general language of the "no reduction" clause. The fact that the company unilaterally paid more than it was required to under the CBA should not bind the company to continue to do so in the future. Those kinds of benefits should be negotiated at the bargaining table, which this was not.

Source: Adapted from *Rod's Food Products v. Teamsters, Local 630,* 116 LA 1734 (2002).

(continued)

(Continued)

QUESTIONS

1. What do you think would be the "fair" way to resolve this case? Should the company be required to pay 5/8 employees double time even though that benefit has never been negotiated, and so, arguably, the company has never received any exchange for this benefit? Or should those employees who have in good faith accepted overtime work believing they would be paid double time, even though their contract did not say they would, have to give up this benefit and get nothing in return?
2. Should the company have waited to bring up this issue when the CBA was being renegotiated? Does it change your answer to know that the CBA was not to be renegotiated for three years?
3. The parties did not know why the company began paying double time to the 5/8 employees. If the practice began as an error on the part of a payroll clerk, would that fact change your opinion as to how to decide this case?

Case Study 7-2 Incentive Pay

The company had an incentive pay rate in place that could increase the employees' pay by 30 percent over their base pay. Citing changed circumstances, the employer eliminated the incentive pay for one department. The union appealed. The collective bargaining agreement (CBA) in place at the time of the grievance reserved all management rights to the company unless restricted by the language of the agreement.

Article V of the agreement established wages to be paid and specifically continued during the term of the agreement "all incentive rates" in existence at the time of the agreement, excepting only the company's right to "establish new incentive rates or to adjust existing incentive rates" under certain conditions listed in the agreement. Those conditions included changes, modifications, or improvements made in equipment involved in an incentive pay area; new or changed standards of manufacturing; and changes in job duties of those affected by incentive pay.

Procedures on how the company was to proceed to establish new or changed incentive rates were also included in Article V of the agreement, unless changes to the incentive rates were a result of the changed circumstances previously cited. If this was the case, employees affected by the changes were given the right to grieve the application of the changed incentive rate. When the incentive pay was totally eliminated for one department, the union grieved on behalf of those affected employees.

It was the company's position that significant changes of equipment and operations in the affected department authorized the unilateral elimination of the incentive pay under the agreement. A new mechanical device had eliminated the need for fracture tests of a furnace. The employees in the department had been reduced from 6 Head Operators, 22 Attendant Carburizing, and 4 Recorder Optical Pyrometers to 3 Head Operators and 4 Attendants. The classification of Recorder Optical Pyrometer was completely eliminated because the duties were no longer needed. The company's interpretation of the contract language was that these changed circumstances allowed the company to eliminate unilaterally the incentive pay for the remaining employees.

The union's position was that the CBA contemplated the incentive pay being kept in place as part of the employees' wages, and the company could not unilaterally eliminate the incentive pay. New or changed rates could be negotiated as circumstances dictated, but eliminating the pay completely was not allowed.

The following are the relevant contract provisions:

ARTICLE V—WAGES

A. Wage Rates

[S]uch hourly wage rates, together with all incentive rates now in existence, which altogether constitute the wage structure applicable to existing occupations in effect on August 28, 1983, shall remain in effect during the term of this agreement, except as any of such rates may be changed, adjusted, or supplemented in the manner prescribed in this Article . . .

B. New and Changed Rates

It is recognized that the company, at its discretion, may also find it necessary or desirable from time to time to establish new incentive rates or to adjust existing incentive rates because of any of the following circumstances:

1. Changes, modifications, or improvements made in equipment, material, or product. If there is any such change, modification, or improvement in existing equipment or material or on an existing product, the company may change the elements of the rate or rates affected by such change, modification, or improvement but will not change the elements not affected by such change, modification, or improvement.
2. New or changed standards of manufacture in (a) processes; (b) methods; and (c) quality.
3. Changes in the duties of an occupation covered by incentive rates that affect the existing incentive standards.

Whenever it is claimed by any employee that any of the changes or events have occurred that are outlined in Paragraphs 1, 2, and 3 of the preceding Section B of this Article V, any employee who is affected thereby, either (1) by the production of product or (2) by being employed on an occupation affected by such claimed changes or events outlined in said paragraphs, may request the establishment of a new rate by discussing such request with his supervisor. In the event that no agreement is reached in respect to the employee's request, grievance may be filed by such employee within ten calendar days after such changes or events have occurred.

If, as the result of a grievance being processed under this Section B, it is determined that the company did not have the right to establish a new or adjusted rate, the rate structure in effect prior to the new or adjusted rate shall be reinstated as of the effective date of the new or adjusted rate. The company will calculate retroactive payment to the extent possible under the applicable rate structure.

Source: Adapted from *Timken Co.*, 85 LA 377 (1985).

QUESTIONS

1. Did the changes made in the department satisfy the circumstances cited in the agreement that would allow the company to eliminate the incentive pay?
2. Did the affected employees have a legitimate grievance under the CBA's language?
3. If you were the arbitrator, would you allow the company to eliminate the incentive pay? Explain your answer.

Key Terms and Concepts

ability to pay *270*
arena bargaining *266*
back-loaded contract *258*
base compensation *275*
concession bargaining *264*
costing *274*
cost-of-living adjustment (COLA) *258*
deferred wage rate increases *257*
exempt *254*
front-end loading *257*
job evaluation *271*
legacy costs *266*
lump-sum payment *263*
"me-too" agreements *253*
nonexempt *254*
pattern bargaining *253*
pay equity *248*
pay for time worked *247*
piece-rate system *256*
piecework *248*
prevailing wage *255*
productivity theory *269*
profit sharing *260*
pyramiding *255*
roll-up *276*
Scanlon plan *261*
standard rate *256*
two-tier wage system *262*
value-added concept *269*
variable wage formula *261*
wage reopener *258*
wage surveys *273*

Review Questions

1. What are the general wage concerns that management and employee representatives bring to the negotiating table?
2. Why have profit-sharing plans replaced COLAs in some recently negotiated agreements?
3. Why have unions and employers negotiated more wage concessions in recent years?
4. How can wage surveys be effectively used in collective bargaining?
5. Why are labor and management negotiators likely to respond to consideration of the company's ability to pay higher wages?
6. What are the pros and cons of two-tier pay systems?
7. Why must labor and management be able to determine accurately the cost of wage proposals?
8. How should negotiators treat the roll-up costs when negotiating wage changes?
9. Why might union negotiators favor front-end loaded over deferred wage increases? Are there potential drawbacks?
10. Why do you think profit-sharing and lump-sum provisions have increased in usage in recent years, whereas COLAs and wage reopeners have decreased in use?

YOU BE THE ARBITRATOR

Scheduling Saturday as Part of the Workweek

Article II—Union-Management Relations—Section 2.5 Management (in pertinent part): Except as specifically abridged or limited by the express provisions of this Agreement or any supplementary agreement that may hereafter be made, the Employer retains all the rights, powers and authority exercised or had by it prior to the time the Employer entered into its first collective bargaining agreement with this Union. Without limiting the generality of the foregoing, it is understood that the rights retained by management include, but are not limited to, the following: the right to plan, determine, direct and control bakery operations and the extent thereof; . . . and the right to control the workforce . . . the assignment and scheduling of work; . . .

Article V—Working Hours and Other Conditions of Employment
Section 5.1 Workday and Workweek—(B) Production Workweek (in pertinent part): The basic workweek for all bakery employees shall consist of five (5) eight (8) hour workdays for a total of forty (40) hours . . . The basic workweek shall be from 12:01 A.M. Sunday and end at midnight (12:00 A.M.) Saturday.
Section 5.3—Weekly and Daily Guarantees — (B): A minimum of eight (8) hours of work shall be guaranteed to all full-time employees under this Agreement who report for work in any one day, except that the minimum guarantee shall be only four (4) hours with respect to work requested on the sixth and seventh day of the workweek.

Section 5.4—Work Schedules (in pertinent part): The Employer reserves the right to determine working schedules and the number and starting times of working shifts . . .

Section 5.5—Overtime and Other Premium Pay—

(A) Overtime *(in pertinent part):* . . . Overtime at the rate of time and one-half (1-1/2) the employee's regular straight time hourly rate . . . shall be paid for work performed . . . (4) On the sixth consecutive day of work. Overtime at the rate of double (2x) the employee's regular straight time hourly rate . . . shall be paid for all work performed on the seventh consecutive day of work. No overtime shall be payable for Saturday or Sunday work as such.

(B) Sunday Work: Any employee who is assigned to a work schedule that does not provide for two (2) consecutive days off shall be credited with one (1) earned work credit share for each Sunday worked under any non-consecutive day work schedule.

(D) Extra Day Work (9): Saturday and Sunday work which is regularly scheduled as part of the basic workweek shall not be considered extra day work for purposes of seniority claiming.

Letter of Understanding Calculation of Double Time Pay to Bakery Workers Who Work Seven Consecutive Days (page 50 of the Agreement) (in pertinent part): Section 5.5 of the Collective Bargaining Agreement provides for the payment of double the employee's regular straight time rate of pay for all work performed on the seventh consecutive day of work. It has been the past practice to combine two workweeks in order to allow employees to have seven consecutive days of work. Normally the employee's pay period, as set by Payroll, runs from Sunday through Saturday and then a new week starts . . .

Facts

The employer is a wholesale baker and sells bakery products to others. The employer purchased the wholesale bakery assets of the former employer and is a successor employer that assumed the existing agreement. The employer employs 125 production employees, whose basic workweek for at least 14 years has been Sunday, Monday, Wednesday, Thursday, and Friday, with Tuesday and Saturday as days off. To meet increased customer demand, the employer opened a second bun line so that fresh buns would be baked on Saturday for pickup by 5 A.M. Sunday.

The employer posted bids for the new line, which showed the basic workweek for the new production employees to be Sunday, Tuesday, Wednesday, Thursday, and Saturday, and the days off would be Monday and Friday. Seventeen or 18 production employees work the second bun line and were affected by the new workweek. Two employees filed a grievance on behalf of the bakery employees affected by the new workweek schedule. The grievance charges that the employer violated the Article 5, Section 5.1 B, of the agreement by starting the workweek on Saturday at 4 P.M.

Issue

Did the employer violate the collective bargaining agreement by scheduling Saturday as a part of the basic workweek?

Position of the Parties

The employer contended that it is permitted to make Saturday part of the basic workweek by the clear language of the agreement. The employer argued that pursuant to Article V, Section 5.1(B), the basic workweek is clearly intended to be a seven-day period, beginning at 12:01 A.M. Sunday and ending at midnight Saturday. Furthermore, the letter of understanding confirms this by stating the workweek runs from "Sunday through Saturday." Therefore, the employer may, under the management rights provision, change the basic workweek to include Saturday. The employer argued that a week is seven consecutive days usually beginning on Sunday and ending on Saturday and uses the *Random House Dictionary* to support that definition. Thus, the workweek necessarily runs through midnight Saturday, just before the 12:01 A.M. Sunday starting time. According to common usage, midnight is part of the day that is ending, not part of the day that is beginning. Therefore, it argued "midnight Saturday" means the midnight between Saturday and Sunday and not the midnight between Friday and Saturday. "Midnight" Saturday comes at the end of the day and is followed by Sunday. The reference to "12:00 A.M." is a misunderstanding of how to designate midnight because noon and midnight are technically neither "A.M." nor "P.M." Noon is generally considered to be 12:00 P.M. and midnight to be 12:00 A.M. Under a prior arbitration proceeding, the arbitrator found that the collective bargaining agreement prohibited the use of a past practice to change the meaning of the agreement and that because the employer was a successor-employer who adopted the agreement and did not negotiate it, it was even more necessary to interpret and apply the parties' written agreement according to the plain and ordinary meaning of its language.

The union argued that Article V, Section 5.1(B), which provides that "the basic workweek shall be from 12:01 A.M. Sunday and end at midnight (12:00 A.M.) Saturday" does not permit the employer to make Saturday part of the basic workweek since Saturday is specifically excluded from the definition of the basic workweek as provided by this clear and unambiguous language. Under this language the production workweek ends 12:00 A.M. Friday night and begins again at 12:01 A.M. Sunday morning. If the negotiators had intended to have Saturday as part of the basic workweek, the language would read that the workweek would start at 12:01 Saturday morning. "A.M." is morning before noon, and 12:00 A.M. is the morning of Saturday and not the morning of Sunday. In support of this position, the union cites *Webster's Dictionary*, which defines "A.M." as "ante meridian, before noon: used to designate the time from midnight to noon," and "P.M." as "post meridian, after noon: used to designate the time from noon to midnight." The union further argues that there has been a long-standing past practice of at least 14 years that establishes that Saturday cannot be a part of the basic workweek because it is a scheduled day off for the production employees. The production employees have always had Saturday as a scheduled day off and have always been paid premium time when they have been required to work on Saturdays. The prior arbitration award did not preclude the examination of past practice in this instance because it is used to support and define the clear meaning of the agreement. Furthermore, the letter of understanding refers to a payroll issue, does not define the basic workweek, and does not override the specific provisions of the agreement that define the basic workweek.

QUESTIONS

1. As arbitrator, what would be your award and opinion in this arbitration?
2. Identify the key, relevant section(s), phrases, or words of the collective bargaining agreement (CBA), and explain why they were critical in making your decision.
3. What actions might the employer and/or the union have taken to avoid this conflict?

Source: Adapted from *North Baking Co.,* 116 LA 1788 (2002).

CHAPTER 8

Employee Benefits

Nearly 1,500 machinists went on strike against the Space and Defense Systems unit of Boeing, like these IAM members from LL 2766 in Huntsville, Alabama. *Source:* AP Images.

Chapter Outline

Every advance in this half-century: Social Security, civil rights, Medicare, aid to education—came with the support of American labor.

JIMMY CARTER (38TH U.S. PRESIDENT)

LABOR NEWS

New Health Care Law

Employee health benefits are *the issue* of concern to most union and management negotiators today. Employee benefits were often called "fringe benefits" in the past because their total costs were only a small portion of the total compensation package provided in labor agreements. Skyrocketing increases in the 1980s and 1990s, and employer demands that employees pay a greater share of the costs, made health care the most common issue behind labor strikes from 2000 to today.

U.S. presidential polls in 2008 indicated that health care is the top domestic issue on the minds of voters. Why? For over 50 years most U.S. workers, union and nonunion, received employer-provided health care with minimum or no cost to them. Then skyrocketing cost increases caused employers and unions to search for cost control methods such as HMOs, PPOs, flexible spending plans, and so on. But no magic pill, as it were, was found, and the standard employer-provided plan began to disappear.

U.S. employers offering *any health care benefit* fell from about 90 percent in the 1980s to below 60 percent by 2008. Employee-paid copayments rose sharply as did deductibles: $500 or larger deductibles were paid by only 14 percent of workers in 2000 but were paid by over 38 percent in 2010. Families bore a large portion of health insurance cost increases—the average U.S. family paid about $6,000 in 2000—which doubled to $12,000 in 2007! Presidential candidates and even the American Association of Retired Persons (AARP) began to urgently call for action by the federal government.

In 2010 President Barak Obama signed the Affordable Care Act after considerable debate and with the support of most congressional Democrats, most labor leaders, and the AARP, as well as others, but no congressional Republicans. It will take years for the long-term effects of the bill, especially for its effect on the costs of health care, to be known. The act contained several key provisions:

- Adult children remain under their parents' insurance to age 26.
- Individuals without insurance in 2014 pay $750/year fine.
- Expanded benefits coverage for 32 million Americans.
- Small businesses with less than 25 employees (and average wages of $50,000) receive tax credits.
- Insurance companies' new plans must cover full cost of preventive care and cannot deny preexisting conditions.
- Individuals over age 65 receive more care at a lower price.
- Expanded Medicare drug benefits with 50 percent cost reduction on brand name drugs.

Source: Adapted from Chad Terhune and Laura Meckler, "A Turning Point for Health Care," *Wall Street Journal* (July 27, 2007), pp. A1, 13; and Shailagh Murray and Lori Montgomery, "House Passed Health Care Reform Bill," *The Washington Post* (March 23, 2010), p. A1.

Today, negotiated employee benefits, once referred to as "fringe benefits," represent a critical part of the total economic package. Employers may easily find that between 25 and 45 percent of the total economic package now consists of benefits rather than direct compensation. In fact, management negotiators may adopt a "zero-sum bargaining" approach. In this approach, all economic items—wages, health care, pensions, and other benefits—are traded against each other to create a zero or fixed amount increase instead of negotiating benefits separate from wages, as was customary in the past. Thus, in terms of collective bargaining, management often strives to meet an overall compensation budget goal.[1] Yet benefits are not usually designed to meet the same employee objectives as the wage portion of the negotiated agreement. From the employee standpoint, the wage portion of the economic package provides income needed for the necessities of life, such as food, shelter, and clothing, and is exchanged for their labor. Management, by comparison, views wages as a means of attracting, retaining, and motivating employees and therefore maximizing their productivity.

Benefits, however, provide less certain motivational and productivity advantages to management. Thus today the cost of more expensive benefits such as health care, pension, and paid time off is more likely to be in question. Recently negotiated agreements produced dramatic shifts in the two most expensive types of employee benefits for employees in large and medium-size organizations. The area of health benefit plans saw a substantial shift away from fee-for-service plans, which accounted for over 67 percent of all plans in 1990 to less than 20 percent by 2010. During the same time, nontraditional health care plans, including health maintenance organizations (HMOs) and preferred provider organizations (PPOs), increased to 73 percent of all plans offered (HMOs, 33 percent; PPOs, 40 percent). In most of these newer plans, employees were required to contribute a greater portion of the costs than had been the case in their prior fee-for-service plans. Employers today continue to try to negotiate a shift in total health care cost to their employees, and unions resist that shift.

The second dramatic shift in benefits occurred in the area of retirement plans. Although the proportion of all employees covered by an employer retirement plan remained at about 80 percent, the shift away from defined benefit plans and toward defined contribution plans and other plans have increased.[2] The shift continues through today when the number of employees covered by defined benefit plans has dropped to 54 percent, although more union workers are covered by defined benefit plans (73 percent) than nonunion workers (16 percent).[3]

REQUIRED BENEFITS

Some employee benefits are required by law and are therefore not negotiated. However, both labor and management representatives need to be cognizant of these benefits and their impact on other benefits that can be negotiated. Some negotiated benefit plans are designed to supplement those required by law to guarantee the employee a greater level of benefit.

Unemployment insurance, Social Security, and workers' compensation are three costly and important government-required benefits. Unemployment insurance programs have been operating since 1938. States provide unemployed workers with benefits by imposing payroll taxes on employers. The amount paid normally varies according to the state's unemployment rate. The unemployed person must have worked for a certain period of time and must register with the state bureau of employment to receive benefits.

About 97 percent of all workers are included in the federal and state **unemployment insurance** system. Employers pay a payroll tax on each employee's wages. There are no federal standards for benefits, qualifying requirements, benefit amounts, or duration of benefits; the states each develop their own formulas for workers' benefits. Under all state laws, a worker's benefit rights depend on work experience during a "base period" of time. Most states require a claimant to serve a waiting period before receiving benefits.[4] Workers are usually required to be available for work, able to work, and seeking work actively to receive benefits. Claimants are disqualified for voluntarily leaving without good cause, discharge for misconduct, or refusal to accept suitable work. In 2007, for example, members of the Local 45B Glass Molders and Pottery Workers Union were denied state unemployment benefits because they had been on strike for three months. An Ohio hearing officer made that decision even though the OPW Fueling Company had declared a lockout and hired permanent replacement workers because those actions came after the strike had started. The workers lost $350 per week in unemployment benefits and only received $112 per week in union strike pay funds.[5]

UNEMPLOYMENT INSURANCE

Established in 1935 and funded through payroll taxes paid by employers, the program is designed to provide compensation, after a brief waiting period, to those employees who have been laid off from employment. Recipients are expected to seek employment actively.

In 1935, Congress established the *Social Security* system to provide supplemental income to retired workers. Initially intended to supplement private, often union-negotiated pension plans, Social Security would help retirees live in dignity and comfort. Employers and employees who pay an equal amount of taxes into the system carry the cost of the system, which then uses the funds to pay benefits to currently retired individuals. Technically, Social Security taxes are

Federal Insurance Contributions Act (FICA) taxes. Management often points out that the employees pay only half the cost of the system yet receive all the benefits.

Another phase of the Social Security system was added to provide disability, survivor, and Medicare benefits. To become eligible for retirement benefits, individuals born after 1928 must contribute for 40 quarters (ten full years). Required contributions to receive medical benefits vary according to age.

Since the Social Security Revision Act of 1972, the benefits paid to retirement income recipients have increased each year by a percentage equal to the increase in the consumer price index. This automatic and liberal increase has been one of the main causes of the shaky financial condition of the Social Security system.[6] It has also provided management's primary weapon in not increasing employees' private pensions. Employers complain that Social Security taxes have increased each year along with raised salaries because the tax is a percentage of the employees' salary. In addition, Congress raised the employers' and employees' Social Security tax rate from 4.8 percent in 1970 to 7.65 percent in 1990.[7]

WORKERS COMPENSATION

A program designed to provide employees with assured payment for medical expenses or lost income due to injury on the job.

Laws requiring **workers compensation** were enacted by states to protect employees and their families against permanent loss of income and high medical bills because of accidental injury or illness on the job. The primary purpose of most state laws is to keep the question of the cause of the accident out of court. The laws ensure employees payment for medical expenses or lost income. Workers compensation primarily consists of employer contributions into a statewide fund. A state industrial board then reviews cases and determines employee eligibility for compensation for injury on the job.

NEGOTIATED BENEFITS

The law does not require most benefits included in labor agreements, although most are mandatory issues for negotiations. However, any such paid benefits must be gained at the negotiating table. In general, these benefits can be grouped into four categories as illustrated in Table 8-1: (1) income maintenance, (2) employee health care, (3) pay for time not worked, and (4) premium pay. A fifth group includes employee services.

TABLE 8-1 Benefit Issues

Type of Issue	Issue	Relevant Items
Required	Social Security	
	Unemployment insurance	
	Workers' compensation	
Negotiated	Income maintenance plans	Pensions
		Wage employment guarantees
		Supplemental unemployment benefits (SUB) plans
		Guaranteed income stream (GIS)
		Severance pay
		Death and disability
	Employee health care	Health insurance
		Dental, optical, prescription drugs
		Alcohol and drug treatment
		Wellness programs
		Employee assistance programs
	Pay for time not worked	Paid holidays
		Paid vacations
		Sick leave
		Paid leaves

TABLE 8-1 *(Continued)*

Premium pay	Reporting pay Shift differential Call-in pay/on-call pay Bilingual skills Travel pay
Employee services	Flexible benefit plans Child care Credit union Education assistance

INCOME MAINTENANCE PLANS

Income maintenance provisions have become commonplace in collective bargaining agreements. These plans are negotiable and include supplemental unemployment benefits, severance pay (also called dismissal or termination pay), and wage employment guarantees (WEGs). In addition, these plans protect employees from financial disruptions. Private pension plans provide for income during retirement, along with Social Security.

Pension Plans

A pension is a guaranteed monthly payment to a former employee during retirement. The **pension plan** benefit began in the United States after the Civil War when former Union Army soldiers were given payments for their service. Then a few companies began offering pensions as a new benefit. One of the first private pension plans was offered by Procter & Gamble in Cincinnati, Ohio, to employees in its soap plants. Unions began negotiating pension benefits during World War II when a national wage freeze made it impossible to negotiate higher hourly wages, and pension plans gradually became a common benefit in the workplace. Since the 1980s, however, the number of employers offering pension plans has continuously declined. In 1985, about 112,208 plans were covered by the Pension Benefit Guarantee Corporation, whereas in 2005 only about 29,000 were covered, a 75 percent drop!

PENSION PLAN

The way a pension, which guarantees a monthly payment to a former employee during retirement, is structured.

Cost Containment

Employers striving to cut personnel costs that affect their bottom line have either simply terminated their pension plans or converted them to cash balance plans. In addition, new employers have not started plans. Employers in severe financial trouble have used the U.S. bankruptcy laws to avoid paying pensions owed to retired and current employees. Others, such as AK Steel, have asked unions to agree to major concessions to avoid bankruptcy and thus preserve their pension plans. Therefore, employee pension plans, a fixture in the American workplace as late as the 1980s, is today a vanishing part of the American dream for union and nonunion workers alike.[8] Private pension plans today are one of the most prized and most expensive employee benefits. In the early stages of the U.S. labor movement, the benefit provided motivation for senior employees to remain with the organization and thus increase their retirement income. Later, both labor and management negotiators accepted management's obligation to provide income to employees beyond their productive years. Acceptance of this obligation occurred largely as a result of a 1949 decision by the Supreme Court, *Inland Steel Company v. NLRB*,[9] in which the Court declared that pension plans are mandatory collective bargaining subjects. Today, pension plans are still provided in most labor contracts.[10]

Public Sector Pensions

Like their private sector counter parts, many local and state governments today are searching for ways to reduce skyrocketing pension costs. In San Francisco, for example, the city's annual

Ballot measures before voters in San Francisco and Bakersfield proposed reducing the pensions of future public employee hires in efforts to rein in public pension costs. *Source:* ZUMA Press/ Newscom.

DEFINED BENEFIT PLAN

An employer-sponsored retirement plan in which employee benefits are paid based on a formula using factors such as salary and duration of employment. Usually there are restrictions on when and how the plans can be accessed without penalties. The amount of the retirement is fixed and the employee knows the amount.

DEFINED CONTRIBUTION PLAN

A retirement plan in which a certain amount or percentage of money is set aside each year by a company for the benefit of the employee. There are restrictions as to when and how the plans can be accessed without penalties. There is no way to know how much the plan will ultimately give the employee upon retiring. The amount contributed is fixed, but the benefit is not.

pension cost for current and retired workers more than doubled in just five years from 2005 to 2010, from $419 to $1.2 billion! Some changes only affect new workers. In Bakersfield, California, for example, future police officers and firefighters would be hired under a "2 at 50" plan—meaning retirees receive 2 percent of their final salary at age 50 for each year of service, which would be a 50 percent cut from the current "3 at 50"! Many public officials in other states and cities, also looking for ways to cut pension costs, are watching California closely since it was the California tax revolt, Proposition 13, that started a similar wave of tax law changes across the United States.[11] In addition to private and public sector pension plans, those controlled by unions have reported underfunding during the Great Recession. In 2009, for example, Service Employees International Union National Industry Pension Fund was put in the "red zone" by federal regulators because it had only 74 percent of the funds needed to pay the earned benefits of its members. The Teamsters at 59 percent and United Food and Commercial Workers Union at 58 percent were even worse. The federal government "rule of thumb" is that any fund under 80 percent is "endangered" and below 65 percent is "critical." The SEIU fund had been in great financial shape at 103 percent shortly before the economic recession. The Pension Benefit Guarantee Corporation, however, also reported that the stock market decline could not be solely blamed for the funds' decline—poor management and union officer benefits were also noted as potential causes.[12]

Traditional Pension Plans

The two "traditional" types of plans are distinguished by how their benefits are determined. A traditional **defined benefit plan** (73 percent of contracts) on retirement provides a stipulated, fixed amount of income, usually paid monthly. The exact amount is determined by a benefit formula (see p. xx) and is based on years of service and base pay. The second traditional type of plan is a **defined contribution plan**, which is less common in labor contracts (27 percent) but far

Article 23
Pension

23.1

Grocery Pension Hourly Contributions—The Employer agrees to make a contribution of one dollar and eleven cents ($1.11) per hour on all straight-time hours worked for employees hired on or before October 16, 1989. (Tier I) Effective for employees hired after October 16, 1989, the contribution rate shall be eighty-five cents (.85) per hour after eighteen (18) full months of employment. (Tier II) The contributions requirement will begin on the first of the month following the individual employee having completed the required period of employment. Contributions shall also be made on hours for which employees receive holiday pay and vacation pay. No contribution shall be made on hours worked in excess of forty (40) per week. Employees hired after October 27, 2004 shall have a forty-five cents (.45) per hour contribution made on their behalf based on the above eligibility requirements. (Tier III)

Kroger and UFCW Local 1099 have agreed to a set of pension contribution and benefits changes. This includes an increase in the Employer contribution of .10 per hour for participants in all three tiers effective January 1, 2008, and a new benefit accrual rate of $17.11 for Tier II participants effective for service on and after January 1, 2008.

	1/1/07	1/1/08
Tier I	1.01	1.11
Tier II	.75	.85
Tier III	.35	.45

FIGURE 8-1 Pension Article. *Source:* Agreement between the Kroger Co. and the United Food and Commercial Workers International Union AFL–CIO, 2007–2010. Used by permission.

more common in nonunion employers. Under these plans the employer makes a specified dollar contribution to an account in a managed fund, and the retirement benefit depends on the investment gains or losses by the fund, as in the Kroger Co.–United Food and Commercial Workers Union example in Figure 8-1, which provides for a defined hourly contribution.

The example also includes three "tiers" of contributions based on hire date, similar to "two-tier" pay systems. Because the benefits depend on the investment performance of the fund, the worker is not guaranteed a specific amount of income on retirement. Some contracts provide other pension options in addition to a defined benefit or defined contribution plan. Two other forms of pension plans are tax-deferred retirement savings plans: 401(k) plans and cash balance plans. *Tax-deferred 401(k) accounts* have grown in popularity from their creation so that by 2005, 77 percent of agreements provide for them, usually in combination with a defined benefit plan. The specifics of an IRS Tax Code Section 401(k) vary, but most provide an employer match (at a ratio of 1:1 or 1:2) of a worker's voluntary contribution up to a fixed percentage of salary, usually 6 percent. Employers and unions have viewed 401(k) accounts favorably as a means of increasing a worker's retirement income, but only if the worker chooses to participate by providing funds.

The Enron Corporation, however, in 2001 changed the universal appeal of 401(k) accounts. Enron had matched employee contributions to 401(k) accounts with company stock and then froze those accounts and transferred them to another provider as the company revealed a huge loss of $638 million. Company executives managed to divest most of their own holdings before the fall in stock price, but thousands of workers were left with company stock accounts that were worthless. Thousands of other employers, unions, and their members realized the practical dangers of some 401(k) retirement accounts that put "all their eggs in one basket" as Enron had done. In addition, the substantial fall in stock prices from 2000 to 2002 also caused people to realize the volatility of these accounts.

Cash balance plans are the newest and fastest growing type of retirement plans and are found in 10 percent of collective bargaining contracts. Under these plans, often designed to supplement a defined benefit plan, the employer contributes a fixed percentage of workers'

CASH BALANCE PLANS

A type of defined-benefit pension plan under which an employer credits a participant's account with a set percentage of his or her yearly compensation plus interest. The investment performance of the fund does not affect the final benefits to be received by the participant upon retirement. Unlike the regular defined benefit plan, the cash balance plan is maintained on an individual account basis, much like a defined contribution plan.

income to a hypothetical account and guarantees it will grow at a fixed rate. Thus, the benefit grows more quickly than the traditional defined benefit plan and provides a more predictable benefit.[13] Many employers, in recent years, including IBM, AT&T, Xerox Corporation, Cigna, and Delta Air Lines, have converted their traditional pension plans to cash balance plans in efforts to reduce their pension liability. These plans are usually less attractive to employees and typically reduce their retirement benefits by 20–40 percent in comparison with their former plan.[14]

ESOP: An Alternative Retirement Plan

An employee stock ownership plan (ESOP) provides a unique alternative to a company in financial trouble or in need of improved employer–employee relations. An ESOP can act as a kind of retirement benefit plan. For example, since 1988, Houchens Industries Inc. has operated as a 100 percent employee-owned company. As the company makes money, it pays down outstanding debt and distributes shares of stock to employees, instead of retirement funds. Upon retiring, the employee sells the shares back to the company. Houchens began operations in 1919 with one grocery store in Bowling Green, Kentucky, and today is one of the largest ESOPs in the nation. In 2006, Houchens's sales exceeded $200 million from over 400 stores, as well as construction, insurance, and manufacturing units. In 2007, it purchased Hilliard Lyons, the financial services firm, with $1.9 billion from its sale of Commonwealth Brands, the fourth largest U.S. cigarette producer to British Imperial Tobacco Group PLC.[15]

Employee Retirement Income Security Act

EMPLOYEE RETIREMENT INCOME SECURITY ACT (ERISA)
The first comprehensive reform law passed to protect employee pensions. Additionally, it places strict regulations on private pension plans and protects the vested rights of employees' beneficiaries.

PENSION BENEFIT GUARANTEE CORPORATION (PBGC)
Established within the Department of Labor to encourage voluntary employee pension continuance when changing employment by providing portability, the right of an employee to transfer tax-free pension benefits from one employer to another.

In 1974, Congress passed the **Employee Retirement Income Security Act (ERISA)**, also known as the Pension Reform Act. The law was passed in response to alleged abuses and incompetence in some private pension plans. ERISA provided a sweeping reform of pension and benefit rules. The lengthy and complicated law primarily affects the following aspects of pension planning:

1. Employers are required to count toward vesting all service from age 18 and to count toward earned benefits all earnings from age 21. (Prior to the Retirement Equity Act of 1984, accrual toward vesting began at age 22 and toward earnings at age 25.)
2. Employers must choose from among three minimum vesting standards (Sec. 203).
3. Each year employers must file reports of their pension plans with the U.S. secretary of labor for approval. New plans must be submitted for approval within 120 days of enactment.
4. The **Pension Benefit Guarantee Corporation** (PBGC) was established within the Department of Labor to encourage voluntary employee pension continuance when changing employment. This is accomplished by providing *portability*, the right of an employee to transfer tax-free pension benefits from one employer to another. The PBGC also assumes the pension plans from employers with underfunded plans in financial difficulties.

   This provides an important safety net for retired and active workers who might otherwise lose their entire pension benefits. For example, in 2005, the PBGC assumed the underfunded retirement plans of United Airlines mechanics, ramp workers, and flight attendants. The plans covered over 120,000 workers and included a $9.8 billion underfunded liability, the largest in the 30-year history of the PBGC. United Airlines took the action to avoid bankruptcy. The PBGC assumption of the pension plans almost guarantees the workers will receive lower benefits than they expected.[16] In 2009 the PBGC, in an unprecedented move, pressured General Motors into paying "top-ups" to retired Delphi UAW retirees so that they would receive the pensions promised them by GM when it spun off the parts division. The PBGC, which had taken over the Delphi pension fund, said it could not pay the promised levels with the assets given by GM when Delphi was spun off.

GM provided "top- ups" or increased pension benefits to retired Delphi workers, as promised, but not to non-union retirees. *Source:* AP Images.

The top-ups, much to the resentment of retired nonunion Delphi workers, was paid only to former union workers.[17]

5. Pension plan members are permitted to leave the workforce for up to five consecutive years without losing service credit and allowed up to one year maternity or paternity leave without losing service credit.[18]

Issues in Pension Negotiations

VESTING The conveying of employees' nonforfeitable rights to share in a pension fund is termed **vesting**. Many individuals never receive private pension funds because they leave employers before working enough years to become vested.

VESTING

The process by which an employee accrues nonforfeitable rights over employer contributions that are made to the employee's qualified retirement plan account. Generally, nonforfeitable rights accrue based on the number of years of service performed by the employee.

Section 203 of ERISA provides that employers choose from among three alternatives of retirement age and service. One alternative is to provide 100 percent vested rights after five years of service. The other two provide less than 100 percent vested rights with fewer years of service. Union negotiators are very interested in the plan chosen by management. However, no single plan is always preferred by employees.

QUALIFIED PLAN A *qualified plan* generally refers to a plan that meets standards set by the Internal Revenue Service (IRS). By qualifying under the IRS provisions, an employer can deduct pension contributions made to the qualified plan as business expenses for tax purposes. This, of course, is a major reason employers seek to qualify their pension plans whenever possible. Employees, however, also benefit because they do not pay taxes on any dollars either they or the employer invest in the plan under current income. Instead, income taxes are paid when the retirement benefits are received. A *nonqualified plan* would not provide the tax advantages of the qualified plan but would be required to meet the strict guidelines set by the IRS.

CONTRIBUTORY PLANS All pension plans are either contributory or noncontributory. In a *contributory plan*, the employer pays a portion of the funding and the employee pays the other portion. The percentage paid by employer and employee becomes of keen interest during collective bargaining. Also of interest is the type of benefit plan provided. In a *noncontributory plan*, the employer pays all the administrative and funding costs. Therefore, the question of how much is to be paid by the employer does not arise during collective bargaining; rather, the benefit package provided by the plan becomes the central issue.

AGE OR SERVICE REQUIREMENT Most pension plans require a minimum age or years of service before an employee becomes eligible to receive retirement benefits. The plan may simply require a minimum age such as 55 or 60 at which the retired employee begins receiving benefits or a minimum of 25 or 30 years of service. Other plans require a minimum of both, such as 25 and 60, meaning 25 years of service and 60 years of age. Under such a plan, the employee who began work with the company at age 20 must work for 40 years before becoming eligible to receive retirement benefits, even though he or she could become eligible at age 45 under the service requirement. Some systems provide for an option of retirement minimums. For example, an employee may receive 50 percent of the benefits if he or she retires at age 55, 70 percent at age 60, 80 percent at age 62, or 100 percent at age 65. Management realizes that the percentages and ages can be changed to motivate employees to retire at an earlier age or to stay with the company longer. A similar type of provision can be created for years of service. The minimum age or service requirement is an item of great interest during contract negotiations. If union membership is heavy with senior employees close to retirement, changing the minimum requirement becomes an even greater goal of the union negotiators.

DISQUALIFICATIONS ERISA allows a pension plan to suspend pension payments of a retired member who reenters the job market to protect participants against their pension plan being used, in effect, to subsidize low-wage employers who hire plan retirees to compete with and undercut the wages and working conditions of employees covered by the plan. In a 2004 Supreme Court case, *Central Laborers' Pension Fund v. Heinz, et al.*,[19] the anticut provision was interpreted, however, to protect accrued benefits from *after-retirement* changes. Heinz retired from the construction industry after accruing enough pension credits to qualify for early retirement payments under a "service-only" multiemployer pension plan that pays him the same monthly benefit he would have received had he retired at the usual age. The plan prohibits such beneficiaries from certain "disqualifying employment" after they retire, suspending monthly payments until they stop the forbidden work. When Heinz retired, the plan defined "disqualifying employment" to include a job as a construction worker but not as a supervisor, the job Heinz took. Subsequent to Heinz's retirement and entry into his job, the plan expanded its definition of disqualifying employment to include any construction industry job and stopped Heinz's payments. Heinz sued to recover the suspended benefits, claiming that the suspension violated the "anticutback" rule of ERISA, which prohibits any pension plan amendment that would reduce a participant's accrued benefit. The Court held that imposing new conditions on rights to benefits already accrued violates the anticutback rule.

BUYOUT Employers wishing to downsize the number of union workers or replace some higher-paid workers with newly hired lower-tier workers may negotiate an early retirement provision with a union. For example, in 2006, a General Motors buyout offer led to a reduction of 34,000 workers who received a bonus of $39,000 to $140,000 in addition to their normal pensions. Because such programs are usually voluntary and help keep the employer competitive, unions may not oppose their implementation but will want to negotiate the exact terms of a program.[20]

BENEFIT FORMULA Perhaps the most important pension item in a defined benefit plan is the benefit formula, in which benefits due each retiree are calculated. A common benefit would appear as follows:

$$\text{Benefit dollars} = \text{Years of service} \times \text{Base pay} \times \_\_\_\_ \%$$

The three variables of importance in the formula are years of service, employee's base pay, and a percentage to be applied. The percentage is usually a fixed figure that is seldom negotiated to change; 2–3 percent is often used, but the percentage can be as high as 5 percent or as low as 1 percent. The individual employee determines the number of years of service. The determination of the base pay, therefore, becomes critical to many contract negotiations. For many years, base pay was defined as the average of the employee's annual gross wage received. However, in recent years, with high inflation causing rapid salary increases as well as moves through promotion and transfer, base pay often receives other definitions.

Wage Employment Guarantees

In recent years, union negotiators have fought vigorously for an income maintenance benefit previously provided only to white-collar workers—that of guaranteed income throughout the year regardless of available hours of work or actual work performed. Union negotiators feel that their members should also have the security and convenience of regular pay periods. The problems and frustrations of fluctuating income make the guaranteed wage a high priority for many union leaders.

Wage employment guarantees (WEGs) ensure employees a minimum amount of work or compensation during a certain period of time, usually for the life of the contract. Normally all full-time employees who have at least one year's service are eligible. The UAW contracted a guaranteed wage in its agreement with Ford Motor Company in 1967, a major step for union negotiators in the industry. Today WEGs appear in 16 percent of all agreements.[21] A wage employment guaranteed provision might read, "All regular, full-time employees shall be guaranteed a minimum of 40 hours of work per week or compensation in lieu of work being provided."

WAGE EMPLOYMENT GUARANTEES (WEGs)

A contract negotiation assuring employees a minimum amount of work or compensation during a specified amount of time.

When negotiating to provide a guaranteed annual wage, management often will insist on an **escape clause** to suspend the guarantee for production delays beyond the control of management, such as natural or accidental disasters, voluntary absences, employee discharge, or strikes.

ESCAPE CLAUSE

A contract provision that allows either negotiating party to be released from a specific provision of a collective bargaining agreement, under certain conditions.

Supplemental Unemployment Benefits

In the 1950s, steel and automobile industry union leaders began to negotiate for **supplemental unemployment benefits (SUB) plans**. These plans provide additional income to supplement state unemployment benefits to employees who are laid off. Union negotiators normally contend that state unemployment benefits do not enable employees to maintain adequately their style of living. SUB plans are designed to be directly supplemental; employees receive a certain percentage of their gross pay for a maximum number of weeks when unemployed. For example, if each employee subjected to a layoff during the period of the contract receives 75 percent of normal base pay, with the company providing the additional funds necessary to the employee's state unemployment benefits, an employee making about $532 a week would receive a total of $400. This 75 percent figure would include $300 per week of state unemployment benefits, with the remaining $100 provided by the company.

SUPPLEMENTAL UNEMPLOYMENT BENEFITS (SUB) PLANS

Plans that provide additional income to supplement state unemployment benefits to employees who are laid off.

Some negotiated SUB plans provide only 50–75 percent of gross pay; few go beyond 75 percent. Most provide the additional unemployment benefits for at least a period equal to the state's unemployment, often exceeding up to one year in length. Employees must have at least one year's service before they are eligible for SUB benefits; they do not receive such benefits if they are on strike or under disciplinary action. Most SUB plan provisions include the escape clauses discussed in the previous section.

Management usually strongly opposes implementing a SUB plan. Management negotiators emphasize that the company already pays into the state unemployment fund as required by law and that union leaders should lobby their state legislature to increase those funds. Management also argues that additional unemployment benefits decrease its ability to make technological changes and to provide new equipment and processes because of the additional benefits paid to displaced employees.

Although some SUB plans were negotiated as early as 1923 by Procter & Gamble and 1932 by Nunn Shoe Company, the great increase in the number of plans providing coverage for employees came after the 1955 negotiated SUB plan between the Ford Motor Company and the UAW. Today most plans are within the primary metals, transportation, electrical, rubber, and auto industries.[22]

Severance Pay

SEVERANCE PAY

A lump sum or a dispersal of payments given to employees who are permanently separated from the company through no fault of their own.

Severance pay, sometimes called dismissal pay, is income provided to employees who have been permanently terminated from the job through no fault of their own. Although similar to SUB in its appearance and formula for provision in determining benefits, severance pay is given under quite different circumstances. SUB pay enables the employee who is temporarily laid off to feel minimum impact from the layoff and anticipate a return to work and full pay. Employees who receive severance pay, however, realize that they have no hope for future work with the company. It is not normally provided to employees who are terminated for just cause or who quit.

The purpose of severance pay is to cushion the loss of income because of plant closing, merger, automation, or subcontracting of work. Union negotiators contend that management should shoulder some of the financial burden while the employee is seeking other permanent work.

The provision of severance pay and advance notice of layoffs varies by industry. It is most common in industries that have incurred past layoffs during hard economic times, such as manufacturing (74 percent of all contracts) and utilities; contracts for professional and technical employees seldom (16 percent) provide severance pay and advance notice.[23]

The amount of severance pay is usually specified by a formula guaranteeing a percentage of base pay determined by number of years of service with the company. For example, the contract provision in Figure 8-2 provides 16 hours of pay for each year of service. To be eligible, employees may be required to have a minimum number of years of service, usually one, except in a case of disability. Management negotiators have been somewhat more sympathetic to severance pay provisions because management controls its cost completely. However, as the economy, technology, and mergers force changes in many of our industries, management negotiators may be likely to resist further increases in severance pay provisions.

If severance pay is included in an agreement, it is considered an employee right. In the case of a merger, plant closing, relocation, or the sale of the company, the liability for severance pay may become a most important issue. Court decisions have upheld the legal right of employees to receive severance pay from the parties involved. In such cases severance pay owed workers is generally regarded as a legal liability of the company.[24] Unions have a legal right to file suit on behalf of employees denied negotiated severance pay under the Labor Management Relations Act, Section 301.[25]

Article XVI
General Provisions

Section 1—Severance Provision

In the event the Company decides to permanently close C. Lee Cook, severance pay will be granted to each active (on the payroll) employee in the Machinists Bargaining Union in an amount equal to sixteen (16) hours pay at his/her regular hourly rate at the time of closing for each year of continuous service with C. Lee Cook. "Active" is defined for the purposes of severance pay, as meaning any employee on the active payroll of C. Lee Cook on the date of the Company announcement of shutdown plans, and any employee on approved medical leave of absence at that time; or any employee in a laid-off status then and not recalled actively prior to such announcement. The severance will be made available no later than seven (7) calendar days of the last day of operation of C. Lee Cook.

FIGURE 8-2 Severance Pay Article. *Source:* Agreement between C. Lee Cook Division, Dover Resources, Inc. and Lodge No. 681, International Association of Machinists and Aerospace Workers AFL–CIO, 2007–2012. Used by permission.

Even though the former employees of Enron were nonunion, the AFL–CIO said it helped them recover severance pay because 'unions exist to improve the lives of working families. *Source:* David Phillip/AP Images.

In 2002 the AFL–CIO filed suit and paid all legal fees on behalf of the 4,200 former Enron workers. The unusual support followed the historic financial collapse of Enron after the company refused to pay severance pay to former workers, while top executives received millions in bonuses. After several months in federal court, Enron and its creditors agreed to pay $34 million in severance pay, up to $13,500 per worker. Even though the workers were nonunion, the AFL–CIO supported them because "unions exist to improve the lives of working families," according to Vice President Linda Chavez-Thompson.[26]

Death and Disability Plans

Union leaders have also strongly negotiated for death and disability benefits to supplement Social Security. The negotiated benefit may provide for coverage up to a maximum, or it may provide benefits independent of others received by the employee. The need for negotiators to be very specific about what is provided by these benefits is illustrated in Case 8-1, in which misunderstandings about a program led to arbitration. However, negotiators are aware of the benefits made available on death or disability to employees by the Social Security system, and employers remind union officials that they contribute to the Social Security system and therefore provide funding for its death and disability benefits as well as those received through the collective bargaining process. An example of the negotiated benefit is included in the following agreement between Duke Energy Company Ohio, Inc. and the International Brotherhood of Electrical Workers:[27]

> ARTICLE V
>
> Section 27. The Company will provide each employee with Term Life Insurance in the amount of two (2) times the employee's straight time annual salary.

The company commonly bears the entire premium cost of death and disability insurance. However, often it may be negotiated that employees will be offered additional group insurance through the group plan at reduced rates. Union members, of course, often benefit from such a plan by an amount greater than the premium paid by the company in their behalf. Usually the company can obtain group insurance at a rate cheaper than each individual could purchase on his or her own.

CASE 8-1

Disability Pension

The agency's pension plan and agreement for the employees provided that an applicant for disability pension would be subject to a medical examination and evaluation by the agency doctors to determine whether the applicant was qualified for a disability pension. The decision, however, would be made by the Disability Pension Board, which is made up of three representatives from the company and three representatives from the union.

The employee in this case became disabled and was unable to drive a bus, which was her job. The employee had been diagnosed by her own doctor as suffering from temporomandibular joint syndrome (TMJ). The employee applied for disability pension, and the board voted on her application. The six-member panel was deadlocked: The three company trustees voted no, and the three union trustees voted yes. The position of the union was that the employee suffered from permanent disability and, under the collective bargaining agreement, should be allowed a pension.

The applicable provision of the collective bargaining agreement stated that employees with ten years or more of service who become permanently physically or mentally incapable of performing their job could retire and begin receiving benefits. Any such pensioner who regains his (or her) health or mental capacity will have his pension discontinued, and he will be restored to his former position with full seniority rights.

The union pointed out that although the collective bargaining agreement pension rules required an employee to be examined by an agency physician when applying for permanent disability, the decision of whether the employee qualified was left to the trustees. The trustees had admitted that they did not take into consideration the opinions of the employee's private physicians that the employee suffered from TMJ and could be considered permanently disabled.

The position of the company, however, was that the examination by the agency physician failed to decide conclusively the issue of the permanency of the disability. On the basis of one examination, the agency physician determined that the employee was unable to drive a bus at that time but could not find any physical impairment that would justify classifying the employee's condition as permanent disability.

Decision

The arbitrator found that to rely only on the agency physician, who had admittedly performed a relatively short and cursory exam, was not sufficient. The arbitrator found that the grievant did meet the disability requirement under the pension plan and should be awarded pension benefits.

Source: Adapted from *Bi-state Development Agency,* 90 LA 91 (1987).

Tips from the Experts

Union

What are the three best benefits employees can try to get from their employers?

1. Employment security (as opposed to job security)
2. Family coverage (health insurance, appropriate leave opportunities, child care, and elder care)
3. Opportunity for employee growth through retraining, promotion, education, literacy, and recognition for performance

Management

What three benefits should an employer avoid?

1. COLA (cost-of-living adjustment) or any other benefit plan with fixed benefits unrelated to costs or a future plan with fixed entitlement
2. Discretionary overtime
3. Premium pay for time not worked or any other pay for nonproductive time, such as on-call pay

Employee life insurance plans are included in more than 65 percent of negotiated plans. Most provide a specific benefit, often $10,000.[28] Another common type of benefit provides an amount directly related to the employees' annual earnings. Plans that relate the amount to earnings most often provide a maximum benefit equal to total yearly earnings; some provide twice the earnings.[29] The cost of life insurance coverage is paid entirely by the employer in most agreements.

HEALTH CARE

Employee health benefits today are *the issue* for many employees, unions, and employers. Double-digit annual cost increases and premium hikes over the past 20 years caused health care to become a most common issue behind union-called strikes in recent years. Both unions and employers are concerned over the annual cost of employee health care—$12,600.00 per U.S. worker in 2011! Health care issues are also complex and thus more difficult to negotiate at the bargaining table. Issues to be negotiated include (1) benefit coverage, (2) deductibles, (3) monthly premiums, (4) copayments, and (5) choice of health care provider.

Health insurance benefits are found in most collective bargaining agreements (97 percent), and in terms of total labor costs they rank second only to wages and salaries for most employers. The most commonly found provisions provide for hospitalization (97 percent), prescription drugs (96 percent), physician visits (96 percent), mental health (93 percent), dental care (90 percent), and vision care (73 percent). Dental and vision care, less common only ten years ago (43 percent of contracts in 1993), have increasingly appeared in more contracts until today they are provided in 90 percent of 2011 contracts. Overall management negotiators have been willing to negotiate better health insurance benefits—which are then often provided to nonunion employees as well, including management. Both sides recognize the need for employees and their families to have access to health care, which may be unobtainable or very expensive if purchased outside an employer group plan. Health care plans usually specify an initial deductible, a family deductible, copayments, and maximum coverage. Most employers provide a choice of health insurance plans to employees, including one or more options under each of the three most common forms of coverage:[30]

1. Preferred provider organizations (PPOs) are available to 74 percent of union workers. A PPO is a contract among the employer, insurance carriers, hospitals and health care providers, dentists, and physicians that provides specific services at a discount in exchange for a guaranteed number of patients.
2. Health maintenance organizations (HMOs) are available to 62 percent of union workers. An HMO is a medical facility that provides routine checkups, shots, and treatments as well as maternity care, vision testing, and so on, usually at a lower total annual cost to families than a typical insurance plan, and that requires a monthly charge per family.
3. Traditional fee-for-service or indemnity plans are available to 48 percent of union workers.

Health Care Cost Containment

Controlling health care cost increases is a major negotiation issue, sometimes resulting in difficult choices for both unions and employers. For example, the 11,000 members of the United Food and Commercial Workers Union (UFCW) Local 1099 authorized a "Hollywood" strike, or show of solidarity through a short two- to three-day strike against the Kroger Company. As contract talks reached an impasse, Kroger ran full-page newspaper ads announcing it was accepting applications for temporary replacement workers. The UFCW members picketed Kroger stores and called on customers to pressure management. For over 36 years, Kroger and the UFCW Local 1099 had experienced harmonious labor relations. What caused the disruption

Containing health care costs is a primary concern for both management and union negotiators. *Source:* © FORGET Patrick/SAGAPHOTO.COM/Alamy.

of harmonious relations? Although wage and pension issues were also unresolved, health care was the core issue. In the end Kroger agreed to lower prescription copays, and no increases in employee premiums.[31]

Why has this particular fringe benefit taken on so much importance? Employers in the United States experienced ten fold increase in family coverage health care premiums ($1,094–$12,600) in only ten years, 2000–2011, and that was on top of ten years of significant increases! Thus all parties involved have expressed a new willingness to find cost-containment measures.[32] The single most important health care issue is usually what portion of the total cost the employer will pay and what portion the employees will pay. For employers, the issue of health care cost containment is critical because if costs are allowed to increase, they can quickly rise faster than any other personnel cost. Thus, 95 percent of labor contracts require union workers to directly share some of the costs, primarily through three methods: copayments, deductibles, and monthly premium contributions. Over 95 percent of all contracts include cost-containment methods, and most include several. In recent years the requirement to use generic drugs, preadmission testing for hospital stays, utilization reviews, and pretax spending accounts have rapidly increased because of employer demands. However, at the bargaining table the specifics of the cost-sharing plan typically receive greater attention than the addition or alteration of a cost-containment method. Management negotiators are seldom willing to consider changing a cost-containment method because they are aimed primarily at duplication and unnecessary costs. Union negotiators are generally sympathetic to management's efforts to cut excess costs—as long as the cost-sharing specifics are reasonable from their perspective.[33]

Behavior Modification Programs

A relatively new method of cost containment that is likely to be supported by both management and union negotiators is called "behavior modification"—a term that has been common in psychology for many years, but now applied to health care. Behavior modification programs generally include cash incentives to workers given when they complete, for example, (1) routine health risk assessments, (2) smoking cessation programs, (3) weight reduction programs, (4) exercise regimes. Studies indicate that cash incentives above $200 do positively modify workers' behaviors over a long period of time and thus produce healthier employees, and save employers costs.[34]

Health Reimbursement Arrangements

In 2006, the Ford Motor Company paid about $1,200 per vehicle manufactured in health care benefits. Alan Mulally, Ford CEO, stated frankly, "We simply cannot add that amount to a vehicle and remain competitive." As a result, in 2008, Ford Motor Company stopped providing group health care insurance to 57,000 salaried (nonunion) retirees and their spouses and instead began to provide each $1,800 in a **Health Reimbursement Arrangement (HRA)**. Those employees then decide when to use their HRA fund to pay for medical expenses, which may be supplemented by Medicare. An HRA is similar to a 401(k) pension fund in that an employer contributes a fixed amount of tax-deferred money into an account and then the employee or retiree chooses when to use the funds to pay for medical expenses. In 2007, Kellogg Company, Keebler unit, and Chrysler started similar HRA plans. The HRA provides the employer with a certain fixed cost for health care.[35] Under IRS regulations, an HRA must be funded solely by an employer and cannot include voluntary employee salary reduction. Employees are reimbursed tax free for qualified medical expenses. An HRA may, however, be offered together with a Health Savings Account (HSA).

HEALTH REIMBURSEMENT ACCOUNTS (HRA)

Similar to a 401(k) pension fund in that an employer contributes a fixed amount of tax-deferred money into an account for the employee to use for medical expenses.

A Health Savings account is a tax-exempt trust administered by a bank, insurance company, or other IRS-approved organization. Both employees and employers make tax deductible contributions to an HSA. Account balances may be carried over from one year to the next, and earned interest is tax free. Another advantage to employees is that an HSA is "portable": It can be transferred from one employer to another.[36] HSAs were introduced in 2004 as a way for employers to provide more affordable health care. The primary goal is to lower health insurance costs and premiums by giving the employee more control over how funds are spent and an incentive to *save* funds for future needs. In 2008, the maximum contributions are $2,900 for individuals and $5,800 per family. The fact that funds can be carried over from one year to the next gives HSAs a distinct advantage over flexible spending accounts. Thus, an HSA may be viewed as a health care retirement account.[37]

Domestic Partners

In recent years some unions have sought health care benefits for the domestic partners of their members. The partners in such provisions may or may not be limited to same-sex partners. The provisions usually require specific evidence that the partner has shared housing for a minimum period of time. In 2007, for example, the University of Cincinnati and American Association of University Professors (AAUP) agreed to a new contract that contained full health care benefits (and tuition benefits) to domestic partners for the first time. The university chief labor negotiator, Bill Johnson, noted the change should cause a less than 1 percent increase in health care claims. The university believed the change in benefit would make it more competitive in recruiting and retaining faculty.[38]

Voluntary Employees Beneficiary Association

A **Voluntary Employees Beneficiary Association (VEBA)** under U.S. Internal Revenue Code Section 501(c) (9) is an organization created for the purpose to pay life, sick, accident, and similar benefits to members or their dependents or beneficiaries. The members must have an employment-related common bond, such as an employer or affiliated employers, coverage under one or more collective bargaining agreements, or membership in a labor union.[39] A VEBA operates in a similar manner to a pension fund. Employers contribute a specific amount of money each year to accounts for their employees. The employer contributions are

VOLUNTARY EMPLOYEES BENEFICIARY ASSOCIATION (VEBA)

An organization for members who have an employment-related common bond, or coverage under one or more collective bargaining agreements, or membership in a labor union, to pay life, sick, accident, and similar benefits. A VEBA operates similar to a pension fund in that employers contribute a specific amount of money each year to accounts for their employees.

tax deductible as operating expenses and earn tax-free interest in the VEBA.[40] Employers can contribute their own stock to the plan that is less expensive, but then, if the VEBA is administered by a union like the 2007 UAW–GM, Ford, Chrysler trust, the union may become a major stockholder in the company. The UAW VEBA made headlines in 2007 because the auto companies had been the U.S. icon for the traditional health care plan that was started by GM and the UAW in 1950. Also the new UAW VEBA with about $70 billion in assets became the largest VEBA in the United States.

VEBAs, however, are not new concepts. A 1928 federal law first provided for tax-exempt trusts to fund life, health, and accident benefits to its members. It allows both employers and employees to contribute to a trust. About a third of large U.S. employers have established VEBAs, including Duke Energy Corporation, Conagra Foods, and Texas Instruments, as well as recently established ones by Procter & Gamble Company in 2005, the Kellogg Company in 2007, and the UAW–GM, Ford, Chrysler 2007 VEBA for retirees. GM had previously established a VEBA to fund health benefits for current employees.[41]

VEBAs provide employers the following advantages: (1) current tax deductions for contributions to cover expenses that are not currently required; (2) latitude in choosing plan benefits; (3) funds grow tax deferred and have no penalties for early withdrawals; (4) benefits can be passed to family members free of income, estate, and gift taxes; and (5) the assets are protected from creditors in case of employer bankruptcy, of special interest to unions.

Some VEBA critics, however, point out the one created by Caterpillar, Inc., in 1998. The giant equipment manufacturer set up a VEBA health care trust to defray and control retiree medical costs. By 2004, the trust ran out of money and had to increase retiree monthly premiums by $281 per person.[42]

Wellness Programs

WELLNESS PROGRAM
Any of a variety of employer-sponsored programs designed to enhance the employee's well-being, such as stress management, cancer detection, exercise programs, and complete physical fitness centers.

Negotiated **wellness programs** have increased in collective bargaining agreements. In 2008, 55 percent of public sector CBAs and 37 percent of private sector CBAs contained at least two of the common benefits:

- Smoking cessation
- Exercise programs
- Weight control
- Nutrition education
- Physical exams
- Stress management
- Back care[43]

Most are expanded physical fitness or alcohol and drug rehabilitation programs, but many complete wellness programs include stress management, high blood pressure detection, cancer detection and treatment, and individualized exercise programs. Many wellness programs today are created or expanded as a health care cost containment measure. They focus on individual interventions with employees designed to identify and reduce risky behaviors such as smoking, overeating, and lack of exercise, as well as early detection of illnesses through regular checkups.[44]

The DaimlerChrysler–United Auto Workers wellness program began in the 1980s with the then Chrysler Corporation and has evolved into a model of labor–management cooperation. The program is run by the six-person labor and management Wellness Advisory Council and involves over 90,000 UAW workers at 35 different DaimlerChrysler locations nationwide. It won the prestigious C. Everett Koop National Health Award in 2000 and was the first labor–management partnership to win the award. The objectives of the program include the number of annual employee health-risk assessments, employee satisfaction surveys, and research by an outside agency. The program provides free on-site awareness, education, and maintenance in several key health areas, including nutrition, exercise, injury prevention, mental health, driver safety, and smoking cessation. Employees may voluntarily attend workshops and receive individual counseling. Family members, retirees, and other workers are also allowed to participate.

The program has been widely accepted by employees and has grown until the following milestones were reached:[45]

1. Thirty-six percent of eligible employees volunteered to participate in health-risk appraisals.
2. Ninety-five percent of employees who did participate were satisfied with the program.
3. Driving habit risks decreased by 42 percent.
4. Significantly lowered health risks were reported by 4,184 employees.
5. Smoking risks decreased 27 percent.
6. High-risk alcohol consumption decreased by 39 percent.
7. Mental health risks decreased significantly.

Both union and management negotiators often view a company-provided physical fitness plan or wellness program as a desirable addition to the workplace. Thus, the issue at the negotiating table may be reduced to who designs, runs, and pays for the program. What do workers think? A Ford Motor Company employee and UAW member noticed the positive effect on morale: "They've taken out 500 lockers and put in exercise equipment, and two hourly employees get paid to run the room. Those things help make the camaraderie stronger."[46]

Employee Assistance Programs

Beginning in the early 1970s, the number of **employee assistance programs** (EAPs) in contracts have increased significantly. In 2008, 82 percent of public sector CBAs and 65 percent of private sector CBAs contained at least one of the following EAP benefits:[47]

EMPLOYEE ASSISTANCE PROGRAMS (EAPs)

Company-sponsored programs designed to assist employees in resolving personal problems, such as stress, finances, and alcoholism, that may adversely affect job performance and attendance.

- Alcoholism
- Drug Abuse
- Marital difficulties
- Financial problems
- Emotional problems
- Legal problems

The number increased because many labor relations managers believe that they can save money by helping employees resolve personal problems that affect job performance. EAPs also provide the union with evidence of management's concern for employees' well-being, which should be a strong boost to employee relations. But the primary reason for more company-sponsored EAPs is that they may enhance a company's profitability by reducing absenteeism, turnover, tardiness, accidents, and medical claims.[48]

Many EAPs grew from alcohol treatment programs. The typical program addresses psychological and physical problems, including stress, chemical dependency (alcohol and drug), depression, marital and family problems, financial problems, health, anxiety, and even job boredom. The procedure in virtually all EAPs is problem identification, intervention, and treatment and recovery.

An example of a successful referral program is the EAP at Bechtel Power Corporation in San Francisco. When a supervisor believes an employee's performance has been adversely affected by personal problems, the supervisor phones the EAP office. (An alternative first step would be an employee self-referral.) Once the supervisor and EAP specialist discuss the particulars of the situation—performance record, absenteeism, and so on—the supervisor is normally advised to suggest that the employee use the EAP. It is carefully explained to the employee that participation is voluntary and does not affect the discipline process, which may be implemented if required by poor work. Strict confidentiality is guaranteed.[49]

Unions have often taken an active role in designing EAPs. Usually both labor and management agree that the troubled employee is a valuable asset and, if rehabilitated, can remain a valuable employee after treatment. However, neither the union nor management views the EAP as an alternative to the disciplinary process and at some point an employee may be forced to choose between treatment and termination.

The Consolidated Omnibus Budget Reconciliation Act

CONSOLIDATED OMNIBUS BUDGET RECONCILIATION ACT (COBRA)

A law that provides for the continuation of medical and dental insurance for employees, spouses, and dependents in the event of an employee's death, termination, divorce, or other loss of health care eligibility.

A federal law titled the **Consolidated Omnibus Budget Reconciliation Act (COBRA)** was passed in 1986. This law provides for the continuation of medical and dental insurance for employees, spouses, and dependents in the event of termination of employment, death of the employee, divorce, legal separation, or reduction of hours, which results in the loss of group health plan eligibility. An employee or the employee's dependents must elect this coverage and pay 100 percent of the full cost of the plan selected. The intent of this law is to alleviate gaps in health care coverage by allowing the employee or beneficiary to elect to continue medical or dental insurance for up to 18 or 36 months, depending on the circumstances of their employment separation. The passage of the act was a major victory for unions, which had been seldom able to obtain similar provisions from employers at the bargaining table.

Under COBRA, one of the six events requiring an employer to continue group health coverage is termination of employment or a reduction in hours. Under federal regulations, a strike qualifies as such an event; thus, management is required to provide continued health care coverage to striking employees and their families at the employees' expense. COBRA also requires management to notify in writing each employee and spouse of the right to continue coverage. The employee then has 60 days to choose continued coverage. If the employee chooses to continue coverage, under COBRA, the employer must provide the same group health care coverage that was provided before the strike.[50]

PAY FOR TIME NOT WORKED

What has become one of the most sought-after employee benefits by union members is **pay for time not worked** on the job, or paid leave. Employees today have come to expect to be paid for holidays and vacations as well as many other absences. These time-off-with-pay components of labor agreements are many and varied and include the following:

Holidays
Vacations
Jury duty
Civic duty
Military duty
Funeral leave
Marriage leave
Maternity/paternity/family leave
Sick leave
Wellness leave (no sick leave used)
Blood donation
Grievance and contract negotiations
Lunch, rest, and break periods

TABLE 8-2 Percentage of U.S. Workers with Access to Paid Leave Benefits, 2005

Type of Paid Leave	Holidays (%)	Sick Leave (%)	Vacation (%)	Funeral Leave (%)	Jury Duty (%)	Military (%)	Family Leave: Paid (%)	Family Leave: Unpaid (%)
Union	87	61	86	82	83	55	6	89
Nonunion	47	58	77	66	68	47	8	90

Source: U.S. Bureau of Labor Statistics, *National Compensation Survey* (Washington, DC: Bureau of Labor Statistics, 2005), p. 22.

Personal leave/anniversary of employment

Sabbatical leave[51]

Union business

In general, as illustrated in Table 8-2, a greater percentage of union workers than nonunion workers receive paid leave for different reasons.

Profile 8-1

Law Benefits Former Workers at Nuclear Plants

In the 1940s and 1950s, the U.S. Department of Energy (DOE) constructed several atomic weapons plants. Upgrades and maintenance of the plants continued for decades. Since then, thousands of workers from those sites, including many International Brotherhood of Electrical Workers (IBEW) members, have suffered major illnesses, especially cancer, which is believed to have been caused by toxic exposure at the DOE plants. In July 2001, a new federal program, the Energy Employees Occupational Illness Compensation Program Act, became law, offering compensation benefits to workers who

The Energy Employees Occupational Illness Compensation Program Act in 2001 paid $121 million in benefits to 1,647 former IBEW members who worked at atomic energy plants and suffered cancer and other work –related illnesses. *Source:* Smileus/ShutterStock.

(continued)

have suffered from illnesses associated with their work at one of the atomic plants. In less than a year, 1,647 claims totaling $121 million were paid out under the act, with many workers receiving $150,000 lump-sum payments.

One IBEW business manager, Gary Seaz, worked at the Paducah, Kentucky, plant in the 1970s and, like many of the 150 IBEW electricians who worked at the plant, has been diagnosed with cancer. Seaz recalled, "We had no idea of the hazard that existed. Many local union members have come down with cancer." According to the U.S. Department of Labor, workers exposed to radiation may have contracted cancer, beryllium sensitivity, chronic beryllium disease, or chronic silicoses. Claimants can get information at one of nine DOE centers around the nation.

Source: "Benefits Available for Employees of Nuclear Weapons Facilities," *IBEW Journal* (April 2002), pp. 14–15.

Paid Holidays

More than 99 percent of labor agreements provide for paid holidays. Union negotiators' demand for increased paid holidays has been great and continues to increase the average number of paid holidays provided by the agreements. In 1950, the average number of paid holidays in labor agreements was three; now, almost 60 years later, the average is closer to 11.[52] However, the average number in agreements has remained steady at about 11 from 1986 to 2008. Most contracts provide for between 8 and 13 paid holidays, as illustrated in Table 8-3. Normally, employees required to work on holidays receive double or even triple pay in the contract provision. In the chemical, hotel, and restaurant industries, which operate every day, employees may be given double pay for working holidays and another day off during the following week. If a holiday falls during an employee's paid vacation, the employee usually receives an extra day of scheduled vacation. Employees on layoff during a paid holiday usually do not receive pay for that holiday. Vacation pay provisions can be the source of conflict, as you can see in Case 8-2.

TABLE 8-3 Trend in Number of Paid Holidays (frequency expressed as percentage of contracts)

	1957	1966	1975	1986	1995	2008
None specified	1	1	1	2	1	—
Fewer than 7	36	16	6	3	4	13
7–7½	48	39	10	6	4	9
8–8½	12	31	12	8	7	11
9–9½	4	7	29	9	12	11
10–10½	4	7[a]	20	23	18	15
11–11½	—	—	12	18	24	13
12–12½	—	—	10[b]	14	16	11
13 or more	—	—	—	19	16	16
Average	**6.2**	**7.6**	**9.1**	**10.4**	**10.5**	**11**

[a]10 or more

[b]12 or more

Source: Bureau of National Affairs, *Basic Patterns in Union Contracts*, 14th ed. (Washington, DC: Bureau of National Affairs, 1995), p. 58; and see also U.S. Bureau of Labor Statistics, *National Compensation Survey* (Washington, DC: Bureau of Labor Statistics, 2005), p. 23.

CASE 8-2

Vacation Pay

For many years, the company operated several cigarette-manufacturing facilities in Louisville, Kentucky. In February 1999, the company announced that it planned to phase out the production of cigarettes in the Louisville area. The final production date was in July 2000. However, employees were laid off in various stages prior to the final closing.

The collective bargaining agreement (CBA) between the union and the company provided for a one-week summer vacation and a one-week Christmas vacation for all bargaining unit employees. Generally, production at the facilities was halted during the two vacations, and employees were paid one week of vacation pay pursuant to the CBA. For both vacation shutdowns, the practice of the company has been to pay the vacation pay on the last scheduled day of work prior to the shutdown. The CBA requires that employees be "actually on the payroll at the time of the specific vacation period" to receive shutdown vacation pay. The employer scheduled the summer shutdown so that it included the Fourth of July holiday. The dates of the vacation period varied, depending on the employee's place in the production process. Those employees who process tobacco at the beginning of the production cycle began their vacation on the Friday prior to the week of the Fourth of July and returned on a Monday, and employees who hold jobs later in the production sequence began vacation on Monday of the week of the Fourth of July and returned on Tuesday.

In 2000, the last day of production prior to the summer shutdown was Thursday, June 29, 2000, so the union understood the shutdown began on June 30, 2000. The employees performed regular duties on June 29. On June 30, the employees being laid off did not perform regular duties but reported to the plant to attend to various administrative matters related to their layoff. These employees were compensated for a full day of work for June 30, 2000, but were not paid vacation pay for the 2000 summer vacation shutdown. The company considered that the effective layoff date for the employees was July 1, 2000. The company concluded that these employees were not *on the payroll during the vacation shutdown period* and therefore were not entitled to the vacation pay for the summer shutdown because the start date for the summer shutdown was Monday, July 3, not Friday, June 30.

In 1999, the Christmas shutdown began on December 24, 1999. A group of employees was laid off in December 1999. Their last day of work was December 23, 1999, with an effective layoff date of January 1, 2000. These employees were paid for the Christmas shutdown because the company considered these employees to be employed during the shutdown.

The union argues that although Article VI, Part 2, of the CBA says that only employees "on the payroll" are entitled to vacation shutdown pay, the term "on the payroll" is not defined in the agreement.

The CBA does not specify whether an employee must be on the payroll during the entire vacation period or only at the beginning of the vacation period. Also unanswered is the question of when a laid-off employee is to be removed from the payroll. For these reasons, Article VI, Part 2, is ambiguous when applied to the facts in this case. Furthermore, the company sent a letter to employees who were to be laid off in June 2000. The letter provided that their last day of work would be June 30, 2000, with a layoff date of July 1, 2000. The "Summer Plant Shutdown Schedule" provides that the shutdown began as of the close of business on June 29, 2000. The employees worked on June 29, 2000, and were scheduled to report for work on June 30, 2000, and were paid their regular wages for that day. Therefore, the company considered the employees to be on the payroll on June 30, 2000. Because they were on the payroll on the first day of the scheduled summer shutdown, they should have received the vacation pay for that week.

The company contended that with the practice to vary the "extra" day the employees get during the summer shutdown by including the Fourth of July, the summer vacation shutdown begins on a Friday for some and a Monday for others. So in 2000, the employees who reported to work on Friday, June 30, would start their "summer shutdown week" on Monday, July 3. As the laid-off employees were not on the payroll on Monday, July 3, they were not eligible for the shutdown vacation pay. The laid-off employees who left the company in December 1999 had an effective layoff date of December 31, 1999. The shutdown week at Christmas that year began on December 23. Those employees were clearly on the payroll as of the start date of the winter shutdown.

(*continued*)

Decision

The judge found the position of the company inconsistent. The company notified the laid-off employees that their last day of work would be June 30, a Friday, and they would be removed from the payroll on July 1, a Saturday. And yet the company argued that because the employees worked on Friday, their next "work day" would have been Monday, July 3. The company wanted to use workdays for calculation of the vacation shutdown but used calendar days for determining the date that employees could be removed from the payroll. The judge further noted that there was no indication as to, absent the layoff, which of the employees would have begun their vacation on Friday and which on Monday. The judge determined that the notice to the employees that the "shutdown" would begin on June 30 was binding on the company as to all the laid-off employees and that, because they were on the payroll as of that date, they were entitled to vacation pay.

Source: Adapted from *Phillip Morris USA v. The Bakery, Confectionery, Tobacco Workers and Grain Millers International Union,* 116 LA 1650 (2002).

FLOATING HOLIDAY

A paid holiday that may be used at the employee's discretion or when mutually agreed to by the employee and management.

MONDAY HOLIDAY PROVISION

Based on a federal government practice, moving the observance of a holiday that has a specific date, such as a President's birthday, to the closest Monday in order to give employees a three-day week-end.

The **personal day, or floating holiday**, started in the rubber industry. Floating holiday provisions allow the selection of the day on which the holiday is observed to be left to the discretion of the employee or to be agreed on mutually between management and the employee. Management has resisted the concept of a floating holiday on the theory that there is little difference between a floating holiday and an additional vacation day.

Many labor agreements have observed the **Monday holiday provision** of the federal government. The observance of Monday holidays is, in theory, designed to give employees more three-day weekends during the year for additional rest and relaxation. In practice, however, the Monday holiday has increased absenteeism, the chief administrative problem caused by paid holidays. Employees can easily see that being absent on Friday or Tuesday would provide them a four-day weekend or almost a complete week's vacation.

An agreement provision for a paid holiday should specify the following:

1. ***Eligibility.*** As illustrated in the duPont agreement, Figure 8-3, Section 2(b), employee eligibility, which requires employees to work the last working day before the holiday and the first scheduled working day after the holiday, helps minimize the problem of employees stretching holiday periods.
2. ***Holiday rate.*** If employees are scheduled to work on what was agreed to be a paid holiday, they will receive premium pay, as in Section 1 of Figure 8-4.
3. ***Which days are paid holidays.*** The days determined to be paid holidays should be specified in the agreement as in Section 1 of Figure 8-4.
4. ***Holidays falling on nonwork days.*** As specified in Figure 8-4, provisions for the holiday should be made in case the holiday falls on a nonwork day, such as a Sunday.

Paid Vacations

The practice of providing employees with paid vacations in labor agreements has become not only commonly accepted but also expected by union employees. About 86 percent of labor contracts in 2005 provided for paid vacations of two to six weeks' duration.[53] Employers believe that, unlike paid holidays, paid vacations are effective in increasing employee productivity. Employees, by taking a physical and mental break from the workplace, are able to return to work refreshed and rejuvenated.

Four types of vacation plans are commonly negotiated: the graduated plan, the uniform plan, the ratio-to-work plan, and the funded plan. By far the most popular type of plan is the *graduated plan*, which provides an increase in the number of weeks of vacation according to

Article VII
Holiday Pay

Section 1. An employee who works on any one of the holidays listed below shall be paid, subject to the further provisions of Section 3 of this Article, overtime pay at one and one-half (1) times his regular rate for hours worked in addition to a holiday allowance equivalent to his regularly scheduled working hours not to exceed two and one-half (2) times his regular often will such holiday hours worked, whichever yields the greater pay.

New Year's Day	Labor Day
*Washington's Birthday	Thanksgiving Day
Good Friday	Day after Thanksgiving Day
Memorial Day	Christmas Eve
**July Third	Christmas Day
July Fourth	

*A Choice of either Washington's Birthday or Martin Luther King's Birthday will be offered provided the COMPANY and UNION have not agreed, prior to December 31 of the preceding year, that another day shall be designated as a holiday in lieu of either Washington's Birthday or Martin Luther King's Birthday.
**July Third shall be one of the recognized holidays except when July Fourth falls on Thursday in which case July Fifth shall be the holiday.

When any of the foregoing holidays, except Christmas Eve or July Third fall on Sunday, the following Monday will be observed as the holiday. When Christmas Eve or July Third falls on Sunday, the following Tuesday will be observed as the holiday. When any of the foregoing holidays fall on Saturday, the preceding Friday shall be observed as the holiday for all employees who normally are scheduled to work Monday through Friday. Saturday shall be designated as the holiday for all other employees. When Christmas Day or July Fourth falls on Saturday, and is observed on Friday by employees normally scheduled to work Monday through Friday, the December Twenty-Fourth holiday or the July Third holiday shall be observed on the preceding Thursday.

Holiday hours shall correspond to the hours of the regular workday.

Employees will be informed at least one (1) week in advance if they are expected to work on a holiday.

Section 2. Pay for hours equivalent to regularly scheduled hours not to exceed eight (8), at the employee's regular rate, shall be paid to an employee for each of the holidays designated above on which he does not work, provided such employee:

a. Does not work the holiday for the reason that:

  1. He is required by Management to take the day off from work solely because it is a holiday, or

  2. The holiday is observed on one of his scheduled days of rest (an employee on vacation, leave of absence, or absent from work for one (1) week or more due to a shutdown of equipment or facilities or conditions beyond Management's control shall not be considered as having "scheduled days of rest" during such periods of absence), and

b. Works on his last scheduled working day prior to the holiday and on his next scheduled working day following the holiday, except when the employee has been excused from work by Management.

If an employee who is scheduled to work on the holiday fails to work, he will receive no pay for the holiday if his absence is not excused.

FIGURE 8-3 Holiday Pay Provision, duPont-Neoprene Craftsmen Union Agreement. *Source:* Agreement between E.I. duPont de Nemours and Neoprene Craftsmen Union, 1994, pp. 20–22.

Article 13
Vacations

13.1 Vacation Schedule—Employees will be entitled to vacation pay based upon the following schedule:

***Years of Continuous Service**	**Weeks Vacation**
1 year	1 week
3 years	2 weeks
7 years	3 weeks
14 years	4 weeks
18 years	5 weeks
25 years	6 weeks

*Continuous service shall include all service as a part-time and/or full-time employee without a break.

13.2 Eligibility for Vacation—Eligibility for an employee's first vacation (one week) and for any increase in vacation will be determined by their anniversary date. Arrangements must be made to permit employees to enjoy such earned vacations between the actual anniversary date and the end of the year in which it occurs. Where necessary, vacations due in the 12th and 13th periods may be carried over to the first period of next year. Employees who completed the required service prior to January 1 of any year are eligible for vacations as of that date. After an employee has qualified for the amount of vacations as stipulated in Section 13.1 above, they automatically qualify for that amount of vacation as of January 1 of each year, provided the employee has worked one scheduled work day up to eight (8) hours in that year. Lay Off Status—Employees who are on lay off or leave of absence at the end of a calendar or anniversary year will not be entitled to vacation and vacation pay for service for said year until their return to work. Their vacation will be subject to the reductions outlined under paragraph 13.6.

13.4 Scheduling Vacation—Choice of vacation dates will be granted on the basis of seniority by classification . . . The Employer will post a vacation schedule in each store effective December 1 of each year. The employees will exercise their preference by January 15 of each year. A complete vacation schedule shall be posted in each store within fifteen (15) days . . .

13.5 Holiday Occurring During Vacation—If one of the holidays set forth in Article 12, Sections 12.1 and 12.2 occurs during any week of an employee's vacation, they shall receive holiday pay as set forth in Article 12 of this Agreement, in addition to their vacation pay for such week.

FIGURE 8-4 Vacation Provision. *Source:* Agreement between the Kroger Co. and the United Food and Commercial Workers International Union AFL-CIO, 2007–2010. Used by permission.

length of service. This is the most common type of vacation plan. The average number of days provided in contracts in 2005 based on servic is as follows:

Service (year)	Number of Vacation Days (days)
1	8.9
3	11.5
5	13.9
10	17.6
15	20.2
20	22.7
25	24.5

Source: The U.S. Bureau of Labor Statistics, *National Compensation Survey* (Washington, DC: Bureau of Labor Statistics, 2005), p. 24.

The *uniform vacation plan* provides all workers with the same length of vacation. This is most commonly found in manufacturing firms that shut down for specified periods to retool or change product lines, giving employees vacations during the shutdown. The *ratio-to-work plan*, commonly found in the printing and transportation industries, relates the length of vacation to the number of hours or days the employee works during a given time period, usually the year preceding the allocation of vacation. The *funded plan* requires employers to contribute to a vacation fund from which employees may draw vacation pay during periods when no work is available. This is most often found in the construction and apparel industries.

An example of a graduated vacation plan in the agreement between the Kroger Company and the United Food and Commercial Workers Union is provided in Figure 8-4.

This example includes several provisions that should be specified in the labor agreement, including the eligibility for vacation leave and pay, how long the employee has to be with the company to qualify, and any other requirements for vacation leave. Duration of vacation leave must be determined along with any additional vacation pay, such as premium pay or bonuses. Also, the scheduling of vacations, a critical aspect of the contract, must be specified. Normally, scheduling is done on the basis of seniority, as in the Kroger Company example; however, management may try to retain some right in the determination of employee scheduling so that adequate skills and abilities can be maintained in the workplace. Note that the Kroger Co. example in Figure 8-4 includes the language: "least affect the operation of stores . . . " which gives management flexibility.

Determining the annual cost of any negotiated increase in the number of vacation days or holidays is relatively straightforward. One common method is to multiply the number of additional vacation or holiday hours by the base wage rate of employees covered. Another method would be to determine the appropriate percentage of the amount charged to the holiday or vacation pay account from the previous fiscal year. For example, if the company estimates that employees averaged 11 days of paid vacation in the previous year at a total cost of $1,200,000, then the average cost per day was $109,090. Thus, if one additional vacation day is negotiated, the total cost for the next year will be $1,309,090.[54] One problem in determining the cost of additional vacation or holiday benefits is that the cost of continuing production as usual is not provided in the two alternatives. Industries such as chemical and utility companies that provide around-the-clock service require many employees to work on holidays for premium rates. Thus, it may be necessary to add additional factors to the estimate of negotiated increases in vacation and holiday pay.[55]

Sick Leave

Sick leave is often accrued by employees at a specific rate, such as one day per month from the first day of permanent employment. The subject of many arbitration cases, sick leave is intended to provide for continuation of employment when employees are physically unable to report for work. To minimize grievances and other problems associated with sick leave provisions, the labor agreement should specify the procedure for taking sick leave: the time sick leave must be reported by during the beginning of the work shift and what verification by a physician or other individuals is required, a definition of "sick," and the accumulation rights. Some contracts provide that unused sick leave can be accumulated without any maximum to cover employees who require extended sick leave for serious illnesses. A doctor's certification is usually needed only when an employee uses extended sick leave. Many contracts also specify a maximum number of days of sick leave that can be accumulated by an employee.

SICK LEAVE

Time off allowed an employee because of illness or injury, with the provision of continued employment when the employee is able to report back to work.

Paid Leaves of Absence

Most agreements provide for paid leaves of absence for a variety of other purposes, including military service, education, and union business as well as personal reasons. Personal leave may result from a variety of causes, such as jury duty, appearing as a witness in a court case, or attending a family funeral. In negotiations for a funeral leave benefit, it is important to specify for which family members the leave should apply. Personal leave may also include the awarding of personal days that employees may take without specifying why they missed work or giving advance notice. Military leave is often negotiated for employees in the United States Armed Forces Reserve Units.

PREMIUM PAY

PREMIUM PAY

Wages that exceed the standard or regular pay rate given an employee for work performed under undesirable circumstances, such as overtime hours, weekend work, holiday work, or dangerous and hazardous circumstances.

Virtually all labor agreements provide a specific work schedule and require **premium pay** for any hours worked beyond the normal schedule. More than 67 percent of labor agreements provide for premium pay for Saturdays and Sundays that are not part of the normally scheduled workweek, and 99 percent provide for specified overtime premium pay rates on either a weekly or a daily basis.[56] Overtime premiums are often provided on a daily basis for time over eight hours. Such additional pay was termed "penalty pay" in the past because it was intended to discourage employers from requiring employees to work additional hours or weekends. Today employers are anxious to maintain their rights in scheduling additional hours so that overtime costs in premium payments can be minimized.

Negotiated increases in overtime in premium pay benefits cannot easily be costed because the actual cost increase per year will be determined by management's scheduling of overtime hours. Therefore, to make the best estimation of negotiated cost increases, multiply the percentage increase in the benefit by last year's total dollars allocated to that particular benefit. For example, if management spent an additional $550,000 in overtime pay and the overtime rate is increased by 5 percent during the next year, the additional cost of the increase to management will be $27,500 annually.

PYRAMIDING OF OVERTIME

The payment of overtime on top of another overtime rate that occurs if the same hours of work qualify for both daily and weekly overtime payment. Most contracts prohibit this type of payment.

The **pyramiding of overtime** pay is prohibited in most contracts. Pyramiding is the payment of overtime on overtime, which can occur if the same hours of work qualify for both daily and weekly overtime payment. In contracts that prohibit pyramiding, provisions specifying how such hours will be paid are usually included.

How overtime work is distributed among employees is also discussed in most labor contracts. The most common provision is a general statement to the effect that overtime will be distributed equally as far as practical. Other provisions assign overtime on the basis of seniority or by rotation. Many agreements limit overtime distribution to employees within a department, shift, job classification, or those specifically qualified.[57]

SHIFT DIFFERENTIAL

Additional hourly rates of pay provided to employees who work the least desirable hours.

Premium pay for other undesirable work situations may also be negotiated. **Shift differentials** are negotiated additional hourly rates of pay provided to employees who work the least desirable hours. Usually specified in cents per hour in the labor agreement, the cost of the increase in a shift differential would be calculated similarly to that of an overtime premium pay increase. More than 90 percent of all late-shift factory workers receive a shift differential premium over their day-shift counterparts. A significant 2007 research study of mostly nurses and airline crews found higher rates of breast and prostate cancer among women and men whose shift started after dark. The International Agency for Research on Cancer, of the World Health Organization, decided the research results were enough to add overnight shift work as a probable carcinogen. The higher cancer rates, however, do not prove that overnight work causes cancer; other related factors may contribute to the higher rate. Why the potential link between cancer and shift work? Researchers suspect the disruption of the circadian rhythm: The body's biological clock may be the reason. The hormone melatonin that suppresses cancerous tumors is usually produced at night while the body is at rest. Graveyard shift work, therefore, may disrupt that production.[58]

REPORTING PAY

The minimum payment guaranteed for employees who report for work, even if work is not available, provided they have not been given adequate notice not to report to work.

Other forms of premium payments similar to shift differentials include reporting pay, call-in pay, and on-call pay. **Reporting pay** is the minimum payment guaranteed employees who report for work even if work is not available. If employees have not been given adequate notice An to work, usually of 24 hours, they are eligible to receive either the minimum amount of work or payment usually equal to four hours of scheduled work as seen in this example from an agreement between Miller Brewing Company and Teamsters Local 97[59]:

ARTICLE XVI

Report-In Pay

Any employee who reports for work and who has not been notified not to work shall be granted four (4) hours of work or pay therefore. Notice in this Section means that the Company will telephone the employee at the number on file with the Company.

A supplemental payment given to employees called back to work before they were scheduled is usually termed **call-in pay**. Most labor agreements provide a lump-sum amount or an amount equal to a minimum number of hours of pay for employees called in during other than scheduled work hours. Thus, employees receive a bonus for being called in before their next normal reporting time.

CALL-IN PAY

A supplemental payment given to employees called back to work before they are normally scheduled to return.

On-call or *standby pay* is given to workers available to be called in if needed. This type of pay is commonly negotiated in companies such as the chemical industry or airlines that must provide continuous production or service. Usually a lump-sum amount is paid to employees on a daily basis when they must be available to work, whether they are called in or not.

Bilingual Language Skills

The 1996 agreement between the National Treasury Employees Union and the U.S. Treasury Department provided premium pay of 5 percent to about 7,000 customs agents who are bilingual. The new premium pay provision was one of the first in U.S. collective bargaining agreements. Other employers agreeing to pay a bilingual premium pay include Delta Airlines to flight attendants and MCI, which pays a 10 percent bonus to workers who are required to speak a second language more than half the time. In general, more unions are pressing for new bilingual premium pay if the skill is needed a substantial percentage of the time in job-related communication.[60]

Travel Pay

In industries that require workers to travel regularly to different job sites, a premium is paid for excessive travel. The construction industry may provide, for example, a specified home office and a "free zone" of several miles from that office in which workers will travel to sites for free. Beyond that zone, they receive a premium as in this provision from the contract between Tri-State Contractors Association and the District Council of Carpenters:[61]

ARTICLE 10—TRAVEL PAY

Branch Office. Ashland, Kentucky

Travel pay on all jobs covered by this Agreement are as outlined below, and all miles shall be measured from the office of Millwright Local 1031 by use of the most direct route, using only improved or hard surface, non-toll roads.

5 miles free zone

All jobs outside the free zone shall be $.25 per hour additional for each hour paid.

EMPLOYEE SERVICES

A wide variety of employee services have been negotiated in labor agreements. In general, they are not as commonly found as the previously discussed employee benefits; however, most labor agreements provide for at least a few employee services. Some of the more traditional employee services include sponsoring social and recreational activities, such as picnics and athletic events. The cost of these services has been reexamined in recent years because only a relatively small percentage of employees use them.

Subsidized food services are a popular employee benefit. Both labor and management believe that providing dining facilities, low-cost meals, or vending machine products minimizes time away from the job spent on breaks or at mealtime in addition to improving employees' diets. Company-sponsored credit unions are another employee service often sought by union negotiators. Although a credit union is normally operated completely independently from the employer, the employer's cooperation in establishing it and providing payroll deductions is critical and must be negotiated.

In recent years, some of the newer employee services negotiated include work-related costs, such as transportation to and from the job; free or subsidized home computers; legal services; and elder care.

Flexible Benefit Plans

FLEXIBLE BENEFIT PLANS

Negotiated in lieu of fixed benefits, employees can choose the benefits that fit their needs among a designated list and within a price established by the contract. Usually includes medical insurance, vacation, pensions, and life insurance.

An alternative to negotiating a fixed combination of employer-provided benefits is a **flexible benefit plan**. In a typical flexible benefit plan, employees are allowed to choose the benefits they believe will best meet their needs. Their choices are limited to the total cost the employer has agreed to pay in the collective bargaining agreement. Thus, for example, employees may be given a monthly benefit-dollar figure and told that they can allocate the dollars to the benefits they select from a list. In many programs, employees may exceed their benefit limit, but they must pay the difference between what the employer provides and the cost of what they wish, or if employees choose to allocate fewer dollars than their maximum, they may be allowed to keep all or part of the savings as additional monthly income.

Flexible benefit plans have had an on-again, off-again, on-again life. In the 1960s, *cafeteria plans*, which also allowed employees to choose some benefits from a "menu" of benefits, started to spread among employers. However, the cafeteria approach ran into problems. Employees found it confusing and difficult to make decisions, and employers (without today's computer programs) found the administration of the programs expensive and difficult.

Today, however, flexible benefit plans have become commonplace for several reasons. A 2005 study by TowersPerrin found that 68 percent of employers with plans believe they help provide a positive organizational identity and culture.[62] The primary reason employers are switching from fixed to flexible plans, in addition to better meeting their employees' needs, is to contain their medical costs. In fact, flexible benefit plans may be the most effective means employers have of containing medical costs.

With a flexible benefit workers make individual choices—as they do in cafeterias. *Source:* © JLP/Jose L. Pelaez/Corbis.

An important feature of a flexible plan is the opportunity for each employee to spend employer dollars as personally desired. By contrast, many so-called flexible plans are fixed. They either offer the employee the opportunity to choose among limited alternatives or offer a "take-it-or-leave-it" approach. For example, the employer offers to pay a portion of an employee's medical insurance if the employee pays the balance. But if the employee does not choose medical insurance (possibly because of a spouse's coverage), then the employer's contribution is lost. A true flexible plan credits the employee with the employer's share, which could be applied to another benefit.

ADVANTAGES OF FLEXIBLE PLANS Originally created to better meet the needs of employees, flexible plans have become increasingly effective in matching employees' needs to their benefit plan. Among the advantages of flexible plans are the following:

1. ***Control benefit costs.*** Of employers with flexible plans, 78 percent reported that a major objective in their initiating a plan was to contain rising health care costs. With health care costs continuing to rise, this effective containment method is likely to spread among employers.
2. ***Improve benefits offered.*** Employers can better meet the needs of their employees by expanding the variety of benefits offered to employees. Child care is a good example: Employers can pay a portion or all of the cost of providing child care at an off-site facility through a voucher system. In choosing the coverage, employees must either reduce the coverage of another benefit or have the increased cost deducted from their pay. (Employers generally, however, provide a portion of child care.)
3. ***Attract and retain employees.*** The changing workforce is causing employers in some industries to consider flexible benefits as a tool in the recruitment and retention of employees. Just as flexible work schedules can be used to attract and keep employees, flexible benefit plans can be included in recruitment and advertising.
4. ***Avoid duplicate coverage.*** Another aspect of the changing labor force is the increased number of working married couples with duplicate benefit coverage from separate employers. Flexible benefit plans may allow a married couple to save thousands of dollars in wasted duplicate coverage.[63]

Child care is one of the fastest growing employee benefits in labor contracts.
Source: MCT via Getty Images.

Child Care

Although many employers have addressed the child care needs of their employees, child care, according to the National Labor Relations Board (NLRB), is not a mandatory subject for collective bargaining. As the workforce continues to include more single parents and dual-career couples, the direct link between employment and child care might cause the NLRB to reconsider its position. A survey conducted by the U.S. Department of Labor listed the following *employer benefits* from a child care policy:

1. Greater ability of the employer to keep and attract good employees
2. Less employee absenteeism
3. A lower job turnover rate
4. Improved employee morale

Employer-sponsored child care programs are varied.

CHILD CARE CENTERS Some employers provide in-house child care services by establishing a child care center in the workplace. The company must have available space and a sufficient number of interested employees for this service to work. Often, smaller employers join together and create a nonprofit center off the premises for all employees. A number of employers choose to participate in their employees' child care needs by providing financial assistance. Employees can afford quality child care with the assistance offered by the employer. Many communities lack the resources necessary to provide quality child care, however, and employers often find it necessary to actually provide the centers.[64]

Elder Care Programs

A relatively new benefit in labor contracts is the support for *elder care programs*. Elder care is defined as assistance for employees who must care for older relatives not able to fully care for themselves. U.S. employees are increasingly challenged with caring for aging relatives. The demand has caused the number of employers offering some form of elder care benefit to increase to almost 25 percent of all large U.S. organizations. Verizon Communications Inc., for example, offers benefits to full-time and part-time employees. Employers have increased the benefit because it reduces absenteeism and worker stress.[65]

Employer-sponsored programs may include the following:

- Information services including legal, retirement, and estate planning
- Referral services for in-home caregiving programs
- Geriatric evaluation and counseling
- Flexible work schedules, part-time work, and time-off policies
- Long-term care insurance for elderly relatives and employees/spouses[66]
- In-home emergency care

Considering the demographics of the American workforce, it is a benefit likely to appear increasingly as a new priority issue for unions. In fact, a 2002 survey of Communication Workers of America (CWA) members found that 20 percent thought they would face elder care needs. Two of the first unions to have negotiated elder care benefits include the CWA and the Hotel and Restaurant Employees (HERE) Union. The benefits negotiated by the two differ in structure and represent two of the more common forms of the negotiated elder care provisions.

First, the CWA and Lucent Technologies in a five-year contract provided for annual contributions to a Family Care Development Fund (FCDF). Employees cannot obtain funds from the FCDF directly but rather can request grants to centers that provide elder care to their family members. Lucent contributes $1.5 million annually to the fund, and more than 330 grants totaling $11 million were awarded in five years. The contract also provides for an elder care referral program to employees seeking assistance. A second major type of elder care provision was negotiated by HERE with over 50 San Francisco hotels. First negotiated in 1994, the provision was partially intended to help the hotels reduce tardiness and absenteeism, which employees reported were partially caused by elder care obligations. Under the contract provision, the hotels contribute 18 cents per hour worked by the employees to a trust fund. Employees with eligible relatives must "win" one of the 100 slots through a lottery to receive the $150-per-month assistance benefit. Eligible relatives include spouse, parent, domestic partner, father-in-law, mother-in-law, or grandparent.[67]

Credit Unions

One of the oldest and most common employee services is the credit union. Most agreements provide that the employer will initiate a payroll deduction process, but the union assumes responsibility for enrolling members, investing funds, and administering the program. In general, employers wish to stay apart from the process and have "the credit union assume complete responsibility."[68]

PUBLIC SECTOR BENEFITS ISSUES

Public employers provide many of the same employment benefits offered in the private sector. For most public employers, income maintenance plans include only pension and death and disability plans. Wage guarantees, supplemental employee benefits, guaranteed income stream plans, and severance pay are not provided to public employees as an acknowledgment that tax dollars cannot be used to pay for nonservice. Medical care plans offered are similar to those in the private sector, and public employers and employees face the same problem with escalating costs as do employers in the private sector.

Vacations, holidays, sick leave, and paid leave of absences for such reasons as jury duty and military leave are commonly found in public sector agreements. Premium pay provisions are usually found in agreements covering employees in public safety areas, such as fire, police, and emergency medical services.

One significant area of difference between public and private sector benefits is in the prevalence of defined benefit pension plans. Historically, public safety employees did not participate in the Social Security system. Therefore, nearly a third of all public employees relied solely on their pensions for retirement income. To match the retirement of an employee from the private sector who receives an average of 59 percent of final salary from a combination of benefits from a defined *contribution pension plan* and *Social Security*, the public employee receives 60 percent of final compensation from a defined benefit pension plan. In addition, many public pension plans provide health care benefits to retirees until they qualify for Medicare. In recent years sharply rising pension and health care benefits for retirees of state, county, and city governments has caused a budget crisis for many of them. For example, in one state, local governments in 1988 paid 19 percent of salaries of fire, police, and emergency medical service (EMS) workers into the state pension fund. By 2008, only 20 years later, the costs had risen to 34 percent and were estimated to increase to 61 percent by 2013! Newport, Kentucky, Finance Director Greg Engelman said of the rise: "It's like a meteor and you can't get out of the way!" In reality, governments have only poor choices: reduce services, raise taxes, change traditional "20 years and out" full pensions, or underfund pensions.[69]

Summary

Once called only "fringe," employee benefit costs have constantly risen for several decades and today are a sizable part of employee compensation. The four most expensive types of benefits in agreements are (1) income maintenance, (2) medical care, (3) pay for time not worked, and (4) premium pay. Still, a variety of employee benefits have increased in recent years as employees and union leaders initiate new benefits in labor negotiations. By necessity, some benefits are unique to particular industries. For example, the agreement between the UAW and Ford Motor Company includes a safety belt user program that pays $10,000 to the beneficiary of a participant who dies in an automobile accident while "properly using a qualified passenger restraint."[70]

Today the top benefit issues in most contract negotiations are health care and pensions. The health care issues include who will pay for it, which plans are to be offered, and how spiraling costs will be contained. Retirement plans are a close second to health care as a major benefit concern, with the concern being, again, who will pay for them and which type of plans will be offered. These two very expensive benefits are often among the top priorities of both union and management.

CASE STUDIES

Case 8-1 Paid Leaves of Absence

The collective bargaining agreement between the company and the union contained the following provisions:

> *Overtime/Compensatory Time:* . . . Employees may elect to use compensatory time off in lieu of a cash payment. Compensatory time is paid at time and one-half. The scheduling of compensatory time, if such be elected by the employee, must be approved by the employee's supervisor. . . .
>
> *Eligibility for Sick Leave:* . . . Each permanent employee who has earned sick leave credits shall be eligible for sick leave for any period or absence from employment which is due to illness . . . of members of the immediate family (defined as . . . children of the employee or his/her spouse. . . .)

The company allowed employees who worked overtime to either be paid time and a half for each hour worked or earn time off at the rate of one and one-half hour for each hour worked. The employees accrued eight sick days and ten vacation days a year.

Prior to February 13, 1995, employees were allowed to use compensatory time when they were absent because of illness, and prior approval for the use was not always required. However, on February 13, 1995, the company issued a directive stating, "Supervisors will no longer approve utilizing compensatory time for sick leave absences. An exception may be made by a supervisor if the employee does not have any sick leave hours available but does have a compensatory balance."

The employee's son became ill on February 28, and she left a note for her supervisor that she might not be in on March 1. She did, in fact, take the day off. On March 2, she called in and said she would not be at work and said she would be using a vacation day. When she filled out her time sheet, she listed March 1 as a compensatory day. On the basis of the company's directive, her supervisor required the employee to use a sick day for March 1 but allowed the use of a vacation day for March 2. The union pursued this grievance on her behalf.

The union's position was that a past practice of allowing the employees to use compensatory time for leaves due to illness without the prior approval of the supervisor had been established and that the company could not change that practice unilaterally. The employees had acquired a "benefit" through that past practice, and the collective bargaining agreement (CBA) did not give the company the right to take away that benefit.

The company position was that the past practice argument was not controlling in this case. Rather, the precise language of the CBA required the use of sick leave for illness and required a supervisor's approval for use of compensatory time. Because the CBA is definitive, past practice does not create additional rights. In addition, the management rights clause of the agreement allows the company to make changes in the way it manages the workplace. Controlling leave time would be included under that clause.

Source: Adapted from *Sheboygan County,* 105 LA 605 (1995).

QUESTIONS

1. The union claimed that the employees lost a benefit when the company changed the use of compensatory time for illness. In light of the fact that the use was permitted if the employee had no sick leave available, how were the employees damaged?
2. The company paid employees the same wage whether the time was credited against accrued sick leave, compensatory time, or vacation. Why would the employer care which leave was used?
3. As the arbitrator, give your reasons for ruling in the union's favor. Now give your reasons for ruling in the company's favor.

Case 8-2 Employee Benefits

The company offers its employees a two-option health and benefit plan. These plans are self-insured by the company, and a third party calculates the health insurance premiums. Premiums are calculated annually in late August on the basis of information from the preceding June–July period. Open enrollment for the employees for the next year are held in October to become effective for the following January.

Premium sharing by employees began on January 1, 1995. Under the collective bargaining agreement (CBA) that expired on August 12, 1999, employees paid an amount equal to 10 percent of the monthly premium. The CBA specified that those rates would be $18 for employees with no dependents (category 1), $36 for employees with one dependent (category 2), and $48 for employees with two or more dependents (category 3). These rates were 10 percent rounded to the nearest dollar of the third-party actuarial calculation of $180 for category 1, $355 for category 2, and $475 for category 3.

The current CBA, which became effective August 13, 1999, changed the premium sharing from 10 to 11 percent for the employees and set out premium sharing rates of $21, $41, and $54, respectively, for the three levels of coverage based on the 1999 premiums. In October 1999, however, the company announced that the premium share levels would be $23, $46, and $61, respectively. The union protested these rates. The union then filed an unfair labor practice charge with the NLRB alleging that the company unilaterally changed the terms of the CBA by increasing the premium sharing amount over the stated amounts.

Discussion

The relevant provision of the CBA stated as follows:

> Health Care and Welfare Benefits—Two-Option Plan ("TOP")
>
> *Premium Sharing:* Effective January 1, 2000, for employees and dependents, there will be a monthly premium sharing equal to 11 percent of the monthly premium for three (3) levels of coverage: (1) employee, (2) employee plus one dependent, and (3) employee plus two or more dependents. Based on 1999 premiums for the TOP, this is (1) $21 for the employee, (2) $41 for employee plus one dependent, and (3) $54 for the employee plus two or more dependents per month. Each year in October the rate for the next year will be announced. In no case shall the premium share dollar amounts increase by more than 10 percent per year rounded to the nearest whole-dollar amount.

The union argued that the company violated that section of the CBA because the amounts announced by the company in October exceeded the amounts in the CBA of $21, $41, and $54, which should have been the 2000 rates. And, the union argued, the amounts in the CBA were the amounts the union membership understood they would be charged for the employee share of premiums for the year 2000, when they voted on and approved the CBA.

The company argued that the operative language in that section of the CBA was "based on 1999 premiums." It was clear from the use of that phrase that the dollar amounts for the employees' share of the premiums in the CBA were there for illustrative purposes only, not to establish the 2000 rates. And even if the CBA was ambiguous, the company's past practice was not. Each year the company counted on its third-party administrator to calculate the health insurance premiums on the basis of information from the preceding year June through July. That calculation was available in October for the open enrollment period, and the premiums took effect on January 1. The initial premiums that would take effect under the CBA approved in August would not be known until October. The union had to know that the rates in the CBA were there as examples only.

Source: Adapted from *Sandia National Laboratories v. Atomic Projects and Production Workers,* 115 LA 1482 (2001).

QUESTIONS

1. Premiums for health insurance have had a tendency to increase appreciatively from year to year. Has the union negotiated a "good" benefit provision for its members? Explain.
2. Do you think that the union's interpretation of the CBA language was reasonable? Explain.
3. Do you think the company should have made the language of the CBA provision more specific so that the union members voting on the contract would understand exactly what the premiums would be? Explain.

Key Terms and Concepts

call-in pay *312*
cash balance plans *291*
Consolidated Omnibus Budget Reconciliation Act *304*
defined benefit plan *290*
defined contribution plan *290*
employee assistance programs *303*
Employee Retirement Income Security Act *292*
escape clause *295*
flexible benefit plans *313*
floating holiday *307*
Health Reimbursement Arrangement (HRA) *301*
Monday holiday provision *309*
on-call pay *312*
Pension Benefit Guarantee Corporation *292*
pension plan *289*
personal day *307*
premium pay *311*
pyramiding of overtime *312*
reporting pay *312*
severance pay *296*
shift differentials *312*
sick leave *311*
supplemental unemployment benefits (SUB) plans *295*
unemployment insurance *287*
vesting *293*
Voluntary Employees Beneficiary Association (VEBA) *301*
wage employment guarantees *295*
wellness programs *302*
workers compensation *288*

Review Questions

1. How can negotiators reduce health care costs and maintain good health care benefits?
2. In recent years, management negotiators have increased their resistance to increases in private pension plan funding. Why?
3. Why might workers be ineligible for retirement funds from a private pension plan even though they have worked all their lives?
4. What is meant by eligibility in a holiday clause?
5. Why do workers try to negotiate wage employment guarantees? Supplemental unemployment benefits (SUBs)?
6. Who is responsible for COBRA payments?
7. What type of health care plans are normally negotiated? How can a health maintenance organization (HMO) be considered as an alternative to such plans? What are the purposes of HMOs?
8. Why do employees today place a high priority on paid time off? How has the Monday holiday caused administrative problems? How can holiday provision problems be minimized?
9. What paid leaves of absence are usually provided by labor agreements?
10. Why does management dislike pyramiding of overtime?

YOU BE THE ARBITRATOR
Not Working a 40-Hour Week

ARTICLE 3
HOURS OF WORK AND OVERTIME:

Employees covered by this Agreement are to work a normal workweek of 40 hours and a normal workday of 8. Each employee shall be entitled to one (1) full day of rest per week, which shall be twenty-four (24) consecutive hours. All work performed in excess of the normal workday or in excess of the normal workweek, or on a day off, shall be paid one and one-half (11/2) times the straight hourly wage plus regular day's pay, or one and one-half (11/2) times the daily rate of pay, whichever is the higher. Doorman does not get paid for lunch hour.

ARTICLE 12
DISCIPLINE

The Company shall have the right to discipline or discharge employees for just cause. Any disciplinary action taken for minor infractions shall be progressive and will include:

a. written warning
b. written reprimand
c. suspension
d. discharge

Facts

The grievant is a night-shift doorman of an apartment building. He is required to work an eight-hour day. Beginning in August 1999, the grievant was sent a letter containing the caption "Second Warning," which spelled out specific instances when he was away from his post for at least a half hour. He was reminded in the letter that his work hours were 3 P.M. to 11 P.M., with an hour off for dinner and reasonable bathroom breaks. Other than that, he was expected to be at the door. In July 2001, a new collective bargaining agreement (CBA) was entered into that changed the grievant's work shift to 3 P.M. to 12 P.M., with an unpaid hour for dinner. In August 2001, the company's vice president ("VP") sent a registered letter to the grievant in which she pointed out that he was not working a full 40-hour week. She concluded that letter by stating to him, "Effective immediately, you will work an eight-hour day and a 40-hour week. If you continue to work a short week, you will be suspended without pay." The VP had observed that in addition to the unpaid dinner hour, the grievant was regularly away from his post for 15- or 30-minute periods. This August 2001 letter did not contain any language indicating that it was a warning. In October 2001, the VP asked the building superintendent to document the actual hours being worked by the grievant. The superintendent monitored videotape records from security cameras in the building and documented the grievant's actual hours of work. He showed that the grievant was not working eight hours during his nine-hour shift. The VP sent another letter to the grievant in which she advised him that he was being suspended for a one-week period. The union contends that this suspension was not for proper cause and filed this grievance.

Issue

Was there proper cause to suspend the grievant?

Position of Parties

The company states that the CBA is clear and unambiguous and that it required that employees work an eight-hour day. The grievant has a history of not working the required number of hours in a workday, and he was warned in August 2001 that if he continued not working a full eight-hour day, he would face the consequences of a disciplinary suspension.

It is the union's position that the company is required to provide employees full and adequate notice of an offense before discipline can take place and that it failed to do so in this case. When the grievant received a warning in 1999, the letter was clearly labeled as a warning. The letter the VP sent to the grievant in August 2001 did not spell out that it was a warning letter. Further, under the contract that was in effect prior to July 2001, the grievant worked a shift beginning at 3 P.M. and ending at 11 P.M. In July 2001, the shift changed, and it ended at midnight with an unpaid dinner hour. The union argues that no one from management ever explained these changes to the grievant and thus that management was to blame for the grievant's misunderstanding of the work hours.

QUESTIONS

1. As arbitrator, what would be your award and opinion in this arbitration?
2. Identify the key, relevant section(s), phrases, or words of the collective bargaining agreement (CBA), and explain why they were critical in making your decision.
3. What actions might the employer and/or the union have taken to avoid this conflict?

Source: Adapted from *Sagamore Owners,* 116 LA 1574.

CHAPTER 9

Job Security and Seniority

Chapter Outline

Employers in the railroad industry contract talks propose to consolidate engineers, conductors, switchmen, signalmen, firemen, and oilers into a generic "transportation employee" category. The unions oppose the proposal because it would eliminate minimum crew sizes, which are based on a certain number of each craft working on each train and, therefore, would reduce the number of union jobs. Thus, the core issue for the 155,000 union employees and the five largest U.S. railroads was *job security*. *Source:* © Joe Sohm/Chromosohm/Stock Connection.

> *The issue is jobs. You can't get away from it: jobs!*
>
> STUDS TERKEL (PULITZER PRIZE–WINNING AUTHOR)

LABOR NEWS

Railroad Unions, Carriers Clash Over Jobs

The contract talks between the five largest U.S. railroads and the unions that represent about 155,000 employees focused on one issue—job security. Don Hahs, president of the Brotherhood of Locomotive Engineers and Train men, which represents about 30,000 engineers and other railroad workers, said the key issue was the employers' proposal to do away with the traditional crafts, which most unions are based on, and consolidate them into a "transportation employee" category under one collective bargaining agreement. The unions oppose the proposal for three primary reasons: (1) The elimination of minimum crew sizes (based on a certain number of each craft working on each train) would reduce the number of union jobs; (2) the railroad unions are largely organized by crafts (engineers, conductors, switchmen, signalmen, firemen, oilers, and maintenance of way), and the consolidation into one job category would cause conflict among the unions; and (3) safety—the reduction from two workers (engineer, conductor) to one (transportation employee) on most trains may present a public safety problem.

Robert Allen, chairman of the National Carriers Conference Committee, which represents Burlington Northern and Santa Fe Railway Co., CSX Transportation, Kansas City Southern Co., Norfolk Southern Railway Co., and Union Pacific, believes the current contract requires more workers than are needed on today's modern trains, which are guided by improved technology. Consolidating employee crafts and reducing crew sizes is the goal of the carriers, according to Allen, and "when we can safely operate with one person, that's what we're after."

After two years of negotiations, a new five-year contract (2007–2012) provides the job security sought by the union, as well as wage increases and a cap on health insurance premiums. "We were able to keep the carriers (management) at bay," said Hahs.

Source: Adapted from "Unions Fight Freight Rail Carriers' Bargaining Proposals," *2005 Source Book on Collective Bargaining* (Washington, DC: Bureau of National Affairs, 2005), p. 107. Available at www.ble.org. Accessed February 8, 2008.

JOB SECURITY

Over the years, workers' interests and demands regarding job security have never waned. Together with wages and benefits, union negotiators view job security as a top priority in both good and bad economic times. Many view job security as simply meaning the guarantee of work. However, in reality it means much more, including the rights to remain employed during times of layoffs, rights to promotion opportunities, and to a fair hearing in cases involving discipline, as well as the need to have work performed by employees within the company rather than subcontracting or increasing the use of automatic equipment. The ultimate job security employment situation occurs in some other countries where, after a probationary period, employees are guaranteed a job with good wages and benefits for their entire careers as long as they continue to produce satisfactorily. At the other end of the job security continuum are the hypothetical situations in which management might fire, promote, or lay off employees without rationale or consideration for experience and productivity. Negotiating for better wages or working conditions would be meaningless if management could, without reason or with biased intentions, terminate employees or remove jobs from the workplace. As Studs Terkel said about job security and seniority in the chapter-opening quote—"the issue is jobs. You can't get away from it: jobs!"

For example, a three-year-long and often bitter labor dispute between Anheuser-Busch (makers of Budweiser and Michelob) and the International Brotherhood of Teamsters (which includes bottlers, brewers, mechanics, and truck drivers) ended in July 1999 with a new four-year contract. In one case, after more than two years of failed negotiations, Anheuser-Busch imposed its final offer—paying the average Teamster, with overtime, $66,000 a year.

Why did the union reject an offer that included the highest pay in the brewing industry? Job security. The members wanted a job security provision and struck the St. Louis plant when negotiations reached an impasse.[1]

INDUSTRIAL JURISPRUDENCE

The system of rules and regulations that labor and management fashion to define their specific employment rights and obligations in the workplace.

The concept of job security has also been termed **industrial jurisprudence** by Sumner Slichter. His concept contains the primary ingredients of job security in today's collective bargaining: seniority as a determining factor in layoffs, promotions, and transfers; control of entrance to the organization or trade; seniority as a determining factor in job assignments; negotiated management change and work methods and introduction of new machinery; and negotiated wage rates.[2] Industrial jurisprudence generally embodies the principle that a single individual or group of top management officials will not determine the operation of the organization. Instead, the employees are given some rights to guarantee input into important decisions regarding their employment.

The ultimate labor–management conflict over job security is a basic and important one. Management believes that it needs to have a free hand in the operation of the workplace to maximize profits and exercise its abilities. In contrast, labor believes that employee experience and skills are critical to productivity. Employees require some protection against unreasonable managers as well as guarantees that important decisions, such as promotions and layoffs, will be made rationally and that favoritism or union busting will be avoided.

LAST-HIRED, FIRST-FIRED

Senioirty-based procedure for the order of layoff and recall to keep the most experienced employees.

Beginning in the 1930s, seniority-based procedures, such as the **last-hired, first-fired rule**, became common layoff and recall decision criteria. Various theories support this rule, including the human capital theory, in which employees increase their productivity with experience and rational employers want to retain the more productive employees; the implicit contract theory, in which the career strategy of employers encourages employees to commit themselves to steady productive work (thus, laying off senior employees would cause worker distrust in any career planning); and the internal labor market theory, in which collective bargaining produces rules and procedures to ease the tension between the parties. Seniority-based layoff procedures are a prime example of such rules in limiting management's actions and increasing employee loyalty.[3]

The Great Recession of 2008 caused hundreds of thousands of workers to be permanently laid off. Permanent layoffs are of particular concern to employees because layoffs result in

The "last-hired, first-fired" rule is often used in layoffs because the employees' past job performance is not an issue. *Source:* Steve Miller/AP Images.

significant reductions in earnings over the course of employees' work lives. Thus, employees have even stronger expectations that, during economic downswings, employers will reward loyalty.[4] The last-hired, first-fired rule has caused lower permanent turnover rates among union workers in comparison with nonunion workers along with more frequent temporary layoffs in the union sector because of senior union members' preference for short layoffs, allowing them to maintain their seniority.[5]

Job security can be provided through a number of contract provisions. About 95 percent of contracts contain one of the job security provisions listed in Table 9-1, and most contain three or more. In general, contracts with larger unionized workforces contain more job security provisions. Job security, along with wages, health care, and pension benefits, often ranks as one of the top negotiation priorities, especially during hard economic times.[6] However, union negotiators may claim that, in contrast to wages and benefits, job security provisions may not become direct costs to an employer over the life of a contract; they may only determine which workers are promoted, trained, given scheduling preferences, and so on.

SENIORITY

A **seniority system** is a set of rules governing the allocation of economic benefits and opportunities on the basis of service with one employer.[7] It is by far the most commonly negotiated means of measuring service and comparing employees for promotion and layoff–recall decisions, thus providing job security.

SENIORITY SYSTEMS

A set of rules and procedures within an agreement that determine the allocation of certain job situations including promotion, layoff and recall, as well as certain economic benefits based on length of service.

Seniority is perhaps the most important measure of job security to employees, and the issue of seniority is popular among unions and viewed as critical to job security. Seniority is highly visible because it is so easy to define and measure. Normally, it is calculated in terms of days, beginning with the employee's date of hire and, with a few exceptions, continues over the years during the employee's tenure. Union negotiators will vehemently claim that management, in the absence of a job seniority system, will make promotion, layoff, and other decisions solely on the basis of possible short-run cost savings or individual biases rather than on the objective criteria that seniority easily provides. These criteria include the employee's loyalty to the company and his or her skills and productivity, which increase with time spent on the job.

TABLE 9-1 Types of Job Security Provisions in Contracts

	Percentage of Employees				
		By Industry		By Size of Bargaining Unit	
	All Employees	Manufacturing	Nonmanufacturing	Large	Small
Layoff and recall rights	68%	73%	63%	73%	65%
Promotion	67	72	62	72	64
Subcontracting restrictions	56	52	60	61	55
Advance notice of shutdown	56	63	49	52	59
Transfer rights	45	40	49	64	36
Successorship	38	39	37	39	38
Flexible work scheduling	27	15	40	34	24
Professional development program	16	3	29	27	9
Retraining program	13	15	11	23	
Shared work	5	2	9	11	3

Source: Adapted from The Bureau of National Affairs, *2002 Source Book on Collective Bargaining* (Washington, DC: BNA, Inc., 2002), p. 59. Used by permission. Copyright © 2002 by the Bureau of National Affairs, Inc.

Management may argue that time worked on the job is only one measure and the employee's performance record (as well as other criteria, especially performance appraisals completed by supervisors) should be considered. However, performance appraisal systems often depend heavily on supervisors' objectivity and ability to evaluate individual performance honestly and thoroughly, which is often very difficult. Therefore, performance appraisals are often viewed by unions as subjective and do not guarantee employees the objectivity and consistency they expect when promotion or layoff decisions are made.

To define fully the concepts of seniority, it may be helpful to distinguish between unionized and nonunionized employer–employee relationships. Seniority systems are not required by federal or local laws, nor are they an inherent right of employees. However, seniority is a mandatory subject in the collective bargaining process. Strict formal seniority systems are commonplace in virtually all unionized organizations, but they are rare among nonunion employers. However, nonunion employers often consider seniority a factor when making promotion or other employment decisions. In most of the contracts surveyed, seniority played a critical role in the determination of promotion, transfer, and layoff decisions.[8]

CALCULATION OF SENIORITY

In general, seniority is considered to be the process of giving preference in employment decisions on the basis of the length of continuous service with the company. When seniority is involved in promotion considerations, it may be defined as preference in employment on the basis of the length of continuous service and the ability and fitness of the employee to perform the job. New employees generally begin acquiring seniority on the date they are first hired. In the case of two or more employees hired on the same date, the exact time of hire or the alphabetical listing of their last names may determine seniority. Often, however, seniority is not awarded to employees until after the probationary period, even though they begin accruing seniority from their date of first hire.[9] The contract clause that specifically defines seniority can be quite fairly detailed. Some clauses may be fairly brief, such as the following seniority provision from the agreement between Anaconda Aluminum Company and the Aluminum Workers Trades, AFL-CIO:

> *Section 1.* Plant seniority is defined as an employee's length of continuous service at Anaconda Aluminum Company, division of the Anaconda Company, Columbia Falls reduction plant in Columbia Falls, Montana.
>
> *Section 2.* Departmental seniority is defined as employee's length of continuous service in a department of the plant.
>
> *Section 3.* Granted leaves of absence, vacations, and jury duty will not be considered as a break in service. The applicable federal and state laws shall determine reemployment rights of employees who enter the armed forces.[10]

Seniority List

SENIORITY LIST

A company list used to identify employees in a bargaining unit according to their length of continuous employment.

Most agreements require the company prepare and post a **seniority list** so there will be no question about employee, department, or plant-wide seniority. There must be total agreement as to the exact calculation and order of employees on seniority lists. The method of displaying seniority lists is usually a matter for local negotiation between labor and management. Many contracts provide that seniority lists are updated on a regular basis and contain the employee's name, occupational group or department, any specific skilled trades, date of entry, and related seniority. Any disputes over seniority lists are usually taken through the grievance procedure for resolution, as seen in Case 9-1.

CASE 9-1

Dovetailing Seniority Lists

Employees worked for an unincorporated division, Division 1, of the company. The company also operated a second incorporated division in another state, Division 2. Each division had a separate collective bargaining agreement (CBA).

The company announced plans to relocate the Division 2 operations and workers to Division 1. It proposed to "dovetail" (i.e., integrate) the Division 2 seniority list into the Division 1 seniority list. The alternative would have been to "end-tail" the Division 2 workers, that is, treat them as new employees and eliminate their Division 2 seniority. The workers at the Division 1 plant filed a grievance protesting the dovetailing proposal, and the matter was submitted to arbitration.

The basic dispute that drove the arbitration was whether Division 1 and Division 2 were separate "employers" or whether the company should be considered the "employer" of the workers at both divisions. Under both CBAs, the term "employer" was defined as the division, "seniority" as "continuous service with the employer," and the company was not mentioned by name.

The company argued that it was the employer for both divisions. It pointed out that Division 1 was not a separate legal entity. It operated out of the same facility as the company until 1987. The two divisions had the same president and the same accounting and administrative staff. Both divisions had substantially the same working conditions and pay rates. And virtually all the work was interchangeable between workers in the two divisions.

The employees of Division 1 argued that neither of the CBAs provided for the consolidation of the two divisions and that a "no-modification" clause in both contracts precluded the dovetailing of the seniority lists.

Decision

The arbitrator found, nonetheless, that the company had the authority to dovetail the two seniority lists. First, the arbitrator determined that the company was the de facto employer of the workers at both divisions based on the history of company's development, the shared administrative and executive operations of the two divisions, and the fact that "Division 1" was merely an unregistered trade name, not a separate legal entity.

And although the two CBAs did not explicitly provide for dovetailing, they did not preclude it either. Allowing for dovetailing was a permissible interpretation of the agreement under the changed circumstances presented by the consolidation of work. As the arbitrator noted, the "grievance and arbitration procedures are part and parcel of the ongoing process of collective bargaining. It is through these processes that the supplementary rules of the plant are established."

Source: Adapted from *Division 1 v. R.W.F. Inc.*, 144 LRRM 2649 (1993).

Depending on the particular labor agreement, seniority rights are vested within a variety of employee units. The most common unit is **plant-wide seniority**, in which an individual employee receives credit that becomes applicable whenever that employee competes with any other employee from another unit for the same position. Plant-wide seniority first appeared in the E. I. duPont and Neoprene Craftsmen Union contract in 1943. That year, according to union negotiator Archie V. Carrell, it was the top priority of the members, who wanted job security over members of a new production unit being acquired. Thus, the provision in 1943 stated that "with respect to reduction of force," seniority shall be determined by "length of continuous service at the plant," therefore providing security to current union members over those of the new unit.[11] All employees of the new unit, therefore, began with zero seniority like those of Division 2 in Case 9-1.

Other common seniority units include departmental, trade, classification, and companywide. In a **departmental seniority system**, employees accrue seniority according to the amount of time they worked within a particular department, and that seniority credit is valid only within that department.[12] For example, an employee with 11 years seniority in Department X could not successfully compete with an employee with seven years in Department Y for an open position in Department Y.

Classification seniority, similar to departmental seniority, provides for employee seniority only within the same job classification. Companywide seniority systems combine all employees from various locations and types of facilities. When two employees compete for an open position in a companywide system, individual experience, length of service, and related departments or job classifications are not considered, only the seniority with the company. This provision makes companywide seniority the most impractical and infrequently used.

Companies often use a seniority system combining plant-wide seniority with departmental seniority, thus giving two different forms of seniority. Plant-wide seniority may be used for determining layoffs, vacations, and other specific benefits. Departmental seniority is often used to determine eligibility for a promotion or a transfer so employees with specific skills and related job experience can be considered for new positions. However, in the case of layoffs, it is often believed that employees' total work experience, and therefore their plant-wide seniority, is the most important job security factor.

In situations involving layoffs, seniority systems often use bumping (63 percent of all contracts). **Bumping** occurs when employees with greater seniority whose jobs have been phased out have the right to displace employees with less seniority. Most bumping clauses require that bumping employees be as qualified as the junior employee.[13] For example, in one case, an arbitrator denied a more senior employee the right to bump a junior employee because the agreement specified that to bump another employee a person must be qualified to perform the work. The senior employee had been fired for poor performance and then reinstated. When he tried to bump a junior employee, the company denied his request. The arbitrator upheld the denial, citing the agreement language because the senior employee was not as qualified as the junior employee.[14]

BUMPING

A procedure commonly used during layoffs, in which employees with greater seniority whose jobs are eliminated displace employees with lesser seniority. Bumping is more often used in companies with plant wide seniority in unskilled jobs.

Seniority and the Americans with Disabilities Act

In a historic decision, the Supreme Court ruled that an employee is not entitled to a job assignment as a reasonable accommodation of his or her disability under the Americans with Disabilities Act (ADA) if the assignment would conflict with the rules of a seniority system. The decision in *U.S. Airways, Inc. v. Barnett* supported seniority systems when they are in conflict with the ADA in a similar situation. In the case, Barnett, a freight handler, injured his back and then used his seniority to transfer to the mailroom. Two senior employees exercised their seniority, however, and bumped Barnett from the mailroom. Barnett asked to remain in the mailroom as a reasonable accommodation of his disability. U.S. Airways declined his request because it would have been counter to the seniority system in the contract. The Equal Employment Opportunity Commission concluded that U.S. Airways had discriminated against Barnett by denying him reasonable accommodation. The Supreme Court, however, held that the requested accommodation was in conflict with the rules of a bona fide and established seniority system and thus was not a reasonable accommodation.[15] Thus the Supreme Court upheld seniority rights over employee rights under the ADA when they come in conflict.

Under the GM–UAW master contract, UAW workers from a GM plant in Baltimore were given superseniority over all other workers—both new employees and those transferred to the GM Shreveport, Louisiana, plant when it first opened. Many of the UAW workers deeply resented the Baltimore workers' superseniority and called them "Baltimorons" because of their higher seniority rights.[16]
Source: Steve Ruark/AP Images.

Superseniority

Union officers and committee personnel may be given preferred seniority rights for layoff and recall situations. Often referred to as **superseniority**, it is granted in the collective bargaining agreement so that union stewards and other labor officials will continue to work during periods of layoff, thus enabling the union to continue to operate effectively. When agreeing to superseniority for the union, management may ensure that certain labor relations personnel be similarly protected against layoffs. Some superseniority clauses require that protected union officials have the ability to perform available work or that superseniority is provided only within departments or job classifications. Others limit superseniority to those union officials who perform steward duties, such as grievance processing and contract administration.[17] Superseniority may also be given in unique situations involving a national contract and local plants.

SUPERSENIORITY

The special seniority rights granted to union officers and committee personnel that override ordinary seniority during layoffs and recall situations in order to maintain active union representation within the company.

The value of superseniority depends on the frequency and degree of layoffs typically experienced by the company. In some cases, it is virtually meaningless because union stewards and officials have high levels of seniority from their many years of experience with the union and company.

The labor agreement should explicitly specify under what conditions an employee might lose seniority. Virtually all contracts provide that employees lose seniority if they voluntarily quit or are discharged. Employees who do not report back to work after a vacation or other leave of absence for an excessive period of time may also be deprived of their seniority. Usually employees on layoff retain and accumulate seniority for a period of time specified within the agreement.

PROMOTIONS

Management often disagrees with the use of seniority as the sole factor in promotion decisions. The Bureau of National Affairs estimates that seniority is a determining factor in promotional policies as provided by collective bargaining agreements in 67 percent of labor contracts. However, only 5 percent call for promotion decisions based on seniority as the sole determiner.

Another 49 percent provide that the most senior individual will receive promotion among those equally qualified, and 40 percent provide seniority as one factor along with "skill and ability, with management determining ability."[18]

Some contract clauses that allow promotion according to seniority simply state that promotions to fill vacancies or new job positions on a permanent basis are based on length of service within the company and employee skill and ability. Determining which employees have the required skill and ability can be difficult and subjective. Management generally contends that promotion should be based on an employee's individual performance and required skills as well as length of service.

When labor agreements provide that promotional decisions will be made according to seniority and job skills, it is difficult to determine the weight of each factor and the measurement of individual skills. Although seniority is a factor in promotion decisions in most labor contracts, it is usually not considered to be as important as the ability to perform the job. Quite frequently, ability becomes the dominant factor. When management decides to promote a less senior employee on the basis of higher demonstrated ability, employee grievances may result. Management must prove that the junior employee has greater ability to perform the job, as measured by tests, past performance, training, and so on.

Managers may argue that making important promotional decisions solely on length of service takes away employee incentive. Employees will tend to perform at the status quo, knowing they cannot be promoted before all the senior employees and that, when their turn comes, no one can take the promotion away from them. Labor leaders point out that seniority can be measured objectively and easily. Therefore, promotion decisions based on seniority are far less subject to supervisor bias or the inability to assess individual performance and skills correctly.

Arbitrators have generally held that management has the right to judge, weigh, and determine qualifications as long as the methods are fair and nondiscriminatory. However, if a clause provides that seniority alone is the deciding factor, then management cannot promote a "better qualified" person if the senior employee is "capable of doing the work." When ability and seniority are equal factors, arbitrators generally allow management the right to make the selection, subject to a union challenge that the decision was unreasonable (given the facts), capricious, arbitrary, or discriminatory. In most disputed cases, the employer's decision is supported, and when the position is a supervisory one, management has unquestioned authority. However it is important to note that contract clauses dealing with promotion apply only to positions within the bargaining unit.[19] Why? It is generally held that management has complete authority to "select its own"—meaning managers. And, unless clearly restricted by the agreement, it is also generally held that management has the right to fill temporary vacancies in the bargaining unit caused by illness, vacations, and so forth.

Job Bidding

JOB BIDDING

The process of a company posting notices of new job positions to give permanent employees the opportunity to apply. Bids are based on plant seniority and competency and fall into three categories: (1) up-bid, a bid from a lower to a higher pay grade; (2) down-bid, a bid from a higher to a lower pay grade; and (3) lateral bid, a bid from one classification to another classification in the same pay grade.

It is quite common for the **job bidding** process to be detailed in the labor agreement to minimize misunderstandings and grievances and to increase employee morale. An example of the detailed job bidding process follows in the agreement between C. Lee Cook Division, Dover Resources, and the International Association of Machinists and Aerospace Workers, AFL-CIO, 2007–2012:[20]

ARTICLE XII

Seniority

Section 6—Job Bidding

A. The Company will post classification openings on the bulletin board for a period of three workings days. Bids will be accepted on all classification openings plus any classification not posted. Pre-bids will be accepted on all classifications and must specify job classification desired. Pre-bids will be purged on February 1st of each year.

After the three-day posting bid period, the posted opening will be filled from bids on hand, including pre-bids. Any jobs that become open as a result of filling the posted job will be filled from the bids and pre-bids on hand at the time of posting. If any employee leaves the newly assigned job for any reason, as second, third, and etc., selection will be made from the remaining original bids until a successful applicant is found or a new hire could result.

B. Qualifications will be based on the following:
 1. Seniority
 2. Skill and Ability
 3. Experience

 If Nos. 2 and 3 are equal, No. 1 will prevail. Seniority shall be on the basis of classification seniority first, if any exists among those employees bidding on the job and Plant-wide seniority second, if no classification seniority exists.

C. Job Bidding—Pay Rate. In job bidding, the employee's pay rate will be determined as follows:
 1. Employee bidding **upward**:
  a. An employee bidding upward will be paid his present rate.
 2. Employee bidding **laterally**:
  a. A rated employee bidding laterally will be paid the bottom of the "A" rate.
  b. A trainee bidding laterally will enter the classification at his present rate of pay.
 3. Employee bidding **downward**:
  a. Employee whose present rate of pay is higher than the "A" rate of the job to which he has bid, will enter the new classification at the bottom of the "A" pay rate.
 4. Any employee may bid back into a classification in which he has classification seniority. If his previous rate, plus contract increases, was higher than the bottom of the "A" rate, this will be his new rate. If less, Item No. 2a or b will apply.

D. Multi-Job Bids. When a job bid is posted for more than one opening in a classification, and two or more employees covered by the contract bid on it, the seniority dates entering the new job classification will be staggered so as to maintain the same seniority status that exists plant wide among these employees accepting the jobs.

E. Employees will be limited to a combination of three bids in any one-year period. These will consist of upward, lateral, or downward bids. Where any employee signs a job bid, is offered the job, and refuses (the job), he will be charged with one of the three allowed bids. When more than one job is posted with the same date, employees will be charged with only one bid regardless of how many of the posted jobs he may be offered.

LAYOFF AND RECALL RIGHTS

Agreements often specify seniority as the sole decision criterion in **layoff** and **recall** situations. Employers may argue that ability should be a greater factor in determining layoff and recall of employees. However, because layoff and recall situations are usually seen as temporary, management's argument against the use of seniority is considerably weakened. Also, in layoff and recall situations, there is less of a question of the employee's ability because he or she had been performing the job satisfactorily before a layoff occurred. Thus, management has little room to argue that seniority is a more valid criterion in layoff and recall than in promotion decisions.

LAYOFF AND RECALL RIGHTS

Contract provisions that specify how seniority, ability, and other factors will be used to determine the order of employee temporary job layoffs and job recalls.

In most labor contracts, probationary employees are to be laid off first, with further layoffs made in accordance with plant-wide seniority as necessary. Laid-off employees may be given the opportunity to exercise their plant-wide seniority and bump employees at the bottom of the seniority list rather than be laid off. When skilled trades or other specialized job classifications are involved, layoffs commonly occur by seniority within the trades or classifications. Most agreements also provide that the company gives reasonable notice and reasons for upcoming layoffs to the unions. If the workforce is increased after a layoff, contracts usually provide that laid-off employees be recalled according to plant-wide seniority for appropriate jobs.

Profile 9-1

Teacher Layoffs: Based on Seniority or Merit?

The 2008 Great Recession brought to the forefront an issue which had been simmering for years. The issue? How should K–12 teachers be laid off—according to seniority or merit? State budgets in many states with K–12 teacher unions such as California, Ohio, New York, Illinois, and New Jersey faced historic deficits and thus hundreds of layoffs resulted. In most states union agreements required that layoffs be decided solely by seniority, also the most common criteria in private sector agreements. Thus the newest teachers would be let go first under the "last in, first out" criteria of seniority. In Illinois, however, a new state law permits the use of merit as a criterion, and thus the least competent teacher to be let go first.

Supporters of the use of seniority only point out its advantages; it rewards loyalty, layoffs are not the fault of those involved, and in many cases merit is difficult to determine—for example 99 percent of Chicago's teachers are rated "excellent" or "superior," only 1 percent "unsatisfactory"—and finally seniority is easy to calculate and use as a criteria. Supporters of using merit to decide layoffs, however, believe that principals know who are the worst teachers and if given the authority could make the decisions based on merit. In addition, according to Kate Walsh, of the National Council on Teacher Quality, "weeding out the weakest teachers and keeping the most effective" makes the most sense. Arizona is the only state to ban the use of seniority in cases of layoff and recall, although other states make teacher performance, or merit, a factor in hiring and promotion decisions, as well as seniority, and may follow Arizona's lead in layoffs.

Source: Adapted from Pat Wingert and Evan Thomas, "Chicago's Lesson in Layoffs," *Newsweek* (July 26, 2010), p. 41.

A hot issue in education is which criteria, seniority or merit, should be used in cases of teacher layoffs. Which would you support? *Source:* ZUMA Press/Newscom.

Contract layoff procedures may fall into four general categories: (1) layoff based entirely on seniority, (2) layoff based on seniority among those employees who management feels are capable of performing the work, (3) layoff based on seniority only if ability and other factors are equal among affected employees, and (4) the least common criteria, layoff based on past performance. See Profile 9-1 for a discussion of these controversial criteria. When the last three methods of layoff and recall procedures are used, grievances are likely to be filed because of the subjectivity of determining an employee's ability to perform work, especially when bumping is used and employees are performing new jobs.[21] If a contract provides that seniority and equal ability will govern in layoff and recall decisions, arbitrators are likely to interpret *equal* as meaning not exactly equal but relatively equal. When contracts provide that ability should be part of the determination in layoff and recall decisions, arbitrators' awards have suggested that certain guidelines be considered.[22] Some of the guidelines include the following:

1. When seniority is considered a governing criterion if ability to perform the work is relatively equal, then only the employee's seniority should be considered.[23]
2. A junior employee could be given preference over a senior employee if the senior requires a much greater amount of supervision in performing the job.[24]
3. Senior employees can be required to demonstrate ability to perform the work by passing a test that would qualify them for jobs held by junior employees.[25]

In cases involving temporary or emergency layoffs, management is often given more flexibility in selecting employees than in indefinite layoffs. If the contract does not specify differences in procedure involving temporary layoffs and indefinite layoffs, arbitrators have generally held that ordinary layoff procedures must be followed even where the lack of work lasted only a few hours or one to two days. However, the more common ruling of arbitrators in such situations has been that cumbersome seniority rules need not be followed to the letter in a brief layoff. Arbitrators have even held that in layoffs caused by emergency breakdowns or natural or unforeseen disasters, seniority rules can be disregarded if necessary. However, if the application of seniority rules in the contract does not cause a hardship during the emergency, the employer is advised to follow the contract layoff procedures.[26] The following is a concise layoff and recall contract clause setting forth the procedure and notification requirements and possible emergency exceptions:[27]

ARTICLE XII

Section 5—Layoff Procedure

- **A.** When it becomes necessary to decrease the work force, the following provisions shall be applicable:
  1. Probationary employees shall be the first to be laid off.
  2. Additional layoffs, if necessary, shall be on a Plant-wide basis in reverse order of seniority.
  3. When a cutback is necessary, the procedure will be to determine where every employee would be rolled up into the new classification structure. When established, the reduction will be by classification seniority.
  4. Any employee involved in a reduction of the working force with more than three (3) years plant-wide seniority may exercise his right to bump at the time of the layoff another employee in any classification (excluding labor grades within classifications where no seniority is accrued), provided he has more classification seniority than the lowest senior man in that classification.
- **B.** Employees removed from the classifications(s) as listed in Items 3 and 4 will then be placed in the vacancies created by the Plant-wide Seniority layoff. Such placements in the vacated jobs shall be on the same selection basis as job bidding. Jobs will not be posted.

C. Recall. An employee who has been laid off is subject to reemployment (recall) when work becomes available on the following basis:
1. Job openings to be filled will be posted and made available to working employees through the job bidding procedure.
2. If no bids are received, laid-off employees will be recalled on the basis of Plant-wide Seniority.

Typically, the only exceptions to the use of seniority as the total or partial determinant in layoff and recall decisions occur when probationary employees are laid off first without any discussion of ability to perform or in cases involving superseniority when union officials are laid off last.

Layoffs and Affirmative Action Plans

Regarding seniority rights involving layoffs by companies or governmental agencies subject to court-ordered affirmative action plans, the Supreme Court, in *Firefighters Local Union No. 1784 v. Stotts*,[28] upheld a seniority system, even though the resulting layoffs adversely affected blacks hired under a consent decree to remedy past discrimination. The Court would not allow the consent decree, which had not dealt with the layoff issue, to be given preference over a collectively bargained seniority system. Labor leaders generally defend the protection afforded by seniority systems as necessary to preserve a basic negotiated job right. They argue that changed hiring practices giving women and blacks more job opportunities will eventually lead to their seniority in the various systems. Increased employment and secure job rights will accomplish the desired affirmative action goals without adversely affecting the senior worker. Since the **Stotts case** seniority rights have generally been upheld over Affirmation Action rights in cases of layoffs when the two are in conflict.

STOTTS CASE

Supreme Court upheld a CBA seniority system even though the layoffs adversely affected blacks hired under a court order to remedy past discrimination.

ADVANCED NOTICE OF SHUTDOWN

Worker Adjustment and Retraining Notification Act

WARN ACT

Commonly known as the Plant Closing Act, WARN became effective in 1989 and generally requires employers to provide 60 days of advance written notice to employees and communities of either a plant closing or mass layoffs.

In 1989, the **Worker Adjustment and Retraining Notification Act (WARN)**, more commonly known as the Plant Closing Act, became effective.[29] The general purpose of the law is to "warn" workers and local communities of plant closing or mass layoff decisions by requiring employers to provide advance notice in either situation. The U.S. Chamber of Commerce strongly opposed the plant closings bill. However, corporate officials at Ford Motor Company, Eastman Kodak, Whirlpool Corporation, and other companies noted that WARN mandates less notice than most firms have voluntarily given workers.[30]

The act requires employers to provide 60 days' advance written notice of either a plant closing or a mass layoff once the decision is made by management. A plant closing is defined as the permanent shutdown of a single site or one or more operating units that causes an employment loss of 30 days or more for 50 or more employees, excluding part-time workers. The law requires written notification even when other employees remain working if 50 or more are included in the shutdown. Advance notice of a temporary shutdown decision is required if the action affects, for more than six months, at least 50 employees and 33 percent of all employees—or whenever 500 or more employees are affected. Advance written notice of 60 days is also required when mass layoff decisions will affect at least 50 full-time workers and 33 percent of all employees or whenever 500 or more are affected.

Employers covered by the act include most private sector and nonprofit organizations that employ 100 or more full-time workers. Federal, state, and local government operations are not included in the law. Major exemptions from the law include sudden and unforeseen economic circumstances, natural disasters, and faltering companies actively raising capital to keep a facility open.

The greatest advantage of advance notification is that workers and their community are given time to prepare for the action. For example, workers near retirement may inquire about the status of their pension and decide to retire without unnecessary psychological strain. Other workers may choose to enter retraining programs offered by the employer or community agencies, and some will secure new jobs and thus avoid weeks or months of unemployment. In some cases, the additional notice can provide the time necessary for community, union, and company leaders to find a means of keeping the plant open. A most persuasive argument is simply the humanitarian issue. Studies show that the incidence of alcoholism, suicide, child abuse, ulcers, and heart attacks increases to an alarming extent when workers are subject to plant closure.[31]

In another case, the Court found that, because the federal act had no time limitations on the bringing of a suit under it for failure to comply with its provisions, the laws in each state would be applied to determine the timeliness of the lawsuit. This interpretation will mean that in one state an employee might have one year to bring a suit against the employer for failure to notify of a plant closing and that in another state an employee could have five years.[32]

DETERMINING ABILITY

In general, the burden of proof is placed on the employer to show that a bypassed senior employee is not competent for the job during promotions or layoff or recall actions. However, employers are not required to show that junior employees are more competent. When seniority and ability are given practically equal weight in contract clauses, arbitrators expect the employer to prove whether the ability factor was given greater weight than the seniority factor. In general, even though arbitrators may speak in terms of burden of proof when management's decision regarding a passed-over employee's ability is challenged, both parties are expected to produce any evidence supporting their respective positions.[33]

Although it is generally agreed that management has the right to determine how ability is to be measured in cases involving promotion or layoff and recall decisions, there is no federal law or agreed-on formula to specify exactly how such decisions should be made. Management generally uses a variety of factors to determine the ability to perform a job, including performance, tests, a trial period, disciplinary records, merit evaluations, and education, as long as they are job related.[34] The specific factors may be limited by the contract clause prevailing in a given situation. However, the absence of any such clause gives management the freedom to determine its own factors and measurements. The factors or criteria most commonly used to determine an employee's ability to perform the job and make decisions of promotion or recall can be found in Table 9-2.

COMPANY MERGERS

When separate companies or different entities merge, how the seniority lists of the two are combined becomes a critical question. The merger must specify which principle of combining seniority lists will be used. For example, in 2009, Delta and Northwest airlines negotiated a merger. But they needed the support of the Air Line Pilots Association, which represented the pilots of both airlines and had successfully derailed a hostile takeover of Delta by US Airways. The merger would make the new airline the largest in the world. The task for the union leaders of the two airlines was to choose a method of merging the seniority lists that would satisfy their members. The merged seniority list is critical because it determines job losses, pay, work schedules, and the size of aircraft the pilots fly. Thus, it was important to both the unions and the airlines to find a fair method of merging the two seniority lists.[35]

Over the years mergers have utilized at least five common methods of combining the seniority lists of merged employees. One of the most commonly used methods is the **Surviving group principle**, in which seniority lists are merged by adding the names of the employees of the acquired company to the bottom of the acquiring company. Thus, all the employees of the acquiring company receive greater seniority consideration than any employee of the acquired company.

SURVIVING GROUP PRINCIPLE

Seniority lists are merged by adding the names of the employees of the acquired company to the bottom of the acquiring company.

TABLE 9-2 Factors Commonly Utilized to Determine Employee Ability to Perform

1.	Tests	Include written, oral, behavioral (work samples), physical ability, assessment center, decision making.
2.	Experience	Direct experience on the job or experience with similar individual tasks or job functions.
3.	Trial period	Temporary period in which applicant is provided opportunity so he/she can perform the job satisfactorily.
4.	Supervisor opinion	Includes ratings of quality of work, job knowledge, cooperation, initiative, and ability to follow orders.
5.	Education	Job-related training, technical training, and formal education.
6.	Production record	As a measure of ability and motivation, may be given high priority or even used as sole criteria.
7.	Attendance record	Past poor attendance may be reason for an employee being passed over.
8.	Discipline record	Past record of disciplinary actions may be considered.
9.	Physical ability	Job-related physical fitness test results may be considered if it may limit employee's ability to perform the job.
10.	Attitude	Attitude as exhibited by behaviors such as cooperation with others, willingness to perform new tasks, customer relations.

Source: Adapted from Frank Elkouri and Edna Elkouri, *How Arbitration Works*, 6th ed. (Washington, DC: Bureau of National Affairs, 2003), pp. 883–921.

LENGTH OF SERVICE PRINCIPLE

Two seniority lists are combined and length of service is considered regardless of with which company the employees formerly worked.

FOLLOW THE WORK PRINCIPLE

Seniority lists maintain previously earned seniority on separate seniority lists when their work with the merged company can be separately identified.

ABSOLUTE RANK PRINCIPLE

Seniority list maintains employees' ranking position from prior seniority list on merged list.

RATIO-RANK PRINCIPLE

Seniority lists combined by establishing a ratio based on the total number of employees in the two groups to be merged.

Another method, the **length of service principle**, is used when an employee's length of service is considered, regardless of which company he or she worked for before the merger; therefore, the two seniority lists are combined, with no employee losing any previously earned seniority. With the **follow the work principle**, employees are allowed to continue previously earned seniority on separate seniority lists when their work with the merged company can be separately identified. The **absolute rank principle** gives employees rank positions on the merging seniority lists equal to their rank position on the prior seniority lists. Therefore, two employees are ranked first, followed by two ranked second, followed by two ranked third, and so on.

The **ratio-rank principle** combines seniority lists by establishing a ratio based on the total number of employees in the two groups to be merged. If group A has 150 employees and group B has 50 employees, the ratio is 3:1, and of the first four places on the new seniority lists, the three ranked highest in group A are given positions 1, 2, and 3, and the highest ranked position in group B are given rank 4.[36]

Any one principle, especially length of service, may be selected, or a combination of methods may be used to combine seniority lists of merged units or companies, with weight given to the different principles. For example, in a case involving the merging two airline pilot seniority lists, one-third weight was given to the ratio-rank principle and two-thirds to the length of service principle.[37]

Mergers can also cause problems when one employer has a bargaining unit for a certain job classification, and the other employer is nonunion. For example, when Delta Airlines and northwest Airlines merged in 2009 the 14,000 flight attendants at Delta were not unionized, but the 7,000 flight attendants at Northwestern belonged to the Association of Flight Attendants union. The merger agreement recognized and maintained the bargaining unit and the existing agreement, but also imposed Delta policies after the merger. This led to a grievance filed by the union over the dress policies imposed by Delta over the former Northwest flight attendants. The grievance concerned the lack of availability of dress sizes over 18, and the requirement that orthopedic shoes must be worn with slacks. The union asked that the dress size maximum be increased to 28. Management claimed safety concerns were the reason for the 18 maximum. Delta denied the grievance and maintained policies that were in place before the merger.[38]

Subcontracting, Outsourcing, and Relocating

Although few problems arise when there are specific contract restrictions on management's rights to subcontract, management's insistence on freedom in this area often leads to grievances. A grievance over management's right to subcontract (or **outsource**) work during the agreement often results in arbitration. In the past, many arbitrators held that management has the right to subcontract work through independent contractors; however, in recent years, arbitrators have somewhat restricted this practice.

What is subcontracting? It has been termed the "twilight zone" of management rights in collective bargaining, and both labor and management consider it a headache. Basically, **subcontracting** and **outsourcing** may be defined as arranging to make goods or perform services with another firm that could be accomplished by the bargaining unit employees within the employer's current facilities.[39] The decision was made, however, in a 1964 Supreme Court ruling, *Fibreboard Paper Products Corp. v. NLRB,* that subcontracting is a mandatory subject for collective bargaining.[40]

SUBCONTRACTING/ OUTSOURCING

The arrangement by an employer to have another firm make goods or perform work that could be accomplished by the employer's own bargaining unit employees, usually because the subcontracted work can be done more efficiently or for less cost.

Contract provisions limiting subcontracting may carry over to new employers, as when the Communication Workers of America won a $6 million settlement from AT&T over subcontracting. The 130 workers who won reinstatement of their jobs claimed that AT&T had violated the subcontracting clause contained in their agreement with Pennsylvania Bell. The breakup of the Bell system shifted the workers to AT&T, where they were laid off, and their work, primarily wiring and installation of telephones, was contracted out. The union won reinstatement of their jobs and back pay for the 130 workers and, in addition, it won back pay for another 900 workers and resolved more than 100 pending arbitration cases.[41]

An example of a contract clause limiting the ability of management to subcontract is provided in Figure 9-1. This example is typical in that it allows management to subcontract work but only for less than 500 hours—probably for seasonal rush periods, and not if the subcontracting would cause layoffs.

Outsourcing as a threat to job security is a threat to many unions today and causes them to negotiate a **scope clause** in new contracts. A scope clause like the one negotiated by the International Association of Machinists and Aerospace Workers (IAMAW) with Comair in their 2005–2009 agreement prohibits the company from outsourcing mechanical work while any member of the union is on furlough. The IAMAW had witnessed the Delta Air Lines layoff of 2,000 nonunion mechanics and the shift of work to outside companies only a month earlier.[42] Thus the machinists union feared their furloughed employees would be replaced by laid-off nonunion Delta mechanics.

SCOPE CLAUSE

Provision that prohibits outsourcing bargaining unit work while any union member is in layoff status.

Management's right to subcontract is usually judged by arbitrators against the recognition of the bargaining unit, seniority, wages, and other clauses within the agreement. Standards of

Article V

Section 19.

(a) The Company agrees to notify the Business Manager of the Union, on a quarterly basis, of the hiring of any outside contractors to do planned work normally done by the regular employees covered by this Agreement that may exceed 500 hours of time. It is the Company's intention that any contractors performing work on behalf of the Company do so safely and competently.

(b) In instances where it is necessary to contract for equipment, during periods of emergency, such equipment will be manned by regular Company employees if and when they are available and qualified to operate such equipment.

(c) It is the sense of this provision that the Company will not contract any work which is ordinarily done by its regular employees, if as a result thereof, it would become necessary to lay off any such employees.

FIGURE 9-1 Subcontracting Provision. *Source:* Agreement between Duke Energy Ohio, Inc. and Local Union 1347 International Brotherhood of Electrical Workers, AFL-CIO, 2006–2009. Used by permission.

The Duke Energy Company's CBA with IBEW only allows the company to bring in outside contractors during emergencies, such as storm power outages, and for fewer than 500 hours. *Source:* Chuck Burton/AP Images.

reasonableness and good faith are applied in determining whether subcontracting has violated clauses in the contract. In general, management's right to subcontract is recognized; provided it is exercised in good faith and no specific contract restriction exists. Arbitrators often recognize that signing a contract does not establish an agreement that all the jobs will continue to be performed by members of the bargaining unit unless this condition is specified within the contract. However, the company cannot undermine the unit by subcontracting for the sole purpose of getting rid of work done by union employees in favor of nonunion employees who are paid lower wages.

An issue intertwined with subcontracting is management's decision to relocate work previously done at one location by union workers to another location that is generally nonunion. A Supreme Court decision in 1981, *First National Maintenance Corporation v. NLRB*, said that a management decision to eliminate work previously done by union workers was not a mandatory bargaining issue if the decision to eliminate the work was for economic reasons.[43] Case 9-2 is a typical grievance about subcontracting.

CASE 9-2

Subcontracting

Until January 1982, the company was in the business of installing and servicing equipment on trucks and selling parts. Since the 1950s, the employees had been classified as mechanic welders, painters, and utility men and were covered by collective bargaining agreements. It is undisputed that the company had been losing money since 1979 and that by 1981 three of the four remaining unit employees were on layoff status.

In 1981, the company was approached by two individuals with an offer to take over the company's mounting and service work under a subcontract. An agreement was worked out, and the company hired the two parties as independent contractors for providing mounting and service work. The company was to lease its facilities and equipment to them. The subcontractor was to pay a percentage of the company's rent and utility bills and to provide various kinds of liability and other insurance. The company reserved the right to hire other subcontractors but reserved no right to exercise control over the employees of the subcontractor. The company notified its employees and the union of the subcontract agreement, citing the dire economic conditions that required the subcontract. The union grieved the layoff of employees as a violation of the contract, protesting that outside employees were performing work normally done by members of the bargaining unit. While the grievance was in progress, the union conducted an audit of the company's books and confirmed that the company was in a poor financial condition. The union offered to consider wage concessions to get the laid-off employees back to work, but the company declined because it deemed the concessions insufficient to address the cash flow problems. The company, citing the reversal by the National Labor Relations Board (NLRB) of the *Milwaukee Spring* decision, stated that before it can be found a company has violated the act by subcontracting during the term of the contract, a specific term contained in the contract must be identified that prohibits such subcontracting. In addition, under the *Otis Elevator Company* case, a management decision to subcontract was not subject to mandatory bargaining because the essence of the decision turned on a change in the nature or direction of the business and not on labor costs.

The company stated that its decision to contract out service work turned not on labor cost but on a significant change in the nature and direction of the business; therefore, the company had no duty to bargain. The company's decision to subcontract was to reduce its overhead cost across the board so it could remain in business. To that end, the subcontractor agreed to pay a specified percentage of the rent paid by the company for use of the premises, plus a monthly fee for the rental of the equipment. In addition, the subcontractor agreed to pay a specified percentage of utility bills, to produce liability insurance, and to maintain workers' compensation and other insurance. The company had made a decision to abandon its service and mounting operations. Therefore, on the basis of *Otis Elevator*, the company had no duty to bargain regarding its subcontracting decision.

Decision

Although the NLRB agreed that the company did not have to bargain its decision to subcontract, it found that the company unlawfully failed to bargain with the union about the effects of the subcontracting decision on union employees. The NLRB found that the company's notice to the union that the subcontract had been entered into, and its failure to meet with the union and laid-off employees for two months after the subcontract, was not sufficient notice and a meaningful opportunity to bargain with the union about the effect of subcontracting on unit employees. The employees were awarded back pay, as is the customary remedy in such cases.

Source: Adapted from *Gar Wood Detroit Truck Equipment,* 118 LRRM (1985).

The NLRB decided in *Milwaukee Spring II*[44] and in *Otis Elevator II*[45] that the decision to relocate work for economic reasons was akin to eliminating work for economic reasons and, therefore, was not a mandatory bargaining subject. Nonetheless, although a decision to relocate either all or part of the business for economic reasons is not a mandatory subject of bargaining, a company must bargain over the *effects* of such a decision.[46]

In *Dubuque Packing Co. v. NLRB*, however, the NLRB modified its position. Noting that a decision to relocate, subcontract, or outsource work rather than to eliminate work was not a change in the scope of the enterprise itself, just a decision to do the same work with other workers, the board found that it was a mandatory bargaining subject.[47] Generally, unless an agreement contains specific language barring subcontracting, a union has difficulty stopping it. They are generally not successful in winning arbitration cases based on a mere implication that it harms the bargaining unit. This view on subcontracting changed in recent years; once consistently limited by arbitrators, now subcontracting is a common practice.[48]

Tips from the Experts

Union

What are some practical protections against employers' relocating, outsourcing, or subcontracting?

1. Good contract language is the best protection against these employer actions. Good language would ensure no loss of jobs as the result of any of these actions during the life of the contract.
2. Include processes for meaningful union input into the debate prior to these decisions being made and into plans to ensure no adverse effects on present employees from such decisions if they are made.
3. Address plans for retraining and redeployment of existing staff if necessary, outplacement services, severance packages, reemployment rights, insurance and pension protections, and reasonable notice of any adverse action.

Management

What are the best ways an employer can outsource, relocate, or subcontract without violating the law or a collective bargaining agreement?

1. Retain specific management rights in each area in the collective bargaining agreement with no restrictions or limitations.
2. Develop a credible business plan for when outsourcing, relocating, or subcontracting is necessary, in conjunction with budgeting, marketing, production, sales organizations, and so on, with buy-in from all who assist in its development, which is defensible to the employees, the media, the public, and whatever board, arbitrator, or judge will ultimately hear the issue.
3. Give timely and appropriate notice to union leadership and then to employees as well.

EMPLOYEE TEAMS

A large portion of the work within most organizations occurs within groups. Most jobs do not exist in isolation but instead involve both formal work groups (departments, sections, and etc.) and informal groups of employees whose strong friendships affect their working relationships. The effectiveness of these **employee teams** can be critical to the success of the entire organization.

EMPLOYEE TEAMS

Employee involvement that creates an environment in which people have an impact on decisions and actions that affect their workplace, not the terms and conditions of their employment. Characterized by workplace decision making by truly empowered, intact employee teams for whom managers provide consultation and assistance in how the work is to be done.

A major reason for the frequent use of groups is synergy, which occurs when the production of the whole (group) is greater than the sum of the parts (individuals). When people work together in a group, they exchange ideas, learn from each other, and motivate each other to achieve more than they typically achieve when working in isolation. The heart of this interaction is the social mingling of the group. Employees build strong friendships with each other; in fact, often their best friends are their coworkers. Thus, when a group develops a successful working interaction, synergy occurs, and more can be achieved as a group than the members could achieve working individually. This enhanced productivity occurs in three primary areas:[49]

1. ***Decision making.*** Without a designated leader who is looked to for most decisions, groups often make better decisions than the member would if acting alone.
2. ***Problem solving.*** Through the exchange of ideas and sharing of information, groups usually solve common problems better than individuals who are limited to their own knowledge and experience.
3. ***Creativity.*** Groups are more willing to make innovative or creative changes in their tasks because they have the support of members.

In many organizations, formal groups of employees responsible for an identifiable work process, a specific project, or solving a problem are called employee teams or committees. These groups were once called the "productivity breakthrough of the 1990s," even though the first ones—such as those at General Foods in Topeka, Kansas—had been in existence for more than 20 years.[50] A 2004 study on employee teams noted that surveys of *Fortune* 1,000 companies indicate at least 68–70 percent use employee teams. Major users include Ford, Procter & Gamble, Federal Express, Levi Strauss, and Westinghouse. Most companies have reported that teams increased productivity, quality of products, and innovation. However, others have reported no gains in these areas and even negative outcomes from changing to teams. The research study found that the level of autonomy provided to a team and the structural context—work rules, policies, and procedures—might be significant predictors of the success of teams within an organization.[51] We refer to all these groups as teams.

Union Response to Employee Teams

Union leaders and members have varied greatly in their responses to the creation of self-directed employee teams. At a Ford Motor Company assembly plant, the creation of self-directed teams has made the facility "a much better place to work," according to J. R. "Buddy" Hoskinson, union cochairman of the UAW–Ford Education Development and Training Programs. "In the old days we punched a time card and had no say in what was going on. . . . We'd just do what we had to get by." But today Hoskinson credits the self-directed teams, which have no direct supervision and devise their own work schedules, with creating a "new sense of pride. . . . We know we're doing the best we can do."

In general, the team concept and similar workplace programs designed to increase employee involvement, such as "high performance work systems," are designed to increase productivity and employer loyalty by giving workers greater input into daily decision making. Some union critics of the team concept, however, believe that it undermines union legitimacy, workers' belief that the union gives them solidarity through a sense of community, and their belief that the union is effective in protecting their economic interests. This concern is critical to unions because to a large extent employees join and remain in unions because they view them as a legitimate means of protecting their economic interests and providing a social community.

A unique 2007 case study of UAW team members at the GM Shreveport, Louisiana, truck assembly plant provided insight into the issue of whether or not employees' participation in teams affects their perception of their union. The Shreveport plant is unique because it was unionized without a union election. Some employees at the start were UAW employees transferred from other plants; others were "locals" who were hired into the team concept from the start. Based on survey responses as well as in-depth interviews, the study found that workers' attitudes toward the team concept were greatly affected by whether or not they entered the plant under the team concept, in which case they held more positive views, or if they were transferred from a nonteam plant, in which case they held more negative views. And those who had entered under the team concept, and only worked under the team concept, did indicate weaker support of the union than those who had transferred from a traditional unionized plant. In addition, the study found that working under the team concept weakened employee support for the union, even among union members transferred in years ago from traditional, unionized plants. A key issue for those workers unhappy with the team concept was that it weakened seniority, a historical basis of union solidarity. Thus, the study confirms union fears that members working under a team system may have weaker perceptions of their union.[52]

The results from organizations that have adopted employee teams or high performance work practices (HPWPs) over the past 20 years have been mixed. Although HPWPs in some cases have produced increased organizational performance, and increased worker job satisfaction from more flexible job design teamwork and greater decision making, others have not produced the expected outcomes. In these cases, increased earnings and productivity did not materialize (with many possible causes), and workers' concerns about job security and wages/benefits were high, as reported at the GM-Shreveport plant. In cases in which unions and their members experienced a "full" partnership with management, the outcomes were more likely to be positive than when unions adopted a "watchdog" or limited cooperation approach. A critical factor that may affect the outcomes from a union–management cooperative teamwork or HPWP approach is the level of external market pressures. If external competition, domestic or foreign, is high, then often management cannot deliver the higher economic benefits and job security expected by union members, and instead they must continually press for reduced costs and greater productivity. Unions, therefore, may find that in the face of a potential plant closing or layoffs, they are "coerced to cooperate."[53] This climate can produce the classic labor–management conflict: management's need for higher profits and reduced costs versus the union's goal of maintaining job security and negotiating greater economic benefits for its members.

In 1998, the Teamsters union won a long-sought agreement from United Parcel Service to end "Team Concept" programs. The Teamsters believed the "real purpose [of the teams]" appeared to restrict workers' rights under collective bargaining.[54] The National Labor Relations Board and the courts have generally agreed with critics who have considered employee involvement programs and self-directed work teams as potentially unlawful under Section 8(a)(2) of the Wagner Act. In general, for a violation to occur it must be shown that (1) the entity created by the program is a "labor organization" and (2) the employer dominates or interferes with the formation or administration of that labor organization or contributes support to it. A committee or group is generally considered a "labor organization" if employees participate in it and at least one purpose is to "deal with" the employer on issues of grievances, labor disputes, wages, work rules, or hours of employment. The "dealing" must involve give and take—as in collective bargaining. If the employer simply says yes or no to employee proposals (often the case with committee quality circles) or if an employee group can decide such issues by itself (often the case with self-directed teams), then the element of dealing is missing, and the group is probably not a labor organization.

With regard to the second criterion for violation—employer domination or interference—Section 8(c) of the Wagner Act allows an employer to voice an opinion on labor–management issues but not to create or initiate a labor organization. Thus, an employer can suggest the idea of committees or work teams, but employees must be free to adopt or reject the concept (as did the Union Pacific workers). In cases involving employers' suggesting the creation of employee teams, motive may be considered a factor. Although Section 8(a)(2) of the Wagner Act does not require the presence of an antiunion motive; it condemns any interference or domination.[55] Some "employee–management" teams have been in existence for years and avoid any criticism. How? See Profile 9-2.

The National Labor Relations Board (NLRB) in two historic decisions has limited the creation of employee committees or teams by its strict interpretation of the NLRA. Employee teams having the authority to make decisions and act without obtaining employer approval are not illegal labor organizations.[56] If joint labor–management teams or committees are created to

Profile 9-2

Employee Teams at Kaiser Permanente

A provision in the national collective bargaining agreement between Kaiser Permanente and the Coalition of Kaiser Permanente Unions provides for the establishment of 1,793 teams of workers across the country. The teams include about 55,516 employees in unit-based teams. John August, the union's executive director, said the teams perform a "derivative of collective bargaining" by developing lower cost programs that provide better patient care. Examples of how the teams have worked successfully include the following:

- ***Healthy bones program.*** A team developed a method of identifying patients of high risk of broken bones and treated them before they suffered a fracture. The program lowered the number of broken bones by 37 percent and saved over $39 million in the first year.
- ***High blood pressure.*** A Denver team composed of a nurse, doctor, pharmacist, and medical assistant developed a new method of using electronic records to identify at-risk patients and allowed them to be seen without appointment. After only two years the program experienced a control rate of 70 percent (patients with high blood pressure in check), saved 11 lives, and over $512,000.
- ***Congestive heart failure.*** A team in Hawaii developed a new approach to treating patients with diabetes and congestive heart failure that led to a 70 percent reduction in such admissions.

Source: Adapted from "Integrated Care Used by Kaiser, Unions Touted as Reform Model," BNA Reports, *2010 Source Book on Collective Bargaining* (Washington, DC: Bureau of National Affairs, 2010), p. 119.

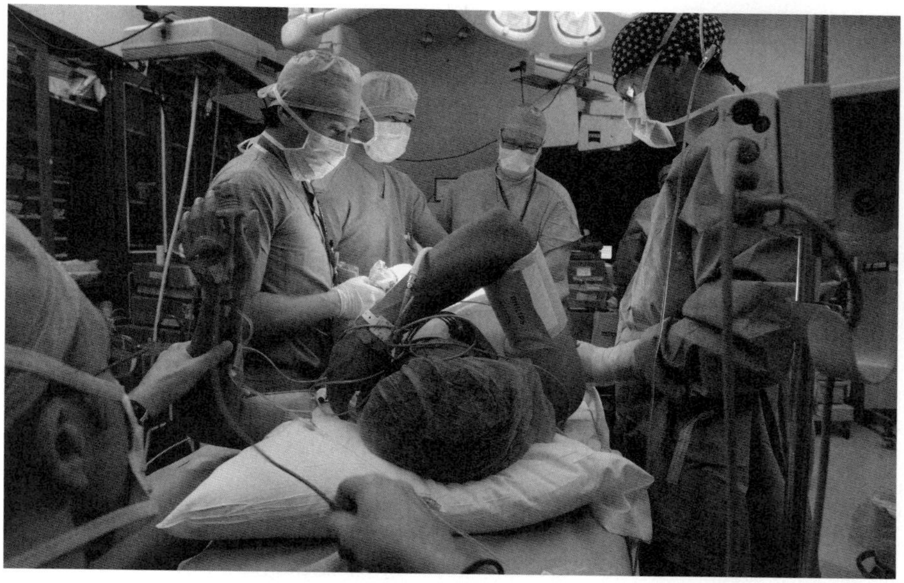

The CBA between Kaiser Permanente, the health care provider, and its unions provides for 1,793 employee teams with over 55,000 workers. The teams are formed to develop methods of better patient care and cost reductions. *Source:* © Michael Macor/San Francisco Chronicle/ Corbis.

consider employment issues and a union represents the employees, the union must be involved in the creation of the groups. If such groups are created, they should be voluntary and contain more union members than management. In addition, the board has ruled that an employee committee with delegated managerial authority does not take on the union's role to "deal with" management because they are management.

SUCCESSORSHIP

If there is a change in either a collective bargaining representative or an employer, parties to an unexpired collective bargaining agreement may not be certain of their status. This situation may exist when the union becomes decertified, because of a schism, merger, or change in union affiliation, or if the union simply becomes defunct and is replaced. Changes in management can occur when the sale of all or part of a business occurs because of a merger or corporation consolidation or if the corporation is reorganized. The courts refer to these situations as **successorship**.

SUCCESSORSHIP

The status of the collective bargaining relationship between an employer and the union when a change in the ownership of the organization or a change in a union occurs.

The law on successorship provides that if there is a genuine change in the collective bargaining representative, the existing collective bargaining contract, even if unexpired, is not binding on the successor representative. If a genuine change of employer exists but the employing industry remains substantially the same, the successor employer is required to recognize the existing collective bargaining unit and its representative but is not bound by the agreement.

The Supreme Court for the first time offered a test for determining the circumstances under which the **successorship doctrine** applies in *Fall River Dyeing v. National Labor Relations Board.*[57] A new company, Fall River Dyeing, acquired the plant, equipment, and remaining inventory of a textile dyeing and finishing plant (Sterlingware Corporation). The union that had represented the production employees of Sterlingware sought and was refused recognition by Fall River Dyeing. The union filed an unfair labor practice charge, and the NLRB upheld its claim. The Supreme Court upheld the NLRB decision and imposed a bargaining duty on Fall River Dyeing under the successorship doctrine. The Court in its decision suggested three factors that must be present for the successorship doctrine to apply to the purchaser of a business employing union members:[58]

1. ***Substantial continuity.*** The successor substantially continues the business operations of the predecessor. Factors considered include the purchase of real property, equipment, and

Employees may lose their negotiated wages, benefits, and working conditions when a change in ownership occurs, such as when British Petroleum (BP) replaced Texaco. *Source:* Paul Sancya/AP Images.

inventory; employing workers on essentially the same jobs; employing the same supervisors; and continuing the predecessor's product line. In general, not all factors must be present for substantial continuity.

2. ***Appropriate bargaining unit.*** The bargaining unit(s) of employees must remain appropriate after the change of employers. Job duties and operational structure are critical in this determination. Significant change in the nature of jobs performed or in the means of operation may mean the unit is no longer appropriate.
3. ***Predecessor's workers.*** The new employer hires a majority of its employees from the predecessor.

Successor Employer Rights

The new employer has several important rights even as a successor employer, including (1) the right to hire its own workers (although it may not discriminate against workers of the predecessor because of union status), (2) the right to disregard the predecessor's collective bargaining agreement, and (3) the right to set the initial terms of employment, such as wages, benefits, and working conditions, without consulting the union.[59] The NLRB qualified prior rulings concerning a successor employer's refusal to rehire the predecessor's employees because of their union status in *Planned Building Services.* The board held that if a successor employer could show it would not have hired the employees even in the absence of its acknowledged union animus, it would not be guilty of an unfair labor practice.[60]

In a 2009 decision, a U.S. Court of Appeals sought to clarify what is sometimes called the "perfectly clear" successor concept. The court stated if and only if a new employer has made it "perfectly clear" to the predecessor's employees that their employment status would remain unchanged if they accepted employment with the new employer, then the successor is not entitled to change terms of employment within a CBA without bargaining with the union. This is because, noted the court, a successor employer ordinarily may set terms for hiring the predecessor's employees. The U.S. Supreme Court in a precedent case, *Burns*, had ruled that a successor employer, except in the rare case (e.g., the "perfectly clear" successor), is not bound by the provisions of a CBA negotiated by the predecessor employer. In the 2009 case, which involved a Long Beach California nursing home, the Appeals Court noted that the new employer had notified the employees that if rehired, their status would be "at will" and that their wages, benefits, policies, and employment conditions were subject to change under new terms of employment. In addition they were informed of the elimination of the grievance/arbitration process. Thus the judge found "no employee could have failed to understand that significant changes were underfoot," and the new employer was not a "perfectly clear" successor and was lawfully able to set new working conditions under the successorship doctrine.[61]

A successor employer also may be obligated to remedy an unfair labor practice committed by its predecessor. If it is a true successor, and if it had notice of the unfair labor charge, the NLRB may require the new owner to remedy the unfair labor practice by, for example, reinstating an employee and providing back pay.[62]

A successor employer may be obligated to arbitrate the grievances filed under the predecessor's collective bargaining agreement. So, although a successor employer is not bound by the prior employer's collective bargaining agreement, it is bound to arbitrate violations. If the collective bargaining agreement contained a successor clause that stated the predecessor employer agreed to "require" a purchaser of the company to honor the collective bargaining agreement and did not do so, a union may be able to force the successor employer to honor that agreement through arbitration.[63]

The NLRB further delineated the successorship doctrine in the *Canteen Company* case. In this case, the NLRB found that the employer was obligated to bargain with the union about terms of employment. The employer had acquired a unionized plant from another company. The employer then interviewed and offered jobs to some employees and discussed possible new provisions with the union. The NLRB found that by making job offers to some employees and discussing the compensation package with the union, the employer had "demonstrated a clear intention" to hire a majority of its new workforce from among the workforce of the former employer; thus, it had violated the National Labor Relations Act by not bargaining with the union.[64]

BANKRUPTCY. Cases that involve the bankruptcy of an employer organization are unique legal situations because the NLRA conflicts with Chapter 11 of the U.S. federal bankruptcy code. The major difference between the two is the NLRA does not allow for a breach of an existing CBA due to financial hardship, while Chapter 11 does allow for a bankruptcy judge to reject an existing CBA. Bankruptcy courts have exclusive jurisdiction over a reorganization proceeding, and they have granted petitions by employers to reject an existing CBA about 68 percent of the time. Furthermore, judges assume once a CBA expires, it is over and done with and there is no obligation to maintain current wages, benefits, or other contract provisions. Thus the use of federal bankruptcy courts to terminate existing agreements has become a more realistic alternative to employers in recent years, especially during hard financial times.[65]

EMPLOYEE ALCOHOL AND DRUG TESTING

The use of alcohol and drug testing of job applicants and employees has become a complicated and critically important job security issue. Management often claims that employee use of alcohol and illegal drugs is a problem that must be contained.

President Ronald Reagan launched a federal government "drug-free workplace" campaign that started the testing of job applicants and employees. By 2003, it was estimated that about 25 million people in the United States were tested annually, and millions more were subject to a possible test because of an accident or other cause. Drug test screens typically detect opiates, cocaine, barbiturates, methamphetamine, and marijuana. According to the American Management Association, approximately 61 percent of all employers screen job applicants, and 50 percent test employees. According to the American Council for Drug Education, substance abusers, compared with nonabusers, are ten times more likely to miss work, 3.6 times more likely to be involved in an on-the-job accident, five times as likely to file a workers' compensation claim, have three times the health care costs, and have 33 percent lower productivity.[66] Illegal drug use continues to be a major workplace problem, despite greater testing by employers and unions.

The U.S. Department of Labor estimates that substance abuse costs American businesses over $100 billion per year or about $740 per employee through higher absenteeism (30 days per year average), higher rate of on-the-job accidents, lower productivity, greater criminal behavior, and greater health care costs. The industry with the highest rate of substance abuse is the construction industry. A 2006 report of construction companies found that 85 percent had drug-testing programs. Companies with testing programs reported reductions in drug-related accidents of between 10 and 60 percent. One company reported a reduction in insurance premiums from $1.2 million annually to $206,000.[67]

In two landmark decisions, the NLRB ruled that the alcohol and drug testing of current employees is a mandatory subject of bargaining; thus, any such program must be negotiated with the union.[68] The NLRB reasoned that the test results could affect a worker's job security and therefore constituted a condition of employment; thus, the testing requires bargaining. Management may generally require any applicant to submit to a drug-screening test, unless limited by a state law. Employers, in a statement of policy, may express their desire to hire only qualified applicants, and because the use of drugs may adversely affect job performance, they can choose to hire only applicants who pass a screening test. Today many unions have instituted drug testing for their officers and personnel as well as apprenticeship program applicants. For example, in 2005, the International Brotherhood of Electrical Workers instituted a drug-testing program for its own personnel and negotiated an agreement with the National Electrical Contractors' Association that required local unions to institute programs.[69]

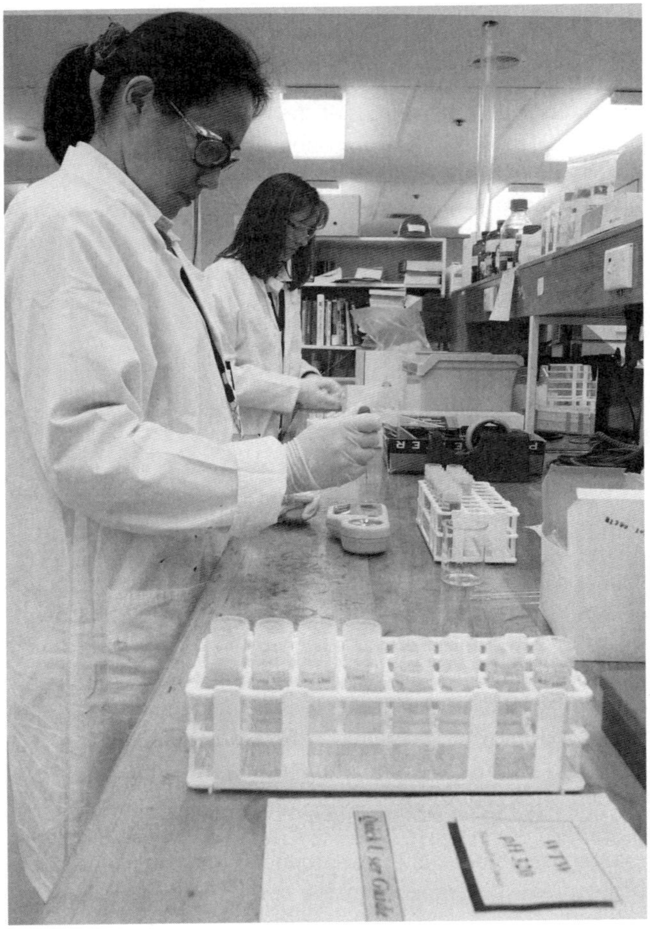

Worker drug-testing programs have become common in contracts in recent years. The NLRB ruled that employee drug testing is a mandatory bargaining subject. However, negotiation issues such as employee privacy, test validity, and when drug testing should occur make it a complicated issue. *Source:* Rick Rycroft/AP Images.

Management's desire to screen all job candidates may increase because of several factors: (1) the increased use of drugs within all segments of society, (2) the reluctance of previous employers to report suspected or known drug usage of former employees for fear of litigation, and (3) the employer's liability for the negligent hiring of employees.

Six common types of drug testing are used by employers:[70]

1. Preemployment testing
2. Reasonable suspicion testing
3. Routine fitness-for-duty testing
4. Post-accident testing
5. Random testing
6. Follow-up to rehabilitation (after returning to work from drug/alcohol treatment) testing

In general, drug testing follows these steps:

1. The employee or potential employee receives a letter from his employer indicating the time, date, and location of the test and a description of what will happen if the employee tests positive or refuses to participate.
2. On the day of the test, the employee provides a urine and/or hair sample either at the workplace or at a clinic.
3. The sample is collected and sent to a certified testing laboratory. During the collection and testing processes, a "Chain of Custody" form is used to ensure no tampering of the samples.
4. The test results are reported to a Medical Review Officer (MRO). The MRO is a licensed physician who has knowledge of substance abuse disorders and has received the appropriate medical training to interpret and evaluate an individual's positive test result as it relates to the employee's medical history and/or any other biomedical information.
5. If the result is positive, a confirmation test is performed. All samples confirmed as positive are referred to an MRO for interpretation.
6. Results are reported to the employer.

CASE 9-3

Drug Testing

The company and union are parties to a collective bargaining agreement (CBA) with arbitration provisions. The CBA specifies that, in arbitration, in order to discharge an employee, the company must prove it has "just cause." Otherwise, the arbitrator will order the employee reinstated. The arbitrator's decision is final.

Smith worked for the company as a member of a road crew, a job that required him to drive heavy truck-like vehicles on public highways. As a truck driver, Smith was subject to Department of Transportation (DOT) regulations requiring random drug testing of workers engaged in "safety-sensitive" tasks. Smith tested positive for marijuana. The company sought to discharge him. The union went to arbitration, and the arbitrator concluded that Smith's positive drug test did not amount to just cause for discharge. Instead, the arbitrator ordered Smith's reinstatement with conditions. Smith had to accept a suspension of 30 days without pay, participate in a substance abuse program, and undergo drug tests at the discretion of company for the next five years. Smith passed four random drug tests.

But in July 1997, he again tested positive for marijuana. The company again sought to discharge Smith. The union again went to arbitration, and the arbitrator again concluded that Smith's use of marijuana did not amount to just cause for discharge in light of two mitigating circumstances. Smith had been a good employee for 17 years and had made a credible appeal

(continued)

concerning a personal/family problem that caused this current relapse into drug use. The arbitrator ordered Smith's reinstatement with new conditions. Smith had to accept a new suspension without pay, this time for slightly more than three months; reimburse the company and the union for the costs of both arbitration proceedings; continue to participate in a substance abuse program; continue to undergo random drug testing; and provide the company with a signed, undated letter of resignation to take effect if Smith tested positive for drugs within the next five years.

The company brought suit in federal court seeking to have the arbitrator's award vacated, arguing that the award contravened a public policy against the operation of dangerous machinery by workers who test positive for drugs. The district court, although recognizing a strong regulation-based public policy against drug use by workers who perform safety-sensitive functions, held that Smith's conditional reinstatement did not violate that policy. The Court of Appeals for the Fourth Circuit also affirmed the arbitration award, and the company appealed to the Supreme Court.

The Supreme Court considered the company's claims that considerations of public policy make the arbitration award unenforceable. In considering this claim, however, the Court held that the CBA itself called for Smith's reinstatement because both employer and union have granted to the arbitrator the authority to interpret the meaning of the contract's language. Therefore, the arbitrator's award must be treated as if it represented an agreement between the company and the union. The Court then had only to decide whether a contractual requirement to reinstate the employee is so contrary to public policy that it would fall within the legal exception that makes a CBA unenforceable.

The question before the Court, then, was not whether Smith's drug use itself violates public policy but whether the agreement to reinstate him does so. To put the question more specifically, does a contractual agreement to reinstate Smith with specified conditions run contrary to an explicit, well-defined, dominant public policy?

In the company's view, federal laws regarding drug use by workers in the transportation field embody a strong public policy against drug use by transportation workers in safety-sensitive positions and in favor of random drug testing to detect that use. The company argued that reinstatement of a driver who has twice failed random drug tests would undermine that policy—to the point where a judge must set aside an employer–union agreement requiring reinstatement.

In the union's view, these same federal laws promote rehabilitation as a critical component of any testing program, stating that rehabilitation "should be made available to individuals, as appropriate." The DOT regulations specifically state that a driver who has tested positive for drugs cannot return to a safety-sensitive position until (1) the driver has been evaluated by a "substance abuse professional" to determine if treatment is needed, (2) the substance abuse professional has certified that the driver has followed a rehabilitation program, and (3) the driver has passed a return-to-duty drug test. In addition, the driver must be subject to at least six random drug tests during the first year after returning to the job. Neither the act nor the regulations forbids an employer to reinstate in a safety-sensitive position an employee who fails a random drug test once or twice.

Decision

The Court noted that the law on drug testing embodied several relevant policies. As the company pointed out, these include policies against drug use by employees in safety-sensitive transportation positions and in favor of drug testing such employees; and as the union noted they also include a policy favoring rehabilitation of employees who use drugs. But these relevant statutory and regulatory provisions must be weighed against the labor law policy that favors arbitration.

The award violated no specific provision of any law or regulation. It was consistent with DOT rules requiring completion of substance abuse treatment before returning to work. It does not preclude the company from assigning Smith to a non-safety-sensitive position until Smith completes the prescribed treatment program. The award is also consistent with the act's rehabilitative concerns because it requires substance abuse treatment and testing before Smith can return to work.

The Court noted that reasonable people could differ as to whether reinstatement or discharge is the more appropriate remedy in this case. But as both the employer and the union have agreed to entrust this remedial decision to an arbitrator, the Court could find no law or legal precedent of an explicit, well-defined, dominant public policy to which the arbitrator's decision runs contrary. Therefore, the Court affirmed the lower-court decisions in upholding the arbitrator's decision.

Source: Adapted from *Company Associated Coal v. United Mine Workers,* 165 LRRM 2865 (2000).

Employee Attitudes toward Drug Testing

Unions' institutional response to drug-testing programs originally focused on the struggle over bargaining duties; that is, could an employer institute a drug-testing program unilaterally? After the NLRB ruled that such policies have to be negotiated, unions were faced with the responsibility of representing their members' views on drug testing at the bargaining table. In the atmosphere created by the federal government's "War on Drugs," less than a strong antidrug attitude was considered unpatriotic. Knowing that, unions focused no longer on *whether* drug testing would be done but on *how* it would be done.

Of the three policies, the use of random testing has raised the strongest criticisms by unions, largely on the basis of an employee's right to privacy. However, as discussed in a later section, because of the random testing policies in the public sector and in industries regulated by the federal government, such as in the defense and transportation industries, the legal barriers to random testing have largely been removed.

Still, private sector unions may resist random testing programs and insist on a probable-cause or an accident-related program. Drug testing only when there is "probable cause" is a policy that will often be more readily acceptable by employees. Probable-cause testing has also received support from the courts and from arbitrators when the test has been given because of a reasonable suspicion of drug use. A supervisor's reasonable suspicion based on absenteeism, erratic behavior, or poor work performance can generally be accepted as a reason to test.

A major accident involving employees can be considered an immediate probable-cause situation and can thus invoke required testing of all employees involved. The Supreme Court in the *Skinner* case upheld the federal government regulation requiring railroads to test all crew members after major train accidents.[71] The Court held that private railroads subject to federal regulations had to comply with the requirement that all members of a train crew be tested after a major train accident. Both blood and urine tests are required.

Here are several negotiation issues regarding the probable-cause testing process and the use of test results.

1. ***Valid testing procedure.*** The burden of proof is clearly on management in questions regarding the use of confidential, fair, and valid testing procedures. Proper testing procedures include the use of an approved, certified laboratory with state-of-the-art tests. To guard against "false-positive" results leading to unfair discipline or other actions, a second confirming test should be required. The testing procedure should also specify a "chain of custody" of the specimen. In *Amalgamated Transit Union*, for example, an employee fired for a positive drug test was able to show that the company failed to protect the chain of custody of the drug sample, rendering it useless to the disciplinary proceedings.[72]

2. ***On-the-job impairment.*** In cases involving discipline as a result of a positive drug test, an employee or union may contend that the tests prove the presence of a drug in the employee's body but not on-the-job use or on-the-job impairment. Indeed, in *Shelby County Health Care Center*, the relevant provision of the contract limited drug- or alcohol-related major offenses to drug or alcohol use on the employer's premises or being "under the influence." A fired employee was reinstated because, although his drug test was positive, there was no on-the-job impairment.[73]

There is concern that positive drug tests involving illegal drugs might be used to discipline an employee for the illegal activity involved in obtaining and possessing the drug regardless of the on-the-job effect. The employer's position is that an employee who engages in such illegal activity is not a fit employee. To date, however, arbitrators and courts often require a nexus between the employee's drug use and the behavior in the workplace before just cause for discipline is found. Such a relationship should not be difficult to find in most cases.

For example, in *Boise Cascade Corp.*, a drug-screening test was done on an employee after his involvement in an auto accident. Although the test found the presence of marijuana, the level was so low that there was no finding of intoxication. The arbitrator, however, upheld the company's 60-day suspension and requirement that the employee join the employee assistance program. The arbitrator pointed to the employer's drug program, which the union had never challenged, that allowed for disciplinary action "if drugs are detected." No on-the-job impairment was necessary.[74]

3. *Refusal to be tested.* Management can usually sustain the termination of an employee for failure to take a drug test in cases of probable cause. In *Warehouse Distribution Centers*, the employer was told that his employee had been seen in a car in the company parking lot "blowing a joint." On the basis of that report, the employee was directed to have a drug test taken, but the employee refused. The collective bargaining agreement provided for disciplining an employee who refused to take a drug test if there is suspicion of drug use. The arbitrator found sufficient grounds for the employer's suspicion and upheld the firing.[75] However, if no probable cause is found for the test, an employee is within his or her rights to refuse to take the test as a protest against an unwarranted invasion of privacy. In *Gem City Chemicals*, management unilaterally added a drug screen to a negotiated annual "physical examination for environmental effects." There was no demonstrated drug problem at the plant. The grievant refused to submit to the test as part of his annual physical and was discharged for his refusal. The arbitrator reinstated the employee because requiring the test under that circumstance was not reasonable.[76]

And just as with other dischargeable offenses, the employee must be warned that failure to submit to testing will result in discharge. After a truck accident, a supervisor who smelled beer on the driver's breath asked him to take a blood alcohol test. The driver at first agreed and accompanied the supervisor to the hospital. However, before the test he changed his mind and declined to take the test. The arbitrator found no evidence that the supervisor made it clear to the employee that failure to take the test would result in disciplinary action, and the employee was reinstated.[77]

4. *Supervisor training.* A program that includes the training of all supervisors to recognize the typical signs of employee drug use is important if probable cause is the basis of testing. Any challenge to the reasonableness of a supervisor's request for a test is likely to be discounted if the supervisor has participated in an appropriate training program.[78] Although many supervisors may be able to detect alcoholic intoxication, detection of drug abuse is more difficult to recognize without training.

Whether unions are indeed representing their members' views in negotiating drug-testing programs was the subject of an interesting survey. In 1989, 930 union members were surveyed on their attitudes toward various drug-testing programs. Approximately 29 percent of those surveyed had drug-testing programs in their workplace; 71 percent did not. The survey hoped to discover whether union members' attitudes regarding drug-testing programs were greatly influenced by their own personal workplace experience or whether the attitudes among union members were fairly uniform.[79]

SOCIAL MEDIA USAGE

A major new job security issue appearing in more newly negotiated agreements and in more discipline cases is employees' use of social media such as Facebook, Twitter, and YouTube. Employers, in both private and public sectors, are increasingly adopting policies to limit the use of social media—both in and out of the workplace. The failure to follow such a work rule under many existing CBAs is treated as a case of employee misconduct, and can lead to suspension or even termination. Unions thus may strive to negotiate a specific new contract provision that deals with social media. Teamsters' special counsel James A. McCall recommends that such provisions include the following:[80]

- Description of acceptable use of social media tracking technology
- Notice to workers warning them of such tracking
- Union access to information obtained through tracking
- The inclusion of an "on-off switch" on the tracking technology to protect workers who take home equipment and are allowed to use it for personal business

The employers' right to use technology to ensure employees on the job are working and not using technology for nonwork purposes versus employees' rights to privacy and not having monitoring technology used for illegitimate purposes is at the heart of the social media issue. In one case, a city fire department lieutenant used the department's e-mail to send "sexually suggestive" messages to the wife of a subordinate with whom he was having an affair. When the city found the e-mails, it terminated the lieutenant for violating the city's e-mail use policy—which applied to all city workers. The union grieved arguing the city had no rule against "fraternization among employees." The arbitrator noted that absent any specific contract language applying to the case, "while it is a fundamental principle of workplace justice that an employee's private life is none of the employer's concern," the lieutenant's conduct clearly violated the city's policy against sexually oriented email messages. The arbitrator upheld the termination.[81]

PUBLIC SECTOR SECURITY ISSUES

As discussed in Chapter 3, public unions and their members are concerned that to lower their personnel costs, governments will turn to outsourcing full-time public sector jobs. In Indianapolis, for example, outsourcing reduced the city's number of public employees by 40 percent in only three years. Sunnyvale, California, used a temporary Manpower company for 25 percent of its workforce. Some states, such as Pennsylvania, have developed their own pool of temporary workers, and large state community college systems use as many as 66 percent contract workers instead of full-time faculty.

In addition to outsourcing both the National Education Association (NEA) and the American Federation of Teachers (AFT) have cited "school voucher" programs as a major concern for the public employee. Critics of public schools have advocated tuition voucher programs, which provide families with public funds that could be used for private school tuition, including religious-based school tuition. Advocates of school vouchers contend that giving families a choice will force public schools to improve to stay competitive.[82] The NEA and AFT argue that the lack of public oversight of private schools undermines accountability to the public for the expenditure of tax dollars.

Finally, as a result of the Great Recession of 2008, public sector unions are watching developments around the country as angry taxpayers complain about the size and expense of government.

Summary

Job security and seniority are vital to collective bargaining agreements. Both labor and management strongly believe that they must maintain certain rights where job security affects the employee's ability to keep his or her job and successfully compete for higher positions. Seniority, or length of service with the organization, and the employee's ability to perform the job successfully are the two primary factors considered in layoff and promotion situations for both union and nonunion companies. An effective job security system also requires that the labor agreement contain a fair and just discipline and grievance system so that management's decisions regarding promotion or layoff and recall can be properly disputed by labor.

Seniority systems have generally been used because they are easy to develop and provide an objective, unambiguous means of considering employees when job openings occur. The theory behind using seniority is that if the employees are approximately equal in ability, then the employee who has the greatest length of service should be given the opportunity first. This practice is commonplace in nonunion as well as union organizations. Unfortunately, there are not always objective measures of ability to perform. The difficulty lies in determining the relative ability of competing employees. Seniority systems and employee feelings of job security are meaningless unless contract provisions limit management's ability to subcontract work. Without such provisions, management can subcontract work temporarily and force severe hardships on employees, causing them to leave and lose their seniority. Certainly, although union leaders agree that subcontracting is necessary in some situations, it can and has been used to undermine labor unions.

If a change in employers occurs, the successor is not bound by existing collective bargaining agreements. Also, if a genuine change in business has occurred, the new employer is not required to recognize the union. Public sector unions try to use a successorship provision to make sure its members do not lose their jobs to outside contractors.

The use of an alcohol- and drug-testing program on current employees covered by a collective bargaining agreement must be negotiated at the bargaining table. Unions generally agree only to probable-cause testing and strongly object to random testing of all workers. Both sides express great interest in several aspects of any testing program, including the testing procedure, on-the-job impairment, and basis for probable-cause testing.

Employees are finding that more and more employers are adopting policies to limit the use of social media in the workplace, while such new technologies offer employers an opportunity to watch the activities of employees more closely.

Public sector unions worry that in hard economic times the public is willing to have many of their jobs outsourced or eliminated altogether.

CASE STUDIES

Case Study 9-1 Relocating Work without Bargaining

The company is a family-owned business founded in 1943. Schultz is the company's president and part owner. The company began manufacturing caliper pins, which are used in the production of automobile disc brakes, at its Michigan facility in late 1994. Deciding that caliper pins would be the critical product line for the future of the company, the company received a $3 million industrial development revenue bond from Michigan Strategic Fund (MSF) in March 1996. For federal tax purposes, a borrowing under an MSF agreement must be for a specific project at a specific location. Under the company's MSF agreement, the project site was the Michigan facility, and the project was the renovation of that facility and the purchase and installation of new machinery, including machinery for use in the production of caliper pins. Because the purpose of the MSF was to strengthen the state economy, the company had to give assurances of a reasonable intent to install the machinery at the project site and to maintain it there during the term of the loan. If the company decided to move equipment purchased under the MSF agreement from the site, the company would have to redeem an amount of the bonds equivalent to the value of the relocated machinery "contemporaneously" with the movement of machinery. After receiving the MSF loan, the company renovated its facility and purchased new machinery to meet its goal of increased caliper production. As part of the renovation, the company converted an area of approximately 2,300 square feet in the facility, known as the "blue room," into a caliper pin production area.

In December 1995, the company also applied for tax abatement from Plymouth Township. The tax abatement was to apply to the new machinery that the company would use in its caliper pin production and required that the machinery remain within the township. The company submitted its tax abatement application on May 31, 1996, and the tax abatement was granted on January 29, 1997.

On May 10, 1996, the company signed a lease to acquire 10,800 square feet of space in Louisville, Kentucky. The company sent its caliper pin customer in the Louisville area—an announcement of its intent to open a warehouse and distribution facility in Louisville.

In June 1996, the company held a meeting for all employees at the Elks Club across the street from the Plymouth facility to tell them about the company's future plans. Schultz discussed the company's plans for increased personnel and machinery. He forecast that the company's caliper pin sales would go from approximately $1.5–$6 million and that the caliper pin business might be relocated to Louisville to be closer to the company's customer base.

Schultz did not mention any specific date for the relocation, however, and he did not state that a definite decision had been made to move the caliper pin operation.

Between October and December 1996, Schultz said he generally discussed with the caliper pin customer whether it would be prudent to move the company's caliper pin operation to Louisville. Schultz testified that he wanted to know whether the company's largest caliper pin customer thought it would be wise to undertake such a move. Schultz further testified that he decided independently in late December 1996 to relocate the caliper pin operation to Louisville, and he made this decision primarily because Louisville was closer to the company's main caliper pin customer.

In February 1997, the union began its organizing drive at the company's Michigan facility. The union presented Schultz with a signed employee document that set out the rights of employees under Section 7 of the act and explained what specific acts would be illegal during the union's organizing campaign. On March 6, the union filed its election petition with the board. The union gave Schultz a document titled "Sensible Rules for a Fair Election," which was signed by 50 employees. Schultz read the document but would not sign it. It is undisputed that the company was aware of the campaign because employees openly wore union buttons to show their support for the UAW. The election was held on April 17, and the union was certified as the exclusive collective bargaining representative of the unit employees on April 25. In May, a UAW staff representative was assigned to assist the newly certified union obtain its first collective bargaining agreement with the company, which at the time of this grievance had not been done.

Sometime in March, before the election, Schultz walked over to two of the unit employees while they were working in the blue room. He asked, "Do you know what's going on around here?" They both responded no. He then said, "Well, if a union gets in here, a lot of people could be laid off." He placed his hand on one worker's shoulder and said, "If the union gets in here, you can be laid off." In late March or early April, and again prior to the election, the company's comptroller came up to a group of employees as they were discussing the pros and cons of the union and said to the group, "You know that there are changes that are going to be made when the union is voted in, and there may or may not be jobs left. Nothing is in stone, nothing is permanent."

On June 3, a company manager asked the owner of an equipment moving company to come to the Plymouth plant to look at certain machines that were to be moved to another facility. During a tour of the facility, he was asked whether there would be any labor problems if the equipment were relocated. The company manager stated that he did not believe there would be a problem, and he said he wanted the equipment moved from the Plymouth facility to Louisville on July 4.

On June 24, the moving company owner telephoned the union representative and told him of his visit to the company's Plymouth facility and informed him that the company wanted him to move six machines from the Plymouth facility to Louisville on July 4. On June 27, the union representative met with Schultz at the Plymouth facility. During the meeting, he told Schultz that he had heard rumors that the company planned to move some of its equipment and operations to the south. Schultz responded, "That may be something that may have to be considered in the future, but as it stood right then, there were no immediate plans to move anything out of the plant."

On July 2, Schultz informed his customer that the company was relocating its caliper pin operation to Louisville. Then, on July 3, Schultz held an employee meeting at the Plymouth facility. He informed the employees that because of overcrowding in the blue room and the caliper pin customers were closer to Louisville, it was necessary to implement a reduction of employees because of the transfer of the caliper pin operation to the company's Louisville facility. Schultz explained that it would be necessary to lay off 33 employees—those who had been hired since January 1995. Schultz added that applications would be accepted from anyone who was interested in applying for a job in Louisville. Also on July 3, the union representative received a fax transmission from Schultz concerning the move of the caliper pin operation from the Plymouth facility to Louisville.

(continued)

The union representative responded,

> I specifically asked you [at the June 27 meeting] about any plans the company might have to move work from Plymouth to your facilities in the south. You did not indicate any such plans. Six days later, I now receive your letter announcing the company's "gradual realignment of its core business" and the news you are moving 29 jobs to Kentucky. I find it hard to believe that you were not aware of this plan when we spoke last Friday.

Also on July 3, the union president received a call from a company employee who informed him of the just-announced layoff of company employees. He decided that the union would put up an informational picket line at the Plymouth facility on July 4. Early on July 4, the company manager contacted a moving company and asked them to begin to move the equipment immediately.

A vice president in the commercial loan department of the bank that loaned the company the $3 million testified without contradiction that he learned in September that the company had acquired a facility in Louisville and that it had transferred machinery valued at over $1 million to that facility from Plymouth. He advised Schultz that the bonds had to be redeemed to the value of the machinery moved out of state. On November 7, the company redeemed $1.3 million of the bonds with funds borrowed on a short-term loan. On its year-end tax return for 1997, the company notified Plymouth Township that machinery that had been subject to the tax abatement had been moved out of state.

The union filed an unfair labor charge against the company for unilaterally implementing a decision to relocate bargaining unit work and for discrimination because it was clear the decision to relocate the union work was in response to the employees exercising their right to organize and bargain collectively.

Discussion

Applying the analysis set out in *Dubuque Packing Co.*, the union argued that the relocation decision was a mandatory subject of bargaining; that labor costs, both direct and indirect, were a factor in the company's decision to relocate the caliper pin operation; and that the union could have offered labor cost concessions that could have persuaded the company, had it been notified and permitted to submit bargaining proposals prior to July 3, to retain the caliper pin manufacturing work at the Plymouth facility.

The union further argued that the relocation and layoffs were discriminatorily motivated and therefore violated Section 8(a)(3) of the act. The union pointed out that the evidence does not support Schultz's testimony that he made the relocation decision in December 1996, some two months before the union came on the scene. It was not coincidental that the company implemented the relocation and layoffs on July 3 and 4, less than three months after the union had won the election and been certified as the bargaining representative of the company's employees. Thus, the timing of the relocation and layoffs, shortly after the employees' union activities culminated in the union's election victory and certification, and the company's knowledge of its employees' union activities support the union's contention that the relocation and layoffs were unlawfully motivated.

Furthermore, Schultz and the comptroller implied loss of employment if the union won the election. Their unsupported statements that layoffs could occur and that there might or might not be jobs left if the union got in are evidence of antiunion animus. Schultz was the president of the company and therefore in a position to carry out the threatened layoffs if the union won the election. In these circumstances, the mere fact that he may have visited the facility only once a week does not lessen the impact of his threat. The company comptroller's threats were credible to the employees because she was fully informed of the company's financial condition.

The union also pointed out that the company originally announced that it intended to use the Louisville facility as a warehouse and distribution center. It was only after the union had been certified and immediately prior to the relocation that the company leased additional space at a second facility in Louisville so it could relocate the caliper pin machinery from Plymouth to Louisville. The employees' union activities were a motivating factor in the company's decision to relocate the caliper pin operation to Louisville. The company's entering into the MFS agreement in 1996 evidences the company's intention to maintain its caliper pin operation at the Plymouth facility for the indefinite future. It was only after a bank official notified the company of the redemption obligation over two months after the relocation that the company took steps to remedy the problem. Even then, it could only redeem the bonds through a short-term loan. The company's careful preparations to get the MSF loan with its announced intent to keep the caliper pin operation in Plymouth—preparations that occurred prior to the union's appearance—stand in sharp contrast to the company's sudden breach of the terms of the agreement in July—after the union came on the scene—and to its abrupt departure from its avowed intent to keep the caliper pin operation in Plymouth. The union contended that this dramatic change proved that the union's appearance was a motivating factor in the company's relocation decision.

The company's intent to keep the caliper pin operation in Plymouth before the onset of the union campaign is also evidenced by its successful efforts to gain tax abatement from Plymouth Township for the caliper pin machinery. Less than six months after receiving the tax abatement, however, and less than three months after the union won the election, the company moved that machinery out of Plymouth Township. This sudden departure from the company's documented intention to keep the caliper machinery in Plymouth proves that the appearance of the union was a motivating factor in the company's decision to relocate that machinery. Finally, the union pointed out the company's stealth in carrying out the relocation—its refusal to inform the union representative that the relocation was imminent despite his request he be so informed and its sudden secreting of the equipment out of the Plymouth facility over the July 4 holiday—are further evidence of the company's desire to avoid and be rid of the union. The company's stealth in relocating the equipment is further evidenced by its failure to inform its caliper pin customer in the Louisville area of the relocation until only a few days before it occurred.

In its defense, the company pointed out that even if an antiunion animus is found, the company could not be found to have engaged in an unfair labor practice if it would have taken the same action regardless of the union activity. The company then reiterated that Schultz discussed the possibility of moving the caliper pin operation to Louisville with his customer in the fall of 1996, before the organizing campaign, and that he contended he made the relocation decision in December 1996. And he reminded the court that as early as June 1996, long before the organizing campaign, he informed his employees there was a possibility that the work would move to Louisville.

Furthermore, Schultz asserted that the reasons for making the relocation decision—that the blue room was overcrowded and the company's caliper pin customers were in the Louisville area—were valid reasons that supported his decision to move.

Source: Adapted from *Vico Products Co. v. NLRB,* 170 LRRM 1124 (2001).

QUESTIONS

1. The union argues that the company's efforts to borrow low-interest bonds and to get tax breaks to build and operate in Michigan support their position that the motivating factor in moving to Kentucky was antiunion animus. Do you agree?
2. The company's defense, that Schultz made the decision to move the company before the organizing campaign got started, was supported only by his own testimony. If you were told that the hearing officer who conducted the hearing and heard the testimony believed Schultz, would it change your opinion of the defense? Why or why not?
3. Kentucky, like Michigan, is not a right-to-work state, so union organizing in a plant in Kentucky is as likely as in Michigan. The company's decision to move from Michigan seems to have been both complicated and expensive. Do you think that the company made such a decision mainly to avoid a unionized workforce?

(continued)

Case Study 9-2 Drug Testing

The company and the union had negotiated a typical substance abuse prevention and treatment program in their collective bargaining agreement. It prohibited the use of legally obtained drugs and alcohol if such use adversely affected the employee's job performance. It also prohibited the sale, purchase, transfer, use, or possession of illegal drugs "on the work premises or while on employer business." It allowed for testing in the following circumstances: for reasonable cause, after on-the-job accidents or incidents, for safety-sensitive jobs, and for reinstatement after treatment for drug or alcohol abuse. The collective bargaining agreement also stated, in a separate article, the general principle that "there is no intent to intrude upon the private lives of employees."

The employee tested positive for an illegal substance after an on-the-job accident and was enrolled in an inpatient treatment program. At the completion of the program, he was reinstated subject to the normal provisions that he would continue with aftercare treatment and submit to random testing for three years. The employee was a member of a work crew that reported to work on a regular schedule and was not subject to being called in. In fact, if he chose not to report to work with his crew, there was no penalty. The employee had been called for a random drug test and had been tested eight times, all of which were negative. The ninth time he was called, he was contacted at home on a day he was not scheduled to work and was told to report for a drug test. In this instance, he tested positive, and the company dismissed him. The union appealed.

The union position was that the collective bargaining agreement prohibited intrusion into the private lives of employees, the drug policy prohibited only on-the-job impairment or abuse, and random testing can be used only in relationship to the workplace (i.e., when the employee is, should be, or may be reporting to work, at work, or about to leave work). The employee was not scheduled to work, was not on the employer's premises or business, and was not subject to being called in to work. His reinstatement agreement to submit to random drug tests meant only those types of random tests consistent with the substance abuse policy (i.e., for on-the-job impairment).

The company's position was that because some employees can be called into work at any time, the conduct of random testing needs to be on a 24-hour-a-day, 7-day-a-week basis; the union had not previously objected, and a past practice can be argued; the employee had violated the collective bargaining agreement by drug use on the job and had agreed to submit to random testing for three years in order to be reinstated, so an argument can be made that his testing then is job related; and this employee could elect not to report to work on any given day, so this reinforces the need to be able to test him on his off-duty time.

Source: Adapted from *New Orleans Steamship Association,* 105 LA 79 (1995).

QUESTIONS

1. As the arbitrator, give your reasons for ruling in the union's favor. Then give your reasons for ruling in the employer's favor.
2. Argue for and against a decision by the employer in this case to insist on expanding the drug program to include the prohibition of sale, possession, or use of illegal substances on the employee's own time.

Key Terms and Concepts

absolute rank principle *336*
bumping *328*
employee teams *340*
follow the work principle *336*
industrial jurisprudence *324*
job bidding *330*
last-hired, first-fired rule *324*
layoff *331*
length of service principle *336*

Review Questions

1. Why is seniority considered a critical issue? What are the advantages and disadvantages of using a seniority system?
2. In layoffs involving K–12 teachers, should seniority or merit be the determining factor? Explain why.
3. Describe the different methods by which labor agreements might consider seniority in a promotion decision.
4. Why is seniority often used in layoff and recall actions? Specifically, how do contract clauses provide for the consideration of seniority in such decisions?
5. Under what circumstances might the employer bypass a senior employee and promote a junior employee when the labor agreement contains a seniority clause?
6. Why has management's right to subcontract work been the subject of many grievances?
7. What are the key issues in an employee alcohol- and drug-testing program?
8. How does the successorship doctrine affect union security?
9. Should employers be able to limit employees' use of social media? What might be reasonable limits?
10. When is a successor employer required to recognize a union from the previous employer's business?
11. Why has the use of "employee teams" been so controversial? What are the pros and cons?

YOU BE THE ARBITRATOR

Subcontracting Work or Union Busting?

ARTICLE XXV
CONTRACTING WORK

If for any reason the Company desires to contract or subcontract out work, it may do so; however, the Company agrees not to use such contracting or subcontracting as a union-busting tactic.

It is not the Company's intent to contract or subcontract work within a branch location while employees who are qualified to do the work within the branch are on layoff status, except as required by business necessity.

Facts

The employer marketed and sold both large (PBX) and small (key) telephone systems for institutional customers and provided the service and maintenance of those systems after installation. The employer's extensive warehouse and depot operation was responsible for the storage and staging areas for (1) some PBX and almost all key systems, (2) materials and parts stocking for technicians' trucks, and (3) critical spare and replacement parts for both PBS and key systems. In the mid-1990s, to become a competitive survivor in the collapsing telecommunications industry, the employer adopted a strategic survival plan that included the dramatic centralization of its distribution operations. The strategic plan called for closing five local warehouses and reducing the size of several others. Following discussions with the union in January 1996, the employer began to implement the centralizing strategic plan. Some material handler positions were eliminated, but although it had no contractual obligation to do so under the terms of the collective bargaining agreement (CBA), the employer successfully placed all the affected employees within its operations. Around the same time, the employer entered into a number of third-party vendor (TPV) contracts. These TPVs provided services that the employer's warehouse workers could not perform, a 24/7/365 delivery system for critical spare and replacement parts and the storing and staging of PBX equipment. In the fall of 2000, the employer, which had continued to lose money, refined its strategic plan to focus on its service and maintenance agreements and dramatically cut back on its sales and installation role. Ultimately, this led to consolidating the entire employer's 59 warehouses and depots into three locations and the layoff of hundreds of employees. Eleven laid-off material handlers who were not placed within the operation filed a grievance charging that the employer had violated the subcontracting clause of the CBA.

Issue

Did the employer have a business necessity to subcontract work that the laid-off employees could perform, or was it union busting?

Position of the Parties

According to the union, the laid-off employees were fully qualified to provide the services being performed by the TPVs. They had historically performed the full range of work, including the storage and staging of the large PBX equipment, albeit infrequently, and the delivery of critical spare and replacement parts. The union admitted that the employer did not provide the same 24/7/365 operation the TPV did, but the employees were under an "on-call" system so that they could perform timely deliveries just as well as the TPV. The union pointed out that the employer's decision to consolidate and eliminate warehouses resulted in not having the physical facilities that would have allowed the employees to perform their jobs. It was like a taxicab company that sells all its taxis and then subcontracts with another taxi company to transport its customers. Clearly, the employer's actions were nothing but union busting. Further, the union contended that the employer could not prove it had a business necessity for consolidating its warehouse operation and laying off the employees because it still had considerable losses after the 2000 changes. Clearly, according to the union, the real reason for the layoffs and subcontracting was to bust the union.

According to the employer, it had no antiunion animus. It had, in fact, consulted with the union as its strategic plan was put into place and had made an effort to place laid-off employees within the confines of its scaled-back operations. The TPV contracts had been entered into prior to the 2000 consolidation plan and prior to the last CBA negotiations of the employer with the union. The TPV work did not increase after execution of the 2000 strategic plan; rather, the employer's work changed so that its growth was in the service and maintenance operations and not its warehousing operations. In other words, there was a decrease in the employer's overall warehousing operation, and the decrease came totally from the employee side of its operation, not the contractual side of its operation. So although there was a loss on the employee side, there was no gain on the contractual side. Therefore, its subcontracting did not violate the CBA. Furthermore, the TPVs were in place when the current CBA was negotiated. If the union had wanted to "undo" the existing subcontracts, it should have brought it up at the negotiating table. The employer contended that the laid-off workers were not qualified to do the work of the TPVs because the employer did not have the facilities to house/move the PBX systems, and the "call-in" of workers could not meet the efficiency of the 24/7/365 of the TPVs. Finally, the employer contended that the savings in changing its core work from supplying equipment to servicing and maintaining the systems proved that there was a business necessity for the changes it made, including the closing of the warehouses and its subcontracting.

QUESTIONS

1. As arbitrator, what would be your award and opinion in this arbitration?
2. Identify the key, relevant section(s), phrases, or words of the collective bargaining agreement (CBA), and explain why they were critical in making your decision.
3. What actions might the employer and/or the union have taken to avoid this conflict?

Source: Adapted from *Nexitra,* 116 LA 1780.

PART IV The Labor Relations Process in Action

CHAPTER 10

Unfair Labor Practices and Contract Enforcement

Thousands of University of California union workers on nine campuses picketed in protest during contract talks. UC officials filed an unfair labor practice charge against the AFSMCE union. In 2010 Californian PERB dismissed the charges. *Source:* Newscom

Chapter Outline

> *Employees covered by the Act are protected from certain types of employer and union misconduct and have the right to attempt to form a union where none currently exists.*
>
> NATIONAL LABOR RELATIONS BOARD

LABOR NEWS

Unfair Labor Charges Filed Against AFSCME Union

The University of California filed unfair labor practice charges against the American Federation of State, County and Municipal Employees Union (AFSCME). The union represents about 11,000 patient care employees who work in UC medical centers in California. The charges claim the union failed to "bargain in good faith" during contract negotiations. In addition, the charges claim the union failed to participate in impasse procedures in good faith and exhibited a disregard for patients and their families.

At the center of the university's charges was a response to AFSCME's unwillingness to bargain over the union's distribution of leaflets to patients and visitors to the UC medical centers. The leaflet distribution was a violation of the university's long-standing policy against handing out leaflets for any purpose. The university stated the policy was designed to provide safe access to the facilities and to protect the rights of patients and their families. That refusal to follow the policy, and actively distribute the leaflets during contract negotiations, led the university to file the unfair labor practice charge against AFSCME for failure to bargain in good faith. The medical centers affected include the University of California medical centers in San Francisco, Los Angeles, Davis, Irvine, and San Diego. The California Public Employment Relations Board (PERB) in 2010 dismissed the unfair labor practice charge filed by the university. The PERB decision noted that the AFSCME leafleting action was in fact a violation of the contract. However, when confronted by university officials, the union members agreed to move their activity, and thus their conduct was "just an isolated breach of the contract" and thus not a failure to "bargain in good faith," which might have constituted an unfair labor practice.

Source: Adapted from "UC Files Unfair Labor Charges Against AFSMCE," *UCSF Today* (February 22, 2008), p. 1; and State of California PERB Decision No. 2105-H (April 21, 2010). Available at www.perb.ca.gov. Accessed August 30, 2011.

As explained throughout this text, the National Labor Relations Act (NLRA) gives most private sector employees the right to organize and to choose their representatives; it also requires employers to meet with the employee representatives and make an honest effort to reach agreement on workplace issues. The act protects the right of employees to strike and limits the employer's retaliatory powers. And although the interest of management and labor usually focuses on the months of negotiations necessary to arrive at a collective bargaining agreement, the negotiated agreement itself is implemented over a much longer period. It is that period of implementation that tests the quality of its terms and the willingness of the parties to abide by the contract.

UNFAIR LABOR PRACTICES (ULPS)

Certain actions taken by employers or unions that violate the NLRA. Such acts may be investigated by the NLRB.

The NLRA, as with any law, requires effective enforcement. This chapter details how to recognize violations of the act, known as an **unfair labor practices** or ULPs, and how the National Labor Relations Board and federal courts take action on those violations. The authority of the NLRB in such cases is also discussed. This chapter also includes an overview of the rights of individuals within unions.

The primary objective of the NLRA is to encourage collective bargaining in order to minimize industrial strife that adversely affects the free flow of commerce. (Section 1.) To that end, the act gave employees certain protected rights. Section 7 of the act, as amended by the Taft-Hartley Amendments, enumerates these rights:

1. To self-organize
2. To form, join, or assist labor organizations or to refrain from such union activities
3. To bargain collectively through representatives of their own choosing
4. To engage in other concerted activities for the purpose of collective bargaining or other mutual aid or protection
5. To refrain from any or all of the preceding rights[1]

The act in Section 8(a) also lists activities considered unfair labor practices in violation of those rights by employers:

1. Interference with, restraint, or coercion of employees in rights guaranteed under Section 7 (Subsection (1))
2. Domination or interference with the formation or administration of a labor union (Subsection (2))
3. Discrimination against union members for their union membership (Subsection (3))
4. Discrimination against an employee for pursuing the rights under the act (Subsection (4))
5. Refusal to bargain collectively with representatives of its employees[2] (Subsection (5))

Also in Section 8(b) of the act, activities considered unfair labor practices by labor organizations are listed:

1. Restraint or coercion of employees in rights guaranteed under Section 7 (Subsection (1))
2. Discrimination against an employee for not engaging in union activities (Subsection (2))
3. Refusal to bargain in good faith with the employer (Subsection (3))
4. Conducting secondary strikes or boycotts, or strikes to dislodge another union (Subsection (4))
5. Requiring a closed shop (Subsection (5))
6. Demanding "make work" jobs (Subsection (6))
7. Certain picketing activities (Subsection (7))

It may be helpful to think of unfair labor practices in two major categories: first, unfair labor practices that occur during a union organizational campaign, and second, unfair labor practices that occur during the negotiations of a collective bargaining agreement and during the life of that agreement.

INTERFERENCE WITH EMPLOYEES' RIGHT TO ORGANIZE

The process for establishing a bargaining unit and gaining recognition by conducting an election is detailed in Chapter 4. As pointed out in that chapter, there are "do's and don'ts" by both employers and unions during such activity. The first unfair labor practice listed in the NLRA for both sides prohibits actions that interfere, restrain, or coerce employees in the exercise of their right to unionize or not to unionize. To determine an unfair labor practice by an employer of this right, the NLRB must find that the employer's action interfered with, restrained, or coerced an activity under a reasonable probability test.

The NLRB's reasonable probability test eliminates the need to prove actual interference, restraint, or coercion by the employer if it can be shown that the activity tends to interfere with the free exercise of protected rights.[3] The courts, however, distinguish between inherently discriminatory or destructive violations of employee rights, when an employer could foresee the unlawful consequences, and those not so blatantly in violation. A hostile motive may be necessary to establish proof of an unfair labor practice if the activity itself can be objectively viewed as nondestructive. The kind of practice that most often evokes the need to prove intent is one motivated by a legitimate and substantial business justification.[4] In such cases, an actual intent to frustrate the purposes of the act must be found to warrant an unfair labor practice charge. Employers' historical resistance to having their employees represented by unions has created an extensive list of do's and don'ts by employers and unions during representation elections, as previously detailed in Chapter 4. Following is a more detailed look at how violations of those do's and don'ts may be unfair labor practices.

Unfair Labor Practices That Interfere With Organizing a Bargaining Unit

Employees have the right to "organize" into labor organizations. The first step in organizing is to talk to other employees about the issues involved in unionizing, and the "pros and cons" of unions. Employees have the right to organize, but in many cases, the exercise of that right directly opposes the employer's right to maintain a work environment. The courts have devised rules based on the NLRB's opinion that working time is for work, to balance the two interests. Organizing activities that are protected under the National Labor Relations Act include the following:

1. ***Solicitation and distribution.*** Employees are allowed to solicit support for a union from their fellow employees during nonworking times. This includes lunchtime, break time, rest periods, and before and after the regular workday. The Supreme Court in *Republic Aviation* said that an employer rule prohibiting union solicitation by employees outside working time, even on the employer's property, was an unfair labor practice as an unreasonable impediment to self-organization.[5] Employees are limited, however, in the distribution of union literature. Generally such distribution is restricted to nonworking times and areas. The board based this decision on employers' representations that such literature could clutter the workplace. The board has held, however, that the distribution by off-duty employees of union literature in nonworking areas, such as in company parking lots, is clearly protected by the act and that an employer commits an unfair labor practice prohibiting such activity unless the prohibition is justified by business reasons.[6] However, the board adopted a blanket rule for employers in retail businesses, such as department stores and restaurants, saying they may prohibit union solicitation by employees in areas where the public is invited even during an employee's nonworking time.[7] And the board concluded that the special characteristics of hospitals justified similar treatment because the primary function of a hospital is patient care and that a tranquil atmosphere is essential to the carrying out of that function. In order to provide this atmosphere, hospitals may be justified in imposing somewhat more stringent prohibitions on solicitation than are generally permitted. *For example*, a hospital may be warranted in prohibiting solicitation even on nonworking time in strictly patient care areas, such as the patients' rooms, operating rooms, and places where patients receive treatment, such as x-ray and therapy areas.[8]

The courts, however, have long viewed organizing by an employee and organizing by a nonemployee, or union organizer, as distinct when deciding on the right of access to employer premises. Originally, nonemployee union organizers could be barred from coming onto the employer's property to solicit support for a union if there were other ***reasonable means*** to reach employees. For example, if there was one location from which the employees entered or exited the property so that the union organizer had the ability to speak with all of the employees, the company's rule was not an unfair labor practice. However, with the decision in the *Lechmere* case, the Supreme Court decided that an employer would not be committing an unfair labor practice when barring a nonemployee access to its property if there was ***any other means*** to reach the employees.[9] Lechmere owned a retail store in a shopping plaza and was part owner of the plaza's parking lot. Lechmere employees used this lot to park their vehicles during their shifts. This parking lot was separated from a public highway by a strip of land which was almost entirely public property. Local union organizers, not employees of Lechmere, attempted to organize Lechmere employees by placing promotional handbills on the windshields of cars parked in the employee area of the lot. Lechmere denied the organizers access to the lot. This act caused the organizers to instead distribute their handbills and picket from the strip of public land between the lot and the highway. Justice Clarence Thomas wrote in his opinion that the nonemployee union organizers had reasonable access to the employees *outside* the employer's property; because such access existed, there was to be no "balancing" of the employer–employee rights used in other cases.

A landmark federal appeals court decision reaffirmed the *Lechmere* decision and, to a certain extent, expanded it. In *UFCW Local No. 880 v. NLRB*, the court ruled against a union's request to find the employer, a retail store, guilty of an unfair labor practice when the employer refused the union access to its parking lot to distribute boycott information to the store's customers. Relying on the *Lechmere* reasoning, the court noted that *the availability of mass media alone to reach the store's customers* gives the union a *reasonable alternative* to what the court termed "trespass access."[10]

An employer may implement a **no-solicitation** policy for employees during both work and nonwork hours if that policy extends to all types of solicitation. If it is applied only to union solicitation, it is likely to be an unfair labor practice. For example, several employees at an Oklahoma manufacturing plant were disciplined for soliciting support for the United Steelworkers union on company time. The employer had a nonsolicitation policy that prohibited workers from distributing literature or soliciting during work hours. The court in *Webco Industries, Inc. v. NLRB*[11] upheld the NLRB decision that the employer had committed an unfair labor practice not because the policy was unlawful, but because the employer allowed other types of solicitation such as group sales of candy and cookies, sports pools, and fantasy football.[12] However, in *Cleveland Real Estate Partners v. NLRB*,[13] the federal court held that the employer did not discriminate against unions when it excluded handbills favoring one union over another or employer materials over union materials but allowed charities to solicit on its property.

NO-SOLICITATION POLICY

Employer policy that bars on-site solicitation of employees for a specific purpose. Generally unfair if only applied to union activity

2. *Union buttons or insignias.* Another protected activity is the wearing of union buttons or insignias. This right is balanced against the employer's right to conduct business. If a button or insignia should in particular circumstances cause a disturbance, present a health hazard, distract workers, cause damage to a product, or offend or distract customers, it may be prohibited. The NLRB in 1985, however, refused to allow an employer to discharge a construction employee who had a union insignia sticker on his helmet because no special circumstance existed to make the removal necessary to maintain production or discipline or to ensure safety.[14]

3. *Bulletin boards and meeting halls.* Employees have no statutory right to use an employer's bulletin board. However, if the employees are allowed access to the bulletin board, the employer cannot censor the material to exclude union solicitation. In addition, a union may negotiate the use of a bulletin board for union business, such as this example:

An employee has the right to wear union buttons or insignias in most circumstances. *Source:* Getty Images.

ARTICLE X

Bulletin Boards

The Company shall supply on its premises and in a prominent place, one bulletin board for the use of the Union. The Union agrees to sign all its notices and present them to the Director of Operations. The Union has the right to post notices in the following categories:

1. Notices of Union recreational and social affairs.
2. Notices of Union elections.
3. Notices of Union appointments and results of Union elections.
4. Notices of Union meetings.

Notices outside this category must not be posted unless approved by the management.[15]

Meeting halls fall under the same rule. If access has been allowed to employees on an unrestricted basis, use by employees for union organization cannot be the only exception. Also, if the physical location of the business makes other meeting places inaccessible and the employer does not normally give employees access to the hall, his or her subsequent refusal might result in an unfair labor practice charge. In one case, the NLRB found an unfair labor practice when the company denied the union access to employee mailboxes that the union had been using to distribute literature for 40 years. Although the company claimed that the union could reach employees by other means, their denial was found discriminatory because other groups were allowed access to the mailboxes.[16]

4. *E-mail solicitation.* Section 7 of the NLRB clearly affects employer rights to regulate electronic mail (e-mail) use. Employees have the right not to be discriminated against by their employer for engaging in discussions relating to wages, hours, and working conditions, assuming the discussions do not violate a legitimate employer policy regarding the use of work time or equipment. An NLRB decision in 2007 restricted the use of e-mail solicitations by unions. The board held that it is legal for an employer to prohibit union-related e-mail if the employer has a policy banning employees from using the employer's e-mail for other "non-job-related" solicitations for outside organizations. The decision overturned several prior board decisions that had made it illegal for an employer to impose such a ban on union-related e-mail if it let employees use e-mail for personal communications. The NLRB reasoned that a distinction can be made between *personal* e-mail use, such as "for-sale" notices or birthday announcements, and *organizational* e-mail purposes, such as union material. Unions see the decision as a significant setback in their communication efforts. The NLRB ruling involved a Eugene, Oregon, newspaper, *The Register-Guard*, and e-mail messages sent by the president of the Newspaper Guild.[17]

5. *Employer rules.* Employer rules that prohibit employees from discussing wages, benefits, and conditions of employment may be an unlawful restriction of employee rights under Section 7 of the NLRA. However, in *Lutheran Heritage Village-Livonia Home, Inc.*,[18] the NLRB reversed its prior position and ruled that rules prohibiting "abusive and profane language," "harassment," and "verbal, mental and physical abuse" were lawful. Employers, according to the NLRB, have the right to establish such rules for the similar purpose of maintaining a civil workplace and to avoid liability under federal and state laws. In similar cases, the NLRB upheld employer rules that prohibit fraternization on or off duty, dating, or becoming overly friendly with a client's employee.[19]

TYPICAL UNFAIR LABOR PRACTICES IN AN ORGANIZING CAMPAIGN Through its rulings over the years, the NLRB has determined that certain activities during an election that constitute violations of the act include the following:

1. *Campaign propaganda and misrepresentation.* In the conduct of representation elections, the board routinely ignores rhetoric, realizing that it is part of any election campaign and usually will be disregarded by employees in making decisions. But such an attitude is flexible if the rights of the parties to an untrammeled choice are in jeopardy. In *Midland National Life Insurance Company*, the NLRB stated that it would intervene in cases in which forgery would render the voters unable to discern the propagandistic nature of a publication.[20] Also, an employer was found to have interfered with an election when it provided a $250 prize to the employee who scored highest on a test that determined knowledge of the process used in decertifying a union.[21]

The board often sees misleading information on wage and fringe benefit data, proffered by the union to encourage unionization, as exaggeration, but if viewed by the courts as more serious, it can cause the election to be invalidated.[22] The board has also found that a flyer circulated by the union that guaranteed it was illegal for the company to close or threaten to close the plant if the union won the election was a piece of union campaign literature that the voters could evaluate for themselves and not a reason to void an election.[23]

2. *Threats and loss of benefits.* Unlike mere campaign rhetoric, the actual reduction or withholding of benefits as a method of combating an organizational drive constitutes interference. Direct threats of economic reprisals issued to thwart a representation election will result in an unfair labor practice finding. These include discharge, loss of pay or benefits, more onerous working conditions, and threats of plant closure, physical violence, or permanent replacement of strikers. It is more difficult to ascertain an unfair labor practice when threats of reprisals or promises of benefits are merely implied. In 2000 in *Springs Industries*, the NLRB ruled that when an employer threatens to close a plant if the union wins a representation election, that the assumption is the threat will make the rounds of the workplace, thereby tainting an election. However, in a 2004 NLRB (3 to 2) decision, *Springs Industries* was overruled. In *Crown Bolt, Inc.*, the NLRB decided that if a threat of plant closure were made to a single employee, an election would not be overturned without evidence that the threat was actually disseminated throughout the workforce.[24]

Under the *Gissel* case, an employer is not prohibited from communicating general views about unionism or predictions of the effect of unionization on the company as long as such predictions involve consequences outside the employer's control.[25] The Supreme Court added a subjective test of what the speaker intended and the listener understood to ensure that veiled threats would not coerce employee actions. To determine the coercive nature of a statement, a court should examine the total context in which the statement is made. Elements to be reviewed include the presence or absence of other unfair labor practice incidents, the actual content of the communication, the exact language used, the employer's history of dealing with unions, and the identity of the speaker.[26]

3. *Promise or grant of benefit.* The promise of economic benefits by the employer if employees reject unionization will violate the National Labor Relations Act, as will the promise or grant of economic benefits during an organizational campaign to influence the outcome of an election or to discourage organizational activities. The fact that there is no direct link between receipt of the benefit and a vote against the union is unimportant; the courts look to the implication of such largesse. The employee may be impressed with the power of the employer's discretion to give and presumably take away benefits. However, the granting of benefits during a union campaign has not always been held a violation of the act. The board does not favor a per se approach but examines each case within context. For example, the board refused to assume without specific proof that an employer's unilateral grant of improved health insurance caused a decertification of the union.[27] Clearly, offering money while urging a vote in a particular way will be considered coercive. In other cases, the board has found interference when salary increases were made in the context of repeated references to unionization, made effective just before an election, or announced before an election when there was no particular reason to do so.[28] However, a salary increase has been found not to interfere with the employee's right to organize when the timing, amount, and application of the increase were consistent with past practice.[29]

4. *Interrogation and polling of employees.* The NLRB originally viewed all employer interrogation of employees as to union sympathy as unlawful per se for two reasons: Such interrogation instills a fear of discrimination in the mind of the employee, thereby restraining freedom of choice, and no purpose could be served by such inquiry except to identify employees with union sympathies. The courts, however, chose not to view employee interrogation as a per se violation and instead examined it within the context of the inquiry. As a result, the board set its standard for polling of employees in *Struksnes Construction Co.*:

> Absent unusual circumstances, the polling of employees by an employer will be violative of Section 8(a)(1) of the act unless the following safeguards are observed: the purpose of the poll is to determine the truth of a union's claim of majority, this purpose is communicated to the employees, assurances against reprisals are given, the employees are polled by secret ballot, and the employer has not engaged in unfair labor practices or otherwise created a coercive atmosphere.[30]

GOOD-FAITH REASONABLE DOUBT

An NLRB rule that provides an employer who entertains a good-faith reasonable doubt that the employees support the incumbent union may request an election, withdraw recognition and refuse to bargain with that union, or conduct an informal poll of employees.

A long-standing NLRB precedent provides that an employer who entertains a **good-faith reasonable doubt** whether a majority of its employees support an incumbent union has three options:

- To request a formal board-supervised election
- To withdraw recognition from the union and refuse to bargain
- To conduct an internal poll of employee support for the union

In the 1998 decision of *Allentown Mack Sales & Service, Inc. v. NLRB*,[31] the Supreme Court held the "good-faith reasonable doubt" test for employer polling to be consistent with the National Labor Relations Act. The reasonable doubt standard is the same one used to support a representation petition (RM) that is used when an employer questions if a labor organization continues to represent a majority of the employees.[32] And the NLRB held that in determining whether an employer had a good-faith uncertainty under *Allentown Mack*, statements by known union opponents to the effect that other unnamed employees opposed union representation were entitled to "little weight."[33]

Individual or isolated questioning of employees is not a per se violation of the act. Tests of noncoercive questioning are whether an employer has a legitimate interest in the information sought, the employee is assured that no reprisals will result from the answer, and there is no evidence of coercion in the interrogation itself. Such interrogation can arise when an employer attempts to prepare a defense for an NLRB unfair labor practice proceeding. However, if under all the circumstances the interrogation reasonably tends to restrain or interfere with employees in the exercise of their rights, it will be held unlawful (see Case 10-1). Previously, the board had held that questioning of open and well-known union adherents was inherently coercive, but under its decision in *Rossmore House*, the totality of the circumstances must now be examined to determine if a violation has occurred.[34]

CASE 10-1

Unlawful Interrogation

The company is in the business of selling automotive replacement parts at wholesale from 11 warehouses and distribution centers in the eastern United States. Early on the morning of May 12, 1994, the plant manager summoned an employee to his office and asked whether she had heard rumors about the union. When she replied that she had, the plant manager asked what he could do to stop the union and if getting rid of a particular supervisor whom the workers disliked would help. The employee said she did not know, and the conversation ended.

The union charged the company with an unfair labor practice because asking the employee whether the union could be stopped if he terminated the disliked supervisor constituted an unlawful offer to improve working conditions in violation of Section 8(a)(1). In addition the union alleged that the conversation was an unlawful interrogation.

The company contended that there was no coercion during this conversation inasmuch as the plant manager was unaware that the employee had signed a union card, he had spoken with her a number of times over the years, and he "trusted" her.

An employer violates Section 8(a)(1) when it interrogates an employee about the union where the questioning reasonably tends to restrain, coerce, or interfere with employees' rights guaranteed by the act. To determine whether the inquiry is coercive, the board considers the following factors: the background, the nature of the information sought, the identity of the questioner, and the place and method of interrogation.

Decision

Applying these factors to the plant manager's interrogation of the employee, the board found that the union amply demonstrated coercion on the part of the company of the type prohibited by Section 8(a)(1). As of May 12, 1994, the employee was not an open and active union supporter. On that date, the plant manager, the highest management official at the facility, summoned her to his office for no purpose other than to ask her about the union and, during the course of the brief conversation, unlawfully promised to improve working conditions to stop the union effort. Where the interrogation is accompanied by threats or other violations of Section 8(a)(1), as this one was, there can be no question as to the coercive effect of the inquiry.

Source: Adapted from *Parts Depot, Inc. v. NLRB,* 170 LRRM 1005 (2000).

5. *Surveillance.* Surveillance in almost any form has been held a violation of the unfair labor practices section of the National Labor Relations Act. The board has such an aversion to surveillance that it will uphold findings even if the employees know nothing about it or the surveillance was only an employer's attempt to foster an impression of scrutiny. Encouraging surveillance and eavesdropping by union members has also been condemned by the NLRB.

6. *Poll Activity.* The NLRB prohibits any electioneering at or near the polls in a campaign. In fact, in *Milchem, Inc.*, the board applied a strict rule that conversations between company or union officials in the polling area are prohibited regardless of what is discussed. Although the exact distance within this rule varies, the board often sets a radius of 100 feet around the polls.

7. *24-Hour Rule.* In a 1953 case, *Peerless Plywood Co.*,[35] the board detailed a **24-hour rule**, which it has maintained for more than 50 years. The 24-hour rule prohibits employers and unions from making organizational campaign speeches on company time to large assemblies of employees within 24 hours of a scheduled election—the 24-hour rule. However, such meetings within 24 hours of an election do not violate these rules if voluntarily attended on the employee's own time. Employers may assemble their employees and speak to them on company time if it is prior to 24 hours to the election and if the employer does not prevent, by rigid no-solicitation rules, access to the employees by the union representatives.

24-HOUR RULE

This NLRB rule prohibits employers and unions from making organizational campaign speeches on company time to assemblies of employees within 24 hours of a scheduled election.

On election day, prolonged conversations between either party and the voters are prohibited, as are traditional campaign activities at the polling place. For example, election-day raffles have been held to be illegal because of the potential to taint an election[36]. In recent studies of employee participation in representative elections, some questions have been raised as to what degree even a legal campaign discourages participation.[37] If an employee perceives that an election will be won or lost regardless of his or her vote, that employee may choose not to vote at all.[38]

UNION INTERFERENCE WITH AN ORGANIZING CAMPAIGN The activities that concern representation elections, including the 24-hour rule, electioneering near polls, and coercion, apply equally to unions and employers. In addition, unions, under Section 8(b)(1)(A) of the National Labor Relations Act, are prohibited from the threat or use of violence against unsupportive employees. Threats, if made by union organizers or merely supportive employees, may cause the

NLRB to overturn an election.[39] For example, in *United Broadcasting Co. of New York*, a union steward told an employee he would be blacklisted and could never work again in New York: The union victory was overturned.[40]

Examples of unfair labor practices during union organizing campaigns can be found in Table 10-1.

TABLE 10-1 Organizational Campaign

Unfair Labor Practice	Not an Unfair Labor Practice
Organizing a Bargaining Unit	
Not letting employees solicit union support outside of working time on employer's premises	Not letting employees solicit union support during working time on or off of employer's premises
Not letting nonemployees solicit union support outside of working time on employer's premise if there is absolutely no other way to reach employees	Not letting nonemployees solicit union support outside of working time on employer's premise if union has any other access
Not letting employees distribute union material outside of working time in nonworking areas	No-leafleting policy applies equally to distribution of all types of material
Restricting employees' display of union buttons which do not interfere with employer's business	Restricting employees' display of union buttons if it causes a hazard
Not allowing use of a bulletin board and meeting halls for union business	Not allowing use of a bulletin board and meeting halls for any non-job-related business
Not allowing use of company e-mail for union business	Not allowing use of company e-mail for any "non-job-related" business and/or allowing use of company e-mail only for personal use
Union picketing for recognition for longer than 30 days without filing an election petition	
Election Campaign Activity: Employer and Union	
Misrepresentation in campaign literature using forgery or fraud	Campaign literature that exaggerates facts
Direct threats of economic reprisals during a campaign	Communicating general views about possible economic consequence of unionization
Promising or granting benefits during a campaign	Granting benefits during campaign consistent with past practice as to timing and amount
Threats (by union) to employees that they will lose their jobs unless they support the union	
Engaging in picket line misconduct, such as threatening, assaulting, or barring nonstrikers from the employer's premises	
Interrogating or polling employees as to union sympathy	Interrogating or polling employees under a "good-faith reasonable doubt" as to majority support for union
Surveillance and eavesdropping	
Electioneering near polls	Electioneering outside a 100 foot radius from polls
Campaign speeches on company time within 24 hours of an election	Campaign speeches on employee's own time 24 hours of an election if attendance is voluntary

Employer Domination and Interference

Under the National Labor Relations Act, in addition to campaign-related violations, employers' domination of and assistance to labor organizations are also *employer unfair labor practices.* This provision obviously reflects the historical aversion to company unions of the 1930s that were used to discourage outside union organization. The National Labor Relations Act views employer interference in the internal workings of a union as a threat to the employees' free exercise of guaranteed rights.

The unlawful domination and assistance pertains only to labor organizations. Employee recreation committees, credit unions, social clubs, and the like may be initiated and supported by the employer without violation. Once a labor organization is identified, the board looks for prohibited domination or support. *Support* is mere assistance to a favored union, whereas domination means actual control of the union. An employer-created organization falls within the prohibited controls section of the act.

Employee Teams and the NLRA

The National Labor Relations Board (NLRB) in two historic decisions has limited the creation of employee committees or teams by its strict interpretation of the Wagner Act. In the **Electromation case**, the board found that the company illegally created and dominated a labor organization.[41] The case involved the Electromation Company of Elkhart, Indiana, a nonunion electrical parts manufacturer. The employer crafted six "action committees" to deal with the employees on various issues. The committees contained members of both management and hourly workers and were charged with developing proposals for management's consideration. Issues considered by the action committees included pay, absenteeism, and attendance bonus programs. The Teamsters union had begun an organizing drive at the company about the time the committees were created. The NLRB ruled that the company clearly violated Section 8(a)(2) of the National Labor Relations Act by creating the action committees. The board decided that the committees had been formed for the purpose, at least in part, of "dealing with" the employer over conditions of employment.

ELECTROMATION CASE

A Supreme Court case in which the Court ruled that the employer-created "work committees" comprising both employees and managers that met to discuss working conditions were a violation of the National Labor Relations Act.

In the 1993 landmark *duPont* case, the NLRB ordered the company to dismantle seven committees of labor and management representatives that had been established to work on safety and recreation issues at the Deepwater, New Jersey, plant.[42] The board ruled that the company had illegally bypassed the plant's union by setting up the committees and thus violated the Wagner Act. This was the board's first ruling on labor–management committees in a unionized plant. The board did note that "brainstorming" sessions might be held if decisions are made by a majority vote and management representatives are in the minority.

From these cases and others, it can be concluded, in general, that employee teams having the authority to make decisions and act without obtaining employer approval are not illegal labor organizations.[43] If joint labor–management teams or committees are created to consider employment issues and a union represents the employees, the union must be involved in the creation of the groups. If such groups are created, they should be voluntary and contain more union members than management.

A decision by the NLRB, however, appears to signal a possible departure from the board's holdings in *Electromation* and *duPont*. Under *Electromation* the board had a consistent, restrictive approach to employee committee issues. This approach lasted throughout the 1990s and until mid-2001, when *Crown Cork & Seal*[44] was decided. Crown Cork & Seal Company, an aluminum can manufacturing plant, employed approximately 150 employees who were not represented by a union. From the time the plant opened, it operated under an employee–management system in which substantial authority was delegated to employees to operate the facility through their participation on numerous standing committees. These employee participation committees consisted of employees and managers and made decisions concerning a broad range of matters, including production, quality, training, attendance, safety, and maintenance. Committees also decided certain disciplinary issues. The board found the employee committees lawful on the grounds that none of the committees were "dealing" with management because "dealing" is not present where a committee's purpose is to perform managerial functions. Indeed, the board found that an employee committee with delegated managerial authority does not "deal with" management because they are management.

Domination of a union may also be found when the employer does not create a union. The employer's behavior toward an existing union may result in the employees' freedom of choice being unlawfully infringed. Courts have found domination when supervisors solicited union membership, the employer's attorney acted for the union in drafting its constitution and bylaws, and the employer allowed union officials on company time and property to pursue a union organization drive. Tests for domination are subjective from the standpoint of the employees.[45] Another violation of this section is employer interference by friendly cooperation with the creation or operation of a labor organization. A suggestion in and of itself by an employer that a union be formed is not an unfair labor practice, but interference may be found if the suggestion is timed to counter an organizational drive by an outside union. After a union has been recognized, a violation may occur if supervisors and company executives who gained membership status prior to their promotions remain in the union.

Employer Support and Assistance

Although domination and control of a labor organization clearly violate the act, support and assistance of a labor organization by the employer present a different problem. Often the suspect activities may be a manifestation of the employer's legal cooperation with the union. If the support does not have any effect on the employees' exercise of their rights guaranteed by the act and is trivial, no violation will be found.

Assistance or support that does violate the NLRA is employer aid to one of two competing unions. The employer can unlawfully favor one union by giving direct assistance to its campaign drive, by allowing it exclusive use of company facilities, by supplying the union with employee names to aid in a raid of the other union's membership, and by assessing and collecting union dues without signed authorization cards. Prior to 1982, continuing to recognize an incumbent union when an election challenge is pending would have been a violation of the act. The board determined in that year that the mere filing of a representation petition by an outside union does not require or permit an employer to withdraw from bargaining with the incumbent union.[46] Financial support of a union, either directly by donating money or indirectly by, for instance, allowing the union to receive the profits from company-owned vending machines, are other violations of the support and assistance provisions.

DISCRIMINATION AGAINST UNION MEMBERS

Discrimination against employees, based on their union activities, is an unfair labor practice and an obvious deterrent to successful collective bargaining. A violation of the act occurs when an employer encourages or discourages membership in any labor organization by hiring or tenure practices or by using membership as a term or condition of employment.

Discrimination occurs when a union member is treated differently from a nonunion worker because he or she is involved in union activity. In general, the fact that a particular incident took place is not an issue. It is easy to ascertain that a refusal to hire, a discharge, or a change in an employment condition has occurred. The question for the board to resolve is whether the action was motivated by a desire to encourage or discourage union membership and thereby discriminate against the member. **Antiunion animus** is found when the employer's conduct is not motivated, or at least is not entirely motivated, by legitimate and substantial business reasons but by a desire to penalize or reward employees for union activity or the lack of it.

ANTIUNION ANIMUS

When an employer's conduct is not motivated, or at least not entirely motivated, by legitimate and substantial business reasons but by a desire to penalize or reward employees for union activity or the lack of it.

An employer has a right to select employees and take disciplinary action to maintain good business conditions. The NLRB must weigh claims of discrimination by the employee against claims by the employer that certain actions were taken for cause.

Discrimination cases fall into two categories. In a **dual-motive discrimination case**, two explanations for the action complained of can be offered by the employer. One constitutes a legitimate business reason, and the other is a reason prohibited under the act. In a **pretext discrimination case**, the employer puts forth only the legitimate business reason, but the complainant asserts that the prohibited reason is the true cause for the action. Approximately 60 percent of the unfair labor practice cases presented to the board involve a charge of discrimination for union activity. Prior to 1980, the board's test in these cases was to decide if the antiunion animus of the employer played a part in the complaint. If so, the employer was found to have violated the act. Since then, however, the board has required the employee to present a prima facie case that the antiunion animus of the employer played a substantial or motivating role in the complaint before requiring the employer to justify the action taken.[47]

DUAL-MOTIVE DISCRIMINATION CASE

A case in which the employer puts forth two explanations for taking an action against an employee—one constitutes a legitimate business reason and the other is a reason prohibited under the NLRA as an unfair labor practice.

PRETEXT DISCRIMINATION CASE

An unfair labor practice charge in which an employer puts forth a legitimate business reason for taking an action, but the employee asserts that the true reason is one prohibited under the NLRA.

Discriminatory acts by the employer in compliance with a union shop provision in a collective bargaining agreement do not violate the act. The act specifically allows a collective bargaining agreement to require that new employees join the union within 30 days of employment.

Applicants for jobs as well as persons already employed are protected by the act. The language "discrimination in regard to hire" could stand no other interpretation. Therefore, it is an unfair labor practice for an employer to refuse to hire an applicant because of union activities. It is also a violation to offer employment on the condition that the applicant will not join or participate in a union. As discussed in Chapter 4, union "salts" have, to some extent, been treated differently than other union members seeking employment. The Supreme Court ruled in *NLRB v. Town and Country Electric*[48] that regardless of one's relationship with one's union, each employee of the nonunion company has rights under the National Labor Relations Act. If the employee is doing the work asked by his or her employer, union activities cannot be used against the employee.[49] The lower court had ruled that paid union organizers, or "salts," were not employees in the true meaning of the act and thus did not have the right to organize and engage in collective bargaining. The rationale provided by the lower court was that paid organizers served the union's interests and not the interests of the employer. In disagreeing, however, the Supreme Court noted that (1) paid union organizers fall within the definition of "employee," (2) individuals can be employed by two employers without losing their employee status, and (3) an employee has the right to attempt to persuade fellow employees to support or join a union.[50] The protection of salting as an effective organizing tool has been diminished by these rulings of the NLRB: A union interfered with employees' right not to organize by granting "salts" preference dispatching treatment in a hiring hall over other members who were not willing or able to act as salts;[51] limited back-pay awards to those discriminated against in a salting case because there is no presumption in salting cases that the employee would have stayed with the employer for any significant length of time even if hired;[52] and required that an applicant's genuine interest in securing employment must be proven to sustain an unfair labor practices charge. It provided a two-prong test for ascertaining such interest (1) the individual, or someone particularly designated by the individual, has to actually apply for a position and (2) the application must reflect that the applicant is sincerely seeking employment.[53]

Obvious acts of discrimination against employees regarding wages, hours, and working conditions may lead to charges of unfair labor practices. As discussed earlier, withholding benefits pending union recognition elections is an unfair labor practice if the purpose is to influence the election. Discrimination can arise when an employer treats striking employees differently from nonstriking employees. For example, discrimination may be found if an employer announces that he or she will pay vacation benefits under an expired agreement to returning strikers, nonstriking workers, and strike replacements but not to strikers.

Examples of when an employer commits an unfair labor practice by attempting to take over a labor organization and when an employer is guilty of discriminating against union members can be found in Table 10-2.

TABLE 10-2 Employer Interference with Union and Discrimination

Unfair Labor Practice	Not an Unfair Labor Practice
Employer Interference with Labor Organizations	
Company created employee group which "deals with" the employer on issues of grievances, labor disputes, wages, work rules, or hours of employment	Company created employee group to performs managerial duties
Company participation in union's internal activities	
Company support of one union over another	
Discrimination in Employment	
Taking employment action against employee because of union status	Taking employment action against employee because of union status *and* a legitimate business reason so that antiunion animus is not the substantial reason for the action (dual-motive discrimination)
Taking employment action against employee citing legitimate business reason	Taking employment action against employee and union status is the real reason (pretext discrimination)
Refusing to hire because of union activities	Not hiring "salts" when the applicant(s) is not genuinely interested in getting the job
Hiring on condition applicant will not join union	
Treating striking employees different from nonstriking employees	

PROTECTED CONCERTED ACTIVITIES

CONCERTED ACTIVITY

Any legitimate action taken by employees to further their common but not individual interests, such as wages, hours, and working conditions.

Employers that discriminate against employees for engaging in concerted activities violate the interference, restraint, or coercion provisions of the unfair labor practices section of the act and also violate the discrimination for purposes of discouraging union membership provision. **Concerted activity** is any action by employees to further legitimately their common interests pursued on behalf of or with other employees and not solely by and on behalf of an individual.[54] The most common form of concerted activity is the *strike*. Concerted activity need not involve union leadership or membership to be protected. To establish concerted activity, certain elements must exist: The issue involved must be work related, the goal should be to further a group interest, a specific remedy or result is sought, and the act itself must not be unlawful or improper.

The work-relatedness requirement is not stringently applied. The board has found many activities protected under the act:

1. Employees assisting another employer's personnel to unionize
2. Union resolution condemning employer's opposition to another union's strike
3. Union support of workers' compensation law changes
4. Union lobbying against the National Immigration Policy
5. Union lobbying against right-to-work laws[55]

However, as seen in Case 10-2, the courts do not always agree with the NLRB's findings.

CASE 10-2

Employer's Unfair Labor Practice: Retaliation

The company, an industrial general contractor, received a contract to modernize a steel mill near the beginning of 1987. According to the company, various unions attempted to delay the project because the company's employees were nonunion. The company and the mill operator filed suit against those unions based on the following basic allegations:

1. The unions had lobbied for adoption and enforcement of an emissions standard despite having no real concern the project would harm the environment.
2. The unions had passed out handbills and picketed at the company's site—and also encouraged strikes among the employees of the company's subcontractors—without revealing reasons for their disagreement.
3. The unions had filed an action in state court alleging violations of the Health and Safety Code to delay the construction project and raise costs.
4. The unions had launched grievance proceedings against the company's joint venture partner based on inapplicable collective bargaining agreements.

Initially, the company and the mill operator sought damages under Section 303 of the Labor–Management Relations Act, which provides a cause of action against labor organizations for injuries caused by secondary boycotts prohibited under Section 158(b)(4). But after the court granted the unions' motion for summary judgment on the company's lobbying- and grievance-related claims, it amended the complaint to allege that the unions' activities violated Sections 1 and 2 of the Sherman Antitrust Act, which prohibit certain agreements in restraint of trade, monopolization, and attempts to monopolize.

The court dismissed the amended complaint because it realleged claims that had already been decided. The appeals court affirmed the dismissal of the company's antitrust claim because the unions had antitrust immunity when lobbying officials or petitioning courts and agencies, unless the activity was a sham. The company did not argue that the unions' litigation activity had been objectively baseless but maintained that "the unions had engaged in a pattern of automatic petitioning of governmental bodies . . . without regard to . . . the merits of said petitions."

In the meantime, two unions had lodged complaints against the company with the NLRB, and after the federal proceedings ended, the board's general counsel issued an administrative complaint against the company, alleging that it had violated Section 8(a)(1) of the National Labor Relations Act by filing and maintaining the federal lawsuit. Section 8(a)(1) prohibits employers from restraining, coercing, or interfering with employees' exercise of rights related to self-organization, collective bargaining, and other concerted activities.

The NLRB ruled that the company's federal lawsuit had been unmeritorious because all of the company's claims were dismissed or voluntarily withdrawn with prejudice. The board then examined whether the company's suit had been filed to retaliate against the unions for engaging in activities protected under the National Labor Relations Act. The board first concluded that the unions' conduct was protected activity and then decided that the company's lawsuit had been unlawfully motivated because it was directed at protected conduct and necessarily tended to discourage similar protected activity. The NLRB also found evidence of retaliatory motive because the company's Labor–Management Relations Act claims had an utter absence of merit and had been dismissed on summary judgment. The NLRB found that the company had committed an unfair labor practice because the suit it brought was unsuccessful and retaliatory. The company appealed to the Supreme Court.

(continued)

Decision

The Supreme Court reversed the judgment, however, holding that the same application of the First Amendment that kept the unions from being found in violation of the Sherman Antitrust Act for lobbying efforts prevented the company from being charged with an unfair labor practice. Under the First Amendment, citizens are allowed the right to "petition" their government. Joining together to lobby elected officials, which certainly unions do, is a protected activity and cannot be found to have violated the Sherman Antitrust Act. Likewise, "petitioning" the government includes the right to seek redress with the court system. So that filing a well-founded, albeit unsuccessful, lawsuit, even if it would not have been commenced but for the company's desire to retaliate against the unions for exercising rights protected by the National Labor Relations Act, is a protected activity under the First Amendment.

The case, being reversed and decided on constitutional grounds and not under the NLRA, was sent back to the NLRB for review of the unfair labor practice charge. The NLRB ruled that an employer exercising protected First Amendment rights, that is, bringing a reasonably based lawsuit, could not be charged with an unfair labor practice just because the lawsuit had been brought for a retaliatory reason against a union and was, ultimately, unsuccessful.

Source: Adapted from *BE & K Construction Company v. NLRB,* 170 LRRM 2225 (2002); and *BE & K Construction Company*, 351 NLRB No. 29 (September 29, 2007).

Unprotected concerted activities occur when the employees are violent, act in breach of contract, or engage in activities otherwise prohibited by the act, such as jurisdictional strikes or secondary boycotts. Employees can lose the protection of Section 7's concerted activities if they take actions disproportionate to the grievance involved. Disparaging an employer's product without clarification of the context of the dispute is such an action.

STRIKES A strike is a type of concerted activity protected under the act if it is called for economic reasons (an *economic strike*) or to protest unfair labor practices (*unfair labor practice strike*). Any retaliation against employees participating in a primary strike is therefore an unfair labor practice. For example, if a union member was fired for union activities, workers could stage a strike until the discriminatory practice was remedied.

The circumstances that cause workers to strike and form a picket line are often tense and thus can easily provoke strikers to "let off steam," an impulse that can easily lead to serious misconduct. Workers on strike may resort to conduct that the employer believes is improper—conduct that causes damage to property or, in some cases, even bodily harm. The NLRB has held that activities of striking employees constitute serious misconduct when they "reasonably tend to coerce or intimidate employees."[56] The application of this standard has led the courts and the NLRB to consider *physical acts or threats of physical harm directed at nonstriking employees (called* **scabs***) to be serious and warrant possible discharge*. Actions that have been ruled as serious misconduct include the throwing of rocks or eggs, vandalizing a supervisor's car, carrying a gun or a club on the picket line, and threatening physical harm.[57] In *Clear Pine Mouldings, Inc.*,[58] the NLRB ruled that verbal threats alone could warrant the discharge of a striker who, while carrying a gun, threatened to kill a nonstriking employee. In most cases, the isolated instance of obscenities or name-calling alone is not considered serious strike misconduct. If an employer fires striking employees because of serious misconduct, the employer is not required to show that all the employees engaged in the activity if they were "actively cooperating" in the misconduct. And violent activity can result in the removal of the participants from the protection of the National Labor Relations Act. An examination of misconduct cases led one labor attorney to conclude that arbitrators are generally tolerant of strikers' misconduct, particularly if the employer provoked the incident.[59]

SCABS

Workers who cross picket lines to work when union employees are on strike.

This distinction between how striking employees are treated as a result of either an economic or an unfair labor practice strike was established by a Supreme Court decision in 1938.[60] As discussed in Chapter 6, the Court decided employers could permanently replace striking workers without violating the (then three-year-old) Wagner Act. The Court noted that although Section 13 of the National Labor Relations Act prohibits the interference with employees' right to strike, an employer has the right to continue the operations of a business and replace strikers. Three NLRB decisions which modified the Court's ruling held that employers cannot permanently replace strikers who are striking over an unfair labor practice, strikers who apply for reinstatement unconditionally must be placed on a "waiting list" and hired as jobs become available, and employers cannot grant pay raises to replacements not offered to strikers.[61]

ILLEGAL STRIKES Strikes undertaken by unlawful means or purposes are not legal, and employees can be fired. Unlawful means of conducting a strike include the following:

1. ***Sit-down strike.*** A takeover of the employer's property. This action is seen as a violation of the owner's property rights.
2. ***Wildcat strike.*** An economic strike conducted by a minority of the workers without the approval of the union and in violation of a no-strike clause in an existing contract. Although courts try to discourage such actions to ensure the continued credibility of the union, these strikes may be sanctioned if actually called to protect one of the union's aims.[62]
3. ***Partial strike.*** Various types of job actions, such as a work slowdown or refusal to work overtime. This action is seen as a violation of the owner's property rights.
4. ***Sickout.*** An organized effort to have workers call in sick. In the 1990s, the fastest growing type of job action was the **sickout**. In December 1998, for example, Trans World Airlines was forced to cancel 240 flights after the flight attendants all called in sick during the week of Christmas. In an age when most labor unions try to avoid strikes if possible, the sickout is a good alternative job action. The action sends a clear message to the employer and can cause real inconvenience and loss of income. However, unlike when workers go out on an economic strike, they are not out long enough to be replaced with new permanent employees. Public sector unions, usually under no-strike laws, used sickouts more often than private sector unions in past years. But private sector unions have increasingly used the tactic as a show of strength and to protest stalled contract negotiations. They can be most effective when used by employees who cannot be easily replaced.[63]

SICKOUT
An illegal partial strike in which employees call in sick to protest a working condition.

In the absence of an absolute strike, the employer cannot replace the workers to keep the operation going, although the employer continues to be responsible for the workers' wages.

The National Labor Relations Act requires that a union desiring to terminate or modify an existing contract may not strike for 60 days after giving written notice to the employer or before the termination date of the contract, whichever occurs later. Also, the appropriate federal and state mediation agencies must be notified within 30 days. Any strike held during the 60-day period is unlawful.

The National Labor Relations Act outlaws some consequences for which workers might strike. The following are unlawful ends that make a strike illegal:

1. ***Jurisdictional strike.*** Called because two unions are in dispute as to whose workers deserve the work. For example, an electrical union could strike a construction site in protest of laborers being used to unload electrical supplies.
2. ***Featherbedding strike.*** When a union tries to pressure the employer to make work for union members through the limitation of production, increasing the amount of work to be performed, or other make-work arrangements.
3. ***Recognitional strike.*** When a strike is called to gain recognition for another union if a certified union already represents employees.[64]

Prominent U.S. Strikes

The number of major economic strikes (1,000 or more workers) has declined sharply in recent years—to a record low of only 11 in 2010. However, a few significant strikes which have attracted the news media and permanently affected U.S. labor–management relations are summarized in Table 10-3.

TABLE 10-3 Major US Strikes 1983 to Present

The 1983 and 1989 Telephone Workers Strikes	Nearly 700,000 unionized telephone workers broke a 12-year labor peace on August 7, 1983. This strike was partially the result of an order by a federal judge to divest AT&T into 22 local operating companies. Management's ability to endure the strike by means of automated equipment and longer shifts of supervision was something new—telescabbing, using modern technology as a substitute for labor during a called strike.
The 1986–1987 Steel Industry Negotiations	For the first time in 30 years, the major U.S. steelmakers decided in the spring of 1986 not to bargain jointly. The prior use of coordinated bargaining enabled all the major steel producers to negotiate common wage rates and benefits with the United Steelworkers of America.
The 1993 United Mine Workers Strike	In early May 1993, the United Mine Workers began a selective strike against coal producers after contract negotiations failed to result in a new master agreement with the Bituminous Coal Operators Association. The primary goal of the union during the talks was to stem the coal operators' practice of opening new nonunion mines.
The 1994 Baseball Players Strike	The most disastrous strike in sports history canceled the 1994 World Series and cost the sport many fans and significant revenue (see Chapter 1).
The 1996 General Motors Strike	A local labor dispute in one plant eventually crippled the world's largest automobile company. UAW local in Dayton, Ohio, went on strike over outsourcing, the employer practice of giving business to nonunion suppliers that usually eventually means fewer union jobs. The strike gained national prominence and historical significance because the Dayton General Motors plant supplied 90 percent of the brakes for GM cars and trucks. Thus, within weeks, more than 72,000 workers at 21 of GM's 29 North American auto assembly plants were idled at a cost of $45 million per day.
The 1997 UPS Strike	The Teamsters union strike idled over 180,000 workers and crippled delivery of packages worldwide. A central issue was part-time versus full-time jobs. The union won 10,000 new full-time jobs and focused national attention on this issue. After the strike the Teamsters kept pressure on UPS to add the promised new full-time jobs. One successful method used by the union was to ask its members online (www.teamsters.org) to help identify exactly where full-time jobs were needed (see Figure 10-4).
The 2001 Comair Strike	Comair, once one of the most successful of the regional U.S. airlines, began an 89-day strike in the spring of 2001 by the Airlines Pilots Association, costing Comair and parent company Delta Airlines almost $500 million in expenses and lost revenue. In addition 2,400 nonpilot employees were laid off because of the strike. With the strike settled in June 2001, Comair had slowly begun to rebuild when the aftermath of September 11, 2001, severely hit the entire airline industry and stalled Comair's recovery.

TABLE 10-3 *(Continued)*

The 2003–2004 Southern California Grocery Chain Lockout and Strike	In October 2003, contract negotiations between the United Food and Commercial Workers Union and Kroger's West Coast grocery chains (Albertsons, Vons, and Ralphs) broke down over health care costs. A bitter 20-week strike caused Kroger Company to lose over $337 million in one quarter and cost over 70,000 workers in 860 stores from San Diego to San Luis Obispo almost five months of income. Kroger cited the need to lower operating costs to compete with the nation's largest food retailer, Walmart, which is nonunion and estimated to have substantially lower personnel costs. The new contract, approved in February 2004, contained a "two-tiered" system of wages and health care benefits, with employees hired after October 5, 2003, placed on a lower tier. The union tried unsuccessfully to resist the two-tier approach.
The 2007–2008 Writers Guild Strike	The Writers Guild of America, representing over 12,000 television and movie writers in Hollywood as well as the East Coast, struck the Alliance of Motion Picture and Television producers. The strike was the first in 20 years by the writers and affected millions of movie fans and TV viewers, and cost the entertainment industry over $500 million in lost commercial revenues. The key issue was the writers' demand for a greater percentage of DVD, download, and online revenues.

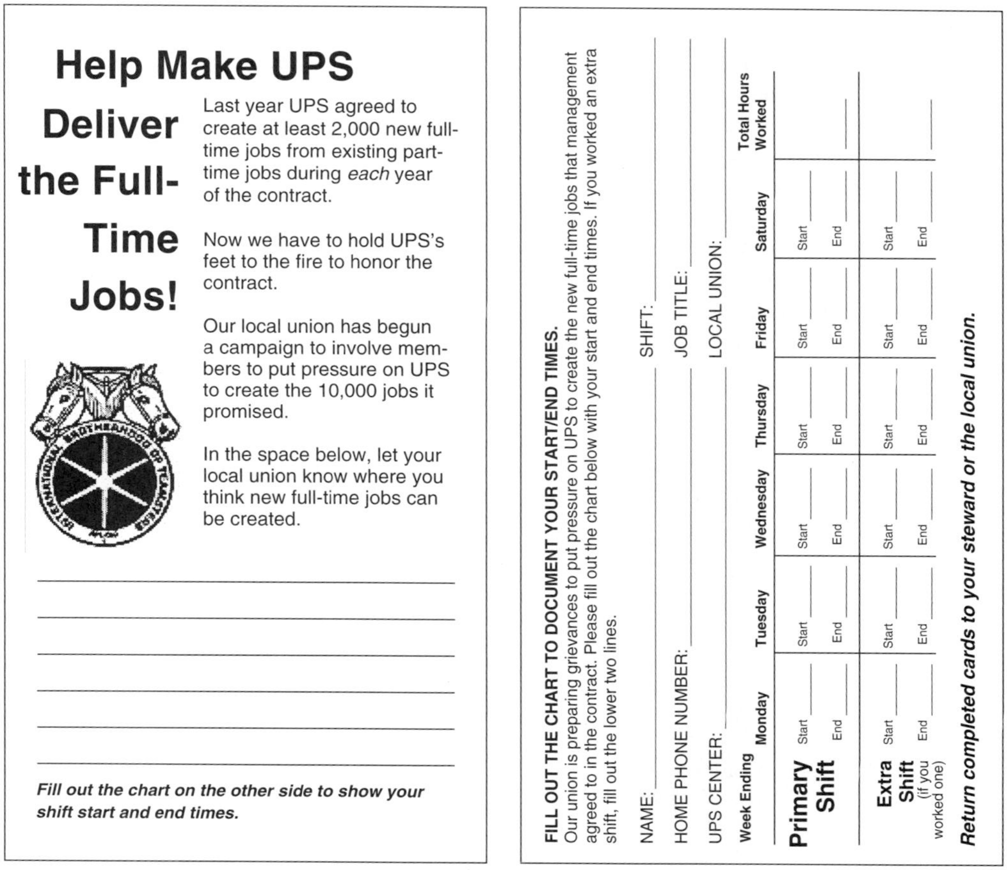
Help Make UPS Deliver the Full-Time Jobs!

Last year UPS agreed to create at least 2,000 new full-time jobs from existing part-time jobs during *each* year of the contract.

Now we have to hold UPS's feet to the fire to honor the contract.

Our local union has begun a campaign to involve members to put pressure on UPS to create the 10,000 jobs it promised.

In the space below, let your local union know where you think new full-time jobs can be created.

Fill out the chart on the other side to show your shift start and end times.

FILL OUT THE CHART TO DOCUMENT YOUR START/END TIMES.
Our union is preparing grievances to put pressure on UPS to create the new full-time jobs that management agreed to in the contract. Please fill out the chart below with your start and end times. If you worked an extra shift, fill out the lower two lines.

NAME: ______ SHIFT: ______
HOME PHONE NUMBER: ______ JOB TITLE: ______
UPS CENTER: ______ LOCAL UNION: ______

Week Ending	Monday	Tuesday	Wednesday	Thursday	Friday	Saturday	Total Hours Worked
Primary Shift	Start ___ End ___	Start ___ End ___	Start ___ End ___	Start ___ End ___	Start ___ End ___	Start ___ End ___	
Extra Shift (if you worked one)	Start ___ End ___	Start ___ End ___	Start ___ End ___	Start ___ End ___	Start ___ End ___	Start ___ End ___	

Return completed cards to your steward or the local union.

Front of Palm Card Back of Palm Card

FIGURE 10-1 Teamster Online Appeal to Members. *Source:* Available at www.teamsters.org/98ups.

Weingarten Rule

WEINGARTEN RULE

A Supreme Court ruling that a union employee has the right to request the presence of a union official during a meeting with management if the meeting may involve a discipline issue.

The U.S. Supreme Court in the case *NLRB v. Weingarten, Inc.*[65] adopted what is today one of the most important concerted activity rights provided employees by the NLRA. The Court held that employees under Section 7 of the NLRA are entitled to have a union representative present during an investigatory interview where the employee fears the interview may result in their receiving discipline. However, under this **Weingarten Rule**, while an employee has the right to union representation during an investigatory interview, such representation is limited by the employer's right to conduct the interview. The role of the union representative is to protect the employees without interfering with the legitimate rights of the employer, without turning the interview into an adversarial contest. The role of the union representative therefore is seen to lie somewhere between mandatory silence and adversarial confrontation. The employer cannot request that the union representative remain silent during the interview. The union representative may advise the employee against answering questions that are perceived to be abusive, misleading, badgering, confusing, or harassing.[66]

The Court reasoned that employee representation is appropriate due to the NLRA's purpose of eliminating the inequality of power between the employer and the employee. However, the Court also noted that the employer is not obligated in any way to bargain with the union representative. If an employer denies an employee a union representative, the NLRB under the Weingarten Rule will usually grant a "make-whole" remedy, including reinstatement, back pay, and the removal of all related discipline records, except in discipline cases involving "just cause." The employer cannot discipline an employee for the union representative's conduct, but may discipline the representative.

The original *Weingarten* decision has been narrowed by subsequent board decisions. For example, the union employee cannot refuse to attend a meeting with management without a union representative because until the meeting begins, the employee cannot know it is an investigatory interview,[67] and a union steward can be expelled from an investigatory interview if the steward interferes with the employer's legitimate right to investigate.[68] Thus, management can request some meetings with employees without a steward present and is not obligated under *Weingarten* to tell employees when they do have the right to have their steward present. The general purpose for having a steward present when a disciplinary situation may be discussed is to (1) provide a witness, (2) provide the employee with assistance of a person experienced in such situations, and (3) advise the employee about what to say and not say. The International Brotherhood of Teamsters provides their members printed cards with language to use if management asks about a potential disciplinary situation. The card reads, "If this discussion could in any way lead to my being disciplined or terminated, or affect my personal working conditions, I request that my union representative, officer, or steward be present at the meeting. Without representation, I choose not to answer any questions."[69]

Tips from the Experts

Union Most Common Unfair Labor Practices

What are the most common unfair labor practices unions should avoid, and how can it do so?

A. Charge: 8(b)(1), interfering with employees rights under Seciton 7. In states where unions can negotiate union shop provisions, employees must become a union member or at least pay a lawful fee representing the cost of being represented. Unions can seek the employee's suspension, discharge, or other punishment for not being a union member but not if the employee has paid or offered to pay the applicable fees. Union officials have to be very careful to respect the employee's right not to be a union member.

B. Charge: 8(b)(2), discriminting against an employee for not engaging in union activities. A union must fairly represent all of the employees covered by a collective bargaining agreement in the grievance and arbitration procedures. Union officials must be diligent in investigating and pursuing employees' rights, especially for nonunion employees to avoid a charge of failing in that duty. If the grievance is not worth pursuing, make sure that fact is documented and that a union member's similar grievance was treated the same way.

Management

What are the most common unfair labor practices management should avoid, and how can it do so?

A. Charge: 8(a)(3), discriminating against a union sympathizer/organizer/officer as regards discipline, especially termination. Avoid by either not touching those persons for violations of work rules (which makes managing the workforce very difficult) or (preferably) being doubly cautious in enforcing violations of work rules by such persons, that is, making absolutely certain that the violation and similar treatment for nonunion violators is well documented before taking action.

B. Charge: 8(a)(5), refusal to bargain/surface bargain intentionally or inadvertently, such as in unilaterally implementing a drug and alcohol policy. Avoid by scheduling sufficient numbers of negotiation sessions, being prepared and willing to make and listen to proposals, making some movement on at least some issues, not making public announcements either before bargaining commences or during the process (prior to impasse) that "X" is the company's position and that the union can go fly a kite or whatever if it thinks it will get any more, and so on. With respect to the inadvertent stuff, make sure human resources and legal are working together in the implementation of any new or major changes to current policies or benefits to ensure no unintentional unilateral changes in terms or conditions of employment.

C. Charge: 8(a)(1), interference with employees in the exercise of their Section 7 rights. Avoid soliciting information, spying, or crossing over the line in an organizing campaign. Make sure thorough supervisory training is repeated regularly and supported by an adequately staffed and respected labor relations department. Make certain the labor relations department is available for immediate assistance when necessary.

In 2004, the NLRB reversed a previous NLRB decision[70] that had extended the *Weingarten* right to employees in nonunion workplaces. That previous opinion found such activity protected under the act for all employees because it provided employees with the opportunity to act in concert to address their mutual concerns. The board in *IBM, Corp.*,[71] however, asserted that in nonunion workplaces coworkers do not represent the interests of the entire workforce, have no official status as a union representative, thus they cannot redress the imbalance of power between employer and employee, and may compromise the confidentiality of the interview. Therefore, employees who work in a nonunion organization do not have the right to request that a coworker be present in an investigatory interview.

Union Restraint or Coercion of Employees

Unfair labor practice standards were applied to labor organizations to enforce an employee's right to refrain from union activities, which was granted by the Taft-Hartley Amendments. This right includes protection to work without restraint from strikes, to refuse to sign union dues check offs, and not to be coerced into accepting a particular union or any union at all.

The amendments did not impair the right of a labor organization to prescribe its own rules on members in good standing. And if a union shop provision is part of a current collective bargaining agreement, an employee can be compelled to join the union after being hired and to pay dues or fees to retain employment. Nonetheless, in *Pattern Makers League v. National Labor Relations Board,* the Supreme Court held that a union was guilty of an unfair labor practice when it attempted to fine its members for resigning from the union and returning to work during a strike. The Court believed that such fines were an attempt to compel membership in the union in violation of Section 8(b)(1)(A) of the act.[72]

Only a labor organization or its agent can violate the section of the amendments prohibiting unfair labor practices by unions. Actions by individual employees not sanctioned by a union cannot subject the employee to an unfair labor practice charge. Coercion may also take the form of "pink sheeting"—a practice where union officials pressure organizers into disclosing sensitive personal information—recorded on pink pieces of paper. The organizers are then strongly urged to tell their personal stories of abuse or neglect to workers they were trying to organize in order to gain their support. While Unite Here, a union formed in 2004 by the merger of Unite, an apparel workers union, with Here, a hotel and restaurant employees union, adopted new guidelines against pink sheeting, several of its organizers reported that it was common practice for the aggressive, fast-growing union. One Tampa International Airport Unite Here organizer, Julia Rivera, complained that she was ordered to tell her personal story of sexual abuse again and again to workers and that "it was sick, it was horrible." Ms. Rivera left Unite Here to work for Workers United in Florida.[73]

Specific union activities that have been deemed to be in violation of the amendments include the following:

1. Physical assaults or threats of violence directed at employees or their relatives
2. Threats of economic reprisals
3. Mass picketing that restrains the lawful entry or leaving of a worksite
4. Causing or attempting to cause an employer to discriminate against employees
5. Discriminating provisions in collective bargaining agreements (union shop being an exception), for example, superseniority clauses for union members that do not exist for a legitimate purpose[74]

Unfair labor practices concerning protected concerted effort can be found in Table 10-4.

TABLE 10-4 Protected Concerted Activities

Unfair Labor Practice	Not an Unfair Labor Practice
Protected Concerted Activities	
Taking action against workers for primary strike for economic reasons or to protest unfair labor practice	Taking action against striking workers who are engaged in illegal strikes such as secondary strikes or boycotts, sit-down strike, wildcat strike, partial strike, sickout
Replacing striking workers with permanent employees during an unfair labor practice strike	Replacing striking workers with permanent employees during an economic strike
Unions striking under an existing contract	Unions striking under an existing contract after giving employers 60 days' notice and mediation agency 30 days' notice
Participating in a jurisdictional strike; featherbedding strike; or strike targeting another certified union	
Denying union representation at an investigatory meeting that may result in discipline (Weingarten rule)	
Employee Right to Refrain from Union Activity	
Fining employees who have validly resigned from the union for engaging in protected concerted activities following their resignation or for crossing an unlawful picket line	
Seeking the suspension, discharge, or other punishment of an employee for not being a union member even if the employee has paid or offered to pay a lawful initiation fee and periodic fees thereafter	

DUTY TO BARGAIN IN GOOD FAITH

The National Labor Relations Act established a national policy to encourage collective bargaining as a way to eliminate or to mitigate industrial strife obstructing commerce. Employees seek strength in numbers by joining employee organizations to ensure equal bargaining powers. Under the act, union organizing is a right—protected and preserved. However, once that right is exercised, a duty is placed on both the union and the employer to proceed to bargain in good faith.

Nature of the Duty

The Wagner (National Labor Relations) Act made it an unfair labor practice for an employer to refuse to bargain with representatives of his employees. The NLRB, in enforcing that provision—**the duty to bargain in good faith**—imposed a good-faith efforts test as a condition for compliance with this duty. The comprehensive inclusion of unions in the unfair labor practices by the Taft-Hartley Amendments placed an equal obligation to bargain in good faith on employees. In addition, the amendments clarified what "bargaining" was under the act: to meet at reasonable times; to confer in good faith with respect to rates of pay, wages, hours of employment, or other conditions of employment; and to execute a written contract if the parties reach an agreement. However, the obligation to bargain does not compel either party to agree to a proposal or to make a concession.

DUTY TO BARGAIN IN GOOD FAITH

Reasonable efforts demonstrated by both management and labor during contract negotiations. Generally, it requires both sides to meet, confer, and make written offers. It does not require either side to concede or agree on any issue but rather to show reasonable intent to reach an agreement.

The "good faith" criteria established by the board goes farther and includes the following:

1. Active *participation* in deliberations with an *intention* to find a basis for agreement
2. A sincere *effort* to reach a common ground
3. Binding agreements on *mutually acceptable* terms[75]

The board found indications of bad faith in bargaining if employers (1) met directly with employees outside the bargaining process to reach an agreement not sanctioned by their representatives; (2) made unilateral changes in terms or conditions of employment; (3) refused to make counterproposals; or (4) refused to put the agreement in writing even after all issues were agreed to.[76] Examples of bad-faith bargaining on the part of a union include (1) refusing to sign an agreement the union and employer have come to terms on and (2) insistence on being recognized as the exclusive bargaining agent for an inappropriate unit or when majority status is not held.

Totality of Conduct Doctrine

TOTALITY OF CONDUCT DOCTRINE

A test or review of the total bargaining process used to determine if a negotiating party has acted in good faith, as opposed to isolated acts that may have occurred during negotiations. Generally requires some "give and take" by a negotiating party to warrant good faith.

As the employer is mandated to negotiate while employees seek to negotiate, it is generally the employer who is judged on its "good faith." A test, known as the **totality of conduct doctrine**, is applied to determine the fulfillment of the **good-faith bargaining obligation**. If, in total conduct, a party has negotiated with an open mind in a sincere attempt to reach an agreement, isolated acts will not prove bad faith. However, actions that are not per se unfair labor practices may indicate bad-faith bargaining when viewed in the totality of the bargaining process.

Boulwarism is a "take-it-or-leave-it" bargaining technique. Its name derives from Lemuel R. Boulware, a vice president for the General Electric Company, who negotiated for that company. His strategy was to refuse to bargain with the union while sending management's offer directly to the workers. Using this technique, a company presents a comprehensive contract proposal that, in its opinion, has included all that is necessary or warranted. This form of negotiation eliminates any need to compromise in the employer's mind. Such a proposal is presented at the outset with the understanding that nothing is being held back for later trading, and employees are notified it is a final offer. This practice places the employer in the untenable position of not being able to negotiate. The NLRB declared an attitude of boulwarism a violation of the duty to bargain. It noted that although the formality of bargaining is followed—no illegal or nonmandatory subjects are insisted on, and intent to enter into an agreement is exhibited—there exists no serious intent to adjust differences and to reach a common ground.

BOULWARISM

A collective bargaining approach in which management presents its entire proposal as its final offer, holding nothing back for further negotiations. This approach lacks any "give and take" in bargaining.

Negotiators bargaining in "good-faith" exchange proposals at a negotiation table. *Source:* © REBECCA COOK/Reuters/Corbis.

A 1964 decision (confirmed in 1969) involving this procedure as practiced by the General Electric Company gave the NLRB a chance to examine the technique in detail. The company had examined all relevant facts and had anticipated union demands. It actively communicated its position to employees prior to the negotiation session. It presented what it considered a fair and firm offer; although representations were made that new information could alter its position. The company was found to have failed in its duty to bargain in good faith because it failed to furnish information requested by the union; it had attempted to bypass the international union and to bargain directly with local unions; it had presented a take-it-or-leave-it insurance proposal; and it had, in its overall attitude and approach as evidenced by the totality of its conduct, failed in the good-faith test.[77]

By the examination of the totality of conduct, the court expanded the understanding of the duty to bargain collectively by emphasizing the collective nature of the duty as contained in the National Labor Relations Act. Involvement is a bilateral procedure, allowing both parties a voice in the agreements reached. It is in direct opposition to the intent and purpose of the act for a party to assume the role of decision maker; an exchange of options must be presented and received with an open mind.

The technique of boulwarism, although most often used by an employer, has also been used by unions. In *Utility Workers (Ohio Power Company)*, the board found a union violating the duty to bargain in good faith when the union insisted that identical offers be made to several bargaining units and conditioned acceptance in any single unit on submission of identical offers to all units.[78]

Surface Bargaining

SURFACE BARGAINING

The act by either party of simply going through the motions of negotiating without any real intention of arriving at an agreement. Surface bargaining is a violation of the duty to bargain in good faith.

Another violation of the good-faith duty can be evidenced by **surface bargaining**, that is, simply going through the motions without any real intention of arriving at an agreement. A totality test is used to determine surface bargaining. Surface bargaining can occur when a party has rejected a proposal and offered its own and does not attempt to reconcile the differences, or it can be used when a party's only proposal is the continuation of existing practices.[79] Surface bargaining often occurs in cases of first contract negotiations after a heated representation election. For example, in one instance in the initial bargaining session after a successful representation election, the employer refused to provide the union with requested information, threatened employees with job loss, and did in fact terminate two union supporters. The NLRB sought and won an injunction against the employer for engaging in surface bargaining.[80]

Extensive negotiation in and of itself will not justify a finding of surface bargaining because the National Labor Relations Act does not compel parties to agree to proposals or to make concessions. Hard bargaining on a major issue does not exhibit bad faith because a party is not required to yield on a position fairly maintained. Even if the parties exhibit open hostility, surface bargaining may not be charged if the totality of the bargaining process complies with the dictates of the act.

The NLRB uses these factors when considering an unfair labor charge for surface bargaining:

1. Prior bargaining history of the parties
2. Parties' willingness to make concessions
3. The character of exchanged proposals and demands
4. Any dilatory tactics used during negotiations
5. Conditions imposed by either party as necessary to reaching an agreement
6. Unilateral changes made during the bargaining process in conditions subject to bargaining
7. Communications by employer to individual employees
8. Any unfair labor practices committed during bargaining[81]

DELAYING TACTICS The NLRB in its totality review considers the degree to which either party stalls or uses *delaying tactics* to avoid collective bargaining. Obviously, a complete refusal to meet and to bargain violates the act. Scheduling meetings infrequently or canceling scheduled meetings can also evidence bad faith. Prolonged discussions on formalities designed to thwart the collective bargaining process are considered bad faith. The number or length of negotiation sessions alone cannot determine good or bad faith, but the NLRB frequently reviews meeting history to determine an employer's charge of bad faith. Also, although there is no hard-and-fast rule as to how many or how long sessions should be, a review of case decisions shows the board's preference for frequent meetings—79 in 11 months, 11 in 5 months, 11 in 4 months, and 37 in 10 months.[82]

As described in Chapter 7, the Great Recession of 2008 ushered in another era of concession bargaining. Good-faith negotiations means that the parties must seriously work to resolve differences and reach a common understanding. But this duty does not require either party to agree to the other's demands or to make a concession. So while it is not unlawful for an employer to insist on concessions from its union by asking the employees to give up gains made under previous agreements, it may be difficult to reach agreement. When the parties reach an impasse, employees have the right to strike and the employer has the right to unilaterally imposing its pre-impasse proposals, including a reduction of wages and benefits. So in concession bargaining the employees are presented with a unique challenge. If they agree, they will give up pay or benefits previously won in negotiations, but by continuing to negotiate, they maintain the status quo, which means they might have higher wages and benefits during bargaining than under a new contract. Consequently, unions may have a vested interest in prolonging the bargaining process. Delays in a declaration of impasse, a declaration which would free management to implement concessions unilaterally, tend to strengthen the bargaining power of unions rather than that of employers.

UNILATERAL CHANGES BY EMPLOYER Employers may be guilty of bad faith if they unilaterally change conditions, such as employees' wages, rates of pay, or hours of employment, during contract negotiations. One employer violated the act when it unilaterally rescinded a long-standing practice of allowing employees to participate in blood drives during paid work time after an impasse.[83] The NLRB has ruled in decertification situations, however, that there must be a causal connection between the unilateral change in benefits and the employee dissatisfaction with the union.[84] The act seeks to avoid this attempt to bypass the union and to deal directly with employees.

However, there are exceptions to this rule. If an impasse is reached that is not the result of the employer's bad faith, unilaterally imposing contract terms and conditions that are reasonably comprehended within its pre-impasse proposals is not evidence of bad faith. This ability to unilaterally impose changed working conditions at impasse is a judicial invention used to reconcile the dual mandate of the act, that is, to enforce the duty of good-faith bargaining while not compelling parties to accept agreements or make concessions. The NLRB is regularly called upon to determine if the employer's unilateral change in pay or working conditions of its union employees was a result of an actual impasse. In *Taft Broadcasting*, 163 N.L.R.B. 475 (1967), the board enunciated specific factors which would become the standard the courts looked to when evaluating impasse as a matter of law. The factors include the following: (1) the good faith of the parties in the negotiations, (2) the bargaining history, (3) the length of negotiations, (4) the importance of the issues over which there is disagreement, and (5) the contemporaneous understanding of the parties as to the state of negotiations. The presence of good faith throughout the negotiation process is necessary to a finding of true impasse. Only if the parties have demonstrated the willingness to compromise on at least some issues will a court accept the premise that continuing to negotiate will not result in agreement on the still remaining issues.

BYPASS THE UNION Bypassing the bargaining representation by attempting to *negotiate directly with employees* is often held as a violation of the duty to bargain in good faith. The courts, in reviewing the National Labor Relations Act, found it was the employer's duty to recognize the union and conduct negotiations through the union rather than deal directly with employees. This is an obligation even if the employer traditionally had contracts with individual workers. The collective bargaining contract supersedes such contracts.[85] One very important exception to this rule is that if during contract negotiations a union refuses a final offer, the employer may communicate that offer directly to employees.

AUTHORITY TO SETTLE The good-faith test includes the duty to send negotiators to the table with sufficient authority to carry on meaningful negotiations. All attempts to delay commitment by the recourse of management representatives to check with some final authority are scrutinized closely for evidence of bad faith. However, the obligation of the union representative to take a contract back for a vote of union members before acceptance is not a violation of the duty to bargain in good faith.

COMMITTING UNFAIR LABOR PRACTICE Unfair labor practices during contract negotiations evidence bad faith. Threats to close a plant or to engage in discriminating layoffs during bargaining have been held to be in bad faith. To encourage the decertification of a union or to assist employees in the decertification process has also been found to obstruct the bargaining process.

Duty to Furnish Information

The employer has a **duty to furnish information** to the union, enabling it to carry on the negotiation process. Often, the employees are unable to collect relevant data about an employer's business without the employer's cooperation. If the National Labor Relations Act did not support this duty to furnish information, much of the collective bargaining process would be futile. As with the duty to bargain, the duty to furnish information arises only after a request for information is made in good faith. A union may be subject to a charge of an unfair labor practice if it requests information only to harass or humiliate the employer.

1. ***Relevancy.*** Within liberal interpretations, the NLRB has said that information requested must be relevant to the union's right to represent its members. The union need not prove that the particular information requested is related to a currently discussed item if the subject matter is part of the overall negotiations.

2. *Financial information of company.* When an employer claims financial inability to meet a union wage demand, the financial information of the employer's company becomes relevant. The Supreme Court held that if such a claim by the employer is important enough to be made at the table, it requires some proof of its accuracy.[86] The board has extended this rule to actual claims of financial inability. Refusal to grant wage increases because the employer claims it could not stay competitive or would lose the profit margin was held by the board to invoke financial inability. Therefore, financial data become relevant. In the absence of such a claim, an employer's financial records can be denied the union's bargaining team. The employer may see nondisclosure of financial information as a reaffirmation of management prerogative and by the employees as an obstacle to effective bargaining.[87] In a very narrow interpretation of previous Court decisions, the NLRB has denied a union's right to financial information when the employer merely claimed it could not meet the union's wage demands and stay competitive.[88] A later federal court opinion, however, ruled that an employer had asserted an "inability to pay" when it said that "competitive pressures" prevented it from agreeing to union contract demands.[89]

3. *Prompt delivery of information in workable form.* Bad faith may be evidenced if requested information is not delivered in a timely manner or is delivered in an unreasonable, useless form. An employer may claim that compiling requested data is unduly burdensome, but he or she must be flexible and should suggest alternatives. If the information is given in a form generally accepted in business, a union's request for a different form will not be binding on the employer. And when the employer allows the union access to all its records, it need not furnish information in a more organized form.

4. *Information that must be furnished.* Almost all areas touching on mandatory bargaining have been open to union requests for information. However, employers frequently refuse requests by the union to furnish wage information. The board, supported by lower courts and the Supreme Court, has found little if any justification for such refusals. The statutory requirement that wages be subject to collective bargaining extends to wages paid to particular employees, to groups of employees, and to methods of computing compensation. The union's right to information may include employees even outside the bargaining unit or in other plants operated by the employer.

RIGHTS AND PROHIBITED CONDUCT DURING THE TERM OF A CONTRACT

Certain rights and duties arise during the term of a contract. These include the duty to bargain during a contract term, and the duty to refrain from prohibited economic activities.

Duty to Bargain during the Contract Term

The standards for good-faith collective bargaining contained in the National Labor Relations Act include the duty to bargain during the contract term under certain circumstances. The duty, however, is not absolute. The language of the act provides that a party cannot be required to discuss or agree to terminate or modify the contract during its term. In addition, the contract under which parties operate may limit the duty in the following ways:

ZIPPER CLAUSE

A provision of a collective bargaining agreement that restricts either party from requiring the other party to bargain on any issue that was not previously negotiated in the agreement for the term of the contract.

1. *Zipper clause.* The **zipper clause** is an abbreviated form of the waiver provision in a collective bargaining agreement, sometimes referred to as a "wrap-up" clause, considered to denote waiver of the right of either party to require the other to bargain on any matter not covered in an agreement during the life of the contract, thus limiting the terms and conditions of employment to those set forth in the contract. A clause of this type is the following zipper clause contained in the 2007–2011 Agreement between Louisville/Jefferson County Metro Government and Fraternal Order of Police, Lodge 614:

> **ARTICLE 39**
>
> **Entire Agreement**
>
> *Section 1.* Metro Government and the Lodge shall not be bound by any requirement, which is not specifically stated in this Agreement. Specifically, but not exclusively Metro Government and the Lodge are not bound by any past practices or understandings of Metro Government or the Lodge, or their predecessors. The parties agree that only those items contained in this Agreement constitute the entire agreement and respective rights of the parties.
> *Section 2.* The Lodge and Metro Government agree that this Agreement is intended to cover all matters referred to in Article 2 and that during the term of this Agreement, neither Metro Government nor Lodge will be required to negotiate on any further matters affecting these or other subjects not specifically set forth in this Agreement.[90]

OPENER CLAUSE

An agreement provision that allows future negotiations during the term of the contract on specific mandatory issues such as wages or health care.

2. *Opener clause*. This clause allows negotiations to take place during the contract term on certain mandatory items. Most clauses provide for the reopening of negotiations on only one specific issue, whereas the remainder of the contract is closed to discussions. The most common issue specified in reopeners is wages; specific benefits are also common issues.[91] For example,

> **Article XX**
>
> *Section 2.* This Agreement shall be reopened by either party for the purpose of adjusting the increase in the base hourly rate of pay, and only the hourly rate of pay; upon receiving a written request, the parties will meet within ten days.

SEVERABILITY CLAUSE

A CBA provision that keeps all other provisions in the agreement in place should one provision become null and void.

3. *Severability clause.* Most contracts contain a severability clause that protects the rest of the contract should one section come into conflict with state or federal law. Such a clause usually provides that the offending section becomes null and void or that, as in the following Article XIV from the agreement between duPont Co. and the Neoprene Craftsmen Union, the section must be renegotiated as needed:

> **ARTICLE XIV**
>
> **Suspension of Provisions of Agreement**
>
> *Section 1.* If during the life of this agreement there shall be in existence any applicable rule, regulation or order issued by governmental authority, which shall be inconsistent with any provision of this agreement, such provision shall be modified to the extent necessary to comply with such law, rule, regulation, or order.[92]

Union Demand to Negotiate During a CBA

A question of bargaining during the contract term may arise when the union seeks to add new items not covered under the contract. This situation highlights the two competing views of collective bargaining. One view is that the collective bargaining agreement does not end the collective bargaining process. It is a continuous process, albeit with rules as to how the process should proceed. Many people believe that the grievance-arbitration procedures are a part of that process because those decisions shape the administration of the contract and therefore its terms.

The opposite view is that the collective bargaining process must be completed with the signing of the contract to give meaning to the contract terms. Because bargaining should encompass all subjects, the final agreement should settle all subjects either explicitly or implicitly between the parties.

Under this view, the grievance-arbitration procedure only interprets the contract and adds nothing to its terms. The NLRB's attitude to a union demand for bargaining on a new mandatory bargaining item during a contract term seems to be that, without a zipper clause, if the item is not contained in the contract and was not discussed during negotiations, the employer has a duty to bargain on that item.[93]

Employer's Unilateral Action During a Contract Term

Most often the question of the duty to bargain during a contract term arises as a result of unilateral action by the employer. Depending on the circumstances, such action may be deemed an unfair labor practice as a breach of that duty to bargain. The question of whether a substantive or procedural provision of a contract was violated arises when an employer takes unilateral action during a contract term and makes a change in some condition of employment. If the employer's action changes a stated term of the contract, the answer is simple. The employer has committed an unfair labor practice. However, if under a broad management rights clause the employer takes an action that affects employees in a manner not contemplated by the contract, disagreement as to breach obviously occurs. For example, an employer committed an unfair labor practice when it installed hidden surveillance cameras and disciplined or discharged 16 workers recorded engaging in misconduct. But although the NLRB found the employer's unilateral action in installing the cameras violated the act, it overruled prior board decisions and refused to order reinstatement or back pay for the workers caught misbehaving.[94]

As a rule, the NLRB considers charges of unfair labor practice by a union against an employer for taking unilateral action a matter for arbitration and, under the *Collyer* decision, will defer its jurisdiction to the arbitrator.

Even under a management rights clause in which the final decision is the employer's, a contract may contain a requirement that the union must be consulted before any action. An employer who violates this procedural requirement is in breach of the contract and of his or her duty to bargain during its duration.

Prohibited Economic Activity During a Contract Term

To use economic pressure as a means to enforce a contract obviously is not the preferred method, as evidenced by the support given arbitration in court decisions. A union slowdown or strike countered by an employer lockout or mass dismissal seems at odds with the National Labor Relations Act's aim of promoting industrial peace. But to use economic activity, or at least the ability to resort to economic activity, is a key element in the success of the collective bargaining process.

As discussed earlier, the use of economic weapons, strikes, and other concerted activity during recognition campaigns and during negotiations are familiar tactics. Although use of economic power to enforce an existing contract has become increasingly rare because of mandatory grievance and arbitration procedures and no-strike clauses in labor agreements, such action has not disappeared. The Supreme Court, in the ***Boys Market* case**, upheld an injunction against a union that struck over an arbitrable grievance despite a no-strike clause and a mandatory grievance procedure.[95] But the Court noted that not all such strikes would be enjoined. It adopted strict standards from an earlier case:

BOYS MARKET CASE

A case in which the Supreme Court upheld an injunction against a union that struck an employer despite a no-strike clause in its contract. The Court also ruled that an employer is ordered to arbitrate while seeking a court injunction against a union striking in violation of a no-strike clause.

> When a strike is sought to be enjoined because it is over a grievance which both parties are contractually bound to arbitrate, the district court may issue no injunctive order until it holds that the contract does have that effect; and the employer should be ordered to arbitrate, as a condition of his obtaining an injunction against the strike. Beyond this, the district court must, of course, consider whether issuance of an injunction would be warranted under ordinary principles of equity—whether breaches are occurring and will continue, or have been threatened and will be committed; whether they have caused or will cause irreparable injury to the employer; and whether the employer will suffer more from the denial of an injunction than will the union from its issuance.[96]

Thus, a union does have an effective weapon despite a no-strike clause if the grievance does not factually come under the contract arbitration procedure, if the employer is not willing to arbitrate, and if the employer cannot show where he or she has suffered irreparable injury from the breach of the no-strike obligation.

The Supreme Court later upheld the right of a union to engage in a sympathy strike pending an arbitrator's decision on whether such a strike was forbidden under the particular no-strike clause of the labor agreement.[97] The strike had been called in support of another union properly engaged in an economic strike. Although the arbitration procedure could be invoked to decide the scope of the no-strike clause, the Court would not allow the union's strike to be enjoined pending that decision. The NLRB, in its decision in *Indianapolis Power and Light Company*,[98] attempted to create a presumption that broad no-strike clauses were intended to cover sympathy strikes, but the U.S. Court of Appeals overruled that presumption in 1986 in *International Brotherhood of Electrical Workers, Local 387 v. National Labor Relations Board*.[99] The court said a no-strike clause must be interpreted according to the terms of the particular collective bargaining agreement, the bargaining history, and the past practices of the parties to determine its application to sympathy strikes.

The National Labor Relations Act, as amended by Taft-Hartley and Landrum-Griffin, outlawed four specific economic pressure techniques that unions might try to use during the term of a contract: secondary boycotts, hot cargo agreements, jurisdictional disputes, and featherbedding.

SECONDARY BOYCOTTS Section 8(b)(4) of the National Labor Relations Act prohibits a union from engaging in or from inducing others to engage in a strike or boycott aimed against the goods or services of one employer so as to force the employer to cease doing business with another employer. This prohibition was a response to the labor movement's use of the **secondary boycott** to affect employer A by exerting economic pressure on those who do business with employer A. Primary economic activity such as a boycott by employees against an employer is not prohibited by this section, nor is a secondary boycott with an objective that is not statutorily forbidden.

SECONDARY BOYCOTT

Union pressure exerted on a neutral party indirectly related to the primary employer. The neutral party then exerts pressure against the primary employer.

PRIMARY BOYCOTT

A legally permissible action against the employer directly involved in collective bargaining that involves pressure on others to withhold purchases of the employer's goods or services.

The Supreme Court attempted to give guidance on the distinction between a primary and a secondary boycott. A **primary boycott** occurs when persons who normally deal directly with the work involved are encouraged to withhold their services. This type of boycott is not prohibited and includes, for example, appeals to replacement workers or delivery people not to cross a picket line or appeals to employees of subcontractors not to continue work essential to the operation. Even if the picketing takes place at the work site of the secondary employer, it may be protected if the work involved is the object of the dispute.

In 1988, the Supreme Court gave a significant victory to labor unions by ruling that union members may hand out leaflets in a secondary boycott action. The case, *De Bartola Corp. v. Florida Gulf Coast Trades Council*,[100] involved a union's distributing handbills in a shopping mall. The handbills asked customers not to shop at any of the stores in the mall because a construction company hired to build a new mall store was paying substandard wages. The mall was owned by the De Bartola Corporation, which then filed a complaint with the NLRB charging the union with engaging in a secondary boycott against the mall stores. The NLRB and a U.S. circuit court ruled in favor of De Bartola and ordered the union to cease and desist the action. The Supreme Court reversed the decision on the grounds that peaceful handbilling urging a customer boycott was not prohibited by Section 8 of the National Labor Relations Act when unaccompanied by picketing. The key difference between this case and previous cases was the act of handbilling without picketing. The Court declared that picketing was qualitatively different and produced different consequences. Although the Court noted that both picketing and handbilling could have detrimental effects on a neutral third party, prohibiting peaceful and truthful handbilling raised questions of First Amendment rights.[101]

The use of banners by a union outside of a secondary business, however, was upheld in 2005 by the U.S. Ninth Circuit Court of Appeals in *Overstreet v. United Brotherhood of Carpenters & Joiners of America*.[102] The Circuit Court held that Section 8(b)(4) of the NLRA if

Workers are legally permitted to boycott the employer they directly have a dispute with to put business pressure on the employer. *Source:* Noah Berger/AP Images.

used to prohibit a union's bannering activity would be a violation of the union's First Amendment free speech rights. The court decided that since the 4- by 15-foot banners that read "SHAME ON (name of neutral retailer)" and "LABOR DISPUTE" did not obstruct the business or contain a fraudulent message, and was a reasonable distance from the entrances, it was not an unlawful secondary boycott. The case involved the United Brotherhood of Carpenters union, which set up the signs in front of 18 retail sites where the retailers conducted business with any of three construction contractors that hired nonunion workers.[103]

A union may be held liable for any actual damages resulting from an unlawful secondary boycott sustained by the secondary or primary employer.

SHOP-INS A new form of secondary boycotting was demonstrated in 1995 by a union in Massachusetts. The Teamsters union was in a labor dispute with a beer distributor, August A. Busch & Co. of Massachusetts, Inc. The union conducted three *shop-ins* involving three different retail establishments that carried Busch products. The shop-ins involved anywhere from 50 to 125 union members converging on the stores at the same time; buying small items, such as gum or snacks; and paying with large-denomination bills.

The results were crowded parking lots, delays in service, and the loss of regular customers. The union did not engage in any information sharing; that is, it did not leaflet or express an opinion regarding Busch. Nor was it actually picketing. An unfair labor practice charge was made against the union, and the NLRB found this activity to be prohibited as a secondary boycott. Clearly the shop-in was conducted to pressure the retailers not to use Busch products. There was no communication to the public about Busch that would have been protected under the First Amendment.[104]

HOT CARGO AGREEMENT **Hot cargo agreement** refers to a negotiated contract provision stating that union members of one employer need not handle nonunion or struck goods of other employers. Court decisions after passage of the Taft-Hartley Amendments basically allowed such agreements, stating that the prohibition against secondary boycotts did not prohibit an employer and union from voluntarily including a hot cargo clause in their agreement, but such a provision was not an absolute defense against an unfair labor practice charge. If inducements of employees prohibited by Section 8(b)(4) of the National Labor Relations Act in the absence of a hot cargo provision occurred, the inducements would still violate the act.

HOT CARGO AGREEMENT
A negotiated contract provision stating that union members of one employer have the right to refuse to handle nonunion or struck goods of other employers.

Clauses completely prohibiting an employer from subcontracting are valid. But a clause forbidding subcontracting with nonunion employers may be a violation if it is aimed at a union's difference with another employer and is not designed to protect union standards. A work-preservation clause is lawful if the object of the clause is to protect and preserve work customarily performed by employees in the unit. This is true even if it involves refusing to handle certain cargo as long as it is the cargo that is refused and not the employer making the cargo. The aim of the clause must be to protect the actual employees of the bargaining unit and not union members as a group.

HOT CARGO AND SWEATSHOPS The Landrum-Griffin Act clouds union concerns over the operation of foreign sweatshops. The Garment Industry Proviso in Section 8(e) of the National Labor Relations Act allows labor organizations representing the apparel industry to require garment industry employers—known as jobbers—to do business only with union shops. It exempts the garment industry from the provision of the act that makes it an unfair labor practice for labor organizations to force employers to stop handling products of nonunion employers or hot cargo agreements. The garment industry's labor agreement requires jobbers who use contractors to hire union shops. But it also allows those who use nonunion shops or who use low-cost factories outside the United States to pay a "liquidated damage" penalty to the union. Garment unions have collected more than $160 million in liquidated damages.[105]

FEATHERBEDDING Another prohibited activity is featherbedding, which, according to Section 8(b)(6) of the National Labor Relations Act, is "to cause an employer to pay . . . for services not performed or not to be performed."[106] The featherbedding section is rarely used unless a union tries to cause an employer to pay for services neither performed nor intended to be performed. In such cases the NLRB may order the union to reimburse the employer and cease the unlawful activity.[107] The Supreme Court may uphold a negotiated agreement to provide pay for make-work if the work was actually done regardless of its value to the employer.

Some examples of unfair labor practices during negotiations and under a collective bargaining agreement are summarized in Table 10-5.

TABLE 10-5 Unfair Labor Practices During Bargaining and During Term of Contract

Unfair Labor Practice	Not an Unfair Labor Practice
Duty to Bargain in Good Faith	
Refusing to meet for the purpose of negotiating an agreement	
Boulwarism—"take it or leave it" approach with no give and take exchange is bad faith	
Surface bargaining—going through the motions with no intent to reach agreement is bad faith	Hard bargaining on mandatory issues even if parties can't reach agreement
Employer's unilateral change in conditions of employment during negotiations	Employer's unilateral change in conditions of employment after reaching "no-fault" impasse
Negotiating directly with employees	Communicating "final offer" union rejected to all employees
Not sending negotiators to table with sufficient authority to have meaningful negotiations is evidence of bad faith	Union negotiators having to take proposals back to union membership for final vote
Refusing to sign an agreement after reaching consensus	

TABLE 10-5 *(Continued)*

Duty to Furnish Information	
Employer refusing to provide financial information when claiming inability to pay	Employer refusing to provide financial information if *not* claiming inability to pay
Delay in furnishing information or furnishing it in useless form	Providing information in form generally accepted in business
Refusing to provide information employer does not consider relevant to negotiations	
Union requesting information to harass or humiliate employer	
During Term of Contract	
Union strike when CBA has no-strike clause and grievance procedure	Union strike when CBA has no-strike clause and grievance procedure but disputed issue is not grievable
Refusing to bargain under an "opener clause"	
Refusing to bargain on new mandatory item raised by union if not contained in contract or discussed during negotiations	Refusing to bargain under a "zipper clause"
Unilateral change in terms and conditions of employment by employer during term of contract	Unilateral change in terms and conditions of employment by employer during term of contract if valid under management rights clause
Unions engaging in secondary boycotts—picketing 3rd party to influence 2nd party	Unions only leafleting, not picketing, in secondary boycott to pressure 3rd party to influence 2nd party
Unions engaged in "shop-in" to disrupt 3rd party business	
Union forcing employers to refrain from handling products of nonunion employers in absence of hot cargo agreement in CBA	Forcing employers in the garment industry to refrain from handling products of nonunion employers even in absence of hot cargo agreement in CBA
Striking to force featherbedding	
Refusing to process a grievance because an employee is not a member of the union in states where union security clauses are not permitted.	

THE AUTHORITY OF THE NLRB

UNFAIR LABOR PRACTICES An unfair labor practice charge comes to the NLRB through procedures similar to election petitions. The party claiming injury files an appropriate form with a regional office of the NLRB (see Figure 10-2 and Figure 10-3). An initial investigation is held, and if merit is found to the charge and the regional director cannot convince the parties to settle, a hearing is held before an administrative law judge. The decision of the administrative law judge may be appealed to the NLRB, which decides the case through a subpanel of three members randomly selected by its executive secretary.[108]

A party who disagrees with an NLRB decision can appeal to a federal court. Recent statistics, however, show that less than 3 percent of the unfair labor practice cases brought to the NLRB actually ended up in a litigation process, either in the NLRB or in federal court. The study demonstrated how cases are resolved through the NLRB process. When a complaint is filed, it is

FORM EXEMPT UNDER 44 U.S.C 3512

FORM NLRB-501
(9-07)

UNITED STATES OF AMERICA
NATIONAL LABOR RELATIONS BOARD
CHARGE AGAINST EMPLOYER

DO NOT WRITE IN THIS SPACE	
Case	Date Filed / /

INSTRUCTIONS:
File an original together with four copies and a copy for each additional charged party named in item 1 with NLRB Regional Director for the region in which the alleged unfair labor practice occurred or is occurring.

1. EMPLOYER AGAINST WHOM CHARGE IS BROUGHT

a. Name of Employer		b. Number of workers employed
c. Address *(Street, city, state, and ZIP code)* -	d. Employer Representative	e. Telephone No. ( ) - Fax No. ( ) -
f. Type of Establishment *(factory, mine, wholesaler, etc.)*	g. Identify principal product or service	

h. The above-named employer has engaged in and is engaging in unfair labor practices within the meaning of section 8(a), subsections (1) and *(list subsections)* ______________________ of the National Labor Relations Act, and these unfair labor practices are practices affecting commerce within the meaning of the Act, or these unfair labor practices are unfair practices affecting commerce within the meaning of the Act and the Postal Reorganization Act.

2. Basis of the Charge *(set forth a clear and concise statement of the facts constituting the alleged unfair labor practices)*

3. Full name of party filing charge *(if labor organization, give full name, including local name and number)*

4a. Address *(Street and number, city, state, and ZIP code)* -	4b. Telephone No. ( ) - Fax No. ( ) -

5. Full name of national or international labor organization of which it is an affiliate or constituent unit *(to be filled in when charge is filed by a labor organization)*

6. DECLARATION
I declare that I have read the above charge and that the statements are true to the best of my knowledge and belief.

By ______________________
(signature of representative or person making charge)

____
(Print/type name and title or office, if any)

(fax) ( ) - ______________________

Address ______________________ - ( ) - ______ / /
(Telephone No.) *(date)*

WILLFUL FALSE STATEMENTS ON THIS CHARGE CAN BE PUNISHED BY FINE AND IMPRISONMENT (U.S. CODE, TITLE 18, SECTION 1001)

PRIVACY ACT STATEMENT

Solicitation of the information on this form is authorized by the National Labor Relations Act (NLRA), 29 U.S.C. § 151 *et seq.* The principal use of the information is to assist the National Labor Relations Board (NLRB) in processing unfair labor practice and related proceedings or litigation. The routine uses for the imformation are fully set forth in the Federal Register, 71 Fed. Reg. 74942-43 (Dec. 13, 2006). The NLRB will further explain these uses upon request. Disclosure of this information to the NLRB is voluntary; however, failure to supply the information will cause the NLRB to decline to invoke its processes.

FIGURE 10-2 National Labor Relations Board Charge Against Employer

FORM NLRB-508
(9-07)

FORM EXEMPT UNDER 44 U.S.C 3512

UNITED STATES OF AMERICA
NATIONAL LABOR RELATIONS BOARD
CHARGE AGAINST LABOR ORGANIZATIONS OR ITS AGENTS

DO NOT WRITE IN THIS SPACE	
Case	Date Filed / /

INSTRUCTIONS: File an original together with four copies and a copy for each additional charged party named in item 1 with NLRB Regional Director for the region in which the alleged unfair labor practice occurred or is occurring.

1. LABOR ORGANIZATION OR ITS AGENTS AGAINST WHICH CHARGE IS BROUGHT

a. Name	b. Union Representative to contact
c. Telephone No. ( ) - Fax No. ( ) -	d. Address *(Street, city, state, and ZIP code)*

e. The above-named organization(s) or its agents has *(have)* engaged in and is *(are)* engaging in unfair labor practices within the meaning of section 8(b), subsection(s) *(list subsections)* ____ ____ ____ ____ ____ ____ ____ ____ __of the National Labor Relations Act, and these unfair labor practices are unfair practices affecting commerce within the meaning of the Act, or these unfair labor practices are unfair practices affecting commerce within the meaning of the Act and the Postal Reorganization Act.

2. Basis of the Charge *(set forth a clear and concise statement of the facts constituting the alleged unfair labor practices)*

3. Name of Employer		4. Telephone No. ( ) - Fax No. ( ) -
5. Location of plant involved *(street, city, state and ZIP code)*		6. Employer representative to contact
7. Type of establishment *(factory, mine, wholesaler, etc.)*	8. Identify principal product or service	9. Number of workers employed
10. Full name of party filing charge		
11. Address of party filing charge *(street, city, state and ZIP code.)*		12. Telephone No. ( ) - Fax No. ( ) -

13. DECLARATION

I declare that I have read the above charge and that the statements therein are true to the best of my knowledge and belief.

By ______________________________
(signature of representative or person making charge)

____
(Print/type name and title or office, if any)

(Fax) ( ) - __________

Address ______________________________ ( ) - __________ / /
(Telephone No.) *(date)*

WILLFUL FALSE STATEMENTS ON THIS CHARGE CAN BE PUNISHED BY FINE AND IMPRISONMENT (U.S. CODE, TITLE 18, SECTION 1001)

PRIVACY ACT STATEMENT

Solicitation of the information on this form is authorized by the National Labor Relations Act (NLRA), 29 U.S.C. § 151 *et seq.* The principal use of the information is to assist the National Labor Relations Board (NLRB) in processing unfair labor practice and related proceedings or litigation. The routine uses for the information are fully set forth in the Federal Register, 71 Fed. Reg. 74942-43 (Dec. 13, 2006). The NLRB will further explain these uses upon request. Disclosure of this information to the NLRB is voluntary; however, failure to supply the information will cause the NLRB to decline to invoke its processes.

FIGURE 10-3 National Labor Relations Board Charge Against Labor Organization or its Agents

assigned to an agent of the regional director in the NLRB region with jurisdiction over the parties. The agent is under tight time restraints to investigate the charges and make a recommendation to the regional director. Statistics show that the decision of a regional director to issue a complaint or not almost always determines the ultimate outcome of the charges. With that in mind, the practice of the NLRB regional directors is to let the parties know which way the decision is going to go and to give the losing party a choice of withdrawing (if the charging party is going to lose) or offering a settlement (if the charged party is going to lose).[109] The success of this precharging process can be seen in the statistics in Figure 10-4 showing the disposition of NLRB cases in a typical year in which some withdrawals and dismissals were resolved before complaints were issued.

Section 10(j): Court Injunctions

SECTION 10(j) INJUNCTION

The section of the NLRA that allows the board to seek a federal court injunction in situations in which the action of a union or the employer might cause substantial harm to the other side.

Section 10(j) of the National Labor Relations Act permits the NLRB to seek a federal court injunction in situations in which the action of the union or employer might cause substantial harm to the other side. The court, in response, can then order either party to resume or desist from a certain action. In general, the NLRB must demonstrate that the unfair labor practice, if left alone, will irreparably harm the other side before a final NLRB decision can be administered, or "justice delayed is justice denied." For example, in 2009 a federal district court issued a Section 10(j) injunction against an employer, Vincent/Metro Trucking LLC, and ordered it to resume collective bargaining with the United food and Commercial Workers Union Local 789. The courts stated the injunction was "essential, just, proper and appropriate" because the NLRB was investigating unfair labor practices, and unless the injunction was issued, the employer's potentially illegal actions were likely to continue. The union had requested the telephone and fax

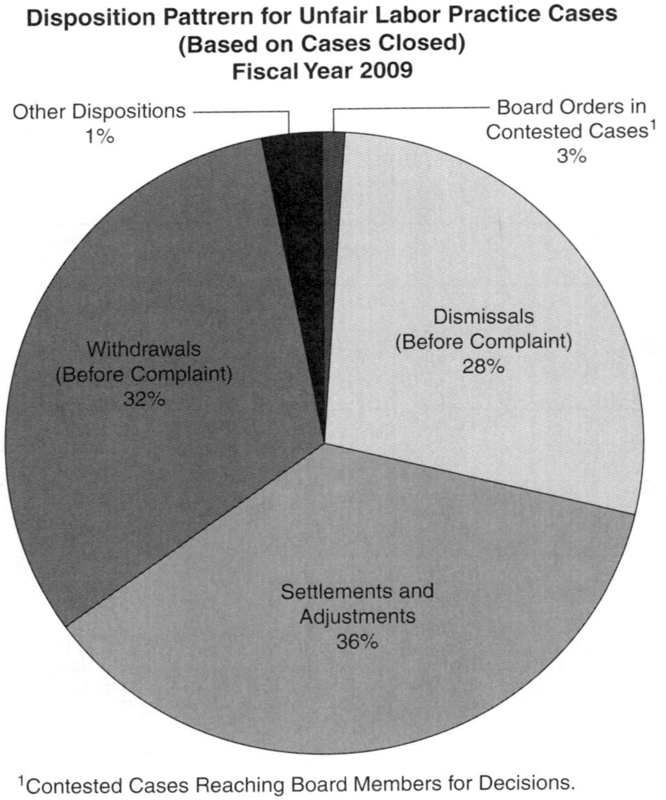

FIGURE 10-4 Dispositions of NLRB Cases, 2009. *Source:* "Seventy-Fourth Annual Report of the National Labor Relations Board for Fiscal Year ending September 30, 2009," p. 6. Available at http://www.nlrb.gov.

In 2009 a federal court issued an injunction against Vincent/Metro Trucking LLC and required it to resume collective bargaining with the local UFCW union. *Source:* © Doug Berry/Corbis.

numbers and addresses of employees, which the employer had not provided, and at the same time held meetings with the employees in an attempt to bypass the union.[110]

In the 1994–1996 baseball strike players would have found their abilities slipping with increasing age; thus U.S. District Court judge Sonia Sotomayor ordered the owners to abide by the old contract and to "play ball" until a new contract was reached. Some baseball fans believed that the NLRB saved the game!

Most Section 10(j) cases fall within the following 13 categories:[111]

1. Union organizing campaign interference
2. Subcontracting work to outside employers
3. Withdrawing recognition of the union
4. Undermining or denigrating the members of the union's bargaining team
5. Granting exclusive representation to a minority union
6. Successor employer refusing to recognize and bargain
7. Bad-faith conduct during negotiations
8. Picketing violence
9. Strike or picketing notice or waiting period violations
10. Employer refusal to allow protected activity on private property
11. Retaliation for NLRB processes
12. Closedown of operations during litigation
13. Union coercion to achieve unlawful object

The number of Section 10(j) injunctions issued by the NLRB, however, has declined sharply since 2000 under the Bush-appointed NLRB. Section 10(j) gives the NLRB, at its discretion, one of its most powerful tools: to obtain quick injunctive relief against a wide variety of unfair labor practices, committed by either an employer or a labor organization. In practice, however, most injunctions are applied against employers in cases involving the employer's refusal to bargain with a newly certified union (about half of the cases) or employee termination or discipline cases. In 1995, the NLRB issued Section 10(j) injunctions in 104 cases, the highest total in the 70-year history of the board. In 2004, however, only 14 injunctions were authorized by the NLRB, the lowest number in over 30 years.[112]

CONTRACT ENFORCEMENT BY NLRB Once the parties have agreed and entered into a collective bargaining agreement, disputes can still disrupt the workplace. The CBA is a contract and as such can be enforced through court proceedings as any other contract; enforced through adherence to grievance and arbitration procedures as discussed in Chapters 11 and 12; through the economic self-help pressure activities discussed earlier; or in some cases enforced through an unfair labor practice action by the NLRB.

Violation of a provision of a collective bargaining agreement is not in and of itself an unfair labor practice. Therefore, enforcement and interpretation of a contract provision might come within the jurisdiction of the board **only** if the matter also involves a violation of an unfair labor practice provision. The board may be involved in contract enforcement if the contract has incorporated a statutory obligation it already has jurisdiction to enforce or if a contract has incorporated an unlawful provision it is called on to invalidate.

For example, if an employer is accused of refusing to bargain during the term of the contract by making a unilateral change in the wage structure or other term of employment, by subcontracting work, and by refusing to supply information the union seeks, and if the employer claims that the contract justifies his or her action, the NLRB can interpret the *lawful contract clause*. The board is called on to investigate and determine the validity of the employer's claim.

The board's interpretive power might also be apparent in a case involving a union security clause or the provisions of a grievance procedure in which a contract is used by an employer or a union to defend the discharge or disciplining of an employee and that employee claims a violation of the National Labor Relations Act.

In representation cases, a party may claim that proper interpretation of a contract places him or her under its protection and provisions. Thus, the NLRB's definition of the parties to a collective bargaining agreement or the appropriate unit of employees who should be represented by a union can have great impact.

The NLRB may *invalidate a contract or clause* if it finds that the union acted under an erroneous though good-faith claim that it had majority representation, in a successorship situation in which one union has dissolved or merged with another, or when a business has changed hands. Contract clauses impinging on areas prohibited by the act will come before the board for validity tests. Items tested include union security clauses, discriminatory provisions, hot cargo clauses (in which union members refuse to handle goods from a nonunion employer), and breach of a union's duty of fair representation. Also, a petition and election for representation not barred by an existing contract may invalidate an existing contract.

Court and NLRB Deferral to Arbitration

Prior to the Taft-Hartley Amendments, employers and unions could sue in state court for breach of contract if one party believed the other party violated a collective bargaining agreement. Most state courts viewed the collective bargaining agreement as a legally enforceable obligation. Unions could obtain injunctions to restrain employers from violation of wage provisions or to require employers to abide by a union shop agreement. The employer could obtain an injunction against strikes in breach of a valid no-strike clause. Still, contract enforcement for the employer was difficult because many labor unions were not incorporated. In some states such unincorporated organizations could not be sued; thus, the employer had to sue each union member individually. Even if the unincorporated union could be sued for specific injunctive relief, monetary damages might not be available. The Taft-Hartley Amendments were an attempt to lessen the unions' power by allowing access to federal courts on suits for collective bargaining contract violations. The amendments specifically recognized labor unions as entities that could be sued and held liable for monetary damages.

Having established that the courts could effectively enforce labor agreements, the Supreme Court looked to the grievance and arbitration provisions found in most agreements and called for specific performance of an employer's promise to arbitrate.[113] The Court felt that the agreement to arbitrate grievance disputes was the employer's trade-off for the union's agreement not to strike.

The role of arbitration and court enforcement of contract agreements was specifically outlined in the **Lincoln Mills case** and three cases known as the **Steelworkers Trilogy.**[114] These cases held that when a collective bargaining agreement contains an arbitration provision, the function of a court is limited to a review of whether the issue to be arbitrated is governed by the contract. Any doubt as to the coverage should be resolved in favor of arbitration. Unless the arbitrator's award is ambiguous, the courts should enforce it even if the court would not have decided the substantive issue in the same way. The Court gave almost complete deference to arbitration as a means of contract enforcement by limiting its own review of an arbitration award to whether the issue under arbitration is in the agreement.

LINCOLN MILLS CASE

A landmark decision in which the Supreme Court ordered an employer to arbitrate grievances as provided for in a collective bargaining agreement, stating that an employer's agreement to arbitrate grievance disputes was a trade-off for the union's agreement not to strike.

STEELWORKERS' TRILOGY

Three 1960 Supreme Court rulings that upheld the grievance arbitration process and limited judicial intervention.

The *Misco* case is an example of the Supreme Court's deferral to arbitration. In the *Misco* case, the Company's work rules listed as cause for discharge the possession or use of a controlled substance on company property. An employee covered by the collective labor agreement was apprehended by police in the backseat of someone else's car on the company parking lot. There was marijuana smoke in the air of the car and a lighted marijuana cigarette in the front-seat ashtray. A police search of the employee's own car on the lot revealed marijuana gleanings. Management discharged the employee for violation of the disciplinary rule. The employee grieved, and an arbitrator later upheld the grievance and ordered reinstatement. The arbitrator concluded that the cigarette incident was insufficient proof that the grievant was using or had possessed marijuana on company property. At the time of discharge, the company was not aware of the fact that marijuana was found in the employee's own car, and the arbitrator refused to accept that claim into evidence. The lower court vacated the arbitration award ruling that reinstatement would violate the public policy against the operation of dangerous machinery by persons under the influence of drugs. The Supreme Court reversed, however, holding that the court of appeals exceeded the limited authority possessed by a court reviewing an arbitrator's award under a collective bargaining agreement. The Court stated that absent fraud by the parties or the arbitrator's dishonesty, reviewing courts in such cases are not authorized to reconsider the merits of an arbitrator's award. The Court also stated that the collective bargaining agreement left evidentiary matters to the arbitrator: The arbitrator's finding of fact is conclusive.[115] Since the *Misco* decision, fewer federal or district courts have overturned an arbitration decision on public policy grounds.[116]

The NLRB also defers its jurisdiction in certain unfair labor practice cases to an arbitration procedure established under the contract. In the ***Collyer* case**, the NLRB agreed to defer jurisdiction if there was a stable collective bargaining relationship between the parties, the party defending the charge was willing to arbitrate the issue, and the dispute centered on the contract and its meaning.[117] The board also decided to defer to an arbitration award if the arbitration procedure met the following criteria:

1. ***Fair and regular proceedings.*** That the proceedings are the equivalent of due process, affording parties an opportunity to be heard, cross-examine witnesses, be represented by counsel, and have an unbiased decision maker.
2. ***Agreement to be bound.*** Both parties must agree to abide by the arbitrator's decision. A hearing over the parties' objections would not be honored.
3. ***Award not repugnant to purposes and policies of the act.*** Even if due process is followed, the arbitrator's award can be invalidated if it violates the purposes of the National Labor Relations Act. For example, an arbitrator upheld a dismissal of an employee for being disloyal, but his so-called disloyalty was in seeking help from the NLRB. The board did not uphold that award.
4. ***Unfair labor practice to be considered by arbitrator.*** The actual issue surrounding the unfair labor practice must be reviewed and decided by the arbitrator, or the NLRB will not defer to the award. Deciding other issues between the parties is immaterial.
5. ***Facts are presented.*** The arbitrator was generally presented with the facts relevant to resolving the unfair labor practice.[118]

PUBLIC SECTOR UNFAIR LABOR PRACTICES AND CONTRACT ENFORCEMENT

Federal Government

For 1.1 million federal government employees represented by unions worldwide, the Federal Labor Relations Authority (FLRA) is the independent government agency charged with administering federal labor–management relations. Included in that role is adjudicating unfair labor practice claims involving federal government agencies. Modeled after the National Labor Relations Act, the Federal Labor Relations Act creates rights and obligations on the part of management and unions in a federal government workplace represented by a labor union. The Federal Service Labor–Management Relations Statute (Civil Service Reform Act of 1978, Title VII) enumerates the following unfair labor practices for an agency:

1. Interference with, restraint, or coercion of employees in rights guaranteed under the statute;
2. Discrimination against union members for their union membership;
3. Domination or interference with the formation or administration of a labor union;
4. Discrimination against an employee for pursuing the rights under this statute;
5. Refusal to consult or bargain collectively with representatives of its employees as required by the statute;
6. Fail to or refuse to cooperate in impasse procedures and impasse decisions as required by the statute;
7. Enforce any rule or regulation in conflict with an applicable collective bargaining agreement if the agreement was in effect before the date the rule or regulation was prescribed; or
8. Fail or refuse to comply with any provision of the statute.

The statute also details the following unfair labor practices for labor organizations under the statute:

1. Interfere with, restrain, or coerce any employee in the exercise of any right under the statute;
2. Cause or attempt to cause an agency to discriminate against any employee in the exercise by the employee of any right under the statute;
3. Coerce, discipline, fine, or attempt to coerce a member of the labor organization as punishment, as reprisal, or for the purpose of hindering or impeding the member's work performance or productivity as an employee or the discharge of the member's duties as an employee;
4. Discriminate against an employee with regard to the terms or conditions of membership in the labor organization on the basis of race, color, creed, national origin, sex, age, preferential or nonpreferential civil service status, political affiliation, marital status, or handicapping condition;
5. Refuse to consult or negotiate in good faith with an agency as required by the statute;
6. Fail or refuse to cooperate in impasse procedures and impasse decisions as required by the statute;
7. Call, or participate in, a strike, work stoppage, or slowdown, or picketing of an agency in a labor–management dispute if such picketing interferes with an agency's operations, or condone such activity by failing to take action to prevent or stop such activity; or
8. Otherwise fail or refuse to comply with any provision of the statute.[119]

The FLRA's enforcement power in unfair labor practice cases is similar to that of the NLRB; it may order the agency or labor organization to cease and desist from continuing an unfair labor practice; require the parties to renegotiate a collective bargaining agreement in accordance with the order of the Authority and require that the agreement be given retroactive effect; and/or require reinstatement with back pay of an employee.

As noted earlier, the NLRB has fairly limited authority in contract enforcement. Violation of a provision of a collective bargaining agreement is not in and of itself an unfair labor practice. Therefore, a contract violation only comes under NLRB jurisdiction if the matter also involves a violation of an unfair labor practice provision. But the Authority has jurisdiction in all the arbitration awards appealed to it regardless of the issue involved. The authority performs a quasi-judicial role, and it determines whether the arbitrator's award is contrary to any law, rule, or regulation or is deficient on other grounds similar to those applied by federal courts in private sector labor–management relations.[120]

State and Local Governments

Most bargaining statutes specify unfair labor practices on the part of both the employer-government and the labor organization modeled on the NLRA. The only significant difference is that it is considered an unfair labor practice in most jurisdictions that recognize public sector collective bargaining for employees to participate in a strike. (See Chapter 3.)

INDIVIDUAL RIGHTS WITHIN UNIONS

Duty of Fair Representation in contract negotiations

The certified union for a bargaining unit is granted an exclusive right under the National Labor Relations Act to represent all the employees in that unit, members and nonmembers alike. Individuals within that bargaining unit may not contract privately with the employer but must be represented by the recognized bargaining agent. The exclusivity rule giving the union the right to represent all members, however, is essential to the union's ability for proper representation at the bargaining table. Along with this right goes the duty to represent fairly all the employees of the unit. Under its duty of fair representation, a union must consider all the employees in the bargaining unit when negotiating an agreement and must make an honest effort to serve their interests. This must be a good-faith effort, without hostility or arbitrary discrimination to represent union and non-union alike. But the end result of such negotiations may still unevenly affect one, several, or a class of employees without the union's being considered in breach of its duty.

RIGHT TO REFRAIN FROM UNION ACTIVITIES The NLRA gives employees the right to refrain from union activities. Individual employees who may have voted in a minority against the union still find their employment contract affected by the negotiations. Although the union has a duty to represent all employees fairly during the negotiation process, absent a showing of actual hostile discrimination, the court will accept a wide range of "reasonableness" when a question of a breach of that duty arises.

UNION SECURITY CLAUSES Originally the National Labor Relations Act allowed an employer to make an agreement with a union to require union membership as a prior condition of employment—that is, the closed shop. All forms of union security were permitted as long as the agreement was made with a bona fide union representing the bargaining unit. Closed shop clauses became common in collective bargaining agreements. Although these clauses protected and promoted the growth of unions, abuses of the system against individuals who were denied job opportunities led to the Taft-Hartley Amendments. These amendments made the closed shop an unfair labor practice and added the right *not* to organize and engage in union activity. Although union shop clauses still could be negotiated and enforced against existing employees, the employee need only pay dues to abide by that contract clause; no other activity was required. The amendments also allowed state right-to-work laws to outlaw even the union shop requirement.

The union hiring hall is another practice that appears to give equal consideration to union and nonunion personnel. Although a hiring hall operating as a closed shop was technically outlawed by the amendments, a union can still negotiate a contract clause that requires the employer to hire through the union's exclusive referral system. It is then up to the nonunion individual to claim and prove discriminatory referrals.

Negotiating clauses to compel union membership are not the only prohibited behavior violating the individual employee's right to refrain from union activity. The courts consider union intimidation, reprisals, or threats against employees as restraint and coercion. In a leading Supreme Court case, *Steele v. Louisville and N.R.R.*, a black railroad fireman asked the Court to set aside a seniority agreement negotiated by his union because it discriminated against minorities who were part of the bargaining unit.[121] Although the Railway Labor Act under which the union had exclusive rights to bargain for the employees did not explicitly do so, the Court held that the act implicitly imposed a duty on the union to exercise its powers fairly on behalf of all those it acted for. Later court decisions found that the National Labor Relations Act imposed that same duty on its unions.

In 1998, the Court upheld its decision in *Vaca* in *Marquez v. Screen Actors Guild, Inc., et al.*, and held that a union does not breach the duty of fair representation by negotiating a union security clause that includes statutory language that incorporates an employee's right not to "join" the union and to pay only for representational activities.[122] In a historic Supreme Court case, *Bowen v. The U.S. Postal Service*, the Court apportioned the damages due the wrongfully discharged employee between the union and the employer by using the date of a hypothetical arbitration decision.[123] All back pay prior to that hypothetical date was due from the employer; all back pay from that date to the time of settlement was due from the union. The Court reasoned that if the employee had been properly represented, the employer's liability would have ended at the arbitration decision. All back-pay benefits from that point forward were caused and should be paid by the union.

Employees' "right to refrain" from supporting a union includes (1) the right to refrain from joining a union, (2) the right to resign union membership at any time, and (3) the right to stop paying full union dues and pay only the financial core, which includes only the costs of collective bargaining. When an employee joins a union, however, he or she is subject to the internal rules of the union and may be fined and even sued in court. As an example, unions often fine members who cross a picket line during a strike. However, unions can discipline only their voluntary members, and those members are free to leave the union at any time. Many employees wrongfully believe that they must remain a union member to keep their jobs. However, formal union membership cannot be required—they can only be required to pay the financial core or agency fee. But union members and nonmembers are still within the bargaining unit and thus covered by the terms of any negotiated agreement, including wages, benefits, and working conditions. Because a union can discipline only those employees who are voluntary members, those who refrain from joining or leave a union are not subject to any form of discipline a union may impose on its members.[124]

FAIR REPRESENTATION IN CONTRACT ENFORCEMENT A far more litigious area concerning fair representation is in contract enforcement. An employee must use the grievance procedure controlled by the union, but the employee does not have an absolute right to have a grievance pursued. In *Vaca v. Sipes*, the Supreme Court noted that a procedure giving the union discretion to supervise the grievance machinery and to invoke arbitration establishes an atmosphere for both parties to settle grievances short of arbitration.[125] The parties are assured that similar grievances receive similar treatment; thus, problem areas under the collective bargaining agreement can be isolated and perhaps resolved. Therefore, a breach of the duty to represent an employee fairly occurs only if the union's conduct toward the member is *arbitrary, discriminatory, or in bad faith*. Grievance arbitration has become the most common method of enforcing each party's promise to abide by the contract. That promise to arbitrate is enforceable by either the employer or the union. Fitting the individual into that arbitration system involves balancing conflicting interests. The National Labor Relations Act adopted the doctrine of majority rule when it granted a union exclusive representation rights if selected by most unit members. The courts confirmed this doctrine by giving the collective agreement precedence over the individual employment contract. To balance the power of the union, the court recognized the union's duty to represent all its employees.

But there remained a question of whether an individual employee could arbitrate against both or either party. In *Vaca v. Sipes*, *Hines v. Anchor Motor Co., Inc.*, and *Bowen v. U.S. Postal Service*, the Supreme Court indicated that the individual has no absolute right to have a grievance arbitrated and that the union is liable to the employee only if, in processing and settling that grievance, it violates its fair representation duty.[126]

In contract administration issues, the duty of fair representation is breached when a union's conduct is arbitrary, discriminatory, or in bad faith. A union may not arbitrarily ignore a meritorious grievance or process it in a perfunctory manner. Yet proof of the merit of a grievance is not enough under this test: Arbitrary or bad-faith actions must also be proved.

The subjective nature of the fair representation test has left unions with "Hobson's choice." If a union cannot be reasonably certain that its honest and rational decision not to pursue a grievance to arbitration will withstand a *Vaca* challenge, the arbitration process will be so burdened that its effectiveness and financial viability will be undermined. At the same time, the *Vaca* rule ensures an individual that although there is no absolute right to arbitrate a grievance, the union cannot behave in a capricious fashion.[127]

Summary

Employer unfair labor practices impede the collective bargaining process. Unfair labor practices, as contained in the National Labor Relations Act, include interference with employees in the exercise of their rights, domination of an employee union, discrimination against union members, and refusal to bargain. The act imposed a duty to bargain in good faith on both the employer and the labor organization. That good faith is evidenced by the total conduct of the parties toward the collective bargaining process.

Because the NLRA guarantees employees the right to refrain from union activities, attempts by labor unions to coerce employees to join may be a ULP violation. A union must fairly represent all its members, union and nonunion alike, and a breach of that duty is an unfair labor practice. The Weingarten Rule provides members an important right—to have a steward present as a witness and advisor during a discipline meeting with management.

CASE STUDIES

Case Study 10-1 Unfair Labor Practice by an Employer

The employer manufactures automobile parts and supplies those parts to major auto manufacturers. The UAW filed a representation petition to unionize the employer's workforce. Between November 14, 1994, when the petition was filed, and January 12, 1995, when the election was held, the employer did the following:

1. The human resources director distributed a letter to employees asserting that two-thirds of the 600 plants that had closed in their state over the past 20 years had been unionized.
2. The employer distributed an article concerning Ford's decision to move a parts contract from a supplier whose workforce had gone out on strike, emphasizing that the striking union was the UAW.
3. Around Christmas, the employer relocated production of a Ford part to another one of its plants at a location not subject to the pending election petition. The employer offered no explanation for the move.

4. The employer told the employees that negotiations on a renewal contract with a customer were being held in abeyance until the outcome of the union election, although the customer also had issues of quality and delivery to discuss.
5. The employer displayed large photo posters of closed manufacturing plants and distributed a letter noting that all the plants had been unionized.
6. On January 9, 1995, the president of the company sent a letter to employees telling of his concern that its manufacturing partners would become nervous and go elsewhere if the company developed "a reputation for not being dependable because of labor problems, a UAW-led strike, or even the possibility of a strike every time the contract comes up for renewal."
7. On January 10, 1995, the division manager told employees that the employer was concerned about the impact of the union vote on its manufacturing customers. On January 9 and 10, one such customer did a very visible "walk-through" inspection of the facility accompanied by numerous managers.

When the ballots were counted, the union lost 196 to 154. The union filed an unfair labor charge against the employer, charging that its campaign tactics had violated the National Labor Relations Act and invalidated the results.

Source: Adapted from *SPX Corporation*, 151 LRRM 1300 (1995).

QUESTIONS

1. Which, if any, of the employer's actions might the court find violated the National Labor Relations Act and therefore might cause the election to be set aside?
2. Recognizing that this election took place in 1995, do you think the court might find that the employees could have seen through the employer's tactics and voted the way they wanted despite the employer's actions?
3. Would you have been swayed by the employer's actions to the point you could not have voted with "freedom of choice"?

Case Study 10-2 Unfair Labor Practice by a Union

A decertification election was held at a plant owned by a Japanese company. The appeal to the NLRB by the company and one employee was that the election, in which the decertification petition was defeated, be set aside on the basis of the union's unfair labor practice. The company and the petitioning employee charged that the union's patterns of threats and intimidation, as well as its racially oriented acts, were so extensive and persuasive that they prevented the employees' exercise of free choice.

The company presented testimony at the hearing regarding the following activities:

1. An employee's tires were slashed after he had been identified in the union's newsletter as withdrawing his union membership. In addition, one of his wheels fell off when he left work; he discovered that the lugs had been removed and were only a few feet from where the car had been parked.
2. Another employee, who had headed up the decertification petition, received numerous anonymous obscene telephone calls.
3. A union steward intimidated an employee along the roadway by slowing down so the employee would pass and then speeding up and quickly slamming on the brakes, causing the employee to do the same and swerve to avoid an accident. The union steward had used

the same harassing highway tactics on another employee who was driving with her daughter and five grandchildren.

4. One employee was followed home and found her fuel line cut the next day.
5. Another employee discovered a scratch down the entire side of her car, which had been parked at the plant.
6. An employee wearing a "Vote No" button was threatened with physical harm by a fellow employee.
7. Several employees received intimidating telephone calls at their homes from both union agents and anonymous callers. The employees' children answered some of the calls, and threatening statements were then made to the children.
8. Two employees were overheard discussing the rumors of threats surrounding the campaign, and one of the employees said, "Sometimes it takes this kind of thing to get the point across."
9. At two union organizing meetings, at which more than 100 employees were present, a union official ended his speech with the following quote: "We beat the Japs after Pearl Harbor, and we can beat them again." Anti-Japanese graffiti appeared on bathroom walls, and a steward wore a shirt and work tags printed with the phrases "Remember Pearl Harbor" and "Japs go home."

The union's position was that it should not be charged with an unfair labor practice because of the alleged activities of individuals who were not acting at the union's direction. Union membership and support for the union can cause emotions to run high; it happens in every election. But no evidence indicated that the employees were prevented from exercising their free choice in the election itself. The anti-Japanese statements were unfortunate but mere rhetoric. Such rhetoric violates none of the established NLRB standards for conducting a fair election.

Source: Adapted from *YKK (U.S.A.), Inc.*, 115 LRRM 1186 (1984).

QUESTIONS

1. Would you set aside the election results and order another election? Explain your answer.
2. How could the union have stopped individuals from the intimidating actions that allegedly went on in this case?
3. Does the racial nature of the rhetoric involved in this case put a heavier burden on the union than does the usual rhetoric about an employer? Explain your answer.

Key Terms and Concepts

antiunion animus *370*
Boys Market case *387*
Boulwarism *381*
Collyer case *397*
concerted activity *372*
dual-motive discrimination case *371*
duty to bargain in good faith *381*
duty to furnish information *384*
Electromation case *369*
good-faith reasonable doubt *366*
hot cargo agreement *389*
Lincoln Mills case *397*
no-solicitation policy *363*
opener clauses *386*
pretext discrimination *371*
primary boycott/secondary boycott *388*
scabs *374*
severability clause *386*
Section 10(j) injunction *394*
sickout *375*
Steelworkers' Trilogy *397*
surface bargaining *382*
totality of conduct doctrine *381*
unfair labor practice *360*
Weingarten rule *378*
zipper clause *385*
24-hour rule *367*

Review Questions

1. What might the NLRB consider to be a breach of the good-faith bargaining principle?
2. How does the NLRB review an unfair labor practice charge of surface bargaining?
3. What is the Weingarten rule? For what purpose did the Supreme Court adopt the rule?
4. What are the rules that employers and union organizers must follow during an organizational campaign?
5. When is an employer illegally discriminating against employees because of their union activities?
6. What union activities are prohibited under the Taft-Hartley unfair labor practices provision?
7. By what methods can collective bargaining agreements be enforced?
8. How did the *Steelworkers Trilogy* help clarify the role of arbitration and court enforcement of contracts?
9. What individual rights do employees have within the collective bargaining process?
10. Why does management often desire to add a zipper clause to a CBA?

YOU BE THE ARBITRATOR

Refusing to Arbitrate

ARTICLE IV
GRIEVANCE PROCEDURE

3. If the grievance is not resolved at the conference as provided for In STEP TWO above, then either party may request, in writing, within fifteen (15) days of the conference that the matter proceed in accordance with ARTICLE V. Failure of either party to give such written notice shall waive the rights to proceed in accordance with ARTICLE V.

ARTICLE V
ARBITRATION

1. Disputes concerning contract interpretation, the disposition of assets, the right of sale, the right to control the number of hours that the plant be open or closed down either for lack of business or for economic reasons, or matters which involve management decision or business judgment shall not be subject to arbitration. Procedural questions of compliance with the contract shall be subject to judicial determination and not arbitration. Either party may seek judicial relief with regard to any of the foregoing.

Any other disputes concerning working conditions, safety or other matters not excluded herein, shall be subject to arbitration; provided a written notice has been given as provided in ARTICLE IV, Section 3 above. The Company and the Union shall attempt by mutual agreement to appoint an arbitrator, then either party may request a panel of arbitrators to be submitted by the Federal Mediation and Conciliation Service, State Conciliation Service or American Arbitration Association, and an arbitrator shall be selected from such panel by the process of each party alternately eliminating one of the suggested names until there remains only one name on the panel. . . .

Facts

The Union and Employer are parties to a written collective-bargaining agreement (the CBA) covering a 30-member unit of production employees at a plant in Yuma, Arizona.

The CBA has a no-strike, no-lockout provision and requires that all disputes and grievances be resolved under the grievance procedure in the agreement. The CBA includes a two-step formal grievance procedure prior to either arbitration or judicial enforcement. The CBA requires that formal grievances at step one and step two to be in writing, describe the facts, state the remedy sought, and identify the sections of the CBA claimed to have been violated.

The Union filed four grievances, none of which were resolved at Step two. The issues grieved were (1) a performance memo issued to an employee for having a negative and uncooperative attitude and suspending her for three days, (2) an employee being improperly hired and paid from the piece rate pool generated by senior unit employees, (3) an operator improperly given a share of group piecework pay for work done by other unit employees, (4) a written warning issued to the entire crew for asserted violations of company policy and a work rule.

The Union sent separate letters to the State Mediation and Conciliation Service requesting a panel of arbitrators for each grievance. Each of the letters stated, inter alia, "This matter is a labor dispute involving interpretation and application of a collective-bargaining agreement."

The Employer refused to arbitrate these grievances, contending that they were not subject to arbitration under the CBA.

Issue

Was the Employer's refusal to arbitrate the grievances an unfair labor practice?

Union Position

An employer's refusal to arbitrate grievances, pursuant to a collective-bargaining agreement, violates Section 8(a)(5) of the act if the employer's conduct amounts to a unilateral modification or wholesale repudiation of the collective-bargaining agreement. The Union charged that the Employer's refusal to arbitrate grievances in this case was both an unlawful contract modification and an unlawful unilateral change. In refusing to arbitrate the grievances, the Employer relied on the narrow language of the arbitration clause, which excludes from arbitration disputes concerning contract interpretation or matters which involve management decision or business judgment. The Union asserts that the grievances at issue here were not excluded by the language of the contact, and that even assuming that there was some arguable basis for the Employer's position, the Employer was required to arbitrate the arbitrability of the grievances. The Union further argues that the Employer's conduct is a "wholesale" repudiation of the arbitration procedure.

Employer Position

It is well settled that arbitration is a matter of contract, and a party cannot be required to submit to arbitration any dispute that the party has not agreed to submit. The CBA in this case contains a very narrow arbitration clause, expressly excluding, inter alia, "[d]isputes concerning contract interpretation . . . management decision or business judgment." The Employer contended that the four grievances concerned contract interpretation, management decisions, or business judgment and were therefore excluded from the arbitration provision. The Union itself initially took the position that the four grievances involved contract interpretation; the Union's letters requesting the arbitration of those grievances stated that the "matter is a labor dispute involving interpretation and application of a collective-bargaining agreement." Given the nature of the grievances and the Union's own characterization of the four grievances as involving contract interpretation, the Employer was under no obligation to arbitrate the four grievances.

QUESTIONS

1. As arbitrator, what would be your award and opinion in this arbitration?
2. Identify the key, relevant section(s), phrases, or words of the collective bargaining agreement (CBA), and explain why they were critical in making your decision.
3. What actions might the employer and/or the union have taken to avoid this conflict?

Source: ACS, LLC and United Food and Commercial Workers International Union, Local 1096, 345 NLRB No. 87 (2005).

CHAPTER 11

Grievance and Disciplinary Procedures

Chapter Outline

The Hotel Association of New York City reported a 44 percent increase in grievances being filed by the New York Hotel Trades Council in anticipation of new contract negotiations. A contract settlement avoided a strike and provided funds to resolve hundreds of grievances. Fears of a harmful strike by hotel workers were eased, and the New York hotel industry experienced a period of peace and growth with occupancy rates of over 90 percent in 2010 and the opening of 44 new hotels. *Source:* Stewart Cohen/Photolibrary.com.

We will never have civilization until we have learned to recognize the rights of others.

WILL ROGERS (AMERICAN NEWS REPORTER, AUTHOR, COLUMNIST, HUMORIST)

LABOR NEWS

New York Hotel Strike Avoided

The Hotel Association of New York City negotiated with the New York Hotel Trades Council union that represents thousands of employees at 149 hotels. The Hotel Association reported that the union filed 597 grievances in the previous calendar year—an increase of 44 percent over the prior year. The substantial increase in the number of grievances was largely over increased workloads according to Peter Ward, president of the New York Hotel Trades Council, and foreshadowed the new negotiations in 2006 as the prior five-year contract expired. The union president emphasized that the substantial increase in grievances filed during the term of a contract was a strong indication of the area the union members would want to focus on in the new contract negotiations. The union strike fund of $13 million was growing rapidly and raised fears of a strike that could cripple the New York hotel and tourism industry.

The workload grievances included complaints of unsafe working conditions and employees being required to work through scheduled breaks. The core of the workload issue is the expanded duties, including cleaning coffeepots and triple-sheeting mattresses while being required to clean the same number of rooms—14 per day. It is estimated that at $20 per hour, New York's desk clerks and room attendants are among the highest paid in the industry. Ward would like to have more of his approximately 1,000 unemployed union members hired by the hotels. In the previous eight years the union was involved in recovering over $12 million in back pay for members in workload grievance cases.

A historic six-year contract was signed that avoided a strike and provided three years of 4 percent wage increases followed by three years of 3.5 percent increases, or a total of 22.5 percent. Health care, safety, and back pay to settle hundreds of grievance disputes were also included in the new contract. Under the new industry-wide agreement, grievances may be sent to arbitration for resolution. One labor leader noted, "New York City is booming and is where the dream of good hotel jobs comes true." For example, in 2010, 44 new hotels opened in New York, and overall occupancy averaged over 90 percent.

Source: Adapted from Lisa Fickenscher, "Hotel Union Sets Targets for Contract," *Crain's New York Business 21,* no. 39 (September 26, 2005), pp. 1–3. Used by permission. Also see www.hotelworkersrising.org. Accessed August 3, 2010.

In the day-to-day administration of a collective bargaining agreement, the majority of time is spent on grievance handling.[1] The **grievance procedure** is the core of the continuous collective bargaining process. An employer's refusal to process grievances is a violation of the NLRA. The extreme importance of a good grievance procedure has been described as the "lifeblood of a collective bargaining relationship."[2]

Regardless of the completeness and clarity of the labor agreement, disagreements do arise during the life of the contract. Thus, a grievance procedure, a previously agreed-on procedure to resolve such disputes, must be provided in the agreement. The grievance handling process must settle disputes arising during the term of the agreement; if it does not, strikes, lockouts, or other work disruptions may result. A **grievance** is often defined as any perceived violation of a contract provision. This definition could be broadened to include any complaint by an employee against an employer and vice versa. One arbitrator provided a classic definition: "If a man thinks he has a grievance, he has a grievance."[3] However, a more precise definition might include any formal complaint lodged by persons who believe they have been wronged.[4] A grievance is not a *gripe*, which is generally defined as a complaint by an employee concerning an action by management that does not violate the contract, past practice, or law. For example, an employee may only have a gripe if his supervisor speaks to him in a harsh tone, but when the supervisor assigns him work outside his job classification, he may have a grievance.

GRIEVANCE

Any formal complaint filed by an employee or union concerning any aspect of the employment relationship. A grievance is generally a perceived violation of a contract provision.

Fortunately, most collective bargaining agreements contain provisions similar to Figure 11-1 and delineate a grievance procedure that consists of a specified series of four or five procedural steps that aggrieved employees, unions, and management representatives

Article 8
Grievance and Arbitration Procedure

8.1 Grievance Procedure—Should any "grievance" arise over the interpretation or application of the contents of this Agreement, there shall be an earnest effort on the part of both parties to settle same promptly through the following steps. The term "grievance" comprehends any complaint, difficulty, disagreement or dispute between the Employer and the Union or any employee covered by this Agreement, and which complaint, difficulty, disagreement or dispute pertains to the interpretation or application of any and all provision of this Agreement.

Step 1 By conference between the aggrieved employee, the job steward or both and/or a representative of the Union and the manager of the store. If the grievance is not settled, it shall be reduced to writing with copies to the Union and Employer and referred within ten (10) days to Step 2, unless such time period is mutually extended by the Union, and the zone manager.

Step 2 By conference between the representative of the Union and zone manager. If this Step does not settle the grievance, it shall be referred within ten days to Step 3, unless such time period is mutually extended by the Union and zone manager.

Step 3 By conference between the business representative and/or the executive officer of the Union, the Human Resource Manager and/or a representative delegated by the Employer. In the event the grievance is not settled in this Step, a written response will be exchanged by the parties within twenty (20) days from the Step 3 conference unless otherwise mutually agreed to.

Step 4 In the event that the last Step fails to settle satisfactorily the grievance, and either party wishes to submit it to arbitration, the party desiring arbitration must so advise the other party in writing within forty-five (45) days from Step 3 written response, or the grievance will be considered settled in Step 3.

8.2 Timeliness of Grievances—No grievance will be considered or discussed unless the outlined procedure has been followed, and the grievance presented within ten (10) days, except a grievance arising from an error in the rate of pay may be presented within two (2) years.

Grievances may arise of a general nature affecting or tending to affect an employee or employees. Such grievances may be initiated at any of the above steps deemed appropriate by the parties.

FIGURE 11-1 Grievance Procedure. *Source*: Agreement between the Kroger Co. and the United Food and Commercial Workers International Union AFL-CIO (2007–2010). Used by permission.

must follow when a complaint arises. Typically, the grievant is provided with a systematic set of appeals through successively higher levels of union and management representatives. The fact that most contracts provide for specific grievance procedures clearly indicates that although both sides try to develop a clear and precise document during the contract negotiation process, some areas will be subject to misunderstanding during the life of the contract. Indeed, as shown in Case 11-1, the grievance procedure itself is sometimes the subject of a grievance.

The signing of a contract spells out a new relationship between labor and management, and the agreement specifies a new set of rules legally binding labor and management during the life of the contract. The formal grievance process agreed on in the contract provides for the administration of the contract. Although the number and contents of the procedural steps in a formal grievance process vary from contract to contract, most grievance processes involve three to five steps.

CASE 11-1

Untimely Filing of a Grievance

The grievance procedure in this case contains four steps with a time period of seven calendar days at each step. For example, Step 1 of the grievance procedure states that the union has seven calendar days to present a grievable incident to management. If the grievance is not resolved in Step 1, then the union has seven calendar days to prepare a grievance form and move it to Step 2, and so on. At Step 4, if the grievance is not resolved, the union is required to prepare a written notice of intent to arbitrate and has 14 calendar days to do so. The contract specifies that the notice of intent to arbitrate shall be sent by certified mail with return receipt requested, and the postmark shall govern compliance with the time limit. The union is also required to obtain a listing of possible arbitrators from the Federal Mediation and Conciliation Service (FMCS), meet with the company, and select an arbitrator.

On November 4, 1993, a meeting occurred between the union business agent and the employer's human resources manager (HRM) concerning the discharge of two employees. The meeting was within the seven-day time period required in the contract. During the arbitration hearing, the union business agent testified that on November 9, 1993, he had hand-delivered the "intent to arbitrate" document to the company's HRM. Also, during the arbitration, the HRM testified that he did not remember receiving such a document from the union. On November 15, 1993, the union forwarded a request for an arbitration panel to the FMCS. On December 28, 1993, the union business agent approached the company's HRM with a list of arbitrators. At that time (December 28, 1993), the HRM informed the union for the first time that a grievance had not been properly filed. The union argued that Step 1 of the grievance procedure became Step 4 because of the nature of the grievance (the two employees had been discharged) and that an intent to arbitrate had been filed in a timely manner. The parties continued to disagree with respect to both whether the grievance was filed and its timeliness.

In November 1994, at an arbitration hearing to resolve this issue, the arbitrator was asked to make a finding as to the timeliness issue. If the grievance was determined to be timely, then the grievance would be heard on its merits. Otherwise, the matter would be dismissed. During the arbitration hearing, the company argued that a written grievance was not filed in a timely manner and that the parties' labor agreement specifically states the following: "If the grieving party fails to process the grievance in accordance with the requirements of this article, the grievance is waived."

The collective bargaining agreement further states that the "arbitrator may not add to, detract from, or alter in any way, the provisions of the agreement."

Decision

The arbitrator ruled that the union had failed to follow the requirements of the grievance procedure, and the grievance was denied.

Source: Adapted from *Los Alamos Protection Technology,* 104 LA 23.

STEPS IN A GRIEVANCE PROCEDURE

The number of steps and the exact process specified varies from contract to contract. However, most CBAs contain 3–5 steps with binding arbitration as the last step, which ensures the issues will be resolved.

Step 1: Employee, Steward, Supervisor

The initial step in a grievance procedure usually instructs the employee to discuss the grievance with the shop steward or go directly to the supervisor. The employee has the legal right to do the latter; the supervisor must resolve the grievance consistent with the contract. The supervisor must also notify the union of the grievance. The shop steward, however, is usually the first person contacted. Therefore, the steward must be experienced in handling grievance matters and be familiar with the terms of the contract and its provisions. The steward must also be able to recognize grievances containing some merit as well as those that are trivial and should be dropped. A steward will encourage and help the employee to pursue a legitimate grievance and in some cases must convince the employee that a grievance contains no merit.

The extent to which grievances are resolved at the *lowest possible level* is an important indicator of effective grievance handling and a measure of peaceful labor relations. One means of attaining resolution at the lowest possible level is the use of feedback from previous grievance cases. The outcome of previous similar cases provides cues to both parties that tend to focus their discussion and provide a faster resolution of the grievance. In general, the purpose of feedback is not to "set precedent" but to provide both parties with an array of possible likely solutions.[5] In practice, if both sides introduce the results of previous similar grievances at the first level of grievance discussions, a compromise may well be reached more quickly than if they wait until the issue goes to arbitration.

Step 2: Written Grievance

If steward and employee agree that the grievance has some merit and should be pursued, then the grievance is reduced to writing. At this point, the grievance is said to have moved from the informal to the formal stage. The steward and employee complete a grievance form within a specified period, usually 48 hours of the occurrence or within the time limit specified in the contract. The process of writing out the complaint forces the grievant to set forth the facts, contract provisions, and contingencies early on in the process.

Most company and union representatives believe it is important to formalize the grievance in written format at this stage.[6] Once the grievance has been reduced to writing, the steward and the employee meet with the supervisor to discuss the grievance in an honest effort to settle the matter quickly. Both sides can assess the strengths and weaknesses of the claim. Most grievances containing little merit are dropped at this stage.

The steward normally investigates the grievance to provide documented facts on the case. The pertinent facts are written on a grievance form such as the one in Figure 11-2. A good rule for remembering the crucial facts in a grievance is the **"5Ws" rule**:

"5 Ws" RULE

Assembling crucial facts in a grievance what happened, where did it happen, when did it happen, why is the complaint a grievance, and who was involved.

- What happened?
- Where did it happen?
- When did the event take place?
- Why is the complaint a grievance?
- Who was involved? (Witnesses?)

The written grievance is delivered to the supervisor, and a meeting of the three parties is held (the shop steward is occasionally accompanied by a personnel or industrial relations representative). In discussing the grievance, all the parties make an attempt to settle the matter at that point. Research indicates that most grievances are settled in this step of the grievance process. If the grievance cannot be resolved at this stage, the employee usually may choose to appeal.

Step 3: Shop Steward, Department Head

When the shop steward and supervisor cannot resolve the grievance, then it may be appealed to the next higher level of management and union representative, usually within seven calendar days. At this

GRIEVANCE NUMBER _10–003_ DATE FILED _4/23/10_ UNION _Local 1233_
NAME OF GRIEVANT(S) _Davis, Henry_ CLOCK # _0379_
DATE CAUSE OF GRIEVANCE OCCURRED _4/20/10_
CONTRACTUAL PROVISIONS CITED _Articles III, VII, and others_
STATEMENT OF THE GRIEVANCE:

On April 20, Foreman George Moore asked Henry Davis to go temporarily to the Rolling Mill for the rest of the turn. Davis said he preferred not to, and that he was more senior to others who were available. The foreman never ordered Davis to take the temporary assignment. He only requested that Davis do so.

Davis was improperly charged with insubordination and suspended for three days. The foreman did not have just cause for the discipline.

RELIEF SOUGHT:

Reinstatement with full back pay and seniority.

GRIEVANT'S SIGNATURE _Henry Davis_ DATE _4/22/10_
STEWARD'S SIGNATURE _Jim Bob Smith_ DATE _4/22/10_

STEP 1

DISPOSITION:

Foreman Moore gave Davis clear instructions to report temporarily to the Rolling Mill for the remainder of the shift. Davis refused to do so and was warned that it could result in discipline. When he again refused the foreman's directive, he was disciplined.

The discipline was for just cause. The grievance is rejected.

SIGNATURE OF EMPLOYER REPRESENTATIVE _Paul Roberts_ DATE _4/26/10_ ______ Grievance Withdrawn or √ Referred to Step 2
SIGNATURE OF UNION REPRESENTATIVE _Jim Bob Smith_ DATE _4/28/10_

FIGURE 11-2 A Standard Grievance Record Form Step I

point, the union representative continues to be the shop steward or business agent. However, the management representative usually represents a higher level and may be a plant superintendent or department head. At this stage, the two sides review the written grievance and try to reach a resolution.

Step 4: Union Grievance Committee, Director of Personnel and Industrial Relations

At this step the plant manager or department head may be assisted by the director of personnel and industrial relations in reviewing the grievance from a management perspective. As with the second step, they review the written grievance and discuss the case with the employee's representatives. The two sides continue to try to resolve the grievance honestly rather than go to the final stage of the process—final and binding arbitration. At this point, a plant-wide union grievance committee that may further appeal the answer to Step 5, usually within 30 calendar days, reviews the employee's grievance. This final step is more expensive, represents a failure to reach an agreement in the matter, and brings greater tension to the grievance. Both sides realize that they may completely lose the case before an independent arbitrator.

Step 5: Arbitration

Approximately 98 percent of all collective bargaining agreements provide for a binding arbitration as the final step in the handling of grievances.[7] The contract provisions usually include that either management or labor may request arbitration as a final step in resolving the grievance. This request must be made within a specified period, such as 30 calendar days of the receipt of the answer of Step 4. The outside independent arbitrator studies the evidence and listens to the arguments of both sides before rendering a decision. The arbitrator's decision, as agreed on in the collective bargaining contract, is final and binding on both parties and can be appealed to the courts only on the grounds of collusion, if the arbitrator's award exceeded his or her authority, or if the arbitrator's decision was not based on the essence of the labor agreement.[8] Profile 11-1 explains how a new "expedited grievance-arbitration" process works for the U.S. Postal Service.

Profile 11-1

New Grievance-Arbitration Process Relieves Gridlock at the U.S. Postal Service

In 2001, the U.S. Postal Service had one of its worst financial years—a $2.4 billion loss. The causes for the financial failure included higher fuel costs, revenues that fell short of estimates, and a "grievance gridlock." About 210,000 grievances were pending under a grievance system that has been negotiated among the National Association of Letter Carriers (NALC), the American Postal Workers Union (APWU), the National Postal Mail Handlers Union (NPMHU), and the U.S. Postal Service at costs of more than $200 million per year to operate. It required over 300 outside arbitrators to settle just the grievances that reached the final step in the resolution process, not the hundreds of thousands that are resolved before that step.

Why was the grievance system in a state of gridlock? Employees said that supervisors are too domineering and that they complain employees are paid too much and work too little. Supervisors complained that employees file grievances just to annoy them. But Anthony Vegliante, vice president of labor relations for the Postal Service, notes that postal workers, like most public sector employees, cannot legally strike and do not receive profit sharing or some other private sector economic perks, and thus they turn to the grievance system to air their complaints. And the significant backlog of cases, he noted, created underlying tensions that harmed productivity because people felt their issues should be heard in a timely manner.

In April 2002, USPS and NALC, representing approximately 234,000 postal employees, announced a new Joint Dispute Resolution Process. The new process is faster, more efficient, and focuses on addressing and resolving disputes at the lowest levels of the organization. It places a premium

After years of "grievance gridlock" a new grievance process reduced grievances sent to arbitration by 59 percent! *Source:* © David R. Frazier Photolibrary, Inc. / Alamy.

on teaching dispute resolution skills to individuals responsible for grievance handling at the lowest steps of the process. This ensures that disputes are resolved when it is appropriate to do so. The Joint Dispute Resolution Process was piloted in 19 sites across the country and reduced the number of cases appealed to arbitration by 59 percent. A five-year collective bargaining agreement with NALC, signed in 2002, incorporated the new grievance-arbitration procedure, replacing an old process that no longer met the parties' needs. This was the first major restructuring of the grievance-arbitration procedure in more than 20 years. "The best part of the new system is that both groups, the Postal Service and the Union, share the responsibility. If we measure it against the past, it's been very successful," said Vincent R. Sombrotto, president of the National Association of Letter Carriers, AFL-CIO. "Under the old system, someone had to win and someone had to lose. This way, the two parties can work to achieve a win-win. It's better for employees and it's better for the Postal Service," said Vegliante.

And in 2005, a Memorandum of Understanding was entered into with APWU to improve the grievance-arbitration process by streamlining the handling of cases. The agreement included such steps as holding grievances that were the same or substantially similar to a grievance already pending at the national level until those grievances were resolved, and moving a "Direct Appeal" grievance to regular or expedited arbitration immediately. The APWU represents approximately 260,000 postal workers.

Source: Adapted from Rick Brooks, "Mail Disorder: Blizzard of Grievances Joins a Sack of Woes at U.S. Postal Service," *Wall Street Journal* (June 22, 2001), pp. A1, A4. Available at www.apwu.org and www.usps.com. Accessed March 2, 2008.

FUNCTIONS OF GRIEVANCE PROCEDURES

Formal grievance procedures are the most common tool to resolve conflicts arising between labor and management during the life of the agreement. In general, the functions provided by a grievance procedure are as follows.

1. ***Conflict management resolution.*** Before grievance procedures and arbitration became popular, employees and unions often used strikes, slowdowns, or other disruptive actions to resolve complaints over the interpretation of labor agreements. Without grievance procedures, issues would often be resolved by a test of strength, harmful both to management and to the union, rather than the facts of the case. The use of grievance procedures to resolve complaints has greatly improved the labor relations process.
2. ***Agreement clarification.*** All agreements contain a certain amount of unintentional ambiguity that results in questions requiring contract interpretation. The dynamics of the employer–employee relationships cannot be fully anticipated by the parties at the bargaining table; thus, negotiating language often must be applied to unforeseen situations. Several of the "You Be the Arbitrator" cases at the end of chapters in this text contain issues that arose at least in part due to vague, incomplete, or competing contract provisions.
3. ***Communication.*** Grievance procedures provide a vehicle for individual employees to express their problems and perceptions. They offer employees a formal process to air perceived inequities in the workplace.
4. ***Due process.*** The most widely heralded function of grievance procedures is that of a neutral, third-party intervention. Most grievance procedures provide a fair and equitable due process containing binding arbitration as a final step, and some include grievance mediation as a step before arbitration. Without this process, management would likely have an upper hand in most grievance situations. However, employee and union strikes would be heightened and economic measures used to balance management's authority.
5. ***Strength enhancement.*** The grievance mechanism helps unions develop employee loyalty and trust. Grievance processing emphasizes union presence and strength during the term of the collective bargaining agreement and reminds employees of the union efforts to protect their interests. The formal grievance also strengthens management and labor's communication skills because first-level stewards and supervisors are almost always involved in the initial step of the grievance procedure. The two sides come to better understand each other's perspectives and develop a closer working relationship.[9]

EMPLOYEE MISCONDUCT

EMPLOYEE MISCONDUCT

A wide range of offenses ranging from serious, such as fighting or threatening others, to minor offenses, such as failing to punch a timecard, can be considered examples of misconduct.

In labor relations the term "misconduct" applies to a broad spectrum of offenses, ranging from relatively minor ones, such as discourteous behavior, to major ones, including theft and picket line violence. A basic maxim or premise established early in the history of U.S. labor relations is that incidents of **employee misconduct** should be viewed as either (1) *serious offenses*, which under normal circumstances warrant immediate discharge without the necessity of prior warnings or attempts at corrective action, or (2) *minor offenses*, which call for attempts at corrective action and do not call for discharge for the first offense. However, minor offenses can, when repeated despite warnings, lead to discharge.

Employee misconduct cases that are decided by arbitration often are won or lost not because of questions of guilt or innocence but because of (1) management's consistent enforcement of the rules that are involved in the case, (2) management's compliance with the disciplinary procedures in the contract, (3) an employee's work history, and (4) an employee's length of service with the company. According to the Bureau of National Affairs' *Grievance Guide*, 12th ed. (2008), the most common examples of employee misconduct and key factors considered by arbitrators in deciding the cases include the following.[10]

1. ***Damaging company property.*** A person's deliberate and malicious intent is the primary factor in considering the appropriate discipline. The relative value of the damage has relatively little significance. Immediate discharge is usually upheld even in cases of low property value when intent is deliberate.
2. ***Discourtesy.*** Employees, especially those who serve the public, are expected to be courteous and solicitous toward coworkers and members of the public. Employee discourtesy is generally accepted as just cause for disciplinary action. Customer complaints about rude behavior can be used as sufficient reason for termination, even when they are anonymous.
3. ***Dishonesty.*** Proof "beyond a reasonable doubt," a higher standard than in most misconduct cases, is required to uphold a discharge because of dishonesty. A higher standard of evidence is required because the accused worker has a greater inability to become reemployed (after a discharge due to dishonesty) than for any other cause.
4. ***Dress and grooming.*** Management has the right to set dress and grooming standards for reasons of public image, job safety, and the health of workers, coworkers, and customers. However, workers have the right to unwarranted interference by management. Thus, dress and grooming standards must be clear and consistently enforced and reasonably related to a "business need," which may include distraction owing to revealing attire.
5. ***E-mail and technology issues.*** Employers increasingly monitor employees' use of e-mail and the Internet in efforts to reduce personal and inappropriate use. Unions realize e-mail is a fast and inexpensive means of communicating with members—and workers they are trying to organize. Employers generally should develop and communicate policies that make it clear to all employees that their e-mail communication and Internet use are not private but instead are the property of the employer. Section 7 of the NLRA protects the communications of both union and nonunion employees who might discuss wages, hours, working conditions, and so on. However, in the *Register–Guard* case[11] the NLRB supported a company policy that e-mail was "not to be used to solicit outside organizations (unions)" but allowed *other* personal uses. The NLRB noted that "Section 7 does not provide employees an automatic right to use company email" because it is employer property, but that company policy cannot single out union uses of e-mail. The U.S. Court of Appeals for the District of Columbia reversed certain aspects of that ruling, however, in finding that the company's policy was not discriminatory to the union. However, the enforcement of that policy against a union employee who used the company e-mail was discriminatory because the e-mail was not a solicitation and did not call for action but

merely discussed a union-related event.[12] The use of e-mail, however, will likely be reviewed again by the NLRB for a more definitive decision.

6. ***Gambling.*** In most organizations, gambling, such as sports pools or lunch-hour poker, is ignored. However, employees involved in illegal bookmaking or numbers operations may be discharged, particularly if they have been given prior warning.
7. ***Garnishment.*** Management may discharge employees who violate rules concerning the garnishment of their wages. However, such rules must be based on employer cost, liability, and inconvenience. Less severe penalties may be decided on the basis of the employee's length of service, work record, and efforts to resolve the debt.
8. ***Horseplay.*** Although joking and playing pranks is usually tolerated, acts of horseplay that involve a high risk of serious injury may warrant a serious penalty. Only acts that are premeditated, malicious, and done with evil intent with knowledge of possible injuries or property damage will likely warrant discharge for the first incident (see Case 11-2).
9. ***Off-duty misconduct.*** In general, management may not discipline an employee for off-duty misconduct because employees have a right to privacy in their private lives. However, employees may be discharged or given lesser penalties if their off-duty misconduct (1) creates publicity that harms the organization's public image, (2) creates difficulty for an employee to perform his or her job, or (3) causes other employees to refuse to work with the employee. Examples of discharges include an employee convicted of manslaughter for fatally beating a 71-year-old woman and an employee who ignored written warnings and continued to park his car on residential streets, invoking the "wrath" of local residents.
10. ***Moonlighting.*** Holding a second job or moonlighting during an employee's off time can be a cause for discharge, particularly if the labor contract includes a relevant provision. Discharge actions are most likely upheld if the case involves (1) an employee's impaired performance, such as absenteeism, tardiness, poor productivity, or inability to work overtime; (2) a conflict of interest because of the second employer being viewed as a competitor; or (3) fraudulently taking a leave of absence to work at another job.
11. ***Sleeping and loafing.*** In general, sleeping on the job warrants discharge, particularly when it causes danger to employees or equipment. However, management in such cases must prove the employee was actually sleeping and not just resting with eyes closed. In addition, management must strictly and consistently enforce a no-sleeping work rule.

In some cases even "horseplay" on the job can result in termination for a first offense, as in the "Gooseplay" case. *Source:* Compassionate Eye Foundation/Janie Airey/OJO Images Ltd.

Sleeping during lunch breaks or rest periods is generally permissible unless it causes the employee not to return to work on time.

12. ***Violence.*** The increased number of workplace violence incidents that have led to the injury or death of coworkers or supervisors has caused employers to take the issue more seriously in recent years. Many employers, therefore, have developed serious or "zero-tolerance" policies covering not only violent acts and fighting but also threats of violence, bullying, and "uncivil" behavior. Arbitrators have generally held that management has the right to invoke discipline, including termination, in such cases. In cases where the violence was clearly provoked, including fighting, arbitrators have imposed lesser penalties. They will also likely consider other factors, such as the length of service and work record of the employee, whether the act consisted of a single blow or a series of deliberate acts, whether the blow was with a dangerous weapon, the effect of the act on other employees, and the emotional stability of the employee.

CASE 11-2

"Gooseplay"

The events in this case occurred in the context of the eighth organizational campaign conducted at the company's Berea, Kentucky, facility. So far as the record shows, no prior unfair labor practices have been committed at this plant.

The company has a pond on its property, and in September hundreds of ducks and geese are there. A goose wandered into the work area of employee Rowlett, who picked up the goose by its feet and told other employees that it wanted to sign a union card to join the union. Employee Poff wrote "Vote Yes" on a small card, attached it to a string about two feet long, and placed the sign over the goose's head while Rowlett held it. Rowlett then proceeded to drive the goose through the plant on a forklift truck. The record shows that a Canada goose weighs approximately 14 pounds and has a five-foot wingspan.

At the conclusion of the goose escapade, the company sent Rowlett and Poff home early. The company conducted an investigation and collected statements from witnesses. Rowlett and Poff were given the opportunity to explain their conduct, but they declined to participate in the investigation. After considering all the information it compiled, the company discharged Rowlett and Poff. The basic reasons for the discharge decision were that the employees' behavior did not meet adult expectations, posed a safety hazard to them as well as to others, and disrupted production activities of the plant.

The employees sued the company for unfair labor practice in discharging them, claiming that it was because they were union members supporting the organizational campaign.

The administrative law judge (ALJ) appeared to recognize that the National Labor Relations Act did not protect the goose incident because she said the employees' conduct should have a disciplinary consequence. She concluded, however, that the discipline imposed was unlawfully motivated; that is, she found that antecedent lawful union activity, not the "goose" incident, was the reason for the discharge. As evidence of this, she pointed to antiunion statements in the company's employee handbook and the fact that the only types of dischargeable offenses in the company prior to this had involved dishonesty, attendance problems, and sexual activity on the job.

The company appealed.

Discussion

The National Labor Relations Board (NLRB) found that the record, when fairly considered as a whole, did not contain substantial evidence of antiunion animus. It is true that the company's employee handbook expressed the view that a union "could seriously impair the relationship between the company and the employees and could retard the growth of the company and the progress of the employees." The NLRB has held that statements such as these, although alone not rising to the level of unfair labor practices, may still be used to show animus.

However, the ALJ failed to accord weight to the significant countervailing evidence. No antiunion comments were made to the discharged employees. No unfair labor practices were committed in the previous organizational campaigns conducted at the Berea plant. The same employee handbook that the ALJ relied on as evidence of animus expressly acknowledged the right of the employees to join a union if they wished. In sum, the company's opposition to unionization is not sufficient, in the circumstances of this case, to warrant the inference that it would unlawfully terminate these employees because of their union support or activities.

The company's officials involved in the investigation and/or decision-making aspects of this incident consistently, albeit in different words, explained their actions as concerns for maintaining safety, production, and discipline in the plant.

Having reviewed the record, the NLRB found no basis for finding that these concerns were not the foundation for the company's decision to suspend and discharge both Poff and Rowlett. Finally, the NLRB rejected the ALJ's finding that these discharges constituted disparate treatment because the only earlier incidents of employee misconduct that resulted in discharge involved dishonesty, attendance problems, and sexual activity on the job. It is true that the record contains no evidence of previous incidents of "gooseplay" resulting in termination. However, an essential ingredient of a disparate treatment finding is that other employees in similar circumstances were treated more leniently than the alleged discriminatee was treated. The NLRB found no record of a similar incident that the company tolerated. Thus, it concluded that there is no evidence of disparate treatment.

Decision

The complaint was dismissed because the union failed to establish by a preponderance of the evidence that the company was unlawfully motivated in suspending and discharging Poff and Rowlett.

Source: Adapted from *NACCO Materials Handling Group Inc., v. NLRB,* 170 LRRM 1139.

Minor Offenses

Incidents of employee misconduct that are generally considered minor offenses include loafing during working hours, failure to attend meetings, attending to personal business during working hours, failure to keep a time card, minor insubordination, carelessness, and, perhaps most important, poor work performance. Under most labor agreements the penalty for a minor offense is determined by how often it has occurred. Such a system of **progressive discipline** usually includes several levels of penalties for minor offenses, such as the following:

First offense—oral warning

Second offense—written warning

Third offense—second written warning and suspension without pay

Fourth offense—termination

PROGRESSIVE DISCIPLINE

A discipline system for addressing minor employee misconduct that usually includes several levels of penalties such as warnings, reprimands, suspensions, and, finally, termination. The objective is to inform an employee of inappropriate behavior and enable the employee to correct such behavior without serious or permanent consequences.

The objectives of a system of progressive levels of penalties are to inform employees of their inappropriate behavior, advise them of the correct behavior, and allow them to correct it without serious consequences. It is assumed that the cause of the problem is lack of awareness or motivation and not ability, and therefore the employee can choose to correct the behavior in the future. Thus, a CBA may specify if the behavior is not repeated within a certain period of time, such as six months, the incident(s) usually is removed from the employee's record. However, repeated incidents of even unrelated minor offenses can lead to termination because the employee is unwilling or unable to stop his or her behavior.

The right of the Company to discharge and discipline employees is recognized, but such action will only be taken for just cause.

Section 1. Commission of the following acts shall constitute just cause for disciplinary action, up to and including discharge:

1. Dishonesty, such as stealing from the Company or other employees, falsification of time records, punching time cards of other employees, or furnishing false information for personnel records.
2. Performing willful destructive acts harmful to persons or property.
3. Interfering with or obstructing production, or attempting to do so.
4. Conviction of a felony or a crime.
5. Gross negligence on Company premises or in line of duty resulting in injury, loss, or damage to persons or property.
6. Insubordination, including refusal or deliberate failure to perform work assignments on instructions given by supervisors.
7. Fighting, horseplay, or any other form of disorderly conduct.
8. Bringing intoxicants onto the Company's premises or consuming intoxicants while on duty, or reporting to work under the influence of intoxicants.
9. Being away from the job or out of work area without the permission of the supervisor.
10. Possessing dangerous weapons on Company property.
11. Excessive unexcused absences and tardiness (more than two days per month).
12. Deliberate violations of safety rules or sanitation rules, or repeated refusal or failure to observe such rules.
13. Operating any machine, equipment, or vehicle without instruction or permission.
14. Participating in the unnecessary wasting of materials.
15. Sleeping on duty.
16. Failure or refusal to cooperate with other workers.

Section 2. The list in Section. 1 of acts which shall constitute just cause for discharge is not exhaustive, and the failure to enumerate any specific act above shall in no way be interpreted to infer that other acts other than enumerated above may not also constitute just cause of discharge.

FIGURE 11-3 Article XXI Discharge and Discipline. *Source:* Adapted from an Agreement between AFL-CIO Local 2501, Kentucky State District Council of Carpenters and Anderson Wood Products Company, Inc., 1999–2002.

Serious Offenses

Contracts often contain provisions that specify certain actions can lead to immediate discharge for the first offense. Figure 11-3 is an example of such a provision from an agreement between AFL-CIO carpenters' local union and Anderson Wood Products Company, Inc. It lists 16 specific examples that can lead to discharge, but "such action will only be taken for just cause." Section 2 of the agreement also notes that the list of 16 acts is not exhaustive; other acts may also lead to discharge for just cause. The purpose of listing the 16 most common acts is to warn employees about those specific acts and thus, it is hoped, remove any doubt they may have as to the outcome should they commit one of those acts. It is also important to realize that the union has agreed to the acts listed in the contract.

LAST CHANCE AGREEMENT

Agreement between the union and the employer that allows an employee who was fired for misconduct his/her job back with the condition that if the employee violates the LCA he/she will be discharged without right of an appeal.

Last Chance Agreement

When an employee's misconduct becomes unacceptable, a **last chance agreement** (LCA) among the employer, union, and employee can be negotiated. Last chance agreements, however, are not viewed the same by all labor experts. One view is that an LCA is separate from the collective bargaining agreement and will be strictly enforced. That is, the employee will be terminated if the LCA is violated. A second view of LCAs is that they represent a mutually accepted modification of the collective bargaining agreement in which the employer has forfeited the right to immediate discharge, in favor of giving the employee a last chance, and the employee has given up the right to arbitrate or litigate a potential termination in favor of retention within the specifics of the LCA. Generally the written agreement describes the conduct that led to the potential termination, specific policy violations, and specific work requirements that if not met will lead to termination in the future, as well as the employee's forfeit of arbitration or litigation rights. The agreement may include an expiration date.[13] In general, courts have upheld LCAs. For example, in *Mayo v. Columbia University*, a federal judge ruled that Columbia University did not violate the Age Discrimination Act by terminating an employee who failed to meet the terms of an LCA. The court upheld the LCA when it found that the employee had been terminated for a nondiscriminatory, work-related reason and therefore failed to meet the conditions of the LCA.[14]

DISCIPLINARY PROCEDURES

A primary objective of a grievance process is to provide employees with a fair review and, if necessary, an appeal of disciplinary actions taken by management. Regardless of size or industry, every company at some time must administer corrective discipline. Certain employees may need such attention only once or twice in their careers and quickly respond to fair procedures; others may never correct their behavior and will exhaust any progressive disciplinary process. However, other employees must believe the disciplined employee was given a fair chance and equitable punishment. To maintain good labor relations, both labor and management should strive for fair and effective disciplinary policies.

Employers need a comprehensive and effective discipline system to maintain control over the workforce. Otherwise, satisfactory employee attendance, conduct, and productivity cannot be achieved. A well-structured and uniformly enforced discipline program also may reduce employee discontent, along with any manager's tendency to treat employees in an arbitrary or biased manner. Employees are more satisfied when they know what consequences to expect from rule violations and when they see **disciplinary procedures** administered consistently.[15]

DISCIPLINARY PROCEDURES

Processes that are usually designed to set standards of performance and work rules, and apply discipline (up to termination) when those standards are not followed, in a fair and consistent manner. The general purpose of the procedures is to reduce the number of violations.

Labor and management officials want to minimize the use of disciplinary actions, but both realize such actions will be needed in some situations. Therefore, virtually all collective bargaining agreements outline a disciplinary procedure.

Other than the economic benefits of a labor agreement, the disciplinary process may be the most vital aspect of a labor–management relationship. Management views the right and ability to discipline its employees effectively as the heart of maintaining a productive workforce. If one employee can accidentally or willfully violate work rules, the total result could be very costly. For example, if one employee continues to neglect wearing protective goggles because they are uncomfortable or inconvenient, others may follow because they think the rule has been relaxed. The eventual penalty is Occupational Safety and Health Administration (OSHA) citations and fines or possibly an individual's loss of eyesight in an accident because of one minor infraction.

Any degree of discipline—even if it is only an oral warning—is both stressful and embarrassing to the employee because of the economic and psychological penalties of possible layoff or termination. If such discipline is not warranted by the facts of the situation, if the employee is ignorant of any wrongdoing, or if the penalty is unusually harsh, other employees will react very negatively. Protection from biased or thoughtless supervisors in disciplinary matters has been a prime motive behind many union organizing campaigns.

A critical aspect of the disciplinary procedure is the face-to-face counseling provided by the supervisor. Such encounters can become explosive and often lead to subjective and emotional behavior. Employees may feel that they need a union to protect them against what they perceive as unfair supervisory actions.

A variety of disciplinary policies may be provided in the labor contract. The Bureau of National Affairs suggests management and labor officials use the following policies.[16]

Disciplinary Procedure

1. ***Explain company rules.*** Orientation courses, employee handbooks, bulletin board notices, e-mails, and other devices may be used to bring work rules to the attention of employees.
2. ***Get the facts.*** Investigate fairly and objectively by interviewing witnesses to ensure that both sides of a story are presented. Circumstantial evidence, personality factors, and unproven assumptions cannot be easily defended before arbitrators. Determine if substantial evidence is present.
3. ***Give adequate warning.*** Most grievance warning steps are given to the employee in writing; however, all warnings, even oral warnings, should be noted in the employee's personnel record. Copies of warning notices should go to the union.
4. ***Ascertain motive.*** People usually have a reason for what they do. Seldom do employees intentionally and maliciously violate rules. The penalty should be adjusted to the degree the employee's action was intentional.
5. ***Consider the employee's past record.*** Before taking disciplinary action, consider the employee's past record. Take into account both a good work record and seniority, especially in cases of minor offenses. Previous unrelated offenses should not be given heavy consideration.
6. ***Discipline without discharge.*** Wherever possible, avoid the use of discharge. Only when there is no hope of future improvement or the offense is severe should discharge be used. Consider the employee's length of service, past work record, and if appropriate using a last chance agreement.
7. ***Act in a timely fashion.*** Issue discipline in a timely manner, within a reasonable period after the misconduct, for example 24 hours. In most cases, the further removed the disciplinary meeting is from the event, the less productive the discussion.

The Labor–Management Relations Act, in addition to civil and antidiscrimination laws, provides restrictions on employee discipline. The act prohibits disciplinary action against employees for union-related activity. Most related charges of such employer actions arise from union organizing campaigns. The second most common source of unfair discipline charges arises from conflict between the union steward and management. The steward must file the grievances of union members and advocate their point of view. In this situation, the NLRB may view disciplinary actions against the steward as an unfair labor practice. Thus, employers should have a uniformly applied and well-documented disciplinary program they can defend against possible claims of unfair labor practice discrimination.[17]

Grounds for Discharge

Employees may be terminated or discharged for "cause" or "just cause" for specific offenses. Most contracts specify the offenses that are sufficient grounds for immediate discharge, but they also provide for an appeal procedure in that event. The contract may require that the union be notified in advance of a discharge or that a predischarge hearing be held with the employee and union present. The most common grounds for discharge specified in contracts include those listed in Table 11-1. An example of a "violation of leave" grievance is seen in Case 11-3. In cases involving the termination of an employee, the union often insists on taking the case through all the procedural steps to arbitration in an effort to save the employee's job. Management exercises extreme care to follow the steps of the disciplinary process exactly because the decision and process steps are likely to be challenged. Arbitrators generally view a discharge as the "workplace equivalent of capital punishment" and therefore expect both parties to adhere carefully to the letter and spirit of the contract.[18]

TABLE 11-1 Common Grounds for Immediate Discharge

1. Unsatisfactory work performance
2. Unauthorized absence
3. Insubordination (one major occurrence or persistent minor occurrences)
4. Dishonesty or theft of employer property
5. Failure to follow safety rules
6. Impaired work performance due to the influence of alcohol or drugs
7. Conviction of job-related crime
8. Workplace violence
9. Unauthorized strike participation
10. Violation of work rules

CASE 11-3

Just Cause

The company posted a notice on October 24 scheduling the grievant, along with other employees, to report a half hour early on October 28 to attend a United Way meeting. The half hour would be scheduled overtime and paid as such. The grievant saw the notice, made no attempt to discuss the matter with his supervisor, and failed to report at the time stated in the notice. The grievant reported at his regular work time. The company put a discipline memo in his personnel file for failure to report to work for scheduled overtime. The memo noted that the grievant had not reported to work as scheduled and warned that further disciplinary action would result if he continued to violate the contract. The employee grieved the disciplinary action on the basis that he should not be required to attend a United Way meeting because he did not agree with the principles espoused by United Way.

It was the company's position that the company was within its rights to require the employee to report a half hour early for work and to attend the United Way meeting on company time. Furthermore, the failure of the employee to report to work on time was in violation of a contract provision. The company adhered to the established principle that the employee should "obey now, grieve later." The company argued that the employee should have attended the meeting and then grieved the factual issue of whether the company had the right to compel attendance at the United Way meeting. It was the union's position that, although the union was supportive of the United Way activity and participated with the company in the annual United Way drive, the company did not have the right to compel the attendance of the employee at the meeting.

Decision

The arbitrator found that the issue in the case was whether the company had the right to compel the grievant's attendance at a United Way meeting. Although it is a well-established rule that the employer has the right to direct the workforce—and this company had the right under its contract with the union to schedule overtime with appropriate notice—the exercise of its management rights must reasonably relate to the operation of the employer's enterprise. It was the arbitrator's belief that the United Way drive was not reasonably related to the company's operation. So, although the company may request attendance by the employees at a meeting and be willing to pay overtime, it did not have the authority to require attendance at the meeting. The arbitrator did not accept the company's position that the grievant should have reported to work and grieved the issue later because that basic premise, "work now, grieve later," is relevant only when it allows the company's operation to continue during a dispute

(Continued)

with a grievant. Because the United Way meeting was in no way related to the employer's ability to keep his operation going, there was no requirement that the employee delay his disagreement with the requirement.

Source: Adapted from *Green Bay Packing,* 87 LA 1057.

GRIEVANCE MEDIATION

GRIEVANCE MEDIATION

The use of a neutral third party as one step in a grievance procedure. The mediator, in a confidential process, facilitates the parties developing a resolution of the grievance themselves and thus avoiding arbitration.

Most collective bargaining agreements include procedures to resolve grievances that arise during the life of the contract, with binding arbitration as the last step. Increasingly, contracts provide for **grievance mediation** as a voluntary last step *before* arbitration if it is acceptable to both parties—because generally mediation to be successful is a voluntary process in which both parties seek a neutral third party to assist them in finding a settlement. The following CBA example provides mediation as the fourth step in a grievance procedure:

> ARTICLE VII
>
> **Grievance Procedure**
>
> Step 4. Mediation may be used in place of traditional arbitration provided that this option is acceptable to the Company and the Union. If either party rejects mediation, it will be moved to Step 5, arbitration. In the event mediation is chosen, the parties will mutually agree on a mediator at that time.

The process provides the opportunity for a neutral third party, such as a mediator from the FMCS (Federal Mediation and Conciliation Service), state, or local mediation services to assist the parties in reaching their own settlement of the dispute before it reaches arbitration.

Grievance mediation is a supplement to or a single step in a contractual grievance resolution process but should *not* be viewed as a substitute for the process. The mediator cannot resolve the dispute by making a binding decision but rather works with both parties to achieve a mutually acceptable settlement of the grievance. To request a mediator, both parties must submit a signed written request that outlines the issues involved.

Grievance mediation often provides several advantages to the process of resolving disputes: (1) faster resolution of issues compared to arbitration; (2) both parties, grievant and manager, have the opportunity to present their case to a neutral third party without the possibility of losing as they might in a binding arbitration; (3) even if the process does not lead to a settlement, both parties can better evaluate the strengths and weaknesses of their cases before proceeding to arbitration; (4) the FMCS or state offices provide the service without charge to the parties so that, if a settlement is reached, the costs of arbitration can be

Tips from the Experts

Arbitrator

What are the three best ways to ensure a fair grievance procedure if you are the employer or the union?

1. Conduct a full and adequate investigation into the facts and circumstances. Give the employee an opportunity to explain why he or she should not be disciplined, or the employer the chance to explain why the discipline imposed did not violate the agreement or past practice.
2. Make full disclosures at the earliest possible grievance step. Disclose the issues, the facts, the documents to be presented, and the names of the witnesses and what they will offer as testimony.
3. Do not rely on the other side to make the case for you. Develop a theory of the case, with witnesses and documents ready to support it.

avoided, and (5) the mediation process is confidential—the mediator assures the parties that he/she will not discuss any aspect of their case with anyone else. The process the FMCS uses in grievance mediation is somewhat different from that of arbitration; thus, the documents prepared and statements made in grievance mediation *cannot* be used during subsequent arbitration proceedings. Both parties must usually agree to the 10 FMCS Guidelines for Grievance Mediation in Figure 11-4.[19]

The process of grievance mediation generally follows one of two formats: (1) the mediator meets with both parties separately and jointly to determine the issues, priorities, and barriers. Then the mediator may present to each side the likely outcome if the grievance progresses to arbitration, or (2) instead of predicting outcomes, the mediator meets jointly and separately with the parties and uses an interest-based process to seek a mutually agreeable settlement that the parties fashion themselves. For example, a union might trade its demand for back pay (low priority) in exchange for reinstatement (high priority).[20] A 2005 study of 3,387 cases over a 24-year period produced significant findings that support the use of grievance mediation in comparison to arbitration:[21]

- ***Cost savings.*** The average cost of mediation per case was $672 compared to $3,202 per arbitration.
- ***Time savings.*** The average time required to mediate a case was 43.5 days—compared to 473 days to arbitrate a case.
- ***Satisfaction with process.*** The participants who were "highly satisfied" with interest-based mediation included 89 percent management, 68 percent union, and 47 percent grievants.
- ***Increased ability to resolve grievances.*** Participants (83 percent) indicated they were better able to resolve future grievances because they learned how to communicate better. In addition, 65 percent indicated that the use of interest-based grievance mediation had led to a better union–management relationship thanks to a more cooperative atmosphere and the use of mediation techniques.

In recent years grievance mediation has increasingly been combined with expedited arbitration. This combination resolves the major disadvantage of grievance mediation in settling

1. The grievant is entitled to attend the mediation.
2. Unless the collective bargaining agreement provides for mediation within the grievance procedure, the parties must waive any time limits while the grievance mediation step is being utilized.
3. The grievance mediation process is informal and the rules of evidence do not apply. No record, stenographic, or tape recordings of the meetings will be made.
4. The mediator's notes are confidential and will be destroyed at the conclusion of the grievance mediation meeting. FMCS is a neutral agency, created to mediate disputes, and maintains a policy of declining to testify for any party, either in court proceedings or before government regulatory authorities.
5. The mediator will use problem-solving skills to assist the parties, including joint and separate caucuses.
6. The mediator has no authority to compel a resolution.
7. If the parties cannot resolve the problem, the mediator may provide the parties in joint or separate session with an oral advisory opinion.
8. If the parties cannot resolve the grievance, they may proceed to arbitration according to the procedures in their collective bargaining agreement.
9. No statement given by either party as part of the grievance mediation process, nor any documents prepared for a mediation session, can be used during arbitration proceedings.
10. The parties must agree to hold FMCS and FMCS mediators harmless for any claim of damage arising from the mediation process.

FIGURE 11-4 Guidelines for Grievance Mediation. *Source: FMCS Grievance Mediation: Problem Solving in the Workplace* (Washington, DC: U.S. Government Printing Office, 2001).

labor disputes—the possibility of no settlement. For example, the National Mediation Board, which is responsible for resolving labor disputes in the railroad and airline industries, will send the case to expedited arbitration if a grievance mediation is not successful, sometimes through web conferencing to even further reduce costs and obtain a faster decision.[22]

PUBLIC SECTOR GRIEVANCE ISSUES

Although differences exist between public and private sector labor relations, there are similarities. A major similarity is that the collective bargaining agreements of both sectors are often influenced by the personalities of the negotiators and their abilities to improve their bargaining power relative to the other party.[23] Also, grievances in the two sectors are generally processed in the same manner.

The expense of grievance arbitration is of concern to employers in the public sector just as it is to those in the private sector. A study was done on the attitudes of union stewards toward filing grievances in the public sector to see whether costs could be reduced. It was demonstrated that grievance rates tended to be reduced when management negotiators were perceived as accommodating rather than combative during negotiations. Grievance rates tended to increase or decrease depending on whether union stewards perceived their union members to be combative or cooperative toward their government managers. The study also found that if an informal method of communication existed, fewer grievances were filed. Surprisingly, the clarity of a collective bargaining agreement had little effect on the number of grievances filed. If the relationship between the parties tended to be combative or cooperative, disagreements over contract language followed that same pattern.[24] See Profile 11-2 for some of the approaches used in the federal government to counter the time and expense of typical grievance arbitration resolution techniques.

In the area of discipline and dismissal, however, public sector labor law has developed along completely different lines because of the constitutional protection afforded government employees. When government acts at any level to discipline or dismiss an employee, a form of state action has occurred. The power of the state over an individual is curtailed by the Bill of Rights, and if any constitutionally protected right is infringed on by the discipline

Profile 11-2

FLRA Collaboration and Alternative Dispute Resolution Activities

The Federal Labor Relations Authority is actively engaged in the labor–management Collaboration and Alternative Dispute Resolution Program (CADR). CADR is dedicated to reducing the costs of conflict in the federal service. This agency-wide program, launched in 1996, provides overall coordination of the use of alternative dispute resolution techniques in every step of labor–management disputes—from investigation and prosecution to the adjudication of cases and resolution of bargaining impasses.

The initiatives include the following:

1. Resolving unfair labor practice and representational disputes by the Office of General Counsel using facilitation, training, and educational services delivered jointly to both management and union representatives on the federal labor relations law, interest-based bargaining, alternative dispute resolution, and relationship building and intervention.
2. Operating an Unfair Labor Practice Trial Settlement Project administered by the Office of Administrative Law Judges; this assigns a judge or a settlement attorney to conduct settlement conference negotiations with the parties before trial. The initial pilot of this project resulted in an 80 percent settlement rate.
3. Resolving impasses in collective bargaining agreement negotiations through the Federal Service Impasses Panel using procedures that include mediation, fact-finding, written submissions, and arbitration to move the parties toward voluntarily resolving the impasses short of a written decision and order from the panel.

Source: Adapted from "FLRA News." (2000). Available at www.flra.gov. Accessed October 15, 1999.

or dismissal of an employee, that employee has a valid claim against the governmental entity regardless of contractual rights. Examples of constitutionally protected rights include the following:

1. Privilege against self-incrimination
2. Freedom of association
3. Right to participate in partisan politics
4. Freedom of expression

These constitutionally protected rights, as well as specific statutes allowing government employees to appeal to various courts, have assured public employees of multiple forms of relief not available to private sector employees. Although this protection tends to weaken the grievance-arbitration system, it guarantees the rights of the individual over those of the unions.[25]

Summary

Grievance procedures and the mediation and arbitration of disputes provide important tools to collective bargaining. Without such procedures, labor and management, as well as the community, would suffer greatly from alternative actions such as strikes and walkouts. In addition, the effective resolution of grievances prevents "grievance gridlock" and low employee morale and productivity. Instead, issues such as a supervisor's disciplining an employee, as well as instances of "letting off steam," as it were, can be decided logically. Contract provisions that specify how situations involving employee misconduct will be handled are included in most contracts. Serious offenses usually lead to immediate termination, whereas minor offenses are treated by a progressive discipline policy.

The Supreme Court and the NLRB have given sufficient authority to negotiated grievance procedures and the use of arbitration as a final step, making the practices commonplace and effective. However, specific steps to be used in employee grievances should be detailed in the labor agreement. Grievance mediation reduces the need for arbitration as a final step and should be considered when possible. In addition, in comparison to arbitration, mediation is less expensive, faster, and produces more satisfactory results. A key reason for the success of grievance mediation is that, unlike arbitration, both parties participate in developing a mutually agreeable settlement, not one that is imposed by a judge or arbitrator, and thus neither party can "lose" a decision.

CASE STUDIES

Case Study 11-1 Insubordination of a Police Officer While in Pursuit of a Stolen Vehicle

The city's police department has a procedure that establishes guidelines for police officers who are in pursuit of the occupants of another vehicle. A section of the pursuit policy states that a shift commander is to be assigned as management supervisor of each pursuit and has the authority to terminate a pursuit when public safety is at risk.

Patrol officers became involved in a pursuit when a man pointed a rifle at his wife, threatened her, discharged the rifle, and then, in a vehicle he had stolen, fled from investigating police officers. Sergeant D, who had been assigned as managing supervisor, monitored the pursuit and finally ordered it terminated. Police Officer A, however, continued to follow the suspect, despite having been told by both Sergeant D and Sergeant C to stop the pursuit. Officer A apprehended the suspect when the suspect's automobile "broke down." The city charged Officer A with a violation of the pursuit procedure and suspended him for one day without pay.

At an arbitration hearing, Officer A testified that he was concerned the suspect's automobile would break down and because the suspect had committed a felony (stealing a

(Continued)

vehicle) and was armed, he might engage in a carjacking. Officer A further testified of his oath to protect the public and his belief that the public was in danger from the suspect. Officer A also testified that his emergency lights and siren were not in operation while he followed the suspect, and he never attempted to close the gap on the suspect's automobile; thus, he was not in pursuit.

The city argued that Officer A had failed to obey the orders of two sergeants to terminate a pursuit and should be disciplined for his failure to obey their orders.

Source: Adapted from *City of San Antonio,* 95 ARB 5066.

QUESTIONS

1. Was Officer A in pursuit of the suspect's vehicle?
2. As an arbitrator, would you uphold or deny the grievance?
3. Would you change the punishment of Officer A from a one-day suspension to that of a written warning?
4. What is the value to the police command in disciplining Officer A?

Case Study 11-2 Sleeping On the Job

The grievant has been employed by the Company as a truck driver of an all-wheel drive, articulating dump truck which he operated in conjunction with other pieces of equipment. While sitting in a loading area at the preparation plant he was being loaded by a long-armed loader; he was observed by a supervisor leaning back with his head against the box behind the seat with his eyes closed and his mouth open. The truck was running, and it was out of gear with the safety brake on, as prescribed by the safety procedures. He was suspended in compliance with the labor agreement—a 24–48-hour meeting was properly held, and he was terminated on March 11, 2009, for sleeping on the job.

The Company contended that this was the third such incident involving the grievant. In the previous summer, the supervisor found the grievant asleep while sitting in his truck as it was being loaded. The motor was running, it was out of gear, and the safety brake was on. The supervisor had the loader bump the truck, and when the startled grievant eyeballed the supervisor, the supervisor shook his finger at him and shook his head to let him know he was caught sleeping and that it was not permitted.

On September 17, 2008, the grievant was observed sleeping for an extended period of time while being loaded by a backhoe. In this instance the supervisor physically mounted the truck and opened the cab door to a very startled awakened employee. Again, the motor was running, it was out of gear, and the safety brake was on. A written safety observation card which stated "EMPLOYEE WAS ASLEEP" was issued to the grievant. In addition, a counseling session was held with the grievant and his Union Steward. The Company and the Union Stewart informed the grievant that if he were caught asleep again, he would be discharged. The Company informed him if he had physical problems, he should get a doctor's excuse and he stated he had no problems.

A third occurrence of the grievant being found sleeping on the job was evidenced on March 3, 2009, as the supervisor was walking past the grievant's truck while it was being loaded. The supervisor had walked completely around the truck and was not seen or noticed by the sleeping grievant. The cab of the truck has a clear 180-degree open view through its windows. The supervisor and the backhoe operator observed the grievant asleep for several minutes. The Supervisor reported the incident to Management, and the grievant was discharged for sleeping on the job.

The Company argued that a third sleeping on the job violation, while in the cab of a running piece of heavy equipment, is more than just cause for termination. This is a work area where there is high foot traffic and is frequented with numerous smaller vehicles and other equipment that is constantly on the move. Sleeping on the job is a very dangerous act.

The Union argued that there was no record of the first "sleeping on the job" incident reported by the supervisor. The supervisor's statement that he believed it occurred sometime in the summer is insufficient to establish occurrence. If this is such a critical incident, which warrants immediate discharge, it seems unreasonable that in one instance it would be treated with just the shaking of a finger. This incident is unrecorded and should not be considered as evidence against the grievant.

There is no denial of the second incident as the grievant states he does not know if he was asleep or not. He was startled by the supervisor jumping on his truck and became disoriented as a result. He was arguably asleep, however, and was counseled by his Steward to be extremely careful in the future. It is easy to shut your eyes and relax for a few minutes while your truck is being loaded. The truck was locked out with the parking brake and cannot move; thus there is no immediate danger of any kind.

In the incident of March 3, 2009, the truck was parked at an odd angle with the left front of the truck angled down. In order not to slide off the seat, the grievant had to totally extend his left leg and brace it against the corner of the bottom of the left door. This put him in a reclining position forcing his head back against the black box mounted behind the seat. One must remember the seat in this vehicle is in the middle; thus the downhill angle of the truck forced the grievant to appear to be lying back in a reclining position. *Appearance of asleep is not asleep as charged.* Furthermore, the Union noted that the Company's treatment of the grievant for the previous similar incident was only a safety observation and counseling; no discipline was involved. The Union did not have the backhoe driver testify at the hearing.

Source: Adapted from *Dickenson-Russell Coal Company, LLC and United Mine Workers of America, Local Union No. 7950*, 126 LA (BNA) 517 (2009).

QUESTIONS

1. Should the Company's treatment of the grievant for the first two "sleeping on the job" incidents influence the outcome in this case? Explain.
2. Did the Company have just cause to dismiss the grievant for violating safety rules when in each instance cited, the truck was out of gear with the safety break on?
3. Is the union's argument that the grievant just "appeared to be sleeping" creditable in the absence of any testimony of support by the backhoe driver, a fellow union member?

Key Terms and Concepts

"5 Ws" rule *410*
disciplinary procedures *419*
employee misconduct (minor and serious offenses) *414*
grievance *407*
grievance mediation *422*
grievance procedures *407*
last chance agreement *418*
progressive discipline *417*

Review Questions

1. Why might both management and a union agree to a last chance agreement?
2. Explain a typical grievance procedure.
3. Describe how the concepts of authority and influence affect the grievance process.
4. Explain the steps of a grievance process. Why do these steps exist?
5. Discuss how disciplinary procedures affect the labor–management relationship.
6. What are the advantages and disadvantages of grievance mediation?
7. Why is progressive discipline used in misconduct cases involving minor offenses?
8. What serious misconduct offenses should always result in discharge?

YOU BE THE ARBITRATOR
Employee Writing Threats

SECTION XXIV COMPANY RULES

Company rules include but are not limited to those listed in APPENDIX "D" of this Agreement. Reasonable changes or additions to these rules may be made from time to time and the Company shall notify the Union of the same prior to the notification to all employees. By the publishing of these rules and notification of changes and additions, it shall be considered that employees will have complete knowledge of the rules. The employees shall abide by the Company's rules and practices; however, the Union may question the reasonableness of any new rule.

APPENDIX D RULES FOR EMPLOYEE CONDUCT

Rules for acceptable conduct of employees are necessary for the orderly operation of the Courtland Mill and for the benefit and protection of the right, safety, and security of all employees and the Company.

These rules, and others which may be established from time to time, are hereby published to provide and promote understanding of what is considered unacceptable conduct in order to promote a safe, orderly, and efficient operation of the Mill.

Any employee who commits any of the following acts or other acts which are properly and customarily the subject of disciplinary action may be disciplined, including discharge from employment, either after a warning or immediately without warning, depending on the seriousness, nature, and circumstances of the violation(s). Repeated violations of the same rule, or compounded violations of more than one, shall be cause for accelerated disciplinary action . . .

7. Deliberately damaging, destroying, mutilating, or defacing tools, equipment, or any property of the Company or of another employee . . .

22. Threatening, intimidating, coercing other employees; interfering with the activities of another employee in the performance of his work; or directing abusive, vile or insulting remarks to or about another employee on Company premises at any time.

Supplemental Agreement—Memorandum of Under-standing Sub-Foreman Statements (in pertinent part)

A bargaining unit employee set-up to Sub-foreman will continue to have and to accrue all benefits he or she has as a bargaining unit employee during the time he or she is set-up to Sub-foreman.

Facts

The company employed approximately 1,800 production workers represented by three unions. As a result of a change in how its production was done, it announced a downsizing of production workers and some supervisory staff. It accorded the three unions an opportunity to comment on the downsizing plan, which two unions did. One union did not and protested by asking its members not to bid on the sub-foreman jobs as they became available. Employee R, a union member, chose to bid and was given a sub-foreman job. Employee R became the object of union harassment in the form of X-rated graffiti on the bathroom walls. Many of the writings contained threats as well. One bathroom wall had the following: "Watch your back R, you M——F——er. R has an A——whipping coming and soon." The company sent copies of the graffiti and samples of handwritings of a number of workers it suspected to a handwriting expert who determined that the grievant had written the graffiti. The grievant, a 20-year employee, was notified that he was suspected of writing the threats on the bathroom walls and was suspended. He and his union representative met with management, and after confirming that the handwriting sample the company had provided the expert was the grievant's handwriting, he was told he was terminated. He asked management to reconsider and give him a suspension or a last-chance letter rather than dismiss him. Management declined to do so, stating that his request for leniency was tantamount to an admission of guilt. The grievant denied that he was guilty, but he was dismissed. He filed this grievance. At his hearing, management's handwriting expert testified that the grievant was the writer of the graffiti. But the union's handwriting expert testified that the grievant was not the writer of the graffiti.

Issue

Did the company have just cause to discharge a 20-year employee for writing threats against another employee on bathroom walls?

The Position of the Parties

The company's position was that the grievant was fired for just cause because he violated the company rules regarding threats and destroying company property that were a part of the collective bargaining agreement (CBA). Further more, the company's workplace violence policy had a zero-tolerance level. The company had suspected the grievant because he had brought Employee R up on charges with the union for taking the sub-foreman position. After the handwriting expert had identified the grievant as the responsible party and he was told he was fired, his reaction was to ask for a lesser penalty. Only after he was denied a reprieve did he say he was not guilty of the offense. The grievant's actions warranted the ultimate penalty of discharge because the company cannot tolerate the kind of hostile work environment the threats of violence created.

The union's position is that the grievant alone did not create the hostile work environment that existed in the plant. The company had to share responsibility for that because of its downsizing. And, after 20 years of service without incident, the grievant deserved better treatment. First of all, the union's handwriting expert testified that the grievant was not the writer of the graffiti. Second, the grievant had correctly pressed his complaint about Employee R when he brought him up on charges within the union. There was no testimony that the grievant had done anything else that could have been called harassment of Employee R. The union contended that the company had not demonstrated it had just cause to dismiss the grievant.

QUESTIONS

1. As arbitrator, what would be your award and opinion in this arbitration?
2. Identify the key, relevant section(s), phrases, or words of the collective bargaining agreement (CBA), and explain why they were critical in making your decision.
3. What actions might the employer and/or the union have taken to avoid this conflict?

Source: Adapted from *Champion International Co. v. Paper, Allied Industrial, Chemical and Energy Workers International Union,* 115 LA 27.

CHAPTER 12

The Arbitration Process

Chapter Outline

Today many U.S. employers require employees to sign employment arbitration agreements that require arbitration, rather than the courts, to resolve employment disputes. In 2009, in response to employee–rights groups' complaints that such agreements unfairly restrict the rights of workers, the Arbitration Fairness Act was introduced in the U.S. Congress. The act if passed in the future will make employment and consumer arbitration agreements invalid and unenforceable. *Source:* Photos.com/ Jupiter Images.

When will mankind be convinced and agree to settle their difficulties by arbitration?

BENJAMIN FRANKLIN (U.S. FOUNDING FATHER AND SIGNER OF THE DECLARATION OF INDEPENDENCE)

LABOR NEWS

Arbitration of Employment Disputes on the Rise

U.S. employers are increasingly using arbitration to resolve disputes with their employees. The use of employment arbitration has risen partly in response to rising litigation costs and large jury awards in cases involving race, sex, and disability discrimination. Although the use of arbitration originated in labor–management settings, it has spread to less unionized industries including retail, restaurants, financial services, and law. About 20 percent of U.S. employers now require employees to sign an arbitration agreement mandating them to use arbitration to resolve any employment disputes that may arise. In some cases a signed agreement may not be needed.

For example, a Missouri court ruled that an employee was bound by an arbitration agreement even though she had not signed it because she continued to work after the employer mailed her a copy of the arbitration policy. Judges generally prefer arbitration as a means of reducing their caseload. Employers generally support the use of arbitration to resolve cases more quickly and in a more private manner and to avoid large damage awards. Plaintiff lawyers and some union leaders have opposed employment arbitration because they believe workers win fewer cases and receive smaller awards when they do prevail. The Arbitration Fairness Act of 2009 was introduced in the U.S. Congress and would have made mandatory employment arbitration agreements unlawful. The legislation did not pass but will likely be introduced again because opponents continue to criticize what they perceive are abuses of arbitration agreements in employment.

Source: Nathan Koppel, "When Suing Your Boss Is Not an Option," *Wall Street Journal* (December 18, 2007), p. D1.

The first mention of labor **arbitration** in American labor history dates to a clause in the constitution of the Journeymen Cabinet-Makers of Philadelphia in 1829.[1] The earliest recorded arbitration hearing occurred in 1865 when ironworkers in Pittsburgh arbitrated their wages.[2] The first known case in which an outside arbitrator was used occurred in 1871 in eastern Ohio. The Committee of the Anthracite Board of Trade (an association of coal operators) and the Committee of Workingmen's Benevolent Association (the coal miners' union) retained the services of Judge William Ewell of Bloomsburg, Pennsylvania, to settle their dispute on "discharging men for their connection with the Workingmen's Benevolent Association." The results were successful in that the parties accepted and implemented Judge Ewell's recommendation.

ARBITRATION

A process in which the parties involved agree to submit an unresolved dispute to a neutral third party, whose decision is final and binding.

Today virtually all labor contracts provide for arbitration as the last step in the grievance procedure. As the agreement between GE Aviation and the International Association of Machinists and Aerospace Workers, AFL-CIO, in Figure 12-1 illustrates, arbitration clauses commonly include specifics as to when arbitration will be used, which provisions in the agreement are subject to arbitration, which are not subject to arbitration, and the timetable of events; the fact that the decision of the arbitrator is "final and binding"; and how the fee will be divided between the parties. Some agreements also provide for an "expedited arbitration" process for specified types of cases, such as termination, for just cause. In such cases the normal arbitration process is shortened, and the arbitrator may only issue a decision or award, without an explanatory opinion statement.

TYPES OF ARBITRATION

Two major types of arbitration exist with respect to labor disputes: interest arbitration and rights arbitration. **Interest arbitration** resolves conflicts of interest over the establishment of the terms and conditions of employment that are negotiated through collective bargaining and formalized in union contracts. A breakdown in these collective bargaining negotiations can result in a strike. Interest arbitration avoids or ends strikes. As discussed in Chapter 2, the development of interest arbitration can be attributed to the government's desire to protect the public interest by preventing

INTEREST ARBITRATION

A process used to resolve an impasse in negotiations in which the parties submit the unresolved items to a neutral third party to render a binding decision.

Article XXII
Arbitration

Any grievance which remains unsettled having been fully processed pursuant to the provisions of the Article XXII shall notwithstanding the Company right to refuse to arbitrate grievances, as reserved in Article XXIV (2), be submitted to arbitration upon written request of either the Union or the Company, provided such request is made within thirty days after the final decision of the Company has been given to the Union pursuant to Article XXII, and provided such request directly raises an issue which is either: a disciplinary penalty, consisting of a warning notice, a suspension, or a discharge, which penalty is imposed on or after the effective date of this Agreement and is claimed to have been imposed without just cause; or a non-disciplinary termination occurring after the effective date of this Agreement; or a claimed violation of one of the provisions of this Agreement.

Any grievance which remains unsettled after having been fully processed pursuant to the provisions of Article XXII, and which involves any issue not included among those specified as subject to arbitration in paragraph (1) of this Article, may be submitted to arbitration only if the Company and the Union first mutually agree in writing to do so.

If, within ten days following the request for arbitration of such a grievance, the Company and the Union cannot mutually agree upon an arbitrator, they may jointly request the Federal Mediation and Conciliation Service to submit a panel of seven names from which an arbitrator shall be chosen. Upon receipt of such panel, representatives of the Company and the Union shall strike in alternate turn one of the names from the panel list until six names have been so struck, whereupon the arbitrator whose name remains shall be deemed to be the arbitrator selected by mutual agreement of the parties. A second panel may be requested by mutual agreement of the parties.

The award of an arbitrator so selected upon any grievance so submitted to him/her shall be final and binding upon all parties to this Agreement. The arbitrator shall have no authority to add to, detract from, or in any way alter the provisions of this Agreement.

The fees and expenses of the arbitrator, as well as the cost of furnishing the hearing room, shall be borne equally by the Company and the Union.

FIGURE 12-1 Arbitration Provision. *Source:* Agreement between General Electric Aviation and Lodge No. 912, International Association of Machinists and Aerospace Workers, AFL-CIO, 2007–2011. Used by permission.

or ending strikes in key industries, such as the Coal Strike of 1902. Interest arbitration is still frequently used in the construction industry to resolve collective bargaining disputes. The United Steelworkers of America adopted an elaborate form of interest arbitration, known as the Experimental Negotiating Agreement, in the 1970s as a means of avoiding the long and costly strikes that had made the industry vulnerable to foreign competition. The agreement was in place for nearly a decade and is credited with raising the average wage of steelworkers.[3] Major League Baseball uses a variant of interest arbitration, in which an arbitrator chooses between the two sides' final offers, to set the terms for contracts for players who are not eligible for free agency.

Interest arbitration in the private sector is voluntary—the parties can choose arbitration as an alternative to a strike if desired. Most interest arbitration in the United States occurs in the public sector under compulsory statutes as discussed later in this chapter. Private sector negotiators are generally reluctant to give up their right to strike and to turn over their decision-making authority to a third party. Case 12-1 offers an example of one dissatisfied participant. The voluntary nature of interest arbitration in the private sector may change, however, if the Employee Free Choice Act is approved by Congress. Union organizers have long complained that under the current labor law, even after a majority of employees vote for union representation, only 56 percent of them achieves a first contract after two years. The EFCA includes a process for ensuring that once employees vote for a union, they will get a first contract. It provides for negotiations and mediation as the first step in the process and arbitration for those that fail to reach an agreement on their own. Experience in the public sector shows that only a small minority, in most cases well under 10 percent, of negotiations end up requiring an arbitration decision. In areas where public

CASE 12-1

Arbitrability in Major-League Sports

The Major League Baseball Players Association (Association) filed grievances against the Major League Baseball Clubs (Clubs), claiming the Clubs had colluded in the market for free-agent services, in violation of the industry's collective bargaining agreement. A free agent is a player who may contract with any Club rather than one whose right to contract is restricted to a particular Club. The case resulted in a finding of collusion by the Clubs, and damages were awarded in the amount of $280 million. The Association and Clubs entered into a Settlement Agreement (Agreement) regarding the distribution of the fund for claims relating to a particular season or seasons. The Agreement provided that players could seek an arbitrator's review of the distribution plan. The arbitrator would determine "only whether the approved framework and the criteria set forth therein have been properly applied in the proposed Distribution Plan."

Steve Garvey, a retired, highly regarded first baseman, submitted a claim for damages of approximately $3 million, alleging that his contract with the San Diego Padres was not extended because of collusion. The Association rejected Garvey's claim because he presented no evidence that the Padres actually offered to extend his contract. Garvey objected, and an arbitration hearing was held. At the arbitration, he presented a June 1996 letter from the president of the Padres that contained the offer to extend Garvey's contract through the 1989 season but then refused to negotiate with Garvey because of collusion. The arbitrator denied Garvey's claim, and in his decision he explained that he doubted the credibility of the statements in the letter because, he noted, in the original arbitration the president of the Padres had denied collusion and had testified the Padres simply were not interested in extending Garvey's contract.

Garvey asked the federal district court to vacate the arbitrator's award, alleging that the arbitrator violated the framework by denying his claim. The district court denied the motion. The Court of Appeals for the Ninth Circuit, however, granted the motion and reversed the arbitrator's decision. The court acknowledged that judicial review of an arbitrator's decision in a labor dispute is extremely limited. But it held that review of the merits of the arbitrator's award was warranted in this case because the arbitrator's refusal to credit the president's letter was "inexplicable" and "border[ed] on the irrational" because a panel of arbitrators in the original proceedings had concluded that the owners' prior testimony was false; that is, the testimony that they did not collude had been rejected by that arbitration. The court found that the record provided "strong support" for the truthfulness of the 1996 letter and directed the lower court to vacate the award. The lower court remanded the case to the arbitration panel for further hearings, and Garvey appealed, arguing that the arbitrator had nothing more to decide because the court of appeals had already found that the 1996 letter was controlling. The court of appeals agreed and directed that the arbitration panel simply enter an award to Garvey in an appropriate amount. Both the Association and the Club appealed the Court of Appeals' overruling of the arbitrator's award to the U.S. Supreme Court, which agreed to hear the case.

Discussion

The Supreme Court noted that Section 301 of the Labor Management Relations Act guided its decision because the controversy involved rights under an agreement between an employer and a labor organization. Garvey's specific allegation was that the arbitrator violated the scheme for resolving players' claims for damages, which was to remedy the Clubs' breach of the collective bargaining agreement. The Court noted that judicial review of a labor-arbitration decision pursuant to such an agreement is very limited. Courts are not authorized to review the arbitrator's decision on the merits even if there are allegations that the decision rests on factual errors or misinterpretation of the parties' agreement. Under the *Steelworkers Trilogy,* it is only when the arbitrator strays from interpretation and application of the agreement that the decision may be

(Continued)

held unenforceable by the Court. When an arbitrator resolves disputes regarding the application of a contract and no dishonesty is alleged, the arbitrator's improvident, even silly, fact-finding does not provide a basis for a reviewing court to refuse to enforce the award.

As the Court had previously ruled in the *Misco* case, even in the very rare instances when an arbitrator's procedural aberrations rise to the level of misconduct, the court must not settle the merits of the case but should simply vacate the award and leave open the possibility of further arbitration proceedings under the terms of the negotiated agreement.

In this case, the Court of Appeals erred when it overturned the arbitrator's decision because it disagreed with the arbitrator's factual findings with respect to the credibility of the 1996 letter. The arbitrator was construing a contract and acting within the scope of his authority, and established law precludes a court from resolving the merits of the parties' dispute on the basis of its own factual determinations, no matter how erroneous the arbitrator's decision.

The Supreme Court reversed the Court of Appeals' decision and sent Garvey back to the arbitrator for further proceedings.

Source: Adapted from *Major League Baseball Players Association v. Steve Garvey,* 532 U.S. 504 (2001).

sector employees have the right to resolve collective bargaining conflicts through arbitration, the vast majority of contracts are still settled voluntarily rather than through arbitration.

RIGHTS ARBITRATION

The submission to arbitration for the interpretation or application of current contract terms. In grievance cases, the arbitration involves the rights of the parties involved under the terms of the contract.

Rights arbitration, or **grievance arbitration**, involves interpretation of a party's "rights" or the application of a particular provision under an existing contract. Rights arbitration is found in almost every labor agreement and used far more than interest arbitration today. Grievance arbitration became popular during World War II, when most unions had adopted a no-strike pledge. The War Labor Board, which attempted to mediate disputes over contract terms, pressed for inclusion of grievance arbitration in collective bargaining agreements. The Supreme Court subsequently made labor arbitration a key aspect of federal labor policy. Rights arbitration deals with the allegation that an existing collective agreement has been violated or misinterpreted. Most collective bargaining agreements set out a procedure for the handling of disputes and differences. The idea is that parties should be obliged to meet at different steps in their own specific grievance procedure to review and discuss the grievance. However, often the parties cannot resolve disputes and need to use arbitration. A common example involves the discipline and discharge of employees. Most union contracts specify that employees can only be disciplined and discharged with just cause, so grievances are frequently filed over whether or not a specific instance of discipline or discharge was consistent with the requirements of just cause. An arbitrator might rule that the discharge was consistent with just cause and therefore stands or that management violated a principle of just cause, and therefore the grievant is entitled to be reinstated to his or her job, perhaps with back pay. Other examples include questions of whether or not the contractual provisions were followed in layoffs or promotions, whether or not a specific employee was eligible for vacation pay, or whether or not management has the right to subcontract work.

Demand for Rights Arbitration

There are no prescribed rules for grievance arbitration as there are in the judicial process. Arbitration procedures should be based on the wishes and the needs of the parties involved to the extent possible within the judgment of the arbitrator. The arbitration process is more private and therefore unique to the parties, as compared with the public judicial process. Also, the grievance arbitration procedure involves more sophisticated and knowledgeable parties than those in most judicial proceedings, and the arbitrator, in most cases, is more knowledgeable than the judge. Figure 12-2 is a typical example of a demand for a contract interpretation or rights arbitration.

FIGURE 12-2 Demand for Arbitration

American Arbitration Association
Dispute Resolution Services Worldwide

LABOR ARBITRATION RULES
Demand for Arbitration

MEDIATION: Please consult the AAA regarding mediation procedures. If you would like the AAA to contact the other parties and attempt to arrange a mediation, please check this box ☐

Name of Respondent ☐Employer or ☐Union			Name of Representative (if known)		
Contact Person			Name of Firm (if applicable)		
Address:			Representative's Address:		
City	State	Zip Code	City	State	Zip Code
Phone No.		Fax No.	Phone No.		Fax No.
Email Address:			Email Address:		

The named claimant, a party to an arbitration agreement dated ____________________, which provides for arbitration under the Labor Arbitration Rules of the American Arbitration Association, hereby demands arbitration.

Nature of Grievance:

Name of Grievant(s) (if applicable):

Claim or Relief Sought:

REMINDER: You can file your case online by visiting the AAA's website at www.adr.org. Please select "AAA Webfile" from the list of side menu options. You may also wish to visit the "Labor" "Focus Area" for a complete list of our administrative services and procedures, including our Expedited Procedures.

AMOUNT OF FILING FEE ENCLOSED WITH THIS DEMAND (please refer to the rules for the appropriate fee) $

THE FILING PARTY REQUESTS THAT HEARINGS BE HELD AT THE FOLLOWING LOCALE: ____________________

You are hereby notified that copies of our arbitration agreement and this demand are being filed with the American Arbitration Association office located in ____________________, with a request that it commence administration of the arbitration. Under the rules, you may file an answering statement within ten days after notice from the AAA.

Signature (may be signed by a representative) Date:			Name of Representative		
Name of the Claiming ☐Union or ☐Employer			Name of Firm (if applicable)		
Address (to be used in connection with this case):			Representative's Address:		
City	State	Zip Code	City	State	Zip Code
Phone No.		Fax No.	Phone No.		Fax No.
Email Address:			Email Address:		

To begin proceedings, please send two copies of this Demand and the Arbitration Agreement or relevant contract language, along with the filing fee as provided for in the Rules, to the AAA. Send the original Demand to the Respondent.

AAA Customer Service can be reached at 800-778-7879

Although many labor disputes are clearly suitable for arbitration, judgment must be exercised in deciding whether to arbitrate a particular dispute. Factors to be considered are the merits of the case, the importance of the issue, the effect of winning or losing the dispute, the possibilities of settlement, and psychological and face-saving aspects. The most popular use of labor arbitration is interpreting applications of the collective bargaining agreements. However, labor arbitration is not always the solution. Management will hesitate to arbitrate issues it considers to be its sole prerogative, such as determining methods of production, operating policies, and finances. Labor likewise considers the settlement of an internal union conflict as a topic in which management should not participate.[4]

HISTORY AND LEGAL STATE OF ARBITRATION

LINCOLN MILLS CASE
A landmark decision in which the Supreme Court ordered an employer to arbitrate grievances as provided for in a collective bargaining agreement, stating that an employer's agreement to arbitrate grievance disputes was a trade-off for the union's agreement not to strike.

As discussed in Chapter 10, state and federal courts have the authority to enforce collective bargaining agreements. In doing so, the Supreme Court in the ***Lincoln Mills* case** required specific performance of an employer's promise to arbitrate in a collective bargaining agreement.[5] The Court felt that the agreement to arbitrate grievance disputes was the employer's trade-off for the union's agreement not to strike. The role of arbitration and court enforcement of contract agreements was more specifically outlined in three Supreme Court cases known as

STEELWORKERS TRILOGY

Three 1960 Supreme Court rulings that upheld the grievance arbitration process and limited judicial intervention.

the **Steelworkers Trilogy**.[6] These cases held that the function of a court is limited to a review of whether the issue to be arbitrated is governed by the contract. Any doubt as to the coverage should be resolved in favor of arbitration. Unless the arbitrator's award is ambiguous, the courts should enforce it even if the court would not have decided the substantive issue in the same way:

> The 1960 *Steelworkers Trilogy* expanded vastly upon the foundation laid in *Lincoln Mills*. Arbitration was acknowledged as the preferred, superior forum for contract interpretation and enforcement. The powers of an arbitrator were held to be bounded by the restrictions of the "four corners of the contract" but arbitral actions were largely immunized from judicial review. As repeatedly stated thereafter, arbitration became the cornerstone of the rapidly arising edifice housing the federal law of the labor agreement.[7]

The Court gave almost complete deference to arbitration as a means of contract enforcement by limiting its own review of an arbitration award to whether the issue under arbitration is in the agreement.

In a study of federal and district court decisions for the 30 years following the *Steelworkers Trilogy*, it was found that the courts deferred to the arbitration process 70–74 percent of the time.

These four cases established the following five principles to govern the arbitration of grievances under collective bargaining:[8]

1. Arbitration is a matter of contract. The parties are not required to arbitrate a dispute that they have not agreed to submit to arbitration. The courts determine whether there is a duty to arbitrate a dispute.
2. In determining whether there is a duty to arbitrate a dispute, the courts should not examine the merits of the underlying grievance, even if it appears to be frivolous.
3. In labor contracts with an arbitration clause, there is a presumption of arbitrability unless there is positive assurance that the arbitration clause is not susceptible to an interpretation that covers the dispute. Doubts should be resolved in favor of coverage.
4. As long as an arbitration award is based on the bargaining agreement, a court should enforce the award without examining its correctness.
5. In interpreting the labor agreement, the arbitrator is not limited to the words of the contract. The arbitrator may consider factors such as past practice, parol evidence, and the common law of the shop.

Three important issues have evolved from the *Lincoln Mills* and the *Steelworkers Trilogy* cases: the principle of general arbitrability, situations in which the contract has expired or the ownership of the company has changed, and whether the duty to arbitrate survives a change in company ownership:[9]

1. ***General arbitrability.*** The courts have consistently enforced the principle that if the contract provides for the arbitration of grievances, then a grievance is presumed to be arbitrable as long as the agreement does not exclude the topic under consideration.
2. ***Expired contracts or changes in ownership.*** The U.S. Supreme Court has ruled that the duty to arbitrate can extend beyond the life of the contract. A post-expiration grievance is arbitrable only when it involves facts and events that occurred before the expiration of a CBA, when the action infringes a right vested under the agreement, or when the normal principles of contract interpretation show that the disputed contractual right survives the remainder of the agreement.
3. ***Successorship.*** The U.S. Supreme Court has also ruled that a successor employer is not required to adopt the substantive terms of the predecessor agreement, but that the

successor inherits the contractual duty to arbitrate as long as there is "substantial continuity" between the old and the new companies.

In summary, the rulings by the Supreme Court on the duty to arbitrate make it clear that if the parties' labor agreement requires the arbitration of grievances, then it will be difficult to avoid arbitration, even in situations where the CBA has expired, a new owner becomes the employer (successor), or the issue is not explicitly discussed in the CBA.

The Supreme Court acknowledged the superiority of arbitration in resolving labor–management disputes under collective bargaining agreements by stating the following:

> The labor arbitrator performs functions which are not normal to the courts; the considerations which help him fashion judgments may indeed be foreign to the confines of courts. The parties expect that his judgments of a particular grievance will not only reflect what the contract says but, insofar as the collective bargaining agreement permits, such factors as the effect upon productivity of a particular result, its consequence to the morale of the shop, his judgment whether detentions will be heightened or diminished. For the parties' objective in using the arbitration process is primarily to further their common goal of uninterrupted production under the agreement, to make the agreement meet their specialized needs. The ablest judge cannot be expected to bring the same experience and confidence to bear upon the determination of a grievance because he cannot be similarly informed.[10]

The arbitrator's role, however, is not unlimited. Beginning with the *Steelworkers Trilogy*, the Supreme Court limited the arbitrator's role to the interpretation and application of the collective bargaining agreement. The Court held that although an arbitrator may look outside the contract for guidance, "he does not sit to dispense his own brand of industrial justice."[11] The courts stressed that arbitrators' decisions, as long as they are based on interpretation of the contract, should be final and binding and not questioned by the courts. For example, in 1986, the Seventh Circuit Court upheld an arbitrator's decision and overturned a district court's reversal of that decision. In this case, an employee of E. I. duPont de Nemours & Company, during a nervous breakdown, attacked fellow employees and damaged company property. The arbitrator had concluded that the incident was a result of a mental breakdown (not drug use as the company contended) and would most likely not recur. The Seventh Circuit Court upheld the arbitrator's decision, which had been vacated by the district court. The court stated, "So long as the arbitrator interpreted the contract in making his award, his award must be affirmed even if he clearly misinterpreted the contract."[12]

Another advantage of arbitration over litigation is the final and binding provision contained in most agreements to arbitrate grievances. This provides a final step for settling labor disputes in comparison with the court process requiring a series of lengthy appeals and many steps before a final decision. In addition, the technical rules of evidence found in the courtroom need not be applied to the proceedings. Arbitration hearings are less formal than litigation, and the advocates need not have legal training.

For most of the 50-plus years since the *Steelworkers Trilogy* cases, judges have refused to review the merits of an arbitration award. Why? Former Michigan Law School dean Theodore St. Antoine answered that question:

> Put most simply, the arbitrator is the parties' officially designated "reader" of the contract. He (or she) is their joint alter ego for the purpose of striking whatever supplementary bargain is necessary to handle the unanticipated omissions of the initial agreement. Thus, a "misinterpretation" or "gross mistake" by the arbitrator becomes a contradiction in terms. In the absence of fraud or an overreaching of authority on the part of the arbitrator, he is speaking for the parties and his award is their contract.[13]

The arbitrator in the role of interpreting and applying the provisions of a collective bargaining agreement is often required to look outside of the "four corners" of the agreement itself. Disputes arise because the parties cannot agree on the meaning of the written agreement. In most cases that reach arbitration, there is some ambiguity in the language of the contract, or events that were not anticipated when the contract was negotiated have caused the contract to be applied in a way the parties may not have agreed. In those instances, the arbitrator is not just the "reader" of the contract but is, in fact, the judge of what the parties really *meant* in the agreement. The arbitrator will usually rely upon past practice, common law of the shop, or parol evidence to reach that judgment.

PAST PRACTICE

A recognition of the bargaining history of the two parties involved in a dispute to determine their respective rights in arbitration.

Past practice is recognition of the bargaining history of the two parties involved in the dispute. For example, a collective bargaining agreement states that a holiday that falls on a Sunday will be observed on the following Monday, but is silent as to whether a holiday that falls on a Saturday will be observed on the preceding Friday. The employer, however, has always done so. One year, the employer decides *not* to observe the holiday and the union appeals. Relying on past practice, the arbitrator would decide that the employees had come to rely upon this "practice" and therefore even though the contract was silent on the issue, the practice had become a condition of employment upon which the employees could rely.

COMMON LAW OF THE SHOP

A recognition of the bargaining history of those in the same industry to determine the respective rights of the parties involved in a labor dispute.

The **common law of the shop** is recognition of the bargaining history of those in the same industry as opposed to the actual parties in a particular case. For example, some large manufacturers "schedule" employees' vacations by closing the plant for an established week each year. An arbitrator might uphold a decision by an employer that produces parts for a manufacturing plant, even if the parts employer's agreement was unclear as to whether or not management had the right to change the vacation scheduling process.

PAROL EVIDENCE

Evidence that is not contained within the four edges of the collective bargaining agreement but which may be considered by the arbitrator to interpret terms of the agreement but which may be considered by the arbitrator to interpret terms of the agreement and find or clarify ambiguities within the agreement.

Parol evidence in labor arbitration cases refers to evidence, oral or otherwise, that is not contained within the four edges of the collective bargaining contract. In other words, it is evidence of discussions or writings that happened prior to or outside of the bargaining process that are not referenced in the final collective bargaining agreement itself. In basic contract law, the terms of a final written agreement between two parties cannot be interpreted or contradicted by evidence of anything that happened before the contact was finalized—or "parol evidence." For example, two parties enter into an agreement on the sale and purchase of a house. The contract clearly states that none of the house's appliances are a part of the transaction. After the buyer moves in, however, she sues the seller claiming that an earlier version of the contract provided that the seller would leave the dishwasher. The court will not allow the buyer to present such evidence. The assumption is that the agreement as contained in the formal written document both parties signed *is* the agreement of the parties that should be enforced.

However, collective bargaining agreements have special qualities that make some contract principles inapplicable. First, often the parties negotiating a union contract are not drafting the final agreement. Second, unlike ordinary contracts, collective bargaining agreements are often intentionally silent on significant matters. In order to be of a readable length, collective agreements must be written in generalized language that is capable of capturing the myriad relationships between management and labor. Third, collective bargaining doesn't stop with the signing of an agreement; it is a continuous process, beginning with the negotiation of a contract through the life of the contract with almost daily interpretations and administration of its provisions. Because of the unique nature of the collective bargaining agreement, arbitrators often rely upon parol evidence to ascertain the true meaning of the written labor agreement. Such evidence is usually not admitted for the purpose of varying or contradicting the actual written language recorded in the labor agreement. Generally parol evidence is used in the following ways:

1. To aid in the interpretation of existing terms. For example, an arbitrator is asked to determine what kind of offenses the parties meant by "Discipline for *minor* offenses will be progressive" when the contract did not include any definition of "minor." The arbitrator

allowed the union to present a number of *prior contracts* between the parties that had listed examples of offenses subject to progressive discipline.

2. Show that in light of all the circumstances surrounding the making of the contract, the contract is actually ambiguous. For example, an arbitrator is asked to determine whether employees received pay for travel time based on a provision of the contract that states "if you are 'called in/called out' to work outside you normal work schedule . . . you will receive overtime pay for *all* hours worked." The union testified that they believed the "all" included travel time because in the negotiations, the parties often referred to provisions in the company's "Employee Handbook" to explain proposals, and under the handbook's identical language, employees were paid for travel time. Therefore, the union believed that was the agreement of the parties. The arbitrator allowed introduction of the "Employee Handbook" even though it is parol evidence.
3. Resolve an ambiguity in the contract. For example, an arbitrator is asked to determine whether there was a valid contract in effect on January 1, 2005, when the cover page of the CBA said, "Date of Agreement: January 1, 2005–March 31, 2008," but the first sentence of the CBA stated, "This is an Agreement by and between . . . effective April 13, 2005." The arbitrator allowed introduction of *prior CBAs* between the parties to determine whether the cover page or the language inside the document was used in the past to define the term.

ARBITRATION OF STATUTORY RIGHTS IN UNION AND NONUNION CASES

In *Alexander v. Gardner-Denver*, the Supreme Court addressed the application of an arbitration clause to the pursuit of an individual's statutory rights even if the individual is covered by an arbitration provision in a collective bargaining agreement.[14] In that case the Court ruled that an individual could not be precluded from suing under the civil rights laws just because his claim had gone through arbitration under the collective bargaining agreement. The Court was articulating a public policy exception to labor arbitration provisions.

Title VII Cases

The principle stated by the Court in the *Gardner-Denver* case is clear: Individuals may exercise a legal right based on external law that is independent of their rights under a collective bargaining agreement.[15] An individual who takes a grievance to arbitration that involves an EEO (equal employment opportunity) matter could be entitled to a trial if he or she loses in arbitration.

In 1998, the Supreme Court again took up the issue of whether an employee subject to a collective bargaining agreement with a compulsory arbitration clause is required to take a discrimination dispute to arbitration rather than pursue the claim in federal court. In *Wright v. Universal Maritime Service Corp.*, a longshoreman was refused employment following a settlement of a claim for permanent disability.[16] When he filed suit under the Americans with Disabilities Act, the lower court dismissed the case because the longshoreman failed to pursue his claim under the contract's arbitration procedure. The Supreme Court reversed the lower-court decision on the grounds that the arbitration provision did not contain a "clear and unmistakable" waiver of the employee's right to pursue his antidiscrimination claim in federal court.[17] And at least one federal court has ruled that a waiver of an individual statutory right by a collective bargaining agreement is nonnegotiable, making it an illegal bargaining item.[18]

Although seeming to uphold *Gardner-Denver*, some observers note that the decision follows the reasoning of the Court in *Gilmer v. Interstate/Johnson Lane Corporation*.[19] In *Gilmer*, the Court upheld compulsory arbitration of an age discrimination claim under an employee-signed employment agreement that covered termination for any reason. Although *Gilmer* did not involve an arbitration clause in a collective bargaining agreement, the holding in *Wright* would indicate that if a collective bargaining agreement arbitration provision "clearly and unmistakably" includes antidiscrimination claims. In *Penn Plaza v. Pyett*, the U.S. Supreme Court in 2009 ruled that a collective bargaining agreement that "clearly and unmistakably" requires employees to arbitrate claims under the Age Discrimination in Employment Act (ADEA) is enforceable. The opinion of the court included the justification that "nothing in the text of the ADEA prohibited arbitration of discrimination suits" and that the "broad sweep" of the NLRA makes collective bargaining agreements and their arbitration provisions enforceable. The decision pleased many employers who disliked the idea of employees getting two sources of recourse—first a grievance under the CBA, and then a federal lawsuit to win their case. Employees, however, may not like the idea that the CBA negotiated by their union now may waive their right as an individual to file a federal lawsuit.[20] The *Pyett* decision therefore permits employers and unions to bargain away the right of individual members of the bargaining unit to pursue individual claims of discrimination in federal court if a provision in the CBA "clearly and unmistakably" requires them to arbitrate such claims. Therefore, instead of federal judges, labor arbitrators will decide cases involving federal discrimination laws, a field in which they may or may not have experience.[21]

The Federal Arbitration Act and Individual Employment Agreements

In the United States, three statutes govern the private sector arbitration of disputes: the 1947 Labor Management Relations Act (LMRA), which provides for the arbitration of disputes involving collective bargaining agreements as discussed in this chapter; the 1926 Railway Labor Act (RLA), which has jurisdiction over disputes between employees and a carrier in the railroad and airline industries; and the 1925 Federal Arbitration Act (FAA), also called the United States Arbitration Act.[22] The U.S. Supreme Court reinterpreted the FAA in a series of cases in the 1980s and 1990s to cover the full scope of interstate commerce. In the process, the Court held that the FAA preempted many state laws covering arbitration, some of which had been passed by state legislatures to protect their consumers against powerful corporations.

The Federal Arbitration Act[23] governs commercial arbitration situations such as business–business, employer–employee, and buyer–seller situations. The FAA provides the parties involved with guidelines and enforcement mechanisms for arbitrated disputes. The act enables one party to force the other party to arbitrate a dispute when an agreement to arbitrate exists between the two parties. The U.S. Supreme Court stated that with the FAA, Congress "declared a national policy favoring arbitration" over the more expensive, slower court litigation process. The act also provides that an arbitration award can be confirmed by a court judgment.[24]

The Supreme Court expanded its *Gilmer* decision when it ruled that individual employment agreements that contain arbitration clauses could be enforced under the Federal Arbitration Act (FAA). In *Circuit City Stores Inc. v. Adams*, the employee had signed an employment application with Circuit City that included a provision agreeing to settle any and all "claims, disputes, or controversies arising out of or relating to my . . . employment . . . exclusively by final and binding arbitration.[25] By way of example only, such claims include claims under federal, state, and local statutory or common law, including . . . the Civil Rights Act." Two years later, the employee filed an employment discrimination lawsuit against Circuit City, and Circuit City filed suit to require him to submit to final and binding arbitration. The court of appeals ruled that because the FAA excluded coverage of "contracts of employment of seamen, railroad employees, or any other class of workers engaged in foreign or interstate commerce," the clause was not enforceable. The Supreme Court disagreed. It held that the exclusion language of the FAA ought to be narrowly interpreted to apply only to transportation workers. The Court held the following:

> "[A]rbitration agreements can be enforced under the FAA without contravening the policies of congressional enactments giving employees specific protection against discrimination prohibited by federal law; as we noted in *Gilmer,* "[b]y agreeing to arbitrate a statutory claim, a party does not forgo the substantive rights afforded by the statute; it only submits to their resolution in an arbitral, rather than a judicial forum."[26]

As a result of the U.S. Supreme Court decision in the Circuit City case, many nonunion employees are bound by employment arbitration agreements. *Source:* William T Kane / Getty Images.

The Supreme Court also upheld a mandatory arbitration provision in a nonemployment case that might have repercussions on employment arbitrations. In *Green Tree Financial Corp. Alabama v. Randolph*, the plaintiff claimed that because the arbitration clause was silent about the costs for such arbitration, she was effectively precluded from pursuing her statutory claim under the Truth in Lending Act for fear of incurring excessive costs.[27] The Court ruled that a party seeking to avoid an arbitration agreement must demonstrate the likelihood of incurring prohibitive costs, not just the possibility. And in February 2008, the Supreme Court held that a challenge to the validity or legality of a contract that has an arbitration clause must be decided by the arbitrator not another state court or agency because the FAA has preempted state laws in this area.[28]

Profile 12-1

Arbitration of Nonunion Employment Disputes

In 1991, the U.S. Supreme Court held for the first time that predispute employment arbitration agreements are enforceable just like any other contracts. Since then, many employers have drafted arbitration agreements for their employees and applicants. Some of these are simple stand-alone agreements in which the employer and employees agree to arbitrate rather than litigate any disputes that might arise in the future. Other agreements involve overreaching by the employer—as when an employer attempts to waive or restrict employees' ability to recover damages, to impose onerous filing fees or other costs, or to choose the arbitrator without the employee's participation. Courts generally have struck down arbitration agreements that involve employer overreaching.

Some more progressive employers, however, have gone in the opposite direction, and have designed comprehensive dispute-resolution programs for their nonunion workforces. The premise behind these programs is that both employers and employees are better off if they are able to amicably resolve their differences without having to go to court, and that both sides benefit if the programs are truly fair.

The Anheuser-Busch Program

One example of a hugely successful program is Anheuser-Busch, the beer manufacturer which controls over half the U.S. market, and is a wholly owned subsidiary of

(continued)

Anheuser-Bush, the beer manufacturer, provides employees a three-step dispute-resolution program which includes mediation and binding arbitration.
Source: © Michael Newman / PhotoEdit.

Belgium-based Anheuser-Busch InBev. Anheuser-Bush implemented an innovative dispute-resolution program in 1997. Anheuser-Busch encourages employees to resolve work-related disputes informally with their managers or the H.R. Department. When such informal efforts do not resolve the dispute, there is a three-step process.

Step 1: Employee and Management Discussion In Level One, Local Management Review, the dispute-resolution procedures vary by subsidiary or department, but all involve the employee and members of the management team specially trained in dispute resolution.

Step 2: Mediation Level Two is nonbinding mediation with a mediator jointly selected by the employee and the company. The employee pays a $50 filing fee, and the company pays for the mediator and for the employee's wages during the mediation.

Step 3: Arbitration Level Three is binding arbitration with an arbitrator jointly selected by the employee and the company. The employee pays a $125 filing fee, and the company pays for the arbitrator and the wages of the employee and any employee-witnesses during the arbitration hearing. The arbitrator's decision is final and binding on both the company and the employee. Employees must agree to this dispute-resolution program as a condition of employment.

Results

Results from the first ten years of the program indicate it has been beneficial to both employees and management. Of the claims submitted to Anheuser-Busch's dispute-resolution program, 95 percent are resolved in Level One, 4 percent are resolved in Level Two, and only 1 percent progress to Level Three. Anheuser-Busch's both legal and administrative cost of resolving employment disputes declined approximately 50 percent following implementation of the program, and that reduction has held steady over time. Level One disputes were resolved in an average of four weeks, Level Two disputes in six months, and Level Three disputes in 15 months. Win rates for employees at Level Three were slightly higher than would be expected in litigation, though the amount recovered was lower. Figures for win rates and recovery amounts probably is not reliable, however, both because of the small number of disputes that made it to Level Three and because the claims that made it to that level were not necessarily representative of claims that otherwise would have been litigated (e.g., comprehensive dispute-resolution programs enable employers to identify, and settle early, cases that an employee might otherwise have won in litigation).

Source: Richard A. Bales and Jason N. W. Plowman, "Compulsory Arbitration as Part of a Broader Employment Dispute Resolution Process: The Anheuser-Busch Example," *Hofstra Law Review 26,* no. 1 (2010). Used by Permission.

SELECTING THE ARBITRATOR

Both labor and management pay the arbitration fees and have a hand in the choice of arbitrator; he or she is not an outside party imposed on them to resolve disputes. The arbitrator's jurisdiction evolves from the contract negotiated by the two parties. Therefore, the arbitrator's performance must generally be satisfactory; the parties can dispense with an incompetent arbitrator. The arbitrator is well aware that he or she provides a service for a fee and is expected to meet certain professional standards. Unlike litigation, both parties have the ability to participate in the selection of the arbitrator. This is recognized as a great advantage over the litigation process, in which the parties have little or no input in the selection of a judge. In fact, both parties can easily access thousands of arbitration awards by arbitrator, by employer, and by union or subject matter. Thus, they know a great deal about possible arbitrator candidates and their thoughts in similar cases.[29]

Because of the very real need to keep both parties satisfied with arbitration decisions, arbitrator decisions and awards are far from uniform on almost any issue.[30] However, no two grievance situations are the same. The arbitrator may be a permanent umpire chosen beforehand by labor and management to decide disputes arising during the life of the collective bargaining agreement. However, most arbitrations take place ad hoc, with arbitrators selected to hear disputes case by case. Permanent arbitration can help provide a stable union–management relationship. With their knowledge of the specific language of a contract, the personalities involved, and past labor relations, permanent arbitrators can quickly participate, provide immediate assistance, and resolve disputes much faster than the courts in most situations.[31] Collective bargaining agreements with arbitration normally provide for the selection process of arbitrators. If a permanent arbitrator is not designated in the contract, then an impartial agency is often agreed on as a source of arbitrators. The American Arbitration Association and the Federal Mediation and Conciliation Service agencies are the most frequent sources of arbitrators.

The arbitrator would be required to follow the contract language regardless of any personal opinion as to the reasonableness of the agreement language if the intent of the provision is clear.

Contract provisions often call for arbitrators (one or a panel) to be selected from the American Arbitration Association or the FMCS Office of Arbitration Services. *Source:* bikeriderlondon/ ShutterStock.

However, the language is often ambiguous, and the arbitrator must interpret the provision in question.

By interpreting contract language, arbitrators are often sources of future contract language. Collective bargaining agreements can be drafted with general language to be flexible. Sometimes the parties at the bargaining table are purposely vague in some areas to reach agreement in others. At other times, simply because of the size and complexity of an agreement, inconsistent provisions are a source of contention after the contract is signed. Arbitrators therefore are called on to resolve disputes arising from the contract language. In the absence of clear and unambiguous contract language, an arbitrator is guided by basic contract interpretation principles derived from the common law of contracts:

1. Honor the intent of the parties.
2. Interpret the agreement as a whole.
3. Give effect to all terms of the agreement.
4. Give undefined terms reasonable definitions.
5. Avoid absurd results by considering reason and equity.

ARBITRATOR'S AWARD

The arbitrator's decision in a grievance case, presented in written format and signed by the arbitrator. Examples of awards include back pay and reinstatement of job or benefits.

By following those rules, an arbitrator crafts an "award" that often includes an interpretation of a collective bargaining agreement. To some extent, an **arbitrator's award** interpreting contract language becomes part of the contract. A prior arbitration award that contains a well-reasoned opinion and involves the same parties, the same contract, and the same issues is entitled to great weight in subsequent arbitrations. This creates a disincentive for a party dissatisfied with the outcome of arbitration from repeating the same issue before another arbitrator in the hopes of getting a different result.[32]

In addition, in cases where the parties have had the opportunity to negotiate subsequent contracts and to make changes in contract language that has been interpreted in arbitration and fail to do so, the parties may be held to have adopted the award as a part of the contract. Indeed, the binding force of an award may even be strengthened by such renegotiation without change because the opportunity exists in negotiations to alter, amend, or modify any arbitral interpretation that does not reflect the intent of the parties.[33]

Arbitration Services

One source of arbitration panels is the Federal Mediation and Conciliation Services' Office of Arbitration Services (OAS). The responsibilities of the OAS include the following:

- Maintaining a roster of arbitrators qualified to hear and decide labor questions in labor–management disputes
- Providing the parties involved in collective bargaining agreements with a list of experienced panels of arbitrators
- Appointing arbitrators following their selection by the involved parties

The OAS maintains a roster of approximately 1,641 private arbitrators. The maintenance of this roster requires establishment of and adherence to high standards of qualification. The OAS boasts of experienced practitioners with backgrounds in collective bargaining and labor–management relations. Panels are selected on the basis of geographic location, professional affiliation, occupation, experience in various industries, and issues or other specified criteria requested by the parties. In 1996, the OAS submitted 30,066 panels to requesting parties in both the private and the public sectors. Table 12-1 shows the number of OAS panel requests from 2005 through 2009.

Qualifications of Arbitrators

Arbitrators are not required to have any specific educational or technical training unless specified in the collective bargaining agreement. But the qualifications of an arbitrator are key to a

TABLE 12-1 OAS Arbitration Panel Services

Activity	2005	2006	2007	2008	2009
Panel Requests	15,370	15,572	14,287	14,444	14,072
Panels Issued[a]	16,787	16,854	16,264	15,717	16,692
Arbitrators Appointed	7,592	6,860	6,485	6,568	6,496

[a]Frequently, the labor–management parties request more than one panel for arbitration cases, resulting in an increase in the number of panels issued over the number of requests received.

Source: Federal Mediation and Conciliation Service. *Sixty-Second Annual Report* (Washington, DC: Author, 2010), p. 8. Available at http://www.fmcs.gov. Accessed September 5, 2010.

successful system. If rigid qualifications are required, it may become very difficult to find an available arbitrator.

Various characteristics, including experience, education, occupation, and visibility, have been identified as affecting arbitrator selection. Both labor and management prefer arbitrators with specific attributes. Research indicates that age and experience are the most significant demographic factors affecting arbitrator decisions. Surprisingly, though, labor lawyers have not been able to distinguish between the decisions of experienced and inexperienced arbitrators.[34]

In addition to these demographic variables, other variables affecting arbitrator selection include visibility, such as public speaking and professional association membership, and past arbitration decisions. All three appear to determine which arbitrator might be selected for a case. Empirical data indicate that visibility in the community may be the single most important variable.[35] In addition to visibility, a 2000 study of arbitrator behaviors found that arbitrators who use more procedural justice methods (process and procedures used during hearings) are perceived to be fairer by the participants. In addition, those who use more interactional justice methods (treat the participants with respect, candor, and a lack of prejudice) are more acceptable and likely to be chosen for future cases.[36]

Arbitrators are secured from a wide variety of backgrounds and include attorneys, public officials, judges, and university professors. Elkouri and Elkouri in *How Arbitration Works* outline some general qualifications of an arbitrator:

1. ***Impartiality.*** Although no one can be absolutely free from bias or prejudice, the arbitrator is expected to divest himself or herself from personal inclinations during an arbitration, even though he or she decides cases according to his or her own judgment. The elements of honesty and impartiality are the most critical qualifications, and the arbitrator must always be able to be up front with both parties. Otherwise, he or she might not be selected again.
2. ***Integrity.*** Arbitrators are expected to be of the highest integrity. Both parties can review backgrounds and affiliations of prospective arbitrators; personal, financial, or business interests in the affairs of either party are primary considerations. The Code of Ethics for Arbitrators requires the arbitrator to disclose any association or relation that might reasonably bring any doubt to his or her objectivity. Records of past decisions and whether the arbitrator has expressed strong opinions in favor of either labor or management are also reviewed. Arbitrators are expected to exercise fairness and good judgment in issuing awards and not just to please both sides by splitting awards.
3. ***Ability and expertise.*** A labor–management arbitrator should have a broad background of social and economic experience. Maturity of judgment and a quick, analytical mind are also necessary. The arbitrator is not expected to be a subject-matter specialist; such an expert may be difficult or impossible to find. Both parties may prefer someone with general business or financial expertise, as well as significant arbitration experience.
4. ***Legal training.*** Labor–management arbitrators are often lawyers. Legal training may help an arbitrator to be objective and to analyze and evaluate facts without personal bias.

Profile 12-2

William C. Heekin is a labor arbitrator/ADR neutral based in Cincinnati, Ohio. Presently, he is on the arbitration and fact-finding rosters maintained by the Federal Mediation and Conciliation Service (FMCS), the National Mediation Board (NMB), the City of Louisville, Kentucky Labor/Management Committee, and the Ohio State Employee Relations Board (SERB). He graduated from Xavier University in 1977 with a B.A. in economics and in 1983 received a J.D. from Northern Kentucky University/Salmon P. Chase School of Law. From 1979 to 1983, he was the Labor Tribunal Administrator in the Cincinnati regional office of the American Arbitration Association (AAA). From 1983 to 1985, he interned with Arbitrator Charles L. Mullin in Pittsburgh, Pennsylvania, while beginning a career as a labor arbitrator/ADR neutral. In 1989, he became a member of the National Academy of Arbitrators (NAA). In 2003, he founded the Arbitration and Mediation Service (AMS), a private firm dedicated to strengthening the ADR, an institutional framework with a primary focus on labor arbitration. From 1997 to 2003, he participated in a number of international development projects regarding the transition to a democratic government/free market economy in several countries located in Central and Eastern Europe. This was under the sponsorship of the American Bar Association, Central East European Law Initiative (ABA/CEELI) and funded by the United States Agency for International Development (USAID).

Arbitration is a form of alternative dispute resolution (ADR) which, like mediation, involves the intervention of a third-party neutral. As with mediation, arbitration is normally faster and less expensive than litigation. It is usually voluntary and thus not Court-ordered or required by statute as exists in Ohio regarding public sector safety forces. Most often, labor arbitration is used by way of a grievance procedure/arbitration clause contained in a collective bargaining agreement (CBA). Thus, it is normally used to resolve a contract or "rights" dispute pertaining to the interpretation and/or application of a CBA. Unlike with mediation, labor arbitration, which is reflective of the "Common Law" tradition, has established standards and procedures. Since arbitration is comparable to litigation in that it involves the adjudicative process, where the parties do not retain decision-making authority over the outcome, there is a hearing where witnesses are called and document evidence submitted. Accordingly, unlike in mediation, which involves the legislative process, arbitration results in a final and binding decision being made by an outside labor arbitrator based on the merits.

William C. Heekin is a highly acclaimed arbitrator with international experience. *Source:* William Heekin.

However, not all lawyers make good arbitrators, nor are all good arbitrators lawyers. The lawyer who is overly concerned with technical rules of evidence may be ineffective.[37] Profile 12-2 includes the background and beliefs of a successful labor arbitrator.

Tripartite Arbitration Board

TRIPARTITE ARBITRATION BOARD

An arbitration board composed of one or more members representing management, an equal number representing labor, and a neutral member who serves as chairperson.

The labor agreement may provide for multiple arbitrators. A **tripartite arbitration board** usually has one or more members selected by management, an equal number of members selected by labor, and a neutral member who serves as chairperson. The labor and management members act as partisans or advocates for their respective sides, and in essence, the neutral chairperson becomes a single arbitrator. The panel chair plays a unique role in the arbitration process. It is the chair's duty to keep the other arbitrators informed about all aspects of the case so they can make informed decisions. One panel member may be assigned the duty to outline all issues to be decided and circulate relevant information among the panel members. This outline serves as a "road map" of the issues in dispute.[38]

Tripartite boards sometimes do not reach decisions unanimously. Collective bargaining agreements, therefore, often stipulate that a majority award of the board is final and binding. Some agreements may even give the neutral member the sole right and responsibility for making the final decision. The advantage of using a tripartite board rather than a single arbitrator is to provide the neutral member with valuable advice and assistance from the partisan members. Each party may be able to give to the neutral arbitrator a more realistic and informed picture of the issues involved than may be given by formal presentation of the issues. The disadvantage of such a board, of course, is the additional time and expense incurred.[39] The following is an example of a panel selection procedure specified in a CBA:

> **ARTICLE 27**
>
> **Section 2**
>
> If the issue cannot be resolved by the Joint Conference Committee, a panel of seven (7) impartial arbitrators will be promptly secured from the Federal Mediation and Conciliation Service. The employer and the union shall each have the right to reject two arbitrators from the panel of seven impartial arbitrators. The remaining three individuals shall be the arbitrators and their decision shall be final and binding on the employer, the union, and the employees. Expenses incurred in any arbitration under the provision of this article will be borne equally by the employer and the union.

DETERMINING ARBITRABILITY

The basic concept of arbitrability suggests that some disputes and conflicts are not subject to arbitration. The power to determine whether arbitration is proper, the breadth of contractual issues, and whether any other issues limit the ability of an arbitrator to resolve a dispute may be called **arbitrability**.[41] If both parties in a dispute submit the dispute to arbitration, there is no question of arbitrability because a submission by both parties identifies their agreement to go to arbitration. However, if only one party invokes the arbitration clause in a collective bargaining agreement by notice of intent to arbitrate a dispute, the other party may resist the intent to arbitrate on the grounds that the dispute is not arbitrable. Such a challenge to arbitrability is presented either to the arbitrator or to the courts. Although most questions of arbitrability are left in the hands of the arbitrator, they may be taken to the courts. The courts may be involved with arbitrability in one of three ways:

ARBITRABILITY
The challenge of whether a disputed issue is subject to arbitration under the terms of the contract.

1. The party challenging arbitrability may seek a temporary injunction or stay of arbitration, pending determination of arbitrability.
2. The party demanding arbitration may seek a court order compelling the other party to arbitrate when the applicable law upholds agreements to arbitrate future disputes; the latter party then raises the issue of arbitrability.
3. The issue of arbitrability may be considered when an award is taken to court for review or enforcement unless the parties have clearly vested the arbitrator with exclusive and final right of determining arbitrability or unless the right to challenge arbitrability is held by the court to have been otherwise waived under the circumstances of the case.[42]

The Supreme Court in the ***Warrior & Gulf* case** declared that congressional policy in favor of settlement of disputes through arbitration restricts the judicial process and strictly confines it to questions of whether the reluctant party agreed to arbitrate the grievance in the collective bargaining contract. A labor–management agreement to arbitrate therefore should not be denied unless a court is absolutely positive that the arbitration clause in the collective bargaining contract is not susceptible to interpretation covering the dispute. Any doubt in questions of arbitrability should be resolved in favor of the grievance being arbitrated.[43] Case Study 12-2 at the end of the chapter illustrates a possible exception to this rule.

In general, the arbitrator may rule on the question of arbitrability. That ruling is not subject to reversal by the courts as long as the arbitrator is applying the contract and acting within the scope of his or her authority. For example, in 2004, the arbitrator in the *Republic Waste Services* case ruled that regardless of the merits of the case, which involved termination of an employee, he did not have the authority to arbitrate it. His lack of authority was owing to the fact that the prior agreement had expired in January, the employee was fired in April, and the new contract started in July. The new contract did not contain a "retroactivity" clause, and the employer argued the question of arbitrability because the contract was not in effect when the employee was fired, and thus it could not be compelled into arbitration.[44]

DOUBLE JEOPARDY A bus driver departed from his scheduled stop five minutes early and was given a six-day suspension. He accepted the suspension and returned to work afterward. About a week after he returned to his route, he was informed that because of his history of running ahead of schedule and deviating from his route, he was terminated for his record of numerous offenses. The employer's discipline code included specific infractions, including running ahead of schedule, which could result in termination after four offenses in the period of a year. The driver's offense was his fourth within a year.

DOUBLE JEOPARDY

A concept borrowed from criminal law for the principle that a person cannot be punished twice for the same offense based on the same conduct.

The union, however, grieved the driver's termination under the principle of **double jeopardy**. The union argued that his six-day suspension, which he served, was the disciplinary action decided by management for the last offense, and the termination decision was a second disciplinary action for the same offense and therefore amounted to "double jeopardy," or two penalties for the same offense.

The arbitrator pointed out that the union did not contest the fact that the driver committed a code violation or that the employer had the right to discipline the driver, and that the disciplinary action chosen could have been termination because it was his fourth offense within a year. However, the union did contest management's decision to impart a second disciplinary action for the same offense. The arbitrator pointed out that the employer knew his record at the time the suspension was imposed and presented no facts to support why a second disciplinary action was justified. The arbitrator noted that the principle of "double jeopardy" is well known in labor and employment relations and a commonly accepted principle. Thus, the arbitrator applied the principle and concluded that the employer lacked sufficient cause to levy the second penalty of termination.[45]

An arbitrator returned a bus driver to his job after his employer first suspended, then fired him for the same infraction. The arbitrator invoked the principle of "double jeopardy" in ruling that the employer could not punish the employee twice for the same offense. *Source:* Tina Fineberg/AP Images.

HEARING PROCEDURES

The arbitrator fixes the date of the hearing after consulting with both sides and makes the necessary arrangements. The hearing procedure for the arbitration of a grievance normally follows a certain series of steps:

1. An opening statement by the initiating party (except that the company goes first in discharge or discipline cases)
2. An opening statement by the other side
3. The presentation of evidence, witnesses, and arguments by the initiating party
4. A cross-examination by the other side
5. The presentation of evidence, witnesses, and arguments by the defense
6. A cross-examination by the initiating party
7. A summation by the initiating party (optional)
8. A summation by the other side (optional)
9. Filing of briefs (optional)
10. The arbitrator's award[46]

Opening Statement

The opening statement lays the groundwork for the testimony of witnesses and helps the arbitrator understand the relevance of oral and written evidence. The statement should clearly identify the issue, indicate what is to be proved, and specify the relief sought. Sometimes parties present the opening statement in writing to the arbitrator, with a copy given to the other side. Usually, the opening statement is also made orally so appropriate points can be highlighted and given emphasis if doing so would be to the advantage of the presenting side.[47]

Rules of Evidence

Strict legal **rules of evidence** are not usually observed unless expressly required by the parties. The arbitrator determines how the hearing is run and how evidence is presented: In arbitration, the parties have submitted the matter to persons whose judgment they trust, and it is for the arbitrators to determine the weight or credibility of evidence presented to them without restrictions as to rules of admissibility that would apply in a court of law.[48]

In general, any pertinent information or testimony is acceptable as evidence if it helps the arbitrator understand and decide the issue. Arbitrators are usually extremely receptive to evidence, giving both parties a free hand in presenting any type they choose to strengthen and clarify their case.[49] The arbitrator decides how much weight to give evidence in making a decision.

Assessing Credibility of Witnesses

Included in the weighing of evidence is the arbitrator's need to assess witness credibility. An arbitrator is both judge and jury in deciding an arbitration. Conducting a fair hearing and at the same time trying to arrive at the truth from the facts presented demands keen analysis. Psychological studies regarding eyewitness testimony offer arbitrators helpful guidelines for such analysis.

An arbitrator must be aware of the following:

1. The most confident witness is not necessarily the most accurate.
2. Demeanor alone cannot reveal that a witness is lying.
3. Biases because of race, sex, or ethnic stereotyping must be eliminated.
4. The occupation or social class of a witness does not guarantee veracity.

In addition, studies indicate the following regarding the ability of a witness to recall information:

1. The more often and the longer an observer sees an event, the more accurate the recall. This factor must be weighed against the possibility that the observer's familiarity with a situation causes the person to see what he or she expects to see from past experience.
2. Witnesses are not very accurate in estimating the duration of an event or the height, distance, or speed relevant to an event. The more emotionally charged the event, the less accurate the recall.
3. A witness's personal biases may cloud both the memory and the perception of an event.
4. Memory dims as time passes, and "after-acquired" information becomes incorporated into this memory.[50]

Presenting Documents, Photographs, and Videos

Most arbitration cases provide for the presentation of essential documents. Most important, of course, are those sections of the collective bargaining agreement that have some bearing on the grievance. Other documentation might include records of settled grievances, jointly signed memoranda, official minutes of contract negotiation meetings, personnel records, office reports, and organizational information. Documentary evidence is usually presented to the arbitrator, with a copy made available to the other party, but it is also explained orally to emphasize its importance.[51] Photographs and videos as well as written documents can provide excellent evidence. In fact, experienced arbitrators encourage the use of visual evidence that can be worth "a thousand words" in understanding a dispute. Visual aids should be carefully identified with date, location, and the identification of the key persons involved.[52]

Examination of Witnesses

Each party depends on the direct examination of its own witnesses during an arbitration hearing. The witness is identified and qualified as an authority on the facts to which he or she will testify and is generally permitted to tell his or her story without interruptions and without the extensive use of leading questions as in legal cases. The witness in an arbitration proceeding is rarely cut off, and some arbitrators even ask the witness whether he or she wants to add anything to the testimony as relevant to the case. Arbitrators generally uphold the right of cross-examination of witnesses but not as strongly as the courts. The arbitrator also does not usually limit the rights of parties to call witnesses from the other side for cross-examination. However, opinion is split concerning the right of the company to call the grievant as a witness. One side believes that the application of the privilege against self-incrimination should apply in arbitration proceedings, even though there is no applicable constitutional privilege. The opposing view is that the privilege against self-incrimination in the field of criminal law is not present in grievance cases.[53]

Summation

Before the hearing is closed by the arbitrator, both sides are given equal time for closing statements. This is the last chance for each side to convince the arbitrator and to refute all the other side's arguments. Each side can summarize the situation and emphasize relevant facts and issues.[54]

Arbitrator's Award and Opinion

The *arbitrator's award* is the arbitrator's decision in the grievance case. Awards are usually short, presented in written format, and signed by the arbitrator. Even if an oral award is rendered, the arbitrator usually produces a written award later. Awards usually include the arbitrator's decision on each remedy sought by the party filing the grievance.

The arbitrator also often presents a written **arbitrator's opinion** stating the reasons for the decision. This opinion is separate from the award and clearly indicates where the opinion ends and the award begins. It is generally felt that a well-reasoned opinion can contribute greatly to the acceptance of the award. The Supreme Court has emphasized the need for arbitrator opinions and encouraged their use. Such opinions should be solidly based on the contract's terms, answer all the questions raised in the arbitration without raising new questions, and address all the arguments raised in the hearing, especially those of the losing party.[55]

ARBITRATOR'S OPINION

An arbitrator's written statement discussing the reasons for the decision in the case.

CASE PREPARATION

When a grievance has reached the point of arbitration, both parties have probably gone through several steps of discussion in negotiations to resolve the issue. The issues disputed by the parties usually have been fairly well defined by the time the case reaches arbitration. To prepare the case for arbitration, the American Arbitration Association recommends the following steps in hearing preparation:

1. Study the original statement of the grievance and review its history through every step of the grievance machinery.
2. Carefully examine the initiating grievance paper (submission or demand) to help determine the arbitrator's role. It might be found, for instance, that although the original grievance contains many elements, the arbitrator, under the contract, is restricted to resolving only certain aspects.
3. Review the collective bargaining agreement from beginning to end. Often clauses that at first glance seem to be unrelated to the grievance are found to have some bearing.
4. Assemble all necessary documents and papers at the hearing. When feasible, make postdated copies for the arbitrator and the other party. If some of the documents are in the possession of the other party, ask in advance that they be brought to the arbitration. Under some arbitration laws, the arbitrator has the authority to subpoena documents and witnesses if they cannot be made available in any other way.
5. If you think the arbitrator should visit the plant or job site for on-the-spot investigation, make plans in advance. The arbitrator should be accompanied by representatives of both parties.
6. Interview all witnesses. They should certainly understand the whole case and particularly the importance of their own testimony.
7. Make a written summary of each proposed witness's testimony. This summary is useful as a checklist at the hearing to make sure nothing is overlooked.
8. Study the other side of the case. Be prepared to answer the opposing evidence and arguments.
9. Discuss your outline of the case with others in your organization. Another's viewpoint often discloses weak areas or previously overlooked details.
10. Read as many articles and published awards as you can on the general subject matter and dispute. Although awards by other arbitrators or other parties have no binding present value, they may help clarify the thinking of parties and arbitrators alike.[56]

Decision Criteria

In surveys conducted by the National Academy of Arbitrators, some interesting facts on how arbitrators decide cases were analyzed. The major criteria used by arbitrators did not change over the 12-year period. The following three factors were used most by arbitrators in both groups:

1. ***Labor contract language.*** If the labor agreement provides clear and specific directives, obviously this is the first factor that arbitrators use.
2. ***Past practice.*** In the absence of clear contract language, arbitrators rely on the parties' past practice to decide.
3. ***Fairness.*** Arbitrators felt some latitude to decide an issue in a fair and reasonable way regardless of contract language and past practices.

The next five factors were not used by arbitrators in the same order, but they were used often:

1. ***Industry practice.*** Even if the parties have no past practice in a particular area, the industry may have some consistent approach to an issue that an arbitrator can use.
2. ***Other arbitration awards.*** Precedent does not bind arbitrators, but they do often review other arbitrator awards for guidance.
3. ***Future labor relations.*** Occasionally an arbitrator decides an issue on what he or she believes will further the labor–management relationship.
4. ***State or federal law.*** If relevant, adherence to or violation of state or federal law determines the outcome of arbitration.
5. ***Social mores and customs.*** Seldom is an arbitration award decided on the basis of customs outside the workplace.[57]

As a counterweight to the findings on how arbitrators decide cases, a New York State Bar Association survey of labor and management attorneys found considerable criticism of some arbitrators' styles. Three-fourths of the 345 respondents felt that arbitrators should not consider outside factors in deciding a case. Such factors as the political fallout of a decision, a possible strike, or alleged abuse of power were not appropriate considerations. The respondents also believed that an arbitrator should not help one side even if that side has poor representation at the arbitration hearing.[58] The critical importance of addressing only the precise issue(s) in a dispute cannot be overstated. The arbitrator must avoid *obiter dictum*—remarks irrelevant to the decision—and confine the opinion and award to the case brought to arbitration.[59]

JUST CAUSE

Although both labor and management strive to produce a contract that results in as few disagreements as possible, contractual disputes do arise. Some of these, of course, end up in arbitration after other avenues for resolution have been explored. Historically, certain contractual issues seem to develop an agreed-on solution mechanism that eventually enables both parties to resolve their dispute before arbitration is needed. However, many issues simply cannot be easily resolved with any contractual language and therefore must go to arbitration for final resolution. Table 12-2 lists typical contract issues in arbitration with the Federal Mediation and Conciliation Services'

TABLE 12-2 Arbitration Issues

	2007	Percentage of Cases	2008	Percentage of Cases
Total Number of Issues	**2,172**	**100**	**2,066**	**100**
General Issues	**243**	**11**	**267**	**13**
Seniority	**241**	**11**	**264**	**13**
Promotion and upgrading	20		26	
Layoff bumping and recall	32		36	
Other seniority	21		46	
Working conditions	16		15	
Discrimination	13		14	
Management rights	82		77	
Scheduling of work	45		39	
Work assignments	12		11	
Economic Wage Rates and Pay Issues	**157**	**7**	**146**	**7**
Wage issues	155		145	
Overtime pay	2		1	

TABLE 12-2 *(Continued)*

Fringe Benefits Issues	**76**	**4**	**63**	**3**
Health and welfare	25		24	
Pensions	11		6	
Other fringe issues	40		33	
Discharge and Disciplinary Issues	**728**	**34**	**762**	**37**
Technical Job Issues	**54**	**2**	**28**	**1**
Job posting and bidding	38		18	
Job evaluation	11		9	
Job classification	5		1	
Scope of Agreement	**31**	**1**	**31**	**2**
Subcontracting	24		27	
Jurisdictional disputes	7		4	
Arbitrability of Grievances	**275**	**13**	**228**	**11**
All Other	**367**	**17**	**277**	**13**

Source: Federal Mediation and Conciliation Service, *Sixty-First Annual Report* (Washington, DC: Author, 2009), pp. 9–10. Available at http://www.fmcs.gov. Accessed September 5, 2010.

Office of Arbitration Services. The most common issue was discipline and discharge—which often focuses on **just cause**, a critical although vague concept in labor relations.

JUST CAUSE
Sufficient or proper reasons for which management has the right to discipline or discharge employees.

Most collective bargaining agreements provide that management has the right to discipline or discharge employees for just cause. Arbitrator Clarence R. Deitsch noted the importance of just cause provisions in agreements: "Protection from arbitrary and capricious discipline has remained the rock-solid foundation upon which all other negotiated benefits have been based."[60] Thus, he reasoned, bargaining unit members' negotiated wages, benefits, and working conditions are at risk unless the labor contract contains a provision requiring that employees can only lose them for a good, proper, or just cause—or simply a good reason. In addition, Deitsch has judged cases in recent years in which employers have pressed for an "end run" around just cause clauses by arguing that an employee under a seniority clause should not only lose seniority but employment as well. This most commonly occurs when an employee "walks away" from the job or is absent without notification for three consecutive working days.[61]

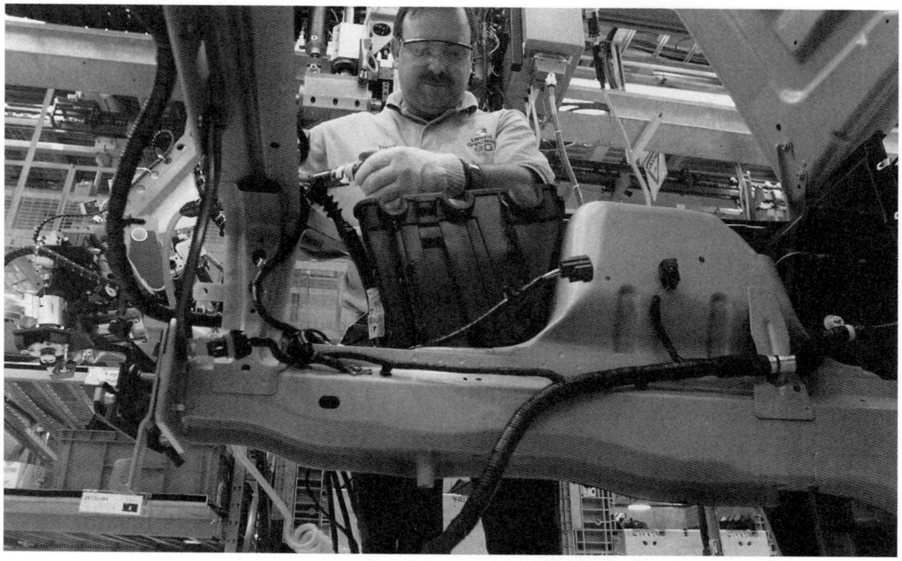

The equal treatment of all employees who may violate a work rule is a critical factor in determining "just cause" for employee discipline. For example, all employees who do not wear required safety goggles on the job should receive the same discipline. *Source:* Al Goldis /AP Images.

CASE 12-2

Just Cause at Ball-Icon

A 20-year maintenance electrician employed by Ball-Icon Glass Packaging Corporation was discharged after he physically attacked his supervisor, who allegedly had pushed the employee and slapped his face while giving him a new work assignment. Several coworkers prevented the employee from attempting to throw the supervisor over a catwalk railing (the employee and supervisor were on a catwalk approximately 30 feet from floor level).

During arbitration, the supervisor alleged that the electrician previously had threatened to beat him up and also had threatened to kill him. The current plant manager testified that there were morale problems between the supervisor and his employees. The former plant manager testified that the electrician had complained about his supervisor several times and on one occasion had said, "If things don't change, somebody is going to get hurt."

The company contended that the discharge should be upheld because the electrician assaulted his supervisor, who could have been seriously injured or killed. "No employee has the right to physically assault his supervisor with the intent to do serious bodily harm or cause death to him," the company argued.

The union's position was that the electrician was provoked. The supervisor had systematically harassed the electrician over the past four years, the union contended, and the company's inability to control the situation after it was brought to management's attention several times "puts the responsibility squarely on the company's shoulders."

Decision

Arbitrator Marlin Volz ruled that, although fighting with a supervisor is a serious disciplinary offense, the manner in which the supervisor assigned the work to the electrician had triggered the offense. Arbitrator Volz noted several factors in the employee's favor: an exceptionally good work record for 20 years, no prior disciplinary offenses, three consecutive years of perfect attendance, and no record of difficulties getting along with other supervisors.

Volz ruled that Ball-Icon did not have sufficient just cause to discharge the electrician and restored the electrician to his job with back pay.

Source: Adapted from *Ball-Icon Glass Packaging Corporation,* 98 LA 1.

Although most labor and management negotiators can agree on the general concept, specifying exactly what constitutes just cause appears impossible. Some contracts specify the exact grounds that constitute just cause and usually include other less specific provisions that are open to dispute. The inability to specify exactly which employee offenses constitute just cause is a major reason why employee discipline and discharge procedures continue to be one of the most frequently arbitrated contractual issues.[62] The overwhelming majority of discipline cases also involve disagreement over the concept of just cause. Case 12-2 presents an unusual set of circumstances leading to an employee discharge later found to be unjust.

An example of the just cause provisions appears in the agreement between the National Conference of Brewery and Soft Drink Workers and Teamsters Local No. 745 and the Jos. Schlitz Brewing Company, Longview, Texas:

> **ARTICLE V**
>
> **Section 1**
>
> The right of the company to discharge, suspend, or otherwise discipline in a fair and impartial manner for just and sufficient cause is hereby acknowledged. Whenever employees are

discharged, suspended, or otherwise disciplined, the union and the employees shall promptly be notified in writing of such discharge, suspension, or other disciplinary action and the reason therefore. No discipline, written notice of which has not been given to the union and the employee, nor any discipline which has been given more than twelve months prior to the current act, shall be considered by the company in any subsequent discharge, suspension, or other disciplinary action.

Section 2

If the union is dissatisfied with the discharge, suspension, or other disciplinary action, the questions as to whether the employee was properly discharged, suspended, or otherwise disciplined shall, upon request of the union, be reviewed in accordance with the grievance procedure set forth.

Seven Tests of Just Cause for Discipline

In employee discipline and discharge cases arbitrators commonly apply the **just cause** standard in deciding the case. While the particular facts and circumstances of each case are important for the arbitrator to determine if management acted fairly, many arbitrators apply the "seven tests of just cause for discipline" developed by arbitrator Adolph M. Koven in deciding a case:

1. ***Adequate warning.*** Is the employee given adequate, oral or printed, warning as to the consequences of his conduct? Employees should be warned by the employer as to punishments either in the contract, handbook, or other means in disciplinary cases. Certain conducts such as insubordination, drunkenness, or stealing are considered so serious that employees are expected to know they will be punishable. Was the rule reasonably related to efficient and safe operation of the organization?
2. ***Prior investigation.*** Did management investigate the case before administering the discipline? Thorough investigation should have normally been made before the decision to discipline. When immediate action is required, the employee should be suspended pending investigation with the understanding that he or she will be returned to the job and paid for time lost if found not guilty.
3. ***Evidence.*** Did the investigation produce substantial evidence or proof of guilt? It is not required that evidence be conclusive or beyond reasonable doubt, except when the misconduct is of such a criminal nature that it seriously impairs the chances for future employment of the person accused of wrongdoing.
4. ***Equal treatment.*** Were all employees judged by the same standards, with rules applied equally? If past enforcement was lax, management should not suddenly begin to crack down without a new warning. The same penalty, however, may not be always given because it may be a second offense, or other factors may logically suggest a different punishment.
5. ***Reasonable penalty.*** Was the penalty reasonably related to the seriousness of the offense and the past record of the employee? The level of the offense should be related to the level of the penalty, and the employee's past record should be taken under consideration.
6. ***Rule of reason.*** Was the rule or order reasonably related to efficient and safe operations? Even in the absence of specific provisions, a collective bargaining agreement protects employees against unjust discipline. Employees may reasonably challenge any company procedure that threatens to deprive employees of their negotiated rights.
7. ***Internal consistency.*** Was management enforcement of the rule or procedure consistent? The company should not selectively enforce codes of conduct against certain employees. Enforcement should be fair and objective. An arbitrator carefully reviews the past practice of management in similar cases.[63]

The more common remedies used by arbitrators in overturning management actions in discipline and discharge cases often include a **make whole remedy** such as reinstatement with back pay, without back pay, or with partial back pay, with other rights and privileges remaining unimpaired; commuting the discharge to suspension for a specified period of time or further reducing the penalty to only a reprimand or a warning; and reversing management's assessment of suspension because the arbitrator believes the penalty is too severe. Back pay is usually ordered consistent with the elimination of suspension.[64] Most arbitrators apply accepted common law with contracts not specifying just cause, which usually means that management action is subjected to tests of prior standards and procedural requirements. If the action meets both criteria, it will generally be found to be a valid prerogative of management.[65]

Case 12-3 describes a situation in which an employee was discharged because his absences placed him in the "worst 2 percent" of all employees and the arbitrator decided to reinstate the employee with back pay.

CASE 12-3

Absenteeism at Weber Aircraft

Weber Aircraft's labor agreement contains a no-fault attendance policy that specifies that after 80 hours of absences, an employee is subject to discharge. Vacation time, approved medical leaves, special situation absences, or holidays are not counted against the employee. On February 26, 1992, grievant A received a written notice that his 1990 and 1991 absences placed him "in the worst 2 percent of all employees in the entire plant with respect to attendance and that a failure to maintain an acceptable attendance may result in discharge without any additional warnings." The labor agreement also specifies that an employee is to be notified when 64 of the allowed 80 hours of absences are used.

Beginning in 1990, grievant A experienced heart problems and high blood pressure, which occasioned considerable absence from work during 1990 and 1991 while on approved medical leave. After these absences, grievant A received the February 26, 1992, warning letter. On March 31, 1992, grievant A was granted a medical leave of absence relating to a cyst problem. Grievant A had a cyst removed from his leg and originally believed that this procedure would not result in any loss of work. However, the stitches broke open, and A had to seek and obtain medical leave again. Grievant A's hour bank was not charged for the approved medical leave relating to the cyst problem. Beginning in June 1992, Grievant A experienced considerable discomfort and symptoms (blood in his urine) related to a prostate condition. He continued to work with this discomfort until he left work at approximately 10:30 A.M. on June 15, 1992, to visit a doctor. A's shift began at 7 A.M., and he had obtained approval from his supervisor to leave work. His doctor advised him to take off work until June 22, 1992. On the morning of June 16, 1992, A's wife (also a company employee) took a slip signed by A's doctor to the plant nurse, who advised that A should apply for medical leave. The nurse advised A's wife that he probably would not be granted a second medical leave but the company would charge vacation time for the medical leave and A would not be charged for an absence. On June 17, 1992, A received a telephone call from his supervisor advising that his medical leave had not been approved, his allowable absence hours were exhausted, and he was discharged. The company argued that it could not operate efficiently without the assurance that employees, within reason, will report to work. Numerous arbitral decisions were cited by the company in which an employer has the general right to discharge an employee for chronic excessive absenteeism.

Decision

Arbitrator Daniel Jennings ruled that the employer was not justified in discharging A because his work record reflected "genuine hard luck and real illnesses" rather than

Tips from the Experts

Arbitrator

What are the three most common violations by employers of the "just cause" provision of a collective bargaining agreement?

1. Assuming that the company's rule-making authority abolished the contractual obligation to observe just cause in imposing discipline. It does not necessarily follow that because a unilaterally promulgated rule is reasonable on its face and uniformly applied that all the just cause requirements have been met and the penalty is automatically justified.
2. Failing to observe an employee's Weingarten rights. Whenever an employee is summoned to an interview with management that he or she reasonably believes is likely to result in discipline, he or she is entitled to union representation if a request is made.
3. Failing to afford the employee procedural due process. This action would include such elements as giving adequate notice of a rule, conducting an adequate and thorough investigation before imposing discipline, and imposing discipline for the purpose of correcting conduct and not punishing.

What are the three most common errors unions make in challenging a "just cause" discharge?

1. Failing to screen the facts and circumstances or to assess properly the company's case. Before deciding to proceed with the grievance, the union needs to be thorough in its investigation and assess the possibility of losing or setting a harmful precedent.
2. Failing to offer successful post-discharge evidence of rehabilitation. In cases involving discharge for drug and alcohol use, a union can demonstrate to the arbitrator the rehabilitation of the employee discharged.
3. Relying on uncorroborated hearsay evidence or bad precedents. A union should carefully screen its evidence for corroboration and its precedents when citing prior arbitration awards to make sure they support the union's position.

frequently recurring illnesses that would indicate a sickly state that might be permanent. Arbitrator Jennings noted (1) that A's problems (high blood pressure, cyst, and prostate problems) were not permanent and that no evidence was introduced to suggest the grievant suffered from an illness that would prevent him from returning to work on a regular basis; (2) that although the company had warned A on February 26, 1992, it had failed to discipline him for subsequent illnesses or to warn him that his employment was in jeopardy; in fact, the company had granted a medical leave for the period March 25, 1992, through April 6, 1992; (3) that the company had failed to notify A that he had expended 48 hours of his allowable 80 absence hours; and (4) that the company had failed to honor its agent, the plant nurse, who had given assurances that A's absences since June 15, 1992, would not be counted against him.

The award of arbitrator Jennings was to uphold A's grievance; A was reinstated and received back pay.

Source: Adapted from *Weber Aircraft,* 100 LA 417.

ARBITRATION ISSUES IN THE PUBLIC SECTOR

Interest Arbitration

In the public sector, interest arbitration is often compulsory, that is, required by law, which echoes the rationale of preventing strikes that harm the public interest. At least 20 states and the federal government deny government employees the right to strike and instead require interest arbitration. These compulsory arbitration laws are especially prevalent among occupations deemed essential, such as police officers, firefighters, and prison guards. Legislation that allows public sector collective bargaining but prohibits strikes often details the procedures available to resolve an impasse. Mediation is provided in almost all states with collective bargaining in the public sector. As with the private sector, the mediator has no independent

In the public sector, workers essential to serve the public often are denied the right to strike, by law, and therefore the laws also require the use of interest arbitration to settle contract negotiations that go to impasse. *Source:* Glynnis Jones/ ShutterStock.

authority but uses acquired skills to bring the parties back together. It has been suggested that the mediator represent the public's interest at the bargaining table. Such a role does not facilitate resolution of a dispute.

Fact-finding and advisory arbitration can be far more successful in the public sector than the private sector because of political pressures. Under fact-finding and advisory arbitration, an unbiased third party examines the collective bargaining impasse and issues findings and recommendations. The findings may move the process by simply eliminating the distrust a party feels for the other party's facts or figures. Reasonable recommendations may also pressure a party to accept an offer that otherwise would not have been considered.

Interest arbitration allows a panel to make a *final and binding decision* on a negotiation dispute and has been used in the public sector to resolve impasses. However, the legality of allowing a third party to set the terms of the contract has been questioned in light of the sovereignty doctrine discussed in Chapter 3.[66] The use of a compulsory mechanism such as final and binding interest arbitration seems incompatible with collective bargaining. A fundamental tenet of American industrial relations is that the bargaining outcome be determined by the parties to the greatest extent possible. Interest arbitration violates that tenet by substituting a third party's decision for that of the negotiating parties. Interest arbitration can become a substitute for the arduous demands of bargaining and can discourage the concessions so necessary to negotiations.[67] Furthermore, a third party's decision removes the inherent authority of public officials to determine policies, in this case, concerning public employment issues.

Rights Arbitration

Rights arbitration in the public sector is treated much like the private sector as shown in Case 12-4. As in Case 12-4, the authority of the arbitrator in rights arbitration is limited by the terms and conditions of the collective bargaining agreement. If a public agency agrees to arbitrate employment decisions using the "just cause" standard, then the arbitrator generally has the authority to reinstate a public employee if that standard is violated. However, courts have overturned an arbitrator's decision to reinstate an employee because the arbitrator felt the discipline was too severe stating, "If an arbitrator finds that one of the enumerated grounds for dismissal has been proved, the arbitrator may not substitute his judgment of what the penalty should be for that of the school district."[68]

CASE 12-4

Public Safety and Random Drug Tests

Oklahoma City, Oklahoma ("City"), in its collective bargaining agreement ("CBA") with the American Federation of State, County and Municipal Employees ("Union"), required employees with Commercial Driver's Licenses (CDLs) to submit to random drug testing pursuant to Federal Statutes and the U.S. Department of Transportation rules for public employers. Employees who test positive for drugs or alcohol are subject to "suspension, demotion, or termination . . . determined based on the employee's total work record, including but not limited to, any prior drug or alcohol problems." The CBA's Drug Policy also included an Employee Assistance Program to which employees could be required to participate in as a condition of continued employment.

The Grievant had been employed by the City for 19 years and had an excellent work record. As a driver in the Street and Drainage Maintenance Division of the Public Works Department, he was required to have a CDL and to submit to random drug tests. In May 2001, he was selected for a random test, for the fourth time in one and a half years, and tested positive for marijuana. Following a predetermination hearing in which the grievant offered no defense to the results of the test, the City discharged the Grievant. The Union appealed the City's action, and an arbitration hearing was held.

The City contended that the grievant was required to have a CDL, the random drug-testing policy for CDL drivers was valid, and the grievant tested positive for marijuana use. The grievant did not challenge the test at the time or avail himself of his right to have the sample tested by a different lab. The City defended its decision to dismiss the grievant as an appropriate act because it cannot tolerate the abuse of controlled substances that represents a threat to public safety and its "accountability to its citizens." The City contended that its decision in this case to dismiss the grievant rather than impose a lesser discipline was after due consideration of the grievant's "total work record." The relevant "work record" for the City to consider, according to the testimony of the city officials, was whether the offending employee was or was not required to have a CDL. In other words, nothing in the grievant's 19 years of service was relevant to the City's determination other than the CDL requirement. The City maintained that since 1998 there was a City rule that employees with CDLs who test positive for drug use be dismissed. Therefore, the grievant was not treated differently than other employees. Finally, the City argued that unless the City has violated a specific provision of the CBA or abused its discretion, the Arbitrator should not substitute his decision for the City's as to the proper discipline for a public employee for failing a drug test.

The Union contended that the City's random drug-testing procedures were suspect because the grievant was one of 500 employees subject to testing, and yet he was tested four times in one and a half years. More importantly, the drug test did not indicate that the grievant was impaired or under the influence of drugs while at work. The Union further contended that the discharge did not meet the "just cause" test because the City failed to follow progressive discipline and treated the grievant differently from other City employees. The Union presented the Arbitrator with proof that of the 48 City employees with CDLs who had tested positively for drugs in the preceding three years, 13 were demoted to nondriving positions and not discharged. Finally, the Union argued that the City violated the CBA because it did not consider the Grievant's "total work record" of 19 years of exemplary performance but only considered the fact that the grievant was required to have a CDL for his position.

The City countered that its decision to demote other employees for the same offense was irrelevant in that some of the demotions were necessary because the procedures followed in those cases were flawed and would not have withstood a challenge by the offending employees. The

City noted that even if it had decided that demotion was proper in this case, there was no funded nondriver position available for the grievant.

Decision

Arbitrator Dr. Daniel F. Jennings declined to take a position on the issues raised by the Union as to the validity of the actual drug test taken by the grievant as there was insufficient evidence presented at the hearing on the test. The Arbitrator did find that there was sufficient evidence to determine that the City *has not always discharged* employees with CDLs who test positive for drugs or alcohol; although there was insufficient evidence to determine whether there was disparate treatment in this case because the circumstances of the other incidents were not presented at the hearing.

The Arbitrator then considered whether the City had "just cause" to impose the severest penalty available to it and addressed the City's contention that the Arbitrator should not substitute his judgment for that of the City in deciding the appropriate punishment. The Arbitrator relied on other arbitration opinions by other arbitrators as justification for overturning the disciplining of an employee. One arbitrator ruled: "Taking the supreme penalty against an employee without due consideration for a long unblemished record goes to the very heart of 'just cause.' " While another held, "[M]ost arbitrators exercise the right to change or modify a penalty if it is found to be improper or too severe, . . . This right is deemed to be inherent in the arbitrator's power to discipline and in his authority to finally settle and adjust the dispute before him."

Arbitrator Jennings found that the grievant had an excellent work record for 19 years, and the City, in imposing the discipline, should have considered it. Therefore, he held that the City lacked "just cause" to terminate the grievant and ordered that he be reinstated in a nondriving position at the same pay as an Equipment Operator I, even if such a position had to be created for him. He also awarded the grievant back pay, less a two-month suspension, which the Arbitrator deemed the appropriate penalty for the grievant in this case.

Source: City of Oklahoma City, 116 LA 1117.

Summary

The arbitration process has been developed and refined over many years. The selection of an arbitrator or board of arbitrators is generally specified in the labor agreement. The hearing procedure, however, which is not bound by legal precedent, is quite flexible and subject to the arbitrator's discretion. The courts have generally left the questions of arbitrability and case decisions to arbitrators.

A great variety of important and complex issues are referred to arbitration. The issue of just cause for employee discipline or discharge is difficult to define within the contract and in most cases involves emotional situations. Drug testing for substance abuse presents unique problems for an arbitrator to resolve. Seniority and absenteeism are deceptively simple yet important contractual issues. Disagreements over incompetence, holiday pay, and management rights are also common arbitration subjects.

In recent years the number of nonunion employees covered by employment arbitration agreements has rapidly increased until the number has exceeded the number of employees who have the right to arbitration under collective bargaining agreements. Thus, the use of arbitration and not litigation to settle employment disputes has become commonplace in the nonunion sector, as it has been in the unionized sector for decades.

CASE STUDIES

Case Study 12-1 Drug and Alcohol Testing

The company is an insulation subcontractor that performs maintenance work for duPont. For several decades, the company had a collective bargaining agreement with a union that included employees who were sent to a duPont plant for maintenance work. The contract in effect between the company and the union had no reference to a drug-testing or substance abuse program. Before 1986, the company had never required its employees to submit to drug testing. In 1986, however, the company received a letter from duPont stating that duPont was developing a substance abuse policy and requiring its subcontractors to develop a similar policy to include testing procedures.

The company instituted a drug program similar to duPont's and sent it to the union for its information. The company notified the union that it was willing to meet to discuss the plan. At the meeting, the union met not only with its company but also with representatives from duPont concerning the drug program. The written policy stated that "the use, possession of, being under influence of, or the presence in the person's system of prohibitive drugs and unauthorized alcoholic beverages is prohibited on any company work location." Under the policy, all new employees of the company were required to sign consent forms for testing as a condition of employment. The company implemented the drug-testing policy but only as it related to the duPont plant. The union instructed its members to sign the forms consenting to drug testing with the statement that they were signing under duress.

The grievant in this case was referred to the duPont plant by the company for its maintenance work in April 1987. The employee, along with four other fellow employees, submitted to a urine test. The grievant's test was sent to the screening facility, and the initial test resulted in a positive finding of marijuana. The chain of custody for the test was not established, and the level of marijuana found in the test was extremely low. Nonetheless, the grievant was dismissed. The position of the company was that duPont made it mandatory for subcontractors to adopt minimum requirements for drug testing and that such minimum requirements for new employees were not unreasonable. The company further contended that, although it did not agree to negotiate with the union, the company gave the union ample time to study the program's policy.

The union believed that the company's policy was really duPont's policy and was adopted despite the union's disapproval solely because duPont had insisted on it. The union contended that the company made no effort to assure the union that the policy or the enforcement of the policy was reasonable, fair, or accurate. The cutoff level for a positive test result was unreasonable because it did not indicate either on-the-job impairment or consistent use of marijuana. The company did not examine the grievant's prior work record or the fact that there was no prior history or evidence of drug impairment on the job. In fact, the company could not even prove that the specimen tested was the grievant's. The union further contended that even if the results of the test proved the employee was using marijuana, on the basis of her past work history, she should be given an opportunity to correct her conduct and be treated in a fair and consistent way. Discharge was clearly not appropriate.

Source: Adapted from *Young Insulation Group,* 90 LA 341.

QUESTIONS

1. Did the company have a legitimate business reason for instituting a drug-testing program during the term of a contract?
2. Did the company conduct the drug-testing program properly?
3. As the arbitrator, would you reverse or uphold the dismissal of the grievant? Explain your answer.

(Continued)

Case Study 12-2 Arbitrability

In September 1981, the union grieved the company's announced intention to lay off 79 employees from its Chicago location. The union contended there was no lack of work at that site, and under the contract the company can lay off from the site only when there is a lack of work. Despite the grievance, the company laid off the employees and transferred approximately 80 employees from other locations to the Chicago location.

The union demanded that the dispute be arbitrated, and the company refused. The company claimed that the "management functions" clause of the contract gives it the prerogative to determine "lack of work" and that as long as it lays off in the order prescribed by the contract, there is nothing to arbitrate. The union contended that certain provisions of the contract modified the "management functions" clause and requested the court to order arbitration.

The lower court found there were arguable issues to arbitrate and ordered the parties to arbitrate the arbitrability issue; in other words, an arbitrator would decide whether she had jurisdiction under the contract of the issue in dispute.

Before this could happen, the company appealed the lower court's ruling. The company argued that the lower court erred in not simply deciding whether the dispute was subject to arbitration. It contended that under the *Steelworkers Trilogy* cases, the courts, not the arbitrator, must decide whether the issue is subject to arbitration. The company proposed the following points:

1. Arbitration is a matter of contract, and parties cannot be forced to submit issues to arbitration that they have not agreed to submit.
2. Unless the contract clearly provides otherwise, arbitrability is a judicial determination.
3. In deciding arbitrability, the court is not to decide on the merits of the claim.
4. Where the contract has an arbitration clause, the presumption is for arbitrability.

The lower court pointed out, however, that the exception to the rule is found when deciding the arbitrability of the case would also involve the court in interpreting the substantive provisions of the labor agreement.

The union's position was that the layoffs were subject to arbitration, and they pointed to sections of the labor agreement to prove this. The "management functions" clause, the "adjustment to the working force" clause, and the "arbitration" clause must be read together and interpreted. The court could not decide arbitrability in this case without interpreting these sections and therefore deciding the substantive issue. It is for an arbitrator to decide the substantive issues.

Source: Adapted from *Communication Workers of America v. Western Electric,* 751 F.2d 203.

QUESTIONS

1. Should the court decide whether there is an issue to arbitrate, or should an arbitrator? Why?
2. Give the reasons you think arbitration is a superior resolution process to court action in contract disputes.
3. Give the reasons you think a court action is a superior resolution process to arbitration in contract disputes.

Key Terms and Concepts

arbitrability *447*
arbitration *431*
arbitrator's award *444*
arbitrator's opinion *451*
common law of the shop *438*
double jeopardy *448*
interest arbitration *431*
just cause *453*
Lincoln mills case *435*
make whole remedy *456*
parol evidence *438*
past practice *438*
rights arbitration *434*
rules of evidence *449*
Steelworkers Trilogy 436
tripartite arbitration board *446*
Warrior & Gulf case *447*

Review Questions

1. Describe how the legal foundation for arbitration as it exists today in the United States was developed.
2. Discuss the five principles that govern the arbitration of grievances under collective bargaining.
3. Explain how the change in ownership of a company affects the duty to arbitrate.
4. What is the process normally used in the selection of an arbitrator? How does the selected arbitrator interpret ambiguous contract provisions?
5. How is binding arbitration superior to the courts in settling labor disputes? How does it differ from mediation and conciliation?
6. What information can be presented as evidence during arbitration proceedings? What are the usual hearing procedures?
7. Can a party harm its own case during arbitration proceedings? If it can, explain how.
8. How does an arbitrator determine that a company had just cause for taking a disciplinary action? What remedy might an arbitrator choose if a company did not have just cause?
9. What are the advantages and disadvantages of using arbitration to settle nonlabor issues such as consumer complaints, employee–employer disputes, and so on?
10. Discuss the issues an arbitrator might use in deciding a discharge case involving drug abuse.

YOU BE THE ARBITRATOR

Can a "Just Cause" Standard Be Satisfied without Proving Fault?

CBA ARTICLE XXIII DISCIPLINE

A. The employer may establish and publish reasonable rules and regulations governing the conduct of employees, as are necessary for the proper operation of the facilities and the proper care of residents.

1. Any discipline imposed for infractions of these rules and regulations will be corrective and progressive in nature with the objective of helping the employee improve. . . .

D. Should it be determined by the Home, or by the arbitrator appointed in accordance with the arbitration procedure, that the employee has been suspended or discharged unjustly, the Home shall reinstate the employee and pay full compensation at the regular rate of pay for the time lost.

Facts

The employer is a nursing home in the state of Minnesota. The state of Minnesota has implemented a policy for the return of unused Schedule III medications from nursing homes to pharmacies, a protocol to ensure the integrity of the drug being returned. When drugs for one reason or another are left over at the end of a one-week cycle at the employer's nursing home, they are returned to the dispensing pharmacies in accordance with that protocol.

During the Thursday to Friday night shift, the four drug carts, one from each wing of the nursing home, are collected by the charge nurse and (at least until recently, with the assistance of a Trained Medication Aide) the drug trays are then sorted and the amounts being returned recorded and then placed in large blue canvas transfer bags for return to the dispensing pharmacies. Prior to their return to the pharmacies, the bags are stored in the 400-wing "med room." The room contains a locked drug cabinet for storing Schedule II medications and also has a lock on the door to the room. The nursing home stores the unlocked bags for pickup in the locked med room.

It came to the attention of the employer that there was a discrepancy in the records concerning how much medication had been returned to the pharmacies from one of the grievant's shifts. The grievant was a charge nurse on the graveyard shift. An investigation was initiated. Witnesses were questioned regarding access to keys to the meds room. Testimony indicated that the investigation concluded that each Licensed Professional Nurse charge nurse had a key, as did the four LPNs on the day shift and the Registered Nurses and DK, the nurse secretary; there was no inventory of the total number of keys, nor was there any sort of "sign-in/sign-out" system for the keys. No other conclusion regarding the missing medication was reached. The grievant received a letter from her employer indicating that she was being terminated "due to discrepancy in the amount of medication returned to the pharmacies after the exchange done on the nights you were charge nurse. Records indicate that the number of individual pills documented for return is less than the amount received by the pharmacy." The grievant appealed her termination.

Issue

Can the "just cause" standard, which governs discipline and discharge of employees in the bargaining unit, be satisfied without proving fault on the part of the grievant?

Position of the Parties

The employer contended it had just cause to dismiss the grievant. It did not contend that the grievant took the missing medications or knows who did. Rather, it contends that as charge nurse she had the responsibility to correctly account for and return unused medications, and her failure to do so or to supervise others to do so properly put the nursing home's license at risk. The employer pointed to the grievant's job description, which requires her to be licensed and to function under the standards of the nursing profession and in compliance with all the nursing home's rules and regulations. The employer held the grievant to a "strict liability" theory; that is, if there were discrepancies in the tallies, no matter what the explanation might be for such discrepancies, the grievant was responsible.

The union's position was that the employer did not have just cause to discharge the grievant. Although the grievant acknowledged that as the nurse in charge of the building at night she had a duty to try to explain any discrepancies in the drug tallies, she testified that it had not been her understanding that her failure to be able to explain the discrepancies was grounds for termination. The discrepancies in the drug count could have been caused by any number of things not under the control of the grievant. There is no meaningful difference between "for cause," "just cause," "discharged unjustly," and similar such phrases. "Just cause" references and provisions have evolved in the workplace and in arbitration decisions over time to the point of having certain characteristics and requirements in common, which are generally applicable to all grievance disputes. As a general proposition, expressions in contracts referring to "just cause" exclude discipline and discharge for mere whim or caprice. They are, obviously, intended to include those things for which employees have traditionally been fired. The employer in this case has disciplined the grievant for something that occurred—discrepancy in drug count—without proving that the grievant did anything wrong. The grievant should be returned to her position.

QUESTIONS

1. As arbitrator, what would be your award and opinion in this arbitration?
2. Identify the key, relevant section(s), phrases, or words of the collective bargaining agreement (CBA), and explain why they were critical in making your decision.
3. What actions might the employer or the union have taken to avoid this conflict?

Source: Adapted from *Lutheran Care Center*, 116 La 1795 (Arb. 2002).

CHAPTER 13

Comparative Global Industrial Relations

In China a wave of worker strikes and unrest was highlighted by a May 17, 2010, strike. It took place at Honda's China factories when hundreds of workers walked off their jobs and Honda was forced to close four assembly plants. The strikes were led by a new generation of Chinese workers who demand higher wages and benefits. *Source:* AP Images.

Chapter Outline

Only free men can negotiate, prisoners cannot enter into contracts. Your freedom and mine cannot be separated.

NELSON MANDELA (PRESIDENT OF SOUTH AFRICA AND CIVIL RIGHTS LEADER)

LABOR NEWS

China Labor Unrest at Honda Plants

A new labor movement in China is led by a new generation of young, educated workers who know their rights and are demanding higher wages and better working conditions. The movement is aided by 787 million mobile-phone users and 348 million Internet users who use technology to organize and to learn their rights under a new 2008 national law that guarantees safer working conditions and double pay for overtime. In the past authorities quickly fired labor leaders to settle labor issues, but a very tight labor market and a new generation of workers less tolerant of such actions have changed the labor climate. Instead, according to Harley Seyedin, president of the American Chamber of Commerce in China, "The days of cheap labor are gone!"

On May 17, 2010, the labor unrest in China surfaced when young, mostly women, workers demonstrated and struck several Honda facilities in China. The unrest was triggered by one woman at the Zhongshan plant who was denied entry by a security guard because she wore her identity badge improperly on her shirt. When she complained the guard pushed her to the ground and other employees began demonstrating, which led to a general strike of the 1,700 workers. Management told workers they would forgive them if they returned to work and signed a "no strike" promise. Management also tried hiring replacement workers, but the acute labor shortage in China caused that to fail. The strike lasted for eight days as workers demanded the following:

- Wage increases of 89 percent—to equal the male-dominated Foshan plant
- The right to form their own union, independent of the national union which is forbidden in China
- Changes in policies that do not allow workers to talk while on the job and require them to ask for passes to go to the bathroom.

Because Honda has a "zero inventory" policy, the strike quickly shut down Honda's other four Chinese factories. The May strike was followed by others in China including one at Atsumitec, a Honda supplier, that resulted in a 45 percent wage increase for workers plus performance bonuses, and another in Zhongshan that idled over 1,000 workers.

The Chinese government eventually brought the parties together to settle the issues. Workers were able to democratically elect 16 representatives to collectively bargain for them, and prominent Chinese labor scholar Professor Chang Kai was brought in to facilitate the talks. On June 4, 2010, the shop stewards and management settled an agreement that provided for substantial gains, including increased wages of 35 percent for permanent workers and 70 percent for trainees, a promise of no reprisals for the union leaders, and new work policies.

Shortly after the Honda strikes, workers at Toyota plants in China also went on strike and secured substantial wage increases. Labor scholars believe that the strikes may begin a new wave of worker unrest in China over poor wages and benefits, subminimum wages paid to trainees, excessive overtime, and the lack of independent labor unions.

Source: Adapted from Keith Bradsher, "A Labor Movement Stirs in China," *The New York Times* (June 10, 2010), p. A1; and Dexter Roberts, "A New Labor Movement in China is Born," *Bloomberg Businessweek* (June 14–20, 2010), pp. 7–8.

Business conducted on an international scale is commonplace. Its impact on the labor movement, in this country and around the world, is significant. This chapter discusses how the cycle of globalization in the twenty-first century, unlike previous cycles, has resulted in a complex system of worldwide investment, technology, deregulation, and flexible labor markets. These worldwide labor markets have become both competitors with and companions to the U.S. labor movement. A comprehensive review of international labor relations and collective bargaining theories and practices around the world is beyond the scope of this text. However, it is necessary to have a basic understanding of how labor relations developed in representative nations and of the current state of labor relations and collective bargaining around the world. This chapter focuses primarily on industrial relations in Great Britain, Canada, and Australia; on the European Union—Germany, France, and Italy; and on the Far East nations of Japan and China. The International Labour Organization, a common thread for industrial relations in many nations, is also examined within the context of the worldwide labor movement and globalization.

GLOBALIZATION

Globalization is the pervasive integration of economies and societies around the world as a result of unprecedented changes in communications, transportation, and computer technology.[1] Globalization results in increased competition. For example, the production of automobiles, which for nearly a century was concentrated geographically at a national level, is now done at a global level, with cars that are being assembled from component parts that are produced by suppliers in dozens of countries. The internationalization of production directly affects the collective bargaining environment. With companies easily able to operate in the international arena, not only the actual transfer of an enterprise from one country to another adversely affects unionized employees, but the mere threat of doing so can also significantly change power relations at the bargaining table. In addition, workers bargaining at a national level may find that they have inadequate access to information about the international financial position and corporate plans of their employer or that the employer's representative has no real decision-making power. In such circumstances, the real content and meaning of collective bargaining can be seriously reduced. One view is that the effective realization of the right to collective bargaining requires that it too be conducted at the international level.[2] Some unions and multinational corporations are addressing the need for a more global approach to labor relations by entering into international agreements as outlined in Profile 13-1, International Framework Agreements.

GLOBALIZATION

Refers not only to the expansion of international trade in goods and services but also to the degree of interdependence that goes along with the integration of production across national boundaries and the resulting increase in international investment by multinational enterprises.

The term *globalization* means many things to many people. For the purposes of this text, it refers not only to the expansion of international trade in goods and services but also to the degree of interdependence that goes along with the integration of production across national boundaries and the resulting increase in international investment by multinational enterprises.[3] In this section, we examine the components of globalization that have impacted the employer–employee relationship. These components include foreign investments, multinational enterprises, the import and export of goods and services, deregulation, and the technological revolution.

Foreign Direct Investment

International economic interdependence has been driven over the past 30 years by a dramatic growth of ***foreign direct investment*** **(FDI)**. FDI is a category of international investment made by a direct investor (a resident entity in one country) in a direct investment enterprise (an enterprise resident in another country) with the objective of establishing a lasting interest. Until the 1970s, international economic activity was mostly in the form of *exchange* of goods and services between nation-states where products were made in one country and then transported to another. Since that time, companies have moved production to other countries, resulting in a significant increase in the movement of capital in the global economy.

Multinational Enterprises

This trend toward foreign direct investment has a concomitant increase in the role multinational enterprises play in the world economy. Because an important share of the investment and world trade takes place within multinational enterprises, their operation affects labor relations around the world. A company is not a **multinational enterprise** just because it sells exports overseas; it has to have actually moved part of its operations to another country by investing abroad. Lowering economic barriers between nations opens up enormous new possibilities for multinational companies and the growing number of national businesses connected to them. Parent firms

MULTINATIONAL ENTERPRISE

An entity that operates in more than one nation for a significant portion of its business, that may export products, and that may have actually moved part of its operations to another country by investing abroad. Also called transnationals.

Profile 13-1

International Framework Agreements (IFA)

What do Volkswagen, DaimlerChrysler, Renault, and BMW, all global automotive industry giants, have in common with IKEA, the Swedish furniture company? These international companies have joined dozens of others in entering into International Framework Agreements as explained in this article from the International Metalworkers' Federation:

International Framework Agreements (IFAs) are negotiated between a transnational company and the trade unions of its workforce at the global level. It is a global instrument with the purpose of ensuring fundamental workers' rights in all the target company's locations. Thus, IFAs are negotiated on a global level but implemented locally. Generally, an IFA recognizes the ILO Core Labour Standards. In addition, the company should also agree to offer decent wages and working conditions as well as to provide a safe and hygienic working environment. Furthermore, there is an agreement that suppliers must be persuaded to comply and, finally, the IFA includes trade unions in the implementation. Transnational business operations and a global economy raise issues that go beyond the reach of national legislation. Through IFAs, the ILO's Core Labour Standards can be guaranteed in all facilities of a transnational company, which is especially helpful in transitional and developing countries, where legislation is sometimes insufficient, poorly enforced, or antiworker. For transnational companies, IFAs can secure good relations with trade unions and contribute to a positive public image. More and more companies increasingly see the need to respond to the growing ethical concerns of consumers and investors. For trade unions, IFAs are a way to promote workers' rights in the global arena. The arrangement guarantees influence and the possibility of a dialogue that is mutually beneficial. Unlike unilateral Codes of Conduct, IFAs emphasize implementation, which paves the way for actual improvements.

Source: International Metalworkers' Federation, *NewsLetter* (January 7, 2003). Available at www.imfmetal.org. Accessed October 1, 2005. Used with permission.

and foreign affiliates of multinational enterprises (MNEs) now account for 25 percent of global output.[4]Although the main impact of employment is on national/local companies that are subcontractors or otherwise linked to MNEs, total direct employment of foreign employees has been increasing.

Financial Markets

After World War II, a money exchange rate system was put into place to provide a degree of international exchange rate stability. It resulted in the creation of international financial institutions such as the International Monetary Fund (IMF) and the World Bank. The Bretton Woods exchange rate system collapsed in the 1970s, and flexible exchange rates were introduced.[5] Many national controls on the movement of investment capital were removed, followed by deregulation of the financial sector. The result has been significant movement of capital around the world, with increased cross-border lending, and development of new and restructured financial institutions.[6]

Over the years, the International Confederation of Free Trade Unions (ICFTU) has sought to introduce new international regulations of those financial processes to dampen speculation and to reduce the risk of large-scale financial collapse. The ICFTU has suggested reform of the IMF and World Bank, so that their programs promote good governance, respect for human rights and fundamental labor standards, increased employment, poverty reduction, and the provision of public services in key areas.

Deregulation and Liberalization

As a result of global, regional, and bilateral trade and investment negotiations, countries have lowered barriers to trade and investment by liberalizing trade quotas, tariffs, and, as discussed earlier, deregulated national capital controls. This deregulation and liberalization trend is worldwide. Major financial institutions, such as the IMF and the World Bank, encourage and facilitate the introduction of free-market-based economic policies in their programs. A broadening of the global market saw some developing countries, particularly in Asia, receive a great deal of investment and support for their exports. With the collapse of the Soviet bloc, many Eastern European countries increased their participation in and exposure to the global market as well.

Developing countries have also moved toward a market economy, many of them under the pressure of the structural adjustment programs of the IMF or the World Bank. Economic reforms often involve privatization of large state-owned enterprises and a reduction of public services. One of the main driving forces responsible for the increase in global trade has been the creation of a framework of intergovernmental trade agreements at global and regional levels, which are covered later in this chapter.

Trade Unions

All the changes brought about by globalization—the restructuring of production through new technology, the opening of financial and labor markets, and deregulation and the liberalization of national laws regarding trade—have allowed organizations to concentrate on their core business and to outsource nonessential functions previously done by in-house workers. Modifications in work organization, spurred by the search for more flexible and responsive work methods, have resulted in more contract and part-time work. In addition, the labor market has been doubled with the entry of China, India, and the former Soviet countries into the world economy.[7] These factors are affecting traditional employment relations and the exercise of collective bargaining rights. Flexible work patterns make it more difficult to organize workers; subcontracting arrangements have begun to resemble commercial relationships rather than employer–employee relationships.

Globalization has presented significant challenges to workers and their trade unions:

- Government deregulation has challenged nation-centered systems whose national social and economic policies helped create a degree of social justice and economic equity.
- The international institutions lack a framework in place that can deal effectively with issues of justice and equity.
- Capital is much more mobile than workers, so different forms of business organization and relationships have been created that shift employment and threaten collective bargaining relationships.
- MNEs, which can be rootless, introduce new management methods and sometimes threaten to relocate to countries with lower social or environmental standards and no independent trade unions.
- New forms of work organization have been established such as outsourcing, subcontracting, contract labor, and various other forms of nontraditional employment.
- Competitiveness and flexibility are still the main objectives for most enterprises in the global environment, which put workers into increasingly fierce competition for keeping their jobs, exert pressure on social safety nets, and undermine workers' rights.

The challenge facing trade unions in the era of globalization is to ensure that structural change and adaptation are achieved without compromising the goals of full employment and social justice.[8]

WORLDWIDE LABOR MOVEMENT

Industrial Revolution

The **industrial revolution** began in England in the early 1800s and developed there and in the United States in similar fashion. In fact, the industrial revolution's impact on other nations has certain common features regardless of when the industrialization began, although

INDUSTRIAL REVOLUTION

Through invention and innovation, enterprises substituted machinery for human labor and by using new chemical and metallurgical process harnessed new forms of energy to fuel production. This resulted in the emergence of factories with large concentrations of workers in an interdependent production process that required a hierarchy style of management and a clear division of labor.

industrialization was tempered by national experiences and economic influences. The industrial revolution, through invention and innovation, substituted machinery for human labor and by using new chemical and metallurgical process harnessed new forms of energy to fuel production. This resulted in the emergence of factories with large concentrations of workers in an interdependent production process that required a hierarchy style of management and a clear division of labor.[9]

The industrial revolution caused the widespread movement of people from rural to urban areas, as well as immigration from the Old World to the New World as discussed in Chapter 2. In England and in Europe, employment was characterized as a "status" relationship such as tenant farmers and peasants in feudal relationships with landed gentry or apprentices and indentured servants tied to master craftsmen engaged in cottage industries such as weaving or metallurgy. The migration of labor into urban areas to work in mines, mills, and factories changed the labor market from one of "status" between master and servant to one of "contract" between employer and employee. The need for workers, worker mobility, and the increased proportion of people working for wages caused labor to be seen as a commodity, and its purchase and sale became a cost of doing business.[10]

Democratic Revolution

The political revolutions of the late eighteenth century in the United States and in France coincided with the industrial revolution. France's revolution had a dramatic influence in Europe because France shared its feudal tradition with its neighboring nations, and the impact of a new political and social order anchored with the idea of people governing themselves threatened centuries of tradition.

The transformation of the United States into a democracy was easier because it had no feudal past or rigid patterns of class inequality, with the notable exception of slavery. The growth of democratic ideas and political liberalization in France, as well as Germany, Sweden, Italy, the Austro-Hungarian Empire, and Russia through the nineteenth century, coupled with the development of a middle class through industrialization, led to a demand for *industrial democracy*. Workers, who were questioning the continuation of the "divine right of kings" in the political arena, began to question the autocracy and denial of basic human rights in the mills and factories.[11]

Capitalist Revolution

The third revolution of the late nineteenth century was the rise of capitalism and the spread of the market economy. Adam Smith, in *The Wealth of Nations*[12] published in 1776, the same year as the American Declaration of Independence, challenged the mercantile system of economic monopoly by asserting that a market economy would produce national prosperity. Mercantilism is the economic theory that a nation's prosperity depends on the amount of its capital, represented by bullion, and by the volume at which its exports exceed its imports. A mercantile system of economics requires a protectionist role of government in encouraging exports and discouraging imports, generally through the use of tariffs.

According to Smith, however, a nation's prosperity relies on its people as a strategic asset for economic development and a source of prosperity through a more productive use of human capital. Smith believed that a market economy, which is characterized by the principles of free trade, competition, and choice, would spur economic development and reduce poverty. Smith explained that by increasing the division of labor, there would be greater productivity and the development of machinery, as well as the development of new skills and trades among workers.[13] Smith claimed that if given a free hand, an individual would invest a resource, for example, land or labor, to earn the highest possible return on it. Such self-interest, if allowed to flourish, would drive a nation's economy toward prosperity. Smith is credited with creating

capitalism from his market economy philosophy because capitalism is about allowing self-interest, profit making, and market forces to have free play.

CAPITALISM

A market economy characterized by the principles of free trade, competition and choice, and noninterference by government.

The creation of private property (i.e., private ownership of the means of production and their use for personal profit) was a cornerstone of capitalism and the source of a new labor relationship. Employers paid a group of people—employees—to provide labor in the form of work, and a market for "labor" was created. This labor market was the result of the interplay between the employer's demand for labor and the worker's supply of labor. Labor markets could be in geographic areas over which competition for labor took place or within categories of labor such as skilled or unskilled. The wage relation was the negotiation, either formal or informal, over what work labor was willing to perform and what the employer was willing to pay for that work. Wages to the employer represented a cost that affected the enterprise's production cost and profit. Wages to the employees were a source of income and the means for survival. Capitalists wanted to have labor at the lowest possible price, and workers, the suppliers of labor, wanted the highest possible price. This created the basic conflict of interests between capital and labor. However, because without cooperation nothing would be produced and no wages would be earned, capital and labor in a capitalistic economy have an incentive to cooperate.

The need for collective action and the formation of trade unions came about because when the parties are negotiating their wage relation, they are "equals," but once the relationship is established, the employer becomes the "boss." The boss has an interest in regulating how the work is performed to make sure it is efficient and effective. And because the effort expended by labor is to a degree discretionary by the employees, the boss uses various methods and practices to elicit the maximum amount of work from labor, such as providing supervision, granting incentives, or imposing penalties. At the end of the 1800s and in the early 1900s, large numbers of unemployed workers in major industrial nations allowed employers to pay little and treat workers poorly. The outgrowth of this mistreatment in the United Kingdom (U.K.) and Europe, as in the United States, was the rise of collective action, by the creation of trade unions, by the use of worker strikes, and, at times, by violence. Capitalism, although the constant economic theory in U.S. labor relations, competed with other economic theories as the industrial revolution spread. Table 13-1 details such other economic and social theories that influenced the path of other nations' industrial relations.

TABLE 13-1 Economic/Social Movements Influencing Global Industrial Relations

Manchester School	The economic theory that agreed with the noninterference maxim of capitalism but without an emphasis on human capital.
Capitalism	The economic theory that a nation's prosperity relies on a more productive use of human capital and that by increasing the division of labor there would be greater productivity, the development of new machinery and of new skills and trades among workers. A capitalist or market economy is characterized by the principles of free trade, competition, and choice and noninterference by government.
Mercantilism	The economic theory that a nation's prosperity depends on the amount of its capital, represented by bullion, and by the volume at which its exports exceed its imports. A mercantile system of economics requires a protectionist role of government in encouraging exports and discouraging imports, generally through the use of tariffs.
Neoliberalism	Neoliberalism refers to a political and economic philosophy that deemphasizes or rejects government intervention in the economy, focusing instead on achieving progress and even social justice by encouraging free-market methods and fewer restrictions on business operations and economic development.

(continued)

TABLE 13-1 *(Continued)*

Chartism	Chartism was a short-lived political movement in England based on the demand for voting rights and the political representation of the working class in Parliament. It won support from a wide variety of workers and even from lower-middle-class radicals and was regarded a threat to the established order. In 1842, it engineered a general strike against the proposal of the cotton manufactures to cut wages by 25 percent because of the severe trade depression. The government responded with mass arrests of Chartist leaders, who were put on trial for "levying war against the Queen" and exiled.
Syndicalism	The organizers' pre–World War I strikes were inspired by syndicalism, which advocated mass strikes and rapid trade union recruitment as a means to overcome employers' actions.
Fabian Society	The Fabians aimed for democratic socialism. Believing that voters could be persuaded of socialism's justice, they sought to achieve reform by education, stimulating debate through lectures and discussions initiated by democratically accountable and educated professionals. The Fabian Society maintained its independence from the Labour Party, although it helped to create the Labour Representation Committee in 1900. Trade union militancy from 1910 to 1926 and the unemployment climate and depression of the 1930s diminished the attractiveness of Fabian Society, but the seeds for a more political labor movement had been sown.
Progressivism	A broadly based reform movement that reached its height early in the twentieth century. It arose as a response to the vast changes brought by industrialization, the spread of the factory system, and the growth of cities.

Growth of Trade Unions

At their conception, trade unions in the United States, U.K., and Europe were seen as having three roles: (1) their market function was to represent and advance the employment interests of its members through collective bargaining as workplace representatives; (2) their class function was to fight battles for the rights and interests of all workers to increase workers' status and power in the economic and political systems; and (3) their social function was to improve the overall quality of life of workers, promoting greater social justice, better schools, and health care. In the United States, unions made the choice to focus on just representation in the workplace, whereas in the U.K. and Europe, they tended to embrace all three to some degree, making the history and direction of the industrial relations in Europe all the more complex.

Most governments have displayed one or more of three distinct attitudes in reaction to unionization of workers: suppression, tolerance, and encouragement.[14] Early in the development of their industrial economy, most countries worked to *suppress* unions and the notion of collective bargaining. In Great Britain at the beginning of the industrial revolution, the Combination Acts, passed in 1799 and 1800, made a union of employees illegal as a conspiracy to restrain trade. In France, a 1791 law that forbade employee combinations—ostensibly to prevent any organization from coming between the government and the workers—was actually used to suppress unions. In the late nineteenth and early twentieth centuries, when industrialization reached Germany, Russia, and Japan, these nations passed laws suppressing or banning unions. Some developing countries just emerging into the industrial world have not directly banned unions but have attempted to suppress collective bargaining. The governments of Ghana, Nigeria, and Singapore, for example, supported unions legislatively but limited their authority.

Great Britain and the United States, however, from as early as the 1830s, began to *tolerate* unions, primarily because unions continued to function despite antiunion attitudes. The ability or desire to keep workers from organizing lost support as these countries experienced economic growth. As representatives of the working masses, unions became powerful political forces that could not be ignored.[15] In addition, both nations had budding middle classes that had embraced progressive moral and political agendas, some from a desire to avoid labor unrest that would threaten their newly found prosperity.

Industrial nations fighting World War I, and subsequently World War II, found it necessary to marshal capital and labor for the war effort. Governments found that what "capital" wanted in exchange was money and what labor wanted was collective bargaining. Largely as a result of this need, through law or policy, the United States and Britain mandated collective bargaining, although other countries continued to resist it. As a nation's economy fluctuates, its attitude toward unions and collective bargaining fluctuate. Governments *encourage* collective bargaining when it is perceived as having a positive effect on the economy.[16] But they discourage it when the economy is struggling. This was the case in the interwar period between the world wars (1919–1938) when there was a massive global economic recession. The Great Depression was by far the largest sustained decline in industrial production and productivity in the century and a half for which economic records had been kept. Its impact was felt throughout the entire industrialized world and with their trading partners in less developed nations. Nations' individual responses to trade unions during this period are discussed later. As for international response to trade unions, the League of Nations attempted to address the need for stability of labor markets by the creation of the International Labour Organization.

INTERNATIONAL LABOUR ORGANIZATION

The signers of the Treaty of Versailles in 1919, which ended World War I, formed the **International Labour Organization (ILO)** as a parallel organization to the League of Nations. The mission of the League was to keep the peace between nations, and the mission of the ILO was to keep the peace within societies threatened by class divisions within countries. Before the war in Europe, the fear that continued worker unrest could lead to increased labor radicalism, support for the Marxist class struggle, and the abolition of capitalism created a labour problem that needed to be addressed.[17] A contributing cause for World War I was the imperialistic, territorial, and economic rivalries that had been intensifying from the late nineteenth century, particularly among Germany, France, Great Britain, Russia, and Austria-Hungary. These issues, imperialist and nationalist, seemed to have been moderated by the advance of industrialization and economic prosperity. Many Europeans counted on the deterrent of war's destructiveness to preserve the peace. But that did not happen.

INTERNATIONAL LABOUR ORGANIZATION (ILO)
Created as a parallel organization to the League of Nations with a mission to keep the peace withing societies threatened by class divisions between capital and labor.

After the war, these nations hoped to address the humanitarian, political, and economic issues that had been prominent prior to and during the war by the creation of the ILO and by adopting labor standards to improve the conditions of workers.[18] The humanitarian goal of the ILO was to end the exploitation of workers in industrialized countries; the political goal was to moderate unrest caused by clashes between workers and the owners; and the economic goal was to establish international standards to improve the workplace so that countries that adopted social reforms would still be competitive.

The creation of the ILO was not without difficulties. Samuel Gompers, president of the American Federation of Labor (AFL), served as chair of the drafting committee charged with formulating the special labor clauses for the treaty. Consistent with his AFL philosophy, Gompers advocated an international organization that would foster support for the workers' right to organize and collective bargaining as the solution to the labor problem, rather than an organization that advocated for political and economic reforms. Many trade unionists and social reformers from Europe believed the ILO had to do more to reform society as well as the workplace if it was to accomplish its purpose of fostering industrial peace. The industrialized countries wanted a set of labor standards that applied to everyone, whereas countries beginning industrialization wanted some leeway to foster their development. There was a question of how

In 1941, President Franklin D. Roosevelt addressed 250 delegates of the International Labour Organization in the East Room of the White House. *Source:* © Bettmann/ CORBIS.

colonial territories were going to be affected, and some nations warned they would not join the ILO unless a strong statement condemned racial segregation in participating nations.

A compromise plan proposed by the British gained acceptance.[19] To satisfy the European interests, the ILO was housed in Geneva, Switzerland, and its mission included political lobbying to improve employer–worker relations. All nation-states in the League of Nations were automatic members. The United States never joined the League of Nations, so it was not an initial participant in the ILO.

Nine principles written into the ILO Constitution defined its philosophy:

- Labor should not be treated as a commodity.
- Workers have the right to organize.
- Workers should get a reasonable wage to maintain a reasonable standard of living.
- Work should be limited to an 8-hour day or a 48-hour week.
- One day of rest each week.
- No child labor.
- Equal pay for equal work.
- Equitable treatment of immigrants.
- Enforcement of labor laws.

TRIPARTITE ORGANIZATIONAL STRUCTURE

Unique ILO governance structure in which governments, employers, and workers are equal parties.

The ILO had a unique **tripartite organizational structure** that brought together representatives of not only the participating governments but also employers and workers as equal parties in its governance. The main work of the ILO was to enact international conventions and recommendations regarding labor. *Conventions* would be submitted for ratification to the nation-states and on ratification would be binding; *Recommendations* were suggested provisions submitted for nation-states to consider. The first International Labour Conference resulted in six International Labour Conventions covering hours of work, unemployment, maternity protection, night work for women, and the minimum age for young workers. Since that time, the ILO has issued 185 conventions and 195 recommendations.[20]

In 1998, the ILO adopted a *Declaration on Fundamental Principles and Rights at Work* to ensure that social progress goes hand in hand with economic progress and development.

The Declaration commits member states to respect and promote principles and rights in four categories: freedom of association and the effective recognition of the right to collective bargaining, the elimination of forced or compulsory labor, the abolition of child labor, and the elimination of discrimination in employment. A Global Report each year provides a dynamic global picture of the current situation of the principles and rights expressed in the Declaration. The Global Report is an objective view of the global and regional trends on the issues relevant to the Declaration and serves to highlight those areas that require greater attention. In the Global Report "Your Voice at Work," issued in 2000,[21] the ILO focused on collective bargaining and the standards and principles regarding collective bargaining embodied in the ILO Convention 87, "Freedom of Association and Protection of the Right to Organize," adopted in 1948, and Convention 98, "Right to Organize and Collective Bargaining," adopted in 1949.

Those conventions endorsed good-faith collective bargaining as a fundamental right of all workers, private and public, except those in the armed services and the police. Some of the overriding principles can be summarized as follows:

- Collective bargaining should be undertaken by independent workers' organizations not under the control of employers or governments.
- The collective bargaining process should include bargaining over the terms and conditions of employment and the relationship between the parties.
- The agreements reached should be binding on the parties.
- A trade union that represents a majority or high percentage of the workers may enjoy exclusive bargaining rights.
- Conciliation and mediation can be a part of collective bargaining, but compulsory arbitration on the terms and conditions in agreements is contrary to the principle of voluntary collective bargaining.
- Legislation intending to annul, modify, or restrict the agreement of the parties, particularly as it relates to wage agreements, is also contrary to the principle of voluntary collective bargaining.

The Global Report concluded that three interrelated priorities should guide the promotional work by the ILO: (1) ensuring that all workers can form and join a trade union of their choice without fear of intimidation or reprisal and that employers are also free to form and join independent associations; (2) encouraging an open and constructive attitude by private business and public employers to the chosen representation of workers, including the development of agreed methods of bargaining and complementary forms of cooperation concerning terms and conditions of work; (3) recognition by governments that respect for fundamental principles and rights at work contributes to stable economic, political, and social development in the context of international economic integration, the fostering of democracy, and the fight against poverty.[22]

ANGLOPHONE COUNTRIES

Although the United States, Great Britain, Canada, and Australia have a common heritage, share a language, and legal and political systems, their industrial relations developed in some unique ways. In this section, we compare their evolution and their status today.

Great Britain

As discussed earlier, the industrial revolution began in Great Britain largely because it had the technological means, government encouragement, and a large and varied trade network via its river system. The development of a large inland water-transport network was perhaps the most important factor behind the industrial revolution in Great Britain.[23] The first factories appeared in 1740, concentrating on textile production. Such English inventions as the flying shuttle and carding machines and the spinning jenny integrated with a new source of power, the steam engine, resulted in more than 100,000 power looms in Great Britain and Scotland between 1790 and 1830. But the industrial revolution had brought with it abuses and hardships on workers. As a medical doctor described such a workplace in the early 1830s,

> The operatives are congregated in rooms and workshops during the twelve hours in the day, in an enervating, heated atmosphere, which is frequently loaded with dust or filaments of cotton. . . . They are drudges who watch the movements, and assist the operations of a mighty material force. . . . The preserving labor of the operative must rival the mathematical precision, the incessant motion, the exhaustless power of the machine.[24]

Whereas previously workers had joined together to form skilled trade unions, the industrial revolution spurred widespread unionization of semiskilled and unskilled laborers as a reaction to low wages, long hours, and deplorable conditions. Trade unions developed rapidly, especially in the factory-based textile industry. There were also attempts to form general unions of all workers irrespective of trade as a means for protecting and improving workers' living standards and for changing the political and economic order of society. Table 13-1 lists a number of movements in Britain's labor history that influenced the path of its trade unionism.

TRADES UNION CONGRESS

Federation of labour unions founded in Great Britain in 1868 to represent trade unionists. Currently has 56 affiliated unions representing 6.2 million workers.

In 1868, the **Trades Union Congress** was founded and because of the extension of the right to vote, trade unions began to have success in lobbying for laws protecting workers. The Employers and Workmen Act of 1875 modified the old Master and Servant Law so employers too could be sued for breach of contract; the 1874 Factory Act set a ten-hour limit on the working day; and the 1871 Trade Union Act recognized unions as legal entities entitled to protection under the law.

Between 1888 and 1918, membership in trade unions grew from 750,000 to 6.5 million, and unionism within the unskilled, semiskilled, white-collar, and professional workforces spread

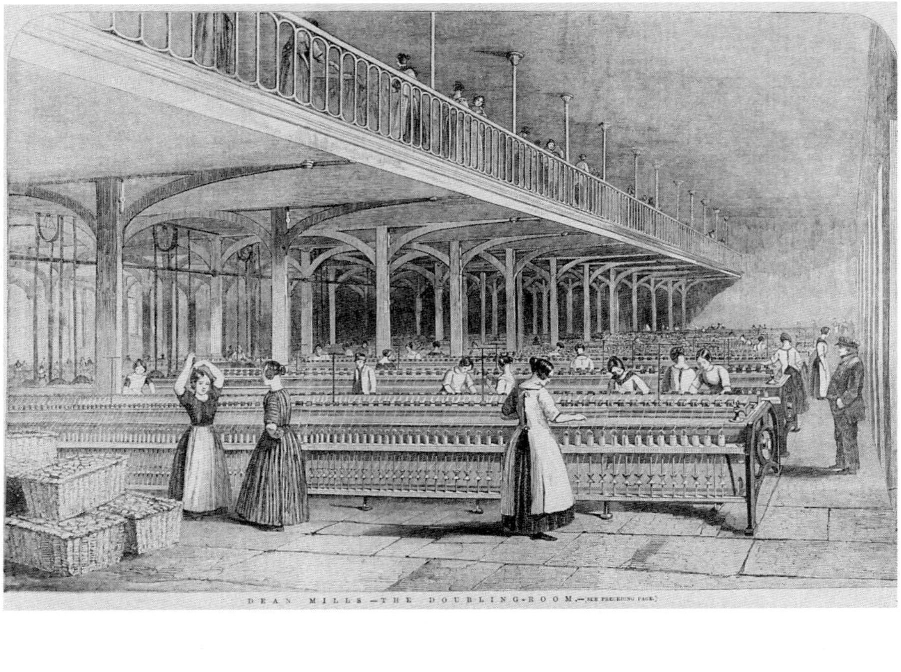

DEAN MILLS—THE DOUBLING-ROOM.—(SEE PRECEDING PAGE.)

The interior of the doubling-room at Dean Mill, Halliwell, England, in 1851 is an example of some of the innovations in textile production in England at the start of the industrial revolution. *Source:* © Bettmann/CORBIS All Rights Reserved.

rapidly. The strength of the movement was seen in its huge May Day 1890 demonstration in favor of the eight-hour day. Employers, who were threatened by the unions' obvious strength, engineered court decisions that outlawed peaceful picketing and enabled them to sue unions for losses during strikes. Despite these measures, the militancy of unions during the prewar years led to a wave of strike action, dubbed "the great unrest."[25]

The World War I accentuated divisions within the labor movement as labor's rank and file continued to press for economic and political reforms while labor's leaders aligned more with the government in its war effort. The gulf between the two generated its own structures in the form of the **Shop Stewards Movement and Workers' Committees.** Shop stewards of today can trace their origins to this wartime period, during which rank-and-file workers rather than union officials kept effective trade unionism alive in the face of their leaders' preoccupation with the war effort.[26]

SHOP STEWARDS MOVEMENT AND WORKERS' COMMITTEES

In Britain worker committees formed during World War I, when divisions within the labor movement—with rank and file interested in reforms and labor leaders interested in supporting war effort—created a need for new representation.

The British labor movement in the early 1920s was influenced by the following beliefs: Capitalism's decline was inevitable, labor and capital have opposing interests, capitalism should be replaced by socialism, and strikes should be used for both economic and political ends. Great Britain, reacting to what it believed was an untenable position, created the Whitley Committee to study the causes of labor unrest. The committee recommended collective bargaining by independent trade unions and endorsed a system of joint councils to provide for joint consultation by employers and unions.[27]

The first majority Labour government gained prominence as a part of Winston Churchill's coalition government during World War II. In the election of 1945, it gained a majority of the members of Parliament, resulting in a Labour Party prime minister and cabinet. The Labour government inherited the severe economic problems of postwar Europe and responded by passing the following legislation involving labor:

- Nationalized the ailing coal, gas, and electric industries; the iron and steel industry; and the Bank of England, resulting in more than 2 million people becoming public sector employees.
- Extended social benefits instituting the "cradle-to-grave" welfare system with sick leave and unemployment benefits, workers' compensation, and universal health care.

From 1965 to 1979, the British trade union movement was supported by the creation of a Royal Commission on Trade Unions and Employers Associations (the Donovan Commission), which endorsed collective bargaining rights and Britain's traditional approach to minimal legal regulations of unions and bargaining.[28] This traditional approach, characterized by an absence of statutory regulation, is termed *voluntarism* or a collective laissez-faire system. Under voluntarism, a union and an employer or an employers' association can agree to be a party to a collective bargaining agreement, and the contract can extend for as long as the parties agree, although wages are generally negotiated annually. The collective bargaining agreement's terms and conditions cover all the individuals in the bargaining unit, even if they are not in the union. Laissez-faire in British labor relations came to an end with the election of the Conservative government headed by Prime Minister Margaret Thatcher. During Thatcher's term in office, a number of changes occurred in labor–management relations when legislation was passed that

- narrowed a union's immunity from labor injunctions
- outlawed secondary strikes
- restrained picketing
- required a secret election of the union membership before calling a strike
- prohibited a closed shop

With the election of a Labour government in 1997, led by Prime Minister Tony Blair, unions hoped for a change in attitude. But the major aspects of Thatcher's legislation remained in place. Blair's government opted into the European Union EU's protocols on employment standards involving hours of work, parental leave, and the creation of work councils. The Employment Act of 2002 was enacted to ensure the following:

- Enhance employees' parental leave rights
- Guarantee parental flextime
- Curtail employment appeal rights by requiring the losing party to pay the cost of the appeal
- Establish minimal grievance procedures for collective bargaining agreements to reduce the caseload of employment courts
- Grant fixed-term, or contract, employee protections comparable with regular employees
- Require consultation with employee representatives before layoffs

These legislative enactments have largely supplanted the long-established voluntarism in Britain's labor relation's history.

Canada

Canada in the late 1880s and early 1900s confronted the same labor unrest as the United States and Great Britain because of the deplorable working conditions associated with the early stages of industrialization. The Winnipeg General Strike in 1919 and fears of Bolshevism led to the appointment of the Royal Commission on Industrial Relations, which cited as its charge, "[T]he duty of considering and making suggestions for establishing permanent improvement in the relations between employers and employees, whereby, through close contact and joint action, they can improve existing industrial conditions and devise means for their continual review and betterment."[29] The Royal Commission identified unemployment as the most important condition causing industrial unrest; condemned the treatment of labor as a commodity to be bought and sold at a price determined by supply and demand; and endorsed a collective voice for workers, although it had both a majority position, which endorsed independent unions, and a minority position accepting employer-created representation plans.

Up until the World War II, Canada's economy was still largely rural, centered on resource extraction industries of mining and timber, rather than manufacturing. This inhibited the growth of a large urban-based, wage-earning labor force. And because of Canada's reliance on a few key industries, its economy was more vulnerable to the disruptive effects of strikes and labor conflict. For these reasons, Canada's labor relations developed to discourage the adversarial scheme of trade unionism and collective bargaining and to encourage cooperation and unity of interest between employers and employees to promote efficiency in production and peace in labor relations. This strategy combined British-style voluntarism in union recognition, American-style welfare capitalism, and Australian-style government-mandated mediation and fact-finding.

As the percentage of union membership steadily declined in the United States beginning in the 1940s, the pattern was reversed in Canada, where more collectivist traditions led to more favorable political attitudes toward unions and thus a growth in the union movement. Another contributing factor is Canada's governmental and legal environment. Canada's system of federated government vests most employment matters in the ten provinces. Its federal authority, except in times of crisis, is limited to about 10 percent of its workers in federal civil service and national industries such as transportation and telecommunications.[30] This fragmented system means that employers and unions have to contend with varying local labor laws. Quebec province, which still enjoys its French heritage, and Ontario province have the largest share of Canada's union members.[31]

Canadian law on both the federal and the provincial levels mirrors the protections found in the U.S. National Labor Relations Act. Workers have the right to form unions and to elect exclusive bargaining agents, employers must meet with unions for the purpose of collective bargaining, grievance procedures and arbitration are mandated, and strikes during the term of a contract are prohibited. Canadian labor boards have the authority to (1) certify unions without formal elections; (2) make quick, final decisions on unfair labor practice cases; and (3) impose first contracts when employers refuse to bargain with a new union. Canadian labor laws have also provided *public sector* unions a stronger position by giving them the right to strike (in most instances) and the right to compulsory arbitration.

A Federal Government Task Force in 1998 endorsed Canada's collective bargaining system as a "balance between labour and management; between social and economic values; between the various instruments of labour policy; between rights and responsibilities; between individual and democratic group rights; and between the public interest and free collective bargaining."[32]

Traditionally, the fate of labor relations in Canada followed that of the United States. In fact, in 1966, the percentage of workers in unions in the two countries was almost identical. In recent years, however, that has not been the case. Canadian union density increased and decreased later than the United States or U.K., peaking in the mid-1980s and declining less severely, so that by 2000 its density was 30 percent overall and over 80 percent in the public sector, which was higher than in either the United States or the U.K. and actually double the United States in overall union density.[33]

The Canadian Auto Workers (CAW) union is the largest private sector union in Canada. In 1985, the CAW split from the U.S. United Auto Workers (UAW) union to become an independent union. Since that year, the UAW has experienced declining membership while the new Canadian union more than doubled its membership from 120,000 members to over 260,000 members today. The CAW successfully expanded into other industries such as education, health care, retail, railways, airlines, hotels, and transportation. Because of this growth, CAW's former president Basil "Buzz" Hargrove became a national figure in Canada. In addition to growth, the CAW has (1) made wage gains by retaining cost-of-living increases and resisting wage concessions, or lump-sum payments and profit sharing, typical of U.S. labor agreements; (2) resisted long-term contracts, which by policy it called "the new concession," and (3) negotiated same-sex spousal recognition for paid leaves and benefits.[34]

Australia

Australia, like Canada, had a long history of British colonial rule and largely reflected British cultural, political, and legal systems. But Australia's industrial relations developed in a unique manner. In opposition to the Anglo-American preference for voluntarism in labor relations, Australia adopted a federal compulsory conciliation and arbitration system in 1904, which gave legal protection to collective bargaining but requires trade union and employer associations to submit disputed contract terms to a state tribunal for conciliation and, if necessary, binding arbitration.[35] This system was in place for most of the twentieth century, but amid the economic difficulties of the 1980s, both labor and employers sought to decentralize collective bargaining and adopt enterprise (company or industry specific) bargaining.[36]

Australian labor relations are governed by the **Workplace Relations Act (WRA)**. The key elements of the WRA include the following:

WORKPLACE RELATIONS ACT (WRA)

Australian labor law reform that includes streamlined award and unfair-dismissal system; emphasis on enterprise bargaining; and curbs on strikes.

- A streamlined "award" system (CBAs)
- More emphasis on enterprise bargaining
- Curbs on union power
- Restrictions on strikes
- A streamlined unfair-dismissal system that limits frivolous appeals and compensation claims

Under the WRA, the Australian system of industrial relations is still a centralized model, characterized by industry-wide or company *awards* (similar to U.S. collective bargaining agreements), which are negotiated by company, union, and sometimes government officials and then submitted to the Australian Industrial Relations Commission (AIRC) for ratification or resolution of differences.[37] Such awards establish minimum wages and working conditions for specific categories of workers.[38] Individual companies and their employees or unions may negotiate supplemented "over award" wage benefits based on market conditions. These benefits, when registered with the AIRC, are known as a Certified Agreement if it covers most or all of a company's workforce or an Australian Workplace Agreement (AWA) if it covers an individual employee.

The WRA also barred *closed shops*, where an individual has to be a member of a union to be hired and eliminated preference clauses, which required an employer to give a preference to specified individuals. Under the WRA, unions and workers are prohibited from striking companies engaged in interstate commerce, except when they are negotiating a new enterprise agreement. The strike must also concern a matter specifically related to the negotiations. This is known as "protected action" during a "bargaining period." Industrial disputes are then intended to be settled via conciliation and, if necessary, compulsory arbitration by the AIRC. When unions do strike outside a bargaining period, they can be sued by employers for damages, and union officials and individual strikers can be held personally liable.

Eighty percent of all Australian wage and salary earners are covered by the awards system, with the greatest proportion of employees receiving overaward payments through some form of enterprise agreement. Despite efforts by the federal government to promote the use of AWAs, the vast majority of employers still prefer enterprise agreements or awards.

Although enterprise bargaining is likely to continue to dominate the industrial relations scene for years to come, the ACTU believes that enterprise bargaining has run its course in Australia and has been arguing that workers are unlikely to benefit any further from decentralized bargaining. The union movement sees the future in terms of a return to industry-wide bargaining as the only way to provide increased significant new benefits to workers, especially in view of the weakening of the award system.

EUROPEAN UNION NATIONS

The European Union

EUROPEAN UNION

A regional body made up of 27 member states on the continent of Europe that delegate their sovereignty on questions of joint interest to common institutions, which represent the interests of the EU as a whole. However, the EU member states are not one single new nation.

The **European Union (EU)** is a unique regional body made up of 27 member states that delegate their sovereignty on questions of joint interest to common institutions, which represent the interests of the EU as a whole. However, the EU member states are not one single new nation. The mission of the EU is to integrate the economies of the member states, to "lay the foundations for an ever closer union," to raise the living standards of its citizens, to remove obstacles to concerted action, and to promote a high level of employment and of social protection. As of 2010 no member has ever withdrawn from the EU. However, the May 2010, $147 billion bailout of Greece by the EU through the IMF caused many to question the economic viability of the EU. In Spain, for example, the country's largest union, Comisiones Obreras, which represents 2.6 million public sector employees, conducted a strike in which 75 percent of the members participated, the largest number in the country's history. The 2010 strike was to protest the Spanish government's response to the economic recession which hit both Greece and Spain particularly hard. The Spanish government announced a 5 percent wage cut and a freeze in pension contributions in an effort to balance the budget. The union was concerned that these economic cuts were only the first steps in a broader national effort to change labor laws and harm workers' rights.[39]

The EU's priority objective has been the political and economic integration of Europe through a gradual elimination of customs barriers and an introduction of common external tariffs. As explained in an EU publication:

> The EU's foundational agreement is a pact between sovereign nations that have resolved to share a common destiny and to pool an increasing share of their sovereignty. It concerns the things that European peoples care most deeply about: peace, security, participatory democracy, justice and solidarity. This pact is being strengthened and confirmed all across Europe: half a billion human beings have chosen to live under the rule of law and in accordance with age-old values that center on humanity and human dignity.[40]

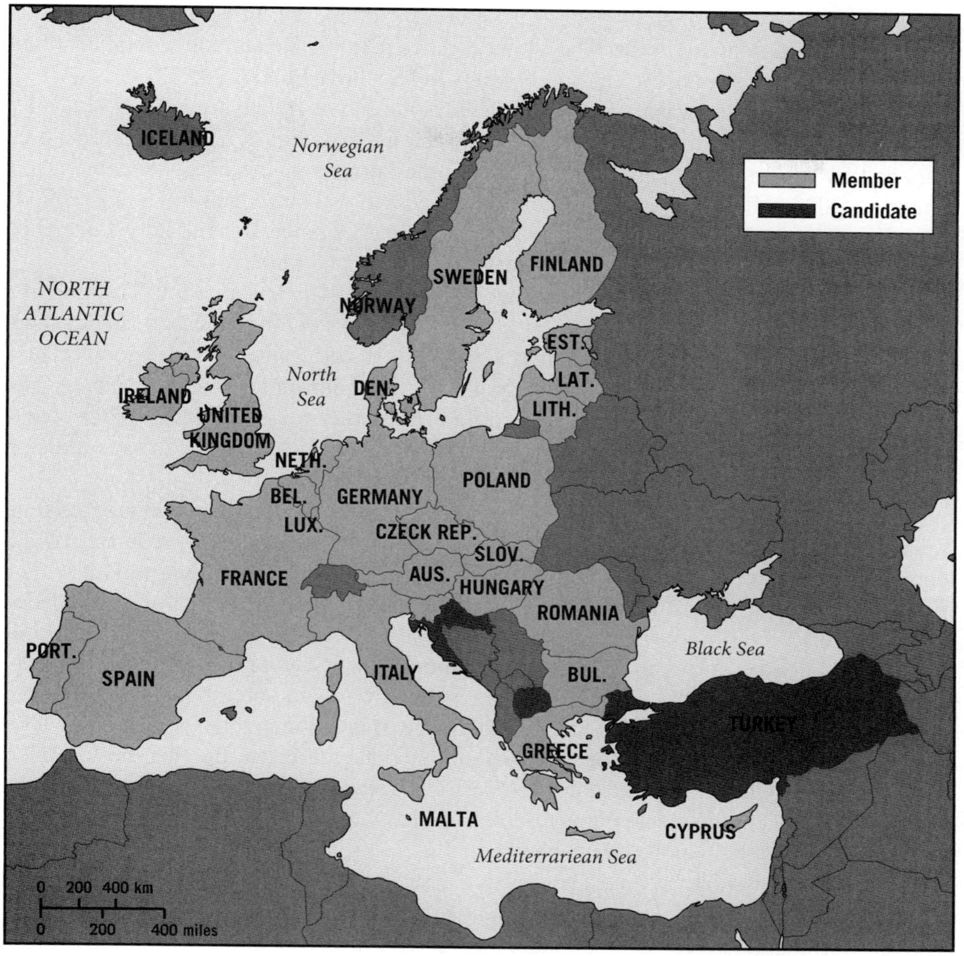

FIGURE 13-1 European Union Countries. *Source:* Available at http://www.cia.gov/library/publications/the-worldfactbook. Accessed September 29, 2010.

Five EU institutions—the European Parliament, the Council, the Commission, the Court of Justice, and the Court of Auditors—hold responsibility for making and administering EU policy. The EU, headquartered in Brussels, includes Belgium, Germany, France, Italy, Luxembourg, the Netherlands, Austria, Denmark, Finland, Greece, Ireland, Portugal, Spain, Sweden, the United Kingdom, Cyprus, the Czech Republic, Estonia, Hungary, Latvia, Lithuania, Malta, Poland, Slovakia, Slovenia, Bulgaria, and Romania. As a politician from one of the new member states put it, "Europe has finally managed to reconcile its history with its geography,"[41] as seen on the map of EU member states in Figure 13-1.

In economic, trade, and monetary terms, the EU has become a major world power. It has considerable influence within international organizations such as the World Trade Organization (WTO), the United Nations (UN), and at world summits on the environment and development. The EU dates its beginning to 1957 when its member states began removing trade barriers and forming a "common market." In 1967, a single Council of Ministers as well as the European Parliament was created to govern the Common Market. Originally, the members of the European Parliament were chosen by the national parliaments, but in 1979 the first direct elections were held, allowing the citizens of the member states to vote for the candidate of their choice. Since then, direct elections have been held every five years.

TREATY OF MAASTRICHT
Enhanced the European Union through intergovernmental cooperation and adding new forms of cooperation between the member states, particularly on defense and in the area of justice and home affairs.

The **Treaty of Maastricht** (1992) enhanced the EU by introducing intergovernmental cooperation to the existing "Community" system and adding new forms of cooperation between the member states, particularly on defense and in the area of justice and home affairs. Economic and political integration within the EU has resulted in member countries developing common policies in a very wide range of fields—agriculture, culture, consumer affairs, the environment, energy, transportation, and trade. The EU negotiates major trade and aid agreements with other countries and is developing a Common Foreign and Security Policy.

The Single Market was formally completed at the end of 1992 when the EU decided to adopt economic and monetary union (EMU), through the introduction of a single European currency managed by a European Central Bank. The single currency—the euro—became a reality on January 1, 2002, when euro notes and coins replaced national currencies in 15 of the 27 countries of the European Union (Belgium, Germany, Greece, Spain, France, Ireland, Italy, Luxembourg, the Netherlands, Austria, Portugal, Finland, Slovenia, Cyprus, and Malta).

The completion of the Single Market affected the EU's trade policy. The import restrictions that EU countries had been allowed to maintain were steadily abolished, as was the internal distribution of "sensitive" imports such as textiles, steel, cars, and electronic goods. The EU is a single trading bloc, and it is home to nearly half a billion consumers with a relatively high average level of income. As such, it is a very attractive market for exporters in other countries. In terms of trade and investment, the EU is the main partner of the United States and the only one with which it enjoys a stable relationship.

The European Commission recognizes three European-wide industrial relations unions as "social partners" in the EU social dialogue: the European Trade Union Confederation (ETUC) for labor and the Union of Industrial and Employers' Confederations of Europe (UNICE) and the European Center of Enterprises with Public Participation and Enterprises of General Economic Interest (CEEP) for employers.[42] ETUC, CEEP, and UNICE are the primary liaison bodies that advise and lobby the European Commission on employment and labor concerns. The commission is required to consult with its social partners when it wants to submit proposals in a particular social field. Unions within the EU face the challenge of operating at the supranational level, in an effort to influence common EU social and economic policy directly affecting their interests.

The Social Charter contained in the Maastricht Treaty sets forth an action program to protect workers' rights in employment contracts, collective bargaining, health and safety in the workplace, consultation and participation, parental leave, and social protection. Workers' rights, especially during corporate downsizing, became a hot political issue during the 1990s. The EU borrowed from its members' experiences, especially French and German, to guarantee workers and their unions the right to information and consultation before large-scale layoffs could occur and to institutionalize work councils within companies. **Works councils** are permanent elected bodies of workforce representatives or in some instances joint committees with employer's representatives, established on the basis of law or collective bargaining agreements with the overall task of promoting cooperation within the enterprise. Their task is for the benefit of both the employees and the enterprise by maintaining good and stable employment conditions and increasing the welfare and security of employees and their understanding of enterprise operations, finance, and competitiveness. The EU directive on works councils specifies it is to provide employees with rights to information and consultation, and it directs member states to ensure that the employees' representatives, when carrying out their functions, enjoy adequate protection against dismissal. These are the information and consultation rights:

WORKS COUNCILS

Permanent elected bodies of workers representatives or in some instances joint committees with employers representatives, established on the basis of law or collective bargaining agreements with the overall task of promoting cooperation within the enterprise.

- Information on the recent and probable development of the company's activities and economic situation
- Information and consultation on the situation, structure, and probable development of employment within the company and on any anticipatory measures envisaged, in particular, where there is a threat of layoffs
- Information and consultation, with a view to reaching an agreement, on decisions likely to lead to substantial changes in the company or in contractual relations with the company

For a summary of works councils in the EU15 countries see Table 13-2.

Organized labor is well established in the EU throughout its member states,[43] although union membership has dwindled in most EU nations. Changes in the composition of the labor force,

TABLE 13-2 Work Councils in EU-15 Regulations on Employee Information and Consultation

Country	Definition
Austria	Elected by the workforce, represents all employees within an enterprise consistently employing five or more workers. Exercises the workplace-level consultation and codetermination rights conferred by law on the workforce as a whole.
Belgium	With the workplace health and safety committee, a works council is the main form of employee participation and representation in an undertaking with 100 or more employees. It is a joint bipartite body composed of representatives elected by workers in the enterprise and representatives appointed by the employer from among managerial staff, who may not outnumber the employees' representatives.
Denmark	Joint body with equal management/workforce representation set up under a cooperation agreement with the purpose of promoting cooperation and employee involvement at individual workplace level. The employee representatives may not be a member of a trade union.
Finland	Works councils are not a part of the national regulation on cooperation within undertakings. The Act on Personnel Representation in the Administration of Undertakings only provides employee representation on the company administrative bodies.
France	Joint body composed of the company's CEO and employee representatives elected by the workforce, of private companies with more than 50 employees. They receive information, respond to formal consultation by the employer, and manage cultural activities for which they have a budget at their disposal.
Germany	Employee representation body that applies to establishments that are organized under private law. The works council has a number of participation rights, consisting of rights to information, consultation, and codetermination.
Greece	Voluntary organs of employee representation and participation in enterprises with at least 50 employees or 20 employees for enterprises that have no trade union. The function of the works councils is participatory and consultative and is aimed at improving working conditions in conjunction with the growth of the company.
Ireland	No statutory work council system.
Italy	Works councils are created by the trade unions, which also define their regulations based on the national sectoral collective agreement. Works councils generally exercise information and consultation rights.
Luxembourg	Employee Committees are made up of employee representatives whose function is to protect employee rights and interest through their right of information and consultation. In addition Joint Works Committees are bodies composed of both employee and employer representatives and exercise codetermination rights over company policy and management decision.
The Netherlands	Body composed of employees within an enterprise that has the task of promoting the interest both of the enterprise and of its workforce. The main rights given to works councils by law are the right of access to information, advisory powers, the right of consent (i.e., the veto right on a number of related matters), and the right to propose initiatives.
Norway	The working environmental committees are compulsory bipartite bodies composed of an equal number of employee and employer representatives. The various duties of these committees include considering questions in areas such as rationalism schemes, work process, and working time arrangements. In addition, work councils are compulsory in companies with more than 100 employees. Employees may also demand the establishment of a work council in companies with fewer than 100 employees.

(continued)

TABLE 13-2 *(Continued)*

Spain	The committee is made up of elected worker representatives. It has defined information and consultation rights, but no right to codetermination. Duties include monitoring the implementation of labor laws and related discipline.
Sweden	There is no system of statutory works councils in Sweden, nor are such bodies established on a voluntary basis. Workplace employee participation and representation is based on the role of trade unions and their codetermination rights.
United Kingdom	There is no system of statutory works councils in the U.K. Trade unions are the primary vehicle for the consultation of employees. However there is legislation providing for consultation of employees over certain issues. In addition, "joint consultative committees," based on collective agreements or voluntary practice, remain significant.

Source: Mark Carley, Annalisa Baradel, and Christian Welz, *Works Council, Workplace Representation and Participation Structures* (© European Foundation for the Improvement of Living and Working Conditions, 2004), pp. 1–38, 6–8. Used with permission.

including women, temporary and part-time workers, and foreign workers, have required trade unions to change from traditional methods of advocacy. At the present time, the overwhelming majority of collective bargaining agreements are still negotiated and signed at the *national level or lower.* However, the increasing integration of the national economies into a European one (including the introduction of the euro) is opening new methods for *transnational labor–management relations.* Steelworkers in Germany and the Netherlands have jointly negotiated a labor contract, and ETUC is developing resources to allow its affiliates and its 11 European industry federations to compare agreements made in other parts of the EU to improve on their negotiations. To date, ETUC, UNICE, and CEEP have signed three European "framework agreements," dealing with parental leave, part-time work, and fixed-term contracts. These agreements are much more general than a normal collective bargaining agreement and only set general frameworks for further negotiations on national levels (see Profile 13-1).

Germany

For Germany the coming of the industrial revolution, democracy, and capitalism was not a gradual transition but was concentrated in the last half of the 1800s. Earlier in that century, the German principalities, ruled by monarchs and supported by a serf system, were challenged by bloody and unsuccessful revolts. The successful uniting of Germany in 1872 did create an elected Parliament, albeit selected by landowners only, and a chancellor appointed by a hereditary monarch.[44] A severe economic slump in Germany that coincided with its emerging industrialization caused Germany to reject Adam Smith's brand of capitalism and Great Britain's form of democracy for a state socialism. This state socialism emphasized the role of government in regulating the market economy rather than the laissez-faire touted by capitalists. In its feudal tradition, Germany's state socialism included a safety net of welfare programs (called *Soczialpoletik*[45]), but such programs failed to suppress the inevitable labor problem that accompanied the abuses of the industrial system. When the working classes began to embrace the socialism of Karl Marx and to form radical anarchist political parties, Germany enacted an Anti Socialist Law that banned all political meetings and trade unions associated with socialist groups.[46] After that the trade unionists adopted the threefold agenda rejected by U.S. unions of representation at the bargaining table, participating within the economic and political systems, and pursuing social justice for all workers.

Nonetheless, just as the United States and U.K. had cooperated with labor when two world wars and a worldwide depression threatened their democracies, German industrialists began to cooperate with trade unions during the World War I, which continued through Germany's defeat and the abdication by the kaiser. In 1918, trade unions and industrialists signed the Stinnes-Legien Agreement to preserve a representative democracy and a market economy, followed by legislative guarantees for workers' rights. But during World War II, Adolf Hitler and the Nazi Party abolished labor unions and persecuted its leadership. After World War II, Germany's modern industrial relations system was created.

Briefly, in Germany employees are represented in three ways:

- ***Trade unions*** negotiate collective bargaining agreements that are primarily concerned with wages. Collective bargaining takes place nationally or regionally with a particular industry. These centralized negotiations usually take place annually and result in "pattern" or fairly uniform results.[47] Such collective agreements, however, are only legally binding on the employers who are a part of the association negotiating the agreement and the actual members of the trade union,[48] although employers generally apply the contract to all workers.
- ***Work councils*** negotiate working conditions that are location specific and enforce the collective bargaining agreement. Work councils, at the company or enterprise level, participate in the day-to-day operation of the collective bargaining agreement. The members are elected by all employees and represent them in mandated consultations with the particular employer. Employers have to consult with work councils before taking certain employment action such as dismissals, layoffs, or changes in benefits. Work councils can seek wage increases above the collective bargaining agreement entered into on the national level.
- ***Codetermination law***, in firms with 2,000 or more employees, requires that the company's supervisory board contain a certain number of employee representatives. **Codetermination** means that unions and employees have a say in company policy, as well as sharing responsibility for the firm.

CODETERMINATION

In Germany, a system which requires a company's supervising board to have employee representatives giving unions and employees a say in policy and a stake in company's success.

The pressure on German trade unions intensified with the fall of the Berlin Wall. Suddenly, an entire country, East Germany, had to be integrated into the economic, political, and social fabric of West Germany. Policy makers underestimated the scope of unemployment, antiquated means of production and infrastructure, and environmental damage in West Germany, as well as the negative impact through the loss of the former Soviet Union's foreign trade system. The East German trade unions, which had been closely aligned with the communist regime, dissolved, and an influx of new members to West German trade unions did not improve working conditions as had been hoped. Globalization and membership in the EU have added more challenges to Germany by the internationalization of employee relations and the creation of European work councils. Table 13-2 describes the range of work councils in the EU.

France

Industrial relations in France are characterized by a strong legacy of class conflict, anarcho-syndicalism, and communism within the labor movement; employer opposition to power sharing, which caused a slow development of collective bargaining rights; and extensive state involvement through legal regulations. The evolution of French collective bargaining is consistent with its cultural heritage. It has been a grant of power from the state (previously represented by royalty) to the *social partners*—employers (previously represented by the nobility) and employees (previously represented by the feudal system). Industrialization started in the early 1800s, followed by the growth of craft unions and then national federations of labor. After World War I, France enacted favorable collective bargaining legislation that increased union membership. In reaction to the Great Depression, France initiated the Popular Front, which paralleled Franklin Roosevelt's New Deal. France emerged after World War II as a major economic power with large, technologically equipped companies, and an active labor movement.

The French system of employee relations is unique in that it emerged from the anarchists and revolutionary socialists within the labor movement (anarcho-syndicalism), which led to a working-class culture distrustful of government and employers and bitter that class divisions still existed. Employers have exacerbated the situation by their hold on the reins of authority as a claim of right unfettered by their need for labor. All French governments of whatever persuasion have advocated for the freedom of social partners to negotiate terms and conditions of employment through collective bargaining, but all have also seriously intervened by passing legislation governing those very terms. Reciprocally, employers' associations and unions exert serious pressure on political parties and the government to obtain through legislation what they cannot get through bargaining.[49]

Collective bargaining legislation names the employers' and employees' bodies that have "representative" status; establishes the terms under which bargaining is valid; specifies what subjects are open to negotiation; and details most bargaining practices (e.g., the law places an obligation to negotiate annually on pay and on job classifications every five years). Additionally, the state is directly responsible for a series of decisions regarding the minimum wage, hours of work, employment status, and terms and conditions for layoffs. Frequently, the content of collective agreements is merely a repackaging of the wording of general statutory frameworks.

Negotiations can be carried out at all levels of economic activity, national, sector, or company, as long as recognized bodies take part in them. All employees in a sector or company are covered by an agreement through a state-approved *extension*. Companies that are not even members of the employers' association that entered into the agreement are still covered by a sector-level agreement once the government has extended it. As a general rule, the government always extends sector-level agreements when they comply with statutory criteria and have been signed by recognized bodies. Because of the extension of sector-level agreements by the Ministry of Labour, despite a union membership of less than 10 percent, it is estimated that around 90 percent of private sector employees in France are covered by sector-level agreements. This system of extension explains the dichotomy for France between *union density*, which is the percentage of workers in the workforce who are union members, and *collective bargaining coverage*, which is the percentage of workers in the workforce who are covered by a collective bargaining agreement (see Figure 13-2, Union Density/Collective Bargaining Coverage).

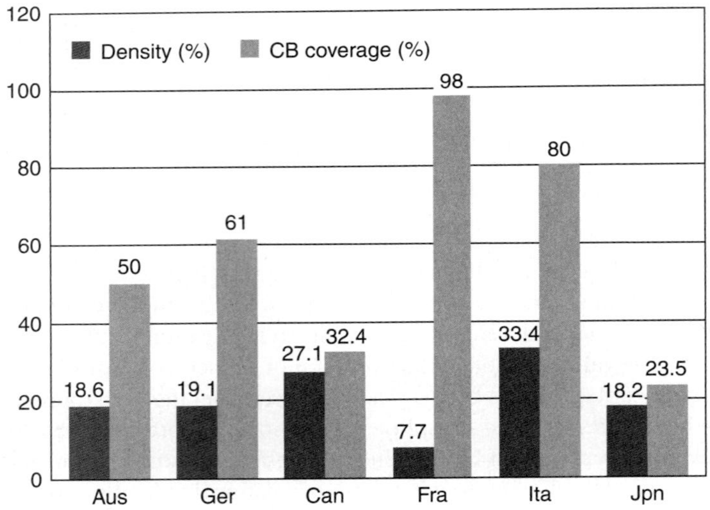

FIGURE 13-2 Union Density/Collective Bargaining Coverage, 2007–2008. *Source: OECD Employment Outlook,* Organization for Economic Co-operation and Development (2004). Available at http://www.oecd.org. Accessed September 2010; "Collective Bargaining, A Positive Force for the Greater Good," *CWA News 67*, no. 2 (March 2007), p. 3; and "Collective Bargaining," European Trade Union Institute. Available at http://www.worker-participation.eu. Accessed September 2010.

French president Nicolas Sarkozy, after his 2007 election victory, began questioning his nation's labor laws. Eric Woerth, his budget minister, has stated that France is still in the "Stone Age" of labor relations. He cited the World Economic Forum's Global Competitiveness Index, which ranks France's labor market 129th out of 131 countries.

The first labor target of Sarkozy was the retirement requirement of public transport workers, who responded with a crippling nine-day strike in 2007. Sarkozy proposed increasing the number of years for some public employees to retire from 37.5 to 40 years. A public opinion survey showed 82 percent of French citizens supported the change. The workers ended the strike after nine days and a loss of hundreds of millions in lost productivity because French workers were unable to get to their jobs. The proposed change in retirement years remains unresolved.

Sarkozy promised to continue his attack on Frances' *Code du travail*, or labor laws, which were largely written in the 1960s and provide a cradle-to-grave social contract for workers. Other key targets include the national 35-hour workweek, early retirement, and employers' ability to fire or lay off workers owing to profitability.[50] Sarkozy was elected in May 2007 largely on his promise of labor law reform. His election came only a year after his predecessor, Jacques Chirac, tried to change a labor law, and his effort resulted in over a million workers staging protests all over France, including the Place de la Bastille, where the 1789 French Revolution began (see Profile 13-2). After 15 days, Chirac cancelled the new law that would have allowed employers to fire new workers under the age of 26 without reason. Will Sarkozy be able to achieve labor law changes despite worker protests?

Profile 13-2

Youth Labor Law Ignites Protests across France

Over a million French teenage workers, union members, and retirees jammed the streets of Paris, France, on March 27, 2006, to protest a new labor law. The protests centered outside the Place de la Bastille, where the historic 1789 French Revolution began over 200 years before, and they followed several weeks of similar protests. The French labor law that ignited the protests made it easier for employers to fire young workers. However, some observers, including Serge July, director of the French newspaper *Liberation*, believe the protests are also about the new French "free-market system," which is supported by only 36 percent of the French population, compared to 71 percent in the United States and 74 percent in China, according to a poll conducted by the University of Maryland Program on International Policy Attitudes.

The protests coincided with a one-day national strike conducted by French trade unions that closed schools, factories, rail and air traffic, and even the Eiffel Tower. Protests also occurred in other French cities across the country. In Montpellier, a city in the south of France, protestors took down a statue of former socialist Jean Jaurès, claiming it represented their "mourning of the rise of capitalism." Hundreds of protestors were arrested, and in Paris riot, police were forced to use water cannons and tear gas to disperse thousands of protestors who began throwing bottles and stones at the police.

Prime Minister Dominique de Villepin stood firmly behind the new law, despite national polls showing his government with only a 20 percent favorable rating. The new law had allowed employers to fire workers under the age of 26 without reason during the first two years of work. Called "the first contract," the law was known as CPE in France and is designed to lower national unemployment, estimated at 9.6 percent for all workers and 23 percent for workers under age 26. The rationale behind the law was that employers would be more likely to hire additional workers if they knew they were not required to keep them. Previously it was almost impossible for employers to fire workers unless they committed "grievous mistakes" or the company faced bankruptcy, and even then a worker could go to court where judges usually ruled in favor of the worker.

On April 10, 2006, former President Chirac "caved in to" the protesters and canceled the law. The announcement was seen as a major political blow to Villepin, who had hoped to succeed Chirac as president of France.

(*Continued*)

After over a million French teenage workers, union members, and retirees protested a new labor law in the streets of Paris, President Jacques Chirac cancelled the implementation of the act, which critics said would have made it easier for employers to fire young workers. *Source:* Remy Gabalda/AP Images.

Source: Adapted from Andrew Higgins, "Liberté, Précarité: Labor Law Ignites Anxiety in France," *Wall Street Journal* (March 28, 2006), pp. A1, A8; John Leicester, "Labor Law Protests Widen in France," *Associated Press* (March 29, 2006); and Christine Ollivier, "France Rescinds Labor Law; Protesters Win," *Louisville Courier Journal* (April 11, 2006), p. A4.

Italy

Modern Italy can be traced to the influence of the French Revolution in 1789, which spurred liberal Italians to push for unification of the various city-states that occupied the Italian peninsula. The Italian unification movement, known as the *Risorgimento*, led to final unification in 1861. Unification combined a group of wealthier northern regions with historical and cultural ties to Austria, Switzerland, and France with a group of southern regions linked to North Africa.

The new nation faced many serious problems. A large debt, few natural resources, and almost no industry or transportation facilities combined with extreme poverty. During the 1880s, in Italy as in other European countries, a socialist movement began to develop among workers in the cities. Despite the fact that some economic and social progress took place before World War I, Italy during those prewar decades, in an attempt to increase its international influence and prestige, joined in an alliance with Germany and Austria and tried unsuccessfully to conquer Ethiopia and Libya. After the outbreak of World War I in 1914, Italy remained neutral for almost a year and then finally joined the Allies. Aside from a few victories in 1918, Italy suffered serious losses of men, materiel, and morale, and under the treaties that followed the war, Italy received only a small part of the territories it had expected. These disappointments produced a powerful wave of nationalist sentiment against the Allies and the Italian government. Italy was plunged into deep social and political crisis by the war, and the 1919 elections suddenly made the Socialist and the new Popular (Catholic) parties the largest in parliament. In the midst of these unsettled conditions, Benito Mussolini, a former revolutionary socialist, founded a new movement called *fascism.* In the 1930s, the Italian army invaded and conquered Ethiopia and Albania, sent troops to support Francisco Franco in the Spanish Civil War, established the Rome-Berlin Axis with Adolf Hitler, and entered World War II on Germany's side. Mussolini's war effort met with setbacks and defeats on all fronts so that when the Allies invaded Sicily, Mussolini was forced to resign. Italy then joined in the war against Germany.

Between 1945 and 1948, Italians abolished the monarchy in favor of a republic and adopted a new constitution. The Italian nation emerged from the disaster of fascism and war under the leadership of its largest political party, the Christian Democrats, which stressed industrial growth, agricultural reform, and close cooperation with the United States and the Vatican. In the late 1970s and early 1980s, Italy, along with other Western nations, experienced chronic inflation and unemployment. Labor unrest, frequent government scandals, and the violence of extremists all contributed to a volatile political situation.

In the 1990s, Italy faced significant challenges as voters demanded political, economic, and ethical reforms. New political forces and new alignments of power emerged in the 1994 national elections, which swept media magnate Silvio Berlusconi and his "Freedom Pole" coalition into office, his first time as prime minister. A series of center-left coalitions dominated Italy's political landscape between 1996 and 2001 when national elections returned Berlusconi to power at the head of the five-party center-right "Freedom House" coalition. Because of a poor showing in regional elections, he was again forced to resign in April 2005 and form a new government, which was the 60th government since the liberation of Italy.[51]

Industrial relations in Italy are governed by its constitution, acts of Parliament, regional laws, customs and practice, and also European Union (EU) measures affecting employment and any adopted recommendations and conventions of the International Labour Organization. The Constitution

- Recognizes trade union freedom and collective bargaining (Article 39)
- Recognizes the right to strike (Article 40)
- Recognizes employee participation in enterprises (Article 46)
- Recognizes the right to work (Article 4)
- Charges the republic with a duty to protect labor (Article 35)
- Establishes the right to pay based on quantity and quality of work (Article 36)
- Calls for the registration of trade unions for the purpose of extending the terms of labor agreements to all workers in the industry, union and nonunion, known as an ***erga omnes*** effect.

ERGA OMNES

In Italy, collective bargaining agreements that apply to all workers in a bargaining unit and all employees in industries are covered by it if the trade union is properly registered.

The Workers' Statute guarantees the freedom of opinion, the right to form and join unions, and the right to carry on union activity at the workplace. It provides trade union representation in firms with more than 15 workers and includes the right to collective bargaining at the company or production facility level, as well as the right to call a strike at company level. Companies may not take actions to suppress union activity. Employers and unions are involved in determining the overall direction of general policy with respect to legislative activity and economic policy and planning.

Reform of Italian labor law to enhance the match between labor demand and supply, relating primarily to job placement services and forms of employment, culminated in June 2003, with the approval of a draft decree enacting a new law on employment and the labor market, the so-called Biagi reform, named after Italian Labor Ministry consultant Marco Biagi, whose assassination in 2002 is linked with the reform law, discussed in Profile 13-3.

As a result of the Biagi Law reform measure, collective bargaining negotiations have begun to address and regulate the use of some of these new forms of employment. They include an agreement on part-time work negotiated at the local level that provides incentives for companies to increase the number of part-time staff and give workers time off with pay according to the premium for overtime work established by the sectoral collective agreement. The first national agreement on coordinated freelance contracts in outsourced call centers and a company-level

Profile 13-3

Marco Biagi, International Labor Martyr

In the United States, the violence that accompanied the fledgling labor movement in the nineteenth century produced regrettable but infrequent incidents of deaths among labor leaders. Such incidents, however, are far removed from today's labor movement. But it would seem the same is not true in Italy. On March 19, 2002, terrorists, claiming to be from the "Red Brigades," murdered Marco Biagi, an Italian labor law and industrial relations expert, who was working with the Italian Labor Ministry on labor law reforms. Three years prior to this, terrorists who identified themselves as "Red Brigades" claimed to have murdered Massimo D'Antona, who also advised the government on labor reforms. Biagi was consulting on a proposal to reform the Italian labor market by changing the protections offered laid-off or fired workers under a system that makes a third of Italy's 21 million workers virtually invulnerable to firing. On the day of his death, Biagi had published an article in Italy's leading business newspaper arguing that Italy needed to change its welfare system to catch up with Europe's biggest economies.

Marco Biagi, 50, was shot dead March 2002 in Bologna, Italy. Biagi worked as an adviser for the Italian Labour Ministry on controversial labor reform proposals. *Source:* BARACCHI-BENVENUTI/AFP/Newscom.

Biagi, a professor of labor law at the University of Modena and a consultant to the EU, was a member of the Italian Socialist Party but had worked with the center-right government of Prime Minister Silvio Berliusconi because he knew that Italy needed to change its labor market. As Biagi biked home from work, he was gunned down by two men on motorcycles outside his home, just steps away from his wife and child and just months after his security escort had been discontinued after threats over his work on a Milan employment pact.[52]

agreement that established a committee on working hours and an "hours bank" in which workers can accumulate overtime hours are additional innovations.[53]

CONCERTAZIONE

Involvement of employees and employers in the design of economic policy with the Italian government promoted by the formal adoption of tripartite agreements or pacts.

The involvement of *social partners*—employers and employees—in the design of economic policy, the so-called ***concertazione*** of the Italian government, has been promoted by the formal adoption of tripartite agreements, or *pacts*. Such agreements were signed between labor unions, employers associations, and the government in 1995 to target pension reform; in 1996 to reform the labor market and promote worker education and training; in 1998 to set up a new system of three-way industrial relations, including local authorities; and in 2002 with the goal of reforming the nation's labor market and employment benefits. That bargaining structure was established by a tripartite pact as a framework for income policy and new rules for the wage bargaining system. The *Protocol on Labour Costs of July 1993* provides for a two-tier wage bargaining system: At the national industry level, collective bargaining agreements are valid for four years on the terms and conditions of employment and for two years for wages and economic benefits and are intended to set minimum wage levels; and at the company or firm level, agreements are valid for four years and may link pay to company profits and increases in productivity.[54] National agreements are binding for all employers in a sector under a principle known as *erga omnes*.[55] In theory, consistent with this two-tiered approach to bargaining, economic decisions at the national level are to be influenced by external measures regarding the competitive position of the affected industry and the rate of inflation. At the company level, pay is linked to the performance achieved in relationship to the expectations of the parties.

In the face of continuing difficulties in the Italian economy, industry has proposed new action strategies that require reform of the production system—mainly by means of large investments in research and in the development of infrastructures—and the resumption of meaningful dialogue with the trade unions and the government. Amid the apparent stagnation of Italian industry, these events can be interpreted as signaling a renewed commitment by trade unions and employers' associations to participate with the government in the definition of economic and social policies, which may prove crucial for the Italian economic system to improve its competitiveness.[56]

FAR EAST

Western industrialization took place primarily in a laissez-faire setting, not under direct government direction or patronage. An entrepreneurial middle class moved the industrialization process forward, which in turn created a distinctive and relatively homogeneous working class. This working class was able to organize into trade unions to protect its interests. Western governments did not "create" unions. Western industrial relations systems reached maturity in the twentieth century, long after the commencement of the industrial revolution and at a time when democratic political systems were more or less in place. The industrial relations systems that developed were underpinned by a value system based on democratic principles, a balance between employers and employees, and relatively minimal government intervention. In such an environment, collective bargaining and freedom of association were logical developments.

In contrast, the majority of Asian countries were subject to foreign occupation, so no indigenous entrepreneurial middle class of any significance emerged that could have spearheaded the industrialization process. During the colonial period, governments assumed a dominant role, which was maintained by the post-independence governments. Only after the industrialization process had been in operation for some time did an entrepreneurial class emerge to take over some part of the government's role in economic activity. In Japan and China, for example, the governments nurtured and assisted in the development of these entrepreneurial classes and provided them with protection from competition until they achieved international competitiveness. The economic development and its imperatives, then, were government and not entrepreneurial driven.

Japan

Contrary to most aspects of Japanese society, the Japanese system of labor relations is not the product of years of tradition. Japan's industrialization began in the 1880s with ownership of a majority of its enterprises concentrated in powerful family groups, which later became the powerful ***keiretsu*** group of holding companies. Keiretsu is a loose conglomeration of companies organized around a single bank for their mutual benefit. The companies sometimes, but not always, own equity in each other. These families ran their factories in a paternalistic tradition, not unlike U.S. company towns of the same era. Although some trade unions were around before World War II, they had very little impact. After the war during the occupation of Japan by Allied forces, the Japanese labor movement was encouraged, so by 1949, 55.8 percent of the workforce was unionized. In Japan as elsewhere, however, union membership hovered around 30 percent from the 1950s to the 1970s, fell to 20 percent in the early 1980s, and in 2003, the unionization rate dropped to 19.6 percent.[57]

KEIRETSU

In Japan, a conglomeration of companies organized around a single bank for their mutual benefit.

THREE KEY PREMISES OF JAPANESE LABOR RELATIONS. The Japanese system of labor relations can be summarized as having three key premises. The first key premise is the concept of lifetime employment, which is not so much a guaranteed benefit as a result of how enterprises are organized. Regular employees enter a firm with the expectation that they will be kept on until they reach the mandatory retirement age of 60. These employees are hired not for specific jobs or occupations but as company employees, knowing the employer will exhaust all other measures before laying these regular employees off. Japanese firms compete with each other every spring to recruit the best of the new university and high school graduates as regular employees. The desirability of each graduate is normally determined as much by the prestige attached to his or her university or school as by academic record.

The second key premise is the traditional Japanese wage system based on seniority. New employees are given a monthly salary based on the individual's level of educational attainment but not job assignment. This sum automatically rises at least annually in accordance with a published table on the basis of length of service. Japan also has a distinctive bonus system, under which workers are given bonuses twice yearly (June and December). These bonuses are described as a deferred salary payment and constitute a significant portion of the workers' annual income. The amount of the bonus, which is either negotiated with a union or based on custom, traditionally is not tied to profits.[58]

The third key premise is that although Japanese labor unions are organized into three tiers—enterprise-based unions, industry-level unions, and national federations—more than 90 percent are enterprise-based unions. These company unions engage in collective bargaining and consultation with company management. Together, these three management methods, lifetime employment, seniority-based pay, and company unions, served as a mechanism in which both managers and employees could develop their knowledge and ability within the company in the security of the practice of long-term stable employment. The result was that expertise and know-how was accumulated within the organization.

In recent years, Japanese companies have shifted toward a wage system that links performance and bonuses to overall corporate profits because Japanese businesses now face increasing global competition and the need to motivate their workers.

Japan is increasing the scope of its employment legislation to deal with the new economic and social conditions. A council established by Japan's government called for legal reform in the employment/labor field to encourage labor mobility, industrial structure transformation, and diversified working patterns. Lawmakers in 2003 added an explicit clause that (1) required employers to have just cause when dismissing employees; (2) increased the maximum duration of a fixed-term labor contract from one to three years (five years for workers engaged in highly specialized duties and those ages 60 and above); (3) extended the period from one to three years that a worker may be "dispatched" and the types of job dispatched workers (i.e., temporary workers) can engage in; (4) granted local public bodies the right to provide free job placement services; (5) increased the contribution rate for the unemployment insurance program; (6) lowered the maximum amount of unemployment benefits; (7) enabled a panel of a judge and two labor experts to provide rapid, specific solutions for labor disputes; and (8) extended the retirement age until age 65.

The constitution of Japan provides for freedom of association, the right to organize, and the right to act collectively. The courts have interpreted the right to act collectively as extending to the right to strike. The Trade Union Law protects Japanese workers in exercising autonomous self-organization for the purpose of collective action, defines collective action as the right to engage in union activities and the right to strike, and allows unions and employers to negotiate with each other and to conclude collective bargaining agreements. The Trade Union Law proscribes an employer's refusal to bargain collectively as an unfair labor practice.

Japanese labor unions basically have a "triplicate structure," enterprise labor unions organized at each business, industrial trade unions organized as loose federations of enterprise union members by industry, and national centers made up of the industry trade unions at the national level (a typical example is the Japanese Trade Union Confederation, *Rengo*).

Collective bargaining is practiced widely in Japan on the terms and conditions of employment. However, issues affecting management and production, such as new plant and equipment and subcontracting, usually are resolved through regular consultations between the unions and management. The Japanese joint consultation system provides a means for continual information sharing and communication. Joint consultation committees are made up of both senior corporate executives and high-level union officials. These committees do not conduct wage negotiations, but it is common for the enterprise to share confidential business and financial information with the union through these committees before wage negotiations. The approach of Japanese employers and unions to a cooperative collective bargaining process through information sharing has resulted in more employment security but more moderate wage increases.[59]

Collective bargaining negotiations normally do not cover wages, which are negotiated separately during the Spring Wage Offensive (***shunto***). The Spring Wage Offensive has occurred annually since 1955. During shunto, enterprise-based unions in each industry conduct negotiations simultaneously with their companies. The objectives of shunto are to provide each individual union with a greater bargaining power and to distribute wage increases proportionally across the industry. Recently, shunto negotiations have shifted away from wages to job security because of the current economic situation.

SHUNTO

The Spring Wage Offensive in Japan, at which wages are negotiated separate from other collective bargaining. During *shunto* enterprise-based unions in each industry simultaneously conduct negotiations with their companies. The objectives of *shunto* are to provide each individual union with a greater bargaining power and to distribute wage increases proportionally across the industry.

Rengo, formed in 1989 with the merger of public and private sector unions, is the largest national trade union organization in Japan, representing over 7 million members, almost two-thirds of Japanese organized labor. In 2000, 11.4 million of an eligible 53.8 million Japanese workers were unionized. The most important role of the national trade unions is their participation in politics. Rengo represents the labor sector on various government advisory bodies and actively takes part in decision-making processes concerning labor policy.

China

For centuries China, the third largest country in the world occupying a fifteenth of the world's landmass, stood as a leading civilization, outpacing the rest of the world in the arts and sciences. But in the nineteenth and early twentieth centuries, the country was beset by civil unrest, major famines, military defeats, and foreign occupation. After World War II, the Communists under Mao Zedong established an autocratic socialist system that imposed strict controls over everyday life.

In late 1978, Deng Xiaoping and other leaders began moving the economy from a sluggish, inefficient, centrally planned economy to a more market-oriented system. Although the system still operates within a political framework of strict state control, the economic influence of nonstate organizations and individual citizens has been steadily increasing. China replaced old collectives with a system of household and village responsibility in agriculture, increased the authority of local officials and plant managers in industry, permitted a wide variety of small-scale enterprises in services and light manufacturing, and opened the economy to increased foreign trade and investment. The result has been a quadrupling of the gross domestic product (GDP) since 1978 and an amazing growth in foreign trade (Table 13-3). Measured on purchasing power parity (PPP) basis, China in

TABLE 13-3 Growth of China's Foreign Trade (1996–2008) (Unit USD$ 1 billion)

Year	Imports	Exports
1996	151.05	138.83
1998	183.71	140.24
2000	249.20	225.09
2002	325.60	295.17
2004	593.40	561.40
2006	791.50	968.90
2008	1,233.10	1,428.60

Source: *China Statistical Yearbook*, China Statistics Press, 2010; General Administration of Customers of the PRC, China's Customs Statistics from Chinability at www.chinability.com.

2010 stood as the second largest economy in the world after the United States. In only thirty short years after Xiaoping's economic reforms, China's exports increased from $9.75 billion in 1978 to $1,428.6 billion in 2008.

SOCIALIST MARKET ECONOMY

In China, economic system in which state retains ownership of the means of production but wages, prices, and employment would be allowed to develop in the private sector.

China has benefited from globalization in the Internet industry and has a lead in the absorption of technology and a rising prominence in world trade. For example, China posted an 11.4 percent economic growth in 2007—more than twice the world average of 4.9 percent.[60] The transition toward a market economy has led to changes in the labor relations environment. The starting point of China's industrial relations system was an economy based on the state ownership of the means of production and strict centralized control of wages, prices, and employment. This planned economy was able to reconcile the interests of workers, managers, and the state with an administrative framework guaranteed by the central government. China initially attempted to develop a "**socialist market economy**" in which state ownership of the means of production would be retained but the control of wages, prices, and employment would be relaxed and a private sector would be allowed to develop.[61] China revised that economic model to strongly favor state-owned enterprises, granting them preferential access to capital, technology, and markets, and, at the same time, to allow foreign investment, resulting in foreign firms claiming much of China's industrial exports.[62] China relaxed its guarantees of employment, wages, and welfare as these **state-owned enterprises (SOEs)** became subject to competitive market pressures, and the central government turned over responsibility for economic management and financial solvency to the SOEs.

STATE-OWNED ENTERPRISES

In China, state-owned businesses which enjoy preferential access to capital, technology, and markets as well as protection from private sector competition.

This transformation challenged trade unions in China because they had been a part of the socialist system, not as workers' representatives but performing state functions in the workplace. The All-China Federation of Trade Union's constitution had described their role as "transmission belts between the [communist] party and the masses."[63] They focused on the day-to-day shop floor problems to ensure the success of the enterprise while educating the workers and making sure they were not exploited. With entry into the global economy, jobs and living standards have

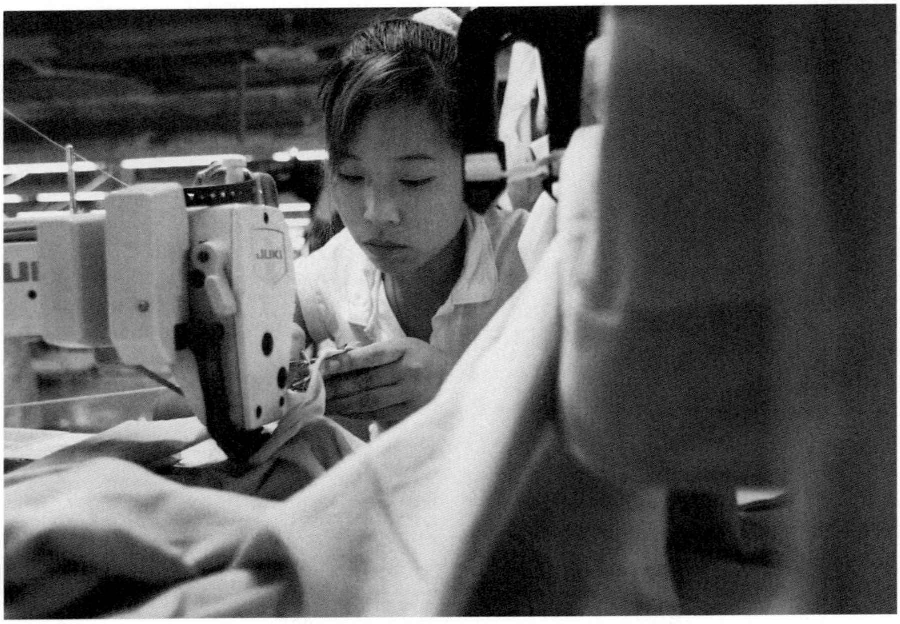

A Chinese woman sews shirts at the Youngor Group's textile factory in Ningbo, in China's Zhejiang province. *Source:* © REINHARD KRAUSE/Reuters/Corbis.

become subordinate issues to SOEs being competitive. So the growing divergence of interest between employers (the state) and employees has led to increased worker unrest. Thus, in China, as in the countries discussed earlier, the emergence of trade unions as worker representatives, and not the representatives of employers, has been as a result of labor unrest.

Philosophically, China's industrial relations within its socialist market economy have a fundamental difference from industrial relations within capitalist economies. According to the theory of the socialist market economy, state ownership of the enterprise means the "employers" are really custodians of the interests of the entire society. The trade union, then, is not supposed to represent the employees *against* the employer, but the entire enterprise, just as the employers do. Therefore, collective contracting and resolution of disputes were nonadversarial, resolved on the basis of the common interest of the whole.[64] That philosophy began to change somewhat with the transition to a capitalist market economy, albeit made up primarily of SOEs. These enterprises had to cover their costs and realize a profit to finance future development, which refocused their attention from the collective good to the bottom line. Trade unions found their roles somewhat enhanced as actual representatives of the employees rather than just transition belts between the government and the workers.

In the past, trade unionism in China, as in other "new" economies, suffered from its inability to pressure employers, be they either SOEs or foreign investors, without resorting to conflict tactics that might provoke social unrest and renewed repression, as had been experienced after the Tiananmen Square incident in 1989.

However, a new labor movement in China that surfaced when workers went on strike at Honda and Toyota plants has caused many companies to change their labor relations practices and policies, raise wages and benefits, and improve working conditions. Some Chinese production workers are comparing their pay with their counterparts in Japan—a substantial pay gap that may be an ominous sign for Chinese employers. The tight job market combined with a more militant, young, educated workforce has caused employers like Honda, Toyota, Daimler AG, Yum Brands Inc. (KFC and Pizza Hut), and Compal Electronics—the world's largest manufacturer of PCs—to offer performance-based bonuses as well as other economic improvements to attract and retain Chinese workers. One dramatic incident caused Hon Hai Precision Industry—the world's largest contract manufacturer of electronics (Apple and Hewlett-Packard)—to initiate labor improvements. In 2010 ten of Hon Hai's workers jumped to their deaths to focus attention on the plight of their coworkers.[65]

Profile 13-4

China Walmart Stores Organized with U.S. Labor Assistance

On August 16, 2006, Walmart, the U.S. retailer with a history of antiunion policies, signed an agreement allowing the formation of unions in its China stores. Joe Hatfield, chief executive of Walmart, Asia, said, "I fully anticipate working collaboratively with leadership from All China Federation of Trade Unions (ACFTV) and union organizations at all levels to create a model working relationship." The decision was a complete reversal of Walmart's hostile union policy in past years. It is quite ironic because Walmart, the U.S.-based retail giant, opened the door to unions in communist China, whereas it has successfully kept out unions in the United States. Within months, the ACFTU established unions at 62 Walmart stores in 30 China cities. Under Chinese law, however, the unions do not have collective bargaining or strike rights.

The historic event came largely as the result of (1) a new 2005 China labor law that gives unions more powers to organize workers and (2) a two-year focused effort by U.S.

(Continued)

Even though Walmart announced it would not allow its stores in China to unionize, the All-China Federation of Trade Unions (ACFTU), with over 130 million members, successfully organized 62 Walmart stores by the end of 2007. *Source:* Remy Gabalda/AP Images.

labor leader Andy Stern, president of Service Employees International Union (SEIU), to organize Walmart stores in China. A key point in the process came in November 2005 when a delegation from the Chinese union flew to the United States. At a dinner in San Francisco they complained that workers in Nanjing, China, had made more than 20 attempts to meet with Walmart management—without success. The SEIU team suggested that instead they begin meeting with workers at their homes, bus stops, or restaurants. The idea worked, and the ACFTU leaders found a Walmart employee to lead the organizational effort. Ke Yunlong, a 30-year-old frozen meats worker in Jingiang, agreed to lead the union efforts. Yunlong, with the assistance of the ACFTU, held the first Walmart China union meeting on July 29, 2006. The ACFTU officials made a written promise to workers that if they were fired for union-related activity, the union would find them a similar-paying job. The union then began sending organizers to the entrance of the store to catch workers before shifts and sign them as members. The banner above Yunlong on July 29, 2006, read, "Determined to take the road to develop trade unionism with Chinese characteristics."

Source: Adapted from Mei Fong and Kris Maher, "U.S. Labor Leader Aided China's Wal-Mart Coup," *Wall Street Journal* (June 22, 2007), pp. A1, 8; and UNI, Commerce home page. Available at www.union-network.org. Accessed February 28, 2008.

Summary

Globalization in the twenty-first century has increased competition among nations for investment, technology, and labor. The international trade union movement has been seen as a uniting force, able, perhaps, to institutionalize worker protections within various political and legal systems. In studying labor relations around the world, a comparison can be made between a number of countries and the United States in the way the labor movement grew from industrialization. When the industrial revolution began, whether in England in the early 1800s or in Japan a century later, the unskilled workers needed to fuel the industries were vulnerable to being treated as a commodity. So although industrialization brought progress and prosperity, workers found it necessary to band together to make sure they could reap benefits from both.

Great Britain had for years followed a voluntary approach to labor relations, which focused on a union and an employer's agreement to engage in collective bargaining, rather than legislative fiats. That situation changed somewhat in the 1980s when Prime Minister Margaret Thatcher outlawed secondary strikes, limited picketing, and prohibited a closed shop. Australia's industrial relations system uses compulsory conciliation and arbitration to resolve collective bargaining impasses. Prior to the 1980s, most of the time wages and terms of conditions of employment were established across industries once an "award" was arrived at by negotiators or imposed by the arbitrator. Australia modernized its system by streamlining the award system and emphasizing enterprise rather than industry-wide bargaining. Canada combined British-style voluntarism in recognition of unions, American-style welfare capitalism in labor benefits laws, and Australian-style government-mandated mediation and fact-finding for its industrial relations.

In Europe, oligarchies and democracies, capitalists and socialists, caused the labor movement to embrace a threefold agenda: representing employees and advancing their employment interests through collective action, increasing workers' protections through active engagement in the political process, and improving the lives of workers through the promotion of welfare and education agendas. The EU has become a powerful economic and political entity through its Single Market and Social Charter principles. However, it is still struggling to increase labor mobility despite linguistic and cultural differences, problems with benefit portability, and inconsistent training and education standards.

Japan had been subject to foreign occupation so that when the industrial revolution arrived, it had no indigenous entrepreneurial middle class to finance and grow needed industries. So powerful families, with the help of the government, became the entrepreneurs and opened and ran the factories with the government's help. The Allies fostered the labor movement in Japan after World War II. China has emerged as the second largest world economy after moving to a market-oriented system. In recent years Chinese workers demanded and received substantially higher wages and benefits.

And although it is not a significant player in the history of the labor movement in the United States, the International Labour Organization is a 70-year-old organization dedicated to the key principles of the labor movement: Labor is not a commodity, workers have the right to organize into unions, and workers have the right to bargain with their employers about wages and the terms and conditions of their employment. ILO's international standards bring focus and unity to the labor movement around the world, particularly in developing nations.

CASE STUDIES

Case Study 13-1 Freedom of Movement

Regulation (EEC) No 1612/68 of the European Union Council of October 15, 1968 on freedom of movement for workers within the Community Article 7(1) and (2) reads as follows:

1. A worker who is a national of a Member State may not, in the territory of another Member State, be treated differently from national workers by reason of his nationality in respect of any conditions of employment and work, in particular as regards remuneration, dismissal, and should he become unemployed, reinstatement or reemployment;
2. He shall enjoy the same social and tax advantages as national workers.

According to the law of Germany on child-raising allowance and parental leave, any permanent resident or any person who is ordinarily a resident of Germany who has a dependent child and has no full-time employment can claim a child-raising allowance. In addition, nationals of the EU Member States from countries having a common border with Germany are also entitled to the child-raising allowance, provided they are engaged in more than minor employment in Germany. Finally, the spouse resident in another Member State of a person working in the civil service or a public-law employment in Germany may receive child-raising allowance. The Court had previously held that Germany's child-raising allowance constitutes a social advantage within the meaning of Article 7(2).

The Plaintiff is an Austrian national married to a German national who previously lived in Germany. They now live in Austria with their three children, and her husband works in Germany as a civil servant. Bavaria refused to grant Ms. Hartmann the child-raising allowance provided for under German law for her three children. The grounds for the refusal to grant the child-raising allowance were that the Plaintiff was not a resident in Germany and did not work there.

Two questions were presented to the court for a preliminary ruling. First:

> "Is a German national who, while continuing his service as a post office official in Germany, moved his permanent residence from Germany to Austria and has since then carried on his occupation as a border worker to be regarded as a migrant worker within the meaning of Regulation (EEC) No 1612/68?"

The German government, the U.K. government, and the Commission of the European Communities, in their written observations, and the Netherlands government, at the hearing, submitted that only the movement of a person to another Member State *for the purpose of*

(continued)

carrying on an occupation should be regarded as having exercised the right of freedom of movement for workers protected by EU agreements. A person such as the Plaintiff's husband, who never left his employment in the Member State of which he is a national and merely transferred his residence to the Member State of his spouse, could not therefore benefit from the EU Community provisions on freedom of movement for workers.

The Plaintiff's response was that just because her husband settled in Austria for reasons not connected with his employment does not justify refusing him the status of migrant worker that he acquired when, following the transfer of his residence to Austria, he made full use of his right to freedom of movement for workers by going to Germany to carry on an occupation there. Plaintiff's husband falls within the scope of the provisions of the EC Treaty on freedom of movement for workers, and hence of the Regulation.

This was the second question:

> "Does it constitute indirect discrimination within the meaning of Article 7(2) of Regulation No 1612/68 if the non-working spouse of the person mentioned in Question 1, who lives in Austria and is an Austrian national, was excluded from receiving German child-raising allowance in the period in question because she did not have either her permanent or ordinary residence in Germany?"

The German and U.K. governments observed that it would be unfair to allow a border worker whose residence and workplace are in different Member States to enjoy the same social advantages in both Member States and to combine them. To avoid that risk, and in view of the fact that the Regulation does not contain any coordinating rules to avoid the stacking of benefits, the possibility of "exporting" child-raising allowance to the frontier worker's Member State of residence could be excluded. As explained by the parties, the German child-raising allowance constitutes an instrument of national family policy intended to encourage the birth-rate in that country. The primary purpose of the allowance is to allow parents to care for their children themselves by giving up or reducing their employment in order to concentrate on bringing up their children in the first years of their life. The German government adds essentially that child-raising allowance is granted in order to benefit persons who, by their choice of residence, have established a real link with German society. It says that, in that context, a residence condition such as that at issue in the main proceedings is justified.

The Plaintiff argues that her husband's status of frontier worker does not in any way prevent him from being able to claim the equal treatment prescribed by Article 7(2) in relation to the grant of social advantages. The Court has already held that frontier workers can rely on the provisions of Article 7 on the same basis as any other worker to whom that article applies. The Plaintiff as the spouse of a worker who falls within the scope of the Regulation, is an indirect beneficiary of the equal treatment granted to migrant workers by Article 7(2). Consequently, the benefit of German child-raising allowance can be extended to her if that allowance constitutes for her husband a "social advantage" within the meaning of Article 7(2).

The Plaintiff notes that a benefit such as German child-raising allowance, which enables one of the parents to devote himself or herself to the raising of a young child, by meeting family expenses, benefits the family as a whole, whichever parent it is who claims the allowance. The grant of such an allowance to a worker's spouse is capable of reducing that worker's obligation to contribute to family expenses, and therefore constitutes for him, or her, a "social advantage" within the meaning of Article 7(2). Further, that article provides that a migrant worker is to enjoy the same social and tax advantages in the host Member State as national workers. Since child-raising allowance is a "social advantage" within the meaning of that provision, a migrant worker in a situation such as this, and consequently his spouse, must, for the reasons mentioned earlier, be able to enjoy it on the same basis as a national worker. Regardless of whether the aims pursued by the German legislation could justify a national rule based exclusively on the criterion of residence, it must be observed that the German legislature did not confine itself to a strict application of the residence condition for the grant of child-raising allowance but allowed exceptions under which frontier workers who carry on an occupation in Germany but reside in another Member State can claim German child-raising allowance if they carry on an occupation of a more than minor extent.

Source: Adapted from *Gertraud Hartmann v. Freistaat Bayern,* Case C-212/05, Court of Justice of European Union (Grand Chamber), July 18, 2007.

QUESTIONS

1. How should the court decide this case to support the European Union's commitment to labor mobility between Member States? Explain.
2. Contrast and compare the situations of compelling Germany to grant child-raising benefits to the plaintiff, a resident of Austria, with the state of Illinois granting state unemployment benefits to a resident of Indiana.

Case Study 13-2 Discrimination against Union Official

The Trade Unions International of Public and Allied Employees filed a complaint with the ILO Committee alleging violations of trade union rights in France. The union explained that Mr. Laganier, administrator at the National Institute of Statistics and Economic Studies (INSEE), had been detached to the Ministry of Industry for seven years. On his return from leave he found furniture removers in his office and learned that he was being sent back to his office of origin without his superiors having requested it. Although the official reason given for the measure was that of budgetary restrictions, the union added that Laganier had cost the Ministry of Industry nothing because he continued to be paid by the INSEE. The union stated that Laganier has been transferred not in his capacity as an official with INSEE, but as general secretary of a trade union, and the move was a violation of trade union rights in complete contradiction with ILO Conventions Nos. 98 and 135. According to the union, it was part of a more general, large-scale offensive against the trade union rights of public servants, organized by the French government.

In its reply the government stated that the director of the Office of the Minister of Industry had communicated the decision of Laganier's return to his former office to his superiors. According to the government, the reason for the return was the reorganization of the services of the Ministry of Industry, which required a reduction in the number of permanent officials on loan from INSEE. Naturally Laganier was paid by INSEE, but there is an overall limitation on loaned officials so there are organizational ramifications for placements. Furthermore, the government pointed out that this decision was by no means an exceptional one because it fell within the normal career development process of INSEE administrators, who are placed at the disposal of the Ministry of Industry on a purely temporary basis. The case of Laganier, who had been attached to the Ministry for over seven years, was, according to the government, analogous to that of all other INSEE administrators recruited at the same time or earlier, without exception, and they, like him, had returned to this body after spending several years working for the Ministry of Industry. The government added that the official's departure had no effect on the CGT's representation within the ministry. It concluded by stating that freedom of association was fully respected in this ministry, as in other departments, under the provisions of the prime minister's circular dated September 14 relating to the exercise of trade union rights in the public service.

The union responded that ILO has always taken the view that one of the fundamental principles of freedom of association is that workers should enjoy adequate protection against all acts of antiunion discrimination in respect of their employment—dismissal, transfer, downgrading, and other prejudicial measures—and that this protection is particularly desirable in the case of trade union officials because, to carry out their trade union functions in full independence, they must have the assurance they will not be victimized by virtue of their trade union office. Furthermore, the ILO considers that the existence of basic legislation forbidding acts of antitrade union discrimination is

(continued)

insufficient if such legislation is not accompanied by effective procedures ensuring its practical application. Thus, when a worker considers that he has been a victim of antitrade union practices, he should be able to appeal to a tribunal or to another authority independent of the parties.

The government responded that, based on the provisions of the prime minister's circular previously mentioned, the representatives of trade union organizations subjected to discrimination regarding their progression in their careers "may in particular defend themselves before administrative courts against . . . individual decisions prejudicial to the collective interests of public officials." The union in this case did not appeal the decision of the ministry with the appropriate French court so this case should not be before the ILO Committee. The ILO Committee, although not bound by any rule that national procedures of redress must be exhausted before it will hear such complaints, will consider that a national remedy before an independent tribunal whose procedure offers appropriate protections, has not been pursued.

Source: Adapted from *The Trade Unions International of Public and Allied Employees v. Government of France,* Case No. 866, Report No. 168, International Labour Organization.

QUESTIONS

1. What are some of the reasons that the ILO does not defer to national procedures, such as U.S. courts defer to arbitration, before hearing a labor complaint?
2. If the practice of the Ministry of Industry had been to return loaned personnel on a routine basis, give some of the reasons why the union in this case would have believed Laganier was being discriminated against.

Key Terms and Concepts

capitalism *471*
codetermination *485*
concertazione 490
erga omnes 489
European Union (EU) *481*
globalization *467*
Industrial revolution *469*
International Labour Organization (ILO) *473*
keiretsu 491
multinational enterprise *467*
Shop Stewards Movement and Workers' Committees *477*
shunto 493
socialist market economy *494*
state-owned enterprise (SOE) *494*
Trades Union Congress *477*
Treaty of Maastricht *481*
tripartite organizational structure *474*
Workplace Relations Act (WRA) *480*
works councils *482*

Review Questions

1. What are the key components of globalization, and how can they influence collective bargaining?
2. Discuss the challenges that globalization presents to trade unions and how trade unions are responding.
3. Why did the industrial revolution, the democratic revolution, and the rise of capitalism result in different labor movements in Anglophone, European, and Far East countries?
4. Using one of the countries described in this chapter, discuss how its government attempted to suppress, then tolerate, and then support unions and why.
5. Why was the International Labour Organization created, and what influenced its structure and its mission?
6. What beliefs of the British labor movement influenced its post–World War I development?
7. Compare and contrast the industrial relations system in the United States, Canada, and Australia.
8. Describe the various ways European work councils are organized and their purpose.
9. Explain the reasons for a dichotomy in European countries between union membership and collective bargaining coverage.
10. Labor union membership dropped in most nations after the 1950s. What were the common reasons in the countries discussed in this chapter, and what were the unique reasons?
11. Why and how is the Japanese tradition of lifetime employment changing?
12. What recent events led to higher wages in China?

YOU BE THE ARBITRATOR
Minimum Wage

PARAGRAPH 1 (1) MINIMUM WAGE

The Law on the Posting of Workers extends certain collective agreements to employers established outside Germany and to their workers posted to Germany. That provision is worded as follows:

> The legal rules resulting from a collective agreement governing the construction industry which is declared to be universally applicable . . ., which relate to minimum pay, including pay for overtime . . . shall also apply . . . to an employment relationship linking an employer established outside Germany and his employee working within the territory covered by that collective agreement. . . .
>
> [T]he collective agreement on the minimum wage provides that the minimum wage consists of the hourly pay provided for by that agreement and the bonus granted to workers in the construction industry, which together make up the total hourly pay under the agreement. . . . [A]llowances and supplements paid by an employer, with the exception of the general bonus granted to workers in the construction industry, were not to be regarded as constituent elements of the minimum wage. . . . those supplements include in particular allowances in respect of overtime, night and Sunday work or work on public holidays, in addition to bonuses for travel and for heavy work.

Facts

It is an obligation of the member states to the European Union to ensure that employers from other countries that have posted their workers within the member state's borders follow the host country's minimum wage laws. This obligation stems from the promotion of freedom of movement for workers and nondiscrimination against another member state's citizens. The EU Commission investigated a complaint lodged against the Federal Republic of Germany that it was not enforcing the minimum wage law because it was not including in the calculation of the minimum wage all allowances and supplements paid by the employer. By not including those allowances and supplements, the foreign employer was required to pay its workers a higher minimum wage than German employers were required to pay. Specifically, the omitted allowances included bonuses for a 13th and 14th salary months, holiday pay, contributions to retirement accounts, bonuses for the quality of the work performed, and bonuses for dirty, heavy, or dangerous work.

Issue

Did Germany apply the correct method for comparing the minimum rate of pay due under German law and the amount of pay actually paid by the employer established in another member state to its posted employees?

The Position of the Parties

According to the commission, employers established in other Member States may be obliged, under the provisions applicable in those states, to provide other elements of pay in addition to the normal hourly pay. For example, an employer in the U.K. may be required to compensate its construction workers posted outside the U.K. for any medical bills they are required to pay because they would not have access to U.K.'s universal health care coverage while outside the U.K. Under the German legislation, such payments cannot be taken into account for the purpose of calculating the minimum wage. The commission contends that the failure to take into account allowances and supplements results in higher wage costs than those that German employers are required to pay to their employees and that employers established in other Member States are thus prevented from offering their services in Germany. Although the commission agrees that the Member State to the territory of which a worker is posted is allowed to determine the minimum rate of pay applicable within its borders, a Member State cannot, in comparing that rate and the wages paid by employers established in other Member States, impose its own payment structure on that employer.

According to the German government, it recognizes allowances and supplements paid by an employer that do not alter the relationship between the service provided by the worker and the payment that he receives. By contrast, allowances and supplements that do alter the balance between the services provided by the worker and the consideration that he receives in return cannot, according to the German rules, be recognized as forming part of the minimum wage and cannot be treated as constituent elements of that wage rate. The German government argues that hours worked that involve requirements of a particularly high degree of quality, or that involve special constraints or dangers, have a greater economic value than that of normal working hours and that the bonuses relating to such hours must not be taken into account in the calculation of the minimum wage. If those amounts were taken into account for the purposes of that calculation, the worker would be deprived of the economic value corresponding to those hours of work.

QUESTIONS

1. As arbitrator, what would be your award and opinion in this arbitration?
2. Identify the key, relevant section(s), phrases, or words of the collective bargaining agreement (CBA), and explain why they were critical in making your decision.
3. What actions might the employer and/or the union have taken to avoid this conflict?

Source: Adapted from *Commission of the European Communities v. Federal Republic of Germany,* Case C-341/02, April 14, 2005.

APPENDIX A

Texts of Statutes

National Labor Relations Act

Also cited NLRA or the Act; 29 U.S.C. §§151–169
[Title 29, Chapter 7, Subchapter II, United States Code]

FINDINGS AND POLICIES

SECTION 1. [§151.] The denial by some employers of the right of employees to organize and the refusal by some employers to accept the procedure of collective bargaining lead to strikes and other forms of industrial strife or unrest, which have the intent or the necessary effect of burdening or obstructing commerce by (a) impairing the efficiency, safety, or operation of the instrumentalities of commerce; (b) occurring in the current of commerce; (c) materially affecting, restraining, or controlling the flow of raw materials or manufactured or processed goods from or into the channels of commerce, or the prices of such materials or goods in commerce; or (d) causing diminution of employment and wages in such volume as substantially to impair or disrupt the market for goods flowing from or into the channels of commerce.

The inequality of bargaining power between employees who do not possess full freedom of association or actual liberty of contract and employers who are organized in the corporate or other forms of ownership association substantially burdens and affects the flow of commerce, and tends to aggravate recurrent business depressions, by depressing wage rates and the purchasing power of wage earners in industry and by preventing the stabilization of competitive wage rates and working conditions within and between industries.

Experience has proved that protection by law of the right of employees to organize and bargain collectively safeguards commerce from injury, impairment, or interruption, and promotes the flow of commerce by removing certain recognized sources of industrial strife and unrest, by encouraging practices fundamental to the friendly adjustment of industrial disputes arising out of differences as to wages, hours, or other working conditions, and by restoring equality of bargaining power between employers and employees.

Experience has further demonstrated that certain practices by some labor organizations, their officers, and members have the intent or the necessary effect of burdening or obstructing commerce by preventing the free flow of goods in such commerce through strikes and other forms of industrial unrest or through concerted activities which impair the interest of the public in the free flow of such commerce. The elimination of such practices is a necessary condition to the assurance of the rights herein guaranteed.

It is declared to be the policy of the United States to eliminate the causes of certain substantial obstructions to the free flow of commerce and to mitigate and eliminate these obstructions when they have occurred by encouraging the practice and procedure of collective bargaining and by protecting the exercise by workers of full freedom of association, self-organization, and designation of representatives of their own choosing, for the purpose of negotiating the terms and conditions of their employment or other mutual aid or protection.

DEFINITIONS

SEC. 2. [§152.] When used in this Act [subchapter]—

1. The term "person" includes one or more individuals, labor organizations, partnerships, associations, corporations, legal representatives, trustees, trustees in cases under title 11 of the United States Code [under title 11], or receivers.
2. The term "employer" includes any person acting as an agent of an employer, directly or indirectly, but shall not include the United States or any wholly owned Government corporation, or any Federal Reserve Bank, or any State or political subdivision thereof, or any person subject to the Railway Labor Act [45 U.S.C. §151 et seq.], as amended from time to time, or any labor organization (other than when acting as an employer), or anyone acting in the capacity of officer or agent of such labor organization.
   [Pub. L. 93–360, §1(a), July 26, 1974, 88 Stat. 395, deleted the phrase "or any corporation or association operating a hospital, if no part of the net earnings inures to the benefit of any private shareholder or individual" from the definition of "employer."]
3. The term "employee" shall include any employee, and shall not be limited to the employees of a particular employer, unless the Act [this subchapter] explicitly states otherwise, and shall include any individual whose work has ceased as a consequence of, or in connection with, any current labor dispute or because of any unfair labor practice, and who has not obtained any other regular and substantially equivalent employment, but shall not include any individual employed as an agricultural laborer, or in the domestic service of any family or person at his home, or any individual employed by his parent or spouse, or any individual having the status of an independent contractor, or any individual employed as a supervisor, or any individual employed by an employer subject to the Railway Labor Act [45 U.S.C. §151 et seq.], as amended from time to time, or by any other person who is not an employer as herein defined.
4. The term "representatives" includes any individual or labor organization.
5. The term "labor organization" means any organization of any kind, or any agency or employee representation committee or plan, in which employees participate and which exists for the purpose, in whole or in part, of dealing with employers concerning grievances, labor disputes, wages, rates of pay, hours of employment, or conditions of work.
6. The term "commerce" means trade, traffic, commerce, transportation or communication among the several States, or between the District of Columbia or any Territory of the United States and any State or other Territory, or between any foreign country and any State, Territory, or the District of Columbia, or within the District of Columbia or any Territory, or between points in the same State but through any other State or any Territory or the District of Columbia or any foreign country.
7. The term "affecting commerce" means in commerce, or burdening or obstructing commerce or the free flow of commerce, or having led or tending to lead to a labor dispute burdening or obstructing commerce or the free flow of commerce.
8. The term "unfair labor practice" means any unfair labor practice listed in section 8 [section 158 of this title].
9. The term "labor dispute" includes any controversy concerning term, tenure or conditions of employment, or concerning the association or representation of persons in negotiating, fixing, maintaining, changing, or seeking to arrange terms or conditions of employment, regardless of whether the disputants stand in the proximate relation of employer and employee.
10. The term "National Labor Relations Board" means the National Labor Relations Board provided for in section 3 of this Act [section 153 of this title].
11. The term "supervisor" means any individual having authority, in the interest of the employer, to hire, transfer, suspend, lay off, recall, promote, discharge, assign, reward, or discipline other employees, or responsibly to direct them, or to adjust their grievances, or effectively to recommend such action, if in connection with the foregoing the exercise of such authority is not of a merely routine or clerical nature, but requires the use of independent judgment.

12. The term "professional employee" means—

a. any employee engaged in work (i) predominantly intellectual and varied in character as opposed to routine mental, manual, mechanical, or physical work; (ii) involving the consistent exercise of discretion and judgment in its performance; (iii) of such a character that the output produced or the result accomplished cannot be standardized in relation to a given period of time; (iv) requiring knowledge of an advanced type in a field of science or learning customarily acquired by a prolonged course of specialized intellectual instruction and study in an institution of higher learning or a hospital, as distinguished from a general academic education or from an apprenticeship or from training in the performance of routine mental, manual, or physical processes; or

b. any employee, who (i) has completed the courses of specialized intellectual instruction and study described in clause (iv) of paragraph (a), and (ii) is performing related work under the supervision of a professional person to qualify himself to become a professional employee as defined in paragraph (a).

13. In determining whether any person is acting as an "agent" of another person so as to make such other person responsible for his acts, the question of whether the specific acts performed were actually authorized or subsequently ratified shall not be controlling.

14. The term "health care institution" shall include any hospital, convalescent hospital, health maintenance organization, health clinic, nursing home, extended care facility, or other institution devoted to the care of sick, infirm, or aged person.

[Pub. L. 93–360, §1(b), July 26, 1974, 88 Stat. 395, added par. (14).]

NATIONAL LABOR RELATIONS BOARD

SEC. 3. [§153.]

(a) [Creation, composition, appointment, and tenure; Chairman; removal of members] The National Labor Relations Board (hereinafter called the "Board") created by this Act [subchapter] prior to its amendment by the Labor Management Relations Act, 1947 [29 U.S.C. §141 et seq.], is continued as an agency of the United States, except that the Board shall consist of five instead of three members, appointed by the President by and with the advice and consent of the Senate. Of the two additional members so provided for, one shall be appointed for a term of five years and the other for a term of two years. Their successors, and the successors of the other members, shall be appointed for terms of five years each, excepting that any individual chosen to fill a vacancy shall be appointed only for the unexpired term of the member whom he shall succeed. The President shall designate one member to serve as Chairman of the Board. Any member of the Board may be removed by the President, upon notice and hearing, for neglect of duty or malfeasance in office, but for no other cause.

(b) [Delegation of powers to members and regional directors; review and stay of actions of regional directors; quorum; seal] The Board is authorized to delegate to any group of three or more members any or all of the powers which it may itself exercise. The Board is also authorized to delegate to its regional directors its powers under section 9 [section 159 of this title] to determine the unit appropriate for the purpose of collective bargaining, to investigate and provide for hearings, and determine whether a question of representation exists, and to direct an election or take a secret ballot under subsection (c) or (e) of section 9 [section 159 of this title] and certify the results thereof, except that upon the filling of a request therefor with the Board by any interested person, the Board may review any action of a regional director delegated to him under this paragraph, but such a review shall not, unless specifically ordered by the Board, operate as a stay of any action taken by the regional director. A vacancy in the Board shall not impair the right of the remaining members to exercise all of the powers of the Board, and three members of the Board shall, at all times, constitute a quorum of the Board, except that two members shall constitute a quorum of any group designated pursuant to the first sentence hereof. The Board shall have an official seal which shall be judicially noticed.

(c) **[Annual reports to Congress and the President]** The Board shall at the close of each fiscal year make a report in writing to Congress and to the President summarizing significant case activities and operations for that fiscal year.

(d) **[General Counsel; appointment and tenure; powers and duties; vacancy]** There shall be a General Counsel of the Board who shall be appointed by the President, by and with the advice and consent of the Senate, for a term of four years. The General Counsel of the Board shall exercise general supervision over all attorneys employed by the Board (other than administrative law judges and legal assistants to Board members) and over the officers and employees in the regional offices. He shall have final authority, on behalf of the Board, in respect of the investigation of charges and issuance of complaints under section 10 [section 160 of this title], and in respect of the prosecution of such complaints before the Board, and shall have such other duties as the Board may prescribe or as may be provided by law. In case of vacancy in the office of the General Counsel, the President is authorized to designate the officer or employee who shall act as General Counsel during such vacancy, but no person or persons so designated shall so act (1) for more than forty days when the Congress is in session unless a nomination to fill such vacancy shall have been submitted to the Senate, or (2) after the adjournment sine die of the session of the Senate in which such nomination was submitted.

[The title "administrative law judge" was adopted in 5 U.S.C. §3105.]

SEC. 4. [§154. ELIGIBILITY FOR REAPPOINTMENT; OFFICERS AND EMPLOYEES; PAYMENT OF EXPENSES]

(a) Each member of the Board and the General Counsel of the Board shall be eligible for reappointment, and shall not engage in any other business, vocation, or employment. The Board shall appoint an executive secretary, and such attorneys, examiners, and regional directors, and such other employees as it may from time to time find necessary for the proper performance of its duties. The Board may not employ any attorneys for the purpose of reviewing transcripts of hearings or preparing drafts of opinions except that any attorney employed for assignment as a legal assistant to any Board member may for such Board member review such transcripts and prepare such drafts. No administrative law judge's report shall be reviewed, either before or after its publication, by any person other than a member of the Board or his legal assistant, and no administrative law judge shall advise or consult with the Board with respect to exceptions taken to his findings, rulings, or recommendations. The Board may establish or utilize such regional, local, or other agencies, and utilize such voluntary and uncompensated services, as may from time to time be needed. Attorneys appointed under this section may, at the direction of the Board, appear for and represent the Board in any case in court. Nothing in this Act [subchapter] shall be construed to authorize the Board to appoint individuals for the purpose of conciliation or mediation, or for economic analysis.

[The title "administrative law judge" was adopted in 5 U.S.C. §3105.]

(b) All of the expenses of the Board, including all necessary traveling and subsistence expenses outside the District of Columbia incurred by the members or employees of the

Board under its orders, shall be allowed and paid on the presentation of itemized vouchers therefore approved by the Board or by any individual it designates for that purpose.

SEC. 5. [§155. PRINCIPAL OFFICE, CONDUCTING INQUIRIES THROUGHOUT COUNTRY; PARTICIPATION IN DECISIONS OR INQUIRIES CONDUCTED BY MEMBER] The principal office of the Board shall be in the District of Columbia, but it may meet and exercise any or all of its powers at any other place. The Board may, by one or more of its members or by such agents or agencies as it may designate, prosecute any inquiry necessary to its functions in any part of the United States. A member who participates in such an inquiry shall not be disqualified from subsequently participating in a decision of the Board in the same case.

SEC. 6. [§156. RULES AND REGULATIONS] The Board shall have authority from time to time to make, amend, and rescind, in the manner prescribed by the Administrative Procedure Act [by subchapter II of chapter 5 of title 5], such rules and regulations as may be necessary to carry out the provisions of this Act [subchapter].

RIGHTS OF EMPLOYEES

SEC. 7. [§157.] Employees shall have the right to self-organization, to form, join, or assist labor organizations, to bargain collectively through representatives of their own choosing, and to engage in other concerted activities for the purpose of collective bargaining or other mutual aid or protection, and shall also have the right to refrain from any or all such activities except to the extent that such right may be affected by an agreement requiring membership in a labor organization as a condition of employment as authorized in section 8(a)(3) [section 158(a)(3) of this title].

UNFAIR LABOR PRACTICES

SEC. 8. [§158.]

a. **[Unfair labor practices by employer]** It shall be an unfair labor practice for an employer—

(1) to interfere with, restrain, or coerce employees in the exercise of the rights guaranteed in section 7 [section 157 of this title];

(2) to dominate or interfere with the formation or administration of any labor organization or contribute financial or other support to it: Provided, That subject to rules and regulations made and published by the Board pursuant to section 6 [section 156 of this title], an employer shall not be prohibited from permitting employees to confer with him during working hours without loss of time or pay;

(3) by discrimination in regard to hire or tenure of employment or any term or condition of employment to encourage or discourage membership in any labor organization: Provided, That nothing in this Act [subchapter], or in any other statute of the United States, shall preclude an employer from making an agreement with a labor organization (not established, maintained, or assisted by any action defined in section 8(a) of this Act [in this subsection] as an unfair labor practice) to require as a condition of employment membership therein on or after the thirtieth day following the beginning of such employment or the effective date of such agreement, whichever is the later, (i) if such labor organization is the representative of the employees as provided in section 9(a) [section 159(a) of this title], in the appropriate collective-bargaining unit covered by such agreement when made, and (ii) unless following an election held as provided in section 9(e) [section 159(e) of this title] within one year preceding the effective date of such agreement, the Board shall have certified that at least a majority of the employees eligible to vote in such election have voted to rescind the authority of such labor organization to make such an agreement: Provided further, That no employer shall justify

any discrimination against an employee for nonmembership in a labor organization (A) if he has reasonable grounds for believing that such membership was not available to the employee on the same terms and conditions generally applicable to other members, or (B) if he has reasonable grounds for believing that membership was denied or terminated for reasons other than the failure of the employee to tender the periodic dues and the initiation fees uniformly required as a condition of acquiring or retaining membership;

(4) to discharge or otherwise discriminate against an employee because he has filed charges or given testimony under this Act [subchapter];

(5) to refuse to bargain collectively with the representatives of his employees, subject to the provisions of section 9(a) [section 159(a) of this title].

b. [Unfair labor practices by labor organization] It shall be an unfair labor practice for a labor organization or its agents—

(1) to restrain or coerce (A) employees in the exercise of the rights guaranteed in section 7 [section 157 of this title]: Provided, That this paragraph shall not impair the right of a labor organization to prescribe its own rules with respect to the acquisition or retention of membership therein; or (B) an employer in the selection of his representatives for the purposes of collective bargaining or the adjustment of grievances;

(2) to cause or attempt to cause an employer to discriminate against an employee in violation of subsection (a)(3) [of subsection (a)(3) of this section] or to discriminate against an employee with respect to whom membership in such organization has been denied or terminated on some ground other than his failure to tender the periodic dues and the initiation fees uniformly required as a condition of acquiring or retaining membership;

(3) to refuse to bargain collectively with an employer, provided it is the representative of his employees subject to the provisions of section 9(a) [section 159(a) of this title];

(4) (i) to engage in, or to induce or encourage any individual employed by any person engaged in commerce or in an industry affecting commerce to engage in, a strike or a refusal in the course of his employment to use, manufacture, process, transport, or otherwise handle or work on any goods, articles, materials, or commodities or to perform any services; or (ii) to threaten, coerce, or restrain any person engaged in commerce or in an industry affecting commerce, where in either case an object thereof is—

(A) forcing or requiring any employer or self-employed person to join any labor or employer organization or to enter into any agreement which is prohibited by section 8(e) [subsection (e) of this section];

(B) forcing or requiring any person to cease using, selling, handling, transporting, or otherwise dealing in the products of any other producer, processor, or manufacturer, or to cease doing business with any other person, or forcing or requiring any other employer to recognize or bargain with a labor organization as the representative of his employees unless such labor organization has been certified as the representative of such employees under the provisions of section 9 [section 159 of this title]: Provided, That nothing contained in this clause (B) shall be construed to make unlawful, where not otherwise unlawful, any primary strike or primary picketing;

(C) forcing or requiring any employer to recognize or bargain with a particular labor organization as the representative of his employees if another labor organization has been certified as the representative of such employees under the provisions of section 9 [section 159 of this title];

(D) forcing or requiring any employer to assign particular work to employees in a particular labor organization or in a particular trade, craft, or class rather than to employees in another labor organization or in another trade, craft, or class, unless such employer is failing to conform to an order or certification of the Board determining the bargaining representative for employees performing such work:

Provided, That nothing contained in this subsection (b) [this subsection] shall be construed to make unlawful a refusal by any person to enter upon the premises of any employer (other than his own employer), if the employees of such employer are engaged in a strike ratified or approved by a representative of such employees whom such employer is required to recognize under this Act [subchapter]: Provided further, That for the purposes of this paragraph (4) only, nothing contained in such paragraph shall be construed to prohibit publicity, other than picketing, for the purpose of truthfully advising the public, including consumers and members of a labor organization, that a product or products are produced by an employer with whom the labor organization has a primary dispute and are distributed by another employer, as long as such publicity does not have an effect of inducing any individual employed by any person other than the primary employer in the course of his employment to refuse to pick up, deliver, or transport any goods, or not to perform any services, at the establishment of the employer engaged in such distribution;

(5) to require of employees covered by an agreement authorized under subsection (a)(3) [of this section] the payment, as a condition precedent to becoming a member of such organization, of a fee in an amount which the Board finds excessive or discriminatory under all the circumstances. In making such a finding, the Board shall consider, among other relevant factors, the practices and customs of labor organizations in the particular industry, and the wages currently paid to the employees affected;

(6) to cause or attempt to cause an employer to pay or deliver or agree to pay or deliver any money or other thing of value, in the nature of an exaction, for services which are not performed or not to be performed; and

(7) to picket or cause to be picketed, or threaten to picket or cause to be picketed, any employer where an object thereof is forcing or requiring an employer to recognize or bargain with a labor organization as the representative of his employees, or forcing or requiring the employees of an employer to accept or select such labor organization as their collective-bargaining representative, unless such labor organization is currently certified as the representative of such employees:

(A) where the employer has lawfully recognized in accordance with this Act [subchapter] any other labor organization and a question concerning representation may not appropriately be raised under section 9(c) of this Act [section 159(c) of this title],

(B) where within the preceding twelve months a valid election under section 9(c) of this Act [section 159(c) of this title] has been conducted, or

(C) where such picketing has been conducted without a petition under section 9(c) [section 159(c) of this title] being filed within a reasonable period of time not to exceed thirty days from the commencement of such picketing: Provided, That when such a petition has been filed the Board shall forthwith, without regard to the provisions of section 9(c)(1) [section 159(c)(1) of this title] or the absence of a showing of a substantial interest on the part of the labor organization, direct an election in such unit as the Board finds to be appropriate and shall certify the results thereof: Provided further, That nothing in this subparagraph (C) shall be construed to prohibit any picketing or other publicity for the purpose of truthfully advising the public (including consumers) that an employer does not employ members of, or have a contract with, a labor organization, unless an effect of such picketing is to induce any individual employed by any other person in the course of his employment, not to pick up, deliver, or transport any goods or not to perform any services.

Nothing in this paragraph (7) shall be construed to permit any act which would otherwise be an unfair labor practice under this section 8(b) [this subsection].

c. [Expression of views without threat of reprisal or force or promise of benefit] The expressing of any views, argument, or opinion, or the dissemination thereof, whether in written, printed, graphic, or visual form, shall not constitute or be evidence of an unfair labor practice under any of the provisions of this Act [subchapter], if such expression contains no threat of reprisal or force or promise of benefit.

d. [Obligation to bargain collectively] For the purposes of this section, to bargain collectively is the performance of the mutual obligation of the employer and the representative of the employees to meet at reasonable times and confer in good faith with respect to wages, hours, and other terms and conditions of employment, or the negotiation of an agreement or any question arising thereunder, and the execution of a written contract incorporating any agreement reached if requested by either party, but such obligation does not compel either party to agree to a proposal or require the making of a concession: Provided, That where there is in effect a collective-bargaining contract covering employees in an industry affecting commerce, the duty to bargain collectively shall also mean that no party to such contract shall terminate or modify such contract, unless the party desiring such termination or modification—

(1) serves a written notice upon the other party to the contract of the proposed termination or modification sixty days prior to the expiration date thereof, or in the event such contract contains no expiration date, sixty days prior to the time it is proposed to make such termination or modification;

(2) offers to meet and confer with the other party for the purpose of negotiating a new contract or a contract containing the proposed modifications;

(3) notifies the Federal Mediation and Conciliation Service within thirty days after such notice of the existence of a dispute, and simultaneously therewith notifies any State or Territorial agency established to mediate and conciliate disputes within the State or Territory where the dispute occurred, provided no agreement has been reached by that time; and

(4) continues in full force and effect, without resorting to strike or lockout, all the terms and conditions of the existing contract for a period of sixty days after such notice is given or until the expiration date of such contract, whichever occurs later.

The duties imposed upon employers, employees, and labor organizations by paragraphs (2), (3), and (4) [paragraphs (2) to (4) of this subsection] shall become inapplicable upon an intervening certification of the Board, under which the labor organization or individual, which is a party to the contract, has been superseded as or ceased to be the representative of the employees subject to the provisions of section 9(a) [section 159(a) of this title], and the duties so imposed shall not be construed as requiring either party to discuss or agree to any modification of the terms and conditions contained in a contract for a fixed period, if such modification is to become effective before such terms and conditions can be reopened under the provisions of the contract. Any employee who engages in a strike within any notice period specified in this subsection, or who engages in any strike within the appropriate period specified in subsection (g) of this section, shall lose his status as an employee of the employer engaged in the particular labor dispute, for the purposes of sections 8, 9, and 10 of this Act [sections 158, 159, and 160 of this title], but such loss of status for such employee shall terminate if and when he is reemployed by such employer. Whenever the collective bargaining involves employees of a health care institution, the provisions of this section 8(d) [this subsection] shall be modified as follows:

a. The notice of section 8(d)(1) [paragraph (1) of this subsection] shall be ninety days; the notice of section 8(d)(3) [paragraph (3) of this subsection] shall be sixty days; and the contract period of section 8(d)(4) [paragraph (4) of this subsection] shall be ninety days.

b. Where the bargaining is for an initial agreement following certification or recognition, at least thirty days' notice of the existence of a dispute shall be given by the labor organization to the agencies set forth in section 8(d)(3) [in paragraph (3) of this subsection].

c. After notice is given to the Federal Mediation and Conciliation Service under either clause (A) or (B) of this sentence, the Service shall promptly communicate with the parties and use its best efforts, by mediation and conciliation, to bring them to agreement. The parties shall participate fully and promptly in such meetings as may be undertaken by the Service for the purpose of aiding in a settlement of the dispute.

[Pub. L. 93–360, July 26, 1974, 88 Stat. 395, amended the last sentence of Sec. 8(d) by striking the words "the sixty-day" and inserting the words "any notice" and by inserting before the words "shall lose" the phrase ", or who engages in any strike within the appropriate period specified in subsection (g) of this section." It also amended the end of paragraph Sec. 8(d) by adding a new sentence "Whenever the collective bargaining . . . aiding in a settlement of the dispute."]

e. [Enforceability of contract or agreement to boycott any other employer; exception] It shall be an unfair labor practice for any labor organization and any employer to enter into any contract or agreement, expressed or implied, whereby such employer ceases or refrains or agrees to cease or refrain from handling, using, selling, transporting or otherwise dealing in any of the products of any other employer, or cease doing business with any other person, and any contract or agreement entered into heretofore or hereafter containing such an agreement shall be to such extent unenforceable and void: Provided, That nothing in this subsection (e) [this subsection] shall apply to an agreement between a labor organization and an employer in the construction industry relating to the contracting or subcontracting of work to be done at the site of the construction, alteration, painting, or repair of a building, structure, or other work: Provided further, That for the purposes of this subsection (e) and section 8(b)(4)(B) [this subsection and subsection (b)(4)(B) of this section] the terms "any employer," "any person engaged in commerce or an industry affecting commerce," and "any person" when used in relation to the terms "any other producer, processor, or manufacturer," "any other employer," or "any other person" shall not include persons in the relation of a jobber, manufacturer, contractor, or subcontractor working on the goods or premises of the jobber or manufacturer or performing parts of an integrated process of production in the apparel and clothing industry: Provided further, That nothing in this Act [subchapter] shall prohibit the enforcement of any agreement which is within the foregoing exception.

f. [Agreements covering employees in the building and construction industry] It shall not be an unfair labor practice under subsections (a) and (b) of this section for an employer engaged primarily in the building and construction industry to make an agreement covering employees engaged (or who, upon their employment, will be engaged) in the building and construction industry with a labor organization of which building and construction employees are members (not established, maintained, or assisted by any action defined in section 8(a) of this Act [subsection (a) of this section] as an unfair labor practice) because (1) the majority status of such labor organization has not been established under the provisions of section 9 of this Act [section 159 of this title] prior to the making of such agreement, or (2) such agreement requires as a condition of employment, membership in such labor organization after the seventh day following the beginning of such employment or the effective date of the agreement, whichever is later, or (3) such agreement requires the employer to notify such labor organization of opportunities for employment with such employer, or gives such labor organization an opportunity to refer qualified applicants for such employment, or (4) such agreement specifies minimum training or experience qualifications for employment or provides for priority in opportunities for employment based upon length of service with such employer, in the industry or in the particular geographical area: Provided, That nothing in this subsection shall set aside the final proviso to section 8(a)(3) of this Act [subsection (a)(3) of this section]: Provided further, That any agreement which would be invalid, but for clause (1) of this subsection, shall not be a bar to a petition filed pursuant to section 9(c) or 9(e) [section 159(c) or 159(e) of this title].

g. **[Notification of intention to strike or picket at any health care institution]** A labor organization before engaging in any strike, picketing, or other concerted refusal to work at any health care institution shall, not less than ten days prior to such action, notify the institution in writing and the Federal Mediation and Conciliation Service of that intention, except that in the case of bargaining for an initial agreement following certification or recognition of the notice required by this subsection shall not be given until the expiration of the period specified in clause (B) of the last sentence of section 8(d) of this Act [subsection (d) of this section]. The notice shall state the date and time that such action will commence. The notice, once given, may be extended by the written agreement of both parties.

[Pub. L. 93–360, July 26, 1974, 88 Stat. 396, added subsec. (g).]

REPRESENTATIVES AND ELECTIONS

SEC. 9. [§159.]

a. **[Exclusive representatives; employees' adjustment of grievances directly with employer]** Representatives designated or selected for the purposes of collective bargaining by the majority of the employees in a unit appropriate for such purposes, shall be the exclusive representatives of all the employees in such unit for the purposes of collective bargaining in respect to rates of pay, wages, hours of employment, or other conditions of employment: Provided, That any individual employee or a group of employees shall have the right at any time to present grievances to their employer and to have such grievances adjusted, without the intervention of the bargaining representative, as long as the adjustment is not inconsistent with the terms of a collective-bargaining contract or agreement then in effect: Provided further, That the bargaining representative has been given opportunity to be present at such adjustment.

b. **[Determination of bargaining unit by Board]** The Board shall decide in each case whether, in order to assure to employees the fullest freedom in exercising the rights guaranteed by this Act [subchapter], the unit appropriate for the purposes of collective bargaining shall be the employer unit, craft unit, plant unit, or subdivision thereof: Provided, That the Board shall not (1) decide that any unit is appropriate for such purposes if such unit includes both professional employees and employees who are not professional employees unless a majority of such professional employees vote for inclusion in such unit; or (2) decide that any craft unit is inappropriate for such purposes on the ground that a different unit has been established by a prior Board determination, unless a majority of the employees in the proposed craft unit votes against separate representation or (3) decide that any unit is appropriate for such purposes if it includes, together with other employees, any individual employed as a guard to enforce against employees and other persons rules to protect property of the employer or to protect the safety of persons on the employer's premises; but no labor organization shall be certified as the representative of employees in a bargaining unit of guards if such organization admits to membership, or is affiliated directly or indirectly with an organization which admits to membership, employees other than guards.

c. **[Hearing on questions affecting commerce; rules and regulations]** (1) Whenever a petition shall have been filed, in accordance with such regulations as may be prescribed by the Board—

   (a) by an employee or group of employees or any individual or labor organization acting in their behalf alleging that a substantial number of employees (i) wish to be represented for collective bargaining and that their employer declines to recognize their representative as the representative defined in section 9(a) [subsection (a) of this section], or (ii) assert that the individual or labor organization, which has been certified or is being currently recognized by their employer as the bargaining representative, is no longer a representative as defined in section 9(a) [subsection (a) of this section]; or

(b) by an employer, alleging that one or more individuals or labor organizations have presented to him a claim to be recognized as the representative defined in section 9(a) [subsection (a) of this section]; the Board shall investigate such petition and if it has reasonable cause to believe that a question of representation affecting commerce exists shall provide for an appropriate hearing upon due notice. Such hearing may be conducted by an officer or employee of the regional office, who shall not make any recommendations with respect thereto. If the Board finds upon the record of such hearing that such a question of representation exists, it shall direct an election by secret ballot and shall certify the results thereof.

(2) In determining whether or not a question of representation affecting commerce exists, the same regulations and rules of decision shall apply irrespective of the identity of the persons filing the petition or the kind of relief sought and in no case shall the Board deny a labor organization a place on the ballot by reason of an order with respect to such labor organization or its predecessor not issued in conformity with section 10(c) [section 160(c) of this title].

(3) No election shall be directed in any bargaining unit or any subdivision within which, in the preceding twelve-month period, a valid election shall have been held. Employees engaged in an economic strike who are not entitled to reinstatement shall be eligible to vote under such regulations as the Board shall find are consistent with the purposes and provisions of this Act [subchapter] in any election conducted within twelve months after the commencement of the strike. In any election where none of the choices on the ballot receives a majority, a run-off shall be conducted, the ballot providing for a selection between the two choices receiving the largest and second largest number of valid votes cast in the election.

(4) Nothing in this section shall be construed to prohibit the waiving of hearings by stipulation for the purpose of a consent election in conformity with regulations and rules of decision of the Board.

(5) In determining whether a unit is appropriate for the purposes specified in subsection (b) [of this section] the extent to which the employees have organized shall not be controlling.

d. [Petition for enforcement or review; transcript] Whenever an order of the Board made pursuant to section 10(c) [section 160(c) of this title] is based in whole or in part upon facts certified following an investigation pursuant to subsection (c) of this section and there is a petition for the enforcement or review of such order, such certification and the record of such investigation shall be included in the transcript of the entire record required to be filed under section 10(e) or 10(f) [subsection (e) or (f) of section 160 of this title], and thereupon the decree of the court enforcing, modifying, or setting aside in whole or in part the order of the Board shall be made and entered upon the pleadings, testimony, and proceedings set forth in such transcript.

e. [Secret ballot; limitation of elections] (1) Upon the filing with the Board, by 30 per centum or more of the employees in a bargaining unit covered by an agreement between their employer and labor organization made pursuant to section 8(a)(3) [section 158(a)(3) of this title], of a petition alleging they desire that such authorization be rescinded, the Board shall take a secret ballot of the employees in such unit and certify the results thereof to such labor organization and to the employer.

(2) No election shall be conducted pursuant to this subsection in any bargaining unit or any subdivision within which, in the preceding twelve-month period, a valid election shall have been held.

PREVENTION OF UNFAIR LABOR PRACTICES

SEC. 10. [§160.]

a. **[Powers of Board generally]** The Board is empowered, as hereinafter provided, to prevent any person from engaging in any unfair labor practice (listed in section 8 [section 158 of this title]) affecting commerce. This power shall not be affected by any other means of adjustment or prevention that has been or may be established by agreement, law, or otherwise: Provided, That the Board is empowered by agreement with any agency of any State or Territory to cede to such agency jurisdiction over any cases in any industry (other than mining, manufacturing, communications, and transportation except where predominately local in character) even though such cases may involve labor disputes affecting commerce, unless the provision of the State or Territorial statute applicable to the determination of such cases by such agency is inconsistent with the corresponding provision of this Act [subchapter] or has received a construction inconsistent therewith.

b. **[Complaint and notice of hearing; six-month limitation; answer; court rules of evidence inapplicable]** Whenever it is charged that any person has engaged in or is engaging in any such unfair labor practice, the Board, or any agent or agency designated by the Board for such purposes, shall have power to issue and cause to be served upon such person a complaint stating the charges in that respect, and containing a notice of hearing before the Board or a member thereof, or before a designated agent or agency, at a place therein fixed, not less than five days after the serving of said complaint: Provided, That no complaint shall issue based upon any unfair labor practice occurring more than six months prior to the filing of the charge with the Board and the service of a copy thereof upon the person against whom such charge is made, unless the person aggrieved thereby was prevented from filing such charge by reason of service in the armed forces, in which event the six-month period shall be computed from the day of his discharge. Any such complaint may be amended by the member, agent, or agency conducting the hearing or the Board in its discretion at any time prior to the issuance of an order based thereon. The person so complained of shall have the right to file an answer to the original or amended complaint and to appear in person or otherwise and give testimony at the place and time fixed in the complaint. In the discretion of the member, agent, or agency conducting the hearing or the Board, any other person may be allowed to intervene in the said proceeding and to present testimony. Any such proceeding shall, so far as practicable, be conducted in accordance with the rules of evidence applicable in the district courts of the United States under the rules of civil procedure for the district courts of the United States, adopted by the Supreme Court of the United States pursuant to section 2072 of title 28, United States Code [section 2072 of title 28].

c. **[Reduction of testimony to writing; findings and orders of Board]** The testimony taken by such member, agent, or agency or the Board shall be reduced to writing and filed with the Board. Thereafter, in its discretion, the Board upon notice may take further testimony or hear argument. If upon the preponderance of the testimony taken the Board shall be of the opinion that any person named in the complaint has engaged in or is engaging in any such unfair labor practice, then the Board shall state its findings of fact and shall issue and cause to be served on such person an order requiring such person to cease and desist from such unfair labor practice, and to take such affirmative action including reinstatement of employees with or without back pay, as will effectuate the policies of this Act [subchapter]: Provided, That where an order directs reinstatement of an employee, back pay may be required of the employer or labor organization, as the case may be, responsible for the discrimination suffered by him: And provided further, That in determining whether a complaint shall issue alleging a violation of section 8(a)(1) or section 8(a)(2) [subsection (a)(1) or (a)(2) of section 158 of this title], and in deciding such cases, the same regulations and rules of decision shall apply irrespective of whether or not the labor organization affected is affiliated with a labor organization national or international in scope. Such order may further require such person to make reports from time to time showing the extent to which it has complied with the order. If upon the preponderance of the testimony taken the Board shall not be of the opinion that the person named in the complaint has engaged in or is engaging in any such unfair labor practice, then the Board shall state its findings of fact and shall issue an order dismissing the said complaint. No order of the Board shall require the reinstatement of any individual as an employee who has been suspended or discharged, or the payment to him of any back pay, if such individual was suspended or discharged for cause. In case the evidence is presented before a member of the Board, or before an administrative law judge or judges thereof, such member, or such judge or judges, as the case may be, shall issue and cause to be served on the parties to the proceeding a proposed report, together with a recommended order, which shall be filed with the Board, and if no exceptions are filed within twenty days after service thereof upon such parties, or within such further period as the Board may authorize, such recommended order shall become the order of the Board and become affective as therein prescribed.

[The title "administrative law judge" was adopted in 5 U.S.C. §3105.]

d. **[Modification of findings or orders prior to filing record in court]** Until the record in a case shall have been filed in a court, as hereinafter provided, the Board may at any time, upon reasonable notice and in such manner as it shall deem proper, modify or set aside, in whole or in part, any finding or order made or issued by it.

e. **[Petition to court for enforcement of order; proceedings; review of judgment]** The Board shall have power to petition any court of appeals of the United States, or if all the courts of appeals to which application may be made are in vacation, any district court of the United States, within any circuit or district, respectively, wherein the unfair labor practice in question occurred or wherein such person resides or transacts business, for the enforcement of such order and for appropriate temporary relief or restraining order, and shall file in the court the record in the proceeding, as provided in section 2112 of title 28, United States Code [section 2112 of title 28]. Upon the filing of such petition, the court shall cause notice thereof to be served upon such person, and thereupon shall have jurisdiction of the proceeding and of the question determined therein, and shall have power to grant such temporary relief or restraining order as it deems just and proper, and to make and enter a decree enforcing, modifying and enforcing as so modified, or setting aside in whole or in part the order of the Board. No objection that has not been urged before the Board, its member, agent, or agency, shall be considered by the court, unless the failure or neglect to urge such objection shall be excused because of extraordinary circumstances. The findings of the Board with respect to questions of fact if supported by substantial evidence on the record considered as a whole shall be conclusive. If either party shall apply to the court for leave to adduce additional evidence and shall show to the satisfaction of the court that such additional evidence is material and that there were reasonable grounds for the failure to adduce such evidence in the hearing before the Board, its member, agent, or agency, the court may order such additional evidence to be taken before the Board, its member, agent, or agency, and to be made a part of the record. The Board may modify its findings as to the facts, or make new findings, by reason of additional evidence so taken and filed, and it shall file such modified or new findings, which findings with respect to question of fact if supported by substantial evidence on the record considered as a whole shall be conclusive, and shall file its recommendations, if any, for the modification or setting aside of its original order. Upon the filing of the record with it the jurisdiction of the court shall be exclusive and its judgment and decree shall be final, except that the same shall be subject to review by the appropriate

United States court of appeals if application was made to the district court as hereinabove provided, and by the Supreme Court of the United States upon writ of certiorari or certification as provided in section 1254 of title 28.

f. **[Review of final order of Board on petition to court]** Any person aggrieved by a final order of the Board granting or denying in whole or in part the relief sought may obtain a review of such order in any United States court of appeals in the circuit wherein the unfair labor practice in question was alleged to have been engaged in or wherein such person resides or transacts business, or in the United States Court of Appeals for the District of Columbia, by filing in such court a written petition praying that the order of the Board be modified or set aside. A copy of such petition shall be forthwith transmitted by the clerk of the court to the Board, and thereupon the aggrieved party shall file in the court the record in the proceeding, certified by the Board, as provided in section 2112 of title 28, United States Code [section 2112 of title 28]. Upon the filing of such petition, the court shall proceed in the same manner as in the case of an application by the Board under subsection (e) of this section, and shall have the same jurisdiction to grant to the Board such temporary relief or restraining order as it deems just and proper, and in like manner to make and enter a decree enforcing, modifying and enforcing as so modified, or setting aside in whole or in part the order of the Board; the findings of the Board with respect to questions of fact if supported by substantial evidence on the record considered as a whole shall in like manner be conclusive.

g. **[Institution of court proceedings as stay of Board's order]** The commencement of proceedings under subsection (e) or (f) of this section shall not, unless specifically ordered by the court, operate as a stay of the Board's order.

h. **[Jurisdiction of courts unaffected by limitations prescribed in chapter 6 of this title]** When granting appropriate temporary relief or a restraining order, or making and entering a decree enforcing, modifying and enforcing as so modified, or setting aside in whole or in part an order of the Board, as provided in this section, the jurisdiction of courts sitting in equity shall not be limited by sections 101 to 115 of title 29, United States Code [chapter 6 of this title] [known as the "Norris-LaGuardia Act"].

i. **Repealed**.

j. **[Injunctions]** The Board shall have power, upon issuance of a complaint as provided in subsection (b) [of this section] charging that any person has engaged in or is engaging in an unfair labor practice, to petition any United States district court, within any district wherein the unfair labor practice in question is alleged to have occurred or wherein such person resides or transacts business, for appropriate temporary relief or restraining order. Upon the filing of any such petition the court shall cause notice thereof to be served upon such person, and thereupon shall have jurisdiction to grant to the Board such temporary relief or restraining order as it deems just and proper.

k. **[Hearings on jurisdictional strikes]** Whenever it is charged that any person has engaged in an unfair labor practice within the meaning of paragraph (4)(D) of section 8(b) [section 158(b) of this title], the Board is empowered and directed to hear and determine the dispute out of which such unfair labor practice shall have arisen, unless, within ten days after notice that such charge has been filed, the parties to such dispute submit to the Board satisfactory evidence that they have adjusted, or agreed upon methods for the voluntary adjustment of, the dispute. Upon compliance by the parties to the dispute with the decision of the Board or upon such voluntary adjustment of the dispute, such charge shall be dismissed.

l. **[Boycotts and strikes to force recognition of uncertified labor organizations; injunctions; notice; service of process]** Whenever it is charged that any person has engaged in an unfair labor practice within the meaning of paragraph (4)(A), (B), or (C) of section 8(b) [section 158(b) of this title], or section 8(e) [section 158(e) of this title] or section 8(b)(7) [section 158(b)(7) of this title], the preliminary investigation of such charge shall be made forthwith and given priority over all other cases except cases of like character in the office where it is filed or to which it is referred. If, after such investigation, the officer or regional attorney to whom the matter may be referred has reasonable cause to believe such charge is true and that a complaint should issue, he shall, on behalf of the Board, petition any United States district court within any district where the unfair labor practice in question has occurred, is alleged to have occurred, or wherein such person resides or transacts business, for appropriate injunctive relief pending the final adjudication of the Board with respect to such matter. Upon the filing of any such petition the district court shall have jurisdiction to grant such injunctive relief or temporary restraining order as it deems just and proper, notwithstanding any other provision of law: Provided further, That no temporary restraining order shall be issued without notice unless a petition alleges that substantial and irreparable injury to the charging party will be unavoidable and such temporary restraining order shall be effective for no longer than five days and will become void at the expiration of such period: Provided further, That such officer or regional attorney shall not apply for any restraining order under section 8(b)(7) [section 158(b)(7) of this title] if a charge against the employer under section 8(a)(2) [section 158(a)(2) of this title] has been filed and after the preliminary investigation, he has reasonable cause to believe that such charge is true and that a complaint should issue. Upon filing of any such petition the courts shall cause notice thereof to be served upon any person involved in the charge and such person, including the charging party, shall be given an opportunity to appear by counsel and present any relevant testimony: Provided further, That for the purposes of this subsection district courts shall be deemed to have jurisdiction of a labor organization (1) in the district in which such organization maintains its principal office, or (2) in any district in which its duly authorized officers or agents are engaged in promoting or protecting the interests of employee members. The service of legal process upon such officer or agent shall constitute service upon the labor organization and make such organization a party to the suit. In situations where such relief is appropriate the procedure specified herein shall apply to charges with respect to section 8(b)(4)(D) [section 158(b)(4)(D) of this title].

m. [Priority of cases] Whenever it is charged that any person has engaged in an unfair labor practice within the meaning of subsection (a)(3) or (b)(2) of section 8 [section 158 of this title], such charge shall be given priority over all other cases except cases of like character in the office where it is filed or to which it is referred and cases given priority under subsection (1) [of this section].

INVESTIGATORY POWERS

SEC. 11. [§161.] For the purpose of all hearings and investigations, which, in the opinion of the Board, are necessary and proper for the exercise of the powers vested in it by section 9 and section 10 [sections 159 and 160 of this title]—

(1) [Documentary evidence; summoning witnesses and taking testimony] The Board, or its duly authorized agents or agencies, shall at all reasonable times have access to, for the purpose of examination, and the right to copy any evidence of any person being investigated or proceeded against that relates to any matter under investigation or in question. The Board, or any member thereof, shall upon application of any party to such proceedings, forthwith issue to such party subpoenas requiring the attendance and testimony of witnesses or the production of any evidence in such proceeding or investigation requested in such application. Within five days after the service of a subpoena on any person requiring the production of any evidence in his possession or under his control, such person may petition the Board to revoke, and the Board shall revoke, such subpoena if in its opinion the evidence whose production is required does not relate to any matter under investigation, or any matter in question in such proceedings, or if in its opinion such subpoena does not describe with sufficient particularity the evidence whose production is required. Any member of the Board, or any agent or agency designated by the Board for such purposes, may administer oaths and affirmations, examine witnesses, and receive evidence. Such attendance of witnesses and the production of such evidence may be required from any place in the United States or any Territory or possession thereof, at any designated place of hearing.

(2) [Court aid in compelling production of evidence and attendance of witnesses] In case on contumacy or refusal to obey a subpoena issued to any person, any United States district court or the United States courts of any Territory or possession, within the jurisdiction of which the inquiry is carried on or within the jurisdiction of which said person guilty of contumacy or refusal to obey is found or resides or transacts business, upon application by the Board shall have jurisdiction to issue to such person an order requiring such person to appear before the Board, its member, agent, or agency, there to produce evidence if so ordered, or there to give testimony touching the matter under investigation or in question; and any failure to obey such order of the court may be punished by said court as a contempt thereof.

(3) Repealed

[Immunity of witnesses. See 18 U.S.C. §6001 et seq.]

(4) [Process, service, and return; fees of witnesses] Complaints, orders, and other process and papers of the Board, its member, agent, or agency, may be served either personally or by registered or certified mail or by telegraph or by leaving a copy thereof at the principal office or place of business of the person required to be served. The verified return by the individual so serving the same setting forth the manner of such service shall be proof of the same, and the return post office receipt or telegraph receipt therefor when registered or certified and mailed or when telegraphed as aforesaid shall be proof of service of the same. Witnesses summoned before the Board, its member, agent, or agency, shall be paid the same fees and mileage that are paid to witnesses in the courts of the United States, and witnesses whose depositions are taken and the persons taking the same shall severally be entitled to the same fees as are paid for like services in the courts of the United States.

(5) [Process, where served] All process of any court to which application may be made under this Act [subchapter] may be served in the judicial district wherein the defendant or other person required to be served resides or may be found.

(6) [Information and assistance from departments] The several departments and agencies of the Government, when directed by the President, shall furnish the Board, upon its request, all records, papers, and information in their possession relating to any matter before the Board.

SEC. 12. [§162. OFFENSES AND PENALTIES] Any person who shall willfully resist, prevent, impede, or interfere with any member of the Board or any of its agents or agencies in the performance of duties pursuant to this Act [subchapter] shall be punished by a fine of not more than $5,000 or by imprisonment for not more than one year, or both.

LIMITATIONS

SEC. 13. [§163. RIGHT TO STRIKE PRESERVED] Nothing in this Act [subchapter], except as specifically provided for herein, shall be construed so as either to interfere with or impede or diminish in any way the right to strike, or to affect the limitations or qualifications on that right.

SEC. 14. [§164. CONSTRUCTION OF PROVISIONS]

(a) **[Supervisors as union members]** Nothing herein shall prohibit any individual employed as a supervisor from becoming or remaining a member of a labor organization, but no employer subject to this Act [subchapter] shall be compelled to deem individuals defined herein as supervisors as employees for the purpose of any law, either national or local, relating to collective bargaining.

(b) **[Agreements requiring union membership in violation of State law]** Nothing in this Act [subchapter] shall be construed as authorizing the execution or application of agreements requiring membership in a labor organization as a condition of employment in any State or Territory in which such execution or application is prohibited by State or Territorial law.

(c) [Power of Board to decline jurisdiction of labor disputes; assertion of jurisdiction by State and Territorial courts]

(1) The Board, in its discretion, may, by rule of decision or by published rules adopted pursuant to the Administrative Procedure Act [to subchapter II of chapter 5 of title 5], decline to assert jurisdiction over any labor dispute involving any class or category of employers, where, in the opinion of the Board, the effect of such labor dispute on commerce is not sufficiently substantial to warrant the exercise of its jurisdiction: Provided, That the Board shall not decline to assert jurisdiction over any labor dispute over which it would assert jurisdiction under the standards prevailing upon August 1, 1959.

(2) Nothing in this Act [subchapter] shall be deemed to prevent or bar any agency or the courts of any State or Territory (including the Commonwealth of Puerto Rico, Guam, and the Virgin Islands), from assuming and asserting jurisdiction over labor disputes over which the Board declines, pursuant to paragraph (1) of this subsection, to assert jurisdiction.

SEC. 15. [§165.] Omitted.

[Reference to repealed provisions of bankruptcy statute.]

SEC. 16. [§166. SEPARABILITY OF PROVISIONS] If any provision of this Act [subchapter], or the application of such provision to any person or circumstances, shall be held invalid, the remainder of this Act [subchapter], or the application of such provision to persons or circumstances other than those as to which it is held invalid, shall not be affected thereby.

SEC. 17. [§167. SHORT TITLE] This Act [subchapter] may be cited as the "National Labor Relations Act."

SEC. 18. [§168.] Omitted.

[Reference to former sec. 9(f), (g), and (h).]

INDIVIDUALS WITH RELIGIOUS CONVICTIONS

SEC. 19. [§169.] Any employee who is a member of and adheres to established and traditional tenets or teachings of a bona fide religion, body, or sect which has historically held conscientious objections to joining or financially supporting labor organizations shall not be required to join or financially support any labor organization as a condition of employment; except that such employee may be required in a contract between such employee's employer and a labor organization in lieu of periodic dues and initiation fees, to pay sums equal to such dues and initiation fees to a nonreligious, nonlabor organization charitable fund exempt from taxation under section 501(c)(3) of title 26 of the Internal Revenue Code [section 501(c)(3) of title 26], chosen by such employee from a list of at least three such funds, designated in such contract or if the contract fails to designate such funds, then to any such fund chosen by the employee. If such employee who holds conscientious objections pursuant to this section requests the labor organization to use the grievance-arbitration procedure on the employee's behalf, the labor organization is authorized to charge the employee for the reasonable cost of using such procedure.

[Sec. added, Pub. L. 93–360, July 26, 1974, 88 Stat. 397, and amended, Pub. L. 96–593, Dec. 24, 1980, 94 Stat. 3452.]

Labor-Management Relations Act

Also cited LMRA; 29 U.S.C. §§141–197

[Title 29, Chapter 7, United States Code]

SHORT TITLE AND DECLARATION OF POLICY

SECTION 1. [§141.]

(a) This Act [chapter] may be cited as the "Labor Management Relations Act, 1947." [Also known as the "Taft-Hartley Act."]

(b) Industrial strife which interferes with the normal flow of commerce and with the full production of articles and commodities for commerce, can be avoided or substantially minimized if employers, employees, and labor organizations each recognize under law one another's legitimate rights in their relations with each other, and above all recognize under law that neither party has any right in its relations with any other to engage in acts or practices which jeopardize the public health, safety, or interest. It is the purpose and policy of this Act [chapter], in order to promote the full flow of commerce, to prescribe the legitimate rights of both employees and employers in their relations affecting commerce, to provide orderly and peaceful procedures for preventing the interference by either with the legitimate rights of the other, to protect the rights of individual employees in their relations with labor organizations whose activities affect commerce, to define and proscribe practices on the part of labor and management which affect commerce and are inimical to the general welfare, and to protect the rights of the public in connection with labor disputes affecting commerce.

TITLE I, Amendments to

National Labor Relations Act

29 U.S.C. §§151–169 (printed above)

TITLE II

[Title 29, Chapter 7, Subchapter III, United States Code]

CONCILIATION OF LABOR DISPUTES IN INDUSTRIES AFFECTING COMMERCE; NATIONAL EMERGENCIES

SEC. 201. [§171. DECLARATION OF PURPOSE AND POLICY] It is the policy of the United States that—

(a) sound and stable industrial peace and the advancement of the general welfare, health, and safety of the Nation and of the best interest of employers and employees can most satisfactorily be secured by the settlement of issues between employers and employees through the processes of conference and collective bargaining between employers and the representatives of their employees;

(b) the settlement of issues between employers and employees through collective bargaining may be advanced by making available full and adequate governmental facilities for conciliation, mediation, and voluntary arbitration to aid and encourage employers and the representatives of their employees to reach and maintain agreements concerning rates of pay, hours, and working conditions, and to make all reasonable efforts to settle their differences by mutual agreement reached through conferences and collective bargaining or by such methods as may be provided for in any applicable agreement for the settlement of disputes; and

(c) certain controversies which arise between parties to collective-bargaining agreements may be avoided or minimized by making available full and adequate governmental facilities for furnishing assistance to employers and the representatives of their employees in formulating for inclusion within such agreements provision for adequate notice of any proposed changes in the terms of such agreements, for the final adjustment of grievances or questions regarding the application or interpretation of such agreements, and other provisions designed to prevent the subsequent arising of such controversies.

SEC. 202. [§172. FEDERAL MEDIATION AND CONCILIATION SERVICE]

(a) **[Creation; appointment of Director]** There is created an independent agency to be known as the Federal Mediation and Conciliation Service (herein referred to as the "Service," except that for sixty days after June 23, 1947, such term shall refer to the Conciliation Service of the Department of Labor). The Service shall be under the direction of a Federal Mediation and Conciliation Director (hereinafter referred to as the "Director"), who shall be appointed by the President by and with the advice and consent of the Senate. The Director shall not engage in any other business, vocation, or employment.

(b) **[Appointment of officers and employees; expenditures for supplies, facilities, and services]** The Director is authorized, subject to the civil service laws, to appoint such clerical and other personnel as may be necessary for the execution of the functions of the Service, and shall fix their compensation in accordance with sections 5101 to 5115 and sections 5331 to 5338 of title 5, United States Code [chapter 51 and subchapter III of chapter 53 of title 5], and may, without regard to the provisions of the civil service laws, appoint such conciliators and mediators as may be necessary to carry out the functions of the Service. The Director is authorized to make such expenditures for supplies, facilities, and services as he deems necessary. Such expenditures shall be allowed and paid upon presentation of itemized vouchers therefor approved by the Director or by any employee designated by him for that purpose.

(c) **[Principal and regional offices; delegation of authority by Director; annual report to Congress]** The principal office of the Service shall be in the District of Columbia, but the Director may establish regional offices convenient to localities in which labor controversies are likely to arise. The Director may by order, subject to revocation at any time, delegate any authority and discretion conferred upon him by this Act [chapter] to any regional director, or other officer or employee of the Service. The Director may establish suitable procedures for cooperation with State and local mediation agencies. The Director shall make an annual report in writing to Congress at the end of the fiscal year.

(d) **[Transfer of all mediation and conciliation services to Service; effective date; pending proceedings unaffected]** All mediation and conciliation functions of the Secretary of Labor or the United States Conciliation Service under section 51 [repealed] of title 29, United States Code [this title], and all functions of the United States Conciliation Service under any other law are transferred to the Federal Mediation and Conciliation Service, together with the personnel and records of the United States Conciliation Service. Such transfer shall take effect upon the sixtieth day after June 23, 1947. Such transfer shall not affect any proceedings pending before the United States Conciliation Service or any certification, order, rule, or regulation theretofore made by it or by the Secretary of Labor. The Director and the Service shall not be subject in any way to the jurisdiction or authority of the Secretary of Labor or any official or division of the Department of Labor.

FUNCTIONS OF THE SERVICE

SEC. 203. [§173. FUNCTIONS OF SERVICE]

(a) **[Settlement of disputes through conciliation and mediation]** It shall be the duty of the Service, in order to prevent or minimize interruptions of the free flow of commerce growing out of labor disputes, to assist parties to labor disputes in industries affecting commerce to settle such disputes through conciliation and mediation.

(b) **[Intervention on motion of Service or request of parties; avoidance of mediation of minor disputes]** The Service may proffer its services in any labor dispute in any industry affecting commerce, either upon its own motion or upon the request of one or more of the parties to the dispute, whenever in its judgment such dispute threatens to cause a substantial interruption of commerce. The Director and the Service are directed to avoid attempting to mediate disputes which would have only a minor effect on interstate commerce if State or other conciliation services are available to the parties. Whenever the Service does proffer its services in any dispute, it shall be the duty of the Service to promptly put itself in communication with the parties and to use its best efforts, by mediation and conciliation, to bring them to agreement.

(c) **[Settlement of disputes by other means upon failure of conciliation]** If the Director is not able to bring the parties to agreement by conciliation within a reasonable time, he shall seek to induce the parties voluntarily to seek other means of settling the dispute without resort to strike, lockout, or other coercion, including submission to the employees in the bargaining unit of the employer's last offer of settlement for approval or rejection in a secret ballot. The failure or refusal of either party to agree to any procedure suggested by the Director shall not be deemed a violation of any duty or obligation imposed by this Act [chapter].

(d) **[Use of conciliation and mediation services as last resort]** Final adjustment by a method agreed upon by the parties is declared to be the desirable method for settlement of grievance disputes arising over the application or interpretation of an existing collective-bargaining agreement. The Service is directed to make its conciliation and mediation services available in the settlement of such grievance disputes only as a last resort and in exceptional cases.

(e) **[Encouragement and support of establishment and operation of joint labor management activities conducted by committees]** The Service is authorized and directed to encourage and support the establishment and operation of joint labor management activities conducted by plant, area, and industrywide committees designed to improve labor management relationships, job security, and organizational effectiveness, in accordance with the provisions of section 205A [section 175a of this title].

[Pub. L. 95–524, §6(c)(1), Oct. 27, 1978, 92 Stat. 2020, added subsec. (e).]

SEC. 204. [§174. CO-EQUAL OBLIGATIONS OF EMPLOYEES, THEIR REPRESENTATIVES, AND MANAGEMENT TO MINIMIZE LABOR DISPUTES]

(a) In order to prevent or minimize interruptions of the free flow of commerce growing out of labor disputes, employers and employees and their representatives, in any industry affecting commerce, shall—

(1) exert every reasonable effort to make and maintain agreements concerning rates of pay, hours, and working conditions, including provision for adequate notice of any proposed change in the terms of such agreements;

(2) whenever a dispute arises over the terms or application of a collective-bargaining agreement and a conference is requested by a party or prospective party thereto, arrange promptly for such a conference to be held and endeavor in such conference to settle such dispute expeditiously; and

(3) in case such dispute is not settled by conference, participate fully and promptly in such meetings as may be undertaken by the Service under this Act [chapter] for the purpose of aiding in a settlement of the dispute.

SEC. 205. [§175. NATIONAL LABOR-MANAGEMENT PANEL; CREATION AND COMPOSITION; APPOINTMENT, TENURE, AND COMPENSATION; DUTIES]

(a) There is created a National Labor-Management Panel which shall be composed of twelve members appointed by the President, six of whom shall be selected from among persons outstanding in the field of management and six of whom shall be selected from among persons outstanding in the field of labor. Each member shall hold office for a term of three years, except that any member appointed to fill a vacancy occurring prior to the expiration of the term for which his predecessor was appointed shall be appointed for the remainder of such term, and the terms of office of the members first taking office shall expire, as designated by the President at the time of appointment, four at the end of the first year, four at the end of the second year, and four at the end of the third year after the date of appointment. Members of the panel, when serving on business of the panel, shall be paid compensation at the rate of $25 per day, and shall also be entitled to receive an allowance for actual and necessary travel and subsistence expenses while so serving away from their places of residence.

(b) It shall be the duty of the panel, at the request of the Director, to advise in the avoidance of industrial controversies and the manner in which mediation and voluntary adjustment shall be administered, particularly with reference to controversies affecting the general welfare of the country.

SEC. 205A. [§175A. ASSISTANCE TO PLANT, AREA, AND INDUSTRYWIDE LABOR MANAGEMENT COMMITTEES]

(a) **[Establishment and operation of plant, area, and industrywide committees]** (1) The Service is authorized and directed to provide assistance in the establishment and operation of plant, area, and industrywide labor management committees which—

a. have been organized jointly by employers and labor organizations representing employees in that plant, area, or industry; and
b. are established for the purpose of improving labor management relationships, job security, organizational effectiveness, enhancing economic development, or involving workers in decisions affecting their jobs including improving communication with respect to subjects of mutual interest and concern.

(2) The Service is authorized and directed to enter into contracts and to make grants, where necessary or appropriate, to fulfill its responsibilities under this section.

(b) **[Restrictions on grants, contracts, or other assistance]** (1) No grant may be made, no contract may be entered into, and no other assistance may be provided under the provisions of this section to a plant labor management committee unless the employees in that plant are represented by a labor organization and there is in effect at that plant a collective bargaining agreement.

(2) No grant may be made, no contract may be entered into, and no other assistance may be provided under the provisions of this section to an area or industrywide labor management committee unless its participants include any labor organizations certified or recognized as the representative of the employees of an employer participating in such committee. Nothing in this clause shall prohibit participation in an area or industrywide committee by an employer whose employees are not represented by a labor organization.

(3) No grant may be made under the provisions of this section to any labor management committee which the Service finds to have as one of its purposes the discouragement of the exercise of rights contained in section 7 of the National Labor Relations Act (29 U.S.C. §157) [section 157 of this title], or the interference with collective bargaining in any plant, or industry.

(c) [Establishment of office] The Service shall carry out the provisions of this section through an office established for that purpose.

(d) [Authorization of appropriations] There are authorized to be appropriated to carry out the provisions of this section $10,000,000 for the fiscal year 1979, and such sums as may be necessary thereafter.

[Pub. L. 95–524, §6(c)(2), Oct. 27, 1978, 92 Stat. 2020, added Sec. 205A.]

NATIONAL EMERGENCIES

SEC. 206. [§176. APPOINTMENT OF BOARD OF INQUIRY BY PRESIDENT; REPORT; CONTENTS; FILING WITH SERVICE] Whenever in the opinion of the President of the United States, a threatened or actual strike or lockout affecting an entire industry or a substantial part thereof engaged in trade, commerce, transportation, transmission, or communication among the several States or with foreign nations, or engaged in the production of goods for commerce, will, if permitted to occur or to continue, imperil the national health or safety, he may appoint a board of inquiry to inquire into the issues involved in the dispute and to make a written report to him within such time as he shall prescribe. Such report shall include a statement of the facts with respect to the dispute, including each party's statement of its position but shall not contain any recommendations. The President shall file a copy of such report with the Service and shall make its contents available to the public.

SEC. 207. [§177. BOARD OF INQUIRY]

a. **[Composition]** A board of inquiry shall be composed of a chairman and such other members as the President shall determine, and shall have power to sit and act in any place within the United States and to conduct such hearings either in public or in private, as it may deem necessary or proper, to ascertain the facts with respect to the causes and circumstances of the dispute.
b. **[Compensation]** Members of a board of inquiry shall receive compensation at the rate of $50 for each day actually spent by them in the work of the board, together with necessary travel and subsistence expenses.
c. **[Powers of discovery]** For the purpose of any hearing or inquiry conducted by any board appointed under this title, the provisions of sections 49 and 50 of title 15, United States Code [sections 49 and 50 of title 15] (relating to the attendance of witnesses and the production of books, papers, and documents) are made applicable to the powers and duties of such board.

SEC. 208. [§178. INJUNCTIONS DURING NATIONAL EMERGENCY]

a. **[Petition to district court by Attorney General on direction of President]** Upon receiving a report from a board of inquiry the President may direct the Attorney General to petition any district court of the United States having jurisdiction of the parties to enjoin such strike or lockout or the continuing thereof, and if the court finds that such threatened or actual strike or lockout—
(i) affects an entire industry or a substantial part thereof engaged in trade, commerce, transportation, transmission, or communication among the several States or with foreign nations, or engaged in the production of goods for commerce; and
(ii) if permitted to occur or to continue, will imperil the national health or safety, it shall have jurisdiction to enjoin any such strike or lockout, or the continuing thereof, and to make such other orders as may be appropriate.
b. **[Inapplicability of chapter 6]** In any case, the provisions of sections 101 to 115 of title 29, United States Code [chapter 6 of this title] [known as the "Norris-LaGuardia Act"] shall not be applicable.

c. **[Review of orders]** The order or orders of the court shall be subject to review by the appropriate United States court of appeals and by the Supreme Court upon writ of certiorari or certification as provided in section 1254 of title 28, United States Code [section 1254 of title 28].

SEC. 209. [§179. INJUNCTIONS DURING NATIONAL EMERGENCY; ADJUSTMENT EFFORTS BY PARTIES DURING INJUNCTION PERIOD]

(a) **[Assistance of Service; acceptance of Service's proposed settlement]** Whenever a district court has issued an order under section 208 [section 178 of this title] enjoining acts or practices which imperil or threaten to imperil the national health or safety, it shall be the duty of the parties to the labor dispute giving rise to such order to make every effort to adjust and settle their differences, with the assistance of the Service created by this Act [chapter]. Neither party shall be under any duty to accept, in whole or in part, any proposal of settlement made by the Service.

(b) **[Reconvening of board of inquiry; report by board; contents; secret ballot of employees by National Labor Relations Board; certification of results to Attorney General]** Upon the issuance of such order, the President shall reconvene the board of inquiry which has previously reported with respect to the dispute. At the end of a sixty-day period (unless the dispute has been settled by that time), the board of inquiry shall report to the President the current position of the parties and the efforts which have been made for settlement, and shall include a statement by each party of its position and a statement of the employer's last offer of settlement. The President shall make such report available to the public. The National Labor Relations Board, within the succeeding fifteen days, shall take a secret ballot of the employees of each employer involved in the dispute on the question of whether they wish to accept the final offer of settlement made by their employer as stated by him and shall certify the results thereof to the Attorney General within five days thereafter.

SEC. 210. [§180. DISCHARGE OF INJUNCTION UPON CERTIFICATION OF RESULTS OF ELECTION OR SETTLEMENT; REPORT TO CONGRESS] Upon the certification of the results of such ballot or upon a settlement being reached, whichever happens sooner, the Attorney General shall move the court to discharge the injunction, which motion shall then be granted and the injunction discharged. When such motion is granted, the President shall submit to the Congress a full and comprehensive report of the proceedings, including the findings of the board of inquiry and the ballot taken by the National Labor Relations Board, together with such recommendations as he may see fit to make for consideration and appropriate action.

COMPILATION OF COLLECTIVE-BARGAINING AGREEMENTS, ETC.

SEC. 211. [§181.]

(a) For the guidance and information of interested representatives of employers, employees, and the general public, the Bureau of Labor Statistics of the Department of Labor shall maintain a file of copies of all available collective bargaining agreements and other available agreements and actions thereunder settling or adjusting labor disputes. Such file shall be open to inspection under appropriate conditions prescribed by the Secretary of Labor, except that no specific information submitted in confidence shall be disclosed.

(b) The Bureau of Labor Statistics in the Department of Labor is authorized to furnish upon request of the Service, or employers, employees, or their representatives, all available data and factual information which may aid in the settlement of any labor dispute, except that no specific information submitted in confidence shall be disclosed.

EXEMPTION OF RAILWAY LABOR ACT

SEC. 212. [§182.] The provisions of this title [subchapter] shall not be applicable with respect to any matter which is subject to the provisions of the Railway Labor Act [45 U.S.C. §151 et seq.], as amended from time to time.

CONCILIATION OF LABOR DISPUTES IN THE HEALTH CARE INDUSTRY

SEC. 213. [§183.]

(a) **[Establishment of Boards of Inquiry; membership]** If, in the opinion of the Director of the Federal Mediation and Conciliation Service, a threatened or actual strike or lockout affecting a health care institution will, if permitted to occur or to continue, substantially interrupt the delivery of health care in the locality concerned, the Director may further assist in the resolution of the impasse by establishing within 30 days after the notice to the Federal Mediation and Conciliation Service under clause (A) of the last sentence of section 8(d) [section 158(d) of this title] (which is required by clause (3) of such section 8(d) [section 158(d) of this title]), or within 10 days after the notice under clause (B), an impartial Board of Inquiry to investigate the issues involved in the dispute and to make a written report thereon to the parties within fifteen (15) days after the establishment of such a Board. The written report shall contain the findings of facts together with the Board's recommendations for settling the dispute, with the objective of achieving a prompt, peaceful, and just settlement of the dispute. Each such Board shall be composed of such number of individuals as the Director may deem desirable. No member appointed under this section shall have any interest or involvement in the health care institutions or the employee organizations involved in the dispute.

(b) **[Compensation of members of Boards of Inquiry]** (1) Members of any board established under this section who are otherwise employed by the Federal Government shall serve without compensation but shall be reimbursed for travel, subsistence, and other necessary expenses incurred by them in carrying out its duties under this section.

(2) Members of any board established under this section who are not subject to paragraph (1) shall receive compensation at a rate prescribed by the Director but not to exceed the daily rate prescribed for GS-18 of the General Schedule under section 5332 of title 5, United States Code [section 5332 of title 5], including travel for each day they are engaged in the performance of their duties under this section and shall be entitled to reimbursement for travel, subsistence, and other necessary expenses incurred by them in carrying out their duties under this section.

(c) **[Maintenance of status quo]** After the establishment of a board under subsection (a) of this section and for 15 days after any such board has issued its report, no change in the status quo in effect prior to the expiration of the contract in the case of negotiations for a contract renewal, or in effect prior to the time of the impasse in the case of an initial bargaining negotiation, except by agreement, shall be made by the parties to the controversy.

(d) **[Authorization of appropriations]** There are authorized to be appropriated such sums as may be necessary to carry out the provisions of this section.

TITLE III

[Title 29, Chapter 7, Subchapter IV, United States Code]

SUITS BY AND AGAINST LABOR ORGANIZATIONS

SEC. 301. [§185.]

(a) **[Venue, amount, and citizenship]** Suits for violation of contracts between an employer and a labor organization representing employees in an industry affecting commerce as defined in this Act [chapter], or between any such labor organization, may be brought in any district court of the United States having jurisdiction of the parties, without respect to the amount in controversy or without regard to the citizenship of the parties.

(b) [Responsibility for acts of agent; entity for purposes of suit; enforcement of money judgments] Any labor organization which represents employees in an industry affecting commerce as defined in this Act [chapter] and any employer whose activities affect commerce as defined in this Act [chapter] shall be bound by the acts of its agents. Any such labor organization may sue or be sued as an entity and in behalf of the employees whom it represents in the courts of the United States. Any money judgment against a labor organization in a district court of the United States shall be enforceable only against the organization as an entity and against its assets, and shall not be enforceable against any individual member or his assets.

(c) [Jurisdiction] For the purposes of actions and proceedings by or against labor organizations in the district courts of the United States, district courts shall be deemed to have jurisdiction of a labor organization (1) in the district in which such organization maintains its principal offices, or (2) in any district in which its duly authorized officers or agents are engaged in representing or acting for employee members.

(d) [Service of process] The service of summons, subpoena, or other legal process of any court of the United States upon an officer or agent of a labor organization, in his capacity as such, shall constitute service upon the labor organization.

(e) [Determination of question of agency] For the purposes of this section, in determining whether any person is acting as an "agent" of another person so as to make such other person responsible for his acts, the question of whether the specific acts performed were actually authorized or subsequently ratified shall not be controlling.

RESTRICTIONS ON PAYMENTS TO EMPLOYEE REPRESENTATIVES

SEC. 302. [§186.]

(a) [Payment or lending, etc., of money by employer or agent to employees, representatives, or labor organizations] It shall be unlawful for any employer or association of employers or any person who acts as a labor relations expert, adviser, or consultant to an employer or who acts in the interest of an employer to pay, lend, or deliver, or agree to pay, lend, or deliver, any money or other thing of value—

(1) to any representative of any of his employees who are employed in an industry affecting commerce; or

(2) to any labor organization, or any officer or employee thereof, which represents, seeks to represent, or would admit to membership, any of the employees of such employer who are employed in an industry affecting commerce;

(3) to any employee or group or committee of employees of such employer employed in an industry affecting commerce in excess of their normal compensation for the purpose of causing such employee or group or committee directly or indirectly to influence any other employees in the exercise of the right to organize and bargain collectively through representatives of their own choosing; or

(4) to any officer or employee of a labor organization engaged in an industry affecting commerce with intent to influence him in respect to any of his actions, decisions, or duties as a representative of employees or as such officer or employee of such labor organization.

(b) [Request, demand, etc., for money or other thing of value] (1) It shall be unlawful for any person to request, demand, receive, or accept, or agree to receive or accept, any payment, loan, or delivery of any money or other thing of value prohibited by subsection (a) [of this section].

(2) It shall be unlawful for any labor organization, or for any person acting as an officer, agent, representative, or employee of such labor organization, to demand or accept from the operator of any motor vehicle (as defined in part II of the Interstate Commerce Act [49 U.S.C. §301 et seq.]) employed in the transportation of property in commerce, or the employer of any such operator, any money or other thing of value payable to such organization or to an officer, agent, representative, or employee thereof as a fee or charge for the unloading, or in connection with the unloading, of the cargo of such vehicle: Provided, That nothing in this paragraph shall be construed to make unlawful any payment by an employer to any of his employees as compensation for their services as employees.

(c) [Exceptions] The provisions of this section shall not be applicable (1) in respect to any money or other thing of value payable by an employer to any of his employees whose established duties include acting openly for such employer in matters of labor relations or personnel administration or to any representative of his employees, or to any officer or employee of a labor organization, who is also an employee or former employee of such employer, as compensation for, or by reason of, his service as an employee of such employer; (2) with respect to the payment or delivery of any money or other thing of value in satisfaction of a judgment of any court or a decision or award of an arbitrator or impartial chairman or in compromise, adjustment, settlement, or release of any claim, complaint, grievance, or dispute in the absence of fraud or duress; (3) with respect to the sale or purchase of an article or commodity at the prevailing market price in the regular course of business; (4) with respect to money deducted from the wages of employees in payment of membership dues in a labor organization: Provided, That the employer has received from each employee, on whose account such deductions are made, a written assignment which shall not be irrevocable for a period of more than one year, or beyond the termination date of the applicable collective agreement, whichever occurs sooner; (5) with respect to money or other thing of value paid to a trust fund established by such representative, for the sole and exclusive benefit of the employees of such employer, and their families, and dependents (or of such employees, families, and dependents jointly with the employees of other employers making similar payments, and their families, and dependents): Provided, That (A) such payments are held in trust for the purpose of paying, either from principal or income or both, for the benefit of employees, their families, and dependents, for medical or hospital care, pensions on retirement or death of employees, compensation for injuries or illness resulting from occupational activity or insurance to provide any of the foregoing, or unemployment benefits or life insurance, disability and sickness insurance, or accident insurance; (B) the detailed basis on which such payments are to be made is specified in a written agreement with the employer, and employees and employers are equally represented in the administration of such fund, together with such neutral persons as the representatives of the employers and the representatives of employees may agree upon and in the event the employer and employee groups deadlock on the administration of such fund and there are no neutral persons empowered to break such deadlock, such agreement provides that the two groups shall agree on an impartial umpire to decide such dispute, or in event of their failure to agree within a reasonable length of time, an impartial umpire to decide such dispute shall, on petition of either group, be appointed by the district court of the United States for the district where the trust fund has its principal office, and shall also contain provisions for an annual audit of the trust fund, a statement of the results of which shall be available for inspection by interested persons at the principal office of the trust fund and at such other places as may be designated in such written agreement; and (C) such payments as are intended to be used for the purpose of providing pensions or annuities for employees are made to a separate trust which provides that the funds held therein cannot be used for any purpose other than paying such pensions or annuities; (6) with respect to money or other thing of value paid by any employer to a trust fund established by such representative for the purpose of pooled vacation, holiday, severance or similar benefits, or defraying costs of apprenticeship or other training programs: Provided, That the requirements of clause (B) of the proviso to clause (5) of this subsection shall apply to such trust funds; (7) with respect to money or other thing of value paid by any employer to a pooled or individual trust fund established by such representative for the purpose of (A) scholarships for the benefit of employees, their families, and dependents for study at educational institutions, or (B) child care centers for preschool and school age dependents of employees: Provided, That no labor organization or employer shall be required to bargain on the establishment of any such trust fund, and refusal to do so shall not constitute an unfair labor practice: Provided further, That the requirements of clause (B) of the proviso to clause (5) of this subsection shall apply to such trust funds; (8) with respect to money or any other thing of value paid by any employer to a trust fund established by such representative for the purpose of defraying the costs of legal services for employees, their families, and dependents for counsel or plan of their choice: Provided, That the requirements of clause (B) of the proviso to clause (5) of this subsection shall apply to such trust funds: Provided further, That no such legal services shall be furnished: (A) to initiate any proceeding directed (i) against any such employer or its officers or agents except in workman's compensation cases; or (ii) against such labor organization, or its parent or subordinate bodies, or their officers or agents, or (iii) against any other employer or labor organization, or their officers or agents, in any matter arising under the National Labor Relations Act, or this Act [under subchapter II of this chapter or this chapter]; and (B) in any proceeding where a labor organization would be prohibited from defraying the costs of legal services by the provisions of the Labor-Management Reporting and Disclosure Act of 1959 [29 U.S.C. §401 et seq.]; or (9) with respect to money or other things of value paid by an employer to a plant, area, or industrywide labor management committee established for one or more of the purposes set forth in section 5(b) of the Labor Management Cooperation Act of 1978.

[Sec. 302(c)(7) was added by Pub. L. 91–86, Oct. 14, 1969, 83 Stat. 133; Sec. 302(c)(8) by Pub. L. 93–95, Aug. 15, 1973, 87 Stat. 314; and Sec. 302(c)(9) by Pub. L. 95–524, Oct. 27, 1978, 92 Stat. 2021.]

(d) [Penalty for violations] Any person who willfully violates any of the provisions of this section shall, upon conviction thereof, be guilty of a misdemeanor and be subject to a fine of not more than $10,000 or to imprisonment for not more than one year, or both.

(e) [Jurisdiction of courts] The district courts of the United States and the United States courts of the Territories and possessions shall have jurisdiction, for cause shown, and subject to the provisions of rule 65 of the Federal Rules of Civil Procedure [section 381 (repealed) of title 28] (relating to notice to opposite party) to restrain violations of this section, without regard to the provisions of section 17 of title 15 and section 52 of title 29, United States Code [of this title] [known as the "Clayton Act"], and the provisions of sections 101 to 115 of title 29, United States Code [chapter 6 of this title] [known as the "Norris-LaGuardia Act"].

(f) [Effective date of provisions] This section shall not apply to any contract in force on June 23, 1947, until the expiration of such contract, or until July 1, 1948, whichever first occurs.

(g) [Contributions to trust funds] Compliance with the restrictions contained in subsection (c)(5)(B) [of this section] upon contributions to trust funds, otherwise lawful, shall not be applicable to contributions to such trust funds established by collective agreement prior to January 1, 1946, nor shall subsection (c)(5)(A) [of this section] be construed as prohibiting contributions to such trust funds if prior to January 1, 1947, such funds contained provisions for pooled vacation benefits.

BOYCOTTS AND OTHER UNLAWFUL COMBINATIONS

SEC. 303. [§187.]

(a) It shall be unlawful, for the purpose of this section only, in an industry or activity affecting commerce, for any labor organization to engage in any activity or conduct defined as an unfair labor practice in section 8(b)(4) of the National Labor Relations Act [section 158(b)(4) of this title].

(b) Whoever shall be injured in his business or property by reason of any violation of subsection (a) [of this section] may sue therefor in any district court of the United States subject to the limitation and provisions of section 301 hereof [section 185 of this title] without respect to the amount in controversy, or in any other court having jurisdiction of the parties, and shall recover the damages by him sustained and the cost of the suit.

RESTRICTION ON POLITICAL CONTRIBUTIONS

SEC. 304. REPEALED. [See sec. 316 of the Federal Election Campaign Act of 1972, 2 U.S.C. §441b.]

SEC. 305. [§188.] Strikes by Government employees. Repealed.

[See 5 U.S.C. §7311 and 18 U.S.C. §1918.]

TITLE IV

[Title 29, Chapter 7, Subchapter V, United States Code]

CREATION OF JOINT COMMITTEE TO STUDY AND REPORT ON BASIC PROBLEMS AFFECTING FRIENDLY LABOR RELATIONS AND PRODUCTIVITY

SECS. 401–407. [§§191–197.] Omitted.

TITLE V

[Title 29, Chapter 7, Subchapter I, United States Code]

DEFINITIONS

SEC. 501. [§142.] When used in this Act [chapter]—

(1) The term "industry affecting commerce" means any industry or activity in commerce or in which a labor dispute would burden or obstruct commerce or tend to burden or obstruct commerce or the free flow of commerce.

(2) The term "strike" includes any strike or other concerted stoppage of work by employees (including a stoppage by reason of the expiration of a collective-bargaining agreement) and any concerted slowdown or other concerted interruption of operations by employees.

(3) The terms "commerce," "labor disputes," "employer," "employee," "labor organization," "representative," "person," and "supervisor" shall have the same meaning as when used in the National Labor Relations Act as amended by this Act [in subchapter II of this chapter].

SAVING PROVISION

SEC. 502. [§143.] [Abnormally dangerous conditions] Nothing in this Act [chapter] shall be construed to require an individual employee to render labor or service without his consent, nor shall anything in this Act [chapter] be construed to make the quitting of his labor by an individual employee an illegal act; nor shall any court issue any process to compel the performance by an individual employee of such labor or service, without his consent; nor shall the quitting of labor by an employee or employees in good faith because of abnormally dangerous conditions for work at the place of employment of such employee or employees be deemed a strike under this Act [chapter].

SEPARABILITY

SEC. 503. [§144.] If any provision of this Act [chapter], or the application of such provision to any person or circumstance, shall be held invalid, the remainder of this Act [chapter], or the application of such provision to persons or circumstances other than those as to which it is held invalid, shall not be affected thereby.

APPENDIX B

Collective Bargaining Simulation

The process of collective bargaining is dynamic and exciting! It is both an art and a science. The purpose of this simulation is to provide students the opportunity to apply the concepts, terms, and negotiation tactics and strategies to an actual labor agreement. The authors, based on their combined many years of teaching collective bargaining classes as well as many more years of professional negotiation experience, believe the traditional classroom experience can be greatly enhanced by the addition of students' hands-on experiences of negotiating a labor agreement. The simulation is designed to provide a practical, in-class understanding of the collective bargaining process.

The nature of the real-world collective bargaining is two teams sitting across the table from each other with the objective of negotiating an agreement that meets the interests of their party and is acceptable to the other side. This process can be easily simulated in the classroom environment by teams of students. To maximize the feel of a real-world situation, the situational analysis of the renegotiation of an agreement is provided in this appendix and the complete actual agreement (as well as the expired prior agreement) is available online from the publisher at www.prenhall.com/carrellheavrinsimulation.com. Questions about the simulation can be directed to the text authors, who negotiated the actual new agreement, at carrellm@nku.edu. Students are encouraged to use the collective bargaining processes, strategies, and skills presented in Chapters 5 and 6, as well as the economic concepts presented in Chapters 7, 8, and 9.

HOW TO USE THIS SIMULATION

This simulation can be successfully used in only a few hours or several days. Based on many years of experience teaching with collective bargaining simulations, the authors suggest following these stages:

Step 1: Introduction. The course instructor divides the class into an even number of three- to five-member labor and management student teams. The teams are then given adequate time to carefully review the situational summary provided, the actual agreement, and the relevant chapters of the text.

Step 2: Preparation. Student teams determine their individual roles. Suggested roles include chief negotiator (the only member able to make/accept formal, written proposals), assistant chief negotiator (responsible for developing the "framing" of each proposal and writing each formal proposal), financial advisor (the "numbers" person who estimates costs of individual economic proposals, as well as the total cost of all agreed/proposed issues), business agent (keeps minutes of all negotiation sessions, proposals, and counterproposals), and researcher (responsible for researching recent agreements within the region and by similar bargaining units to provide supportive information during negotiations). Teams then develop a list of economic and noneconomic issues they will propose, as well as a list they expect the other side to propose, their opening position on each issue, and their desired position on each issue.

Step 3: Opening Session. Labor and management teams meet across the table, and each side makes an opening statement. Ground rules are agreed on, and finally initial economic and noneconomic demands are exchanged (unless another process is determined in the ground rules) and explained.

Step 4: Negotiation Sessions. Proposals and counterproposals are exchanged until agreement is reached on all mandatory issues presented in the opening session or an impasse is declared. This stage normally requires several meetings of one to three hours each. Chief negotiators are encouraged to sign and date all agreed proposals.

Step 5: Final Agreement. A final agreement that includes the exact written language of all issues that have been successfully negotiated is committed to writing and signed by the chief negotiators. The instructor then leads a class discussion of the agreement(s).

Simulation Rules

1. During their first team meeting, the members of each team agree to hours outside of class in which they can all meet each day or week to plan and prepare for their negotiation sessions. If the simulation runs for eight weeks, three hours per week outside of class is recommended.
2. Team members each play their roles to the best of their ability. They only negotiate in good faith and strive to negotiate the best, most realistic agreement. Members generally follow the information provided in the summary, but they may also use additional information related to their research and others ideas.
3. Team members do not consult with members of any other team, past or present.
4. Teams make reasonable cost estimates of economic proposals based on the information provided in the summary as well as outside information gained through research. In addition they do not delay negotiations because they lack more economic data.
5. At the end of the time allowed by the instructor, teams either reach a written agreement on all issues or declare an impasse. No contract extension is possible. The written agreement should list each article of the current agreement with all words that have been deleted shown ~~marked through with a line~~. <u>All new words or numbers should be underlined</u>. Any articles or sections that have not been changed can be listed as "no change."

Summary of the Labor–Management Situation

On June 30, 2007, the three-year labor agreement between Louisville/Jefferson County Metro Government (management, hereafter called "Metro") and the River City Fraternal Order of Police Lodge # 614 (the union, hereafter called "FOP") expired. As contract negotiations began on March 30, 2007, the atmosphere between the FOP and Metro might be described as cordial, but tense, and far more tense than past negotiations in recent memory. The FOP, with 1,175 members in the bargaining unit, was the largest of 27 bargaining units recognized by Metro government, and thus the negotiations would be closely watched by all the other unions as well as nonunion employees. The officers and sergeants represented by the FOP believed they had taken a step backward in the last negotiation—the first since the merger of city and county governments and thus the first since the merger of the former city and county FOP Lodges. Both sides anticipated a difficult negotiation process, and thus they added new negotiators to their teams.

Although the current collective bargaining agreement (Art. 6, Sec. 3) as well as state law provided a "no-strike" situation for the FOP, the FOP members, like many police departments, enjoyed a high level of public support, which helped level the playing field, or provided negotiating leverage, between the two sides. The FOP hoped to gain increases that would make up for lost buying power realized over the past three years of low negotiated annual increases. The FOP has historically demanded a traditional, distributive bargaining process at the table, and it has resisted past attempts at "two-tier" wage increases or benefits because of a strong sense of solidarity and equity among the members. When pressured by Metro, the FOP has appealed for, and often received, at least moderate public support.

State law requires that the Metro Government operate each year with a balanced budget, and both sides realize that Metro's tax revenues have been flat and even experienced a decline of about 2 percent in recent months because of local and national economic conditions. Over the past 20 years, Metro revenues averaged 4 percent very consistently, but the stagnant national economy caused an unexpected $9 million shortfall in the current year's revenues that led to a hiring freeze and midyear budget cuts in all departments, as well as the possibility of employee layoffs. Members of the FOP, however, were not subject to layoff because the current contract contains a "no-layoff" clause.

In 2003, during the first round of labor negotiations as a new merged government, Metro adopted a "formula" for determining the annual pay increase to propose to bargaining groups. The initial contract with the FOP and all other contracts settled by Metro with its labor unions had the "formula" increase: a percentage increase equal to half of the percentage increase in tax revenue with a guaranteed 2 percent, which is the same as Article 24, Section 2, 3 of the expiring FOP contract.

At the start of the simulation, the course instructor will provide confidential information to each labor and management team which is a list of the economic issues and priorities developed by the parties themselves in the actual negotiation. The confidential lists can be used by the teams to determine their negotiation strategies. The lists of issues and priorities, as well as the entire 2007–2011 Agreement, are provided in the Instructor's Manual.

APPENDIX C

Labor Media Guide

Labor relations is a field that is rich with a number of movies and documentaries that can "bring to life" the human element and circumstances of American labor history. Therefore we recommend that a course in labor relations and collective bargaining be enhanced by the use of media, either in the classroom or outside. The following is a mixture of award-winning documentaries, popular Hollywood first-run movies, and other unique media which focus on labor events and are available on DVD and thus can be easily used in most classrooms or downloaded and viewed directly on a computer. For each film the Instructor's Manual also contains suggested scenes, labor issues presented, suggested relevant text chapters, and relevant discussion questions.

1. *Norma Rae.* (20th Century Fox Films, 1979, 118 minutes)

Summary: This popular Hollywood movie, which stars Sally Field in the Academy Award–winning title role, is considered by some to be the classic American labor movie. The film is based on the true events experienced by a union organizer in a J. P. Stevens & Co. textile mill in South Carolina—at that time the largest employer in the state. By viewing the hardships endured by Norma Rae, a struggling single mother of young children, students can better understand why she risks her job and much more to gain recognition from management.

2. *American Dream.* (Miramax Films, 1990, ISBN 0-7888-5043-1).

Summary: Academy Award winner for Best Documentary. If students see only one labor film—this is the one! This landmark film is unique among the best labor films because it contains all footage of a historical, economic strike by members of United Food and Commercial Workers Union, Local P-9, at the Austin, Minnesota, Hormel plant in 1986. After management reduces hourly wages from $10.69 to $8.25, local union leaders propose the first economic strike in 52 years—which is solidly supported by the membership and community at first, but in the end replacement workers are hired, and only 20 percent of the strikers are recalled. Scenes, some graphic, were filmed as they happened and thus provide thought-provoking and powerful insight into the strategies of both sides, and the issues and emotions of the people involved.

3. *The "Wooblies"* (1979, ISBN 0-7670-8966-9, 90 minutes)

Summary: An outstanding docudrama on the class struggle during the turn of the century (1900) of the International Workers of the World (IWW)—The "Wooblies"—and big business. The film includes interviews with aged IWW members who were present at early events, including the 1912 Lawrence, Massachusetts, strike; 1913 Patterson, New Jersey, strike; and 1916 Everett, Washington, free speech fight. It also shows numerous newspaper articles about the events as well as a black-and-white film footage of the times. The basic theme is the struggle between big business and the working class. Students find the firsthand accounts from elderly members of the union especially interesting.

4. *Harlan County U.S.A.* (The Criterion Collection, 1976, 103 minutes)

Summary: One of the most popular documentaries about labor history, this Academy Award–winning production shows the struggles and violence between coal miners and the Eastover mining company, a division of Duke Power Company in Harlan county, Kentucky, in 1973. The realistic nature of the documentary makes the film an excellent choice for the classroom or assigned outside viewing. The film catalogs the yearlong strike by United Mine Workers of America (UMWA) against the Brookside Mine, which evolves into the hiring of scabs, court-ordered injunctions, police intervention, picket lines, and violence. At one point wives of the miners decide to join the acts, which adds an interesting dynamic to the struggle. The historical plight of coal miners in Appalachia is presented to provide context to the activities.

5. *The Molly Maguires* (Paramount Studio, 1970, 123 minutes)

Summary: This Hollywood first-run movie stars Sean Connery and Richard Harris in a reenactment of the mine bombing by the Molly Maguires in 1877. The plot of the movie includes Richard Harris hired as a spy by the owners to infiltrate the Molly Maguires group to identify them for the owners. Scenes of the workers in the mines are realistic and portray the unsafe and hard-working conditions of the day. The mine workers are constantly watched by armed guards who utilize violence on occasion. Today the Molly Maguires are U.S. labor history legends; however, it is debated by historians if they were a secret group of the Ancient Order of Hiberians, an Irish benevolent society, simply union organizers, or in fact Pinkerton agents hired by the mining company. They may have been "guilty as hell" of violent acts against the company, or they may have been framed and executed for acts they did not commit!

6. *The Golden Cage: A Story of California's Farmworkers* (Filmmakers Library, 1989)

Summary: A documentary of the plight of migrant farmworkers in California. Excellent historical footage of the workers' living conditions and fights with the owners of the agricultural companies. Includes the history of the United Farm Workers (UFW) and its fight to negotiate contracts with the owners despite the lack of federal laws. A moving non-Hollywood film with historical footage, interviews, and newspaper clippings. The role of Cesar Chavez in organizing the union is presented.

7. *Jimmy Hoffa* (A & E Television Biography, 2000)

Summary: An A&E made for television biography provides a balanced look at the life of Teamsters Union president Jimmy Hoffa. Actual footage from the moving U.S. Senate hearings involving Senators John F. Kennedy and Robert F. Kennedy as well as their dislike for Hoffa and his eventual imprisonment are highlighted in the film. Hoffa's ties to organized crime as well as his personal family life are included. Interviews with Hoffa's son and daughter provide alternative insights into the man.

8. *Harry Bridges—A Man and His Union* (MW Productions, 1992, Title ID: 0236211; 1 hour)

Summary: A biography of the charismatic, liberal labor leader who headed the powerful International Longshoremen and Warehouse Union from the 1930s to the 1970s. Bridges was a lightening rod for both pro- and antilabor movement activists. Prosecuted by three U.S. presidents, Bridges was convicted by a federal jury for lying about his Communist Party membership—but the conviction was later overturned.

9. *Coalmining Women* (www.APPALSHOP.org, 1982, 2007 40 minutes)

Summary: Excellent docudrama about women coal miners who worked in a male-dominated industry and the problems they endured. Interviews with the women coal miners both at home and in the mines provide a moving insight into their unique roles, and general insights into the coal-mining industry.

10. *On the Waterfront* (Columbia Pictures, 1954, ISBN 0-7678-0427-9, 108 minutes)

Summary: Winner of 8 Academy Awards including Best Picture and Best Actor (Marlon Brando), this Hollywood classic provides insights into the gang-ridden waterfront of the 1950s. The powerful cast also includes Eva Marie Saint, Karl Malden, Lee J. Cobb, and Rod Steiger. Brando as Terry Malloy unknowingly sets up a neighborhood friend for murder because he had been talking with the Crime Commission. The film is based on the novel *Crime on the Waterfront* by Malcom Johnson and details shady and violent activities of East coast longshoremen, the International Longshoreman's association, and organized crime. In one scene Brando delivers the powerful lines, "I could've been a contender. I could have been somebody." It became one of the classics of Hollywood films.

11. *Newsies* (Walt Disney Production, 1992, 125 minutes)

Summary: A Walt Disney movie which has attained cult status among younger students due to the star actors (Luke Edwards, Bill Pullman, Ann-Margaret, and Robert Duvall) and popular songs. The plot of the movie is typical Hollywood—poor newsboys in New York must unionize to fight newspaper owners William Randolph Hearst and Joseph Pulitzer. The 3,000 newsboys stage a selective strike against the newspaper magnets. Their organizing drive is based loosely on the 1899 Trolleyman's strike and violence. The focus of the newsboys' strike is their demand that they only pay a half cent for each newspaper, which they sold for a penny. In the end Governor Theodore Roosevelt steps in on the side of the newsboys to prevent the strike from spreading to other child laborers.

12. *Teamster Boss: The Jackie Presser Story* (HBO Home Video, 1999, 111 minutes)

Summary: The riveting story of one of the most important labor leaders of the 1980s. The film stars Brian Dennehy as Jackie Presser, the Teamster leader who started from humble beginnings as a bowling alley manager and rises, thanks largely to his father Bill Presser, a powerful Teamster leader, to lead the powerful Teamster union. When threatened by the Mob, after the disappearance of Jimmy Hoffa, Presser becomes an FBI informant and strives to clear the union of Mob ties and changes the union process of elections. The film also stars Eli Wallach, Maria Alonso, Jeff Daniels, and Tony Lo Bianco.

ENDNOTES

Chapter 1

1. Gerald G. Somers, ed., *Collective Bargaining: Contemporary American Experience* (Madison, WI: Industrial Relations Research Association, 1980), pp. 553–56.
2. Scott A. Kruse, "Giveback Bargaining: One Answer to Current Labor Problems?" *Personnel Journal 62,* no. 4 (April 1983), p. 286.
3. National Labor Relations Act, Sec. 7, [§ 157] (1935).
4. Joe Barrett, "Two Cities in Fight Over Factory Jobs at Mercury," *The Wall Street Journal* (September 4, 2009), p. A6.
5. Pieter A. Grobler, Surette Warnich, Michael R. Carrell, Norbert F. Elbert, and Robert D. Hatfield, *Human Resource Management in South Africa,* 4th ed. (Andover, UK: Cengage Learning, 2011), pp. 482, 483.
6. Albert Rees, *The Economics of Trade Unions* (Chicago: University of Chicago Press, 1977), p. 30.
7. Michael H. LeRoy, "State of the Unions: Assessment by Elite American Labor Leaders," *Journal of Labor Research 13,* no. 4 (Fall 1992), pp. 371–79.
8. Peter A. Bamberger, Avraham N. Kluger, and Ronena Suchard, "The Antecedents of Union Commitment—A Meta-Analysis," *Academy of Management Journal 42,* no. 3 (1999), pp. 304–18.
9. Jonathan A. Segal, "Keeping Norma Rae at Bay," *H.R. Magazine* (August 1996), pp. 111–17.
10. Randall G. Holcombe and James D. Gwartney, "Unions, Economic Freedom, and Growth," *Cato Journal 30,* no. 1 (Winter 2010), pp. 1–23.
11. Gary Chaison, "Union Membership Attrition," *Monthly Labor Review 133,* no. 1 (January 2010), p. 76.
12. James A. Walker, "Union Membership in 2007: A Visual Essay," *Monthly Labor Review* (October 2008), pp. 1–39.
13. Richard Feldman and Michael Betzold, *End of the Line: Autoworkers and the American Dream* (New York: Weidenfeld & Nicolson, 1988), p. 6.
14. Jack Fiorito, "The State of Unions in the United States," *Journal of Labor Research 28,* no. 1 (Winter 2007), p. 46.
15. Robert J. Flanagan, "Has Management Strangled U.S. Unions?" *Journal of Labor Research 26,* no. 1 (Winter 2005), pp. 33–63.
16. Michelle Amber, *2007 Source Book on Collective Bargaining* (Washington, DC: Bureau of National Affairs, 2007), pp. 175–76.
17. Mark Fitzgerald, "Can't We All Just Get Along?" *Editor & Publisher 136,* no. 27 (July 14, 2003), pp. 10–17.
18. David Moberg, "Labor Debates Its Future," *The Nation 280,* no. 10 (March 14, 2005), pp. 11–16.
19. Ed McKenna, "Teamsters Target DHL," *Traffic World* (April 25, 2005), p. 30.
20. Ed Watkins, "Storm Warnings," *Lodging Hospitality 60,* no. 14 (October 2004), p. 4.
21. John E. Lyncheski, "Keeping the Unions at Bay," *Nursing Home Long Term Care Management 51,* no. 5 (May 2002), pp. 44–51.
22. Joe Carlson, "Labor Comes on Strong," *Modern Healthcare 39,* no. 13, (March 30, 2009), p. 12.
23. "Labor-Management Relationships at Utilities, Airlines," *2007 Source Book on Collective Bargaining* (Washington, DC: Bureau of National Affairs, 2007), pp. 117–18.
24. *San Manuel Indian Bingo and Casino v. NLRB*, 475 F.3d. 1306 (C.A. D.C. 2007).
25. James P. Sweeney, "U.S. Labor Laws Apply to Tribes, Court Says," *San Diego Union-Tribune* (February 10, 2007), p. A1.
26. Susan R. Hobbs, "UAW Members Ratify Landmark Contract With Native American—Owned Casino," BNA Reports, *2010 Source Book on Collective Bargaining* (Washington, DC: Bureau of National Affairs, 2010), pp. 129–33.
27. Daniel Kiley, "Labor's New Roll of the Dice," *Business Week* (December 24, 2007), p. 37.
28. Anne Marie Squeo, "How Longshoremen Keep Global Wind at Their Backs," *Wall Street Journal* (July 27, 2006), pp. A1, 12.
29. Robert L. Aronson, "Unionism among Professional Employees in the Private Sector," *Industrial and Labor Relations Review 38,* no. 3 (April 1985), pp. 352–64.
30. John Eckberg, "Union Review Finds Janitors in Poverty," *Cincinnati Enquirer* (March 9, 2005), p. D2.
31. Majorie Valbrun, "To Reverse Declines, Unions are Targeting Immigrant Workers," *The Wall Street Journal* (May 27, 1999), p. A1.
32. Neal E. Boudette, "Honda and UAW Clash Over New Factory Jobs," *Wall Street Journal* (October 10, 2007), p. A1.
33. Jeff Ball, "UAW's Reception in Alabama Mercedes Plant Is Sour," *Wall Street Journal* (January 31, 2000), p. A15.
34. Bill Wolfe, "UPS Freight Workers Sign Up for Teamsters," *Louisville Courier-Journal* (January 26, 2008), p. A1.
35. Harry C. Katz, Thomas A. Kochan, and Kenneth R. Gobelle, "Industrial Relations Performance and QWL Programs: An Interplant Analysis," *Industrial and Labor Relations Review* 37, no. 1 (October 1983), pp. 3–17.
36. Federal Mediation and Conciliation Service, *Interest-based Bargaining: A Different Way* (Washington, DC: FMCS, 1999).
37. Mike Bozer, "Union OKs Deal with AK Steel," *Cincinnati Enquirer* (September 7, 2005), p. D1.
38. Paul D. Staudohar, "Labor-Management Cooperation at NUMMI," *Labor Law Journal* (January 1991), pp. 57–63; and Martha Groves, "Rolling On: GM-Toyota Plant Prospers amid Auto Industry Slump," *Los Angeles Times* (December 12, 1991), pp. D1–D2.
39. Richard Verrier, "SAG Members, Finally, Approve Contract," *The Los Angeles Times* (June 9, 2009), p. A.1.

40. Lucy May, "Pilots from Other Airlines Show Unity," *Business Courier* (January 12, 2007), p. 5.
41. Miriam Pawel, "Union Seeks Boycott of Gallo Wines," *Los Angeles Times* (June 14, 2005). Available at www.ufw.org. Accessed February 8, 2008.
42. Paul D. Staudohar, *The Sports Industry and Collective Bargaining* (New York: ICR Press, 1986), pp. 1–7.
43. Ibid.
44. See *Curtis C. Flood v. Bowie K. Kuhn, et al.*, 407 U.S. 258, 32 L.Ed. 2d 728, 92 S.Ct. 2099 (1972).
45. Staudohar, *The Sports Industry*, pp. 20–29.
46. Ronald Blum, "Average Salary for Players in Arbitration Declines," *Associated Press.* Available at www.sports.com/mlb/news. Accessed February 19, 2005.
47. U.S. Constitution, art. I sec. 8 (1787).
48. 29 U.S.C. sec. 157 (1982).
49. 29 U.S.C. sec. 158(a) (1982).
50. 28 U.S.C. sec. 152 (1982).
51. Ludwig Teller, *Labor Disputes and Collective Bargaining,* Vol. 2 (New York: Baker, Voorhis & Co., 1940), p. 688.
52. "Liebman Hopes Board Will Take More Dynamic Approach," BNA Reports, *2010 Source Book on Collective Bargaining* (Washington, DC: Bureau of National Affairs, 2010), pp. 93, 94.
53. Press Release, National Labor Relations Board (June 17, 2010). Available at www.nlrb.gov. Accessed June 18, 2010.
54. 29 U.S.C. sec. 152 (1) (1982).
55. 341 NLRB No. 138, (2004).
56. *Concrete Form Walls, Inc.*, 346 NLRB No. 80 (April 13, 2006).
57. *EEOC v. Arabian American Oil Co.* (ARAMCO) 499 U.S. 244 (1991).
58. Todd Keihley, "Does the National Labor Relations Act Extend to Americans Who are Temporarily Abroad?" *Columbia Law Review 105,* no. 7 (November 2005), pp. 2135–70.
59. U.S. Congress, 39 U.S.C. sec. 1209 (1982).
60. *National Labor Relations Board v. Cabot Carbon Co.,* 360 U.S. 203, 79 S.Ct. 1015, 3 L.Ed. 2d 1175 (1959).
61. *San Diego Building Trades Council v. Garmon,* 359 U.S. 236, 76 S.Ct. 773, 3 L.Ed. 2d 775 (1959); *Amalgamated Association of Street, Electric Railway & Motor Coach Employees v. Lockridge,* 403 U.S. 224, 91 S.Ct. 1909, 29 L.Ed. 2d 473 (1971); *Sears, Roebuck & Co. v. San Diego District Council of Carpenters,* 98 S.Ct. 1745, 56 L.Ed. 2d 209 (1978); and *Tamburelli v. Comm-Tract Corporation,* 67 F.3d 973 (1st Cir. 1995).
62. *Smith v. Evening News Association,* 371 U.S. 195, 51 LRRM 2646 (1962); and Local 174, *Teamsters v. Lucas Flour Co.,* 369 U.S. 95, 49 LRRM 2717 (1962).

Chapter 2

1. Foster Rhea Dulles and Melvyn Dubofsky, *Labor in America, A History,* 4th ed. (Arlington Heights, IL: Harlan Davidson, 1984), p. 1.
2. Ibid., pp. 32, 70–73.
3. Robert Asher and Charles Stephens, eds., *Labor Dividend: Race and Ethnicity in United States Labor Struggles 1835–1960* (Albany, NY: State University of New York Press, 1990), pp. 154–58.
4. Maurice F. Neufeld, "The Persistence of Ideas in the American Labor Movement: The Heritage of the 1830s," *Industrial and Labor Relations Review 35,* no. 2 (January 1982), p. 212.
5. John R. Commons, *History of Labor in the United States,* Vol. 2 (New York: Macmillan, 1946), pp. 7–8.
6. Joseph G. Rayback, *A History of American Labor* (New York: The Free Press, 1966), pp. 120–22.
7. Dulles and Dubofsky, *Labor in America,* pp. 111–12; Rayback, *A History of American Labor,* 1966, pp. 131–33.
8. Samuel Yellen, *American Labor Struggles* (New York: Harcourt Brace, 1936), pp. 3–38.
9. Joseph G. Rayback, *A History of American Labor* (New York: Macmillan, 1959), p. 135.
10. Ron Panko, "Underwriting Strike Insurance," *Bests Review 100,* no. 10 (October 2001), pp. 32–33.
11. Yellen, *American Labor Struggles,* pp. 39–71.
12. Richard O. Bayer and Herbert M. Morris, *Labor's Untold Story* (New York: United Electrical Radio and Machine Workers of America, 1955), pp. 98–99, by permission of United Electrical and Radio Machine Workers.
13. Ibid., p. 99; see Dulles and Dubofsky, *Labor in America,* pp. 116–18.
14. Dulles and Dubofsky, *Labor in America,* p. 135.
15. Joseph Adler, "The Past as Prologue? A Brief History of the Labor Movement in the United States," *Public Personnel Management 35,* no. 4 (Winter 2006), pp. 311–29.
16. Sherman Antitrust Act, 15 U.S.C. sec. 1 (1892).
17. Bayer and Morris, *Labor's Untold Story,* p. 131.
18. Ibid., p. 119.
19. J. Robert Constantine, "Eugene V. Debs: An American Paradox," *Monthly Labor Review 114,* no. 8 (August 1991), pp. 30–33.
20. Stuart Bruce Kaufman, "Birth of a Federation: Mr. Gompers Endeavors Not to Build a Bubble," *Monthly Labor Review 104,* no. 11 (November 1981), p. 24.
21. Rayback, *A History of American Labor,* 1966, pp. 194–26.
22. Alice Kessler-Harris, "Trade Unions Mirror Society in Conflict between Collectivism and Individualism," *Monthly Labor Review 110,* no. 8 (August 1989), pp. 34–35.
23. Judith Nielsen, from the papers of Stanley Eston, archived at the University of Idaho. Accessed August 18, 2011.
24. Rayback, *A History of American Labor,* 1966, pp. 238–39; Gary N. Chaison, *Unions in America* (Thousand Oaks, CA: Sage, 2006), p. 10.
25. Dulles and Dubofsky, *Labor in America,* p. 214.
26. Juliet H. Mofford, "Women in the Workplace: Labor Unions," *Women's History Magazine* (Spring/Summer 1996).
27. Ludlow Massacre, From the United Mine Workers of America, with a link to the Ludlow Monument listing the names of the victims. Available at http://222.umwa.org/history/ludlow-massacre.shtml). Accessed August 18, 2011.

28. Rayback, *A History of American Labor,* 1959, pp. 54–57.
29. David P. Twomey, *Labor Law and Legislation* (Cincinnati, OH: South-Western, 1980), pp. 7–8.
30. *Commonwealth v. Hunt*, 45 Mass. (4 Met.) III (1842).
31. Bayer and Morris, *Labor's Untold Story,* p. 131.
32. Erdman Act, 30 Stat. 424 (1898), amended by P.L. 6, 38 Stat. 103 (1913); referenced in 45 U.S.C. sec. 101 (1976).
33. Rayback, *A History of American Labor,* 1966, p. 212.
34. Clayton Act, ch. 323, sec. 1, 6, and 7, 38 Stat. 730 (1914); referenced in 15 U.S.C. sec. 12, 17, and 18 (1982).
35. Theodore Kheel, *Labor Law* (New York: Matthew Bender, 1988), chap. 5, p. 24.
36. *Duplex Printing Press Co. v. Deering*, 254 U.S. 443, 41 S.Ct. 172, 65 L.Ed. 349 (1921); *Redford Cut Stone Co. v. Journeymen Stone Cutters' Association*, 274 U.S. 37, 47 S.Ct. 522, 71 L.Ed. 916 (1927).
37. Railway Labor Act, 45 U.S.C. sec. 151 (1976).
38. *Texas and New Orleans Railroad Co. v. Brotherhood of Railway & Steamship Clerks*, 281 U.S. 548 (1930).
39. Ibid., p. 570.
40. David Moberg, "On 75th Anniversary of Railway Labor Act, We Need to Protect Workers' Rights," *The Progressive Media Project* (May 15, 2001). Available at www.progressive.org; Morgan O. Reynolds and D. Eric Schansberg, "At Age 65, Retire the Railway Labor Act," *Regulation 14,* no. 3 (Summer 1991). Available at www.cato.org.
41. Davis-Bacon Act, Title 40 U.S.C.A. sec. 276a (1931).
42. Norris–La Guardia Act, 29 U.S.C. sec. 101 (1982).
43. National Industrial Recovery Act, Pub.L. 67, 48 Stat. 195 (1933); referenced in 7 U.S.C. sec. 601 (1982).
44. *Schechter Poultry Corp. v. United States,* 295 U.S. 495, 55 S.Ct. 837, 79 L.Ed. 893 (1937).
45. Patrick Hardin, ed., *The Developing Labor Law,* 3rd ed. (Washington, DC: Bureau of National Affairs, 1992), pp. 12–13.
46. Ibid., p. 28.
47. National Labor Relations Act, 29 U.S.C. sec. 151 et seq. (1982).
48. *Associated Press v. National Labor Relations Board*, 301 U.S. 103 (1937); and *National Labor Relations Board v. Jones & Laughlin Steel Corporation,* 301 U.S. 1, 57 S.Ct. 615, 81 L.Ed. 893 (1937).
49. Walsh-Healy Act, Title 29 U.S.C.A. sec. 557; and (1936) Title 41 U.S.C.A. secs. 35–45.
50. Fair Labor Standards Act, 29 U.S.C. sec. 201 (1982).
51. War Labor Disputes Act, Pub.L. 89, 57 Stat. 163 (1943).
52. *Thornhill v. Alabama,* 310 U.S. 88 (1940); and *Milk Drivers Local 753 v. Meadowmoore Dairies, Inc.*, 312 U.S. 287 (1941).
53. Darren Bell, "Understanding Recent Changes in the FLSA," *Intercom 52,* no. 4 (April 2005), pp. 25–27.
54. Hardin, *The Developing Labor Law,* p. 35.
55. Labor-Management Reporting and Disclosure (Landrum-Griffin) Act, 29 U.S.C. sec. 401 et seq. (1982).
56. William W. Osborne, Jr., *All You Need to Know about the History of Labor Union Law* (Washington, DC: BNA Books, 2003), pp. 56–58.
57. Neil W. Chamberlain, *Sourcebook on Labor* (New York: McGraw-Hill, 1964), pp. 26–29.
58. Labor-Management Reporting and Disclosure (Landrum-Griffin) Act.
59. *Transportation Workers Local 525,* 317 N.L.R.B. 62, 149 L.R.R.M. 1222 (1995).
60. *Wirtz v. Hotel, Motel & Club Employees Union, Local 6,* 391 U.S. 492 (1968).
61. Wilma B. Liebman, "Decline and Disenchantment: Reflections on the Aging of the National Labor Relations Board," *Berkeley Journal of Employment & Labor Law 28,* no. 2 (2007), pp. 569–89.
62. The Employee Free Choice Act, H.R. 800 (2007).
63. George McGovern, "My Party Should Respect Union Ballots," *Wall Street Journal* (August 8, 2008), p. A13.
64. Adrienne E. Eaton and Jill Kriesky, "NLRB Elections Versus Card Check Campaigns: Results of a Worker Survey," *Industrial and Labor Relations Review 62,* no. 2 (January 2009), p. 157.
65. Susan J. T. Johnson, "First Contract Arbitration: Effects on Bargaining and Work Stoppages," *Industrial and Labor Relations Review 63,* no. 4 (July 2010), p. 585.
66. Dulles and Dubofsky, *Labor in America,* p. 86.
67. Ibid., p. 96.
68. Rayback, *A History of American Labor,* 1966, pp. 122–23; Norman Hill, "Forging a Partnership between Blacks and Unions," *Monthly Labor Review 100,* no. 8 (August 1987), pp. 38–39.
69. Michael Flug, "Organized Labor and the Civil Rights Movement of the 1960s: The Case of the Maryland Freedom Union," *Labor History 31,* no. 3 (Summer 1990), pp. 322–46.
70. U.S. Department of Labor, Employment and Earnings (2009).
71. Rayback, *A History of American Labor,* 1966, pp. 120–22.
72. Philip S. Foner, *Women and the American Labor Movement,* Vol. 1 (New York: Free Press, 1979), pp. 290–300.
73. Ibid., Vol. 2, 1980, p. 327.
74. Paul Johnston, "Outflanking Power, Reframing Unionism: The Basic Strike of 1999–2001," *Labor Studies Journal 28,* no. 4 (Winter 2004), pp. 1–24.

Chapter 3

1. "The Labor Movement," *Workforce 81,* no. 1 (January 2002), p. 27.
2. Jack Blackburn and Gloria Busman, *Understanding Unions in the Public Sector* (Los Angeles, CA: Institute of Industrial Relations University of California, 1977), p. 51; U.S. Census Bureau, *Labor Union Membership by Sector*. Available at www.allcountries.org/uscensus. Accessed October 8, 2010. U.S. Bureau of Labor Statistics
3. Congressional Budget Office, *The Federal Workforce: Its Size, Cost and Activities* (Washington, DC: Congress of the United States, 1977), p. 8.
4. U.S. Department of Education, *10 Facts About K-12 Education Funding*, Washington, DC, 2005. Available at www2.ed.gov/about/overview/fed/10facts/index.html. Accessed October 8, 2010.

5. Congressional Budget Office, *The Federal Workforce.*
6. Benjamin Aaron et al., *Public-Sector Bargaining* (Washington, DC: Bureau of National Affairs, 1979), p. 46.
7. Richard Kearney, *Labor Relations in the Public Sector,* 4th ed. (Boca Raton, FL: CRC Press, 2009), p. 14.
8. Joseph Adler, "The Past as Prologue? A Brief History of the Labor Movement in the United States," *Public Personnel Management 35,* no. 4 (Winter 2006), pp. 311–29.
9. Fraternal Order of Police Grand Lodge. Available at www.grandlodgefop.org. Accessed October 8, 2010.
10. Kearney, *Labor Relations in the Public Sector,* p. 15.
11. David Lewin and Shirley B. Goldenberg, "Public Sector Unionism in the U.S. and Canada," *Industrial Relations 19,* no. 3 (Fall 1980), pp. 239–56.
12. Jerry Wurf, "Establishing the Legal Right of Public Employees to Bargain," *Monthly Labor Review 92,* no. 7 (July 1969), p. 66.
13. Henry Campbell Black, *Black's Law Dictionary,* 4th ed. (St. Paul, MN: West, 1968), p. 1568.
14. *McLaughlin v. Tilendis,* 398 F.2d 287 (7th Cir., 1968).
15. Eileen Norcross, "Public-Sector Unionism: A Review," Mercatus Center Working Paper No. 11-26, George Mason University, May 2011. Available at http://www.scribd.com/doc/56268043/PUBLIC-SECTOR-UNIONISM-a-review. Accessed August 20, 2011.
16. Kearney, *Labor Relations in the Public Sector,* p. 53.
17. Murray Comarow, "The Demise of the Postal Service," *COSMOS Journal* (2002). Available at http://www.cosmos-club.org/web/journals/2002/comarow.html. Accessed October 9, 2010.
18. *American Federation of Government Employees, AFL-CIO, et al., v. Gates,* 486 F.3d 1316, 181 L.R.R.M. (BNA) 3153 (2007).
19. *National League of Cities v. Usery,* 426 U.S. 833 (1976).
20. *Garcia v. San Antonio Metropolitan Transit Authority,* 469 U.S. 528 (1985).
21. *Alden v. Maine,* 527 U.S. 706 (1999).
22. *United States v. Lopez,* 514 U.S. 549 (1995).
23. For an overview of state and local legislation, see Aaron et al., *Public-Sector Bargaining,* pp. 191–23; Nels E. Nelson, "Public Policy and Union Security in the Public Sector," *Journal of Collective Negotiations in the Public Sector 7,* no. 2 (1978), pp. 87–17.
24. Available at www.juj.org/news/update. Accessed January 4, 2007.
25. *Davenport v. Washington Education Association* 127 S. CT. 2372, 181 LRRM (2007).
26. Jess Bravin, "High Court Allows a Curb on Union Political Activity," *Wall Street Journal* (June 15, 2007), p. A3.
27. National Education Association. Available at www.nea.org. Accessed October 11, 2010.
28. Available at www.seui.org. Accessed October 11, 2010.
29. Available at www.teamsters.org. Accessed October 12, 2010.
30. National Education Association, www.nea.org and American Federation of Teachers. Available at www.aft.org. Accessed January 20, 2008.
31. *Utility Workers Local 111 (Ohio Power),* 203 NLRB 230, 238 (1973) enfd. 490 F. 2d 1383 (6th Cir. 1974).
32. *Fraternal Order of Police, et al. v. Prince George's County, Maryland,* —F.Supp.2d—, 2009 WL 2516788 (D.Md.)
33. *FOP v. Prince George's County,* p. 21.
34. Roger L. Bowlby and William R. Shriver, "The Behavioral Interpretation of Bluffing: A Public Sector Case," *Labor Law Journal 32,* no. 8 (August 1981), pp. 469–73.
35. *Service Employees' International Union, AFL-CIO, Local 556 v. Department of the Army, Headquarters, U.S. Army Support Command, Fort Shafter, Hawaii,* 1 FLRA No. 64 (1979)
36. *Abood v. Detroit Board of Education,* 431 U.S. 209 (1977).
37. James E. Martin, "Employee Characteristics and Representation Election Outcomes," *Industrial and Labor Relations Review 38,* no. 3 (April 1985), pp. 365–76.
38. Aaron et al., *Public-Sector Bargaining,* p. 151.
39. Eugene H. Becker, "Analysis of Work Stoppages in the Federal Sector, 1962–81," *Monthly Labor Review 105,* no. 8 (August 1982), pp. 49–53.
40. Theodore W. Kheel, "Resolving Deadlocks without Banning Strikes," *Monthly Labor Review 92,* no. 7 (July 1969), p. 62.
41. John M. Capozzola, "Public Employee Strikes: Myths and Realities," *National Civic Review 68,* no. 4 (April 1979), pp. 178–88.
42. Randy Steele, "The Rise of PATCO," *Flying 109* (March 1982), p. 35.
43. Ibid.
44. Herbert R. Northrup, "The Rise and Demise of PATCO," *Industrial and Labor Relations Review 37,* no. 2 (January 1984), pp. 167–84.
45. *Mountain Valley Education Association v. Maine School Administrative District,* 655 A. 2d 348 (1995). See also *Wasco County v. AFSCME,* 613 P. 2d 1067 (1980).
46. *M&M Building & Electrical Service,* 262 N.L.R.B. 1472 (1982).
47. *Montgomery County Council of Supporting Services Employees, Inc. v. Board of Education,* 354 A. 2d 781 (1976).
48. Kenneth P. Swan, "Public Bargaining in Canada and the U.S.: A Legal View," *Industrial Relations 19,* no. 3 (Fall 1980), pp. 272–91.
49. David B. Lipsky and Harry C. Katz, "Alternative Approaches to Interest Arbitration: Lessons from New York City," *Public Personnel Management 35,* no. 4 (Winter 2006), p. 267.
50. Kearney, *Labor Relations in the Public Sector,* p. 287.
51. 5 U.S.C. sec. 7122 (1982).
52. G. Pascal Zachary, "Two-Edged Sword: Some Public Workers Lose Jobs as Agencies Outsource," *Wall Street Journal* (August 6, 1996), pp. A1, 6.
53. Kevin R. Kosar, "Privatization and the Federal Government: An Introduction," *CRS Report for Congress* (December 28, 2006), p. 1.
54. "Privatization: Pros and Cons," *AFSCME* (1999). Available at www.afscme.org. Accessed October 26, 1999.

55. Erika Hayasaki, "Charter Academy Shuts 60 Schools," *Los Angeles Times* (August 16, 2004), p. B1.
56. Kosar, "Privatization and the Federal Government," pp. 6–12.
57. "Fighting Privatization: Strategies," *AFSCME* (1999). Available at www. afscme.org. Accessed October 26, 1999.
58. "Vouchers and the Accountability Dilemma," *American Federation of Teachers* (1999). Available at www.aft.org. Accessed October 26, 1999; "Vouchers," *National Education Association* (1999). Available at www.nea.org. Accessed October 26, 1999.
59. Ibid.
60. No. 00–1751, decided June 27, 2002.
61. *National Treasury Employees Union (NTEU) et al. v. Von Raab,* 57 LA 4338 (March 21, 1989); *Skinner v. Railway Labor Executive's Association,* 57 LA 4324 (March 21, 1989).
62. Fighting for Opportunity, *School Choice Yearbook 2009–10* (Washington, DC: Alliance for School Choice, 2010), p. 17. Available at www.allianceforschoolchoice.org. Accessed October 13, 2010.
63. Charles Idelson, "Special Election: Just Say No!" *Revolution: The Journal for RNs and Patient Advocacy 6,* no. 5 (2005), pp. 9–10.
64. Chris Edwards. "Public Sector Unions and the Rising Costs of Employee Compensation," *Cato Journal 3,* no. 1 (Winter 2010), p. 87.
65. Leslie Eaton, Ryan Knutson, and Philip Shishkin, "States Shut Down to Save Cash," *Wall Street Journal* (September 4, 2009), pp. A1, 6.
66. Daniel Massey, "Public Unions Face Growing Firestorm: Seen Thriving at Private Sector's Expense; Local Pols on Warpath," *Crain's New York Business* (June 11, 2010), p. 1.
67. Ibid.
68. Tim Martin, "Granholm Proposes Retirement Plan to Cut Costs," *The Oakland Press* (January 30, 2010). Available at www.theoaklandpress.com. Accessed October 16, 2010.
69. Claire Heininger, "Gov. Chris Christie Accuses N.J. Teachers' Union of 'Using Students Like Drug Mules' In School Elections," *New Jersey Real-Time News* (April 19, 2010). Available at www.nj.com. Accessed October 16, 2010.
70. Lise Valentine and Richard H. Mattoon, "Public and Private Sector Compensation: What is Affordable in this Recession and Beyond?—A Conference Summary," *Chicago Fed Letter,* no. 262a (May 2009), pp. 1–4.
71. Jeffrey Keefe, "Debunking the Myth of the Overcompensated Public Employee," *Economic Policy Institute Briefing Paper #276* (September 15, 2010), p. 5.

Chapter 4

1. *May Department Stores Co. v. National Labor Relations Board,* 326 U.S. 376, 66 S. Ct. 203, 90 L. Ed. 145 (1945).
2. Agreement between Duke Energy Ohio, Inc. and Local Union 1347 International Brotherhood of Electrical Workers, AFL-CIO, 2006–2009. Used by permission.
3. Stephen I. Schlossberg and Judith A. Scott, *Organizing and the Law,* 4th ed. (Washington, DC: Bureau of National Affairs, 1991), pp. 216–17.
4. James L. Perry and Harold L. Angle, "Bargaining Unit Structure and Organizational Outcomes," *Industrial Relations 20,* no. 1 (Winter 1981), pp. 47–59.
5. *Short Stop Inc.,* 192 NLRB 184, 78 LRRM 1087 (1971); *Mock Road Super Duper Inc.,* 156 NLRB 82, 61 LRRM 1173 (1966); *Wil-Kil Pest Control,* 440 F.2d 371 (7th Cir. 1971); *National Labor Relations Board v. Saint Francis College,* 562 F.2d 246 (3rd Cir. 1977); *National Labor Relations Board v. Action Automotive,* 469 U.S. 490, 118 LRRM 2577 (1985).
6. *M.B. Sturgis,* 331 NLRB 1298 (2000).
7. Karyn-Siobhan Robinson, "Temp Workers Gain Bargaining Rights," *HR News Online* (Washington, DC: Society for Human Resource Management, September 18, 2000).
8. *H.S. Care LLC, d/b/a Oakwood Care Center and N&W Agency, Inc.,* 343 NLRB 76 (2004).
9. Cases cited, in order of listing, are *General Electric,* 107 NLRB 21, 33 LRRM 1058 (1953); *T.C. Wheaton Co.,* 14 LRRM 142 (1944); *Safety Cabs, Inc.,* 173 NLRB 4, 69 LRRM 1199 (1968); *Land Title Guarantee & Trust Co.,* 194 NLRB 29, 78 LRRM 1500 (1971).
10. *Globe Machinery & Stamping Co.,* 3 NLRB 294, 1-A LRRM 1122 (1937); *Short Stores, Inc.,* 192 NLRB 184, 78 LRRM 1087 (1971).
11. Harold S. Roberts, *Dictionary of Industrial Relations,* 3rd ed. (Washington, DC: Bureau of National Affairs, 1986), p. 243.
12. *Bendix Products Corporation,* 3 NLRB 682 (1937).
13. *National Labor Relations Board v. Delaware-New Jersey, Ferry Co.,* 128 F.2d 130 (3rd Cir. 1941).
14. Schlossberg and Scott, *Organizing and the Law,* p. 219.
15. *Milwaukee City Cir. LLC,* 354 NLRB 77 (September 21, 2009).
16. *Tidewater Oil Co. v. National Labor Relations Board,* 358 F.2d 363 (2d Cir. 1966).
17. Mark Schoeff, "Supervisor Bill Likely to Face Battle in Senate," *Workforce Management* (October 8, 2007), p. 18.
18. *National Labor Relations Board v. Yeshiva University,* 444 U.S. 672 (1980); see also Clarence R. Dietsch and David A. Dilts, "NLRB v. Yeshiva University: A Positive Perspective," *Monthly Labor Review 106,* no. 7 (July 1983), pp. 34–37; Marsha Huie Ashlock, "The Bargaining Status of College and University Professors under the National Labor Relations Laws," *Labor Law Journal 35,* no. 2 (February 1984), pp. 103–11.
19. John Graves, "Scenes from the Picket Lines," *Chronicle of Higher Education* (May 13, 2005), pp. A8–A10.
20. Patrick Hardin, ed., *The Developing Labor Law*, 3rd ed. (Washington, DC: Bureau of National Affairs, 1992), pp. 463–64.
21. *Mallinckrodt Chemical Works*, 162 NLRB 387, 64 LRRM 1011 (1967); see also *Airco, Inc.,* 273 NLRB 53, 118 LRRM 1053 (1984).
22. Hardin, *The Developing Labor Law,* pp. 464–66.

23. *Stephens Produce,* 515 F.2d 1373, 89 LRRM 2311 (8th Cir. 1975); Hardin, *The Developing Labor Law,* pp. 467–68.
24. *Manor Healthcare Corp.,* 285 NLRB 224 (1987).
25. *Prince Telecom,* 347 NLRB 73 (July 31, 2006); *Rental Uniform Service,* 330 NLRB 334 (1999).
26. *Trane, an Operating Unit of American Standard Companies,* 339 NLRB 106 (2003).
27. *Kroger Limited Partnership, d/b/a Hilander Foods,* 348 NLRB 82 (November 30, 2006).
28. Richard R. Carlson, "The Origin and Future of Exclusive Representation in American Labor Law," *Duquesne Law Review 30,* no. 4 (Summer 1992), pp. 779–67.
29. *National Labor Relations Board v. Beck Engraving Co.,* 522 F.2d 475 (3d Cir. 1975).
30. Jeffrey S. Bosley, "NLRB Provides Long-Awaited Guidance Concerning Enforceability of Labor Agreements Between Project Developers and Construction Unions," *Employment Relations Law Journal 34,* no. 2 (Autumn 2008), pp. 103–11.
31. *Glens Falls Building and Construction Trades Council, et al.,* 350 NLRB 42 (2007).
32. *American Hospital Association v. NLRB,* 499 U.S. 606 (1991).
33. Joe Ward, "Unions, Nurses Mutually Attracted," *Courier-Journal* (April 16, 1989), pp. E1, E3; Joe Ward, "Hospitals Boost Pay Benefits of Nurses, Other Workers," *Courier-Journal* (April 20, 1989), p. B10; Associated Press, "Board Issues Final Rules That Unions Say Will Help Hospital Organizing," *Courier Journal* (April 21, 1989), p. F1; See also John Thomas Delaney and Donna Sockell, "Hospital Unit Determination and the Preservation of Employee Free Choice," *Labor Law Journal 39,* no. 5 (May 1988), pp. 259–72; Cynthia A. Shaw, "Appropriate Bargaining Units in the Health Care Industry," *The Labor Lawyer 5,* no.4 (Fall 1989), pp. 787–23.
34. *NLRB v. Health Care & Retirement Corporation,* 511 U.S. 571 (1994).
35. *NLRB v. Kentucky River Community Care, Inc.,* 121 S. Ct. 1861 (2001).
36. *Oakwood Healthcare, Inc.,* 348 NLRB 37 (September 29, 2007).
37. *Golden Crest Healthcare Center,* 348 NLRB 39 (September 29, 2007).
38. Victor G. Devinatz, "Union Organizing Trends on the Question of Post—Industrial Unions in the Early 21st Century," *Labor Law Journal 59,* no. 3 (Fall 2008), pp. 265–271.
39. The Associated Press, "Unions Campaigning Against Breakup of Los Angeles," *Cincinnati Enquirer* (June 23, 2002), p. A15.
40. E. Edward Herman and Alfred Kuhn, *Collective Bargaining and Labor Relations* (Englewood Cliffs, NJ: Prentice Hall, 1981), p. 101.
41. Jonathan A. Segal, "Keeping Norma Rae at Bay," *HR Magazine* (August 1996), pp. 111–19.
42. *Industrial Workers of the World* (August 2002). Available at www.iww.org. Accessed October 30, 2004.
43. "Workers Routinely Subject to Threats Over Organizing Activity, EPI Study Says," BNA Reports, *2010 Source Book on Collective Bargaining* (Washington, DC: Bureau of National Affairs, 2010), pp. 149, 150.
44. "Labor Relations and You at the Wal-Mart Distribution Center #6022," Prepared by Orsan Mason, September 1991, United Food and Commercial Workers (August 2002). Available at www.ufcw.org. Accessed August 2002.
45. "Wal-Mart: A Manager's Toolbox to Remaining Union Free," United Food and Commercial Workers (August 2002). Available at www.ufcw.org. Accessed August 2002.
46. Roberts, *Dictionary of Industrial Relations,* p. 668
47. Theodore Kheel, *Labor Law* (New York: Matthew Bender, 1988), chap. 7A, p. 20.
48. *Trustees of Columbia University,* 350 NLRB No. 54 (2007) .
49. Kheel, *Labor Law,* chap. 13, pp. 3–4.
50. *Fessler & Bowman, Inc.,* 341 NLRB 122 (2004).
51. 107 NLRB 427, 33 LRRM 1151 (1953); *Rodac Corp.,* 231 NLRB 261, 95 LRRM 1608 (1977).
52. Roberts, *Dictionary of Industrial Relations,* p. 101.
53. "University of Baltimore Employees Win Runoff," *AFL-CIO* (June 2002). Available at www.aflcio.org., Accessed June 17, 2002.
54. *General Shoe Corporation,* 77 NLRB 24 (1948).
55. Peter J. Caldwell, "Campaign Promises in NLRB Election," *Labor Law Journal 56,* no. 4 (Winter 2005), pp. 243–45
56. Joel Cutcher-Gershenfeld and Patrick McHugh, "Finding That Most New Bargaining Units Achieve Contracts Contradicts Other Reports," *2005 Source Book on Collective Bargaining* (Washington, DC: Bureau of National Affairs, 2005), p. 139.
57. "Seventy-Fourth Annual Report of the National Labor Relations Board for Fiscal Year Ending," (September 30, 2009), pp. 130–32. Available at www.nlrb.gov. Accessed October 20, 2010.
58. David Wessel, "Some Workers Gain with New Union Tactics," *Wall Street Journal* (January 3, 2002), p. A1.
59. "Serving the Young, Joining AFSCME," *AFSCME* (June 2002). Available at www.afscme.org. Accessed June 17, 2002.
60. *Pope Maintenance Corp.,* 227 NLRB 326, 94 LRRM 1135 (1976).
61. "Contract Interpretation, Neutrality Discussed at ABA Meeting," *2005 Source Book on Collective Bargaining* (Washington, DC: Bureau of National Affairs, 2005), p. 117.
62. "Parties Weigh in an NLRB Case Involving Neutrality Agreement," *2007 Source Book on Collective Bargaining* (Washington, DC: BNA, 2007), pp. 129–30.
63. Mark Schoeff, Jr., "Mixed Outlook for Genetics, Card-Check Bills," *Workforce Management 86,* no. 4 (2007), p. 3.
64. *National Labor Relations Board v. Gissel Packing Co.,* 395 U.S. 575, 71 LRRM 2481 (1969).
65. *Gourmet Foods,* 270 NLRB 578, 116 LRRM 1105 (1984); overruling *United Dairy Farmers* 257 NLRB 772, 107 LRRM 1577 (1981); *Conair Corp.* 261 NLRB 1189, 110 LRRM 1161 (1982).

66. Bureau of National Affairs, *2007 Source Book on Collective Bargaining* (Washington, DC: Bureau of National Affairs, 2007), p. 121.
67. *Dana Corp.,* 351 NLRB 28 (September 29, 2007).
68. *Wurtland Nursing & Rehabilitation Center*, 351 NLRB 50 (September 29, 2007).
69. James B. Dworkin and Marian Extejt, "Why Do Workers Decertify Their Unions? A Preliminary Investigation," Academy of Management, Proceedings of the 39th Annual Meeting (August 7–11, 1979), p. 244.
70. Clyde J. Scott and Edwin W. Arnold, "Deauthorization and Decertification Elections," *Working USA 7,* no. 3 (Winter 2003–4), pp. 6–20.
71. Ibid.
72. *Rhode Island State Labor Relations Bd. of City of Woonsocket, 3 Public Employee Bargaining* (CCH) 43,730 (R.I., 1984).
73. Douglas E. Ray, Jennifer Gallagher, and Nancy A. Butler, "Regulating Union Representation Election Campaign Tactics: A Comparative Study of Private and Public Sector Approaches," *Nebraska Law Review 66* (1987), pp. 532–61.
74. Richard R. Carlson, "The Origin and Future of Exclusive Representation in American Labor Law," *Duquesne Law Review 30,* no. 4 (Summer 1992), pp. 779–867.

Chapter 5

1. *Local 65–B, Graphic Commons Conference of the International Brotherhood of Teamsters v. NLRB*, 7th Circuit Court, No. 08-4045 (July 10, 2009).
2. Patrick J. Cleary, *The Negotiation Handbook* (Armonk, NY: M.E. Sharpe, 2001), pp. 20–21.
3. Roger Fisher, William Ury, and Bruce Patton, *Getting to Yes,* 2nd ed. (New York: Penguin Books, 1991), pp. 28, 29.
4. Charles S. Loughran, *Negotiating a Labor Contract: A Management Handbook* (Washington, DC: Bureau of National Affairs, 1992), p. 184
5. Herb Cohen, *You Can Negotiate Anything* (New York: Bantam Books, 1980), pp. 91–98.
6. Fisher, Ury, and Patton, *Getting to Yes.*
7. C. Marlene Fiol, Edward J. O'Connor, and Herman Aguinis, "All for One and One for All? The Development and Transfer of Power across Organizational Levels," *Academy of Management Review 26,* no. 2 (April 2001), pp. 224–42.
8. Deepak Malhotra, "Make Your Weak Position Strong," *Negotiation 8,* no. 7 (2005), pp. 1–4.
9. Peter B. Stark and Jane Flaherty, *The Only Negotiating Guide You'll Ever Need* (New York: Broadway Books, 2003), pp. 17–20.
10. Cohen, *You Can Negotiate Anything*.
11. Cleary, *The Negotiation Handbook,* p. 15.
12. Steven Greenhouse, "UPS and Teamsters Reach Deal for a 25% Raise," *New York Times* (July 17, 2002), p. A10.
13. Milton Rokeach, *The Nature of Human Values* (New York: Free Press, 1973). See also, John Stevenson, "Exploring Workplace Values," *Journal of Vocational Education and Training 51,* no. 3 (1999), pp. 335–54.
14. Ibid.
15. Roger Scruton, *A Dictionary of Political Thought* (New York, NY, 2007), p. 156.
16. Peter C. Cramton and J. Gregory Dees, "Promoting Honesty in Negotiation: An Exercise in Practical Ethics," *Business Ethics Quarterly 3,* no. 4 (1993), pp. 1–23.
17. Roy J. Lewicki and Robert J. Robinson, "Ethical and Unethical Bargaining Tactics, An Empirical Study," in Carrie Menkel-Meadow and Michael Wheeler, eds., *What's Fair, Ethics for Negotiators* (San Francisco, CA: John Wiley & Sons, Inc., 2004), pp. 221–45.
18. J. Gregory Dees and Peter C. Cramton, "Shrewd Bargaining on the Moral Frontier: Toward a Theory of Morality in Practice," *Business Ethics Quarterly 1,* no. 2 (1991), pp. 135–67.
19. Steven P. Cohen, "Negotiation as a Paradigm for Business: Ethical Negotiations Lead to Ethical Business," *The Negotiator Magazine* (October 2002). Available at http:// www.negotiatormagazine.com. Accessed August 23, 2011.
20. Lewicki and Robinson, "Ethical and Unethical Bargaining Tactics," pp. 226–27 and 232.
21. Michael R. Carrell and Christina Heavrin, *Negotiating Essentials: Theory, Skills and Practices* (Upper Saddle River, NJ: Pearson Education Inc., 2008), pp. 194–202.
22. Jerome T. Barrett and John O'Dowd, *Interest-Based Bargaining: A User's Guide*, (Victoria, BC: Trafford Publishing 2005), pp. 41–45.
23. Richard E. Walton and Robert B. McKersie, *A Behavioral Theory of Labour Negotiations* (New York: McGraw-Hill, 1965).
24. W. David Rees and Christine Porter, "Negotiation: Mystic Art or Identifiable Process?" *Industrial and Commercial Training 29,* no. 5 (1997), pp. 153–57.
25. Susan Cross and Robert Rosenthal, "Three Models of Conflict Resolution: Effects on Intergroup Expectancies and Attitudes," *Journal of Social Issues 55,* no. 3 (1999), pp. 561–80.
26. Ibid.
27. David A. Lax and James K. Sebenius, "Anchoring Expectations," *Negotiation 7*, no. 9 (September 2004), pp. 9–11.
28. Charles Craver, *The Intelligent Negotiator* (New York: Random House, 2002), p. 41.
29. Ibid., pp. 41–42.
30. Patricia Findlay, Alan McKinlay, Abigail Marks, and Paul Thompson, "Collective Bargaining and New Work Regimes: Too Important to be Left to Bosses," *Industrial Relations Journal 40,* no. 3 (2009), pp. 235–51.
31. *Negotiation* (Boston, MA: Harvard Business School Publishing, 2003), pp. 110–14.
32. G. Richard Shell, *Bargaining for Advantage* (New York: Viking Penguin, 1999), pp. 39–51.
33. "Being Fair and Getting What You Want," *Negotiation 7,* no. 2 (2004), p. 12.
34. Fisher, Ury, and Patton, *Getting to Yes,* pp. 153–57.
35. Gary A. Ballinger and Kevin W. Rockmann, "Chutes Versus Ladders: Anchoring Events and a Punctuated—Equilibrium

Perspective on Social Exchange Relationships," *Academy of Management Review 35,* no. 3 (2009), p. 373.

36. Robert B. Cialdini, *Influence: The Psychology of Persuasion* (New York: Harper Publishing, 2006), pp. 1–4.
37. Kathy Domenici and Stephen W. Littlejohn, *Mediation,* 2nd ed. (Prospect Heights, IL: Waveland Press, 2001), pp. 84–8.
38. Max H. Bazerman, "Picking the Right Frame: Make Your Offer Seem Better," *Negotiation 7,* no. 10 (2004), pp. 9–11.
39. William Ury, *Getting Past No* (New York: Bantam Books, 1991), pp. 59–71.
40. Cross and Rosenthal, "Three Models of Conflict Resolution," pp. 564–66.
41. *Negotiation,* pp. 2–11.
42. Russell Korobkin, "Against Integrative Bargaining," *Case Western Law Review 58,* no. 4 (2008), pp. 1323–42.
43. Craver, *The Intelligent Negotiator,* pp. 85–87.
44. Ibid.
45. Bureau of National Affairs, *2002 Sourcebook on Collective Bargaining* (Washington, DC: BNA Press, 2002), p. 37.
46. Federal Mediation and Conciliation Service, *Interest-Based Bargaining: A Different Way to Negotiate* (Washington, DC: Federal Mediation and Conciliation Service, 1999), pp. 1–36.
47. Susan Black, "Bargaining: It's in Your Best Interest," *American School Board Journal* (April 2008), pp. 52–54.
48. Barrett and O'Dowd, *Interest-Based Bargaining,* pp. 69–89.
49. Ira B. Lobel, "Is Interest-Bargaining Really New?" *Dispute Resolution Journal 55,* no. 1 (2000), pp. 9–17.
50. *Negotiation,* pp. 57–60.
51. Theodore H. Kheel, *The Keys to Conflict Resolution,* (New York: Four Walls Eight Windows Publications, 1999), pp. 16–17.
52. Colonel Vince Robison, Louisville Metro Police Department, unpublished theory, February 14, 2008.
53. Michael R. Carrell and Christina Heavrin, *Negotiating Essentials: Theory, Skills and Practices* (Upper Saddle River, NJ: Pearson Education Inc., 2008), pp. 194–202.
54. Stewart Levine, *Getting to Resolution* (San Francisco, CA: Berrett-Koehler Publications, 1998), pp. 143–47.
55. Frederick Rose, "Longshoremen Are Expected to Reject Contract," *Wall Street Journal* (August 28, 1996), p. A2.

Chapter 6

1. Bureau of National Affairs, *Basic Patterns in Union Contracts,* 14th ed. (Washington, DC: BNA Books, 1995), p. 3.
2. "Employers Urged to Take a Fresh Look at Negotiations Approach," Bureau of National Affairs, *2007 Source Book on Collective Bargaining* (Washington, DC: BNA, 2007), p. 109.
3. 29 U.S.C. sec. 159(a) (1982).
4. *National Labor Relations Board v. Wooster Division of the Borg-Warner Corp.,* 356 U.S. 342, 78 S.Ct. 718, 1 L.Ed. 2d 823 (1958).
5. *Ford Motor Co. v. NLRB,* 441 U.S. 488 (1979).
6. Donald Peterson and Harvey Boller, "Hidden Surveillance Cameras: A Mandatory Subject for Bargaining?" *Employee Relations Law Journal 31,* no. 3 (Winter 2005), pp. 56–64.
7. Ann C. Hodges, "Bargaining for Privacy in the Unionized Workplace," *International Journal of Comparative Labor Law and Industrial Relations 22,* no. 2 (2006), pp. 147–82.
8. E. J. Dannin, "Statutory Subjects and the Duty to Bargain," *Labor Law Journal* (January 1988), pp. 442–45.
9. *Allied Chemical & Alkali Workers Local Union No. 1 v. Pittsburgh Plate Glass Company,* 404 U.S. 157 (1971).
10. Mairead E. Connor, "The Dubuque Packing Decision: New Test for Bargaining Over Decision."
11. Donna Sockell, "The Scope of Mandatory Bargaining: A Critique and a Proposal," *Industrial and Labor Relations Review 40,* no. 1 (October 1986), pp. 19–34.
12. *Fibreboard Paper Products Corp. v. National Labor Relations Board,* 379 U.S. 203 (1964), pp. 210–23; *First National Maintenance Corp. v. National Labor Relations Board,* 452 U.S. 666 (1981), pp. 677–89; and see also *Otis Elevator Company,* 269 NLRB 891 (1984).
13. *W. W. Cross & Co. v. National Labor Relations Board,* 174 F.2d 875 (1st Cir. 1949).
14. Bureau of National Affairs, *Basic Patterns in Union Contracts,* p. 49.
15. Kevin B. Zeese, *Drug Testing Legal Manual* (New York: Clark Boardman Company, 1988), chap. 4, pp. 14–15; Johnson Bateman Company, 295 NLRB 26 (1989).
16. Bureau of National Affairs, *Basic Patterns in Union Contracts,* p. 4.
17. Bruce E. Kaufman, "Bargaining Theory, Inflation, and Cyclical Strike Activity in Manufacturing," *Industrial and Labor Relations Review 34,* no. 3 (April 1981), pp. 333–55; and Bruce E. Kaufman, "Inter-Industry Trends in Strike Activity," *Industrial Relations 22,* no.1 (Winter 1983), pp. 45–57.
18. Michael D. Moberly, "Striking a Happy Medium: The Conversion of Unfair Labor Practice Strikes to Economic Strikes," *Berkeley Journal of Employment & Labor Law 22,* no. 1 (2001), pp. 131–74.
19. The Associated Press, "Not Just GM at Stake in Strike," *Cincinnati Enquirer* (September 27, 2007), pp. A1, 7.
20. Mike Boyer, "Union Thinks Over Smart Talks," *Cincinnati Enquirer* (June 12, 2002), p. D1.
21. Carlos Tejada, "With Jobs and Business at Stake, Labor Talks Are Growing Longer," *Wall Street Journal* (August 22, 2003), p. A1.
22. *Noel Corp. v. National Labor Relations Board,* 82 F.3d 1113 (D.C. Cir. 1996).
23. "Breakthrough at Bridgestone," *America at Work* (November/December 1996), p. 5.
24. Jonathan K. Kramer and Thomas Hyclak, "Why Strikes Occur: Evidence from the Capital Markets," *Industrial Relations 41,* no. 1 (January 2002), pp. 80–93.
25. *North Carolina Fuel Company v. National Labor Relations Board,* 645 F.2d 177 (3d Cir. 1981).

26. Frederick J. Bosch and Paul A. Tufano, "Establishing a Uniform Standard for Striker Misconduct in Arbitration Cases," *Labor Law Journal* (September 1988), pp. 629–33.
27. 268 NLRB 173, 115 LRRM 1113 (1984).
28. Bosch and Tufano, "Establishing a Uniform Standard," pp. 629–33.
29. John P. Kohl and David B. Stephens, "Labor Relations, Replacement Workers during Strikes: Strategic Options for Managers," *Personnel Journal 65,* no. 4 (April 1986), pp. 93–98.
30. Moberly, "Striking a Happy Medium," p. 138.
31. "Labor Letter," *Wall Street Journal* (June 8, 1993), p. A1.
32. "British Airline Workers Back after Walkout," *Chicago Tribune* (August 13, 2005), p. 2.
33. Linda Stockman Vines, "High Court Upholds NLRB Strike Replacement Policy," *HR News* (June 1993), p. 10.
34. *NLRB v. Mackay Radio and Telegraph Co.,* 304 U.S. 333 (1938).
35. William T. Krizner, "The Mackay Doctrine," *Labor Law Journal* (June 1998), pp. 997–1007.
36. George S. Roukis and Mamdouhj I. Farid, "An Alternative Approach to the Permanent Striker Replacement Strategy," *Labor Law Journal* (February 1993), pp. 80–91.
37. Paul Johnston, "Outflanking Power, Reframing Unionism: The Basic Strike of 1999–2001," *Labor Studies Journal 28,* no. 4 (Winter 2004), pp. 1–24.
38. Bruce Schreiner, the Associated Press, "Nurses to Vote on Offer," and *Cincinnati Enquirer* (December 4, 2007), p. B5.
39. Richard L. Lippke, "Government Support of Labor Unions and the Ban on Strike Replacements," *Business and Society Review 109,* no. 2 (Summer 2004), pp. 127–51.
40. Goldie Blumenstyk, "Yale University Workers End Strike," *Chronicle of Higher Education* (October 3, 2003), p. A27.
41. David S. Bradshaw, "Labor Relations, How to Put Teeth into a Labor Injunction," *Personnel Journal 64,* no. 10 (October 1985), pp. 80–85.
42. *Overstreet v. United Brotherhood of Carpenters,* U.S. 9th Cir. Ct. (July 8, 2005).
43. Stephanie N. Mehta, "Declining Power of Picket Lines Blunts New York Maintenance Worker's Strike," *Wall Street Journal* (January 17, 1996), p. B1.
44. Mike Boyer, "NuTone Locks Out Union Workers," *Cincinnati Enquirer* (July 19, 2005), p. D2.
45. *American Shipbuilders,* 380 U.S. 300, 58 LRRM 2672 (1965).
46. George S. Roukis and Mamdoah Farid, "Balancing Partisan Bargaining Interests Requires More Than Labor Law Reform," *Labor Law Journal* (February 1991), pp. 67–80.
47. Agreement between C. Lee Cook Division, Dover Resources, Inc. and Lodge No. 681, International Association of Machinists and Aerospace Workers AFL-CIO, 2007–2012. Used by permission.
48. Bureau of National Affairs, *Basic Patterns in Union Contracts,* pp. 91–93.
49. Ibid., p. 94.
50. Peter Perl, "Steel Firms Start Crucial Labor Talks," *Washington Post* (March 19, 1986), pp. K1, K7.
51. Charles B. Craver, *Effective Legal Negotiation and Settlement,* 5th ed. (Danvers, MA: Matthew Bender, 2005), p. 492.
52. Thomas Kochan and Joel Cutcher-Gershenfeld, "FMCS Announces Results of Third Customer Survey," *FMCS NEWSLETTER* (2004). Available at www.fmcs.gov. Accessed July 28, 2010.
53. John R. Stepp, Robert P. Baker, and Jerome T. Barrett, "Helping Labor and Management See and Solve Problems," *Monthly Labor Review 105,* no. 9 (September 1982), pp. 15–20.
54. "Labor-Management Tensions High; Need for Mediation Services Strong, FMCS Finds," *2005 Source Book on Collective Bargaining* (Washington, DC: Bureau of National Affairs, 2005), p. 145.
55. Craig A. Olson and Barbara L. Rau, "Learning from Interest Arbitration: The Next Round," *Industrial and Labor Relations Review 50* (January 1997), pp. 237–51.
56. *Basic Agreement, 2007–2011 between Major League Clubs and the Major League Baseball Players Association* Available at www.mlbplayers.mlb.com. Accessed August 25, 2011, p. 14.
57. Maury Brown, "2010 MLB Salary Arbitration Players See Pay Change 107%," *Business of Sports Network* (2011). Available at www.bizofbaseball.com. Accessed July 30, 2010.
58. *H. J. Heinz Co. v. National Labor Relations Board,* 311 U.S. 514, 51 S.Ct. 320, 85 L.Ed. 309 (1941).
59 29 U.S.C. sec. 158(b)(1982).
60. David A. Dilts and Clarence Deitsch, *Labor Relations* (New York: Macmillan, 1983), p. 152.
61. Shaun G. Clark, "Rethinking the Adversarial Model in Labor Relations: An Argument for Repeal of Section 8(a)(2)," *Yale Law Journal 96* (1987), pp. 2021–50.
62. George Will, "Wisconsin's Liberals Failed to Stop Walker," *The Cincinnati Enquirer* (August 25, 2011), p. A7.
63. Patrick Hardin, ed., *The Developing Labor Law,* 3rd ed. (Washington, DC: Bureau of National Affairs, 1992), p. 1496.
64. S. M. Crampton, J. W. Hodge, and J. M. Mishra, "The Use of Dues for Political Activity—Current Status," *Public Personnel Management 31,* no. 1 (Spring 2002), p. 126.
65. *California Saw & Knife Works,* 320 NLRB 11, 151 LRRM 1121 (1995).
66. 373 U.S. 734 (1963).
67. *Electrical Workers Local 48,* 342 NLRB No. 10 (2004).
68. *NLRB v. IBEW*, 425 F. 3d 1035 (C.A. 7th, 2005).
69. 108 F.3d 1415 (U.S. 1998); see also The Cornell University Legal Information Institute. Available at supct.law.cornell.edu/supct/html/94.947.25 (July 23, 1999).

70. *Davenport, et al. v. Washington Education Association*, 127 S.Ct. 2372 (2007).
71. States with right-to-work laws include the following:

Alabama	Nevada
Arizona	North Carolina
Arkansas	North Dakota
Florida	Oklahoma
Georgia	South Carolina
Idaho	South Dakota
Iowa	Tennessee
Kansas	Texas
Louisiana	Utah
Mississippi	Virginia
Nebraska	Wyoming

72. Raymond Hogler, Steven Shulman, and Stephan Weiler, "Right-to-Work Legislation, Social Capital, and Variations in State Union Density," *Review of Regional Studies 34,* no. 1 (2004), pp. 95–111.
73. Kheel, *Labor Law,* chap. 42, p. 2; Norman Hill, "The Double-Speak of Right-to-Work," AFL-CIO *American Federationist 87* (October 1980), pp. 13–16.
74. Barry T. Hirsch, "The Determinants of Unionization: An Analysis of Interarea Differences," *Industrial and Labor Relations Review 33,* no. 2 (January 1980), pp. 147–61.
75. Kenneth A. Kovach, "National Right-to-Work Law: An Affirmative Position," *Labor Law Journal* (May 1977), pp. 305–14.
76. Raymond Hogler, Steve Shulman, and Stephan Weiler, "Right-to-Work Laws and Business Environment: An Analysis of State Labor Policy," *Journal of Managerial Issues 16,* no. 3 (Fall 2004), pp. 289–304.
77. William A. Wines, "An Analysis of the 1986 'Right-to-Work Referendum in Idaho,' " *Labor Law Journal* (September 1988), pp. 622–28.
78. Thomas M. Carroll, "Right to Work Laws Do Matter," *Southern Economic Journal 5,* no. 2 (October 1983), pp. 494–509.
79. Wines, "An Analysis of the 1986 'Right-to-Work Referendum in Idaho,' " pp. 622–28.
80. Emin M. Dinlersoz and Ruben Hernandez-Murillo, "Did 'Right-to-Work' Work for Idaho?" *Review 84,* no. 3 (May/June 2002), pp. 29–43.
81. Henry S. Farber, "Nonunion Wage Rates and the Threat of Unionization," *Industrial and Labor Relations Review 58,* no. 3 (April 2005), pp. 348–49.
82. Raymond L. Hogler, "The 2008 Defeat of the Right-to-Work in Colorado: Is it the End of Section 14 (B)?" *Labor Law Journal 60,* no. 1 (Spring 2009), pp. 5–16.
83. Ibid.
84. Bureau of National Affairs, *Basic Patterns in Union Contracts,* 14th ed. (Washington, DC: BNA Books, 1995), pp. 1–3.
85. Bureau of National Affairs, *2002 Source Book on Collective Bargaining* (Washington, DC: Bureau of National Affairs, 2002), p. 33.
86. Blumenstyk, "Yale Workers End Strike."
87. Marvin Hill, Jr., and Anthony V. Sinicrope, *Management Rights* (Washington, DC: Bureau of National Affairs, 1986), p. 3.
88. Bureau of National Affairs, *Basic Patterns in Union Contracts,* pp. 79–81.
89. Hill and Sinicrope, *Management Rights,* pp. 4–5.
90. Arthur J. Goldberg, "Management's Reserved Rights: A Labor View," *Proceedings of the 9th Annual Meeting of the National Arbitration Association 118* (1956), pp. 120–21.
91. Agreement between the Kroger Co. and the United Food and Commercial Workers International Union AFL-CIO, 2007–2010. Used by permission.
92. Hill and Sinicrope, *Management Rights,* pp. 6–7.
93. Paul Prasow and Edward Peters, *Arbitration and Collective Bargaining: Conflict Resolution in Labor Relations,* 2nd ed. (New York: McGraw-Hill, 1983), pp. 33–34.
94. *Fibreboard Corp.,* 379 U.S. 203 (1964).
95. *First National Maintenance,* 452 U.S. 666 (1981).
96. *Otis Elevator Co.,* 269 NLRB 891, 115 LRRM 1281 (1984).
97. *Dubuque Packing Co.,* 303 NLRB 66 (1991).
98. Connor, "The Dubuque Packing Decision."
99. Bureau of National Affairs, *Basic Patterns in Union Contracts,* pp. 79–82.
100. *Auciello Iron Works, Inc. v. National Labor Relations Board,* 517 U.S. 781 (1996).
101. Stephen I. Schlossberg and Judith A. Scott, *Organizing and the Law,* 4th ed. (Washington, DC: BNA Books, 1991), p. 285.
102. Bernard F. Ashe, "Current Trends in Public Employment," *Labor Lawyer 2,* no. 2 (Spring 1986), pp. 277–98.
103. Ibid.
104. Kenneth P. Swan, "Public Bargaining in Canada and the U.S.: A Legal View," *Industrial Relations 19,* no. 3 (Fall 1980), pp. 272–91.
105. Fritz Ihrig, "Labor Contract Negotiations: Behind the Scenes," *Personnel Administrator 31,* no. 4 (April 1986), pp. 55–60.

Chapter 7

1. Chris Berger and Donald Schwab, "Pay Incentives and Pay Satisfaction," *Industrial Relations 19,* no. 2 (Spring 1980), p. 206.
2. Michael R. Carrell, "A Longitudinal Field Assessment of Employee Perceptions of Equitable Treatment," *Organizational Behavior and Human Performance 21,* no. 1 (1978), pp. 108–18.
3. Julie Moran Alterio and Jerry Gleeson, "Worker/CEO Pay Gap Widens," *The Cincinnati Enquirer* (December 30, 2002), p. B6; see also www.aflcio.org/corporatewatch. Accessed February 23, 2008.

4. Scott McCartney, "Livid over Executive Pay, AMR Unions May Balk at Cuts," *Wall Street Journal* (April 18, 2002), p. B1.
5. Bruce E. Kaufman, "Models of Union Wage Determination: What Have We Learned Since Dunlap and Ross?" *Industrial Relations 41,* no. 1 (January 2002), pp. 110–58. *UAW-Chrysler Newsgram* (October 1996), pp. 2–3.
6. Martha Bryson Hodel, "Union Miners Ratify Deal," *Associated Press* (New York: Associated Press, December 23, 2001).
7. Stephen Franklin, "Garbage Strikers Smelling Like Rose," *Chicago Tribune* (Chicago, IL: The Tribune Company, October 12, 2003), pp. 4–1, 4–4.
8. Bureau of National Affairs, *2002 Source Book on Collective Bargaining* (Washington, DC: Bureau of National Affairs, 2002), p. 33.
9. Clare Ansberry, "Union Approves Five-Year Pact with U.S. Steel," *Wall Street Journal* (May 20, 2003), p. B1.
10. Bureau of National Affairs, *2007 Source Book on Collective Bargaining* (Washington, DC: 2007), pp. 165–84.
11. Lawrence F. Katz and Alan B. Krueger, "The Effect of the Minimum Wage on the Fast Food Industry," *Industrial and Labor Relations Review 46,* no. 1 (October 1992), pp. 6–21; David Card, "Using Regional Variation in Wages to Measure the Effects of the Federal Minimum Wage," *Industrial and Labor Relations Review 46,* no. 1 (October 1992), pp. 22–37; and David Card, "Do Minimum Wages Reduce Employment? A Case Study of California 1987–89," *Industrial and Labor Relations Review 46,* no. 1 (October 1992), pp. 6–54.
12. Bureau of National Affairs, *Basic Patterns in Union Contracts* (Washington, DC: BNA Books, 1995), pp. 50–53.
13. Dan Klepal and Tim Bonfield, "Pact with Nurses Averts a Walkout," *Cincinnati Enquirer* (June 29, 2002), p. B4.
14. "Workers Risk Injury, Illness from Long Hours, Labor Argues," *2005 Source Book on Collective Bargaining* (Washington, DC: Bureau of National Affairs, 2005), p. 121.
15. Laura Baverman, "Ohio Pay Rules Could Boost Cost of CPS Building Plans," *The Business Courier* (November 30, 2007), p. 4.
16. John C. Richardson, "Prevailing Wage Laws a Boon, Not a Threat," *Los Angeles Times* (March 10, 1991), p. D1.
17. Bruce Shearer, "Piece Rates, Fixed Wages and Incentives: Evidence from a Field Experiment," *Review of Economic Studies 71,* no. 2 (2004), pp. 513–34.
18. Agreement between UAW and Chrysler Corporation, 1997–1999. Available at http://chryslerlabortalks07.com/Media_Briefing_Book.pdf. Accessed August 26, 2011.
19. U.S. Department of Labor Statistics (2007). Available at http://data.bls.gov/pdq/SurveyOutputServlet. Accessed August 26, 2011.
20. Sanford M. Jacoby, "Cost-of-Living Escalators Became Prevalent in the 1950s,"*Monthly Labor Review 108,* no. 5 (May 1985), pp. 32–33.
21. Bureau of National Affairs, *2002 Source Book on Collective Bargaining,* p. 37.
22. Bureau of National Affairs, *Basic Patterns in Union Contracts,* p. 119.
23. "Pay Day: Typical Ford Worker Gets $1,200 for Profit-Sharing," *Courier-Journal* (March 13, 1986), p. B8; and "Auto Workers Will Feel Pinch of Lower or No Profits," *Bakersfield Californian* (February 20, 1990), p. 87.
24. Matthew Dolan, "UAW Signals Key Shift On Pay," *The Wall Street Journal* (June 10, 2011), pp. B1, 4.
25. Douglas Frasier, speech at the University of Louisville, April 22, 1986.
26. Michael R. Carrell and Christina Heavrin, *International Municipal Lawyers Association Conference Proceedings,* Miami, FL (October 2009).
27. Harold S. Roberts, *Dictionary of Industrial Relations,* 3rd ed. (Washington, DC: Bureau of National Affairs, 1986), p. 645.
28. Robert J. Schulhof, "Five Years with a Scanlon Plan," *Personnel Administrator 24* (June 1979), pp. 55–62, and see also Shaun G. Clark, "Rethinking the Adversarial Model in Labor Relations: An Argument for Repeal of Section 8(a) (2)," *Yale Law Review 96* (1987), pp. 2021–50.
29. John Savage, "Incentive Programs at Nucor Corporation Boost Productivity," *Personnel Administrator 22* (August 1981), pp. 33–36.
30. "The Revolutionary Wage Deal at G.M.'s Packard Electric," *Business Week* (August 29, 1983), p. 54.
31. Jere Downs, "New UAW Contracts May Have Wide Effect," *Louisville Courier-Journal* (December 16, 2007), p. D1.
32. Matthew Dolan, "Ford to Begin Hiring at New Lower Wages," *The Wall Street Journal* (January 26, 2010), p. B1.
33. *2008 District Council 37 Memorandum of Economic Agreement* (2008). Available at http://www.dc37.net/dc37contracts/economic.html. Accessed September 29, 2010.
34. Bureau of National Affairs, *2002 Source Book on Collective Bargaining,* pp. 37–38.
35. The Associated Press, "Workers OK Pact with Unit of Kroger," *Cincinnati Enquirer* (March 8, 2005), p. D2.
36. "The Double Standard That's Setting Worker against Worker," *BusinessWeek* (April 8, 1983), p. 70.
37. Dee-Ann Durbin and Tom Krisher, "UAW Perks Not as Sweet as Before," *The Associated Press* (June 21, 2010).
38. Sharon Terlep, "Union's Giveback Isn't Yet Helping GM," *The Wall Street Journal* (May 17, 2010), p. B1
39. Thomas D. Heetderks and James E. Martin, "Employee Perceptions of the Effects of a Two-Tier Wage Structure," *Journal of Labor Research 7,* no. 3 (Summer 1991), pp. 279–95.
40. Bureau of National Affairs, *Basic Patterns in Union Contracts,* p. 113.
41. Fay Hansen, "Wages Head South," *Workforce Management 84,* no. 2 (February 2005), pp. 71–72.
42. Bureau of National Affairs, *2005 Source Book on Collective Bargaining,* p. 179.
43. Bureau of National Affairs, "Give-Backs Highlight Three Major Bargaining Agreements," *Personnel Administrator 28,* no. 1 (January 1983), pp. 33–35.
44. "Employers Will Seek Concessions in Benefits, May Make Them on Wages, BNA Report Finds," *2005 Source Book on*

Collective Bargaining (Washington, DC: Bureau of National Affairs, 2005), pp. 37–38.
45. Harry B. Stang, "Laboring Under Health Care Reform," *HR Magazine 55,* no. 7 (July 2010), p. 16.
46. Bureau of National Affairs, *Report on Labor Relations in an Economic Recession: Job Losses and Concession Bargaining* (Washington, DC: Bureau of National Affairs, 1982), pp. 56–59.
47. Carrell and Heavrin, *International Municipal Lawyers Association Conference Proceedings.*
48. "Communication Called Essential for Bargaining in Tough Times," BNA Reports, *2010 Source Book on Collective Bargaining* (Washington, DC: Bureau of National Affairs, 2010), p. 91.
49. Tom Krisher, "Auto Talks Target Labor Costs," The Associated Press, *Cincinnati Enquirer* (August 8, 2007), p. A6.
50. Mark Schuster, "The Impact of Union-Management Cooperation on Productivity and Employment," *Industrial and Labor Relations Review 36,* no. 4 (1983), pp. 415–30.
51. Staff report, "Chronicle, Union Reach Tentative Deal on Concessions," *The San Francisco Chronicle* (March 10, 2009), p. C4.
52. "Negotiated Settlements Called Preferable to Court-Imposed Cuts," *2005 Source Book on Collective Bargaining* (Washington, DC: Bureau of National Affairs, 2005), p. 115.
53. Mark Plovnick and Gary Chaison, "Relationships between Concession Bargaining and Labor-Management Cooperation," *Academy of Management Journal 28,* no. 3 (September 1985), pp. 697–704.
54. Nick Bunkley, "Union Intends to Benefit as US Automakers Turn Around," *The New York Times* (May 16, 2010), p. A1.
55. Gary N. Chaison and Mark S. Plovnick, "Is There a New Collective Bargaining?" *California Management Review 28,* no. 4 (1986), pp. 54–61.
56. Jere Downs, "84% of UAW Members voted Against Contract Proposals," *The Courier-Journal* (October 31, 2009), p. A1, 4.
57. Joann S. Lublin, "Cost-Cutting Airlines Grapple with Issues of Executive Pay," *Wall Street Journal* (January 29, 2005), pp. B1, B9.
58. Cliff Peale, "UC Professors Union OKs Contract, But Has Concerns," *Cincinnati Enquirer* (October 5, 2007), p. B7.
59. "Utility Workers Union of America . . . Protest Out of Control Executive Pay," *Economics Week* (June 18, 2010), p. 175.
60. Judy L. Ward, "Firms Forcing Employees to Repay Some Costs If They Quit Too Soon," *Wall Street Journal* (July 16, 1985), p. A30.
61. James Pilcher, "Comair's Pilots Vote on Pay Freeze," *Cincinnati Enquirer* (February 20, 2005), pp. A1, A10.
62. Susan Carey and Scott McCartney, "Airlines Big Profits Raise Unions' Expectations," *Wall Street Journal* (January 10, 1997), p. A2.
63. David W. Belcher, *Wage and Salary Administration* (Upper Saddle River, NJ: Prentice-Hall, 1982), pp. 106–13.
64. Bureau of National Affairs, *Grievance Guide,* 11th ed. (Washington, DC: BNA Books, 2003), pp. 463–68.
65. Ibid., pp. 236–43.
66. Michael H. Granof, *How to Cost Your Labor Contract* (Washington, DC: Bureau of National Affairs, 1973), pp. 4–5.
67. Ibid., p. 33.
68. Cascio, *Costing Human Resources,* p. 102.
69. Granof, *How to Cost Your Labor Contract,* p. 34.
70. Frederick L. Sullivan, *How to Calculate the Manufacturer's Costs in Collective Bargaining* (New York: AMACOM, 1980), pp. 23–26.

Chapter 8

1. Bureau of National Affairs, *2007 Source Book on Collective Bargaining* (Washington, DC: Bureau of National Affairs, 2007), p. 111.
2. U.S. Department of Labor, *Employee Benefits Survey* (Washington, DC: U.S. Department of Labor, 1999).
3. Bureau of Labor Statistics, U.S. Department of Labor, *National Compensation Survey* (Washington, DC: Superintendent of Documents, U.S. Government Printing Office, 2005), p. 5.
4. James M. Rosbrow, "Unemployment Insurance System Marks Its 50th Anniversary," *Monthly Labor Review 108,* no. 9 (September 1985), pp. 21–28.
5. Mike Boyer, "Ruling Denies Jobless Benefits to OPW Workers," *Cincinnati Enquirer* (December 14, 2007), p. A13.
6. Jerry Flint, "The Old Folks," *Forbes 125,* no. 4 (February 18, 1980), pp. 51–56.
7. Dale Detlefs, *1984 Guide to Social Security* (Louisville, KY: Meidinger and Associates, 1984), pp. 6–9.
8. James Pilcher, "Fear Over Pensions: Workers Fret as Systems Bear Strain," *Cincinnati Enquirer* (November 6, 2005), pp. J1, J7.
9. *Inland Steel Co. v. NLRB,* 170 F.2d 247 (CA7 1948).
10. Bureau of National Affairs, *Basic Patterns in Union Contracts,* 14th ed. (Washington, DC: Bureau of National Affairs, 1995), p. 27.
11. Barry Horstman, "Public Pensions in Peril," *The Cincinnati Enquirer* (June 27, 2010), pp. A1, 10.
12. "Union Pension Funds in the Red," *The Wall Street Journal* (July 27, 2009), p. A.14.
13. Bureau of National Affairs, *2002 Source Book on Collective Bargaining* (Washington, DC: Bureau of National Affairs, 2002), pp. 51–53, 103.
14. Ellen E. Schultz, "New Pension Plan Attracts Firms Despite Criticism," *Wall Street Journal* (October 5, 2004), p. D2.
15. Bruce Schreiner, "Employee-owned Houchens Expanding at a Rapid Pace," The Associated Press, *Cincinnati Enquirer* (November 24, 2007), p. A7.
16. Susan Carey, "UAL's Pension Takeover May Prompt a Strike," *Wall Street Journal* (July 1, 2005), p. B3.
17. Mary Williams Walsh, "Salaried Workers Benefits Shrink, but Others Don't," *The New York Times* (October 27, 2009), p. B1.

18. Retirement Equity Act of 1984, Pub. L. 98–397, 98 Stat. 1426 (August 23, 1984).
19. *Central Laborers' Pension Fund v. Heitz, et al.,* No. 02–891, 541 U.S. (2004).
20. John D. Stoll, "GM Starts First Phase of Buyouts," *Wall Street Journal* (December 19, 2007), p. A13.
21. Bureau of National Affairs, *Basic Patterns in Union Contracts,* p. 41.
22. Ibid., p. 44.
23. Cristina Pita, "Advance Notice and Severance Pay Provisions in Contracts," *Monthly Labor Review 119,* no. 7 (July 1996), pp. 43–50.
24. Martin Joy Galvin and Michael Robert Lied, "Severance: A Liability in Waiting?" *Personnel Journal 65,* no. 6 (June 1986), pp. 126–31.
25. *UAW v. Roblin Industries,* 114 LRRM 2428 (Mich. Cir. 1984).
26. "ENRON Workers Win Severance Fight," *AFL-CIO* (June 2002). Available at http://www.uupinfo.org/voice/summer/labor.html. Accessed August 27, 2011.
27. Agreement between Duke Energy Ohio, Inc. and Local Union 1347 International Brotherhood of Electrical Workers, *AFL-CIO* (2006–2009). Used by permission.
28. The U.S. Bureau of Labor Statistics, *National Compensation Survey,* pp. 5–23.
29. Allan P. Blostin, "Is Employer-Sponsored Life Insurance Declining Relative to Other Benefits?" *Monthly Labor Review 104,* no. 7 (September 1981), pp. 31–3.
30. Bureau of National Affairs, *2002 Source Book on Collective Bargaining,* pp. 44–7.
31. John Eckberg, "Kroger, Union Reach a Deal," *Cincinnati Enquirer* (November 2, 2007), p. A1.
32. "Health Premiums Rose 9.2% in 2005," *HR Focus 82,* no. 11 (2005), pp. 12–21.
33. Bureau of National Affairs, *2002 Source Book on Collective Bargaining,* pp. 43–8.
34. Cliffe Peale, "Benefits Now Tied to Behavior Modification," *The Cincinnati Enquirer* (February 28, 2010), p. G1.
35. Chad Terhune and Laura Meckler, "A Turning Point for Health Care," *Wall Street Journal* (July 27, 2007), pp. A1, A13.
36. U.S. Internal Revenue Service, *Publication 969: Health Savings Accounts* (2006).
37. Victoria E. Knight, "A Healthy Aid to Retirement," *Wall Street Journal* (January 5–6, 2008), p. B2.
38. Cliff Peale, "UC Domestic Partners Win Perks," *Cincinnati Enquirer* (October 25, 2007), p. B1.
39. Ellen E. Schultz and Theo Francis, "What Might GM Retiree Fund Mean at Other Firms?" *Wall Street Journal* (September 27, 2007), p. A14.
40. U.S. Internal Revenue Service, *Publication 969* (2006).
41. Lance Wallach, "Benefits of Forming a VEBA," *The CPA Journal* (September 2003), p. 12.
42. David Welch and Nanette Byrnes, "GM's Health Plan Could Be Contagious," *Business Week* (October 8, 2007), p. 37.
43. Eli R. Stoltztus, "Access to Wellness and EAPs in the U.S.," *BNA 2010 Source Book on Collective Bargaining* (Washington, DC: Bureau of National Affairs, 2010), pp. 389–93.
44. William J. Angelo, "Wellness Program Cures Rising Health-Care Costs," *Engineering New-Record 253,* no. 3 (2004), p. 13.
45. Jennifer Hutchins, "Labor and Management Build a Prescription for Health," *Workforce 80,* no. 3 (2001), pp. 50–52.
46. Richard Feldman and Michael Betzold, *End of the Line: Autoworkers and the American Dream* (New York: Weidenfeld & Nicolson, 1988), p. 21.
47. Stoltztus, "Access to Wellness and EAPs in the U.S.," p. 376.
48. Ibid.
49. Roger K. Good, "What Bechtel Learned Creating an Employee Assistance Program," *Personnel Journal 63,* no. 9 (September 1984), pp. 80–86.
50. Melissa Praffitt Reese, "Strikes and the Obligation to Continue Group Health Care Coverage under COBRA," *Labor Law Journal 39,* no. 11 (November 1988), pp. 766–70.
51. Bureau of National Affairs, *Grievance Guide,* 11th ed. (Washington, DC: Bureau of National Affairs, 2003), p. 111.
52. The U.S. Bureau of Labor Statistics, *National Compensation Survey.*
53. Ibid., p. 22.
54. Michael Granof, *How to Cost Your Labor Contract,* (Washington DC: BNA Book, 1973), pp. 45–51.
55. Ibid., pp. 50–1.
56. Ibid., p. 22.
57. Ibid.
58. Kurt Straif, Robert Baan, Yann Grosse, and Beatrice Secretan, et al., "Carcinogenicity of Shift Work," *The Lancet Oncology 8,* no. 12 (2007), pp. 1065–66.
59. Agreement between Miller Brewing Company and Teamsters Local 97, 2000–2003.
60. Peter Fritsch, "Bilingual Employees Are Seeking More Pay, and Many Now Get It," *Wall Street Journal* (November 13, 1996), pp. A1, A6.
61. Agreement between District Council of Carpenters and Tri-State Contractors Association, 2001–2004.
62. Towers Perrin, Employee Benefits/TowersPerrin Flexible Benefits Research 2005.
63. Michael R. Carrell, Norbert F. Elbert, and Robert Hatfield, *Human Resource Management,* 5th ed. (Upper Saddle River, NJ: Prentice Hall, 1995), pp. 472–75.
64. Carol Ann Diktaban, "Employer Supported Child Care as a Mandatory Subject of Collective Bargaining," *Hofstra Labor Law Journal 8,* no. 2 (1991), p. 385.
65. M. P. McQueen, "Employers Expand Elder-Care Benefits," *Wall Street Journal* (July 27, 2006), p. D1.
66. Richard F. Federico, "Elder Care Benefits Cry Out for Better Communication," *Employee Benefit News 18,* no. 1 (2004), pp. 36–41.
67. Bureau of National Affairs, "Growing Demand for Eldercare Programs Ensures Their Survival," pp. 153–54.

68. Agreement between Ziniz, Inc. and Kentucky State District Council of Carpenters, Millwrights, Conveyors, and Machinery Erectors, 1995–1999, p. 23.
69. Dan Hassert, "The Public Pension Squeeze," *Cincinnati Post* (April 14, 2007), pp. A1, A14.
70. Agreement between Ford Motor Company and the UAW, 1996, p. 241.

Chapter 9

1. Agreement between Anheuser-Busch, Inc. and the International Brotherhood of Teamsters (1999–2004). Available at www.teamsters.org. August 1999. Accessed August 30, 1999.
2. Sumner H. Slichter, *Union Policies and Industrial Management* (Washington, DC: Brooklyn Institute, 1941), pp. 1–5.
3. Daniel Cornfield, "Seniority, Human Capital, and Layoffs: A Case Study," *Industrial Relations 21,* no. 3 (Fall 1982), pp. 352–64.
4. William Cooke, "Permanent Layoffs: What's Implicit in the Contract?" *Industrial Relations 20,* no. 2 (1981), pp. 186–92.
5. Francine Blau and Lawrence Kahn, "Unionism, Seniority, and Turnover," *Industrial Relations 22,* no. 3 (1983), pp. 362–73.
6. Bureau of National Affairs, *2002 Source Book on Collective Bargaining* (Washington, DC: Bureau of National Affairs, 2002), p. 58.
7. Maryellen Kelley, "Discrimination in Seniority Systems: A Case Study," *Industrial and Labor Relations Review 36,* no. 1 (1982), pp. 40–41.
8. Bureau of National Affairs, *Basic Patterns in Union Contracts,* 14th ed. (Washington, DC: BNA Books, 1995), p. 85.
9. Stephen Cabot, *Labor Management Relations Manual,* 1981 Supplement (Boston: Warren, Gorham, Lamont, 1981), chap. 15, p. 1.
10. Agreement between Anaconda Aluminum Co. and Aluminum Workers Trades Council of Columbia Falls, AFL-CIO (1980), p. 6.
11. Agreement between E. I. duPont Co. and the Affiliated Chemical Workers of Kentucky (1943).
12. Cabot, *Labor Management Relations Manual,* chap. 15, p. 4.
13. Bureau of National Affairs, *Basic Patterns in Union Contracts,* p. 69.
14. "Unqualified Worker Has No Bumping Rights," *Labor Relations Bulletin 746* (May 2003), p. 3.
15. Jonathan Daird Bible, "*U.S. Airways v. Barnett:* Seniority Systems and the ADA," *Labor Law Journal 53,* no. 2 (2002), pp. 61–68.
16. *Gulton Electro-Voice, Inc.,* 266 NLRB 406, 112 LRRM 1361 (1983).
17. Bureau of National Affairs, *Basic Patterns in Union Contracts,* p. 86.
18. Bureau of National Affairs, *Grievance Guide,* 12th ed. (Washington, DC: Bureau of National Affairs, 2008), pp. 361–69.
19. Agreement between C. Lee Cook Division, Dover Resources, Inc. and Lodge No. 681, International Association of Machinists and Aerospace Workers AFL-CIO, 2007–2012. Used by permission.
20. Bureau of National Affairs, *Grievance Guide,* 12th ed. (2008), p. 239.
21. Ibid.
22. *Bethlehem Steel Co.,* 1924 LA 820 (1955).
23. *Copeo Steel & Engineering Co.,* 12 LA 6 (1979).
24. *Metallab, Inc.,* 65 LA 1191 (1975).
25. Bureau of National Affairs, *Grievance Guide,* 12th ed. (Washington, DC: Bureau of National Affairs, 2008), pp. 244–45.
26. Agreement between C. Lee Cook Division, Dover Resources, Inc. and Lodge No. 681, International Association of Machinists and Aerospace Workers AFL-CIO, 2007–2012. Used by permission.
27. *Firefighters Local Union No. 1784 v. Stotts,* 467 U.S. 561 (1984).
28. P. L. 100–379, 102 Stat. 895, August 14, 1988.
29. "Reagan Succumbing to Politics, Decides against Vetoing Plant Closings Measure," *Wall Street Journal* (August 3, 1988), p. A3.
30. Paul D. Staudohar, "New Plant Closing Laws Aids Workers in Transition," *Personnel Journal 68,* no. 1 (January 1989), pp. 87–90.
31. *North Star Steel Co. and Thomas et al. v. USWA,* 115 S.Ct. 1927 (1995).
32. Frank Elkouri and Edna Asper Elkouri, *How Arbitration Works,* 6th ed. (Washington, DC: Bureau of National Affairs, 2003), pp. 877–79.
33. Bureau of National Affairs, *Grievance Guide,* 12th ed. (2008), pp. 371–79.
34. "Pilots Get Merger Details," *The Cincinnati Enquirer* (February 12, 2008), p. A7.
35. Thomas Kennedy, *Labor Arbitration and Industrial Change* (Washington, DC: Bureau of National Affairs, 1963), pp. 1–34.
36. Elkouri and Elkouri, *How Arbitration Works,* p. 870.
37. Kelly Yamanouchi, "Delta's Red Dresses Don't Fit, Union Says," *Cincinnati Enquirer* (July 17, 2009), p. C2.
38. Walter Baer, *Winning in Labor Arbitration* (Columbus, OH: Crain, 1982), p. 20.
39. *Fibreboard Paper Products Corp. v. NLRB,* 130 NLRB 1558 (1961).
40. "Union Wins $6 Million Settlement with AT&T," *Louisville Courier-Journal* (January 10, 1987), p. B1.
41. James Pilcher, "Mechanics OK Comair Pact with 2% Raise," *Cincinnati Enquirer* (April 29, 2005), p. 8.
42. *First National Maintenance Corp.,* 452 U.S. 666 (1981).
43. *Milwaukee Spring Division of Illinois Coil Spring Co.* (I), 718 F.2d 1102 (7th Cir. 1983); (II), 268 NLRB 601 (1984).
44. *Otis Elevator,* 269 NLRB 891, 115 LRRM 1281 (1984).
45. Patrick Hardin, ed., *The Developing Labor Law,* 3rd ed. (Washington, DC: Bureau of National Affairs, 1992), pp. 916–18.

46. *Dubuque Packing Co. v. NLRB,* 303 NLRB 66, 137 LRRM 1185 (1991).
47. Bureau of National Affairs, *Grievance Guide,* 12th ed. (2008), pp. 465–83.
48. Marvin E. Shaw, *Group Dynamics: The Psychology of Small Group Behavior,* 2nd ed. (New York: McGraw-Hill, 1976).
49. S. Dillingham, "Topeka Revisited," *Human Resource Executive 4,* no. 5 (May 1990), pp. 55–58.
50. Jasmine Tata and Sameer Prasad, "Team Self-Management, Organizational Structure, and Judgments of Team Effectiveness," *Journal of Managerial Issues 16,* no. 2 (Summer 2004), pp. 248–65.
51. John Eric Baugher, "Union Legitimacy and the Team Concept: A Case Study of Workers' Attitudes," *Sociological Inquiry 77,* no. 2 (May 2007), pp. 136–65.
52. Nicolas Bacon and Paul Blyton, "Union Co-operation in a Context of Job Insecurity: Negotiated Outcomes from Teamworking," *British Journal of Industrial Relations 44,* no. 2 (June 2006), pp. 215–37.
53. The International Brotherhood of Teamsters (August 1, 1999). Available at www.teamsters.org/98ups/news. Accessed August 1, 2999.
54. Harold J. Datz, "Employee Participation Programs and the National Labor Relations Act—A Guide for the Perplexed," presented at the Ninth Annual Labor and Employment Law Institute, University of Louisville, Louisville, KY (1992).
55. *Electromation,* NLRB Case No. 25-CA-19818 (1991).
56. *Fall River Dyeing v. National Labor Relations Board,* 107 S. Ct. 2225 (1987).
57. Robert F. Mace, "The Supreme Court's Labor Law Successorship Doctrine after Fall River Dyeing," *Labor Law Journal 39,* no. 2 (1988), pp. 102–9.
58. Hardin, *The Developing Labor Law,* pp. 779–80.
59. *Planned Building Services,* 347 NLRB No. 64 (July 31, 2006).
60. Susan J. McGolrick, "D.C. Circuit Overturns NLRB Ruling that S & F Was 'Perfectly Clear' Successor," BNA Reports, *2010 Source Book on Collective Bargaining* (Washington, DC: Bureau of National Affairs, 2010), p. 337–40.
61. Steven B. Goldstein, "Protecting Employee Rights in Successorship," *Labor Law Journal 44,* no. 1 (January 1993), pp. 18–29.
62. Celestine J. Richards, "The Efficacy of Successorship Clauses in Collective Bargaining Agreements," *Georgetown Law Journal 79* (1991), p. 1549.
63. *NLRB v. Canteen Company,* 317 NLRB 1052 (1995).
64. "NLRB has Backseat in Bankruptcy," BNA Reports, *2010 Source Book on Collective Bargaining* (Washington, DC: Bureau of National Affairs, 2010), p. 94.
65. Maria M. Perotin, "Drug Tests for Jobs Waning?" *Knight Ridder News Service* (May 26, 2003), pp. B5, B8.
66. R. Edward Minchin, Charles R. Giagola, Kelo Guo, and Jennifer L. Lanquell, "Case for Drug Testing of Construction Workers," *Journal of Management in Engineering 22,* no. 1 (2006), pp. 43–50.
67. *Johnson-Bateman Co.,* 295 NLRB 26 (1989).
68. Ann C. Hodges, "Bargaining for Privacy in the Unionized Workplace," *International Journal of Comparative Labor Law and Industrial Relations 22,* no. 2 (2006), p. 170.
69. Texas Workers' Compensation Commission, "Study on Drug-free Workplace," *Report to the Texas Legislature and the Research and Oversight Council,* Austin, TX (2003).
70. *Skinner v. Railway Labor Executives Association,* 109 S. Ct. 1402 (1989).
71. *Pacific Motor Trucking,* 86 LA 497 (1986); and *Amalgamated Transit Union, Local 1433 and Phoenix Transit System,* 87–2 ARB Paragraph 8510 (1987).
72. *Shelby County Health Care Center,* 90 LA 1225 (1988).
73. *Boise Cascade Corp.,* 90 LA 105 (1987).
74. *Warehouse Distribution Centers,* 90 LA 979 (1987).
75. *Gem City Chemicals,* 86 LA 1023 (1986).
76. *Signal Delivery Services, Inc.,* 86 LA 7S (1986).
77. *Consolidated Coal Co.,* 87 LA 111 (1986).
78. Michael H. LeRoy, "The Presence of Drug Testing in the Workplace and Union Member Attitudes," *Labor Studies Journal 16,* no. 4 (1991), pp. 33–42.
79. S. J. McGolrick, L. C. LaBrecque, and J. C. Walthall, "Workplace Monitoring Examined," BNA Reports, *2010 Source Book on Collective Bargaining* (Washington, DC: Bureau of National Affairs, 2010), p. 100.
80. "Firing Employee Who Sent Sexually Charged Email OK'd," BNA Reports, *2010 Source Book on Collective Bargaining* (Washington, DC: Bureau of National Affairs, 2010), p. 255.
81. "Vouchers and the Accountability Dilemma," American Federation of Teachers (October 26, 1999). Available at www.aft.org. Accessed October 26, 1999; and "Vouchers," *National Education Association* (October 26, 1999). Available at www.nea.org. Accessed October 26, 1999.
82. Baugher, "Union Legitimacy and the Team Concept," p. 142.

Chapter 10

1. 29 U.S.C. sec. 157 (1982).
2. 29 U.S.C. sec. 158(a) (1982).
3. *Cooper Thermometer Co.,* 154 NLRB 502, 59 LRRM 1767 (1965); and *American Freightways Co.,* 124 NLRB 646, 44 LRRM 1202 (1959).
4. *National Labor Relations Board v. Preston Feed Corp.,* 309 F.2d 346 (4th Cir. 1962).
5. *Republic Aviation,* 324 U.S. 793, 16 LRRM 620 (1945).
6. *St. Luke's Hospital,* 300 NLRB 836, 837 (1990); see also *PPG Industries,* 351 NLRB 1049, 1051 (2007).
7. *Marriott Corp. (Children's Inn),* 223 N.L.R.B. 978 (1976).
8. *St. John's Hospital & School of Nursing, Inc.,* 222 N.L.R.B. 1150 (1976).
9. *Lechmere, Inc. v. NLRB,* 112 S.Ct. 841 (1992); see also Roger C. Hartley, "The Supreme Court's 1991–92 Labor & Employment Law Term," *Labor Lawyer 8,* no. 4 (Fall 1992), p. 757.
10. *UFCW Local No. 880 v. NLRB,* 151 LRRM 2289 (1996).
11. *Webco Industries, Inc. v. NLRB,* 217 F.3d 1306 (2000).
12. "Nonsolicitation Policy is a Non-Starter," *Labor Relations Bulletin,* no. 718 (January 2001), p. 1.

13. *Cleveland Real Estate Partners v. NLRB,* 95 F. 3d 457 (6th Cir. 1996).
14. *Malta Co.*, 276 NLRB 171 (1985).
15. Agreement between C. Lee Cook Division, Dover Resources, Inc. and Lodge No. 681, International Association of Machinists and Aerospace Workers AFL-CIO, 2007–2012. Used by permission.
16. *The Cincinnati Enquirer,* 279 NLRB 149 (1986).
17. Steven Greenhouse, "Board Restricts Union Use of Email," *New York Times* (December 22, 2007). *The Guard Publishing Company, d/b/a/ The Register-Guard,* 351 NLRB No. 70 (December 16, 2007).
18. *Lutheran Heritage Village-Livonia Home, Inc.*, 343 NLRB No. 75, 2004 WL 2678632 (November 19, 2004).
19. William Corbett, "The Narrowing of the National Labor Relations Act," *Berkeley Journal of Employment & Labor Law 27,* no. 1 (2006), pp. 41–7.
20. *Midland National Life Ins. Co. v. National Labor Relations Board,* 263 NLRB 24, 110 LRRM 1489 (1982).
21. *Houston Chronicle Publishing Co.*, 293 NLRB 38 (1989).
22. James P. Swann, Jr., "Misrepresentation in Labor Union Elections," *Personnel Journal 59,* no. 11 (November 1980), pp. 925–26.
23. *U-Haul of Nevada,* 341 NLRB No. 26 (2004).
24. *Crown Bolt, Inc.,* 343 NLRB No. 86 (2004).
25. *National Labor Relations Board v. Gissel Packing Co.,* 395 U.S. 575, 71 LRRM 2481 (1969).
26. Gary L. Tidwell, "The Supervisor's Role in a Union Election," *Personnel Journal 62,* no. 8 (August 1983), pp. 640–45.
27. *Saint Gobain Abrasives, Inc.*, 342 NLRB No. 39 (2004).
28. James H. Hopkins and Robert D. Binderup, "Employee Relations and Union Organizing Campaigns," *Personnel Administrator 25,* no. 3 (March 1980), pp. 57–61.
29. *Automated Products, Inc.,* 242 NLRB 424, 101 LRRM 1208 (1979).
30. *Struksnes Construction Co.,* 165 NLRB 1062, 1063, 65 LRRM 1385 (1967).
31. *Allentown Mack Sales & Service, Inc. v. NLRB,* 522 U.S. 359 (1998).
32. Peter J. Hurtgen, "Recent Decisions and Current Issues before the Board," *Labor Law Journal* (June 1998), pp. 1031–36.
33. *MSK Corp.,* 341 NLRB No. 11 (2004).
34. *Rossmore House,* 269 NLRB 1176, 116 LRRM 1025 (1984).
35. *Peerless Plywood Co.,* 107 NLRB 427, 33 LRRM 1151 (1953); and *Rodac Corp.,* 231 NLRB 261, 95 LRRM 1608 (1977).
36. *Atlantic Limousine Inc. v. Teamsters Local 331,* 165 LRRM 1001 (August 14, 2000).
37. Herbert G. Heneman, III, and Marcus H. Sandver, "Predicting the Outcome of Union Certification Elections: A Review of the Literature," *Industrial and Labor Relations Review 36,* no. 4 (July 1983), p. 555.
38. Richard N. Block and Myron Roomkin, "Determinants of Voter Participation in Union Certification Elections," *Monthly Labor Review 105,* no. 4 (April 1982), pp. 45–47.
39. Stephen I. Schlossberg and Judith A. Scott, *Organizing and the Law*, 4th ed. (Washington, DC: Bureau of National Affairs, 1991), pp. 322–24.
40. *United Broadcasting Co.,* 248 NLRB 403, 103 LRRM 1421 (1980).
41. *Electromation,* NLRB Case No. 25-CA-19818 (1991).
42. *E. I. duPont de Nemours Company v. Chemical Workers Association, Inc.,* 311 N.L.R.B. 88 (1993), 143 LRRM 1121 (1993) (corrected at 143 LRRM [268]).
43. *General Foods Corp.,* 231 NLRB 1232, 1235 (1977).
44. *Crown Cork & Seal,* 334 NLRB No. 92 (2001).
45. *Federal-Magul Corp., Coldwater Distributors Center Division v. National Labor Relations Board*, 394 F.2d 915 (Mich. Cir. 1968).
46. *RCA del Caribe, Inc.,* 262 NLRB 963, 110 LRRM 1369 (1982); and *Bruckner Nursing Home,* 262 NLRB 955, 110 LRRM 1374 (1982).
47. David Vaughn, "Mixed Motives in Unfair Labor Practices," New York University, 35th Annual National Conference on Labor (New York: Matthew Bender, 1983), pp. 169–94.
48. *NLRB v. Town & Country Elec., Inc.,* 516 U.S. 85 (1995).
49. "Paid Union Organizers," *Labor Law Reports 107,* no. 468 (August 1995).
50. John M. Capron, "A Saline Solution to the Salting Problem," *Employee Relations Law Journal 30,* no. 4 (Spring 2005), pp. 12–19.
51. *Electrical Workers IBEW Local 48,* 342 NLRB No. 10 (2004).
52. *Oil Capitol Sheet Metal, Inc.,* 349 NLRB No. 118 (2007).
53. *Toering Electric Co.,* 351 NLRB No. 18 (2007).
54. *Meyers Industries v. Prill,* 268 NLRB 493 (1984); and *Meyers Industries, Inc. II,* 281 NLRB 118 (1986).
55. Patrick Hardin, ed., *The Developing Labor Law,* 3rd ed. (Washington, DC: Bureau of National Affairs, 1992), pp. 137–46.
56. *North Carolina Fuel Company v. National Labor Relations Board,* 645 F.2d 177 (3d Cir. 1981).
57. Frederick J. Bosch and Paul A. Tufano, "Establishing a Uniform Standard for Striker Misconduct in Arbitration Cases," *Labor Law Journal* (September 1988), pp. 629–33.
58. *Clear Pine Mouldings, Inc.,* 268 NLRB 173, 115 LRRM 1113 (1984).
59. Bosch and Tufano, "Establishing a Uniform Standard," pp. 629–33.
60. *NLRB v. Mackay Radio and Telegraph Co.,* 304 U.S. 333 (1938).
61. William T. Krizner, "The Mackay Doctrine," *Labor Law Journal* (June 1998), pp. 997–1007.
62. Hardin, *The Developing Labor Law,* p. 1112.
63. Emily Nelson and J. C. Conklin, "Leary of Strikes, More Workers Stage Sickouts," *Wall Street Journal* (February 12, 1999), pp. B1, B4.
64. Hardin, *The Developing Labor Law,* pp. 1115–20.
65. *NLRB v. Weingarten, Inc.,* 420 U.S. 251 (1975).
66. Jodie Meade Michalski, "Knowing When to Keep Quiet: Weingarten on the Limitations on Representative Participation,"

Hofstra Labor & Employment Law Journal 26, no. 1 (Fall 2008), pp. 163–92.

67. *Roadway Express, Inc.*, 246 NLRB 1127 (1979); and Neil N. Bernstein, "Weingarten: Time for Reconsideration," *Labor Lawyer 6,* no. 4 (Fall 1990), pp. 1005–27.
68. *New Jersey Bell Telephone Co.*, 308 NLRB 32 (August 18, 1992); and Christopher J. Martin, "Some Reflections on Weingarten and the Free Speech Rights of Union Stewards," *Employee Relations Law Journal 18,* no. 4 (Spring 1993), pp. 647–53.
69. Teamsters (August 1, 1999). Available at www.org/99 resources/. Accessed August 1, 1999.
70. *Epilepsy Foundation v. NLRB,* 168 LRRM 2673 (CA DC 2001).
71. *IBM Corp.*, 341 NLRB No. 148 (2004).
72. *Pattern Makers League v. National Labor Relations Board,* 473 U.S. 95, 119 LRRM 2928 (1985). For analysis, see Beverly A. Williams, "Pattern Makers' League v. National Labor Relations Board: Individual Autonomy v. Union Solidarity," *Rutgers Law Review 39* (Fall 1986), pp. 197–16.
73. Steven Greenhouse, "Some Organizers Protest Their Union's Tactics," *The New York Times* (November 11, 2009), p. B1.
74. Hardin, *The Developing Labor Law,* pp. 178–84.
75. *National Labor Relations Board v. Montgomery Ward & Co.*, 133 F.2d 676, 686, 12 LRRM 508 (9th Cir. 1943).
76. Ludwig Teller, *Labor Disputes and Collective Bargaining,* Vol. 2 (New York: Baker, Voorhis, 1940), p. 884.
77. *National Labor Relations Board v. General Electric Co.*, 418 F.2d 736, 72 LRRM 2530 (2d Cir. 1969) cert. denied, 397 U.S. 965, 73 LRRM 2600 (1970).
78. *Utility Workers (Ohio Power Co.),* 203 NLRB 230, 83 LRRM 1099 (1973).
79. *U.S. Gypsum Co.*, 200 NLRB 132, 82 LRRM 1064 (1972).
80. Bureau of National Affairs, *2007 Source Book on Collective Bargaining* (Washington, DC: Bureau of National Affairs, 2007), p. 121.
81. Theodore Kheel, *Labor Law* (New York: Matthew Bender, 1988), chap. 16, pp. 26–31.
82. Hardin, *The Developing Labor Law,* p. 635, n. 317.
83. *Verizon New York, Inc.*, 339 NLRB No. 6 (2003).
84. *Saint Gobain Abrasives, Inc.*, 342 NLRB No. 39 (2004).
85. *JI Case v. National Labor Relations Board,* 321 U.S. 332, 64 S.Ct. 576, 88 L. Ed. 762 (1944).
86. *National Labor Relations Board v. Truitt Manufacturing Co.*, 351 U.S. 149, 38 LRRM 2024 (1955).
87. Robert E. Block, "The Disclosure of Profits in the Normal Course of Collective Bargaining: All Relevant Information Should Be on the Table," *Labor Lawyer 2,* no. 1 (Winter 1986), pp. 47–74.
88. *Nielsen Lithographing Co.*, 305 NLRB 90, 138 LRRM 1444 (1988); and Reid Canon and Kathryn Ernst Noecker, "The Employer's Duty to Supply Financial Information to the Union: When Has the Employer Asserted an Inability to Pay?" *Labor Lawyer 8,* no. 4 (Fall 1992), p. 815.
89. *Efrain Rivera-Vego, et al. v. Conagra, Inc.*, 70 F.3d 153 (1st Cir. 1995).
90. Collective Bargaining Agreement between Louisville/Jefferson County Metro Government and the Fraternal Order of Police, Lodge 614, July 1, 2007–June 30, 2011.
91. Bureau of National Affairs, *Basic Patterns in Union Contracts,* pp. 2–3.
92. Agreement between E. I. duPont de Nemours and Company and the Neoprene Craftsmen Union (1994), p. 28.
93. *N.L.R.B. v. Communications Workers of America, AFL-CIO, Local 1170,* 474 F.2d 778, 82 L.R.R.M. 2101 (2nd Cir. 1972) citing *Jacobs Manufacturing Company,* 94 NLRB 1214 (1951).
94. *Anheuser-Busch, Inc.*, 351 NLRB No. 40 (September 29, 2007).
95. *Boys Market, Inc. v. Retail Clerks Union Local 770,* 398 U.S. 235, 90 S. Ct. 1583, 26 L. Ed. 2d 199 (1970).
96. *Sinclair Refining Company v. Atchison,* 370 U.S. 195, 82 S. Ct. 1328, 8 L. Ed. 440 (1962).
97. *Buffalo Forge Company v. United Steelworkers of America,* 428 U.S. 397, 96 S. Ct. 3141, 49 L. Ed. 2d 1022 (1976).
98. *Indianapolis Power and Light Company,* 276 NLRB 211 (1985).
99. *IBEW Local 387 v. NLRB,* No. 85–7129 (9th Cir., May 6, 1986).
100. *De Bartola Corp. v. Florida Gulf Coast Trades Council,* 56 USLW 4328 (1988).
101. Samuel A. DiLullo, "Secondary Boycotts: Has the Court Gone Too Far or Maybe Not Far Enough?" *Labor Law Journal 40,* no. 6 (1989), pp. 376–81.
102. *Overstreet ex rel. NLRB v. United Brotherhood of Carpenters & Joiners of America,* 409 F.3d 1199 (9th Cir. 2005).
103. Jeff Vlasek, "Hold Up the Sign and Lie Like a Rug: How Secondary Boycotts Received Another Lease on Life," *Journal of Corporate Law 32,* no. 1 (2006), pp. 179–95.
104. *Pye v. Teamsters Local 122,* 149 LRRM 3089 (1st Cir. 1995).
105. Dominic Bencivenga, "1959 Sweatshops Law," *New York Law Journal* (August 13, 1998), pp. 1–4.
106. National Labor Relations Act, Section 8(b)(6) (1947).
107. Schlossberg and Scott, *Organizing and the Law,* p. 110.
108. Donald L. Dotson, "Processing Cases at the NLRB," *Labor Law Journal* (January 1984), pp. 3–9.
109. Matthew M. Franckiewicz, "How to Win NLRB Cases: Tips from a Former Insider," *Labor Law Journal* (January 1993), pp. 40–47.
110. *Ostus v. Vincent/Metro Trucking LLC, D. Minn., No. 09-1726* (August 14, 2009).
111. Clifford M. Coen, Sandra J. Hartman, and Dinah M. Payne, "NLRB Wields a Rejuvenated Weapon," *Personnel Journal* (December 1996), pp. 85–7.
112. William B. Gould IV, "The NLRB at Age 70: Some Reflections on the Clinton Board and the Bush II Aftermath," *Berkeley Journal of Employment & Labor Law 26,* no. 2 (2005), pp. 309–18.
113. *Textile Workers Union v. Lincoln Mills,* 353 U.S. 448, 40 LRRM 2113 (1957).
114. *United Steelworkers v. American Mfg. Co.*, 363 U.S. 564, 46 LRRM 2414 (1960); *United Steelworkers v. Warrior & Gulf*

Navigation Co., 363 U.S. 574, 46 LRRM 2416 (1960); and *United Steelworkers v. Enterprise Wheel & Car Corp.,* 363 U.S. 593, 46 LRRM 2423 (1960).

115. *United Paperworkers International Union, AFL-CIO v. Misco, Inc.,* 484 U.S. 29, 108 S. Ct. 364 (1987).
116. Michael H. LeRoy and Peter Feuille, "The Steelworkers Trilogy and Grievance Arbitration Appeals: How the Federal Courts Respond," *Industrial Relations Law Journal 13,* no. 1 (1992), pp. 78–120; see also *American Postal Workers Union, AFL-CIO v. U.S. Postal Service,* 52 F.3d 359 (1995).
117. *Collyer Insulated Wire,* 192 NLRB 837, 77 LRRM 1931 (1971).
118. *Spielberg Manufacturing Company,* 112 NLRB 1080, 36 LRRM 1152 (1955); see also Frank Elkouri and Edna Asper Elkouri, *How Arbitration Works,* 6th ed. (Washington, DC: Bureau of National Affairs, 2003), pp. 534–36.
119. 5 U.S.C. sec. 7116 (1982).
120. 5 U.S.C. sec. 7122 (1982).
121. *Steele v. Louisville and N.R.R.,* 323 U.S. 192, 15 LRRM 708 (1944).
122. *Marquez v. Screen Actors Guild, Inc., et al.,* 124 F.3d 1034 (U.S. 1998).
123. *Bowen v. The U.S. Postal Service,* 112 LRRM 2281 (1983).
124. Rossie D. Alston, Jr., and Glenn M. Taubman, "The Rights and Responsibilities of Employees Confronted with Union Discipline," *Labor Law Journal* (December 1998), pp. 1214–24.
125. *Vaca v. Sipes,* 386 U.S. 171, 64 LRRM 2369 (1967).
126. Ibid.; *Hines v. Anchor Motor Co., Inc.,* 424 U.S. 554, 91 LRRM 2481 (1976); and *Bowen v. U.S. Postal Service,* 112 LRRM 2281 (1983).
127. See George W. Bohlander, "Fair Representation: Not Just a Union Problem," *The Personnel Administrator 25,* no. 3 (1980), pp. 36–40, 82.

Chapter 11

1. David Lewin and Richard B. Peterson, "A Model for Measuring Effectiveness of the Grievance Process," *Monthly Labor Review 106,* no. 4 (1983), pp. 47–49.
2. Frank Elkouri and Edna Asper Elkouri, *How Arbitration Works,* 6th ed. (Washington, DC: Bureau of National Affairs, 2003), pp. 198–99.
3. *Cudahy Packing Co.,* 7 LA G45, G46 (1947).
4. Elkouri and Elkouri, *How Arbitration Works,* p. 201.
5. Thomas B. Knight, "Feedback and Grievance Resolution," *Industrial and Labor Relations Review 39,* no. 4 (July 1986), pp. 585–98.
6. Harold Davey, Mario Bognanno, and David Estenson, *Contemporary Collective Bargaining,* 4th ed. (Upper Saddle River, NJ: Prentice Hall, 1982), p. 169.
7. Bureau of National Affairs, *Basic Patterns in Union Contracts,* 14th ed. (Washington, DC: BNA Books, 1995), p. 35.
8. See the *Steelworkers Trilogy* cases: *United Steelworkers of America v. Enterprise Wheel & Car Corp.,* 80 S.Ct. 1358, 34 LA 569 (1960); *United Steelworkers of America v. American Mfg. Co.,* 363 U.S. 566–567 (1960); and *United Steelworkers of America v. Warrior & Gulf Navigation Company,* 363 U.S. 582 (1960).
9. Steven Briggs, "The Grievance Procedure," *Personnel Journal 60,* no. 6 (June 1981), pp. 471–74.
10. Bureau of National Affairs, *Grievance Guide* (2008), pp. 67–157.
11. *The Guard Publishing Company d/b/a The Register-Guard and Eugene Newspaper Guild, CWA Local 37194,* 351 NLRB No. 70 (2007).
12. *Guard Publishing Co. v. N.L.R.B.,* 571 F.3d 53 (D.C. 2009).
13. Bureau of National Affairs, *2007 Source Book on Collective Bargaining* (Washington, DC: Bureau of National Affairs, 2007), p. 107.
14. *Mayo v. Columbia University,* 2003 U.S. Dist. LEXIS 5639 (2003).
15. Stephen Cabot, *Labor-Management Relations Manual* (Boston, MA: Warren, Gorham, Lamont, 1979), chap. 16, pp. 1–2.
16. Bureau of National Affairs, *Grievance Guide* (2008), pp. 7–8.
17. Cabot, *Labor-Management Relations Manual,* chap. 16, pp. 3–5.
18. T. L. Stanley, "Running at Peak Performance," *Supervision 66,* no. 3 (2005), pp. 10–13.
19. *FMCS Grievance Mediation: Problem Solving in the Workplace* (Washington, DC: U.S. Government Printing Office, 2001).
20. Stephen B. Goldberg, "How Interest-Based, Grievance Mediation Performs over the Long Term," *Dispute Resolution Journal 59,* no. 4 (2004–2005), pp. 8–15.
21. Ibid.
22. Ken May, "Union—City Relationships, NMB Use of Technology," BNA Reports, *2010 Source Book on Collective Bargaining* (Washington, DC: Bureau of National Affairs, 2010), pp. 95, 96.
23. Richard B. Freeman and Carey Ichniowski, "Introduction: The Public Sector Look of Unionism," in Richard B. Freeman and Carey Ichniowski, eds., *When Public Sector Workers Unionize* (Chicago, IL: University of Chicago Press, 1988), pp. 50–97.
24. Michael J. Duane, "To Grieve or Not to Grieve: Why Reduce It to Writing?" *Public Personnel Management 20,* no. 1 (1991), pp. 83–90.
25. David L. Dilts and Clarence K. Deitsch, "Arbitration Lost: The Public Sector Assault on Arbitration," *Labor Law Journal 35,* no. 3 (1984), pp. 182–88.

Chapter 12

1. Edwin Witte, *Historical Survey of Labor Arbitration* (Ithaca, NY: Cornell University Press, 1952), pp. 29–33.
2. Ibid.
3. "Bernie Kleiman, "A Lifetime of Dedication to USW and Our Members," *USW@Work 2,* no. 1 (Winter 2007), pp. 26–27.
4. Frank Elkouri and Edna Elkouri, *How Arbitration Works,* 6th ed. (Washington, DC: Bureau of National Affairs, 2003), pp. 106–7.

5. *Textile Workers Union v. Lincoln Mills,* 353 U.S. 448, 40 LRRM 2113 (1957).
6. *United Steelworkers v. American Mfg. Co.,* 363 U.S. 564, 46 LRRM 2414 (1960); *United Steelworkers v. Warrior & Gulf Navigation Co.,* 363 U.S. 574, 46 LRRM 2416 (1960); and *United Steelworkers v. Enterprise Wheel & Car Corp.,* 363 U.S. 593, 46 LRRM 2423 (1960).
7. Benjamin Aaron et al., The *Future of Labor Arbitration in America* (New York; American Arbitration Association, 1976), p. 56.
8. Charles J. Coleman and Theodora T. Haynes, *Labor Arbitration: An Annotated Bibliograph*y (Ithaca, NY: ILR Press, 1994), pp. 10–22.
9. Arnold M. Zack, *Handbook for Grievance Arbitration: Procedural and Ethical Issues* (New York: Lexington Books, 1992), pp. 76–93.
10. *United Steelworkers of America v. Warrior & Gulf Navigation Co.,* 363 U.S. 574, 80 S.Ct. 1347 (1960).
11. *Steelworkers v. Enterprise Wheel & Car Corp.*, 363 U.S. 593 (1960).
12. *E. I. duPont de Nemours & Co. v. Grasselli Employees Independent Association of East Chicago, Inc.,* No. 85–1577 (7th Cir., May 9, 1986).
13. Theodore St. Antoine, "Judicial Review of Labor Arbitration Awards: A Second Look at *Enterprise Wheel* and Its Progeny," *Michigan Law Review 75,* no. *1137* (1977), p. 1140.
14. *Alexander v. Gardner-Denver,* 415 U.S. 36 (1974).
15. *Harrell Alexander, Sr. v. Gardner-Denver Co.*, 415 U.S. 36, 944 S.Ct. 101 (1974); and *W. R. Grace and Co., v. Local Union 759, International Union of the United Rubber Cork, Linoleum and Plastic Workers of America,* 461 U.S. 757, 103, S.Ct. 2177 (1963).
16. *Wright v. Universal Maritime Service Corporation,* 525 U.S. 70 (1998).
17. Ibid.
18. *Airline Pilots v. Northwest Airlines,* 199 F. 3d 477 (D.C. Cir. 1999), reinstated 211 F. 3d 1312 (D.C. Cir. 2000), cert. den. 531 U.S. 1011 (2000).
19. *Gilmer v. Interstate/Johnson Lane Corp.,* 500 U.S. 20 (1991); and George M. Sullivan, "Alexander v. Garner Denver: Staggered but Still Standing," *Labor Law Journal 48,* no. 1 (March 1999), pp. 43–51.
20. *14 Penn Plaza v. Pyett,* 129 S. Ct. 1456, 105 FEP Cases 1441 (2009).
21. David P. Twomey, "The Supreme Court *14 Penn Plaza, LLC v. Pyett* Decision: Impact and Fairness," *Labor Law Journal 61,* no. 2 (Summer 2010), pp. 55–67.
22. Elkouri and Elkouri, *How Arbitration Works,* pp. 49–51.
23. The Federal Arbitration Act, 9 U.S.C. 1–16 (2000), first enacted in 1925.
24. Teresa L. Elliott, "Conflicting Interpretations of the One-Year Requirement On Motions to Confirm Arbitration Awards," *Creighton Law Review 38,* no. 3 (2005), pp. 661–89.
25. *Circuit City Stores Inc. v. Adams,* 532 U.S. 105 (2001).
26. Ibid.
27. *Green Tree Financial Corp.-Alabama v. Randolph,* 531 U.S. 79 (2000).
28. *Preston v. Ferrer,* 128 S.Ct. 978, U.S. NO. 06–1463 (February 20, 2008).
29. Theodore W. Kheel, *The Keys to Conflict Resolution* (New York: Four Walls Eight Windows, 1999), pp. 88–89.
30. Elkouri and Elkouri, *How Arbitration Works,* p. 116.
31. Kheel, *The Keys to Conflict Resolution,* p. 90.
32. *T.J. Maxx,* 113 LA 533 (1999).
33. *Flathead County Commissioners,* 97 LA 350 (1991).
34. Nels Nelson and Earl Curry, "Arbitrator Characteristics and Arbitral Decisions," *Industrial Relations 20,* no. 3 (1981), pp. 312–17.
35. Steven Briggs and John Anderson, "An Empirical Investigation of Arbitrator Acceptability," *Industrial Relations 19,* no. 2 (1980), pp. 163–73.
36. Richard A. Posthuma, James B. Dworkin, and Maris S. Swift, "Arbitrator Acceptability: Does Justice Matter?" *Industrial Relations 39,* no. 2 (2000), pp. 313–35.
37. Elkouri and Elkouri, *How Arbitration Works*, pp. 182–88.
38. Judith B. Ittig and Michael J. Baynard, "Thirty Steps to Better Arbitration," *Dispute Resolution Journal 59,* no. 3 (2004), pp. 41–45.
39. Elkouri and Elkouri, *How Arbitration Works* (2003), pp. 155–58.
40. Agreement between the Mechanical Contractors Association and Plumbers and Gas Fitters Local Union No. 107, 1979–1982, p. 21.
41. Steven C. Bennett, "The Developing American Approach to Arbitrability," *Dispute Resolution Journal 58,* no. 1 (2003), pp. 8–23.
42. Elkouri and Elkouri, *How Arbitration Works,* p. 279.
43. *United Steelworkers of America v. Warrior & Gulf Navigation Co.,* 80 S.Ct. 1347, 1352–1353 (1960).
44. *Republic Waste Services,* 119 LA 1105 (2004).
45. *Transit Authority of River City,* 118 LA 939 (2003); and "Two Penalties for One Offense Prohibited by Double Jeopardy," *2005 Sourcebook on Collective Bargaining* (Washington, DC: Bureau of National Affairs, 2005), p. 247.
46. American Arbitration Association, *Labor Arbitration Procedures and Techniques* (New York: American Arbitration Association, 1978), pp. 17–20.
47. Ibid.
48. *Instrument Workers v. Minneapolis Honeywell Co.,* 54 LRRM 2660, 2661 (1963).
49. Stephen Cabot, *Labor-Management Relations Manual* (Boston, MA: Warren, Gorham, Lamont, 1979), chap. 18, p. 6.
50. Margaret A. Lareau and Howard R. Sacks, "Assessing Credibility in Labor Arbitration," *Labor Lawyer 5,* no. 3 (1989), pp. 151–93.
51. Theodore W. Kheel, *Labor Law,*(New York, NY: Matthew Bender, 1986), chap. 24, p. 55.
52. Ittig and Baynard, "Thirty Steps to Better Arbitration."
53. Cabot, *Labor-Management Relations Manual,* chap. 18, pp. 7–8.
54. Kheel, *Labor Law,* chap. 24, p. 56.
55. Roger I. Abrams and Dennis R. Nolan, "Arbitral Craftsmanship and Opinion Writing," *Labor Lawyer 5,* no. 2 (1989), pp. 195–222.

56. Kheel, *Labor Law,* chap. 24, pp. 50–51.
57. Daniel F. Jennings and A. Dale Allen, Jr., "How Arbitrators View the Process of Labor Arbitration: A Longitudinal Analysis," *Labor Studies Journal 18,* no. 1 (1993), pp. 41–50.
58. Howard Stiefel, "The Labor Arbitration Process: Survey of the New York State Bar Association Labor and Employment Law Section," *Labor Lawyer 8,* no. 4 (1992), pp. 971–83.
59. Kheel, *The Keys to Conflict Resolution,* pp. 90–91.
60. Clarence R. Deitsch, "Seniority Clauses: An End Run Around Just Cause?" *Dispute Resolution Journal 59,* no. 4 (2004–2005), pp. 30–4.
61. Ibid.
62. Wallace B. Nelson, "The Role of Common Law in Just Cause Disputes," *Personnel Journal 58,* no. 8 (1979), pp. 541–43.
63. Bureau of National Affairs, *Grievance Guide,* 12th ed. (Washington, DC: Bureau of National Affairs, 2008), pp. 4–7.
64. Elkouri and Elkouri, *How Arbitration Works*, p. 1235.
65. Nelson, "The Role of Common Law in Just Cause Disputes," pp. 541–43.
66. Kenneth P. Swan, "Public Bargaining in Canada and the U.S.: A Legal View," *Industrial Relations 19,* no. 3 (1980), pp. 272–91.
67. David E. Bloom, "Is Arbitration Really Compatible with Bargaining?" *Industrial Relations 20,* no. 3 (1981), pp. 233–44; and see also Patricia Compton-Forbes, "Interest Arbitration Hasn't Worked Well in the Public Sector," *Personnel Administrator 29,* no. 2 (1984), pp. 99–104.
68. *School Committee of Beverly v. Geller,* 435 Mass. 223 (2001).

Chapter 13

1. Thomas L. Friedman, *The World Is Flat: A Brief History of the Twenty First Century* (New York: Farrar, Straus and Giroux, 2005), pp. 48–172.
2. Juhani Lonnroth, "Global Employment Issues in the Year 2000," *Monthly Labor Review 117,* no. 9 (1994), pp. 5–15.
3. Helmut Wagner, "Implications of Globalization for Monetary Policy," IMF Working Papers (2001 International Monetary Fund), pp. 1–63. Available at www.imf.org. Accessed October 2005.
4. Stephen J. Kobrin, "Sovereignty@Bay: Globalization, Multinational Enterprise, and the International Political System," in Alan Rugman and Thomas Brewer, eds., *The Oxford Handbook of International Business* (Oxford, England: Oxford University Press, 2001), pp. 181–205.
5. Greg Bamber, Russell D. Langsbury, and Nick Wailes, eds., *International and Comparative Employment Relations: Globalisation and the Developed Market Economies* (Thousand Oaks, CA: Sage, 2004), p. 211.
6. *A Trade Union Guide to Globalization,* 2nd ed. (Brussels, Belgium: International Confederation of Free Trade Unions (ICFTU), 2004), pp. 1–172, 13.
7. Howard Guille, "Unions have no future if they do not become truly global institutions," *Social Alternatives 28,* no. 1 (2009), pp. 37–41.
8. Michael Mussa, "Factors Driving Global Economic Integration." Presented in Jackson Hole, Wyoming, symposium sponsored by the Federal Reserve Bank of Kansas City on "Global Opportunities and Challenges," (August 25, 2000). Available at www.imf.org. Accessed October 2005.
9. Friedman, *The World Is Flat,* p. 9.
10. Bruce E. Kaufman, *The Global Evolution of Industrial Relations: Events, Ideas and the IIRA* (Geneva: International Labour Office, 2004), p. 16.
11. Ibid. p. 20.
12. Adam Smith, *An Inquiry into the Nature and Causes of the Wealth of Nations* (New York: Oxford University Press, 1998).
13. Ibid., pp. 12–13.
14. Roy J. Adams, "Regulating Unions and Collective Bargaining: A Global, Historical Analysis of Determinants and Consequences," *Comparative Labor Law Journal 14,* no. 3 (1993), pp. 272–300.
15. Ibid.
16. Adams, "Regulating Unions and Collective Bargaining," p. 282.
17. Kaufman, *The Global Evolution of Industrial Relations,* p. 77.
18. Lee Swepston, "The Future of ILO Standards," *Monthly Labor Review 117,* no. 9 (1994), pp. 16–23.
19. Kaufman, *The Global Evolution of Industrial Relations,* pp. 204–5.
20. Swepston, "The Future of ILO Standards," p. 16.
21. International Labour Office, *Your Voice at Work.*
22. Bernard Gernigon, Alberto Odero, and Horacio Guido, "ILO Principles Concerning Collective Bargaining," *International Labour Review 139,* no. 1 (2000), pp. 33–55.
23. Laurence Waterhouse, "Surveying the British Canal System," *US Hydro* (2001), pp. 1–13. Available at www.thsoa.org/ hyol/5_4.pdf. Accessed September 24, 2005.
24. Kaufman, *The Global Evolution of Industrial Relations,* p. 25.
25. Ibid., p. 52.
26. Mary Davis, "The Union Makes Us Strong: TUC History Online," *Centre for Trade Union Studies*. Available at London Metropolitan University Web site, www.unionhistory.info. Accessed September 2005.
27. Kaufman, *The Global Evolution of Industrial Relations,* p. 199.
28. Ibid., p. 383.
29. Ibid., p. 278.
30. Ibid., p. 416.
31. *International and Comparative Employment Relations,* pp. 91–115.
32. Kaufman, *The Global Evolution of Industrial Relations,* p. 422.
33. Ibid., p. 421.
34. Jonathan Eaton and Anil Verma, "Does 'Fighting Back' Make a Difference? The Case of the Canadian Auto Workers Union," *Journal of Labor Research 27,* no. 2 (2006), pp. 187–212.
35. Ibid., p. 290.
36. Joo-Cheong Tham, "The Framework of Australian Labour Law and Recent Trends in 'Deregulation,'" Paper presented at The Japan Institute for Labour Policy and Training (JILPT) Comparative Labor Law Seminar (Tokyo, 2004), pp. 37–50.
37. Bahman Bahrami, "Australian Labor Relations: The Recent Developments," *Labor Law Journal 47,* no. 5 (1996), pp. 327–41.

38. Tham, "The Framework of Australian Labour Law."
39. Daniel De La Puente and Jonathon House, "Spanish Workers Protest Austerity," *The Wall Street Journal* (June 9, 2010), p. A 10.
40. Pascal Fontaine, *Europe in 12 Lessons* (Luxembourg: Office for Official Publications of the European Communities, 2004), pp. 1–68.
41. Ibid., p. 54.
42. Bureau of International Affairs, U.S., "Foreign Labor Trends: European Union," *Federal Publications* (2003). Paper 100 pp. 1–25. Available at digitalcommons.ilr.cornell.edu. Accessed August 30, 2011.
43. Ibid., p. 19.
44. Kaufman, *The Global Evolution of Industrial Relations,* p. 20.
45. Ibid., p. 474.
46. Ibid., p. 32.
47. *International and Comparative Employment Relations,* pp. 232–34.
48. Rolf Wank, "The Mechanism for Establishing and Changing Terms and Conditions of Employment," Paper presented at the Japan Institute for Labour Policy and Training (JILPT) Comparative Labor Law Seminar (Tokyo, 2004), pp. 59–72.
49. Christian Dufour, "Questionnaire for EIRO Comparative Study on Changes in the National Collective Bargaining Systems Since 1990—Case of France," *EIROnline* (May 2005). Available at http://www.eiro.eurofound.eu.int/2005/03/study/ index.html. Accessed October 2005. See also Christian Dufour, "Bargaining in France in 2001: The End of an Unusual Era," in G. Fayertag, ed., *Collective Bargaining in the EU Member-States* (Brussels: European Trade Union Institute, 2002); and Christian Dufour, "Mandating: Precursor of a New Practice in Employee Representation or Destructive Force?" in Daugareilh Isabelle and Pierre Iriart, eds., *Lessons Learned from the Reduction of Working Time* (Cedex: *Maison Des Sciences de l'Homme d'Aquitaine* 2004), pp. 255–65.
50. Emma Vandore, "France Appears Willing to Try Stepping Out of Labor 'Stone Age,' " Associated Press (December 24, 2007).
51. *International and Comparative Employment Relations,* pp. 148–53.
52. David Dukcevich, "Italian Labor Reformer Murdered," *Forbes* (March 20, 2002). Available at www.forbes.com. Accessed September 2005.
53. Diego Coletto and Livio Muratore, "2004 Annual Review for Italy," *EIROnline* (July 2005). Available at http://www.eiro.eurofound.eu.int/about/2005/01/feature/it0501209f.html. Accessed October 2005.
54. Michele Tiraboschi and Maurizio Del Conte, "Recent Changes in the Italian Labour Law," Paper presented at the Japan Institute for Labour Policy and Training (JILPT) Comparative Labor Law Seminar (Tokyo, 2004), pp. 85–93.
55. *International Reform Monitor, Social Policy, Labour Market Policy and Industrial Relations,* 9th ed. (Gütersloh, Germany: Bertelsmann Stiftung, October 2005). Available at http://en.bertelsmann-stiftung.de/foundation. Accessed October 2005.
56. Diego Coletto, Fondazione Regionale Pietro Seveso, and Livio Muratore, Ires Lombardia, "2004 Annual Review for Italy," *European Industrial Relations Observatory (EIRO).* Available at http://www.eiro.eurofound.eu.int/structure.html. Accessed October 2005.
57. Mitsuru Yamashita, "Japanese Labor-Management Relations in an Era of Diversification of Employment Types: Diversifying Workers and the Role of Labor Unions," *Japan Labor Review 2,* no. 1 (2005), pp. 105–17, 107.
58. "Japan 2002," *Foreign Labor Trends* (U.S. Department of Labor, Bureau of International Labor Affairs, 2002). Available at http://www.dol.gov/ILAB/media/reports. Accessed October 2005.
59. Motohiro Morishma, "Information Sharing and Collective Bargaining in Japan: Effects on Wage Negotiations," *Industrial and Labor Relations Review 44,* no. 3 (1991), pp. 469–85.
60. Available at www.chinaview.cn. Accessed August 13, 2008.
61. Simon Clark, "Post Socialist Trade Unions: China and Russia," *Industrial Relations Journal 36,* no. 1 (2005), pp. 2–18.
62. George J. Gilboy, "The Myth behind China's Miracle," *Foreign Affairs 83,* no. 4 (2004), pp. 33–48.
63. Sarosh Kuruvilla, "Change and Transformation in Asia Industrial Relations," *Industrial Relations 41,* no. 2 (2002), pp. 171–228.
64. Clarke, "Post Socialist Trade Unions," p. 8.
65. Juliet Ye and Juro Osawa, "Foreign Firms Act on Labor in China," *The Wall Street Journal,* (June 15, 2010), pp. B. 1, 2.

INDEX